BRADFORD'S POCKET CROSSWORD SOLVER'S DICTIONARY

Collins

HarperCollins Publishers
Westerhill Road
Bishopbriggs
Glasgow
G64 2QT
Great Britain

First Edition 2008

© Anne R. Bradford 2008

Reprint 10 9 8 7 6 5 4 3 2

The Author hereby asserts her
moral rights to be identified as the
author of this work.

ISBN 978-0-00-726109-3

Collins® is a registered trademark of
HarperCollins Publishers Limited

www.collinslanguage.com

A catalogue record for this book is
available from the British Library

Technical support and typesetting
by Thomas Callan

Printed in Great Britain by
Clays Ltd, St Ives plc

Author's Preface

Cryptic crosswords are a challenge from the setter to the solver, and it helps to have lateral thinking. Those who enjoy cryptics probably also enjoy riddles and excruciating puns. The word puzzles, particularly acrostics, which were popular even before the advent of the crossword some eighty years ago, were very often in the form of a riddle.

The setter's intent is usually to mislead the solver, so the first step is to try to decide which word or set of words in the clue represent the definition. A verb is often an indicator as to the secondary wordplay, possibly suggesting an anagram or that one part of the solution lies within another. A favourite clue which I encountered many years ago is: *Pineapple rings in syrup (9)*. Here the definition could be either 'pineapple' or 'syrup', but few synonyms for pineapple spring to mind and for the most part they have too few letters. The word 'rings' could be a noun *or* a verb, and now the penny begins to drop – a word for pineapple surrounds (rings) the word 'in' and eureka! – Grenad-in-e, a syrup.

The *Bradford's Pocket Dictionary* helps, when needed, by giving possible synonyms for nouns, useful for non-cryptic crosswords, too, and also shows when a word may indicate an anagram or some other form of construction. Use it to good effect.

Anne R. Bradford 2008

Solving Crossword Clues

Crossword puzzles tend to be basically 'quick' or 'cryptic'. A 'quick' crossword usually relies on a one- or two-word clue which is a simple definition of the answer required. Many words have different meanings, so that the clue 'ball' could equally well lead to the answer 'sphere', 'orb', or 'dance'. The way to solve 'quick' crosswords is to press on until probable answers begin to interlink, which is a good sign that you are on the right track.

'Cryptic' crosswords are another matter. Here the clue usually consists of a basic definition, given at either the beginning or end of the clue, together with one or more definitions of parts of the answer. Here are some examples taken from all-time favourites recorded over the years:

1. '*Tradesman who bursts into tears*' (**Stationer**)

    Tradesman is a definition of *stationer*. *Bursts* is cleverly used as an indication of an anagram, and *into tears* is an anagram of *stationer*.

2. '*Sunday school tune*' (**Strain**)

    Here *Sunday* is used to define its abbreviation *S*, *school* is a synonym for *train*, and put together they give *strain*, which is a synonym of *tune*.

3. '*Result for everyone when head gets at bottom*' (**Ache**)
    (used as a 'down' clue)

    This is what is known as an '& lit' clue, meaning that the setter has hit on a happy composition which could literally be true. *Everyone* here is a synonym for *each*, move the *head* (first letter) of the word to the *bottom*, and the answer is revealed, the whole clue being the definition of the answer in this case.

4. '*Tin out East*' (**Sen**)

    In this example, *tin*, implying 'money', requires its chemical symbol *Sn* to go *out*(side) *East*, or its abbreviation, *E*, the whole clue being a definition of a currency (*sen*) used in the East.

5. *'Information given to communist in return for sex'* (**Gender**)

   Information can be defined as *gen*; *communist* is almost always *red*, *in return* indicates 'reversed', leading to *gen-der*, a synonym for *sex*.

6. *'Row about no enclosure of this with sardines'* (**Tin-opener**)

   Row is a synonym for *tier*, *about* indicates 'surrounding', *no enclosure* can be *no pen*, leading to *ti-no pen-er*, and another '& lit' clue.

7. *'Cake-sandwiches-meat, at Uncle Sam's party'* (**Clambake**)

   Meat here is *lamb*, *sandwiches* is used as a verb, so we have *C-lamb-ake*, which is a kind of party in America. *Uncle Sam* or *US* is often used to indicate America.

8. *'Initially passionate meeting of boy and girl could result in it'* (**Pregnancy**)

   Initially is usually a sign of a first letter, in this case 'p' for *passionate* + *Reg* (a boy) and *Nancy* (a girl), and another clever '& lit'.

With 'cryptic' clues the solver needs to try to analyse the parts to see what he or she is looking for – which word or words can be the straight definition, and which refer to the parts or hint at anagrams or other subterfuges. Whilst it would be unrealistic to claim total infallibility, practice has shown that in most crosswords some 90% of the answers are to be found in this work.

Anne R. Bradford

How to Use the Dictionary

This dictionary is the result of over fifty years' analysis of some 300,000 crossword clues, ranging from plain 'quick' crosswords requiring only synonyms to the different level of cryptic puzzles. Therefore the words listed at each entry may be connected to the keyword in various ways, such as:

- a straightforward synonym

- a commonly associated adjective

- an associated or proper noun

- a pun or other devious play on words

Keywords are listed alphabetically; in cases where the heading consists of more than one word, the first of these words is taken to be the keyword, and in cases where the end of a word is bracketed, the material up to the opening bracket is taken to be the keyword. Keywords marked with the symbol ▶ refer the user to other entries where additional information may be found. Keywords marked with the symbol ▷ give leads to anagrams and other ploys used by crossword setters. If the keywords found in the clue do not lead directly to the required answer, the solver should look under words given as cross-references to other entries. These are indicated by the symbol >, with the cross-referenced word shown in capitals.

Some additional entries have been divided into two parts – a general entry similar to the standard entries which appear elsewhere, and a panel entry which contains a list of more specific or encyclopedic material. So, for example, the entry 'Artist(ic)' includes not only a list of general words connected with 'Artist' or 'Artistic' in some way, such as 'Bohemian', 'Cubist', 'Fine' and 'Virtuoso', but also a panel with the heading 'Artists' containing a list of the names of specific artists, such as 'Bellini', 'Constable', and 'Rembrandt'. For added help, the words in these panels are arranged by length, with all three-letter words grouped together in alphabetical order, then all four-letter words, then all five-letter words, and so on.

About the Author

Anne Bradford's love of words began to make itself evident even in her schooldays, when, as Head Girl of her school, she instituted a novel punishment – instead of making rulebreakers write lines, she had them write out pages from a dictionary, on the grounds that this was a more useful exercise. Little did she know this was soon to be her own daily routine!

In time, crosswords became a magnificent obsession for Anne. All lovers of crosswords can understand the irresistible lure of solving them, but Anne's interest went much deeper than most people's, and when she stopped work in 1957 to have her first child, she found herself starting to note down answers to particularly tricky clues as an aid to memory, in case she should come across them again in another puzzle. It was from this simple beginning that this crossword dictionary evolved.

Over the space of 25 years, Anne continued to build on her collection of solutions, analysing every crossword clue as she solved it and adding it to her steadily growing bank of entries. This unique body of material eventually reached such proportions that she had the idea of offering it to her fellow crossword-solvers as a reference book, and since then, the book has gone from strength to strength, providing valuable help to countless cruciverbalists over a number of editions.

Anne Bradford continues to devote time each day to solving crosswords, averaging some 20 a week – both quick and cryptic – and still avidly collects new solutions for her *Crossword Solver's Dictionary* at a rate of around 150 a week, compiling each solution by hand (without the use of a computer!). This latest edition therefore includes much new material, gleaned by a true crossword lover who not only solves crosswords but, as an active member of the Crossword Club, can offer the user an insight into the mind of a cunning crossword compiler.

The Crossword Club

If you are interested in crosswords, you might like to consider joining
the Crossword Club. Membership is open to all who enjoy tackling
challenging crosswords and who appreciate the finer points of clue-
writing and grid-construction. The Club's magazine, Crossword, contains
two prize puzzles each month. A sample issue and full details are
available on request.

The Crossword Club
Coombe Farm
Awbridge
Romsey, Hants.
SO51 OHN
UK

email: bh@thecrosswordclub.co.uk
website address: www.thecrosswordclub.co.uk

Aa

A, An Ack, Adult, Ae, Alpha, Angstrom, Argon, D, Ein, Her, If, L, One, Per, They

Abandon(ed), Abandonment Abdicate, Abnegate, Abort, Adrift, Amoral, Apostasy, Back down, Cade, Cancel, Castaway, Corrupt, Decommission, Defect, Derelict, > **DESERT**, Desuetude, Discard, Disown, Dissolute, Ditch, Drop, Dump, Elan, Evacuate, Expose, Flagrant, Forhoo(ie), Forhow, Forlend, Forsake, Gomorra, Immoral, Jack(-in), Jettison, Jilt, Leave, Loose, Louche, Maroon, Old, Orgiastic, Profligate, Quit, Rat, Relinquish, Renounce, Reprobate, Scrap, Shed, Sink, Strand, Vacate, Waive, Wanton, Yield

Abase Degrade, Demean, Disgrace, Grovel, > **HUMBLE**, Kowtow, Lessen

Abate(ment) Allay, Appal, Decrescent, Diminish, Lyse, Lysis, Moderate, Reduce, Remit, > **SUBSIDE**

▷ **Abate** *may indicate* a contention

Abbey Abbacy, Bath, Buckfast, Cloister, Downside, Fonthill, Fountains, Glastonbury, Je(r)vaulx, Medmenham, Melrose, Minster, Nightmare, Northanger, Priory, Rievaulx, Tintern, Westminster, Whitby, Woburn

Abbot Aelfric, Archimandrite, Brother, Friar

Abbreviate, Abbreviation Abridge, Ampersand, Compendium, Condense, Curtail, > **SHORTEN**, Sigla

Abdicate, Abdication Cede, Disclaim, Disown, Resign

Abdomen Belly, C(o)eliac, Epigastrium, Gaster, Hypochondrium, Paunch, Pleon, > **STOMACH**, Tummy, Venter

Abduct(ed), Abduction Enlèvement, Kidnap, Rapt, Ravish, Shanghai, Steal

Abet(tor) Aid, Back, Candle-holder, Second

Abeyance, Abeyant Dormant, Shelved, Sleeping, Store

Abhor(rent) > **DETEST**, > **HATE**, Loathe, Shun

Abide Dwell, Inhere, > **LAST**, Lie, Live, Observe, Remain, Stand, Tarry

Ability Aptitude, Calibre, Capacity, Cocum, > **COMPETENCE**, Efficacy, ESP, Facility, Faculty, Ingine, Instinct, Lights, Potential, Prowess, Savey, Savoir-faire, Savv(e)y, Skill, Talent

Abject Base, Craven, Grovel, Humble, Servile, Slave

Able Ablins, Accomplished, > **ADEPT**, Aiblins, Apt, Capable, > **COMPETENT**, Fere, Proficient, Seaman, Yibbles

Abnormal(ity) Anomalous, Atypical, > **DEVIANT**, Dysfunction, Ectopic, Erratic, Etypical, Freakish, Odd, Preternatural, > **QUEER**, Sport, Unnatural, Varus

Abode Domicile, Dwelling, Habitat, > **HOME**, Lain, Libken, Midgard, Remain

Abolish, Abolition(ist) Annihilate, Annul, Axe, > **BAN**, D, Delete, Destroy, Eradicate, Erase, Extirpate, John Brown, Nullify, Repeal, Rescind

Abominable, Abominate, Abomination Bane, Cursed, > **HATE**, Nefandous, Nefast, Revolting, Snowman, Vile, Yeti

Aboriginal, Aborigine Boong, Bushmen, Gin, Indigenous, Lubra, Maori, Mary, Myall, Siwash, Vedda(h)

Abound(ing) Bristle, Copious, Enorm, Rife, Teem

About A, Almost, Anent, Around, C, Ca, Circa, Circiter, Concerning, Encompass, Environs, Going, Near, Of, On, Over, Re, Regarding, Soon at

▷ **About** *may indicate* one word around another

Above Abune, Over, Overhead, Overtop, Owre, Sopra, Superior, Supra-, Upon

Abrade, Abrasive Carborundum®, Chafe, Emery, Erode, File, Garnet paper, > GRATE, Rub, Sand, Scrape

Abreast Alongside, Au courant, Au fait, Beside, Level, Up

Abridge(ment) Audley, Compress, Condense, Cut, Digest, Dock, Epitome, Pot, Shorten, Trim

Abroad Afield, Away, Distant, Forth, Out, Overseas

▷ **Abroad** *may indicate* an anagram

▷ **Abrupt** *may indicate* a shortened word

Abrupt(ly) Bold, Brusque, Curt, Gruff, Offhand, Premorse, Prerupt, Short, Staccato, Terse

Abscond Decamp, Desert, Elope, Flee, Levant, Welch

Absence, Absent(ee), Absent-minded(ness) Abs, Abstracted, Away, Distant, Distracted, Distrait, Exile, Hookey, Mitch, Scatty, Skip, Truant, Vacuity, Void, Wool-gathering

Absolute(ly) Bang, Complete, Dead, Deep-dyed, Downright, Fairly, Implicit, Ipso facto, Just, Mere, Mondo, Nominative, Plenary, Plumb, Quite, Real, Sheer, Total, Truly, Unmitigated, Unqualified, Utter, Veritable, Very

Absolve, Absolution Clear, Exculpate, Excuse, Pardon, Shrive

Absorb(ed), Absorbent, Absorbing, Absorption Assimilate, Autism, Blot, Consume, Desiccant, Devour, Digest, Dope, Drink, > ENGROSS, Imbibe, Ingest, Intent, Merge(r), Occlude, Occupy, Porous, Preoccupation, Rapt, Sorbefacient, Spongy, Unputdownable

Abstain(er), Abstemious, Abstinence, Abstinent Band of Hope, Celibacy, Chastity, Continent, Desist, Eschew, Forbear, Forgo, Maigre, Nazarite, Nephalism, Rechab(ite), Refrain, Resist, Sober, Temperate, TT

Abstract(ed), Abstraction Abrege, Abridge, Academic, Appropriate, Brief, Deduct, Digest, Discrete, Epitome, Essence, Metaphysical, Musing, Notional, Précis, Prepossessed, Prescind, Resumé, Reverie, Stable, Steal, Summary, Tachism

Absurd(ity) Apagoge, Fantastic, Farcical, Folly, Inept, Irrational, Laputan, Ludicrous, Nonsense, Paradox, Preposterous, Ridiculous, Silly, Solecism, Stupid, Toshy

Abundance, Abundant A-gogo, Ample, Bounty, Copious, Excess, Flood, Flush, Fouth, Fowth, Fruitful, Galore, Lashings, Mickle, Mine, Mint, Oodles, Opulent, Over, Plenitude, Plenteous, > PLENTIFUL, Plenty, Pleroma, Plethora, Plurisie, Prolific, Relative, Replete, Rich, Rife, Routh, Rowth, Sonce, Sonse, Store, Tallents, Teeming, Tons, Uberous

Abuse, Abusive Assail, Billingsgate, Blackguard, Flak, Fustilarian, Fustil(l)irian, Hail, Insult, Invective, Limehouse, Maltreat, Miscall, Misuse, Obloquy, Opprobrium, Philippic, Rail, Rampallian, Rate, Rayle, Revile, Satire, Scarab(ee), Scurrilous, Slang, Slate, Sledging, Snash, Solvent, Tirade, Vilify, Violate, Vituperation

Abut Adjoin, Border, Touch

Academic(ian) A, Della-Cruscan, Don, Erudite, Fellow, Hypothetic(al), Immortals, Literati, Master, Pedantic, PRA, RA, Reader, Rector

Academy Athenaeum, Dollar, Loretto, Lyceum, Military, St Cyr, Sandhurst, Seminary, West Point

Accelerate, Acceleration, Accelerator Bevatron, Collider, Cyclotron, G, Gal,

Gun, Hasten, Increase, Linac, Linear, Rev, Speed, Stringendo, Synchrotron

Accent(ed), Accentuate Acute, Beat, Breve, Brogue, Bur(r), Circumflex, Cut-glass, Doric, Drawl, Enclitic, Enhance, Grave, Hacek, Intonation, Kelvinside, Long, Macron, Martelé, Morningside, Mummerset, Nasal, Orthotone, Oxford, Oxytone, Pitch, Rhythm, Stress, Tittle, Tone, Twang

Accept(able), Acceptance, Accepted A, Accede, Admit, Adopt, Agree, Allow, Approbate, Bar, Believe, Buy, Can-do, Common, Consent, Cool, Cosher, Decent, Done, Grant, Kosher, Meet, Obey, On, Pocket, Putative, Settle, Stand, Swallow, Take, Tolerate, U, Wear, Widespread

Access(ible) Avenue, Card, Come-at-able, Credit, Door, Entrée, > ENTRY, Fit, Ingo, Key, Passe-partout, Password, Random, Recourse, Remote, Sequential, Spasm, Wayleave

Accessory, Accessories Abettor, Addition, Aide, Ally, Ancillary, Appendage, Appurtenance, Attribute, Bandanna, Bells and whistles, Cribellum, Findings, Staffage, Trappings, Trimming

Accident(al) Adventitious, Bechance, Blowdown, Blunder, Calamity, > CHANCE, Circumstance, Contingency, Contretemps, Crash, Disaster, Fall, Fluke, Hap, Hit and run, Mischance, Mishap, Promiscuous, Rear-ender, Shunt, Smash, Smash-up, Spill, Stramash, Wreck

Acclaim Accolade, Applaud, Brava, Bravo, Cheer, Eclat, Fame, Fanfare, Hail, Kudos, Ovation, Praise, Salute

Accolade Award, Honour, Palm, Token

Accommodate, Accommodation Adapt, B and B, Bedsit, Berth, Board, Botel, Bunkhouse, Camp, Chalet, Compromise, Crashpad, Flotel, Gaff, Gite, Grace and favour, Homestay, Hostel, Hotel, House, Lend, Loan, Lodge, Lodgement, Motel, > OBLIGE, Parador, Pension, Quarters, Rapprochement, Recurve, Room, Sorehon, Stabling, Stateroom, Steerage, Storage, Wharepuni

▷ **Accommodating** *may indicate* one word inside another

Accompany(ing), Accompanied (by), Accompaniment, Accompanist Accessory, Alberti, And, Attend, Chaperone, Chum, Concomitant, Consort, Continuo, Descant, > ESCORT, Harmonise, Herewith, Obbligato, Obligate, Obligato, Trimmings, Vamp

Accomplice Abettor, Aide, > ALLY, Collaborator, Confederate, Federarie, Partner, Shill, Stale

Accomplish(ed), Accomplishment Able, > ACHIEVE, Arch, Attain, Clever, Complete, Done, Effect, Master, Over, Perform, Polished, Realise, Ripe, Savant

Accord(ingly), According to After, Agree, Ala, Allow, As per, Attune, Chime, Consensus, Give, Grant, Harmony, Jibe, Meet, Sort, Thus

Accost Abord, Approach, Greet, Hail, Importune, Molest, Solicit, Tackle

Account(s) AC, Audit, Battels, Behalf, Bill, Cause, Charge, Chronicle, Current, Deposit, Discretionary, Enarration, Expense, Explain, Exposition, Ledger, Long, Memoir, Narration, Procès-verbal, Reason, Recital, Regest, Register, > REPORT, Repute, Resumé, Sake, Suspense, Swindlesheet, Tab, Tale, Thesis, Version

Accountable Responsible

Accountant Auditor, CA, Cost, Liquidator, Reckoner

Accumulate, Accumulation Adsorb, Aggregate, > AMASS, Augment, Backlog, Collect, Gather, Hoard, Lodg(e)ment, Pile, Uplay

Accuracy, Accurate(ly) Bang-on, Cocker, > CORRECT, Dead-on, Fair, Fidelity, Minute, Precise, Right, Spot-on, True, Word-perfect

Accusation, Accuse(d) Allege, Arraign, Attaint, Bill, Blame, Censure, Challenge, Charge, Criminate, Denounce, Dite, Gravamen, Impeach, Incriminate, Panel, Suspect, Tax, Threap, Threep, Traduce, Wight, Wite, Wyte

Accustom(ed) Acquaint, Attune, Enure, General, Habituate, Inure, Wont, Woon

Ace(s) Basto, Dinger, > **EXPERT**, Jot, Master, Mournival, One, Quatorze, Spadille, Spadill(i)o, Spot, Tib, Virtuoso, Wonderful

Ache, **Aching** Aitch, Die, Long, Mulligrubs, Nag, Otalgia, Pain, Stitch, Yearn, Yen

Achieve(ment) Accomplish, Acquisition, Attain, Come, Compass, > **EFFECT**, Exploit, Feat, Fulfil, Gain, Hatchment, Realise, Satisfice, Satisfy, Stroke, Succeed, Triumph, Trock, Troke, Truck

Acid(ity) Acrimony, Corrosive, Drop, EPA, Etchant, Hydroxy, Reaction, Ribosomal, Ribozyme, Solvent, Sour, Tart, Trans-fatty, Vinegar, Vitriol

Acknowledge(ment) Accept, Admit, Allow, Answer, Avow, Confess, Grant, Mea culpa, Nod, Own, Receipt, Recognise, Respect, Righto, Roger, Salute, Ta, Touché, Wilco

Acoustic(s) Harmonics, Sonics

Acquaint(ance), **Acquainted** Advise, Cognisant, Enlighten, Familiar, > **INFORM**, Knowledge, Nodding, Notify, Tell, Versed

Acquire, **Acquisition** Acquest, Earn, Ern, Gain, > **GET**, Land, Obtain, Procure, Purchase, Steal, Take-over, Usucap(t)ion

Acquit(tal) Assoil, Cleanse, Clear, Exonerate, Free, Loose, Loste, Pardon

Acrid, **Acrimony** Bitter(ness), Empyreuma, Rough, Sour, Surly

Acrobat(s), **Acrobatics** Equilibrist, Gymnast, Ropedancer, Splits, Trampoline, Tumbler

Across A, Ac, Athwart, Opposite, Over, Through

Act(ing), **Action**, **Acts** A, Affirmative, Antic, Assist, Auto, Barnstorm, Behave, Business, Camp, Case, Cause, Charade, Conduct, Deal, > **DEED**, Detinue, Do, Enabling, Excitement, Exert, Exploit, Factory, Feat, Feign, Function, Furthcoming, Habeas corpus, Homestead, Identic, Impersonate, Industrial, Juristic, Litigate, Locutionary, Measure, Method, Movement, Mutiny, Navigation, Perform(ance), Play, Positive, Practice, Pretence, Private, Procedure, Process, Qui tam, Reflex, Represent, Rising, Secondary, Serve, Showdown, Shtick, Simulate, Suit, Terminer, Test, Theatricise, Transitory, Treat, Truck, Turn, Union, War

Activate Arm, Goad, Spark, Spur, Stur, Styre, Trigger

Active, **Activist**, **Activity** A, Agile, Alert, At, Athletic, Brisk, Busy, Cadre, Deedy, DIY, Do(ing), Dynamited, Dynamo, Ecowarrior, Effectual, Energetic, Energic, Exercise, Extra-curricular, Floruit, Fluster, Game, Go-go, Goings-on, Hum, Hyper, Leish, Licht, Live, Mobile, Motile, Nimble, Ongo, On the go, Op, Operant, Play, Rambunctious, Residual, Sprightly, Springe, Spry, Sthenic, Surge, Third house, Vacuum, Voice, Wick, Wimble

Actor(s), **Actor-like** Agent, Alleyn, Artist, Ashe, Barnstormer, Benson, Betterton, Burbage, Cast, Character, Company, Diseur, Donat, Gable, Garrick, Gielgud, Guiser, Ham, Hamfatter, Heavy, Histrio(n), Jay, Juve(nile), Kean, Luvvie, MacReady, Mime, Mummer, Olivier, Performer, Player, Playfair, Roscian, Roscius, Savoyard, Sim, Stager, Strolling, Super, Thespian, Tragedian, Tree, Tritagonist, Trouper, Understudy, Wolfit

Actress Bankhead, Duse, Ingenue, Pierrette, Siddons, Soubrette, Terry, West

Actual(ity), **Actually** De facto, Entelechy, Literal, Live, Material, Real, Real-life, True, Very

Acute Astute, Dire, Fitché, > **INTENSE**, Keen, Quick-witted

Adage Aphorism, Gnome, Maxim, Motto, Paroemia, Proverb, Saw, Saying, Truism

Adamant Inexorable, Obdurate, Rigid, Unbending

Add(ed), **Addendum**, **Adder** Accrue, Adscititious, > **APPENDIX**, Attach, Cast, Coopt, Dub, Ech(e), Eik, Eke, Elaborate, Embroider, Enhance, Fortify, Insert, Lace, Reckon, Score, Spike, Sum, Summate, Tot(e), Total

Addict(ion), Addicted Abuser, Acidhead, Buff, Devotee, Etheromaniac, Fan, Fiend, Freak, Hophead, Hype, Jones, Joypopper, Junkie, Mainliner, Mania, Need, Pillhead, Pillpopper, Pothead, Shithead, Slave, Space-cadet, Speedfreak, User, Wino

Addition(al) Also, And, Codicil, Encore, Etc, > **EXTRA**, Increment, New, Odd, On, Other, Padding, Plus, PS, Rider, Spare, Suffix, Supplementary, Top-up

Address, Address system Accommodation, > **ATLAS**, Call, Dedication, Delivery, Diatribe, Discourse, Lecture, Orate, Poste-restante, Salute, Sermon, Speech, Tannoy®

Adept Able, Adroit, Dab, Deacon, Don, > **EXPERT**, Fit, Handy, Mahatma

Adequate Condign, Does, Due, Egal, Equal, Ere-now, Passable, Proper, > **SUFFICIENT**, Tolerable, Valid

Adhere(nt), Adherence, Adhesive Allegiance, Ally, Bond, Burr, Child, Cling, Conform, Dextrin, Disciple, Epoxy, Follower, Glue, Gum, Jain(a), Mucilage, Partisan, Resin, Sectator, Servitor, Sticker, Supporter, Synechia, Waterglass

Adjacent, Adjoining Bordering, Conterminous, Contiguous, Handy, Nigh

Adjourn(ment) Abeyance, Delay, > **POSTPONE**, Prorogate, Recess, Rise, Suspend

Adjunct Addition, Aid, Ancillary, Rider

Adjust(able), Adjustment, Adjuster Accommodate, Adapt, Attune, Coapt, Dress, Ease, Fit, Gang, Gauge, J'adoube, Modify, Modulate, Orientate, Prepare, Reduce, Regulate, Scantle, Sliding, Suit, Tram, Trim, True, Tune, Tweak

▷ **Adjust** *may indicate* an anagram

Ad-lib Wing it

Administer, Administration, Administrator Adhibit, Anele, Apply, Arrondissement, Bairiki, Control, > **DIRECT**, Dispence, Dispense, Executive, Intendant, Intinction, > **MANAGE**, Regime, Registrar, Run, Secretariat, Steward

Admirable, Admiration, Admire(d), Admirer Clinker, Clipper, Conquest, Crichton, Esteem, Estimable, > **EXCELLENT**, Flame, Fureur, Ho, Iconise, Idolater, Laudable, Partisan, Regard, Ripping, Toast, Tribute, Venerate, Wonder

Admission, Admit(ting), Admittance Accept, Access, Agree, Allow, Avow, Concede, > **CONFESS**, Enter, Entrée, Entry, Estoppel, Grant, Induct, Ingress, Initiate, Intromit, Ordain, Owe, Own, Recognise, Tho(ugh), Yield

Admonish, Admonition Chide, Lecture, Moralise, Rebuke, > **SCOLD**, Tip, Warn

Ado Bother, Bustle, Fuss

Adolescent Developer, Grower, Halflin, Juvenile, Neanic, Teenager, Veal, Youth

Adopt(ed) Accept, Affiliate, Assume, Embrace, Espouse, Father, Foster, Mother

Adoration, Adore Homage, Love, Pooja(h), Puja, Revere, Venerate, Worship

Adorn(ed), Adornment Attrap, Banderol, Bedeck, Bedight, Bejewel, Caparison, Clinquant, Deck, Dight, Drape, Embellish, Emblaze, Emblazon, Embroider, Enchase, Equip, Festoon, Flourish, Furnish, Garnish, Grace, Graste, Ornament, Riband, Tattoo, Tatu, Tinsel

Adroit Adept, Clever, Dextrous, Expert, Skilful

Adulate, Adulation Flatter(y), Praise, > **WORSHIP**

Adult Amadoda, Grown-up, Man, Mature, Upgrown, X

Advance(d) A, Abord, Accelerate, Ante, Approach, Assert, Charge, Develop, Extreme, Fore, Forge, Forward, Get on, Haut(e), Impress, Imprest, Incede, Late, Lend, > **LOAN**, March, Mortgage, Overture, Pass, Piaffe, Posit, Postulate, Precocious, Prefer, Prest, Process, Progress, > **PROMOTE**, Propose, Propound, Ripe, Rise, Sub, Submit, Tiptoe

Advantage(ous) Accrual, Aid, > **ASSET**, Avail, Batten, Benefit, Bisque, Boot, Edge, Emolument, Expedient, Exploit, Favour, Fruit, Gain, Grouter, Handicap, Handle,

Head-start, Help, Interess, Interest, Lever(age), Odds, One-up, Percentage, Plus, Privilege, Prize, Purchase, Salutary, Strength, Toe-hold, Use, Van, Whiphand

Adventure(r), Adventuress Argonaut, Assay, Buccaneer, Casanova, Conquistador, Emprise, Enterprise, Escapade, Filibuster, Gest, Lark, Mata Hari, Mercenary, Merchant, Picaresque, Picaro, Risk, Routier, Rutter, Swashbuckler, Vamp, Voyage

Adversary Cope(s)mate, Enemy, Foe

Adverse, Adversity Calamity, Cross, Down, Harrow, Misery, Reversal, Setback, Untoward, Woe

Advert(ise), Advertisement, Advertising Ad, Allude, Bark, Bill, Circular, Classified, Coign(e), Coin, Commercial, Copy, Display, Dodger, Flysheet, Hype, Jingle, Madison Avenue, Mailshot, Noise, > **NOTICE**, Parade, Placard, Plug, Promo, Promote, Promulgate, Prospectus, Puff, Quoin, Refer, Sky-write, Splash, Stunt, Subliminal, Teaser, Throwaway, Tout, Trailer, Trawl

Advice Conseil, Counsel, > **GUIDANCE**, Guideline, Information, Invoice, Opinion, Read, Recommendation, Re(e)de

Advise(d), Adviser, Advisable Acquaint, CAB, Counsel, Enlighten, Expedient, Inform, Instruct, Mentor, Oracle, Peritus, Prudent, > **RECOMMEND**, Tutor, Urge, Wise

Advocate(d) Agent, Argue, Attorney, Back, Devil's, Exponent, Gospel, Lawyer, Move, Paraclete, Peat, Peddle, Pleader, Pragmatist, Preach, Proponent, Syndic, Urge

Aerial Antenna, Dipole, Dish, Ethereal, Loop, Parabolic

Aerodrome *see* **AIRPORT**

Aerofoil Spoiler

▶ **Aeroplane** *see* **AIRCRAFT**

Affable Amiable, Avuncular, Benign, Suave, Urbane

Affair(s) Amour, Business, Concern, Current, Event, Fight, Go, Intrigue, Matter, Pash, Pi(d)geon, Pidgin, Ploy, Relationship, Res, Romance, Shebang, Subject, Thing

Affect(ed), Affectation, Affection(ate) Air, Alter, Breast, Camp, Chi-chi, Concern, Crazy, Endearment, Euphuism, Foppery, Hit, Ladida, Lovey-dovey, Mimmick, Minnick, Minnock, Mouth-made, Phoney, > **POSE**, Poseur, Precieuse, Preciosity, Pretence, Spoilt, Stag(e)y, Storge, Susceptible, Sway, Tender, Twee, Unction, Unnatural

Affiliate, Affiliation Adopt, Associate, Merge, Unite

Affinity Bro, Kin(ship), Penchant, Rapport, Tie

Affirm(ative), Affirmation Assert, Attest, Maintain, Predicate, Protestation, Uh-huh, > **VERIFY**

Afflict(ed), Affliction Asthma, Cross, Cup, Curse, Disease, Furnace, Harass, Hurt, Lumbago, Molest, Nosology, Palsy, Persecute, Pester, Plague, Scourge, Smit, Sore, > **SORROW**, Stricken, Teen, Tene, Tic, Tribulation, > **TROUBLE**, Unweal, Visitation, Woe

Affluence, Affluent Abundance, Fortune, Opulence, Wealth

Afford Bear, Manage, Offer, Provide, Spare

Affront Assault, Defy, Facer, > **INSULT**, > **OFFEND**, Outrage, Scandal, Slight, Slur

Afraid Adrad, Alarmed, Chicken, Fearful, Funk, Rad, Regretful, Scared, Timorous, Windy, Yellow

Africa(n) Abyssinian, Akan, Angolan, Ashanti, Baganda, Bambara, Bantu, Barbary, Barotse, Basotho, Basuto, Beento, Bemba, Beninese, Berber, Biafran, Bintu, Black, Boer, Botswana, Cairene, Carthaginian, Chewa, Chichewa, Congo(l)ese, Cushitic, Damara, Dinka, Duala, Dyula, Efik, Eritrean, Ethiopian,

Fang, Fanti, Fingo, Flytaal, Fula(h), Gabonese, Galla, Gambian, Ganda, Gazankulu, Grikwa, Griqua, Gullah, Hamite, Hausa, Herero, Hottentot, Hutu, Ibibi, Ibo, Igbo, Impi, Kabyle, Kaf(f)ir, Kenyan, Khoikhoi, Kikuyu, Kongo, Lango, Lesotho, Liberian, Libyan, Lowveld, Lozi, Luba, Luo, Maghreb, Maghrib, Malawi, Malian, Malinke, Mande, Mandingo, Masai, Mashona, Matabele, Mende, Moor, Moroccan, Mossi, Mozambican, Mswahili, Munt(u), Mzee, Nama, Nama(qua), Namibian, Negrillo, Nguni, Nilot(e), Nubian, Nuer, Nyanja, Oromo, Ovambo, Pedi, Pied noir, Pondo, Rastafarian, Rhodesian, San, Shilluk, Shluh, Shona, Shono, Somali, Songhai, Sotho, Soweto, Sudanese, Susu, Swahili, Swazi, Temne, Tiv, Tonga, Transkei, Transvaal, Tshi, Tsonga, Tswana, Tuareg, Tutsi, Twi, Ugandan, Venda, Voltaic, Waswahili, Wolof, X(h)osa, Yoruban, Zairean, Zulu

After(wards) About, At, Behind, Beyond, Eft, Epi-, > LATER, On, Past, Rear, Since, Sine, Subsequent

Afterimage Photogene

▷ **After injury** *may indicate* an anagram

Afternoon A, Arvo, PM, Postmeridian, Undern

Afterpiece, Afterthought Addendum, Codicil, Epimetheus, Exode, Footnote, Note, PS, Supplement

Again Afresh, Agen, Anew, Back, Bis, De novo, Ditto, Do, Eft, Eftsoons, Encore, Iterum, More, Moreover, O(v)er, Re-, Recurrence, Reprise, Than, Then

Against A, Anti, Beside, Con, Counter, Gainsayer, Into, Nigh, On, Opposing, To, V, Versus

Age(d), Ages, Aging Ae, Aeon, Antique, Chellean, Cycle, Dark, Eon, Epact, Epoch(a), Era, Eternity, Generation, Golden, Heroic, Ice, Iron, Jurassic, Kalpa, Mature, Middle, Millennium, Neolithic, New, Paleolithic, Period, Senescence, Space, Stone

Agency, Agent Ambassador, Bailiff, Broker, Bureau, Catalyst, Cat's paw, Complexone, Consul, Countryside, Crown, Dating, Developing, Disclosing, Distributor, Doer, Double, Emissary, Envoy, Escort, Estate, Exciseman, Executor, Factor, Forwarding, Free, G-man, Go-between, Hand, House, Implement, Indian, Influence, Instrument, Intermediary, Law, Legate, Literary, Magic bullet, Means, Medium, Mercantile, Mole, Narco, Nerve, OO, Oxidizing, Parliamentaire, Parliamentary, Patent, Penetration, Pinkerton, Press, Proxy, Realtor, Reducing, Rep(resentative), Reuters, Riot, Road, Runner, Salesman, Secret (service), Shipping, Solvent, Spy, Tass, Third party, Ticket, Training, Travel, UNESCO, Virino, Voice, Wetting, Wire service

Agenda Business, Programme, Remit, Schedule

Aggravate Annoy, Inflame, Irk, Needle, Nettle, Provoke, Try, Vex

Aggression, Aggressive, Aggressor Attack, Belligerent, Bullish, Butch, Defiant, Enemy, Feisty, Foe, Gungho, Hawk, Invader, Militant, On-setter, Pushing, Rambo, Rampant, Shirty, Truculent, Wild

Agile Acrobatic, Deft, Lissom(e), Nifty, Nimble, Quick, Spry, Supple, Swank

Agitate(d), Agitation, Agitator Activist, Ado, Agitprop, Boil, Bolshie, Bother, Churn, Commotion, Convulse, Distraught, > DISTURB, Ebullient, Emotion, Excite, Extremist, Fan, Ferment, Firebrand, Fluster, Frenzy, Fuss, Goad, Heat, Hectic, Lather, Militant, Perturb, Pother, Rattle, Restless, Rouse, Ruffle, Seethed, Stir(-up), Tailspin, Tizzy, Toss, Tremor, Trouble, Turmoil, Twitchy, Welter, Whisk

▷ **Agitate** *may indicate* an anagram

Agonise, Agony Ache, Anguish, Ecstasy, Heartache, > PAIN, Torment, Torture

Agree(ing), Agreed, Agreement Accede, Accept, Accord, Acquiescence, Allow, Amen, Analogy, Assent, Ausgleich, Aye, Cartel, Chime, Coincide, Collective, Compact, Comply, Concert, Concord(at), Concur, Conform, > CONSENT, Contract, Convection, Correspond, Covenant, Cushty, Deal, Deffo, Entente, Equate,

Agreeable | 8

Gentleman's, Harmony, Homologous, Knock-for-knock, League, Like-minded, National, Nod, Nudum pactum, Okay, Pact, Pair, Plant, Prenuptial, Procedural, Productivity, Repurchase, Right(o), Roger, Sanction, Service, Side, Square, Standstill, Substantive, Suit, Sympathy, Synchronise, Tally, Technology, Trade, Treaty, Union, Unison, Wilco, Yea, Yes

Agreeable Amene, Harmonious, Pleasant, Sapid, Sweet, Well-disposed, Willing, Winsome

▷ **Ague(ish)** *may indicate* an anagram

Ahead Anterior, Before, Foreship, Forward, Frontwards, Onward, Up

Aid(s), **Aide** Accessory, Adjutant, Assist, Decca, > **DEPUTY**, Galloper, Grant, Help, Key, Legal, Lend-lease, Monitor, Optophone, PA, Relief, Serve, Slim, Succour, Support, Visual

Ail(ment) Affect, Afflict(ion), Complaint, Croup, Disease, Malady, Narks, Pink-eye, Pip, Sickness

Aim Approach, Aspire, Bead, Bend, End, Ettle, Eye, Goal, Hub, Intent, Level, Mark, Mission, Object, Plan, Plank, Point, Purpose, Reason, Sake, Seek, Sight(s), Target, Tee, Telos, Train, View, Visie, Vizy, Vizzie

Aimless Drifting, Erratic, Haphazard, Random, Unmotivated

Air(s), **Airer**, **Airy** Ambience, Atmosphere, Attitude, Aura, Bearing, Ether(eal), Expose, Inflate, Lift, Lullaby, Madrigal, Manner, Melody, Mien, Ozone, Parade, Screen, Serenade, Shanty, > **TUNE**, Ventilate, Wind

Aircraft, **Airship** Aerodyne, Aerostat, Angels, AST, Auster, Autoflare, Autogiro, Autogyro, Aviette, Avion, Biplane, Blimp, Brabazon, Bronco, Camel, Canard, Canberra, Chaser, Chopper, Coleopter, Comet, Concorde, Convertiplane, Corsair, Crate, Cropduster, Cyclogiro, Delta-wing, Dirigible, Doodlebug, Drone, Eagle, F, Ferret, Fixed-wing, Flying wing, Fokker, Freedom-fighter, Freighter, Galaxy, Glider, Gotha, Gyrodyne, Gyroplane, Hang-glider, Harrier, Hawkeeze, Heinkel, Helicopter, Hercules, Hunter, Hurricane, Interceptor, Intruder, Jet star, Jumbo, Jump-jet, Kite, Lancaster, Liberator, Lifting-body, Messerschmitt, Microlight, Microlite, MIG, Mirage, Monoplane, Mosquito, Moth, Multiplane, Nightfighter, Nightflider, Oerlikon, Orion, Ornithopter, Orthopter, Parasol, Penguin, Phantom, > **PLANE**, Provider, Prowler, Ramjet, Rigid, Rotaplane, Runabout, Scramjet, Semi-rigid, Skyhawk, Sopwith, Sopwith Camel, Spitfire, SST, Starfighter, Starlifter, Stealth bomber, STOL, Stratocruiser, Stratotanker, Stuka, Super Sabre, Sweptwing, Swing-wing, Tankbuster, Taube, Taxiplane, Thunderbolt, Thunderchief, Tomcat, Tornado, Tracker, Trident, Tri-jet, Triplane, Turbo-jet, Turbo-prop, Turboramjet, Vigilante, Viking, Viscount, Voodoo, VTOL, Wild weasel, Zeppelin

Aircraftsman, **Airman** AC, Aeronaut, Kiwi, LAC, RAF

Airline, **Airway** Aeroflot, Anthem, BAC, BEA, Duct, Larynx, Lot, SAS, S(ch)norkel, TWA, Weasand(-pipe), Windpipe

▶ **Airman** *see* AIRCRAFTSMAN; FLIER

Airport Drome, Entebbe, Faro, Gander, Gatwick, Heliport, Idlewild, Kennedy, Landing strip, Lod, Luton, Lympne, Orly, Rotor-station, Runway, Shannon, Stansted, Stolport, Vertiport, Wick

Air-tight Hermetic, Indisputable, Sealed

Akin Alike, Cognate, Congener, Kindred

Alabaster Oriental

Alarm Alert, Arouse, Bell, Bleep, Caution, Dismay, False, Fricht, Fright, Ghast, Larum, Panic, Perturb, Rouse, Siren, Smoke, Startle, Tirrit, Tocsin, Warn, Yike(s)

Alas Ah, Alack, Ay, Eheu, Ha, Haro, Harrow, Io, Lackadaisy, Lackaday, O, Oh, Ohone, O me, Waesucks, Waly, Well-a-day, Wellanear, Wel(l)away, Woe

Albatross Alcatras, Golf, Gooney(-bird), Omen, Onus

Alchemic, **Alchemist**, **Alchemy** Adept, Brimstone, Faust(us), Hermetic(s), Multiplier, Quicksilver, Sal ammoniac, Sorcery, Spagyric, Spagyrist, Witchcraft

Alcohol(ic) Acrolein, Aldehyde, Bibulous, Booze, Borneol, Catechol, Cetyl, Chaptalise, Cholesterol, Choline, Citronellol, Cresol, Diol, Dipsomaniac, Drinker, Ethal, Ethanol, Ethyl, Farnesol, Firewater, Fusel-oil, Geraniol, Glycerin(e), Grain, Hard, Inebriate, Inositol, Isopropyl, Lauryl, Linalool, Mannite, Mannitol, Mercaptan, Mescal, Methanol, Meths, Nerol, Phytol, Propyl, Rotgut, Rubbing, Sorbitol, Sphingosine, Spirits, Sterol, Wino, Xylitol

Alcove Apse, Bay, Bole, Dinette, Niche, Recess

Ale, **Alehouse** Audit, Barleybree, Beer, Humpty-dumpty, Lamb's wool, Light, Morocco, Nappy, Nog, Nogg, October, Purl, Real, Stout, Swats, Tiddleywink, Tipper, Whitsun, Wort, Yard, Yill

Alert Arrect, Astir, Attentive, Aware, Gleg, Gogo, Intelligent, Qui vive, Red, Scramble, Sharp, Sprack, Sprag, Stand-to, Vigilant, Volable, Wary, Watchful

Alga(e) Anabaena, Blanketweed, Chlorella, Conferva, Desmid, Diatom, Dulse, Heterocontae, Isokont, Jelly, Nostoc, Pleuston, Pond scum, Prokaryon, Protococcus, Seaweed, Spirogyra, Star-jelly, Stonewort, Ulothrix, Ulotrichales, Valonia, Volvox, Zooxanthella

Algebra Boolean, Linear, Quadratics

Alias Aka, Epithet, Moni(c)ker, Pen-name, Pseudonym

Alibi Excuse, Watertight

Alien(ate), **Alienation** A-effect, Amortise, Disaffect, Ecstasy, Estrange, ET, Exotic, External, Foreign, Hostile, Martian, Metic, Outlandish, Philistine, Repugnant, Strange(r)

Alight Alowe, Availe, Detrain, Disembark, Dismount, In, Lambent, Land, Lit, Perch, Pitch, Rest, Settle

Align Arrange, Associate, Collimate, Dress, Juxtapose, Marshal, Orient

▸ **Alike** *see* LIKE

Alimentary Oesophagus, Pharynx

Alive Alert, Animated, Breathing, Extant, Quick

Alkali(ne), **Alkaloid** Antacid, Apomorphine, Base, Bebeerine, Berberine, Betaine, Borax, Brucine, Capsaicin, Codeine, Colchicine, Emetin(e), Ephedrine, Gelsemin(in)e, Guanidine, Harmaline, Harmin(e), Hyoscine, Lobeline, Lye, Narceen, Narceine, Nicotine, Papaverine, Piperine, Potash, Quinine, Reserpine, Rhoeadine, Scopolamine, Soda, Sparteine, Thebaine, Theobromine, Theophylline, Tropine, Veratrin(e), Vinblastine, Vincristine, Yohimbine

All A, > ENTIRE, Entity, Finis, Omni, Pan, Quite, Sum, > TOTAL, Toto, Tutti, Whole

All at once Holus-bolus, Suddenly

Allay Calm, Lessen, Quieten, Soothe

Allegation, **Allege** Assert, Aver, Claim, Obtend, Plead, Purport, Represent, Smear

Allegiance Faith, Foy, Loyalty

Allegory, **Allegorical** Apologue, Fable, Mystic, Myth, Parable

Alleviate Allege, Calm, Mitigate, Mollify, Palliate, > RELIEVE, Temper

Alley Aisle, Blind, Bonce, Bowling, Corridor, Ginnel, Lane, Laura, Marble, Passage, Tin Pan, Vennel, Walk, Wynd

Alliance Agnation, Axis, Bloc, Cartel, Coalition, Combine, Compact, Federacy, > LEAGUE, Marriage, NATO, Syndicate, Union

Alligator Al(l)igarta, Avocado, Cayman

Allocate, **Allocation** Allot, Apportion(ment), Earmark, Placement, Ration,

Share, Zone

Allot(ment), **Allow(ance)**, **Allowed**, **Allowing** Alimony, Allocation, Although, Award, Budget, Confess, Discount, Excuse, Grant, Indulge, Latitude, Let, Licit, Pension, > **PERMIT**, Portion, Quota, Ration, Rebate, Sanction, Share(-out), Stipend, Suffer, Though, Tolerance, Yield

▶ **Allow** *see* ALLOT

Alloy Albata, Alnico®, Amalgam, Babbit, Bell-metal, Billon, Brass, Britannia metal, Bronze, Cermet, Chrome(l), Compound, Constantan, Cupronickel, Duralumin®, Electron, Electrum, Gunmetal, Invar®, Kamacite, Latten, Magnalium, Magnox, Marmem, Mischmetal, Mix, Monel®, Nicrosilal, Nimonic, Nitinol, Occamy, Oreide, Orichalc, Ormolu, Oroide, Osmiridium, Paktong, Pewter, Pinchbeck, Platinoid, Potin, Shakudo, Shibuichi, Similor, Solder, Spelter, Steel, Stellite®, Tambac, Terne, Tombac, Tombak, Tutenag, Zircal(l)oy, Zircoloy

▷ **Alloy** *may indicate* an anagram

Allright A1, Assuredly, Fit, Hale, Hunky(-dory), OK, Safe, Tickety-boo, Well

All the same Nath(e)less, Nevertheless

Allude, **Allusion** Hint, Imply, Innuendo, Mention, Refer, Reference, Suggest

Allure, **Alluring** Agaçant(e), Charm, Circe, Decoy, Glam, Glamour, Magnet(ic), SA, Seduce, Seductive, Tempt, Trap, Trepan, Vamp

Alluvium Carse

Ally, **Allied** Accomplice, Agnate, Aide, Alley, Alliance, Backer, Belamy, Cognate, Colleague, Dual, German(e), Holy, Marble, Marmoreal, Partner, Plonker, Related, Taw, Unholy

Almanac Calendar, Clog, Ephemeris, Nostradamus, Whitaker's, Wisden, Zadkiel

Almost Anear, Anigh, Most, Near, Nigh(ly), Ripe, Une(a)th, Virtually, Well-nigh, Welly

Alms Awmous, Charity, Dole, Handout

Alone Hat, Jack, Lee-lane, Onely, Secco, Separate, Single, Singly, Sola, Solo, Solus, Unaccompanied, Unaided, Unholpen

Along, **Alongside** Abeam, Aboard, Abreast, Apposed, Beside, By, Parallel

Alphabet ABC, Black-out, Brahmi, Braille, Cyrillic, Deaf, Devanagari, Estrang(h)elo, Futhark, Futhorc, Futhork, Glagol, Glagolitic, Glossic, Grantha, Hangul, Horn-book, International, ITA, Kana, Kanji, Katakana, Kufic, Latin, Manual, Nagari, Og(h)am, Pangram, Phonetic, Pinyin, Romaji, Roman, Runic, Signary, Syllabary

Alpine, **Alps** Australian, Bernese, Cottian, Dinaric, Gentian, Graian, Julian, Laburnum, Lepontine, Maritime, Matterhorn, Pennine, Rhaetian, Savoy, Southern, Transylvanian, Tyrol

Also Add, And, Eke, Item, Likewise, Moreover, Too, Und

Altar, **Altar-cloth**, **Altarpiece** Dossal, Dossel, Polyptych, Retable, Shrine, Tabula

Alter Adapt, Adjust, Bushel, Change, Correct, Customise, Evolve, Falsify, Lib, Modify, Modulate, Mutate, Recast, Revise, Transpose, Up-end, > **VARY**

Alternate, **Alternating**, **Alternation**, **Alternative** Boustrophedon, Bypass, Exchange, Instead, Metagenesis, > **OPTION**, Ossia, Other, Rotate, Solidus, Staggered, Systaltic, Tertian, Variant

▷ **Alter(native)** *may indicate* an anagram

▷ **Alternately** *may indicate* every other letter

Although Admitting, Albe(e), All-be, But, Even, Howsomever, Whereas, While

Altitude Elevation, Height

▷ **Altogether** *may indicate* words to be joined

Altruistic Heroic, Humane, Philanthropic, Selfless, Unselfish
Alumnus Graduate, OB
Always Algate(s), Ay(e), Constant, E'er, Eternal, Ever(more), Forever, I, Immer, Sempre, Still
Amass Accumulate, Assemble, Collect, Heap, Hoard, Pile, Upheap
Amateur(s) A, AA, Armchair, Beginner, Corinthian, Dilettante, Diy, Ham, Inexpert, L, Lay, Novice, Tiro, Tyro
Amaze(d), Amazement, Amazing Astonish, Astound, Awhape, Cor, Criv(v)ens, Dumbfound, Flabbergast, Gobsmack, Goodnow, Grace, Incredible, Magical, Monumental, O, Open-eyed, Open-mouthed, Perplex, Poleaxe, Pop-eyed, Stagger, Stupefaction, Stupendous, Thunderstruck
Ambassador Diplomat, Elchee, Elchi, Eltchi, Envoy, HE, Internuncio, Ledger, Legate, Leiger, Minister, Nuncio, Plenipo, Plenipotentiary
Ambience Aura, Milieu, Setting
Ambiguous, Ambiguity Amphibology, Cryptic, Delphic, Double, Enigmatic, Epicene, Equivocal, Loophole, Weasel words
Ambit Scope
Ambition, Ambitious Aim, Aspiring, Careerism, Drive, Emulate, Goal, Go-getter, High-flier, Keen, Office-hunter, Purpose, Pushy, Rome-runner
Amble Meander, Mosey, Pace, Saunter, Stroll
Ambulance, Ambulanceman Blood-wagon, Pannier, Van, Yellow-flag, Zambu(c)k
Ambush(ed) Ambuscade, Bushwhack, Embusque, Latitant, Lurch, Perdu(e), Trap, Waylay
Amen Ammon, Approval, Inshallah, Verify
Amend(ment) Alter, Change, Expiate, Fifth, Redress, Reform, Repair, Restore, > REVISE, Satisfy
▷ **Amend** *may indicate* an anagram
America(n) Algonki(a)n, Algonqu(i)an, Am, Caddo, Cajun, Carib, Chicano, Chickasaw, Copperskin, Digger, Doughface, Down-easter, Federalist, Flathead, Fox, Gringo, Interior, Joe, Jonathan, Latino, Mistec, Mixtec, Native, Norteno, Olmec, Paisano, Salish, Stateside, Statesman, Statist, Tar-heel, Tico, Tupi, Uncle Sam, US(A), WASP, Yankee, Yanqui
Amethyst Oriental
Amiable Friendly, Genial, Gentle, Inquiline, Sweet, Warm
Amid(st) Among, Atween, Between, Inter, Twixt
Amine Putrescine, Spermine
Amiss Awry, Ill, Up, Wrong
Ammunition Ammo, Buckshot, Bullets, Chain-shot, Grenade, Round, Shot, Slug, Tracer
Among Amid(st), In, Within
Amorous(ly) Erotic, Fervent, Lustful, Warm
Amount Come, Dose, Element, Figure, Lashings, Levy, Lot, Number, Ocean, Pot(s), Premium, Price, Quantity, Quantum, Span, Stint, Throughput, Volume, Whale, Wheel
Amphibian, Amphibious Amb(l)ystoma, Amtrack, Anura, Axolotl, Batrachian, Caecilia, Caecilian, Desman, Eft, Frog, Guana, Hassar, Mermaid, Mudpuppy, Newt, Olm, Proteus, Rana, Salamander, Salientia, Seal, Tadpole, Urodela(n), Urodele, Weasel
Amphitheatre Bowl, Coliseum, Colosseum, Ring, Stage
Ample Bellyful, Copious, Enough, Generous, Good, Large, Opulent, Profuse, Rich,

Roomy, Round, Uberous, Voluminous

Amplifier, Amplify Booster, Double, Eke, Enlarge, Hailer, Laser, Loud hailer, Maser, Megaphone, Push-pull, Solion, Transistor, Treble

Amulet Charm, Fetish, Pentacle, Talisman, Tiki, Token

Amuse(ment), Amusing(ly) Caution, Disport, Diversion, Divert, Drole, Droll, Game, Gas, Glee, Hoot, Killing, Levity, Light, Occupy, Pleasure, Popjoy, Priceless, Rich, Scream, Slay, Solace, > **SPORT**, Tickle, Titillate

▶ **An** see A

Anaesthetic, Anaesthetise, Anaesthetist Analgesic, Avertin®, Benzocaine, Bupivacaine, Chloroform, Cocaine, Epidural, Ether, Eucain(e), Freeze, Gas, General, Halothane, Jabber, Ketamine, Lignocaine, Local, Metopryl, Morphia, Novocaine, Number, Opium, Orthocaine, Procaine, Stovaine, Trike, Urethan(e)

Analogous, Analogy Akin, Corresponding, Like, Parallel, Similar

Analyse(r), Analysis Alligate, Anagoge, Anatomy, Assess, Breakdown, Construe, Emic, Eudiometer, Examine, Fourier, Harmonic, Parse, Process, Qualitative, Quantative, Quantitative, Rundown, Scan(sion), Semantics, Sift, Spectral, Systems, Test

▷ **Analysis** may indicate an anagram

Analyst Alienist, Jung, Psychiatrist, Shrink, Trick cyclist

Anarchist, Anarchy Black Hand, Bolshevist, Chaos, Kropotkin, Provo, Rebel, Revolutionary, Trotskyite

Anatomy, Anatomist Bones, Framework, Histology

Ancestor, Ancestral, Ancestry Adam, Avital, Descent, Extraction, For(e)bear, Gastraea, Humanoid, Lin(e)age, Parent, Proband, Profectitious, Progenitor, Propositus, Roots, Sire, Tree

Anchor(age) Atrip, Bower, Cell, Deadman, Drag, Eremite, Grapnel, Hawse, Hermit, Kedge, Killick, Killock, Laura, Mud-hook, Nail, Ride, Roads(tead), Root, Scapa Flow, Sheet, Spithead, Stock

Ancient Antediluvian, Archaic, Auld-warld, Early, Gonfanoner, Historic, Hoary, Iago, Immemorial, Lights, Neolithic, Ogygian, Old-world, Primeval, Primitive, Pristine, Ur, Veteran

And Als(o), Ampassy, Ampersand, Amperzand, Ampussyand, Besides, Et, Furthermore, 'n', Plus, Und

Anecdote(s) Ana, Exemplum, Story, Tale, Yarn

Anew De integro, De novo

Angel(s) Abdiel, Adramelech, Apollyon, Archangel, Ariel, Arioch, Asmadai, Azrael, Backer, Banker, Beelzebub, Belial, Benefactor, Cake, Cherub, Clare, Deva, Dominion, Dust, Eblis, Falls, Gabriel, Guardian, Hierarchy, Host, Investor, Israfel, Ithuriel, Lucifer, Power, Principality, Raphael, Recording, Rimmon, Seraph, Spirit, St, Throne, Uriel, Uzziel, Virtue, Watcher, Zadkiel, Zephiel

Angelica Archangel

Anger, Angry > **ANNOY**, Bile, Black, Bristle, Choler(ic), Conniption, Cross, Dander, Displeased, Dudgeon, Enrage, Exasperation, Face, Fury, Gram, Heat, Horn-mad, Incense, Inflame, Infuriate, Iracund, Irascible, Ire, Kippage, Livid, Mad, Monkey, Moody, Nettle, Pique, Provoke, Radge, Rage, Rampant, Ratty, Renfierst, Rile, Roil, Rouse, Sore, Spleen, Steam, Stroppy, Tamping, Tantrum, Tarnation, Teen(e), Temper, Tene, Tooshie, Vex, Vies, Waspish, Waxy, Wound up, Wrath, Wroth, Yond

Angle(d), Angular Acute, Altitude, Argument, Aspect, Axil, Azimuthal, Canthus, Cast, Catch, Chiliagon, Coign, Complementary, Conjugate, Contrapposto, Corner, Cos, Critical, Deidre, Diedral, Diedre, Dihedral, Elbow, Elevation, Ell, Fish, Fish-hook, Fork, Geometry, Gonion, Hade, Hip, In, L, Laggen, Laggin, Mitre, Oblique, Obtuse, Parallax, Pediculate, Perigon, Piend, Pitch, Plane, Quoin,

Radian, Rake, Re-entrant, Reflex, Right, Sally, Sine, Sinical, Solid, Steeve, Steradian, Supplementary, Sweepback, Trotline, Vertical, Viewpoint, Washin, Weather

Anglican(s) CE-men, Conformist, Episcopal

Angora Goat, Mohair, Rabbit

Anguish(ed) Agony, Distress, Gip, Gyp, Hag-ridden, Heartache, Misery, > PAIN, Pang, Sorrow, Throes, > TORMENT, Torture, Woe

Animal(s) Acrita, Anoa, Armadillo, Atoc, Bag, Bandog, Barbastel, Beast, Bestial, Brute, Cariacou, Carnal, Chalicothere, Coati, Creature, Criollo, Critter, Fauna, Felis, Gerbil, Herd, Ichneumon, Jacchus, Jerboa, Kinkajou, Klipdas, Mammal, Marmoset, Marmot, Menagerie, Moose, Noctule, Oribi, Parazoon, Pet, Protozoa, Pudu, Quagga, Rac(c)oon, Rhesus, Sensual, Sloth, Stud, Tarsier, Teledu, Urson, Waler, Xenurus, Yapock, Zerda, Zoo

Animate(d), Animation Activate, Actuate, Arouse, Biophor, Ensoul, Excite, Fire, Hot, Inspire, Live, Morph, Mosso, Rouse, Spritely, Verve

Animosity Enmity, Friction, Hostility, Malice, Pique, Rancour

Ankle Coot, Cuit, Cute, Hock, Hucklebone, Knee, Malleolus

Annal(s) Acta, Archives, Chronicles, Register

Annex(e) Acquire, Add, Affiliate, Attach, Codicil, Extension, Subjoin

Annihilate Destroy, Erase, Exterminate, Slay

Anniversary Birthday, Feast, Jubilee, Obit, Yahrzeit

Announce(r), Announcement Banns, Bellman, Biil(ing), Blazon, Bulletin, Communiqué, Decree, Divulgate, Gazette, Herald, Hermes, Inform, Intimate, Meld, Newsflash, Post, Preconise, Proclaim, Promulgate, Pronunciamente, Publish, Release, > REPORT, Speaker(ine), State, Trumpet

Annoy(ance), Annoyed, Annoying Aggravate, Aggrieve, Anger, Antagonise, Badger, Bother, Bug, Bugbear, Chagrin, Disturb, Drat, Fash, Fleabite, Frab, Fumed, Gall, Harass, Hatter, Hector, Hip, Huff, Hump, Incense, Irk, > IRRITATE, Miff, Mischief, Molest, Nag, Nark, Nettle, Noisome, Peeve, Pesky, Pester, Pipsqueak, Pique, Rankle, Rats, Resentful, Ride, Rile, Roil, Rub, Shirty, Tiresome, Tracasserie, Try, Vex

Annual, Annuity Book, Etesian, > FLOWER, Half-hardy, Hardy, Pension, Perpetuity, Rente, Tontine, Yearbook, Yearly

Annul(ment) Abolish, Abrogate, Cashier, Cassation, Dissolution, Irritate, Negate, Repeal, Rescind, Reversal, Revoke, Vacatur, > VOID

▷ **Anomaly** *may indicate* an anagram

Anon Again, Anew, Later, Soon

Anonymous Adespota, Anon, A.N.Other, Faceless, Grey, Impersonal, Somebody, Unnamed

Answer(ing), Answer(s) Acknowledge, Amoebaean, Ans, Antiphon, Because, Comeback, Crib (sheet), Defence, Echo, Key, Lemon, Light, No, Oracle, Rebuttal, Rebutter, Rein, Rejoin(der), Repartee, Reply, Rescript, Respond, Response, Retort, Return, Riposte, Serve, Sol, Solution, Solve, Verdict, Yes

Ant(s), Anthill Amazon, Army, Bull(dog), Carpenter, Colony, Driver, Dulosis, Emmet, Ergataner, Ergates, Fire, Formic, Formicary, Myrmecoid, Myrmidon, Nasute, Neuter, Pharaoh, Pismire, Sauba, Soldier, Termite, Thief, Velvet, White, Wood

Ante Bet, Punt, Stake

Ant-eater Aardvark, Echidna, Edental, Manis, Numbat, Pangolin, S(e)ladang, Spiny, Tamandu, Tamandua, Tapir

Antelope Addax, Blackbuck, Blaubok, Blesbok, Bloubok, Bluebuck, Bongo, Bontebok, Bubal(is), Bushbuck, Chamois, Chikara, Dikdik, Duiker, Duyker,

Dzeren, Eland, Elk, Gazelle, Gemsbok, Gerenuk, Gnu, Goral, Grysbok, Hartbees, Hartebeest, Impala, Inyala, Kaama, Kid, Klipspringer, Kob, Kongoni, Koodoo, Kudu, Lechwe, Madoqua, Nagor, Nilgai, Nilgau, Nyala, Nylghau, Oribi, Oryx, Ourebi, Pale-buck, Pallah, Prongbuck, Pronghorn, Puku, Pygarg, Reebok, Reedbuck, Rhebok, Sable, Saiga, Sasin, Sassaby, Serow, Sitatunga, Situtunga, Steenbok, Steinbock, Stemback, Stembok, Suni, Takin, Thar, Topi, Tragelaph, Tsessebe, Waterbuck, Wildebeest

Antenna Aerial, Dipole, Dish, Horn, Sensillum, TVRO

Anterior Anticous, Earlier, Front, Prior

Anthem Hymn, Introit, Isodica, Marseillaise, Motet(t), National, Psalm, Responsory, Song, Theme, Tract

Anthology Album, Ana, Chrestomathy, Digest, Divan, Florilegium, Garland, Pick, Spicilege

Anti Against, Agin, Con, Hostile

Anti-bacterial, **Antibiotic** Actinomycin, Bacitracin, Cephalosporin, Cloxacillin, Colistin, Doxorubicin, Doxycycline, Drug, Erythromycin, Gentamicin, Gramicidin, Griseofulvin, Interferon, Interleukin, Kanamycin, Lincomycin, Lineomycin, Methicillin, Mitomycin, Neomycin, Nystatin, Opsonin, Oxacillin, Oxytetracycline, Penicillin, Polymixin, Rifampicin, Rifamycin, Spectinomycin, Streptomycin, Streptothricin, Terramycin®, Tetracycline, Tyrocidine, Tyrothricin

Antibody Agglutinin, Amboceptor, Antitoxin, Blocker, Isoagglutinin, Lysin, Monoclonal, Precipitin, Reagin

Antic(s) Caper, Dido, Frolic, Gambado, Hay, Prank, Shenanigan, Stunt

Anticipate, **Anticipation** Antedate, Augur, Await, Drool, > EXPECT, Forecast, Foresee, Forestall, Foretaste, Hope, Intuition, Prevenancy, Prolepsis, Prospect, Type

Anticlimax Bathos, Deflation, Letdown

Antidote Adder's wort, Alexipharmic, Angelica, Antivenin, Bezoar, Contrayerva, Cure, Emetic, Guaco, Mithridate, Nostrum, Orvietan, Remedy, Ribavirin, Senega, Theriac(a), (Venice)-Treacle

Antimonopoly Trust buster

Antipasto Caponata

Antipathy Allergy, Aversion, Detest, > DISLIKE, Enmity, Repugnance

Antiquated, **Antique**, **Antiquarian** Ancient, Archaic, A(u)stringer, Bibelot, Curio, Dryasdust, FAS, Fog(e)y, Fogram(ite), Fossil, Old-fangled, Ostreger, Relic

Antiseptic Acriflavine, Carbolic, Cassareep, Creosote, Disinfectant, Eupad, Eusol, Formaldehyde, Guaiacol, Iodine, Phenol, Sterile, Thymol, Tutty

Antisocial Hostile, Ishmaelitish, Misanthropic

Antithesis Contrary, Converse, Opposite

Antivitamin Pyrithiamine

Anvil Bick-iron, Block, Incus, Stiddie, Stithy

Anxiety, **Anxious** Angst, Brood, Care(ful), Cark, Concern, Disquiet, Dysthymia, Fanteeg, Fantigue, Fantod, Fraught, Grave, Heebie-jeebies, Hypochondria, Inquietude, Jimjams, Jumpy, Reck, Restless, Scruple, Solicitous, Stress, Suspense, Sweat, Tension, Trepidation, Twitchy, Unease, Unquiet, Upset, Uptight, White-knuckle, Worriment

Any Arrow, Ary, Some

Anybody, **Anyone** One, Whoso, You

Anyhow Anyway, Leastways

Anything Aught, Oucht, Owt, Whatnot

▷ **Anyway** *may indicate* an anagram

Apart Aloof, Aside, Asunder, Atwain, Beside, Separate

Apartment Ben, Condominium, Digs, Duplex, Flat, Insula, Mansion, Paradise, Penthouse, Pied-a-terre, Quarters, Room, Simplex, Solitude, Suite, Unit

Apathetic, **Apathy** Accidie, Acedia, Incurious, Languid, Lethargic, Listless, Lobotomized, Pococurante, Torpid

Ape(-like), **Apeman** Anthropoid, Barbary, Big-foot, Catarrhine, Copy, Dryopithecine, Gelada, Gibbon, Gorilla, > IMITATE, Magot, Mimic, Orang, Paranthropus, Pongo, Proconsul, Simian, Simulate, Yowie

Apex Acme, Culmen, Keystone, Knoll, Knowe, Summit, Vortex

Aphorism Adage, Epigram, Gnome, Proverb, Sutra

Aphrodisiac, **Aphrodite** Cytherean, Erotic, Idalian, Paphian, Philter, Philtre, Spanish fly, Urania, Yohimbine

Apology Excuse, Justifier, Mockery, Oops, Pardon, Scuse

Apostle, **Apostolic** Cuthbert, > DISCIPLE, Evangelist, Johannine, Jude, Matthew, Pauline, Spoon, Twelve

Appal(ling) Abysmal, Affear(e), Dismay, Egregious, Frighten, Horrify, Piacular, Tragic

▷ **Appallingly** *may indicate* an anagram

Apparatus Appliance, Caisson, Clinostat, Condenser, Cryostat, Defibrillator, Device, Digester, Ebullioscope, Effusiometer, Electrograph, Electrophorus, Electroscope, Equipment, Gadget, Helioscope, Hemocytometer, Hodoscope, Holophote, Hydrophone, Incubator, Injector, Instrument, Lease-rod, Microreader, Mimeograph, Oscillograph, Oxygenator, Pasteuriser, Percolator, Phonometer, Phytotron, Potometer, Proto®, Pulmotor®, Radiosonde, Replenisher, Respirator, Respirometer, Resuscitator, Retort, Set, Snorkel, Spirophore, Stellarotor, Steriliser, Still, Switchgear, Tackle, Tackling, Talk-you-down, Teleprinter, Transformer, Transmitter, Ventouse, Wheatstone's bridge

Apparel Attire, Besee, > COSTUME, Garb, Raiment, Wardrobe, Wardrop

Apparent(ly) Ap, Clear, Detectable, Manifest, Ostensible, Outward, Overt, Plain, Prima facie, Semblance, Visible

▷ **Apparent** *may indicate* a hidden word

Apparition Dream, Eidolon, Fetch, Ghost, > ILLUSION, Phantom, Shade, Spectre, Visitant, Wraith

Appeal(ing) Ad, Beg, Cachet, Catchpenny, Charisma, Charm, Cri de coeur, Cry, Entreat, Entreaty, Epirrhema, Fetching, Invocation, It, O, Oomph, Plead, SA, Screeve, Solicit, SOS, Suit

Appear(ance) Advent, Air, Arrival, Aspect, Brow, Debut, Emerge, Enter, Facade, Feature, Garb, Guise, Hue, Image, Loom, > MANNER, Mien, Occur, Outward, Phenomenon, Physiognomy, Presence, Represent, Rise, Seem, Semblance, Show, Spring, View, Visitation

Appease(ment) Allay, Calm, Danegeld, Mitigate, Munichism, Pacify, Placate, Propitiate, Satisfy, Soothe, Sop

Append(age) Adjunct, Codpiece, Hanger-on, Lobe, Lug, Tail, Tentacle, Uvula

Appendix Addendum, Apocrypha, Codicil, Grumbling, Label, Pendant, Pendent, Rider, Schedule, Vermiform

Appetite, **Appetitive**, **Appetise(r)** Antepast, Antipasto, Aperitif, Appestat, Bhagee, Bhajee, Bulimia, Bulimy, Canapé, Concupiscence, Concupy, Crudités, Dim-sum, Entremes(se), Entremets, Flesh, Hunger, Limosis, Malacia, Meze, Nacho, Orectic, Orexis, Passion, Pica, Polyphagia, Relish, Tapa(s), Titillate, Twist, Yerd-hunger, Yird-hunger

Applaud, **Applause** Bravo, > CHEER, Clap, Claque, Eclat, Encore, Extol, Olé, Ovation, Praise, Root, Tribute

Apple Alligator, Baldwin, Balsam, Biffin, Blenheim orange, Bramley, Charlotte, Codlin(g), Cooker, Costard, Crab, Custard, Eater, Granny Smith, Greening, Jenneting, John, Jonathan, Leather-coat, Love, Mammee, Medlar, Nonpareil, Pearmain, Pippin, Pomace, Pome(roy), Pomroy, Pyrus, Quarantine, Quarenden, Quar(r)ender, Quarrington, Redstreak, Reinette, Rennet, Ribston(e), Ruddock, Russet, Seek-no-further, Snow, Sops-in-wine, Sturmer, Sugar, Sweeting, Thorn, Toffee, Winesap

Application, Apply, Appliance(s) Address, Adhibit, Appeal, Appose, Assiduity, Barrage, Blender, Devote, Diligence, Dressing, Exercise, Foment, Implement, Inlay, Lay, Lotion, Ointment, Petition, Plaster, Poultice, Put, Resort, Rub, Sinapism, Stupe, Truss, > USE, White goods

Appoint(ee), Appointment Advowson, Assign, Berth, Date, Delegate, Depute, Designate, Dew, Due, Executor, Induction, Installation, Make, Name, > NOMINATE, Nominee, Office, Ordain, Position, Post, Posting, Rendezvous, Room, Set, Tryst

▷ **Appointed** *may indicate* an anagram

Appraise, Appraisal Analyse, > EVALUATE, Gauge, Judge, Tape, > VALUE, Vet

Appreciate, Appreciation Acknowledgement, Cherish, Clap, Dig, Endear, Esteem, Gratefulness, Increase, Prize, Realise, Regard, Relish, Rise, Sense, Stock, Taste, Thank you, Treasure, > VALUE

Apprehend, Apprehension Afears, Alarm, Arrest, > CATCH, Collar, Fear, Grasp, Insight, Intuit, Perceive, Quailing, See, Take, Toey, Trepidation, Uh-oh, Unease, Uptake

Apprehensive Jumpy, Nervous, Uneasy

Apprentice(ship) Article, Cub, Devil, Garzone, Improver, Indent(ure), Jockey, L, Learner, Lehrjahre, Novice, Noviciate, Novitiate, Printer's devil, Pupillage, Trainee, Turnover

Approach(ing), Approachable Abord, Access, Accost, Advance, Anear, Appropinquate, Appulse, Avenue, Close, Come, Converge, Cost(e), Drive, Driveway, Fairway, Feeler, Gate, Imminent, Line, Near, Nie, Overture, Pitch, Procedure, Road, Run-up, Verge

Appropriate Abduct, Abstract, Annex, Apposite, Apt, Asport, Assign, Bag, Borrow, Collar, Commandeer, Commensurate, Confiscate, Convenient, Due, Embezzle, Expedient, Fit, Germane, Good, Happy, Hijack, Hog, Jump, Just, Meet, Nick, Pilfer, Pocket, Pre-empt, Proper, Right, Seize, Sequester, Sink, Snaffle, Steal, Suit, Swipe, Take, Timely, Trouser, Usurp

Approval, Approve(d) Adopt, Allow, Amen, Applaud, Attaboy, Aye, Blessing, Bravo, Credit, Dig, Endorse, Favour, Hear hear, Hubba-hubba, Imprimatur, Initial, Kitemark, Laud, Nod, Okay, Olé, Orthodox, Plaudit, Rah, Ratify, Rubber-stamp, Sanction, Stotter, Thumbs-up, Tick, Tribute, Yay, Yes

Approximate(ly), Approximation Almost, Circa, Close, Coarse, Estimate, Guess, Imprecise, Near, Roughly

Apron Barm-cloth, Bib, Blacktop, Brat, Bunt, Canvas, Fig-leaf, Pinafore, Pinny, Placket, Stage, Tablier, Tier

Apt(ly) Apposite, Appropriate, Apropos, Ben trovato, Capable, Evincive, Fit, Gleg, Happy, Liable, Prone, Suitable, Tends

Aptitude Ability, Bent, Faculty, Flair, Gift, Skill, Talent, Tendency

Aquamarine Madagascar

Aqueduct Canal, Channel, Conduit, Hadrome, Xylem

Arab(ian), Arabia, Arabic Abdul, Algorism, Ali, Baathist, Bahraini, Bahrein, Bedouin, Druse, Druz(e), Effendi, Fedayee(n), Gamin, Geber, Hashemite, Himyarite, Horse, Iraqi, Jawi, Lawrence, Mudlark, Nabat(a)ean, Omani, PLO,

Rag(head), Saba, Sab(a)ean, Saracen, Semitic, Sheikh, UAR, Urchin, Yemen

Arbiter, Arbitrator ACAS, Censor, Daysman, Judge, Ombudsman, Ref(eree), Umpire

Arbitrary Despotic, Haphazard, Random, Wanton

Arboreal, Arbour Bower, Dendroid, Pergola, Trellis

Arc Azimuth, Bow, Carbon, > **CURVE**, Flashover, Fogbow, Halo, Octant, Quadrant, Rainbow, Reflex, Trajectory

Arcade Amusement, Burlington, Cloister, Gallery, Loggia, Triforium

Arcane Esoteric, Obscure, Occult, Orphism, Recherché, Rune, Secret

Arch(ed) Acute, Admiralty, Arblaster, Arcade, Archivolt, Camber, Chief, Counterfort, Crafty, Cross-rib, Ctesiphon, > **CUNNING**, Curve, Fallen, Flying buttress, Fog-bow, Gothic, Hance, Haunch, Instep, Intrados, Keystone, Lancet, Lierne, Limb-girdle, Marble, Norman, Ogee, Ogive, Pelvic, Portal, Proscenium, Relieving, Roguish, Roman, Safety, Saucy, Segmental, Shouldered, Skew, Soffit, Span, Squinch, Stilted, Trajan, Triumphal, Vault

Archaeological, Archaeologist Carter, Dater, Dig, Evans, Layard, Leakey, Mycenae, Petrie, Pothunter, Wheeler, Woolley

Archangel Azrael, Gabriel, Israfeel, Israfel, Israfil, Jerahmeel, Michael, Raguel, Raphael, Sariel, Satan, Uriel

Archbishop Anselm, Augustine, Cosmo, Cranmer, Davidson, Dunstan, Ebor, Elector, Hatto, Lanfranc, Lang, Langton, Laud, Metropolitan, Primate, Temple, Trench, Tutu, Whitgift

Archer Acestes, Bow-boy, > **BOWMAN**, Cupid, Eros, Hood, Philoctetes, Sagittary, Tell, Toxophilite

Archetype Avatar, Model, Pattern

Architect(ure), Architectural Baroque, Bauhaus, Bricolage, Byzantine, Composite, Corinthian, Data-flow, Domestic, Doric, Early English, Flamboyant, Georgian, Gothic, Ionic, Landscape, Lombard, Moorish, Moresque, Mudejar, Naval, Neoclassical, Neo-gothic, Norman, Palladian, Perpendicular, Planner, Romanesque, Saxon, Spandrel, Spandril, Tudor, Tuscan

Archive(s) Muniment, PRO, Records, Register

Arctic Estotiland, Frigid, Hyperborean, In(n)uit, Inupiat, Polar, Tundra

Ardent, Ardour Aflame, Aglow, Boil, Broiling, Burning, Fervent, Fervid, Fiery, Flagrant, Heat, Het, > **HOT**, In, Mettled, Mettlesome, Passion(ate), Perfervid, Rage, Spiritous, Vehement, Warm-blooded, Zealous, Zeloso

Are A

Area Acre, Aleolar, Apron, Are, Bailiwick, Belt, Catchment, Centare, Centre, Development, Disaster, District, Domain, Eruv, Extent, Goal, Grey, Growth, Hectare, Henge, Hide, Input, Landmass, Latitude, Locality, Metroplex, Milieu, No-go, Parish, Penalty, Place, Plot, Precinct, Province, Purlieu, Quad, Quarter, Range, Redevelopment, > **REGION**, Rest, Sector, Service, Shire, Sterling, Subtopia, Support, Target, Technical, Terrain, Territory, Theatre, Tract, Tundra, Urban, White, Yard, Zone

Arena Circus, Cockpit, Dohyo, Field, Maidan, Olympia, > **RING**, Stadium, Tiltyard, Venue

Argue, Argument Altercation, Argy-bargy, Bandy, Beef, Blue, Conflict, Contend, Contest, Cosmological, Debate, Difference, Dilemma, Dispute, Dissent, Exchange, Expostulate, Free-for-all, Logic, Moot, Patter, Plead, Polylemma, Propound, Quarrel, Quibble, > **REASON**, Remonstrate, Row, Run-in, Spar, Straw man, Summation, Teleological, Tiff, Transcendental, Wrangle

Aria Ballad, Cabaletta, Melody, Song

Arise Appear, Develop, Emanate, Emerge, Upgo, Wax

Aristocracy, Aristocrat(ic) Blood, Classy, Debrett, Duc, Elite, Gentry, Grandee, High-hat, Nob, Noble, Optimate, Patrician, Tony, U-men, Upper-crust, Well-born

Arm(ed), Arms Akimbo, Arsenal, Bearing, Brachial, Branch, Bundooks, Canting, Cove, Crest, Embattle, Equip, Escutcheon, Fin, Firth, Frith, Gnomon, Halbert, Hatchment, Heel, Heraldic, Inlet, Jib, Krupp, Limb, Loch, Long, Member, Olecranon, Pick-up, Quillon, Radius, Ramous, Rocker, Rotor, SAA, Secular, Side, Small, Spiral, Tappet, Tentacle, Timer, Tone, Transept, Tremolo, Ulnar, > **WEAPON**, Whip

▷ **Arm** *may indicate* an army regiment, etc.

Armadillo Dasypod, Dasypus, Pangolin, Peba, Pichiciago, Tatou(ay), Xenurus

Armour(ed) Ailette, Armet, Barbette, Beaver, Besagew, Bevor, Brasset, Brigandine, Buckler, Byrnie, Camail, Cannon, Casspir, Cataphract, Chaffron, Chain, Chamfrain, Chamfron, Chausses, Corium, Cors(e)let, Couter, Cuirass, Cuish, Cuisse, Culet, Curat, Curiet, Cush, Defence, Fauld, Garniture, Gear, Genouillère, Gorget, Greave, Habergeon, Hauberk, Jack, Jambeau, Jazerant, Jesserant, Lamboys, Mail, Mentonnière, Nasal, Panoply, Panzer, Pauldron, Petta, Placcat, Placket, Plastron, Poitrel, Poleyn, Pouldron, Sabaton, Secret, > **SHIELD**, Solleret, Spaudler, Tace, Tank, Taslet, Tasse(t), Thorax, Tonlet, Tuille, Vambrace, Vantbrass, Visor, Voider

Army Arrière-ban, BEF, Church, Colours, Confederate, Crowd, Federal, Fyrd, Golden (Horde), Horde, Host, IRA, Land, Landwehr, Legion, Line, Military, Militia, Multitude, Para-military, Red, SA, Sabaoth, Salvation, Sena, Service, Soldiers, Standing, Swarm, TA, Territorial, Volunteer, War, Wehrmacht

▷ **Army** *may indicate* having arms

Aroma(tic) Allspice, Aniseed, Aryl, Balmy, Coriander, Fenugreek, Fragrant, Odorous, Pomander, Spicy, Vanillin, Wintergreen

Around About, Ambient, Circa, Near, Peri-, Skirt, Tour

▷ **Around** *may indicate* one word around another

Arouse, Arousal Alarm, > **EXCITE**, Fan, Fire, Incite, Inflame, Must(h), Needle, Provoke, Stole, Urolagnia, Waken

Arrange(r), Arrangement Adjust, Array, Attune, Bandobast, Bundobust, Concert, Concinnity, Configuration, Design, Display, Dispose, Do, Edit, Engineer, Fix, Foreordain, Formation, Grade, Ikebana, Layout, Marshal, Modus vivendi, Orchestrate, Orchestration, Ordain, > **ORDER**, Ordnance, Organise, Pack, Pattern, Perm, Permutation, Plan, Position, Prepare, Prepense, Quincunx, Redactor, Regulate, Run, Schedule, Schema, Scheme, Set, Settle, Sort, Spacing, Stereoisomerism, Stow, Straighten, Style, System, Tactic, Taxis, Transcribe

▷ **Arrange** *may indicate* an anagram

Array(ed) Attire, Deck, Herse, Marshal, Muster

Arrear(s) Aft, Ahint, Backlog, Behind, Debt, Owing

Arrest(ed), Arresting Abort, Alguacil, Alguazil, Ament, Apprehend, Attach, Attract, Blin, Book, Bust, Caption, Capture, Cardiac, Catch, Check, Citizen's, Collar, Detain, False, Furthcoming, Hold, House, Knock, Lift, Nab, Nail, Nick, Nip, Nobble, Pinch, Pull, Restrain, Retard, Riveting, Round-up, Run-in, Salient, Sease, Seize, Stasis, Stop, Sus(s)

Arrival, Arrive, Arriving Accede, Advent, Attain, Come, Get, Happen, Hit, Inbound, Influx, Johnny-come-lately, Land, Natal, Nativity, Reach, Strike

Arrogance, Arrogant Assumption, Bold, Bravado, Cavalier, Cocksure, Disdain, Dogmatic, Effrontery, Haughty, Haut(eur), High, Hogen-mogen, Hoity-toity, Hubris, Imperious, Morgue, Overweening, Presumption, Proud, Side, Surquedry, Toploftical, Uppity, Upstart

Arrow, Arrow-head Acestes, Any, Ary, Bolt, Dart, Filter, Flechette, Missile, Pheon, Pointer, Quarrel, Reed, Sagittate, Shaft, Sheaf

Arsenal Ammo, Armo(u)ry, Depot, Magazine, Side

Arson(ist) Firebug, Pyromania

Art(s), **Arty**, **Art school**, **Art style** Abstract, Applied, Arte Povera, Bauhaus, Bloomsbury, Bonsai, Bricart, Brut, Chiaroscuro, Clair-obscure, Clare-obscure, Clip, Cobra, Commercial, Conceptual, Constructivism, Contrapposto, Craft, Cubism, Cunning, Dada, Daedal(e), Deco, Decorative, Dedal, De Stijl, Die Brucke, Diptych, Divisionism, Expressionism, Fauvism, Feat, Fine, Finesse, Flemish, Folk, Futurism, Genre, Graphic, Impressionist, Jugendstil, Kakemono, Kano, Ka pai, Kinetic, Kirigami, Kitsch, Knack, Liberal, Mandorla, Mannerism, Martial, Minimal, Montage, Motivated, Music, Nabis, Nazarene, Neoclassical, Neo-impressionism, New Wave, Norwich, Nouveau, Optical, Origami, Orphic cubism, Orphism, Outsider, Performance, Perigordian, Plastic, Pointillism, Pop, Postimpressionism, Postmodern, Practical, Pre-Raphaelite, Primitive, Psychedelic, Public, Quadratura, Quadrivium, Relievo, Sienese, > **SKILL**, Still-life, Supremation, Surrealism, Synchronism, Tachism(e), Tatum, Tenebrism, Toreutics, Trecento, Trivium, Trompe l'oeil, Trouvé, Tsutsumu, Useful, Verism, Virtu, Visual, Vorticism

▷ **Art** *may indicate* an -est ending

▷ **Artefact** *may indicate* an anagram

Artery Aorta, Carotid, Coronary, Duct, Femoral, Iliac, Innominate, M1, Pulmonary, Route

Artful Cute, Dodger, Foxy, Ingenious, Quirky, Sly, Subtle, Tactician

Article(s) A, An, Apprentice, Column, Commodity, Definite, Feature, Indefinite, Indenture, Item, Leader, Paper, Piece, Pot-boiler, Sidebar, Specify, The, Thing, Thirty-nine, Treatise, Ware

Articulation, **Articulate(d)** Clear, Diarthrosis, Distinct, Eloquent, Enounce, Express, Fluent, Gimmal, Hinged, Jointed, Lenis, Limbed, Lisp, Pretty-spoken, Pronounce, Utter, Vertebrae, Voice

Artifice(r), **Artificial** Bogus, Chouse, Dodge, Ersatz, Factitious, Finesse, Guile, Hoax, In vitro, Logodaedaly, Man-made, Mannered, Opificer, Pretence, Prosthetic, Pseudo, Reach, Ruse, Sell, Sham, Spurious, Stratagem, > **STRATEGY**, Synthetic, Theatric, > **TRICK**, Unnatural, Wile, Wright

Artillery Battery, Cannon, Fougade, Fougasse, Guns, Mortar, Ordnance, Pyroballogy, RA, Rafale, Ramose, Ramus, Train

Artisan Craftsman, Joiner, Journeyman, Mechanic, Pioner, Pyoner, Workman

Artist(ic) Bohemian, Cartoonist, Colourist, Cubist, Dadaist, Daedal(e), Deccie, Decorator, Etcher, Fine, Gentle, Gilder, ICA, Impressionist, Limner, Linear, Maestro, Master, Miniaturist, > **MUSICIAN**, Nazarene, Oeuvre, Orphism, > **PAINTER**, Pavement, Paysagist, Piss, Plein-airist, Primitive, RA, Romantic, Screever, Sien(n)ese, Tachisme, Trapeze, Trecentist, Virtuose, Virtuoso

Artless Candid, Ingenuous, Innocent, Naive, Open, Seely

Art nouveau Jugendstil

As Aesir, Als, Arsenic, Coin, Eg, Forasmuch, Kame, Qua, Ridge, 's, Since, So, Thus, Ut, While

As before Anew, Ditto, Do, Stet

Ascend(ant), **Ascent** Anabasis, Climb, Dominant, Escalate, Gradient, Pull, Ramp, Rise, Sclim, Sklim, Slope, Up, Upgang, Uphill, Uprise, Zoom

Ascertain Determine, Discover, > **ESTABLISH**, Prove

Ascribe Assign, > **ATTRIBUTE**, Blame, Imply, Impute

As good as Equal, Tantamount

Ash(es), **Ashy** Aesc, Aizle, Cinders, Cinereal, Clinker(s), Easle, Embers, Kali, Pallor, Pearl, Pozz(u)olana, Prickly, Rowan, Ruins, Sorb, Tephra, Urn, Varec, Wednesday, Witchen, Yg(g)drasil(l)

Ashamed Abashed, Embarrassed, Hangdog, Mortified, Repentant, Shent

Ashore Aland, Beached, Grounded, Stranded

Asia(n), Asiatic Balinese, Bengali, Cantonese, E, Evenki, Ewenki, Gook, Hun, Hyksos, Indian, Korean, Kurd, Lao, Malay, Mongol, Naga, Negrito, Nepalese, Pushtu, Samo(y)ed, Shan, Siamese, Sogdian, Tamil, Tibetan, Turanian, Turk(o)man

Aside Apart, By, Despite, Private, Separate, Shelved, Sotto voce

Ask Beg, Beseech, Cadge, Demand, Desire, Enquire, Entreat, Evet, Implore, Intreat, Invite, Newt, Petition, Prithee, Pump, Quiz, Request, Rogation, Seek, Solicit, Speer, Speir, Touch

Askance Asconce, Askew, Oblique, Sideways

Asleep Dormant, Inactive, Napping

Aspect Angle, Bearing, Brow, Face, Facet, Facies, Feature, Look, Mien, Nature, Outlook, Perfective, Perspective, Side, > VIEW, Visage, Vista

Aspersion Calumny, Innuendo, Libel, Slander, Slur, Smear

Asphalt Bitumen, Blacktop, Gilsonite®, Pitch, Uinta(h)ite

Aspirant, Aspirate, Aspiration, Aspire Ambition, Breath, Buckeen, Challenger, Desire, Dream, Endeavour, Ettle, Goal, H, Hope(ful), Pretend, Pursue, Rough, Spiritus, Wannabe(e), Yearn

Assail(ant) Assault, Batter, Bego, Belabour, Bepelt, Beset, Bombard, Impugn, Oppugn, Pillory, Ply, Revile

Assassin(ate), Assassination Booth, Brave, Bravo, Brutus, Casca, Frag, Gunman, Highbinder, Hitman, Killer, Ninja, Sword, Thuggee, Tyrannicide

Assault Assail, Assay, Attack, Battery, Bombard, Hamesucken, Indecent, Invasion, Mug, > RAID, Stoor, Storm, Stour, Stowre

Assemble, Assembly Audience, Ball, Chapter, > COLLECTION, Company, Conclave, Convention, Convocation, Convoke, Council, Court, Diet, Folkmote, Forgather, Gather(ing), General, Group, Levee, Loya jirga, Mass, > MEETING, Moot, Muster, National, Panegyry, Parishad, Parliament, Primary, Quorum, Rally, Reichstag, Resort, Sanghat, Sejm, Senate, Society, Synagogue, Synod, Tribunal, Troop, Unlawful, Vidhan Sabha

Assent Accede, Acquiesce, Agree, Amen, Aye, Comply, Concur, Nod, Placet, Sanction, Yea, Yield

Assert(ing), Assertion Affirm, Allege, Constate, Contend, > DECLARE, Ipse-dixit, > MAINTAIN, Pose, Predicate, Proclaim, Protest, Thetical

Assess(ment) Affeer, Appraise, Estimate, Evaluate, Gauge, Guesstimate, > JUDGE, Levy, Measure, Perspective, Rating, Referee, Scot and lot, Tax, Value, Weigh

Asset(s) Advantage, Capital, Chattel, Fixed, Intangible, Liquid, Plant, Property, Resource, Talent, Virtue

Assign(ation), Assignment Allocate, > ALLOT, Apply, Aret, Ascribe, Attribute, Award, Date, Dedicate, Duty, Errand, Fix, Grant, Impute, Point, Quota, Refer, Transfer, Tryst

Assimilate(d) Absorb, Blend, Digest, Esculent, Fuse, Imbibe, Incorporate, Merge

Assist(ance), Assistant Acolyte, Adjunct, Aid(e), Ally, Alms, Attaché, Busboy, Cad, Collaborate, Counterhand, Dresser, Facilitate, Factotum, Famulus, Gofer, > HAND, Help, Henchman, Legal aid, Offsider, Omnibus, Reinforce, Relief, Second, Server, Servitor, Sidesman, Stead, Subsidiary, Suffragan, > SUPPORT, Usher

Associate, Association Accomplice, Affiliate, Alliance, Attach, Bedfellow, Brotherhood, Cartel, Chapel, Club, Combine, Comrade, > CONNECT, Consort(ium), Correlate, Crony, Fellow, Fraternise, Guild, Hobnob, Join, League,

Liaison, Member, Mix, Partner, Relate, Ring, Stablemate, Syndicate, Trade, Union, Word

▷ **Assorted** *may indicate* an anagram

Assuage Allay, Appease, Beet, Calm, Ease, Mease, Mitigate, Mollify, Slake, Soften

Assume, **Assuming**, **Assumption** Adopt, Affect, Arrogate, Attire, Axiom, Believe, Don, Donné(e), Feign, Hypothesis, Lemma, Occam's Razor, Posit, Postulate, Preconception, Premise, Premiss, Presuppose, Pretentious, Principle, Putative, Saltus, Suppose, Surmise, Take

▷ **Assumption** *may mean* attire

Assure(d), **Assurance** Aplomb, Aver, Belief, Calm, > CERTAIN, Confidence, Confirm, Earnest, Gall, Guarantee, Pledge, Poise, Warranty

Asteroid Ceres, Eros, Hermes, Hygiea, Juno, Pallas, Star, Starfish

Astonish(ed), **Astonishing**, **Astonishment**, **Astound** Abash, Admiraunce, Amaze, Banjax, Bewilder, Confound, Corker, Crikey, Daze, Donnert, Dum(b)found, Dumbstruck, Flabbergast, Gobsmack, Open-eyed, Open-mouthed, Phew, Rouse, Singular, Stagger, Startle, Stupefaction, Stupefy, Stupendous, Surprise, Thunderstruck, Wow

Astray Abord, Amiss, Errant, Lost, Will, Wull

Astride Athwart, Spanning, Straddle-back

Astringent Acerbic, Alum, Catechu, Gambi(e)r, Harsh, Kino, Rhatany, Sept-foil, Severe, Sour, Styptic, Tormentil, Witch-hazel

Astrologer, **Astrology** Archgenethliac, Chaldean, Culpeper, Faust, Figure-caster, Genethliac, Lilly, Moore, Nostradamus, Soothsayer, Starmonger, Zadkiel

Astronaut Cosmonaut, Gagarin, Glenn, Lunarnaut, Spaceman, Spacer

Astronomer, **Astronomy**, **Astronomical** Almagest, Aristarchus, Bessel, Bradley, Brahe, Callipic, Cassini, Celsius, Copernicus, Eddington, Encke, Eratosthenes, Eudoxus, Flamsteed, Galileo, Hale, Halley, Herschel, Hewish, Hipparchus, Hoyle, Hubble, Huggins, Jeans, Kepler, Laplace, Leverrier, Lockyer, Lovell, Meton, Omar Khayyam, Oort, Planetology, Ptolemy, Radio, Reber, Roche, Schwarzschild, Sosigenes, Tycho Brahe, Urania

Astute Acute, Canny, Crafty, Cunning, Downy, Perspicacious, Shrewd, Subtle, Wide, Wily

As well Additionally, Also, Both, Even, Forby, Too

Asylum Bedlam, Bin, Bughouse, Frithsoken, Funny-farm, Girth, Grith, Haven, Institution, Lunatic, Madhouse, Magdalene, Nuthouse, Political, Rathouse, Refuge, Retreat, Sanctuary, Shelter, Snake-pit

Asymmetric(al) Lopsided, Skew

Atheist Doubter, Godless, Infidel, Sceptic

Athlete, **Athletic(s)** Aglle, Agonist, Blue, Coe, Discobolus, Field, Gymnast, Jock, Leish, Miler, Milo, Nurmi, Olympian, Pacemaker, Runner, Sportsman, Sprinter, Track

Atlas Linguistic, Maps, Range, Silk

▷ **At last** *may indicate* a cobbler

Atmosphere Aeropause, Air, Ambience, Aura, Chemosphere, Elements, Epedaphic, Ether, F-layer, Geocorona, Ionosphere, Lid, Magnetosphere, Mesosphere, Meteorology, Miasma, Ozone, Thermosphere, Tropopause, Troposphere, Upper, Vibe(s)

Atom(ic), **Atoms** Boson, Electron, Excimer, Gram, Ion, Iota, Isobare, Isotone, Isotope, Ligand, Molecule, Monad, Monovalent, Muonic, Nuclide, Particle, Pile, Radionuclide, Side-chain, Steric, Substituent

Atomiser Airbrush

Atone(ment) Aby(e), Acceptilation, Appease, Expiate, Redeem, Redemption, Yom Kippur

▷ **At random** *may indicate* an anagram

Atrocious, Atrocity Abominable, Brutal, Diabolical, Flagitious, Heinous, Horrible, Monstrous, Outrage, Vile

▷ **At sea** *may indicate* an anagram

Attach(ed), Attachment Accessory, Adhesion, Adhibition, Adnate, Adnation, Adscript, Affix, Allonge, Bolt, Bro, Byssus, Covermount, Devotement, Devotion, Distrain, Glue, > JOIN, Obconic, Pin, Snell, Stick, Tie, Weld

Attack(ing), Attacker Affect, Airstrike, Alert, Apoplexy, Assail, Assault, Batten, Belabour, Beset, Blitz(krieg), Bombard, Bout, Broadside, Campaign, Charge, Clobber, Club, Counteroffensive, Coup de main, Denounce, Feint, Fit, Foray, Iconoclast, Incursion, Inroad, Invade, Inveigh, Lampoon, Let fly, Maraud, Molest, Mug, Offensive, Onfall, Onrush, Onset, Onslaught, Oppugn, Panic, Pillage, Polemic, Pre-emptive, Push, Raid, Sandbag, Savage, Seizure, Siege, Skitch, Snipe, Sortie, Storm, Strafe, Strike, Thrust, Tilt, Vituperate, Wage, Zap

Attain(ment) Accomplish, Arrive, Earn, Fruition, Get, Land, Reach

Attempt Bash, Bid, Burl, Crack, Debut, Effort, Endeavour, Essay, Go, Mint, Nisus, Seek, Shot, Shy, Stab, Strive, > TRY, Venture, Whack, Whirl

Attend(ance), Attendant Accompany, Batman, Bearer, Chaperone, Courtier, Entourage, Equerry, Escort, Esquire, Footman, Gillie, Hear, > HEED, > LISTEN, Marshal, Note, Outrider, Page, Presence, Respect, Satellite, Second, Steward, Trainbearer, Valet, Visit, Wait, Watch, Zambuck

Attention, Attentive Achtung, Assiduity, Court, Coverage, Dutiful, Ear, Gallant, Gaum, Gorm, Heed, Mind, Notice, Present, Punctilio, Qui vive, > REGARD, Tenty, Thought

Attest Affirm, Certify, Depose, Guarantee, Notarise, Swear, > WITNESS

Attic Bee-bird, Garret, Greek, Koine, Loft, Mansard, Muse, Salt, Solar, Soler, Sollar, Soller, Tallat, Tallet, Tallot

Attire Accoutre, Adorn, Apparel, Clobber, > DRESS, Garb, Habit

Attitude Air, Aspect, Behaviour, Demeanour, Light, > MANNER, Mindset, Nimby, Outlook, Pose, Posture, Propositional, Sense, Song, Stance, Tone, Viewpoint

Attorney Advocate, Counsellor, DA, Lawyer, Proctor, Prosecutor

Attract(ion), Attractive Bait, Becoming, Bewitch, Bonny, Catchy, Charisma, > CHARM, Cute, Dish(y), > DRAW, Engaging, Entice, Eye-catching, Fascinate, Fetching, Heartthrob, Hunky, Inviting, Loadstone, Looker, Luscious, Magnet(ism), Photogenic, Picturesque, Sexpot, Sideshow, Striking, Taking, Tasteful, Winning, Winsome

Attribute Accredit, Allot, Ap(p)anage, Ascribe, Asset, Credit, Gift, Impute, Lay, Metonym, Owe, Quality, Refer, Shtick

Aubergine Brinjal, Brown Jolly, Egg-plant, Mad-apple

Auburn Abram, Chestnut, Copper, Vill(age)

Auction(eer) Barter, Bridge, Cant, Dutch, Hammer, Outcry, Outro(o)per, Roup, Sale, Subhastation, Tattersall, Vendue

Audacious, Audacity Bald-headed, Bold, Brash, Cheek, Chutspah, Der-doing, Devil-may-care, Effrontery, Face, Hardihood, Indiscreet, Insolence, Intrepid, Neck, Nerve, Rash, Sauce

Audience, Auditorium Assembly, Court, Durbar, Gate, House, Interview, Pit, Sphendone, Tribunal

Audit(or) Accountant, Check, Ear, Examine, Inspect, Listener

Auger Miser

Augment(ed) Boost, Eche, Eke, Ich, Increase, Supplement, Swell, Tritone

Augury Ornithoscopy

Aunt(ie) Agony, Augusta, Beeb, Giddy, Naunt, Sainted, Tia

Aura Aroma, Mystique, Nimbus, Odour, Vibrations

Austere, Austerity Astringent, Bleak, Dantean, Hard, > HARSH, Moral, Plain, Rigour, Stern, Stoic, Stoor, Strict, Vaudois, Waldensian

Australia(n) Alf, Antipodean, Aussie, Balt, Banana-bender, Bananalander, Billjim, Canecutter, Cobber, Currency, Darwinian, Digger, Gin, Godzone, Gumsucker, Gurindji, Koori, Larrikin, Myall, Norm, Ocker, Oz, Pintupi, Roy, Sandgroper, Strine, Wallaby, Yarra-yabbies

Austrian Cisleithan, Tyrolean

Authentic(ate) Certify, Echt, Genuine, Honest, Notarise, Official, Real, Sign, Test, True, Validate

Author(ess) Anarch, Auctorial, Inventor, Me, Parent, Volumist, Wordsmith, > WRITER

▷ **Author** *may refer to* author of puzzle

Authorise(d), Authorisation Accredit, Clearance, Empower, Enable, Exequatur, Imprimatur, Legal, Legit, > LICENCE, Official, OK, Passport, > PERMIT, Plenipotentiary, Sanction, Sign, Stamp, Warrant

Authority, Authoritarian, Authoritative Canon, Charter, Circar, Cocker, Commission, Commune, Crisp, Definitive, Domineering, Dominion, Establishment, Ex cathedra, Expert, Fascist, Free hand, Gravitas, Hegemony, Inquirendo, Jackboot, Licence, Magisterial, Mandate, Mantle, Mastery, Name, Oracle, Permit, > POWER, Prefect, Prestige, Pundit, Remit, Right, Rod, Say-so, Sceptre, Sircar, Sirkar, Source, Supremacy, Unitary, Warrant

Autobiography Memoir

Autocrat(ic) Absolute, Caesar, Cham, Despot, Neronian, Tsar, Tyrant

Automatic, Automaton Android, Aut, Browning, Deskill, Instinctive, Machine, Mechanical, Pistol, Reflex, Robot, RUR, Zombi

Auxiliary Adjunct, Adjuvant, Adminicle, Aide, Be, Feldsher, Have, Helper, Ido

Avail(able) Benefit, Dow, Eligible, Going, Handy, On call, Open, Pickings, > READY, Serve, Use, Utilise

Avalanche Deluge, Landfall, Landslide, Landslip, Lauwine, Slide, Slip, Snowdrop

Avarice, Avaricious Cupidity, Golddigger, Greed, Money-grubbing, Pleonexia, Sordid

Avenge(r) Eriny(e)s, Eumenides, Goel, Kurdaitcha, Punish, Redress, Requite, > REVENGE, Wreak

Avenue Alley, Arcade, Channel, Corso, Cradle-walk, Hall, Mall, Passage, Vista, Way, Xyst(us)

Average Adjustment, Av, Batting, Dow Jones, Mean, Mediocre, Middle-brow, Middling, Moderate, Norm, Par, Run, Soso, Standard

Averse, Aversion, Avert Against, Antipathy, Apositia, Disgust, Distaste, Hatred, Horror, Opposed, Phobic, Scunner

Avert Avoid, > DEFLECT, Forfend, Parry, Ward

Aviator Airman, Alcock, Bleriot, Brown, Earhart, Flier, Hinkler, Icarus, Johnson, Lindbergh, Pilot

Avid > EAGER, Greedy, Keen

Avoid(er), Avoidance Abstain, Ba(u)lk, Boycott, Bypass, Cop-out, Cut, Dodge, Duck, Elude, Escape, Eschew, Evade, Evitate, Evite, Fly, Forbear, Gallio, Hedge, Miss, Obviate, Parry, Prevaricate, Scutage, Secede, Shelve, Shun, Sidestep, Skirt, Spare, Spurn, Waive

Avow(ed) Acknowledged, Affirm, Declare, Own, Swear

Await Abide, Bide, Expect, Tarry

Awake(ning) Aware, Conscious, Conversion, Fly, Rouse, Vigilant

Award Academy, Accolade, Addoom, Allot, Alpha, Aret(t), Bafta, Bestow, Bursary, Cap, Clasp, Clio, Crown, Emmy, Exhibition, Grammy, Grant, Medal, Meed, Mete, Oscar, Palme d'or, Premium, Present(ation), > PRIZE, Scholarship, Tony, Trophy, Yuko

Aware(ness) Alert, Cognisant, Conscious, Conversant, ESP, Est, Hep, Hip, Informed, Liminal, Onto, Panaesthesia, Prajna, Presentiment, Samadhi, Scienter, Sensible, Sensile, Sensitive, Sentience, Streetwise, Vigilant, Wot

Away Absent, Afield, Apage, Avaunt, By, For-, Fro(m), Go, Hence, Off, Out, Past

▷ **Away** *may indicate* a word to be omitted

Awe(d) D(o)ulia, Dread, Fear, Intimidate, Loch, Overcome, Popeyed, Regard, Respect, Reverent, Scare, Solemn

Awful(ly) Alas, Deare, Dere, Dire, Fearful, Horrendous, O so, Piacular, Terrible

▷ **Awfully** *may indicate* an anagram

Awkward Angular, Bolshy, Bumpkin, Clumsy, Complicated, Corner, Crabby, Cubbish, Cumbersome, Cussed, Embarrassing, Farouche, Fiddly, Fix, Gangly, Gauche, Gawky, Handless, Howdy-do, Inconvenient, Inept, Kittle-cattle, Lanky, Loutish, Lurdan(e), Lurden, Maladdress, Mauther, Mawr, Naff, Nasty, Ornery, Perverse, Refractory, Slummock, Spot, Sticky, Stiff, Stroppy, Stumblebum, Swainish, Uneasy, Ungainly, Unwieldy, Wry

Awry Agley, Askew, Cam, Kam(me), Wonky

Axe Abolish, Adz(e), Bill, Celt, Chop(per), Cleaver, Gisarme, Gurlet, Halberd, Halbert, Hatchet, Ice, Palstaff, Palstave, Partisan, Piolet, Retrench, Sax, Sparth(e), Sperthe, Spontoon, Thunderbolt, Tomahawk, Twibill

Axeman Bassist, Guitarist

Axe-shaped Securiform

Axiom Adage, Motto, Peano's, Proverb, Saw, Saying

Aye Eer, Ever, Yea, Yes

Bb

B Bachelor, Black, Book, Born, Boron, Bowled, Bravo

Babble(r) Blather, Chatter, Gibber, Haver, Lallation, Lurry, Prate, Prattle, Runnel, Tonguester, Twattle, Waffle

Baboon Ape, Bobbejaan, Chacma, Dog-ape, Drill, Gelada, Hamadryas, Mandrill, Sphinx

Baby Bairn, Blue, Bub, Bunting, Duck, Grand, Infant, Jelly, Neonate, Nursling, Pamper, Papoose, Preverbal, Sis, Small, Sook, Suckling, Tar, Test tube, Tot, Wean

Bachelor BA, Bach, Benedict, Budge, Celibate, En garçon, Pantagamy, Parti, Single, Stag

Bacillus Comma, Germ, Micrococcus, Virus

Back(ing), Backward Abet, Accompany, Addorse, Again, Ago, Anticlockwise, Arear, Arrear, Assist, Backare, Bankroll, Buckram, Champion, Chorus, Consent, Defender, Dorsal, Dorse, Dorsum, Dos, Ebb, Empatron, Encourage, Endorse, Finance, Frae, Fro, Fund, Gaff, Help, Hind, Historic, La-la, Late, Notaeum, Notal, Notum, On, Patronise, Poop, Pronotum, Punt, Rear(most), Retral, Retro(grade), Retrogress, Retrorse, Return, Rev, Reverse, Ridge, Root, Shy, Spinal, Sponsor, Stern, > **SUPPORT**, Sweeper, Tail, Telson, Tergum, Third, Thrae, Tonneau, Ulu, Uphold, Verso, Vie, Vo, Wager, Watteau

▷ **Back(ing)** *may indicate* a word spelt backwards

Backbone Chine, Grit, Guts, Mettle

Backchat Lip, Mouth, Sass

Backer Angel, Benefactor, Patron, Punter, Seconder, Sponsor

Backgammon Acey-deucy, Lurch, Tick-tack, Trick-track, Tric-trac, Verquere

Background Antecedence, Fond, History, Horizon, Setting, Ulterior

Backslide(r), Backsliding Apostate, Lapse, Regress, Relapse, Revert

Bacon Danish, Essayist, Flitch, Francis, Gammon, Lardo(o)n, Pancetta, Pig, Pork, Rasher, Roger, Spec(k), Streaky, Verulam

Bacteria, Bacterium Aerobe, Bacilli, Bacteriological, > **BUG**, Cocci, Culture, > **GERM**, Intestinal flora, Listeria, Lysogen, Microbe, Mother, MRSA, Packet, Pasteurella, Pathogen, Proteus, Pus, Salmonella, Septic, Serotype, Serum, Spirilla, Spore, Staph, Strep(tococcus), Superbug, Vibrio

Bad, Badness Addled, Chronic, Crook, Defective, Diabolic, Dud, Duff, Egregious, Execrable, Faulty, Heinous, Ill, Immoral, Inferior, Injurious, Lither, Mal, Naughty, Nefandrous, Nefarious, Nice, Off, Ominous, Oncus, Onkus, Piacular, Poor, Rank, Ropy, Scampish, Scoundrel, Sinful, Spoiled, Turpitude, Useless, Wack, Wick, > **WICKED**

▷ **Bad(ly)** *may indicate* an anagram

Badge Brassard, Brooch, Button, Chevron, Cockade, Cockleshell, Cordon, Crest, Emblem, Ensign, Epaulet, Episemon, Fáinne, Film, Flash, Garter, Gorget, ID, Insignia, Kikumon, Mark, Mon, Rosette, Scallop, Shield, Shouldermark, > **SIGN**, Symbol, Tiger, Token, Vernicle, Vine-rod, Wings

Badger > **ANNOY**, Bait, Bedevil, Beset, Brock, Browbeat, Bug, Bullyrag, Cete, Dassi(e), Ferret, Gray, Grey, > **HARASS**, Hassle, Hog, Honey, Hound, Nag, Pester,

Plague, Provoke, Ratel, Ride, Roil, Sow, Teledu, Wisconsin

Bad luck Ambs-ace, Ames-ace, Deuce-ace, Hoodoo, Jinx, Jonah, Shame, Voodoo

Bad-tempered Carnaptious, Curmudgeon, Curnaptious, Curst, Grouchy, Grum(py), Irritable, Moody, Patch, Splenetic, Stroppy

Baffle(d), Baffling Anan, Balk, Bemuse, Bewilder, Confound, Confuse, Elude, Evade, Floor, Flummox, Foil, Fox, Get, Hush-kit, Mate, Muse, Mystify, Nark, Nonplus, Pose, Puzzle, Stump, Throw, Thwart

Bag(gage), Bags Acquire, Alforja, Amaut, Amowt, Besom, Bladder, Blue, Body, Bulse, Buoyancy, Caba(s), Caecum, Capture, Carpet, Carrier, Carryall, Case, Cecum, Clutch, Cly, Cod, Cool, Corduroy, Crone, Crumenal, Cyst, Daypack, Dilli, Dilly, Dime, Diplomatic, Ditty, Doggy, Dorothy, Douche, Duffel, Dunnage, > **EFFECTS**, Excess, Flannels, Flotation, Follicle, Game, > **GEAR**, Gladstone, Grab, Grip, Gripsack, Grow, Holdall, Ice, Impedimenta, Jelly, Jiffy®, Kill, Lavender, Meal-poke, Minx, Mixed, Monkey, Musette, Muzzle, Mystery, Nap, Net, Nunny, Overnight, Oxford, Packsack, Pantaloons, Plastic, Plus fours, Pochette, Pock(et), Pocketbook, Poke, Politzer's, Poly(thene), Port(manteau), Portmantle, Portmantua, Post, Pot, Pouch, Pounce, Pudding, Punch, Purse, Rake, Red, Reticule, Ridicule, Rucksack, Sabretache, Sac(cule), Sachet, Sack, Saddle, Sag, Satchel, Scent, Scrip, Scrotum, Sea, Shopper, Sick, Slattern, Sleeping, Sponge, Sporran, Stacks, Sugar, Survival, Tea, Tote, > **TRAP**, Trews, Trollop, Trouse(r), Tucker (box), Udder, Unmentionables, Valise, Vanity, Viaticals, Waist, Wallet, Water, Weekend, Win, Woolpack, Work, Ziplock

Bagpipe Chorus, Cornemuse, Drone, Musette, Pibroch, Piffero, Skirl, Sourdeline, Uillean, Zampogna

Bail(er), Bailment Bond, Ladle, Mainpernor, Mainprise, Mutuum, Scoop

Bailiff Adam, Beagle, Bum, Factor, Grieve, Land-agent, Philistine, Reeve, Steward, Tipstaff, Water

Bait Badger, Berley, Brandling, Burley, Chum, Dap, Decoy, Entice, Gentle, Harass, Incentive, Lobworm, Lug(worm), Lure, Mawk, > **RAG**, Ragworm, Teagle, Tease

Bake(r), Baked, Baking Alaska, Batch, Baxter, > **COOK**, Fire, Kiln-dry, Roast, Scorch, Shirr

Balance Account, Beam, Counterpoise, Counterweight, Equate, Equilibrium, Equipoise, Equiponderate, Even, Gyroscope, Gyrostat, Isostasy, Launce, Libra, Librate, Meet, Otolith, Peise, Perch, Peyse, Poise, > **REMAINDER**, Remnant, Residual, Rest, Scale, Spring, Stand, Steelyard, Symmetry, > **TOTAL**, Trial, Trim, Tron(e)

Balcony Circle, Gallery, Loggia, Mirador, Moucharaby, Porch, Sundeck, Tarras, Terrace, Veranda(h)

Bald, Baldness Alopecia, Apterium, Awnless, Barren, Calvities, Coot, Crude, Egghead, Fox-evil, Glabrous, Hairless, Madarosis, Open, Peelgarlic, Pilgarlic(k), Pollard, Psilosis, Slaphead, Smoothpate, Tonsured

Bale Bl, Bundle, Evil, Pack, Truss

Ball(s) Agglomerate, Alley, Ally, Ammo, Aniseed, Beach, Bead, Beamer, Bobble, Bolus, Bosey, Bouncer, Break, Cap, Cherry, Chinaman, Clew, Clue, Cotill(i)on, Cramp, Croquette, Crystal, Cue, Curve, Daisy-cutter, > **DANCE**, Delivery, Dollydrop, Gazunder, > **GLOBE**, Glomerate, Googly, Gool(e)ys, Goolies, Grub, Gutta, Gutter, Hank, Hop, Inswinger, Ivory, Knur(r), Leather, Leg-break, Lob, Long-hop, Marble, Masque(rade), Medicine, Minié, Moth, Nur(r), O, Off-break, Off-spin, Outswinger, Overarm, Pea, Pellet, Pill, Pompom, Prom, Puck, Quenelle, Rissole, Rover, Rundle, Seamer, Sneak, Sphere, Spinner, Testes, Tice, Witches, Wood, Yorker

Ballast Kentledge, Makeweight, Stabiliser, Trim, Weight

Ballerina Coryphee, Dancer, Pavlova

Ballet, Ballet movement, Ballet-system Bolshoi, Checkmate, Développé,

Écarté, Firebird, Giselle, Kirov, Laban

Ballistic Wildfire

Balloon(ist) Aeronaut, Aerostat, Airship, Bag, Barrage, Billow, Blimp, Bloat, Dirigible, Dumont, Fumetto, Hot air, Lead, Montgolfier, Pilot, Rawinsonde, Weather, Zeppelin

Ballot Election, > POLL, Referendum, Suffrage, Ticket, Vote

Balm(y) Anetic, Arnica, Balsam, Calamint, Fragrant, Garjan, Gilead, Gurjun, Lemon, Lenitive, > MILD, Mirbane, Myrbane, Nard, Oil, Opobalsam, Ottar, Redolent, Remedy, Soothe, Spikenard, Tolu, Unguent

Balsam Canada, Copaiba, Copaiva, Nard, Peruvian, Resin, Spikenard, Tamanu, Tolu(ic), Touch-me-not, Tous-les-mois, Turpentine

Ban Abolish, Accurse, Anathema, Black(ing), Censor, Debar, D-notice, Embargo, Estop, Excommunicate, Forbid, For(e)say, For(e)speak, Gate, Green, Moratorium, No, Outlaw, Prohibit, Proscribe, Taboo, Tabu, Test, Veto

Banal Corny, Flat, Hackneyed, Jejune, Mundane, Platitudinous, > TRITE, Trivial

Banana(s) Abaca, Hand, > MAD, Musa, Plantain, Split

Band(s) Alice, Anadem, Armlet, Belt, Border, Braid, Brake, Brass, Brassard, Brassart, Caravan, CB, Channel, Chromosome, Circlet, Citizen's, Cohort, Collar, Collet, Combo, Company, Conduction, Corslet, Coterie, Crew, Deely boppers, Elastic, Endorse, Energy, Facia, Falling, Fascia, Ferret, Ferrule, Fess, Filament, Fillet, Frequency, Frieze, Frog, Frontlet, Galloon, Gamelan, > GANG, Garage, Garland, Garter, Gasket, Gaskin, Geneva, Gird, Girth, Guard, > HOOP, Hope, Iron, Jazz, Jug, Kitchen, Label, Lytta, Maniple, Massed, Military, Mourning, Noise, One-man, Orchestra, Pack, Pass, Patte, Pipe, Plinth, Property, Puttee, Rib, Ribbon, Rim, Ring, Robbers, Rubber, Sash, Scarf, Screed, Sect, Shadow, Sheet, Shoe, Snood, Steel, Strake, Strap, Stratum, String, Stripe, Swath(e), Tape, Tendon, Tie, Tippet, Tourniquet, Train, Troop, Troupe, Tumpline, Turm, Tyre, Unite, Valence, Vitrain, Vitta, Wanty, Wedding, Weeper, Welt, With(e), Wristlet, Zona, Zone

Bandage Bind, Dressing, Fillet, Lint, Pledget, Roller, Sling, Spica, Swaddle, Swathe, T, Tape, Truss, Wadding

Bandit Apache, Bravo, Brigand, Desperado, Outlaw, Pirate, Rapparee, > ROBBER, Turpin

Bane Curse, Evil, Harm, Poison

Bang(er) Amorce, Big, Cap, Chipolata, Clap, Cracker, Crock, Explode, Flivver, Fringe, Haircut, Heap, Implode, Jalopy, Maroon, Rattletrap, Report, Sausage, Sizzler, Slam, Thrill, Wurst

Bangle Anklet, Armlet, Bracelet, Kara

Banish(ment) Ban, Deport, Depose, Exile, Expatriate, Expel, Extradition, Forsay, Maroon, Ostracise, > OUTLAW, Relegate, Rusticate

Bank(ing) An(n)icut, Asar, Backs, Bar, Bay, Bk, Blood, Bluff, Bottle, Brae, Brim, Bund, Camber, Cay, Central, Chesil, Clearing, Cloud, Commercial, Cooperative, Data, Depend, Deposit, Dogger, Down, Dune, Dyke, Earthwork, Escarp, Fog, Gene, Giro, Glacis, Gradient, Gradin(e), Hele, Hill, Home, Incline, Jodrell, Land, Left, Lender, Levee, Link, Memory, Merchant, Mound, Nap, National, Nore, Overslaugh, Parapet, Penny, Piggy, Pot, Private, Rake, Ramp, Rampart, Reef, > RELY, Reserve, Rivage, Riverside, Rodham, Row, Sandbar, Savings, Shallow, Shelf, Side, Slope, Soil, Sperm, Staithe, State, Sunk, Telephone, Terrace, Terreplein, Tier, Vault, West, World

Banker Agent, Financial, Fugger, Gnome, Lombard, Medici, > RIVER, Rothschild, Shroff

▷ **Banker** *may indicate* a river

Bankrupt(cy) Break, Broke, Bung, Bust, Cadaver, Carey Street, Crash, Debtor,

Deplete, Duck, Dyvour, Fail, Fold, Insolvent, Receivership, Ruin, Rump, Scat, Sequestration, Skatt, Smash

▷ **Bankrupt** *may indicate* 'red' around another word

Banner Banderol(e), Bandrol, Bannerol, > **FLAG**, Gumphion, Labarum, Oriflamme, Sign, Streamer

Banquet Beanfeast, Dine, Feast, Junket, Spread

Banter Badinage, Borak, Chaff, Dicacity, Dieter, Jest, > **JOKE**, Persiflage, Picong, Rag, Rally, Ribaldry, Roast, Tease

Baptise(d), Baptism, Baptist Affusion, Amrit, Christen, Dip, Dipper, Dopper, Dunker, Illuminati, Immersion, Sprinkle, Tinker

Bar(s) Angle-iron, Asymmetric, Axletree, Bail, Ban, Baulk, Beam, Bilboes, Billet, Bistro, Blackball, Blacklist, Block(ade), Bloom, Bolt, Boom, Bottega, Brasserie, Buffet, Bull, Bumper, But, Buvette, > **CAGE**, Came, Cantina, Capo, Capstan, Cocktail, Coffee, Colour, Counter, Cramp(on), Crow, Crush, Currency, Dive, Draw, Drift, Dumbbell, Espresso, Estop(pel), Except, Exclude, Fen, Fid, Flinders, Forbid, Foreclose, Forestall, Fret, Gad, Grate, Grid, Grog-shop, Hame, Handspike, Heck, > **HINDRANCE**, Horizontal, Hound, Impediment, Ingot, Inn, Inner, Judder, Juice, Karaoke, Kickstand, Knuckleduster, Latch, Let, Lever, Limbo, Line, Local, Lounge, Macron, Mandrel, Mandril, Measure, Menu, Milk, Muesli, Mullion, Nail, Nanaimo, No-go, Norman, Obstacle, Onely, Outer, Oxygen, Parallel, Perch, Pile, Pinch, Pole, Private, Prohibit, Pub, Public, Rabble, Rack, Rail, Ramrod, Rance, Reach, Restrict, Rib, Risp, Rod, Roll, Roo, Rung, Saddle, Salad, Saloon, Sans, Save, Saving, Scroll, Shaft, Shanty, Shet, Shut, Singles, Skewer, Slice, Slot, Snack, Snug, Spacer, Spar, Speakeasy, Spit, Splinter, Sprag, Status, Stave, Stick, Stretcher, Stripe, Sway, Swee, T, Tap(-room), Tapas, Taphouse, Tavern(a), Temple, Toll, Tombolo, Tommy, Tool, Torsion, Tow, Trace, Trangle, Transom, Trapeze, Trundle, Type, Vinculum, Wall, Ward, Wet, Whisker, Window, Wine, Wire, Wrecking, Z, Zed

Barb(ed) Bur(r), Fluke, Harl, Herl, > **HOOK**, Jag(g), Jibe, Pheon, Prickle, Ramus, Tang, Vexillum

Barbarian, Barbaric Boor, Fifteen, Foreigner, Goth, Heathen, Hottentot, Hun, Inhuman, Lowbrow, Outlandish, Philistine, Rude, Savage, Tartar, Tatar(ic)

Barbecue Braai vleis, Cook-out, Flame-grill, Grill, Hangi, Hibachi, Roast, Spit

Barber Epilate, Figaro, Scrape(r), Shaver, Strap, Todd, Tonsor, Trimmer

Bare, Bare-headed Adamic, Aphyllous, Bald, Barren, Blank, Bodkin, Cere, Décolleté, Denude, Hush, Lewd, Marginal, Moon, > **NAKED**, Open, Plain, Scant, Sear, Stark, Uncase, Uncover, Unveil

Barely Hardly, Just, Merely, Scarcely, Scrimp

Bargain(ing) Barter, Braata, Chaffer, Champerty, > **CHEAP**, Collective, Contract, Coup, Deal, Dicker, Distributive, Effort, Find, Go, Haggle, Higgle, Horse-trade, Huckster, Integrative, Option, > **PACT**, Plea, Productivity, Scoop, Snip, Steal, Supersaver, Time, Trade, Trock, Troke, Truck, Wanworth, Wheeler-dealing

Barge Birlinn, Bucentaur, Budgero(w), Butty, Gabbard, Gabbart, Galley-foist, Hopper, Intrude, Jostle, Keel, Lighter, Nudge, Obtrude, Pra(a)m, Ram, Scow, > **SHIP**, Trow, Wherry

▷ **Barge** *may indicate* an anagram

Bark Angostura, Ayelp, Bass, Bast, Bay, Bowwow, Canella, Cascara, Cassia, China, Cinchona, Cinnamon, Cork, Cortex, Honduras, Kina, Kinakina, Liber, Myrica, Peel, Pereira, Peruvian, Quebracho, Quest, Quillai, Quina, Quinquina, Rind, Salian, Sassafras, Scrape, > **SHIP**, Skin, Tan, Tap(p)a, Waff, Waugh, Woof, Wow, Yaff, Yelp, Yip

Bar-keeper, Barmaid, Barman Advocate, Ale-wife, Bencher, Hebe, Luckie, Lucky, Tapster, Underskinker

Barley (water) Awn, Bear, Bere, Bigg, Malt, Pearl, Truce

Barn Bank, Byre, Cowshed, Dutch, Grange, Skipper, Tithe

Barnacle Acorn, Cypris, Goose(neck), Limpet

Baroque Gothic, Ornate, Rococo

▷ **Baroque** *may indicate* an anagram

Barrack(s), **Barracking** Asteism, Boo, Cantonment, Casern(e), Cat-call, Garrison, Heckle, Irony, Quarters

Barrage Balloon, Fusillade, Heat, Salvo

Barrel Bl, Butt, Cade, Capstan, Cascabel, Cask, Clavie, Drum, Hogshead, Keg, Kibble, Morris-tube, Organ, Pièce, Run(d)let, Tan-vat, Thrall, Tierce, Tun, Vat, Wood

Barren Addle, Arid, Badlands, Blind, Blunt, Clear, Dry, Eild, > **EMPTY**, Farrow, Hirstie, Jejune, Sterile, Unbearing, Waste, Wasteland, Wilderness, Yeld, Yell

Barrier Bail, Barrage, Bayle, Block, Breakwater, Cauld, Checkrail, Cheval de frise, Chicane, Cordon (sanitaire), Crash, Crush, > **DAM**, Defence, Drawgate, Dyke, Fence, Fraise, Gate, Heat, Hedge, Hurdle, Mach, Obstruct, Pain, Rail(-fence), Rampart, Restraint, Revetment, Roadblock, Screen, Skreen, Sonic, Sound, Spina, Stockade, Thermal, Tollgate, Trade, Transsonic, Turnpike, Turnstile, > **WALL**

Barrister Advocate, Attorney, Counsel, Devil, Lawyer, Rumpole, Serjeant(-at-law), Silk, Templar, Utter

Barrow Dolly, Handcart, Henge, How, Hurley, Kurgan, Molehill, Mound, Pushcart, Tram, Trolley, Truck, Tumulus

Barter Chaffer, Chop, Dicker, > **EXCHANGE**, Haggle, Hawk, Niffer, Sco(u)rse, Swap, > **TRADE**, Traffic, Truck

Base Alkali, Bed, Beggarly, Billon, Bottom, Camp, Degenerate, Degraded, Dog, Down, E, > **ESTABLISH**, Floor, Foot, Foothold, Footstall, Found, Fundus, Harlot, Ignoble, Infamous, Install, Lewis, > **LOW**, > **MEAN**, Nefarious, Nook, Partite, Patten, Platform, Plinth, Podium, Premise, Ptomaine, Purin(e), Rascally, Rests, Ribald, Root, Servile, Shameful, Shand, Sheeny, Socle, Soda, Staddle, > **STAND**, Station, Substrate, Ten, Torus, Turpitude, Unworthy, Vile

Bash Belt, Clout, Go, Hit, Rave, Shot, Slog, Strike, Swat, Swipe

Bashful Awed, Blate, Coy, Modest, Retiring, Shamefast, Sheep-faced, Sheepish, > **SHY**

Basic, **Basis** ABC, Abcee, Alkaline, Aquamanale, Aquamanile, Crude, > **ESSENTIAL**, Fiducial, Fond, Fundamental, Ground(work), Gut, Integral, Intrinsic, Logic, Nitty-gritty, No-nonsense, Primordial, Principle, Radical, Rudimentary, Spit-and-sawdust, Staple, Substance, Underlying, Uracil

Basin Artesian, Bidet, Bowl, Canning, Catch, Cirque, Corrie, Cwm, Dish, Dock, Great, Lavabo, Laver, Minas, Monteith, Pan, Park, Piscina, Playa, Porringer, Reservoir, Scapa Flow, Slop, Stoop, Stoup, Tank, Tidal

Bask Apricate, Revel, Sun, > **WALLOW**

Basket, **Basket-work** Bass, Bassinet, Bread, Buck, Cabas, Car, Cob, Coop, Corbeil(le), Corf, Creel, Cresset, Dosser, Fan, Flasket, Frail, Gabian, Hamper, Hask, Junket, Kipe, Kit, Leap, Maund, Mocuck, Moses, Murlain, Murlan, Murlin, Osiery, Pannier, Ped, Petara, Pottle, Punnet, Rip, Scull, Scuttle, Seed-lip, Skep, Skull, Trug, Van, Wagger-pagger(-bagger), Waste(-paper), Wicker(-work), Will(e), Wisket

Basketball Tip-off

Bass Alberti, Ale, Alfie, B, Continuo, Deep, El-a-mi, Fish, Low, Ostinato, Serran

▷ **Bastard** *may indicate* an anagram

Bat, **Batter**, **Batting**, **Batsman**, **Batty** Ames, Assail, Barbastelle, Baton, Blink, Close, Cosh, Crackers, Dad, Die Fledermaus, Eyelid, Flittermouse, Grace, Hatter, Haywire, Hit, Hobbs, Hook, Horseshoe, In, Ink mouse, Kalong, Language, Man, Mastiff, Maul, May, Mormops, Myopic, Nictate, Nictitate,

Night, Nightwatchman, Noctilio, Nora, Opener, Pinch-hit, Pipistrel(le), Poke, Pummel, Racket, Racquet, Ram, Rearmouse, Ruin, Sauch, Serotine, Sledge, Stick, Stonewall, Striker, Swat, Vampire, Viv, Whacky, Willow, Wood

Batch Bake, Bunch

Bath(room) Aerotone, Aeson's, Bagnio, Bain-marie, Bed, Blanket, Blood, Bubble, Caldarium, Cor, Dip, En suite, Epha, Foam, Hammam, Hip, Hummaum, Hummum, Jacuzzi®, Laver, Mik vah, Mud, Mustard, Piscina, Plunge, Salt, Sauna, Shower, Sitz, Slipper, Soak, Spa, Sponge, Steam, Stew, Stop, Tepidarium, Therm, Tub, Turkish, Tye, Vapour, Whirlpool, Wife

Bathe, Bathing Bay(e), Beath, Bogey, Bogie, Dip, Dook, Embay, Foment, Immerse, Lave, Lip, Skinny-dip, Souse, Splash, Stupe, > swim, Tub, > wash

Baton Mace, Rod, Sceptre, Staff, Truncheon

▷ **Bats, Batting** *may indicate* an anagram

Battalion Bn, Corps, Troop

Batter(ed) Bombard, Bruise, Buffet, Decrepit, Pound

Battery Artillery, Drycell, Field, Henhouse, Nicad, Pra(a)m, Solar, Troop, Voltaic, Waffle

Battle(s), Battleground Action, Affair, Ben, Clash, Cockpit, Combat, > conflict, Encounter, Engagement, Field, > fight, Fray, Front, Joust, Royal, Sarah, Sciamachy, Skiamachy, Spurs, Stoor, Stour, Stowre, Theatre, Wage, > war

Battle-axe Amazon, Bill, Gorgon, Halberd, Ogress, Sparth(e), Termagant, Termagent, Turmagant, Turmagent

Battlement Barmkin, Crenellate, Merlon, Rampart

Battleship Carrier, Destroyer, Dreadnought, Gunboat, Man-o'-war, Potemkin

Bauble Bagatelle, Gaud, Gewgaw, Trifle

Bawl Bellow, Gollar, Howl, Weep

Bay Ab(o)ukir, Arm, Baffin, Bantry, Bark, Bell, Bengal, Bight, Biscay, Bonny, Botany, Broken, Byron, Cardigan, Chesapeake, Cove, Covelet, Creek, Daphne, Delagoa, Discovery, Dvina, False, Famagusta, Fleet, Frobisher, Fundy, Galway, Gdansk, Georgian, Glace, Golden, Green, Harbour, Hawke's, Herne, Horse, > howl, Hudson, Inlet, James, Jervis, Laura, Laurel, Lobito, MA, Manila, Massachusetts, Narragansett, Niche, Oleander, Oriel, Pegasus, Pigs, Poverty, Recess, Red, Roan, Shark, Sick, Sligo, Suvla, Tampa, Tasman, Thunder, Tralee, Ungava, Vae, Voe, Waff, Wash, Yowl

Bazaar Alcaiceria, Emporium, Fair, Fete, Market, Pantechnicon, Sale, Sook, Souk

Beach Bondi, Coast, Ground, Hard, Lido, Littoral, Machair, Miami, Plage, Sand, Seaside, Shingle, Shore, Strand, Waikiki

Beacon Belisha, Fanal, Lightship, Need-fire, Pharos, Racon, Radar, Radio, Signal

Bead(s), Beaded Aggri, Aggry, Baily's, Bauble, Blob, Bugle, Chaplet, Crab-stones, Drop, Droplet, Gaud, Paternoster, Poppet, Poppit, Prayer, Rosary, Tear, Wampum(peag), Worry

Beak AMA, Bailie, Bill, Cad, Cere, Coronoid, Gar, JP, Kip(p), Magistrate, Master, Metagnathous, Mittimus, Nasute, Neb, Nose, Pecker, Prow, Ram, Rostellum, Rostrum

Beam(ing) Arbor, Balance, Bar, Ba(u)lk, Binder, Boom, Bowstring, Box, Breastsummer, Broadcast, Bum(p)kin, Cantilever, Carline, Carling, Cathead, Collar, Crosshead, Crosspiece, Deck, Girder, Grin, Hammer, Hatch, I, Irradiate, Joist, Ke(e)lson, Landing, Laser, Lentel, Lintel, Manteltree, Molecular, Needle, Outrigger, Particle, Pencil, Principal, Purlin, Putlock, Putlog, Radio, > rafter, > ray, Rayon, Refulgent, Rident, Ridgepole, Rood, Roof-tree, Sandwich, Searchlight, Shaft, Shine, Shore, Sleeper, Smile, Stanchion, Stemson, Sternpost, Straining, Streamer, Stringer, Stringpiece, Summer, Support, Tailing, Tie, Timber,

Transom, Trave, Trimmer, Truss, Universal, Walking, Weigh-bauk, Yard, Yardarm

Bean Abrus, Adsuki, Arabica, Berry, Black, Black-eye, Borlotti, Broad, Bush, Butter, Cacao, Calabar, Castor, Cocoa, Coffee, Cow-pea, Fabaceous, Fava, Flageolet, French, Frijol(e), Garbanzo, Gram, Haricot, Harmala, Head, Horse, Jack, Jumping, Kidney, Lablab, Lentil, Lima, Locust, Molucca, Moth, Mung, Nelumbo, Nib, Noddle, Ordeal, Pichurim, Pinto, Runner, Snap, Soy(a), String, Sugar, Tonga, Tonka, Tonquin, Urd, Wax, Winged

Bear(er), Bear lover Abide, Abrooke, Andean, Arctic, Arctophile, Baloo, Balu, Beer, Bigg, Breed, Brook, Brown, Bruin, Brunt, > **CARRY**, Cave, Churl, Cinnamon, Coati-mondi, Coati-mundi, Cub, Demean, Dree, Ean, > **ENDURE**, Engender, Exert, Fur-seal, Gonfalonier, Great, Grizzly, Hack, Ham(m)al, Harbinger, Have, Hold, Honey, Humf, Hump(h), Jampani, Keb, Kinkajou, Koala, Kodiak, Koolah, Lioncel(le), Lionel, Lug, Mother, Nandi, Nanook, Owe, Paddington, Panda, Polar, Pooh, Rac(c)oon, Roller, Rupert, Russia, Sackerson, Seller, Shoulder, Sit, Sloth, Spectacled, Stand, Stay, Stomach, > **SUFFER**, Sunbear, Sustain, Targeteer, Teddy, Teem, Thole, Throw, Tolerate, Tote, Transport, Undergo, Upstay, Ursine, Water, Whelp, White, Wield, Woolly, Yield

Beard(ed) Arista, Awn, Balaclava, Barb, Beaver, Charley, Charlie, Confront, Defy, Face, Five o'clock shadow, Fungus, Goatee, Hair(ie), Hairy, Hear(ie), Imperial, Kesh, Mephistopheles, Outface, Peak, Rivet, Stubble, Vandyke, Whiskerando, Whiskery, Ziff

▷ **Bearhug** *may indicate* Teddy or similar around a word

Bearing(s) Air, Allure, Aspect, Babbitt, Ball, Behaviour, Bush, Carriage, Deportment, Direction, E, Endurance, Gait, Hatchment, Haviour, Hugger-mugger, Manner, Mascle, Middy, Mien, N, Needle, Nor, Pheon, Port, Presence, Reference, Relevant, S, Tenue, Thrust, W, Yielding

▷ **Bearing** *may indicate* compass points

Beast > **ANIMAL**, Behemoth, Brute, Caliban, Caribou, > **CREATURE**, Dieb, Dragon, Dzeren, Gayal, Genet, Grampus, Hog, Hy(a)ena, Jumart, Kinkajou, Lion, Mammoth, Marmot, Mastodon, Mhorr, Oliphant, Oryx, Panda, Potto, Quagga, Rac(c)oon, Rhytina, Rother, Sassaby, Steer, Sumpter, Teg, Wart-hog, Yahoo, Yak, Yale, Zizel

Beat(ing), Beaten, Beater Anoint, Arsis, Athrob, Bandy, Bang, Baste, Bastinado, Batter, Battue, Belabour, Belt, Bepat, Best, Blatter, Bless, Cadence, Cane, Chastise, Clobber, Club, Clump, Conquer, Cream, Cuff, Curry, Debel, > **DEFEAT**, Ding, Donder, Dress, Drub, Excel, Fatigue, Faze, Feague, Feeze, Fibbed, Flagellate, Flail, Flam, Float, Flog, Floor, Flush, Fly, Fustigate, Hollow, Horsewhip, Ictus, Knock, Knubble, Lace, Laidy, Lambast(e), Larrup, Lash, Laveer, Lay, Lick, Lilt, Lounder, Mall, Malleate, Mersey, Nubble, Outclass, Outdo, Outflank, Outstrip, Palpitate, Pash, Paste, Pommel, Pound, Prat, Pug, Pulsate, Pulse, Pummel, Pun, Quop, Raddle, Ram, Ratten, Resolve, Retreat, Rhythm, Ribroast, Round, Ruff(le), Scourge, Slat, Smite, Soak, Sock, Strike, Swinge, Systole, Taber, Tabor, Tact, Tala, Tattoo, Thesis, Thrash, Thresh, Throb, Thud, Thump, Thwack, Tick, Tired, Top, Torture, Trounce, Tuck, Verberate, Vibrate, Wallop, Wappend, Welt, Wham, Whip, Whisk, Whitewash, Wraught, Ybet, Yerk, Yirk

▷ **Beaten-up** *may indicate* an anagram

Beaut(y) Advantage, Belle, Camberwell, Charmer, Colleen, Corker, Dish, Glory, Houri, Hyperion, Lana, Monism, Picture, Pride, Pulchritude, Purler, Sheen, Smasher, Stunner

Beautiful, Beautify Bonny, Bright, Embellish, Enhance, Fair, Fine, Ornament, Pink, Smicker, Specious, To kalon

Beaver Beard, Castor, Eager, Grind, Oregon, Rodent, Sewellel

Because (of) As, Forasmuch, Forwhy, Hence, In, Inasmuch, Sens, Since

Beckon Gesture, Nod, Summons, Waft, Wave

Become, Becoming Apt, Besort, Decent, Decorous, Enter, Fall, Fit, Flatter, Get, Go, Grow, Happen, Occur, Seemly, Suit, Wax, Worth

Bed(ding), Bedstead Air, Allotment, Amenity, Apple-pie, Arroyo, Base, Bassinet, Berth, Bottom, Box, Bundle, Bunk, Caliche, Camp, Carrycot, Channel, Charpoy, Cill, Cot(t), Couch(ette), Counterpane, Couvade, Coverlet, Cradle, Crib, Cross, Cul(t)ch, Day, Divan, Doona, Doss, Duvet, Erf, False, Feather, Filter, Fluidized, Flying, Four-poster, Futon, Gault, Greensand, Hammock, Inlay, Kago, Kang, Kip, Knot, Knot garden, Layer, Lazy, Lilo®, Litter, Marriage, Mat, Matrix, Mattress, Murphy, Nap, Nest, Nookie, Oyster, Pad, Paillasse, Pallet, Palliasse, Pan, Parterre, Patch, Pavement, Pay, Pig, Plank, Plant, Plot, Procrustean, Puff, Quilt, Retire, Rollaway, Roost, Rota, Sack, Scalp, Settle, Shakedown, Sill, Sitter, Sleep, Sofa, Standing, Stratum, Stretcher, Sun, Tanning, Test, Thill, Trough, Truckle, Trundle, Twin, Wadi, Wady, Ware, Water, Wealden, Wedding

Bed-bug B, B flat, Chinch, Flea, Louse, Vermin

Bedchamber, Bedroom Boudoir, Chamber, Cubicle, Dorm(itory), Dormer, Dorter, Ruelle, Ward

▷ **Bedevilled** *may indicate* an anagram

Bee Athenia, Bumble, Carpenter, Cuckoo, Deseret, Drone, Drumbledor, Dumbledore, Group, Hiver, Honey, Humble, Killer, King, Lapidary, Leaf-cutter, Mason, Queen, Solitary, Spell, Spell-down, Swarm, Worker

Beech Hornbeam, Mast, Tree

Beef(y) Baron, Bleat, Brawny, Bresaola, Bull(y), Bullock, Carpaccio, Charqui, Chateaubriand, Chuck, Complain, Corned, Filet mignon, Groan, Grouse, Hough, Jerk, Liebig, Mart, Mice, Mousepiece, Muscle, Neat, Ox, Pastrami, Peeve, Porterhouse, Rother, Sauerbraten, Sey, Silverside, Sirloin, Stolid, Stroganoff, Tournedos, Tranche, Undercut, Vaccine

Beer Ale, Alegar, Amber fluid, Bantu, Bitter, Black, Bock, Chaser, Draught, Drink, Dry, Entire, Export, Gill, Ginger, Granny, Grog, Guest, Heavy, Herb, Home-brew, Kaffir, Keg, Kvass, Lager, Lambic, Lite, Lush, Malt, March, Middy, Mild, Mum, Near, Nog, October, Pils(e)ner, Pint, Pony, Porter, Real, Root, Saki, Scoobs, Sherbet, Skeechan, Small, Spruce, Stingo, Stout, Swanky, Swats, Swipes, Switchel, Table, Taplash, Tinnie, Tipper, Tshwala, Tube, Wallop, Wheat, Zythum

Beet Blite, Chard, Fat-hen, Goosefoot, Mangel(wurzel), Spinach

Beetle Ambrosia, Argos tortoise, Asiatic, Bacon, Bark, Batler, Bee, Blister, Bloody-nosed, Boll weevil, Bug, Bum-clock, Buprestus, Burying, Bustle, Buzzard-clock, Cabinet, Cadelle, Cane, Cantharis, Cardinal, Carpet, Carrion, Chafer, Christmas, Churchyard, Click, Clock, Cockchafer, Cockroach, Colorado, Darkling, Deathwatch, Devil's coach-horse, Diving, Dor(r), Dor-fly, Dumbledore, Dung, Elater, Elytron, Elytrum, Firefly, Flea, Furniture, Glow-worm, Goliath, Gregor, Ground, Hammer, Hangover, Hercules, Hop-flea, Hornbug, Impend, Japanese, Jewel, June, Ladybird, Ladybug, Larder, Leaf, Leather, Longhorn, Mall(et), Maul, May-bug, Oil, Overhang, Pinchbuck, Potato, Project, Protrude, Rhinoceros, Roach, Rosechafer, Rove, Scarab(ee), Scavenger, Scurry, Sexton, Skelter, Sledge(-hammer), Snapping, Snout, Spanish fly, Spider, Stag, Tiger, Tumble-bug, Turnip-flea, Typographer, VW, Water, Weevil, Whirligig, Wireworm, Woodborer

Before(hand) A, Advance, Ante, Avant, By, Coram, Earlier, Early, Ere, Erst(while), > **FORMER**, Or, Pre, Previously, Prior, Pro, Sooner, Till, To, Until, Van, Zeroth

Befriend Assist, Cotton, Fraternise, Support

Beg(gar), Beggarly, Begging Ask, Badgeman, Beseech, Bey, Blighter, Blue-gown, Cadge, Calendar, Crave, > **ENTREAT**, Exoration, Flagitate, Fleech, Gaberlunzie, Gangrel, Hallan-shaker, Implore, Impoverish, Lackall, Lazar(us),

Lazzarone, Maund, Mendicant, Mump, Niggardly, Panhandle, Pauper, Penniless, > PLEAD, Pled, Pray, Prig, Prog, Rag, Randy, Ruffler, Schnorr(er), Screeve, Scrounge, Shool(e), Skelder, Skell, Solicit, Sue, Supplicate, Thig(ger), Toe-rag, Touch, Undo, Whipjack

Begin(ner), **Beginning** Ab ovo, Alpha, Author, B, Black, Cause, Clapdash, Commence, Daw, Dawn, Deb, Debut, Embryo, Enter, Exordium, Fall-to, Genesis, Germ, Go, Greenhorn, Inaugural, Inception, Inchoate, Incipient, Incipit, Initial, Initiate, Intro, L, Lead, Learn, Learner, Logos, Nascent, Neophyte, > NOVICE, Onset, Ope(n), Ord, > ORIGIN, Outbreak, Pose, Prelim(inary), Primer, Rookie, Seed, Set, > START, Startup, Takeoff, Tenderfoot, Tiro, To-fall, Tyro, Yearn

Behave, **Behaviour**, **Behaving** Act, Conduct, Convenance, Decorum, Demean, Do, Etepimeletic, Ethics, Horme, > MANNER, Nature, Netiquette, Noblesse oblige, Obey, Praxeology, Quit, React, Response, Strong meat, Tribalism

Behind(hand) Abaft, Aft(er), Ahind, Ahint, Apoop, Arear, Arere, Arrear, Astern, Beneath, Bottom, Bum, Buttocks, Croup, Derrière, Fud, Late, Overdue, Prat, > REAR, Slow, Tushie

Being Cratur, Creature, Ens, Entia, Entity, Esse, Essence, Existence, Human, Man, Metaphysics, Mode, Nature, Omneity, Ontology, > PERSON, Saul, Soul, Subsistent, Substance, Wight

Belch Boak, Boke, Brash, Burp, Emit, Eruct, Rift, Spew, Yex

Belgian Flemish, Walloon

Belief, **Believe**, **Believed**, **Believer**, **Believing** Accredit, Bigot, Buy, Conviction, Credence, Credit, Creed, Cult, Culture, Deem, Deist, Doctrine, Doxy, Faith, Gnostic, Heterodoxy, Hold, Holist, Idea, Islam, Ism, Ludism, Messianist, Methink, Notion, > OPINION, Ovist, Pantheism, Persuasion, Physicism, Pluralism, Presumption, Religion, Reputed, Seeing, Superstition, Tenet, Theist, Think, Threap, Threep, Trinitarian, Trow, Trust, Unitarian, Wear, Wis(t)

Belittle Cheapen, Decry, Depreciate, Derogate, Discredit, Disparage, Humble, Slight

Bell(s) Angelus, Ben, Bob, Bow, Bronte, Cachecope, Canterbury, Carillon, Chime, Crotal, Curfew, Daisy, Diving, Division, Gong, Grandsire, Jar, Low, Lutine, Passing, Pavilion, Peal, Peter, Pinger, Ring, Roar, Sacring, Sanctus, Tailor, Tantony, Tenor, Tent, Tintinnabulum, Toll, Tom, Triple, Tubular, Vair

Bellow(s) Buller, Holla, Holler, Moo, Rant, Rave, Roar, Saul, Thunder, Troat, Tromp(e), Trumpet, Windbag

Belly Abdomen, Alvine, Bag, Beer, Bunt, Calipee, Celiac, Coeliac, Kite, Kyte, Pod, > STOMACH, Swell, Tum(my), Venter, Wame, Weamb, Wem(b), Womb

Belong, **Belonging(s)** Apply, Appurtenant, Chattels, Effects, Inhere, Intrinsic, Paraphernalia, Pertain, > PROPERTY, Relate, Traps

Beloved Alder-lief, David, Dear, Esme, Inamorata, Joy, Lief, Pet, Popular, Precious

Below Beneath, Inf(erior), Infra, Nether, Sub, Under, Unneath

Belt(ed) Baldric(k), Band, Bandoleer, Bandolier, Baudric(k), Bible, Black, Cartridge, Chastity, Clitellum, Clobber, Commuter, Conveyor, Copper, Cotton, Crios, Equator, Fan, Gird(le), Girt, Inertial, Judoka, Kuiper, Larrup, Life, Lonsdale, Mitre, Orion's, Orogenic, Polt, Pound, Roller, Safety, Sam Browne, Sash, Seat, Speed, Stockbroker, Storm, Strap, Stratosphere, Surcingle, Suspender, Swipe, Taiga, Tear, Tore, Tract, Van Allen, Wanty, Webbing, Wing, Zodiac, Zone, Zoster

Bemoan > LAMENT, Mourn, Sigh, Wail

Bemuse Infatuate, Stonn(e), Stun, Stupefy, Throw

Bench Banc, Bink, Counter, Court, Cross, Exedra, Form, Knifeboard, Magistrates, Pew, Rusbank, Settle, Siege, Stillage, Thoft, Thwart, Treasury, Trestle

Bend(er), **Bending**, **Bends** Angle, Arc, Arch, Articular, Bight, Binge, Buck(le),

Bust, Camber, Carrick, Chicane, Circumflect, Corner, Crank(le), Cringe, > **CROOK**, Curl, Curve, Diffraction, Dog-leg, Elbow, Engouled, Epinasty, Es(s), Falcate, Fawn, Flex(ural), Flexion, Flexure, Fold, Geller, Geniculate, Genu, Genuflect, Grecian, Hairpin, Hinge, Hook, Horseshoe, Hunch, Inflect, Knee(cap), Kneel, Knot, Kowtow, Mould, Nutant, Ox-bow, Plash, Plié, Ply, Recline, Reflex, Retorsion, Retortion, Retroflex, Riband, S, Scarp, Souse, Spree, Spring, Stave, Stoop, Swan-neck, Twist, U, Ups(e)y, Uri, Wale, Warp, > **YIELD**, Z

▷ **Bendy** *may indicate* an anagram

Beneath Below, Sub, Under, Unworthy

Benefactor Angel, Backer, Barmecide, Carnegie, Donor, Maecenas, > **PATRON**, Promoter

Beneficial, **Beneficiary**, **Benefit**, **Benefice** > **AID**, Alms, Avail, Behalf, Behoof, Behove, Bonus, Boon, Boot, Charity, Collature, Commendam, Commensal, Devisee, Disablement, Dole, Donee, Endorsee, Enure, FIS, Fringe, Housing, Incapacity, Incumbent, Inheritor, Injury, Inure, Invalidity, Living, Manna, Maternity, Ménage, Neckverse, Pay, Perk, Perquisite, Plus, Portioner, Postulate, Prebend, Profit, Sake, Salutary, Sanative, Sickness, Sinecure, Spin-off, Stipend, Supplementary, Symbiotic, Unemployment, Use, Usufruct

Benevolence, **Benevolent** Charitable, Clement, Humanitarian, Kind, Liberal, Philanthropy

Benign Affable, Altruistic, Gracious, Kindly, Trinal

Bent Akimbo, Bowed, Brae, Coudé, Courb, Crooked, Curb, Determined, Dorsiflex, Falcate, Fiorin, Flair, Habit, Heath, Inclination, Ingenium, Intent, Leant, Peccant, Penchant, Ply, Reclinate, Redtop, Scoliotic, Talent, Taste

▷ **Bent** *may indicate* an anagram

Bequeath, **Bequest** Bestow, Chantr(e)y, Demise, Endow, Heirloom, > **LEAVE**, Legacy, Mortification, Pittance, Transmit, Will

Berate(d) Censure, Chide, Jaw, Reproach, Scold, Slate, Vilify

Bereave(d), **Bereavement** Deprive, Loss, Mourning, Orb, Sorrow, Strip, Widow

Berry Allspice, Bacca, Cubeb, Fruit, Goosegog, Haw, Pepo, Pimento, Pottage, Rhein, Rhine, Sal(l)al, Slae, Sloe, Sop, Tomatillo

Berserk Amok, Baresark, Frenzy, Gungho, Rage

Berth Anchorage, Bunk, Cabin, Couchette, Dock, Moor, Seat, Space

Beseech Beg, Crave, Entreat, Implore, Invoke, Obsecrate

Beset Amidst, Assail, Assiege, Badger, Bego, Environ, Harry, Perplex, Scabrid, Siege

Beside(s) Adjacent, Alone, And, At, Au reste, Else, Forby(e), Moreover, Next, On, Withal

Besiege(d) Beset, Best(ed), Blockade, Gherao, Girt, Invest, Obsess, Plague, Surround

▷ **Besiege** *may indicate* one word around another

Besot(ted) Dotard, Infatuate, Intoxicate, Lovesick, Stupefy

Best A1, Ace, Aristocrat, Beat, Choice, Cream, Creme, Damnedest, Deluxe, Elite, Eximious, Finest, Flower, Foremost, Greatest, Ideal, Optima, Outdo, Outwit, Overcome, Peak, Peerless, Pick, Pink, Plum, Purler, Ream, Super, The, Tiptop, Top, Topper, Transcend, Wale

Bet(ting), **Betting System** A cheval, Ante, Back, Banco, Double, Flutter, Gaff, Gamble, Go, Hedge, Impone, Lay, Long shot, Martingale, Mise, Note, Pari-mutuel, Perfecta, Pip, Punt, Quadrella, Quinella, Ring, Risk, Saver, Set, Spec, Sport, Stake, Tattersalls, Tatts, Totalisator, Totalise, Tote, Treble, Triella, Trifecta, > **WAGER**, Yankee

Betray(al), **Betrayer** Abandon, Abuse, Belewe, Cornuto, Desert, Divulge, Dob, Double-cross, Giveaway, Grass, Judas, Renegade, Renege, Rumble, Sell, Sellout,

Shop, Sing, Sinon, Stab, Traditor, Traitor, Treachery, Treason, Turncoat

Betroth(ed), Betrothal Assure, Engage, Ensure, Espouse, Fiancé(e), Pledge, Subarr(h)ation

Better Abler, Amend, Apter, Bigger, Buck, Cap, Fairer, Gambler, Gamester, Imponent, Improve, Meliorate, Mend, Outdo, Outpoint, Preponderate, Punter, Race-goer, Reform, Superior, Surpass, Throw, Top, Turfite, Worst

Between Amid, Bet, Betwixt, Inter, Interjacent, Linking, Mesne, Twixt

Beverage Ale, Cocoa, Coffee, Cordial, Cup, > DRINK, Nectar, Tea

Bevy Flock, Group, Herd, Host

Beware Cave, Fore, Heed, Mind, Mistrust

Bewilder(ed), Bewilderment Amaze, Baffle, Buffalo, Confuse, Consternation, Daze, Flummox, Mate, Maze, Mystify, Perplex, Stun, Taivert, Will, Wull

Beyond Above, Ayont, Besides, Farther, Outwith, Over, Thule, Trans, Ulterior

Bias(ed) Angle, Bent, Discriminatory, Imbalance, One-sided, Partial, Parti pris, Partisan, Penchant, Predilection, > PREJUDICE, Prepossess, Skew, Slope, Tendency, Warp

Bible Alcoran, Alkoran, Antilegomena, Apocrypha, Authority, AV, Avesta, Bamberg, Book, Breeches, Coverdale, Cranmer, Cromwell, Douai, Douay, Family, Gemara, Geneva, Gideon, Good book, Goose, Gospel, Hexapla, Itala, Italic, King James (version), Leda, Mazarin(e), Midrash, Missal, Murderer, NT, Omasum, OT, Pentateuch, Peshito, Peshitta, Peshitto, Polyglot, Psalter, Revised Version, RSV, RV, Scriptures, Septuagint, Stomach, Talmud, Tanach, Tantra, Targum, Taverners, Tyndale, Vinegar, Vulgate, Whig, Wyclif(fe), Zurich

Bicker Argue, Bowl, Brawl, Coggie, Dispute, Tiff, Wrangle

Bicycle, Bike(r) Bone-shaker, Coaster, Dandy-horse, Draisene, Draisine, Hobby, Mixte, Moped, Mount, Mountain, Ordinary, Pedal, Penny-farthing, Raleigh®, Roadster, Safety, Scooter, Spin, Tandem, Velocipede

Bid(der), Bidding system Acol, Apply, Call, Canape, Command, Contract, Declare, Double, Gone, Invite, Misère, Nod, NT, > OFFER, Order, Pass, Pre-empt, Proposal, Puffer, Redouble, Summon, Take-over, Tell, Tender, Vied

Big Beamy, Bulky, Bumper, Burly, Cob, Enormous, Fat, Ginormous, Gross, > LARGE, Loud, Massive, Mighty, Obese, Stonker, Thumping, Tidy, Vast, Whacker, Whopper

Bighead Ego

Bigot(ed) Chauvinist, Dogmatist, Fanatic, Hide-bound, Intolerant, Racialist, Wowser, Zealot

Bigshot, Bigwig Cheese, Nob, Swell, > VIP

Bile, Bilious(ness) Cholaemia, Choler, Gall, Icteric, Melancholy, Scholaemia, Venom

Bilge Leak, Pump, Rot, Waste

Bill(y) Ac(c), Accommodation, Accompt, Account, Act, Ad, Addition, Barnacle, Beak, Becke, Budd, Buffalo, Can, Carte, Chit(ty), Cody, Coo, Coronoid, Demand, Dixy, Docket, Double, Due, Exactment, Fin, Finance, Foreign, Gates, Goat, Hybrid, Invoice, Kaiser, > LAW, Lawin(g), Legislation, Liam, Liar, List, Measure, Menu, Neb, Ness, Nib, > NOTE, Notice, Pork barrel, Portland, Poster, Private, Programme, Public, Reckoning, Reform, Rostral, Rostrum, Score, Short, Shot, Show, Sickle, Silly, Sparth(e), Sperthe, Spoon, Sticker, Tab, Tomium, Trade, Treasury, True, Twin, Victualling, Willy

Billiards, Billiards player, Billiards stroke Bar, Cueist, Jenny, Massé, Pool, Potter, Pyramids, Snooker, Whitechapel

Billow Roil, Roller, Rule, Surge, Swell, Wave

Bin Bing, Box, Container, Crib, Hell, Receptacle, Snake-pit, Stall, Wagger-pagger, Wheelie, Wheely

Bind(er), **Binding** Adherent, Adhesive, Alligate, Apprentice, Astrict, Astringent, Bale, Bandage, Bandeau, Bandster, Bias, Brail, Burst, Calf, Chain, Cinch, Circuit, Clamp, Colligate, Complain, Cord, Cummerbund, Drag, Edge, Embale, Enchain, Engage, > FASTEN, Fetter, Gird, Girdle, Hay-wire, Hold, Incumbent, Indenture, Iron, Keckle, Lash(er), Law-calf, Leash, Ligament, Ligature, Mail, Marl, Morocco, Muslin, Obi, Obligate, Oblige, Oop, Organdie, Oup, Parpen, Perfect, Pinion, Raffia, Restrict, Ring, > ROPE, Sheaf, Spiral, Strap, Stringent, Swathe, Tape, Tether, Thirl, Thong, Three-quarter, Tie, Tree-calf, Truss, Twine, Valid, Whip, Withe, Yapp, Yerk, Yoke

Binge Bat, Beano, Bend(er), Blind, Carouse, > DRINK, Drinking-bout, Party, Riot, Soak, Souse, Spree, Toot, Tout

Bingo Beano, Housey-housey, Lotto, Tombola

Binocular(s) Glasses, OO, Stereoscope

Biographer, **Biography** Boswell, CV, Hagiography, History, Life, Memoir, Plutarch, Potted, Prosopography, Suetonius, Vita

Biology, **Biologist** Cladistics, Mendel, Phenetics

Birch Birk, Cane, Cow, Flog, Hazel, Kow, Larch, Reis, Rice, Rod, Silver, Swish, Twig, Whip, Withe

Bird(s) Al(l)erion, Bertram, Brood, Damsel, Doll, Early, Flier, Fowl, Gal, > GIRL, Grip, Hen, Left, Pecker, Pen, Poultry, Quod, Raptor, Roaster, Sis, Skirt

▷ **Bird** *may indicate* a prison sentence

Bird-watcher Augur, Twitcher

Birth Burden, Congenital, Delivery, Drop, Extraction, Genesis, Jataka, Lineage, Nativity, Origin, Parage

Birthday Anniversary, Genethliac

Birthmark Blemish, Mole, Mother-spot, Naevus, Stigmata

Birthright Heritage, Mess, Patrimony

Biscuit Abernethy, Bath-oliver, Bourbon, Butterbake, Charcoal, Cookie, Cracker, Cracknel, Crispbread, Dandyfunk, Digestive, Dunderfunk, Fairing, Flapjack, Florentine, Garibaldi, Gingersnap, Hardtack, Kiss, Lebkuchen, Macaroon, Marie, Mattress, Nut, Oliver, Osborne, Parkin, Perkin, Petit four, Pig's ear, Poppadom, Poppadum, Pretzel, Ratafia, Rusk, Shortbread, Sweetmeal, Tack, Wafer, Zwieback

Bishop Aaronic, Abba, Aidan, Ambrose, Bench, Berkeley, Bp, Cambrensis, Cantuar, Chad, Coverdale, Diocesan, Dunelm, Ely, Eparch, Episcopate, Eusebian, Exon, Golias, Hatto, Henson, Latimer, Lord, Magpie, Metropolitan, Norvic, Odo, Ordainer, Patriarch, Peter, Piece, Polycarp, Pontiff, Prelate, Priest, Primate, Primus, Proudie, RR, Sleeve, Suffragan, Titular, Tulchan, Weed

Bison Bonas(s)us, Buffalo, Ox, Wisent

Bit Baud, Cantle(t), Chad, Cheesecake, Chip, Crumb, Curb, Curn, Drib, Excerpt, Fraction, Haet, Hate, Ion, Jaw, Jot, Mite, Modicum, Morsel, Mote, Mu, Nit, Ort, Ounce, Pelham, Peni, Penny, > PIECE, Port, Rap, Rare, Ratherish, Scintilla, Scrap, Section, Shaving, Shiver, Shred, Smidgen, Snaffle, Snatch, Snippet, Soupcon, Spale, Speck, Splinter, Spot, Suspicion, Tad, Tait, Tate, Threepenny, Trace, Unce, Whit

Bite(r), **Biting**, **Bitten** Caustic, Chelicera, Chew, Eat, Engouled, Erose, Etch, Gnash, Gnat, Hickey, Hickie, Incisor, Knap, Masticate, Midge, Molar, Mordacious, Mordant, Morsel, Morsure, Nibble, Nip(py), Occlude, Pium, Premorse, Rabid, Sarcastic, Sharp, Shrewd, Snap, Tart

Bitter(ness) Absinth, Acerb, Acid, Acrimonious, Ale, Aloe, Angostura, Bile, Caustic, Eager, Ers, Fell, Gall, Keen, Marah, Maror, Myrrh, Pique, Rancorous, Rankle, Resentful, Sarcastic, Sardonic, Snell, Sore, Spleen, Tart(aric), Venom,

Verjuice, Virulent, Vitriolic, Wersh, Wormwood

Bizarre Antic, Curious, Eccentric, Exotic, Fantastic, Gonzo, Grotesque, Odd, Off-the-wall, Outlandish, Outré, Pythonesque, Queer, Strange, Surreal, Weird

▷ **Bizarre** *may indicate* an anagram

Black(en), Blackness, Black-out Atramental, B, BB, Bess, Blae, Carbon, Charcoal, Cilla, Coloured, Coon, Cypress, Darkie, Darky, Death, Denigrate, Dinge, Dwale, Ebon(y), Eclipse, Ethiop, Fuzzy-wuzzy, Geechee, Graphite, Heben, Hole, Ink(y), Ivory, Japan, Jeat, Jet, Jim Crow, Kohl, Malign, Market, Melanic, Melano, Moke, Moor, Muntu, Myall, Negritude, Negro, Niello, Niger, Nigrescent, Nigritude, Obliterate, Obscure, Outage, Oxford, Piceous, Pitch, Platinum, Pongo, Prince, Pudding, Quashee, Raven, Sable, Sambo, Scab, School, Sheep, Sloe, Solvent, Sombre, Soot, Sooterkin, Spode, Spook, Stygian, Swart(y), Swarth(y), Tar, Uncle Tom, Weeds

Blackberry Acini, Bramble, Mooch, Mouch

Blackbird Crow, Jackdaw, Ousel, Raven

Blackjack Billie, Billy, Cosh, Flag, Sphalerite, Tankard, Truncheon, Vingt(-et)-un

Blackmail(er) Bleed, Chantage, Chout, Exact, Extort, Ransom, Strike, Vampire

Blackout ARP, Eclipse, Faint, Swoon

Black sheep Neer-do-well, Reprobate

Blacksmith Brontes, Burn-the-wind, Farrier, Forger, Harmonious, Shoer, Vulcan

Blade Acrospire, Bilbo, Brand, Brown Bill, Cleaver, Co(u)lter, Cutlass, Dandy, Espada, Faible, Foible, Forte, Gleave, Gouge, Guillotine, Hydrofoil, Lance, Leaf, Man, Mouldboard, Oar, Palmetto, Peel, Propeller, Rachilla, Rapier, Razor, Rip, Rotor, Scimitar, Scull, Skate, Spade-, Spatula, Spatule, Spear, Spoon, Stiletto, Stock, > **SWORD**, Symitar, Toledo, Vane, Vorpal, Web

Blame(worthy) Accuse, Censure, Condemn, Confound, Decry, Fault, Guilt, Inculpate, Odium, Rap, Reproach, Reprove, Stick, Thank, Twit, Wight, Wite, Wyte

Blameless Innocent, Irreproachable

Blanch Bleach, Etiolate, Scaud, Whiten

Bland Anodyne, Mild, Pigling, Sleek, Smooth, Suave, Unctuous

Blank Cartridge, Empty, Erase, Flan, Lacuna, Mistigris, Planchet, Shot, Space, Tabula rasa, > **VACANT**

Blanket Afghan, Bluey, Chilkat, Counterpane, Cover, General, Kaross, Mackinaw, Manta, Obscure, Overall, Poncho, Quilt, Rug, Saddle, Sarape, Security, Serape, Shabrack, Smog, Space, Stroud, Wagga, Wet, Whittle

Blast(ed) Blight, Blore, Blow, Bombard, Dang, Darn, Dee, Drat, Dynamite, Explode, Fanfare, Flaming, Flurry, Fo(e)hn, Gale, Gust, Parp, Pryse, Rats, Scarth, Scath(e), Sere, Shot, Sideration, Skarth, Tantara, Toot, Tromp(e), Trump(et), Volley

Blatant Flagrant, Hard-core, Noticeable, Strident, Vulgar

Blaze(r) Beacon, Bonfire, Burn, Cannel, Conflagration, Firestorm, > **FLAME**, Flare, Glare, Jacket, Low(e), Lunt, Palatinate, Race, Ratch, Star, Sun, Tead(e)

Bleach Agene, Blanch, Chemic, Chloride, Decolorate, Etiolate, Keir, Kier, Peroxide, Whiten, Whitster

Bleak Ablet, Bare, Blay, Bley, Dour, Dreary, Dreich, Raw, Wintry

Bleed(er), Bleeding Cup, Ecchymosis, Epistaxis, Extravasate, Fleam, Haemorrhage, Leech, Menorrhagia, Menorrh(o)ea, Metrorrhagia, Milk, Purpura, Root-pressure

Blemish Birthmark, Blot, Blotch, Blur, Botch, Defect, Flaw, Mackle, Mark, Mote, Naevus, Scar, Smirch, Spot, Stain, Sully, Taint, Tash, Vice, Wart, Wen

Blend(ing) Amalgam, Coalesce, Commix, Contemper, Contrapuntal, Counterpoint, Electrum, Fuse, Go, Harmonize, Hydrate, Interfuse, Interlace, Liquidise, Meld, Melt, > **MERGE**, Mingle, Mix, Osmose, Portmanteau, Scumble, Sfumato, Synalepha

▷ **Blend** *may indicate* an anagram

Bless(ing), **Blessed(ness)** Amen, Approval, Asset, Beatitude, Benedicite, Benediction, Benison, Benitier, Bensh, Bismillah, Boon, Brachah, Brocho, Consecrate, Cup, Damosel, Darshan, Elysium, Ethereal, Felicity, Gesundheit, Gwyneth, Holy (dam), Kiddush, Luck, Macarise, Mercy, Mixed, Sain, Saint, Sanctify, Sanctity, Urbi et orbi, Xenium

Blight Afflict, Ague, Bespot, Blast, Destroy, Eyesore, Rot, > **RUIN**, Rust, Shadow, Viticide, Wither

Blimey Coo, Cor, Crimini, O'Riley, Strewth

Blind(ness), **Blind spot** Amaurosis, Amblyopia, Artifice, Austrian, Beesome, Bisson, Blend, Blotto, Carousal, Cecity, Chi(c)k, Cog, Concealed, Dazzle, Eyeless, Feint, Festoon, Gravel, Hemeralopia, Hood, Jalousie, Legless, Meropia, Mole, Nyctalopia, Onchocerciasis, Persian, Persiennes, Pew, Prestriction, Rash, Roller, Scotoma, Seel, Shade, Shutter, Snow, Stimie, Stimy, Stymie, Sun, Teichopsia, Typhlology, Venetian, Word, Yblent

Blindfold Bandage, Hoodwink, Muffle, Seal, Wimple

Blink(er), **Blinkered**, **Blinking** Bat, Bluff, Broken, Flash, Haw, Idiot, Insular, Nictate, Owl-eyed, Owly, Twink, Wapper, Wink

Bliss(ful) Beatitude, Bouyan, Composer, Delight, > **ECSTASY**, Eden, Happy, Ignorance, Married, Millenium, Nirvana, Paradise, Rapture, Sion, Tir-na-nog, Valhalla, Wedded

Blister(ed), **Blistering** Blab, Blain, Bleb, Bubble, Bullate, Epispastic, Herpes, Pemphigus, Phlyctena, Scorching, Tetter, Vesicant, Vesicle

Blitz Attack, Bombard, Onslaught, Raid

Blizzard Buran, Gale, Snowstorm, Whiteout

Bloat(er) Buckling, Puff, Strout, Swell, Tumefy

Blob Bead, Bioblast, Drop, Globule, O, Spot, Tear

Bloc Alliance, Cabal, Cartel, Party

Block(er), **Blockage**, **Blocked**, **Blocking** Altar, Anvil, Ashlar, > **BAR**, Barricade, Barrier, Brake, Breeze, Brick, Briquette, Building, Bung, Bunt, Choke, Chunk, Clint, Clog, Clot, Cloy, Compass, Congest, Constipated, Cylinder, > **DAM**, Dead-eye, Debar, Dentel, Dentil, Die, Dit, Embolism, Encompass, Fipple, Hack-log, High-rise, Hunk, Ileus, Impasse, Impede, Impost, Ingot, Insula, Interrupt, Investment, Jam, Lingot, Lodgment, Log-jam, Lump, Ministroke, Nog, Oasis®, Obstacle, > **OBSTRUCT**, Occlude, Pad, Page, Parry, Pile-up, Plinth, Pre-empt, Prevent, Ram, Scotch, Sett, Siege, Stalemate, Stap, Starting, Stenosis, Stimie, Stimy, Stone, Stonewall, Stop, Stumbling, Stymie, Tamp, Thwart, Tower, Tranche, Trig, Triglyph, Writer's

Bloke Beggar, Chap, Cove, Fellow, Gent, Man, Oik

Blond(e) Ash, Cendré, Fair, Goldilocks, Platinised, Platinum, Strawberry, Tallent, Towhead

Blood(y) Ancestry, Bally, Blue, Blut, Claret, Clot, Cruor, Cup, Ecchymosis, Ensanguine, Epigons, Factor, Haemal, Ichor, Introduce, Kin, Knut, Menses, Nut, Opsonin, Parentage, Persue, Pigeon's, Plasma, Platelet, Properdin, Pup, Race, Rare, Red, Rh negative, Rh positive, Ruby, Sang, Serum, Show, Stroma, Toff, Welter

Bloodless Anaemic, Isch(a)emic, Wan, White

Blood money Eric

Blood-sucker Asp, Dracula, Flea, Gnat, Ked, Leech, Louse, Mosquito, Parasite,

Reduviid, Sponger, Tick, Vampire(-bat)

Bloom(er), Blooming Anthesis, Bally, Blossom, Blow, Blush, Boner, Dew, Error, Film, Florescent, Flowery, Flush, Gaffe, Glaucous, Heyday, Knickers, Loaf, Miscalculation, Out, Pruina, Rationals, Reh, Remontant, Rosy, Underwear

▷ **Bloomer** *may indicate* a flower

Blossom Blow, Burgeon, Festoon, Flourish, Flower, May, Orange, Pip

Blot Atomy, Blob, Cartel, Delete, Disgrace, Eyesore, Obscure, Smear, Smudge, Southern, Splodge, Splotch

Blotch(y) Blemish, Giraffe, Monk, Mottle(d), Spot, Stain

Blouse Choli, Garibaldi, Gimp, Guimpe, Middy, Sailor, Shirtwaist, Smock, Tunic, Windjammer

Blow(er) Bang, Bash, Bat, Bellows, Biff, Billow, Blip, Bloom, Brag, Breeze, Buffet, Burst, Calamity, Clap, Clat, Claut, Clip, Clout, Clump, Conk, Coup, Cuff, Dad, Daud, Dev(v)el, Dint, Douse, Dowse, Etesian, Facer, Fan, Fillip, Gale, Grampus, Gust, Hammer, Haymaker, Hit, Hook, Ictus, Impact, Insufflate, Karate, Kibosh, Knuckle sandwich, KO, Lame, Lander, Lick, Muff, Northerly, Noser, Oner, One-two, Paddywhack, Pash, Phone, Piledriver, Plague, Plug, Plump(er), Polt, Pow, Puff, Punch, Purler, Rats, Rattler, Rib-roaster, Roundhouse, Sas(s)arara, Scat, Settler, Short, Sideswipe, Side-winder, Sis(s)erary, Skiff, Skite, Skyte, Slat, Slog, Slug, Snot, Sock, Sockdolager, Southwester, Spanking, Spat, Spout, Squall, Squander, Stripe, Stroke, Stunning, Sufflate, Supercharger, Swash, Swat, Swinger, Telephone, Thump, Thwack, Tingler, Tootle, Trump(et), Tuck, Undercut, Upper-cut, Waft, Wallop, Wap, Waste, Welt, Whammy, Whang, Whap, Wheeze, Whiffle, Whirret, > **WIND**, Winder, Wipe

Blow-out Binge, Bloat, Exhale, Feast, Feed, Flat, Lava, Nosh-up, Snuff, Spiracle, > **SPREAD**

Bludgeon Bully, Club, Cosh, Cudgel, Sap

Blue(s) Adult, Aquamarine, Azure, Beard, Berlin, Bice, Bleuâtre, Blow, Bottle, Butterfly, Caesious, Cambridge, Cantab, Celeste, Cerulean, Clair de lune, Cobalt, Copenhagen, Cornflower, Coventry, Cyan, Danish, Danube, Dejected, Dirty, Disconsolate, Doldrums, > **DOWN**, Duck-egg, Eatanswill, Eggshell, Electric, Firmament, Fritter, Gentian, Germander, Glaucous, Glum, Heliotrope, Hump, Indecent, Indigo, Indol(e), Iron, Isatin(e), Lapis lazuli, Lavender, Lewd, Lionel, Low, Mazarine, Methylene, Midnight, Mope, Morose, Murder, Nattier, Naughty, Navy, Nile, Ocean, Off-colour, Oxford, Peacock, Periwinkle, Perse, Petrol, Porn, Powder, Prussian, Rabbi, Ribald, Riband, Right, Ripe, Robin's egg, Royal, Sad, Sapphire, Saxe, Saxon(y), Scurrilous, > **SEA**, Shocking, Sky, Slate, Smalt(o), Smutty, Sordid, Spirit, Splurge, Squander, Stafford, Steel, Stocking, Teal, Thenard's, Tony, Tory, Trist, True, Turquoise, Ultramarine, Unhappy, Urban, Washing, Watchet, Wedgwood®, Welkin, Woad

▷ **Blue** *may indicate* an anagram

Bluebell Blawort, Blewart, Campanula, Harebell

Bluebottle Blawort, Blewart, Blowfly, Blowie, Brommer, Brummer, Cop, Cornflower, Fly, Policeman

Blueprint Cyanotype, Draft, Plan, Recipe

Bluff(ing) Blunt, Cle(e)ve, Cliff, Clift, Crag, Fake, Flannel, Frank, Hal, Headland, Height, Hoodwink, Kidology, Pose, Precipice, Steep, Trick

Blunder(er), Blundering Betise, Bévue, Bish, Bloomer, Blooper, Boob, Bull, Bumble, Clanger, Clinker, Cock-up, Err, Faux pas, Floater, Flub, Fluff, Gaff(e), Goof, Howler, Inexactitude, Irish, Josser, Malapropism, > **MISTAKE**, Mumpsimus, Slip, Solecism, Stumble, Trip

Blunt(ed), Bluntly Abrupt, Alleviate, Bate, Bayt, Brash, Brusque, Candid, Deaden, Disedge, Downright, Forthright, Frank, Hebetate, Mole, Morned,

Obtund, Obtuse, Outspoken, Pointblank, Rebate, Retund, Retuse, Roundly, Snub, Straight-out, Stubby

Blur(ring) Cloud, Confuse, Fog, Fuzz, Halation, Mackle, Macule, Stump, Tortillon

Blush(ing) Colour, Cramoisy, Crimson, Erubescent, Erythema, Incarnadine, > REDDEN, Rouge, Ruby, Rutilant

Bluster(ing), Blusterer, Blustery Arrogance, Bellow, Blore, Hector, Rage, Rant, Rodomontade, Roister, Sabre-rattler, Squash, Swagger, Vapour, Wuthering

Boar Barrow, Calydonian, Erymanthian, Hog, Pentheus, Sanglier, Sounder, Tusker

Board(s), Boarding Abat-voix, Admiralty, Banker, Barge, Beaver, Billet, Bristol, Bulletin, Catchment, Centre, Cheese, Chevron, Circuit, Committee, Counter, Cribbage, Dagger, Dart, Daughter, Deal, Directors, Diving, Draft, Draining, Drawing, Embark, Embus, Emery, Enter, Entrain, Fare, Fascia, Featheredge, Fibro, Full, Gibraltar, Gutter, Hack, Half, Half-royal, Hawk, Hoarding, Idiot, Instrument, Ironing, Kip, Lag, Ledger, Lodge, Magnetic, Malibu, Masonite®, Match, Mill, Mortar, Moulding, Notice, Otter, Ouija, Palette, Pallet, Panel, Parochial, Particle, Patch, Pedal, Peg(board), Pension, Planch(ette), Plank, Ply(wood), Quango, Running, Sandwich, Sarking, Scaleboard, School, Screed, Sheathing, Shelf, Shingle, Side-table, Sign, Skirting, Sleeve, Snow, Sounding, Splasher, Spring, Stage, Strickle, Stringboard, Supervisory, Surf, > TABLE, Telegraph, Thatch, Theatre, Trencher, Verge, Wainscot, Wobble

▷ **Board** *may refer to* chess or draughts

Boarder Interne, PG, Roomer

Boarding house Digs, Lodgings, Pension

Boast(er), Boasting Big-note, Blew, Blow, Blowhard, Bluster, Bobadil, Bounce, Brag, Braggadocio, Breeze, Crake, Crow, Fanfaronade, Gas, Gascon(nade), Glory, Hot air, Jactitation, Line, Ostent(atious), Prate, Rodomontade, Scaramouch, Skite, Swagger, Swank, Tall, Thrasonic, Vainglory, Vaunt, Yelp

Boat Canal, Dragon, Eight, Four, Foyboat, Gravy, Hooker, Jolly, Lapstrake, Launch, Lymphad, Mackinaw, Monohull, Narrow, Outrigger, Pair-oar, Pedalo, Pont, Puffer, Sailer, Sauce, Shallop, > SHIP, Skiff, Slogger, Swing, Tender, Torpid, Vaporetto, > VESSEL, Weekender

Boatman Bargee, Charon, Cockswain, Coxswain, George, Gondolier, Harris, Hoveller, Phaon, Voyageur, Waterman, Wet-bob

Bob Acres, Beck, Curtsey, Deaner, Dip, Dock, Dop, Duck, Float, Hod, Hog, Jerk, Page-boy, Peal, Plumb, Plummet, Popple, Rob, S, Shingle

Bobby Bluebottle, Busy, Copper, Flatfoot, Patrolman, Peeler, Pig, > POLICEMAN

Body, Bodies, Bodily Administration, Amount, Anatomic, Astral, Barr, Board, Bouk, Buke, Bulk, Cadaver, Cadre, Carcase, Carnal, Caucas, Chapel, Chapter, Chassis, Clay, Cohort, Column, Comet, Committee, Contingent, Corpor(e)al, Corps, Corpse, Corpus, Corse, Cytode, Detail, Earth, Flesh, Frame, Fuselage, Goner, > GROUP, Hull, Inclusion, Lich, Like, Lithites, > MASS, Militia, Moit, Mote, Mummy, Nacelle, Nucleole, Nucleolus, Pack, Personal, Phalanx, Pineal, Plant, Platelet, Platoon, Politic, Posse, Purview, Quango, Relic(t), Ruck, Senate, Solid, Soma, Sound-box, Spinar, Spore, Squadron, Square, Staff, Stiff, Syndicate, Torso, Trunk, Turm, Ulema

▷ **Body** *may indicate* an anagram

Bodyguard Amulet, > ESCORT, Gentleman-at-arms, House-carl, Minder, Praetorian, Protector, Retinue, Schutzstaffel, > SHIELD, SS, Triggerman, Varangian, Yeomen

Boffin Brain

Bog(gy) Allen, Can, Carr, Clabber, Fen, Gents, Glaur, Hag, Lair, Loo, Machair, Marsh, Mire, Morass, Moss(-flow), Mud, Muskeg, Peat, Petary, Quag, Serbonian, Slack, Slade, Slough, Spew, Spouty, Stodge, Sump, Vlei, Washroom, WC, Yarfa, Yarpha

Bog(e)y Boggart, Bug(aboo), Bugbear, Chimera, Eagle, Poker, Scarer, Spectre, Troll

Bohemian Arty, Beatnik, Gypsy, Hippy

Boil(er), Boiled, Boiling (point) Anthrax, Blain, Botch, Brew, Bubble, C, Coction, Cook, Cree, Dartre, Decoct, Ebullient, Foam, Furuncle, Gathering, Hen, Herpes, Kettle, Leep, Ligroin, Pimple, Poach, Poule, Rage, Reflux, Samovar, Seethe, Simmer, Sod, Sore, Stew, Stye, Tea-kettle

Boisterous Gilp(e)y, Gusty, Hoo, Knockabout, Noisy, Rambunctious, Randy, Riotous, Rorty, Rough, Stormy, Termagant, Turbulent, Wild

Bold(ly), Boldness Brash, Brass, Bravado, Bravery, Bravura, Brazen, Crust, Daredevil, Defiant, Derring-do, Familiar, Free, Hardihood, Heroics, High-spirited, Impudent, Intrepid, Malapert, Mature, Outspoken, Pert, Plucky, Presumptive, Rash, Sassy, Temerity, Unshrinking

Bolt Arrow, Cuphead, Dash, Dead, Eat, Elope, Flee, Gobble, Gollop, Gorge, Gulp, Latch, Levant, Levin, Lightning, Lock, Missile, Pig, Pintle, Ragbolt, Rivet, Roll, Scoff, Slot, Snib, Sperre, Thunder, Toggle, U, Wolf

Bomb(er), Bombing Atom, Attack, B, Blockbuster, Borer, Buzz, Carpet, Cluster, Daisycutter, Deterrent, Doodlebug, Egg, Fission, Flop, Fusion, Grenade, H, Hydrogen, Lancaster, Land-mine, Letter, Liberator, Logic, Megaton, Mills, Minnie, Mint, Molotov cocktail, Mortar, Nail, Napalm, Neutron, Nuclear, Nuke, Parcel, Petar, Petard, Petrol, Pineapple, Pipe, Plaster, Plastic, Prang, Ransom, Robot, Shell, Smoke, Stealth, Stick, Stink, Stuka, Tactical, Terrorist, Time, Torpedo, V1

Bombard(ment) Attack, Battery, Blitz, Cannonade, Drum-fire, Mortar, Pelt, Shell, Stone, Stonk, Strafe, Straff

Bona fide Echt, Genuine

Bond(age) Adhesive, Agent, Bail, Cement, Chain, Compact, Connect, Copula, Corporate, Duty, Escrow, Flemish, Gilt, Hyphen, Ionic, James, Knot, Liaise, Ligament, Link(age), Manacle, Mortar, Nexus, Noose, > **PLEDGE**, Rapport, Shackle, Starr, > **TIE**, Valence, Vinculum, Yearling, Yoke

Bond(s), Bondsman Affinity, Baby, Bail, Bearer, Consols, Coordinate, Covalent, Covenant, Daimyo, Dative, Debenture, Deep-discount, Double, Electrovalent, English, Ernie, Esne, Fetter, Fleming, Flemish, Geasa, Grammy, Granny, Heart, Herringbone, Hydrogen, Income, Investment, Ionic, Junk, Long, Managed, Metallic, Municipal, Nexus, Pair, Peptide, Performance, Post-obit, Premium, Property, Recognisance, Relationship, Revenue, Running, Samurai, Security, Semipolar, Serf, Shogun, Single, Slave, Solder, Stacked, Superglue, Surety, Thete, Treasury, Triple, Vassal, Zebra

Bone(s), Bony Atlas, Axis, Caluarium, Cannon, Capitate, Carpel, Carpus, Catacomb, Centrum, Chine, Clavicle, Cly, Coccyx, Coffin, Concha, Coral, Costa, Coxa, Crane, Cranium, Cuboid, Cunciform, Dib, Dice, Diploe, Endosteal, Femur, Fetter, Fibula, Fillet, Frontal, Funny, Gaunt, Haunch, Hause-bane, Horn, Humerus, Hyoid, Ilium, Incus, Ivory, Kneecap, Knuckle, Lacrimal, Luz, Malar, Malleus, Mandible, Marrow, Mastoid, Maxilla, Medulla, Membrane, Metacarpal, Metatarsal, Nasal, Occipital, Orthopaedics, Os, Ossicle, Palatine, Parasphenoid, Parietal, Patella, Pecten, Pectoral, Pedal, Pelvis, Pen, Percoid, Petrous, Phalanx, Pubis, Rachial, Rack, Radius, Relic, Rib, Sacrum, Scapula, Sclere, Sepium, Sequestrum, Skeleton, Skull, Splint, Splinter, Spur, Stapes, > **STEAL**, Sternum, Stifle, Stirrup, T, Talus, Tarsus, Temporal, Tibia, Tibiotarsus, Tot, Trapezium, True-rib, Tympanic, Ulna, Vertebrae, Whirl, Wish

Bonfire Bale-fire, Beltane, Blaze, Clavie, Pyre

Bonny Blithe, Gay, Merry, Sonsy, Weelfar'd

Bonus Bounty, Bye, Dividend, Hand-out, Lagniappe, No-claim, > **PREMIUM**, Reward, Scrip, Spin-off, Windfall

Book(s), **Bookish**, **Bookwork** Academic, Acts, Album, Amos, Apocalypse, Atlas, Audio, B, Backlist, Bestiary, Bestseller, Bible, Black, Blotter, Blue, Bodice-ripper, Breviary, Caxton, Chron(icles), Chumash, Classic, Closed, Coffee-table, Commonplace, Compendium, Concordance, Cookery, Corinthians, Course, Cyclopedia, Dan(iel), Deuteronomy, Diary, Dictionary, Digest, Directory, Domesday, Doomsday, Eccles, Ecclesiastes, Edda, Encyclopedia, Engage, Enter, Eph, Ephesians, Erudite, Esther, Exercise, Exeter, Exodus, Ezek(iel), Ezra, Folio, Gal, Galatians, Gazetteer, Genesis, Good, Gradual, Guide, Hag(gai), Haggadah, Hardback, Heptameron, Herbal, Hosea, Hymnal, I Ching, Imprint, Incunabula, Isaiah, Issue, Joel, John, Joshua, Jud(ges), Jude, Kama Sutra, Kells, Kings, Lam(entations), Lectionary, Ledger, Leviticus, Lib, Liber, Libretto, Literary, Log, Luke, Macc, Maccabees, Malachi, Manual, Mark, Martyrs, Matthew, Micah, Missal, Monograph, Nahum, Nomenclator, NT, Numbers, Octavo, Omnibus, Open, Order, Ordinal, Ordinary, OT, Page-turner, Paperback, Pass, Pedantic, Penny dreadful, Pharmacopoeia, Philippians, Phrase, Pica, Plug, Polyglot, Pop-up, Porteous, Potboiler, Prayer, Primer, Prompt, Prophet, Proverbs, Psalms, Psalter, Pseudepigraphia, Publication, Quarto, Quire, Rag, Ration, Reader, Red, Reference, Remainder, > RESERVE, Revelations, Road, Romans, Satyricon, Script, Scroll, Sext, Sibylline, Sir, Sketch, Snobs, Softback, Spelling, Statute, Studious, Study, Style, Susanna, Table, Tablet, Talking, Telephone, Teratology, Text(ual), Thriller, Title, Titule, To-bit, Tome, Trade, Transfer, Tripitaka, Twelvemo, Vade-mecum, Veda, Visiting, Visitor's, Vol(ume), Waste, White, Work, Year, Zephadiah

Bookbinder, **Bookbinding** Fanfare, Grolier, Mutton-thumper, Organdie

Book-case Credenza, Press, Satchel

Bookie(s), **Bookmaker** John, Layer, Librettist, Luke, Mark, Matthew, Printer, Ringman, To-bit

Bookkeeper, **Bookkeeping** Clerk, Double entry, Librarian, Posting, Recorder, Satchel, Single-entry

Booklet B, Brochure, Folder

Boom(ing) Baby, Beam, Boost, Bowsprit, Bump, Increase, Jib, Orotund, Prosper, Roar, Sonic, Spar, Thrive, Wishbone

Boon Bene, Benefit, Blessing, Bounty, Cumshaw, Gift, Godsend, Mills, Mitzvah, Prayer, Windfall

Boor(ish) Bosthoon, Chuffy, Churl, Clodhopper, Crass, Goth, Grobian, Hog, Ill-bred, Jack, Keelie, Kern(e), Kernish, Kill-courtesy, Lob, Lout, Lumpen, Ocker, Peasant, Philistine, Trog, Uncouth, Yahoo, Yob

Boost(er) Afterburner, Bolster, Encourage, Fillip, Help, Hoist, Impetus, Increase, Injection, Lift, Promote, Raise, Reheat, Reinforce, Reinvigorate, Spike, Supercharge, Tonic

Boot(s) Addition, Adelaide, Avail, Balmoral, Beetle-crushers, Benefit, Blucher, Bottine, Bovver, Brogan, Brogue, Buskin, Chukka, Cold, Combat, Concern, Cowboy, Denver, Derby, Desert, Dismiss, Field, Finn(e)sko, Finsko, Fire, Galage, Galosh, Gambado, Go-go, Granny, Gum, Hessian, Hip, Jack, Jemima, Lace-up, Last, Mitten, Muchie, Muc(k)luc(k), Pac, Para, Profit, Sabot, > SACK, > SHOE, Surgical, Toe, Tonneau, Tops, Trunk, Ugh, Vibs, Wader, Warm, Weller, Wellie, Wellington, Welly

Booth Assassin, Crame, Kiosk, Polling, Stall, Stand, Voting

Bootlegger Cooper, Coper, Runner

Booty Creach, Creagh, Haul, Loot, Prey, Prize, Spoil(s), Spolia optima, Swag

Booze(r) > DRINK, Liquor, Spree, Tipple

Border(s), **Borderland**, **Borderline** Abut, Adjoin, Apron, Bed, Bind, Bound, Checkpoint, Coast, Cot(t)ise, Dado, Dentelle, > EDGE, Engrail, Fimbria, Frieze,

Fringe, Frontier, Furbelow, Head-rig, Hedgerow, Hem, Herbaceous, Impale, Kerb, Limb, Limbo, Limes, Limit, Lip, List, March, Marchland, > **MARGIN**, Mat, Mattoid, Meith, Mete, Mount, Neighbour, Orle, Pand, Pelmet, Perimeter, Purfle, Purlieu, Rand, Rim, Roadside, Roon, Royne, Rund, Selvage, Side, Skirt, Strand, Strip, Surround, Swage, The Marches, Trench, Valance, Valence, > **VERGE**

▷ **Borders** *may indicate* first and last letters

Bore(d), **Boredom**, **Borer**, **Boring** Aiguille, Anorak, Apathy, Auger, Awl, Beetle, Bind, Bit, Broach, Brog, Bromide, Calibre, Deadly, Drag, > **DRILL**, Dry, Eagre, Eat, Eger, Elshin, Elsin, Endured, Ennui, Ennuye, Foozle, Gim(b)let, Gouge, Gribble, Grind, Had, Heigh-ho, Ho-hum, Irk, Listless, Longicorn, Longueur, Miser, Mole, Nerd, Nuisance, Pall, Penetrate, Perforate, Pest, Pierce, Pill, Probe, Prosaic, Prosy, Punch, Ream(ingbit), Rime, Sat, Screw, Severn, Snooze, Snore, Sondage, Spleen, Sting, Stob, Tedious, Tedium, Termes, Termite, Thirl, Tire, Trocar, Tunnel, > **WEARY**, Well, Wimble, Windbag, Wonk, Woodworm, Worldweary, Yawn

Born B, Free, Great, Nascent, Nat(us), Né(e)

Borneo Kalimantan

Borough Borgo, Pocket, Port, Quarter, Rotten, Township, Wick

Borrow(ed), **Borrowing** Adopt, Appropriate, Cadge, Copy, Eclectic, George, Hum, Scunge, Straunge, > **TAKE**, Touch

Boson Gauge, Squark

Boss(ed), **Bossy** Blooper, Burr, Cacique, Director, Dominate, Gadroon, Headman, Honcho, Hump, Inian, Inion, Jewel, Knob, Knop, Knot, Maestro, > **MANAGER**, Massa, > **MISTAKE**, Mistress, Netsuke, Noop, Nose-led, Omphalos, Overlord, Overseer, Owner, Pellet, Protuberance, Ruler, Run, Stud, Superintendent, Taskmaster, Umbo(nate)

Bother(some) Ado, Aggro, Care, Deave, Deeve, Disturb, Drat, Fash, Fluster, Fuss, Get, Hector, Incommode, Irritate, Moither, Nuisance, Perturb, Pest(er), Pickle, Reke, Todo, > **TROUBLE**

Bottle(s) Ampul(la), Balthasar, Balthazar, Belshazzar, Bundle, Carafe, Carboy, Cock, Cork, Costrel, Courage, Cruet, Cruse, Cucurbital, Cutter, Dead-men, Decanter, Demijohn, Fearlessness, Feeding, Fiasco, Flacket, Flagon, Flask, Goatskin, Gourd, Hen, Imperial, Jeroboam, Klein, Lachrymal, Lagena, Magnum, Matrass, Medicine, Methuselah, Mettle, Nebuchadnezzar, Phial, Pitcher, Rehoboam, Resource, Retort, Salmanazar, Siphon, Split, Vial, Vinaigret(te), Wad, Water, Winchester, Woulfe

▷ **Bottle(d)** *may indicate* an anagram or a hidden word

Bottom Anus, Aris, Arse, Ass, Base, Beauty, Bed, Benthos, Bilge, Breech, Bum, Butt, Buttocks, Croup(e), Croupon, Demersal, Derrière, Doup, Fanny, Floor, Foot, Foundation, Fud, Fundus, Haunches, Hunkers, Hurdies, Keel(son), Kick, Nadir, Podex, Posterior, Pottle-deep, Prat, Pyramus, Rear, Rock, Root, Rump, Seat, Ship, Sill, Sole, Staddle, Tail, Tush, Weaver

Bounce(r), **Bouncing**, **Bouncy** Bang, Blague, Bound, Caper, Dap, Dead-cat, Doorman, Dop, Dud, Eject, Evict, Jounce, Kite, Lie, Lilt, Resilient, Ricochet, Spiccato, Spring, Stot, Tale, Tamp, Verve, Vitality, Yorker, Yump

▷ **Bouncing** *may indicate* an anagram

Bound(er), **Boundary** Adipose, Apprenticed, Articled, Bad, Barrier, Beholden, Border, Bourn(e), Cad, Cavort, Certain, Circumference, Curvet, Decreed, Demarcation, Demarkation, Duty, End, Engirt, Entrechat, Erub, Eruv, Fence, Four, Galumph, Gambado, Gambol, Girt, Hedge, Heel, Held, Hoarstone, Hops, Hourstone, Interface, Jump, Kangaroo, > **LEAP**, Limes, Limit, Linch, Lollop, Lope, Meare, Meer, Mere, Merestone, Mete, Muscle, Obliged, Outward, Pale, Parameter, Perimeter, Periphery, Plate, Prance, Precinct, Purlieu, Redound, Ring-fence, Roller, Roo, Roped, Rubicon, Scoup, Side, Sideline, Six(er), Skip,

Spang, Spring, Sten(d), Stoit, T(h)alweg, Tied, Touchline, Upstart, Vault, Verge, Wallaby

▷ **Bounds** *may indicate* outside letters

Bounty, **Bountiful** Aid, Bligh, Boon, Christian, Generosity, > **GIFT**, Goodness, Grant, Head money, Honorarium, Largess(e), Lavish

Bouquet Aroma, Attar, Aura, Compliment, Corsage, Fragrancy, Garni, Nose, Nosegay, Plaudit, Posy, Spiritual, Spray

Bout Bender, Bust, Contest, Dose, Go, Jag, Match, Spell, Spree, Turn, Venery, Venewe, Venue

Bow(ing), **Bower**, **Bowman** Alcove, Arbour, Arc, Arch, > **ARCHER**, Arco, Arson, Beck, Bend, Boudoir, Clara, Congé(e), Crescent, Crook, Cupid, > **CURVE**, Defer, Dicky, Droop, Duck, Eros, Eye, Fiddle(r), Fiddlestick, Foredeck, Halse, Hawse, Jouk, Kneel, Kotow, Lean, Lout, Nod, Nutate, Obeisance, Paganini, Pergola, Quarrel, Reverence, Salaam, Seamer, Shelter, Slope, Spiccato, Stick, > **SUBMIT**, Tie, Yew, Yield

Bowels Entrails, Guts, Innards, Viscera

▷ **Bower** *may indicate* using a bow

Bowl(ing), **Bowler**, **Bowl over**, **Bowls** B, Basin, Begging, Bicker, Bodyline, Bool, Bosey, Bouncer, Cage-cup, Calabash, Cap, Carpet, Caup, Chalice, Cheese, Chinaman, Christie, Christy, Cog(g)ie, Crater, Cup, Derby, > **DISH**, Dismiss, Dome, Drake, Dumbfound, Dust, Ecuelle, End, Finger, Goldfish, Googly, Grub, Hog, Hoop, Jack, Jeroboam, Jorum, Lavabo, Laver, Leg-spin, Lightweight, Lob, Locke, Monteith, Night, Offbreak, Old, Over-arm, Pace, Pan, Pétanque, Porringer, Pot-hat, Pottinger, Punch, Raku, Rink, Roll, Roundarm, Seam(er), Skip, Skittle(s), Spare, Spinner, Stadium, Stagger, Super, Ten-pin, Tom, Underarm, Underhand, Voce, Wassail, Wood, York(er)

Box(ing) Baignoire, Ballot, Bandbox, Bareknuckle, Bento, Bijou, Bimble, Binnacle, Black, Blue, Bonk, Bunk, Bush, Caddy, Call, Camera, Canister, Case, Cash, Casket, Chest, Chinese, Christmas, Clog, Coach, Coffer, Coffin, Coffret, Coin, Confessional, Cool, Crate, Cuff, Deed, Dialog(ue), Dispatch, Ditty, Dog, Drawer, Encase, Enclose, > **FIGHT**, File, Fist, Fund, Fuse, Fuzz, Glory, Glove, Go-kart, Grass, Hat, Hay, Hedge, Honesty, Humidor, Hutch, Ice, Idiot, Inro, Jewel, Journal, Junction, Jury, Keister, Kick, Kiosk, Kite, Knevell, Ladle, Letter, Light, Live, Locker, Lodge, Loge, Match, Mill, Mitre, Mocuck, Musical, Nest(ing), Omnibus, Orgone, Package, Paint, Pandora's, Patch, Peepshow, Peg, Penalty, Petara, Pew, Phylactery, Pill, Pillar, Pitara, Pix, Poor, Post, Powder, Press, Prompt, Protector, Puff, Pugilism, Pyxis, Register, Ring, Royal, Saggar(d), Sagger, Sand, Savate, Scrap, Seggar, Sentry, Set-top, Shadow, Shoe, Shooting, Signal, Skinner, Skip(pet), Slipcase, Smudge, Soap, Solander, Sound, > **SPAR**, Spice, Spring, Squeeze, Strong, Stuffing, Swell, Telephone, Telly, Tin, Tinder, Tool, Touch, Trunk, Tube, Tuck, TV, Vanity, Vinaigrette, Voice, Weather, Window, Wine, Witness

Boxer Ali, Bantamweight, Bruiser, Bruno, Canine, Carnera, Carpentier, Carthorse, Chinaman, Cooper, Crater, Cruiserweight, Dog, Eryx, Farr, Featherweight, Flyweight, Ham, Heavyweight, Middleweight, Pandora, Pug, Pugil(ist), Rebellion, Rocky, Shadow, Welterweight

Boy(s) Apprentice, Ball, Bevin, Blue-eyed, Breeches, Bub(by), Cabin, Callant, Champagne, Chiel(d), > **CHILD**, Chummy, Cub, Galopin, Garçon, Groom, Ha, Jack, Kid, Klonkie, Knave, Lackbeard, > **LAD**, Loblolly, Loon(ie), Minstrel, Nibs, Nipper, Page, Prentice, Principal, Putto, Rent, Roaring, Shaver, Son, Spalpeen, Sprig, Stripling, Tad, Ted(dy), Tiger, Toy, Urchin, Whipping, > **YOUTH**

▷ **Boy** *may indicate* an abbreviated name

Boycott Avoid, Bat, Black, Blacklist, Exclude, Hartal, Isolate, Ostracise, Shun

Brace(s), **Bracing** Accolade, Couple, Crosstree, Gallace, Gallows, Gallus(es), Gird,

Hound, Invigorate, Pair, Pr, Rear-arch, Rere-arch, Skeg, Splint, Steady, Stiffener, Strut, > **SUPPORT**, Suspenders, Tauten, Tone, Tonic, Two

Bracelet Armil(la), Armlet, Bangle, Cuff, Darbies, Handcuff, Manacle, Manilla

Bracken Brake, Fern, Pteridium, Tara

Bracket Angle-iron, Bibb, Brace, Cantilever, Console, Corbel, Couple, Cripple, Misericord(e), Modillion, Mutule, Parenthesis, Potence, Pylon, Rigger, Sconce, Straddle, Strata, Trivet, Truss

Brag(gart), Bragging Birkie, Bluster, Boast, Bobadil, Braggadocio, Bull, Cockalorum, Crow, Falstaff, Fanfaronade, Gab, Gascon, Hot-air, Loudmouth, Puff, Rodomontader, Skite, Slam, Swagger, Vainglorious, Vaunt

Braid A(i)glet, Aiguillette, Frog, Galloon, Lacet, Plait, Plat, Rickrack, Rick-rack, Ricrac, Seaming-lace, Sennet, Sennit, Sinnet, Soutache, Tress, Trim, Twist, Weave

Brain(s), Brainy, Brain disease, Brain-power Appestat, Bean, Bright, Cerebellum, Cerebrum, Cortex, Dura mater, Encephalon, Fornix, Genius, Gyrus, Harn(s), Head, Hippocampus, Hypothalamus, Insula, Intelligence, IQ, Loaf, Lobe, Mater, Medulla, Mind, Noddle, Noesis, Nous, Peduncle, Pericranium, Pia mater, Pons, Pontile, Sconce, Sense, Sensorium, Striatum, Subcortex, Thalamus

▷ **Brain(s)** *may indicate* an anagram

Brake Adiantum, Air, Bracken, Curb, Disc, Drag, Drum, Fern, Grove, Hydraulic, Nemoral, Overrun, Ratchet, Rein, Shoe, > **SLOW**, Spinney, Sprag, Tara, Thicket, Vacuum

Bramble, Brambly Batology, Blackberry, Boysenberry, Brier, Cloudberry, Rubus, Thorn, Wait-a-bit

Bran Cereal, Chesil, Chisel, Oats, Pollard

Branch(ed), Branches, Branching, Branch Office Affiliate, Antler, Arm, BO, Bough, Cladode, Cow, Dendron, Dept, Diversify, Diverticulum, Divide, Filiate, Fork, Grain, Jump, Kow, Lateral, Limb, Lobe, Loop, Lye, Lylum, Offshoot, Olive, Patulous, Raguly, Ramate, Ramulus, Reis, Rice, Shroud, Special, Spray(ey), Sprig, Spur, Tributary, Turning, Turn-off, Twig, Wattle, Yard

Brand Broadsword, Buist, Burn, Cauterise, Chop, Class, Denounce, Earmark, Ember, Excalibur, Falchion, Faulchin, Faulchion, Idiograph, Iron, Label, Line, > **MARK**, Marque, Sear, Stigma, Sweard, Sword, Torch, Wipe

Brandy Aguardiente, Applejack, Aqua vitae, Armagnac, Bingo, Calvados, Cape Smoke, Cold without, Dop, Eau de vie, Fine, Framboise, Grappa, Mampoer, Marc, Nantes, Nantz, Napoleon, Quetsch, Slivovic(a), Slivovitz, Smoke

Brash Impudent, Pushy, Rain, Rash

Brass(y), Brassware Benares, Brazen, Cheek, Corinthian, Cornet, Dinanderie, Face, Front, Harsh, Horn, Horse, Latten, Lip, Loot, Lota(h), Loud, Matrix, > **MONEY**, Moola(h), Pyrites, Sass, Snash, Sopranino, Talus, Top, Trombone

Brassière Gay deceiver

Brat Bairn, Gait(t), Gamin, Imp, Lad, Terror, Urchin

Brave(ry) Amerind, Apache, Bold, Conan, Corragio, Courage, Creek, Dare, Doughty, Dress, Face, Gallant, Game, Gamy, Gutsy, Hardy, Heroism, Indian, Injun, Intrepid, Lion, Manful, Manly, Nannup, Plucky, Prow(ess), Sannup, Stout, Uncas, Valiant, Valour, Wight

Bravo Acclaim, Bandit, Bully, Desperado, Euge, Murderer, Olé, Spadassin, Villain

Brawl(er) Affray, Bagarre, Bicker, Brabble, Donnybrook, Dust, Fight, Flite, Flyte, Fracas, Fratch, Fray, Melee, Prawl, Rammy, Roughhouse, Scuffle, Set-to, Shindig, Stoush, Tar, Wrangle

Brawn Beef, Burliness, Headcheese, He-man, Muscle, Power, Rillettes, Sinew

Bray Cry, Heehaw, Stamp, Vicar, Whinny

Brazen Bold, Brassy, Flagrant, Impudent, Shameless, Unabashed

Breach Assault, Break, Chasm, Cleft, Gap(e), Infraction, Redan, Rupture, Saltus, Schism, Solution, Trespass, Violate

Bread, Bread crumbs Azym(e), Bagel, Baguette, Bannock, Bap, Barmbrack, Batch, Baton, Brewis, Brioche, Brownie, Bun, Cash, Chal(l)ah, Chametz, Chapati, Cheat, Ciabatta, Cob, Coburg, Corn, Corsned, Croissant, Crostini, Croute, Crouton, Crumpet, Crust, Damper, Dibs, Dika, Doorstep, Flatbread, Focaccia, French, Garlic, Gluten, Graham, Granary, Grissino, Guarana, Hallah, Horse, Host, Indian, Jannock, Johnny-cake, Kaffir, Laver, Leavened, Loaf, Long tin, Manchet, Maori, Milk-sop, > **MONEY**, Monkey, Na(a)n, Pain, Panada, Panary, Pane, Paneity, Paratha, Pikelet, Pit(t)a, Pone, Poppadom, Poultice, Pumpernickel, Puree, Puri, Raspings, Ravel, Roll, Rooty, Roti, Round, Rusk, Rye, Sally Lunn, Simnel, Sippet, Smor(re)brod, Soda, Soft-tommy, Sourdough, Staff of life, Standard, Stollen, Stottie, Sugar, Sweet, Tartine, Tea, Tommy, Twist, Wastel

Break, Break-down, Break-in, Break-up, Broken Adjourn, Bait, Breach, Caesura, Caesure, Cantle, Cark, Cesure, Chinaman, Chip, Cleave, Coffee, Comb, Comma, Commercial, Comminute, Compost, Conk, Crack, Crock, Crumble, Debacle, Demob, Destroy, Diffract, Disintegrate, Disperse, Disrupt, Erupt, Exeat, Fast, Fault, Four, > **FRACTURE**, Fragment, Fritter, Frush, Gaffe, Give, Half-term, Half-time, Hernia, Hiatus, Holiday, Infringe, Interim, Interlude, Intermission, Interrupt, > **INTERVAL**, Irrupt, Knap, Lacuna, Lapse, Leave, Moratorium, Outage, Part, Pause, Playtime, Poach, Polarise, Price, Reave, Recess, Relief, Rend, Respite, Rest, Rift, Ruin, Rupture, Saltus, Schism(a), Secede, Shatter, Shiver, Smash, Snap, Split, Stave, Stop, Stop-over, Stove, Sunder, Tame, Tea-ho, Tear, Time-out, Torn, Transgress, Truce, Vacation, Violate

Breakable Brittle, Delicate, Fissile, Frail, Friable

Breakdown Analyse, Autolysis, Cataclasm, Collapse, Conk, Glitch, Glycolosis, Histolysis, Lyse, Lysis, Ruin

Breaker Billow, Comber, Ice, Roller, Smasher, Surf

Breakfast B, Brunch, Chota-hazri, Continental, Disjune, Kipper, Wedding

Breakwater Groyne, Jetty, Mole, Pier, Tetrapod

Bream Fish, Porgy, Sar(gus), Tai

Breast(s), Breastbone, Breastwork Bazuma, Blob, Bosom, Brave, Brisket, Bristols, Bust, Counter, Diddy, Duddy, Dug, Garbonza, Gazunga, Heart-spoon, Jubbies, Jugs, Knockers, Norg, Nork, Rampart, Redan, Sangar, Stem, Sternum, Sungar, Supreme, Tit, Xiphisternum

Breastplate Armour, Byrnie, Curat, Curiet, Pectoral, Plastron, Rational, Rest, Shield, Thorax, Xiphiplastron

Breath(e), Breathing, Breather Aerobe, Aspirate, Exhalation, Expiration, Flatus, Gasp, Gill, H, Halitosis, Hauriant, Inhale, Inspiration, Lung, Nares, Nostril, Oxygenator, Pant, Pneuma, Prana, Pulmo, Rale, Respire, Respite, Rest, Rhonchus, Scuba, Snorkel, Snuffle, Spiracle, Spirit, Vent, Wheeze, Whiff, Whift, Whisper, Whist, Wind, Windpipe

Breathless(ness) Anhelation, Apnoea, Asthma, Dyspnoea, Emphysema, Orthopnoea, Puffed-out, Tachypnoea, Wheezing

Breech(es) Bible, Buckskin, Chaps, Flog, Galligaskins, Hose, Jodhpurs, Kneecords, Knickerbockers, Plushes, Smallclothes, Smalls, Trews, Trouse(rs), Trusses

Breed(er), Breeding(-place) Bear, Beget, Engender, Eugenics, Lineage, > **MANNERS**, Origin, Procreate, Pullulate, Race, Rear, Seminary, Sire, Species, Stock, Strain, Stud, Tribe

Breeze, Breezy Air, Breath, Brisk, Catspaw, Chipper, Doctor, Fresh, Gentle, Gust, Light, Mackerel, Moderate, Sea, Slant, Sniffler, Tiff, Zephyr

Brew(ery), Brewer, Brewing Ale, Billycan, Brose, Browst, Bummock, Contrive, Dictionary, Ferment, Infusion, Liquor, Malt, Potion, Steep, Yeast, Yill, Zymurgy

Bribe(ry) Backhander, Bonus, Boodle, Bung, Carrot, Dash, Embracery, Get at, Graft, Grease, Hush-money, Insult, Kickback, Oil, Palm, Palm-grease, Palm-oil, Payola, Schmear, Slush, Soap, Sop, Square, Straightener, Suborn, Sweeten(er), Tamper, Tempt, Tenderloin, Vail, Vales

Brick(s), **Brickwork** Adobe, Bat, Bath, Boob, Bullnose, Bur(r), Clanger, Clinker, Closer, Course, Fletton, Gaffe, Gault, Header, Ingot, Klinker, Lateritious, Lego®, Malm, Nogging, Red, Soldier, Sport, Stalwart, Stretcher, Terra-cotta, Testaceous, Tile, Trojan, Trump

Bride(s) Bartered, Danaides, Ellen, Spouse, War, Wife, Ximena

Bridge(head), **Bridge player** Acol, Aqueduct, Auction, Bailey, Balance, Barre, Bascule, Bestride, Brig, Brooklyn, Cantilever, Capo, Capodastro, Capotasto, Catwalk, Chicago, Chicane, Clapper, Clifton, Contract, Counterpoise, Cross, Cut-throat, Deck, Declarer, Drawbridge, Duplicate, Flying, Foot, Four-deal, Gangplank, Gangway, Gantry, Girder, Hog's back, Humber, Humpback, Humpbacked, Ice, Irish, Jigger, Land, Lattice, Leaf, Lifting, Ligger, Link, London, Menai, Overpass, Pivot, Pontifice, Pont Levis, Pontoon, Rainbow, Rialto, Rubber, Sighs, Skew, Snow, > **SPAN**, Spanner, Stamford, Straddle, Suspension, Swing, Tay, Temper, Tête-de-pont, Through, Transporter, Traversing, Trestle, Truss, Turn, Vertical lift, Viaduct, Waterloo, Weigh, Wheatstone, Wire

Bridle Bit, Branks, Bridoon, Bristle, Browband, Curb, Hackamore, Halter, Headstall, Musrol, Noseband, Rein

Brief(s), **Briefing**, **Briefly**, **Brevity** Awhile, Bluette, Brachyology, Breviate, Cape, Compact, > **CONCISE**, Curt, Dossier, Fleeting, Instruct, Laconic, Nearly, Pants, Pennorth, Pithy, Prime, Scant, > **SHORT(EN)**, Short-term, Short-winded, Sitrep, Succinct, Summing, Tanga, Terse, Transient, Undies, Update, Watching

Brigade Boys', Corps, Fire, International, Red, Troop

Bright, **Brightness** Afterglow, Alert, Brainy, Breezy, Brilliant, Brisk, Cheery, Cla(i)re, Clear, Clever, Effulgent, Elaine, Fair, Floodlit, Florid, Garish, Gay, Glad, Glow, Hono(u)r, Light, Lit, Loud, Lucid, Luculent, Lustre, Net(t), Nit, Radiant, Rosy, Scintillating, Sematic, Sharp, Sheeny, Sheer, Shere, Skyre, Smart, Stilb, Sunlit, Sunny, Vive, Vivid, White

Brilliant, **Brilliance** Ace, Blaze, Brainy, Def, Effulgent, Flashy, Galaxy, Gay, Gemmy, Glossy, Inspired, Lambent, Lustre, Mega-, Meteoric, Nitid, Pear, > **RADIANT**, Refulgent, Resplendent, Shiny, Spangle, Splendour, Star, Virtuoso, > **VIVID**, Water

Brim Edge, Lip, Rim, Ugly

Brine Muriatic, Ozone, Pickle, Saline, Salt

Bring Afferent, Bear, Carry, Cause, Conduct, Convey, Earn, Evoke, Fet, Fetch, Hatch, Induce, Land, Produce, Wreak

Bring up Breed, Educate, Exhume, Foster, Nurture, Raise, > **REAR**

Brisk(ness) Active, Alacrity, Alert, Allegro, Breezy, Busy, Chipper, Crank, Crisp, Crouse, Fresh, Gaillard, Galliard, Jaunty, Kedge, Kedgy, Kidge, Lively, Perk, Pert, Rattling, Roaring, Scherzo, Sharp, Smart, Snappy, Spanking, Spirited, Sprightly, Vivace, Yare, Zippy

Bristle, **Bristling**, **Bristly** Arista, Awn, Barb, Birse, Bridle, Chaeta, Flurry, Fraught, Frenulum, Gooseflesh, Hackles, Hair, Hérissé, Horripilation, Seta, Setose, Striga, Strigose, Stubble, Vibraculum, Villus, Whisker

Brit(ish), **Briton(s)**, **Briton** Anglo, Herring, Iceni, Insular, Isles, Limey, Pict, Pom, Rooinek, Saxon, Silurian, UK

Britain Alban(y), Albion

Brittle Bruckle, Crackly, Crimp, Crisp, Delicate, > **FRAGILE**, Frush, Redsear, Shivery, Spall, Spalt

▷ **Brittle** *may indicate* an anagram .

Broach Approach, Open, Raise, Spit, Suggest, Tap, Widen

Broad(ly) Crumpet, Dame, Doll, Doxy, Drab, General, Generic, Largo, Latitudinous, Loose, Outspoken, Ovate, Pro, Roomy, Spatulate, Thick, Tolerant, Wide, Woman

Broadcast(ing), Broadcaster Ad(vertise), Air, Announce, Beam, Breaker, CB, Disperse, Disseminate, Emission, Ham, IBA, OB, On, Outside, Pirate, Programme, Promulgate, Radiate, Radio, Relay, > SCATTER, Scattershot, Screen(ed), SECAM, Seed, Sky, Sow, Sperse, Spread, Sprinkle, Transmission, Ventilate, Wavelength

Brochure Leaflet, Pamphlet, Tract

Broke(n) Bankrupt, Bust(ed), Duff, Evans, Fritz, Insolvent, Kaput, Puckeroo, Shattered, Skint, Stony, Stove, Strapped

▷ **Broken** *may indicate* an anagram

Broker Agent, Banian, Banyan, Go-between, Jobber, Mediator, > MERCHANT, Shadchan, Uncle

Bronze, Bronze age Bell, Bras(s), Brown, Gunmetal, Hallstatt(ian), Helladic, Minoan, Mycenean, Ormolu, Phosphor, Schillerspar, Sextans, Talos, Tan, Third

Brooch Cameo, Clasp, Fibula, Luckenbooth, Ouch, Owche, Pin, Preen, Prop, Spang, Sunburst

Brood(y) Clock, Clutch, Cogitate, Covey, Eye, Eyrie, Hatch, Hover, Incubate, Introspect, Kindle, Litter, Meditate, Mill, Mull, Nest, Nid, Perch, Pet, > PONDER, Repine, Roost, Sit, Sulk, Team

Brook Babbling, Beck, Branch, Burn, Countenance, Creek, Endure, Ghyll, Gill, Kerith, Kill, Pirl, Purl, Rill(et), River, Rivulet, Runlet, Runnel, Stand, Stomach, Stream, Suffer, Tolerate

Broom Besom, Brush, Cow, Genista, Gorse, Greenweed, Knee-holly, Kow, Orobranche, Retama, Spart, Sweeper, Whisk

Brose Atholl, Pease

Broth Bouillon, Brew(is), Cullis, Dashi, Kail, Kale, Muslin-kale, Pottage, Scotch, Skilly, > SOUP, Stock

Brothel Bagnio, Bordel(lo), Cathouse, Corinth, Crib, Den, Honkytonk, Hothouse, Kip, Knocking shop, Seraglio, Stew

Brother(hood) Ally, Bhai, Billie, Billy, Blood, Brethren, Bro, Bud, Comrade, Fellow, Fra, Freemason, Lay, > MONK, Moose, Sib(ling), Theatine, Trappist, Worker

Brow Crest, Forehead, Glabella, Ridge, Sinciput, Tump-line

Brown(ed) Abram, Adust, Amber, Auburn, Bay, Biscuit, Bisque, Bister, Bistre, Bole, Br, Braise, Brindle, Bronzed, Brunette, Burnet, Capability, Caramel, Caromel, Cinnamon, Cook, Coromandel, Dun, Fallow, Filemot, Fulvous, Fusc(ous), Grill, Hazel, Ivor, John, Khaki, Liver, Meadow, Mocha, Mousy, Philamot, Rufous, Rugbeian, Russet, Rust, Scorch, Sepia, Sienna, Soare, Sore, Sorrel, Tan, Tawny, Tenné, Testaceous, Toast, Tom, Umber, Vandyke, Wholemeal, Windsor

Browse(r) Graze, Pasture, Read, Scan, Stall-read, Surf

Bruise Contund, Contuse, Crush, Damage, Ding, Ecchymosis, Frush, Golp(e), Hurt, Intuse, Livedo, Lividity, Mark, Mouse, Pound, Purpure, Rainbow, Shiner, Ston(n), Stun, Surbate

Brush (off), Brushwood Bavin, Brake, Broom, Carbon, Chaparral, Clash, Dandy, Dismiss, Dust, Encounter, Fan, Filbert, Filecard, Firth, Fitch, Frith, Grainer, Hag, Hog, Kiss, Liner, Loofah, Mop, Paint, Pig, Pope's head, Putois, Rebuff, Rice, Rigger, Sable, Scrub, Scuff, Skim, Striper, Thicket, Touch

Brutal, Brute Animal, Beast, Bête, Caesar, Caliban, Cruel, Hun, Iguanodon, Inhuman, Nazi, Nero, Ostrogoth, Pitiless, Quagga, Roughshod, Ruffian, Thresher-whale, Yahoo

Bubble(s), **Bubbly** Air-bell, Air-lock, Barmy, Bead(ed), Bell, Bleb, Blister, Boil, Buller, Cavitate, Champagne, Cissing, Ebullition, Effervesce, Embolus, Enthuse, Espumoso, Foam, > **FROTH**, Gassy, Globule, Gurgle, Head, Mantle, Mississippi, Popple, Rale, Reputation, Roundel, Rowndell, Seed, Seethe, Simmer, South Sea, Vesicle, Widow

Buck (up) Bongo, Brace, Cheer, Dandy, Deer, Dollar, Elate, Encheer, Hart, Jerk, Leash, Male, Ourebi, Pitch, Pricket, Ram, Rusa, Sore, Sorel(l), Sorrel, Spade, Spay(a)d, Staggard, Stud, Wheel

Bucket(s) Bail, Bale, Clamshell, Ice, Kibble, Noria, Pail, Piggin, Scuttle, Situla, Stoop(e), Stope, Stoup, Tub

Buckle Artois, Clasp, Contort, Crumple, Deform, Dent, Fasten, Warp

▷ **Buckle** *may indicate* an anagram

▷ **Bucks** *may indicate* an anagram

Bucolic Aeglogue, Eglogue, Idyllic, Pastoral, Rural, Rustic

Bud(ding), **Buddy** Botoné, Bottony, Bulbil, Burgeon, Clove, Cobber, Deb, Eye, Gem(ma), Germinate, Knosp, Knot, Nascent, Pal, Scion, Serial, Shoot, Sprout, Taste, Turion

Buddha, **Buddhism**, **Buddhist** Abhidhamma, Ahimsa, Amitabha, Anata, Anicca, Arhat, Asoka, Bodhisattva, Dalai Lama, Gautama, Hinayana, Jain, Jataka, Jodo, Mahatma, Mahayana, Maya, Pali, Pitaka, Pure Land, Sakya-muni, Sila, Soka Gakkai, Theravada, Tripitaka, Triratna, Zen(o)

Budge Jee, Move, Stir, Submit

Budget Estimate, Plan, Programme, Shoestring

Buff Beige, Birthday suit, Eatanswill, Fan, Fawn, Nankeen, Nude, Nut, Polish, > **RUB**, Streak

Buffalo African, Anoa, Arna, Asiatic, Bison, Bonasus, Bugle, Cap, Cape, Carabao, Ox, Perplex, Takin, Tamarao, Tamarau, Timarau, Water, Zamouse

Buffer Bootblack, Cofferdam, Cutwater, Fender

Buffet Bang, Blow, Box, Counter, Cuff, Hit, Lam, Maltreat, Perpendicular, Shove, Sideboard, Smorgasborg, Strike, Strook(e)

Bug(s) Arthropod, Assassin, Bacteria, Beetle, Capsid, Chinch, Cimex, Cockchafer, Croton, Damsel, Debris, Dictograph®, Eavesdrop, Harlequin, Hassle, > **INSECT**, Jitter, June, Kissing, Lace, May, Mealy, Micrococcus, Mike, Milkweed, Millennium, Mite, Squash, Tap, Vex, Wheel, Wiretap

Buggy Beach, Car, Cart, Shay, Tipcart, Trap

Bugle, **Bugle call** Chamade, Clarion, Cornet, Hallali, Last post, Ox, Reveille, Taps, > **TRUMPET**, Urus

Build(ing), **Building site** Accrue, Ar(a)eostyle, Assemble, Big, Bricks and mortar, Capitol, Chapterhouse, Colosseum, Commons, Corncrib, Cot, > **CREATE**, Cruck, Curia, Develop, Drystone, Duplex, Edifice, Edify, Erect, Fabric, High-rise, Hut, Infill, Insula, Kaaba, Ken, Linhay, Listed, Low-rise, Lyceum, Minaret, Mould, Observatory, Outhouse, Palazzo, Phalanx, Pile, Portakabin®, Premises, Quonset®, Raise, Ribbon, Rotunda, Skyscraper, Stance, Structure, Synthesis, System, Tectonic, Telecottage, Temple, Tenement, Tower

▷ **Building** *may indicate* an anagram

Bulb Camas(h), Chive, Cive, Corm, Globe, Lamp, Light, Pearl, Scallion, Set, Shallot, Squill

Bulge, **Bulging** Astrut, Bag, Bias, Biconvex, Bug, Bulbous, Bunchy, Cockle, Entasis, Expand, Exsert, Inion, Protrude, Relievo, Rotund, Strout, Strut, > **SWELL**, Tumid

Bulk(y) Aggregate, Ample, Big, Body, Corpulent, Extent, Gross, Hull, Massive, Preponderance, Roughage, Scalar, > **SIZE**, Stout, Vol(ume), Weight

Bull(s), **Bullock**, **Bully** Anoa, Apis, Beef, Blarney, Bluster, Bovine, Brag, Brave, Browbeat, Bucko, Despot, Dragoon, Drawcansir, Englishman, Fancyman, Farnese, Flashman, Flatter, Gold, Gosh, Hapi, Harass, Haze(r), Hector, Hoodlum, Huff, Intimidate, Investor, Irish(ism), John, Killcow, Lambast, Maltreat, Mick(e)(y), Mistake, Mithraism, Mohock, Neat, Papal, Piker, Pistol, Placet, Poler, Rhodian, Roarer, Rot, Ruffian, Sitting, Stag, Strong-arm, Swash-buckler, Taurine, Taurus, Tommy-rot, Tosh, Trash, Twaddle, Tyran(ne), Tyrannise, Tyrant, Zo(bo)

Bulldoze(r) Coerce, Earthmover, Leveller, Overturn

Bullet Balata, Ball, Biscayan, Dumdum, Fusillade, Minié, Minié ball, Missile, Pellet, Plastic, Round, Rubber, Shot, Slug, Tracer

Bulletin Memo, Newsletter, Report, Summary

Bull-fight(er) Banderillero, Banderillo, Corrida, Cuadrilla, Escamillo, Matador, Picador, Rejoneador, Tauromachy, Toreador, Torero

▶ **Bully** *see* **BULL**

Bulwark Bastion, Defence, Rampart, Resistor

Bum Ass, Beg, Prat, Sponge, Thumb, Tramp, Vagabond

Bumble Beadle, Bedel(l)

▷ **Bumble** *may indicate* an anagram

Bump(er), **Bumps** Big, Blow, Bucket, Clour, Collide, Dunch, Fender, Hillock, Immense, Inian, Inion, Joll, Jo(u)le, Jowl, Keltie, Kelty, Knar, Knock, Mamilla, Mogul, Organ, Phrenology, Reveille, Rouse, Speed, Thump

Bumph Loo-roll

Bumpkin Bucolic, Bushwhacker, Clodhopper, Hawbuck, Hayseed, Hick, Jock, Lout, Oaf, Put(t), Rube, Rustic, Yokel, Zany

Bun Barmbrack, Bath, Chelsea, Chignon, Chou, Hot-cross, Huffkin, Mosbolletjie, Roll, Teacake, Toorie, Wad

Bunch Acinus, Anthology, Bob, Botryoid, Cluster, Fascicle, Finial, Flock, > **GROUP**, Hand, Handful, Lot, Lump, Panicle, Raceme, Spray, Staphyline, Tassel, Tee, Truss, Tuft

Bundle Axoneme, Bale, Bavin, Bluey, Bottle, Byssus, Desmoid, Dorlach, Drum, Fag(g)ot, Fascicle, Fascine, Fibre, Fibrovascular, Kemple, Knitch, Lemniscus, Matilda, > **PACK(AGE)**, Parcel, Sack, Sheaf, Shiralee, Shock, Shook, Stook, Swag, Tie, Top, Trousseau, Truss, Vascular, Wad, Wadge, Wap

Bungle(r) Blunder, Blunk, Bodge, Boob, Botch, Bumble, Bummle, Duff, Fluff, Foozle, Foul, Goof, Mess, Mis(h)guggle, Muddle, Muff, Mull, Prat, Screw, Spoil

Bunk(er), **Bunkum** Abscond, Absquatulate, Balderdash, Baloney, Berth, Blah, Bolt, Casemate, Claptrap, Clio, Entrap, Guy, Hazard, History, Hokum, Humbug, Malarky, Rot, Scuttle, Tosh, Trap, Tripe

Bunting Bird, Cirl, Flag, Fringilline, Ortolan, Snow, Streamer, Yellow-hammer, Yowley

Buoy Bell, Breeches, Can, Dan, Daymark, Dolphin, Float, Marker, Nun, Raft, Ring, Seamark, Sonar, Sustain

Buoyant Blithe, Floaty, Resilient

Burden Albatross, Beare, Bob, Cargo, Cark, Chant, Chorus, Cross, Cumber, Drone, Droore, Encumber, Encumbrance, Fa-la, Fardel, Folderol, Fraught, Freight, Gist, Handicap, Hum, Lade, > **LOAD**, Lumber, Millstone, Monkey, Oercome, Onus, Oppress, Put-upon, Refrain, Rumbelow, Saddle, Servitude, Shanty, Substance, Tax, Tenor, Torch, Trouble, Weight, Woe, Yoke

Burdensome Irksome, Onerous, Oppressive, Weighty

Bureau Agency, Agitprop, Cominform, Davenport, Desk, Interpol, Kominform, Marriage, > **OFFICE**

Bureaucracy, Bureaucrat(ic) CS, Impersonal, Jack-in-office, Mandarin, Red tape, Tapist, Wallah

Burgeon(ing) Asprout, Bud, Grow, Sprout

Burgh Parliamentary, Police, Royal

Burglar, Burgle Area-sneak, Cat, Crack(sman), Intruder, Peterman, Picklock, Raffles, Robber, Screw, Thief, Yegg

Burial(place) Catacomb, Charnel, Committal, Crypt, Darga, Funeral, Golgotha, Grave, Interment, Kurgan, Lair, Last rites, Sepulture, Tomb, Vault, Zoothapsis

Burlesque Caricatura, Caricature, Comedy, Farce, Heroicomical, Hudibrastic(s), Hurlo-thrumbo, Lampoon, Macaronic, Parody, Satire, Skimmington, Skit, Spoof, Travesty

Burmese Karen(ni), Naga, Shan

Burn(er), Burning, Burnt Adust, Afire, Alow(e), Ardent, Argand, Arson, Ash, Auto-da-fé, Bats-wing, Beck, Bishop, Blaze, Blister, Brand, Brent, Brook, Bunsen, Caustic, Cauterise, Char, Chark, Chinese, Cinder, Coal, Coke, Combust, Conflagration, Cremate, Crucial, Destruct, Eilding, Ember, Emboil, Fervid, > **FIRE**, Fishtail, Flagrant, Flare, Flash, Fresh(et), Gleed, Gut, Holocaust, Ignite, In, Incendiary, Incinerate, Inure, Inust(ion), Kill, Live, Lunt, Offering, On, Rill, Sati, Scald, Scorch, Scouther, Scowder, Scowther, Sear, Sienna, Singe, Smart, Smoulder, Suttee, Swale, Thurible, Torch, Umber, Urent, Ustion, Wick

Burrow(er), Burrowing Dig, Earth, Fossorial, Gopher, Groundhog, Hole, How, Howk, Mole, Nuzzle, Sett, Tunnel, Viscacha, Warren, Wombat, Worm

Bursar(y) Camerlengo, Camerlingo, Coffers, Grant, Purser, Scholarship, Treasurer

Burst(ing) Blowout, Brast, Break, Dehisce, Disrupt, Dissilient, Ebullient, Erumpent, Erupt, > **EXPLODE**, Fly, Implode, Pop, Sforzato, Shatter, Spasm, Spirt, Split, Sprint, Spurt, Stave, Tetterous

Bury Cover, Eard, Earth, Embowel, Engrave, Enhearse, Graff, Graft, Imbed, Inhearse, Inhume, Inter, Inurn, Landfill, Repress, Sepulture, Sink, Ye(a)rd, Yird

Bus Aero, Bandwagon, Car, Charabanc, Coach, Double-decker, Hondey, Hopper, ISA, Jitney, Mammy-wagon, Rattletrap, Single-decker, Tramcar, Trolley

Bush(y) Bramble, Brier, Bullace, Busket, Calico, Clump, Cotton, Dumose, Firethorn, Hawthorn, Hibiscus, Kapok, Mallee, Matagouri, Mulberry, Outback, Poinsettia, Poly-poly, President, Sallee, Shepherd, Shrub, Sugar, Thicket, Tire, Tod(de)

Bushel Co(o)mb, Homer, Peck, Weight, Wey

Bushwalker Hoon

Business Affair, Agency, Biz, Bus, Cartel, Cerne, Co, Commerce, Company, Concern, Conglomerate, Craft, Duty, Enterprise, Ergon, Establishment, Exchange, Fasti, Firm, Funny, Game, Gear, Hong, Industry, Line, Métier, Monkey, Office, Palaver, Pi(d)geon, Pidgin, Practice, Professional, Racket, Shebang, Shop, Show, To-do, Trade, Traffic, Transaction, Tread, Turnover, Unincorporated, Vocation, Zaikai

Businessman Babbitt, City, Realtor, Taipan, Trader, Tycoon

Busk(er) Bodice, Corset, Entertainer, German-band

Bust Beano, Boob, Brast, Break, Chest, Falsies, Herm(a), Sculp, Shatter(ed), Spree, Statue, Term(inus), To-tear, To-torne, Ups(e)y

▷ **Bust** *may indicate* an anagram

Bustle Ado, Do, Flap, Pad, Scurry, > **STIR**, Swarm, Tournure, Whew

Busy Active, At (it), Deedy, > **DETECTIVE**, Dick, Eident, Employ, Ergate, Eye, Goer, Hectic, Hive, Humming, Occupied, Ornate, Prodnose, Stir, Tec, Throng, Worksome

Busybody Bustler, Meddler, Snooper, Trout, Yenta

But Aber, Bar, Except, However, Merely, Nay, Only, Save, Sed, Simply, Tun

Butcher(y) Cumberland, Decko, Dekko, Flesher, Kill, Killcow, Look, Massacre, Ovicide, Sever, Shambles, Shochet, Shufti, Slaughter, Slay

Butler Bedivere, Bread-chipper, Jeeves, RAB, Rhett, Samuel, Servant, Sewer, Sommelier, Steward

Butt (in) Aris, Barrel, Bunt, Clara, Enter, Geck, Glasgow kiss, Goat, Header, Horn, Jesting-stock, Laughing-stock, Mark, Outspeckle, Pantaloon, Pipe, Push, Ram, Roach, Scapegoat, Snipe, Straight man, Stump, Target, Tun, Ups

Butter Adulation, Billy, Brandy, Butyric, Cocoa, Coconut, Drawn, Flatter, Galam, Garcinia, Ghee, Ghi, Goat, Illipi, Illupi, Kokum, Mahua, Mahwa, Mow(r)a, Nutter, Pat, Peanut, Print, Ram, Scrape, Shea, Spread

▷ **Butter** *may indicate* a goat or such

Buttercup Crow-foot, Crow-toe, Goldilocks, Ranunculus, Reate, Thalictrum

Butterfly Apollo, Argus, Birdwing, Blue, Brimstone, Brown, Cabbage white, Camberwell beauty, Cardinal, Chequered skipper, Cleopatra, Clouded yellow, Comma, Common blue, Dilettante, Eclosion, Emperor, Fritillary, Gate-keeper, Grayling, Hair-streak, Heath, Hesperid, Imaginal, Kallima, Large copper, Large white, Leaf, Marbled-white, Meadow brown, Milk-weed, Monarch, Morpho, Nerves, Orange-tip, Owl, Painted lady, Peacock, Pieris, Psyche, Purple emperor, Red admiral, Ringlet, Silverspot, Skipper, Small white, Speckled wood, Stamper, Sulphur, Swallow-tail, Thecla, Thistle, Tiger swallowtail, Tortoiseshell, Two-tailed pasha, Vanessa, Wall brown, White admiral

Buttocks Arse, Ass, Bahookie, Bottom, Coit, Derrière, Doup, Duff, Fundament, Gluteus maximus, Hinderlan(d)s, Hurdies, Jacksie, Jacksy, Keester, Keister, Nates, Prat, Quoit, Seat

Button(s) Barrel, Bellboy, Fastener, Frog, Hot, Knob, Netsuke, Olivet, Page(boy), Panic, Snooze, Stud, Switch, Toggle

Buttonhole Accost, Detain, Eye, Flower

Buttress Brace, Counterfort, Pier, Prop, Stay, Support

Butty Chum, Oppo

Buy(ing), Buyer Believe, Bribe, Coff, Corner, Customer, Emption, Engross, Monopsonist, Purchase, Shop, Shout, Spend, Take, Trade, Vendee

▷ **Buyer** *may indicate* money

Buzz(er) Bee, Bombilate, Bombinate, Button, Fly, Hum, Rumour, Scram, Whirr, Whisper, Zed, Zing, Zoom

Buzzard Bee-kite, Bird, Buteo, Hawk, Pern, Puttock, Vulture

By Alongside, At, Gin, Gone, In, Near, Neighbouring, Nigh, Of, Past, Per, Through, With, X

Bye-bye Adieu, Farewell, Tata

Bygone Dead, Departed, Past, Yore

Bypass Avoid, Circuit, Coronary, > **DETOUR**, Evade, Ignore, Omit, Shunt, Skirt

By-product Epiphenomenon, Spin-off

Byre Cowshed, Manger, Stable, Trough

Byte Nybble

By the way Incidentally, Obiter

Byway Alley, Lane, Path

Byword Ayword, Phrase, Proverb, Slogan

Cc

C Around, Caught, Celsius, Cent, Centigrade, Charlie, Conservative, San

Cab Boneshaker, Crawler, Drosky, Fiacre, Growler, Hackney, Hansom, Mini, Noddy, Taxi, Vettura

Cabbage(-head), **Cabbage soup** Book choy, Borecole, Brassica, Castock, Cauliflower, Chinese, Choucroute, Cole, Collard, Crout, Kohlrabi, Kraut, Loaf, Loave, Pak-choi, Pamphrey, Sauerkraut, Savoy, Thieve, Turnip, Wort

Cabin Berth, Bibby, Bothy, Box, Cabana, Caboose, Camboose, Coach, Cottage, Crannog, Crib, Cuddy, Den, Gondola, Hovel, Hut, Izba, Lodge, Long-house, Room, Roundhouse, Saloon, Shanty, Stateroom

Cabinet Bahut, Cabale, Case, Closet, Commode, Console, Cupboard, Kitchen, Ministry, Secretaire, Shadow, Shrinal, Vitrine

Cable(way), **Cable-car** Coax(ial), Extension, Flex, Halser, Hawser, Jump leads, Junk, Landline, Lead, Lead-in, Lifeline, Outhaul, Rope, Slatch, Téléférique, > **TELEGRAM**, Telpher(age), Wire

Cackle Cluck, Gaggle, Gas, Haw, Snicker, Titter

Cactus, **Cactus-like** Alhagi, Barel, Cereus, Cholla, Christmas, Dildo, Easter, Echino-, Hedgehog, Jojoba, Maguey, Mescal, Nopal, Ocotillo, Opuntia, Organ-pipe, Peyote, Prickly pear, Retama, Saguaro, Star, Torch-thistle, Tuna, Xerophytic

Cad Base, Boor, Bounder, Churl, Cocoa, Heel, Oik, Rascal, Rotter, Skunk

Cadaver(ous) Body, Corpse, Ghastly, Haggard, Stiff

Cadence Beat, Close, Fa-do, Flow, Lilt, Meter, Plagal, Rhythm

Cadet(s) Junior, OTC, Scion, Syen, Trainee

Cafe(teria) Automat, Bistro, Brasserie, Buvette, Canteen, Commissary, Diner, Dinette, Donko, Estaminet, Filtré, Greasy spoon, Juke joint, Pizzeria, Pull-in, Tearoom, Transport

Cage Bar, Battery, Box, Cavie, Confine, Coop, Corf, Dray, Drey, Enmew, Faraday, Fold, Frame, Grate, Hutch, Mew, Pen, > **PRISON**, Trave

Cake Agnus dei, Angel, Baba, Babka, Baklava, Banbury, Bannock, Barmbrack, Battenberg, Birthday, Brioche, Brownie, Buckwheat bun, Carcake, Cattle, Chapat(t)i, Chillada, Chupati, Chupattie, Chupatty, Clapbread, Clot, Coburg, Corn dodger, Cotton, Croquette, Cruller, Crumpet, Dainty, Devil's food, Drizzle, Dundee, Eccles, Eclair, Fancy, Farl(e), Filter, Fish, Flapjack, Frangipane, Frangipani, Fritter, Galette, Genoa, Gingerbread, Girdle, > **HARDEN**, Hockey, Hoe, Jannock, Jumbal, Jumbles, Koeksister, Kruller, Kuchen, Kueh, Lamington, Lardy, Latke, Layer, Linseed, Macaroon, Madeira, Madeleine, Maid of honour, Marble, Meringue, Millefeuille, Mud, Muffin, Napoleon, Nut, Oatmeal, Oil, Pan, Panettone, Paratha, Parkin, Parliament, Pat, Patty, Pavlova, Petit four, Pikelet, > **PLASTER**, Pomfret, Pone, Pontefract, Poori, Popover, Pound, Profiterole, Puff, Puftaloon(a), Puri, Queencake, Ratafia, Ready-mix, Religieuse, Rice, Rock, Rosti, Roti, Rout, Rum baba, Rusk, Sachertorte, Saffron, Sally Lunn, Salt, Sandwich, Savarin, Scone, Seed, Set, Simnel, Singing-hinny, Slab, Slapjack, Soul, Spawn, Spice, Sponge, Stollen, Stottie, Sushi, Swiss roll, Tablet, Tansy, Tea(bread), Tipsy, Torte, Tortilla, Twelfth, Upside down, Vetkoek, Wad, Wafer, Waffle, Wedding, Wonder, Yeast

▷ **Cake** *may indicate* an anagram

Calculate(d), Calculation, Calculator Abacus, Actuary, Compute(r), Cost, Design, Estimate, Extrapolate, Log, Prorate, Quip(p)u, Rate, > RECKON, Slide-rule, Sofar, Soroban, Tactical, Tell

Calendar Advent, Agenda, Almanac, Chinese, Diary, Fasti, Gregorian, Intercalary, Jewish, Journal, Julian, Luach, Menology, Newgate, New Style, Ordo, Perpetual, Revolutionary, Roman, Sothic

Calf Ass, Bobby, Box, Cf, Deacon, Dogie, Dogy, Freemartin, Golden, Leg, Poddy, Stirk, Sural, Tollie, Tolly, Veal, Vitular

Call(ed), Calling, Call on, Call up Adhan, Appeal, Arraign, Art, Awaken, Azan, Banco, Bawl, Beck, Behote, Bevy, Bid, Boots and saddles, Business, Buzz, Career, Chamade, Cite, Claim, Clang, Clarion, Cleep, Clepe, Close, Cold, Conference, Conscript, Convene, Convoke, Cooee, Cry, Curtain, Dial, Drift, Dub, Evoke, Gam, Go, Hail, Hallali, Haro, Heads, Heave-ho, Hech, Hete, Hey, Hight, Ho, Hot(e), Howzat, Huddup, Hurra(h), Job, Junk, Last (post), Line, Local, Métier, Misère, Mobilise, Mot, Name, Nap, Need, Nemn, Nempt, Nominate, Olé, Page, Phone, Photo, Post, Proo, Pruh, Pursuit, Rechate, Recheat, Retreat, Reveille, Ring, Roll, Rort, Rouse, Route, Sa-sa, Sennet, > SHOUT, Shut-out, Slam, Slander, Slogan, Soho, Sola, SOS, STD, Style, Subpoena, Summon(s), Tails, Tantivy, Taps, Telephone, Term, Toho, Toll, Trumpet, Trunk, Visit, Vocation, Waken, Wake-up, Whoa-ho-ho, Wo ha ho, Yell, Yo, Yodel, Yodle, Yo-ho(-ho), Yoicks, Yoo-hoo

Caller Fresh, Guest, Herring, Inspector, Muezzin, Rep, Traveller, > VISITOR

Callisthenics T'ai chi (ch'uan)

Calm Abate, Allay, Allege, Appease, Ataraxy, Composed, Cool, Doldrums, Easy, Equable, Equanimity, Even, Eye, Flat, Glassy, Halcyon, Loun(d), Lown(d), Lull, Mellow, Mild, Milden, Millpond, Nonchalant, Pacify, Peaceful, Philosophical, Phlegmatic, Placate, Placid, Quell, Quiet, Relax(ed), Repose, Seraphic, Serene, Settle, Sleek, > SOOTHE, Still, Stilly, Subside, Tranquil(lise), Windless

Camel, Camel train Arabian, Artiodactyla, Bactrian, Caisson, Colt, Dromedary, Kafila, Llama, Oont, Sopwith, Tulu

Camera, Camera man Box, Brownie®, Camcorder, Candid, Chambers, Cine, Compact, Disc, Flash, Gamma, Iconoscope, Kodak®, Obscura, Orthicon, Palmcorder, Panoramic, Pantoscope, Pinhole, Polaroid®, Reflex, Schmidt, SLR, Somascope, Speed, Steadicam®, Video

Camouflage Conceal, > DISGUISE, Mark, Maskirovka, War-dress

▷ **Camouflaged** *may indicate* an anagram

Camp(er) Affectation, Aldershot, Banal, Base, Belsen, Bivouac, Boma, Boot, Caerleon, Cantonment, Castral, Colditz, Concentration, David, Death, Depot, D(o)uar, Dumdum, Epicene, Faction, Fat, Flaunt, Gulag, Happy, Health, High, Holiday, L(a)ager, Labour, Lashkar, Leaguer, Low, Manyat(t)a, Oflag, Outlie, Peace, Prison, Side, Siwash, Stagey, Stalag, Stative, Swagman, Tent, Theatrical, Transit, Treblinka, Valley Forge, Work, Zare(e)ba, Zariba, Zereba, Zeriba

Campaign(er) Barnstorm, Battle, Blitz, Blitzkreig, Canvass, Crusade, Drive, Field, Jihad, Lobby, Mission, Promotion, Run, Satyagraha, Smear, Stint, Strategist, Venture, Veteran, War, Warray, Warrey, Whistle-stop

Can(s) Able, Billy, Bog, Capable, Churn, Cooler, Dow, Gaol, Gents, Headphones, Is able, Jug, Karsy, Loo, May, Nick, Pail, Pot, Preserve, > PRISON, Privy, Stir, Tin

Canada, Canadian Abenaki, Acadian, Canuck, Dene, Herring choker, Inuit, Johnny Canuck, Quebeccer, Quebecker, Québecois

Canal Alimentary, Ampul, Anal, Birth, Caledonian, Channel, Conduit, Corinth, Duct, Duodenum, Ea, Enteron, Erie, Foss(e), Gota, Grand (Trunk), Grande Terre, Grand Union, Groove, Gut, Haversian, Kiel, Klong, Labyrinth, Lode, Manchester Ship, Meatus, Midi, Mitelland, Navigation, New York State Barge, Oesophagus,

Panama, Pharynx, Pipe, Pound, Resin, Ring, Root, Scala, Schlemm's, Semi-circular, Ship, Shipway, Spinal, Stone, Suez, Suo, Urethra, Waterway, Welland, Zanja

Canal-boat Barge, Fly-boat, Gondola, Vaporetto

Canary Bird, Grass, Roller, Serin, Singer, Yellow

Cancel Abrogate, Adeem, Annul, Counteract, Countermand, Cross, Delete, Destroy, Erase, Kill, Negate, Nullify, Obliterate, Override, Remit, Repeal, Rescind, Retrait, Revoke, Scrub, Undo, Unmake, Void, Wipe

Cancer(ous) Big C, Carcinoma, Crab, Curse, Kaposi's Sarcoma, Leukaemia, Oat-cell, Tropic, Tumour, Wolf

Candid, **Candour** Albedo, Blunt, Camera, Franchise, Frank, Honesty, Open, Round, Upfront

Candidate(s) Agrege, Applicant, Aspirant, Contestant, Entrant, Field, Nominee, Ordinand, Postulant, Running mate, Stalking horse, Testee

Candied, **Candy** Angelica, Caramel, Cotton, Eryngo, Eye, Glace, Maple, Rock, Snow, Succade, Sugar, > **SWEET**

Candle(stick), **Candelabra** Amandine, Bougie, C(i)erge, Dip, Fetch, Girandole, Hanukiah, Jesse, Lampadary, Light, Menorah, Padella, Paschal, Pricket, Roman, Rushlight, Sconce, Serge, Shammash, Shammes, Slut, Sperm, Tace, Tallow, Tallow-dip, Taper, Torchère, Tricerion, Wax

▸ **Candy** *see* **CANDIED**

Cane Arrow, Baculine, Bamboo, Baste, Beat, Birk, Dari, Dhurra, Doura, Dur(r)a, Ferula, Ferule, Goor, Gur, Jambee, Malacca, Narthex, Penang-lawyer, Pointer, Rat(t)an, Rod, Stick, Sugar, Swagger-stick, Swish, Switch, Swordstick, Tan, Tickler, Vare, Wand, Whangee, Wicker(-work)

Canine Biter, C, Dog, Eye-tooth

Cannibal Anthropophagus, Heathen, Long pig, Ogre, Thyestean

Cannon Amusette, Barrage, Basilisk, Bombard, Breechloader, Carom, Carronade, Chaser, Collide, Criterion, Culverin, Drake, Falcon, Gun, Howitzer, Kiss, Long-tom, Monkey, Nursery, Saker, Stern-chaser, Water, Zamboorak, Zomboruk, Zumbooru(c)k

Canny Careful, Frugal, Prudent, Scot, Shrewd, Slee, Sly, Thrifty, Wice, Wily, Wise

Canoe(ist) Bidarka, Bidarkee, Canader, Dugout, Faltboat, Kayak, Monoxylon, Montaria, Oomiack, Paddler, Piragua, Pirogue, Rob Roy, Woodskin

Canon(ise) Austin, Brocard, Camera, Chapter, Chasuble, Code, Crab, Isidorian, > **LAW**, Line, Mathurin(e), Nocturn, Nursery, Pitaka, Polyphony, Prebendary, Premonstratensian, Rota, Round, Rule, Square, Squier, Squire, Standard, Tenet, Unity

Canopy Awning, Baldachin, Baldaquin, Chuppah, Ciborium, Dais, He(a)rse, Huppah, Majesty, Marquee, Marquise, Pavilion, Shamiana(h), State, Tabernacle, Tent, Tester

Canton District, Quarter

Cantor Haz(z)an

Canvas Awning, Burlap, Dra(b)bler, Lug-sail, Mainsail, Marquee, Oil-cloth, Paint, Raven's-duck, Reef, > **SAIL**, Staysail, Stuns(ai)l, Tent, Trysail, Wigan

Canvass(er) Agent, Doorstep, Drum, Poll, Solicit

▷ **Canvasser** *may indicate* a painter or a camper

Canyon Box, Canada, Defile, Grand, Nal(l)a, Nallah

Cap(ped) Abacot, Amorce, Balaclava, Balmoral, Barret, Baseball, Bathing, Bellhop, Bendigo, Ber(r)et, Biggin, Biretta, Blakey, Blue, Blue-bonnet, Bonnet-rouge, Bycoket, Call, Calotte, Calpac(k), Capeline, Caul, Chaco, Chape, Chapeau, Chaperon, Chapka, Chechia, Cheese-cutter, Cloth, Cockernony, Coif,

Cope, Cornet, Cowl, Cradle, > **CROWN**, Czapka, Davy Crockett, Deerstalker, Dunce's, Dutch, Fatigue, Ferrule, Filler, Flat, Fool's, Forage, Gandhi, Garrison, Gimme, Glengarry, Grannie, Granny, > **HAT**, Havelock, Hummel bonnet, Iceberg, International, Jockey, Juliet, Kalpak, Kepi, Kilmarnock, Kippa, Kippoth, Kipput, Kiss-me(-quick), Knee, Liberty, Lid, Mob, Monmouth, Monteer, Montero, Mor(r)ion, Mortar-board, Muffin, Mutch, Newsboy, Night, Outdo, Pagri, Patellar, Percussion, Perplex, Phrygian, Pile, Pileus, Pinner, Polar, Puggaree, Quoif, Root, Schapska, Shako, Skullcap, Square, Statute, Stocking, Summit, > **SURPASS**, Taj, Tam(-o'-shanter), Thimble, Thinking, Thrum, Toe, Toorie, Top, Toque, Toy, Trenchard, Trencher, Tuque, Turk's, Watch, Wishing, Yarmulka, Yarmulke, Zuchetto

Capable, Capability Able, Brown, Capacity, Competent, Deft, Effectual, Efficient, Firepower, Qualified, Skilled, Susceptible, Up to

Capacitance, Capacity Ability, Aptitude, C, Cab, Competence, Content, Cor, Cubic, Endowment, Function, Limit, Log, Power, Qua, Receipt, Scope, Size, Tonnage, Valence, Vital, Volume

Cape Agulhas, Almuce, Bon, Burnouse, Byron, Calimere Point, Canaveral, Canso, Cloak, Cod, Comorin, Delgado, Dezhnev, Domino, Dungeness, East(ern), Fairweather, Faldetta, Fanion, Fanon, Farewell, Fear, Fichu, Finisterre, Flattery, Good Hope, Guardafui, Harp, Hatteras, Head(land), Helles, Hoe, Hogh, Hook of Holland, Horn, Inverness, Kennedy, Leeuwin, Lindesnes, Lizard, Mant(e)let, Mantilla, Mantle, Matapan, May, Miseno, Mo(z)zetta, Muleta, Naze, Ness, Nordkyn, North, Northern, Ortegal, Palatine, Parry, Pelerine, Peninsula, Point, Poncho, Race, Ras, Ray, Reinga, Roca, Ruana, Runaway, Sable, St Vincent, Sandy, Scaw, Skagen, Skaw, Sontag, Southwest, Talma, Tippet, Trafalgar, Ushant, Verde, Waterproof, Western, Wrath

Capitalise Carpe diem

▷ **Capitalist** *may indicate* a citizen of a capital

Capitals A1, Assets, Block, Boodle, Bravo, Cap, Chapiter, Chaptrel, Doric, Equity, Euge, Excellent, Fixed, Flight, Float, Floating, Fonds, Great, Helix, Human, Initial, Ionic, Lethal, Lulu, Metropolis, Principal, Risk, Rustic, Seat, Seed, Social, Splendid, Sport, Stellar, Stock, Super, Topping, UC, Upper case, Venture, Working

▷ **Capless** *may indicate* first letter missing

▷ **Capriccioso** *may indicate* an anagram

Caprice, Capricious Arbitrary, Boutade, Capernoitie, Conceit, Desultory, Erratic, Fancy, Fitful, Freak, Humoresk, Humoresque, Irony, Mood, Perverse, Quirk, Vagary, Wayward, Whim(sy)

Capsize Overbalance, Purl, Tip, Turn turtle, Upset, Whemmle, Whomble

▷ **Capsized** *may indicate* a word upside down

Capsule Amp(o)ule, Bowman's, Cachet, Habitat, Ootheca, Orbiter, Ovisac, Pill, Spacecraft, Spermatophore, Time, Urn

Captain Ahab, Bligh, Bobadil, Bones, Brassbound, Capt, Chief, Cid, Commander, Condottiere, Cook, Copper, Cuttle, Flint, Group, Hornblower, Kettle, Kidd, Leader, Macheath, Master, Nemo, Old man, Owner, Patroon, Post, Privateer, Protospatharius, Skip(per), Standish, Subah(dar), Subedar, Swing, Trierarch

Caption Heading, Headline, Inscription, Masthead, Sub-title, Title

Captivate(d), Captivating Beguile, Bewitch, Charm, Enamour, Enthrall, Epris(e), Take, Winsome

Captive, Captivity Bonds, Duress, POW, Prisoner, Slave

Capture Abduct, Annex, Bag, Catch, Collar, Cop, Grab, Land, Net, Prize, Rush, Seize, Snabble, Snaffle, Snare, > **TAKE**

Car Astra, Audi, Auto, Banger, Beetle, Berlin, Biza, BL, Bluebird, Bomb, Brake, Bubble, Buffet, Bugatti, Buick, Bumper, Bus, Cab(riolet), Cadillac, Catafalco,

Catafalque, Chariot, Classic, Clunker, Coach, Company, Concept, Convertible, Cortina, Coupé, Courtesy, Crate, Daimler, Diner, Dodgem®, Drag(ster), Drophead, Dunger, Elf, Estate, E-type, Fastback, Fiat, Flivver, Ford, Formula, Freight, Ghost, Gondola, Griddle, GT, Hardtop, Hatchback, Heap, Hearse, Hillman, Hot-rod, Irish, Jalop(p)y, Jamjar, Jammy, Jaunting, Jim Crow, Kart, Kit, Knockabout, Lada, Lagonda, Lancia, Landaulet, Landrover, Lift-back, Limo, Limousine, Merc(edes), MG, Mini, Model T, Morris, Nacelle, Notchback, Observation, Opel, Panda, Parlour, Patrol, Popemobile, Prowl, Racer, Ragtop, Railroad, Rattletrap, Restaurant, Roadster, Roller, Rolls, RR, Runabout, Rust bucket, Saloon, Scout, Sedan, Service, Shooting-brake, Skoda, Sleeper, Sleeping, Soft-top, Speedster, Sports, Squad, Station wagon, Steam, Stock, Stretch-limo, Subcompact, Sunbeam, Tank, Telepherique, Telpher, Three-wheeler, Tin Lizzie, Tonneau, Tourer, Tram, Trolley, Turbo, Two-seater, Vehicle, Veteran, Vintage, Voiture, VW, Wheeler, Wheels

Caravan Caf(f)ila, Convoy, Fleet, Kafila, Safari, Trailer

Carbohydrate Agarose, Carrageenan, Cellulose, Chitin, Dextran, Disaccharide, Glycogen, Heptose, Hexose, Inulin, Ketose, Laminarin, Mannan, Pectin, Pentosan(e), Pentose, Saccharide, Sorbitol, Starch, Sucrose, Sugar

Carcase, **Carcass** Body, Cadaver, Carrion, Corpse, Cutter, Krang, Kreng, Morkin, Mor(t)ling

Card(s), **Cardboard** Ace, Affinity, Amex®, Baccarat, Basto, Bill, Birthday, Bower, Business, Calling, Canasta, Cartes, Cash, Caution, Charge, Chicane, Club, Comb, Compass, Court(esy), Credit, Cue, Dance, Debit, Deck, Deuce, Diamond, Donor, Ecarté, Eccentric, Euchre, Expansion, Flaught, Flush, > **GAME**, Green, Hand, Heart, Honour, Identity, Jack, Jambone, Joker, Kanban, Key, King, Loo, Loyalty, Manille, Matador, Meishi, Mise, Mistigris, Mogul, Mournival, Oddity, Ombre, Pack, Pasteboard, PC, Picture, Placard, Plastic, Playing, Proximity, Quatorze, Queen, Quiz, Red, Rippler, Rove, Scribble, Singleton, Smart, Soda, Solo, Sound, Spade, Spadille, Squeezer, Store, Strawboard, Swab, Swipe, Swish, Switch, Swob, Swot, Talon, Tarok, Tarot, Tease(r), Tenace, Test, Thaumatrope, Ticket, Tose, Toze, Trading, Trey, Trump, Valentine, Visiting, Wag, Weirdie, Wild, Yellow, Zener

Cardigan Jacket, Wam(m)us, Wampus, Woolly

Cardinal Camerlingo, Chief, College, Eight, Eminence, Eminent, Grosbeak, Hat, HE, Hume, Legate, Manning, Mazarin, Newman, Number, Pivotal, Polar, Prelate, Radical, Red, Red-hat, Richelieu, Sacred college, Sin, Spellman, Virtue, Vital, Ximenes

Care(r), **Caring** Attention, Burden, Cark, Caution, Cerne, Cherish, > **CONCERN**, Cosset, Grief, Heed, Intensive, Kaugh, Keep, Kiaugh, Maternal, Mind, Pains, Palliative, Parabolanus, Reck(e), Reke, Respite, Retch, Solicitude, > **TEND**, Tenty, Worry

Career Course, Hurtle, Life, Line, Run, Rush, Speed, Start, Tear, Vocation

▷ **Career** *may indicate* an anagram

Careful(ly) Canny, Chary, Discreet, Gentle, Hooly, Meticulous, Mindful, Pernickety, Provident, Prudent, Scrimp, Studious, Tentie, Tenty, Thorough, Vigilant, Ware, Wary

Careless(ly) Casual, Cheery, Debonair, Easy, Free-minded, Gallio, Improvident, Imprudent, Inadvertent, Insouciance, Lax, Lighthearted, Négligé, > **NEGLIGENT**, Nonchalant, Oversight, Raffish, Rash, Remiss, Resigned, Riley, Slam-bang, Slapdash, Slaphappy, Slipshod, Sloven(ly), Slubber, Taupie, Tawpie, Unguarded, Unmindful, Untenty, Unwary

▷ **Carelessly** *may indicate* an anagram

Caress Bill, Coy, Embrace, Fondle, Kiss, Lallygag, Lollygag, Noursle, Nursle, Pet, Touch

Caretaker Concierge, Curator, Custodian, Guardian, Janitor, Nightwatchman, Sexton, Shammash, Shammes, Superintendent, Verger, Warden

Careworn Haggard, Lined, Tired, Weary

Cargo Bulk, Burden, Fraught, Freight, Lading, Last, > LOAD, Payload, Shipment

Caribbean Belonger, Puerto Rican, Soca, Sokah, Taino, WI

Caricature, Caricaturist Ape, Beerbohm, Burlesque, Caron d'Ache, Cartoon, Cruikshank, Doyle, Farce, Gillray, Rowlandson, Skit, Spy, Travesty

Carnation Dianthus, Malmaison, Picotee, Pink

Carnival Fair, Festival, Fete, Moomba, Revelry

Carol Noel, Sing, Song, Wassail, Yodel

Carousal, Carouse Bend, Birl(e), Bouse, Bride-ale, Compotation, Drink, Mallemaroking, Mollie, Orge, Orgy, > REVEL, Roist, Screed, Spree, Upsee, Upsey, Upsy, Wassail

Carp(er) Beef, Censure, Complain, Crab, Critic, Crucian, Crusian, Gibel, Goldfish, Id(e), Kvetch, Mirror, Mome, Nag, Nibble, Roach, Roundfish, Scold, Twitch, Yerk, Yirk

Carpenter Cabinet-maker, Carfindo, Chips, Fitter, Joiner, Joseph, Menuisier, Quince, Tenoner, Wright

▷ **Carpenter** *may indicate* an anagram

Carpet Aubusson, Axminster, Beetle, Berate, Bessarabian, Broadloom, Brussels, Castigate, Chide, Drugget, Durrie, Kali, Kelim, Khilim, Kidderminster, Kilim, Kirman, Lecture, Lino, Mat, Moquette, Persian, Rate, Red, Reprimand, Reproach, Rug, Runner, Shagpile, Shark, Turkey, Wall-to-wall, Wig, Wilton

Carriage Air, Bandy, Barouche, Bearing, Berlin(e), Bier, Brake, Brit(sch)ka, Britska, Britzka, Brougham, Buckboard, Buggy, Cab, Calash, Calèche, Car, Cariole, Caroche, Carriole, Carryall, Cartage, Chaise, Charet, Chariot, Chassis, Chay, Clarence, Coach, Coch, Composite, Conveyance, Coupé, Curricle, Demeanour, Dennet, Deportment, Désobligeante, Diner, Dormeuse, Dos-a-dos, Do-si-do, Drag, Dros(h)ky, Ekka, Equipage, Fiacre, Fly, Four-in-hand, Gait, Gig, Gladstone, Go-cart, Growler, Gun, Haulage, Herdic, Horseless, Hurly-hacket, Landau(let), Limber, Mien, Non-smoker, Norimon, Observation-car, Phaeton, Pick-a-back, Pochaise, Pochay, Poise, Port(age), Portance, Postchaise, Posture, Poyse, Pram, Pullman, Railcar, Railway, Randem, Rath(a), Remise, Rickshaw, Rockaway, Shay, Sled, Sleeper, Smoker, Sociable, Spider, Stanhope, Sulky, Surrey, Tarantas(s), Taxi, Tender, Tenue, Tilbury, Tim-whiskey, Tonga, Trail, Trap, Vetture, Victoria, Voiture, Wagonette, Waterage, Whirligig, Whisk(e)y

Carrier Airline, Arm, Baldric, Barkis, Barrow, Bomb-ketch, Caddy, Cadge, Camel, Coaster, Conveyor, Escort, Fomes, Fomites, Frog, Grid, Hamper, Haversack, Hod, Janker, Jill, Minority, Nosebag, Noyade, Obo, Packhorse, Pigeon, Porter, Rucksack, Satchel, Schistosoma, Semantide, Sling, Straddle, Stretcher, > TRAY, Vector

Carrion Cadaver, Carcase, Carcass, Flesh, Ket, Stapelia

Carry(ing) Bear, Chair, Convey, Enlevé, Escort, Ferry, Frogmarch, Hawk, Hent, Hump, Kurvey, Land, Pack, Pickaback, Port, Stock, Sustain, Tide over, Tote, > TRANSPORT, Trant, Wage, With, Yank

Cart Bandy, Barrow, Bogey, Buck, Cape, Car(r)iole, Chapel, Democrat, Dog, Dolly, Dray, Furphy, Gambo, Gill, Golf, Governess, Gurney, Hackery, Jag, Jill, Lead, Mail, Pie, Rickshaw, Scotch, Shandry, T, Tax(ed), Telega, Trolley, Tumbrel, Tumbril, Village, Wag(g)on, Wain, Whitechapel

Cartel Duopoly, Ring, Syndicate

Cartilage Gristle

Carton Box, Case, Crate, Sydney, Tub

Cartoon(ist) Animated, Caricature, Comic, Disney, Drawn, Emmet, Garland, Leech, Low, Manga, Mel, Partridge, Popeye, Short, Spy, Strip, Tenniel, Tintin, Trog

Cartridge Blank, Bullet, Cartouche, Doppie, Shell

Carve(d), **Carver**, **Carving** Bas relief, Cameo, Chisel, Cilery, Crocket, Cut, Dismember, Doone, Enchase, Engrave, Entail, Entayle, Fiddlehead, Gibbons, Glyptic, Hew, Incise, Inscribe, Insculp, Intaglio, Netsuke, Nick, Petroglyph, Scrimshaw, Sculp(t), Slice, Tondo, Truncheon, Whittle

Cascade Cataract, Fall, Lin(n), Stream, Waterfall

Case(s), **Casing** Ablative, Accusative, Action, Allative, Altered, Appeal, Aril, Ascus, Assumpsit, Attaché, Basket, Beer, Bere, Bittacle, Blimp, Box, Brief, Bundwall, Burse, C, Ca, Cabinet, Calyx, Canister, Canterbury, Capsule, Cartouch(e), Cartridge, Cause celebre, Cellaret, Chase, Chitin, Chrysalis, Cocoon, Compact, Crate, Croustade, Crust, Dative, Declension, Detinue, Dispatch, Dossier, Dressing, Elytron, Etui, Etwee, Example, Flan, Flapjack, Frame, Genitive, Grip, Hanaper, Hard, Hatbox, Hold-all, Housewife, Hull, Humidor, Husk, Index, Indusium, Instance, Keister, Locative, Locket, Lorica, Manche, Matter, Mezuzah, Nacelle, Nominative, Non-suit, Nutshell, Objective, Oblique, Ochrea, Ocrea, Papeterie, Patient, Pencil, Penner, Phylactery, Plight, Plummer-block, Pod, Port, Possessive, Prima facie, Quiver, Recce, Reconnoitre, Sabretache, Sad, Scabbard, Sheath(e), Shell, Situation, Six-pack, Sporran, Stead, Subjunctive, Suit, Tantalus, Tea-chest, Telium, Test, Theca, Tichborne, Trial, Trunk, Valise, Vasculum, Vocative, Volva, Walise, Walking, Wallet, Wardian, Wing, Writing

Cash Blunt, Bonus, Bounty, Change, Coin, Dosh, Dot, Float, Imprest, Lolly, > **MONEY**, Needful, Ochre, Pence, Petty, Ready, Realise, Rhino, Spondulicks, Stumpy, Tender, Tin, Wampum, Wherewithal

Cashier Annul, Break, Depose, Disbar, Dismiss, Teller, Treasurer

Casino Monte Carlo

Cask(et) Armet, Barrel, Barrico, Bas(i)net, Box, Breaker, Butt, Cade, Casque, Cassette, Drum, Firkin, Galeate, Harness, Heaume, Hogshead, Keg, Leaguer, Octave, Pin, Pipe, Puncheon, Pyxis, Run(d)let, Salade, Sallet, Sarcophagus, Shrine, Solera, Tierce, Tun

Casserole Diable, Osso bucco, Pot, Salmi, Terrine, Tzimmes

Cassette Cartridge, Tape, Video

Cassock Gown, Soutane

Cast (down, off, out), **Casting** Abattu, Actors, Add, Appearance, Bung, Die, Discard, Ecdysis, Eject, Exorcise, Exuviae, Exuvial, Fling, Found, Fusil, Heave, Hob, Hue, Hurl, Impression, Ingo(w)es, Keb, Look, Lose, Mew, Molt, Moulage, Mould, Plaster(stone), Players, Put, Reject, Shed, Shoot, Sling, Slive, Slough, Spoil, Stookie, Tailstock, > **THROW**, Toss, Tot, Warp, Wax, Ytost

▷ **Cast** *may indicate* an anagram or a piece of a word missing

Castaway Adrift, Crusoe, Gunn, Left, Outcast, Selkirk, Stranded

▷ **Cast by** *may indicate* surrounded by

Caste Class, Dalit, Group, Harijan, Hova, Kshatriya, Rank, Sect, Sudra, Varna

Castle(d) Adamant, Arundel, Balmoral, Bamburgh, Bastille, Belvoir, Berkeley, Bouncy, Braemar, Broch, C, Calzean, Canossa, Carbonek, Carisbrooke, Casbah, Chateau, Chepstow, Chillon, Citadel, Colditz, Conwy, Corfe, Culzean, Dangerous, Despair, Doubting, Dunsinane, Edinburgh, Egremont, Eileen Donan, Elephant, Elsinore, Fastness, Fort, Fotheringhay, Glamis, Gormenghast, Harlech, Herstmonceux, Hever, Howard, Kasba(h), Kenilworth, Lancaster, Leeds, Lincoln, Ludlow, Malperdy, Man, More, Mot(t)e, Otranto, Perilous, Rackrent, Raglan, Rook, Schloss, Sherborne, Sissinghurst, Spain, Stirling, Stokesay, Stormont, Stronghold, Tintagel, Trim, Urquhart, Villa, Wartburg, Warwick, Windsor

Casual Accidental, Adventitious, Airy, Blasé, Chance, Flippant, Grass, Haphazard, Idle, Incidental, Informal, Jaunty, Lackadaisical, Nonchalant, Odd(ment), Offhand, Off-the-cuff, Orra, Passing, Promiscuous, Random, Scratch, Sporadic, Stray, Temp, Throwaway

Cat Abyssinian, Alley, Angora, Asparagus, Balinese, Baudrons, Bluepoint, Bobcat, Burmese, Cacomistle, Cacomixl, Caracal, Cheetah, Cheshire, Civet, Clowder, Colourpoint, Cop, Cougar, Dandy, Eyra, Fat, Felid, Feline, Felix, Foss(a), Foumart, Foussa, Genet(te), Gib, Gossip, Grimalkin, Gus, Himalayan, Hipster, Hodge, Jazzer, Kilkenny, Kit, Korat, Lair, Lash, Leopard, Linsang, Lion, Long-hair, Lynx, Maine coon, Malkin, Maltese, Manul, Manx, Margay, Marmalade, Mehitabel, Mewer, Mog, Mouser, Musang, Nandine, Neuter, Nib, Ocelot, Ounce, Painter, Panther, Pard, Pardal, Persian, Pharaoh, Polecat, Practical, Puma, Puss, Rasse, Rex, Ringtail, Rumpy, Russian blue, Scourge, Sealpoint, Serval, Shorthair, Siamese, Sick, Spew, Spue, Swinger, Tabby, Tibert, Tiger, Tigon, Tigress, Tobermory, Tom, Tortoise-shell, Tybalt, Weasel

Catalogue Dewey, Index, Inventory, List, Litany, Magalog, Messier, Ragman, Ragment, Raisonné, Record, Register, Table, Tabulate

Catalyst Accelerator, Agent, Influence, Unicase, Ziegler

Catapult Ballista, Ging, Launch, Mangon(el), Perrier, Petrary, Propel, Scorpion, Shanghai, Sling, Slingshot, Stone-bow, Tormentum, Trebuchet, Wye, Y

Catastrophe Calamity, > DISASTER, Doom, Epitasis, Fiasco, Meltdown

Catch(y), Caught Air, Apprehend, Attract, Bag, Benet, Bone, C, Capture, Chape, Clasp, Cog, Collar, Contract, Cop, Corner, Ct, Deprehend, Detent, Dolly, Engage, Enmesh, Ensnare, Entoil, Entrap, Fang, Field, Fumble, Gaper, Get, Glee(some), Grasp, Had, Hank, Haud, Haul, Hear, Hold, Hook, Inmesh, Keddah, Keight, Kep(pit), Kheda, Kill, Land, Lapse, Lasso, Latch, Lime, Lock, Morse, Nab, Nail, Net, Nick, Nim, Nobble, Noose, Overhear, Overhent, Overtake, Parti, Pawl, Rap, Release, Rope, Round, Rub, Safety, Sean, Sear, See(n), Seize, > SNAG, Snap, Snare, Snig, > SONG, Surprise, Swindle, Tack, Take, Trammel, Trap, Trawl, Trick, Tripwire, Troll, Twig, Understand, Wrestle

Categorise, Category > CLASS, Etic, Genus, Label, Order, Pigeonhole, Range, Taxon

Cater(er) Acatour, Cellarer, Feed, Manciple, > PROVIDE, Serve, Steward, Supply, Victualler, Vivandière

Caterpillar Aweto, Boll worm, Cotton-worm, Cutworm, Eruciform, Geometer, Hop-dog, Hornworm, Inchworm, Larva, Looper, Osmeterium, Palmer, Tent, Webworm, Woolly-bear

Cathedral Basilica, Chartres, Chester, Cologne, Dome, Duomo, Ely, Lateran, Minster, Notre Dame, Rheims, St Paul's, Sens, Wells, Westminster, Winchester

Catholic Broad, Defenders, Doolan, Ecumenical, Fenian, General, Irvingism, Jebusite, Latin, Left-footer, Liberal, Marian, Ostiary, Papalist, Papaprelatist, Papist, Recusant, Redemptionist, Roman, Salesian, Spike, Taig, Te(a)gue, Teigue, Thomist, Tory, Tridentine, Universal, Ursuline, Wide

Cattle(pen) Aberdeen Angus, Africander, Ankole, Aver, Ayrshire, Beefalo, Brahman, British white, Buffalo, Carabao, Charbray, Charol(l)ais, Chillingham, Dexter, Drove, Durham, Fee, Friesland, Galloway, Gaur, Gayal, Guernsey, Gyal, Heard, Herd, Hereford, Highland, Holstein (Friesian), Illawara, Jersey, Kerry, Kine, Kouprey, Kraal, Ky(e), Kyloe, Lairage, Limousin, Lincoln, Longhorn, Luing, Neat, Nout, Nowt, Owsen, Oxen, Piemontese, Rabble, Redpoll, Rother, Santa Gertrudis, Shorthorn, Simment(h)al, Soum, Sowm, Steer, Stock, Store, Stot, Sussex, Tamarao, Tamarau, Teeswater, Welsh black

Caucus Assembly, Cell, Gathering, Race

Caulk Fill, Pitch, Snooze

Causation, **Cause(d)**, **Causes** Aetiology, Agent, Beget, Breed, Bring, Compel, Create, Crusade, Determinant, Due, Effect, Efficient, Encheason, Engender, Factor, Final, First, Flag-day, Formal, Gar(re), Generate, Ideal, Induce, Lead, Lost, Make, Material, Motive, Movement, > OCCASION, Parent, Probable, Provoke, Reason, Root, Sake, Source, Teleology, Topic, Ultimate, Wreak

Caustic Acid, Acrimonious, Alkaline, Burning, Erodent, Escharotic, Moxa, Pungent, Sarcastic, Scathing, Seare, Tart, Vitriol, Waspish, Withering

Caution, **Cautious (person)** Achitophel, Admonish, Ahithophel, Alert, Amber, Awarn, Beware, Cagey, Card, Care, Cave, Caveat, Chary, Circumspect, Credence, Cure, Defensive, Deliberate, Discretion, Fabian, Gingerly, Guard(ed), Heedful, Leery, Prudent, Rum, Scream, Skite, Tentative, Vigilant, Ware, > WARN, Wary, Yellow card

Cave(rn), **Caves**, **Cave-dwelling** Acherusia, Altamira, Antar, Antre, Beware, Cellar, Collapse, Corycian, Den, Domdaniel, Erebus, Fingal's, Fore, Grot(to), Hollow, Jenolan, Lascaux, Look-out, Lupercal, Mammoth, Nix, Pot-hole, Proteus, Sepulchre, Spel(a)ean, Speleology, Spelunker, Speos, Tassili, Vault, Waitomo, Ware, Weem

Caveman Adullam, Aladdin, Fingal, Neanderthal, Primitive, Troglodyte, Troll

Caviare Beluga, Roe, Sevruga, Sturgeon

Cavity Acetabulum, Amygdale, Atrial, Camera, Celom, Chamber, Coelom(e), Concepticle, Concha, Crater, Crypt, Dent, Druse, Enteron, Follicle, Foss, Gap, Geode, Glenoid, Hold, Hole, Lacuna, Locule, Mediastinum, Orbita, Orifice, Pocket, Sinus, Tear, Tympanum, Vacuole, Vein, Ventricle, Vesicle, Vitta, Vomica, Vug, Well

Cease(fire) Abate, Blin, Cut, Desist, Die, Disappear, Halt, Intermit, Lin, Lose, Pass, Refrain, Sessa, > STOP, Truce

Cedar(wood) Arolla, Atlas, Deodar, Incense, Toon

Ceiling Absolute, Barrel, Coffered, Cove, Cupola, Dome, Glass, Lacunar, Laquearia, Limit, Plafond, Roof, Soffit

Celebrate(d), **Celebration**, **Celebrity** Ale, Beanfeast, Besung, Bigwig, Binge, Carnival, Chant, Commemorate, Distinguished, Do, Emblazon, Encaenia, Epithalamion, Epithalamium, Fame, Feast, Fest, Festivity, Fete, Fiesta, Gala, Gaudeamus, Gaudy, Glorify, Grog-up, Harvest home, Hold, Holiday, Honour, Jamboree, Jollifications, Jollities, Jubilee, Keep, Laud, Legend, Lion, Loosing, Lowsening, Maffick, Mardi gras, Mawlid al-Nabi, Monstre sacre, Name, Noted, Nuptials, Observe, Occasion, Orgy, Panathenaea, Praise, Randan, Rejoice, Renown, Repute, Revel, Roister, Saturnalia, Sing, Spree, Star, Storied, Sung, Triumph, Wassail, Wet

Celestial Chinese, Divine, Ethereal, Heavenly, Supernal, Uranic

Celibate, **Celibacy** Bachelor, Chaste, Paterin(e), Rappist, Rappite, Shakers, Single, Spinster

Cell(s), **Cellular** Battery, Bullpen, Cadre, Chamber, Chapel, Crypt, Cubicle, Death, Dungeon, Group, Laura, Padded, Peter, > PRISON, Unit

Cellar Basement, Coalhole, Storm, Vault, Vaut

Celt(ic) Breton, Brython, Druid, Gadhel, Gael, Goidel, Helvetii, Kelt, Taffy, Welsh

Cement Araldite®, Compo, Concrete, Fix, Flaunch, Glue, Grout, Lute, Maltha, Mastic, Mortar, Paste, Pointing, Portland, Putty, Rubber, > STICK, Trass

Cemetery Aceldama, Arenarium, Arlington, Boneyard, Boot Hill, Campo santo, Catacomb, God's Acre, Golgotha, Graveyard, Musall, Necropolis, Père Lachaise, Saqqara, Urnfield

Censor(ious), **Censure** Accuse, Admonition, Animadvert, Appeach, Ban, Banner, Berate, Blame, Blue-pencil, Bowdler, Braid, Cato, Comstockery,

> **CONDEMN**, Critical, Criticise, Damn, Dang, Decry, Dispraise, Edit, Excommunicate, Excoriate, Expurgate, Gag, Obloquy, Rap, Repress, Reprimand, Reproach, Reprobate, Reprove, Satirise, Slam, Slate, Suppress, Tax, Tirade, Traduce, Wig

Cent Bean, Coin, Ct, Penny, Red

Central, **Centre** Active, Amid, Attendance, Axis, Broca's, Bunt, Call, Cardinal, Chakra, Civic, Community, Contact, Core, Cost, Day, Daycare, Dead, Detention, Detoxification, Deuteron, Deuton, Downtown, Drop-in, Epergne, Eye, Field, Focus, Frontal, Garden, Health, Heart, Hotbed, Hothouse, Hub, Incident, Inmost, Internal, Interpretive, Kernel, Kingpin, Law, Leisure, Lincoln, Live, Main, Mecca, Median, Medulla, Mid(st), Music, Nave, Nerve, Nucleus, Omphalus, Pompidou, Profit, Property, Reception, Rehabilitation, Remand, Shopping, Social Education, Storm, Teachers', Trauma, Visitor, Waist, Weather

▷ **Centre** *may indicate* middle letters

Century Age, C, Era, Magdeburg, Period, Ton

Ceramic(s) Arcanist, China, Earthen, Ferrite, Porcelain, Pottery, Sialon, Tiles

Cereal Amelcorn, Barley, Blé, Bran, Buckwheat, Bulgar, Bulg(h)ur, Cassava, Corn, Couscous, Emmer, Farina, Gnocchi, Grain, Granola, Hominy, Maize, Mandioc(a), Mandiocca, Mani(h)oc, Manihot, Mealie, Millet, Muesli, Oats, Paddy, Popcorn, Rye(corn), Sago, Samp, Seed, Semolina, Sorghum, Spelt, Tapioca, Tef(f), Triticale, Wheat, Zea

Ceremonial, **Ceremony** Amrit, Barmitzvah, Chado, Chanoyu, Common Riding, Coronation, Doseh, Durbar, Encaenia, Enthronement, Etiquette, Eucharist, Flypast, Form(al), Gongyo, Habdalah, Havdalah, Havdoloh, Heraldry, Investiture, Matsuri, Maundy, Mummery, Observance, Occasion, Ordination, Pageantry, Parade, Pomp, Powwow, Protocol, Rite, Ritual, Sacrament, Sado, Seder, Service, State, Tea, Unveiling, Usage

Cert(ain), **Certainty** Absolute, Actual, Assured, Banker, Bound, Cast-iron, Cinch, Cocksure, Confident, Convinced, Decided, Exact, Fact, Fate, Indubitable, Inevitable, Infallible, Monte, Nap, One, Positive, Poz, Precise, Shoo-in, Siccar, Sicker, Snip, Some, > **SURE**, Sure-fire, Truth, Yes

Certificate, **Certified**, **Certify** Affirm, Attest, Bene decessit, Bond, Chit, Cocket, Confirm, Credential, Death, Debenture, Depose, Diploma, Docket, Document, Enseal, Gold, Guarantee, Landscrip, Licence, Lines, Medical, MOT, Notarise, Paper, Patent, Proven, Savings, School, Scrip, Scripophily, Share, Stock, Sworn, Talon, Testamur, Testimonial, Treasury, U, Unruly, Voucher, Warrant

Chafe, **Chafing** Chunter, Fray, Fret, Harass, Intertrigo, Irritate, > **RUB**, Seethe, Worry

Chain(ed) Acre's-breadth, Albert, Anklet, Bind, Bond, Bracelet, Bucket, Cable, Catena, Choke, Cistron, Daisy, Decca, Drive, Dynasty, Engineer's, Esses, Fanfarona, Fetter, Fob, Food, Furlong, Gleipnir, Gunter's, Gyve, Markov, Mayor, Micella(r), Micelle, Noria, Pennine, Pitch, Range, Roller, Seal, > **SERIES**, Shackle, Slang, Sprocket, String, Strobila, Team, Tug, Watch

Chair Basket, Bath, Bench, Bentwood, Berbice, Bergère, Birthing, Bosun's, Butterfly, Camp, Cane, Captain's, Carver, Club, Curule, Deck, Dining, Director's, Easy, Electric, Estate, Fauteuil, Fiddle-back, Folding, Frithstool, Garden, Gestatorial, Guérite, High, Jampan, Jampanee, Jampani, Ladder-back, Lounger, Love-seat, Merlin, Morris, Pew, Preside, Recliner, Rocker, Sedan, Stool, Sugan, Swivel, Throne, Wainscot, Wheel, Windsor, Wing

Chairman Convener, Emeritus, Mao, MC, Pr(a)eses, Prof, Prolocutor, Sheraton, Speaker

Chalk(y) Calcareous, Cauk, Cawk, Crayon, Credit, Cretaceous, French, Soapstone, White(n), Whit(en)ing

Challenge(r), **Challenging** Acock, Assay, Call, Cartel, Champion, Confront, Contest, Dare, Defy, Gage, Gauntlet, Glove, Hazard, Hen(ner), Iconoclasm, Impugn, Oppugn, Provoke, Query, Question, Recuse, Sconce, Shuttle, Tackle, Taker, Tall order, Tank, Threat, Vie, Whynot

Chamber(s) Atrium, Auricle, Camarilla, Camera, Casemate, Cavern, Cavitation, Cavity, Cell(a), Chanty, Cloud, Cofferdam, Combustion, Cubicle, Decompression, Dene-hole, Dolmen, Echo, Float, Gas, Gazunder, Hall, Horrors, Hypogea, Ionization, Jerry, Jordan, Kiva, Lethal, Locule, Mattamore, Po(t), Privy, Roum, Serdab, Silo, Spark, Star, Swell-box, Synod, Thalamus, Undercroft, Upper, Utricle, Vault, Ventricle, Zeta

Champ Bite, Chafe, Chew, Chomp, Eat, Gnash, Gnaw, Mash, Morsure, Munch

Champagne Boy, Bubbly, Charlie, Fizz, Gigglewater, Pop, Sillery, Simkin, Simpkin, Stillery, Troyes, Widow

Champion(s) Ace, Adopt, Ali, Apostle, Belt, Campeador, Cid, Cock, Defend, Don Quixote, Doucepere, Douzeper, Dymoke, Enoch, Espouse, Gladiator, Harry, > **HERO**, Horse, Kemp, Kemper(yman), King, Knight, Maintain, Matchless, Messiah, Messias, Neil, Paladin, Palmerin, Peerless, Perseus, Promachos, Proponent, Protagonist, Roland, St Anthony, St David, St Denis, St George, St James, St Patrick, Spiffing, Spokesman, Star, Support, Tribune, Upholder, Victor, Wardog, > **WINNER**, Yokozuna

Chance (upon), **Chancy** Accident, Aleatory, Aunter, Bet, Break, Buckley's, Cast, Casual, Cavel, Contingent, Dice, Earthly, Even, > **FATE**, Fluke, Fortuitous, Fortuity, Fortune, > **GAMBLE**, Game, Hap, Happenstance, Hobnob, Iffy, Kevel, Light, Look-in, Lot, > **LOTTERY**, Luck, Meet, Mercy, Occur, Odds, Opening, Opportunity, Posse, Potluck, Probability, Prospect, Random, Rise, Risk, Serendipity, Slant, Spec, Stake, Stochastic, Sweep, Toss-up, Treble, Turn, Tychism, Ventre, Venture, Wager

Change(able), **Changes**, **Changing** Adapt, Adjust, Agio, > **ALTER**, Amendment, Attorn, Backtrack, Barter, Become, Bob-major, Capricious, Cash, Catalysis, Chop, Cline, Commute, Convert, Coppers, Denature, Departure, Edit, Enallage, Eustatic, Exchange, Find, Flighty, Float, Fluctuate, Flux, Guard, Gybe, Inflect, Innovate, Killcrop, Labile, Make-over, Metabolic, Metabolise, Metamorphosis, Mobile, Modify, Mutable, Mutation, Parallax, Peal, Permute, Protean, Realise, Recant, Rectify, Reform, Refraction, Rest, Revise, Rework, Sandhi, Sd, Seesaw, Shake-out, Shake-up, Shift, Silver, Small, Substitute, Swap, Swing, Switch, Tolsel, Tolsey, Tolzey, Transfer, Transfiguration, Transform, Transition, Transmute, Transpose, Transubstantial, Turn, Uncertain, Upheaval, U-turn, Vagary, Variant, Variation, Vary, Veer, Volatile, Volte-face, Wheel, Wow

▷ **Change(d)** *may indicate* an anagram

Channel Access, Aqueduct, Artery, Beagle, Bed, Billabong, Bristol, Canal, Chimb, Chime, Chine, Chute, Conduit, Culvert, Cut, Cutting, Distribution, Ditch, Drain, Duct, Dyke, Ea, English, Estuary, Euripus, Fairway, Flume, Foss, Funnel, Furrow, Gat, Geo, Gio, Glyph, Gully, Gut, Gutter, Head-race, Ingate, Katavothron, Khor, Kill, Kos, Lane, Leat, Leet, Limber, Major, Meatus, Medium, Minch, Moat, Mozambique, Multiplex, Narrows, North, Penstock, Pentland Firth, Pescadores, Pipeline, Qanat, Race, Rebate, Rigol(l), Rivulet, Sea-gate, Seaway, Sewer, Shunt, Sinus, Sky, Sloot, Sluice, Sluit, Sny(e), Solent, Solway Firth, Sound, Sow, Spillway, Sprue, Strait, Suez, Sure, Swash, Tailrace, Tideway, Trough, Ureter, Watercourse, Yucatan

Chant Anthem, Antiphon, Cantillate, Cantus, Chaunt, Decantate, Euouae, Evovae, Gregorian, Haka, Harambee, Hymn, Intone, Introit, Motet, Pennillion-singing, Psalm, Sing, Slogan, Te deum, Yell

Chaos, **Chaotic** Abyss, Anarchy, Confusion, Disorder, Fractal, Hun-tun, Jumble, Mess, Muss, Shambles, Snafu, Tohu bohu

▷ **Chaotic** *may indicate* an anagram

Chapel Bethel, Bethesda, Beulah, Cha(u)ntry, Ebenezer, Feretory, Galilee, Lady, Oratory, Sacellum, Sistine

▷ **Chaps** *may indicate* an anagram

Chapter Accidents, C, Canon, Cap, Capitular, Ch, Chap, Cr, Division, Episode, Lodge, Phase, Section, Social, Sura(h), Verse

Character(s) Aesc, Alphabet, Ampersand, Ampussyand, Aura, Backslash, Brand, Calibre, Case, Cipher, Clef, Cliff, Climate, Complexion, Contour, Credit, Digamma, Dramatis personae, Eta, Ethos, > **FEATURE**, Fish, Fist, Form, Grain, Grit, Hieroglyphic, Ideogram, Ideograph, Italic, Kern, Kind, La(m)bda, Letter, Logogram, Make-up, Mark, Mu, Nagari, > **NATURE**, Nu, Ogam, Ogham, Pahlavi, Pantaloon, Part, Pehlevi, Person(a), Personage, > **PERSONALITY**, Phonogram, Physiognomy, Protagonist, Psi, Reference, Repute, Rho, Role, Rune, Runic, Sampi, San, Self, Sirvente, Slash, Sonancy, Stamp, Subscript, Superscript(ion), Swung dash, Syllabary, Symbol, Testimonial, Ton(e), Trait, Uncial, Vav, Vee, Waw, Wen

Characterise(d), **Characterism**, **Characteristic(s)** Attribute, Aura, Cast, Colour, Distinctive, Ethos, Facies, Feature, Hair, Hallmark, Has, Headmark, Idiomatic, Idiosyncrasy, Jizz, Lineament, Mien, Nature, Notate, Peculiar, Persona, Point, Property, Quality, Stigma, Strangeness, Streak, Style, Typical, Vein

Charge(s), **Charged**, **Charger** Accusal, Accuse, Aerate, Agist, Allege, Annulet, Arraign, Ascribe, Assault, Baton, Bear, Behest, Blame, Brassage, Brush, Buckshot, Bum rap, Care, Cathexis, Commission, Community, Complaint, Congestion, Cost, Count, Cover, Criminate, Damage, Debit, Delate, Delf, Delph, Demurrage, Depth, Depute, Directive, Dittay, Dockage, Due, Duty, Electric, Electron, Entrust, Entry, Exit, Expense, Fare, Fee, Fill, Fixed, Fleur-de-lis, Floating, Flock, Freight, Fullage, Fuse, Fuze, Gazump, Gravamen, > **HERALDIC**, Hot, Hypothec, Impeach, Impute, Indict, Inescutcheon, Inform, Instinct, Ion, Isoelectric, Last, Lien, Lioncel(le), Lionel, Live, Load, Mandate, Mine, Mount, Objure, Obtest, Onrush, Onslaught, Onus, Ordinary, Orle, Overhead, Pervade, Pew-rent, Plaint, Positive, Premium, Prime, Prix fixe, Q, Rack-rent, Rap, Rate, Red-dog, Rent, Report, Reprise, Roundel, Run, > **RUSH**, Saddle, Service, Specific, Steed, Tariff, Tax, Tear, Terms, Tilt, > **TRAY**, Tressure, Trickle, Trust, Tutorage, Upfill, Vaire, Vairy, Verdoy, Vigorish, Ward, Warhead, Wharfage

Charitable, **Charity** Alms, Awmous, Benign, Caritas, Dole, Dorcas, Eleemosynary, Largesse, Leniency, Liberal, Lion, Love, Mercy, Oddfellow, Openhanded, Oxfam, Pelican, Zakat

Charlock Runch

Charm(er), **Charming** Abracadabra, Abrasax, Abraxas, Allure, Amulet, Appeal, Aroma, Attraction, Beguile, Bewitch, Captivate, Charisma, Circe, Comether, Cute, Cutie, Emerods, Enamour, Enchant, Engaging, > **ENTRANCE**, Fascinate, Fay, Fetish, Grace, Greegree, Gri(s)gris, Hand of glory, Houri, Juju, Magnetic, Mascot, Mojo, Obeah, Obi(a), Periapt, Phylactery, Porte-bonheur, Prince, Quaint, Quark, Ravish, Siren, Smoothie, Spellbind, Suave, Sweetness, Taking, Talisman, Telesm, Tiki, Trinket, Unction, Voodoo, Winsome

▷ **Charming** *may indicate* an anagram

Chart(ed), **Charting** Abac, Bar, Breakeven, Card, Diagram, Eye, Flip, Flow, Gantt, Graph, Histogram, Hydrography, Isogram, Isopleth, List, Magna Carta, > **MAP**, Mappemond, Nomogram, Plot, Portolano, Ringelmann, Social, Table, Timetable, Waggoner, Weather

Charta, **Charter** Book, Covenant, Hire, Lease, Novodamus, Rent

Chase(r), **Chasing** Cannock, Chace, Chevy, Chivy, Ciseleur, Ciselure, Course, Cranbome, Decorate, Drink, Game, Harass, Hound, > **HUNT**, Jumper, Oxo, Pursuit, Race, Scorse, Sic(k), Steeple, Sue, Suit, Wild-goose

Chasm Abyss, Fissure, Gap, Gorge, Gulf, Schism, Yawn

Chaste, Chastity Agnes, Attic, Celibate, Classic, Clean, Florimell, Ines, Innocent, Modesty, Nessa, > **PURE**, Vestal, Virginal, Virtue

Chat, Chatter(box) Babble, Bavardage, Blab(ber), Blether, Campanero, Causerie, Chelp, Chinwag, Clack, Clishmaclaver, Confab(ulate), Converse, Cosher, Coze, Crack, Dialogue, Froth, Gab(ble), Gas, Gossip, Gup, Hobnob, Jabber, Jargon, Jaw, Kilfud, Madge, Mag(pie), Natter, Patter, Pie, Pourparler, Prate, Prattle, Rabbit, Rabble, Rap, Rattle, Scuttlebutt, Shmoose, Talk, Talkee-talkee, Tattle, Twattle, Waffle, Windbag, Witter, Wongi, Yacketyyak, Yak, Yarn, Yatter, Yoking

Cheap Bargain, Base, Catchpenny, Cheesy, Chintzy, Cut-price, Downmarket, Giveaway, Knockdown, Low, Off-peak, Poor, Sacrifice, Shoddy, Stingy, Tatty, Tawdry, Ticky-tacky, Tinpot, Tinselly, Trivial, Undear, Vile

▷ **Cheap** *may indicate* a d- or p- start to a word

Cheat(ers), Cheating Bam, Bamboozle, Beguile, Bilk, Bite(r), Bob, Bonnet, Bucket, Bullock, Cardsharp(er), Charlatan, Chiaus, Chicane(ry), Chisel, Chouse, Clip, Cod, Cog(ger), Colt, Con, Cozen, Crib, Cross, Cross-bite(r), Cuckold, Cully, Defraud, Delude, Diddle, Dingo, Dish, Do, Doublecross, Duckshove, Dupe, Escroc, Faitor, Fiddle, Finagle, Flam, Fleece, Fob, Foister, Fox, Fraud, Gaff, Gip, Glasses, Gum, Gyp, Hoax, Hocus, Hoodwink, Hornswoggle, Horse, Intake, Jockey, Magsman, Mulct, Mump, Nick, Pasteboard, Picaro(on), Poop, Queer, Rib, Rig, Rogue, Rook, Rush, Scam, Screw, Shaft, Sharper, Short-change, Slur, Smouch, Snap, Stack, Stiff, Sting, Swindle, Thimble-rigging, Trepan, Trim, Two-time, Welsh, Wheedle

Check Arrest, Audit, Bauk, Ba(u)lk, Bill, Bridle, Collate, Compesce, Control, Count, Cramp, Cross-index, Curb, Dam, Damp, Detain, Detent, Discovered, Dogs-tooth, Examine, Foil, Frustrate, Halt, Hamper, Hobble, Houndstooth, Inhibit, Jerk, Jerque, Let, Limit, Mate, Monitor, Observe, Overhaul, Party, Perpetual, Prevent, Rain, Reality, Rebuff, Rebuke, Rein, Repress, Reprime, Repulse, Reread, > **RESTRAIN**, Revoke, Saccade, Screen, Service, Setback, Shepherd's, Shorten, Sit-upon, Sneap, Sneb, Snib, Snub, Sound, Spot, > **STEM**, Stop, Stunt, Tab, Tally, Tartan, Tattersall, Test, Thwart, Tick, Trash, Verify, Vet

Cheek(y) Alforja, Audacity, Buccal, Chap, Chollers, Chutzpah, Crust, Flippant, Fresh, Gum, Hussy, Jowl, Lip, Malapert, Malar, Masseter, Neck, Nerve, Noma, Pert, Presumption, Quean, Sass, Sauce, Sideburns, Wang, Yankie, Zygoma

Cheer(s), Cheerful(ness), Cheering Acclaim, Agrin, Applaud, Banzai, Barrack, Blithe, Bonnie, Bravo, Bright, Bronx, Bubbly, Buck, Buoy, Cadgy, Canty, Carefree, Cherry, Chin-chin, Chipper, Chirpy, > **COMFORT**, Crouse, Debonair, Drink, Ease, Elate, Elevate, Enliven, Exhilarate, Festive, Genial, Gladden, Happy-go-lucky, Hearten, Hilarity, Holiday, Hooch, Hoorah, Hurra(h), Huzzah, Insouciance, Jocund, Jovial, Kia-ora, Light-hearted, Lightsome, Lively, Meal, Ovate, Peart, Perky, Please, Praise, Prosit, Rah, Riant, Rivo, Root, Rumbustious, Shout, Sko(a)l, Slainte, Sonsie, Sunny, Ta, Tata, Thanks, Three, Tiger, Tiggerish, Toodle-oo, Warm, Winsome, Yell

Cheese, Cheesy American, Amsterdam, Appenzell, Asiago, Bel Paese, Blue, Boursin, Brie, Caboc, Caerphilly, Camembert, Cantal, Casein, Caseous, Cheddar, Cheshire, Chessel, Chèvre, Colby, Collommiers, Cottage, Cream, Crowdie, Curd, Damson, Danish blue, Derby, Dolcelatte, Double Gloucester, Dunlop, Edam, Emmental(er), Emmenthal(er), Ermite, Esrom, Ewe, Fet(a), Fontina, Fromage frais, Fynbo, Gloucester, Goat, Gorgonzola, Gouda, Gruyère, Halloumi, Hard, Havarti, Huntsman, Ilchester, Islay, Jarlsberg®, Junket, Kebbock, Kebbuck, Kenno, Killarney, Lancashire, Leicester, Limburg(er), Lymeswold®, Macaroni, Mascarpone, Mousetrap, Mozzarella, Mu(e)nster, Mycella, Neufchatel, Oka, Orkney, Paneer, Parmesan, Pecorino, Pont l'Eveque, Port Salut, Pot, Provolone, Quark, Raclette, Rarebit, Reblochon, Rennet, Ricotta, Romano, Roquefort, Sage

Derby, Samso, Sapsago, Skyr, Stilton®, Stone, Stracchino, Swiss, Tilsit, Tofu, Truckle, Vacherin, VIP, Wensleydale

Chef Commis, Escoffier

Chemical Acid, Acrolein, Adrenalin®, Alar, Aldehyde, Alkali, Alum, Amide, Barilla, Bute, Carbide, Caseose, Catalyst, Cephalin, Developer, Dopamine, Encephalin, Fixer, Fluoride, Formyl, Fungicide, Glutamine, Glycol, Halon, Harmin, Heptane, Hexylene, Histamine, Hypo, ICI, Imine, Indican, Interleukin, Natron, Nitre, Oestregen, Olefin, Olein, Oxide, Oxysalt, Pentane, Pentene, Pentyl, Peptide, Phenol, Phenyl, Pheromone, Potash, Potassa, Ptomaine, Reagent, Resorcin, Soup, Strontia, Sulphide, Thio-salt, Trimer, Weedkiller

Chemist(ry) Alchemy, Alchymy, Analyst, Apothecary, Bunsen, Butenandt, Cavendish, Davy, Debye, Dispenser, Druggist, Drugstore, FCS, Gahn, Hevesy, Inorganic, Lavoisier, Liebig, LSA, MPS, Nernst, Newlands, Nobel, Organic, Paracelsus, Pasteur, Pharmacist, Physical, Pothecary, Pottingar, Proust, Prout, RIC, Sabatier, Sanger, Spageric, Spagiric, Spagyric

Cheque Blank, Giro, Gregory, Stumer, Tab, Traveller's

Cherry (tree) Amarelle, Ball, Bigaroon, Bigarreau, Blackheart, Cerise, Cornelian, Gean, Ground, Heart, Jerusalem, Kearton, Kermes, Kermesite, Malpighia, Marasca, Maraschino, May-duke, Maz(z)ard, Merry, Morel(lo), Red, Whiteheart

Chervil Cow-parsley

Chessman Bishop, Black, Castle, Horse, King, Knight, Pawn, Pin, Queen, Rook, White

Chest(y) Ark, Bahut, Bosom, Box, Breast, Buist, Bunker, Bureau, Bust, Caisson, Cap-case, Case, Cassone, Chapel, Chiffonier, Coffer, Coffin, Coffret, Commode, Cub, Hope, Inro, Kist, Larnax, Locker, Lowboy, Medicine, Ottoman, Pectoral, Pereion, Pigeon, Pleural, Safe, Scrine, Scryne, Shrine, Sternum, Tallboy, Tea, Thorax, Toolbox, Trunk, Wangun, Wanigan, War

Chestnut Auburn, Badious, Ch, Chincapin, Chinese, Chinkapin, Chinquapin, Cliché, Conker, Favel(l), Hoary, Marron, Marron glacé, Moreton Bay, Russet, Saligot, Soare, Sorrel, Spanish, Sweet, Water

Chew(ing) Bite, Champ, Chaw, Cud, Gnaw, Gum, Manducate, Masticate, Maul, Meditate, Moop, Mou(p), Munch, Ruminate, Siri(h), Spearmint

Chic Dapper, Elegant, In, Kick, Modish, Posh, Smart, Soigné, Stylish, Swish, Tonish, Trim

Chick(en) Battery, Biddy, Broiler, Cheeper, Chittagong, Chuckie, Clutch, Cochin, Coward, Cowherd, Eirack, Gutless, Hen, Howtowdie, Kiev, Layer, Marengo, Minorca, Niderling, Poltroon, Poot, Poult, Pout, Prairie, Precocial, Quitter, Roaster, Spatchcock, Spring, Squab, Supreme, Timorous, Unheroic, Windy, Wyandotte, Yellow

Chief(tain) Arch, Ardrigh, Boss, Caboceer, Cacique, Calif, Caliph, Capital, Capitan, Capitayn, Capo, Caradoc, Cazique, Ch, Chagan, Dat(t)o, Dominant, Emir, First, Foremost, Geronimo, Grand, Haggis, > **HEAD**, Hereward, Jarl, Kaid, King, Leader, > **MAIN**, Mass, Mugwump, Nizam, Oba, Overlord, Pendragon, Premier, Primal, Prime, Principal, Quanah, Raja(h), Rajpramukh, Rangatira, Ratoo, Ratu, Sachem, Sagamore, Sarpanch, Sudder, Supreme, Tanist, Tank, Top

Child(ish), Childhood, Children Aerie, Alannah, Babe, Baby, Badger, Bairn, Bambino, Bantling, Boy, Brat, Brood, Butter-print, Ch, Changeling, Cherub, Chick, Chickabiddy, Chit, Collop, Cub, Dream, Elfin, Eyas, Foundling, Gangrel, Ge(i)t, Girl, Gyte, Heir, Hurcheon, Imp, Infant, Issue, It, Jailbait, Jejune, Juvenile, Kid(die), Kiddie(wink), Kiddy, Kinder, Lad, Limb, Litter, Littlie, Mamzer, Minion, Minor, Mite, Munchkin, Naive, Nipper, Nursling, Offspring, Papoose, Piccaninny, Pickin, Progeny, Puerile, Puss, Putto, Ragamuffin, Rip, Rug rat, Scion, Smout, Smowt, Sprog, Street arab, Subteen, Ted, Tike, Toddle(r), Tot(tie), Totty, Trot, Tyke, Urchin,

Wean, Weanel, Weanling, Weeny-bopper, Whelp, Younker, Youth

Chill(er), Chilly Bleak, > COLD, Frappé, Freeze, Freon®, Frigid, Frosty, Gelid, Ice, Iciness, Mimi, Oorie, Ourie, Owrie, Parky, Raw, Refrigerate, Rigor, Scare

Chime(s) Bell, Cymar, Jingle, Peal, Semantron, Tink, > TOLL

Chimney (pot), Chimney corner Can, Cow(!), Femerall, Flare stack, Flue, Funnel, Lug, Lum, Smokestack, Stack, Stalk, Tallboy, Tunnel

China(man), Chinese Ami, Amoy, Boxer, Cameoware, Cantonese, Cathay, Celestial, Ch, Chelsea, Chow, Coalport, Cochin, Cock, Confucius, Crackle, Crockery, Delft, Derby, Dresden, Eggshell, Etrurian, Goss, Hakka, Han, Hizen, Hmong, Imari, Kanji, Kaolin, Kuo-yu, Limoges, Manchu, Mandarin, Mangi, Maoist, Mate, Meissen, Min, Ming, Minton, Oppo, Pal, Pareoean, Pekingese, Pe-tsai, Pinyin, Porcelain, > POTTERY, Putonghua, Queensware, Rockingham, Royal Worcester, Seric, Sèvres, Shanghai, Sinic, Spode®, Sun Yat-sen, Tai-ping, Taolst, Teng, Tocharian, Tungus, Uigur, Wal(l)y, Ware, Wedgwood®, Whiteware, Willowware, Worcester, Wu

Chip(s) Bo(a)st, Carpenter, Counter, Cut, Deep-fried, Fish, Flake, Fragment, Hack, Knap, Nacho(s), Nick, Pin, Shaving, Silicon, Spale, Spall, Tortilla, Transputer

▷ **Chip** *may indicate* an anagram

Chirp(y), Chirrup Cheep, Cherup, Chirm, Chirr, Cicada, Peep, Pip, Pipe, Pitter, Stridulate, Trill, Tweet, Twitter

Chisel(ler), Chisel-like Bam, Boaster, Bolster, Bur, Burin, Carve, Cheat, Clip, Drove, Firmer, Gad, Mason, Scalpriform, Scauper, Scorper, Sculpt, Sting

Chit Docket, Girl, Note, Voucher

Chivalry, Chivalrous Brave, Bushido, Courtly, Gallant

Chocolate Aero, Brown, Cacao, Carob, Cocoa, Dragee, Ganache, Neapolitan, Noisette, Pinole, Truffle

Choice, Choose, Choosy, Chosen Adopt, Anthology, Appoint, Aryan, Cherry-pick, Cull, Dainty, Decide, Druthers, Eclectic, Elect, Elite, Esnecy, Fine, Fork, Free will, Hobson's, Leet, Leve, Lief, List, Opt, Option, Or, Ossian, Peach, Peculiar, > PICK, Picking, Plum(p), Precious, Predilect, Prefer, Proairesis, Rare, Recherché, > SELECT, Superb, Try(e), Via media, Volition, Wale

Choir, Choral, Chorister, Chorus Antiphony, Antistrophe, Anvil, Apse, Burden, Dawn, Decani, Faburden, Fauxbourdon, Group, Hallelujah, Harmony, Hymeneal, Motet, Parabasis, Precentor, > REFRAIN, Singing, Strophe, Treble, Triad

Choke(r) Block, Clog, Gag, Silence, Smoor, Smore, Smother, Stifle, Stop, Strangle(hold), Strangulate, > THROTTLE

Choler Yellow bile

Chop(per), Chops, Chopper(s), Choppy Adze, Ax(e), Celt, Charge, Cheek, Chump, Cleave, Côtelette, Cuff, Cutlet, Dice, Fell(er), Flew, Hack, Helicopter, Hew, Ivory, Karate, Lop, Mince, Mouth, Rotaplane, Rough, Suey, Teeth, Wang

Chord(s) Arpeggio, Barré, Common, Diameter, Harmony, Intonator, Nerve, Triad, Vocal

Chorea Sydenham's

Christ > CHRIST, Ecce homo, Messiah, Saviour, X

Christen(ing) Baptise, Launch, Name-day

Christian(ity) Adventist, Albigenses, Beghard, Believer, Cathar(ist), Coptic, Dior, Donatist, D(o)ukhobor, Ebionite, Galilean, Giaour, Gilbertine, Gnostic, Goy, Holy roller, Homo(i)ousian, Jehovah's Witness, Marrano, Melchite, Melkite, Moral, Mozarab, Mutineer, Nazarene, Nestorian, Phalange, Pilgrim, Protestant, Quartodeciman, RC, Sabotier, Scientist, SCM, Traditor, Uniat(e), Unitarian, Waldensian, Wesleyan, Xian, Zwinglian

Christmas(time) Dec, Island, Nativity, Noel, Yuletide

Chronicle(r) Anglo-Saxon, Annal, Brut, Calendar, Diary, Froissart, Hall, History, Holinshed, Logographer, Paralipomena, Parian, > **RECORD**, Register, Stow

Church Abbey, Armenian, Autocephalous, Basilica, Bethel, Bethesda, Brood, Byzantine, CE, Ch, Chapel, Chevet, Clergy, Collegiate, Congregational, Coptic, Delubrum, EC, Ecumenical, Episcopal, Episcopalian, Established, Faith, Fold, Free, High, Kirk, Lateran, Low, Lutheran, Maronite, Methodist, Minster, Moravian, Mormon, Orthodox, Prebendal, Presbyterian, RC, Reformed, Rome, Shrine, Smyrna, Stave, Steeple, Temple, Unification, Wee Free, Western

Churchgoer, Churchman, Churchwarden Azymite, Moonie, Predicant, Predikant, Ruridecanal, Subdeacon, Succentor, Ubiquitarian, Verger

Church house Deanery

Churl(ish) Ill-natured

Cider Drink, Perry, Scrumpy

Cigar(ette), Cigarette cards Beedi(e), Bumper, Burn, Cancer stick, Caporal, Cartophily, Cheroot, Cigarillo, Claro, Coffin nail, Conch, Concha, Corona, Dog-end, Doob, Durry, Fag, Filter-tip, Gasper, Giggle(-stick), Havana, Joint, Locofoco, Long-nine, Loosies, Maduro, Manilla, Panatella, Paper-cigar, Perfecto, Puritano, Reefer, Regalia, Roach, Roll-up, Smoke, Snout, Splif(f), Stog(e)y, Stogie, Stompie, Twist, Weed, Whiff, Zol

Cinch Duck soup

Cinema(s) Art house, Big screen, Biograph, Bioscope, Circuit, Drive-in, Films, Fleapit, Flicks, Megaplex, Movies, Multiplex, Mutoscope, New Wave, Nickelodeon, Nouvelle Vague, Odeon, Plaza, Theatre, Tivoli

Cinnamon, Cinnamon stone Canella, Cassia(bark), Essonite, Hessonite, Spice

Circle Almacantar, Almucantar, Annulet, Antarctic, Arctic, Circassian, Co, Colure, Company, Compass, Corn, Corolla, Coterie, Cromlech, Crop, Cycloid, Cyclolith, Dip, Disc, Dress, Druidical, Eccentric, Ecliptic, Embail, Enclose, Epicyclic, Equant, Equator, Equinoctial, Euler's, Family, Fraternity, Full, Galactic, Girdle, Gloriole, Great, Gyre, Halo, Hoop, Horizon, Hour, Hut, Inner, Inorb, Lap, Longitude, Loop, Magic, Malebolge, Mandala, Meridian, Mohr's, Nimbus, O, Orb, Orbit, Parhelic, Parquet, Parterre, Penannular, Peristalith, Pitch, Polar, Quality, Rigol, > **RING**, Rondure, Rotate, Roundlet, Sentencing, Set, Setting, Small, Sphere, Stemme, Stone, Striking, Surround, Tinchel, Traffic, Transit, Tropic, Turning, Umbel, Upper, Vertical, Vicious, Vienna, Virtuous, Volt, Wheel

Circuit(ous) Ambit, AND, Autodyne, Bypass, Closed, Comparator, Daughterboard, Diocese, Discriminator, Dolby®, Equivalent, Eyre, Gyrator, IC, Integrated, Interface, Lap, Limiter, Logic, Loop, Microprocessor, Motherboard, NAND, NOR, NOT, Open, OR, Perimeter, Phantom, Phase, Printed, Quadripole, Reactance, Ring, Round, Scaler, Series, Short, Smoothing, Three-phase, Tour, Windlass

Circular Annular, Court, Folder, Leaflet, Mailshot, Orby, Round, Spiral, Unending, Wheely

Circulate, Circulation Astir, Bloodstream, Cyclosis, Disseminate, Flow, Gyre, Issue, Mingle, Mix, Orbit, Pass, Publish, Report, Revolve, Rotate, Scope, Spread, Stir, Troll, Utter

▷ **Circulating** *may indicate* an anagram

Circumcise(r), Circumcision Pharaonic

Circumference Boundary, Girth, Perimeter, Size

Circumflex Perispomenon

Circumstance(s), Circumstantial Case, Detail, Event, Fact, Formal, > **INCIDENT**, Mitigating, Precise, Shebang, Situation

Circus, Circus boy Arena, Big top, Flea, Flying, Hippodrome, Marquee, Maximus,

Media, Monty Python, Ring, Three-ring

Cissy Nelly

Cistern Feed-head, Flush-box

Citation, **Cite** Adduce, Allegation, Mention, Name, Quote, Recall, Reference, Repeat, Sist, Summon

Citizen(s), **Citizenship** Burgess, Burgher, Civism, Cleruch, Denizen, Dicast, Ephebe, Franchise, Freeman, Jus sanguinis, Jus soli, Kane, National, Oppidan, Patrial, People, Quirites, Resident, Roman, Second-class, Senior, Snob, Subject, Trainband, Trierarch, Venireman, Voter

Citrus Acid, Calamondin, Cedrate, Lemon, Lime, Mandarin, Min(n)eola, Orange, Pomelo, Tangerine, Ugli

City Agra, Athens, Atlantis, Babylon, Burgh, Carthage, Cosmopolis, Ctesiphon, EC, Empire, Eternal, Forbidden, Gath, Holy, Inner, LA, Leonine, Medina, Megalopolis, Metropolis, Micropolis, Mycenae, NY, Petra, Pompeii, Rhodes, Smoke, Sparta, Tech, Town, Ur, Vatican, Weldstadt

Civil(ian), **Civilisation**, **Civilised**, **Civility** Amenity, Christian, Citizen, Civ(vy), Comity, Courtesy, Culture, Fertile crescent, Humane, Indus Valley, Maya, Municipal, Nok, Polite, Politesse, Secular, Temporal, Urbane

Claim Appeal, Arrogate, Assert, Bag, Challenge, Charge, Darraign(e), Darrain(e), Darrayn, Demand, Deraign, Droit, Encumbrance, Haro, Harrow, Lien, List, Maintain, Nochel, Plea, Pose, Posit, Postulate, Pretence, Pretend, Profess, Pulture, Purport, Puture, Revendicate, Right, Set-off, Sue, Title

Claimant Irredentist, Petitioner, Pot-waller, Pretender, Prospector, Tichborne, Usurper

Clam Bivalve, Cohog, Geoduck, Giant, Gweduc, Littleneck, Mollusc, Mya, Quahang, Quahog, Tridacna, Venus

Clammy Algid, Damp, Dank, Moist, Sticky, Sweaty

Clamp Clinch, Denver boot, Fasten, Grip, Holdfast, Jumar, Pinchcock, Potato-pit, Stirrup, Tread, Vice, Wheel

Clan(sman) Cameron, Clique, Gens, Gentile, Group, Horde, Kiltie, Kindred, Name, Phratry, Phyle, Sect, Sept, Society, Stewart, Stuart, Tribe

Clap(per), **Clapping** Applaud, Blow, Castanet, Chop, Crotal, Dose, Jinglet, Peal, Thunder, Tonant

Clarify, **Clarifier** Clear, Despumate, Dilucidate, Explain, Explicate, Finings, Purge, Refine, Render, Simplify

Clash(ing) Bang, Clangour, Clank, Claver, Coincide, Collide, Conflict, Friction, Gossip, > IMPACT, Incident, Jar, Loud, Missuit, Shock, Showdown, Strike, Swash

Clasp(ing) Address, Agraffe, Barrette, Brooch, Button, Catch, Chape, Clip, Embrace, Fibula, Grasp, Hasp, Hesp, Hook, Hug, Link, Morse, Ochreate, Ouch, Tach(e), Unite

Class(ification), **Classify**, **Classy** Acorn, Arrange, Assort, Bourgeois(ie), Bracket, Brand, Breed, Business, Cabin, Canaille, Caste, > CATEGORY, Chattering, Cheder, CI, Clan, Clerisy, Clinic, Club, Course, Criminal, Dewey, Digest, Division, Economy, Estate, Evening, Faction, First, Form, Genera, Gentry, Genus, > GRADE, Group, Harvard, Heder, Hubble, Ilk, Keep-fit, Kohanga Reo, League, Life, Linn(a)ean, List, Lower, Mammal, Master, Middle, Number, Order, Phonetics, Phylum, Pigeon-hole, Pleb(eian), Proper, Race, Range, Rank, Rate, Rating, Reception, Remove, Salariat, Second, Seminar, Shell, Siege, Social, Sort(ation), Spectral, Steerage, Stratum, Stream, Syntax, Taxonomy, Teach-in, Third, Tony, Tourist, Tribe, Tutorial, > TYPE, U, Universal, Upper, Varna, Water, Working, World, Year

Classic(al), **Classics**, **Classicist** Ageless, Ancient, Basic, Derby, Elzevir, Grecian,

Greek, Humane, Leger, Literature, Pliny, Purist, Roman, Standard, Traditional, Vintage

Clause Apodosis, Article, Condition, Escalator, Escape, Filioque, Four, Golden parachute, Grandfather, Member, Poison-pill, Protasis, Proviso, Reddendum, Reservation, Rider, Salvo, Sentence, Subordinate, Tenendum, Testatum

Claw Chela, Claut, Crab, Dewclaw, Edate, Falcula, Grapple, Griff(e), Hook, Nail, Nipper, Pounce, Scrab, Sere, Talent, Tear, Telson, Unguis

Clay Argil, Blaes, Blaise, Blaize, Bole, Calm, Cam, Caum, Ceramic, Charoset(h), China, Cloam, Clunch, Cob, Earth, Engobe, Fango, Figuline, Fuller's earth, Gault, Glei, Gley, Hardpan, Haroset(h), Illite, Kaolin, Laterite, Lithomarge, Loam, Lute, Malm, Marl, Meerschaum, Mire, Mortal, Mud, Papa, Pipeclay, Pise, Potter's, Pottery, Pug, Saggar(d), Sagger, Seggar, Slip, Slurry, Thill, Till(ite), Varve, Warrant, Warren, Wax

Clean(er), Cleaning Absterge, Besom, Bleach, Bream, Broom, Careen, Catharise, Catharsis, Chaste, Clear, Daily, Debride, Depurate, Deterge(nt), Dhobi, Dialysis, Douche, Dust(er), Eluant, Emunge, Enema, Erase, Ethnic, Evacuant, Evacuate, Expurgate, Fay, Fettle, Fey, Floss, Flush, Full, Grave, Groom, Gut, Heels, Hoover®, Hygienic, Immaculate, Innocent, Launder, Lave, Lustrum, Lye, Mouthwash, Mrs Mop(p), Mundify, Net, Overhaul, Porge, Pull-through, Pumice, Pure, Purgative, Purge, Ramrod, Rebite, Rub, Rump, Scaffie, Scavenge, Scour, Scrub, Shampoo, Snow-white, Soap, Soogee, Soogie, Soojey, Sponge, Spotless, Squeaky, Squeegee, Sterile, Sujee, Swab, Sweep, Vac(uum), Valet, > WASH, Whistle, Wipe

Clear(ance), Clearly Absolve, Acquit, Aloof, Apparent, Bell, Berth, Bold, Bore, Brighten, Bus, Clarify, Crystal, Decode, Definite, Diaphanous, Dispel, Distinct, Downright, Eidetic, Evacuate, Evident, Exculpate, Exonerate, Explicit, Fair, Gain, Headroom, Hyaline, Intelligible, Iron, Laund, Leap, Legible, Limpid, Lucid, Luculent, Manifest, Mop, Neat, Negotiate, Net(t), Observable, Obvious, Ope(n), Overleap, Palpable, Pellucid, Perspicuous, Plain, Play, Pratique, Predy, Pure, Quit, Rack, Realise, Remble, Rid, Ripple, Serene, Sheer, Shere, Slum, Sweep, Thro(ugh), Thwaite, Transire, Translucent, Transparent, Unblock, Vault, Vivid, Well, Windage, Wipe

Clearing Assart, Glade, Opening, Shire, Slash

Clergy(man), Cleric(al) Abbé, Canon, Cantor, Cardinal, Chaplain, Cleric, Clerk, Cloth, Curate, Curé, Deacon, Dean, Ecclesiast(ic), Goliard, Incumbent, Josser, Levite, Ministerial, Ministry, Non-juror, Non-usager, Notarial, Parson, Pastor, Pontifex, Pontiff, Preacher, Prebendary, Precentor, Prelate, Presbyter, Presenter, Priest, Primate, Prior, Proctor, Rabbi, Rector, Red-hat, Reverend, Rome-runner, Scribal, Secretarial, Shaveling, Shepherd, Slope, Spin-text, Squarson, Subdeacon, Theologian, Vartabed, Vicar

Clerk(s) Actuary, Baboo, Babu, Basoche, Cleric, Cratchit, Cursitor, Limb, Notary, Penman, Penpusher, Poster, Prot(h)onotary, Protocolist, Recorder, Scribe, Secretariat, Tally, Vicar, Writer

Clever(ness) Able, Adroit, Astute, Brainy, Bright, Canny, Cool, Cute, Daedal(e), Deft, Genius, Gleg, Ingenious, Intellectual, Know-all, Natty, Nimblewit, Sage(ness), Shrewd, Skilful, Smart(y), Smarty-pants, Souple, Subtle

Cliché Banality, Boilerplate, Commonplace, Corn, Platitude, Saying, Tag

Click(er), Clicking Castanet, Catch, Forge, Pawl, Ratch(et), Snick, Succeed, Tchick, Ticktack

Client Customer, Gonk, John, Patron, Trick

Cliff(s) Beachy Head, Bluff, Cleve, Crag, Craig, Escarp, Palisade, Precipice, Sca(u)r

Climate Atmosphere, Attitude, Continental, Mood, Sun, Temperament, Temperature, Weather

Climax Apex, Apogee, Catastasis, Come, Crescendo, Crest, Crisis, Edaphic, End, Head, Heyday, Orgasm, Top, Zenith

Climb(er) Alpinist, Aralia, Aristolochia, Ascend, Breast, Briony, Bryony, Clamber, Clematis, Clusia, Cowage, Cowhage, Cowitch, Crampon, Creeper, Cucumber, Dodder, Heart-pea, Hedera, Ivy, Kie-kie, Kudzu, Lawyer, Layback, Liana, Liane, > MOUNT, Pareira, Parvenu, Prusik, Rat(t)an, Rise, Scale, Scan, Scandent, Scansores, Sclim, Shin, Shinny, Sklim, Smilax, Social, Speel, Steeplejack, Sty(e), Swarm, Timbo, Tuft-hunter, Udo, Up(hill), Uprun, Vine, Wistaria, With(y)wind, Zoom

Clinch Attach, Ensure, Fix, Rivet, Secure, Settle

Cling(er), Clinging Adhere, Bur(r), Cherish, Cleave, Embrace, Hold, Hug, Ring, Tendril

Clinic Dispensary, Hospital, Hospitium, Mayo

Clint Limestone

Clip(ped), Clipper, Clipping Banana, Barrette, Brash, Bulldog, Butterfly, Cartridge, Clasp, Crocodile, Crop-ear, Crutch, Curt, Curtail, Cut, Cutty Sark, Dag, Dock, Dod, Excerpt, Fleece, Jubilee, Jumar, Krab, Lop, Pace, Paper, Pare, Peg, Prerupt, Prune, Roach, Scissel, Secateur, Shear, Ship, Shore, Shorn, Snip, Spring, Staccato, Tie, Tie-tack, Tinsnips, Topiarist, Trim

Clique Cabal, Clan, Club, Coterie, Faction, Gang, Ring, Set

Cloak(room), Cloaks Aba, Abaya, Abba, Abolla, Amice, Bathroom, Burnous, Capa, Cape, Capote, Caracalla, Cardinal, Cassock, Chasuble, Chimer(e), Chlamydes, Chlamys, Chuddah, Chuddar, Conceal, Cope, Cover, Disguise, Dissemble, Djellaba(h), Domino, Gabardine, Gaberdine, Gal(l)abea(h), Gal(l)abi(y)a(h), Gal(l)abi(y)eh, Gentlemen, Gents, Hall-robe, Heal, Hele, Himation, Hood, Inverness, Jelab, Jellaba, Joseph, Kaross, Manta, Manteel, Mant(e)let, Mantle, > MASK, Mousquetaire, Mozetta, Paenula, Paletot, Pallium, Paludamentum, Pelisse, Pilch, Poncho, Rail, Revestry, Rocklay, Rokelay, Roquelaure, Sagum, Sarafan, Scapular, > SCREEN, Shroud, Swathe, Talma, Toga, Vestiary, Vestry, Visite

Clock Alarm, Ammonia, Analogue, Astronomical, Atomic, Beetle, Big Ben, Biological, Blowball, Body, Bracket, Bundy, Caesium, Carriage, Clepsydra, Cuckoo, Dandelion, Floral, Grandfather, Grandmother, Hit, Knock, Long case, Meter, Repeater, Solarium, Speaking, Speedo, Strike, Sundial, Tell-tale, Time(r), Wag at the wa', Water

Clog Ball, Block, Clam, Crowd, Dance, Fur, Galosh, Golosh, Hamper, Jam, Lump, Mire, Obstruct, Overshoe, Patten

Close(d), Closing, Closure Airless, Alongside, Atresia, Block, Boon, By, Cadence, Clammy, Clap, Clench, Complete, Cone off, Court, Dear, Debar, Dense, > END, Epilogue, Ewest, Finale, Gare, Grapple, Handy, Hard, Hard by, Imminent, Inbye, Infibulate, Intent, Intimate, Lock, Lucken, Marginal, Mean, Miserly, Muggy, Mure, Narre, Narrow, Near, Nearhand, Neist, Nie, Niggardly, Nigh, Nip and tuck, Obturate, Occlude, Occlusion, Oppressive, Parochial, Precinct, Reserved, Reticent, Seal, Secret, Serre, Serried, Serry, Shet, Shut(ter), Shutdown, Silly, Slam, Snug, Stap, Sticky, Stuffy, Sultry, Tailgate, Temenos, Tight, Uproll, Warm, Yard

Closet Cabinet, Confine, Cubicle, Cupboard, Earth, Locker, Safe, Wardrobe, WC, Zeta

Close-up Detail, Fill, Shut, Stop, Zoom

Clot(ting) Clump

Cloth Carmelite, Clergy, Cloot, Clout, > FABRIC, > FELT, Frocking, Frontal, Loin, Lungi, > MATERIAL, Nap, Napery, Napje, Nappie, Needlework, Netting, Pall, Pane, Pilch, Priesthood, Print(er), Rag, Raiment, Roll, Sashing, Scarlet, Serviette, Sheet, Sheeting, Shoddy, Stripe, Tapestry, Tea, Throw, Tissue, Veronica

Clothe(s), Clothing, Clothed Apparel, Array, Attire, Baggies, Besee, Cape, Casuals, Choli, Cits, Clad, Clericals, Clobber, Combinations, Coordinates, Costume, Cour, Cover, Croptop, Dicht, Dight, Don, Drag, > **DRESS**, Duds, Emboss, Endue, Finery, Frippery, Garb, Garments, Gear, Gere, Get-up, Glad rags, Habit, Haute couture, Innerwear, Judogi, Jumps, Layette, Outfit, Pannicle, Raiment, Rami, Rigout, Robes, Samfoo, Samfu, Schmutter, Scungies, Shroud, Slops, Swaddling, Swathe, Swothling, Tackle, Togs, Tracksuit, Trappings, Trousseau, Tweeds, Vernicle, Vestiary, Vestiture, Vestment, Wardrobe, Watteau, Weeds, Workwear, Yclad, Ycled

Cloud(ing), Clouded, Cloudiness, Cloudy Altocumulus, Altostratus, Benight, Cirrocumulus, Cirrostratus, Cirrus, Coalsack, Coma, Crab Nebula, Cumulonimbus, Cumulus, Dim, Dull, Emission nebula, Fog, Fractocumulus, Fractostratus, Funnel, Goat's hair, Haze, Horsehead Nebula, Infuscate, Magellanic, Mare's tail, Milky, Mist, Mushroom, Nacreous, Nephele, Nephelometer, Nepho-, Nimbostratus, Nimbus, Nubecula, Nubilous, Nuée ardente, Obscure, Oort, Overcast, Pall, Pother, Rack, Stain, Storm, Stratocumulus, Stratus, Thunderhead, Turbid, Virga, War, Water-dog, Woolpack, Zero-zero

Clove Chive, Eugenia, Rose-apple, Split

Clover Alfalfa, Alsike, Berseem, Calvary, Cinque, Cow-grass, Hare's foot, Japan, Ladino, Lespedeza, Medic(k), Melilot, Owl's, Rabbit-foot, Serradella, Serradilla, Shamrock, Souple, Sucklers, Trefoil, Trilobe

Clown(ish) Antic, Antick, August(e), Boor, Bor(r)el, Buffoon, Carl, Chough, Chuff, Clout-shoe, Coco, > **COMEDIAN**, Comic, Costard, Daff, Feste, Froth, Girner, Gobbo, Goon, Gracioso, Grimaldi, Harlequin, Hob, Jack-pudding, Jester, Joey, Joker, Joskin, Leno, Merry Andrew, Mountebank, Nedda, Nervo, Peasant, Pickle-herring, Pierrot, Put, Rustic, Slouch, Thalian, Touchstone, Trinculo, Wag, Zany

Club(s), Club-like Adelphi, Airn, Almack's, Alpeen, Apex, Army and Navy, Artel, Association, Athen(a)eum, Baffy, Band(y), Basto, Bat, Bath, Beefsteak, Blackjack, Blaster, Bludgeon, Boodles, Bourdon, Brassie, Brook's, Bulger, C, Card, Carlton, Caterpillar, Cavalry, Chigiriki, Cleek, Clip-joint, Combine, Conservative, Constitutional, Cordeliers, Cosh, Cotton, Country, Crockford's, Cudgel, Devonshire, Disco(theque), Driver, Driving iron, Drones, Fan, Fascio, Garrick, Glee, Golf, Guards, Guild, Hampden, Hell-fire, Honky-tonk, Indian, Investment, Iron, Jacobin, Jigger, Jockey, Junior Carlton, Kennel, Kierie, Kiri, Kitcat, Kiwanis, Knobkerrie, Landsdowne, League, Leander, Lions, Lofter, Luncheon, Mace, Mallet, Mashie, Maul, Mell, Mere, Meri, Mess, Midiron, Monday, National Liberal, Niblick, Night(stick), Nitery, Oddfellows, Patu, Polt, Priest, Provident, Pudding, Putter, RAC, Reform, Ring, Rota, Rotarian, Rotary, Savage, Savile, Shillelagh, Slate, Society, Soroptimist, Sorosis, Spoon, Spot, Spurs, Strike, Strip, Thatched House, Tong, Travellers, Trefoil, Truncheon, Trunnion, Union, United Services, Variety, Waddy, Wedge, White's, Wood, Youth

Clue Across, Anagram, Ball, Charade, Clave, Dabs, Down, > **HINT**, Inkling, Key, Lead, Light, Rebus, Scent, Signpost, Thread, Tip

Clump Cluster, Finial, Knot, Mass, Mot(te), Patch, Plump, Tread, Tuft, Tump, Tussock

▷ **Clumsily** *may indicate* an anagram

Clumsy Artless, Awkward, Bauchle, Bungling, Butterfingers, Calf, Chuckle, Clatch, Clodhopper, Cumbersome, Dub, Dutch, Galoot, Gauche, Gimp, Ham(-fisted), Heavy-handed, Inapt, Inelegant, Inept, Inexpert, Klutz, Lob, Loutish, Lubbard, Lubber, Lummox, Lumpish, Maladroit, Mauther, Mawr, Mawther, Messy, Mor, Nerd, Nurd, Palooka, Plonking, Rough, S(c)hlemiel, Schlemihl, Squab, Stot, Swab, Swob, Two-fisted, Ungain, Unskilful, Unwieldy

Clutch Battery, Brood, Chickens, Clasp, Cling, Eggs, Glaum, Grab, > **GRASP**, Gripe, Nest, Seize, Sitting, Squeeze

Clutter Confusion, Litter, Mess, Rummage

Coach Battlebus, Berlin, Bogie, Bus, Car, Carriage, Chara, Clerestory, Crammer, Diligence, Dilly, Double-decker, Drag, Edifier, Fly, Gig, Hackney, Landau(let), Microbus, Phaeton, Pullman, Railcar, Rattler, Repetiteur, Saloon, Shay, Sleeper, Stage, Surrey, Tally(-ho), Teach(er), Thoroughbrace, Train(er), Tutor, Voiture

Coal Anthracite, Bituminous, Burgee, Cannel, Cherry, Clinker, Coom, Crow, Culm, Eldin, Ember, Fusain, Gathering, Jud, Knob, Lignite, Open-cast, Purse, Sapropelite, Score, Slack, Splint, Vitrain, Wallsend

Coalition Alliance, Bloc, Janata, Merger, Tie

Coarse(ness) Base, Blowzy, Bran, Broad, Common, Crude, Earthy, Fisherman, Foul, Grained, Gross, Ham, Illbred, Indelicate, Low-bred, Plebeian, Rank, Raunchy, Ribald, Rough, Rudas, Rude, Sackcloth, Slob, Sotadic, Vulgar

Coast(al) Barbary, Beach, Causeway, Coromandel, Costa, Drift, Freewheel, Glide, Hard, Ivory, Littoral, Longshore, Maritime, Orarian, Riviera, Seaboard, Seafront, Seaside, > SHORE, Sledge, Strand, Toboggan

Coaster Beermat, Drog(h)er, Mat, Ship

Coat(ing) Abaya, Ab(b)a, Achkan, Acton, Admiral, Anarak, Anodise, Anorak, Balmacaan, Barathea, Bathrobe, Belton, Benjamin, Blazer, Box, British warm, Buff, Buff-jerkin, Car, Chesterfield, Cladding, Claw-hammer, Clearcole, Cloak, Clutch, Cocoon, Coolie, Cover, Covert, Creosote, Crust(a), Cutaway, Doggett's, Dress, Duffel, Duster, Enamel, Encrust, Extine, Fearnought, Film, Fleece, Frock, Fur, Gabardine, Galvanise, Gambeson, Glaze, Grego, Ground, Ha(c)queton, Hair, Happi, Impasto, Inverness, Jack(et), Jemmy, Jerkin, Jodhpuri, Joseph, Jump, Jupon, Lacquer, Lammie, Lammy, Layer, Loden, Mac, Mackinaw, Matinee, Metallise, Morning, Newmarket, Paint, Paletot, Palla, Parka, Parkee, Patinate, Pebbledash, Pelage, Pelisse, Perfuse, Petersham, Plate, Polo, Pos(h)teen, Primer, Prince Albert, Raglan, Redingote, Resin, Resist, Riding, Roquelaure, Sack, Saque, Seal, Sheepskin, Shellac, Sherwani, Silver, Spencer, Sports, Stadium, Surtout, Swagger, Swallowtail(ed), Tabard, Taglioni, Tail, Tar, Teflon, Tent, Top, Trench, Truss, Trusty, Tunic, Tuxedo, Ulster(ette), Veneer, Verdigris, Warm, Wash, Windjammer, Wool, Wrap-rascal, Zamarra, Zamarro, Zinc

Coax Blandish, Blarney, Cajole, Carn(e)y, Cuittle, Flatter, Lure, Persuade, Wheedle, Whillywha(w)

Cobble(s), Cobblers Cosier, Cozier, Mend, Patch, Rot, Snob, Soutar, Souter, Sowter, Stone, Sutor, Twaddle, Vamp

Cobweb(by) Arachnoid, Araneous, Gossamer, Snare, Trap

Cochlear Scala

Cock(y) Alectryon, Ball, Capon, Chanticleer, Chaparral, Erect, Flip, Fowl, France, Fugie, Half, Hay, Jack-the-lad, Jaunty, Penis, Roadrunner, Robin, Rooster, Snook, Strut, Swaggering, Tilt, Turkey, Vain, Valve, Vane

Cockatoo Bird, Corella, Galah, Major Mitchell, Parrot

Cock crow Skreigh of the day

▷ **Cockle(s)** *may indicate* an anagram

Cockney 'Arriet, 'Arry, Bow, Londoner, Londonese

▷ **Cockney** *may indicate* a missing h

Cocktail Alexander, Aperitif, Atomic, Bellini, Bloody Mary, Buck's fizz, Bumbo, Cobbler, Cold duck, Crusta, Daiquiri, Egg-flip, Fustian, Gibson, Gimlet, Harvey Wallbanger, Highball, Julep, Manhattan, Margarita, Martini®, Mix, Molotov, Old-fashioned, Piña colada, Pink lady, Prawn, Punch, Rickey, Rusty nail, Sangaree, Sangria, Sazerac®, Screwdriver, Sherry cobbler, Side-car, Snowball, Spritzer, Stengah, Stinger, Swizzle, Tom Collins, Twist, White-lady

Cod Bag, Cape, Coalfish, Fish, Gade, Gadus, Haberdine, Keeling, Kid, Lob, Man,

Morrhua, Saith, Stockfish, Torsk, Tusk, Whiting

Code, Coding Access, Alphanumeric, Amalfitan, Area, Bar, Binary, Bushido, Canon, Character, Cipher, City, Civil, Clarendon, Codex, Colour, Computing, Condition, Country, Cryptogram, Cryptograph, Dialling, Disciplinary, Dogma, Dress, DX, EBCDIC, Enigma, Error, Escape, Ethics, Fuero, Genetic, Gray, Green Cross, Hammurabic, Highway, Justinian, MAC, Machine, Morse, Napoleon(ic), Object, Omerta, Opcode, Penal, PGP, Pindaric, Postal, Price, Rulebook, Scytale, Signal, Sort, Source, STD, Talmud, Time, TwelveTables, Zip

Coffee, Coffee beans, Coffee pot Arabica, Brazil, Cafetiere, Cappuccino, Decaff, Demi-tasse, Espresso, Expresso, Filter, Gaelic, Gloria, Granules, Instant, Irish, Java, Latte, Mocha, Peaberry, Robusta, Tan, Triage, Turkish

Coffin Bier, Casket, Hearse, Sarcophagus, Shell

Cog(ged) Contrate, Mitre-wheel, Nog, Pinion, Tooth

Cogent Compelling, Forceful, Good, Sound, Telling

Cohere(nt) Agglutinate, Clear, Cleave, Cling, Logical, Stick

Cohort Colleague, Crony, Soldier

Coil(s), Coiled Bight, Bought, Choke, Clew, Clue, Curl, Fake, Fank, Furl, Hank, Helix, Induction, Mortal, Rouleau, Scorpioid, Solenoid, Spark, Spiral, Spiraster, Spire, Tesla, Tickler, Toroid, Twine, Twirl, > **WIND**, Wound, Wreath, Writhe

Coin Base, Bean, Bit, Cash, Change, Copper, Create, Doctor, Dump(s), Fiver, Han(d)sel, Imperial, Invent, Make, Mint, Mite, > **MONEY**, Neoterise, Numismatic, Nummary, Piece, Plate, Proof, Shiner, Slip, Smelt, Specie, Stamp, Strike, Tenner, Unite, Unity

Coincide(nt), Coincidence Accident, Chance, Consilience, Fit, Fluke, Overlap, Rabat(to), Simultaneous, Synastry, Synchronise, Tally

Cold(-blooded) Ague, Algid, Arctic, Austere, Biting, Bitter, Bleak, C, Catarrh, Cauld(rife), Chill(y), Colubrine, Common, Coryza, Ectotherm, Frem(d), Fremit, Frigid, Frost(y), Gelid, Glacial, Hiemal, Icy, Impersonal, Jeel, Nippy, Nirlit, Parky, Passionless, Perishing, Poikilotherm(ic), Polar, Psychro-, Remote, Rheumy, Rigor, Rume, Snap, Snell, Sour, Streamer, Subzero, Taters, Weed, Wintry

Collage Paste up

Collapse Apoplexy, Cave, Conk, Crash, Crumble, Crumple, Debacle, Downfall, Fail(ure), Fall, Fold, Founder, Give, Implode, Inburst, Landslide, Meltdown, Phut, Purler, Rot, Ruin, Scat(ter), Sink, Slump, Stroke, Subside, Sunstroke, Swoon, Telescope, Tumble, Wilt, Zonk

▷ **Collapsing** *may indicate* an anagram

Collar(ed) Arrest, Astrakhan, Bermuda, Bertha, Berthe, Bib, Bishop, Blue, Brecham, Buster, Butterfly, Button-down, Buttonhole, Capture, Carcanet, Chevesaile, Choke(r), Clerical, Collet, Dog, Esses, Eton, Falling-band, Flea, Gorget, Grandad, Hame, Head(stall), Holderbat, Horse, Jabot, Jampot, Karenni, Mandarin, Moran, Mousquetaire, Nab, Nail, Neckband, Necklet, Ox-bow, Peter Pan, Piccadell, Piccadillo, Piccadilly, Pikadell, Pink, Polo, Puritan, Rabato, Rebater, Rebato, Revers, Rollneck, Roman, Ruff, Sailor, Seize, Shawl, Steel, Storm, Tackle, Tappet, Tie-neck, Torque, Turndown, Turtleneck, Vandyke, Whisk, White, Wing, Yoke

Colleague Associate, Bedfellow, Confrère, Mate, Oppo, Partner

Collect(ion), Collective(ly), Collector Accrue, Agglomerate, Aggregate, Album, Alms, Amass, Ana, Anthology, Assemble, Bank, Bow, Budget, Bundle, Burrell, Caboodle, Calm, Cap, Clowder, Compendium, Compile, Congeries, Conglomerate, Covey, Cull, Dossier, Dustman, Earn, Egger, Exaltation, Exordial, Fest, Gaggle, Garner, Gather, Gilbert, Glean, Glossary, Grice, Heap, Herd, Hive, Idant, Jingbang, Kit, Kitty, Levy, Magpie, Meal, Meet, Menagerie, Miscellany, Mish-mash, Montem, Murmuration, Museum, Muster, Nide, Offertory, Omnibus,

Paddling, Pile, Plate, Pod, Post, Prayer, Quest, Raft, Raise, Recheat, Sedge, Serene, Set, Shoe, Siege, Skein, Smytrie, Sord, Sottisier, Sounder, Spring, Stand, Team, Troop, Unkindness, Watch, Whipround, Wisp
▷ **Collection** *may indicate* an anagram

College(s) Academy, All Souls, Ampleforth, Balliol, Brasenose, Business, C, Caius, Campus, CAT, Cheltenham, Clare, Classical, Commercial, Community, Corpus, Downing, Electoral, Emmanuel, Eton, Exeter, Foundation, Girton, Hall, Herald's, Jail, Keble, King's, Lancing, Linacre, Lincoln, LSE, Lycée, Lyceum, Madras(s)a(h), Madressah, Magdalen(e), Medresseh, Merton, Newnham, Nuffield, Oriel, Poly, Polytechnic, Protonotariat, Queen's, Ruskin, St Johns, Saliens, Selwyn, Seminary, Sixth-form, Somerville, Sorbonne, Staff, Tech(nical), Tertiary, Theologate, Training, Trinity, Tug, UMIST, Up, Village, Wadham, Winchester, Yeshwa(h)

Collide, Collision Afoul, Barge, Bird-strike, Bump, Cannon, Carom(bole), Clash, Dash, Fender-bender, Foul, Head-on, Impact, Into, Kiss, Meet, Pile-up, Strike, Thwack

Colony Aden, Cleruchy, Crown, Dependency, Hongkong, Nudist, Penal, Presidio, Proprietary, Rookery, Settlement, Swarm, Termitarium, Zambia

Colour(ed), Colouring, Colours Achromatic, Alizarin(e), Anil, An(n)atta, An(n)atto, Anthocyan, Aquamarine, Arnotto, Auburn, Bay, Bedye, Bice, Bisque, Bister, Bistre, Blee, Blue, Blush, Buff, Burgundy, C, Camel, Cap, Cappagh-brown, Cardinal, Cerise, Chica, Chromatic, Chrome, Complementary, Complexion, Coral, Crayon, Criant, Cyan, Day-Glo®, Distort, Dye, Ecru, Eosin, False, Filemot, Film, Flag, Florid, Flying, French navy, Gamboge, Gouache, Gules, Haem, > **HUE**, Ink, Irised, Isabel, Jet, Kalamkari, Lake, Leer, Lemon, Lilac, Lime, Local, Lovat, Lutein, Magenta, Maroon, Mauve, Metif, Nankeen, Navy, Oatmeal, Ochre, Olive, Or, Orange, Orpiment, Palette, Pastel, Peach, Philamot, Philomot, Pied, Pigment, Pochoir, Polychrome, Primary, Prism, Prismatic, Process, Puke, Queen's, Reddle, Regimental, Reseda, Rince, Riot, Roucou, Rouge, Ruddle, Sand, Secondary, Sematic, Sepia, Shade, Sienna, Solferino, Solid, Spectrum, Startle, Tartrazine, Taupe, Teal, Tenne, Tenny, Tertiary, Tie-dye, Tinc(ture), Tinge, Tint, Titian, Tone, Ultramarine, Umber, Umbrage, Uvea, Vert
▷ **Coloured** *may indicate* an anagram

Colourful Abloom, Brave, Flamboyant, Flowery, Iridescent, Kaleidoscope, Opalescent, Splashy, Vivid

Colourless Albino, Bleak, Drab, Dull, Hyalite, Pallid, Pallor, Wan, White

Column(s), Column foot Agony, Anta, Atlantes, Commentary, Corinthian, Correspondence, Cylinder, Decastyle, Diastyle, Doric, Editorial, Eustyle, Fifth, File, Gossip, Hypostyle, Impost, Lat, Lonelyhearts, Monolith, Nelson's, Newel, Obelisk, Pericycle, Peristyle, Persian, Personal, Pilaster, > **PILLAR**, Pilotis, Prostyle, Rouleau, Row, Spina, Spinal, Spine, Stalactite, Stalagmite, Steering, Stylobate, Systyle, Tabulate, Telamone, Third, Tige, Tore, Torus, Trajan's

Comb(er), Combed, Combing Alveolate, Beehive, Breaker, Card, Copple, Crest, Curry, Dredge, Fine-tooth, Hackle, Heckle, Hot, Kaim, Kame, Kangha, Kemb, Noils, Pecten, Rake, Red(d), Ripple(r), Scribble, Search, Smooth, Tease(l), Toaze, Tose, Toze, Trawl, Wave

Combination, Combine(d), Combining Accrete, Alligate, Ally, Amalgam, Associate, Axis, Bloc, Cartel, Cleave, Clique, Coalesce, Coalition, Concoction, Conflated, Conglomerate, Consortium, Coordinate, Crasis, Fuse, Group, Harvester, Integration, Join, Junta, Kartell, League, Meld, Merge(r), Mingle, Mixture, Perm(utation), Piece, Pool, Quill, Ring, Solvate, Splice, Syncretize, Synthesis, Terrace, Trona, Unite, Valency, Wed
▷ **Combustible** *may indicate* an anagram

Come, Coming (back), Coming out Advent, Anear, Anon, Appear, Approach,

Ar(r), Arise, Arrive, Attend, Debouch, Derive, Future, Happen, Iceman, Issue, Millenarian, Orgasm, Parousia, Pass, Pop, Respond, Second, Via

Come again Eh

Comedian Benny, Buffoon, Chaplin, > CLOWN, Comic, Durante, Emery, Goon, Groucho, Joker, Karno, Leno, Quipster, Robey, Scream, Screwball, Tate, Tati, Wag, Wise, Yell

Comedy Com, Drama, Errors, Farce, Humour, Millamant, Situation, Slapstick, Thalia, Travesty

Comet Geminid, Halley's, Kohoutek, Meteor

Comfort(er), Comforting Amenity, Analeptic, Balm, Bildad, Calm, Cheer, Cherish, Cold, Consolation, Console, Creature, Crumb, Dummy, Ease, Eliphaz, Featherbed, Reassure, Relief, Relieve, Scarf, Solace, Soothe, Succour, Zophar

Comfortable, Comfy Bein, Canny, Cose, Cosh, Cosy, Couthie, Couthy, Cushy, Easy, Gemutlich, Heeled, Homely, Mumsy, Relaxed, Rug, Snug, Tosh, Trig, Warm, Well, Well-to-do

Comic(al) Beano, Buff, Buffo(on), Bumpkin, Buster, Chaplin, Clown, > COMEDIAN, Dandy, Droll, Eagle, Facetious, Fields, > FUNNY, Gagster, Hardy, Horror, Jester, Knock-about, Laurel, Leno, Mag, Manga, Quizzical, Robey, Strip, Tati, Trial, Zany

Command(eer), Commanding, Commandment(s) Behest, Bid, Categorical imperative, Charge, Coerce, Control, Decalogue, Direction, Dominate, Easy, Edict, Fiat, Fighter, Firman, Haw, Hest, Imperious, Instruction, Jussive, Mandate, Mastery, Mitzvah, > ORDER, Precept, Press, Requisition, Rule, Seize, Ukase, Warn, Warrant, Will, Wish, Writ

Commander Ag(h)a, Barleycorn, Bey, Bloke, Blucher, Boss, Brennus, Brig, Caliph, Centurion, Cid, Decurion, Emir, Emperor, Field cornet, Generalissimo, Hetman, Hipparch, Imperator, Killadar, Leader, Manager, Marshal, Master, Meer, Moore, Officer, Overlord, Pendragon, Raglan, Shogun, Sirdar, Taxiarch, Trierarch, Warlord

Commemorate, Commemoration Encaenia, Epitaph, Eulogy, Keep, Memorial, Monument, Plaque, Remember

Comment(ary), Commentator Analyst, Animadvert, Annotate, Comm, Coryphaeus, Critic, Descant, Discuss, Editorial, Essay, Explain, Exposition, Expound, Footnote, Gemara, Gloss(ographer), Glosser, Hakam, Kibitz, Margin, Midrashim, Note, Par, Platitude, Postil, Remark, Scholiast

Commerce, Commercial Ad, Barter, Cabotage, Jingle, Marketable, Mercantile, Mercenary, Merchant, Shoppy, Simony, Trade, Traffic

Commissar People's, Political

Commission(er), Commissioned Brevet, Brokerage, Charge, Charity, Countryside, Delegation, Depute, ECE, Employ, Engage, Envoy, Errand, Factor, High, Husbandage, Job, Kickback, Magistrate, Mandate, Office(r), Official, Ombudsman, Order, Percentage, Perpetration, Place, Poundage, Rake-off, Roskill, Task, Task force, Trust

Commit(al), Commitment Consign, Contract, Decision, Dedication, Delegate, Devotion, Do, Engage, Entrust, Enure, Perpetrate, Pledge, Rubicon

Committee Board, Body, Commission, Council, Group, Joint, Junta, Politburo, Presidium, Propaganda, Samiti, Select, Standing, Steering, Syndicate, Table, Vigilance, Watch

Common(ly), Commoner, Commons Average, Cad, Conventional, Diet, Dirt, Ealing, Eatables, Enclosure, Epicene, Everyday, Familiar, Fare, Folk, General, Green, House, Law, Lay, Low, Mark, Mere, MP, Mutual, Naff, Non-U, Normal, People, Pleb, Prevalent, Prole, Public, Related, Rife, Roturier, Ryfe, Scran, Sense, Shared, Stray, Tie, Trite, Tritical, Tuft, Tye, Use, > USUAL, Vile, Vul(gar), Vulgo, Vulgus, Widespread, Wimbledon

Commonsense Gumption, Nous, Smeddum, Wit

Communal, **Commune** Agapemone, Collective, Com, Meditate, Mir, Phalanstery, Public, Talk, Township

Communicate, **Communication** Ampex, Announce, Baud, Boyau, Cable, Channelling, Conversation, Convey, Cybernetic, E-mail, Expansive, Impart, Infobahn, Inform, Intelsat, Internet, Message, Note, Oracy, Prestel®, Proxemics, Reach, Road, Semiotics, Signal, Tannoy®, Telepathy, Telex, Telstar, Tieline, Transmit, Utraquist

Communism, **Communist** Apparat(chik), Aspheterism, Bolshevist, Com, Comecon, Cominform, Comintern, Commo, Comsomol, Deviationist, Essene, Fourier, Khmer Rouge, Komsomol, Leninite, Maoist, Nomenklatura, Perfectionist, Pinko, Politburo, Red, Revisionism, Soviet, Spartacist, Tanky, Titoist, Trot, Vietcong, Vietminh

Communities, **Community** Alterne, Ashram, Biome, Body, Brotherhood, Clachan, Climax, Coenobitism, Coenobium, Colonia, Colony, Consocies, Ecosystem, EEC, Enclave, European, Frat(e)ry, Kahal, Kibbutz, Mesarch, Neighbourhood, People, Phyle, Public, Pueblo, Seral, Sere, Shtetl, Sisterhood, Society, Street, Town, Tribe, Ujamaa, Village, Virtual, Zupa

Commute(r) Change, Convert, Reduce, Straphanger, Travel

Compact Agreement, Cement, Concise, Conglobe, Covenant, Covin, Coyne, Dense, Entente, Fast, Firm, Flapjack, Hard, Knit, League, Match, Neat, Pledge, Powder, Solid, Terse, Tight, Treaty, Well-knit

Companion(able) Achates, Arm candy, Associate, Attender, Barnacle, Bedfellow, Bonhomie, Bud(dy), Butty, CH, China, Comate, Comrade, Consort, Contubernal, Crony, Cupman, Duenna, Ephesian, Escort, Felibre, > **FELLOW**, Fere, Handbook, Mate, Pal, Pard, Sidekick, Thane, Thegn, Vade-mecum

Company, **Companies** Actors, Artel, Ass, Assembly, Band, Bank, Battalion, Bevy, > **BUSINESS**, Bv, Cahoot, Cartel, Cast, Cavalcade, Chartered, CIA, Circle, City, Close, Club, Co, Conger, Consort, Cordwainers, Core, Corporation, Corps, Coy, Crew, Crowd, Decury, Dotcom, East India, Enterprise, Entourage, Faction, Finance, Fire, > **FIRM**, Flock, Free, Gang, Garrison, Ging, Guild, Haberdashers, Heap, Holding, Hudson's Bay, ICI, Inc, Indie, In-house, Intercourse, Investment, Joint-stock, Limited, Listed, Livery, Management, Maniple, Muster, Order, Organisation, Parent, Plc, Private, Public, Quoted, Rep(ertory), Room, SA, Sedge, Set, Set out, Shell, Siege, Sort, SpA, Stock, Subsidiary, Syndicate, Table, Team, Touring, Troop, Troupe, Trust, Twa, Two(some), Visitor, White

Compare(d), **Comparison** Analogy, Beside, Bracket, Collate, Confront, Contrast, Correspond, Cp, Equate, Liken, Match, Odious, Parallel, Relation, Simile, Weigh

Compartment Bay, Booth, Box, Carriage, Casemate, Cell, Chamber, Cubbyhole, Cubicle, Dog box, Locellate, Loculament, Loculus, Panel, Partition, Pigeonhole, Pocket, Room, Room(ette), Severy, Stall, Till

Compass Ambit, Area, Beam, Bounds, Bow, Gamut, Goniometer, Gyro, Gyroscope, Infold, Magnetic, Needle, Orbit, Perimeter, > **RANGE**, Reach, Rhumb, Room, Scale

Compassion(ate) Aroha, Clemency, Commiseration, Empathy, Humane, Mercy, Pity, Samaritan, Sympathy

Compel(led), **Compulsion**, **Compulsive**, **Compulsory** Addiction, Coact, Coerce, Command, Constrain, Dragoon, Duress, Enforce, Extort, Fain, > **FORCE**, Gar, Make, Mandatory, Oblige, Pathological, Steamroller, Strongarm, Tyrannise

Compensate, **Compensation** Amend(s), Balance, Boot, Comp, Counterbalance, Counterpoise, Damages, Demurrage, Guerdon, Offset, Payment, Recoup, Redress, Reparation, Reprisal, Requital, Restitution, Restore, Retaliation, Salvage, Satisfaction, Solatium, Wergild, X-factor

Compete Contend, Enter, Match, Play, Rival, Vie

Competence, Competent Ability, Able, Adequate, Can, Capacity, Dab, Efficient, Fit, Responsible, Sui juris, Worthy

Competition, Competitive, Competitor Agonist, Bee, Biathlon, Contest, Cup, Drive, Entrant, Event, Field, Gymkhana, Heptathlon, Match, Open, Opponent, Pairs, Panellist, Pentathlon, Player, Puissance, Race, Rally, Repechage, Rival(ise), Rodeo, Show-jumping, Tension, Test, Tiger, Tournament, Tourney, Trial, Triallist, Wap(p)enshaw

Compile(r), Compilation Anthology, Arrange, Collect, Edit, Prepare, Zadkiel

Complain(t), Complainer Adenoids, Affection, Affliction, Alas, Alopecia, Anaemia, Angina, Asthma, Barrack, Beef, Bellyache, Bitch, Bleat, BSE, Carp, Charge, Chorea, Colic, Crab, Cramp, Criticise, Diatribe, Disorder, Dropsy, Epidemic, Ergot, Exanthema, Girn, Gout, Gravamen, Groan, Grouch, Grouse, Growl, Grudge, Grumble, Grutch, Harangue, Hives, Hone, Hypochondria, > ILLNESS, Jeremiad, Lupus, Malady, Mange, Mean(e), Mein, Mene, Moan, Morphew, Mumps, Murmur, Nag, Natter, Neuralgia, Pertussis, Plica, Poor-mouth, Protest, Pyelitis, Rail, Remonstrate, Repine, Rickets, Sapego, Sciatica, Scold, Sigh, Silicosis, Squawk, Staggers, Thrush, Tic, Tinea, Upset, Whimper, Whine, Whinge, Yammer, Yawp

Complete(ly), Completion Absolute, Accomplish, All, Arrant, Attain, Clean, Congenital, Consummate, Crown, Do, End, Entire, Finalise, Finish, Fruition, Fulfil, Full, Full-blown, Hollow, Incept, Integral, In toto, One, Out, Out and out, Perfect, Plenary, Quite, Sheer, Spang, Sum, Teetotal, Thorough, Total, Uncut, Unequivocal, Unmitigated, Whole (hog)

Complex(ity) Abstruse, Compound, Difficult, Electra, Hard, Inferiority, Intricate, Intrince, Involute, Knot, Manifold, Mixed, Multinucleate, Nest, Network, Obsession, Oedipus, Paranoid, Phaedra, Superiority, Syndrome, Web

Complexion Aspect, Blee, Hue, Leer, Temper, Tint, View

Compliance, Compliant, Comply Agree, Assent, Conform, Deference, Hand-in-glove, Obey, Observe, Sequacious, Surrender, Wilco

Complicate(d), Complication Bewilder, Complex, Deep, Elaborate, Embroil, Implex, Intricate, Involve, Inweave, Node, Nodus, Perplex, Ramification, Rigmarole, Tangle, Tirlie-wirlie

▷ **Complicated** *may indicate* an anagram

Compliment(s) Baisemain, Bouquet, Congratulate, Devoirs, Douceur, Encomium, Flatter, Flummery, Praise, Soap, Tribute

Compose(d), Composure Aplomb, Arrange, Calm, Consist, Cool, > CREATE, Equanimity, Even, Face, Improvise, Indite, Lull, Notate, Placid, Poise, Produce, Reconcile, Sangfroid, Sedate, Serenity, Settle, Soothe, Tranquil

Composer Contrapunt(al)ist, Inventor, Maker, Melodist, Musician, Serialist, Symphonist, Triadist, Tunesmith, Writer

▷ **Composing** *may indicate* an anagram

Composition, Compositor Aleatory, Beaumontage, Capriccio, Caprice, Cob, Concerto, Creation, Dite, Essay, Etude, Fantasia, Inditement, Ingredient, Loam, Met, Montage, Morceau, Nonet(te), Opus, Oratorio, Pastiche, Piece, Poem, Polyphony, Printer, Quartette, Raga, Rhapsody, Ship, Sing, Smoot, Sonata, Sonatina, Structure, Symphony, Synthesis, Terracotta, Texture, Toccata, Treatise, Typesetter, Work

Compound, Compound stop Amalgam, Bahuvrihi, Blend, > CAMP, Composite, Constitute, Cpd, Derivative, Mix, Multiply, Racemate, Type

▷ **Compound(ed)** *may indicate* an anagram

Comprehend, Comprehensive All-in, Catch-all, Catholic, Compass,

Compendious, Contain, Exhaustive, Fathom, Follow, General, Global, Grasp, Include, Indepth, Ken, Large, Omnibus, Panoramic, Perceive, School, Sweeping, Thoroughgoing, > UNDERSTAND, Wide

Compress(ed), **Compression**, **Compressor** Astrict, Bale, Coarctate, Contract, Solidify, Squeeze, Stupe, Thlipsis

Compromise Avoision, Brule, Commit, Concession, Endanger, Involve, Settlement, Time-server, Trade off

Computation, **Computer (language)**, **Computer term** ActiveX, Address bus, Ada, Algol, Algorism, Analog(ue), Antialising, Apple (Mac)®, ASCII, Authoring, Autosave, AWK, Backslash, Basic, Bitmap, Bookmark, Boot, Bot army, Breakpoint, Busbar, C, CADMAT, Calculate, Calculus, Chatroom, Checksum, Chip, Clickstream, Clipboard, COBOL, Coder, COL, CORAL, Counter, Cybercafe, Cyber(netics), Dataglove®, Desknote, Desktop, Digital, Domain name, DRAM, Earcon, Earom, Eniac, EPROM, ERNIE, Estimate, Extranet, FAT, Figure, Fileserver, Floptical, Fortran, Freenet, Front-end, GIGO, Gopher, Groupware, HAL, Hardware, High-end, Holmes, Host, Hybrid, Hypermedia, Hypertext, ICL, IDE, Inbox, Inputter, Integrator, Interface, Internet, IT, JANET, Java®, Kludge, Laptop, Linear, Linker, LISP, Logic, LOGO, Macro, Mail merge, Mainframe, Measure, Micro, MIDI, Modem, Morphing, Mouseover, Mung, Network, Neural, Neurochip, Notebook, Number-cruncher, Numlock, Nybble, Object, OCCAM, OCR, On-line, Outbox, Package, Packet sniffer, Pageview, Palmtop, PASCAL, Patch, PC, Pel, Pentium®, Perl, Personal, Phishing, Pixel, Platform, Plug'n'play, Processor, Program, PROLOG, PROM, Proxy server, Public-key, Pushdown, RAM, README file, Read out, Realtime, Reboot, Reckoner, Roque dialler, ROM, Rootserver, Router, Scratchpad, Screensaver, Search engine, Server, Shareware, Shell, Small-talk, Smart, Smurfing, SNOBOL, Soft return, Software, Source, Spim, Spreadsheet, Sprite, SQL, Stand-alone, String, Subroutine, Superserver, Systems, TALISMAN, Tally, Tape streamer, TAURUS, Thick client, Thin client, Time slice, Toggle, Tower, Track(er)ball, Turing machine, Unicode, Unix, Username, Vaccine, Voice response, Voxel, Webbie, Web Board, Web farm, Weblish, Wiki, WIMP, WORM, Wysiwyg, Yottabyte, Zettabyte

Computer programs, **Computer software**, **Computer systems** Abandonware, Acrobat, ActiveX, Agent, Antivirus, Applet, Application, Arpa, ARPANET, Assembler, Autotune, BIOS, Bloatware, Bootstrap, Bot, CADMAT, Cambridge ring, Cancelbot, Careware, Chatbot, Checksum, Client, Columbus, Crippleware, CU See Me, Debugger, Diagnostic, Dictionary, Emacs, ERNIE, Est, Ethernet, Evernet, E-wallet, Executive, Extranet, Extreme, Facemail, Fileserver, Firewall, Firmware, Flash, Freenet, Freeware, Groupware, HAL, HOLMES, Hypermedia, iTunes®, Internet, Intranet, JANET, LAN, Linker, Linux, Loader, Macro, Malware, MARC, Middleware, MIDI, Mmorpg, Neural, Object, OCR, Parser, Payware, Peer-to-peer, Plug-in, Relocator, RISC, Servlet, Shareware, Shovelware, Spellchecker, Spyware, Stand-alone, Stiffware, Systems, Tally, TAURUS, Telnet, Token ring, Translator, Trialware, Unix, Usenet, Utility, Vaporware, WAN, Warez, Web, Web browser, Webcast, Web crawler, Wide-area, WIMP, Windows®, Word processor, Worm

Computer user(s) Alpha geek, Anorak, Brain, Browser, Cast(er), Chiphead, Cyberpunk, Cybersurfer, Digerati, Hacker, Liveware, Luser, Mouse potato, Nerd, Nethead, Netizen, Nettie, Otaku, Pumpking, Troll, White hat

Con(man) Against, Anti, Bunco, Diddle, Dupe, Jacob, Learn, Peruse, Read, Scam, Scan, Steer, Sucker, Swindle

Concede, **Concession** Acknowledge, Admit, Allow, Carta, Charter, Compromise, Confess, Favour, Forfeit, Franchise, Munich, Ou, Owe, Own, Privilege, Sop, Synchoresis

Conceit(ed) Bumptious, Caprice, Carriwitchet, Concetto, Crank, Crotchet,

Device, Dicty, Egomania, Fancy, Fastuous, Fop, Fume, Hauteur, Idea, Notion, Podsnappery, Prig, Princock, Princox, Puppyism, Quiblin, Side, Snotty, Stuck-up, Swellhead, Toffee-nose, Vain(glory), Wind

Conceive, Conceivable Beget, Create, Credible, Imagine, Possible, Surmise

Concentrate(d), Concentration Aim, Bunch, Centre, Collect, Condense, Dephlegmate, Distil, Elliptical, Essence, Extract, Focalise, Focus, Intense, Listen, Major, Mantra, Mass, Molality, Molarity, Potted, Rivet, Samadhi, Titrate, Titre

Concern(ing) About, After, Ail, Altruism, Anent, As to, Bother, Business, Care, Cerne, Company, Disturb, Firm, Going, Heed, In re, Intéressé, Interest, Into, Lookout, > **MATTER**, Mell, Misease, Over, Part, Pidgin, Pigeon, Re, Reck, Regard, Reke, Respect, Retch, Solicitude, Touch, Trouble, Worry

▷ **Concerned** *may indicate* an anagram

Concert (place) Agreement, Benefit, Chamber, Charivari, Cooperation, Device, Dutch, Gig, Hootananny, Hootenanny, Hootnannie, Odeon, Odeum, Pop, Prom(enade), Recital, Singsong, Smoker, Symphony, Together, Unison, Unity, Wit

Concise Compact, Curt, Laconic, Short, Succinct, Terse, Tight

Conclude(d), Conclusion, Conclusive Achieve, A fortiori, Afterword, Amen, Binding, Cease, Clinch, Close, Complete, Dead, Decide, Deduce, > **END**, Envoi, Explicit, Finding, Fine, Finis, > **FINISH**, Foregone, Gather, Illation, Infer, Lastly, Limit, Omega, Peroration, Point, Postlude, Punchline, Reason, Resolve, Settle, Summary, Upshot, Uptie

Concrete, Concretion Actual, Aggregate, Beton, Bezoar, Cake, Calculus, Clot, Dogger, Gunite, Hard, Mass, Minkstone, No-fines, Pile-cap, Positive, Reify, Siporex, Solid, Tangible, Tremie

Condemn(ation) Blame, Blast, Cast, Censor, Censure, Convict, Damn, Decry, Denounce, Deprecate, Doom, Judge, Kest, Obelise, Proscribe, Sentence, Theta, Upbraid

Condense(d), Condenser Abbreviate, Abridge, Capacitator, Compress, Contract, Distil, Encapsulate, Epitomise, Liebig, Précis, Rectifier, Reduce, Shorten, Shrink, Summarise

Condescend Deign, Patronise, Stoop, Vouchsafe

Condiment Caraway, Cayenne, Chutney, Flavour, Kava, Relish, Sambal, Sambol, Sauce, Tracklement, Turmeric, Vinegar

Condition(al), Conditioning Circ(s), Congenital, Connote, Fettle, Going, Hammertoe, Hood, If, Kelter, Kilter, Necessary, Nick, Order, Pass, Pavlovian, Plight, Pliskie, Ply, Point, Position, Predicament, Prepare, Prerequisite, Presupposition, Protasis, Proviso, Provisory, Repair, Reservation, Reserve, Rider, Ropes, Sine qua non, Sis, Standing, State, Sted, Stipulation, String, Sufficient, Term, Tid, Tox(a)emia, Trim, Trisomy, Unless

Condom Cap, Gumboot, Johnny, Letter, Prophylactic, Rubber, Safe, Sheath

Conduct(or), Conductress Accompany, Anode, Arm, Arrester, Bearing, Behaviour, Bus-bar, Cad, Clippie, Coil, Comport, Demean(our), Deportment, Direct, Drive, Editor, Electrode, Escort, Fetch, Hallé, Ignitron, Klemperer, Lark, Lead, Liber, Lightning, Maestro, Mho, Microchip, Nerve, Officiate, Outer, Parts, > **PILOT**, Previn, Prosecute, Rattle, Safe, Sargent, Scudaller, Scudler, Solicit, Solti, Tao, Thermistor, Toscanini, Transact, > **USHER**, Wire, Wood

▷ **Conducting** *may indicate* an '-ic' ending

Conduit Aqueduct, Canal, Carrier, Duct, Main, Pipe, Tube

Cone(s), Conical Cappie, Fir, Moxa, Pastille, Peeoy, Pineal, Pingo, Pioy(e), Puy, Pyramid, Spire, Storm, Strobilus, Taper, Tee, Traffic, Volcanic, Windsock

Confederal, Confederacy, Confederate, Confederation Accessory,

Alliance, Ally, Association, Body, Bund, Bunkosteerer, Cover, Illinois, League, Partner, Union

Confer(ence) Bestow, Cf, Collogue, Colloqium, Colloquy, Congress, Council, Diet, Do, Dub, Fest, Forum, Grant, Huddle, Imparlance, Indaba, Intercommune, Lambeth, Meeting, Munich, Negotiate, Palaver, Parley, Pawaw, Pear, Potsdam, Pourparler, Powwow, Press, Pugwash, Quadrant, Seminar, Settle, Summit, Symposium, Synod, > TALK, Vouchsafe, Yalta

Confess(ion), Confessor Acknowledge, Admit, Agnise, Avowal, Concede, Declare, Disclose, Edward, Own, Recant, Shrift, Shriver, Sing, Whittle

Confide(nce), Confident(ial), Confidant Aplomb, Aside, Assertive, Assured, Bedpost, Belief, Bottle, Certitude, Cocksure, Cocky, Cred, Crouse, Entre nous, Entrust, Faith, Feisty, Gatepost, Hardy, Hope, Hush-hush, Intimate, Morale, Nerve, Pack, Private, Privy, Sanguine, Secret, Secure, Self-possessed, Sub rosa, Sure, Tell, Trust, Unbosom, Under the rose, Vaulting

Confine(d), Confines, Confinement Ambit, Bail, Bale, Cage, CB, Chain, Constrain, Cramp, Crib, Detain, Emmew, Encase, Enclose, Endemic, Enmew, Ensheath, Gate, Immanacle, Immew, Immure, Impound, > IMPRISON, Incommunicado, Inhoop, Intern, Local, Mail, March, Mew, Mure, Narrow, Pen, Pent, Pinion, Poky, Restrict, Rules, Solitary, Trammel

Confirm(ed), Confirmation Addict, Assure, Attest, Bear, Certify, Chrisom, Christen, Chronic, Clinch, Corroborate, Endorse, Homologate, Obsign, OK, Ratify, Sacrament, Sanction, Seal, Strengthen, Ten-four, Tie, Validate, Vouch

Conflict(ing) Agon, Armageddon, Battle, Camp, Clash, Contend, Contravene, Controversy, Disharmony, Encounter, Feud, Fray, Inconsistent, Jar, Lists, Mêlée, Muss, Oppose, Rift, Strife, > STRUGGLE, Tergiversate, War

Conform(ity) Accord, Adjust, Comply, Consistence, Correspond, Normalise, Obey, Observe, Propriety, Standardize, Stereotype(d), Suit, Trimmer, Yield

Confound(ed) Abash, Amaze, Astound, Awhape, Baffle, Bewilder, Blamed, Blasted, Blest, Bumbaze, Contradict, Darn, Drat, Dumbfound, Elude, Floor, Jigger, Mate, Murrain, Nonplus, Perishing, Perplex, Rabbit, Spif(f)licate, Stump, Throw

▷ **Confound** *may indicate* an anagram

Confront(ation) Appose, Beard, Breast, Eyeball, Face, Mau-mau, Meet, Nose, Oppose, Showdown, Tackle

Confuse(d), Confusedly, Confusion Addle, Anarchy, Astonishment, Babel, Baffle, Bedevil, Befog, Befuddle, Bemuse, Bewilder, Blur, Burble, Bustle, Chaos, Cloud, Clutter, Complicate, Debacle, Didder, Disconcert, Disorient, Distract, Dither, Dizzy, Dudder, Dust, Embrangle, Embroglio, Embroil, Farrago, Flap, Flummox, Flurry, Fluster, Fog, Fox, Fuddle, Galley-west, Hash, Havoc, Hazy, Huddle, Hugger-mugger, Hurly-burly, Hurry-skurry, Imbrangle, Imbroglio, > IN CONFUSION, Indistinct, Litter, Lost, Lurry, Maelstrom, Maffled, Mayhem, Maze, Melange, Melee, Mess, Mingle, Mish-mash, Mixtie-maxtie, Mizzle, Moider, Moither, Moonstruck, > MUDDLE, Mudge, Muzzy, Overset, Pellmell, Perplex, Pi(e), Pose, Ravel, Razzle-dazzle, Razzmatazz, Rout, Snafu, Spin, Stump, Stupefy, Tangle, Throw, Topsy-turvy, Tzimmes, Welter, Whomble, Woolly, Woozy

▷ **Confuse(d)** *may indicate* an anagram

Congratulate, Congratulation Applaud, Felicitate, Laud, Mazeltov, Preen, Salute

Congregate, Congregation(alist) Assembly, Barnabite, Body, Brownist, Class, Community, Conclave, Ecclesia, Flock, Fold, Gathering, Host, Laity, Oratory, Propaganda, Synagogue

Congress(man) Assembly, Conclave, Council, Eisteddfod, Intercourse, Legislature, Rally, Senator, Solon, Synod, Vienna

Conjunction Alligation, Ampersand, And, Combination, Consort, Synod, Syzygy, Together, Union

Conk Nose

Connect(ed), Connection, Connector Accolade, Adaptor, Affinity, Agnate, Anastomosis, And, Associate, Attach, Band, Bind, Bridge, Bridle, Cable, Clientele, Coherent, Colligate, Conjugate, Couple, Cross-link, Delta, Dovetail, Drawbar, Fishplate, Fistula, Interlink, Interlock, Join, Jumper, Kinship, Liaison, Lifeline, Link, Marry, Merge, Nexus, On, Online, Pons, Raphe, Rapport, Relate, Relative, Respect, Shuttle, Splice, S-R, Tendon, Through, Tie, Tie-in, Union, Yoke, Zygon

Connive, Connivance Abet, Cahoots, Collude, Condone, Conspire, Plot

Connoisseur Aesthete, Cognoscente, Epicure, Expert, Fancier, Gourmet, Judge, Oenophil

Conquer(or), Conquest Beat, Conquistador, Crush, Debel, Genghis Khan, Hereward, > **MASTER**, Moor, Norman, Ostrogoth, Overcome, Overpower, Overrun, Pizarro, Subjugate, Tame, Tamerlane, Vanquish, Victor

Conscience, Conscientious Casuistic, Heart, Inwit, Morals, Painstaking, Pang, Remorse, Scruple(s), Sense, Superego, Syneidesis, Synteresis, Thorough, Twinge

Conscious(ness) Awake, Aware, Limen, Sensible, Sentient

Consent Accord, Affo(o)rd, Agree, Approbate, Comply, Concur, Grant, Informed, Permit, Ratify, Volens, Yes-but, Yield

Consequence, Consequent(ial) Aftermath, Consectaneous, Corollary, Effect, End, Importance, Issue, Karma, Knock-on, Moment, Outcome, Ramification, Repercussion, > **RESULT**, Sequel

Conservative Blimpish, Blue, C, Cautious, Diehard, Disraeli, Fabian, Hard-hat, Hunker, Old guard, Rearguard, Right(-wing), Square, Thrifty, Tory, True blue, Unionist

Conserve, Conservation(ist) Comfiture, Husband(ry), Jam, Jelly, Maintain, Maintenance, NT, Protect, Save

Consider(able), Consideration Animadvert, Attention, Avizandum, By-end, Case, Cogitate, Contemplate, Count, Courtesy, Debate, Deem, Deliberate, Entertain, Envisage, Factor, Fair, Feel, Heed, Importance, Inasmuch, Judge, Many, Meditate, Muse, Pay, Perpend, Poise, Ponder, Pretty, Rate, Reckon, Reflect, Regard, Respect, See, Several, Solicitous, Song, Speculate, Steem, Study, Substantial, Think, Tidy, Vast, View, Ween, Weigh

Consign(ment) Allot, Award, Batch, Bequeath, Delegate, Deliver, Entrust, Lading, Ship, Transfer

Consist(ent), Consistency Coherent, Comprise, Enduring, Liaison, Rely, Steady

Consolation, Console Ancon, Appease, Balm, Comfort, Relief, Solace

Conspicuous Arresting, Blatant, Clear, Eminent, Glaring, Kenspeck(le), Landmark, Light, Manifest, Patent, Salient, Signal, Striking

Conspiracy, Conspirator, Conspire, Conspiring Cabal, Casca, Cassius, Catiline, Cato St, Cinna, Collaborate, Colleague, Collogue, Collude, Complot, Connive, Covin, Covyne, Guy, In cahoots, Intrigue, Oates, Omerta, > **PLOT**, Ring, Scheme

Constable High, Petty

Constancy, Constant Abiding, Boltzmann, C, Changeless, Chronic, Coefficient, Devotion, Dielectric, Diffusion, Dirac, Eccentricity, Eternal, Faith, Firm, Fundamental, G, Gas, Gravitational, H, Honesty, Hubble's, K, Lambert, Leal(ty), Logical, Loyal, Magnetic, Often, Parameter, Planck's, Pole star, Resolute, Sad, Solar, Staunch, Steadfast, Steady, Time, True, Unfailing, Uniform, Usual

Constellation Andromeda, Antlia, Apus, Aquarius, Aquila, Ara, Argo, Aries,

Auriga, Bootes, Caelum, Canis major, Canis minor, Carina, Cassiopeia, Centaurus, Cepheus, Cetus, Cham(a)eleon, Circinus, Columba, Coma Berenices, Corvus, Crater, Cygnus, Cynosure, Delphinus, Dorado, Draco, Equuleus, Eridanus, Fornax, Galaxy, Gemini, Gru(i)s, Hercules, Hydra, Hydrus, Indus, Lacerta, Leo, Lepus, Libra, Lupus, Lynx, Lyra, Mensa, Monoceros, Musca, Norma, Octans, Ophiuchus, Orion, Pavo, Pegasus, Perseus, Phoenix, Pictor, > **PLANET**, Puppis, Pyxis, Reticulum, Sagitta, Sagittarius, Scorpius, Sculptor, Scutum, Serpens, Sextans, Southern Cross, > **STAR**, Telescopium, Triangulum (Australe), Tucana, Twins, Unicorn, Vela, Virgo, Volans, Vulpecula, Whale

Constituency, Constituent Borough, Component, Element, Part, Seat, Voter
▷ **Constituents** *may indicate* an anagram

Constitute, Constitution(al) Appoint, Charter, Compose, Comprise, Congenital, Creature, Establishment, Form, Fuero, Health, Physique, Policy, Polity, Seat, State, Synthesis

Constrain(ed), Constraint Bind, Bondage, Coerce, Confine, Coop, Curb, Duress(e), Hard, Oblige, Pressure, Repress, Stenosis, Taboo

Constrict(ed), Constriction Bottleneck, Choke, Coarctate, Contract, Cramp, Hour-glass, Impede, Limit, Phimosis, Squeeze, Stegnosis, Stenosis, Thlipsis, Tighten, Venturi

Construct(ion), Constructor, Constructive Build, Compile, Engineer, Erect, Fabricate, Facture, Fashion, Form, Frame, Make, Manufacture, Seabee, Tectonic, Weave

Consult(ant), Consultation Confer, Deliberate, Discuss, Imparl, Peritus, See, Surgery

Consume(r), Consumption, Consumptive Bolt, Burn, Caterpillar®, Decay, Devour, Diner, Eat, Engross, Exhaust, Expend, Feed, Glutton, Hectic, Mainline, Scoff, Spend, Swallow, TB, Use, Waste, Wear

Contact Abut, Adpress, Contingence, Hook-up, Lens, Liaise, Liaison, Meet, Reach, Shoe, > **TOUCH**

Contagious, Contagion Infection, Noxious, Poison, Taint, Variola, Viral

Contain(er) Amphora, Ampulla, Aquafer, Aquifer, Barrel, Bass, Bidon, Bin, Bottle, Box, Buddle, Cachepot, Can, Canakin, Canikin, Canister, Cannikin, Cantharus, Capsule, Carafe, Carboy, Carry, Carton, Case, Cask, Cassette, Chase, Chest, Churn, Coffer, Comprise, Coolamon, Crate, Crater, Crucible, Cup, Cupel, Decanter, Dracone, Dredger, Enclose, Encompass, Enseam, Esky®, Feretory, Flagon, Flask, Gourd, > **HOLD**, House, Igloo, Include, Incubator, Intray, Jar, Jeroboam, Jerrican, Jerrycan, Jug, Keg, Kirbeh, Leaguer, Lekythos, Monkey, Monstrance, Mould, Olpe, Pail, Pinata, Piscina, Pitcher, Pithos, Pod, Pottle, Reliquary, Repository, Restrain, Sac(k), Saggar, Scyphus, Shaker, Situla, Skin, Skip, Snaptin, Spittoon, Stamnos, Tank, Tantalus, Terrarium, Tinaja, Trough, Tub, Tun, Tupperware®, Urn, Vessel, Vinaigrette, Wineskin, Woolpack, Workbag

Contaminate(d) Corrupt, Defile, Flyblown, Impure, Infect, Soil, Stain, Tarnish

Contemporary AD, Coetaneous, Current, Equal, Fellow, Modern, Present, Verism

Contempt(ible), Contemptuous Abject, Ageism, Aha, Arsehole, Bah, BEF, Cheap, Contumely, Crud, Crumb, Cullion, Cynical, Derision, Disparaging, Dog-bolt, Fig, Ignominious, Low, Mean, Measly, Misprision, Paltry, Phooey, Pish, Poxy, Pshaw, Rats, Razoo, Scabby, Scarab, > **SCORN**, Scumbag, Sexism, Shabby, Shithead, Sneeze, Sniff, Snooty, Snot, Soldier, Sorry, Squirt, Squit, Supercilious, Toad, Toerag, Weed, Wretched

Contend(er) Candidate, Claim, Clash, Compete, Cope, Debate, Dispute, Fight, Grapple, Oppose, Stickle, > **STRIVE**, Struggle, Submit, > **VIE**, Wrestle

Content Apaid, Apay, Appay, Blissful, Happy, Inside, Please, Satisfy, Volume

▷ **Content** *may indicate* a hidden word

Contention, **Contentious** Argument, Bellicose, Cantankerous, Case, Combat, Competitive, Perverse, Polemical, Rivalry, Strife, Struggle, Sturt

Contest(ant) Agon, Battle, Beauty, Biathlon, Bout, Catchweight, Challenge, Championship, Combat, Competition, Concours, Darraign, Decathlon, Defend, Deraign, Dogfight, Duel(lo), Entrant, Eurovision, Event, Examinee, Free-for-all, Fronde, Handicap, Heptathlon, Kriegspiel, Lampadephoria, Match, Matchplay, Olympiad, Pancratium, Paralympics, Pentathlon, Pingle, Play-off, Prizer, Race, Rival, Roadeo, Rodeo, Set-to, Skirmish, Slam, Slugfest, Strife, Struggle, Tenson, Tetrathlon, Tournament, Triathlon, Vie, War, With

Continent(al) Abstinent, Asia, Atlantis, Austere, Chaste, Epeirogeny, Euro, Gallic, Gondwanaland, Laurasia, Lemuria, Mainland, Moderate, Pang(a)ea, Shelf, Teetotal, Temperate, Walloon

Continual(ly), **Continuous** Adjoining, Away, Chronic, Connected, Eer, Endlong, Eternal, Ever, Frequent, Incessant, On(going)

Continue, **Continuation**, **Continuing**, **Continuity** Abye, Duration, Dure, During, Enduring, Enjamb(e)ment, Hold, Keep, Last, Link, Onward, Persevere, Persist, Proceed, Prolong, Resume, Sequence, Stand, Subsist, Survive, Sustain, Tenor

▷ **Continuously** *may indicate* previous words to be linked

Contraception, **Contraceptive** Cap, Coil, Condom, Diaphragm, IU(C)D, Loop, Minipill, Oral, Pessary, Pill, Prophylactic, Sheath, Vimule®

Contract(ion), **Contractor** Abbreviate, Abridge, Agreement, Astringency, Bargain, Biceps, Bridge, Builder, Catch, Champerty, Charter, Clonus, Condense, Constringe, Contrahent, Covenant, Cramp, Curtail, Debt, Dwindle, Engage, Entrepreneur, Escrow, Gainsay, Gooseflesh, Guarantee, Hire, Incur, Indenture, Jerk, Knit, Lease, Levator, Make, Miosis, Myosis, Narrow, Party, Promise, Pucker, Purse, Restriction, Shrink, Shrivel, Sign, Slam, Social, Spasm, Specialty, Stenosis, Stipulation, Supplier, Sweetheart, Systole, Tetanise, Tetanus, Tic, Tighten, Tonicity, Treaty, Triceps, Wrinkle, Yellow-dog, Z

Contradict(ion), **Contradictory** Ambivalent, Antilogy, Antinomy, Bull, Contrary, Counter, Dementi, Deny, Disaffirm, Disprove, Dissent, Negate, Oxymoron, Paradox, Sot, Stultify, Sublate, Threap, Threep, Traverse

Contraption Contrivance

Contrarily, **Contrary** Adverse, A rebours, Arsy-versy, But, Captious, Converse, Counter, Crosscurrent, Froward, Hostile, Inverse, Mary, Opposite, Ornery, Perverse, Rebuttal, Retrograde, Wayward, Withershins

Contrast Chiaroscuro, Clash, Compare, Differ, Foil, Relief

Contribute, **Contribution** Abet, Add, Assist, Conduce, Donate, Dub, Furnish, Go, Help, Input, Mite, Offering, Share, Sub, Subscribe, Whack

▷ **Contributing to** *may indicate* a hidden word

Contrive(r) Chicaner, Cook, Devise, Engineer, Frame, Hatch, Intrigue, Machinate, Manage, Manoeuvre, Plan, Procure, Scheme, Secure, Stage, Trump, Weave

Control(ler), **Controllable** Ada, Appestat, Big Brother, Birth, Boss, Bridle, Cabotage, Chair, Check, Christmas tree, Corner, Corset, Cybernetics, Descendeur, Dirigible, Dirigism(e), Dominate, Dominion, Dynamic, Etatiste, Fast-forward, Fet(ch), Finger, Flood, Fly-by-wire, Gain, Gar, Gerent, Govern, Ground, Gubernation, Harness, Have, Heck, Helm, Influence, Influx, Joystick, Knee-swell, Lead, Lever, > **MANAGE**, Martinet, Mastery, Moderate, Mouse, Nipple, Numerical, Operate, Override, Pilot, Placebo, Police, Population, Possess, Power, Preside, Price, Process, Puppeteer, Quality, Radio, Regulate, Regulo®, Rein, Remote, Rent, Repress, Restrain, Rheostat, Ride, Ripple, Rule, Run, School, Servo, Snail,

Solion, Steady, Steer, Stop, Stranglehold, Stringent, Subdue, Subject, Subjugate, Supervise, Suzerain, Sway, Takeover, Thermostat, Throttle, Tiller, Tone, Valve, Weld, Wield, Zapper

Controversial, Controversy Argument, Contention, Debate, Dispute, Eristic(al), Furore, Hot potato

Convenience, Convenient Behoof, Eft, Expedient, Facility, Gain, Gents, > **HANDY**, Hend, Lav, Leisure, Near, Opportune, Pat, Privy, Public, Suitable, Toilet, Use, Well

Convent Cloister, Fratry, Friary, House, Motherhouse, Nunnery, Port-royal, Priory, Retreat

Convention(al) Academic, Accepted, Babbitt, Blackwood, Bourgeois, Caucus, Conclave, Conformity, > **CUSTOMARY**, Diet, Done, Formal, Geneva, Habitude, Iconic, Lingua franca, Meeting, Middlebrow, Middle-of-the-road, More, National, Nomic, Orthodox, Pompier, Proper, Schengen, Staid, Starchy, Stereotyped, Stock, Synod, Uptight, Usage, Warsaw

Conversation(alist), Converse, Conversant Abreast, Antithesis, Board, Buck, Cackle, Causerie, Chat, Chitchat, Colloquy, Commune, Deipnosophist, Dialogue, Discourse, Eutrapelia, Eutrapely, Hobnob, Interlocution, Jaw-jaw, Natter, Opposite, Palaver, Parley, Rap, Rhubarb, Shop, Socialise, > **TALK**, Transpose, Wongi, Word

Conversion, Converter, Convert(ible) Adapt, Alter, Assimilate, Bessemer, Catalytic, Catechumen, Change, Commute, Cyanise, Diagenesis, Disciple, Encash, Exchange, Expropriate, Fixation, Liquid, Marrano, Metanoia, Neophyte, Noviciate, Novitiate, Persuade, Proselyte, Put, Ragtop, Realise, Rebirth, Recycle, Revamp, Souper, Tablet, Transduce, Transmute, Try

▷ **Conversion, Converted** *may indicate* an anagram

Convey(ance) Assign, BS, Carousel, Carry, Charter, Coach, Conduct, Cycle, Deed, Eloi(g)n, Enfeoffment, Grant, Guide, Lease, Litter, Lorry, Mailcar(t), Re-lease, Sac and soc, Tip, Title deed, Tote, Tram, Transfer, Transit, Transmit, Transport, Vehicle

Convict(ion) Attaint, Belief, Bushranger, Certitude, Cockatoo, Cogence, Crawler, Credo, Creed, Criminal, Demon, Dogma, Faith, Felon, Forçat, Lag, Magwitch, > **PERSUASION**, Plerophory, Ring, Trusty, Vehemence, Yardbird

Convince(d), Convincing Assure, Cogent, Doubtless, Luculent, Persuade, Satisfy, Sold, Sure

Convulsion(s), Convulsive Agitate, Clonic, Commotion, Disturb, DT, Eclampsia, > **FIT**, Galvanic, Paroxysm, Spasm, Throe, Tic

Cook(s), Cooker, Cooking Aga®, Babbler, Bake, Balti, Beeton, Benghazi, Bhindi, Bouche, Braise, Broil, Cacciatore, Calabash, Captain, Charbroil, Chargrill, Chef, Coddle, Concoct, Cordon bleu, Cuisine, Devil, Do, Doctor, Dumple, Edit, Escoffier, Fake, Falsify, Fiddle, Flambé, Forge, Fricassee, Fry, Fudge, Greasy, Grill, Haute cuisine, Haybox, Marinière, Meunière, Microwave, Poach, Prepare, Pressure, Ring, Roast, Roger, Sous-chef, Spit, Steam, Stew, Stir-fry, Tandoori, Tire

▷ **Cook** *may indicate* an anagram

Cool(er), Cooling, Coolness Aloof, Aplomb, Calm, Can, Chill, Collected, Composed, Cryogen, Cryostat, Defervescence, Dispassionate, Distant, Esky®, Fan, Frappé, Fridge, Frigid, Frosty, Gaol, Goglet, Ice(box), Jail, Jug, Keel, Phlegm, Prison, Quad, Quod, Refresh, Reserved, Sangfroid, Serene, Skeigh, Stir, Temperate, Thou(sand), Unruffled

Coop Cage, Cavie, Confine, Gaol, Hutch, Mew, Pen, Rip

Cooperate, Cooperation, Cooperative Collaborate, Combine, Conspire, Contribute, Coop, Liaise, Teamwork, Together

Coordinate(d), Coordination Abscissa, Abscisse, Agile, Arrange, Cartesian, Ensemble, Harmony, Nabla, Orchestrate, Ordonnance, Peer, Polar, Synergy, X, Y, Z

Cop(s) Bag, Bull, Catch, Dick, Keystone, Peeler, Peon, > POLICEMAN

Cope Chlamys, Deal, Face, Handle, > MANAGE, Mantle, Meet, Negotiate, Pallium, Poncho

Copy(ing), Copier, Copyist Aemule, Ape, Apograph, Autotype, Calk, Calque, Carbon, Clerk, Clone, Counterpart, Crib, Cyclostyle, Diazo, Ditto, Dyeline, Echo, Echopraxia, Ectype, Edition, Eidograph, Electro, Emulate, Engross, Estreat, Example, Facsimile, Fair, Fax, Flimsy, Forge, > IMITATE, Issue, Manifold, Manuscript, Match, Me-tooer, Milline, Mimeograph®, Mimic, Mirror, MS, Parrot, Photostat®, Plagiarism, Read-out, Replica, Repro, Reproduce, Roneo®, Scribe, Script, Scrivener, Sedulous, Simulate, Spit, Stencil, Stuff, Tenor, Tenure, Trace, Transcribe, Transume, Vidimus, Xerox®

Coral (reef) Alcyonaria, Aldabra, Atoll, Brain, Gorgonia(n), Laccadives, Madrepore, Millepore, Pink, Reef, Sea fan, Sea ginger, Sea-pen, Sea whip, Zoothome

Cord, Cord-like Aiguillette, Band, Bedford, Bind, Boondoggle, Cat-gut, Chenille, Communication, Creance, Drawstring, Flex, Fourragère, Funicle, Gasket, Heddle, Laniard, Lanyard, Ligature, Line, Moreen, Myelon, Net, Ocnus, Piping, Quipo, Quipu, Rep(s), Restiform, Rip, Rope, Sash, Sennit, Service, Spermatic, Spinal, > STRING, Tendon, Tie, Twine, Umbilical, Vocal

Cordon Picket, Ring, Surround

Core Barysphere, Calandria, Campana, Centre, Essence, Filament, Heart, Hub, Nife, Plerome, Quintessence

Cork(ed), Corker Balsa, Bouché, Bung, Float(er), Humdinger, Oner, Phellem, Phellogen, Plug, Seal, Shive, Stopper, Suber(ate)

Corkscrew Bore, Opening, Spiral

Cormorant Duiker, Duyker, Scart(h), Skart(h)

Corn(y) Bajr(a), Banal, Blé, Cereal, Cob, Emmer, Epha, Flint, Gait, Graddan, Grain, Grist, Icker, Indian, Kaffir, Mabela, Maize, Mealie, Muid, Nubbin, Pickle, Pinole, Posho, Rabi, Shock, Stitch, Straw, Thrave, Trite, Zea

Corner Amen, Angle, Bend, Cantle, Canton, Cranny, Dangerous, Diêdre, Elbow, Entrap, Hole, Hospital, Lug, Monopoly, NE, Niche, Nook, NW, Predicament, Quoin, SE, Speakers', Spot, SW, Tack, Trap, Tree, Vertex

Coronation Enthronement

Corporation Belly, Body, Commune, Company, Conglomerate, Guild, Kite, Kyte, Paunch, Stomach, Swag-belly, Tum, Wame, Wem

Corps Body, C, Crew, Diplomatic, Peace, RAC, REME, Unit

Corpse Blob, Body, Cadaver, Carcass, Carrion, Goner, Like, Mort, Relic, Remains, Stiff, Zombi(e)

Correct(ing), Correctly, Correctness, Correction, Corrector Accurate, Alexander, Align, Amend, Aright, Bodkin, Castigate, Chasten, Chastise, Check, Decorous, Diorthortic, Emend, Exact, Fair, Grammatical, Legit, Mend, Preterition, Probity, Proofread, Proper, Propriety, Punctilious, Punish, Rebuke, Rectify, Redress, Remedial, Reprove, Revise, Right(en), Scold, Spot-on, Sumpsimus, Trew, True, U

▷ **Corrected** *may indicate* an anagram

Correspond(ence), Correspondent, Corresponding Accord, Agree, Analogy, Assonance, Coincident, Communicate, Congruence, Counterpart, Equate, Eye-rhyme, Fit, Homolog(ue), Identical, Match, On all fours, One to one, Par, Parallel, Relate, Symmetry, Tally, Veridical, Write

Corridor Air, Aisle, Gallery, Lobby, Passage

Corrode(d), Corrosion, Corrosive Acid, Brinelling, Burn, Canker, Decay, Eat, Erode, Etch, Fret, Gnaw, Hydrazine, Mordant, > ROT, Rubiginous, Rust, Waste

Corrupt(er), Corrupting, Corruption Abuse, Adulterate, Bastardise, Bent, Canker, Debase, Debauch, Decadent, Defile, Degenerate, Depravity, Dissolute, Dry rot, Emancipate, Embrace(o)r, Embrasor, Empoison, Etch, Fester, Gangrene, Graft(er), Immoral, Impure, Inquinate, Jobbery, Leprosy, Malversation, Nefarious, Obelus, Payola, Perverse, Poison, Pollute, Power, Putrid, Ret(t), Rigged, Rot, Scrofulous, Seduce, Sepsis, Septic, Sleaze, Sodom, Sophisticate, Spoil, Suborn, Tammany, Twist, Venal, Vice, Vitiate

Cosmetic Beautifier, Blusher, Bronzer, Eye-black, Eyeliner, Eye-shadow, Face-pack, Foundation, Fucus, Highlighter, Kohl, Liner, Lip gloss, Lip liner, Lipstick, Lotion, Maquillage, Mascara, Mousse, Mudpack, Paint, Pearl-powder, Powder, Reface, Rouge, Talcum, Toner

Cosmos, Cosmic Globe, Heaven, Infinite, Nature, Universe, World

Cost(s), Costly Bomb, Carriage, Charge, Damage, Earth, Escuage, Estimate, Exes, > **EXPENSE**, Hire, Loss, Marginal, Outlay, Overhead, Precious, Price, Quotation, Rate, Sacrifice, Sumptuous, Toll, Unit, Upkeep, Usurious

Costume Apparel, Attire, Camagnole, Cossie, Dress, Ensemble, Get-up, Gi(e), Guise, Judogi, Livery, Maillot, Motley, Nebris, Polonaise, Rig, Surcoat, Tanga, Uniform

Cosy Cosh, Intime, Snug

Cottage(r) Bach, Bordar, Bothie, Bothy, Box, Bungalow, Cabin, Chalet, Cot, Crib, Dacha, Hut, Lodge, Mailer

Cotton Agree, AL, Alabama, Balbriggan, Batiste, Batting, Calico, Candlewick, Ceiba, Chambray, Chino, Chintz, Collodion, Coutil(le), Cretonne, Denim, Dho(o)ti, Dimity, Ducks, Fustian, Galatea, Gossypine, Gossypium, Humhum, Ihram, Jaconet, Lawn, Lea, Lille, Lint, Lisle, Manchester, Marcella, Muslin, Nainsook, Nankeen, Nankin, Pongee, Sea-island, Seersucker, Silesia, Stranded, Surat, T-cloth, Thread, Twig, Upland

Couch Bed, Davenport, Daybed, Express, Grass, Lurk, Palanquin, Palkee, Palki, Quick, Recamier, Sedan, Settee, Sofa, Studio, Triclinium, Word

Cough(ing) Bark, Croup, Expectorate, Hack, Hawk, Hem, Hoast, Kink, Rale, Tisick, Tussis, Ugh, Whooping

Council (meeting), Councillor, Counsel(lor) Achitophel, Admonish, Admonitor, Advice, Advocate, Ahithophel, Alfred, Aread, Assembly, Attorney, Aulic, Board, Body, Boule, Bundesrat, Burgess, Cabinet, Casemate, Committee, Consistory, Corporation, County, Cr, Decurion, Devil, Divan, Douma, Duma, Egeria, Exhort, Greenbag, Hebdomadal, Indaba, Induna, Info, Jirga, Junta, Kabele, Kebele, Kite, Landst(h)ing, Lateran, Leader, Legislative, Majlis, Mentor, Nestor, Nicene, Panchayat, Parish, Powwow, Privy, Provincial, Rede, Reichsrat, Samaritan, Sanhedrim, Sanhedrin, Security, Senate, Shura, Sobranje, Sobranye, Soviet, Syndicate, Synod, Thing, Trent, Tridentine, Trullan, Volost, Whitley, Witan, Witenagemot, Works, Zila, Zillah

Count(ed), Counter, Counting Abacus, Add, Algoriam, Anti, Bar, Basie, Buck, Buffet, Calculate, Cavour, Census, Chip, Compute, Coost, Desk, Dracula, Dump, Earl, Enumerate, Fish, Geiger, Geiger-Muller, Graf(in), Grave, Itemise, Jet(t)on, Landgrave, Margrave, Matter, Merel(l), Meril, Number, Obviate, Olivia, Oppose, Palatine, Palsgrave, Paris, Pollen, Presume, Rebut, > **RECKON**, Refute, Rejoinder, Rely, Retaliate, Retort, Rhinegrave, Scintillation, Score, Sperm, Squail, Statistician, Stop, Sum, Table, Tally, Tell, Tiddleywink, Ugolino, Weigh, Zeppelin

Counterfeit(er) Belie, Bogus, Boodle, Brum, Coiner, Duffer, Dummy, Fantasm, Flash, Forge, Imitant, Phantasm, Phoney, Pseudo, Queer, Rap, Schlenter, Sham, Shan(d), Simulate, Slang, Slip, Smasher, Snide, Spurious

Counties, County Antrim, Armagh, Avon, Barset, Beds, Berkshire, Buteshire, Carlow, Cavan, Ceredigion, Champagne, Clare, Cleveland, Co, Comital, Cork,

Cornwall, District, Donegal, Dorset, Down, Dublin, Durham, Dyfed, Fermanagh, Fife, Flint, Gwent, Gwynedd, Hampshire, Herefordshire, Herts, Hunts, Kent, Kerry, Kesteven, Kildare, Kilkenny, Kincardineshire, Kinrossshire, Kircudbrightshire, Lanarkshire, Laois, Leicestershire, Leitrim, Limerick, Lincolnshire, Loamshire, Londonderry, Longford, Louth, Mayo, Meath, Merionithshire, Merseyside, Metropolitan, Midlothian, Monaghan, Monmouthshire, Montgomeryshire, Moray, Nairnshire, Neath Port Talbot, NI, Norfolk, Northamptonshire, Northumberland, North Yorkshire, Notts, Offaly, Omagh, Oxfordshire, Palatine, Parish, Peeblesshire, Pembrokeshire, Perth(shire), Powys, Radnorshire, Renfrewshire, Roscommon, Ross, Ross and Cromarty, Rutland, Seat, Selkirkshire, Shire, Shropshire, Six, Som(erset), South Glamorgan, Staffordshire, Stirlingshire, Suffolk, Surrey, Sussex, Sutherland, Sy, The Mearns, Tipperary, Torfaen, Tyne and Wear, Tyrone, Vale of Glamorgan, Warwickshire, Waterford, West Glamorgan, West Lothian, Westmeath, West Midlands, Westmoreland, West Sussex, West Yorkshire, Wexford, Wicklow, Wigtownshire, Wilts, Worcs, Yorkshire

Countless Infinite, Innumerable, Myriad, Umpteen, Untold

Country(side), Countrified Annam, Bangladesh, Boondocks, Bucolic, Champaign, Clime, Colchis, Edom, Enchorial, Fatherland, Karoo, Karroo, > **LAND**, Lea, Lee, Mongolia, Motherland, Nation, Parish, Paysage, People, Province, Realm, Region, Republic, Rural, Satellite, Soil, State, Tundra, Weald, Wold, Yemen

Coup Blow, Deal, KO, Move, Putsch, Scoop, Stroke

Couple(r), Coupling Ally, Band, Brace, Bracket, Connect, Duet, Duo, Dyad, Fishplate, Gemini, Geminy, Hitch, Item, > **JOIN**, Marry, Mate, Meng(e), Ment, Ming, Pair, Pr, Relate, Shackle, Tie, Tirasse, Turnbuckle, Tway, Union, Universal, Voltaic, Wed, Yoke

Coupon(s) Ration, Ticket, Voucher

Courage(ous) Balls, Bottle, Bravado, Bravery, Bulldog, Dutch, Fortitude, Gallantry, Game, Gimp, Grit, Gumption, Guts, Heart, Heroism, Lion-heart, Macho, Mettle, Moxie, Nerve, Pluck, Rum, Spirit, Spunk, Stalwart, Steel, Valiant, Valour, Wight

Course(s) Afters, Aim, Aintree, Antipasto, Appetiser, Arroyo, Ascot, Assault, Atlantic, Bearing, Beat, Canal, Career, Chantilly, Chase, Circuit, Consommé, Correspondence, Crash, Current, Curriculum, Cursus, Dessert, Diadrom, Dish, Dromic, Entrée, Fish, Food, Foundation, Going, Goodwood, Greats, Heat, Lane, Lap, Layer, Leat, Leet, Line, Lingfield, Links, Longchamp, Meal, Meat, Mess, Newbury, Newmarket, Nine-hole, Nulla, > **OF COURSE**, Orbit, Period, Policy, PPE, Procedure, Process, Programme, Progress, Pursue, Race, Raik, Refresher, Regimen, Rhumb, Ride, Ring, Rink, Road, Rota, Route, Routine, Run, Rut, Sandown, Sandwich, Semester, Series, Soup, Starter, Stearage, Steerage, Step(s), Stratum, Streak, Stretch, String, Syllabus, Tack, Tanride, Tenor, Track, Trade, Troon, Way

Court(ier) Address, Admiralty, Appellate, Arches, Atrium, Attention, Audience, Audiencia, Aula, Banc, Bar, Basecourt, Bench, Beth Din, Bishop's, Boondock, Camelot, Caravanserai, Cassation, Centre, Chancery, Chase, Clay, Consistory, County, Criminal, Crown, CS, Ct, Curia, Curia Regis, Curtilage, Date, Dedans, Diplock, District, Doctor's Commons, Domestic, Duchy, Durbar, Dusty Feet, En tout cas, Eyre, Federal, Fehm(gericht), Forensic, Forest, Forum, Friars, Fronton, Galleria, Garth, Go steady, Grass, Guildenstern, Halimot(e), Hampton, Hard, High, Hof, Holy See, Hustings, Inferior, Intermediate, Invite, Jack, Justice, Juvenile, Kacheri, Kangaroo, Keys, King, King's Bench, Kirk Session, Knave, Law, Leet, Lobby, Lyon, Magistrate's, Majlis, Marshalsea, Mash, Moot, Old Bailey, Open, Parvis, Patio, Peristyle, Petty Sessions, Philander, Piepowder, Police, Porte, Presbytery, Prize, Probate, Provincial, Provost, Quad, Quarter Sessions, Queen, Queen's

Bench, Retinue, Rosenkrantz, Royal, Sanhedrin, See, Service, Session, Sheriff, Shire-moot, Spoon, Stannary, Star Chamber, Sue, Superior, Supreme, Swanimote, Sweetheart, Thane, Thegn, Traffic, Trial, Tribunal, Vehm, Vestibulum, Walk out, Ward, Wench, Woo, World, Wow, Yard, Youth

Courteous, Courtesy Affable, Agrement, Bow, Comity, Devoir, Etiquette, Genteel, Gracious, Hend, Polite, Refined, Urbanity

Courtly Chivalrous, Cringing, Dignified, Flattering, Refined

Courtyard Area, Cortile, Marae, Patio, Quad

Cousin(s) Bette, Cater, Country, Coz, Cross, German, Kin, Kissing, Robin, Skater

Cover(ed), Covering Adventitia, A l'abri, Amnion, Antependium, Antimacassar, Apron, Aril, Attire, Awning, Barb, Bard(s), Bark, Bedspread, Bestrew, Bind, Blanket, Bodice, Brood, Bubblewrap, Bury, Camouflage, Canopy, Cap, Caparison, Cape, Capsule, Casing, Casque, Catch-all, Caul, Ceil, Ciborium, Cladding, Clapboard, Cleithral, Clithral, Coat, Cocoon, Coleorhiza, Conceal, Cope, Copyright, Cosy, Counterpane, Cour, Covert, Cowl, Curtain, Deadlight, Deck, Deputise, Dividend, Dome, Drape(t), Dripstone, Duchesse, Dust-sheet, Duvet, Eiderdown, Encase, Endue, Enguard, Enlace, Enshroud, Envelop(e), Enwrap, Exoderm(is), Exoskeleton, Extra, Face, Falx, Fanfare, Felting, Fielder, Figleaf, Fingerstall, First-day, Flashing, Fother, Front, Gaiter, Gambado, Grolier, Ground, Hap, Harl, Hat, Hatch, Havelock, Heal, Heel, Hejab, Hele, Hell, Helmet, Hijab, Hood, Housing, Hubcap, Immerse, Incase, Indusium, Inmask, Insulate, Insurance, Insure, Jacket, Lag, Lay, Leap, Leep, Legging, Legwarmer, Lid, Liner, Loose, Manche, Mantle, Mask, Metal, Mount, Muffle, Mulch, Notum, Numnah, Obscure, OC, Occlude, On, Operculum, Orillion, Orlop, Overlay, Palampore, Palempore, Pall, Pand, Parcel, Pasties, Patch, Pebbledash, Pelmet, Periderm, Pillow sham, Plaster, Plate, Pleura, Point, Pseudonym, Pullover, Quilt, Radome, Regolith, Robe, Roof, Roughcast, Rug, Sally, Screen, Serviette, Setting, Sheath, Sheet, Shell, Shelter, Shield, Shrink-wrap, Shroud, Shuck, Skin, Smokescreen, Solleret, Span, Spat, Stand-by, Stifle, Swathe, Tampian, Tampion, Tapadera, Tapis, Tarpaulin, Teacosy, Tectorial, Tegmen, Tegument, Tent, Test(a), Tester, Thatch, Thimble, Thumbstall, Tick(ing), Tile, Tilt, Tonneau, Top, Trapper, Trench, Trip, Turtleback, Twill, Twilt, Umbrella, Upholster, Valance, Veil, Vele, Veneer, Ventail, Vesperal, Vest, Visor, Volva, Wainscot, Waterdeck, Whelm, Whitewash, Wrap, Wrapper, Yapp

Covet(ed), Covetous Avaricious, Crave, Desiderata, Desire, Eager, Envy, Greedy, Hanker, Yearn

Cow, Cowpat Adaw, Alderney, Amate, Appal, Awe, Bovine, Browbeat, Cash, Charolais, Colly, Crummy, Danton, Daunt, Dexter, Dsomo, Dun, Dung, Galloway, Gally, Goujal, Guernsey, Hawkey, Hawkie, Heifer, Hereford, Intimidate, Jersey, Kouprey, Kyloe, Mart, Milch, Mog(gie), Moggy, Mooly, Muley, Mulley, Overawe, Redpoll, Red Sindhi, Rother(-beast), Sacred, Santa Gertrudis, Scare, Simmental, Stirk, Subact, Tath, Teeswater, Threaten, Unnerve, Vaccine, Zebu, Z(h)o

Coward(ly) Bessus, Cat, Chicken, Cocoa, Craven, Cuthbert, Dastard, Dingo, Dunghill, Fraidy-cat, Fugie, Funk, Gutless, Hen, Hilding, Lily-livered, Meacock, Niddering, Nidderling, Nidering, Niderling, Niding, Nithing, Noel, Panty-waist, Poltroon, Pusillanimous, Recreant, Scaramouch, Sganarelle, Slag, Sook, Viliaco, Viliago, Villagio, Villiago, Yellow, Yellow-belly

Cowboy, Cowgirl Buckaroo, Gaucho, Inexpert, Io, Jerrybuilder, Leger, Llanero, Puncher, Ranchero, Ritter, Roper, Vaquero, Waddy, Wrangler

Coy Arch, Coquettish, Mim, Shamefast, > **SHY**, Skittish

Crab(by), Crablike Apple, Attercop, Cancer, Cancroid, Cantankerous, Capernoity, Cock, Coconut, Daddy, Decapoda, Diogenes, Ethercap, Ettercap, Fiddler, Ghost, Grouch, Hard-shell, Hermit, Horseman, Horseshoe, King, Land, Limulus, Mantis, Mitten, Nebula, Ochidore, Oyster, Pagurian, Partan, Perverse,

Podite, Roast, Robber, Rock, Saucepan-fish, Scrawl, Sentinel, Sidle, Soft-shell, Soldier, Spider, Xiphosura, Zoea

▷ **Crab** *may indicate* an anagram

Crack(ed), Cracker(s), Cracking Ad-lib, Admirable, Bananas, Biscuit, Bonbon, Break, Cat, Catalytic, Chap, Chasm, Chat, Chink, Chip, Chop, Clap, Cleave, Cleft, Cloff, Confab, Cranny, Craquelure, Craqueture, Craze, Cream, Crepitate, Crevasse, Crevice, Crispbread, Dawn, Decode, Doom, Dunt, Elite, Fatiscent, Fent, Firework, First-rate, Fisgig, Fissure, Fizgig, Flaw, Flip-flop, Fracture, Go, Graham, Grike, Gryke, Gully, Hairline, Hit, Jibe, Joint, Leak, Liar, Little-endian, Matzo, Moulin, Oner, Peterman, Pore, Praise, Prawn, Quip, Rap, Report, Rhagades, Rictus, Rift, Rille, Rima, Rime, Rimous, Rive, Rock, Saltine, Seam, Snap, Soda, Solve, Split, Squib, Sulcus, Top, Try, Waterloo, Yegg

Cradle Bassinet, Berceau, Cat's, Cot, Crib, Cunabula, Hammock, Knife, Nestle, Rocker

Craft(y) Arch, Art, Aviette, Barbola, Boat, Canal boat, Cautel, Cunning, Disingenuous, Finesse, Fly, Guile, Hydroplane, Ice-breaker, Insidious, Kontiki, Landing, Machiavellian, Mister, Mystery, Oomiack, Reynard, Saic, Shallop, Ship, Shuttle, > **SKILL**, Slee, Sleeveen, Slim, Slippy, Sly, Slyboots, State, Subdolous, Subtil(e), Subtle, Suttle, Triphibian, Umiak, Underhand, Versute, > **VESSEL**, Wile, Workmanship

Craftsman AB, Artificer, Artisan, Artist, Chippy, Cutler, Ebonist, Fabergé, Finisher, Gondolier, Guild, Hand, Joiner, Journeyman, Mason, Mechanic, Morris, Opificer, Wainwright, Wright

Cram(mer) Bag, Candle-waster, Cluster, Craig, Fill, Gag, Gavage, Neck, Pang, Prime, Rugged, Scar(p), Spur, Stap, Stodge, Stow, Swat, Tuck

Cramp(ed) Agraffe, Charleyhorse, Confine, Constrict, Crick, Hamper, Hamstring, Incommodious, Myalgia, Pinch, Poky, Potbound, Restrict, Rigor, Squeeze, Stunt, Tetany, Writer's

Crane Cherry picker, Davit, Demoiselle, Derrick, Gantry, Herd, Heron, Hooper, Ichabod, Jib, Jigger, Rail, Sarus, Sedge, Shears, Sheer, Siege, Stork, Stretch, Whooper, Winch

Cranium Harnpan

Crash Bingle, Collapse, Dush, Fail, Fall, Fragor, Intrude, Linen, Nosedive, Prang, Rack, Ram, Rote, Shunt, Slam, Smash, Thunderclap, Topple

▷ **Crashes** *may indicate* an anagram

Crate Biplane, Box, Case, Ceroon, Crib, Hamper, Tube

Crave, Craving Appetite, Aspire, Beg, Beseech, Covet, Desire, Entreat, Hanker, Hunger, Itch, Libido, Long, Lust, Malacia, Methomania, Orexis, Pica, Polyphagia, Sitomania, The munchies, Thirst, Yearn, Yen

Crayfish Astacology, Gilgie, Jilgie, Yabbie, Yabby

Crayon Chalk, Colour, Conté®, Pastel, Pencil

Craze(d), Crazy Absurd, Ape, Barmy, Bats, Batty, Berserk, Bonkers, Break, Cornflake, Crack(ers), Crackpot, Cult, Daffy, Dement, Derange, Dingbats, Dippy, Distraught, Doiled, Doilt, Doolally, Dottle, Dotty, Fad, Flake, Flaw, Folie, Frantic, Furious, Furore, Gaga, Geld, Gonzo, Gyte, Haywire, Headbanger, Insane, Loco, Loony, Lunatic, Madden, Maenad(ic), Mania, Manic, Mattoid, Meshug(g)a, Nuts, Porangi, Potty, Psycho(path), Rage, Rave, Scatty, Screwball, Skivie, Stunt, Unhinge, Wacko, Wacky, Wet, W(h)acky, Whim, Wowf, Zany

▷ **Crazy** *may indicate* an anagram

Creak(y) Cry, Grate, Grind, Rheumatic, Scraich, Scraigh, Scroop, Seam, Squeak

Cream(y) Barrier, Bavarian, Best, Chantilly, Cold, Crème fraiche, Devonshire, Double, Elite, Foundation, Glacier, Lanolin, Liniment, Lotion, Mousse, Off-white,

Ointment, Opal, Paragon, Pick, Ream, Rich, Salad, Single, Skim, Vanishing

Crease Crumple, > **FOLD**, Lirk, Pitch, Pleat, Popping, Ridge, Ruck(le), Ruga, Rugose, Wrinkle

Create, Creation, Creative Build, Coin, Compose, Devise, Dreamtime, Engender, Establish, Fabricate, Forgetive, Form, Found, Generate, Genesis, Godhead, Ideate, > **INVENT**, Oratorio, Originate, Produce, Shape, Universe

Creature Animal, Ankole, Basilisk, Beast, Being, Chevrotain, Cratur, Critter, Crittur, Man, Nekton, Sasquatch, Sphinx, Whiskey, Wight

Credible, Credit(s), Creditor Ascribe, Attribute, Belief, Billboard, Byline, Carbon, Crawl, Esteem, Extended, Family, Honour, HP, Kite, Kudos, LC, Lender, Mense, Post-war, Probable, Reliable, Renown, Revolving, Shylock, Social, Strap, Tally, Tick, Title, Trust, Weight, Youth

Creep(er), Creeping, Creeps Ai, Aseismic, Cleavers, Crawl, Grew, Grovel, Grue, Heebie-jeebies, Heeby-jeebies, Herpetic, Inch, Insect, Ivy, Nerd, Nuthatch, Pussyfoot, Repent, Reptant, Sarmentous, Sittine, Skulk, Slink, Snake, Sobole(s), Toad, Truckle, Vine, Virginia, Willies

Crepe Blini, Blintz(e), Canton, Pancake

Crescent Barchan(e), Bark(h)an, Fertile, Lune(tte), Lunulate, Lunule, Meniscus, Moon, Red, Sickle, Waxing

Crest(ed) Acme, Chine, Cimier, Cockscomb, Comb, Copple, Crista, Height, Kirimon, Knap, Mon, Peak, Pileate, Pinnacle, Plume, Ridge, Summit, Tappit, Tee, > **TOP**

Crevice Chine, Cranny, Fissure, Interstice, Ravine, Vallecula

Crew Boasted, Company, Core, Eight, Four, Lot, Manners, Men, Oars, Sailors, Salts, Seamen, Team, Teme

Crib Cheat, Cot, Cowhouse, Cratch, Filch, Horse, > **KEY**, Manger, Pony, Purloin, Putz, Shack, Stall, Steal, Trot

Crime Attentat, Barratry, Caper, Chantage, Chaud-mellé, Computer, Corpus delicti, Ecocide, Fact, Felony, Fraud, Graft, Heist, Iniquity, Malefaction, Mayhem, Misdeed, Misdemeanour, > **OFFENCE**, Organised, Ovicide, Peccadillo, Perjury, Pilferage, Rap, Rape, Rebellion, > **SIN**, Tort, Transgression, Treason, Wrong

Criminal Bandit, Bent, Bushranger, Chummy, Con, Cosa Nostra, Counterfeiter, Crack-rope, > **CROOK**, Culpable, Culprit, Delinquent, Escroc, Felon, Flagitious, Forensic, Gangster, Heavy, Heinous, Highbinder, Hitman, Hood(lum), Jailbird, Ladrone, Lag, Larcener, Lifer, Looter, Lowlife, Maf(f)ia, Malefactor, Maleficent, Malfeasant, Mob(ster), Mobster, Ndrangheta, Nefarious, Nefast, Outlaw, Perp(etrator), Racketeer, Receiver, Recidivist, Reprehensible, Rustler, Sinner, Snakehead, Thug, Triad, Underworld, Villain, Wicked, Wire, Yakuza, Yardie, Yegg

▷ **Criminal** *may indicate* an anagram

Criminologist Lombroso

Cringe, Cringing Cower, Creep, Crouch, Fawn, Grovel, Shrink, Sneaksby, Truckle

Cripple(d) Damage, Disable, Game, Hamstring, Handicap, Injure, > **LAME**, Lameter, Lamiter, Maim, Paralyse, Polio, Scotch, Spoil

Crisis Acme, Crunch, Drama, Emergency, Exigency, Fastigium, Fit, Flap, Head, Identity, Make or break, Panic, Pass, Shake-out, Solution, Test

Crisp Brisk, Clear, Crimp, Crunchy, Fresh, Sharp, Short, Succinct, Terse

Critic(al), Criticise, Criticism Acute, Agate, Armchair, Arnold, Attack, Badmouth, Barrack, Berate, Bird, Blame, Boileau, Boo, Captious, Carp, Castigate, Cavil, Censor(ious), > **CENSURE**, Clobber, Comment, Condemn, Connoisseur, Crab, > **CRUCIAL**, Crunch, Dangle, Decisive, Denigrate, Denounce, Deprecate, Desperate, Diatribe, Earful, Exacting, Excoriate, Fastidious, Fateful, Flak, Flay, Fulminous, Harrumph, Important, Impugn, Inge, Inveigh, Judge, Judgemental, Knife-edge, Knock(er), Lash, Leavis, Literary, Masora(h), Mas(s)orete, Nag,

Nasute, Nibble, Nice, Niggle, Overseer, Pan, Pater, Puff, Pundit, Quibble, Rap, Rebuke, Reprehend, Review(er), Rip, Roast, Ruskin, Scalp, Scarify, Scathe, Scorn, Second guess, Serious, Severe, Shaw, Sideswipe, Slag, Slam, Slashing, Slate, Sneer, Snipe, Stick, Stricture, Strop, Tense, Textual, Threap, Touch and go, Urgent, Vet, Vitriol, Watershed

Croak Creak, Crow, Die, Grumble, Gutturalise

Crockery Ceramics, China, Dishes, Earthenware, Ware

▷ **Crocks** *may indicate* an anagram

Crocodile Cayman, File, Garial, Gavial, Gharial, Line, Mugger, River-dragon, Saltwater, Sebek, Teleosaur(ian)

Croft Pightle

Crook(ed) Adunc, Ajee, Awry, Bad, Bend, Bow, Cam, Camsheugh, Camsho(ch), Criminal, Cromb, Crome, Crosier, Crummack, Crummock, Crump, Curve, Elbow, Fraud, Heister, Hook, Indirect, Kam(me), Kebbie, Lituus, Malpractitioner, Shyster, Sick, Skew(whiff), Slick(er), Staff, Swindler, Thraward, Thrawart, Thrawn, Twister, Wonky, Yeggman

▷ **Crooked** *may indicate* an anagram

Crop(s), Cropped Basset, Browse, Cash, Catch, Clip, Craw, Cut, Distress, Dock, Emblements, Epilate, Eton, Foison, Forage, Harvest, Hog, Not(t), Plant, Poll, Produce, Riding, Rod, Root, Shingle, Stow, Succession, Top, Truncate

Cross(ing), Crossbred Angry, Ankh, Ansate, Archiepiscopal, Banbury, Basta(a)rd, Beefalo, Boton(n)e, Burden, Calvary, Cantankerous, Canterbury, Capital, Cattalo, Celtic, Channel, Chi, Chiasm(a), Clover-leaf, Compital, Constantine, Crosslet, Crotchety, Crucifix, Crux, Decussate, Demi-wolf, Dihybrid, Double, Dso(m)o, Dzobo, Eleanor, Encolpion, Faun, Fiery, Fitché, Fleury, Foil, Footbridge, Ford, Frabbit, Fractious, Frampold, Franzy, Funnel, Fylfot, Geneva, George, Grade, Greek, Holy rood, Hybrid, Ill, Imp, Indignant, Interbreed, Intersect, Intervein, Iona, Iracund, Irate, Irked, Iron, Jerusalem, Jomo, Jumart, Kiss, Ladino, Latin, Level, Liger, Lorraine, Lurcher, Maltese, Mameluco, Market, Mermaid, Military, Mix, Moline, Mongrel, Mule, Narky, Nattery, Node, Norman, Northern, Nuisance, Obverse, Ordinary, Orthodox, Overpass, Overthwart, Papal, Patonce, Patriarchal, Pattée, Pectoral, Pedestrian, Pelican, Plus, Pommé, Potence, Potent, Preaching, Puffin, Quadrate, Ratty, Reciprocal, Red, Roman, Rood, Rose, Rouen, Rouge, Rubicon, Sain, St Andrew's, St Anthony's, St George's, St Patrick's, St Peter's, Saltier, Saltire, Satyr, Shirty, Sign, Snappy, Southern, Strid, Svastika, Swastika, T, Tangelo, Tau, Tayberry, Ten, Testy, Thraw, Thwart, Tiglon, Tigon, Times, Transit, Transom, Transverse, Traverse, Tree, Urdé, Vexed, Vext, Victoria, > **VOTE**, Weeping, Whippet, Wry, X, Zebra(ss), Z(h)o, Zobu

▷ **Cross** *may indicate* an anagram

▶ **Crossbeam** *see* **CROSSPIECE**

Cross-examine Grill, Interrogate, Question, Targe

Crosspiece, Cross-bar, Cross-beam, Cross-timber Bar, Cancelli, Footrail, Inter-tie, Lierne, Phillipsite, Putlock, Putlog, Quillon, Serif, Seriph, Stempel, Stemple, Stretcher, Stull, Swingle-tree, Toggle, Transom, Trave, Whiffle-tree, Whipple-tree, Yoke

Crossword Cryptic, Grid, Puzzle, Quickie

Crouch Bend, Cringe, Falcade, Fancy, Lordosis, Ruck, Set, Squat, Squinch

Crow Boast, Brag, Carrion, Chewet, Chough, Corbie, Corvus, Crake, Currawong, Daw, Gorcrow, Hooded, Hoodie, Huia, Jackdaw, Jim(my), Murder, Raven, Rook, Skite, Squawk, Swagger, Vaunt

Crowd(ed) Abound, Army, Bike, Boodle, Bumper, Bunch, Byke, Caboodle, Clutter, Concourse, Congest(ed), Cram, Crush, Crwth, Dedans, Doughnut, Drove, Fill, Flock, Galere, Gate, Gathering, Herd, Horde, > **HOST**, Huddle, Hustle, Jam, Lot,

Mein(e)y, Meinie, Menyie, Mob, Mong, Multitude, Ochlo-, Pack, Pang, Press, Rabble, Raft, Ram, Ratpack, Ring, Ruck, Scrooge, Scrouge, Scrowdge, Scrum, Serr(é), Shoal, Shove, Slew, Slue, Squeeze, Stuff, Swarm, Swell, Three, Throng, Trinity, Varletry

Crown Acme, Bays, Bull, Camp, Cantle, Cap, Capernoity, Cidaris, Civic, Coma, Corona, Cr, Diadem, Ecu, Engarland, Enthrone, Fillet, Garland, Gloria, Haku, Head, Headdress, Instal, Iron, Ivy, Krantz, Laurel, Monarch, Mural, Naval, Nole, Noll, Noul(e), Nowl, Olive, Ore, Ovation, Pate, Peak, Pschent, Sconce, Taj, Tiara, > **TOP**, Triple, Triumphal, Trophy, Vallary, Vertex

Crucial Acute, Critical, Essential, Key, Pivotal, Vital, Watershed

Crude(ness) Bald, Brash, Brute, Coarse, Earthy, Halfbaked, Immature, Incondite, Primitive, Raunch, Raw, Rough, Rough and ready, Rough-hewn, Rough-wrought, Tutty, Uncouth, Vulgar, Yahoo

Cruel(ty) Barbarous, Bloody, Brutal, Dastardly, De Sade, Draconian, Fell, Fiendish, Flinty, Hard, Heartless, Immane, Inhuman, Machiavellian, Neronic, Pitiless, Raw, Remorseless, Stern, Tormentor, Vicious

▷ **Cruel** *may indicate* an anagram

Cruise(r) Busk, Cabin, Nuke, Prowl, Sail, Ship, Tom, Travel, Trip, Voyager

Crumb(le), Crumbly, Crumbs Coo, Decay, Disintegrate, Ee, Fragment, Friable, Law, Leavings, Moulder, Mull, Murl, Nesh, Nirl, Ort, Particle, Ped, Raspings, Rot

Crunch(y) Chew, Craunch, Crisp, Gnash, Grind, Munch, Occlude, Scranch

Crush(ed), Crusher Acis, Anaconda, Annihilate, Bow, Champ, Comminute, Conquer, Contuse, Cranch, Crunch, Defeat, Destroy, Graunch, Grind, Hug, Jam, Knapper, Levigate, Mangle, Mash, Mill, Molar, Mortify, Oppress, Overcome, Overwhelm, Pash, Policeman, Pound, Press, Pulp, Pulverise, Quash, Ruin, Schwarmerei, Scotch, Scrum, Scrumple, Smash, Squabash, Squash, Squeeze, Squelch, Squish, Stamp, Stave, Steam-roll, Stove, Suppress, Telescope, Trample, Tread

Crust(y) Argol, Beeswing, Cake, Coating, Coffin, Continental, Cover, Crabby, Craton, Fur, Gratin, Heel, Horst, Kissing, Kraton, Lithosphere, Osteocolla, Pie, Reh, Rind, Rine, Sal, Salband, Scab, Shell, Sial, Sima, Sinter, Surly, Tartar, Teachie, Terrane, Tetchy, Upper, Wine-stone

Crustacea(n) Amphipod, Barnacle, Cirriped, Copepod, Crab, Crayfish, Cyclops, Cyprid, Cypris, Decapod(a), Entomostraca, Fishlouse, Foot-jaw, Gribble, Isopod, Krill, Lobster, Marron, Nauplius, Ostracoda, Prawn, Sand-hopper, Scampi, Shrimp, Slater, Squilla, Woodlouse

Cry(ing) Aha, Alalagmus, Alew, Banzai, Bark, Battle, Bawl, Bell, Blat, Bleat, Bleb, Blub(ber), Boo, Boohoo, Bray, Bump, Caramba, Caw, Cheer, Chevy, Chirm, Chivy, Clang, Crake, Croak, Crow, Dire, Euoi, Eureka, Evoe, Exclaim, Fall, Field-holler, Gardyloo, Gathering, Geronimo, Gowl, Greet, Halloo, Harambee, Haro, Harrow, Havoc, Heigh, Hemitrope, Herald, Hinny, Hoicks, Holler, Honk, Hoo, Hoop, Hosanna, Hout(s)-tout(s), Howl, Humph, Io, Kaw, Low, Mewl, Mlaou, Miau(l), Miserere, Mourn, Night-shriek, O(c)hone, Oi, Olé, Ow, Pugh, Rallying, Rivo, Sab, Scape, Scream, Screech, Sell, Sese(y), Sessa, > **SHOUT**, Shriek, Slogan, Snivel, Snotter, Sob, Soho, Sola, Squall, Squawk, Street, Tally-ho, Tantivy, Umph, Vagitus, View-halloo, Vivat, Vociferate, Wail, War, Watchword, Waul, Wawl, Weep, Westward ho, Whee(ple), Whimper, Whine, Whinny, Whoa, Whoop, Winge, Wolf, Yammer, Yelp, Yicker, Yikker, Yip, Yippee, Yodel, Yo-heave-ho, Yo-ho-ho, Yoick, Yoop, Yowl

Crypt(ic) Catacomb, Cavern, Chamber, Crowde, Encoded, Favissa, Grotto, Hidden, Obscure, Occult, Secret, Sepulchre, Short, Steganographic, Tomb, Unclear, Undercroft, Vault

Cryptaesthesia ESP

Crystal(lise), Crystal-gazer, Crystalline Allotriomorphic, Baccara(t), Beryl, Candy, Clear, Copperas, Coumarin, Cumarin, Dendrite, Druse, Enantiomorph, Epitaxy, Geode, Glass, Hemitrope, Ice-stone, Jarosite, Lead, Liquid, Love-arrow, Macle, Melamine, Nicol, Orthogonal, Pellucid, Phenocryst, Piezo, Pinacoid, Pinakoid, Prism, Pseudomorph, Purin(e), Quartz, R(h)aphide, R(h)aphis, Rhinestone, Rock, Rotenone, Rubicelle, Scryer, Shoot, Skryer, Snowflake, Sorbitol, Spar, Table, Trichite, Trilling, Watch-glass, Xenocryst

Cub Baby, Kit, Novice, Pup, Whelp

Cubicle Alcove, Booth, Carrel(l), Stall

Cuckoo Ament, Ani, April fool, Bird, Gouk, Gowk, Inquiline, Insane, Koel, > **MAD**, Mental, Piet-my-vrou, Stupid

▷ **Cuckoo** *may indicate* an anagram

Cuddle Canoodle, Caress, Clinch, Embrace, Fondle, Hug, Nooky, Smooch, Smuggle, Snuggle

Cue Cannonade, Catchword, Feed, Half-butt, Hint, Mace, > **PROMPT**, Reminder, Rod, Sign, Signal, Wink

Cuisine Cookery, Food, Menu, Nouvelle

Cult Cabiri, Cargo, Creed, Sect, Worship

Cultivate(d), Cultivation Agronomy, Arty, Civilise, Dig, Dress, Farm, Genteel, Grow, Hoe, Hydroponics, Improve, Labour, Pursue, Raise, Refine, Sative, Sophisticated, Tame, Tasteful, Till, Tilth

Culture(d), Cultural Acheulean, Acheulian, Agar, Art(y), Aurignacian, Azilian, Bel esprit, Brahmin, Capsian, Civil(isation), Ethnic, Experiment, Explant, Gel, Grecian, Hallstatt, Hip-hop, Humanism, Kultur(kreis), La Tène, Learning, Mousterian, Polish, Refinement, Solutrean, Sophisticated, Strepyan, Tissue

Cunning Arch, Art, Artifice, Cautel, Craft(y), Deceit, Deep, Devious, Down, Finesse, Foxy, Insidious, Leery, Machiavellian, Quaint, Skill, Slee(kit), Sleight, Slim, Sly(boots), Smart, Sneaky, Subtle, Vulpine, Wile

Cup(s), Cupped Aecidium, America's, Beaker, Calcutta, Calix, Calyculus, Cantharus, Chalice, Claret, Cotyle, Cruse, Cupule, Cyathus, Cylix, Davis, Demitasse, Dish, Dop, European, FA, Fairs, Final, Fingan, Finjan, Glenoid, Goblet, Grace, Hanap, Horn, Kylix, Loving, Melbourne, Merry, Monstrance, Moustache, Mug, Noggin, Nut, Pannikin, Planchet, Plate, Pot, Procoelous, Quaich, Quaigh, Rhyton, Rider, Ryder, Sangrado, Scyphus, Stirrup, Tantalus, Tass(ie), Tastevin, Tazza, Tea-dish, Tig, Tot, > **TROPHY**, Tyg, UEFA, Volva, World

Cupboard Almery, Almirah, A(u)mbry, Beauf(f)et, Cabinet, Chiffonier, Chiff(o)robe, Closet, Court, Credenza, Dresser, Locker, Press

Cupid Amoretto, Amorino, Archer, Blind, Cherub, Dan, Eros, Love, Putto

Curator Aquarist

Curb Bit, Brake, Bridle, Check, Clamp, Coaming, Dam, Edge, Puteal, Rein, Restrain, Rim, Snub

Cure(d), Curative Amend, Antidote, Antirachitic, Bloater, Cold turkey, Dry-salt, Euphrasy, Ginseng, Heal, Hobday, Jadeite, Jerk, Kipper, Medicinal, Nostrum, Panacea, Park-leaves, > **PRESERVE**, Recover, Recower, Reest, Remede, Remedy, Restore, Salt, Salve, Serum, Smoke, Smoke-dry, Tan, > **TREATMENT**, Tutsan

▷ **Cure** *may indicate* an anagram

Curfew Gate, Prohibit, Proscribe

Curio, Curiosity, Curious Agog, Bibelot, Freak, Inquisitive, Meddlesome, Nos(e)y, Objet d'art, Objet de vertu, Odd, Peculiar, Prurience, Rarity, Rum, > **STRANGE**

▷ **Curious(ly)** *may indicate* an anagram

Curl(s), **Curler**, **Curling**, **Curly** Bonspiel, Cirrus, Coil, Crimp, Crimple, Crinkle, Crisp, Crocket, Earlock, Friz(z), Frizzle, Heart-breaker, Hog, Inwick, Kiss, Leaf, Loop, Love-lock, Outwick, Perm, Pin, Quiff, Repenter, Ringlet, Roll, Roulette, Shaving, Spiral, Spit, Twiddle, > **TWIST**, Wave, Wind

Currant Berry, Raisin, Rizard, Rizzar(t), Rizzer

Currency Cash, Circulation, > **COIN**, Coinage, Decimal, Euro, Finance, Jiao, Kip, Koruna, Monetary, > **MONEY**, Prevalence

▷ **Currency** *may indicate* a river

Current Abroad, AC, Actual, Alternating, Amp(ere), Amperage, California, Canary, Contemporaneous, Cromwell, DC, Direct, Draught, Drift, Dynamo, Ebbtide, Electric, El Nino, Equatorial, Euripus, Existent, Flow, Foucault, Going, Humboldt, I, Immediate, Inst, Intermittent, Japan, Kuroshio, Labrador, Millrace, Modern, Newsy, Now, Ongoing, Present, Prevalent, Race, Rapid, Rife, Rip, Roost, Running, Stream, Thames, Thermal, Thermionic, Tide, Topical, Torrent, Turbidity, Underset, Undertow

Curry Bhuna, Brush, Comb, Cuittle, Dhansak, Fawn, Groom, Ingratiate, Korma, Spice, Tan, Turmeric, Vindaloo

Curse Abuse, Anathema, Badmouth, Ban, Bane, Beshrew, Blast, Chide, Dam(me), Damn, Dee, Drat, Ecod, Egad, Excommunicate, Execrate, Heck, Hex, Imprecate, Jinx, Malison, Maranatha, Mau(l)gré, Mockers, Moz(z), Mozzle, Nine (of diamonds), Oath, Paterson's, Pize, Plague, Rant, Rats, Scourge, 'Snails, Spell, Swear, Upbraid, Weary, Winze, Wo(e)

Curtain(s), **Curtain-rod** Arras, Backdrop, Bamboo, Canopy, Caudle, Cloth, Death, Demise, Drape, Drop, Dropcloth, Dropscene, Fatal, Hanging, Iron, Louvre, Net, Pall, Portière, Purdah, Safety, Scene, Screen, Scrim, Tab, Tormentor, Tringle, Vail, Valance, Veil, Vitrage

Curtsey Bob, Bow, Dip, Dop

Curvature, **Curve(d)**, **Curvaceous**, **Curvy** Aduncate, Arc, Arch, Archivolt, Axoid, Bend, Bow, Camber, Catacaustic, Catenary, Caustic, Cissoid, Conchoid, Contrapposto, Crescent, Cycloid, Entasis, Epinastic, Ess, Evolute, Exponential, Extrados, Felloe, Felly, Geodesic, Gooseneck, Growth, Hance, Helix, Hodograph, Hyperbola, Inswing, Intrados, Isochor, J, Jordan, Laffer, Learning, Lemniscate, Limacon, Lituus, Lordosis, Loxodrome, Nowy, Ogee, Parabola, Pothook, Rhumb, Roach, Rotundate, Scoliosis, Sheer, Sinuate, Spiral, Spiric, Strophoid, Swayback, Tie, Trajectory, Trochoid, Twist, Witch (of Agnesi)

Cushion(s) Air, Allege, Bolster, Buffer, Hassock, > **PAD**, Pillow, Pouf(fe), Pulvillus, Soften, Squab, Upholster, Whoopee

Custodian, **Custody** Care, Claviger, Guard, Hold, Janitor, Keeping, Sacrist, Steward, Trust, Ward

Custom(ised), **Customs (officer)**, **Customary** Agriology, Coast-waiters, Consuetude, Conventional, Couvade, De règle, Douane, Exciseman, Familiar, Fashion, Folklore, > **HABIT**, Lore, Manner, Montem, Mores, Nomic, Octroi, Ordinary, Practice, Praxis, Relic, Rite, Routine, Rule, Sororate, Sunna, Tax, Thew, Tidesman, Tradition, Unwritten, Usance, Used, Usual, Won, Wont, Woon, Zollverein

Customer Client, Cove, Patron, Prospect, Purchaser, Shillaber, Shopper, Smooth, Trade, Trick

Cut(ter), **Cutting** Abate, Abjoint, Abridge, Abscond, Acute, Adeem, Adze, Aftermath, Ali Baba, Amputate, Axe, Bang, Bisect, Bit, Bite, Bowdlerise, Boycott, Brilliant, Broach, Caesarean, Caique, Canal, Cantle, Caper, Carver, Castrate, Caustic, Censor, Chap, Chisel, Chopper, Circumscribe, Cleaver, Clinker-built, Clip, Colter, Commission, Concise, Coulter, Coupé, Crew, Crop, Cruel, Curtail, Deadhead, Decrease, Dicer, Die, Discide, Disengage, Dismember, Dissect,

Division, Divorce, Dock, Dod, Edge, Edit, Embankment, Engraver, Entail, Epistolary, Epitomise, Eschew, Excalibur, Excide, Excise, Exscind, Exsect, Exude, Fashion, Fell, Fillet, Flench, Flense, Flinch, Form, Froe, Frow, Garb, Gash, Grater, Graven, Gride, Gryde, Hack, Handsaw, Hew(er), Ignore, Incision, Incisor, Indent, Intersect, Jigsaw, Joint, Junk, Kerf, Kern, Kirn, Lacerate, Lance, Leat, Lesion, Lin, Lop, Math, Medaillon, Microtome, Milling, Mohel, Mortice, Mortise, Mower, Nick, Not, Notch, Nott, Occlude, Omit, Open, Operate, Oxyacetylene, Padsaw, Pare, Pink, Plant, Pliers, Ploughshare, Pollard, Pone, Power, Precisive, Proin, Quota, Race, Rake off, Rase, Razor, Reap, Rebate, Reduction, Re-enter, Resect, Retrench, Revenue, Ring, Ripsaw, Roach, Rose, Rout, Saddle, Sarcastic, Saw(n), Scarf, Scathing, Scion, Scission, Scissor, Score, Sculpt, Scye, Scythe, Secant, Secateurs, Sect, Sever, Sey, Share(out), Shaver, Shears, Shingle, Ship, Shorn, Short, Shred, Shun, Sickle, Sirloin, Skip, Slane, Slash, Slicer, Slip, Slit, Sloop, Sned, Snee, Snib, Snick, Snip, Snub, Spade, Spin, Spud, Steak, Stencil, Stir, Stramazon, Style, Surgeon, Tailor(ess), Tart, Tenderloin, Tomial, Tonsure, Tooth, Topside, Transect, Trash, Trench, Trenchant, Trepan, Trim, Truant, Truncate, Urchin, Whang, Whittle

▷ **Cut** *may indicate* an anagram

▷ **Cutback** *may indicate* a reversed word

Cute Ankle, Pert, Pretty, Taking

Cutlery Canteen, Flatware, Fork, Knife, Setting, Silver, Spoon, Tableware, Trifid

Cycle, **Cyclist** Anicca, Arthurian, Bike, Biorhythm, Cal(l)ippic, Calvin, Carbon, Carnot, Cell, Circadian, Daisy, Eon, Era, Fairy, Frequency, Heterogony, Indiction, Ko, Krebs, Life, Metonic, Oestrus, Orb, Otto, Pedal, Peloton, Period, Repulp, Revolution, Ride, Roadster, Rota, Round, Samsara, Saros, Scorch, Series, Sheng, Solar, Song, Sonnet, Sothic, Spin, TCA, Trike, Turn, UCI, Water, Wheeler, Wheelman, Wu

Cyclone Storm, Tornado, Typhoon, Willy-willy

Cylinder, **Cylindrical** Clave, Column, Drum, Pipe, Roll, Rotor, Slave, Spool, Steal, Stele, Terete, Torose, Treadmill, Tube

Cyst Atheroma, Bag, Blister, Chalazion, Dermoid, Hydatid, Impost(h)ume, Meibomian, Ranula, Sac, Vesicle, Wen

Dd

Dab(s) Bit, Daub, Fish, Flounder, Pat, Print, Ringer, Smear, Spot, Stupe, Whorl

Dad(dy) Blow, Dev(v)el, Father, Generator, Hit, Male, Pa(pa), Pater, Polt, Pop, Slam, Sugar, Thump

Daffodil Asphodel, Jonquil, Lent-lily, Narcissus

Daft Absurd, Crazy, Potty, Ridiculous, Silly, Simple, Stupid

Dagger(s) An(e)lace, Ataghan, Baselard, Bayonet, Bodkin, Crease, Creese, Da(h), Diesis, Dirk, Double, Dudgeon, Han(d)jar, Hanger, Jambiya(h), Katar, Kindjahl, Kirpan, Kreese, Kris, Lath, Misericord(e), Obelisk, Obelus, Poi(g)nado, Poniard, Puncheon, Sgian-dubh, Skean, Skene(-occle), Stiletto, W(h)inger, Whiniard, Whinyard, Yatag(h)an

Daily Adays, Char, Circadian, Diurnal, Domestic, Guardian, Help, Journal, Mail, Mirror, Paper, Per diem, Quotidian, Rag, Regular, Scotsman, Sun, Tabloid

Dainty Cate(s), Cute, Delicacy, Elegant, Elfin, Entremesse, Entremets, Exquisite, Junket, Lickerish, Liquorish, Mignon(ne), > **MORSEL**, Neat, Nice, Particular, Petite, Pussy, Sunket, Twee

Dairy Creamery, Loan, Parlour

Daisy African, Bell, Felicia, Gowan, Hen and chickens, Livingstone, Michaelmas, Ox-eye, Shasta, Transvaal

Dale(s) Dell, Dene, Dingle, Glen, Vale, Valley

Dam An(n)icut, Arch, Aswan, Bar, Barrage, Barrier, Block, Boulder, Bund, Cabora Bassa, Cauld, Check, Gravity, Hoover, Kariba, Kielder, Ma, Mater, Obstacle, Obstruct, Pen, Stank, > **STEM**, Sudd, Turkey nest, Weir, Yangtze

Damage(d), **Damages**, **Damaging** Bane, Banjax, Bruise, Buckle, Charge, Contuse, Cost, Cripple, Dent, Desecrate, Detriment, Devastate, Devastavit, Estrepe, Fault, Flea-bite, Harm, Havoc, Hit, Hole, Hurt, Impair, Injury, Loss, Mar, Mayhem, Moth-eaten, Nobble, Prang, Price, Retree, Sabotage, Scaith, Scath(e), Scotch, Scratch, Skaith, Smirch, Solatium, > **SPOIL**, Tangle, Toll, Value, Vandalise, Violate, Wear and tear, Wing, Wound, Wreak, Wreck

▷ **Damage(d)** *may indicate* an anagram

Dame Crone, Dowager, Edna, Gammer, Lady, Matron, Nature, Naunt, Partlet, Peacherino, Sis, Title(d), Trot, Woman

Damn(ation), **Damned** Accurst, Attack, Blame, Condemn, Curse, Cuss, Darn, Dee, Execrate, Faust, Hell, Hoot, Jigger, Malgre, Perdition, Predoom, Sink, Swear, Very

Damp(en), **Damping** Aslake, Black, Check, Clam(my), Dank, Dewy, Fousty, Humid, Moist, Muggy, Raw, Rheumy, Rising, Roric, Soggy, Sordo, Sultry, Unaired, > **WET**

Dance(r), **Dancehall**, **Dancing** Astaire, Baladin(e), Ballabile, Ballant, Ballerina, Ballroom, Bayadère, Bob, Body-popping, Caper, Chorus-girl, Contredanse, Corybant, Coryphee, Dervish, Diaghilev, Dinner, Disco, Dolin, Exotic, Figurant, Foot, Gandy, Gigolo, Hetaera, Hetaira, Hoofer, Kick-up, Knees-up, Leap, Maenad, Modern, Nautch-girl, Night, Nijinsky, Nureyev, Oberek, Old-time, Palais, Partner, Pavlova, Petipa, Pierette, Raver, Ring, St Vitus, Salome, Saltatorious, Skipper,

Spring, Step, Strut, Table, Tea, Terpsichore, Tread, Trip(pant), Vogue(ing), Whirl
▷ **Dancing** *may indicate* an anagram

Danger(ous) Apperil, Breakneck, Crisis, Dic(e)y, Dire, Emprise, Fear, Hairy,
Hazard, Hearie, Hot, Insecure, Jeopardy, Lethal, Menace, Mine, Nettle, Nocuous,
Parlous, Pitfall, Precarious, Quicksand, Risk, Serious, Severe, Snag, Tight, Trap

Dangle A(i)glet, Aiguillette, Critic, Flourish, Hang, Loll, Swing

Dank Clammy, Damp, Humid, Moist, Wet, Wormy

Dare, **Dare-devil**, **Daring** Adventure, Bold, Brave, Challenge, Courage,
Da(u)nton, Defy, Durst, Emprise, Face, Gallant, Gallus, Hardihood, Hazard, Hen,
Prowess, Racy, Taunt, Venture

Dark(en), **Darkie**, **Darkness** Aphelia, Aphotic, Apophis, Black, Blind,
Cimmerian, Cloud, Depth, Dim, Dingy, Dirk(e), Dusky, Eclipse, Erebus, Evil, Gloom,
Glum, Inumbrate, Mare, Maria, Melanous, Mulatto, Murk(y), Negro, Night,
Obfuscate, Obscure, Ominous, Ousel, Ouzel, Pall, Phaeic, Pitch-black, Pit-mirk,
Rooky, Sable, Sad, Secret, Shady, Shuttered, Sinister, Solein, Sombre, Sooty,
Sphacelate, Sullen, Swarthy, Tar, Tenebr(i)ous, Tenebrose, Unfair, Unlit, Wog,
Woosel, Yellowboy, Yellowgirl

Darling Acushla, Alannah, Asthore, Beloved, Charlie, Cher, Chéri(e),
Chick-a-biddy, Chick-a-diddle, Chuck-a-diddle, Dear, Dilling, Do(a)ting-piece,
Duck(s), Favourite, Grace, Honey, Idol, Jarta, Jo(e), Lal, Love, Luv, Mavourneen,
Mavournin, Minikin, Minion, Oarswoman, Own, Peat, Pet, Poppet, Precious,
Sugar, Sweetheart, Yarta, Yarto

Dart(er) Abaris, Arrow, Banderilla, Dace, Dash, Deadener, Dodge, Fleat,
Fléchette, Flit, Harpoon, Javelin, Launch, Leap, Scoot, Skrim, Speck, Spiculum,
Strike, Thrust, Wheech

Dash(ing), **Dashed** Backhander, Bally, Blade, Blight, Blow, Buck, Charge, Collide,
Cut, Dad, Dah, Damn, Dapper, Dart(le), Daud, Debonair, Ding, Elan, En, Flair, Fly,
Go-ahead, Hang, Hurl, > **HURRY**, Hustle, Hyphen, Impetuous, Jabble, Jaw, Jigger,
Lace, Line, Minus, Morse, Natty, Nip, Panache, Pebble, Rakish, Ramp, Rash,
Rule, Run, Rush, Sally, Scamp(er), Scart, Scoot, Scrattle, Scurry, Scuttle, Shatter,
Showy, Soupçon, Souse, Spang, Speed, Splash, Splatter, Sprint, Strack, Streak,
Stroke, > **STYLE**, Swung, Throw, Touch

Data(base), **Datum** Archie, Evidence, Facts, Fiche, File, Floating-point, Gen,
Info, Input, Material, Matrix, News

Date(d), **Dates**, **Dating** AD, Age, AH, Almanac, Appointment, Blind, Boyfriend,
Calendar, Carbon, Carbon-14, Computer, Court, Deadline, Engagement, Epoch,
Equinox, Era, Escort, Exergue, Expiry, Fixture, Girlfriend, Ides, Julian, Meet,
Outmoded, Passé, Past, Radio-carbon, Rubidium-strontium, See, System,
Ult(imo)

Daunt Adaw, Amate, Awe, Deter, Dishearten, Intimidate, Overawe, Quail, Stun,
Stupefy, Subdue

Dawdle(r) Dally, Draggle, Drawl, Idle, > **LOITER**, Potter, Shirk, Slowcoach, Troke,
Truck

Dawn Aurora, Cockcrow, Daw, Daybreak, Day-peep, Dayspring, Eoan, Eos, False,
Light, Morrow, Occur, Prime, Start, Sunrise

Day(s) Account, Ahemeral, All Fools', All Hallows', All Saints', All Souls', Anniversary,
Annunciation, Anzac, April Fool's, Armistice, Ascension, Australia, Bad hair, Baker,
Banian, Bastille, Boxing, Calendar, Calends, Calpa, Canada, Civil, Columbus,
Commonwealth, Contango, D, Daft, Date, Decoration, Degree, Distaff, Dog,
Dominion, Duvet, Early, Ember, Empire, Epact, Fast, Fasti, Father's, Feast,
Ferial, Field, Flag, Fri, Gang, Gaudy, Groundhog, Guy Fawkes', Halcyon, High,
Hogmanay, Holy, Holy Innocents', Holy-rood, Hundred, Ides, Inauguration,
Independence, Intercalary, Judgment, Judicial, Kalends, Kalpa, Labo(u)r, Lady,

Lammas, Law(ful), Lay, Leap, Mardi, May, Memorial, Michaelmas, Midsummer, Mon, Morrow, Mother's, Muck-up, Mufti, Mumping, Name, New year's, Nones, Oak-apple, Octave, Open, Orangeman, Pancake, Paper, Pay, Poppy, Pound, Present, Primrose, Pulvering, Quarter, Rag, Rainy, Red-letter, Remembrance, Rest, Robin, Rock, Rogation, Rood(-mas), Rosh Chodesh, Sabbath, Saint's, St Swithin's, St Valentine's, Salad, Sat, Settling, Show, Sidereal, Snow, Solar, Solstice, Speech, Sports, Station, Sun, Supply, Tag, Term, Thanksgiving, Thurs, Ticket, Time, Transfer, Trial, Tues, Twelfth, Utas, Valentine's, Varnishing, VE, Veterans', Victoria, Visiting, VJ, Wed, Wedding, Working

Daydream(er) Brown study, Dwam, Fancy, Imagine, Muse, Reverie, Rêveur, Walter Mitty

Daze(d) Amaze, Bemuse, Confuse, Dwaal, Gally, Muddle, Muzzy, Reeling, > **STUN**, Stupefy, Stupor, Trance

Dazzle(d), **Dazzling** Bewilder, Blend, Blind, Eclipse, Foudroyant, Glare, Meteoric, Outshine, Radiance, Resplendent, Splendour, Yblent

Dead(en) Abrupt, Accurate, Alamort, Asgard, Asleep, Blunt, Bung, Cert, Cold, Complete, D, Deceased, Defunct, Doggo, Expired, Extinct, Gone(r), Inert, Infarct, Late, Lifeless, Muffle, Mute, Napoo, Numb, Obsolete, Obtund, Ringer, She'ol, Smother, Stillborn, True, Utter, Waned

Dead end, **Deadlock** Cut-off, Dilemma, Impasse, Logjam, Stalemate, Stoppage

Deadline Date, Epitaph, Limit

Deadly Baleful, Dull, Fell, Funest, Internecine, > **LETHAL**, Malign, Mortal, Pestilent, Unerring, Venomous

Deal(er), **Dealings**, **Deal with** Address, Agent, Agreement, Allot(ment), Arb, Arbitrageur, Bargain, Breadhead, Brinjarry, Broker, Business, Cambist, Chandler, Chapman, Commerce, Cope, Coup, Cover, Croupier, Dispense, Distributor, Do, Dole, Eggler, Exchange, Fripper, Goulash, Hand(le), Help, Inflict, Insider, Interbroker, Jiggery-pokery, Jobber, Lashing, Lay on, Lay out, Let, Manage, Mercer, Merchant, Mickle, Middleman, Monger, Mort, Negotiate, New, Operator, Package, Pine, Productivity, Pusher, Raft, Raw, Sale, Serve, Side, Sort, Spicer, Square, Stockist, Stockjobber, Takeover, Tape, Timber, Tout(er), > **TRADE**, Traffic, Transaction, Treat, Truck, Wheeler, Wholesaler, Wield, Woolstapler, Yardie

Dear(er), **Dearest**, **Dear me** Ay, Bach, Beloved, Cara, Caro, Cher(e), Cherie, Chuckie, Darling, Duck(s), Expensive, High, Honey(bun), Lamb, Leve, Lief, Lieve, Loor, Love, Machree, Mouse, My, Pet, Steep, Sweet, Toots(ie), Up

Death(ly) Bane, Bargaist, Barg(h)est, Black, Cataplexis, Charnel, Curtains, Cypress, Demise, Departure, Dormition, End, Eschatology, Euthanasia, Exit, Extinction, Fatality, Funeral, Gangrene, Grim Reaper, Hallal, Infarction, Jordan, Lethee, Leveller, Necrosis, Nemesis, Night, Obit, Quietus, Reaper, Sati, Sergeant, SIDS, Small-back, Strae, Sudden, Suttee, Terminal, Thanatism, Thanatopsis, Thanatos

Deathless(ness) Athanasy, Eternal, Eterne, Immortal, Struldberg, Timeless, Undying

Debag Dack

Debase(d) Adulterate, Allay, Bemean, Corrupt, Demean, Depreciate, Dialectician, Dirty, Grotesque, Hedge, Lower, Pervert, Traduce, Vitiate

Debate Argue, Combat, Contention, Contest, Deliberate, Dialectic, Discept, Discuss(ion), > **DISPUTE**, Flyte, Forensics, Moot, Polemics, Reason, Teach-in, Warsle, Wrangle, Wrestle

Debris Bahada, Bajada, Detritus, Eluvium, Moraine, Moslings, Refuse, Ruins, Tephra, Waste

▷ **Debris** *may indicate* an anagram

Debt(or) Alsatia, Arrears, Arrestee, Dr, Due, Floating, Funded, Insolvent, IOU,

Liability, Moratoria, National, Obligation, Poultice, Public, Queer Street, Score, Tie, Unfunded

Debt-collector Bailiff, Forfaiter, Remembrancer

Decadence, Decadent Babylonian, Decaying, Degeneration, Dissolute, Effete, Fin-de-siècle, Libertine

▷ **Decapitated** *may indicate* first letter removed

Decay(ed), Decaying Alpha, Appair, Beta, Biodegrade, Blet, Canker, Caries, Caseation, Crumble, Decadent, Declension, Decline, Decompose, Decrepit, Dieback, Disintegrate, Doat, Doddard, Doddered, Dote, Dricksie, Druxy, Dry rot, Fail, F(o)etid, Forfair, Gangrene, Heart-rot, Impair, Moulder, Pair(e), Plaque, Putrefy, Ret, Rot, Saprogenic, Sap-rot, Seedy, Sepsis, Spoil, Tabes, Wet-rot

Decease(d) Death, Decedent, Demise, Die, Stiff

Deceit(ful), Deceive(r) Abuse, Artifice, Bamboozle, Befool, Bitten, Blind, Bluff, > CHEAT, Chicane, Chouse, Cozen, Cuckold, Defraud, Delude, Diddle, Dissemble, Double-cross, Dupe, Duplicity, False(r), Fast-talk, Fiddle, Flam, Fox, Fraud, Gag, Guile, Gull, Hoax, Hoodwink, Humbug, Hype, Imposition, Inveigle, Invention, Kid, Mislead, Poop, Poupe, Pretence, Punic, Rig, Ruse, Sell, Sham, Sinon, Spruce, Stratagem, Swindle, Swizzle, Trick, Trump, Two-time, Wile

Decency, Decent Chaste, Decorum, Fitting, Healsome, Honest, Kind, Modest, Seemly, Sporting, Wholesome

Deception, Deceptive Artifice, Bluff, Catchpenny, Catchy, Cheat, Chicanery, Codology, > DECEIT, Disguise, Dupe, Duplicity, Eyewash, Fallacious, False, Flam, Fraud, Gag, Gammon, Guile, Have-on, Hocus-pocus, Hokey-pokey, Hum, Hunt-the-gowks, Hype, Ignes-fatui, Ignis-fatuus, Illusion, Insidious, Lie, Moodies, Runaround, Ruse, Sell, Sleight, Smoke and mirrors, Specious, Sting, The moodies, > TRICK, Trompe l'oeil, Two-timing, Underhand

Decide(r), Decided Addeem, Agree, Ballot, Barrage, Cast, Clinch, Conclude, > DECISION, Deem, Definite, Determine, Distinct, Firm, Fix, Jump-off, Mediate, Opt, Parti, Predestination, Pronounced, Rescript, > RESOLVE, Rule, Run-off, See, Settle, Tiebreaker, Try

Decipher(ing) Cryptanalysis, Decode, Decrypt, Descramble, Discover, Interpret

▷ **Decipher(ed)** *may indicate* an 'o' removed

Decision Arbitrium, Arrêt, Crossroads, Crunch, Decree, Fatwa, Fetwa, Firman, Judg(e)ment, Placit(um), Referendum, Resolution, Resolve, Responsa, Ruling, Sentence, Verdict

Decisive Climactic, Clincher, Critical, Crux, Definite, Final, Pivotal

Deck Adorn, Array, Attrap, Bejewel, Boat, Cards, Clad, Daiker, Daub, Decorate, Dizen, Embellish, Equip, Flight, Focsle, Forecastle, Garland, Hang, Helideck, Hurricane, Lower, Orlop, Pack, Platform, Poop, Prim, Promenade, Quarter, Sun, Tape, Upper, Void

Declare, Declaration, Declaim, Decree Absolute, Affidavit, Affirm, Air, Allege, Announce, Assert, Asseverate, Aver, Avow, Balfour, Bann(s), Breda, Dictum, Diktat, Doom, Edict, Enact, Fatwa(h), Fiat, Firman, Go, Grace, Harangue, Insist, Interlocutory, Irade, Law, Mandate, Manifesto, Meld, Mou(th), Nisi, Noncupate, Novel(la), Nullity, Orate, Ordain, Order, Ordinance, Parlando, Pontificate, Proclaim, Profess, Promulgate, Pronounce, Protest, Publish, Rant, Recite, Rescript, Resolve, Rights, Rule, Ruling, SC, Sed, Signify, Speak, Spout, State, Testify, Testimony, UDI, Ultimatum, Unilateral, Vie, Voice, Vouch, Word

▷ **Declaring** *may indicate* a word beginning 'Im'

Decline, Declining Age, Ail, Atrophy, Catabasis, Comedown, Decadent, Degeneration, Degringoler, Deny, Descend, Deteriorate, Devall, Die, Dip, Dissent, Downhill, Downtrend, Downturn, Droop, Dwindle, Ebb, Fade, Fall, Flag, Forbear, Paracme, Quail, Recede, Recession, Refuse, Retrogression, Rot, Rust, Sag, Senile,

Set, Sink, Slide, Slump, Stoop, Wane, Welke, Withdraw, Wither

Decorate(d), Decoration, Decorative Adorn, Angelica, Attrap, Award, Baroque, Beaux-arts, Bordure, Braid, Brooch, Cartouche, Centrepiece, Champlevé, Chinoiserie, Christingle, Cinquefoil, Cloissoné, Crocket, Dentelle, Diamante, Doodad, Dragée, Emblazon, Emboss, Embrave, Enrich, Epergne, Etch, Fancy, Festoon, Filigree, Finial, Fleuron, Floriated, Frieze, Frill, Frog, Furbish, Garniture, Gaud, Goffer, Gradino, Guilloche, Ice, Illuminate, Impearl, Inlay, Intarsia, Intarsio, Interior, Knotwork, Linen-fold, Marquetry, MC, Medal(lion), Moulding, Oath, OBE, Order, > ORNAMENT, Ornate, Orphrey, Ovolo, Paint, Paper, Parament, Pokerwork, Prettify, Prink, Purfle, Rag-rolling, Rangoli, Repoussé, Rich, Ruche, Scallop, Scrimshaw, Set-off, Sgraffito, Soutache, Spangle, Staffage, Stomacher, Strapwork, Tailpiece, Tattoo, TD, Titivate, Tool, Topiary, Trim, Wallpaper

Decoy Allure, Bait, Bonnet, Button, Call-bird, Coach, Crimp, Entice, Lure, Piper, Roper, Ruse, Shill, Stale, Stalking-horse, Stool-pigeon, Tole, Toll, Trap, Trepan

Decrease Decrew, Diminish, Dwindle, Iron, Lessen, Press, Reduce, Rollback, Step-down, Subside, Wane, Wanze

Decree > DECLAIM

Decrepit Dilapidated, Doddery, Failing, Feeble, Frail, Moth-eaten, Tumbledown, Warby, Weak

Dedicate(d), Dedication Corban, Devote, Endoss, Hallow, Inscribe, Oblate, Pious, Sacred, Votive

Deduce, Deduction, Deductive A priori, Assume, Conclude, Consectary, Corollary, Derive, Discount, Gather, Illation, Infer(ence), Reason, Rebate, Recoup, Reprise, Stoppage, Surmise, Syllogism

Deed(s) Achievement, Act(ion), Atweel, Backbond, Charta, Charter, Derring-do, Escrol(l), Escrow, Exploit, Fact(um), Indeed, Indenture, Manoeuvre, Mitzvah, Muniments, Specialty, Starr, > TITLE

Deep(en), Deeply Abstruse, Bass(o), Brine, Briny, Enhance, Excavate, Grum, Gulf, Hadal, Intense, Low, Mindanao, Mysterious, > OCEAN, Profound, Re-enter, Rich, Sea, Sonorous, Throaty, Upsee, Ups(e)y

Deer(-like) Axis, Bambi, Barasing(h)a, Barking, Brocket, Buck, Cariacou, Carjacou, Cervine, Chevrotain, Chital, Doe, Elaphine, Elk, Fallow, Gazelle, Hart, Moose, Mouse, Mule, Muntjac, Muntjak, Musk, Père David's, Pricket, Pudu, Red, Rein, Roe, Rusa, Sambar, Sambur, Selenodont, Sika, Sorel(l), Spade, Spay(d), Spayad, Spitter, Spottie, Stag(gard), Tragule, Ungulate, Virginia, Wapiti

▷ **Defaced** *may indicate* first letter missing

Defame, Defamatory, Defamation Abase, Blacken, Calumny, Cloud, Denigrate, Detract, Dishonour, Impugn, Libel, Mud, Mudslinging, Scurrilous, Slander, Smear, Stigmatise, Traduce, Vilify

Default(er) Absentee, Bilk, Dando, Delinquent, Flit, Levant, Neglect, Omission, Waddle, Welsh

Defeat(ed), Defeatist Beat, Best, Caning, Capot, Codille, Conquer, Counteract, Debel, Defeasance, Demolish, Discomfit, Dish, Ditch, Fatalist, Floor, Foil, Foyle, Hammer, Hiding, Kippered, Laipse, Lick, Loss, Lurch, Marmelize, Master, Mate, Negative, Out, Outclass, Outdo, Outplay, Outvote, Outwit, > OVERCOME, Overpower, Overreach, Overthrow, Overwhelm, Pip, Reverse, Rout, Rubicon, Scupper, Set, Shellacking, Sisera, Squabash, Stump, Tank, Thrash, Thwart, Tonk, Trounce, Vanquish, War, Waterloo, Whap, Whip, Whitewash, Whop, Whup, Wipe-out, Worst

Defect(ion), Defective, Defector Abandon, Amateur, Apostasy, Bug, Coma, Faulty, Flaw, Frenkel, Halt, Hamartia, Kink, Manky, Mote, Natural, Renegade, Renegate, Ridgel, Ridgil, Rig, Rogue, Runagate, Shortcoming, Spina bifida,

Terrace, Treason, Trick, Want, Weakness

Defence, Defend(er), Defensible Abat(t)is, Alibi, Antibody, Antidote, Antihistamine, Apologia, Back, Bailey, Barbican, Barmkin, Barricade, Bastion, Battery, Battlement, Berm, Bridgehead, Bulwark, Calt(h)rop, CD, Champion, Civil, Curtain, Demibastion, Ditch, Embrasure, Hedgehog, Herisson, Hold, J(i)u-jitsu, Justify, Kaim, Keeper, Laager, Laer, Maintain, Martello Tower, Miniment, Moat, Muniment, Outwork, Palisade, Parapet, Rampart, Redan, Redoubt, Resist, Ringwall, > **SHELTER**, Shield, Stonewall, Support, Tenail(le), Testudo, Tower, Trench, Trou-de-loup, Uphold, Vallation, Vallum, Vindicate, Wall, Warran(t)

Defenceless Helpless, Inerm, Naked, Sitting duck, Vulnerable

Defendant Accused, Apologist, Respondent, Richard Roe

Defer(ence), Deferential Bow, Delay, Dutiful, Homage, Morigerous, Obeisant, Pace, Polite, Postpone, Procrastinate, Protocol, Respect, Shelve, Submit, Suspend, Waive, Yield

Defiance, Defiant, Defy Acock, Bold, Brave, Dare, Daring, Disregard, Do or die, Outbrave, Outdare, Recusant, Stubborn, Titanism, Truculent, Unruly

Deficiency, Deficient Absence, Acapnia, Anaemia, Beriberi, Defect, Inadequate, Incomplete, Lack, Scant, Scarcity, SCID, Shortage, Spanaemia, Want

▷ **Deficient** *may indicate* an anagram

Deficit Anaplerotic, Arrears, Defective, Ischemia, Loss, Poor, Shortfall

Define(d), Definition, Definitive Decide, Demarcate, Determine, Diorism, Distinct, Explain, Fix, Limit, Parameter, Set, Tangible, Term

Definite(ly) Classic, Clear, Emphatic, Firm, Hard, Positive, Precise, Specific, Sure, Yes

Deflate Burst, Collapse, Flatten, Lower, Prick

Deflect(or), Deflection Avert, Bend, Detour, Diverge, Divert, Glance, Otter, Paravane, Refract, Snick, Swerve, Throw, Trochotron, Veer, Windage

Deform(ed), Deformity Anamorphosis, Blemish, Crooked, Disfigure, Distort, Gammy, Hammer-toe, Harelip, Mishapt, Mutilate, Polt-foot, Stenosed, Talipes, Valgus, Warp

▷ **Deformed** *may indicate* an anagram

Defraud Bilk, Cheat, Cozen, Gyp, Mulct, Sting, Swindle, Trick

Degrade, Degradation Abase, Cheapen, Culvertage, Debase, Demote, Diminish, Disennoble, Humble, Imbase, Lessen, Lower, > **SHAME**, Waterloo

Degree(s) Aegrotat, As, Azimuthal, BA, Baccalaureate, BCom, BD, B es S, C, Class, D, Doctoral, Engler, Extent, External, F, First, German, Gradation, Grade, Grece, Gree(s), Greece, Gre(e)se, Grice, Griece, Grize, K, Lambeth, Latitude, Letters, Level, Licentiate, MA, Measure, Mediant, Nuance, Peg, PhD, Pin, Poll, Rate, Remove, Second, Stage, Status, Step, Third, Water

Deject(ed), Dejection Abase, Abattu, Alamort, Amort, Chap-fallen, Crab, Crestfallen, Despondent, Dismay, Dispirited, Downcast, Gloomy, Hangdog, Humble, Melancholy

Delay(ed) Ambage, Avizandum, Behindhand, Check, Cunctator, Defer, Demurrage, Detention, Fabian, Filibuster, For(e)slow, Forsloe, Frist, Hesitate, Hinder, Hitch, Hold up, Hysteresis, Impede, Laches, Lag, Late, Laten, Let, Linger, Mora(torium), Obstruct, Procrastinate, Prolong, Prorogue, Remanet, Reprieve, Respite, Retard, Setback, Slippage, Sloth, Slow, > **STALL**, Stand-over, Stay, Stonewall, Temporise, Wait

Delegate, Delegation Agent, Amphictyon, Apostolic, Appoint, Assign, Decentralise, Depute, Devolution, Mission, Nuncio, Offload, Representative, Secondary, Transfer, Vicarial, Walking

Delete Cancel, Cut, Erase, Expunge, Purge, Rase, Scratch, Scrub

Deliberate(ly) Adagio, Consider, Debate, Intentional, Meditate, Moderate, Ponder, Prepensely, Studied, Voulu, Weigh, Witting

Delicacy, **Delicate** Airy-fairy, Beccafico, Canape, Cate, Caviare, Dainty, Difficult, Discreet, Ectomorph, Eggshell, Elfin, Ethereal, Fastidious, Fine, Finespun, Finesse, Flimsy, Fragile, > **FRAIL**, Friand, Gossamer, Guga, Hothouse, Inconie, Incony, Ladylike, Light, Lobster, Nesh, Nicety, Niminy-piminy, Oyster, Reedy, Roe, Sensitive, Soft, Subtle(ty), Sunket, Taste, Tender, Tenuous, Ticklish, Tidbit, Titbit, Truffle

Delicious Ambrosia, Delectable, Exquisite, Fragrant, Goloptious, Goluptious, Gorgeous, Lekker, Lip-smacking, Mor(e)ish, Mouthwatering, Scrummy, Scrumptious, Tasty, Toothsome, Yummy, Yum-yum

▷ **Delight** *may indicate* 'darken'

Delight(ed), **Delightful** Bliss, Chuff, Delice, Dreamy, Elated, Enamour, Enjoyable, Enrapture, Exuberant, Felicity, Fetching, Frabjous, Gas, Glad, Glee, Gratify, Honey, Joy, Overjoy, Please, Pleasure, > **RAPTURE**, Regale, Scrummy, Super, Taking, Turkish, Whacko, Whee, Whoopee, Yippee, Yum-yum

Delinquent Bodgie, Criminal, Halbstarker, Negligent, Offender, Ted

Delirious, **Delirium** Deranged, DT, Frenetic, Frenzy, Insanity, Mania, Phrenetic, Spazz, Wild

Deliver(ance), **Deliverer**, **Delivery** Accouchement, Ball, Birth, Bowl, Caesarean, Consign, Convey, Deal, Escape, Give, Lead, Liberate, Orate, Over, Pronounce, Recorded, Redeem, Release, Relieve, Render, Rendition, > **RESCUE**, Rid, Round(sman), Salvation, Save, Say, Seamer, Sell, Shipment, Speak, Special, Tice, Transfer, Underarm, Underhand, Utter, Wide, Yorker

Dell Dale, Dargle, Dene, Dimble, Dingle, Dingl(e)y, Glen, Valley

Delude, **Delusion** Bilk, Cheat, Deceive, Fallacy, Fool, Hoax, > **MISLEAD**, Trick

Delve Burrow, Dig, Excavate, Exhume, Explore, Probe, Search

Demand(ing) Appetite, Call, Claim, Cry, Dun, Exact, Exigent, Fastidious, Final, Hest, > **INSIST**, Market, Need, Order, Postulate, Pressure, Request, Requisition, Rush, Sale, Stern, Stipulate, Stringent, Summon, Ultimatum, Want

Demean(ing) Comport, Debase, Degrade, Lower, Maltreat

Dement(ed) Crazy, Hysterical, Insane, Mad

Demo March, Parade, Protest, Rally, Sit-in

Democracy, **Democrat** D, Locofoco, Montagnard, Popular, Republic, Sansculotte, Social, Tammany

Demolish, **Demolition** Bulldoze, Devastate, Devour, Floor, KO, Level, Rack, Smash, Wreck

▶ **Demon** *see* **DEVIL**

Demonstrate, **Demonstration**, **Demonstrator** Agitate, Barrack, Display, Endeictic, Evènement, Evince, Explain, Maffick, Manifest, March, Morcha, Ostensive, Portray, Protest, Prove, Provo, > **SHOW**, Sit-in, Touchy-feely

Demoralize Bewilder, Corrupt, Destroy, Shatter, Unman, Weaken

Demote, **Demotion** Comedown, Degrade, Disbench, Embace, Embase, Reduce, Relegate, Stellenbosch

Demure Coy, Mim, Modest, Prenzie, Primsie, Sedate, Shy

Den Dive, Domdaniel, Earth, Hell, Hide-away, Holt, Home, Lair, Lie, Room, Shebeen, Study, Sty, Wurley

Denial, **Deny**, **Denier** Abnegate, Antinomian, Aspheterism, Bar, Contradict, Démenti, Disavow, Disenfranchise, Disown, Forswear, Nay, Negate, Nick, Protest, Refuse, Refute, Renague, Renay, Reneg(e), Renegue, Reney, Renig, Renounce, Reny, Repudiate, Sublate, Withhold

Denote Import, Indicate, Mean, Signify

Denounce, Denunciation Ban, Commination, Condemn, Criticise, Decry, Diatribe, Hatchet job, Hereticate, Proclaim, Proscribe, Shop, Stigmatise, Upbraid

Density Compact, D, Firm, Opaque, Relative, Solid, Spissitude, Tesla, Thick, Woofy

Dent(ed) Batter, Dancette, Depress, Dimple, Dinge, Dint, Nock, V

Dental, Dentist(ry) DDS, Extractor, Kindhart, LDS, Odontic, Periodontic, Toothy

▶ **Deny** *see* DENIAL

Depart(ed), Departing, Departure Abscond, Absquatulate, Bunk, D, Dead, Decession, Defunct, Die, Digress, Divergence, Exit, Exodus, Flight, > GO, Leave, Lucky, Outbound, Remue, Vade, Vamoose, Walkout

Department Achaea, Ain, Aisne, Allier, Angers, Arcadia, Ardeche, Ardennes, Argo, Arrondissement, Arta, Attica, Aube, Aude, Belfort, Branch, Bureau, Calvados, Cantal, Cher, Commissariat, Cote d'Or, Cotes d'Armor, Cotes du Nord, Creuse, Deme, Deux-Sevres, Division, Dordogne, Essonne, Faculty, Finistere, FO, Gard, Gironde, Greencloth, Guadeloupe, Gulag, Hanaper, Isere, Jura, Loire, Lot, Lot-et-Garonne, Ministry, Nome, Nomos, Office, Oise, Orne, Province, Region, Savoie, Secretariat(e), Section, Somme, Sphere, State, Treasury, Tuscany, Var, Vienne, Wardrobe, Yonne

Depend(ant), Dependency, Dependent Addicted, Child, Client, Colony, Conditional, Contingent, Count, Dangle, Fief, Habit, Hang, Hinge, Icicle, Lean, Minion, Pensioner, Relier, Rely, Retainer, Sponge, Subject, Trust, Turn on, Vassal

Dependable Reliable, Reliant, Secure, Solid, Sound, Staunch, Sure, > TRUSTWORTHY

▷ **Deploy(ment)** *may indicate* an anagram

Deport(ment) Address, Air, Banish, > BEARING, Carriage, Demeanour, Mien, Renvoi, Renvoy

Depose, Deposition Affirm, Banish, Dethrone, Displace, Dispossess, Overthrow, Pieta, Testify

Deposit Alluvial, Alluvium, Arcus, Argol, Atheroma, Bank, Bathybius, Bergmehl, Calc-sinter, Calc-tuff, Caliche, Cave-earth, Coral, Crag, Delta, Depone, Diluvium, Evaporite, Fan, File, Firn, Fur, Gyttja, Kieselguhr, Land, Lay, Lodge(ment), Loess, Löss, Measure, Natron, Outwatch, Park, Placer, Plank, Plaque, Put, Repose, Residuum, Saburra, Saprolite, > SEDIMENT, Silt, Sinter, Sludge, Stockwork, Stratum, Surety, Tartar, Terramara, Terramare, Tophus, Turbidite

Depot Barracoon, Base, Camp, Depository, Station, Terminus, Treasure-city, Warehouse

Deprav(ed), Depravity Bestial, Cachexia, Cachexy, > CORRUPT, Dissolute, Evil, Immoral, Low, Rotten, Sodom, Turpitude, Ugly, Vice, Vicious, Vile

Depress(ed), Depressing, Depression Alamort, Amort, Black dog, Blight, Blues, Cafard, Canada, Canyon, Chill, Col, Combe, Couch, Crab, Crush, Cyclone, Dampen, Deject, Dell, Dene, Dent, Despair, Dip, Dismal, Dispirit, Drear, Drere, Dumpish, Exanimate, Flatten, Foss(ula), Fossa, Glen, Gloom, Ha-ha, Hammer, Hilar, Hilum, Hilus, Hollow, Howe, Hyp, Joes, Kettle, Kick(-up), Lacuna, Leaden, Low(ness), Low-spirited, Moping, Neck, Pit, Postnatal, Prostrate, Recession, Re-entrant, Sad, Saddle, Salt-cellar, Salt-pan, Sink, Sinkhole, Sinus, Slot, > SLUMP, Soakaway, Spiritless, Sump, Swag, Swale, Trench, Trough, Vale, Valley, Wallow

Deprivation, Deprive(d) Bereft, Deny, Disenfranchise, Disfrock, Disseise, Disseize, Expropriate, Geld, Have-not, Hunger, Reduce, Remove, Rob, Withhold

Depth F, Fathom, Gravity, Intensity, Isobath, Pit, Profundity

Deputise, Deputy Act, Agent, Aide, Assistant, Commis(sary), Delegate, Legate,

Lieutenant, Locum, Loot, Number two, Proxy, Represent, Secondary, Standby, Sub, Substitute, Succentor, Surrogate, Vicar, Vice, Viceregent, Vidame

Derange(d) Craze, Détraqué, Disturb, Insane, Manic, Troppo, Unhinge, Unsettle

Derelict Abandoned, > DECREPIT, Deserted, Negligent, Outcast, Ramshackle

Deride, **Derision**, **Derisive** Contempt, Gup, Guy, Hoot, Jeer, Mock, Nominal, Raspberry, > RIDICULE, Sardonic, Scoff, Scorn, Snifty, Snort, Yah, Ya(h)boo

Derive, **Derivation**, **Derivative** Ancestry, Creosote, Deduce, Descend, Extract, Get, Kinone, Of, Offshoot, Origin, Pedigree, Secondary

Descend(ant), **Descent** Ancestry, Avail, Avale, Bathos, Blood, Chute, Cion, Decline, Degenerate, Derive, Dismount, Dive, Drop, Epigon, Extraction, Heir, Heraclid, Offspring, Pedigree, Prone, Rappel, Said, Say(y)id, Scarp, Scion, Seed, Shelve, Sien(t), Sink, Stock, Syen, Vest, Volplane

Describe, **Description**, **Descriptive** Blurb, Define, Delineate, Depict, Designate, Draw, Epithet, Exposition, Expound, Graphic, Job, Narrate, Outline, Paint, Portray, Rapportage, Recount, Relate, Report, Sea-letter, Sketch, Specification, Synopsis, Term, Trace

▷ **Describing** may indicate 'around'

Desecrate, **Desecration** Abuse, Defile, Dishallow, Profane, Sacrilege, Unhallow

▷ **Desecrated** may indicate an anagram

Desert(er), **Deserted**, **Desert(s)** Abandon, Apostasy, Arabian, Arid, Arunta, Atacama, AWOL, Badland, Barren, Bug, Bunk, D, Defect, Desolate, Dissident, Due, Empty, Eremic, Factious, Fail, Foresay, Forhoo, Forhow, Forlorn, Forsake, Forsay, Gibson, Gila, Gobi, Great Basin, Great Sandy, Great Victoria, Heterodox, Kalahari, Libyan, Lurch, Merit, Mojave, Nafud, Namib, Negev, Nubian, Ogaden, Painted, Pategonian, Pindan, Rat, Refus(e)nik, Reg, > RENEGADE, Reward, Run, Sahara, Sands, Secede, Simpson, Sinai, Sonoran, Sturt, Syrian, Tergiversate, Turncoat, Void, Wadi, Waste, Worthiness

Deserve(d) Condign, Earn, > MERIT, Well-earned, Worthy

Design(er) Adam, Aim, Architect, Ashley, Batik, Broider, Cardin, Cartoon, Chop, Cloisonné, Create, Cul de lampe, Damascene, Decor, Depict, Devise, Dévoré, Dior, Draft, Embroidery, End, Engine(r), Engineer, Erté, Etch, Fashion, Former, Hepplewhite, Hitech, Iconic, Impresa, Imprese, Intend(ment), Intent(ion), Interior, Layout, Linocut, Logo, Marquetry, Mean, Meander, Modiste, Monogram, Morris, Mosaic, Motif, > PLAN, Plot, Propose, Pyrography, Quant, Ruse, Schema, Scheme, Seal, Sheraton, Sketch, Specification, Stencil, Stubble, Tatow, Tattoo, Tatu, Think, Tooling, Trigram, Vignette, Watermark, Whittle

Desirable, **Desire**, **Desirous** Ambition, Appetite, Aspire, Avid, Best, Cama, Conation, Concupiscence, Covet, Crave, Cupidity, Dreamboat, Earn, Eligible, Epithymetic, Fancy, Gasp, Hanker, Hope, Hots, Hunger, Itch, Kama(deva), Le(t)ch, Libido, List, Long, Luscious, Lust, Mania, Nymphomania, Orectic, Owlcar, Plum, Reck, Request, Residence, Salt, Streetcar, Thirst, Velleity, Vote, Wanderlust, Want, Whim, Will, Wish, Yearn, Yen

Desk Almemar, Ambo, Bureau, Carrel(l), Cash, Check-in, Cheveret, City, Copy, Davenport, Desse, Devonport, Enquiry, E(s)critoire, Faldstool, Lectern, Lettern, Litany, Pay, Pedestal, Prie-dieu, Pulpit, Reading, Roll-top, Scrutoire, Secretaire, Vargueno, Writing

Desolate, **Desolation** Bare, Barren, Desert, Devastate, Disconsolate, Forlorn, Gaunt, Gousty, Moonscape, Waste, Woebegone

Despair, **Desperate**, **Desperation** Acharne, De profundis, Despond, Dire, Extreme, Frantic, Gagging, Giant, Gloom, Hairless, Headlong, Reckless, Unhopeful, Urgent, Wanhope

▶ **Despatch** see DISPATCH

Despise Condemn, Contemn, Forhow, Hate, Ignore, Scorn, Spurn, Vilify, Vilipend

Despite For, Malgré, Notwithstanding, Pace, Though, Venom

Despot(ism) Autarchy, Autocrat, Caesar, Darius, Dictator, Napoleon, Nero, Satrap, Stratocrat, Tsar, Tyrant, Tzar

Dessert Afters, Baked Alaska, Baklava, Bavarian Cream, Bavarois, Bombe, Charlotte, Charlotte russe, Cobbler, Compote, Coupe, Crème brulée, Crème caramel, Entremets, Flummery, Fool, Junket, Kissel, Knickerbocker glory, Kulfi, Marquise, Mousse, Mud pie, Nesselrode, Parfait, Pashka, Pavlova, Peach Melba, > **PUD(DING)**, Sabayon, Sawine, Semifreddo, Shoofly pie, Strudel, Sundae, Syllabub, Tiramisu, Tortoni, Trifle, Vacherin, Zabaglione

Destine(d), Destination Design, End, Fate, Foredoom, Goal, Home, Intend, Joss, Port, Purpose, Weird

Destiny Doom, > **FATE**, Karma, Kismet, Lot, Manifest, Moira, Yang, Yin

Destroy(er) Annihilate, Apollyon, Atomise, Blight, D, Decimate, Deface, Delete, Demolish, Denature, Destruct, Dish, Dismember, Dissolve, Eat, Efface, End, Eradicate, Erase, Exterminate, Extirpate, Fordo, Harry, Iconoclast, > **KILL**, Murder, Obliterate, Overkill, Perish, Predator, Ravage, Raze, Ruin, Saboteur, Scuttle, Slash, Smash, Spif(f)licate, Sterilize, Stew-can, Stonker, Subvert, Undo, Uproot, Vandal, Vitiate, Whelm, Wreck, Zap

Destruction, Destructive Adverse, Bane, Can, Collapse, Deathblow, Deleterious, Devastation, Doom, Downfall, End, Götterdämmerung, Grave, Havoc, Holocaust, Insidious, Internecine, Kali, Lethal, Loss, Pernicious, Rack, Ragnarok, Ravage, Sabotage, Stroy, Wrack

Detach(ed), Detachment Abstract, Alienate, Aloof, Body, Calve, Clinical, Cut, Detail, Discrete, Isolate, Loose, Outlying, Outpost, Patrol, Separate, Sever, Staccato, Stoic, Unfasten, Unhinge

Detail(s), Detailed Annotate, Dock, Elaborate, Embroider, Expatiate, Explicit, Expound, Instance, > **ITEM**, Itemise, Minutiae, Nicety, Particular(ise), Pedantry, Point, Recite, Relate, Respect, Send, Spec, Special, Specification, Technicality

▷ **Detailed** *may indicate* last letter missing

Detain(ee), Detention Arrest, Buttonhole, Collar, Custody, Delay, Detinue, Gate, Glasshouse, Hinder, Intern, Keep, POW, Retard, Stay, > **WITHHOLD**

Detect(or), Detective Agent, Arsène, Asdic, Bloodhound, Brown, Bucket, Busy, Catch, Chan, CID, Cuff, Dick, Discover, Divine, Doodlebug, Dupin, Espy, Eye, Fed, Find, Flambeau, Flic, Fortune, French, Geigercounter, Geophone, Gumshoe, Hanaud, Hercule, Holmes, Interpol, Investigator, Jack, Lecoq, Lupin, Maigret, Minitrack®, Nose, Peeper, PI, Pinkerton, Plant, Poirot, Private eye, Prodnose, Radar, Reagent, Rumble, Scent, Scerne, Sense, Sensor, Shadow, Shamus, Sherlock, Sofar, Sonar, Sonobuoy, Spot, Tabaret, Take, Tec, Thorndyke, Toff, Trace, Trent, Vance, Wimsey, Yard

Deter(rent) Block, Check, Daunt, Dehort, Delay, Dissuade, Prevent, Restrain, Turn-off

Detergent Cleaner, Solvent, Surfactant, Syndet, Tepol, Whitener

Deteriorate, Deterioration Decadence, Degenerate, Derogate, Pejoration, Rust, Worsen

▷ **Deterioration** *may indicate* an anagram

▷ **Determination** *may indicate* 'last letter'

Determine(d), Determination Arbitrament, Ardent, Ascertain, Assign, Assoil, Bent, Condition, Dead-set, > **DECIDE**, Define, Doctrinaire, Dogged, Dour, Drive, Earnest, Fix, Govern, Grit(ty), Headstrong, Hell-bent, Indomitable, Influence, Intent, Judgement, Law, Out, Point, Purpose, Quantify, > **RESOLUTE**, Resolve, Rigwiddie, Rigwoodie, Self-will, Set, Settle, Shape, Stalwart, Steely, Type, Weigh

Detest(able) Abhor, Despise, Execrable, Execrate, Hate, Loathsome, Pestful, Vile
Detonate, Detonator Blast, Explode, Fire, Fuse, Fuze, Ignite, Kindle, Plunger, Primer, Saucisse, Saucisson, Tetryl, Trip-wire
Detour Bypass, Deviate, Divert
Detract Belittle, Decry, Diminish, Discount, Disparage
Devalue Debase, Reduce, Undermine
Devastate Demolish, Destroy, Overwhelm, Ravage, Sack, Waste
Develop(er), Developed, Developing, Development Advance, Breed, Build, Educe, Elaborate, Enlarge, Escalate, Evolve, Expand, Expatriate, Fulminant, Germinate, Gestate, Grow, Hatch, Hypo, Imago, Improve, Incubate, Larva, Mature, Metamorphose, Metol, Pathogeny, Pullulate, Pupa, Pyro, Quinol, Ribbon, Ripe(n), Shape, Soup, Sprawl, Unfold, Upgrow
▷ **Develop** *may indicate* an anagram
Deviant, Deviate, Deviation Aberrance, Abnormal, Anomaly, Brisure, Deflect, Depart, Derogate, Digress, Diverge, Divert, Error, Kurtosis, Pervert, Quartile, Sheer, Solecism, Sport, Stray, Swerve, > TURN, Valgus, Varus, Veer, Wander, Wend
Device Appliance, Artifice, Contraption, Contrivance, Dodge, Emblem, Expedient, Gadget, Gimmick, Gubbins, Instrument, Logo, Mnemonic, Pattern, Plan, > STRATAGEM, Subterfuge, Tactic, Tag, Trademark, Trick
Devil(ish), Demon Abaddon, Afrit, Apollyon, Asmodeus, Auld Hornie, Beelzebub, Belial, Buckra, Clootie, Cloots, Deev, Deil, Demon, Deuce, Diable, Diabolic, Dickens, Div, Drudge, Eblis, Familiar, Fiend, Ghoul, Hornie, Iblis, Imp, Incubus, Infernal, Lucifer, Mahoun(d), Mephisto(pheles), Mischief, Nick, Old Nick, Rahu, Ralph, Satan, Satyr, Scratch, Succubine, Succubus, Tasmanian, Tempter, Wicked, Worricow
Devious Braide, Cunning, Deep, Eel(y), Erroneous, Evasive, Implex, Indirect, Scheming, Shifty, Stealthy, Subtle, Tortuous, Tricky
Devise(d) Arrange, Contrive, Decoct, Hit-on, Imagine, Invenit, Invent, Plot
Devote(e), Devotion(al), Devoted Addiction, Aficionado, Angelus, Attached, Bhakti, Consecrate, Corban, Dedicate, Employ, Fan, Fervid, Fiend, Holy, Hound, Loyalty, Novena, Passion, Pious, Puja, Religioso, Solemn, True, Zealous
Devour(ing) Consume, Eat, Engorge, Engulf, Manducate, Moth-eat, Scarf, Scoff, > SWALLOW
▷ **Devour** *may indicate* one word inside another
Devout Holy, Pious, Reverent, Sant, Sincere
Dew(y) Bloom, Moist, Mountain, Rime, Roral, Roric, Rorid, Roscid, Serene, Tranter
Diagnose, Diagnosis Findings, Identify, Scan, Scintigraphy
Diagonal(ly) Bias, Cater(-corner), Counter, Oblique, Slant, Solidus, Twill
Diagram Argand, Butterfly, Chart, Compass rose, Decision tree, Drawing, Feynman, Figure, Graph, Graphics, Grid, Map, Plan, Plat, Scatter, Schema, Stemma, Stereogram, Venn
Dial(ling) Card, Face, Mug, Phiz, Phone, STD, Visage
Dialect Accent, Burr, Eldin, Erse, Eye, Franconian, Gascon, Geordie, Idiom, Ionic, Isogloss, Jargon, Jockney, Ladin, Lallans, Landsmaal, Langue d'oui, Lingo, Low German, Norman, Norn, Parsee, Patois, Prakrit, Romansch, Scouse, Taal, Tongue, Yenglish, Yinglish
Dialogue Colloquy, Conversation, Critias, Discussion, Exchange, Lazzo, Pastourelle, Speech, Stichomythia, Talk, Upspeak
Diameter Breadth, Calibre, Gauge, Width
Diamond(s), Diamond-shaped Adamant, Black, Boart, Brilliant, Bristol,

Carbonado, Cullinan, D, DE, Delaware, Eustace, Florentine, Hope, Ice, Isomer, Jim, Koh-i-noor, Lasque, Lattice, Lozenge, Paragon, Pick, Pitch, Pitt, Rhinestone, Rhomb, Rock, Rose-cut, Rosser, Rough, Sancy, Solitaire, Spark, Sparklers, Squarial, Suit

Diary, Diarist Chronicle, Dale, Day-book, Evelyn, Hickey, Journal, Kilvert, Log, Nobody, Pepys, Pooter, Record

Dice(r), Dicey Aleatory, Astragals, Bale, Bones, Chop, Craps, Cube, Dodgy, Fulham, Fullams, Fullans, Gourd(s), Highman, Jeff, Shoot, Snake-eyes, Tallmen

▷ **Dick** *may indicate* a dictionary

▷ **Dicky** *may indicate* an anagram

Dictate, Dictator(ial) Amin, Autocrat, Caesar, Castro, Cham, Command, Czar, Decree, Demagogue, Despot, Duce, Franco, Fu(e)hrer, Gauleiter, Hitler, Impose, Lenin, Ordain, Peremptory, Peron, Salazar, Shogun, Stalin, Tell, Tito, Totalitarian, Tsar, Tyrant, Tzar

Dictionary Alveary, Calepin, Chambers, Etymologicon, Fowler, Gazetteer, Glossary, Gradus, Hobson-Jobson, Idioticon, Johnson's, Larousse, Lexicon, Lexis, OED, Onomasticon, Thesaurus, Webster, Wordbook

Die(d), Dying Ache, Cark, Choke, Crater, Croak, Cube, D, Decadent, Desire, End, Evanish, Exit, Expire, Fade, Fail, Forfair, Fulham, Fulhan, Fullam, Go, Highman, Hop, Kark, Long, Morendo, Moribund, Ob(iit), Orb, Pass, Perdendosi, Perish, Peter, Snuff, Solidum, Sphacelation, Stamp, Sterve, Succumb, Suffer, Swage, Swelt, Tine, Wane

Diesel Red

Diet(er) Assembly, Bant(ing), Council, Dail, Eat, Fare, Hay, Intake, Landtag, Lent, Macrobiotic, Parliament, Reduce, Regimen, Reichstag, Slim, Solid, Sprat, Staple, Strict, Tynwald, Vegan, Vegetarian, Weightwatcher, Worms

Differ(ence), Differing, Different(ly) Allo, Barney, Change, Cline, Contrast, Deviant, Diesis, Disagree, Discord, Discrepant, Disparate, Dispute, Dissent, Distinct, Diverge, Diverse, Else, Elsewise, Nuance, Omnifarious, Other, Othergates, Otherguess, Otherness, Otherwise, Separate, Several, Tiff, Unlike, Variform, Various, Vary

Difficult(y) Abstruseness, Ado, Aporia, Arduous, Augean, Badass, Balky, Ballbuster, Bitter, Block, Bolshie, Bother, Catch, Choosy, Complication, Corner, Deep, Depth, Dysphagia, Extreme, Fiddly, Formidable, Gordian, > **HARD**, Hassle, Hazard, Hiccup, Hobble, Hole, Ill, Impasse, Indocile, Intractable, Jam, Kink, Knot, Lurch, Mulish, Net, Nodus, Obstacle, Parlous, Pig, Pitfall, Plight, Predicament, Quandary, Queer St, Recalcitrant, Rough, Rub, Scrape, Scrub, Setaceous, Shlep, Snag, Soup, Steep, Stick, Sticky, Stiff, Strait, Stubborn, Stymie, Ticklish, Tight spot, Trial, Tricky, Troublous, Une(a)th, Uphill, Via dolorosa

Diffuse, Diffusion Disperse, Disseminate, Endosmosis, Exude, Osmosis, Pervade, Radiate, Spread

Dig(s), Digger, Digging, Dig up Antipodean, Australian, Backhoe, Beadle, Bed(e)ral, Billet, Bot, Burrow, Costean, Delve, Enjoy, Excavate, Flea-bag, Fossorial, Gaulter, Gibe, Gird, Graip, Grub, Howk, Jab, Kip, Lair, Like, Lodgings, Mine, Navvy, Nervy, Nudge, Pad, Pioneer, Probe, Prod, Raddleman, Resurrect, Root, Ruddleman, Sap, See, Spade, Spit, Spud, Star-nose, Taunt, Tonnell, Trench, Tunnel, Undermine, Unearth

Digest(ible), Digestion, Digestive Abridgement, Absorb, Abstract, Aperçu, Archenteron, Assimilate, Codify, Concoct, Endue, Epitome, Eupepsia, Eupepsy, Gastric, Indew, Indue, Light, Pandect, Pem(m)ican, Pepsin(e), Peptic, Précis, Salt-cat, > **SUMMARY**

Dignified, Dignify August, Elevate, Exalt, Handsome, Honour, Lordly, Majestic, Manly, Proud, Stately

Dignity Aplomb, Bearing, Cathedra, Decorum, Face, Glory, Grandeur, Majesty, Nobility, Poise, Presence, Scarf

Digress(ion) Deviate, Diverge, Ecbole, Episode, Excurse, Excursus, Maunder, Veer, Wander

Dilate, **Dilation**, **Dilatation** Amplify, Develop, Diastole, Ecstasis, Enlarge, Expand, Increase, Mydriasis, Sinus, Tent, Varix

Dilemma Casuistry, Choice, Cleft, Dulcarnon, Fix, Horn, Predicament, Quandary, Why-not

Diligence, **Diligent** Active, Application, Assiduous, Coach, Conscience, Eident, Industry, Intent, Painstaking, Sedulous, Studious

Dilute, **Dilution** Adulterate, Delay, Diluent, Lavage, Simpson, Thin, Water, Weaken

Dim(ness), **Dimming**, **Dimwit** Becloud, Blear, Blur, Brownout, Caligo, Clueless, Crepuscular, Dense, Dusk, Eclipse, Fade, Faint, Feint, Gormless, Ill lit, Indistinct, Mist, Nebulous, Ninny, Obscure, Overcast, Owl, Pale, Shadow, Unsmart

Dimension Area, Breadth, Extent, Height, Length, Measure, Size, Volume, Width

Diminish(ed), **Diminuendo**, **Diminution**, **Diminutive** Abatement, Assuage, Baby, Calando, Contract, Cot(t)ise, Deactivate, Decrease, Détente, Detract, Disparage, Dissipate, Dwarf, Dwindle, Erode, Fourth, Hypocorism(a), Lessen, Lilliputian, Minify, Minus, Mitigate, Petite, Plgmy, Scarp, Small, Stultify, Subside, Toy, Trangle, Wane, Whittle

Dingy Crummy, Dark, Dirty, Drear, Dun, Fusc(ous), Grimy, Isabel(la), Isabelline, Lurid, Oorie, Ourie, Owrie, Shabby, Smoky

Dining-room Cafeteria, Cenacle, Commons, Frater, Hall, Langar, Refectory, Restaurant, Triclinium

Dinner Banquet, Collation, Feast, Hall, Kail, Kale, Meal, Prandial, Repast

Dinosaur Allosaurus, Brachiosaurus, Brontosaurus, Diplodocus, Hadrosaur, Ichthyosaur(us), Iguanodon, Megalosaur, Plesiosaur, Prehistoric, Pterodactyl, Pterosaur, Sauropod, Smilodon, Stegosaur, Teleosaurus, Titanosaurus, Triceratops, Tyrannosaurus

Diocese Bishopric, District, Eparchate, See

Dip(per) Baptise, Basin, Bathe, Bob, Brantub, Dabble, Dap, Dean, Dib, Diver, Dop, Duck, Dunk, Foveola, Geosyncline, Guacomole, H(o)ummus, Houmous, Hum(m)us, Immerse, Intinction, Ladle, Lucky, Ouzel, Paddle, Rinse, Rollercoaster, Salute, Star, Submerge, Tzatziki, Ursa

Diploma Charter, Parchment, Qualification, Scroll, Sheepskin

Diplomacy, **Diplomat(ic)** Altemat, Ambassador, Attaché, CD, Chargé d'affaires, Consul, DA, Dean, Doyen, El(t)chi, Envoy, Fanariot, Finesse, Gunboat, Legation, Lei(d)ger, Phanariot, Suave, > **TACT**

▷ **Dippy** *may indicate* a bather

Dire Dreadful, Fatal, Fell, Hateful, Ominous, Urgent

Direct(or), **Directly** Administer, Advert, Aim, Airt, Auteur, Board, Boss, Cann, Channel, Charge, Command, Compere, Con(n), Conduct, Control, Cox, Dead, Due, Enjoin, Explicit, Fellini, First-hand, Forthright, Frontal, Guide, Helm, Hitchcock, Immediate, Impresario, Instruct, Kappelmeister, Lead, Lean, Manager, Navigate, Outright, Pilot, Play, Point-blank, Ready, Refer, Régisseur, Rudder, Set, Signpost, Stear, > **STEER**, Straight, Teach, Tell, Truffaut, Vector

Direction Aim, Airt, Arrow, Astern, Bearings, Course, Cross-reference, E, End-on, Guidance, Guide, Heading, Keblah, L, Line, N, Orders, Passim, R, Route, Rubric, S, Sanction, Send, Sense, Side, Slap, Tack, Tenor, Thataway, Trend, W, Way

Directory Crockford, Debrett, Encyclop(a)edia, Kelly, List, Red book, Register

Dirge Ballant, Coronach, Dirige, Epicedium, Knell, Monody, Requiem, Song, Threnody

Dirigible Airship, Balloon, Blimp, Zeppelin

Dirk Dagger, Skean, Whinger, Whiniard, Whinyard

Dirt(y) Begrime, Bemoil, Chatty, Clag, Clarty, Colly, Contaminate, Coom, Crock, Crud, Draggle, Dung, Dust, Earth, Filth, Foul, Gore, Grime, Grufted, Grungy, Impure, Manky, Moit, Mote, Muck, Obscene, Ordure, Pay, Ray, Sculdudd(e)ry, Scum, Scuzzy, Skulduddery, Smirch, Smut(ch), Soil, Sordor, Squalid, Stain, Trash, Unclean, Yucky, Yukky

Disability, **Disable** Cripple, Lame, Maim, Paralyse, Scotch, Wreck

Disadvantage Detriment, Drawback, Handicap, Mischief, Out, Penalise, Penalty, Supercherie, Upstage, Wrongfoot, Zugswang

Disagree(ing), **Disagreeable**, **Disagreement** Argue, Argy-bargy, Bad, Clash, Conflict, Contest, Debate, Differ, Discrepant, Dispute, Dissent, Dissonant, Evil, Fiddlesticks, Friction, Heterodoxy, Pace, Rift

Disappear(ing) Cook, Dispel, Evanesce, Evanish, Evaporate, Fade, Kook, Latescent, Melt, Occult, Pass, Skedaddle, Slope, > VANISH

Disappoint(ment), **Disappointed** Anticlimax, Balk, Chagrin, Comedown, Crestfallen, Delude, Disgruntle, Frustrate, Gutted, Heartsick, Lemon, Letdown, Regret, Sell, Shucks, Sick, Suck-in, Sucks, Swiz(zle), Thwart

Disapproval, **Disapprove** Ach, Animadvert, Boo, Catcall, Censure, Deplore, Deprecate, Expostulate, Frown, Harrumph, Hiss, Napoo, Object, Pejorative, Po-faced, Raspberry, Reject, Reproach, Reprobate, Squint, Tush, Tut, Umph, Veto, Whiss

Disarm(ament), **Disarming** Bluff, Defuse, Demobilise, Nuclear, Winsome

Disarray Disorder, Mess, Rifle, Tash, Undress

Disaster, **Disastrous** Adversity, Apocalypse, Bale, Calamity, Cataclysm(ic), Catastrophe, Debacle, Dire, Doom, Evil, Fatal, Fiasco, Flop, Impostor, Meltdown, Mishap, Pitfall, Rout, Ruin, Shipwreck, Titanic, Tragedy, Wipeout

Disbelief, **Disbelieve(r)** Acosmism, Anythingarian, Atheism, Incredulity, Mistrust, Nothingarianism, Occamist, Phew, Phooey, Puh-lease, Puh-leeze, Question, Sceptic, Voetsak

Disc, **Disk** Bursting, Button, CD, Cheese, Compact, Coulter, Counter, Diaphragm, Dogtag, EP, Epiphragm, Flexible, Floppy, Frisbee®, Gold, Gong, Hard, Harrow, Intervertebral, Laser, LP, Magnetic, Mono, O, Optical, Parking, Paten, Patin, Planchet, Plate, Platinum, Puck, RAM, Rayleigh, Record, Rosette, Roundel, Rowel, Sealed unit, Silver, Slipped, Slug, Stereo, Swash plate, System, Tax, Token, Video, Wafer, Whorl, Winchester, Wink, WORM

Discard(ed) Abandon, Crib, Dele, Jettison, Kill, Leave, Obsolete, Off, Offload, Oust, > REJECT, Scrap, Shuck, Slough, Sluff, Supersede

Discern(ing), **Discernment** Acumen, Acute, Descry, Discrimination, Flair, Insight, Perceive, Percipient, Perspicacity, Realise, Sapient, Scry, See, Skry, > TASTE, Tell, Wate

Discharge Absolve, Acquit, Arc, Assoil, Brush, Cashier, Catarrh, Conditional, Corona, Deliver, Demob, Disembogue, Disgorge, Dismiss, Disruptive, Dump, Efflux, Effusion, Egest, Ejaculate, Eject, Emission, Emit, Enfilade, Evacuate, Excrete, Execute, Exemption, Expulsion, Exude, Fire, Flashover, Flower, Flux, Free, Glow, Lava, Lay off, Leak, Let off, Loose, Maturate, Menses, Mute, Offload, Oust, Pay, Perform, Period, Purulence, Pus, Pyorrhoea, Quietus, Rheum, Sack, Salvo, Sanies, Secretion, Show, Shrive, Snarler, Spark, Suppurate, Teem, Unload, Vent, Void, Water

Disciple(s) Adherent, Apostle, Catechumen, Follower, John, Judas, Luke, Mark, Matthew, Peter, Simon, Son, Student, Thomist, Votary

Disciplinarian, **Discipline** Apollonian, Ascesis, Chasten, Chastise, Correct,

Despot, Drill, Exercise, Feng Shui, Inure, Martinet, Mathesis, Punish, Regimentation, Regulate, School, Science, Spartan, Stickler, Subject, Train, Tutor

Disclaim(er) Deny, Disown, No(t)chel, Recant, Renounce, > REPUDIATE, Voetstoots

Disclose, Disclosure Apocalypse, Confess, Divulge, Expose, Impart, Leak, Manifest, Propale, > PUBLISH, Report, Reveal, Spill, Tell, Unheal, Unhele, Unrip, Unveil

Discomfort Ache, Angst, Dysphoria, Gyp, Heartburn, Pain, Unease

Disconcert(ing) Abash, Confuse, Disturb, Embarrass, Faze, Feeze, Flurry, Nonplus, Phase, Pheese, Pheeze, Phese, > RATTLE, Shatter, Throw, Upset, Wrong-foot

▷ **Disconcert(ed)** *may indicate* an anagram

Disconnect(ed) Asynartete, Detach, Disjointed, Off-line, Sever, Staccato, Uncouple, Undo, Unplug

Discontent(ed) Disquiet, Dissatisfied, Repined, Sour

Discord(ant) Absonant, Ajar, Conflict, Din, Dispute, Eris, Faction, Hoarse, Jangle, Jar, Raucous, Ruction, Strife

▷ **Discord(ant)** *may indicate* an anagram

Discount Agio, Cashback, Deduct, Disregard, Forfaiting, Invalidate, > REBATE, Trade

Discourage(ment) Caution, Chill, Dampen, Dash, Daunt, Demoralise, Deter, Dishearten, Disincentive, Dismay, Dissuade, Enervate, Frustrate, Opposition, Stifle

Discourse Address, Argument, Conversation, Descant, Diatribe, Dissertate, Eulogy, Expound, Homily, Lecture, Lucubrate, Orate, Preach, Relate, Rigmarole, Sermon

Discover(y), Discoverer Amundsen, Anagnorisis, Ascertain, Betray, Breakthrough, Columbus, Cook, Descry, Detect, Discern, Discure, Eureka, > FIND, Heureka, Heuristic, Learn, Locate, Manifest, Moresby, Protege, Rumble, Serendip, Serendipity, Spy, Tasman, Trace, Unearth, Unhale, Unmask, Unveil

▷ **Discovered in** *may indicate* an anagram or a hidden word

Discredit(able) Debunk, Decry, Disgrace, Explode, Infamy, Scandal, Unworthy

Discreet, Discretion Cautious, Circumspect, Freedom, Option, Polite, Politic, Prudence, Prudent, Trait, Wise

Discrepancy Difference, Gap, Lack, Shortfall, Variance

Discriminate, Discriminating, Discrimination Ag(e)ism, Colour bar, Diacritic, Differentiate, Discern, Distinguish, Elitism, Invidious, Nasute, Racism, Secern, Segregate, Select, Sexism, Siz(e)ism, Speciesism, Subtle, Taste

Discuss(ed), Discussion Agitate, Air, Canvass, Commune, Conf(erence), Debate, Dialectic, Dialogue, Dicker, Disquisition, Examine, Handle, Hob and nob, Interlocution, Korero, Moot, Over, Palaver, Parley, Pourparler, Prolegomenon, Quodlibet, Rap, Re, Symposium, Talk, Tapis, Treatment

Disdain(ful) Belittle, Contempt, Coy, Deride, Despise, Geck, Poof, Pooh-pooh, Puh, Sassy, > SCORN, Scout, Sniffy, Spurn, Supercilious

Disease(d) Affection, Ailment, Epidemic, Fever, Infection, Malady, Rot, Scourge, Sickness

▷ **Diseased** *may indicate* an anagram

Disengage(d), Disengagement Clear, Divorce, Liberate, Loosen, Release, Untie

▷ **Disfigured** *may indicate* an anagram

Disgrace Atimy, Attaint, Baffle, Blot, Contempt, Contumely, Degrade, Discredit, Dishonour, Dog-house, Ignominy, Indignity, Infamy, Obloquy, Opprobrium, Scandal, Shame, Shend, Slur, Soil, Stain, Stigma, Yshend

Disgraceful Ignoble, Ignominious, Indign, Infamous, Mean, Notorious, Shameful, Turpitude

▷ **Disgruntled** *may indicate* an anagram

Disguise(d) Alias, Blessing, Camouflage, Cloak, Colour, Conceal, Cover, Covert, Dissemble, Hide, Hood, Incog(nito), Mantle, Mask, Masquerade, Obscure, Peruke, Pretence, Pseudonym, Ring, Travesty, Veil, Vele, Veneer, Visagiste, Vizard

▷ **Disguised** *may indicate* an anagram

Disgust(ing) Ach-y-fi, Ad nauseam, Aversion, Aw, Bah, Cloy, Discomfort, Execrable, Faugh, Fie, Foh, Fulsome, Grody, Irk, Loathsome, Manky, Nauseous, Noisome, Obscene, Odium, Oughly, Ouglie, Pah, Pho(h), Pish, Repel, Repugnant, > **REVOLT**, Revulsion, Scomfish, Scumfish, Scunner, Scuzz, > **SICKEN**, Squalid, Tush, Ugsome, Vile, Yech, Yu(c)k

Dish(y) Allot, Apollo, Ashet, Basin, Belle, Bowl, Chafing, Charger, Cocotte, Cook-up, Cutie, Dent, Dreamboat, Epergne, Flasket, Grail, Kitchen, Laggen, Laggin, Lanx, Luggie, Pan, Pannikin, Paten, Patera, Patin(e), Petri, Plate, Platter, Porringer, Ramekin, Ramequin, Receptacle, Sangraal, Sangrail, Sangreal, Satellite, Saucer, Scallop, Serve, Service, Side, Smasher, Special, Watchglass

Dishevel(led) Blowsy, Blowzy, Daggy, Mess, Rumpled, Touse, Tousle, Touzle, Tumble, Uncombed, Unkempt, Windswept

Dishonest(y) Bent, Crooked, Cross, Dodgy, False, Fraud, Graft, Hooky, Hot, Knavery, Malpractice, Malversation, Shonky, Stink, Twister, Underhand, Venal

Dishonour Defile, Disgrace, Disparage, Ignominy, Seduce, > **SHAME**, Violate, Wrong

Disinfect(ant) Acriflavin(e), Carbolic, Cineol(e), Cleanse, Eucalyptole, Formalin, Fuchsine, Fumigate, Lysol®, Phenol, Purify, Sheep-dip, Terebene

Disjointed Bitty, Incoherent, Rambling, Scrappy

▶ **Disk** *see* DISC

Dislike Allergy, Animosity, Animus, Antipathy, Aversion, Derry, Disesteem, Displeasure, Distaste, Lump, Mind

Dislocate, **Dislocation** Break, Diastasis, Displace, Fault, Luxate, Slip

Dislodge Budge, Displace, Expel, Oust, Rear, Uproot

Disloyal(ty) False, Treason, Unfaithful, Untrue

Dismal Black, Bleak, Cheerless, Dark, Dowie, Drack, Dreary, Funereal, > **GLOOMY**, Grey, Morne, Obital, Sepulchral, Sombre, Sullen, Trist(e), Wae

Dismantle(d), **Dismantling** Derig, Divest, Get-out, Sheer-hulk, Strike, Strip, Unrig

Dismay Amate, Appal, Confound, Consternation, Coo, Daunt, Ha, Horrify, Lumme, Qualms

Dismiss(al) Annul, Ax, Boot, Bounce, Bowl(er), Bum's rush, Cancel, Cashier, Catch, Chuck, Congé, Daff, Discard, Discharge, Expulsion, Fire, Heave-ho, Lay off, Marching orders, Mitten, Och, Prorogue, Push, Recall, Reform, Remove, Road, Sack, Scout, Send, Shoo, Spit, Stump, Via, Walking papers, York

Disobedience, **Disobedient**, **Disobey** Contumacy, Defy, Flout, Insubordination, Rebel, Wayward

Disorder(ly), **Disordered** Ague, Ailment, Anarchy, Ariot, Asthma, Ataxia, Catatonia, Chaos, Clutter, Confuse, Contracture, Defuse, Derange, Deray, Diabetes, Dishevel, Dystrophy, Echolalia, Entropy, Farrago, Grippe, Haemophilia, Huntingdon's chorea, Hypallage, Inordinate, Irregular, ME, Mess, Mistemper, > **MUDDLE**, Muss(y), Neurosis, Oncus, Onkus, Pandemonium, Para-, Psychomatic,

Psychosis, Rile, SAD, Seborrh(o)ea, Shell-shock, Slovenly, Thalass(a)emia, Tousle, Unhinge, Unruly, Upset, Virilism

▷ **Disorder(ed)** *may indicate* an anagram

Dispatch Bowl, Celerity, Consign, Destroy, Dismiss, Expede, Expedite, Express, Gazette, Kibosh, Kill, Missive, Post, Pronto, Remit, Report, > SEND, Ship, Slaughter, Slay

Dispensation, Dispense(r), Dispense with Absolve, Administer, Ax(e), Cashpoint, Chemist, Container, Distribute, Dose, Dropper, Exempt, Handout, Indult, Scrap

Displace(ment), Displaced Antevert, Blueshift, Depose, Disturb, Ectopia, Ectopy, Fault, Heterotopia, Luxate, Move, Oust, Proptosis, Ptosis, Reffo, Stir, Subluxation, Unsettle, Uproot, Valgus, Varus

Display, Display ground Air, Array, Blaze, Blazon, Brandish, Bravura, Depict, Eclat, Epideictic, Etalage, Evidence, Evince, Exhibition, Exposition, Express, Extend, Extravaganza, Exude, Fireworks, Flaunt, Float, Gondola, Hang, Head-down, Head-up, Heroics, LED, Lek, Liquid crystal, Manifest, Mount, Muster, Ostentation, Outlay, Overdress, Pageant, Parade, Paraf(f)le, Peepshow, Pixel, Pomp, Propale, Pyrotechnics, Rode, Rodeo, Roll-out, Scene, Shaw, > SHOW, Sight, Spectacle, Splash, Splurge, Sport, Spree, State, Stunt, Tableau, Tattoo, Tournament, Up, Vaunt, Wear

Displease(d), Displeasure Anger, Dischuffed, Humph, Irritate, Provoke, Umbrage

Dispose(d), Disposal, Disposition Arrange, Bestow, Cast, Despatch, Dump, Eighty-six, Lay(-out), Prone, Sale, Sell, Service, Settle, Stagger

▷ **Disposed, Disposition** *may indicate* an anagram

Disposition Affectation, Attitude, Bent, Bias, Humour, Inclination, Kidney, Lie, Nature, Penchant, Talent, Temper(ament), Trim

Disprove, Disproof Debunk, Discredit, Negate, Rebut, Redargue, Refel, Refute

Dispute(d), Disputant Argue, Barney, Brangle, Cangle, Case, Chaffer, Chorizont(ist), Contend, Contest, Contretemps, Controversy, Debate, Deny, Differ, Discept, Discuss, Eristic, Fray, Haggle, Kilfud-yoking, Lock-out, Militate, Ob and soller, Odds, Oppugn, Plea, Polemic, Pro-and-con, > QUESTION, Rag, Resist, Spar, Stickle, Threap(it), Threep(it), Tiff, Tissue, Variance, Wrangle

Disqualify Debar, Incapacitate, Recuse, Reject, Unfit

Disregard(ed) Anomie, Anomy, Contempt, Disfavour, Flout, Forget, Ignore, Oblivion, Omit, Overlook, Oversee, Pass, Pretermit, Slight, Spare, Violate, Waive

Disreputable, Disrepute Base, Disgrace, Grubby, Louche, Low, Lowlife, Raffish, Ragamuffin, Reprobate, Rip, Scuzz(ball), Seamy, Shady, Shameful, Shy, Sleazy

Disrespect(ful) Contempt, Discourtesy, Impiety, Impolite, Irreverent, Profane, Slight, Uncivil

Disrupt(ion) Breach, Cataclasm, Disorder, Distract, Hamper, Interrupt, Jetlag, Mayhem, Perturb, Quonk, Screw, Upheaval

▷ **Disruption** *may indicate* an anagram

Dissatisfaction Displeasure, Distaste, Humph, Umph

Dissension, Dissent(er), Dissenting Contend, Differ, Disagree, Discord, Dissident, Faction, Heretic, Jain, Lollard, Noes, Non-CE, Non-con(formist), Pantile, Protest, Raskolnik, Recusant, Splinter group, > STRIFE, Vary

Dissertation Essay, Excursus, Lecture, Thesis, Treatise

Dissipate(d) Debauch, Diffuse, Disperse, Dissolute, Gay, Revel, Scatter, Shatter, Squander, Waste

▷ **Dissipated** *may indicate* an anagram

Dissolute Degenerate, Hell, Lax, Libertine, Licentious, Loose, Rake-helly, Rakish, Rip, Roué

▷ **Dissolute** *may indicate* an anagram

Dissolve Deliquesce, Digest, Disband, Disunite, Liquesce, Melt, Terminate, Thaw

Distance Absciss(a), Afield, Apothem, Breadth, Coss, Declination, Eloi(g)n, Farness, Foot, Headreach, Height, Interval, Klick, Kos(s), Latitude, League, Length, Mean, Mileage, Parasang, Parsec, Range, Reserve, Rod, Span, Spitting, Stade, Striking, Way, Yojan

Distant Aloof, Far, Frosty, Icy, Long, Offish, Remote, Tele-, Timbuctoo, Yonder

Distaste(ful) Repugnant, Ropy, Scunner, Unpalatable, Unpleasant, Unsavoury

Distil(late), **Distillation**, **Distiller**, **Distilling** Alcohol, Alembic, Anthracine, Azeotrope, Brew, Condense, Drip, Pelican, Pyrene, Pyroligneous, Rosin, Turps, Vapour

▷ **Distillation** *may indicate* an anagram

Distinct(ive) Apparent, Characteristic, Clear, Different, Evident, Grand, Individual, Peculiar, Plain, Separate, Several, Signal, > **SPECIAL**, Stylistic, Vivid

Distinction Beaut(y), Blue, Cachet, Credit, Diacritic, Difference, Dignity, Diorism, Disparity, Division, Eclat, Eminence, Honour, Lustre, Mark, Mystique, Note, Nuance, OM, Prominence, Quiddity, Rank, Renown, Speciality, Style, Title

Distinguish(ed), **Distinguishing** Classify, Demarcate, Denote, Diacritic, Different(iate), Discern, Discriminate, Divide, Elevate, Mark, Notable, Perceive, Prestigious, Prominent

Distort(ion), **Distorted** Anamorphosis, Bend, Colour, Contort, Contort, Deface, Deform, Dent, Fudge, Helium speech, Jaundiced, Mangle, Misshapen, Pervert, Rubato, Thraw, Twist, > **WARP**, Wow, Wrest, Wring, Wry

▷ **Distort(ed)** *may indicate* an anagram

Distract(ed), **Distraction** Absent, Agitate, Amuse, Avocation, Bewilder, Divert, Éperdu, Forhaile, Frenetic, Lost, Madden, Mental, Nepenthe, Perplex, Upstage

▷ **Distract(ed)** *may indicate* an anagram

Distress(ed), **Distressing** Afflict, Ail, Alack, Anger, Anguish, Antique, Distraint, Dolour, Exigence, Extremity, Grieve, Harass, Harrow, Hurt, Ill, > **IN DISTRESS**, Irk, Misease, Misfortune, Need, Oppress, Pain, Poignant, Prey, Sad, Shorn, Sore, SOS, Straits, Traumatic, > **TROUBLE**, Une(a)th

Distribute(d), **Distribution** Allocate, Allot, Binomial, Busbar, Carve, Chi-square, Colportage, Deal, Deliver(y), Deploy, Dish, Dispense, Dispose, Issue, Lie, Lot, Mete, Out, Pattern, Poisson's, Prorate, Repartition, Serve, Share

▷ **Distributed** *may indicate* an anagram

District Alsatia, Amhara, Arcadia, Ards, Area, Bail(l)iwick, Banat, Barrio, Belt, Canton, Cantred, Classis, Community, Diocese, End, Exurb, Federal, Gau, Ghetto, Hundred, Lathe, Liberty, Locality, Loin, Manor, Metropolitan, > **NEIGHBOURHOOD**, Oblast, Pachalic, Pale, Parish(en), Paroch, Pashalik, Patch, Province, Quarter, Quartier, Rape, > **REGION**, Ride, Riding, Ruhr, Sanjak, Section, Sheading, Sircar, Soc, Soke(n), Stannary, Suburb, Sucken, Talooka, Taluk, Tenderloin, Township, Venue, Vicinage, Walk, Wapentake, Way, Zila, Zillah, Zone

Disturb(ance), **Disturbed** Ado, Aerate, Affray, Agitate, Atmospherics, Autism, Betoss, Brabble, Brainstorm, Brash, Brawl, Broil, Carfuffle, Collieshangie, Concuss, Delirium, Dementia, Derange, Desecrate, Disquiet, Dust, Feeze, Firestorm, Fray, Fret, Harass, Hoopla, Incommode, Infest, Interrupt, Jee, Kerfuffle, Kick-up, Kurfuffle, Muss, Outbreak, Prabble, Ramp, Ripple, Romage, Rook, Roughhouse, Rouse, Ruckus, Ruction, Ruffle, Rumpus, Shake, Shindy, Shook-up, Stashie, Static, Steer, Stir, Sturt, Tremor, Trouble, Turbulent, Unquiet, Unrest, Unsettle, Upheaval, Uproot, > **UPSET**, Vex

▷ **Disturb(ed)** *may indicate* an anagram

Ditch Barathron, Barathrum, Channel, Cunette, Delf, Delph, Dike, Discard, Donga, Drainage, Drop, Dyke, Euripus, Foss(e), Graft, Grip, Gully, Ha(w)-ha(w), Haw-haw, Jettison, Khor, Level, Lode, Moat, Na(l)la(h), Nulla(h), Rean, Reen, Rhine, Rid, Sea, Sheuch, Sheugh, Sike, Sloot, Sluit, Spruit, Stank, Syke, Trench

Dive(r), Diving Armstand, Backflip, Belly-flop, Crash, Dart, Den, Duck, Full-gainer, Half-gainer, Header, Honkytonk, Jackknife, Joint, Ken, Nitery, Nose, Pass, Plummet, Plunge, Plutocrat, Power, Saturation, Scoter, Skin, Sound, Stage, Stoop, Submerge, Swallow, Swan, Swoop, Tailspin, Urinant

Diver(s) Didapper, Duck, Embergoose, Flop, Frogman, Gainer, Grebe, Guillemot, Loom, Loon, Lungie, Many, Merganser, Pearl, Pike, Plong(e), Pochard, Poker, Puffin, Sawbill, Scuba, Snake-bird, Speakeasy, Sundry, Urinator, Various, Zoom

Diverge(nce) Branch, Deviate, Spread, Swerve, Variant, Veer

Diverse, Diversify Alter, Dapple, Different, Interlard, Intersperse, Manifold, Motley, Multifarious, Separate, Variegate, Various, Vary

Diversion, Divert(ing) Amuse, Avocation, Beguile, Deflect, Detour, Disport, Dissuade, Distract, Entertain, Game, Hare, Hobby, Interlude, Pastime, Pleasure, Prolepsis, Ramp, Red-herring, Refract, Reroute, Ruse, Shunt, Sideshow, Sidetrack, Sport, Stalking-horse, Steer, Stratagem, Sway, Switch, Tickle, Upstage, Yaw

▷ **Diverting** *may indicate* an anagram

Divide(d) Apportion, Band, Bipartite, Bisect, Branch, Cantle, Cleft, Comminute, Commot(e), Continental, Counter-pale, Cut, Deal, Demerge, Dimidiate, Estrange, Fork, Great, Indent, Parcel, Part, Polarise, Rend, Rift, Separate, Sever, Share, > sᴘʟɪᴛ, Sunder, Watershed, Zone

Dividend Bonus, Div, Interim, Into, Share

Divine, Divine presence, Divinity Acoemeti, Atman, Avatar, Beatific, Clergyman, Conjecture, Curate, DD, Deduce, Deity, Douse, Dowse, Ecclesiastic, Forecast, Foretell, Fuller, > ɢᴏᴅ, > ɢᴏᴅᴅᴇss, Godhead, Guess, Hariolate, Heavenly, Holy, Immortal, Inge, Isiac, Mantic, Numen, Olympian, Pontiff, Predestinate, Predict, Presage, Priest, RE, Rector, RI, Rimmon, Scry, Sense, Seraphic, Shechinah, Shekinah, Spae, Supernal, Theanthropic, Theologise, Theology, Triune

Division, Divisible Arcana, Arm, Arrondissement, Banat(e), Bar, Branch, Caesura, Canton, Cantred, Cantref, Caste, Category, Chapter, Classification, Cleft, Cloison, Clove, Commune, Compartment, Corps, County, Crevasse, Curia, Department, Dichotomy, Disagreement, Disunity, Fork, Grisons, Gulf, Hedge, Hide, Hundred, Inning, Lathe, Leet, Legion, List, Lobe, Nome, Part, Partition, Period, Pipe, Pitaka, Platoon, Polarisation, Presidency, Quotition, Rape, Region, Reservation, Riding, Schism, Section, Sector, Segment, Sept(ate), Sever, Share, Shed, Shire, Stage, Subheading, Tahsil, Trichotomy, Trio, Troop, Unit, Wapentake, Ward

Divorce(d) Diffarreation, Dissolve, Disunion, Div, Estrange, Get(t), Part, Separate, Sequester, > sᴜɴᴅᴇʀ, Talak, Talaq

Divulge Confess, Disclose, Expose, Publish, Reveal, Split, Tell, Unveil, Utter

Dizziness, Dizzy Beaconsfield, Ben, Capricious, Dinic, Disraeli, Giddy, Giglot, Lightheaded, Mirligoes, Swimming, Vertiginous, > ᴠᴇʀᴛɪɢᴏ, Woozy

Do(es), Doing Accomplish, Achieve, Act, Anent, Beano, Char, Cheat, Chisel, Cod, Con, Cozen, Deed, Dich, Dish, Div, Doth, Dupe, Effectuate, Enact, Execute, Function, Gull, Handiwork, Hoax, Mill, Perform, Same, Serve, Settle, Shindig, Spif(f)licate, Suffice, Thrash, Ut

▷ **Do** *may indicate* an anagram

Dock(er), Docked, Docks Abridge, Barber, Basin, Bistort, Bob, Camber, Canaigre, Clip, Curta(i)l, Cut, Deduct, De-tail, Dry, Floating, Grapetree, Knotweed, Lop, Marina, Moor, Off-end, Pare, Patience, Pen, Pier, Quay, Rhubarb,

Doctor(s) | 116

Rumex, Rump, Seagull, Shorten, Snakeweed, Sorrel, Sourock, Stevedore, Tilbury, Watersider, Wet, Wharf, Yard

Doctor(s) Alter, Arnold, Barefoot, Barnardo, Bleeder, BMA, Bones, Breeze, Bright, Brighton, Brown, Caius, Castrate, Clinician, Cook, Cup(per), Cure(r), Dale, Diagnose, Dr, Erasmus, Extern(e), Fake, Falsify, Family, Faustus, Fell, Finlay, Flying, Foster, Galen, GP, Healer, Homeopath, Houseman, Hyde, Intern, Internist, Jekyll, Jenner, Johnson, Kildare, Lace, Leach, Leech, Linacre, Load, Locum, Luke, Manette, Massage, MB, MD, Medicate, Medico, Minister, Misrepresent, MO, MOH, Molla(h), Moreau, Mulla(h), Neuter, No, Ollamh, Ollav, Panel, Pangloss, Paracelsus, Paramedic, Pedro, PhD, Physician, Pill(s), Practitioner, Quack, Quacksalver, Rabbi, RAMC, Registrar, Resident, Rig, Salk, Saw, Sawbones, School, Slammer, Slop, Spin, Surgeon, Syn, Thorne, Treat, Vet, Water, Watson, Who, Witch

▷ **Doctor(ed)** *may indicate* an anagram

Doctrine Adoptionism, Archology, Cab(b)ala, Calvanism, Chiliasm, Credo, Creed, Dogma, Doxie, Doxy, Esotery, Federalism, Gnosticism, Gospel, Holism, Islam, Ism, Jansenism, Lore, Malthusian, Monroe, Pragmatism, Reformism, Sheria, Shibboleth, Subjectivism, Substantialism, Syndicalism, Synergism, System, Theory, Thomism, Transubstantiation

Document(s), Documentary Bumph, Carta, Certificate, Charter, Contract, Conveyance, Covenant, Daftar, Deed, Diploma, Docket, Doco, Dompass, Dossier, Form, Holograph, Latitat, Logbook, Mandamus, Papers, Production, Ragman, Ragment, Roll, Roul(e), Screed, Waybill, Writ

Dodge, Dodgy Artful, Avoid, Column, Elude, Evade, Evasion, Jink, Jook, Jouk, Racket, Ruse, Shirk, Sidestep, Skip, Slalom, Slinter, Tip, Trick, Twist, Urchin, Weave, Welsh, Wheeze, Wire, Wrinkle

Dog(s) Bowwow, Canes, Canidae, Canine, Feet, Hot, Kennel, Pursue, Shadow, Stalk, Tag, Tail, Top, Tracker, Trail

Dogma(tic) Assertive, Belief, Conviction, Creed, Doctrinal, Ideology, Opinionative, Pedagogic, Peremptory, Pontifical, Positive

Dole Alms, Batta, B(u)roo, Give, Grief, Maundy, Payment, Pittance, Ration, > **SHARE**, Tichborne, Vail, Vales

Doll(y) Barbie®, Bimbo, Common, Corn, Crumpet, Dress, Dutch, Golliwog, Kachina, Kewpie®, Maiden, Marionette, Matryoshka, Maumet, Mommet, Mummet, Ookpik®, Ornament, Parton, Poppet, Puppet, Ragdoll, Russian, Sis(ter), Sitter, Tearsheet, Toy, Trolley, Varden, Washboard

Dollar(s) Balboa, Boliviano, Buck, Cob, Euro, Fin, Greenback, Iron man, Peso, Piastre, Pink, S, Sand, Sawbuck, Sawhorse, Scrip, Smacker, Spin, Wheel

▷ **Dolly** *may indicate* an anagram

Dolphin Amazon, Arion, Beluga, Bottlenose, Cetacean, Coryphene, Delphinus, Grampus, Lampuka, Lampuki, Meer-swine, Porpess(e), Risso's, River, Sea-pig

Dome(-shaped) Cap, Cupola, Dagoba, Geodesic, Head, Imperial, Louvre, Millennium, Onion, Periclinal, Rotunda, Stupa, Tee, Tholos, Tholus, Tope, Vault

Domestic(ate) Char, Cleaner, Dom, Esne, Familiar, Home-keeping, Homely, House, Housetrain, Humanise, Interior, Internal, Intestine, Maid, Menial, > **SERVANT**, Tame, Woman

Dominate, Dominance, Dominant Ascendancy, Baasskap, Bethrall, Clou, Coerce, Control, Henpeck, Maisterdome, Mesmerise, Monopolise, O(v)ergang, Override, Overshadow, Power, Preponderant, Preside, Rule, Soh, > **SUBDUE**, Subjugate, Tower

Dominion Dom, Empire, Khanate, NZ, Realm, Reame, Reign, > **RULE**, Supremacy, Sway, Territory

Domino(es) Card, Fats, Mask, Matador

Don Academic, Address, Assume, Caballero, Endue, Fellow, Garb, Giovanni, Indew, Juan, Lecturer, Prof, Quixote, Reader, Senor, Spaniard, Tutor, Wear

Donate, Donation Aid, Bestow, Contribution, Gift, Give

Done Achieved, Complete, Crisp, Ended, Executed, Had, Over, Spitcher, Tired, Weary

Donkey Ass, Burro, Cardophagus, Cuddie, Cuddy, Dapple, Dick(e)y, Eeyore, Fussock, Genet(te), Jennet, Jerusalem pony, Kulan, Modestine, Moke, Mule, Neddy, Onager, Stupid, Years

Donor Benefactor, Bestower, Settlor

Doofer Thingumabob

Doom(ed) Condemned, Date, Destine, Destiny, > FATE, Fay, Fey, Fie, Goner, Ill-starred, Lot, Predestine, Preordain, Ragnarok, Ruined, Sentence, Spitcher, Star-crossed, Weird

Door(s), Doorstep, Doorway Aperture, Communicating, Drecksill, Dutch, Elephant, Entry, Exit, Fire, Folding, Front, Haik, Hake, Hatch, Heck, Ingress, Jib, Lintel, Louver, Louvre, Muntin, Oak, Open, Overhead, Portal, Postern, Revolving, Rory, Screen, Sliding, Stable, Stage, Storm, Street, Swing, Trap, Up and over, Vomitory, Wicket, Yett

Doorkeeper, Doorman Bouncer, Commissionaire, Guardian, Janitor, Ostiary, Porter, Tiler, Tyler, Usher

Dope Acid, Amulet, Bang, Coke, Crack, > DRUG, Gen, Goose, Info, Narcotic, Nobble, Rutin, Sedate, > STUPID PERSON

Doppelganger Double, Ringer

Dormer Luthern

Dormitory Barrack, Dorter, Dortour, Hall, Hostel, Quarters

Dosage, Dose Administer, Cascara, Draught, Drug, Kilogray, > MEASURE, Physic, Posology, Potion, Powder

Dot(s), Dotted, Dotty Absurd, Bullet, Criblé, Dit, Dower, Dowry, Engrailed, Leader, Lentiginose, Limp, Micro, Occult, Or, Particle, Pixel, > POINT, Polka, Precise, Punctuate, Punctulate, Punctum, Schwa, Semé(e), Set, Speck, Spot, Sprinkle, Stigme, Stipple, Stud, Tap, Tittle, Trema, Umlaut

Dote, Dotage, Doting, Dotard Adore, Anile, Anility, Cocker, Dobbie, Idolise, Imbecile, Pet, Prize, Senile, Tendre, Twichild

Double(s) Amphibious, Ancipital, Bi-, Bifold, Binate, Counterpart, Crease, Dimeric, Doppel-ganger, Dual, Duo, Duple(x), Duplicate, Equivocal, Fetch, Fold, Foursome, Geminate, Gimp, Image, Ingeminate, Ka, Look-alike, Loop, Martingale, Pair, Parlay, Polyseme, Reflex, Replica, Ringer, Run, Similitude, Spit, Trot, Turnback, Twae, > TWIN, Two(fold)

Doubt(ful), Doubter Ambiguous, Aporia, Askance, But, Debatable, Distrust, Dubiety, Dubitate, Hesitate, Hum, Iffy, Incertitude, Misgiving, Mistrust, Precarious, Qualm, Query, > QUESTION, Rack, Scepsis, Sceptic, Scruple, Shady, Shy, Sic, Skepsis, Sus, Suspect, Suss, Thomas, Thos, Umph, Uncertain, Unsure, Waver

Dough(y) Boodle, Cake, Calzone, Cash, Duff, Hush-puppy, Knish, Loot, Magma, Masa, Money, Paste, Pop(p)adum, Ready, Sad, Spondulicks

Doughnut Cruller, Knish, Sinker, Torus

Dour Glum, Hard, Mirthless, Morose, Reest, Reist, Sinister, Sullen, Taciturn

Douse Dip, Drench, Extinguish, Snuff, Splash

Dove Collared, Columbine, Culver, Cushat, Diamond, Doo, Ice-bird, Mourning, Pacifist, > PIGEON, Ring, Rock, Stock, Turtle

Dowdy Frumpish, Mums(e)y, Shabby, Sloppy, Slovenly

Down(s), **Down(beat)**, **Downsize**, **Downward**, **Downy** A bas, Abase, Abattu, Alow, Amort, Bank, Below, Blue, Cast, Catabasis, Chapfallen, Comous, Cottony, Crouch, Darling, Dejected, Dowl(e), Drink, Epsom, Feather, Fledge, Floccus, Flue, Fluff, Fly, Fuzz, Goonhilly, Ground, Hair, Hill, Humble, Humiliate, Lanugo, Losing, Low, Lower, Nap, Oose, Ooze, Owing, Pappus, Pennae, Pile, Plumage, Quash, Repress, Sebum, Thesis, Thistle, Tomentum, Vail, Wretched

Downcast Abject, Chapfallen, Despondent, Disconsolate, Dumpish, Hopeless, Melancholy, Woebegone

Downfall, **Downpour** Cataract, Collapse, Deluge, Fate, Flood, Hail, Onding, Overthrow, Rain, Ruin, Shower, Thunder-plump, Torrent, Undoing, Waterspout

Downright Absolute, Arrant, Bluff, Candid, Clear, Complete, Flat, Plumb, Plump, Pure, Rank, Sheer, Stark, Utter

Downturn Slump

Downwind Leeward

Dowry Dot, Dower, Lobola, Lobolo, Merchet, Portion, Settlement, Tocher

Doze Ca(u)lk, Dove(r), Nap, Nod, Semi-coma, Sleep, Slip, Slumber

Drab Cloth, Dell, Dingy, Dull, Dun, Isabel(line), Lifeless, Livor, Prosaic, Pussel, Quaker-colour, Rig, Road, Slattern, Sloven, Subfusc, Tart, Trull, Wanton, Whore

Draft Cheque, Draw, Ebauche, Essay, Landsturm, Minute, MS, Outline, Plan, Press, Rough, Scheme, Scroll, Scrowle, > **SKETCH**

Drag Car, Drail, Dredge, Drogue, Elicit, Eonism, Epicene, Extort, Hale, Harl, > **HAUL**, Keelhaul, La Rue, Lug, Puff, Pull, Rash, Sag, Schlep, Shoe, Skidpan, Sled, Snig, Sweep, Toke, Tote, Trail, Train, Travail, Travois, Trawl, Treck, Trek, Tump

Dragon Basilisk, Bel, Bellemère, Chaperon(e), Chindit, Draco, Drake, Komodo, Kung-kung, Ladon, Lindworm, Opinicus, Python, Rouge, Wantley, Wivern, Worm, Wyvern

Drain(ed), **Drainage**, **Draining**, **Drainpipe** Bleed, Brain, Buzz, Catchment, Catchwater, Channel, Cloaca, Cundy, Delf, Delph, Dewater, Ditch, Dry, Ea(u), > **EMPTY**, Emulge(nt), Exhaust, Fleet, Grating, Grip, Gully, Gutter, Ketavothron, Kotabothron, Lade, Leach, Leech, Limber, Lose, Milk, Pump, Rack, Rone, Sap, Scupper, Seton, Sew(er), Sheuch, Sheugh, Silver, Sink, Siver, Sluice, Sluse, Soakaway, Sough, Spend, Stank, Sump, Sure, Syver, Tile, Trench, Trocar, Unwater, Ureter, U-trap

Dram Drink, Drop, Portion, Snifter, Tickler, Tiff, Tot, Wet

Drama(tic), **Drama school** Charade, Comedy, Farce, Heroic, Histrionic, Kabuki, Kathakali, Kitchen sink, Legit, Mask, Masque, Mime, Moralities, No, Nogaku, Noh, Piece, Play, RADA, Scenic, Sensational, Singspiel, Stagy, Striking, Tetralogy, Theatric, Thespian, Tragedy, Unities, Wagnerian, Wild

Drape(ry) Adorn, Coverlet, Coverlid, Curtain, Festoon, Fold, Hang, Swathe, Valance, Veil, Vest

Draught(s), **Draughtsman** Aloetic, Breeze, Dam, Design, Drench, Drink, Fish, Gulp, Gust, Haal, Hippocrene, King, Men, Nightcap, Outline, Plan, Potation, Potion, Pull, Quaff, Sketch, Sleeping, Slug, Swig, Tracer, Veronal, Waucht

▷ **Draught** may refer to fishing

Draw (off), **Drawer(s)**, **Drawing**, **Drawn** Adduct, Allure, Attract, Bottom, Cock, Crayon, Dead-heat, Delineate, Derivation, Describe, Doodle, Dr, Draft, Drag, Dress, Educe, Entice, Equalise, Evaginate, Extract, Fetch, Gather, Gaunt, Glorybox, Gut, Haggard, Hale, Halve, Haul, Induce, Indue, Inhale, Lengthen, Limn, Longbow, Lottery, Pantalet(te)s, Panty, Perpetual check, Petroglyph, Protract, Pull, Rack, Raffle, Remark, Scent, Sesquipedalian, Shottle, Shuttle, Siphon, Sketch, Slub, Snig, Spin, Stalemate, Stumps, Sweepstake, Syphon, Tap, Taut, Technical, Tempt, Tenniel, Tie, Till, Toke, Tole, Tombola, Top, Tose, Tow(age), Toze,

Trice, Troll, Tug, Unsheathe, Uplift

▷ **Draw** *may indicate* something to smoke

Drawing Cartoon, Charcoal, Crayon, Dentistry, Detail, Diagram, Elevation, Freehand, Fusain, Graphics, Indraft, Line, Mechanical, Monotint, Orthograph, Pastel, Petroglyph, Profile, Seductive, Sepia, Silverpoint, Study, Technical, Traction, Wash, Working

▷ **Drawn** *may indicate* an anagram

Dread(ed) Angst, Anxiety, Awe, Fear, > HORROR, Redoubt, Thing

Dreadful Awful, Chronic, Dearn, Dire, Formidable, Ghastly, Horrendous, Penny, Sorry, Terrible

Dream(er), **Dream home**, **Dream state**, **Dreamy** Alchera, Alcheringa, Aspire, Desire, Drowsy, Dwa(u)m, Fantast, Fantasy, Faraway, Idealise, Illusion, Imagine, Languor, Mare, Mirth, Moon, Morpheus, Muse, Nightmare, On(e)iric, Pensive, Pipe, Rêveur, Romantic, Somniate, Stargazer, Surreal, Sweven, Trance, Trauma, Vague, Vision, Walter Mitty, Wet

Dreary Bleak, Desolate, Dismal, Doleful, Dreich, Dull, Gloom, Gray, Grey, Oorie, Ourie, Owrie, Sad

Dress(ing), **Dressed** Adorn, Align, Array, Attire, Attrap, Bandage, Black-tie, Bloomer, Blouson, Boast, Bodice, Busk, Caftan, Cheongsam, Chimer, Cimar, Clad, > CLOTHING, Coat, Cocktail, Comb, Compost, Compress, Corsage, Corset, Costume, Court, Curry, Cymar, Deck, Deshabille, Dirndl, Dolly Varden, Dolman, Don, Drag, Dub, Dubbin, Empire, Enrobe, Evening, Fancy, Farthingale, Fatigues, Fertiliser, Fig, Finery, French, Frock, Garb, Garnish, Gauze, Girt, Gown, Gymslip, > HABIT, Italian, Jaconet, Ketchup, Kimono, Line, Lint, Lounger, Mayonnaise, Mob, Morning, Mother Hubbard, Mufti, Mulch, Muu-muu, Oil, Patch, Pinafore, Plaster, Pledget, Plumage, Pomade, Poultice, Prank, Preen, Prepare, Rag, Raiment, Rehearsal, Rémoulade, Rig, Robe, Russet, Sack, Salad, Sari, Sarong, Sartorial, Sauce, Separates, Sheath, Shift, Shirt, Shirtwaister, Smock, Sterile, Stole, Subfusc, Suit, Sundress, Symar, Tasar, Taw, Tent, Thousand Island, Tiff, Tire, Tog, Toga, Toilet, Top, Treat, Trick, Trim, Tunic, Tusser, Tussore, Tuxedo, Uniform, Vest, Vinaigrette, Wear, Wedding, White-tie, Wig

▷ **Dressed up**, **Dressing** *may indicate* an anagram

Dresser Adze, Almery, Bureau, Chest, Couturier, Deuddarn, Dior, Lair, Lowboy, Sideboard, Transvestite, Tridarn, Welsh

Dribble Drip, Drivel, Drop, Slaver, Slop, Trickle

Drift(ing), **Drifter** Becalmed, Continental, Cruise, Current, Digress, Float, Heap, Impulse, Maunder, North Atlantic, Plankton, Purport, Rorke, Slide, Tendence, Tendency, > TENOR, Waft, Wander

Drill(ing) Auger, Bore, Burr, Close order, Educate, Exercise, Form, Hammer, Jackhammer, Jerks, Monkey, Pack, PE, Pierce, Pneumatic, PT, Reamer, Ridge, Seeder, Sow, Square-bashing, Teach, Train, Twill, Twist, Usage, Wildcat

Drink(er), **Drunk(enness)** AA, Absorb, Alky, Bacchian, Bender, Beverage, Bev(v)y, Binge, Blind, Blitzed, Bloat, Blotto, Bombed, Boose, Booze, Bosky, Bottled, Bouse, Bracer, Bumper, Carafe, Carousal, Cat-lap, Chaser, Corked, Crapulous, Crocked, Cuppa, Cut, Demitasse, Dipsomaniac, Double, Down, Drain, Draught, Drop, Ebriate, Elixir, Entire, Eye-opener, Finger, Fou, Fuddled, Full, Half-seas-over, High, Hogshead, Hophead, Imbibe, Indulge, Intemperate, Irrigate, Jag, Jar, Lap, Legless, Lethean, Lit, Loaded, Lord, Lower, Lush(y), Maggoty, Maudlin, Merry, Mortal, Mug, Nog(gin), Obfuscated, Oiled, One, Overshot, Paid, Paint, Partake, Particular, Pickled, Pick-me-up, Pie-eyed, Pint(a), Piss-artist, Pissed, Pisshead, Pisspot, Pixil(l)ated, Potion, Primed, Quaff, Rat-arsed, Ratted, Rolling, Rotten, Rummer, Screwed, Sea, Shebeen, Shotover, Sip(ple), Skinned, Slake, Slewed, Sloshed, Slug, Slurp, Smashed, Snort, Soak, Soused, Sponge,

Squiffy, Stewed, Stimulant, Stinko, Stoned, Sup, Swacked, Swallow, Swig, Swill, Tank, Tiddl(e)y, Tiff, Tight, Tincture, Tipple, Tipsy, Tope, Toss, Usual, Wash, Wat, Well-oiled, Wet, Winebag, Wino, Wrecked, Zonked

Drip Bore, Dribble, Drop, Gutter, IV, Leak, Seep, Splatter, Stillicide, Trickle, Wimp

Drive(r), Driving, Drive out AA, Actuate, Ambition, Backseat, Banish, Beetle, Ca', Cabby, Campaign, Carman, Charioteer, Chauffeur, Coachee, Coact, Crankshaft, Crew, Crowd, Disk, Dislodge, Dr, Drover, Drum, Economy, Eject, Emboss, Energy, Enforce, Engine, Faze, Ferret, Fire, Fluid, Force, Four-wheel, Front-wheel, Fuel, Goad, Hack, Hammer, Haste, Heard, Helmsman, Herd, Hie, Hoon, Hoosh, Hot-rod, Hoy, Hunt, Hurl, Impel, Impetus, Impinge, Impulse, Jehu, Jockey, Juggernaut, Lash, Libido, Lunge, Mahout, Make, Mall, Motor, Motorman, Offensive, Peg, Penetrate, Piston, Power, Propel, Put, RAC, Rack, Ram, Rebut, Ride, Road, Roadhog, Run, Scorch, Screw, Scud, Shepherd, Shoo, Spank, Spin, Spur, Start, Stroke, Sunday, Sweep, Task-master, Teamster, Tee, Test, Thrust, Toad, Tool, Trot, Truckie, Two-stroke, Urge, Urgence, Wagoner, Wood, Wreak

Drivel Balderdash, Blether(skate), Drip, Drool, Humbug, Nonsense, Pap, Rot, Salivate, Slaver

Drizzle Drow, Haze, Mist, Mizzle, Roke, Scouther, Scowther, Serein, Skiffle, Smir(r), Smur, Spit

Droop(y), Drooping Cernuous, Decline, Flag, Languish, Lill, Limp, Lob, Loll, Lop, Nutate, Oorie, Ourie, Owrie, Peak, Ptosis, Slink, Slouch, Weeping, Welk(e), Wilt, Wither

Drop(s), Dropping Acid, Airlift, Apraxia, Bag, Bead, Beres, Blob, Cadence, Calve, Cascade, Cast, Chocolate, Cowpat, Dap, Delayed, Descent, Deselect, Dink, Dip, Downturn, Drappie, Drib(let), Ease, Ebb, Escarp(ment), Fall, Floor, Flop, Fruit, Fumet, Gallows, Globule, Gout(te), Guano, Gutta, Guttate, Instil, Knockout, Land, Minim, Modicum, Muff, Mute, Omit, Pilot, Plonk, Plummet, Plump, Plunge, Plunk, Precepit, Precipice, (Prince) Rupert's, Rain, Scat, Scrap, Shed, Sip, Skat, Spraint, Stilliform, Tass, Taste, Tear, Virga, Wrist

Drop-out Beatnik, Hippie, Hippy

Drought Dearth, Drouth, Lack, Thirst

Drove(r) Band, Crowd, Flock, Herd, Host, Masses, Overlander, Puncher

Drown(ed), Drowning Drook, Drouk, Engulf, Inundate, Noyade, Overcome, Sorrows, Submerge

Drudge(ry) Devil, Dogsbody, Fag, Grind, Hack, Jackal, Johnson, Plod, Scrub, Slave(y), Snake, Sweat, Thraldom, Toil, Trauchle, Treadmill

Drug(ged) Anti-depressant, Bag, Base, Blow, Bolus, Bomber, Boo, Deck, Designer, Dope, Downer, Elixir, Fantasy, Fertility, Fig, Gateway, Hallucinogen, Hard, High, Lifestyle, Line, Load, Mainline, Medicine, Miracle, Nervine, Nobble, Opiate, Painkiller, Paregoric, Parenteral, Pharmaceutics, Pharmacopoeia, Poison, Prophylactic, Psychedelic, Psychodelic, Sedate, Snort, Soft, Spike, Stimulant, Stupefy, Substance, Truth, Upper, Weed, White stuff, Wonder

Drum(mer), Drumming, Drumbeat Arête, Atabal, Barrel, Beatbox, Bodhran, Bongo, Brake, Carousel, Chamade, Conga, Dash-wheel, Devil's tattoo, Dhol, Dr, Drub, Ear, Flam, Kettle, Lambeg, Mridamgam, Mridang(a), Mridangam, Myringa, Naker, Pan, Percussion, Rappel, Rataplan, Reel, Rep, Ridge, Rigger, Roll, Ruff, Ruffle, Salesman, Side, Snare, Steel, Tabla, Tabour, Tabret, Tambourine, Tam-tam, Tap, Tattoo, Thrum, Timbal, Timp(ano), Tom-tom, Touk, Traps, Traveller, Tuck, Tymbal, Tympanist, Tympano, Whim, Work

▷ **Drunken** *may indicate* an anagram

Dry(ing), Drier Air, Anhydrous, Arefaction, Arefy, Arid, Blot, Bone, Brut, Corpse, Crine, Dehydrate, Desiccate, Detox, Drain, Dull, Evaporate, Exsiccator, Firlot, Fork, Harmattan, Hasky, Hi(r)stie, Humidor, Jejune, Jerk, Khor, Kiln, Mummify,

Oast, > **PARCH**, Prosaic, Reast, Reist, Rizzar, Rizzer, Rizzor, Sciroc, Scorch, Sear, Sec(co), Seco, Sere, Shrivel, Siccative, Siroc(co), Sober, Sponge, Steme, Stove, Ted, Thirsty, Thristy, Toasted, Torrefy, Torrid, Towel, Tribble, Trocken, TT, Unwatery, Watertight, Welt, Wilt, Win(n), Wipe, Wither, Wizened, Xeransis, Xerasia, Xero(sis), Xerostomia

Dual Double, Twin, Twofold

Dubious Doubtful, Equivocal, Fishy, Fly-by-night, Hesitant, Iffy, Improbable, Questionable, Scepsis, Sceptical, Sesey, Sessa, > **SHADY**, Suspect, Unlikely

▷ **Dubious** *may indicate* an anagram

Duck(ling), Ducked Amphibian, Avoid, Aylesbury, Bald-pate, Bargander, Bergander, Blob, Blue, Bob, Bufflehead, Bum(m)alo, Canard, Canvasback, Dead, Dearie, Decoy, Dip, Dodge, Dodo, Douse, Drook, Drouk, Dunk(er), Eider, Enew, Escape, Evade, Ferruginous, Flapper, Gadwall, Garganey, Garrot, Golden-eye, Goosander, Greenhead, Hareld, Harlequin, Heads, Herald, Immerse, Jook, Jouk, Long-tailed, Mallard, Mandarin, Muscovy, Musk, Nil, O, Oldsquaw, Paddling, Palmated, Paradise, Pekin(g), Pintail, Plunge, Pochard, Poker, Ruddy, Runner, Rush, Scaup, Scoter, Sheld(d)uck, Shieldrake, Shovel(l)er, Shun, Sitting, Smeath, Smee(th), Smew, Sord, Spatula, Sprigtail, Surf(scoter), Teal, Team, Tufted, Tunker, Velvet scoter, Whistling, Widgeon, Wigeon, Wood, Zero

Duct Bile, Canal(iculus), Channel, Conduit, Epididymus, Fistula, Gland, Lachrymal, Laticifer, Pipe, Tear, Thoracic, Tube, Ureter, Vas deferens

Due(s) Adequate, Arrearage, Claim, Debt, Deserts, Forinsec, Geld, Heriot, Just, Lot, Mature, Owing, Reddendo, Rent, Right, > **SUITABLE**, Thereanent, Toll, Tribute, Worthy

Dug-out Canoe, Shelter, Trench, Trough

Duke(dom) Alva, Clarence, D, Ellington, Fist, Iron, Milan, Orsino, Peer, Prospero, Rohan, Wellington

Dull(ard), Dullness Anorak, Bald, Banal, Barren, Besot, Bland, Blear, Blunt, Boeotian, Boring, Cloudy, Commonplace, Dead (and alive), Deadhead, Dense, Dim, Dinge, Dingy, Ditchwater, Doldrums, Dowf, Dowie, Drab, Drear, Dreich, Dry, Dunce, Faded, Flat, Fozy, Grey, Heavy, Hebetate, Ho-hum, Humdrum, Illustrious, Insipid, Jejune, Lacklustre, Lifeless, Log(y), Lowlight, Mat(t), Matte, Monotonous, Mopish, Mull, Obtund, Obtuse, Opacity, Opiate, Ordinary, Overcast, Owlish, Pall, Pedestrian, Perstringe, Podunk, Prosaic, Prose, Prosy, Rebate, Rust, Slow, Sopite, Staid, Stick, Stodger, Stodgy, Stolid, Stuffy, Stultify, > **STUPID**, Sunless, Tame, Tarnish, Tedious, Ticky-tacky, Toneless, Torpor, Treadmill, Tubby, Vapid, Wonk, Wooden, Zoid

Dumb(ness) Alalia, Aphonic, Crambo, Hobbididance, Inarticulate, Mute, Silent, Stupid

Dummy Comforter, Copy, Effigy, Mannequin, Mock-up, Model, Pacifier, Table, Waxwork

Dump(ing), Dumps Abandon, Blue, Core, Dispirited, Doldrums, Empty, Hole, Jettison, Junk, Scrap, Shoot, Store(house), Tip, Unlade, Unload

Dumpling Dim sum, Dough(boy), Gnocchi, Knaidel, Knish, Norfolk, Quenelle, Suet, Won ton

Dune Areg, Bar, Barchan(e), Bark(h)an, Erg, Sandbank, Seif, Star, Whaleback

Dungeon Bastille, Cell, Confine, Donjon, Durance

Dupe Catspaw, Chiaus, Chouse, Cony, Cully, Delude, Geck, Gull, Hoax, Hoodwink, Mug, Pawn, Pigeon, Plover, Sitter, Sucker, Swindle, > **TRICK**, Victim

Durable Enduring, Eternal, Eterne, Hardy, Lasting, Permanent, Stout, Tough

Duration Extent, Period, Span

Duress Coercion, Pressure, Restraint

During Amid, Dia-, For, In, Over, Throughout, While, Whilst

Dusk(y) Dark, Dewfall, Dun, Eve, Gloaming, Gloom, Owl-light, Phaeic, Twilight, Umbrose

Dust(y) Arid, Ash, Bo(a)rt, Calima, Clean, Coom, Cosmic, Derris, Devil, Duff, Earth, Fuss, Khak(i), Lemel, Limail, Lo(e)ss, Miller, Nebula, Pollen, Pother, Pouder, Poudre, Powder, Pozz(u)olana, Pudder, Rouge, Seed, Shaitan, Slack, Stour, Talc, Volcanic, Wipe

▷ **Dusted** *may indicate* an anagram

Duster Cloth, Feather, Talcum, Torchon

Dutch(man), Dutchwoman Batavian, Boor, Cape, Courage, D(u), Double, Elm, Erasmus, Frow, Kitchen, Knickerbocker, Mynheer, Patron, Sooterkin, Taal, Wife

Dutiful, Duty Active, Ahimsa, Average, Blench, Bond, Charge, Corvee, Customs, Death, Debt, Deontology, Devoir, Docile, Drow, Due, Duplicand, End, Estate, Excise, Fatigue, Feu, Function, Heriot, Homage, Imposition, Impost, Incumbent, Lastage, Likin, Mission, Mistery, Mystery, Obedient, Obligation, Octroi, Office, Onus, Pia, Picket, Pious, Point, Prisage, Probate, Rota, Sentry-go, Shift, Stamp, Stillicide, Stint, Succession, Tariff, > **TASK**, Tax, Toll, Transit, Trow, Watch, Zabeta

Dwarf(ism) Achondroplasia, Agate, Alberich, Andvari, Ateleiosis, Bashful, Belittle, Bes, Black, Bonsai, Brown, Doc, Dopey, Droich, Drow, Durgan, Elf, Gnome, Grumpy, Happy, Hobbit, Homuncule, Hop o' my thumb, Knurl, Laurin, Little man, Man(n)ikin, > **MIDGET**, Mime, Minikin, Minim, Nanism, Nectabanus, Ni(e)belung, Nurl, Overshadow, Pacolet, Pigmy, Pygmy, Red, Regin, Ront, Rumpelstiltskin, Runt, Skrimp, Sleepy, Sneezy, > **STUNT**, Tiddler, Titch, Tokoloshe, Tom Thumb, Toy, Troll, Trow, White

Dwindle Decline, Diminish, Fade, Lessen, Peter, Shrink, Wane

Dye(ing), Dyestuff Alkanet, Anil, Anthracene, Anthraquinone, Archil, Azo(benzine), Bat(t)ik, Camwood, Canthaxanthin, Carthamine, Catechin, Chay(a), Chica, Choy, Cinnabar, Cobalt, Cochineal, Colour, Congo, Corkir, Crocein, Crotal, Crottle, Cudbear, Dinitrobenzene, Direct, Embrue, Engrain, Envermeil, Eosin, Flavin(e), Fuchsin(e), Fustic, Fustoc, Gambi(e)r, Grain, Henna, Hue, Ikat, Imbrue, Imbue, Incardine, Indamine, Indican, Indigo, Indirubin, Indoxyl, Indulin(e), Ingrain, Kamala, Kermes, Kohl, Korkir, Madder, Magenta, Mauvein(e), Myrobalan, Nigrosin(e), Orcein, Orchel(la), Orchil, Para-red, Phenolphthalein, Phthalein, > **PIGMENT**, Primuline, Puccoon, Purpurin, Pyronine, Quercitron, Quinoline, Raddle, Resorcinol, Rhodamine, Rosanilin(e), Safranin(e), Shaya, > **STAIN**, Stone-rag, Stone-raw, Sumac(h), Sunfast, Tannin, Tartrazine, Tie-dye, Tinct, Tint, Tropaeolin, Turnsole, Valonia, Vat, Wald, Weld, Woad, Woald, Wold, Xanthium, Xylidine

▶ **Dying** *see* **DIE**

Dyke Aboideau, Aboiteau, Bund, Devil's, Gall, Offa's

Dynamic Ballistics, Energetic, Forceful, High-powered, Potent

Dynamite Blast, Explode, Gelignite, TNT, Trotyl

Dynasty Angevin, Bourbon, Capetian, Carolingian, Chin(g), Ch'ing, Chou, Era, Habsburg, Han, Hapsburg, Honan, House(hold), Hyksos, Khan, Manchu, Maurya, Merovingian, Ming, Pahlavi, Ptolemy, Qajar, Q'ing, Rameses, Romanov, Rule, Safavid, Saga, Sassanid, Seleucid, Seljuk, Shang, Song, Sui, Sung, Tai-ping, Tang, Tudor, Wei, Yi, Yuan, Zhou

Ee

E Boat, East, Echo, Energy, English, Spain

Each All, Apiece, Ea, > EVERY, Ilka, Per, Severally

Eager(ly) Agog, Antsy, Ardent, Avid, Beaver, Bore, Earnest, Enthusiastic, Fain, Fervent, Fervid, Frack, Gung-ho, Hot, Intent, > KEEN, Perfervid, Race, Raring, Rath(e), Ready, Roost, Sharp-set, Sore, Spoiling, Thirsty, Toey, Wishing, Yare

Eagle Al(l)erion, American, Aquila, Bald, Bateleur, Berghaan, Erne, Ethon, Gier, Golden, Harpy, Legal, Lettern, Ossifrage

Ear(drum), Ear trouble Ant(i)helix, Attention, Audience, Auricle, Cauliflower, Cochlea, Concha, Deafness, External, Glue, Hearing, Inner, Jenkins, Listen, Lug, Otalgia, Otalgy, Otic, Parotic, Pinna, Tragus, Utricle

Earlier, Early Above, Ago, Ahead, AM, Auld, Betimes, Cockcrow, Daybreak, Ex, Germinal, Incipient, Precocious, Precursor, Prehistoric, Premature, Prevernal, Previous, Primeval, Primordial, Prior, Rear, Rudimentary, Soon, Timely, Tim(e)ous

▷ **Early** *may indicate* belonging to an earl

▷ **Early stages of** *may indicate* first one or two letters of the word(s) following

Earmark Allocate, Bag, Book, Characteristic, > RESERVE, Tag, Target

Earn(er), Earnings Achieve, Addle, Breadwinner, Deserve, Gain, Make, Merit, Win

Earnest Ardent, Arle(s)(-penny), Deposit, Fervent, Imprest, Intent, Promise, Serious, Token, Zealous

Earring Drop, Hoop, Keeper, Pendant, Sleeper, Snap, Stud

Earth(y) Antichthon, Art, Capricorn, Clay, Cloam, Cologne, Dirt, Drey, Dust, Eard, Epigene, Foxhole, Friable, Fuller's, Gaea, Gaia, Gault, Ge, Globe, Ground, Horst, Kadi, Lair, Loam, Malm, Mankind, Mantle, Mools, Mould, Mouls, Papa, Pise, Planet, Racy, Rare, Red, Seat, Sett, Sod, > SOIL, Taurus, Telluric, Tellus, Terra, Terrain, Terramara, Terrene, Topsoil, Virgo, Ye(a)rd, Yird

Earthquake Aftershock, Bradyseism, Mercalli, Richter, Seism, Shake, Shock, Temblor

Ease, Easing, Easygoing Alleviate, Carefree, Clear, Clover, Comfort, Content, Defuse, Deregulate, Détente, Facility, Hands down, Informal, Lax, Mellow, Mid(dy), Mitigate, Palliate, Peace, Quiet, Relieve, Reposal, Repose, Soothe

East(erly), Eastward Anglia, Asia, Chevet, E, Fassel, Eassil, Eothen, Eurus, Levant, Orient, Ost, Sunrise

Easter Festival, Island, Pace, Pasch, Pasque

Easy, Easily ABC, Cakewalk, Carefree, Cinch, Cushy, Doddle, Facile, Free, Gift, Glib, Jammy, Lax, Light, Natural, Picnic, Pie, Pushover, Simple, Snotty, Soft, Tolerant, Walk-over, Yare

▷ **Easy** *may indicate* an anagram

Eat(able), Eater, Eating Bite, Bolt, Chop, Consume, Corrode, Edible, Erode, Esculent, Etch, Fare, Feast, > FEED, Fret, Gnaw, Go, Gobble, Graze, Grub, Hog, Munch, Nosh, Nutritive, Omnivore, Partake, Refect, Scoff, Stuff, Sup, Swallow, Take, Taste, Trencherman

Eavesdrop(per) Earwig, Listen, Overhear, Snoop, Tap

Ebb(ing) Abate, Decline, Recede, Sink

Eccentric Abnormal, Cam, Card, Character, Crank, Curious, Dag, Deviant, Dingbat, Ditsy, Ditzy, E, Farouche, Fey, Fie, Freak, Geek, Gonzo, Iffish, Irregular, Kinky, Kook(y), Mattoid, Nutcase, Odd(ball), Offbeat, Off-centre, Original, Outré, > **PECULIAR**, Pixil(l)ated, Queer, Quirky, Quiz, Rake, Raky, Recondite, Rum, Scatty, Screwball, Screwy, Wack(y), Way-out, Weird(o), W(h)acko

▷ **Eccentric** *may indicate* an anagram

Ecclesiastic Abbé, Clergyman, Clerical, Lector, Secular, Theologian

Echinoderm Asteroidea, Basket-star, Brittle-star, Comatulid, Crinoid, Sea-egg, Sea-lily, Sea-urchin, Starfish

Echo Angel, Answer, Ditto, E, Imitate, Iterate, Rebound, Repeat, Repercussion, Reply, Resonant, Respeak, Reverb(erate), Ring, Rote

Eclipse Annular, Block, Cloud, Deliquium, Hide, Lunar, Obscure, Occultation, Outmatch, Outweigh, Overshadow, Penumbra, Solar, Total, Transcend

Ecology Bionomics

Economic(s), **Economise** Budget, Conserve, Eke, Husband, Pinch, Retrench, Scrimp, Skimp, Spare, Sparing

Economy, **Economic(al)**, **Economics** Agronomy, Black, Careful, Cliometrics, Conversation, Frugal, Market, Neat, Parsimony, Retrenchment, Shoestring, Thrift

Ecstasy, **Ecstatic** Bliss, Delight, Dove, E, Exultant, Joy, Lyrical, Rapture, Sent, Trance, Transport

Edda Elder, Prose, Younger

Eden Bliss, Fall, Heaven, Paradise, PM, Utopia

Edge, **Edging**, **Edgy** Advantage, Arris, Border, Bordure, Brim, Brink, Brittle, Brown, Burr, Chamfer, Chimb, Chime, Chine, Coaming, Costa, Cutting, Dag, Deckle, End, Flange, Flounce, Frill, Fringe, Frontier, Furbelow, Gunnel, Gunwale, Hem, Hone, Inch, Inside, Kerb, Knife, Leading, Leech, Limb(ate), Limbus, Limit, Lip, List, Lute, Marge(nt), Margin, Nosing, Orle, Outside, Parapet, Periphery, Picot, Pikadell, Piping, Rand, Rim, Rund, Rymme, Selvage, Selvedge, Sidle, Skirt, Strand, Trailing, Trim, Tyre, Verge, Wear

▶ **Edible** *see* EAT(ABLE)

Edict Ban, Bull, Decree, Decretal, Extravagantes, Fatwa, Interim, Irade, Nantes, Notice, Pragmatic, Proclamation, Ukase

Edit(or), **Editorial** Abridge, Article, City, Cut, Dele, Emend, Expurgate, Garble, Leader, Recense, Redact, Revise, Seaman

▷ **Edited** *may indicate* an anagram

Edith Sitwell

Edition Aldine, Ed, Extra, Hexapla(r), Issue, Limited, Number, Omnibus, Variorium, Version

Educate(d) Baboo, Babu, Enlighten, Evolué, Informed, Instruct, Learned, Noursle, Nousell, Nousle, Nurture, Nuzzle, Polymath, Preppy, Scholarly, School, > **TEACH**, Train, Yuppie

Education(alist) Adult, B.Ed, Classical, Didactics, Heurism, Learning, Mainstream, Montessori, Pedagogue, Pestalozzi, Piarist, Primary, Schooling, Teacher, Tertiary, Upbringing

Edward Confessor, Ed, Elder, Lear, Martyr, Ned, Ted

Eel Conger, Electric, Elver, Hagfish, Lamprey, Launce, Moray, Olm, Sand(ling)

Efface Cancel, Delete, Dislimn, > **ERASE**, Expunge, Obliterate

Effect(s), **Effective(ness)**, **Effectual** Achieve, Acting, Auger, Bags, Belongings, Bit, Causal, Competent, Consequence, Domino, Doppler, Efficacious, Enact,

End, Estate, Functional, Fungibles, Gear, Goods, Greenhouse, Home, Impact, Implement(al), Impression, Knock-on, Moire, Neat, Nisi, Operant, Outcome, Personal, Phi, Position, Potent, Promulgate, Repercussion, > RESULT, Ripple, Side, Sound, Special, Spectrum, Spin-off, Striking, Tableau, Telling, Upshot, Viable, Virtual, Work

Effervescence, Effervescent Bubbling, Ebullient, Fizz

▷ **Effervescent** *may indicate* an anagram

Efficiency, Efficient Able, Capable, Competent, Despatch, Ergonomics, Productivity, Smart, Streamlined, Strong

Effigy Figure, Guy, Idol, Image, Statua, Statue

Effluence, Effluent, Effluvia Air, Aura, Billabong, Discharge, Fume, Gas, Halitus, Miasma, Odour, Outflow, Outrush

Effort Achievement, Attempt, Best, Conatus, Drive, Essay, Exertion, Fit, Herculean, Labour, Molimen, Nisus, Rally, Spurt, Stab, Strain, Struggle, > TRY, Work, Yo

Effrontery Audacity, Brass, Cheek, Face, Gall, Neck, Nerve, Temerity

Effuse, Effusion, Effusive Emanate, Exuberant, Exude, Gush, Lyric, Ode, Outburst, Prattle, Rhapsody, Screed, Spill

Eg As, Example

Egg(s) Abet, Benedict, Berry, Bomb, Caviar(e), Chalaza, Cleidoic, Clutch, Cockney, Collop, Coral, Curate's, Darning, Easter, Edge, Fabergé, Fetus, Flyblow, Foetus, Free-range, Glair(e), Goad, Goog, Graine, Hoy, Incite, Instigate, Layings, Mine, Nit, Oocyte, Oophoron, Ova, Ovum, Prairie oyster, Press, Raun, Roe, Scotch, Seed, Spat, Spawn, Spur(ne), Tar(re), Tooth, Tread(le), Urge, Yelk, Yolk

Egghead Don, Highbrow, Intellectual, Mensa, Pedant

Ego(ism), Egoist Che, Conceit, I, Narcissism, Not-I, Pride, Self, Solipsism, Vanity

Egypt(ian), Egyptologist Arab, Cairene, Carter, Cheops, Chephren, Copt(ic), ET, Goshen, Imhotep, Nasser, Nefertiti, Nilote, Nitrian, Osiris, Ptolemy, Rameses, Syene, Wafd

Eight(h), Eighth day Acht, Byte, Crew, Cube, Nundine, Octa, Octad, Octal, Octastrophic, Octave, Octet, Ogdoad, Okta, Ottava, Ure

Either Also, Both, O(u)ther, Such

Ejaculate Blurt, Discharge, Emit, Exclaim

Eject Bounce, Disgorge, Dismiss, Emit, Erupt, Expel, Oust, Propel, Spew, Spit, Spue, Vent

Eke Augment, Eche, Enlarge, Husband, Supplement

Elaborate Detail, Develop, Enlarge, Florid, Intricate, Ornate

Elan Dash, Drive, Esprit, > FLAIR, Gusto, Lotus, Spirit, Vigour

Elastic(ity) Adaptable, Buoyant, Dopplerite, Elater, Flexible, Give, Resilient, Rubber, Spandex®, Springy, Stretchy, Tone, Tonus

Elastomer Adiprene®

Elate(d), Elation Cheer, Euphoric, Exalt, Exhilarate, Gladden, Hault, Ruff(e), Uplift

Elbow, Elbow tip Akimbo, Ancon, Angle, Bender, Cubital, Hustle, Joint, Jostle, Kimbo, Noop, Nudge, Olecranon, Tennis

Elder(ly), Eldest Ancestor, Ancient, Bourtree, Chief, Classis, Eigne, Geriatric, Guru, Kaumatua, OAP, Presbyter, > SENIOR, Sire, Susanna, Wallwort

Elect(ed), Election(eer), Electoral Choice, Choose, Chosen, Eatanswill, Elite, Gerrymander, Hustings, In, Israelite, Khaki, Opt, Pick, PR, Primary, Psephology, Rectorial, Return, Select, Stump

Electricity Galvanism, HT, Juice, Power, Static

Electrify Astonish, Galvanise, Startle, Stir, Thrill

Elegance, **Elegant** Artistic, Bijou, Chic, Classy, Debonair, Fancy, Finesse, Gainly, Galant, Grace, Luxurious, Polished, Refined, Ritzy, > **SMART**, Soigné(e), Swish, Tall, Urbane

Element(s), **Elementary** Abcee, Abecedarian, Absey, Barebones, Detail, > **ESSENCE**, Essential, Factor, Feature, Fuel, Heating, Ideal, Identity, Milieu, Pixel, Primary, Principle, Rare Earth, Simple, Trace, Transition, Weather

Elephant African, Indian, Jumbo, Mammoth, Mastodon, Oliphant, Pachyderm, Rogue, Tusker, White

Elevate(d), **Elevation**, **Elevator** Agger, Attitude, Cheer, Eminence, Ennoble, Heighten, Hoist, Jack, Lift, Promote, > **RAISE**, Random, Relievo, Ridge, Rise, Sublimate, Up(lift)

Eleven Elf, Legs, Side, Team, XI

Eligible Available, Catch, Fit, Nubile, Parti, Qualified, Worthy

Eliminate, **Elimination** Cull, Delete, Discard, Exclude, Execute, Extirpate, Liquidate, Omit, Preclude, Purge, Rid, Zap

Elite Best, Choice, Crack, > **CREAM**, Elect, Flower, Meritocracy, Ton, U, Zaibatsu

Elm Slippery, Wich, Wych

Elongate Extend, Lengthen, Protract, Stretch

Eloquence, **Eloquent** Articulate, Demosthenic, Facundity, Fluent, Honey-tongued, Oracy, Rhetoric, Vocal

Else(where) Absent, Alibi, Aliunde, Other

Elude, **Elusive** Avoid, Dodge, Escape, > **EVADE**, Evasive, Foil, Intangible, Jink, Slippy, Subt(i)le, Will o' the wisp

Emaciated, **Emaciation** Atrophy, Erasmus, Gaunt, Haggard, Lean, Skinny, Sweeny, Tabid, Thin, Wanthriven, Wasted

Email Flame, Spam

Emancipate, **Emancipation** Deliver, Forisfamiliate, Free, > **LIBERATE**, Manumission, Uhuru

Embankment Bund, Causeway, Dam, Dyke, Earthwork, Levee, Mattress, Mound, Rampart, Remblai, Stopbank

Embargo > **BAN**, Blockade, Edict, Restraint

Embark Begin, Board, Enter, Inship, Launch, Sail

Embarrass(ed), **Embarrassing**, **Embarrassment** Abash, Disconcert, Mess, Pose, Predicament, Shame, Sheepish, Squirming, Straitened

▷ **Embarrassed** *may indicate* an anagram

Embassy Consulate, Embassade, Legation, Mission

Embellish(ed), **Embellishment** Adorn, Beautify, Bedeck, Deck, Decorate, Embroider, Enrich, Garnish, Garniture, > **ORNAMENT**, Ornate

Ember(s) Ash, Cinder, Clinker, Gleed

Emblem(atic) Badge, Bear, Colophon, Daffodil, Device, Figure, Ichthys, Impresa, Insignia, Kikumon, Leek, Lis, Maple leaf, Oak, Rose, Roundel, Shamrock, Sign, Spear-thistle, > **SYMBOL**, Tau-cross, Thistle, Token, Totem(ic), Triskelion, Wheel

Emboss(ed) Adorn, Chase, Cloqué, Engrave, Pounce

Embrace(d) Accolade, Arm, Canoodle, Clasp, Clinch, Clip, Coll, Complect, Comprise, Cuddle, Embosom, Encircle, Enclasp, Enclose, Enfold, Envelop, Espouse, Fold, Grab, Hug, Include, Kiss, Lasso, Neck, Press, Twine, Welcome, Wrap

▷ **Embraces**, **Embracing** *may indicate* a hidden word

Embroider(y) Appliqué, Braid, Brede, Couching, Crewel-work, Cross-stitch, Cutwork, Embellish, Exaggerate, Fag(g)oting, Fancywork, Featherstitch,

Gros point, Handiwork, Lace(t), Needlepoint, Needlework, Orfray, Ornament, Orphrey, Orris, Petit point, Pinwork, Purl, Sampler, Sew, Smocking, Stitch, Stumpwork, Tent

Embryo(nic) Blastocyst, Blastula, Fo(e)tus, Gastrula, Germ, Mesoblast, Origin, Rudiment, Undeveloped

Emend Adjust, Alter, Edit, Reform

Emerge(ncy), Emerging Anadyomene, Arise, Craunch, Crise, Crisis, Crunch, Debouch, Emanate, Erupt, Exigency, Issue, Last-ditch, Need, Outcrop, Pinch, Spring, Stand-by, Strait

▷ **Emerge from** *may indicate* an anagram or a hidden word

Eminence, Eminent Altitude, Cardinal, Distinguished, Grand, Height, Hill, Light, Lion, Lofty, Luminary, Noble, > NOTABLE, Prominence, Renown, Repute, Stature, Tor, > VIP

Emirate Dubai

Emission, Emit Discharge, Emanate, Give, Issue, Utter

Emolument Income, Perk, Remuneration, Salary, Stipend, Tip, Wages

Emotion(al) Anger, Anoesis, Breast, Chord, Ecstasy, Excitable, Feeling, Freak-out, Hysteria, Joy, Limbic, Passion, Reins, Roar, Sensibility, Sensitive, Sentiment, Spirit, Transport, Weepy

Empathy Rapport, Rapprochement, Sympathy

Emperor Agramant(e), Akbar, Akihito, Antoninus, Augustus, Babur, Barbarossa, Bonaparte, Caligula, Caracalla, Charlemagne, Claudius, Commodus, Concerto, Constantine, Diocletian, Domitian, Ferdinand, Gaius, Genghis Khan, Gratian, Hadrian, Heraclius, Hirohito, Imp, Inca, Jimmu, Justinian, Kaiser, Keasar, Kesar, King, Maximilian, Menelik, Mikado, Ming, Mogul, Montezuma, Mpret, Napoleon, Negus, Nero, Nerva, Otho, Otto, Penguin, Peter the Great, Purple, Pu-yi, Rex, Rosco, Ruler, Severus, Shah Jahan, Shang, Sovereign, Sultan, Tenno, Theodore, Theodosius, Tiberius, Titus, Trajan, Tsar, Valens, Valentinian, Valerian, Vespasian, Vitellius

Emphasis, Emphasize, Emphatic Accent, Birr, Bold, Dramatise, Forcible, Foreground, Forzando, Hendiadys, Italic, Marcato, Positive, Sforzando, Underline, Underscore, Vehement

Empire Assyria, British, Byzantine, Domain, Empery, Kingdom, Ottoman, Realm, Reich, Roman

Employ(ment) Business, Calling, Engage, Hire, Occupy, Pay, Practice, Pursuit, Use, Using, Utilise, Vocation

Employee(s) Factotum, Hand, Help, Minion, Payroll, Personnel, Servant, Staff, Staffer, Worker

Employer Baas, Boss, Master, Padrone, User

▷ **Employs** *may indicate* an anagram

Empress Eugenie, Josephine, Messalina, Sultana, Tsarina

Empty Addle, Bare, Barren, Blank, Buzz, Clear, Deplete, Deserted, Devoid, Disembowel, Drain, Exhaust, Expel, Forsaken, Futile, Gut, Hent, Hollow, Inane, Jejune, Lave, Null, Pump, Shallow, Teem, Toom, Tume, Unfurnished, Unoccupied, Vacant, Vacate, Vacuous, Vain, > VOID

▷ **Empty** *may indicate* an 'o' in the word or an anagram

Emulate Ape, Copy, Envy, Equal, Imitate, Match

Enable Authorise, Empower, Potentiate, Qualify, Sanction

Enamel(led), Enamel work Aumail, Champlevé, Cloisonné, Della-robbia, Dentine, Fabergé, Ganion, Lacquer, Polish, Porcelain, Schwarzlot, Shippo, Smalto, Stoved, Vitreous

Encampment Bivouac, Douar, Dowar, Duar, Laager, Laer, Settlement

Encase(d), Encasement Box, Crate, Emboîtement, Encapsulate, Enclose, Obtect

Enchant(ing), Enchanted, Enchantment Captivate, Charm, Delight, Gramary(e), Incantation, Magic, Necromancy, Rapt, Sorcery, Spellbind, Thrill

Enchanter, Enchantress Archimage, Archimago, Armida, Circe, Comus, Fairy, Lorelei, Magician, Medea, Mermaid, Prospero, Reim-kennar, Sorcerer, Vivien, Witch

Encircle(d) Enclose, Encompass, Enlace, Entrold, Gird, Inorb, Introld, Orbit, Pale, Ring, > **SURROUND**

Enclose(d), Enclosing, Enclosure Bawn, Beset, Boma, Box, Cage, Carol, Carrel, Case, Common, Compound, Corral, Court, Embale, Embower, Enceinte, Encircle, Enclave, Enshrine, Fence, Fold, Garth, Haw, Hem, Henge, Hope, Impound, In, Incapsulate, Insert, Interclude, Lairage, Pale, Peel, Pele, Pen(t), Pin, Pinfold, Playpen, Plenum, Rail, Rath, Recluse, Ree(d), Ring, Run, Seal, Sekos, Sept, Seraglio, Serail, Several, Sin bin, Steeld, Stell, Stockade, Sty, > **SURROUND**, Tine, Vibarium, Ward, Wrap, Yard

Encompass Bathe, Begird, Beset, Environ, Include, Surround

Encounter Battle, Brush, Combat, Contend, Cope, Face, Hit, Incur, Interview, > **MEET**, Rencontre, Ruffle, Skirmish

Encourage(ment), Encouraging Abet, Acco(u)rage, Alley-oop, Attaboy, Bolster, Boost, Buck, Cheer, Cohortative, Commend, Dangle, Egg, Embolden, Exhort, Fillip, Fire, Fortify, Foster, Fuel, Gee, Hearten, Heigh, Help, Hortatory, Incite, Nourish, Pat, Patronise, Prod, Push, Reassure, Root, Support, Tally-ho, Uplift, Urge, Yo

Encroach(ment) Impinge, Infringe, Intrude, Invade, Overlap, Overstep, Poach, Trespass, Usurp

Encumber, Encumbrance Burden, Clog, Deadwood, Dependent, > **HANDICAP**, Impede, Load, Obstruct, Saddle

End(ing) Abolish, Abut, Aim, Ambition, Amen, Anus, Arse, Big, Bitter, Bourn(e), Butt, Cease, Climax, Close, Closure, Cloture, Coda, Conclude, Crust, Culminate, Curtain, Curtains, Cut off, Dead, Death, Decease, Denouement, Desinence, Destroy, Determine, Dissolve, Domino, Effect, Envoi, Envoy, Epilogue, Exigent, Expire, Explicit, Extremity, Fatal, Fattrels, Feminine, Final(e), Fine, Finis, > **FINISH**, Finite, Gable, Grave, Heel, Ish, Izzard, Izzet, Kill, Kybosh, Last, Let up, Little, Loose, Masculine, Mill, Nirvana, No side, Ort, Outro, Period, Peter, Pine, Point, Purpose, Quench, Receiving, Remnant, Rescind, Result, Roach, Scotch, Scrag, Shank, Slaughter, Sopite, Split, Sticky, Stub, Surcease, Swansong, Tag, Tail, Tailpiece, Telic, Telos, Term, Terminal, Terminate, Terminus, Thrum, Tip, Toe, Top, Ultimate, Up, Upshot, West, Z

Endeavour Aim, Effort, Enterprise, Strive, Struggle, Try, Venture

Endless Continuous, Ecaudate, Eternal, Eterne, Infinite, Interminable, Perpetual, Undated

▷ **Endlessly** *may indicate* a last letter missing

Endorse(ment) Adopt, Affirm, Approve, Assurance, Back, Confirmation, Initial, Okay, Oke, Ratify, Rubber stamp, Sanction, Second, Sign, > **SUPPORT**, Underwrite, Visa

Endow(ment) Assign, Bequeath, Bestow, Bless, Cha(u)ntry, Dotation, Enrich, Foundation, Gift, Leave, Patrimony, Vest

Endurance, Endure(d), Enduring Bear, Bide, Brook, Dree, Face, Fortitude, Have, Hold, > **LAST**, Livelong, Lump, Patience, Perseverance, Pluck, Ride, Stamina, Stand, Stay, Stomach, Stout, Sustain, Swallow, Thole, Timeless, Tolerance, Undergo, Wear

Enemy Adversary, Antagonist, Boer, Devil, Fifth column, Foe(n), Fone, Opponent, Public, Time

Energetic, Energise, Energy Active, Amp, Animation, Arduous, Cathexis, Chakra, Chi, Dash, Drive, Dynamic, Dynamo, E, Enthalpy, Entropy, EV, Fermi, Fireball, Force, Fructan, Gism, Go, Hartree, Horme, Input, Instress, Internal, > JET, Jism, Jissom, Joie de vivre, Joule, Kinetic, Kundalini, Libido, Luminous, Magnon, Moxie, Nuclear, Orgone, Pep, Phonon, Potency, Potential, > POWER, Powerhouse, QI, Quantum, Rad, Radiant, Radiatory, Rydberg, Sappy, Solar, Steam, Trans-uranic, Verve, Vigour, Vim, Vital, Wave, Zing, Zip

Enervate Exhaust

Enforce(ment) Administer, Coerce, Control, Exact, Implement, Impose

Engage(d), Engagement, Engaging Absorb, Accept, Appointment, Attach, Bespoken, Betrothal, Bind, Book, Busy, Contract, Date, Embark, Employ, Engross, Enlist, Enmesh, Enter, Gear, Gig, Hire, Hold, Interest, Interlock, Lock, Mesh, Met, Occupy, Pledge, Promise, Prosecute, Reserve, Residency, Skirmish, Sponsal, Sponsion, Spousal, Trip, Wage, Winsome

▷ **Engagement** *may indicate* a battle

Engine, Engine part Beam, Bricole, Carburettor, Catapult, Compound, Diesel, Donkey, Dynamo, Fan-jet, Fire, Gas, Ion, Jet, Lean-burn, Light, Locomotive, Machine, Mangonel, > MOTOR, Nacelle, Orbital, Outboard, Petrol, Pilot, Plasma, Podded, Pony, Pug, Pulp, Pulsejet, Push-pull, Radial, Ramjet, Reaction, Reciprocating, Retrorocket, Rocket, Rotary, Scramjet, Search, Side-valve, Stationary, Steam, Tank, Testudo, Traction, Turbine, Turbofan, Turbojet, Turboprop, Two-stroke, V, Vernier, Wankel, Water, Winding

Engineer(ing), Engineers AEU, Arrange, Brunel, De Lessops, Greaser, Heinkel, Junkers, Manoeuvre, Marconi, Marine, Mastermind, McAdam, Operator, Organise, Planner, Repairman, Sapper, Scheme, Siemens, Stage, Stephenson, Telford, Wangle, Wankel, Watt, Whittle

England Albany, Albion, Blighty, John Bull, Merrie

English(man) Anglican, Brit, Bro talk, E, Eng, Estuary, Gringo, John Bull, King's, Limey, Middle, Modern, Norman, Officialese, Oxford, Pidgin, Pom(my), Pommie, Pongo, Queen's, Sassenach, Saxon, Scotic, Shopkeeper, Singlish, Southron, Standard, Wardour Street

Engrave(r), Engraving Aquatint, Blake, Carve, Cerotype, Chalcography, Chase, Cut, Dry-point, Durer, Enchase, Etch, Glyptic, Glyptograph, Hogarth, Impress, Inciser, Inscribe, Intagliate, Lapidary, Mezzotint, Niello, Photoglyphic, Plate, Scrimshandy, Scrimshaw, Steel, Stillet, Stipple, Stylet, Stylography, Xylographer

Engross(ed) Absorb, Engage, Enwrap, Immerse, Monopolise, > OCCUPY, Preoccupy, Prepossess, Rapt, Sink, Writ large

Enhance Add, Augment, Better, Embellish, Exalt, Heighten, Intensify

Enigma(tic) Charade, Conundrum, Dilemma, Gioconda, Mystery, Oracle, Poser, Problem, > PUZZLE, Quandary, Question, Rebus, Riddle, Secret, Sphinxlike, Teaser

Enjoy(able), Enjoyment Apolaustic, Appreciate, Ball, Brook, Delectation, Fruition, Glee, Groove, Gusto, Have, Lekker, Like, Own, Possess, Relish, Ripping, Savour, Taste, Wallow

Enlarge(ment), Enlarger Accrue, Acromegaly, Add, Aneurism, Aneurysm, Augment, Blow-up, Diagraph, Dilate, Exostosis, Expand, Expatiate, Explain, Increase, > MAGNIFY, Piece, Ream, Rebore, Sensationalize, Swell, Telescope, Tumefy, Varicosity

Enlighten(ed), Enlightenment Awareness, Edify, Educate, Explain, Illumine, Instruct, Nirvana, Revelation

Enlist Attest, Conscript, Draft, Engage, Enrol, Induct, Join, Levy, Prest, Recruit, Roster, Volunteer

Enliven(ed) Animate, Arouse, Brighten, Cheer, Comfort, Exhilarate, Ginger,

Invigorate, Merry, Pep, Refresh, Warm

Enmity Animosity, Aversion, Hatred, Malice, Nee(d)le, Rancour

Ennoble(ment) Dub, Elevate, Exalt, Honour, Raise

Enormous Colossal, Exorbitant, Googol, Huge, Humongous, Humungous, > IMMENSE, Jumbo, Mammoth, Mega, Vast

Enough Adequate, > AMPLE, Anow, Basta, Belay, Enow, Fill, Geyan, Nuff, Pax, Plenty, Qs, Sate, Satis, Suffice, Sufficient, Via

Enquire, Enquiring, Enquiry Ask, Check, Curious, Eh, Inquire, Organon, Request, Scan, See, Trial

Enrage(d) > INCENSE, Inflame, Infuriate, Livid, Madden, Wild

Enrich Adorn, Endow, Enhance, Fortify, Fructify, Oxygenate

Enrol(ment) Attest, Empanel, Enlist, Enter, Incept, > JOIN, List, Matriculate, Muster, Register

Ensign Ancient, Badge, Banner, Duster, > FLAG, Gonfalon, Officer, Pennon, Red, White

Enslave(ment) Bondage, Captivate, Chain, Yoke

Ensue Follow, Result, Succeed, Transpire

Entangle(ment) Ball, Elf, Embroil, Encumber, Ensnarl, Entrail, Fankle, Implicate, > KNOT, Mat, Ravel, Retiarius, Trammel

Enter Admit, Broach, Come, Enrol, Infiltrate, Ingo, Insert, Invade, Lodge, Log, Penetrate, Pierce, Record, Submit, Table

Enterprise, Enterprising Adventure, Ambition, Aunter, Dash, Emprise, Free, Goey, Go-getter, Gumption, Industry, Plan, Private, Public, Push, Spirit, Stunt, Venture

Entertain(er), Entertaining, Entertainment Acrobat, Afterpiece, All-nighter, Amphitryon, Amuse, Balladeer, Ballet, Beguile, Burlesque, Busk, Cabaret, Carnival, Cater, Charade, Cheer, Circus, Comedian, Comic, Concert, Conjure, Consider, Cottabus, Crack, Craic, Cuddy, Distract, Divert, Divertissement, ENSA, Extravaganza, Fete, Fleshpots, Floorshow, Foy, Fun, Gaff, Gala, Gas, Gaudy, Gig, Harbour, Harlequin, Have, Hospitality, Host(ess), Impressionist, Interest, Interlude, Intermezzo, Jester, Juggler, Karaoke, Kidult, Kursaal, Lauder, Levee, Light, Masque, Melodrama, Minstrel, Musical, Olio, Opera, Palladium, Panto, Pap, Party, Peepshow, Performer, Piece, Pierrot, Play, Reception, Regale, Review, Revue, Ridotto, Roadshow, Rodeo, Serenade, Showbiz, Sideshow, Singer, Snake-charmer, Soirée, Son et lumière, Striptease, Table, Tamasha, Tattoo, Treat, Variety, Vaudeville, Ventriloquist

Enthuse, Enthusiasm, Enthusiast(ic) Ardour, Buff, Bug, Cat, Cheerleader, Devotee, Ebullience, Ecstatic, Fiend, Fire, Flame, Freak, Furor(e), Get-up-and-go, Gung-ho, Gusto, Hearty, Hype, Into, Keen, Lyrical, Mad, Mania, Muso, Oomph, Outpour, Overboard, Passion, Perfervid, Rah-rah, Raring, Rave, Rhapsodise, Sold, Spirit, Verve, Warmth, Whole-hearted, Zealot, Zest

Entice(ment), Enticing Allure, Angle, Cajole, Carrot, Decoy, Lure, Persuade, Seductive, > TEMPT, Tole, Toll

Entire(ly), Entirety Absolute, All, Complete, Intact, Integral, In toto, Lot, Purely, Systemic, Thorough, Total, > WHOLE

Entity Being, Body, Existence, Holon, Tao, Tensor, Thing

Entrail(s) Bowels, Giblets, Gralloch, Guts, Ha(r)slet, Humbles, Lights, Numbles, Offal, Tripe, Umbles, Viscera

Entrance(d), Entrant, Entry Access, Adit, Anteroom, Arch, Atrium, Attract, Avernus, Bewitch, Charm, Closehead, Contestant, Door, Doorstop, Double, Eye, Fascinate, Foyer, Gate, Ghat, Hypnotise, In-door, Infare, Inflow, Ingress, Inlet, Jaws, Mesmerise, Mouth, Pend, Porch, Portal, Postern, Propylaeum, Propylon,

Reception, Record, Registration, Single, Spellbound, Starter, Stem, Stoa, Stoma, Stulm

Entreat(y) Appeal, Ask, Beg, Beseech, Flagitate, Impetrate, Orison, Petition, Plead, Pray, Precatory, Prevail, Prig, Rogation, Solicit, Sue, Supplicate

Entrepreneur Businessman, Wheeler-dealer

▶ **Entry** *see* ENTRANCE

Entwine Complect, Impleach, Intervolve, Lace, Twist, Weave

Enumerate, Enumeration Catalogue, Count, List, Tell

Envelop(e) Corolla, Corona, Cover(ing), Enclose, Entire, Invest, Involucre, Muffle, Perianth, Sachet, Serosa, Smother, Surround, Swathe

Environment(s), Environmental(ist) Ambience, Entourage, Green, Habitat, Milieu, Setting, Sphere, Surroundings

Envoy Agent, Diplomat, Hermes, Legate, Plenipotentiary

Epic Aeneid, Ben Hur, Beowulf, Calliope, Colossal, Dunciad, Edda, Epopee, Gilgamesh, Homeric, Iliad, Kalevala, Lusiad(s), Mahabharata, Nibelungenlied, Odyssey, Ramayana, Saga

Epicure(an) Apicius, Connoisseur, Gastronome, Glutton, > GOURMAND, Gourmet, Hedonist, Sybarite

Epidemic Pandemic, Pestilence, Plague, Prevalent, Rampant

Epilogue Appendix, Coda, Postscript

Epiphany Twelfthtide

Episode, Episodic Chapter, Incident, Page, Picaresque, Scene

Epistle(s) Lesson, Letter, Missive, Pastoral

Epitome, Epitomise Abridge, Abstract, Digest, Image, Model, Summary, Typify

Epoch Age, Era, Holocene, Miocene, Oligocene, Palaeocene, Period, Pl(e)iocene, Pleistocene

Equable, Equably Calm, Just, Smooth, Tranquil

Equal(ly), Equality, Equal quantities Alike, As, Balanced, Commensurate, Compeer, Egal(ity), Emulate, Equinox, Equiparate, Equity, Even, Even-steven, Fifty-fifty, For, Identical, Identity, Is, Iso-, Isocracy, Level, Level-pegging, Make, Match, Par, Peregal, Rise, Rival, > SO, Square

Equate, Equation(s) Balance, Differential, Dirac, Identity, Parametric, Quadratic, Reduce, Relate, Simultaneous

Equilibrium Balance, Composure, Homeostasis, Isostasy, Poise, Stasis, Tautomerism

Equip(ment), Equipage Accoutrement, Adorn, Apparatus, Apparel, Appliance, Array, Attire, Carriage, Deck, Dight, Expertise, > FURNISH, Gear, Get-up, Graith, Kit, Material, Matériel, Muniments, Outfit, Retinue, Rig, Stock, Stuff, Tack(le), Tool, Turn-out

Equivalence, Equivalent Correspondent, Equal, Same, Tantamount

Equivocate Flannel, Lie, Palter, Prevaricate, Quibble, Tergiversate, Weasel

Era Age, Archaean, C(a)enozoic, Christian, Common, Cretaceous, Decade, Dynasty, Epoch, Hadean, Hegira, Hej(i)ra, Hijra, Jurassic, Lias, Mesozoic, Period, Precambrian, Proterozoic

Eradicate, Erase Abolish, Delete, Demolish, Destroy, Efface, Expunge, Extirp, Obliterate, Purge, Root, Scratch, Uproot

Eratosthenes Sieve

Erect(ion), Erector Build, Construct(ion), Elevate, Hard-on, Perpendicular, Priapism, Prick, Rear, Upright, Vertical

Ergo Argal, Hence, Therefore

Erode, Erosion Corrasion, Denude, Destroy, Deteriorate, Etch, Fret, Wash, Wear, Yardang

Eros, Erotic(a) Amatory, Amorino, Amorous, Aphrodisiac, Carnal, Cupid, Lascivious, Philtre, Prurient, Salacious, Steamy

Err(or) Aliasing, Anachronism, Bish, Blip, Blooper, Blunder, Boner, Bug, Clanger, Comedy, Corrigendum, Fault, Glaring, Heresy, Human, K'thibh, Lapse, Lapsus, Literal, Misgo, Misprint, Misprise, Misprize, Misstep, > **MISTAKE**, Out, Probable, Rounding, Rove, Sampling, Semantic, Sin, Slip, Slip-up, Solecism, Standard, Stray, Trip, Truncation, Typo, Typographical

Errand Chore, Commission, Message, Mission, Sleeveless, Task

Erratic Haywire, Temperamental, Vagary, Vagrant, Wayward

Erroneous False, Inaccurate, Mistaken, Non-sequitur

Erudite, Erudition Academic, Learned, Wisdom

Erupt(ion), Erupture Belch, Brash, Burst, Eject, Emit, > **EXPLODE**, Fumarole, Hives, Lichen, Mal(l)ander, Mallender, Outbreak, Outburst, Papilla, Pustule, Rash

Escape(e), Escapade, Escapist Abscond, Avoid, Bale out, Bolt, Bolthole, Breakout, Caper, Eject, Elope, Elude, Elusion, Esc, Evade, Exit, Fire, Flee, Flight, Frolic, Gaolbreak, Hole, Hoot, Houdini, Hout, Lam, Leakage, Leg-it, Let-off, Levant, Loop(-hole), Meuse, Mews, Muse, Narrow, Near thing, Outlet, Prank, Refuge, Runaway, Scarper, Seep(age), Shave, Slip, Vent, Walter Mitty

Escort Accompany, Attend, Bodyguard, Chaperone, Comitatus, Conduct, Convoy, Cortege, Corvette, Date, Destroyer, Entourage, Frigate, Gallant, Gigolo, Guide, Lead, Outrider, Protector, Retinue, See, Squire, Take, Tend, Usher, Walker

Esoteric Abstruse, Orphic, Rarefied, Recondite, Secret

Especial(ly) Chiefly, Esp, Espec, Outstanding, Particular

Espionage Industrial, Spying, Surveillance

Esprit Insight, Spirit, Understanding, Wit

Essay(s) Article, Attempt, Critique, Disquisition, Dissertation, Endeavour, Paper, Stab, Thesis, Tractate, Treatise, Try

Essayist Addison, Bacon, Columnist, Elia, Ellis, Emerson, Hazlitt, Holmes, Hunt, Huxley, Lamb, Locke, Montaigne, Pater, Prolusion, Ruskin, Scribe, Steele, > **WRITER**

Essence Alma, Atman, Attar, Aura, Being, Core, Element, Entia, Esse, Extract, Fizzen, Flavouring, Foison, Gist, Heart, Hom(e)ousian, Inbeing, Inscape, Kernel, Marrow, Mirbane, Myrbane, Nub, Nutshell, Ottar, Otto, Perfume, Per-se, Pith, Quiddity, Ratafia, Soul, Ylang-ylang

Essential(ly) Basic, Central, Crucial, Entia, Formal, Fundamental, Imperative, In, Indispensable, Inherent, Integral, Intrinsic, Kernel, Key, Lifeblood, Linch-pin, Marrow, Material, Must, Necessary, Need, Nitty-gritty, Nuts and bolts, Part-parcel, Per-se, Prana, Prerequisite, Quintessence, Radical, Requisite, Sine qua non, Vital, Whatness

Establish(ed) Abide, Anchor, Ascertain, Base, Build, Create, Deploy, Embed, Enact, Endemic, Ensconce, Entrench, Fix, > **FOUND**, Haft, Imbed, Ingrain, Instal(l), Instate, Instil, Institute, Inveterate, Ordain, Pitch, Pre-set, Prove, Raise, Root(ed), Set, Stable, Standing, Substantiate, Trad, Trite, Valorise, Verify

Establishment Building, Business, CE, Church, Co, Concern, Creation, Hacienda, Household, Institution, Lodge, Proving ground, Salon, School, Seat, System, Traditional

Estate Allod(ium), Alod, Assets, Commons, Demesne, Domain, Dominant, Dowry, Fazenda, Fee-simple, Fee-tail, Fen, First, Fourth, General, Hacienda, Hagh, Haugh, Having, Hay, Housing, Industrial, Land-living, Latifundium, Legitim, Life, Manor, Messuage, Odal, Personal(ity), Plantation, Press,

> **PROPERTY**, Real, Runrig, Situation, Spiritual, Standing, Talooka, Taluk(a), Temporal, Thanage, Trading, Udal

Esteem(ed), **Estimable** Account, Admiration, Appreciation, Count, Have, Honour, Izzat, Los, Precious, Prestige, Price, Pride, Prize, Rate, > **REGARD**, Respect, Store, Value, Venerate, Wonder, Worthy

▶ **Estimable** *see* **ESTEEM**

Estimate, **Estimation** Appraise, Assess, Calculate, Carat, Conceit, Cost, Esteem, Extrapolation, Forecast, Gauge, Guess, Guess(timate), Opinion, Projection, Quotation, Rate, Rating, Reckon, Regard, Sight, Value, Weigh

Etch(ing) Aquafortis, Aquatint(a), Bite, > **ENGRAVE**, Incise, Inscribe

Eternal, **Eternity** Aeonian, Ageless, Endless, Everlasting, Eviternal, Ewigkeit, Forever, Immortal, Infinity, Never-ending, Perdurable, Perpetual, Sempiternal, Tarnal, Timeless

Ether Atmosphere, Ch'i, Gas, Sky, Yang, Yin

Ethereal Airy, Delicate, Fragile, Heavenly, Nymph

Ethic(al), **Ethics** Deontics, Marcionite, Moral, Principles

Ethiopia(n) African, Amharic, Asmara, Cushitic, Geez, Kabele, Kebele

Etiquette Code, Conduct, > **MANNERS**, Propriety, Protocol, Ps and Qs, Punctilio

Eucalyptus Bloodwood, Coolabah, Gum-tree, Ironbark, Mallee, Marri, Morrell, Sallee, Stringybark, Tewart, Tooart, Tuart, Wandoo

Euphoria, **Euphoric** Cock-a-hoop, Elation, High, Jubilation, Rapture, Rush

Europe(an) Balt, Bohunk, Catalan, Community, Continent, Croat, E, Faringee, Faringhi, Feringhee, Fleming, Hungarian, Hunky, Japhetic, Lapp, Lithuanian, Palagi, Polack, Ruthene, Ruthenian, Serb, Slavonian, Slovene, Topi-Wallah, Transleithan, Tyrolean, Vlach, Yugoslav

Evacuate, **Evacuation** Excrete, Expel, Getter, Planuria, Planury, Scramble, Stercorate, Stool, Vent, Void, Withdraw

Evade, **Evasion**, **Evasive** Ambages, Avoid, Cop-out, Coy, Dodge, Duck, Elude, Escape, Fence, Fudge, Hedge, Loophole, Parry, Prevaricate, Quibble, Quillet, Scrimshank, Shifty, Shirk, Shuffling, Sidestep, Skive, Skrimshank, Stall, Subterfuge, Tergiversate, Waive, Weasel, Whiffler

Evaluate, **Evaluation** Appraise, Assess, Estimate, Gauge, Rate, Review, Waid(e), Weigh

Evangelical, **Evangelist(ical)** Converter, Crusader, Fisher, Gospeller, Happy-clappy, Jesus freak, John, Luke, Marist, Mark, Matthew, Moody, Morisonian, Peculiar, Preacher, Revivalist, Sim(eonite), Stundist, Wild

Evaporate, **Evaporation** Condense, Dehydrate, Desorb, Exhale, Steam, Steme, Ullage, Vaporise

Eve(ning) Dusk, Een, Ene, Erev, Forenight, J'ouvert, Nightfall, Soirée, Subfusc, Subfusk, Sunset, Twilight, Vesperal, Vespertinal, Vigil, Yester

Even(ly), **Evenness** Aid, Albe(a), Albeit, All, Average, Balanced, Clean, Drawn, Een, Ene, Equable, Equal, Erev, Fair, Fair play, Flush, Iron, Level, Level-pegging, Meet, Pair, Par, Plain, Plane, Plateau, Quits, Rib, Smooth, Square, Standardise, Toss-up, Yet

Event Case, Circumstance, Discus, Encaenia, Episode, Fest, Field, Gymkhana, Happening, Heat, Incident, Landmark, Leg, Media, Milestone, Occasion, Occurrence, Ongoing, Outcome, Pass, Regatta, Result, Three-ring circus, Track

Eventual(ity), **Eventually** Case, Contingent, Finally, Future, In time, Nd

Ever Always, Ay(e), Constantly, Eternal, Eviternity

Evergreen Abies, Ageless, Arbutus, Cembra, Cypress, Gaultheria, Ivy, Myrtle, Olearia, Periwinkle, Pinaster, Privet, Thuja, Thuya, Washington, Winterberry

Everlasting Cat's ear, Changeless, Enduring, Eternal, Immortal, Immortelle, Perdurable, Recurrent, Tarnal

Every(one), Everything All, Complete, Each, Ilk(a), Sum, The works, Tout, Tout le monde, Universal, Varsal

Everyday Informal, Mundane, Natural, Ordinary, Plain

Everywhere Omnipresent, Passim, Rife, Throughout, Ubiquity

Evidence, Evident Adminicle, Apparent, Argument, Axiomatic, Circumstantial, Clear, Confessed, Credentials, Direct, Distinct, Document, Empirical, Exemplar, Flagrant, Hearsay, Indicate, Internal, King's, Manifest, Marked, Obvious, Overt, Plain, Premise, Prima facie, Probable, Proof, Queen's, Record, Sign, Smoking gun, State's, Surrebuttal, Testimony, Understandable

Evil Ahriman, Alastor, Amiss, Badmash, Bale, Beelzebub, Budmash, Corrupt, Depraved, Eale, Guilty, Harm, Hydra, Ill, Iniquity, Malefic, Mare, Mischief, Necessary, Night, Perfidious, Rakshas(a), Shrewd, Sin, Turpitude, Vice, Wicked

Evince Disclose, Exhibit, Indicate, Show

Evolution(ary) Countermarch, Development, Growth, Holism, Lamarck, Moner(on), Phylogeny, Turning

▷ **Evolution** *may indicate* an anagram

Evolve Speciate

Ex Former, Late, Quondam, Ten

Exacerbate Aggravate, Embitter, Exasperate, Irritate, Needle

Exact(ing), Exactitude, Exactly Accurate, Authentic, Careful, Dead, Definite, Due, Elicit, Estreat, Even, Exigent, Extort, Fine, Formal, It, Jump, Literal, Literatim, Mathematical, Meticulous, Nice(ty), Pat, Point-device, > **PRECISE**, Require, Slap-bang, Spang, Specific, Spot-on, Strict, T, Verbatim

Exaggerate(d), Exaggeration Agonistic, Amplify, Boast, Brag, Camp, Colour, Distend, Dramatise, > **EMBROIDER**, Goliathise, Hyperbole, Inflate, Magnify, Overdo, Overpaint, Overplay, Overrate, Overstate, Over-the-top, Stretch, Theatrical

Exalt(ed), Exaltation Attitudes, Deify, Dignify, Elation, Enhance, Ennoble, Erect, Extol, Glorify, High, Jubilance, Larks, Lofty, > **PRAISE**, Raise, Rapture, Sublime

Exam(ination), Examine, Examinee, Examiner A-level, Analyse, Analyst, Audit, Autopsy, Baccalauréat, Biopsy, Case, Check-out, Check-up, Collate, Comb, Common Entrance, Consideration, Cross-question, CSE, Deposal, Depose, Disquisition, Dissect, Entrance, Explore, Eyeball, Finals, GCE, GCSE, Going-over, Grade(s), Great-go, Greats, Gulf, Hearing, Inspect, Inter, Interrogate, Interview, Introspection, Jury, Local, Mark, Matriculation, Medical, Mocks, Moderator, Mods, Mug, O-level, Once-over, Oral, Ordeal, Overhaul, Palp(ate), Paper, Peruse, Physical, Post-mortem, Prelim, Probe, Pry, Psychoanalyse, Pump, > **QUESTION**, Quiz, Ransack, Recce, Reconnaissance, Review, Sayer, Scan, Schools, Scrutineer, Scrutinise, Search, Seek, Sift, Sit, Smalls, Sus(s), Test, Trial, Tripos, Try, Vet, Viva

Example Byword, Epitome, Foretaste, > **FOR EXAMPLE**, Illustration, Instance, Lead, Lesson, Model, Paradigm, Paragon, > **PATTERN**, Praxis, Precedent, Prototype, Say, Shining, Showpiece, Specimen, Standard, Touchstone, Type, Typify

Excavate, Excavation, Excavator Burrow, Catacomb, Crater, Delf, Delph, > **DIG**, Dike, Ditch, Dredge, Hollow, JCB, Mine, Pioneer, Pioner, Quarry, Shaft, Sink, Sondage, Stope, Well

Excel(lence), Excellency, Excellent A1, Ace, Admirable, Bangin(g), Beat, Beaut, Better, Blinder, Bodacious, Boffo, Bonzer, Booshit, Boss, Bravo, Brill, Bully, Capital, Champion, Cheese, Choice, Class(y), Classical, Corking, Crack, Crackerjack, Crucial, Daisy, Def, Dic(k)ty, Dilly, Dominate, Doozy,

Elegant, Excelsior, Exemplary, Eximious, Exo, Fab, Fantastic, Five-star, Great, HE, High, Humdinger, Hunky(-dory), Inimitable, Jake, Jammy, Knockout, Laudable, Matchless, Mean, Mega-, Merit, Neat, Noble, Out and outer, Outdo, Outstanding, Overdo, Paragon, Peachy, Prime, Pure, Rad, Rare, Rattling, Ring, Rinsin', Ripping, Ripsnorter, > **SHINE**, Sick-dog, Sik, Spanking, Spiffing, Stellar, Stonking, Stupendous, Sublime, Superb, Super-duper, Superior, Supreme, Swell, Terrific, Tip-top, Top flight, Top-hole, Topnotch, Topping, Virtue, Wal(l)y, War, Way-out, Wicked, Worth

Exceptional Abnormal, Anomaly, Egregious, Especial, Extraordinary, Rare, Ripsnorter, Singular, Special, Uncommon, Zinger

Excess(ive), **Excessively** All-fired, Basinful, Exorbitant, Extortionate, Extravagant, Flood, Fulsome, Glut, Hard, Inordinate, > **LAVISH**, Mountain, Nimiety, OD, Old, OTT, Outrage, Over, Overage, Overblown, Overcome, Overdose, Overkill, Overmuch, Overspill, Over-the-top, Owercome, Plethora, Preponderance, Profuse, Salt, Satiety, Spate, Spilth, Steep, Superabundant, Superfluity, Surfeit, Surplus, Terrific, Troppo, Ultra, Undue, Unequal, Woundily

Exchange Baltic, Bandy, Barter, Bourse, Cambist, Catallactic, Change, Chop, Commute, Contango, Convert, Cope, Corn, Ding-dong, Employment, Enallage, Excambion, Foreign, Inosculate, Interplay, Ion, Labour, Logroll, > **MARKET**, Mart, Needle, Niffer, Paraphrase, PBX, Post, Rally, Rate, Recourse, Rialto, Royal, Scorse, Scourse, Stock, Swap, Switch, Swop, Telephone, Tolsel, Tolsey, Tolzey, > **TRADE**, Traffic, Transfusion, Trophallaxis, Truck

Excitable, **Excite(d)**, **Excitement**, **Exciting** Ablaze, Abuzz, Aerate, Agog, Amove, Animate, Aphrodisiac, Arouse, Athrill, Atwitter, Awaken, Brouhaha, Buck-fever, Climatic, Combustible, Commotion, Delirium, Electrify, Emove, Enthuse, Erethism, Feisty, Fever, Fire, Flap, Frantic, Frenzy, Frisson, Furore, Fuss, Galvanise, Gas, Headiness, Heat, Hectic, Het, Hey-go-mad, Hilarity, Hobson-Jobson, Hoopla, Hothead, Hyped, Hyper, Hysterical, Impel, Incite, Inebriate, Inflame, Intoxicate, Jimjams, Kick, Kindle, Metastable, Must, Neurotic, Oestrus, Orgasm, Overheat, Overwrought, Panic, Passion, Pride, Provoke, Racy, Radge, Red-hot, Rile, Roil, Ruff(e), Rut, Send, Spin, Spur, Startle, Stimulate, Stir(e), Suscitate, Tetany, Tew, Thrill, Titillate, Trickle, Turn-on, Twitter, Upraise, Waken, Whee, Whoopee, Yahoo, Yerk, Yippee, Yoicks

▷ **Excite(d)** *may indicate* an anagram

Exclaim, **Exclamation (mark)** Ahem, Begorra, Blurt, Bo, Ceas(e), Crikey, Criv(v)ens, Dammit, Ecphonesis, Eina, Ejaculate, Eureka, Expletive, Fen(s), Good-now, Haith, Heigh-ho, Hem, Hosanna, Inshallah, Interjection, Oops, Protest, Pshaw, Whoops, Yippee, Zounds

Exclave Cabinda

Exclude, **Excluding**, **Exclusion** Ban, Bar, Block, Debar, Disbar, Eliminate, Ex, Except, Excommunicate, Omit, Ostracise

Excursion Airing, Cruise, Dart, Digression, Jaunt, Junket, Outing, Road, Sally, Sashay, Sortie, Tour, Trip

Excusable, **Excuse** Absolve, Alibi, Amnesty, Condone, Evasion, Exempt, Exonerate, Forgive, Mitigate, Occasion, Out, Overlook, Palliate, > **PARDON**, Pretext, Release, Venial, Viable, Whitewash

Execute(d), **Executioner**, **Executive**, **Executor** Accomplish, Administrate, Behead, Discharge, Finish, Fry, Gar(r)otte, Guardian, Hang, Headsman, Implement, Ketch, Kill, Koko, Lynch, Management, Noyade, Official, Perform, Pierrepoint, Politburo, Top, Trustee

Exempt(ion) Dispensation, Exclude, Free, Immune, Impunity, Indemnity, Quarter, Spare

Exercise(s) Aerobics, Apply, Callanetics®, Cal(l)isthenics, Chi kung, Cloze,

Constitutional, Drill, Employ, Enure, Eurhythmics, Exert, Floor, Gradus, Inure, Isometrics, Kata, Lesson, Limber, Medau, Op, Operation, PE, Ply, Practice, Practise, Press-up, PT, Push-up, Qigong, Shintaido, Sit-up, Solfeggi(o), Step (aerobics), Tai chi (ch'uan), Thema, Theme, Thesis, Train, Use, Warm-up, Wield, Work, Work-out, Xyst(us), Yomp

▷ **Exercise(d)** *may indicate* an anagram

Exert(ion) Conatus, > EFFORT, Exercise, Labour, Operate, Strain, Strive, Struggle, Trouble, Wield

Exhaust(ed), Exhausting, Exhaustion, Exhaustive All-in, Beaten, Beggar, Burn, Burn-out, Bushed, Clapped out, Consume, Deadbeat, Debility, Deplete, Detailed, Dissipate, Done, Drain, Effete, Emission, Empty, End, Enervate, Fatigue, Frazzle, Gruelling, Heat, Heatstroke, Jet-lagged, Jet-stream, Jiggered, Knacker, Mate, Milk, Out, Poop, Powfagged, Puckerood, Rag, Ramfeezle, Rundown, Sap, Shatter, Shot, Shotten, Spend, Spent, Stonkered, Tailpipe, Tire, Use, Used up, Washed-up, Wasted, Waygone, > WEARY, Wind, Worn, Zonked

Exhibit(ion), Exhibitioner Circus, Concours, Demo, Demonstrate, Demy, Diorama, Discover, Display, Evince, Expo, Expose, Fair, Hang, Indicate, Olympia, Pageant, Panopticon, Parade, Present, Retrospective, Salon, Scene, Show(piece), Viewing

Exigency, Exigent Emergency, Pressing, Taxing, Urgent, Vital

Exile Adam, Babylon, Banish, Deport, Emigré, Eve, Expatriate, Exul, Galut(h), Ostracise, Outlaw, Relegate, Tax, Wretch

Exist(ence), Existing Be(ing), Corporeity, Dwell, Enhypostasia, Entelechy, Esse, Extant, Identity, Life, Live, Ontology, Perseity, Solipsism, Substantial, Ubiety

Exit Débouché, Door, Egress, Gate, Leave, Outlet

Exodus Book, Departure, Flight, Hegira, Hejira

Exorbitant Excessive, Expensive, Steep, Tall, Undue

Exotic Alien, Ethnic, Foreign, Outlandish, Strange

Expand, Expanse, Expansion Amplify, Boom, Develop, Diastole, Dilate, Distend, Ectasis, Elaborate, > ENLARGE, Escalate, Grow, Increase, Magnify, Ocean, Snowball, Spread, Stretch, Swell, Wax, Wire-draw

Expatiate Amplify, Descant, Dwell, Enlarge, Perorate

Expect(ant), Expectation, Expected, Expecting Agog, Anticipate, Ask, Await, Due, Foresee, Gravid, Hope, Lippen, Look, Natural, Par, Pip, Pregnant, Presume, Prospect, Require, > SUPPOSE, Tendance, Think, Thought, Usual, Ween

Expedient Advisable, Artifice, Contrivance, Fend, Make-do, Makeshift, Measure, Politic, Resort, Resource, Shift, Stopgap, Suitable, Wise

Expedite, Expedition, Expeditious Advance, Alacrity, Anabasis, Celerity, Crusade, Dispatch, Excursion, Field trip, Hasten, Hurry, Kon-tiki, Pilgrimage, Post-haste, Safari, Speed, Trek, Trip, Voyage

Expel Amove, Dispossess, Egest, Evacuate, Evict, Exile, Exorcize, Hoof, Oust, Out(cast), Void

Expend(iture) Budget, Consume, Cost, Dues, Oncost, Outgo(ing), Outlay, Poll, Squander, Tithe, Toll, Use

Expense(s) Charge, Cost, Exes, Fee, Law, Oncost, Outgoing, Outlay, Overhead, Price, Sumptuary

Expensive Chargeful, Costly, Dear, Executive, Salt, Steep, Upmarket, Valuable

Experience(d) Accomplished, A posteriori, Assay, Blasé, Discovery, Empiric, Encounter, Expert, > FEEL, Felt, Freak-out, Gust, Hands-on, Have, Incur, Know, Learn, Live, Mature, Meet, Mneme, Old hand, Pass, Plumb, Seasoned, See, Senior, Sense, Sensory, Stager, Stand, Street-smart, Streetwise, Taste, Transference, Trial, Trip, Trocinium, Try, Undergo, Versed, Work

Experiment(al) Attempt, Avant-garde, Empirical, Essay, Peirastic, Pilot, Sample, Taste, Tentative, > TRIAL, Try, Venture

Expert(ise) Accomplished, Ace, Adept, Adroit, Arch, Authority, Boffin, Buff, Cambist, Cocker, Cognoscente, Connoisseur, Crack, Dab(ster), Dan, Deft, Don, Egghead, Fundi, Gourmet, Gun, Hotshot, Karateka, Know-all, Know-how, Luminary, Maestro, Masterly, Maven, Mavin, Meister, Nark, Oner, Oneyer, Oneyre, Peritus, Practised, Pro, Proficient, Pundit, Ringer, Savvy, Science, Skill(y), Sly, Specialist, Technique, Technocrat, Ulema, Used, W(h)iz

Expire(d), Expiry Blow, Collapse, Croak, > DIE, End, Exhale, Invalid, Ish, Lapse, Neese, Pant, Sneeze, Terminate

Explain(able) Account, Annotate, Clarify, Conster, Construe, Decline, Define, Describe, Elucidate, Expose, Expound, Extenuate, Gloss, Gloze, Justify, Parabolize, Salve, Solve, Upknit

Explanation, Explanatory Apology, Commentary, Exegesis, Exegetic, Exposition, Farse, Gloss, Gloze, Hypothesis, Key, Note, Preface, Reading, Rigmarole, Solution, Theory

Expletive Arrah, Darn, Exclamation, Oath, Ruddy, Sapperment

Explicit Clean-cut, Clear, Definite, Express, Frank, Outspoken, > PRECISE, Specific

Explode, Explosion, Explosive Agene, Airburst, Amatol, Ammonal, Aquafortis, Backfire, Bang, Bangalore torpedo, Big bang, Blast, Burst, Cap, Cheddite, Chug, Cordite, Cramp, Crump, Cyclonite, Debunk, Detonate, Dualin, Dunnite, Dust, Erupt, Euchlorine, Fireball, Firecracker, Firedamp, Firework, Fulminant, Fulminate, Gasohol, Gelatine, Gelignite, Grenade, Guncotton, Gunpaper, Gunpowder, HE, Jelly, Landmine, Low, Megaton, Melinite, Mine, Nail-bomb, Napalm, Nitroglycerine, Outburst, Payload, Petar(d), Petre, Plastic, Plastique, Pop, Pow, Propellant, Roburite, SAM, Semtex®, Sheet, Shrapnel, Snake, Squib, Tetryl, Thunderflash, Tinderbox, TNT, Tonite, Trinitrobenzene, Trotyl, Volatile, Volcanic, Warhead, Xyloidin(e)

Explore(r), Exploration Amerigo, Amundsen, Baffin, Balboa, Bandeirante, Banks, Barents, Bering, Boone, Burton, Cabot, Cartier, Chart, Columbus, Cook, Cortes, Da Gama, Dampier, Darwin, De Soto, Dias, Diaz, Discover, Dredge, Eric, Eriksson, Examine, Feel, Frobisher, Fuchs, Humboldt, Investigate, Livingstone, Magellan, Map, Marco Polo, Mungo Park, Nansen, Navigator, Pathfinder, Peary, Pioneer, Potholer, Probe, Przewalski, Rale(i)gh, Research, Rhodes, Ross, Scott, Scout, Search, Shackleton, Spaceship, Speke, Stanley, Sturt, Tasman, Vancouver, Vasco da Gama, Vespucci

▷ **Explosive** *may indicate* an anagram

Exponent Advocate, Example, Index, Interpreter, Logarithm

Expose(d), Exposure Air, Anagogic, Bare, Bleak, Blot, Blow, Burn, Debag, Debunk, Denude, Desert, Disclose, Double, Endanger, En prisé, Exhibit, Flashing, Glareal, Indecent, Insolate, Moon, Nude, Object, Open, Out, Over, Propale, Reveal, Showdown, Snapshot, Streak, Strip, Subject, Sun, Time, Uncover, Unmask, Windswept

Expound(er) Discourse, Discuss, Exegete, Explain, Open, Prelict, Red, Scribe, Ulema

Express(ed), Expression, Expressive Air, APT, Aspect, Breathe, Cacophemism, Circumbendimus, Cliché, Colloquialism, Conceive, Concetto, Couch, Countenance, Declare, Denote, Eloquent, Embodiment, Epithet, Explicit, Face, Fargo, Formulate, Good-luck, Gup, Hang-dog, Hell's bells, Idiom, Limited, Locution, Lyrical, Manifest, Metonym, Mien, Mot (juste), Neologism, Non-stop, Orient, Paraphrase, Phrase, Pleonasm, Pony, Precise, Pronto, Put, Quep, Register, Say(ne), Show, Soulful, > SPEAK, State, Strain, Succus, Term, Token, Tone, Topos, Utterance, Vent, > VOICE

Expressionless Blank, Deadpan, Impassive, Inscrutable, Po(ker)-faced, Vacant, Wooden

Expulsion Discharge, Eccrisis, Ejection, Eviction, Exile, Sacking, Synaeresis

Extemporise Ad lib, Improvise, Pong

Extend(ed), Extension Aspread, Augment, Cremaster, Draw, Eke, Elapse, Elongate, Enlarge, Escalate, Expand, Exsert, Fermata, Grow, Increase, Length, Long, Long-range, Long-stay, Long-term, Offer, Outgrowth, Overbite, Overlap, Porrect, Proffer, Prolong, Propagate, Protract, Reach, Retrochoir, Span, Spread, Steso, > **STRETCH**, Substantial, Widen

Extensive, Extent Ambit, Area, Capacious, Catch-all, Compass, Comprehensive, Distance, Large, Length, Limit, Panoramic, Range, Reach, Scale, Size, Spacious, Sweeping, Wide, Widespread

Exterior Aspect, Crust, Derm, Facade, Outer, > **OUTSIDE**, Shell, Surface, Veneer

External Exoteric, Exterior, Extraneous, Foreign, Outer

Extinguish Douse, Dout, Dowse, Extirpate, Obscure, Quash, Quell, Quench, Slake, Snuff, Stifle, Suppress

Extra Accessory, Additament, Addition(al), Additive, Adjunct, And, Annexe, Attachment, Bisque, Bonus, By(e), Debauchery, Encore, Etcetera, Further, Gash, Lagniappe, Left-over, Leg bye, Make-weight, More, Nimiety, Odd, Optional, Out, Over, Perk, Plus, Plusage, Reserve, Ripieno, > **SPARE**, Spilth, Staffage, Sundry, Super, Supernumerary, Supplementary, Suppletive, Surplus, Trop, Undue, Walking-gentleman, Walking-lady, Wide, Woundy

Extract(ion), Extractor Bleed, Breeding, Catechu, Clip, Corkscrew, Decoction, Descent, Distil, Draw, Educe, Elicit, Essence, Excerpt, Extort, Gist, Gobbet, Insulin, Parentage, Passage, Pick, Piece, Pry, Quintessence, Smelt, Suck, Summary, Tap, Trie, Try, Vanilla, Winkle, Worm, Wring

Extraordinary Amazing, Humdinger, Important, Phenomenal, Preternatural, Rare, Singular, Startling, Strange, Unusual

Extravagance, Extravagant, Extravaganza Excessive, Fancy, Feerie, Heroic, High-flown, Hyperbole, Lavish, Luxury, Outré, Prodigal, Profuse, Rampant, Reckless, Riotise, Splash, Splurge, Squander, Sumptuous, Superfluous, Waste

Extreme(ly), Extremist Acute, Almighty, Butt, Desperate, Die-hard, Drastic, Edge, Exceptional, Farthermost, Gross, In spades, > **INTENSE**, Mega-, Opposite, Parlous, Pretty, Radical, Too, Tremendous, Ultimate, Ultra, Utmost, Utter, > **VERY**, Vitally, Wing

▷ **Extreme** *may indicate* a first or last letter

Exuberance, Exuberant Brio, Copious, Ebullient, Effusive, Gusto, Hearty, Lavish, Mad, Profuse, Rumbustious, Skippy, Streamered

Exult(ant) Crow, Elated, > **GLOAT**, Glorify, Jubilant, Paeonic, Rejoice, Triumphant, Whoop

Eye(ful), Eye-ball, Eyes, Eyepiece Evil, Glass, Goggles, Iris, Jack, Keek, Klieg, Lamp, Lazy, Lens, Magic, Mincepie, Mind's, Naked, > **OBSERVE**, Ocellar, Ogle, Optic, Orb, Peeper, PI, Pupil, Regard, Retina, Roving, Sight, Spy, Uvea, Watch, Weather, Windows

Eyesore Blot, Disfigurement, Sty(e)

Eye trouble Amblyopia, Ametropia, Aniseikonia, Anisomatropia, Asthenopia, Astigmatism, Cataract, Ceratitis, Coloboma, Diplopia, Entropion, Exophthalmus, Glaucoma, Hemeralopia, Hemi(an)op(s)ia, Hypermetropia, Iritis, Keratitis, Leucoma, Lippitude, Micropsia, Miosis, Myosis, Nebula, Nyctalopia, Nystagmus, Presbyopia, Retinitis, Scotoma(ta), Stigmatism, Strabismus, Synechia, Teichopsia, Thylose, Thylosis, Trachoma, Tritanopia, Tylosis, Wall-eye, Xeroma, Xerophthalmia

Ff

F Fahrenheit, Fellow, Feminine, Fluorine, Following, Force, Foxtrot

Fable(s) Aesop, Allegory, Apologue, Exemplum, Fiction, Hitopadesa, La Fontaine, Legend, Marchen, Milesian, Myth, Panchatantra, Parable, Romance, Tale

Fabric > CLOTH, Framework

Fabricate, **Fabrication** Artefact, Concoct, Construct, Contrive, Cook, Fake, Figment, Forge, > INVENT, Lie, Porky, Trump, Weave, Web

Fabulous (beast), **Fabulous place** Chimera, Cockatrice, Eldorado, Fictitious, Fung, Gear, Incredible, Jabberwock(y), Legendary, Magic, Manticore, Merman, Mythical, Orc, Phoenix, Roc, Romantic, Sphinx, Unicorn, Unreal, Wyvern

Face, **Facing** Abide, Affront, Ashlar, Ashler, Aspect, Audacity, Brave, Brazen, Caboched, Caboshed, Cheek, Chiv(v)y, Coal, Countenance, Culet, Dalle, Dare, Dartle, Deadpan, Dial, Eek, Elevation, Encounter, Facade, Fat, Favour, Features, Fineer, Fortune, > FRONT, Gardant, Girn, Gonium, Grid, Groof, Groue, Grouf, Gurn, Hatchet, Head-on, Jib, Kisser, Light, Lining, Look, Lore, Mascaron, Meet, Metope, Moe, Mug, Mush, Obverse, Opposite, Outstare, Outward, Pan, Paper tiger, Phisnomy, Phiz(og), Physiognomy, Poker, Puss, Revet, Revetment, Roughcast, Rud, Rybat, Side, Snoot, Socle, Straight, Stucco, Type, Veneer, Vis(age), Visnomy, Withstand, Zocco(lo)

Facetious Frivolous, Jocular, Waggish, Witty

Facile Able, Adept, Complaisant, Ductile, Easy, Fluent, Glib

Facilitate, **Facility** Amenity, Assist, Benefit, Capability, > EASE, Expedite, Fluency, Gift, ISO, Knack, Skill

Fact(s), **Factual** Actual, Case, Correct, Data, Datum, Detail, Info, Literal, Mainor, Nay, Really, Truism, Truth, Veridical, Yes

Faction Bloc, Cabal, Camp, Caucus, Clique, Contingent, Junto, Schism, Sect, Tendency, Wing

Factor Agent, Aliquot, Broker, Cause, Chill, Clotting, Coagulation, Co-efficient, Common, Divisor, Edaphic, Element, F, Feel-good, Growth, House, Intrinsic, Load, Modulus, Power, Q, Quality, Representative, Rh, Rhesus, Risk, Safety, Steward, Wind chill, X

Factory Cannery, Gasworks, Glassworks, Hacienda, Maquiladora, Mill, Plant, Refinery, Sawmill, Steelworks, Sweatshop, Tinworks, Works, Workshop

Faculty Aptitude, Arts, Capacity, Department, Ear, Ease, Indult, Knack, Power, School, Sense, Speech, > TALENT, Teachers, Wits

Fad(dish) Crank, Craze, Cult, Fashion, Foible, Ismy, Thing, Vogue, Whim

Fade(d), **Fading** Blanch, Die, Diminuendo, Dinge, Elapsion, Etiolate, Evanescent, Fall, Filemot, Lessen, Mancando, Pale, Passé, Perdendo(si), Peter, Smorzando, Smorzato, Stonewashed, Vade, Vanish, Wallow, Wilt, Wither

Fag(ging) Chore, Cigarette, Drag, Drudge, Fatigue, Gasper, Homosexual, Menial, Quean, Reefer, Snout, Tire, Toil, Weary

Fail(ing), **Failure** Ademption, Anile, Anuria, Blemish, Blow, Bomb, Bummer, Cark, > COLLAPSE, Conk, Crack up, Crash, Cropper, Debacle, Decline, Defalcation, Default, Defect, Demerit, Die, Dog, Dry, Dud, Fault, Feal, Fiasco, Fink out, Flame out, Flivver, Flop, Flow, Flunk, Fold, Founder, Frost, Glitch, Gutser, Infraction, Lapse, Lemon, Lose, Malfunction, Manqué, Mis-, Miscarry, Miss, Muff, Nerd, No-hoper, No-no, Omit, Outage, Oversight, Pip, Plough, Pluck, Pratfall, Reciprocity, Refer, Refusal, Respiratory, Shambles, Short(coming), Short circuit, Slippage, Smash, Spin, Stumer, Turkey, Vice, Wash-out, Weakness, White elephant, Wipeout

Faint(ness) Black-out, Conk, Darkle, Dim, Dizzy, Dwalm, Fade, Lassitude, Pale, Stanck, Swarf, Swarve, Swelt, Swerf, Swerve, Swoon, Swound, Syncope, Unclear, Wan, Whitish

Fair A(e)fald, Aefauld, Aefwld, Barnet, Bartholomew, Bazaar, Beauteous, Belle, Blond, Bon(n)ie, Bonny, Brigg, Decent, Donnybrook, Equal, Equitable, Evenhanded, Exhibition, Feeing-market, > **FESTIVAL**, Fine, Funfair, Gaff, Gey, Goose, Gwyn, Hiring, Honest, Hopping, Isle, > **JUST**, Kermess, Kermis, Kirmess, Market, Mart, Mediocre, Mela, Mop, Nundinal, Objective, OK, Paddington, Passable, Play, Pro rata, Rosamond, Sabrina, Square, Statute, Straight, Tavistock, Tidy, Tolerable, Tow-headed, Trade, Tryst, Unbias(s)ed, Vanity, Wake, Widdicombe

Fairly Clearly, Enough, Evenly, Midway, Moderately, Pari passu, Pretty, Properly, Quite, Ratherish

Fairy, Fairies Banshee, Befana, Cobweb, Dobbie, Dobby, Elf(in), Fay, Gloriana, Hob, Hop o' my thumb, Leprechaun, Lilian, Mab, Morgane(tta), Morgan le Fay, Moth, Nis, Peri, Pigwidgin, Pigwiggen, Pisky, Pixie, Pouf, Puck, Punce, Sandman, Spirit, Sprite, Sugar-plum, Tink(erbell), Titania, Tooth, Urchin-shows

Faith(ful) Accurate, Achates, Belief, Constant, Creed, Devoted, Doctrine, Faix, Fay, Feal, Fegs, Fideism, Fiducial, Haith, Implicit, Islam, Lay, Loyal, Plerophory, Puritanism, Quaker, Religion, Shema, Solifidian, Staunch, Strict, Troth, > **TRUE**, True-blue, Trust, Truth, Umma(h)

Fake(r), Faking Bodgie, Bogus, Copy, Counterfeit, Duff(er), Ersatz, False, Fold, Fraud, Fudge, Imitation, Imposter, Impostor, Paste, Phoney, Postiche, Pretend, Sham, Spurious, Trucage, Truquage, Truqueur, Unreal

Falcon Gentle, Hawk, Hobby, Kestrel, Lanner(et), Merlin, Nyas, Peregrine, Prairie, Saker, Sakeret, Sparrow-hawk, Stallion, Staniel, Stannel, Stanyel, Tassel-gentle, Tassell-gent, Tercel-gentle

Fall(s), Fallen, Falling Abate, Accrue, Angel, Arches, Astart, Autumn, Boyoma, Cadence, Cascade, Cataract, Chute, Collapse, Crash, Cropper, Cross press, Declension, Decrease, Degenerate, Descent, Dip, Domino effect, Douse, Downswing, Dowse, > **DROP**, Ebb, Firn, Flop, Flump, Folding press, Free, Grabble, Gutser, Gutzer, Horseshoe, Idaho, Iguaçu, Incidence, Kabalega, Kaieteur, Lag, Landslide, Lapse, Lin(n), Niagara, Oct(ober), Owen, Perish, Plonk, Plummet, Plump, Plunge, Prolapse, Purl(er), Rain, Reaction, Relapse, Ruin, Sheet, Sin, Sleet, Snow, Spill, Sutherland, Tailor, Takakkau, Topple, Toss, Trip, Tugela, Tumble, Victoria, Voluntary, Wipeout, Yosemite

Fallacious, Fallacy Elench(us), Error, Idolum, Illogical, Illusion, Pathetic, Sophism, Unsound

▷ **Falling** *may indicate* an anagram or a word backwards

False, Falsify Adulterate, Bastard, Bodgie, Bogus, Braide, Canard, Cavil, Charlatan, Cook, Deceitful, Disloyal, Dissemble, Doctor, Fake, Feigned, Fiddle, Forge, Illusory, Knave, Lying, Meretricious, Mock, Perjury, Pinchbeck, Postiche, Pretence, Pseudo, Roorback, Sham, Specious, Spoof, Spurious, Treacherous, Two-faced, Untrue

Fame, Famous Bruit, Celebrity, Distinguished, Eminent, Glitterati, Gloire, Glory, Greatness, History, Humour, Illustrious, Kudos, Legendary, Luminous, Name, Noted, Notorious, Prestige, Reclamé, Renown, Repute, Rumour, Splendent, Spur, Stardom, Word

Familiar(ise), Familiarity Accustom, Acquaint, Assuefaction, Au fait, Auld, Chummy, Comrade, Conversant, Crony, Dear, Demon, Easy, Free, Friend, Habitual, Homely, Homey, Incubus, Intimate, Known, Liberty, Maty, Old, Old-hat, Privy, Python, Used, Versed, Warhorse

Family Ancestry, Bairn-team, Blood, Breed, Clan, Class, Cognate, Consanguine, Descent, Dynasty, Extended, House(hold), Issue, Kin, Kind, Line, Mafia, Medici, Name, Nuclear, Orange, People, Phratry, Progeny, Quiverful, Race, Sept, Sib(b), Sibship, Stem, Stirps, Strain, Taffy, Talbot, Tribe

Famine Dearth, Lack, Scarcity

▷ **Famished** *may indicate* an 'o' in the middle of a word

Fan(s), Fan-like Admirer, Aficionado, Alligator, Alluvial, Arouse, Bajada, Blow, Cat, Clapper, Claque, Colmar, Cone, Cool, Cuscus, Devotee, Diadrom, Dryer, Enthusiast, Extractor, Fiend, Flabellum, Following, Groupie, Hepcat, Khuskhus, Outspread, Partisan, Punka(h), Rhipidate, Ringsider, Sail, Spread, Supporter, Tail, Tifosi, Ventilate, Votary, Voteen, Washingtonia, Wing, Winnow, Zealot, Zelant

▷ **Fan** *may indicate* an anagram

Fanatic(al) Bigot, Devotee, Energumen, Enthusiastic, Extremist, Fiend, Frenetic, Glutton, Mad, Maniac, Nut, Partisan, Phrenetic, Picard, Rabid, Santon, Ultra, Wowser, Zealot

Fancy, Fanciful Caprice, Chim(a)era, Conceit, Concetto, Crotchet, Daydream, Dream, Dudish, Elaborate, Fangle, Fantasy, Fit, Flam, Florid, Frothy, Guess, Hallo, Idea(te), Idolon, > IMAGINE, Inclination, Lacy, Liking, Maya, Mind, My, Nap, Notion, Ornamental, Ornate, Picture, Pipe dream, Predilection, Reverie, Rococo, Suppose, Thought, Urge, Vagary, Visionary, Ween, Whigmaleerie, Whigmaleery, Whim(sy), Woolgather

▷ **Fancy** *may indicate* an anagram

Fanfare Flourish, Sennet, Show, Tantara, Trump, Tucket

Fantasist, Fantasy, Fantastic Absurd, Antic, Bizarre, Caprice, Chimera, Cockaigne, Cockayne, Escapism, Fab, Fanciful, Grotesque, Hallucination, Kickshaw(s), Lucio, Myth, Outré, Phantasmagoria, Queer, Romance, Unreal, Untrue, > WHIM, Whimsical, Wild

Far Apogean, Away, Distal, Distant, Extreme, Outlying, Remote, Thether, Thither

Fare Apex, Charge, Cheer, Commons, Do, Eat, > FOOD, Go, Passage, Passenger, Rate, Table, Traveller

Farewell Adieu, Adios, Aloha, Apopemptic, Bye, Cheerio, Departure, Godspeed, > GOODBYE, Leave, Prosper, Sayonara, Send off, So long, Toodle-oo, Toodle-pip, Totsiens, Vale, Valediction

Farm(ing), Farmhouse Agronomy, Arable, Bowery, Cold Comfort, Collective, Croft, Cultivate, Dairy, Deep-litter, Emmerdale, Estancia, Extensive, Factory, Fat, Fish(ery), Funny, Geoponical, Grange, Hacienda, Health, Home, Homestead, Husbandry, Intensive, Kibbutz, Kolkhoz, Land, Ley, Loaf, Location, Mains, Mas, No-tillage, Onstead, Orley, Pen, Poultry, Ranch, Rent, Sewage, Shamba, Smallholding, Sovkhoz, Station, Stead(ing), Sted(d), Stedde, Steed, Stock, Subsistence, Tank, Till, Toon, Toun, Town, Wick, Wind

Farmer Boer, Campesino, Carl, Cockatoo, Cocky, Collins Street, Colon, Crofter, Estanciero, Gebur, George, Giles, Hick, Macdonald, Metayer, Nester, NFU, Peasant, Pitt Street, Ryot, Share-cropper, Sodbuster, Squatter, Tenant, Tiller, Whiteboy, Yeoman, Zeminda(r)

Farmhand Cadet, Cottar, Cotter, Cottier, Ditcher, Hand, He(a)rdsman, Hind, Ploughman, Redneck, Rouseabout, Roustabout, Shearer

▶ **Farmhouse** *see* FARM

Farthing Brass, F, Fadge, Har(r)ington, Mite, Q, Quadragesimal, Rag

Fascinate, Fascinating Allure, Attract, Bewitch, > CHARM, Dare, Enchant, Engross, Enthral(l), Fetching, Inthral, Intrigue, Kill, Mesmeric, Rivet, Siren, Witch

Fascist Blackshirt, Blue shirt, Brownshirt, Dictator, Falange, Falangist, Iron Guard, Lictor, Nazi, Neo-nazi, NF, Rexist, Sinarchist, Sinarquist

Fashion(able), Fashioned Aguise, A la (mode), Bristol, Build, Chic, Construct, Convention, Corinthian, Craze, Create, Cult, Custom, Cut, Design, Directoire, Elegant, Entail, Fad, Feat, Feign, Forge, Form, Genteel, Go, Hew, Hip, In, Invent, Kitsch, Look, > MAKE, Manière, Manners, Mode, Mondain(e), Mould, Newgate, Pink, Preppy, Rage, Rate, Sc, Shape, Smart, Smith, Snappy, Snazzy, Stile, Stylar, Style, Swish, Tailor, Ton, Ton(e)y, > TREND(Y), Turn, Twig, Vogue, Way, Wear, With-it, Work, Wrought

Fast(ing), Faster Abstain, Apace, Ashura, Breakneck, Citigrade, Clem, Daring, Double-quick, Elaphine, Express, Fizzer, Fleet, Immobile, Lent, Lightning, Loyal, Maigre, Meteoric, Moharram, Muharram, Muharrem, Pac(e)y, Posthaste, Presto, Pronto, Quadragesimal, Quick, Raffish, Raking, Ramadan, Ramadhan, Rash, Spanking, Speedy, Stretta, Stretto, Stuck, Supersonic, Swift, Tachyon, Thick, Tisha b'Av, Whistle-stop, Yarer, Yom Kippur

Fasten(er), Fastening Anchor, Attach, Bar, Belay, Bind, Bolt, Buckle, Button, Chain, Clamp, Clasp, Click, Clinch, Clip, Cramp, Cufflink, Dead-eye, Diamond-hitch, Dome, Espagnolette, Eye-bolt, Frog, Gammon, Hasp, Hesp, Hook, Lace, Latch, Lock, Moor, Morse, Nail, Netsuke, Nut, Padlock, Parral, Patent, Pectoral, Pin, Preen, Press stud, Reeve, Rivet, Rope, Rove, Seal, > SECURE, Sew up, Shut, Spar, Sprig, Staple, Stitch, Tach(e), Tag, Tape, Tassel, Tether, Tintack, Toggle, U-bolt, Velcro®, Wedge, Zip

Fat(s), Fatten, Fatty Adipic, Bard, Batten, Battle, Blubber, Butter, Calipash, Chubby, Corpulent, Dripping, Embonpoint, Endomorph, Flab, Flesh, Grease, Gross, Lanolin, Lard, Love handles, Margarine, Obese, Oil, Plump, Podgy, Polyunsaturated, Portly, Puppy, Rich, Rolypoly, Rotund, Saturated, Seam(e), Shortening, Stearic, Suet, Tallow, Tomalley, Tub, Unsaturated

Fatal(ism), Fate(s), Fated, Fateful Apnoea, Atropos, Cavel, Chance, Clotho, Deadly, Death, Decuma, Destiny, Doom, End, Fay, Fell, Joss, Karma, Kismet, Lachesis, Lethal, Lot, Meant, Moira, Mortal, Mortiferous, Nemesis, Norn(a), Parca, Pernicious, Portion, Predestination, Skuld, Urd, Verdande, Waterloo, Weird

Father(ly) Abba, Abbot, Abuna, Adopt, Apostolic, Bapu, Begetter, Breadwinner, Brown, City, Curé, Dad, Engender, Founding, Fr, Generator, Genitor, Getter, Governor, Male, Pa, Padre, Papa, Pappy, Parent, Pater(nal), Paterfamilias, Patriarch, Père, Pop(pa), Popper, Priest, Rev, Sire, Stud, Thames, Tiber, William

Fathom Delve, Depth, Dig, F, Plumb, Plummet, Understand

Fatigue Battle, Exhaust, Fag, Jade, Jet lag, ME, Neurosthenia, Overdo, Tire, Weariness, Weary

Fault(y) Arraign, Bad, Beam, Blame(worthy), Blunder, Bug, Cacology, Carp, Culpable, Defect, Demerit, Dip, Dip-slip, Drop-out, Duff, > ERROR, Failing, Flaw, Frailty, Gall, Glitch, Gravity, Henpeck, Hitch, Imperfect, Literal, Massif, > MISTAKE, Nag, Nibble, Niggle, Nit-pick, Oblique, Out, Outcrop, Overthrust, Para, Peccadillo, Rate, Reprehend, Rift, Rupes Recta, San Andreas, Sclaff, Set-off, Short, Slip, Step, Strike, Strike-slip, Technical, Thrust, Trap, Underthrust, Upbraid, Vice

Faux pas Blunder, Boner, Gaffe, Leglen-girth, Solecism

Favour(able), Favoured, Favourite Advance, Advantage(ous), Aggrace, Agraste, Alder-liefest, Approval, Back, Befriend, Behalf, Benign, Bless, Boon, Bribe, Cert, Chosen, Cockade, Curry, Darling, Ex gratia, Fancy, Favodian, Grace, Graste, Gratify, Gree, Hackle, Hot, In, Indulge, Kickback, Minion, Odour, Particular, Peat, Persona grata, Pet, Pettle, Popular, > PREFER, Promising, Propitious, Resemble, Rib(b)and, Roseate, Rose-knot, Rosette, Smile, Toast, Token

Fawn(er), **Fawning** Adulate, Bambi, Beige, Blandish, Brown-nose, Crawl, Creep, Cringe, Deer, Ecru, Flatter, Fleech, Grovel, Ko(w)tow, Lickspittle, Obsequious, Servile, Smarm, Smoo(d)ge, Subservient, Sycophant, Tasar, Toady, Truckle, Tussah, Tusseh, Tusser, Tussore

Fear Angst, Apprehension, Awe, Bugbear, Claustrophobia, Cold sweat, Crap, Cyberphobia, Dismay, Doubt, Drad, Dread, Foreboding, Fright, Funk, Hang-up, Horror, Kenophobia, Mysophobia, Nyctophobia, Ochlophobia, Redoubt, Revere, Taphephobia, Taphophobia, Terror, Trepidation, Willies

Fearful Afraid, Cowardly, Dire, Horrific, Nervous, Pavid, Rad, Redoubtable, Timorous, Tremulous, Windy

Fearless Bold, Brave, Courageous, Gallant, Impavid, Intrepid

Feast Adonia, Agape, Assumption, Banquet, Barmecide, Beano, Belshazzar's, Blow-out, Candlemas, Carousal, Celebration, Dine, Do, Double, Eat, Encaenia, Epiphany, Epulation, Festival, Fleshpots, Fool's, Gaudeamus, Gaudy, Hallowmas, Hockey, Hogmanay, Holy Innocents, Id-al-Adha, Id-al-Fitr, Immaculate Conception, Isodia, Junket, Kai-kai, Lady Day, Lamb-ale, Lammas, Luau, Martinmas, Michaelmas, Movable, Noel, Passover, Pentecost, Pig, Potlatch, Purim, Regale, Revel, Roodmas, Seder, Shindig, Spread, Succoth, Sukkot(h), Tabernacles, Tuck-in, Wayzgoose, Weeks, Yule, Zagmuk

Feat Achievement, Deed, Effort, Exploit, Gambado, Stunt, Trick

Feather(ed), **Feathers** Alula, Barbicel, Boa, Braccate, Cock, Contour, Covert, Crissum, Down, Duster, Filoplume, Fledged, Fletch, Flight, Gemmule, Hackle, Harl, Hatchel, Herl, Lure, Macaroni, Oar, Ostrich, Pen(na), Pin, Pinna, Pith, Plumage, Plume, Plumule, Pteryla, Ptilosis, Rectrix, Remex, Remiges, Rocket-tail, Saddle-hackle, Scapular, Scapus, Semiplume, Sickle, Standard, Stipa, Swansdown, Tectrix, Tertial, Vibrissa, White, Wing covert

Feature(s) Amenity, Appurtenance, Article, Aspect, Attribute, Brow, Character, Chin, Depict, Eye, Eyebrow, Face, Figure, Hallmark, Highlight, Item, Jizz, Landmark, Lineament, Neotery, Nose, Nucleus, Overfold, Phiz(og), Physiognomy, Spandrel, Star, Temple, Trait, Underlip

Fed(eral), **Federation** Agent, Alliance, Axis, Bund, Commonwealth, G-man, Interstate, League, Statal, Union

Fee Charge, Corkage, Dues, Duty, Faldage, Fine, Hire, Honorarium, Mortuary, Mouter, Multure, Obvention, Pay, Premium, Refresher, Retainer, Sub, Transfer, Tribute

Feeble Banal, Characterless, Daidling, Debile, Decrepit, Droob, Effete, Feckless, Flaccid, Footling, Fragile, Geld, Ineffective, Infirm, Jessie, Namby-pamby, Pale, Puny, Sickly, Slender, Slight, Tailor, Tame, Thin, Tootle, Wallydrag, Wallydraigle, Washy, Wastrel, Weak, Weak-kneed, Weak-minded, Weed, Weedy, Wersh, Wet, Wimpish, Worn

Feed(er), **Feeding** Battle, Bib, Browse, Cake, Cater, Cibation, Clover, Dine, Drip, > EAT, Fatten, Fire, Fishmeal, Fodder, Food, Gavage, Graze, Hay, Lunch, Meal, Nourish, Paid, Pecten, Provender, Refect, Repast, Sate, Soil, Stoke, Stooge, Stover, Sustain, Tire, Tractor, Wean

Feel, **Feeling(s)** Aesthesia, Affetuoso, Atmosphere, Compassion, Darshan, > EMOTION, Empathy, Empfindung, Euphoria, > EXPERIENCE, Fellow, Finger, Flaw, Frisk, Grope, Groundswell, Handle, Heart, Heartstrings, Hunch, Intuit, Knock, Know, Palp, Passible, Passion, Pity, Premonition, Presentiment, Probe, Realise, Sensate, Sensation, > SENSE, Sensitive, Sentiment, Spirit, Tactual, Touch, Turn, Undercurrent, Vehemence, Vibes, Zeal

▶ **Feet** *see* FOOT

Feign Act, Affect, Colour, Fake, Malinger, Mime, Mock, > PRETEND, Sham, Simulate

Fel(d)spar Adularia, Albite, Anorthite, Gneiss, Hyalophane, Moonstone, Orthoclase, Petuntse, Petuntze, Plagioclase, Sun-stone

▶ **Feline** *see* CAT

Fell Axe, Chop, Cruel, Deadly, Dire, Dread, Fierce, Hew, Hide, Hill, Inhuman, Knock-down, KO, Lit, Log, Moor, Pelt, Poleaxe, Ruthless, Sca, Shap, Skittle

Fellow(s), Fellowship Academic, Associate, Bawcock, Birkie, Bloke, Bo, Bro, Buffer, Carlot, Cat, Chal, Chap, Chi, China, Cock, Cod(ger), Collaborator, Co-mate, Communion, Companion, Comrade, Confrère, Cove, Cully, Cuss, Dandy, Dean, Dog, Don, Dude, Equal, F, Fogey, Fop, Gadgie, Gadje, Gaudgie, Gauje, Gink, Guy, Joe, Joker, Josser, Lad, Like, M, Mall, Man, Mate, Member, Mister, Mun, Partner, Peer, Professor, Rival, Sister, Sociate, Sodality, Swab, Twin, Waghalter, Wallah

Felt Bat(t), Drugget, Knew, Met, Numdah, Numnah, Pannose, Roofing, Sensed, Tactile, Underlay, Velour

Female (bodies), Feminine, Feminist Anima, Bint, Bit, Dame, Distaff, Doe, F, Filly, Girl, Harem, Hen, Her, Kermes, Lady, Libber, Maiden, Pen, Petticoated, Riot girl, Sakti, Shakti, She, Sheila, Shidder, Soft, Spindle, Thelytoky, -trix, > WOMAN, Yin

▷ **Female, Feminine** *may indicate* an -ess ending

Fence(r), Fencing (position) Bar, Barrier, Botte, Carte, Dogleg, Enclose, Epee, Flanconade, Foils, Fraise, Haha, Hay, Hedge, Hurdle, Iaido, Imbrocate, Kendo, Link, Mensur, Netting, Obstacle, Oxer, Pale, Paling, Palisade, Passado, Pen, Picket, Quart(e), Quinte, Raddle, Rail, Rasper, Receiver, Reset, Ring, Scrimure, Seconde, Sept(um), Septime, Singlestick, Sixte, Stacket, Stockade, Stramac, Stramazon, Sunk, Swordplay, Tac-au-tac, Trellis, Virginia, Wattle, Wear, Weir, Wire

Fend(er) Buffer, Bumper, Cowcatcher, Curb, Mudguard, Parry, Provide, Resist, Skid, Ward, Wing

Fennel Finnochio, Finoc(c)hio, Herb, Love-in-a-mist, Narthex, Ragged lady

Ferment(ation) Barm, Enzym(e), Leaven, Mowburn, Protease, Ptyalin, Seethe, Solera, Stum, Trypsin, Turn, Vinify, Working, Ye(a)st, Zyme, Zymosis, Zymurgy

Fern Acrogenous, Adder's-tongue, Adiantum, Archegonial, Asparagus, Aspidium, Asplenium, Azolla, Barometz, Bird's nest, Bladder, Bracken, Brake, Buckler, Ceterach, Cinnamon, Cryptogam, Cyathea, Cycad, Dicksonia, Elkhorn, Filicales, Filices, Filmy, Grape, Hard, Hart's-tongue, Isoetes, Maidenhair, Marsh, Marsilea, Marsilia, Meadow, Moonwort, Mosquito, Mulewort, Nardoo, Nephrolepis, Ophioglossum, Osmunda, Parsley, Pepperwort, Pillwort, Polypod, Ponga, Pteridology, Pteris, Punga, Rachilla, Rockbrake, Royal, Schizaea, Scolopendrium, Silver, Spleenwort, Staghorn, Sword, Tara, Tree, Venus's hair, Woodsia

Ferry(man) Charon, Convey, Hovercraft, Passage, Plier, Roll-on, RORO, Sealink, Shuttle, Traject, Tranect

Fertile, Fertility (symbol) Battle, Fat, Fecund, Fruitful, Linga, Priapus, Productive, Prolific, Rhiannon, Rich, Uberous

Fertilise(r), Fertilisation Ammonia, Auxin, Bee, Bone-ash, Bone-earth, Bone-meal, Caliche, Caprify, Compost, Fishmeal, Guano, Heterosis, Humogen, Humus, In-vitro, IVF, Kainite, Manure, Marl, Nitrate, Nitre, Pearl-ash, Phosphate, Pollen, Potash, Self, Sham, Stamen, Superphosphate, Top dressing

Fervent, Fervid, Fervour Ardent, Burning, Earnest, Heat, Hwyl, Intense, Keen, Passionate, White-hot, Zeal, Zeloso

Festival, Festive, Festivity Adonia, Aldeburgh, Ale, Al Hijra(h), All Saints' Day, Ambarvalia, Anniversary, Anthesteria, Ashora, Bairam, Baisak(h)i, Bayreuth, Beano, Beltane, Biennale, Candlemas, Carnival, Celebration, Cerealia, Chanuk(k)ah, Childermas, Church-ale, Circumcision, Commemoration, Convivial, Corpus Christi, Corroboree, Crouchmas, Dassehra, Dewali, Dionysia, Divali, Diwali, Doseh, Druid, Easter, Eisteddfod, Encaenia, En fête, Epiphany,

> FAIR, Feast, Feis, Fete, Fiesta, Fringe, Gaff, Gaudy, Gregory, Hallowmas, Hanukkah, Harvest, Hock-tide, Hogmanay, Holi, > HOLIDAY, Holy-ale, Hosay, Hosein, Id-al-fitr, Kermess, Kermiss, Kirmess, Lady-day, Lailat-ul-Qadr, Lammas, Laylat-al-Miraj, Lemural, Lemuria, Lesser Bairam, Lupercalia, Matsuri, Mela, Merry-night, Michaelmas, Miraj, Mod, Navaratra, Navaratri, Noel, Obon, Palilia, Panathenaean, Panegyry, Pardon, Pasch, Passover, Pentecost, Pesa(c)h, Play, Pongal, Pooja(h), Potlach, Puja, Purim, Quirinalia, Revel, Rosh Hashanah, Samhain, Saturnalia, Seder, Semi-double, Shabuath, Shavuath, Shrove(tide), Simchat Torah, Slugfest, Terminalia, Tet, Thargelia, Thesmophoria, Tide, Transfiguration, Up-Helly-Aa, Utas, Vesak, Vinalia, Visitation, Wake, Wesak, Yomtov, Yule(tide)

Fete Bazaar, Champetre, Entertain, > FESTIVITY, Gala, Honour, Tattoo

Fetish(ist) Charm, Compulsion, Idol, Ju-ju, Obeah, Obi(a), Talisman, Totem, Voodoo

Fetter Basil, Bilboes, Chain, Gyve, Hamshackle, Hopple, Iron, Leg-iron, Manacle, Shackle

Feu Tenure

Feud Affray, Clash, Feoff, Fief, Quarrel, Strife

Fever(ish) Ague, Brain, Cabin, Childbed, Dengue, Enteric, Ferment, Frenetic, Glandular, Heatstroke, Hectic, Jungle, Malaria, Marsh, Milk, Parrot, Passion, Pyretic, Rheumatic, Scarlatina, Scarlet, Spring, Sunstroke, Swine, Trench, Typhoid, Yellow(jack)

Few(er) Handful, Infrequent, > LESS, Limited, Scarce, Some, Wheen

Fiancé(e) Betrothed, Intended, Promised

Fiasco Bomb, Debacle, Disaster, Failure, Flask, Flop, Lash-up, Wash-out

Fibre, Fibrous Abaca, Acrilan®, Acrylic, Aramid, Arghan, Backbone, Bass, Bast, Buaze, Bwazi, Cantala, Coir, Constitution, Cotton, Courtelle®, Cuscus, Dralon®, Elastane, Filament, Filasse, Flax, Funicle, Gore-Tex®, Hair, Hemp, Henequen, Henequin, Herl, Istle, Ixtle, Jute, Kapok, Kenaf, Kevlar®, Kittul, Monkey-grass, Monofil, Monomode, Natural, Noil(s), Nylon, Oakum, Orlon®, Peduncle, Piassaba, Piassava, Pita, Pons, Pontine, Pulu, Raffia, Ramee, Rami, Rhea, Roughage, Sisal, Slub(b), Staple, Strick, Sunn-hemp, Tampico, Toquilla, Tow, Viver, Watap, Whisker, Wood pulp

Fickle(ness) Capricious, Change, False, Inconstant, Light, Mutable, Protean, Shifty, Varying, Volatile

Fiction(al), Fictitious Bogus, Cyberpunk, Fable, Fabrication, Pap, Phoney, Romance, Science, Splatterpunk, > STORY

Fiddle(r), Fiddling Amati, Bow, Calling-crab, Cello, Cheat, Crab, Cremona, Croud, Crouth, Crowd, Crwth, Fidget, Fix, Gju, Ground, Gu(e), Jerrymander, Kit, Launder, Nero, Peculate, Petty, Potter, Racket, Rebec(k), Rig, Rote, Sarangi, Saw, Sawah, Scam, Scrape, Scrapegut, Second, Spiel, Strad, Sultana, > TAMPER, Tinker, Trifle, Tweedle(-dee), Twiddle, Viola, > VIOLIN, Wangle

Fidget(y) Fantad, Fanteeg, Fantigue, Fantod, Fike, Fuss, Fyke, Hirsle, Hotch, Jimjams, Jittery, Niggle, Trifle, Twiddle, Twitch, Uneasy

Field(er), Fielding, Fields(man) Aalu, Aaru, Abroad, Aceldama, Aerodrome, Area, Arena, Arish, Arpent, Arrish, Campestral, Campestrian, Catch, Champ(s), Close, Coulomb, Cover, Domain, Electric, Electromagnetic, Electrostatic, Elysian, Entry, Fid, Flodden, Flying, Forte, Fylde, Glebe, Gracie, Gravitational, Grid(iron), Gully, Hop-yard, Ice, Keep wicket, Killing, Land, Landing, Lare, Lay, Lea(-rig), Leg slip, Ley, Line, Long leg, Long-off, Long-on, Longstop, Lords, Magnetic, Mead(ow), Mid-off, Mid-on, Mid-wicket, Mine, Oil, Padang, Paddock, Paddy, Parrock, Pasture, Pitch, Playing, Point, Potter's, Province, Realm, Runners, Salting, Sawah, Scarecrow, Scope, Scout, Shamba, Short leg, Shortstop, Short stop, Silly, Slip,

Sphere, Square leg, Stage, Stray, Stubble, Territory, Tract, Unified, Vector, Visual, W.C., World

▷ **Field** *may indicate* cricket

Field marshal Allenby, Bulow, French, Haig, Ironside, Kesselring, Kitchener, Montgomery, Roberts, Robertson, Rommel, Slim, Wavell

Fiend Barbason, Demon, > **DEVIL**, Enthusiast, Flibbertigibbet, Frateretto, Hellhound, Hobbididance, Mahn, Modo, Obidicut, Smulkin, Succubus

Fierce(ly) Billyo, Breem, Breme, Cruel, Draconic, Dragon, Grim, Hard-fought, Ogreish, Rampant, Renfierst, > **SAVAGE**, Severe, Tigrish, Violent, Wild, Wood, Wud

Fiery Ardent, Argand, Aries, Con fuoco, Dry, Fervent, Hot, Igneous, Leo, Mettlesome, Phlogiston, Sagittarius, Salamander, Zealous

Fiesta Festival, Fete, Gala, Holiday

Fifth Column, Diapente, Hemiol(i)a, Nones, Quint, Sesquialtera

Fig Bania, Benjamin-tree, Caprifig, Fico, Figo, Footra, Fouter, Foutra, Foutre, Hottentot, Moreton Bay, Sycamore, Sycomore, Syncomium, Trifle

Fight(er), Fighting Affray, Aikido, Alpino, Altercate, Bandy, Barney, > **BATTLE**, Bicker, Biffo, Blue, Bout, Box, Brave, Brawl, Bruiser, Bush-whack, Campaign, Chindit, Combat, Conflict, Contest, Crusader, Defender, Dog, Duel, Encounter, Engagement, Extremes, Faction, Fence, Fisticuffs, Fray, Freedom, Free-for-all, Fund, Gladiator, Grap(p)le, Gunslinger, Gurkha, Hurricane, Kite, Lapith, Marine, Med(d)le, Medley, Mêlée, Mercenary, MIG, Mill, Night, Partisan, Pellmell, Pillow, PLO, Press, Pugilist, Pugnacity, Punch up, Repugn, Resist, Ring, Ruck, Ruction, Rumble, Savate, Scold, Scrap, Scrimmage, Scuffle, Shadow, Shine, Skirmish, Slam, Soldier, Spar, Spitfire, Squabble, Straight, Strife, Struggle, Sumo, Swordsman, Tar, Tatar, Toreador, Tussle, Umbrella, War(-dog), War-horse, War-man, Warrior, Wrestle

Figure(s), Figurine Arabic, Aumail, Bas-relief, Body, Build, Caryatid, Cast, Cinque, Cipher, Cone, Cube, Cypher, Decahedron, Digit, Ecorché, Effigy, Eight, Ellipse, Enneagon, > **FORM**, Fusil, Girth, Graph, Hour-glass, Icon, Idol, Ikon, Image, Insect, Intaglio, Integer, Lay, Motif, Nonagon, Number, Numeral, Numeric, Octagon, Octahedron, Outline, Parallelogram, Pentacle, Polygon, Prism, Puppet, Pyramid, Reckon, Repetend, See, > **SHAPE**, Simplex, Statistics, Statue(tte), Telamon, Tetragon, Torus, Triangle, Triskelion, Waxwork

Figure of speech Allegory, Analogy, Antimask, Antimasque, Antimetabole, Antithesis, Asyndeton, Catachresis, Chiasmus, Deixis, Diallage, Ellipsis, Euphemism, Hypallage, Hyperbaton, Hyperbole, Hysteron proteron, Irony, Litotes, Meiosis, Metalepsis, Metaphor, Metonymy, Oxymoron, Paral(e)ipsis, Prosopoea, Simile, Syllepsis, Synecdoche, Taxeme, Tmesis, Trope, Zeugma

Filament Barbule, Byssus, Cirrus, Fibre, Fimbria, Floss, Gossamer, Hair, Hypha, Mycor(r)hiza, Myofibril, Paraphysis, Protonema, > **THREAD**

File, Filing(s) Abrade, Archive, Batch, Binary, Box, Burr, Clyfaker, Coffle, Croc(odile), Crosscut, Data set, Disc, Disk, Dossier, Enter, Floatcut, Generation, Index, Indian, Line, Nail, Pigeon-hole, Pollute, Quannet, Rank, Rasp, Rat-tail, README, Riffler, Risp, Row, Scalprum, Scratch, Single, String, Swarf, Text, Tickler, TIF(F)

Filibuster Freebooter, Hinder, Obstruct, Run on, Stonewall

Fill(ing), Filler Anaplerosis, Balaam, Banoffee, Banoffi, Beaumontag(u)e, Beaumontique, Billow, Bloat, Brick-nog, Brim, Bump, Centre, Charge, Cram, Gather, Gorge, Heart, Imbue, Impregnate, Inlay, Jampack, Line, Mastic, Occupy, Pabulous, Packing, Permeate, Plug, Repletive, Salpicon, Sate, Satisfy, Shim, Stack, Stock, Stocking, Stopping, > **STUFF**, Tales, Teem, Ullage

Fillet(s) Anadem, Annulet, Band, Bandeau, Bandelet, Bone, Cloisonné, Flaunching, Fret, Goujons, Grenadine, Headband, Infula, Label, Lemniscus,

List(el), Mitre, Moulding, Reglet, Regula, Ribbon, Rollmop, Slice, Snood, Sphendone, Stria, Striga, Taeniate, Tape, Teniate, Tournedos, Vitta

Film(s), **Filmmaker**, **Filmy**, **Filming** Acetate, Biopic, Blockbuster, Bollywood, Buddy, Caul, Cel, Cine, Cinerama®, Cliffhanger, Cling, Clip, Deepie, Dew, Diorama, Docudrama, Documentary, Dust, Epic, ET, Exposure, Feature, Fiche, Flick, Floaty, Footage, Gigi, Gossamer, Hammer, Haze, Hollywood, Horror, Kell, Lacquer, Layer, Loid, Mask, Membrane, Microfiche, Mist, Montage, Newsreel, Noir, Oater, Outtake, Panchromatic, Patina, Pellicle, Photo, Plaque, Prequel, Psycho, Quickie, Reel, Release, Rush, Scale, Screen, Scum, Short, Shot, Silent, Skin, Skin flick, Slick, Slo-mo, Snuff, Spaghetti western, Splatter, Studio, Talkie, Tear-jerker, Trailer, Two-shot, Ultrafiche, Video, Video-nasty, Web, Weepie, Weepy, Western

Filter(ing) Clarify, Dialysis, Leach, Percolate, Perk, Seep, Sieve, Skylight, Strain

Filth(y) Addle, Augean, Bilge, Colluvies, Crock, Crud, Defile, Dirt, Dung, Foul, Grime, Lucre, Mire, Muck, Obscene, Pythogenic, Refuse, Slime, Smut(ch), Soil, Squalor, Stercoral, Yuck

Final(e), **Finalise** Absolute, Closing, Coda, Conclusive, Cup, Decider, End, End-all, Eventual, Exam, Extreme, Grand, Last, Net(t), Peremptory, Sew up, Swansong, Terminal, Ultimate, Utter

Finance, **Financial**, **Financier** Ad crumenan, Angel, Back, Banian, Banker, Bankroll, Banyan, Cambism, Chrematistic, Exchequer, Fiscal, Gnome, Grubstake, Monetary, Revenue, Sponsor, Subsidise, Treasurer, Underwrite

Finch Bird, Brambling, Bunting, Canary, Charm, Chewink, Crossbill, Darwin's, Fringillid, Linnet, Marsh-robin, Peter, Serin, Siskin, Spink, Twite

Find(er), **Finding** Ascertain, Come across, Detect, Direction, Discover(y), Get, Hit, Inquest, > **LOCATE**, Meet, Provide, Rumble, Trace, Track down, Trouvaille, Unearth, Verdict

Fine, **Fine words** Amerce, Arts, Assess, Beau(t), Bender, Boss, Brandy, Brave, Braw, Champion, Dainty, Dandy, End, Eriach, Eric(k), Estreat, F, Fair, Famous, Forfeit, Godly, Good(ly), Gossamer, Gradely, Grand, Hair, Hairline, Handsome, Heriot, Hunkydory, Immense, Issue, Keen, Log, Mulct, Nifty, Niminy-piminy, Noble, OK, Oke, > **PENALTY**, Precise, Pure, Relief, Safe, Sconce, Sheer, Sicker, Slender, Spanking, Subtle, Summery, Super, Tax, Ticket(t)y-boo, Tiptop, Topping, Wally, Waly

Finery Braws, Fallal, Frills, Frippery, Gaudery, Ornament, Trinket, Wally, Warpaint

Finger(s), **Fingernail** Dactyl, Digit, Fork, Handle, Index, Lunula, Medius, Name, Nip, Piggy, Pinky, Pointer, Prepollex, Pusher, Ring(man), Shop, Talaunt, Talon, Tot, Trigger, White

Fingerprint(ing) Dabs, Dactylogram, Genetic, Loop, Whorl

Finis, **Finish(ed)**, **Finishing touch** Arch, Blanket, Calendar, Close, Coating, Coda, Complete, > **CONCLUDE**, Crown, Die, Dish, Do, Dope, Dress, > **END**, Epilog(ue), Epiphenomena, Exact, Full, Grandstand, Kibosh, Lacquer, Log off, Matt, Mirror, Neat, Outgo, Outwork, Pebbledash, Peg out, Perfect, Photo, Refine, Ripe, Round, Satin, Settle, Shot, Spitcher, Surface, Terminate, Through, Top out, Up (tie), Veneer, Wau(l)k, Wind-up

Finn(ish) Esth, Huck(leberry), Karelian, Mickey, Mordvin, Suomic, Udmurt, Votyak

Fire(side) Accend, Agni, Animate, Ardour, Arouse, Arson, Atar, Axe, Bake, Bale, Barbecue, Barrage, Beacon, Behram, Blaze, Boot, Brand, Brazier, Brush, Burn, Bush, Chassé, Conflagration, Corposant, Covering, Delope, Discharge, Dismiss, Elan, Electric, Element, Embolden, Ena, Energy, Enfilade, Enkindle, Enthuse, Flak, Flame, Friendly, Furnace, Greek, Gun, Hearth, Hob, Ignite, Inferno, Ingle, Inspire, Kentish, Kiln, Kindle, Launch, Let off, Light, Liquid, Lowe, Pop, Prime, Prometheus, Pull, Pyre, Quick, Rake, Rapid, Red, Red cock, Sack, St Anthony's, St Elmo's,

Scorch, Shell, Shoot, Smudge, Spark, Spirit, Spunk, Stoke, Stove, Strafe, Tracer, Trial, Wake, Watch, Wisp, Zeal

▶ **Firearm** *see* GUN

Fire-break Epaulement, Greenstrip

Firedamp Blower

Fireplace Chimney, Grate, Hearth, Hob, Ingle, Loop-hole, Range

Fireproof Abednego, Asbestos, Incombustible, Inflammable, Meshach, Salamander, Shadrach, Uralite

Firewood Billet, Faggot, Knitch, Tinder

Firework(s) Banger, Bengal-light, Bunger, Cherry bomb, Cracker, Devil, Fisgig, Fizgig, Fountain, Gerbe, Girandole, Iron sand, Jumping Jack, Maroon, Pastille, Peeoy, Petard, Pinwheel, Pioy(e), Pyrotechnics, Realgar, Rocket, Roman candle, Serpent, Skyrocket, Sparkler, Squib, Tantrum, Throwdown, Tourbill(i)on, Volcano, Wheel, Whizzbang

Firm Adamant, Agency, Binding, Business, Collected, Compact, Company, Concern, Concrete, Constant, Crisp, Decided, Determined, Duro, Faithful, Fast, Fixed, Hard, Inc, Oaky, Obdurate, Obstinate, > **RESOLUTE**, Sclerotal, Secure, Set, Siccar, Sicker, > **SOLID**, Stable, Stalwart, Staunch, Ste(a)dfast, Steady, Steely, Steeve, Stern, Stieve, Stiff, Strict, Sturdy, Tight, Tough, Well-knit

First Ab initio, Alpha, Arch, Archetype, Best, Calends, Champion, Chief, Earliest, E(a)rst, Foremost, Former, Front, Head, I, Ideal, Imprimis, Initial, 1st, Kalends, Led, Maiden, No 1, One, Opener, Or, Original, Pioneer, Pole, Premier, Prima, Primal, Prime, Primo, Principal, Prototype, Rudimentary, Senior, Starters, Top, Victor, Yama

First class, **First rate** A1, Crack, Prime, Supreme, Tiptop, Top(notch)

First man Adam, Ask, Premier, President, Yama

▶ **First rate** *see* FIRST CLASS

First woman Embla, Eve, Pandora, Premier

Firth Estuary, Forth, Inlet, Moray, Tay

Fish(ing) Angle, Bob, Cast, Catch, Chowder, Coarse, Cran, Creel, Dredge, Dry-fly, Episcate, Fly, Flying, Fry, Gefilte, Goujons, Guddle, Halieutics, Haul, Ledger, Mess, Net, Otterboard, Overnet, Piscine, Roe, Sashimi, Shoal, Snigger, Sniggle, Spin, Spot, Trawl, Troll, Tub, White

Fish and chips Greasies

Fisher(man) Ahab, Andrew, Angler, Black cat, Caper, High-liner, Liner, Pedro, Peter, Piscator, Rodster, Sharesman, Walton

▶ **Fisherwoman** *see* FISHSELLER

Fishseller, **Fisherwoman** Fishwife, Molly Malone, Ripp(i)er, Shawley, Shawlie

Fissure Chasm, Cleft, Crack, Crevasse, Crevice, Gap, Grike, Gryke, Lode, Rent, Sand-crack, Scam, Vallecula, Vein, Zygon

Fist Clench, Dukes, Hand, Iron, Join-hand, Mailed, Neaf(fe), Neif, Neive, Nief, Nieve, Pud, Punch, Thump

Fit(s), **Fitful**, **Fitting(s)**, **Fitness** Able, Access, Adapt, Ague, Appointment, Appropriate, Apropos, Apt, Bout, Canto, Capable, Condign, Congruous, Convulsion, Decent, Decorous, Dod, Dove-tail, Due, Eligible, Ensconce, Epilepsy, Equip, Expedient, Fairing, Fiddle, Furnishing, Gee, Germane, Hale, Hang, Health, Huff, Hysterics, In-form, Just, Lune, Mate, Meet, Mood, Nest, Paroxysm, Pertinent, Prepared, > **PROPER**, Ready, Rig, Rind, Ripe, Rynd, Seemly, Seizure, Set, Sit, Sort, Sound, Spasm, Spell, Start, Suit(able), Tantrum, Throe, Turn, Up to, Well, Worthy, Wrath

▷ **Fit(ting)** *may indicate* a 't'

Five(s) Cinque, Mashie, Pallone, Pedro, Pentad, Quinary, Quintet, Sextan, Towns, V

Fix(ed), Fixer, Fixative Affeer, Anchor, Appoint, > **ARRANGE**, Assess, Assign, Attach, Bind, Brand, Cement, Clamp, Clew, Clue, Constant, Cure, Decide, Destine, Determine, Do, Embed, Engrain, Establish, Fast, Firm, Fit, Freeze, Hold, Immutable, Imprint, Ingrain, Jag, Jam, Locate, Lodge, Nail, Name, Narcotic, Nobble, Orientate, Peg, Persistent, Pin, Point, Repair, Resolute, Rig, Rigid, Rivet, Rut, Screw, Seat, Seize, Set, Settle, Shoo, Skewer, Splice, Staple, Step, Tie, Weld

Fixture Attachment, Event, Match, Permanence, Unit

Fizz(ed), Fizzy Buck's, Effervesce, Gas, Hiss, Pop, Sherbet, Sod, Soda

Flabbergast(ed) Amaze, Astound, Floor, Thunderstruck

Flabby Flaccid, Lank, Lax, Limp, Pendulous, Saggy

Flag(gy), Flags Acorus, Ancient, Ashlar, Banderol, Banner, Black, Blue Peter, Bunting, Burgee, Chequered, Colour(s), Decline, Droop, Duster, Ensign, Fail, Falter, Fane, Fanion, Gladdon, Gonfalon, Hail, Hoist, Iris, Jack, Jade, Jolly Roger, Kerbstone, Languish, Lis, Old Glory, Orris, Pave(ment), Pennant, Pennon, Peter, Pin, Rag, Red, Red Duster, Red Ensign, Sag, Semaphore, Sink, Slab(stone), Slack, Standard, Stars and bars, Stars and stripes, Streamer, Tire, Tricolour, Union (Jack), Vane, Waft, Whift, White (ensign), Wilt, Wither

Flagon Bottle, Carafe, Jug, Stoop, Stoup, Vessel

Flagrant Egregious, Glaring, Heinous, Patent, Wanton

Flail Beat, Drub, Swingle, Threshel

Flair Art, Bent, Elan, Gift, Knack, Panache, Style, > **TALENT**

Flake Chip, Flame, Flaught, Flaw, Floccule, Flocculus, Fragment, Peel, Scale, Smut, Snow

Flamboyant Baroque, Brilliant, Florid, Garish, Grandiose, Ornate, Ostentatious, Paz(z)azz, Piz(z)azz, Swash-buckler

Flame, Flaming Ardent, Blaze, Fire, Flake, Flambé, Flammule, Glow, Kindle, Leman, Lover, Lowe, Oxyacetylene, Sweetheart

Flank(s) Accompany, Anta, Flange, Flitch, Ilia, Lisk, Loin, Side, Spur

Flannel Blather, Canton, Cloth, Soft-soap, Waffle, Zephyr

Flap(ped), Flapper, Flapping Aileron, Alar, Alarm(ist), Bate, Beat, Bird, Bobbysoxer, Bustle, Chit, Dither, Elevon, Epiglottis, Flag, Flaught, Flutter, Fly, Fuss, Giglet, Hover, > **IN A FLAP**, Labrum, Lapel, Lorna, Lug, Panic, Spin, Spoiler, Tab, Tag, Tailboard, Tailgate, Tiswas, To-do, Tongue, Wave, Whisk

Flare(d), Flare up Bell, Fishtail, Flame, Flanch, Flaunch, Godet, Magnesium, Scene, Signal, Spread, Spunk, Ver(e)y, Widen

Flash(y), Flasher Flare, Flaught, Fulgid, Garish, Gaudy, Gleam, Glisten, Glitzy, Instant, Lairy, Levin, Lightning, Loud, Mo, Raffish, Ribbon, Roary, Scintillation, Second, Sequin, Showy, Snazzy, Spark, Streak, Strobe, Swank(e)y, Tick, Trice, Twinkle, Vivid, Wire

▷ **Flashing** *may indicate* an anagram

Flask(-shaped) Ampulla, Aryballos, Bottle, Canteen, Carafe, Costrel, Cucurbit, Dewar, Erlenmeyer, Fiasco, Flacket, Flacon, Florence, Goatskin, Hip, Lekythos, Matrass, Mick(e)(y), Reform, Retort, Thermos®, Vacuum, Vial

Flat(s), Flatten(ed), Flattener Ancipital, Apartment, Bachelor, Bald, Banal, Beat, Bed-sit, Blow-out, Bulldoze, Callow, Compress, Condominium, Cottage, Dead, Demolish, Double, Dress, Dull, Even, Feeble, Flew, Floor, Flue, Fool, Gaff, Garden, Granny, High-rise, Home-unit, Horizontal, Insipid, Ironed, Jacent, Key, KO, Law, Level, Lifeless, Llano, Marsh, Monotonous, Mud, Nitwit, Oblate, Pad, Pancake, Pedestrian, Penthouse, Pied-à-terre, Plain, Plane, Plat, Plateau, Press, Prone, Prostrate, Recumbent, Rooms, Salt, Scenery, Service, Smooth, Spread-edged, Squash, Studio, Tableland, Tame, Tasteless, Tenement, True, Vapid, Walk-up

Flatter(ing), Flatterer, Flattery Adulate, Beslaver, Blandish, Blarney, Bootlick, Butter, Cajole, Candied, Carn(e)y, Claw(back), Complimentary, Fawn, Flannel, Flummery, Fulsome, Honey, Imitation, Lip-salve, Moody, Palp, Poodle-faker, Puffery, Sawder, Smarm, Soap, Soother, Spaniel, Stroke, Sugar, Sweet talk, Sycophant, Taffy, Toady, Treacle, Unction, Wheedle

Flatulence Belch, Borborygmus, Burp, Carminative, Colic, Gas, Wind

Flaunt Brandish, Flourish, Gibe, Parade, Skyre, Strout, Strut, Wave

Flavour(ed), Flavouring Absinth(e), Alecost, Anethole, Angostura, Anise, Aniseed, Aroma, Bold, Borage, Bouquet garni, Clove, Coriander, Cumin, Dill, Essence, Fenugreek, Flor, Garni, Marinate, Mint, Orgeat, Quark, Race, Ratafia, Relish, Sair, Sassafras, Tack, Tang, Tarragon, > **TASTE**, Tincture, Twang, Vanilla

Flaw Blemish, Brack, Bug, Chip, Crack, Defect, Fallacy, > **FAULT**, Gall, Hamartia, Imperfection, Kink, Lophole, Rima, Spot, Taint, Tear, Thief, Windshake

Flax(en) Aleseed, Blonde, Codilla, Harden, Hards, Herden, Herl, Hurden, Line, Linseed, Lint, Linum, Mill-mountain, Poi, Tow

Flea Aphaniptera, Chigger, Chigoe, Chigre, Daphnid, Hopper, Itch-mite, Lop, Pulex, Sand, Water

Flee Abscond, Bolt, Decamp, Escape, Eschew, Fly, Lam, Loup, Run, Scapa, Scarper, Scram

Fleece, Fleecy Bleed, Coat, Despoil, Flocculent, Golden, Lambskin, Lanose, Pash(i)m, Pashmina, Plot, Pluck, Rifte, Ring, Rob, Rook, Shave, Shear, Sheepskin, Skin, > **SWINDLE**, Toison

Fleet(ing) Armada, Brief, Camilla, Ephemeral, Evanescent, Fast, Flit, Flota, Flotilla, Fugacious, Fugitive, Hasty, Hollow, Lightfoot, Navy, Pacy, Passing, Prison, Spry, Street, Transient, Velocipede

Flesh(y) Beefy, Body, Carneous, Carrion, Corporeal, Corpulent, Creatic, Digastric, Finish, Gum, Hypersarcoma, Joint, Longpig, Lush, Meat, Mons, Muscle, Pulp, Sarcous, Spare tyre, Tissue

Flex(ible), Flexibility Adaptable, Bend(y), Elastic, Genu, Limber, Lissom(e), Lithe, Pliant, Rubbery, Squeezy, Tensile, Tonus, Wieldy, Willing, Wiry

▷ **Flexible, Flexuous** *may indicate* an anagram

Flick(er), Flicks Bioscope, Cinema, Fillip, Film, Flip, Flirt, Flutter, Glimmer, Gutter, Movie, Movy, Snap, Snow, Switch, Talkie, Twinkle, Waver

Flier Airman, Alcock, Amy, Aviator, Blimp, Brown, Crow, Daedalus, Erk, Fur, George, Gotha, Handout, Icarus, Leaflet, Lindbergh, Pilot, RAF, Scotsman, Spec, Speedy

▷ **Flier** *may indicate* a bird

Flight(y) Backfisch, Birdbrain, Bolt, Bubble-headed, Capricious, Charter, Contact, Dart, Departure, Escalier, Escape, Exaltation, Exodus, Fast, Fickle, Flaught, Flibbertigibbet, Flip, Flock, Flyby, Fly-past, Free, Fugue, Giddy, Grese, Gris(e), Guy, Hegira, Hejira, Hejra, Hellicat, Hijra, Lam, Mercy, Milk-run, Mission, Open-jaw, Pair, R(a)iser, Redeye, Ro(a)ding, Rode, Rout, Skein, Sortie, Stairs, Stayre, Steps, Swarm, Test, Top, Tower, Trap, Vol(age), Volatile, Volley, Whisky-frisky, Wing

▷ **Flighty** *may indicate* an anagram

Flimsy Finespun, Gimcrack, Gossamer, Jimcrack, Sleazy, Sleezy, Tenuous, Thin, Weak, Wispy

Flinch Blench, Cringe, Funk, Quail, Recoil, Shrink, Shudder, Start, Wince

Fling Dance, Flounce, Highland, Hurl, Pitch, Shy, Slat, Slug, Slump, Spanghew, Spree, Throw, > **TOSS**

Flint Chert, Firestone, Granite, Hag-stone, Hornstone, Microlith, Mischmetal, Pirate, Rock, Silex, Silica, Stone, Touchstone

Offset, Paillon, Pip, Scotch, Silver, Stooge, Stump, Thwart, Touché

Fold(er), Folding, Folded, Folds Close, Collapse, Concertina, Corrugate, Crease, Crimp, Crinkle, Fan, Frill, Furl, Gather, Jack-knife, Monocline, Nappe, Pintuck, > PLEAT, Ply, Ruck(le), Sheep-pen, Syncline, Tuck, Wrap

Foliage Coma, Finial, Frond, Greenery, Leafage

Follow(er), Following Adhere, After, Agree, Anthony, Attend(ant), Believer, Clientele, Consequence, Copy, Dangle, Disciple, Dog, Echo, Ensew, Ensue, Entourage, Epigon(e), Equipage, F, Fan, Groupie, Heel(er), Henchman, Hereon, Hunt, Man, Merry men, Muggletonian, Myrmidon, Neist, Next, Obey, Pan, Post, Pursue, Rake, Road, Run, Satellite, School, Secundum, Seewing, Segue, Sequel, Seriation, Shadow, Sheep, Sidekick, Stag, Stalk, Stear, Steer, Subsequent, Succeed, Sue, Suivez, Supervene, Tag, Tail, Tantony, Trace, Track, Trail, Train, Use, Vocation, Votary

▷ **Follower** 'a follower' *may indicate* B

Folly Antic, Bêtise, Idiocy, Idiotcy, Imprudence, Lunacy, Mistake, Moria, Unwisdom, Vanity

Fond(ness) Amatory, Ardour, Dote, Keen, Loving, Partial, Tender, Tendre

Fondle Canoodle, Caress, Dandle, Grope, Hug, Nurse, Pet, Snuggle

Food Aliment, Ambrosia, Board, Broth, Bully, Burger, Cate, Cheer, Cheese, Chop, Chow, Collation, Comestible, Commons, Course, > DISH, Eats, Fare, Fodder, Forage, Fuel, Grub, Keep, Manna, Meat, Nosh, Nourishment, Pasta, Provender, Provision, Scoff, Snack, Staple, Stodge, Table, Tack, Takeaway, Trimmings, Tuck(er), Viand, Victuals, Waffle

Fool(hardy), Foolish(ness) April, Berk, Buffoon, Chump, Clot, Clown, Cockeyed, Coxcomb, Delude, Dummy, Dunce, Flannel(led), Folly, Gaby, Gaga, Git, Goat, Goon, Goose, Gubbins, Gull, Halfwit, Idiotic, Imbecile, Inane, Jest, Joke, Kid, Lark, Mislead, Moron, Muggins, Ni(n)compoop, Ninny, Senseless, Soft, Sot, > STUPID, Trifle, Zany

Foot(ing), Footwork, Feet Anap(a)est, Athlete's, Base, Choliamb, Choriamb, Club, Dactyl, Dance, Hoof, Iamb(us), Infantry, Pad, Paeon, Paw, Podium, Shanks's pony, Standing, Tarsus, Terms, Tootsie, Tread, Trench, Trochee, Trotter

Football(er) Back, Barbarian, Ba'spiel, Camp, Centre, Fantasy, FIFA, Flanker(back), Gaelic, Goalie, Gridder, Keeper, Kicker, Libero, Lineman, Lock, Midfield, Pack, Pele, Pigskin, RU, Rugby, Rugger, Rules, Safety, Soccer(oos), Sport, Striker, Sweeper, Table, Total, Touch(back), Wing

Footling Trivial

Footman Attendant, Flunkey, Lackey, Pedestrian, Pompey, Yellowplush

Footpath, Footway Banquette, Catwalk, Clapper, Track

Footprint Ichnite, Ichnolite, Pad, Prick, Pug, Seal, Slot, Trace, Track, Vestige

Footwear Gumboot, > SHOE, Slipper, Sock, Spats, Stocking

Fop(pish) Apery, Barbermonger, Beau, Buck, Cat, Coxcomb, Dandy, Dude, Exquisite, Fallal, Fantastico, Finical, La-di-da, Macaroni, Monarcho, Muscadin, Popinjay, Skipjack, Toff

For Ayes, Because, Concerning, Cos, Pro, Since, To

Forage Alfalfa, Fodder, Graze, Greenfeed, Lucern(e), Pickeer, Prog, Raid, Rummage, Sainfoin, Search

Forbear(ance), Forbearing Abstain, Clement, Endure, Indulgent, Lenience, Lineage, Longanimity, Mercy, Pardon, Parent, Patient, Quarter, > REFRAIN, Suffer, Tolerant, Withhold

Forbid(den), Forbidding Ban, Bar, City, Denied, Don't, Dour, Enjoin, For(e)speak, Gaunt, Grim, Haram, Hostile, Loury, NL, Prohibit, Stern, Taboo, Tabu, Tapu, Tref(a), Verboten, Veto

Force(d), **Forceful**, **Forces**, **Forcible** Agency, Army, Back emf, Bludgeon, Body, Brigade, Bring, Brunt, Bulldoze, Capillary, Centrifugal, Coerce, Commando, Compel, Constrain, Cram, Detachment, Domineer, Dragoon, Drive, Duress(e), Edge, Electromotive, Emphatic, Energetic, Exchange, Expeditionary, Fifth, Fire brigade, Frogmarch, Gendarmerie, Gravitational, Host, Impetus, Impose, Impress, Inertial, Juggernaut, Kinetic, Kundalini, Labour, Land, Legion, Life, Magnetomotive, Make, Manpower, Market, Muscle, Oblige, Od, Old Contemptibles, Orotund, Personnel, Physical, Plastic, Police, Posse, Potent, Pound, Press(gang), Pressure, Prise, Psyche, Pull, Railroad, Rape, Ravish, Reave, Require, SAS, Steam(roller), Stick, Stiction, Strong-arm, Subject, TA, Task, Thrust, Torque, Tractive, Troops, Vehement, Vigorous, Vim, Violence, Vis visa, Vital, Vociferous, Wrench, Wrest, Wring, Zap

▷ **Force(d)** *may indicate* an anagram

▸ **Forebear** *see* FORBEAR

Foreboding Anxiety, Augury, Cloudage, Croak, Feeling, Freet, > OMEN, Ominous, Premonition, Presage, Presentiment, Sinister, Zoomantic

Forecast(er), **Forecasting** Augury, Auspice, Divine, Extrapolation, Horoscope, Metcast, Perm, Precurse, Predict, Presage, Prescience, Prognosis, Prognosticate, Prophesy, Rainbird, Shipping, Soothsay, Spae, Tip, Weather

Forehead Brow, Front(let), Glabella(r), Sincipitum, Temple

Foreign(er) Alien, Arab, Auslander, Barbarian, Easterling, Eleanor, Ethnic, Exclave, Exotic, External, Extraneous, Extrinsic, Forane, Forinsecal, Forren, Fraim, Fremit, Gaijin, German, Gringo, Gweilo, Malihini, Metic, Moit, Mote, Outlander, Outside, Oversea, Peregrine, Remote, > STRANGE, Stranger, Taipan, Tramontane, Uitlander, Unfamiliar, Wog

Foreknowledge Prescience

Foreman Baas, Boss, Bosun, Chancellor, Gaffer, Ganger, Manager, Overseer, Steward, Superintendent, Topsman

Foremost First, Front, Leading, Primary, Prime, Supreme, Van

▷ **Foremost** *may indicate* first letters of words following

Forerunner Augury, Harbinger, Herald, Messenger, Omen, Pioneer, Precursor, Trailer, Vaunt-courier

Foreshadow Adumbrate, Augur, Bode, Forebode, Hint, Portend, Prefigure, Presage, Type

Foresight Ganesa, Prescience, Prophecy, Prospect, Providence, Prudence, Taish, Vision

Forest(ry) Arden, Ashdown, Black, Bush, Caatinga, Charnwood, Chase, Cloud, Dean, Epping, Gallery, Gapo, Glade, Greenwood, Igapo, Jungle, Monte, Nandi, Nemoral, New, Savernake, Selva, Sherwood, Taiga, Urman, Virgin, > WOOD

Forestall Anticipate, Head-off, Obviate, Pip, Pre-empt, Prevent, Queer, Scoop

Foretaste Antepast, Antipasto, Appetiser, Pregustation, Prelibation, Sample, Trailer

Foretell(ing), **Forewarn** Augur, Bode, Caution, Divine, Fatidic, Forecast, Portend, Predict, Premonish, Presage, Prognosticate, Prophecy, Soothsay, Spae

Forethought Anticipation, Caution, Prometheus, Provision, Prudence

Forever Always, Amber, Ay(e), Eternal, Evermore, Keeps

▸ **Forewarn** *see* FORETELL

Foreword Introduction, Preamble, Preface, Proem, Prologue

For example Eg, Say, Vg, ZB

Forfeit Deodand, Fine, Forgo, > PENALTY, Relinquish, Rue-bargain, Sconce

Forge(d), **Forger(y)** Blacksmith, Copy, Counterfeit, Drop, Dud, Fabricate,

Fashion, Foundry, Hammer, Heater, Horseshoe, Ireland, Lauder, Mint, Paper-hanger, Pigott, Progress, Smith(y), Smithery, Spurious, Stiff, Stithy, Stumer, Tilt, Trucage, Truquage, Utter, Valley, Vermeer, Vulcan

Forget(ful), **Forget-me-not** Amnesia, Dry, Fluff, Lethe, Myosotis, Neglect, Oblivious, Omit, Overlook

Forgive(ness), **Forgiving** Absolution, Amnesty, Clement, Condone, Merciful, Overlook, Pardon, Placable, Remission, Remittal

Forgo(ne) Abstain, Expected, Refrain, Renounce, Waive

Fork(ed) Bifurcate, Biramous, Branch, Caudine, Cleft, Crotch, Divaricate, Forficate, Fourchette, Grain, Graip, Morton's, Osmeterium, Prong, Runcible, Tine, Toaster, Tormenter, Tormentor, Trident, Trifid, Tuner, Tuning, Y

Form(s) Alumni, Bench, Bumf, Cast, Ceremonial, Class, Constitute, Coupon, Create, Document, Dress, Experience, Fashion, Feature, Fig, > **FIGURE**, Formula, Free, Game, Gestalt, Hare, Image, Keto, Lexicalise, Logical, Mode, Mood, Morph(ic), Morphology, Mould, Order, Originate, P45, Physique, Protocol, Questionnaire, Redia, Remove, Rite, Ritual, Schedule, Shape, Shell, Stage, Stamp, State, Stereotype, Structure, Style, Symmetry, Ternary, Version

▷ **Form** *may indicate* a hare's bed

Formal Conventional, Dry, Exact, Fit, Literal, Methodic, Official, Pedantic, Precise, Prim, Routine, Set, Starched, Stiff, Stodgy, Tails

Formality Ceremony, Ice, Pedantry, Protocol, Punctilio, Starch

Formation Battalion, Configuration, Diapyesis, Echelon, Eocene, Fours, Growth, Line, Manufacture, Origin, Pattern, Phalanx, Prophase, Riss, Wedge

▷ **Former** *may indicate* something that forms

Former(ly) Ance, Auld, Before, Ci-devant, Earlier, Ere-now, Erst(while), Ex, Late, Maker, Matrix, Old, Once, One-time, Past, Previous, Prior, Pristine, Quondam, Sometime, Then, Umquhile, Whilom

Formidable Alarming, Armipotent, Battleaxe, Fearful, Forbidding, Gorgon, Powerful, Shrewd, Stoor, Stour, Stowre, Sture, Tiger

▷ **Form of**, **Forming** *may indicate* an anagram

Formula(te) Define, Devise, Doctrine, Empirical, Equation, Frame, Incantation, Invent, Kekule, Lurry, Molecular, Paternoster, Prescription, Protocol, Reduction, Rite, Ritual, Stirling's, Structural

Fort(ification), **Fortress** Acropolis, Alamo, Bastille, Battlement, Blockhouse, Burg, Casbah, Castle, Citadel, Earthwork, Fastness, Fieldwork, Garrison, Haven, Kasba(h), Keep, La(a)ger, Pa(h), Peel, Rampart, Ravelin, Redoubt, Salient, Stronghold, Tower

Forthright Candid, Direct, Frank, Prompt

Fortify Arm, Augment, Brace, Casemate, Embattle, Lace, Munify, Steel, > **STRENGTHEN**

Fortitude Endurance, Grit, Mettle, Patience, Pluck, > **STAMINA**

Fortunate Auspicious, Blessed, Blest, Godsend, Happy, > **LUCKY**, Opportune, Providential, Well

Fortune (teller), **Fortune-telling** Auspicious, Bonanza, Bumby, Cartomancy, Chaldee, Cha(u)nce, Destiny, Dukkeripen, Fame, Fate, Felicity, Genethliac, Geomancy, Hap, Hydromancy, I Ching, Lot, Luck, Mint, Motser, Motza, Oracle, Packet, Palmist, Peripety, Pile, Prescience, Pyromancy, Sibyl, Soothsayer, Sortilege, Spaewife, Success, Taroc, Tarok, Tarot, Tyche, Wealth, Windfall

Forum Arena, Assembly, Debate, Platform, Tribunal

Forward(s) Accede, Advanced, Ahead, Along, Arch, Assertive, Assuming, Bright, Early, Flanker, Forrad, Forrit, Forth, Fresh, Future, Hasten, Hooker, Immodest, Impudent, Insolent, Lock, Malapert, On(wards), Pack, Pert, Petulant, Porrect,

Precocious, > **PROGRESS**, Promote, Prop, Readdress, Redirect, Scrum, Send, Stem, To(ward), Van, Wing

Fossil(ised), Fossils Amber, Ammonite, Baculite, Belemnite, Blastoid(ea), Calamite, Ceratodus, Chondrite, Conodont, Cordaites, Derived, Encrinite, Eohippus, Eozoon, Eurypterus, Exuviae, Fogy, Goniatite, Graptolite, Ichnite, Ichnolite, Ichthyodurolite, Ichthyolite, Index, Lingulella, Mosasauros, Nummulite, Olenus, Orthoceras, Osteolepis, Ostracoderm, Petrifaction, Phytolite, Plesiosaur, Pliohippus, Pliosaur, Pterygotus, Pythonomorph, Relics, Reliquiae, Remanié, Sigillaria, Sinanthropus, Snakestone, Stigmaria, Stromatolite, Taphonomy, Titanotherium, Trace, Trilobite, Uintatherium, Wood-opal, Zinganthropus, Zoolite

Foster (child, mother), Fostering Adopt, Cherish, Da(u)lt, Develop, Feed, Forment, Further, Harbour, Incubation, Metapelet, Metaplot, Nourish, Nourse(l), Noursle, Nousell, Nurse, Nurture, Nuzzle, > **REAR**

Foul, Foul-smelling Base, Beray, Besmirch, Besmutch, Bewray, Bungle, Dreggy, Drevill, Enseam, Evil, Feculent, Gross, Hassle, Hing, Mephitic, Mud, Noisome, Olid, Osmeterium, Professional, Putid, Putrid, > **RANK**, Reekie, Rotten, Sewage, Soiled, Squalid, Stagnant, Stain, Stapelia, Technical, Unclean, Unfair, Vile, Violation, Virose

▷ **Foul** *may indicate* an anagram

Found (in) Among, Base, Bed, Bottom, Build, Cast, Emong, Endow, > **ESTABLISH**, Eureka, Institute, Introduce, Met, Occur, Plant, Recovered, Rest, Start, Table

Foundation(s) Base, Bedrock, Cribwork, Establishment, Footing, Girdle, Grillage, Ground, Groundwork, Hard-core, Infrastructure, Institution, Matrix, Pile, Roadbed, Rockefeller, Scholarship, Stays, Substrata, Substructure, Trackbed, Underlie, Underlinen

▷ **Foundations** *may indicate* last letters

Founder Author, Crumple, Fail, Inventor, Iron-master, Miscarry, Oecist, Oekist, Patriarch, Perish, Settle, Sink, Stumble

Fountain Acadine, Aganippe, Bubbler, Castalian, Cause, Conduit, Drinking, Fauwara, Forts, Gerbe, Head, Hippocrene, Jet, Pant, Pirene, Salmacis, Scuttlebutt, Soda, Spring, Trevi, Youth

Four(times), Foursome Cater, Georges, Horsemen, IV, Mess, Quartet, Quaternary, Quaternion, Reel, Tessara, Tessera, Tetrad, Tetralogy, Tiddy, Warp

Fourth Deltaic, Estate, Fardel, Forpet, Forpit, July, Quartet, Quaternary, Quintan, Sesquitertia, Tritone

Fowl Barnyard, Biddy, Boiler, Brahma, Brissle-cock, Burrow-duck, Capon, Chicken, Chittagong, Cob, Cock, Coot, Duck, Ember, Gallinaceous, Gallinule, Game, Guinea, Hamburg(h), > **HEN**, Houdan, Jungle, Kora, Leghorn, Moorhen, Partridge, Pheasant, Pintado, Poultry, Quail, Rooster, Rumkin, Rumpy, Solan, Spatchcock, Spitchcock, Sultan, Sussex, Teal, Turkey, Wyandotte

Fox(y) Alopecoid, Arctic, Baffle, Blue, Charley, Charlie, Corsac, Cunning, Desert, Fennec, Fool, Friend, Fur, Grey, Kit, Lowrie(-tod), Outwit, Pug, Puzzle, Quaker, Red, Reynard, Rommel, Russel, Silver, Skulk, > **SLY**, Swift, Tod, Uffa, Uneatable, Vixen, White, Zerda, Zoril(le), Zorro

Fracas Brawl, Dispute, Mêlée, Prawle, Riot, Rumpus, Shindig, Uproar

Fraction Complex, Improper, Ligroin, Mantissa, Part, Piece, Proper, Scrap, Simple, Some, Vulgar

Fracture Break, Colles, Comminuted, Complicated, Compound, Crack, Fatigue, Fault, Fissure, Greenstick, Hairline, Impacted, Pathological, Pott's, Rupture, Simple, Split, Stress

Fragile Brittle, Crisp, Delicate, Frail, Frangible, Nesh, Slender, Tender, Vulnerable, Weak

Fragment(s) Atom, Bit, Bla(u)d, Brash, Breccia, Brockram, Cantlet, Clastic, Crumb, End, Flinder, Fritter, Frust, Graile, Lapilli, Mammock, Morceau, Morsel, Ort, > **PARTICLE**, Piece, Potshard, Potsherd, Relic, Rubble, Scrap, Segment, Shard, Shatter, Sheave, Shiver, Shrapnel, Skerrick, Sliver, Smithereens, Smithers, Snatch, Splinter

▷ **Fragment of** *may indicate* a hidden word

Fragrance, Fragrant Aromatic, Attar, Bouquet, Conima, Nosy, Odour, Olent, > **PERFUME**, Pot-pourri, Redolent, > **SCENT**, Sent, Spicy, Suaveolent

Frail Brittle, Creaky, Delicate, Feeble, Flimsy, > **FRAGILE**, Puny, Slight, Slimsy, Weak

Frame(work) Angle, Body, Build, Cage, Case, Casement, Casing, Chassis, Cold, Cradle, Fabric, Form, Gantry, Lattice, Louvre, Pergola, Rack, Scaffold, Setting, Skeleton, > **STRUCTURE**, Zimmer®

Franchise Charter, Contract, Liberty, Privilege, Right, Suffrage, Vote, Warrant

Frank(ish) Blunt, > **CANDID**, Direct, Easy, Free, Free-spoken, Honest, Ingenuous, Man-to-man, Merovingian, Natural, Open, Outspoken, Postage, Postmark, Ripuarian, Salian, Sincere, Stamp, Straight, Sty, Upfront

Frantic Demoniac, Deranged, Distraught, Frenzied, Hectic, Mad, Overwrought, Phrenetic, Rabid, Violent, Whirl(ing)

▷ **Frantic** *may indicate* an anagram

Fraternise, Fraternity Affiliate, Brotherhood, Burschenschaft, Consort, Elk, Fellowship, Lodge, Mingle, Moose, Order

Fraud(ulent) Barratry, Bobol, Bubble, Charlatan, Cheat, Chisel, Collusion, Covin, Cronk, Deceit, Diddle, Do, Fineer, Gyp, Humbug, Hypocrite, > **IMPOSTOR**, Imposture, Jiggery-pokery, Jobbery, Liar, Peculator, Piltdown, Pious, Pseud(o), Put-up, Ringer, Rip-off, Roguery, Rort, Scam, South Sea Bubble, Stellionate, Supercherie, Swindle, Swiz(z), Swizzle, Tartuffe, Trick

Fray(ed) Bagarre, Brawl, Contest, Feaze, Frazzle, Fret, Fridge, Ravel, Riot, Scrimmage

Freak Cantrip, Caprice, Chimera, Control, Deviant, Geek, Sport, Teras, Whim, Whimsy

Free(d), Freely Acquit, Assoil, Buckshee, Candid, Canny, Church, Clear, Complimentary, Cuffo, Dead-head, Deregulate, Devoid, Disburden, Disburthen, Disengage, Disentangle, Eleutherian, Emancipate, Enfranchise, Enlarge, Excuse, Exeem, Exeme, Exempt, Exonerate, Extricate, Familiar, Footloose, Frank, French, Gratis, House, Idle, Immune, Independent, Kick, Large, Lavish, Lax, Leisure, Let, Liberate, Loose, Manumit, Open, Parole, Pro bono, Quit(e), Range, Ransom, Redeem, > **RELEASE**, Relieve, Rescue, Reskew, Rick, Rid, Sciolto, Scot, Solute, Spare, Spring, Stald, Stall, Trade, Unlock, Unloosen, Unmew, Unmuzzle, Unshackle, Unsnarl, Untangle, Untie, Untwist, Vacant, Verse, Voluntary

▷ **Free** *may indicate* an anagram

Freedom Abandon, Autonomy, Breadth, Carte blanche, Eleutherian, Exemption, Fear, Fling, Four, Immunity, Impunity, Latitude, Liberty, Licence, Play, Releasement, Speech, Uhuru, UNITA, Want, Worship

Freehold(er) Enfeoff, Franklin, Frank tenement, Seisin, Udal(ler), Yeoman

▷ **Freely** *may indicate* an anagram

Freemason(ry), Freemason's son Craft, Lewis, Lodge, Moose, Templar

Freeze(s), Freezer, Freezing Alcarrazo, Benumb, Congeal, Cool, Cryogenic, Eutectic, Freon®, Frost, Harden, Ice, Lyophilize, Nip, Numb, Paralyse, Regelate, Riss, Stiffen

Freight Cargo, Carriage, Fraught, Goods, Load

French(man), Frenchwoman Alsatian, Basque, Breton, Crapaud, Creole, Dawn, Frog, Gallic(e), Gaston, Gaul, Gombo, Grisette, Gumbo, Huguenot, Joual,

M, Mamselle, Marianne, Midi, Mounseer, Neo-Latin, Norman, Parleyvoo, René, Rhemish, Savoyard

Frenzied, Frenzy Amok, Berserk, Corybantic, Deliration, Delirium, Demoniac, Enrage, Enrapt, Euhoe, Euoi, Evoe, Fit, Fury, Hectic, Hysteric, Lune, Maenad, Mania, Must, Nympholepsy, Oestrus, Phrenetic, Rage

Frequency, Frequent(er), Frequently Attend, Audio, Channel, Common, Constant, Familiar, Formant, FR, Fresnel, Habitué, Hang-out, Haunt, Hertz, High, Incidence, Megahertz, Often, Penetrance, Pulsatance, Radio, Recurrent, Spectrum, Superhigh, Thick

Fresh(en), Freshness Aurorean, Brash, Caller, Chilly, Clean, Crisp, Dewy, Entire, Forward, Green, Hot, Insolent, Lively, Maiden, New, Novel, Quick, Rebite, Recent, Roral, Roric, Rorid, Smart, Span-new, Spick, Sweet, Tangy, Uncured, Verdure, Vernal, Virent

Fret(ful) Chafe, Filigree, Fray, Grate, Grecque, Haze, Impatient, Irritate, Ornament, Peevish, Repine, Rile, Ripple, Roil, Rub, Tetchy, Tracery, Whittle, Worry

Friar(s) Augustinian, Austin, Bacon, Barefoot, Black, Brother, Bungay, Capuchin, Carmelite, Conventual, Cordelier, Crutched, Curtal, Dervish, Dominican, Fra(ter), Franciscan, Frate, Jacobin, Laurence, Limiter, Lymiter, Minim, Minorite, > MONK, Observant, Observantine, Predicant, Recollect, Recollet, Rush, Tuck, White

Friction Attrition, Conflict, Dissent, Drag, Rift, Rub, Stridulation, Tribology, Tripsis, Wear, Xerotripsis

Friend(ly), Friends Ally, Alter ego, Ami(cable), Amigo, Benign, Bosom, Bud(dy), China, Chum, Cobber, Companion, Comrade, Confidant, Cordial, Crony, Damon, Familiar, Gossip, Intimate, Mate, Pal, Pen, Quaker, Sidekick, Sociable, Sport, Steady

Friendliness, Friendship Amity, Bonhomie, Camaraderie, Contesseration, Entente, Platonic, Sodality

Fright(en), Frightened, Frightful Afear, Affear(e), Agrise, Agrize, Agryze, Alarm, Aroint, Aroynt, Ashake, Chilling, Cow, Dare, Da(u)nt, Deter, Eek, Eerie, Faceache, Fear(some), Flay, Fleg, Fleme, Fley, Flush, Gallow, Gally, Ghast, Gliff, Glift, Grim, Grisly, Hairy, Horrid, Horrific, Intimidate, Ordeal, Panic, Scar, Scarre, Scaur, Schrecklich, Sight, Skear, Skeer, Skrik, Spook, Stage, Startle, Terrible, Terrify, Terror, Tirrit, Unco, Windy

Frill Armil, Armilla, Bavolet, Falbala, Furbelow, Jabot, Ornament, Papillote, Ruche, Ruff(le), Tucker, Valance

▷ **Frilly** *may indicate* an anagram

Fringe(s), Fringed Bang, Border, Bullion, Ciliated, Ciliolate, Edge, Fall, Fimbria, Frisette, Laciniate, Loma, Lunatic, Macramé, Macrami, Pelmet, Peripheral, Robin, Ruff, Run, Thrum, Toupee, Toupit, Tzitzith, Valance, Verge, Zizith

Frisk(y) Caper, Cavort, Curvet, Fisk, Flimp, Frolic, Gambol, Search, Skip, Wanton

Fritter Batter, Beignet, Dribble, Dwindle, Fragment, Fribble, Pakora, Potter, Puf(f)taloon, Squander, Waste

Frivolous Butterfly, Empty(-headed), Featherbrain, Flighty, Flippant, Frothy, Futile, Giddy, Idle, Inane, Light, Lightweight, Playboy, Skittish, Trifling, Trivial

Frog Anoura, Anura, Batrachia(n), Braid, Bullfrog, Depression, Fourchette, Frenchman, Frush, Goliath, Hairy, Hyla, Marsupial, Mounseer, Nic, Nototrema, Paddock, Paradoxical, Peeper, Pelobatid, Platanna, Puddock, Puttock, Rana, Ranidae, Tree, Wood, Xenopus

Frolic(some) Bender, Bust(er), Cabriole, Caper, Disport, Escapade, > FRISK(Y), Fun, Galravage, Galravitch, Gambol, Gammock, Gil(l)ravage, Jink, Kittenish, Lark, Play, Prank, Rag, Rand, Rig, Romp, Scamper, Skylark, Splore, Sport, Spree, Tittup, Wanton

From A, Against, Ex, For, Frae, Off, Thrae

Front(al), **Frontman** Antependium, Anterior, Bow, Brass, Brow, Cold, Cover, Dead, Dickey, Dicky, Esplanade, Facade, Face, Fore(head), Forecourt, Foreground, Groof, Grouf, Head, Home, Metope, National, Newscaster, Occluded, Paravant, People's, Plastron, Polar, Popular, Pose, Preface, Pro, Prom, Prow, Sector, Sinciput, Stationary, Tabula, Temerity, Van, Vaward, Ventral, Warm, Western

Frost(ing), **Frosty** Alcorza, Chill, Cranreuch, Cryo-, Freon®, Frigid, Frore(n), Frorne, Glacé, Ground, Hoar, Hore, Ice, Icing, Jack, Mat, Rime, White

Froth(y) Barm, Bubble, Cuckoospit, Despumate, Foam, Frogspit, Gas, Head, Lather, Off-scum, Ream, Saponin, Scum, Seethe, Shallow, Spoom, Spoon, Spume, Sud, Yeasty, Yest

Frugal Meagre, Parsimonious, Provident, Prudent, Scant, Skimpy, Spare, Spartan, Thrifty

Fruit(ing), **Fruit tree**, **Fruity** Accessory, Achene, Akene, Autocarp, Bacciform, Cedrate, Coccus, Compot(e), Confect, Conserve, Crop, Dessert, Drupe, Eater, Encarpus, Etaerio, First, Follicle, Forbidden, Fritter, Harvest, Issue, Orchard, Poof, Product(ion), Pseudocarp, Result, Return, Rich, Ripe, Schizocarp, Seed, Soft, Stoneless, Sweetie, Sweety, Syconium, Syncarp, Utricle, Valve, Wall, Xylocarp, Yield

Fruitful(ness) Calathus, Ephraim, Fat, Fecund, Feracious, Fertile, Productive, Prolific, Uberty, Worthwhile

Frustrate Baffle, Ba(u)lk, Beat, Blight, Bugger, Check, Confound, Dash, Discomfit, Dish, Foil, Hogtie, Outwit, Scotch, Stymie, Thwart

Fry, **Fried** Blot, Brit, Fricassee, Fritter, Frizzle, Parr, Sauté, Small, Spawn, Whippersnapper, Whitebait

Fuddle(d) Drunk, Fluster, Fuzzle, Maudlin, Ta(i)vert, Tosticated, Woozy

▷ **Fuddle(d)** *may indicate* an anagram

Fudge Cook, Doctor, Dodge, Drivel, Evade, Fiddlesticks, Nonsense, Rot, Stop-press

Fuel Anthracite, Argol, Astatki, Avgas, Biodiesel, Biogas, Briquet(te), Bunker, Butane, Candle-coal, Cannel, Coal, Coke, Derv, Diesel, Eilding, Eldin(g), Faggot, Fire(wood), Fossil, Gasohol, Gasoline, Haxamine, Hydrazine, Hydyne, Kerosene, Kerosine, Kindling, Knitch, Lignite, Mox, Napalm, Naphtha, Nuclear, Paraffin, Peat, Propane, Propellant, Stoke, Triptane, Yealdon

Fugitive Absconder, Ephemeral, Escapee, Fleeting, Hideaway, Lot, Outlaw, Refugee, Runaway, Runner, Transient

Fulfil(ment) Accomplish, Complete, Fruition, Honour, Meet, Pass, Realise, > SATISFY, Steed

Full(ness), **Fully** Abrim, Ample, Arrant, Bouffant, Capacity, Chock-a-block, Chocker, Complete, Copious, Embonpoint, Engorged, Entire, Fat, Fed, Fou, Frontal, German, High, Hoatching, Hotch, Mill, Plein, Plenary, Plenitude, Pleroma, Plethora, Replete, Rich, Sated, Satiated, Thorough, Toss, Turgid, Turgor, Ullage, Up, Wau(l)k, Wholly

Fulminate, **Fulmination** Detonate, Explode, Levin, Lightning, Rail, Renounce, Thunder

Fumble Blunder, Faff, Grope, Misfield, Muff

Fume(s) Bluster, Gas, Halitus, Nidor, Rage, Reech, Reek, Settle, Smoke, Stum, Vapours

Fun(ny), **Funny bone** Amusing, Antic, Boat, Buffo, Caper, Clownery, Comedy, Comic(al), Delight, Droll, Frolic, Gammock, Gig, Giocoso, Glaik, Guy, Hilarity, Humerus, Humorous, Hysterical, Jest, Jouisance, Jouysaunce, Killing, Lark, Pleasure, Priceless, Rag, Rich, Rummy, Scream, Sidesplitting, Skylark, Sport, Weird(o), Yell

Function(al) Act, Antilog, Arccos, Arcsine, Arctan, Ceremony, Cosec, Cosh, Cotangent, Cot(h), Discriminant, Dynamic, Exponential, Gibbs, Hamilton(ian), Helmholtz, Hyperbolic, Integrand, Inverse, Job, Logarithm, > OPERATE, Periodic, Quadric, Quantical, Role, Run, Sech, Service, Sine, Sinh, Ste(a)d, Step, Surjection, Tan(h), Tick, Use, Wave, > WORK

Fund(s), Funding, Fundraising Bank, Bankroll, Barrel, Capital, Chest, Consolidated, Emendals, Endow, Evergreen, Finance, Fisc, Fisk, Gild, Hedge, Imprest, Index, Jackpot, Kitty, Managed, Mutual, Nest-egg, Pension, Pool, Pork-barrel, Prebend, Private, Public, Purse, Revolving, Roll-up, Sinking, Slush, Social, Sou-sou, Stabilisation, Stock, Subsidise, Sustentation, Susu, Telethon, Treasury, Trust, Vulture, Wage(s), War chest, Wherewithal

Fundamental(ist) Basic(s), Bedrock, Cardinal, Essence, Grass-roots, Hamas, Nitty-gritty, Organic, Prime, Principle, Radical, Rudimentary, Ultimate

Funeral, Funereal Charnel, Cortege, Dismal, Exequy, Feral, Obit, Obsequy, Sad-coloured, Solemn, Tangi

Fungicide Biphenyl, Bordeaux mixture, Captan, Diphenyl, Ferbam, Menadione, Thiram, Zineb

Fungoid, Fungus Agaric, Amadou, Amanita, Ambrosia, Anthracnose, Apothecium, Asci(us), Asomycete, Aspergillus, Barm, Basidium, Beefsteak, Black, Blackknot, Blewits, Boletus, Bootlace, Bracket, Bunt, Candida, Chantarelle, Chanterelle, Cladosporum, Clubroot, Craterellus, Cryptococcus, Cup, Death-cap, Death-cup, Dermatophytosis, Destroying angel, Discomycetes, Earth-star, Elf-cup, Empusa, Ergot, Eumycetes, Favus, Fuss-ball, Fuzz-ball, Gall, Gibberella, Gill, Honey, Horsehair, Hypersarcoma, Hypha, Imperfect, Ink-cap, Ithyphallus, Jelly, Jew's ear, Liberty cap, Lichen, Magic mushroom, Merulius, Mildew, Milk cap, Monilia, Morel, Mould, Mucor(ales), Mushroom, Mycelium, Mycetes, Mycology, Noble rot, Oak-leather, Oidium, Orange-peel, Penicillium, Pest, Peziza, Phallus, Phycomycete, Pileum, Pore, Prototroph, Puccinia, Puckfist, Puffball, Pythium, Rhizopus, Rhytisma, Russula, Rust, Saccharomyces, Saprolegnia, Saprophyte, Sariodes, Scab, Shoestring, Smut, Sooty mould, Spunk, Stinkhorn, Stipe, Sulphur tuft, Tarspot, Thalline, Thallophyte, Toadstool, Torula, Tremella, Trichophyton, Truffle, Tuckahoe, Uredine, Ustilago, Witches' meat, Wood hedgehog, Yeast, Yellow rust, Zygospore

Funnel Buchner, Chimney, Choana, Flue, Hopper, Infundibulum, Smokestack, Stack, Stovepipe, Tun-dish

Fur Astrakhan, Astrex, Beaver(skin), Boa, Broadtail, Budge, Calabre, Caracul, Castor, Chinchilla, Coonskin, Crimmer, Ermelin, Ermine, Fitchew, Flix, Flue, Fun, Galyac, Galyak, Genet, Kolinsky, Krimmer, Lettice, Minever, Miniver, Mink, Mouton, Musquash, Ocelot, Otter, Pashm, Pean, Pekan, Rac(c)oon, Roskyn, Sable, Sealskin, Sea-otter, Stole, Tincture, Tippet, Vair(e), Victorine, Wolverine, Zibeline, Zorino

Furl Fold, Roll, Stow, Wrap

Furnace Arc, Athanor, Blast, Bloomery, Bosh, Calcar, Cockle, Cremator, Cupola, Destructor, Devil, Finery, Firebox, Forge, Glory-hole, Kiln, Lear, Lehr, Lime-kiln, Oast, Oon, Oven, Producer, Reverberatory, Scaldino

Furnish(ing) Appoint, Array, Deck, Decorate, Endow, Endue, Equip, Feed, Fledge, Gird, Lend, Produce, Provision, Soft, Stock, Supply, Tabaret, Upholster

Furniture Biedermeier, Chattels, Chippendale, Encoignure, Escritoire, Flatpack, Hepplewhite, Insight, Lumber, Moveable, Sheraton, Sideboard, Sticks, Stoutherie, Tire, Unit, Whatnot

Furrow(ed) Crease, Feer, Feerin(g), Furr, Groove, Gutter, Plough, Pucker, Rill(e), Rugose, Rut, Stria, Sulcus, Vallecula, Wrinkle

Further(more), Furthest Additional, Advance, Again, Aid, Also, Besides,

Deeper, Else, Expedite, Extend, Extra, Extreme, Fresh, Infra, Longer, Mo(e), Mow, Other, Promote, Serve, Speed, Then

Furtive(ly) Clandestine, Cunning, Secret, Sly, Sneaky, Stealthy, Stowlins, Stownlins

Fury, Furies, Furious Acharné, Agitato, Alecto, > **ANGER**, Apoplexy, Atropos, Avenger, Eriny(e)s, Eumenides, Exasperation, Frantic, Frenzied, Furor, Incensed, > **IRE**, Livid, Maenad, Megaera, Rabid, Rage, Savage, Tisiphone, Virago, Wood, Wrath, Yond

Fuse(d), Fusion Anchylosis, Ankylosis, Blend, Coalesce, Cohere, Colliquate, Conflate, Encaustic, Endosmosis, Flow, Flux, Match, Merge, Merit, Nuclear, Portfire, Proximity, Rigelation, Run, Saucisson, Slow-match, Syncretism, Syngamy, Tokamak, Unite

Fuss(y) Ado, Agitation, Anile, Ballyho, Bobsie-die, Bother, Br(o)uhaha, Bustle, Carfuffle, Chichi, Coil, Commotion, Complain, Cosset, Create, Cu(r)fuffle, Dust, Faff, Fantad, Fantod, Fiddle-faddle, Finical, Finikin, Hairsplitter, Hoohah, Hoopla, Mither, Niggle, Nit-pick, Old-womanish, Overnice, Palaver, Particular, Perjink, Pernickety, Picky, Pother, Precise, Prejink, Primp, Prissy, Racket, Razzmatazz, Rout, Song, Song and dance, Spoffish, Spoffy, Spruce, Stashie, Stickler, > **STIR**, Stishie, Stooshie, Stushie, Tamasha, To-do, Tracasserie

Futile Empty, Feckless, Idle, Inept, No-go, Nugatory, Null, Otiose, Pointless, Sleeveless, Stultified, Trivial, > **VAIN**

Future(s), Futurist Again, Be-all, Coming, Demain, Hence, Horoscope, Later, Long-range, Offing, Ovist, Prospect, To-be, Tomorrow

Gg

Gad(about), Gadzooks Gallivant, Lud, Rover, Sbuddikins, Sdeath, Traipse, Trape(s), Viretot

Gadget Appliance, Artifice, Device, Dingbat, Dingus, Doodad, Doodah, Doofer, Doohickey, Gismo, Gizmo, Gubbins, Hickey, Jimjam, Notion, Possum, Utility, Widget

Gag Brank, Choke, Estoppel, Joke, Pong, Prank, Silence(r), Smother, Wheeze

Gain(s), Gained Acquire, Appreciate, Attain, Avail, Boot, Bunce, Carry, Catch, Chevisance, Clean-up, Derive, Earn, Edge, Fruit, > GET, Good, Gravy, Land, Lucre, Obtain, Plus, Profit, Purchase, Rake-off, Reap, Thrift, Use, Velvet, Wan, Win, Windfall, Winnings

Gait Bearing, Canter, Pace, Piaffer, Rack, Trot

Galaxies, Galaxy Heaven, Magellanic cloud, Milky Way, Radio, Seyfert, Spiral, Stars

Gale(s) Backfielder, Peal, Ripsnorter, Sea turn, Snorter, Squall, Storm, Tempest, Winder

Gallant(ry) Admirer, Amorist, Beau, Blade, Buck, Cavalier, Chevalier, Cicisbeo, Courtliness, Lover, Prow, Romeo, Sigisbeo, Spark, Valiance

Gallery Accademia, Amphitheatre, Arcade, Belvedere, Catacomb, Cupola, Gods, Hayward, Hermitage, Loft, Loggia, Louvre, Mine, Minstrel, National, Prado, Press, Rogues', Shooting, Strangers', Tate, Uffizi, Veranda(h), Whispering

Galley Bireme, Bucentaur, Caboose, Drake, Galliot, Kitchen, Lymphad, Penteconter, Proof

Gallows Dule-tree, Gibbet, Nub, Tree, Tyburn, Tyburn-tree, Woodie

Galvanometer Tangent

Gambit Manoeuvre, Ploy, Stratagem

Gamble(r), Gambling (place) Back, Bet, Casino, Chance, Dice(-play), Flutter, Mise, Pari-mutuel, Parlay, Piker, Policy, Punter, Raffle, Risk, Roulette, Spec, Speculate, Speculator, Sweep(stake), Throw(ster), Tinhorn, Tombola, Tontine, Two-up, > WAGER

Game(s) Away, Closed, Commonwealth, Computer, Decider, Electronic, Frame, Gallant, Gammy, Ground, Gutsy, High-jinks, Highland, Home, Intrepid, Isthmian, Jeu, > LAME, Match, Middle, Nemean, Numbers, Olympic, On, Open, Panel, Paralympic, Parlour, Perfect, Platform, Play, Plaything, Preference, Pythian, Raffle, Road, Round, Rubber, Saving, Secular, Spoof, Sport, Square, String, Table, Tie-break, Vie, Waiting, Willing

Game, Game birds Bag, Fowl, Grouse, Guan, Hare, Meat, Partridge, Pheasant, Prairie chicken, Ptarmigan, Quail, > QUARRY, Rype(r), Snipe, Spatchcock, Woodcock

Gamete Ootid

Gang Band(itti), Bing, Canaille, Chain, Coffle, Core, Crew, Crue, Elk, Go, Horde, Mob, Nest, Outfit, Pack, Posse, Press, Push, Ratpack, Tribulation, Troop, Yardie

Gangster Bandit, Capone, Crook, Hatchet-man, Highbinder, Hood, Mafioso, Ochlocrat, Skollie, Skolly, Yakuza, Yardie

▶ **Gaol(er)** *see* JAIL(ER)

Gap Breach, Chasm, Chink, Credibility, Day, Embrasure, F-hole, Flaw, Fontanel(le), Generation, Hair-space, Hiatus, Hole, Interlude, Interstice, Lacunae, Loophole, Opening, Pass, Rest, Shard, Sherd, Slap, > SPACE, Spark, Street, Synapse

Garb Apparel, Costume, Gear, Gere, Guise, Ihram, Invest, Leotard, Raiment, Toilet

Garbage Bunkum, Junk, Refuse, Rubbish, Trash

▷ **Garble** *may indicate* an anagram

Garden(ing), Gardens Arbour, Area, Babylon(ian), Bear, Beer, Botanic, Cottage, Covent, Dig, Eden, Floriculture, Gethsemane, Hanging, Hesperides, Hoe, Italian, Kew, Kitchen, Knot, Landscape, Lyceum, Market, Paradise, Parterre, Physic, Pleasance, Plot, Potager, Rockery, Roof, Tea, Topiary, Tuileries, Vauxhall, Window, Winter, Zoological

Gardener Adam, Capability Brown, Jekyll, Landscape, Mary, Nurseryman

Garland Anadem, Anthology, Chaplet, Coronal, Crants, Festoon, Lei, Stemma, Toran(a), Vallar(y), Wreath

Garment Aba(ya), Abba, Alb, Ao dai, Barrow, Blouse, Blouson, Bodice, Body warmer, Bolero, B(o)ub(o)u, B(o)urk(h)a, Breeks, Burnous, Burqa, Busuuti, Caftan, Catsuit, Cerements, Chador, Chasuble, Chimer, Cilice, Cimar, Clout, Cote-hardie, Cotta, Cover-slut, Dalmatic, Dashiki, Dirndl, Djibbah, Doublet, Dreadnought, Ephod, Exomion, Exomis, Fanon, Foundation, Gambeson, G-suit, Habiliment, Habit, Hand-me-down, Himation, Hug-me-tight, Ihram, Izar, Jeistiecor, Jibbah, Jubbah, Jumpsuit, Kaftan, Kanzu, Kaross, K(h)anga, Kittel, Levis, Lingerie, Mandilion, Mandylion, Mantle, Negligee, One-piece, Pallium, Pantihose, Pantyhose, Partlet, Pelerine, Pelisse, Penitential, Peplos, Pilch, Popover, Rail, Ramée, Rami(e), Reach-me-down, Rochet, Rompers, Ruana, Sackcloth, Salopettes, Sanbenito, Sari, Sarong, Scapular, Shroud, Singlet, Slop, Soutane, Step-in, Stola, Stole, Sulu, Surcoat, Surplice, Swimsuit, Tabard, Tank-top, Thong, Toga, Togs, Tunic(le), Unitard, Vestment, Vesture, Waistcoat, Weed, Woolly, Wrapper, Zephyr

Garnish Adorn, Attach, Crouton, Decorate, Gremolata, Lard, Parsley, Sippet, Staffage

Gas(sy) Acetylene, Afterdamp, Air, Ammonia, Argon, Argonon, Arsine, Blah(-blah), Blather, Blether, Bottle(d), Butadiene, Butane, Butene, BZ, Calor®, Chat, Chlorine, Chokedamp, Chrom(at)osphere, CN, Coal(-oil), Crypton, CS, Cyanogen, Damp, Diphosgene, Emanation, Ethane, Ethene, Ether(ion), Ethine, Ethylene, Firedamp, Flatulence, Flatus, Flocculus, Flue, Fluorin(e), Formaldehyde, Gabnash, Greenhouse, H, Halitus, He, Helium, Hot-air, Hydrogen, Ideal, Inert, Jaw, Ketene, Kr(ypton), Laughing, Lewisite, Lurgi, Mace®, Marsh, Methane, Mofette, Mustard, Natural, Ne, Neon, Nerve, Nitrogen, Noble, Nox, O, Olefin(e), Orotund, Oxyacetylene, Oxygen, Perfect, Petrol, Phosgene, Phosphine, Plasma, Poison, Prate, Propane, Propellant, Propene, Propylene, Protostar, Radon, Rare, RN, Sarin, Silane, Solfatara, Stibine, Sulphur dioxide, Synthesis, Tabun, > TALK, Tear, Therm, Thoron, Town, V-agent, Vapour, Waffle, Water, Whitedamp, > WIND, Xenon, Yackety-yak

Gash Incise, Rift, Score, Scotch, > SLASH

Gasp(ing) Anhelation, Apn(o)ea, Chink, Exhale, Kink, Oh, Pant, Puff, Singult, Sob

Gast(e)ropod Cowrie, Cowry, Euthyneura, Glaucus, Harp-shell, Limpet, Mollusc, Murex, Nerita, Nerite, Nudibranch, Opisthobranch, Ormer, Periwinkle, Purpura, Sea-ear, Sea-hare, Slug, Snail, Spindle-shell, Stromb, Whelk

Gate(s), Gateway Alley, Brandenburg, Caisson, Crowd, Decuman, Entry, Erpingham, Golden, Head, Kissing, Lych, Menin, Nor, Pearly, Portal, Portcullis, Postern, Propylaeum, Propylon, Pylon, Starting, Toran(a), Torii, Traitor's, Turnstile, Wicket, Yate, Yet(t)

▷ **Gateshead** *may indicate* 'g'

Gather(ed), **Gathering** Accrue, Amass, Assemble, Bee, Braemar, Cluster, Collate, > COLLECT, Colloquium, Concourse, Conglomerate, Congregate, Conventicle, Corral, Corroboree, Crop, Crowd, Cull, Derive, Eve, Fest, Function, Gabfest, Galaxy, Get together, Glean, Glomerate, Harvest, Hootenanny, Hotchpot, Hui, Husking, In, Infer, Jamboree, Kommers, Learn, Lek, Lirk, Love-in, Meinie, Menyie, Pleat, Plica, Plissé, Pucker, Purse, Raft, Rake, Rally, Reef, Reunion, Round-up, Rout, Ruche, Ruff(le), Salon, Shindig, Shir(r), Shoal, Shovel, Singsong, Social, Spree, Take, Tuck, Vindemiate, Vintage, Wappensc(h)aw

Gauche Awkward, Clumsy, Farouche, Graceless

Gaudy Criant, Fantoosh, Flash, Garish, Glitz(y), Meretricious, Tacky, Tinsel

Gauge Alidad(e), Anemometer, > ASSESS, Bourdon, Broad, Calibre, Denier, Estimate, Etalon, Evaluate, Feeler, Judge, Loading, Manometer, Marigraph, Measure, Meter, Narrow, Ombrometer, Oncometer, Pressure, Rate, Scantle, Size, Standard, Strain, Tape, Tonometer, Tram, Tread, Udometer

Gaunt Haggard, Lancaster, Lean, Randletree, Ranneltree, Rannletree, Rantletree, Rawbone, > THIN, Wasted

Gauze, **Gauzy** Gas mantle, Gossamer, Muslin, Sheer, Tiffany

Gear(ing) Angel, Arrester, Attire, Bags, Bevel, Capital, Clobber, Dérailleur, Differential, Draw, Duds, Engrenage, Epicyclic, Fab, Finery, Granny, Harness, Helical, Herringbone, Hypoid, Involute, Kit, Landing, Lay-shaft, Mesh, Mess, Mitre, Neutral, Overdrive, Ratio, Reverse, Rig, Riot, Rudder, Spur, Steering, Sun and planet, Synchromesh, > TACKLE, Timing, Top, Trim, Tumbler, Valve, Worm(-wheel)

Geld(ing) Castrate, Lib, Neuter, Spado

Gem Baguette, Boule, Brilliant, Briolette, Cabochon, Cachalong, Cairngorm, Carnelian, Cat's eye, Chrysolite, Chrysoprase, Cornelian, Cymophane, Demantoid, Diamante, Diamond, Dumortierite, Emerald, Hawk's eye, Heliodor, Hessonite, Hiddenite, Hyacinth, ID, Idaho, Indicolite, Iolite, Jacinth, Jargo(o)n, Jasper, Jaspis, > JEWEL, Kunzite, Lapis lazuli, Ligure, Marquise, Melanite, Menilite, Moonstone, Morganite, Pearl, Peridot(e), Prase, Pyrope, Rhinestone, Rhodolite, Rubellite, Ruby, Sapphire, Sard, Sardonyx, Scarab, Scarabaeoid, Smaragd, Solitaire, Sparkler, Starstone, Stone, Tiger's eye, Tourmaline, Turquoise, Verd antique

Gemma Bud, Knosp

Gene(tics) Allel(e), Allelomorph, Anticodon, Codon, Creation, Disomic, Episome, Exon, Factor, Genome, Hereditary, Heterogamy, Intron, Mendel, Muton, Operon, Selfish, Terminator

Genealogist, **Genealogy** Armory, Family, Heraldry, Line, Pedigree, Seannachie, Seannachy, Sennachie, Whakapapa

General Agamemnon, Agricola, Agrippa, Alcibiades, Allenby, Antigonus, Antipater, Ataman, Booth, Boulanger, Broad, C in C, Common, Communal, Conde, Cornwallis, Crassus, Current, Custer, De Gaulle, De Wet, Diadochi, Eclectic, Ecumenical, Election, Franco, Gamelin, Gen, GOC, Gordon, Grant, Hadrian, Hannibal, Holofernes, Ike, Inspector, Joshua, Kitchener, Lafayette, Lee, Leslie, Macarthur, Main, Marshall, Montcalm, Napier, Napoleon, Omnify, Overall, Overhead, Patton, Pershing, Pompey, Prevailing, Raglan, Regulus, Rife, Rommel, Scipio, Sherman, Shrapnel, Smuts, Stilwell, Strategist, Tom Thumb, Turenne, > UNIVERSAL, Vague, Wide, Wolfe

Generate, **Generation**, **Generator** Abiogenetic, Age, Beat, Beget, Breeder, Charger, Create, Dynamo, Epigon, Father, Fuel-cell, House, Kipp, Lost, Magneto, Olds, Sire, Spawn, Stallion, Van de Graaff, Yield

Generosity, **Generous** Bounty, Charitable, Free-handed, Handsome, Kind,

Largess(e), > LAVISH, Liberal, Magnanimous, Munificent, Noble(-minded), Open, Open-handed, Open-hearted, Philanthropic, Plump, Profuse, Sporting

▶ **Genetic** *see* GENE

Genial(ity) Affable, Amiable, Benign, Bluff, Bonhomie, Human, Mellow

Genitive Ethical

Genius Agathodaimon, Daemon, Einstein, Engine, Flash, Inspiration, Ka, Michaelangelo, Numen, Prodigy

Genome Prophage

Genre Splatterpunk, Tragedy

Gentle Amenable, Amenage, Bland, Clement, Delicate, Gradual, Grub, Light, Maggot, Mansuete, Mild, Tame, Tender

Gentry County, Landed, Quality, Squir(e)age

Genuflexion Bend, Curts(e)y, Kowtow, Salaam

Genuine Authentic, Bona-fide, Dinkum, Dinky-di, Echt, Frank, Heartfelt, Intrinsic, Jonnock, Kosher, Legit(imate), Nain, Pucka, Pukka, Pure, Pusser, > REAL, Real McCoy, Right, Simon-Pure, Sincere, Square, Sterling, True, Veritable

Germ(s) Bacteria, Bug, Klebsiella, Seed, Spirilla, Strep, Virus, Zyme

German(y) Angle, Anglo-Saxon, Bavarian, Berliner, Boche, Denglish, Franconian, Frank, Fritz, G, Goth, Habsburg, Hans, Hapsburg, Herr, Hun, Jerry, Jute, Kaiser, Kraut, Prussian, Salic, Saxon, Squarehead, Teuton(ic), Visigoth, Wolfgang

Gesticulate, Gesticulation, Gesture(s) Beck(on), Ch(e)ironomy, Mime, Motion, Salute, > SIGN, Signal, Token

Get, Get by, Get On Acquire, Advance, Aggravate, Annoy, Attain, Become, Brat, Bring, Capture, Cop, Cope, Derive, Fet(ch), Fette, Gain, Gee, Learn, Make, Manage, Milk, Net, Noy, > OBTAIN, Peeve, Procure, Progress, Reach, Realise, Rile, Roil, Secure, See, Sire, Twig, Understand, Win

▷ **Getting** *may indicate* an anagram

Getting better Convalescing, Improving, Lysis

Ghastly Gash, Grim, Hideous, Lurid, Macabre, Pallid, Welladay, White

Ghost(ly) Acheri, Apparition, Apport, Caddy, Chthonic, Duende, Duppy, Eerie, Eery, Fantasm, Fetch, Gytrash, Haunt, Hint, Jumbie, Jumby, Larva(e), Lemur, Malmag, No'canny, Paraclete, Pepper's, Phantasm(agoria), Phantom, Revenant, Sampford, Shade, Shadow, Spectre, > SPIRIT, Spook, Trace, Truepenny, Umbra, Vision, Visitant, Waff, Wraith

Giant(ess) Alcyoneus, Alifanfaron, Anak, Antaeus, Archiloro, Argus, Ascapart, Balan, Balor, Bellerus, Blunderbore, Bran, Briareus, Brobdingnagian, Cacus, Colbrand, Colbronde, Colossus, Coltys, Cormoran, Cottus, Cyclop(e)s, Despair, Enceladus, Ephialtes, Eten, Ettin, Ferragus, Gabbara, Galligantus, Gargantua, Géant, Gefion, Geirred, Gigantic, Gog, Goliath, Grim, Harapha, Hrungnir, Hymir, Idris, Jotun(n), Jumbo, Krasir, Lestrigon, Leviathan, Magog, Mammoth, Mimir, Monster, Oak, Og, Ogre, Otus, Pallas, Pantagruel, Patagonian, Polyphemus, Pope, Red, Rounceval, Skrymir, Slaygood, Talos, Talus, Thrym, Titan, Tityus, Tregeagle, Triton, Troll, Tryphoeus, Typhon, Urizen, Utgard, Ymir, Yowie

Gibberish Claptrap, Double Dutch, Greek, Jargon

Gibe Barb, Brocard, Chaff, Fleer, Glike, Jeer, Jibe, Shy, Slant, Wisecrack

Gift(s), Gifted Ability, Alms, Aptitude, Bef(f)ana, Bequest, Blessing, Blest, Bonbon, Bonsel(l)a, Boon, Bounty, Charism(a), Congiary, Corban, Covermount, Cumshaw, Dash, Deodate, > DONATION, Etrenne, Fairing, Flair, Foy, Freebie, Gab, Garnish, Godsend, Grant, Handout, Han(d)sel, Hogmanay, Indian, Knack, Koha, Kula, Lagniappe, Largesse, Legacy, Manna, Ne'erday, Nuzzer, Offering, Parting, Potlatch, > PRESENT, Presentation, Prezzie, Propine, Reward, Sop, Talent, Tongues, Windfall

Gigantic Atlantean, Briarean, Colossal, Goliath, > HUGE, Immense, Mammoth, Rounceval, Titan

Giggle Cackle, Ha, Simper, Snicker, Snigger, Tehee, Titter

Gild(ed), **Gilding** Checklaton, Embellish, Enhance, Inaurate, Ormolu, S(c)hecklaton, Vermeil

Gill(s) Beard, Branchia, Cart, Ctenidium, Jill, Noggin, Spiracle

Gimmick Doodad, Doodah, Hype, Ploy, Ruse, Stunt

Gin Bathtub, Geneva, Genever, Hollands, Juniper, Lubra, Max, Noose, Old Tom, Ruin, Schiedam, Schnapp(s), Sloe, Snare, Springe, Toil, Trap, Trepan, Twankay

Gingerbread D(o)um-palm, Lebkuchen, Parkin, Parliament(-cake)

▶ **Gipsy** *see* GYPSY

Girder Beam, Binder, I-beam, Loincloth, Spar

Girdle Baldric, Cestus, Chastity, Cincture, Cingulum, Corset, Hippolyte, Hoop, Mitre, Sash, Surcingle, Surround

Girl(s) Backfisch, Ball, Bimbo, Bint, Bird, Bit, Bobby-dazzler, Bohemian, Broad, Burd, Call, Charlie, Chit, Chorus, Coed, Colleen, Crumpet, Cutey, Cutie, Deb, Demoiselle, Dish, Doll, Dollybird, Essex, Filly, Flapper, Fluff, Fraulein, Frippet, Gaiety, Gal, Geisha, Gibson, Gouge, Grisette, Hen, Hoiden, Hoyden, Hussy, Judy, Kimmer, Land, Lass(ock), Maid(en), May, Miss(y), Moppet, Nymph(et), Peach, Popsy, Puss, Quean, Queyn, Senorita, Sheila, Shi(c)ksa, Sis(s), Tabby, Trull, Wench

▷ **Girl** *may indicate* a female name

Gist Essence, Kernel, > NUB, Pith, Substance

Give, **Give up**, **Giving** Abandon, Abstain, Accord, Administer, Afford, Award, Bend, Bestow, Buckle, Cede, Confiscate, Dative, Dispense, Dole, > DONATE, Duck, Elasticity, Enable, Forswear, Gie, Impart, Jack, Largition, Render, Resign, Sacrifice, Sag, Spring, Stop, Tip, Vacate, Yeve

Give out Bestow, Dispense, Emit, Exude, Peter

Glacier Aletsch, Crevasse, Drumline, Fox, Franz-Josef, Iceberg, Ice-cap, Icefall, Moraine, Muir, Riss, Serac, Tasman

Glad(ly), **Gladden** Cheer, Fain, > HAPPY, Lief, Willing

Glamour(ise), **Glamorous** Charm, Glitter(ati), Glitz, Halo, It, Prestige, SA, Spell

Glance Allusion, Blink, Browse, Coup d'oeil, Dekko, Glimpse, Lustre, Oeillade, Once-over, Peek, > PEEP, Ray, Ricochet, Scan, Sheep's eyes, Shufti, Shufty, Skellie, Skelly, Snick, Squint, Squiz, Vision

Gland Adenoid, Adrenal, Apocrine, Bartholin's, Bulbourethral, Colleterial, Conarium, Cowper's, Crypt, Digestive, Eccrine, Endocrine, Epiphysis, Exocrine, Goitre, Green, Helocrine, Hypophysis, Ink-sac, Lachrymal, Lacrimal, Liver, Lymph, Mammary, Meibomian, Musk-sac, Nectary, Oil, Osmeterium, Ovary, Pancreas, Paranephros, Parathyroid, Parotid, Parotis, Pineal, Pituitary, Pope's eye, Prostate, Prothoracic, Salivary, Scent, Sebaceous, Silk, Suprarenal, Sweat, Tarsel, Testicle, Testis, Thymus, Thyroid, Tonsil, Uropygial, Vesicle

Glare, **Glaring** Astare, Blare, Dazzle, Flagrant, Garish, Gleam, Glower, Holophotal, Iceblink, Lour, Low(e), Shine, Vivid, Whally

Glass(es), **Glassware**, **Glassy** Amen, Ampul(la), Aneroid, Avanturine, Aventurine, Baccara(t), Barometer, Bifocals, Bins, Bottle, Brimmer, Bumper, Burmese, Burning, Calcedonio, Case, Cheval, Cloche, Cocktail, Cooler, Copita, Cordial, Coupe, Cover, Crookes, Crown, Crystal, Cullet, Cupping, Cut, Dark, Delmonico, Diminishing, Eden, Euphon, Favrile, Fibre, Field, Flint, Float, Flute, Frigger, Frit, Fulgurite, Gauge, Glare, Goblet, Goggles, Granny, Green, Ground, Hand, Highball, Horn-rims, Humpen, Hyaline, Iceland agate, Jar, Jena, Jigger, Lace, Lalique, Laminated, Lanthanum, Latticinio, Lead, Lens, Liqueur, Liquid, Log, Lorgnette, Loupe, Lozen(ge), Lunette, Magma, Magnifying, Metal, Mica,

Middy, Milk, Millefiori, Minimizing, Mirror, Moldavite, Monocle, Mousseline, Multiplying, Murr(h)ine, Musical, Object, Obsidian, One-way, Opal, Opal(ine), Opera, Optical, Pane, Parison, Paste, Pearlite, Pebble, Peeper, Pele, Pele's hair, Perlite, Perspective, Pier, Pince-nez, Pinhole, Pitchstone, Plate, Pon(e)y, Pressed, Prospective, Prunt, Psyche, Pyrex®, Quarrel-pane, Quarry, Quartz, Reducing, Roemer, Ruby, Rummer, Safety, Schmelz, Schooner, Seam, Seidel, Sheet, Silex, Silica, Sleever, Slide, Smalt(o), Snifter, Soluble, Specs, > **SPECTACLES**, Spun, Stained, Stein, Stemware, Stone, Storm, Strass, Sun, Supernaculum, Tachilite, Tachylite, Tachylyte, Tektite, Telescope, Tiffany, Tiring, Toilet, Trifocals, Triplex®, Tumbler, Uranium, Varifocals, Venetian, Venice, Vernal, Vita, Vitrail, Vitreous, Vitrescent, Vitro-di-trina, Volcanic, Watch, Water, Waterford, Weather, Window (pane), Wine, Wire

Glass-house Conservatory, Orangery

Gleam(ing) Blink, Flash, Glint, Glitter, Gloss, Leme, Light, Ray, Relucent, Sheen, Shimmer, > **SHINE**

Glee Exuberance, Joy, Mirth, Song

Glide(away), **Glider**, **Gliding** Aquaplane, Coast, Elapse, Float, Illapse, Lapse, Luge, Microlight, Portamento, Sail, Sailplane, Sashay, Scorrendo, Scrieve, Skate, Ski, Skim, Sleek, Slide, Slip, Swim, Volplane

Glimpse Aperçu, Flash, Glance, Glisk, Stime, Styme, Waff, Whiff

Glint Flash, Shimmer, > **SPARKLE**, Trace, Twinkle

Glisten(ing) Ganoid, Glint, Sheen, Shimmer, > **SHINE**, Sparkle

Glitter(ing) Clinquant, Garish, Gemmeous, Paillon, Sequin, Spang(le), Sparkle, Tinsel

Gloat(ing) Crow, Drool, Enjoy, Exult, Schadenfreude

Globe, **Globule** Ball, Bead, Celestial, Drop, Earth, Orb, Shot, Sphear, Sphere

Gloom(y) Atrabilious, Blues, Cheerless, Cimmerian, Cloud, Crepuscular, Damp, Dark, > **DESPAIR**, Dingy, Disconsolate, Dismal, Dool(e), Drab, Drear, Drumly, Dump(s), Dyspeptic, Funereal, Glum, Grey, Louring, Mirk, Misery, Mopish, Morne, Morose, Murk, Obscurity, Overcast, Sable, Sad, Saturnine, Sepulchral, Solemn, > **SOMBRE**, Stygian, Tenebrous

Glorification, **Glorify** Aggrandise, Apotheosis, Avatar, Bless, > **EXALT**, Halo, Laud, Lionise, Praise, Radiance, Splendour

Glorious, **Gloria**, **Glory** Chorale, Grand, Halo, Hosanna, Ichabod, Kudos, Lustre, Magnificent, Nimbus, Sublime

Gloss(y) Enamel, Gild, Glacé, Japan, Lustre, Patina, > **POLISH**, Postillate, Sheen, Sleek, Slick, Slide, Slur, Veneer, Whitewash

Glove Boxing, Cestus, Dannock, Gage, Gauntlet, Kid, Mitten, Oven, Velvet

Glow(er), **Glowing** Aflame, Aura, Bloom, Burn, Candescence, Flush, Foxfire, Gleam, Halation, Incandescence, Lambent, Luculent, Luminesce, Lustre, Phosphorescence, Radiant, Shine, Translucent, > **WARMTH**

Glue(y) Araldite®, Bee, Cement, Colloidal, Gelatin(e), Ichthyocolla, Isinglass, Paste, Propolis, Size, Spetch

Glum Dour, Livery, Lugubrious, Moody, Morose, Ron, Sombre

Glut Choke, Gorge, Sate, Satiate, Saturate, Surfeit

Glutton(ous), **Gluttony** Bellygod, Carcajou, Cormorant, Edacity, Gannet, Gorb, Gourmand, Gulosity, Gutsy, Lurcher, Pig, Ratel, Scoffer, Sin, Trencherman, Trimalchio, Wolverine

Gnat Culex, Culicidae, Midge, Mosquito

Gnaw(ing) Corrode, Erode, Fret, Lagomorph, Rodent

Gnome Adage, Bank-man, Chad, Cobalt, Financier, Kobold, Motto, Proverb, Saw, Sprite

Go, Going (after, for, off, on, up, etc) Advance, Afoot, Anabasis, Animation, Assail, Attempt, Bash, Bing, Brio, Choof, Clamber, Continuance, Depart, Die, Do, Energy, Fare, Gae, Gang, Gee, Green, Hamba, Hark, Hence, Hie, Imshi, Imshy, Ish, > LEAVE, March, Match, Off, Path, Pep, Perpetual, Ply, Quit, Raik, Repair, Resort, Resume, Run, Scat, Scram, Segue, Shoo, Skedaddle, Snick-up, Sour, Spank, Stab, Success, Transitory, Trine, Try, Turn, Vam(o)ose, Verve, Via, Viable, Wend, Work, Yead, Yede, Yeed, Zap, Zing, Zip

Goad Ankus, Brod, Gad, Incite, > NEEDLE, Prod, Spur, Stimulate, Stimulus, Taunt

Goal(posts) Ambition, Basket, Bourn(e), Destination, Dream, Drop, End, Field, Grail, Mission, Own, Score, Target, Ultima Thule

Goat(-like) Angora, Billy, Buck, Caprine, Cashmere, Hircine, Ibex, Kashmir, Kid, Markhor, Nan(ny)

Gobble Bolt, Devour, Gorge, Gulp, Slubber, Wolf

Go-between Broker, Factor, Intermediate, Link, Mediate, Middleman, Pandarus, Pander, Shuttle

Goblin Bargaist, Barg(h)est, Bodach, Bogey, Bogle, Bogy, Bucca, Croquemitaine, Empusa, Erl-king, Genie, Gnome, Gremlin, Knocker, Kobold, Lutin, Nis(se), Phooka, Phynnodderree, Pooka, Pouke, Puca, Pug, Red-cap, Red-cowl, Shellycoat, Troll, Trow

God(s) Divine, Gallery, Gracious, Light, Maker, Od(d), Principle, Tin, Trinity, Truth, Unknown

Goddess(es) Divine, Muse

Godless Agnostic, Atheistic, Atheous, Impious, Profane

▷ **Going wrong** *may indicate* an anagram

Gold(en) Age, Amber, Apple, Ass, Au, Auriferous, Bough, Bull, Bullion, California, Doubloon, Dutch, Eagle, Electron, Electrum, Emerods, Filigree, Fleece, Fool's, Gate, Handshake, Hind, Horde, Horn, Ingot, Leaf, Lingot, Moidore, Mosaic, Muck, Nugget, Oaker, Obang, Ochre, Ophir, Or, Oreide, Ormolu, Oroide, Pistole, Placer, Pyrites, Red, Reef, Rolled, Silence, Sol, Standard, Stubborn, Talmi, Tolosa, Treasury, White, Yellow

Gold-digger Forty-niner, Prospector

Golfer Alliss, Braid, Cotton, Faldo, Hogan, Pivoter, Rees, Roundsman, Seve, Snead, Teer, Trevino, Wolstenholme, Yipper

Gone Ago, Dead, Defunct, Napoo, Out, Past, Ygo(e), Yod

▷ **Gone off** *may indicate* an anagram

Good(ness), Goody-goody Agatha, Agathodaimon, Altruism, Angelic, Bad, Bein, Benefit, Blesses, Bon, Bonzer, Bosker, Bounty, Brod, Budgeree, Canny, Castor, Civil, Clinker, Common, Coo, Cool, Crack(ing), Credit, Dab, Dandy, Def, Dow, Enid, Estimable, Fantabulous, Finger lickin', First-class, G, Gear, Giffen, Gosh, Guid, Humdinger, Lois, Lor, Ma foi, Nobility, Pi, Plum, Proper, Purler, Rattling, Rectitude, Riddance, Right, Rum, Sake, Salutary, Samaritan, Sanctity, Slap-up, Smashing, Spiffing, St, Suitable, Super, Taut, Tollol, Topping, Valid, Virtue, Virtuous, Weal, Welfare, Whacko, Wholesome, Worthy

Goodbye Addio, Adieu, Adios, Aloha, Arrivederci, Cheerio, Ciao, Farewell, Sayonara, Tata, Toodle-oo, Toodle-pip, Vale

Goods Brown, Cargo, Consumer, Disposable, Durables, Fancy, Flotsam, Freight, Gear, Hardware, Line, Piece, Products, Property, Schlock, Soft, Wares, White

Goodwill Amity, Bonhom(m)ie, Favour, Gree

Goose, Geese Anserine, Barnacle, Bernicle, Blue, Brent, Canada, Capr Barren, Colonial, Daftie, Ember, Gander, Gannet, Golden, Greylag, Grope, Harvest, Hawaiian, Idiot, Juggins, MacFarlane's, Magpie, Michaelmas, Mother, Nana, Nene, Pink-footed, Quink, Roger, Saddleback, Silly, Simpleton, Skein, Snow,

Solan, Strasbourg, Stubble, > STUPID PERSON, Swan, Team, Wav(e)y, Wawa, Whitehead

Goosefoot Allgood, Amarantaceae, Beet, Blite, Fat-hen, Mercury, Orache, Saltbush

Gorge(s) Abyss, Barranca, Barranco, Canyon, Chasm, Cheddar, Cleft, Couloir, Cram, Defile, Donga, Flume, Gap, Ghyll, Glut, Grand Canyon, Grand Coulee, Gulch, Khor, Kloof, Lin(n), Nala, Nalla(h), Nulla(h), Olduvai, Overeat, Pass, Ravine, Staw, > STUFF, Throat, Tire, Tums, Valley, Yosemite

Gorgeous Grand, Splendid, Superb

▶ **Gorilla** *see* MONKEY

Gosh Begad, Begorra, Blimey, Cor, Gadzooks, Gee, Gum, Lor, My, Odsbobs, Odso

Gossip Ana(s), Aunt, Backbite, Cackle, Cat, Causerie, Chat, Chin, Chitchat, Clash, Claver, Cleck, Clish-clash, Clishmaclaver, Confab, Crack, Dirt, Flibbertigibbet, Gab(nash), Gabfest, Gas, Jaw, Loose-tongued, Maundrel, Natter, Noise, Pal, Prattle, Quidnunc, Rumour, Scandal(monger), Schmooze, Scuttlebutt, Shmoose, Shmooze, Talk(er), Tattle, Tittle(-tattle), Twattle, Yatter

Gourmand, Gourmet Apicius, > EPICURE, Gastronome, Gastrosopher, Lickerish, Table, Trencherman, Ventripotent

Govern(or), Government Administer, Alderman, Autarchy, Autocrat, Autonomy, Bencher, Bureaucracy, Cabinet, Caretaker, Coalition, Command, Condiminium, Congress, Constitution, Diarchy, Dinarchy, Dominate, Duarchy, Dulocracy, Dyarchy, Federal, G, Gerontocracy, Gov, Gubernator, Hagiocracy, Helm, Hierocracy, Inspector, Isocracy, Kakistocracy, Kremlin, Legate, Monarchy, Monocracy, Nomocracy, Ochlocracy, Oligarchy, Petticoat, Plutocracy, Polyarchy, Power, Raj, Regency, Regime(n), Reign, > RULE, Senate, Steer, Stratocracy, Sway, Technocracy, Thearchy, Timocracy, Whitehall

Governess Duenna, Eyre, Fraulein, Griffin, Mademoiselle, Prism, Vicereine

Grab Annexe, Bag, Clutch, Cly, Collar, Glaum, Grapnel, Hold, Holt, Rap, Seise, Seize, Swipe

Grace(s), Graceful Aglaia, Amnesty, Anna, Beauty, Become, Benediction, Blessing, Charis(ma), Charites, Charity, Darling, Dr, Elegance, Euphrosyne, Fluent, Gainly, Genteel, Genty, Godliness, Mense, Mercy, Mordent, Omnium, Ornament, Sacrament, Streamlined, Style, Thalia, Thanks, Willowy

Gracious Benign, By George, Charismatic, Generous, Good, Handsome, Hend, Merciful, Polite

Grade, Gradient Alpha, Analyse, Angle, Assort, Beta, Class(ify), Dan, Degree, Delta, Echelon, Gamma, Gon, Gride, Hierarchy, Inclination, Kyu, Lapse, Measure, Order, Ordinary, Rank, Score, Seed, Slope, Stage, Standard, Status

Graduate, Graduation Alumnus, BA, Bachelor, Calibrate, Capping, Incept, Laureateship, Licentiate, LlB, MA, Master, Nuance, Optime, Ovate

Graft Anaplasty, Autoplasty, Boodle, Bribery, Bud, Dub, Enarch, Enrace, Heteroplasty, Imp, Implant, Inarch, Inoculate, Payola, Pomato, Racket, Scion, Shoot, Slip, Transplant, Ympe

Grain(y) Bajra, Bajree, Bajri, Bear, Bere, Boll, Bran, Cereal, Corn, Couscous, Crop, Curn, Curn(e)y, Cuscus, D(o)urra, Extine, Frumentation, Gr, Graddan, Granule, Groats, Grumose, Intine, Kaoliang, Knaveship, Malt, Mashlam, Mashlin, Mashloch, Mashlum, Maslin, Mealie, Millet, Milo, Minim, Mongcorn, Oats, Pickle, Pinole, Pollen, Polynology, Popcorn, Puckle, Rabi, Raggee, Raggy, Ragi, Rhy, Rye, Sand, Scruple, Seed, Semsem, Sorghum, Tola, Touch, Wheat, Wholemeal

Grand(eur), Grandiose Canyon, Epical, Flugel, G, Gorgeous, Guignol, High-faluting, Hotel, Imposing, La(h)-di-da(h), Lordly, Magnificent, Majestic, Palatial, Piano(forte), Pompous, Regal, Splendid, Stately, Stoor, Stour, Stowre, Sture, Sublime, Swell, Tour

Granite Aberdeen, Chinastone, Greisen, Luxul(l)ianite, Luxulyanite, NH, Pegmatite, Protogine

Grant(ed) Accord, Aid, Award, Bestow, Bounty, Bursary, Carta, Cary, Charta, Charter, Concession, > CONFER, Cy, Datum, Endow, Exhibition, Feoff, Lend, Let, Munich, Patent, President, Send, Sop, Subsidy, Subvention, Vouchsafe, Yeven, Yield

Grape(s) Aligoté, Botros, Botryoid, Cabernet, Cabernet Sauvignon, Catawba, Chardonnay, Chenin blanc, Concord, Delaware, Fox, Gamay, Gewurztraminer, Haanepoot, Hamburg(h), Hanepoot, Honeypot, Hyacinth, Lambrusco, Malmsey, Malvasia, Malvesie, Malvoisie, Merlot, Muscadel, Muscadine, Muscat(el), Noble rot, Pinot, Racemose, Raisin, Rape, Riesling, Sauvignon, Scuppernong, Sémillon, Sercial, Shiraz, Sour, Sultana, Sweet-water, Sylvaner, Syrah, Tokay, Uva, Verdelho, Véronique, Vino, Zinfandel

Graph(ic) Bar, Chart, Contour, Diagram, Histogram, Ogive, Picturesque, Pie (chart), Profile, Sonogram, Table, Vivid

Grapple Clinch, Close, Hook, Lock, Struggle, Wrestle

Grasp(ing) Apprehend, Catch, Clat, Claut, > CLUTCH, Compass, Comprehend, Fathom, Get, Grab, Grapple, Greedy, Grip(e), Hent, Hug, Prehend, Prehensile, Raptorial, Realise, Rumble, Sense, Snap, Snatch, Twig, Uptak(e)

Grass(land), Grass roots, Grassy Agrostology, Alang, Alfa(lfa), Arrow, Avena, Bahia, Bamboo, Bang, Barbed wire, Barley, Barnyard, Beard, Bennet, Bent, Bermuda, Bhang, Blade, Blady, Blue(-eyed), Bristle, Brome-grass, Bromus, Buffalo, Buffel, Bunch, Bush, Canary, Cane, Canna, Cannach, Carpet, Cat's tail, Chess, China, Citronella, Cleavers, Clivers, Clover, Cochlearia, Cocksfoot, Cockspur, Cogon, Cord, Cortaderia, Cotton, Couch, Cow, Crab, Culm, Cuscus, Cutty, Dactylis, Danthonia, Dari, Darnel, Deergrass, Dhur(r)a, Diss, Divot, Dogstail, Dog's tooth, Dogwheat, Doob, Doura, Dura, Durra, Eddish, Eel, Eelwrack, Elephant, Emmer, Esparto, Feather, Fescue, Finger, Fiorin, Flinders, Floating, Flote, Fog, Foggage, Foxtail, Gage, Gama-grass, Ganja, Glume, Glumella, Goose, Grama, Green(sward), Hair, Halfa, Harestail, Hassock, Haulm, Hay, Haycock, Heath(er), Hemp, Herbage, High veld, Holy, > INFORM, Jawar(i), Job's tears, Johnson, Jowar(i), Kangaroo, Kans, Kentucky blue, Khuskhus, Kikuyu, Knoll, Knot, Lalang, Laund, Lawn, Lemon, Locusta, Lolium, Lop, Lucern(e), Lyme, Machair, Manna, Marram, Marrum, Mary Jane, Mat, Materass, Matweed, Mead, Meadow (-fescue), Melic, Melick, Millet, Milo, Miscanthus, Monkey, Moor, Nark, Nassella tussock, Nose, Oat, Orchard, Oryza, Painted, Palet, Pamir, Pampas, Panic, Paspalum, Pasturage, Peach, Pennisetum, Pepper, Persicaria, Phleum, Plume, Poa, Porcupine, Pot, Puszta, Quack, Quaking, Quick, Quitch, Ramee, Rami(e), Rat, Rat on, Redtop, Reed, Rescue, Rhodes, Rib, Ribbon, Rice, Rips, Roosa, Rough, Rumble(r), Rusa, Rye, Rye (-brome), Sacaton, Sago, Salt, Savanna(h), Saw, Scorpion, Scraw, Scurvy, Scutch, Sea-reed, Sedge, Seg, Sesame, Sheep's fescue, Shop, Sing, Sinsemilla, Sisal, Sneak(er), Snitch, Snout, Snow, Sorghum, Sour-gourd, Sourveld, Spanish, Spear, Spelt, Spike, Spinifex, Splay, Split, Squeal, Squirrel-tail, Squitch, Stag, Star(r), Stipa, Stool-pigeon, Storm, Sudan, Sugar, Sward, Swath(e), Sword, Tape, Tath, Tea, Tef(f), Tell, Teosinte, Timothy, Toad, Toetoe, Toitoi, Triticale, Triticum, Tuffet, Turf, Tussac, Tussock, Twitch, Veld(t), Vernal, Vetiver, Whangee, Wheat, Whitlow, Windlestraw, Wire, Witch, Wood melick, Worm, Yard, Yellow-eyed, Yorkshire fog, Zizania, Zostera, Zoysia

Grasshopper Cicada, Cricket, Katydid, Locust

Grate(r), Grating Abrade, Burr, Cancelli, Chirk, Crepitus, > FRET, Graticule, Grid, Grill, Guichet, Guttural, Hack, Hearth, Heck, Hoarse, Ingle, Jar, Portcullis, Rasp, Risp, Rub, Ruling, Scrannel, > SCRAPE, Scrat, Shred, Siver, Strident, Syver

Gratuitous, Gratuity Baksheesh, Beer-money, Bonsella, Bonus, Bounty, Cumshaw, Free, Glove-money, Gratis, Tip

Grave(yard) Accent, Arlington, Bass, Bier, Burial, Charnel, Chase, Darga, Demure, Dust, God's acre, Heavy, Heinous, Important, Ingroove, Kistvaen, Kurgan, Mound, Passage, Pit, Sad, Saturnine, Serious, Sober, Sombre, Speos, Staid, Stern, Tomb, Watery

Gravel(ly) Calculus, Channel, Glareous, Grail(e), Grit, Hoggin(g), Murram, Nonplus, Shingle

Gravity Barycentric, G, Geotaxis, Geotropism, Magnitude, Mascon, Specific, Weight

▶ **Gray** *see* GREY

Grease, Greasy Bribe, Creesh, Dope, Dubbing, Elaeolite, Elbow, Enseam, Glit, Lanolin, Lard, Seam(e), Shearer, Sheep-shearer, Smarm, Suint, Unctuous

Great(s), Greater, Greatest Ali, Astronomical, Bully, Colossus, Extreme, Gargantuan, Gran(d), Gt, Guns, Helluva, Immortal, Important, Lion, Macro, Main, Major, Massive, Mega, Mickle, Modern, Much, Muckle, OS, Profound, Rousing, Stupendous, Sublime, Super, Superb, Swingeing, Tall, Titan(ic), Tremendous, Unco, Untold, Utmost, Vast, Voluminous, Zenith

Greed(y) Avarice, Avid, Bulimia, Bulimy, Cupidity, Edacious, Esurient, Gannet, Gare, Gulosity, Killcrop, Lickerish, Mercenary, Piggery, Pleonexia, Rapacity, Selfish, Solan, Voracity, Wolfish

Greek(s) Achaean, Achaian, Achilles, Aeolic, Agamemnon, Ajax, Aonian, Arcadia, Archimedes, Argive, Aristides, Athenian, Attic, Cadmean, Cleruch, Corinthian, Cretan, Delphian, Demotic, Ding, Diomedes, Dorian, Doric, Eoka, Eolic, Epaminondas, Ephebe, Epirus, Euclid, Evzone, Fanariot, Gr, Helladic, Hellene, Hellenic, Homer, Hoplite, Ionian, Isocrates, Italiot(e), Javan, Katharevousa, Klepht, Koine, Lapith, Leonidas, Linear B, Locrian, Lucian, Macedonia, Momus, Nestor, Nike, Nostos, Orestes, Paestum, Patroclus, Pelasgic, Pelopid, Perseus, Phanariot, Pythagoras, Romaic, Samiot, Seminole, Spartacus, Spartan, Stagirite, Strabo, Sybarite, Tean, Teian, Theban, Thersites, Theseus, Thessal(on)ian, Thracian, Timon, Typto, Uniat, Xenophon, Zorba

Green(ery) Apple, Bottle, Callow, Celadon, Cerulein, Chartreuse, Chlorophyll, Chrome, Common, Copper, Crown, Eau de nil, Eco-, Ecofriendly, Emerald, Emerande, Envious, Erin, Fingers, Foliage, Forest, Fundie, Fundy, Glaucous, Goddess, Gretna, Immature, Inexpert, Jade, Lawn, Leafage, Lime, Lincoln, Loden, Lovat, Moss, Naive, New, Nile, Olive, Pea, Peridot, Pistachio, Putting, Raw, Realo, Reseda, Rifle, Rink, Sage, Scheele's, Sludge, Sward, Teal, Tender, Tyro, Unfledged, Uninitiated, Unripe, Uranite, Verdant, Verdigris, Verdure, Vert, Vir(id)escent

Greens Broccoli, Cabbage, Calabrese, Sprout, Vegetable(s)

Greet(ing) Accost, Banzai, Benedicite, Ciao, Hail, Hallo, Handshake, Heil, Herald, Hi, High-five, Hiya, How, Howsit, Jambo, Kia ora, Kiss, Respects, Salaam, Salute, Salve, Shalom, Shalom aleichem, Sorry, Tena Koe, Wave, > WELCOME, Wotcher, Yo

▶ **Gremlin** *see* GOBLIN

Grey(ing), Gray Argent, Ashen, Ashy, Battleship, Charcoal, Cinereous, Dapple, Dorian, Dove, Drab, Glaucous, Gloomy, Gr, Gridelin, Grise, Grisy, Grizzled, Gunmetal, Hoary, Hore, Iron, Leaden, Mouse-coloured, Pearl, Putty, Slaty, Steel

Greyhound Grew, Longtail, Ocean, Saluki, Sapling, Whippet

Grid(dle), Gridiron Bar, Barbecue, Brandreth, Cattle, Dot matrix, Grate, Graticule, Grating, Network, Reseau, Reticle, Roo-bar, Tava(h), Tawa, Windscale

Grief, Grievance, Grieve, Grievous Axe, Bemoan, Bitter, Complaint, Condole, Cry, Dear(e), Deere, Distress, Dole, Dolour, Gram(e), Gravamen, Heartbreak, Hone, Illy, Io, > MISERY, Monody, O(c)hone, Pain, Pathetic, Plaint, Rue, Sorrow, Teen, Tene, Tragic, Wayment, Weeping, Woe, Wrong

Grill(er), Grilling Braai, Brander, Broil, Carbonado, Crisp, Devil, Gridiron, Inquisition, Interrogate, Kebab, Mixed, Pump, Question, Rack, Reja, Yakimona

Grim Dire, Dour, Gaunt, Glum, Gurly, Hard, Stern

▷ **Grim** *may indicate* an anagram

Grimace Face, Girn, Moe, Mop, Moue, Mouth, Mow, Murgeon, Pout

Grime(s), Grimy Colly, Dirt, Peter, Reechie, Reechy, Soil, Sweep

Grin Fleer, Girn, Risus, Simper, Smirk, Sneer

Grind(ing), Grinder Bray, Bruxism, Chew, Crunch, > **CRUSH**, Droil, Gnash, Grate, Graunch, Grit, Kern, Kibble, Levigate, Mano, Mill, Mince, Molar, Muller, Pug, Pulverise, Slog, Stamp, Triturate

Grip(ping), Gripper Ascendeur, Bite, Chuck, Clam, Clamp, Clip, Clutch, Craple, Embrace, Enthral, Get, Grapple, > **GRASP**, Haft, Hairpin, Handhold, Hend, Hold, Hug, Kirby®, Lewis, Obsess, Pincer, Pinion, Prehensile, Purchase, Raven, Rhine, Sally, Sipe, Strain, Streigne, Valise, Vice, Walise, Wrestle

Gripe(s) Colic, Complain, Ditch, Grasp, Griffin, Ileus, Pain, Tormina

Grit(s), Gritty Blinding, Clench, Gnash, Granular, Grate, Guts, Pluck, Resolution, Sabulose, Sand, Shingle, Swarf

Groin Gnarr, Inguinal, Lisk

▷ **Groom** *may indicate* an anagram

Groove(d), Groovy Bezel, Canal, Cannelure, Chamfer, Channel, Chase, Clevis, Coulisse, Croze, Dièdre, Exarate, Fissure, Flute, Fuller, Furr, Furrow, Glyph, Gouge, Kerf, Key-seat, Keyway, Oche, Pod, Rabbet, Race(way), Raggle, Rebate, Rif(f)le, Rigol(l), Rout, > **RUT**, Scrobe, Sipe, Slot, Sulcus, Throat, Track, Trough, Vallecula

Grope(r) Feel, Fumble, Grabble, Hapuka, Ripe, Scrabble

Gross All-up, Coarse, Complete, Crass, Dense, Earthy, Flagrant, Frankish, Gr, Material, Obese, Outsize, Overweight, Pre-tax, Rank, Ribald, Rough, Stupid, Whole

▷ **Gross** *may indicate* an anagram

Grotesque Antic, Bizarre, Fantastic, Fright, Gargoyle, Magot, Outlandish, Rabelaisian, Rococo

Ground(s) Arena, Astroturf, Basis, Bottom, Breeding, Campus, Cause, Common, Criterion, Crushed, Deck, Dregs, Eard, Earth, Epig(a)eal, Epig(a)ean, Epig(a)eous, Footing, Grated, Grist, Grouts, Lees, Leeway, Lek, Lords, Lot, Marl, Mealed, Occasion, Oval, Parade, Pitch, Plat, Plot, Policy, Proving, Quad, > **REASON**, Recreation, Réseau, Ring, Sediment, Slade, Soil, Solum, Stadium, Terra, Terrain, Tract, Turf, Udal, Venue, Waste(land), Yard, Yird

▷ **Ground** *may indicate* an anagram

Group Band, Batch, Beatles, Bee, Bevy, Bloc(k), Body, Camp, Cartel, Category, Cell, Circle, Class(is), Clique, Cluster, Colony, Commune, Community, Congregation, Consort(ium), Contingent, Coterie, Crew, Ensemble, Faction, Genus, Guild, In-crowd, League, Order, Outfit, Panel, Party, Peer, Platoon, Ring, School, Sector, Seminar, Series, Set, Several, Society, Sort, Sub-order, Syndicate, Tribe, Trio, Umbrella, Unit

Grouse Blackcock, Bleat, Caper(caillie), Capercailzie, Covey, Gorcock, Greyhen, Gripe, Growl, Grumble, Hazel-hen, Heath-cock, Heath-hen, Jeremiad, Moan, Moorcock, Moorfowl, Moor-pout, Muir-poot, Muir-pout, Mutter, Natter, Peeve, Pintail, Prairie-hen, Ptarmigan, Resent, Rype(r), Snarl, Spruce, Twelfth, Wheenge, W(h)inge, Willow

Grove Academy, Arboretum, Bosk, Bosquet, Copse, Glade, Hurst, Lyceum, Nemoral, Orchard, Orchat, Silva, Tope

Grow(ing), Grow out, Growth Accrete, Accrue, Acromegaly, Adenoma, Aggrandisement, Angioma, Apophysis, Arborescence, Auxesis, Bedeguar, Boom, Braird, Breer, Burgeon, Car(b)uncle, Cholelith, Chondroma, Compensatory, Condyloma, Crescendo, Crop, Culture, Cyst, Ectopia, Edema, Ellagic, Enate,

Enchondroma, Enlarge, Epinasty, Epitaxy, Excrescence, Exostosis, Expansion, Fibroid, Flor, Flourish, Flush, Gain, Gall, Germinate, Get, Goitre, Hepatocele, Hummie, Hyponasty, Increase, Knur(r), Lichen, Lipoma, Mushroom, Myoma, Nur(r), Oedema, Oncology, Osselet, Osteoma, Polyp, Proleg, Proliferate, Rampant, Scirrhus, Septal, Snowball, Spavin, > **SPROUT**, Stipule, Sympodial, Tariff, Thrive, Tylosis, Vegetable, Wart, Wax, Wox

▷ **Grow(n)** *may indicate* an anagram

Growl(ing) Fremescent, Gnar, Groin, Grr, Gurl, Roar(e), Roin, Royne, Snar(l)

Grub(by) Assart, Bardy, Caddis, Caterpillar, Cheer, Chow, Chrysalis, Dig, Eats, Fare, Fodder, > **FOOD**, Gentle, Groo-groo, Gru-gru, Larva, Leatherjacket, Mawk, Mess, Nosh, Palmerworm, Peck, Pupa, Root(le), Rout, Rowt, Sap, Slave, Stub, Tired, Wireworm, Witchetty, Worm

Gruesome Ghastly, Grisly, Grooly, Horror, Macaberesque, Macabre, > **MORBID**, Sick

Grumble Beef, Bellyache, Bitch, Bleat, Chunter, Croak, Girn, Gripe, Grizzle, Groin, Growl, Moan, Murmur, Mutter, Nark, Natter, Repine, Rumble, Whinge, Yammer

Grump(y) Attercop, Bearish, Cross, Ettercap, Grouchy, Moody, Sore-headed, Surly

Grunt Groin, Grumph, Humph, Oink, Pigfish, Ugh, Wheugh

Guarantee Accredit, Assure, Avouch, Certify, Ensure, Gage, Hallmark, Insure, Mainprise, Money-back, Pignerate, Pignorate, > **PLEDGE**, Plight, Seal, Secure, Sponsion, Surety, Underwrite, > **VOUCHSAFE**, Warn, Warrandice, Warrant(y)

Guard(ed), Guards Advance, Apron, Beefeaters, Blues, Bouncer, Colour, Cordon, Crinoline, Custodian, Duenna, Escort, Fender, Gaoler, Hedge, Home, Horse, Jailer, Keep, Life, Look out, Mask, National, Nightwatch(man), Palace, Patrol, Picket, Point, > **PROTECT**, Provost, Rail, Ride, Screw, Secure, Security, Sentinel, Sentry, Shadow, Shield, Shopping, Shotgun, SS, Switzer, Turnkey, Vambrace, Vigilante, Visor, Ward, Watch (and ward), Watchdog, Watchman, Wire, Yeoman

Guardian Altair, Argus, Curator, Custodian, Custos, Dragon, Gemini, Granthi, Hafiz, Janus, Julius, Miminger, Templar, Trustee, Tutelar(y), Warder, Watchdog, Xerxes

Gue(r)rilla Bushwhacker, Chetnik, Contra, ETA, Fedayee, Gook, Irregular, Khmer Rouge, Komitaji, Maquis, Mujahadeen, Mujaheddin, Mujahed(d)in, Mujahedeen, Mujahideen, Partisan, Red Brigade, Terrorist, Tupamaro, Urban, Viet cong, Zapata

Guess Aim, Aread, Arede, Arreede, Conjecture, Divine, Estimate, Harp, Hazard, Imagine, Infer, Level, Mor(r)a, Mull, Shot, Speculate, Suppose, Surmise, Theorise

Guest(s) Caller, Company, Parasite, Paying, PG, Symbion(t), Symphile, Synoecete, Visitant, > **VISITOR**, Xenial

Guidance, Guide, Guideline, Guiding Advice, Baedeker, Bradshaw, Cicerone, Clue, Conduct, Counsel, Courier, Director(y), > **ESCORT**, Index, Inspire, Itinerary, Key, Landmark, Map, Mark, Mentor, Model, Navigate, Nose, Pilot, Pointer, Ranger, Reference, Rudder, Shepherd, Sign, Sixer, Steer, Template, Train, Waymark

Guild Artel, Basoche, Company, Gyeld, Hanse, Hoastman, League, Society, Tong, Union

Guillotine Closure, Louisiette, Maiden, Marianne

Guilt(y) Angst, Blame, Cognovit, Flagitious, Nocent, Peccavi, Remorse, Wicked

Guitar(ist) Acoustic, Axe(man), Bottleneck, Cithern, Cittern, Dobro®, Fender®, Gittern, Hawaiian, Humbucker, Lute, Plankspanker, Samisen, Sancho, Sanko, Shamisen, Sitar, Spanish, Steel, Uke, Ukulele

Gulf Aden, Aqaba, Bay, Bothnia, California, Cambay, Carpentaria, Chasm, Chihli,

Darien, Exmouth, Fonseca, Hauraki, Honduras, Lepanto, Lingayen, Llofis, Mannar, Martaban, Maw, Mexico, Persian, Queen Maud, Saronic, Sidra, Spencer, Tonkin, Trieste, Tunis

Gull(s) Bonxie, Cheat, Cob(b), Cod, Cozen, Dupe, Fool, Geck, Glaucous, Hoodwink, Laridae, Larus, Maw, Mew, Pickmaw, Pigeon, Queer, Rook, Scaury, Scourie, Scowrie, Sea-cob, Sea-mew, Sell, Simp, Skua, Sucker, Tern, Tystie, Xema

Gullet Crop, Enterate, Maw, Throat, Weasand-pipe

Gully Couloir, Donga, Geo, Gio, Goe, Grough, Gulch, Pit, Rake, Ravine, Sloot, Sluit, Wadi

Gulp Bolt, Draught, Gollop, Quaff, Slug, Sob, > SWALLOW, Swipe, Wolf

Gum (tree) Acacia, Acajou, Acaroid, Agar, Algin, Angico, Arabic, Arabin, Arar, Arctic, Asafoetida, Bablah, Balata, Balm, Bandoline, Bdellium, Benjamin, Benzoin, Bloodwood, Boot, Bubble, Cerasin, Chicle, Chuddy, Chutty, Coolabah, Courbaril, Dextrin(e), Dragon's-blood, Ee-by, Eucalyptus, Frankincense, Galbanum, Gamboge, Gingival, > GLUE, Goat's-thorn, Gosh, Guar, Ironbark, Karri, Kauri, La(b)danum, Lac, Lentisk, Mastic(h), Mucilage, Myrrh, Nicotine, Olibanum, Opopanax, Oshac, Sagapenum, Sarcocolla, Scribbly, Size, Sleep, Spearmint, Spirit, Sterculia, Stringybark, Sugar, Tacamahac, Tragacanth, Tupelo, Xanthan

Gun(fire), Guns Amusette, Archibald, Archie, Arquebus, Automatic, Barker, Baton, Bazooka, Beanbag, Beretta, Big Bertha, Biscayan, Blunderbuss, Bofors, Bombard, Breech(-loader), Bren, Broadside, Brown Bess, Browning, Bulldog, Bullpup, Bundook, Burp, Caliver, Cannonade, Carbine, Carronade, Cement, Chokebore, Coehorn, Colt®, Dag, Derringer, Electron, Elephant, Escopette, Falcon(et), Field, Fieldpiece, Firearm, Fire lock, Flame, Flash, Flintlock, Four-pounder, Fowler, Fowlingpiece, Garand, Gat(ling), Gingal(l), Grease, HA, Hackbut, Half-cock, Harquebus, Heater, Hired, Howitzer, Jezail, Jingal, Kalashnikov, Lewis, Long Tom, Luger®, Machine, Magazine, Magnum, Maroon, Martini-Henry®, Matchlock, Mauser®, Maxim, Metal, Minnie, Minute, Mitrailleuse, Morris Meg, Mortar, Musket(oon), Muzzle-loader, Neutron, Noonday, Oerlikon, Ordnance, Over and under, Owen, Paderero, Paterero, Ped(e)rero, Pelican, Perrier, Petronel, Piece, Pistol(et), Pompom, Pump (action), Punt, Purdey®, Quaker, Radar, Ray, Repeater, Rev, Riot, Rod, Roscoe, Saker, Sarbacane, Self-cocker, Shooter, Sidearm, Siege, Smoothbore, Snapha(u)nce, Spear, Spray, Squirt, Staple, Starting, Sten, Sterculia, Sterling, Stern-cannon, Stern-chaser, Stun, Swivel, Taser®, Tea, Thirty eight, Thompson, Tier, Time, Tommy, Tool, Tupelo, Turret, Uzi, Walther, Wesson, Young, Zip

Gunner, Gunner's assistant Arquebusier, Arsenal, Artillerist, Cannoneer, Cannonier, Culvereineer, Gr, Matross, RA

Gunpowder Charcoal, Saucisse, Saucisson

Gurgle Clunk, Gollar, Goller, Guggle, Ruckle, Squelch

Gush(ing) Blether, Effusive, > FLOOD, Flow, Jet, Outpour, Rail, Regurgitate, Scaturient, Spirt, Spout, Spurt, Too-too

Gust Blast, Blore, Flaught, Flaw, Flurry, Puff, Sar, Waff

Gut(s), Gutty Archenteron, Balls, Beer, Bowel(s), Chitterlings, Cloaca, Disembowel, Draw, Duodenum, Enteral, Enteron, Entrails, Gill, Ileum, Insides, Kyle, Mesenteron, Omental, Omentum, Remake, Sack, Sand, Snell, Stamina, Staying-power, Strip, Thairm, Tripe, Ventriculus, Viscera

Gutta-percha Jelutong, Pontianac, Pontianak

Gutter(ing) Channel, Conduit, Cullis, Grip, Kennel, Rhone, Rigol(l), Roan, Rone, Sough, Spout, Strand, Sweal, Sweel

Guy Backstay, Bo, Burgess, Chaff, Clewline, Decamp, Deride, Effigy, Fall, Fawkes, Fellow, Gink, Josh, Mannering, Parody, Rib, Rope, Scarecrow, Stay, Tease, Vang, Wise

Gym(nasium), **Gymnast(ic)** Acrobat, Akhara, Arena, Dojo, Jungle, Lyceum, Palaestra, PE, PT, Rhythmic, Sokol, Tumbler

Gypsum Alabaster, Gesso, Plaster, Satin-stone, Selenite

Gypsy, **Gipsy** Bohemian, Cagot, Caird, Caqueux, Chai, Chal, Chi, Collibert, Egyptian, Esmeralda, Faw, Gipsen, Gitano, Hayraddin, Lavengro, Meg, Rom(any), Rye, Scholar, Tinker, Traveller, Tsigane, Vagabond, Vlach, Walach, Wanderer, Zigan, Zigeuner, Zincala, Zincalo, Zingaro

Gyrate Revolve, Rotate, > SPIN, Twirl

Hh

H Ache, Aitch, Aspirate, Height, Hospital, Hotel, Hydrant, Hydrogen

Habit(s), **Habitual**, **Habituate**, **Habitué** Accustom, Addiction, Apparel, Assuetude, Bent, Chronic, Clothes, Coat, Consuetude, Custom, Dress, Ephod, Frequenter, Garb, Inure, Inveterate, Motley, Mufti, Nature, Outfit, Practice, Raiment, Regular, Riding, Robe, Routine, Scapular, Schema, Season, Set, Soutane, Suit, Surplice, Toge, Trait, Usual, Way, Won, Wont

Habitat Element, Environment, Haunt, Home, Locality, Station

Hack(er) Chip, Chop, Cough, Cut, Drudge, Garble, Gash, Ghost, Grub-street, Hag, Hash, Hedge-writer, Heel, Hew, Horse, Mangle, Mutilate, Nag, Notch, Pad, Paper-strainer, Penny-a-liner, Pot-boiler, Rosinante, Spurn, Tadpole, Taper, Tussis, Unseam

Hackneyed Banal, Cab, Cliché, Corny, Percoct, Stale, Threadbare, Tired, Trite

Haddock Arbroath smokie, Finnan, Whitefish

Hades Dis, Hell, Orcus, Pit, Tartarus

Haemoglobin Chelate

Hag(-like) Anile, Beldame, Besom, Carlin(e), Crone, Harpy, Harridan, Hell-cat, Hex, Rudas, Runnion, Trot, Witch

Haggard Drawn, > GAUNT, Pale, Rider

Haggle Argue, Badger, > BARGAIN, Barter, Chaffer, Dicker, Horse-trade, Niffer, Palter, Prig

Hail(er) Acclaim, Ahoy, Ave, Bull-horn, Cheer, Fusillade, Graupel, Greet, Hi, Ho, Megaphone, Salue, Salute, Shower, Signal, Skoal, Skol, Sola, Stentor, Storm, Whoa-ho-ho

Hair (cut), **Hair problem/condition**, **Hair style**, **Hairlike**, **Hairline**, **Hairy** Afro, Bang, Barnet, Beard, Bob, Bouffant, Braid, Bristle, Brow, Bun, Bunches, Capillary, Chignon, Coiffure, Cowlick, Crew-cut, DA, Dreadlocks, Fringe, Fur, Lock, Mane, Mohican, Mop, Nape, Pageboy, Perm(anent), Pigtail, Plait, Pompadour, Ponytail, Shingle, Shock, Sideburns, Switch, Thatch, Tonsure, Topknot, Tress, Wig

Hairdresser Barber, Coiffeur, Comb, Crimper, Friseur, Marcel, Salon, Stylist, Trichologist

Hairless Bald, Callow, Glabrate, Glabrous, Irate

Hairpiece Merkin, Strand, Toupee, > WIG

Halcyon Calm, Kingfisher, Mild

Half, **Halved** Bifid, Demi, Dimidiate, Divide, Hemi, Moiety, Semi, Share, Split, Stand-off, Term

Half-wit Changeling, Mome, Simpleton, > STUPID

Hall Anteroom, Atrium, Auditorium, Aula, Basilica, Carnegie, Chamber, Citadel, City, Dance, Dotheboys, Festival, Foyer, Liberty, Lobby, Music, Odeon, Palais, Passage, Salle, Saloon, Tammany, Town, Vestibule, Wildfell

▶ **Hallo** *see* HELLO

Hallucinate, **Hallucination**, **Hallucinogen** Autoscopy, Fantasy, Freak, Illusion, Image, Mirage, Psychedelic

Halo Antheolion, Areola, Aura, Aureola, Corona, Gloria, Gloriole, Mandorla, Nimbus, Rim, Vesica

Halt(er) Abort, Arrest, Block, Brake, Bridle, Cavesson, Cease, Check, Full stop, Game, Hackamore, Heave-to, Hilch, Lame(d), Limp, Noose, Prorogue, Rope, Stall, Standstill, > **STOP**, Stopover, Toho, Whoa

Ham(s) Amateur, Barnstormer, Flitch, Gammon, Haunch, Hock, Hoke, Hough, Hunker, Jambon, Jay, Nates, Overact, Overplay, Parma, Prat, Prosciutto, Tiro, Westphalian, York

Hamlet Aldea, Auburn, Cigar, Dane, Dorp, Hero, Kraal, Stead, Thorp(e), Vill(age), Wick

Hammer(ed), Hammerhead Ballpeen, Ballpein, Beetle, Bully, Bush, Celt, Claw, Flatten, Fuller, Gavel, Hack, Incuse, Kevel, Knap, Madge, Mall(et), Malleate, Martel, Maul, Mjol(l)nir, Nevel, Pane, Pean, Peen, Pein, Pene, Percussion, Piledriver, Plessor, Plexor, Rawhide, Shingle, Sledge, Strike, Tenderizer, Tilt, Trip, Umbre, Water

▷ **Hammered** *may indicate* an anagram

▷ **Hammy** *may indicate* an anagram

Hamper Basket, Cabin, Cramp, Cumber, Delay, Encumber, Entrammel, Hamstring, Handicap, Hobble, Hog-tie, Obstruct, Pad, Pannier, Restrict, Rub, Shackle, Tangle, Trammel, Tuck

Hand(s), Hand over, Hand down, Hand-like, Handwriting Assist(ance), Bananas, Bequeath, Charge, Clap(ping), Club, Clutch, Copperplate, Court, Crew, Cursive, Deal, Deck, Deliver, Devolve, Dukes, Dummy, Fin, Fist, Flipper, Flush, Free, Glad, Graphology, Help, Helping, Impart, L, Man, Manual, Mitt(en), Operative, Pad, Part, Pass, Paw, Post, Pud, R, Script, Signature, Span, Straight, Text, Upper, Whip, Worker

Handbag Caba(s), Grip, Indispensable, Pochette, Purse, Reticule, Valise

Handbook Baedeker, Companion, Enchiridion, Guide, Manual, Vade-mecum

Handcuff(s) Bracelet, Darbies, Irons, Manacle, Mittens, Nippers, Snaps

Handicap Burden, Encumber, Hamper, Impede, Impost, Lame, Liability, > **OBSTACLE**, Off, Restrict, Weigh(t), Welter-race

Handkerchief, Hanky Bandan(n)a, Clout, Kleenex®, Napkin, Nose-rag, Orarium, Tissue, Wipe(r)

Handle(d) Ansate, Bail, Bale, Bitstock, Brake, Broomstick, Cope, Crank, Dead man's, Deal, Doorknob, Dudgeon, Ear, Feel, Finger, Forename, Gaum, Gorm, Grip, Haft, Helve, Hilt, Hold, Knob, Knub, Lug, > **MANAGE**, Manipulate, Manubrium, Maul, Name, Nib, Palp, Paw, Pommel, Process, Rounce, Shaft, Snead, Sneath, Sned, Staff, Staghorn, Stale, Steal(e), Steel, Steil, Stele, Stilt, Stock, Tiller, Title, To-name, Touch, Treat, Use, Whipstock, Wield, Withe

Hand-out Alms, Charity, Dole, Gift, Release, Sample

Handsome Adonis, Apollo, Bonny, Brave, Comely, Dishy, Featuous, Gracious, Liberal

▶ **Handwriting** *see* HAND

Handy(man) Accessible, Close, Convenient, Deft, Dext(e)rous, Digit, Factotum, Jack(-of-all-trades), Near, Nigh, Palmate, Palmist, Ready, Skilful, Spartan, Useful

Hang, Hanger, Hanging(s) Append, Arras, Aweigh, Chick, Chik, Dangle, Darn, Depend, Dewitt, Dossal, Dossel, Dosser, Drape, Droop, Execute, Frontal, Gobelin, Hinge, Hoove, Hove(r), Kakemono, Kilt, Lobed, Loll, Lop, Lynch, Mooch, Noose, Nub, Pend(ant), Sag, Scenery, Scrag, Set, Sit, Sling, Suspend, Suspercollate, Swing, Tapestry, Tapet, Tapis, Toran(a)

Hanger-on Bur, Lackey, Leech, Limpet, Liripoop, Parasite, Satellite, Sycophant, Toady

Hangman, **Hangmen** Bull, Calcraft, Dennis, Derrick, Gregory, Ketch, Marwood, Nubbing-cove, Pierrepoint

Hangover Canopy, Cornice, Crapulence, Drape, DT's, Head, Hot coppers, Katzenjammer, Mistletoe, Tester

Hanker(ing) Desire, Envy, Hunger, Itch, Long, Yearn, Yen

Haphazard Casual, Chance, Higgledy-piggledy, Promiscuous, > **RANDOM**, Rough and tumble, Slapdash, Willy-nilly

Happen(ing), **Happen to** Afoot, Be, Befall, Befortune, Betide, Come, Event(uate), Fall-out, > **OCCUR**, Pan, Pass, Prove, Thing, Tide, Transpire, Worth

Happiness, **Happy** Apposite, Ave, Beatific, Beatitude, Blessed, Bliss, Bonny, Carefree, Cheery, Chuffed, Cock-a-hoop, Dwarf, Ecstatic, Elated, Eud(a)emony, Felicity, Felix, Fortunate, Glad(some), Gleeful, Golden, Goshen, Gruntled, Halcyon, Half-cut, Hedonism, Jovial, Joy, Larry, Light-hearted, Merry, Opportune, Radiant, Rapture, Sandboy, Seal, Seel, Sele, Serene, Sunny, Tipsy, Trigger, Warrior

Harangue Declaim, Diatribe, Lecture, Oration, Perorate, Philippic, Sermon, Speech, Spruik, Tirade

Harass(ed) Afflict, Annoy, Badger, Bait, Beleaguer, Bother, Chivvy, Distract, Dun, Gall, Hassle, Heckle, Hector, Hound, Irritate, Persecute, Pester, Plague, Press, Vex

Harbour(ed) Anchorage, Basin, Brest, Cherish, Dock, Entertain, Herd, Hide, Marina, Mulberry, Pearl, PLA, Port, Quay, Reset, > **SHELTER**, Watemata

Hard(en), **Hardness** Abstruse, Adamant(ine), Bony, Brittle, Bronze, Cake, Calcify, Callous, Cast-iron, Crusty, Difficult, Dour, Ebonite, Endure, Enure, Firm, Flint(y), Geal, Granite, Gruelling, H, HH, Horny, Inure, Iron(y), Knotty, Metallic, Moh, Nails, Obdurate, Osseous, Ossify, Permafrost, Petrify, Raw, Rugged, Ruthless, Set, Severe, Solid, Sore, Steel(y), Steep, Stern, Stoic, Stony, Teak, Temper, Tough, Wooden

Hardship Affliction, Grief, Mill, Mishap, Penance, Privation, Rigour, Trial, Trouble

Hardy Brave, Manful, Oliver, Ollie, Rugged, Sturdy, Thomas

Hare Arctic, Belgian, Doe, Down, Electric, Jugged, Leporine, Malkin, Scut, Snowshoe

Harm(ed), **Harmful** Aggrieve, Bane, Blight, Deleterious, Detriment, Evil, Hurt, Inimical, Injury, Insidious, Maleficent, Malignant, Maltreat, Mischief, Noxious, Pernicious, Sinister, Spoil, Wroken, Wrong

Harmless Benign, Canny, Drudge, Informidable, Innocent, Innocuous, Innoxious, Inoffensive

Harmonious, **Harmonise**, **Harmonist**, **Harmony** Agree(ment), Alan, Assort, Atone, Attune, Balanced, Blend, Chord, Concent, Concentus, Concert, Concinnity, Concord, Congruous, Consonant, Consort, Correspondence, Counterpoint, Descant, Diapason, Diatessaron, Doo-wop, Euphony, Eur(h)ythmy, Faburden, Feng-shui, Jibe, Melody, Musical, Solidarity, Symmetry, Sympathy, Sync, Thorough-bass, Tone, Tune, Unanimity, Unison

Harness(maker) Breeching, Bridle, Cinch, Equipage, Frenum, Gear, Girth, Hitch, Inspan, Lorimer, Loriner, Pad-tree, Partnership, Tack(le), Throat-stop, Trace, Yoke

Harp(sichord) Aeolian, Clairschach, Clarsach, Clavier, Drone, Dwell, Irish, Lyre, Nebel, Trigon, Virginal, Welsh, Zither

Harridan Hag, Harpy, Shrew, Xantippe, Zantippe, Zentippe

Harris Boatman, Isle, Rolf

Harry Aggravate, Badger, Bother, Champion, Chase, Chivvy, Coppernose, Dragoon, Flash, Fret, Hal, Harass, Hassle, Hector, Herry, Houdini, Hound, Lauder, Lime, Maraud, Molest, Nag, Pester, Plague, Rag, Reave, Reive, Rieve, Rile, Tate, Tchick, Torment

▷ **Harry** *may indicate* an anagram

Harsh(ness) Acerbic, Austere, Barbaric, Brassy, Cruel, Desolate, Discordant, Draconian, Glary, Grating, Gravelly, Grim, Gruff, Guttural, Hard, Inclement, Raucle, Raucous, Raw, Rigour, Rude, Scabrid, Screechy, > SEVERE, Sharp, Spartan, Stark, Stern, Stoor, Stour, Stowre, Strict, Strident

Hart Deer, Spade, Spay, Spay(a)d, Venison

Harvest(er), Harvest home Combine, Crop, Cull, Fruit, > GATHER, Hairst, Hawkey, Hay(sel), Hockey, Horkey, In(ning), Ingather, Kirn, Lease, Nutting, Pick, Produce, Rabi, Random, Reap, Shock, Spatlese, Tattie-howking, Thresh, Vendage, Vendange

Hash(ish) Bungle, Charas, Discuss, Garble, Garboil, Hachis, Lobscouse, Mince, Pi(e), Ragout

▷ **Hashed** *may indicate* an anagram

Haste(n), Hastening, Hastily, Hasty Cursory, Despatch, Express, Festinately, Fly, Hare, Headlong, Hie, Hotfoot, > HURRY, Impetuous, Precipitant, Race, Ramstam, Rash, Rush, Scuttle, Speed, Spur, Stringendo, Sudden, Tear, Tilt

Hat(less) Akuba, Ascot, Astrakhan, Balibuntal, Balmoral, Bareheaded, Basher, Beanie, Beany, Bearskin, Beaver, Beret, Billycock, Biretta, Boater, Bollinger, Bonnet, Bowler, Boxer, Brass, Breton, Broad-brim, Busby, Cap, Capotain, Cartwheel, Castor, Chapeau, Cheese-cutter, Chimneypot, Christie, Christy, Claque, Cloche, Cocked, Cockle-hat, Coolie, Cowboy, Crusher, Curch, Deerstalker, Derby, Dolly Varden, Dunstable, Envoy, Fedora, Fez, Flat-cap, Fore-and-after, Gaucho, Gibus, Glengarry, Hard, Hattock, Headdress, Head-rig, Hennin, Homburg, Kamelaukion, Leghorn, Lid, Lum, Matador, Mitre, Mob-cap, Mountie's, Mushroom, Nab, Opera, Pagri, Panama, Petasus, Picture, Pilion, Pill-box, Pilleus, Pilos, Planter's, Plateau, Poke(-bonnet), Pork-pie, Puggaree, Puritan, Ramil(l)ies, Red, Runcible, Safari, Sailor, Shako, Shovel, Silk, Skimmer, Skull-cap, Slouch, Snap-brim, Snood, Sola(-helmet), Solah, Sola-topi, Sombrero, Souwester, Steeple-crown, Stetson®, Stovepipe, Straw, Sugarloaf, Sunbonnet, Sundown, Sunhat, Tam(o'shanter), Tarboosh, Tarb(o)ush, Tarpaulin, Ten-gallon, Terai, Tile, Tin, Tit(fer), Toorie, Top(per), Topee, Topi, Toque, Tricorn(e), Trilby, Turban, Tyrolean, Ugly, Unbeavered, Wide-awake

Hatch(ment), Hatching Achievement, Altricial, Booby, Breed, Brood, Cleck, Clutch, Companion, Concoct, Cover, Devise, Eclosion, Emerge, Escape, Incubate, Set, Trap-door

▷ **Hatching** *may indicate* an anagram

Hate(ful), Hatred Abhor, Abominable, Abominate, Anims, Aversion, Bugbear, Detest, Enmity, Haterent, Loathe, Misogyny, Odium, Phobia, Racism, Resent, Spite, Ug(h), Vitriol

Haughty Aloof, Aristocratic, Arrogant, Disdainful, Fastuous, High, Hogen-mogen, Hoity-toity, Hye, Imperious, Lofty, Paughty, > PROUD, Scornful, Sniffy, Upstage

Haul(age), Haulier Bag, Bouse, Bowse, Brail, Carry, Cart, Catch, Drag, Heave, Hove, Kedge, Loot, Plunder, Pull, Rug, Sally, Scoop, Snig, Touse, Touze, Tow(se), Towze, Transporter, Winch, Yank

Haunt(s) Catchy, Den, Dive, Frequent, Ghost, Hang-out, Honky-tonk, Houf(f), Howf(f), Obsess, Purlieu, Resort, Spot

Havana Cigar

Have, Having Bear, Ha(e), Han, Hoax, Hold, Of, > OWN, Possess, Sell

Haven Asylum, Harbour, Hithe, Hythe, Oasis, Port, Refuge, Refugium, Retreat, Shelter, Tax

Havoc Desolation, Devastation, Hell, Ravage, Waste

▷ **Havoc** *may indicate* an anagram

Hawk(er), Hawkish Accipitrine, Auceps, Badger, Bastard, Buzzard, Caracara, Cast, Cheapjack, Cooper's, Cry, Eagle, Elanet, Eyas, Falcon, Gerfalcon, Goshawk, Haggard, Hardliner, Harrier, Hobby, Keelie, Kestrel, Kite, Lammergeier, Lanner(et), Marsh, Merlin, Monger, Musket, Nyas, Osprey, Ossifrage, Passage, Pearly, Peddle, Pedlar, Peregrine, Ringtail, Sell, Slab, Soar(e), Sorage, Sore(-eagle), Sparrow, Spiv, Staniel, Tallyman, Tarsal, Tarsel(l), Tassel, Tercel(et), Tiersel, Trant(er), Warlike

Hawthorn Albespine, Albespyne, May(flower), Quickset

Hay(cock), Hey Antic, Cock, Contra-dance, Fodder, Goaf, Hi, Kemple, Math, Mow, Pleach, Salt, Stack, Straw, Windrow

Hazard(ous) Breakneck, Bunker, Chance, Danger, Dare, Die, Dye, Game, Gremlin, Guess, Imperil, In-off, Jeopardy, Losing, Main, Moral, Nice, Occupational, Peril, Pitfall, Play, Pothole, Queasy, > RISK, Stake, Trap, Venture, Vigia, Wage, Winning

Haze, Hazy Blear, Cloud, Filmy, Fog, > MIST, Mock, Muzzy, Nebulous, Smog, Tease

▷ **Haze** *may indicate* an anagram

Head(s), Heading, Headman, Head shaped, Heady Apex, Beachy, Bean, Behead, Bill, Block, Bonce, Boss, Brain, Brow, But(t), Cape, Capo, Captain, Caudillo, Chief, Coarb, Coconut, Coma, Commander, Conk, Cop, Coppin, Costard, Crest, Crisis, Crown, Crumpet, Director, Dome, Each, Ear, Figure, Flamborough, Foam, Froth, Hoe, Jowl, Knob, Knowledge-box, Lead(er), Lid, Lizard, Loaf, Loo, Lore, Manager, Mayor, Maz(z)ard, Mull, Nab, Nana, Napper, Ness, Nob, Noddle, Noggin, Noll, Noup, Nowl, Nut, Obverse, Occiput, Onion, Pate, Pater(familias), Patriarch, Point, Poll, Pow, Prefect, President, Principal, Promontory, Provost, Ras, Ream, Scalp, Sconce, Short, Sinciput, Skull, Source, Squeers, Superior, Tete, Throne, Tight, Title, Toilet, Top, Topic

▷ **Head** *may indicate* the first letter of a word

Headdress, Head cover Ampyx, Balaclava, Bandeau, Bas(i)net, Bonnet, Burnous(e), Busby, Calotte, Caul, Chaplet, Circlet, Comb, Cor(o)net, Cowl, Coxcomb, Crownet, Curch, Doek, Dopatta, Dupatta, Fascinator, Fontange, Hat(tock), Helm(et), Juliet cap, Kaffiyeh, Kell, Kerchief, Kuffiyeh, Kufiah, Kufiya(h), Mantilla, Mitre, Mobcap, Modius, Mortarboard, Nubia, Periwig, Pill-box, Plug-hat, Porrenger, Porringer, Romal, Sakkos, Skullcap, Sphendome, Taj, Tarbush, Tiara, Tower, Tulban, Turban, War bonnet, Wig, Wimple

Headland Bill, Cape, Head-rig, Hoe, Hogh, Morro, Naze, Ness, Noup, Promontory, Ras, Ross, Scaw, Skaw

Headline Banner, Caption, Frown, Scare-head, Screamer, Streamer, Title

Headlong Breakneck, Pell-mell, Precipitate, Ramstam, Reckless, Steep, Sudden, Tantivy, Tearaway

▶ **Headman** *see* HEAD

Headphone(s) Cans, Earpiece, Walkman®

Headquarters Base, Command, Depot, Pentagon, Station

▷ **Heads** *may indicate* a lavatory

Headstrong Obstinate, Rash, Stubborn, Unruly, Wayward

Headway Advancement, Headroom, Progress

Heal(ing) Aesculapian, Balsam, Chiropractic, Cicatrise, Cleanse, Cure, Esculapian, G(u)arish, Hele, Knit, Mend, Olosis, Osteopathy, Restore, Sain, Salve, Sanitory, Therapeutic

Healer Asa, Doctor, Homeopath, Naturopath, Osteopath, Sangoma, Shaman, Time

Health(y) Bracing, Chin-chin, Doer, Fit, Flourishing, Gesundheit, Hail, Hale, Hartie-hale, Heart, Holism, Kia-ora, L'chaim, Lustique, Lusty, Medicaid,

Medicare, Pink, Prosit, Robust, Salubrious, Sane, Slainte, Sound, Toast, Tope, Valetudinarian, Vigour, Well, WHO, Wholesome

Heap(ed) Acervate, Agglomerate, Amass, Bing, Bulk, Car, Clamp, Cock, Congeries, Cumulus, Drift, Hog, Jalopy, Lot, Pile, Rick(le), Ruck, Scrap, Slag, Stash, Toorie

Hear(ing) Acoustic, Attend, Audience, Audile, Avizandum, Captain's mast, Catch, Clairaudience, Dirdum, Ear, Harken, Learn, List(en), Oyer, Oyez, Panel

▷ **Hear(say)** *may indicate* a word sounding like one given

Hearsay Account, Gossip, Report, Rumour, Surmise

Heart(en), Heartily, Hearty, Heart-shaped AB, Agood, Auricle, Backslapping, Beater, Bleeding, Bluff, Bosom, Bradycardia, Cant, Cardiac, Centre, Cheer, Cockles, Columella, Cordate, Cordial, Core, Courage, Crossed, Daddock, Embolden, Essence, Gist, H, Hale, Herz, Inmost, Jarta, Kernel, Lepid, Lonely, Memoriter, Mesial, Mid(st), Middle, Nub, Nucleus, Obcordate, Purple, Robust, Root, Sacred, Sailor, Seafarer, Seaman, Sinoatrial, Staunch, Tachycardia, Tar, Ticker, Yarta, Yarto

Hearth Cupel, Fireside, Home, Ingle

Heartless Callous, Cored, Cruel, Three-suited

Heat(ed), Heater, Heating Anneal, Ardour, Arousal, Atomic, Barrage, Blood, Brazier, Calcine, Caloric, Calorifier, Central, Chafe, Convector, Dead, Decay, Dielectric, Dudgeon, Element, Eliminator, Estrus, Etna, Excite, Fan, Ferment, Fever, Fire, Fluster, Fug, Furnace, Het, Hyperthermia, Hypocaust, Immersion, Incalescence, Induction, J, Kindle, Latent, Lust, Normalise, Oestrus, Panel, Prelim, Prickly, Q, Radiant, Radiator, Red, Render, Rut, Salt, Scald, Sizzle, Solar, Space, Specific, Spice, Stew, Storage, Stove, Swelter, Temperature, Tind, Tine, Torrefy, Total, Underfloor, Warming-pan, Warmth, White

Heathen(s) Ethnic, Gentile, Infidel, Litholatrous, Pagan, Pa(i)nim, Paynim, Philistine, Primitive, Profane

▷ **Heating** *may indicate* an anagram

Heave(d) Cast, Fling, Heeze, Hoist, Hump, Hurl, Popple, Retch, Shy, Sigh, Vomit

▷ **Heave** *may indicate* 'discard'

Heaven(s), Heavenly Air, Aloft, Ama, Ambrosial, Asgard, Bliss, Celestial, Celia, Divine, Ecstasy, Elysian, Elysium, Empyrean, Ethereal, Fiddler's Green, Firmament, Hereafter, Himmel, Holy, Leal, Lift, Mackerel, Olympus, Paradise, Pole, Seventh, Shangri-la, Sion, Sky, Supernal, Svarga, Swarga, Swerga, Tur-na-n'og, Uranian, Welkin, Zion

Heavy(weight), Heavily, Heaviness Ali, Dutch, Elephantine, Embonpoint, Endomorph, Grave, Hefty, Last, Leaden, Onerous, Osmium, Pesante, Ponderous, Sad, Scelerate, Stout, Upsee, Ups(e)y, Weighty, Wicked

Heckle Badger, Gibe, Harass, Needle, Spruik

Hedge, Hedging Box, Bullfinch, Enclosure, Equivocate, Haw, Hay, Lay off, Meuse, Mews, Muse, Pleach, Privet, Quickset, Raddle, Sepiment, Shield, Stonewall, Thicket

Hedgehog Gymnure, Hérisson, Tenrec, Tiggywinkle, Urchin

Heed(ed), Heedful Attend, Listen, > MIND, Notice, Observe, Rear, Reck, Regard(ant), Respect, Rought, Tent

Heedless Careless, Incautious, Rash, Scapegrace, Scatterbrain

Heel Cad, Calcaneum, Cant, Careen, Cuban, Dogbolt, Foot, French, Kitten, List, Louse, Rogue, Seel, Spike, Stacked, Stiletto, Tilt, Wedge

Height(en), Heights Abraham, Altitude, Cairngorm, Ceiling, Dimension, Elevation, Embroider, Eminence, Enhance, Golan, H, Hill, Hypsometry, Level, Might, Peak, Procerity, Stature, Stud, Sum, > SUMMIT, Tor

Heir Alienee, Claimant, Coparcener, Dauphin, Devisee, Eigne, Institute, Intitule, Legatee, Parcener, Scion, Sprig, Tanist

▷ **Held by** *may indicate* a hidden word

Hellenic Dorian

Hell(ish) Abaddon, Ades, Agony, Amenthes, Annw(yf)n, Avernus, Below, Chthonic, Dis, Erebus, Furnace, Gehenna, Hades, Heck, Inferno, Malebolge, Naraka, Orcus, Pandemonium, Perditious, Pit, Sheol, Stygian, Tartar(ean), Tartarus, Tophet, Torment

Hello, Hallo, Hullo Aloha, Chin-chin, Ciao, Dumela, Hi, Ho(a), Howdy, Howzit, Yoo-hoo

Helmet Armet, Balaclava, Basinet, Beaver, Burganet, Burgonet, Cask, Casque, Comb, Crash, Galea, Heaume, Knapscal, Knapscull, Knapskull, Montero, Mor(r)ion, Nasal, Pickelhaube, Pith, Plumed, Pot, Salade, Sal(l)et, Shako, Skid-lid, Topee, Topi

Help(er), Helping, Helpful Abet, Accomplice, Adjuvant, Advantage, Aid(ance), Aidant, Aide, Alleviate, Ally, > **ASSIST**, Avail, Back, Befriend, Benefit, Bestead, Boon, Brownie, Char(woman), Coadjutor, Complice, Daily, Dollop, Dose, Forward, Further(some), Go, Hand, Hint, Instrumental, Leg-up, Maid, Mayday, Obliging, Order, Patronage, Ration, Recourse, Relieve, Servant, Serve, Slice, SOS, Stead, Sted, Subserve, Subvention, Succour, Taste, Therapeutic, Use

Helpless(ness) Anomie, Feeble, Impotent, Paralytic

Hen Ancona, Andalusian, Australorp, Biddy, Buff Orpington, Chock, Cochin, Dorking, Eirack, Fowl, Houdan, Langshan, Layer, Leghorn, Orpington, Partlet, Pertelote, Plymouth Rock, Poulard, Pullet, Ree(ve), Rhode Island Red, Sitter, Sultan, Tappit, Welsummer, Wyandotte

Hence Apage, Avaunt, Ergo, Go, Hinc, So, Therefore, Thus

Herald(ic), Heraldry Abatement, Argent, Armory, Azure, Bars, Bend, Bendwise, Blazonry, Bloody Hand, Blue Mantle, Bordure, Caboched, Chevron, Chief, Cicerone, Cinquefoil, Clarenc(i)eux, Compone, Compony, Couchant, Coue, Counter-passant, Couped, Coward, Crier, Difference, Displayed, Dormant, Endorse, Erased, Fecial, Fess(e), Fetial, File, Flory, Forerunner, Gardant, Garter, Golp(e), Gules, Hauriant, Hermes, Issuant, Lionel, Lodged, Lyon, Martlet, Messenger, Mullet, Naiant, Naissant, Nascent, Nombril, Norroy, Opinicus, Or, Ordinary, Pale, Pallet, Paly, Passant, Pile, Portcullis, Potant, Precursor, Proclaim, Purpure, Pursuivant, Quartering, Rampant, Red Hand, Regardant, Roundel, Roundle, Sable, Salient, Scarp, Sea lion, Segreant, Sejant, Statant, Stentor, Subordinary, Trangle, Tressure, Trick, Trippant, Trundle, Umbrated, Urinant, Usher, Verdoy, Vert, Vol(ant), Vorant, Yale

Herb(s) Aconite, Angelica, Anise, Aristolochia, Arugula, Avens, Basil, Bay, Bennet, Bergamot, Borage, Centaury, Chamomile, Chervil, C(h)ive, Cilanto, Comfrey, Coriander, Costmary, Cum(m)in, Dill, Dittany, Echinacea, Eruca, Exacum, Eyebright, Felicia, Fennel, Fenugreek, Ferula, Feverfew, Fireweed, Fluellin, Forb, Garlic, Garnish, Gentian, Germander, Good-King-Henry, Gunnera, Haworthia, Hyssop, Inula, Kalanchoe, Knapweed, Lamb's ears, Laserpicium, Laserwort, Lovage, Madder, Madwort, Mandrake, Marjoram, Maror, Medic, Mint, Moly, Mustard, Oca, Oleraceous, Oregano, Origan(e), Origanum, Ornithogalum, Orval, Parsley, Paterson's curse, Pia, Pipsissewa, Plantain, Purpie, Purslane, Pussytoes, Rest-harrow, Rhizocarp, Rodgersia, Rosemary, Rue, Sage, Salsify, Savory, Senna, Sesame, Soapwort, Sorrel, Southernwood, Spearmint, Staragen, Sweet cicely, Tacca, Tansy, Tarragon, Thyme, Tormentil, Typha, Valerian, Vervain, Weed, Willow, Wormwood, Wort, Yarrow, Yerba

Herbicide Agent Orange, Atrazine, Defoliant, Picloram

Herd(er), Herdsman Band, Corral, Drive, Drover, Flock, Gang, Mob, Pod,

Raggle-taggle, Round-up, Shepherd, Vaquero

Here Adsum, Hi, Hic, Hither, Local, Now, Present

Hereditary, **Heredity** Ancestry, Blood, Breeding, Codon, Eugenics, Genetics, Id(ant), Idioplasm, Mendelism

▷ **Herein** *may indicate* a hidden word

Heresy, **Heretic(al)** Agnoitae, Albi, Albigensian, Apostasy, Arian, Bogomil, Bugger, Cathar, Docete, Dulcinist, Eudoxian, Giaour, Heresearch, Heterodoxy, Lollard, Montanism, Nestorian, Nonconformist, Origen, Patarin(e), Pelagius, Phrygian, Racovian, Rebel, Unitarian, Zendik

Hermaphrodite Androgynous, Gynandromorph, Monochinous, Monoecious

Hermit(age) Anchoret, Anchorite, Ascetic, Ashram(a), Augustinian, Austin, Cell, Cloister, Crab, Eremite, Grandmontine, Marabout, Monk, Museum, Nitrian, Peter, Recluse, Retreat, Sannyasi, Solitary, Troglodyte

Hero(ic) Achilles, Agamemnon, Aitu, Ajax, Alcides, Amadis, Bellerophon, Beowulf, Brave, Champ(ion), Cid, Couplet, Crockett, Cuchulain, Cuchullain, Cyrano, Demigod, Epic, Eponym, Eric, Everyman, Faust, Fingal, Finn, Finn MacCool, Folk, Garibaldi, God, Goody, Great, Hector, Heracles, Hercules, Hiawatha, Howleglass, Hudibrastic, Ideal, Idol, Jason, Kaleva, Kami, Leonidas, Lion, Lochinvar, Lothair, Marmion, Meleager, Nestor, Noble, Oliver, Onegin, Owl(e)glass, Ow(l)spiegle, Paladin, Parsifal, Pericles, Perseus, Priestess, Principal, Resolute, Revere, Rinaldo, Roderego, Roderick, Roland, Rustem, Rustum, Saladin, Sheik, Siegfried, Sigurd, Superman, Tam o'Shanter, Tancred, Tell, Theseus, Tragic, Triptolemus, Tristan, Trist(r)am, Ulysses, Valiant, Vercingetorix, Volsung, White knight

Heroine Andromeda, Ariadne, Candida, Darling, Hedda, Imogen, Isolde, Juliet, Leda, Leonora, Manon, Mimi, Nana, Norma, Pamela, Star, Tess, Una

Herring Bloater, Brisling, Caller, Kipper, Red, Rollmop, Sild, Silt

Hesitant, **Hesitate**, **Hesitation** Balance, Boggle, Cunctation, Delay, Demur, Dicker, Dither, Doubtful, Falter, Halting, Haver, Haw, Mammer, > **PAUSE**, Qualm, Scruple, Shillyshally, Shrink, Stagger, Stammer, Swither, Tarrow, Teeter, Tentative, Um, Ur, Vacillate, Wait, Waver

Hew Ax, Chop, Cut, Hack, Sever

▶ **Hey** *see* HAY

Hiatus Caesura, Gap, Hernia, Interregnum, Lacuna, Lull

Hibernate, **Hibernating** Estivate, Latitant, Sleep, Winter

Hiccup Glitch, Singultus, Snag, Spasm, Yex

Hidden Buried, Cabalistic, Covert, De(a)rn, Doggo, Hooded, Latent, Obscure, Occult, Pentimento, Recondite, Screened, Secret, Shuttered, Sly, Ulterior, Unseen, Veiled, Wrapped

▷ **Hidden** *may indicate* a concealed word

Hide, **Hiding (place)** Abscond, Befog, Bield(y), Box-calf, Burrow, Cache, Camouflage, Ceroon, Coat, Cootch, Cordwain, Couch, Cour, Crop, Curtain, Cwtch, Deerskin, Doggo, Earth, Eclipse, Encave, Ensconce, Enshroud, Envelop, Epidermis, Fell, Flaught, Flay, Gloss over, Harbour, Heal, Heel, Hele, Hell, Hole-up, Incave, Inter, Kip, Kipskin, Lair, Leather, Mai-mai, Mask, Mobble, Nebris, > **OBSCURE**, Parfleche, Pell, Pelt, Plank, Plant, Priest's hole, Robe, Saffian, Screen, Secrete, Shadow, Shellac(k), Shroud, Skin, Spetch, Stash, Strap-oil, Tappice, Thong, Thrashing, Trove, Veil, Wallop, Whang, Wrap

Hideous(ness) Deform(ed), Enormity, Gash, Grotesque, Horrible, Monstrous, Odious, Ugly, Ugsome

High(er), **Highly**, **Highness** Alt(a), Altesse, Altissimo, Apogee, Atop, Brent, Climax, Doped, Drugged, E-la, Elation, Elevated, Eminent, Exalted, Excelsior, Frequency, Gamy, Haut(e), Intoxicated, Lofty, Mind-blowing, Orthian, Prime,

Rancid, Ripe, School, Senior, Sent, Shrill, So, Steep, Stenchy, Stoned, String-out, Strong, Superior, Swollen, Tall, Tension, Tipsy, Top-lofty, Topmost, Treble, Up(per), Very, Wired

▷ **High** *may indicate* an anagram

Highbrow Brain, Egghead, Intelligentsia, Long-hair

Highest Best, Climax, Ne plus ultra, Supreme

Highland(er), Highlands Blue-bonnet, Blue-cap, Cameron, Cat(h)eran, Down, Duniwassal, Dun(n)iewassal, Gael, Kiltie, Plaid(man), Redshank, Riff, Scot, Seaforth, Shire, Teuchter

▶ **High-pitched** *see* HIGH

Highway Alaska, Alcan, Autobahn, Autopista, Autostrada, Flyover, Freeway, Interstate, Motorway, Overpass, Pass, Thoroughfare, Tightrope

Highwayman, Highway robber(y) Bandit, Bandolero, Duval, Footpad, Gilderoy, Jack Sheppard, Latrocinium, MacHeath, Scamp, Skyjacker, Toby, Turpin

Hike(r) Backpack, Bushbash, Bushwalk, Raise, Rambler, Ramp, Rise, Traipse, Tramp, Trape(s), Upraise

Hill(ock), Hills, Hillside Arafar, Areopagus, Aventine, Barrow, Beacon, Ben, Bent, Berg, Beverly, Bluff, Brae, Broken, Bunker, Butte, Caelian, Calvan, Capitol(ine), Cheviots, Chiltern, Chin, Cleve, Cone, Coteau, Crag-and-tail, Crest, Djebel, Drumlin, Dun(e), Eminence, Esquiline, Fell, Gebel, Golan Heights, Golgotha, Gradient, Grampians, Hammock, Height, Helvellyn, Highgate, Horst, How, Hummock, Incline, Inselberg, Janiculum, Jebel, Kip(p), Knap, Knoll, Knot, Kop(je), Koppie, Lammermuir, Lavender, Law, Loma, Low, Ludgate, Mamelon, Man, Mendip, Merrick, Mesa, Monadnock, Monticule, Morro, Mound, Mount Lofty Ranges, Nab, Nanatak, North Downs, Otway Ranges, Palatine, Pennines, Pike, Pingo, Pnyx, Quantocks, Quirinal, Rand, Range, Saddleback, Scaur, Silbury, Sion, Stoss, Tara, Tel(l), Toft, Toot, Tump, Tweedsmuir, Viminal, Wolds, Wrekin, Zion

Hilt Basket, Coquille, Haft, Handle, Hasp, Shaft

Hind(most) Back, Deer, Lag, Rear

Hinder, Hindrance Back, Bar, Block, Check, Counteract, Cumber, Debar, > DELAY, Deter, Hamper, Harass, Holdback, Impeach, Impede, Obstacle, Posterior, Rear, Rein, Remora, Rump, Shackle, Slow, Stunt, Taigle, Thwart, Trammel

Hindi, Hindu(ism) Arya Samaj, Babu, Bania(n), Banyan, Brahman, Brahmin, Dalit, Gentoo, Gurkha, Harijan, Jaina, Kshatriya, Maharishi, Pundit, Rajpoot, Rajput, Rama, Sad(d)hu, Saiva, Sankhya, Shaiva, S(h)akta, Sheik(h), Shudra, Sudra, Swami, Trimurti, Untouchable, Urdu, Vais(h)ya, Varna, Vedanta

Hinge(d) Butt, Cardinal, Cross-garnet, Garnet, Gemel, Gimmer, Joint, Knee, Pivot

▷ **Hinge(s)** *may indicate* a word reversal

Hint Allude, Clew, Clue, Cue, Element, Gleam, Hunch, Imply, Inkle, Inkling, Innuendo, Insinuate, Intimate, Key, Mint, Nuance, Office, Overtone, Pointer, Preview, Scintilla, Shadow, Soupçon, > SUGGEST, Tang, Tip, Touch, Trace, Trick, Wind, Wink, Wisp, Word, Wrinkle

▷ **Hint** *may indicate* a first letter

Hip(pie), Hippy, Hips Cafard, Cheer, Coxa(l), Drop-out, Huck(le), Hucklebone, Hunkers, Informed, Ischium, Sciatic

Hire(d), Hiring Affreightment, Charter, Engage, Fee, Freightage, Job, Lease, Merc(enary), Never-never, Rent, Shape-up, Ticca, Wage

▷ **His** *may indicate* greetings

Hispanic Latino

Hiss Boo, Fizzle, Goose, Hish, Sibilant, Siffle, Sizzle, Swish

Historian Acton, Antiquary, Archivist, Arrian, Asellio, Bede, Biographer, Bryant, Buckle, Camden, Carlyle, Chronicler, Etain, Froude, Gibbon, Gildas, Green, Griot,

Herodotus, Knickerbocker, Livy, Macaulay, Oman, Pliny, Plutarch, Ponsonby, Renan, Roper, Sallust, Starkey, Strachey, Suetonius, Tacitus, Taylor, Thiers, Thucydides, Toynbee, Trevelyan, Wells, Xenophon

History, **Historical** Account, Anamnesis, Annal, Bunk, Case, Chronicle, Clio, Epoch(a), Ere-now, Ever, Heritage, Legend, Life, Mesolithic, Natural, Ontogency, Past, Record

Hit Bang, Bash, Baste, Bat, Bean, Belt, Blip, Blockbuster, Bloop, Blow, Bludgeon, Boast, Bolo, Bonk, Bunt, Clobber, Clock, Clout, Club, Collide, Cuff, Dot, Flail, Flick, Flip, Foul, Fourpenny-one, Fungo, Get, Hay, Head-butt, Home(-thrust), Impact, Knock, Lam, Lob, Magpie, Mug, Pandy, Paste, Pepper, Pistol-whip, Polt, Prang, Punto dritto, Ram, Roundhouse, Sacrifice, Score, Sensation, Six, Skier, Sky, Slam, Slap, Slosh, Smash(eroo), Smit(e), Sock, Spank, Stoush, Straik, Stricken, Strike, Strook, Struck, > **SUCCESS**, Swat, Switch, Thwack, Tip, Tonk, Touché, Undercut, Venewe, Venue, Volley, Wallop, Wham, Wing, Ythundered, Zap, Zonk

Hitch(ed) Catch, Contretemps, Edge, Espouse, Hike, Hirsle, Hoi(c)k, Hotch, Jerk, Lorry-hop, Rub, Sheepshank, Sheet bend, Shrug, Snag, Technical, Thumb

Hoard(ing) Accumulate, Amass, Bill, Cache, Coffer, Eke, Heap, Hoord, Husband, Hutch, Mucker, Plant, Pose, Save, Sciurine, Snudge, Squirrel, Stash, Stock, Store, Treasure

Hoarse(ness) Croupy, Frog, Grating, Gruff, Husky, Raucous, Roar(er), Roopit, Roopy, Throaty

Hoax Bam, Canard, Cod, Do, Doff, Fub, Fun, Gag, Gammon, Gull, Hum, Huntie-gowk, Kid, Leg-pull, Piltdown, Sell, Skit, Spoof, String, Stuff, > **TRICK**

Hob Ceramic, Cooktop, Ferret, Goblin, Lout

Hobble, **Hobbling** Game, Hamshackle, Hilch, Hitch, Lame, Limp, Pastern, Picket, Spancel, Stagger, Tether

Hobby Avocation, Fad, Falcon, Interest, Pastance, Predator, Pursuit, Recreation, Scrimshaw

Hock Cambrel, Dip, Gambrel, Gambril, Gammon, Ham, Heel, Hough, Hypothecate, Pawn, Pledge, Rhenish, Wine

Hoe Claut, Dutch, Grub, Jembe, Nab, Pecker, Rake, Weed

Hog Babiroussa, Babirussa, Boar, Glutton, Guttle, Peccary, Pig, Porker, Road, Shoat, Shott, Whole

Hoist Boom, Bouse, Crane, Davit, Derrick, Gin, Heft, Hills, Jack, Lewis, Lift, Raise, Shearlegs, Shears, Sheerlegs, Sheers, Sway, Teagle, Trice, Whip-and-derry, Wince, Winch, Windas, Windlass

Hold(er), **Holding**, **Hold back**, **up**, **etc** Absorb, Anchor, Belay, Believe, Boston crab, Canister, Cease, Cement, Cinch, Clamp, Clasp, Cling, Clutch, Contain, Delay, Detain, Display, Dog, Embrace, Engross, Er, Fast, Fistful, Frog, Full nelson, Garter, > **GRASP**, Grip, Half-nelson, Hammerlock, Handle, Have, Headlock, Heft, Heist, Hinder, Hitch, Ho(a), Hoy, Hug, Impedance, Impede, Impediment, Incumbent, Intern, Keep, Keepnet, Lease, Maintain, Nelson, Own, Port, Proffer, Rack, Reserve, Rivet, Rob, Save, Scissors, Shelve, Shore, Sleeve, Sostenuto, Stand, Suspend, Tenancy, Tenement, Tenure, Toehold, Tripod, Wristlock, Zarf

Hole(s), **Holed**, **Holey** Albatross, Antrum, Beam, Birdie, Black, Cat, Cave, Cavity, Coal, Coalsack, Crater, Cubby, Dell, Den, Dene, Dog-leg, Dormie, Dormy, Dreamhole, Dry, Dugout, Eagle, Earth, Eye(let), Finger, Foramen, Funk, Gap, Geat, Glory, Gutta, Hag(g), Hideout, Kettle, Knot, Lill, Limber, Loop, Loup, Maar, Moulin, Nineteenth, Oillet, > **OPENING**, Orifice, Ozone, Perforate, Pierce, Pigeon, Pinprick, Pit, Pocket, Pore, Port, Pot, Potato, Priest's, Punctuate, Puncture, Scupper, Scuttle, Situation, Slot, Snag, Snow, Soakaway, Socket, Sound, Spandrel, Spider, Starting, Stead, Stew, Stop, Stove, Swallow, Tear, Touch, Trema, Vent, Voided, Watering, Well, White, Wookey

Holiday(s) Bank, Benjo, Break, Childermas, Ferial, Festa, > FESTIVAL, Fete, Fiesta, Furlough, Gala, Half(term), High, Laik, Leasure, Leave, Leisure, Long, Minibreak, Outing, Packaged, Pink-eye, Playtime, Recess, Repose, Rest, Roman, Seaside, Shabuoth, Shavuot, Stay, Sunday, Trip, > VACATION, Villegiatura, Wake(s), Whitsun

Hollow Alveary, Antar, Antre, Armpit, Boss, Bowl, Cave(rn), Cavity, Chasm, Cirque, Comb(e), Concave, Coomb, Crater, Cup(mark), Dean, Dell, Delve, Den(e), Dent, Dimple, Dingle, Dip, Dish(ing), Empty, Grot(to), Hole, How, Igloo, Incavo, Insincere, Keck(sy), Kex, Mortise, Niche, Orbita, Pan, Pit, Punt, Rut, Scoop, Sinus, Sleepy, Slot, Slough, Socket, Trough

Holy(man), Holiness Adytum, Alliance, Blessed, > DIVINE, Godly, Grail, Halidom, Helga, Hery, Khalif, Loch, Mountain, Orders, Pious, Sacred, Sacrosanct, Sad(d)hu, Saintly, Sanctitude, Sannayasi(n), Santon, Sekos, Sepulchre, Shrine, Starets, Staretz, SV, Tirthankara, War

Holy Books, Holy writing Adigranth, Atharvaveda, Bible, Gemara, Granth, Hadith, Koran, Mishnah, NT, OT, Pia, Purana, Rigveda, Sama-Veda, > SCRIPTURE, Shaster, Shastra, Smriti, Sura(h), Tanach, Writ

Holy building, Holy place Chapel, Church, Kaaba, Penetralia, Synagogue, Temenos, Temple

Homage Bow, Cense, Honour, Kneel, Obeisance, Tribute

Home Abode, Base, Blighty, Burrow, Cheshire, Chez, Clinic, Community, Domal, Domicile, Earth, Eventide, Family, Fireside, Gaff, Goal, Habitat, Harvest, Heame, Hearth, Heme, Hospice, House, In, Lair, Libken, Mental, Mobile, Montacute, Nest, Nursing, Pad, Plas Newydd, Remand, Res(idence), Rest, Starter, Stately, Villa

Homespun Plain, Raploch, Russet, Simple

Homicidal, Homicide Chance-medley, Killing, Manslaughter

Homily Lecture, Pi, Postil, Prone, Sermon

▷ **Homing** *may indicate* coming back

Homogram, Homograph Abac, Heteronym

Honest(y) Aboveboard, Afauld, Afawld, Candour, Clean, Genuine, Incorruptible, Injun, Jake, Legitimate, Lunaria, Lunary, Open-faced, Penny, Probity, Rectitude, Reputable, Righteous, Round, Sincere, Square, Squareshooter, Straight, Trojan, > TRUE, Upright, Upstanding

Honey Comb, Flattery, Hybla, Hymettus, Mel, Melliferous, Nectar, Peach, Popsy-wopsy, Sis, Sugar, Sweetheart, Sweetie

Honeysuckle Lonicera, Woodbind, Woodbine

Honorary, Honour(able), Honours, Honorific Accolade, Ace, Birthday, Blue, CBE, Commemorate, Credit, Dan, Elate, Emeritus, Ennoble, > ESTEEM, Ethic, Face-card, Fame, Fete, Glory, Grace, Greats, Homage, Insignia, Invest, King, Knave, Knight, Kudos, Laudation, Laurels, MBE, Mention, OBE, Pundonor, Queen, Remember, Repute, Respect, Revere, Reward, Ten, Tenace, Titular, Tripos, Venerate, Worship

Hood(ed) Almuce, Amaut, Amice, Amowt, Apache, Balaclava, Bashlik, Biggin, Blindfold, Calash, Calèche, Calyptra, Capeline, Capuccio, Capuche, Chaperon(e), Coif, Cope, Cowl, Cucullate(d), Gangster, Jacobin, Kennel, Liripipe, Liripoop, Mantle, Mazarine, Pixie, Robin, Rowdy, Snood, Trot-cosey, Trot-cozy

Hook(er), Hooked, Hooks Addict, Adunc, Aduncous, Barb(icel), Becket, Butcher's, Cant(dog), Catch, Chape, Claw, Cleek, Clip, Corvus, Crampon, Cromb, Crome, Crook, Crotchet, Cup, Drail, Fish, Gaff, Grapnel, Hamate, Hamose, Hamulus, Heel, Hitch, Inveigle, Kype, Meat, Pot, Prostitute, Snell, Sniggle, Tala(u)nt, Tenaculum, Tenter, Tie, Trip, Uncus, Wanton

Hooligan Apache, Casual, Desperado, Droog, Hobbledehoy, Keelie, Larrikin, Lout,

Ned, Rough(neck), Ruffian, Skollie, Skolly, Tearaway, Ted, Tough, Tsotsi, Yahoo, Yob(bo)

Hoop Bail, Band, Circle, Farthingale, Garth, Gird, Girr, Hula®, O, > RING, Tire, Trochus

Hoot(er) Deride, Honk, Madge, Nose, Owl, Riot, Screech-owl, Siren, Ululate

Hop(per) An(o)ura, Ball, Bin, Cuscus, Dance, Flight, Jeté, Jump, Kangaroo, Leap, Lilt, Opium, Pogo, Saltate, Scotch, Skip, Tremié, Vine

Hope(ful) Anticipate, Aspirant, Contender, Daydream, Desire, Dream, Esperance, Evelyn, Expectancy, Forlorn, Gleam, Pipe-dream, Promising, Roseate, Rosy, Sanguine, Trust, Valley, White, Wish

Hopeless(ness), Hopeless quest Abattu, Anomie, Anomy, Black, Buckley's chance, Despair, Despondent, Forlorn, Goner, Perdu, Pessimist

Horizon Artificial, Event, Scope, Sea-line, Skyline

Horn(y) Advancer, Amalthea, Antenna(e), Baleen, Basset, Bez, Brass, Bugle, Cape, Ceratoid, Cor, Cornet, Cornett, Cornopean, Cornu(a), Cornucopia, Cromorna, Cromorne, Cusp, Dilemma, Flugel-horn, French, Frog, Golden, Gore, Hooter, Hunting, Ivory, Keratin, Klaxon, Lur, Morsing, Mot, Oliphant, Periostracum, Plenty, Post, Powder, Pryse, Shofar, Shophor, Spongin, Tenderling, Trey, Trez, Trumpet, Waldhorn

Hornblende Syntagmatite

Horrible, Horror Aw(e)some, Brat, Dire, Dread(ful), Execrable, Ghastly, Grisly, Gruesome, Hideous, Odious, Shock, Terror, Ugh

Horrid, Horrific, Horrify(ing) Dire, Dismay, Dreadful, Frightful, Ghastly, Gothic, Grim, Grisly, H, Loathy, Odious, Spiteful, Ugly

Hors d'oeuvres Antipasto, Canapé, Carpaccio, Ceviche, Hoummos, Houmus, Hummus, Mez(z)e, Pâté, Smorgasbord, Zak(o)uski

Horse Airer, Bidet, Bloodstock, Carriage, Cut, Cutting, Dark, Doer, Dray, Drier, Drug, Equine, H, High, Hobby, Iron, Knight, Kt, Light, Malt, Outsider, Pack, Pantomime, Plug, Ride, Rocking, Sawbuck, Screen, Selling-plate, Sense, Stalking, Standard-bred, Stayer, Steeplechaser, Stock, Trestle, Vaulting, Willing, Wooden

Horse complaint, Horse disease, Horse trouble Bogspavin, Curb, Dourine, Equinia, Eweneck, Farcy, Fives, Frush, Glanders, Gourdy, Head staggers, Heaves, Hippiatric, Malander, Megrims, Mooneye, N(a)gana, Poll-evil, Quitter, Quittor, Ringbone, Sallenders, Scratches, Seedy-toe, Spavie, Spavin, Strangles, Stringhalt, Surra, Sween(e)y, Thorough-pin, Thrush, Vives, Windgall, Wire-heel, Yellows

Horseman Ataman, Caballero, Cavalry, Centaur, Conquest, Cossack, Cowboy, Death, Dragman, Famine, Farrier, Hobbler, Hussar, Knight, Lancer, Nessus, Ostler, Parthian, Picador, Pricker, Quadrille, Revere, > RIDER, Slaughter, Spahi, Stradiot, Tracer

Horseplay Caper, Polo, Rag, Rant, Romp

Horseshoe(-shaped) Henge, Hippocrepian, King-crab, Lunette, Manilla, Oxbow, Plate

Hose Chausses, Fishnet, Galligaskins, Gaskins, Lisle, Netherstock(ing), Nylons, Panty, Sock, Stockings, Tights, Trunk, Tube

Hospitable, Hospitality Convivial, Entertainment, Euxine, Lucullan, Open house, Philoxenia, Social, Xenial

Hospital Ambulance, Asylum, Barts, Base, Bedlam, Clinic, Cottage, Day, ENT, Field, Guys, H, Home, Hospice, Imaret, Karitane, Lazaretto, Leprosarium, Leprosery, Lock, Loony bin, MASH, Mental, Nosocomial, Pest-house, Polyclinic, San, Scutari, Sick bay, Spital, Spittle, Teaching, UCH

Host(s), Hostess Amphitryon, Army, Barmecide, Chatelaine, Compere, Crowd, Definitive, Emcee, Entertainer, Hirsel, Hotelier, Innkeeper, Laban, Landlady,

Landlord, Legend, Legion, Lion-hunter, Lot, Mass, Mavin, MC, Publican, Quickly, Swarm, Taverner, Throng, Trimalchio

Hostile, Hostility Adverse, Aggressive, Alien, Animus, Bellicose, Bitter, Currish, Diatribe, Feud, Hating, Icy, Ill, Ill-will, Inimical, Inveterate, Oppugnant, Unfriendly, Vitriolic, War

Hot (tempered) Ardent, Big, Blistering, Breem, Breme, Cajun, Calid, Candent, Dog days, Enthusiastic, Facula, Fervid, Feverish, Fiery, Fuggy, Gospeller, In, Incandescent, Irascible, Lewd, Live, Mafted, Mustard, Pepper, Piping, Potato, Randy, Red, Roaster, Scorcher, Sizzling, Spicy, Stewy, Stifling, Stolen, Sultry, Sweaty, Sweltering, Sweltry, Tabasco®, Thermidor, Torrid, Toustie, Tropical, Zealful

Hotchpotch Bricolage, Farrago, Mish-mash, Powsowdy, Welter

Hotel, Hotelkeeper Bo(a)tel, Flophouse, Gasthaus, Gasthof, H, Hilton, Hydro, Inn, Motel, Parador, Posada, Ritz, Roadhouse, Savoy, Tavern

Hothead(ed) Impetuous, Rash, Spitfire, Volcano

Hot-house Conservatory, Nursery, Orangery, Vinery

Hound(s) Afghan, Basset, Beagle, Bellman, Brach, Cad, Canine, Cry, > **DOG**, Entry, Harass, Harrier, Hen-harrier, Javel, Kennet, Lyam, Lym(e), Mute, Otter, Pack, Pursue, Rache, Ranter, Reporter, Saluki, Talbot, True, Tufter

Hour(s) Canonical, Complin(e), Elder's, H, Happy, Holy, Hr, None(s), Orthros, Peak, Prime, Rush, Sext, Small, Terce, Tide, Time, Undern, Vespers, Visiting, Witching, Zero

House(s), Housing, Household(er) Abode, Accepting, Admiralty, Althing, Astrology, Audience, Auditorium, Bastide, Bhavan, Bhawan, Biggin, Bingo, Boarding, Broadcasting, Broiler, Brownstone, Bundestag, Burghley, Bush, Casa, Chalet, Chamber, Chapter, Charnel, Chateau, Chatsworth, Chattel, Chez, Clapboard, Clearing, Coffee, Commercial, Commons, Convent, Cote, Cottage (orne), Council, Counting, Country, Crankcase, Crib, Custom(s), Dacha, Dail, Des res, Discount, Disorderly, Domicile, Dower, Drostdy, Drum, Duplex, Dwelling, Dynasty, Establishment, Fashion, Finance, Firm, Forcing, Frame, Fraternity, Free, Gambling, Gite, Government, Habitat, Habitation, Hacienda, Halfway, Hanover, Harbour, Harewood, Hatfield, Heartbreak, Hearth, Ho, Holyrood, Home, Homestead, Ice, Igloo, Inn, Insula, Issuing, Joss, Kenwood, Keys, Knebworth, Knesset, Lagthing, Lancaster, Lockwood home, Lodging, Longleat, Lords, Lot(t)o, Maison(ette), Malting, Manor, Manse, Mansion, Mas, Meeting, Ménage, Mobility, Montagne, Nacelle, Odelst(h)ing, Open (-plan), Opera, Orange, Osborne, Parliament, Pent, Petworth, Picture, Pilot, Plantagenet, Pole, Post, Prefab, Public, Radome, Ranch, Register, Residence, Rooming, Rough, Russborough, Safe, Sandringham, Schloss, Seanad (Eireann), Semi, Shanty, Sheltered, Show, Social, Software, Somerset, Sporting, Station, Steeple, Stewart, Storey, Stuart, Succession, Syon, Tavern, Tea, Terrace, Theatre, Third, Tied, Tower, Town, Treasure, Tree, Trinity, Trust, Tudor, Upper, Usher, Vaulting, Vicarage, Villa, Wash, Watch, Weather, Weatherboard, Weigh, Wendy, Whare, Wheel, White, Wilton, Windsor, Work, York, Zodiac

Housing Case, Crankcase, Shabrack, Shelter, Slum, Tenement

Hovel Cru(i)ve, Den, Pigsty, Shack, Shanty

However As, But, Leastwise, Sed, Still, Though, Yet

Howl(er) Banshee, Bawl, Bay, Bloop, Clanger, Hue, Mycetes, Ululate, Wow, Yawl, Yowl

Hub Boss, Centre, Focus, Hob, Nave, Pivot, Tee

Hubbub Charivari, Chirm, Coil, Din, Level-coil, Palaver, Racket, Row, Stir

Huckster Hawker, Kidd(i)er, Pedlar

Huddle Cringe, Gather, Hunch, Ruck, Shrink

Hue Colour, Dye, Outcry, Proscription, Steven, Tincture, Tinge, Utis

Huff Dudgeon, Hector, Pant, Pet, Pique, Strunt, Umbrage, Vex

Huge (number) Astronomical, Brobdingnag, Colossal, Enorm(ous), Gargantuan, Giant, > GIGANTIC, Gillion, Ginormous, Humongous, Humungous, Immane, Immense, Leviathan, Lulu, Mega-, Milliard, Octillion, Socking, Titanian, Tremendous, Whacking

Hull Bottom, Framework, Husk, Inboard, Monocoque, Pod, Sheal, Sheel, Shell, Shiel, Shill

▶ **Hullo** *see* HELLO

Hum(ming) Bombilate, Bombinate, Bum, Chirm, Drone, Lilt, Moan, Murmur, Nos(e)y, Pong, Rank, Reek, Sowf(f), Sowth, Stink, Stir, Whir(r), Zing

Human(e), **Humanist**, **Humanity** Anthropoid, Bang, Colet, Earthling, Erasmus, Incarnate, Kindness, Mandom, Merciful, Mortal, Philanthropic, Species, Sympathy, Ubuntu

Humble Abase, Abash, Afflict, Baseborn, Chasten, Cow, Degrade, Demean, Demiss(ly), Lower, Lowly, Mean, > MEEK, Modest, Morigerate, Obscure, Poor, Rude, Small, Truckle

Humbug Berley, Blague, Blarney, Burley, Claptrap, Con, Delude, Flam, Flummery, Fraud, Fudge, Gaff, Gammon, Gas, Guff, Gum, Hoax, Hoodwink, Hookey-walker, Kibosh, Liar, Maw-worm, Nonsense, Shenanigan, Wind

Humdrum Banal, Bourgeois, Monotonous, Mundane, Ordinary, Prosaic, Tedious

Humiliate, **Humiliation**, **Humility** Abase, Abash, Baseness, Degrade, Disbench, Eating crow, Fast, Indignity, Mortify, Put-down, > SHAME, Skeleton, Take-down, Wither

Humorist Cartoonist, Comedian, Jester, Leacock, Lear, Punster, Twain, Wodehouse

Humour, **Humorous** Aqueous, Bile, Blood, Caprice, Cardinal, Chaff, Coax, Cocker, Coddle, Cosher, Cuiter, Cuittle, Daut, Dawt, Dry, Facetious, Fun, Gallows, Ichor, Indulge, Irony, Jocose, Jocular, Juice, Kidney, Levity, Light, > MOOD, Observe, One-liner, Pamper, Phlegm, Pun, Pythonesque, Ribaldry, Salt, Serum, Temper, Trim, Vein, Vitreum, Wetness, Whim, Wit

Hump(ed) Boy, Bulge, Dorts, Dowager's, Gibbose, Gibbous, Hog, Huff, Hummock, Hunch, Pip, Ramp, Tussock

▶ **Humpback** *see* HUNCHBACK

Humus Compost, Leafmould, Moder, Mor, Mull

Hunch, **Hunchback** Camel, Chum, Crookback, Intuition, Kyphosis, Premonition, Quasimodo, Roundback, Urchin

Hundred(s), **Hundredth** Burnham, C, Cantred, Cantref, Cent, Centum, Century, Chiltern, Commot, Desborough, Host, Northstead, Shire, Stoke, Ton, Wapentake

Hungarian, **Hungary** Bohunk, Csardas, Magyar, Nagy, Szekely, Tzigane, Ugric, Vogul

Hunger, **Hungry** Appestat, Appetite, Bulimia, Bulimy, Clem, > CRAVE, Desire, Edacity, Empty, Esurient, Famine, Famish, Fast, Hanker, Hunter, Pant, Peckish, Rapacious, Raven, Ravin, Sharp-set, Unfed, Yaup, Yearn

▷ **Hungry** *may indicate* an 'o' in another word

Hunker Squat

Hunt(er), **Hunting**, **Huntress**, **Huntsman** Chasseur, Dog, Drag(net), Gun, Hound, Lurcher, Nimrod, Predator, Pursue, Quest, Quorn, Ride, Run, Scavenge(r), > SEARCH, Seek, Stalk, Trap, Venerer, > WATCH, Whipper-in, Woodman, Yager

Hunting-call Rechate, Recheat, Tally-ho, View-halloo

Hurdle(r) Barrier, Doll, Fence, Flake, Gate, Hemery, Raddle, Sticks, Wattle

Hurl(ing) Camogie, Cast, Dash, > FLING, Heave, Put(t), Throw, > TOSS

Hurry Belt, Bustle, Chivvy, Chop-chop, Dart, Dash, Drive, Festinate, Fisk, Frisk, Gad, Gallop, Giddap, Giddup, Giddy-up, Hadaway, Hare, Haste, Hie, Hightail, Induce, Mosey, Post-haste, Press, Push, Race, Railroad, > RUSH, Scamper, Scoot, Scramble, Scur(ry), Scutter, Scuttle, Skelter, Skurry, Spank, Speed, Streak, Tear

Hurt(ful) Abuse, Ache, Ake, Bruise, Damage, De(a)re, Disservice, Harrow, Hit, > INJURE, Lesion, Maim, Nocent, Nocuous, Noxious, Noyous, Pain, Pang, Prick(le), Scaith, Wring

Husband(ry), **Husbands** Add, Baron, Breadwinner, Consort, Darby, Ear, Eche, Economy, Eke, Ere, Farm, Gander-mooner, Georgic, Goodman, Groom, H, Hoddy-doddy, Hodmandod, Hubby, Ideal, Man, Manage, Mate, Partner, Polyandry, Retrench, Save, Scrape, Scrimp, Spouse, Squirrel, > STORE, Tillage

Husk(s), **Husky** Acerose, Bran, Draff, Eskimo, Hoarse, Hull, Malemute, Seed, Sheal, Shuck

Hustle(r) Frogmarch, Jostle, Pro, Push, Railroad, Shoulder, Shove, Skelp

Hut(s) Banda, Booth, Bothie, Bothy, Bustee, Cabin, Chalet, Choltry, Gunyah, Hogan, Humpy, Igloo, Mia-mia, Nissen, Pondok(kie), Quonset®, Rancheria, Rancho, Rondavel, Shack, Shanty, Sheal(ing), Shebang, Shed, Shiel(ing), Skeo, Skio, Succah, Sukkah, Tilt, Tolsel, Tolsey, Tolzey, Wan(n)igan, Wi(c)kiup, Wigwam, Wil(t)ja, Wurley

Hybrid Bigener, Bois-brûlé, Catalo, Centaur, Chamois, Chichi, Citrange, Cross, Dso, Funnel, Geep, Graft, Interbred, Jomo, Jumart, Lurcher, Mameluco, Mermaid, Merman, Metis, Mongrel, Mule, Mutation, Ox(s)lip, Percolin, Plumcot, Pomato, Ringed, Tangelo, Tiglon, Tigon, Topaz, Ugli, Zho(mo)

▷ **Hybrid** *may indicate* an anagram

Hydrocarbon Acetylene, Aldrin, Alkane, Alkene, Alkyl, Alkyne, Amylene, Arene, Asphaltite, Benzene, Butadiene, Butane, Butene, Camphane, Camphene, Carotene, Cetane, Cubane, Cyclohexane, Cyclopropane, Decane, Diene, Dioxin, Diphenyl, Ethane, Gutta, Halon, Hatchettite, Heptane, Hexane, Hexene, Hexyl(ene), Indene, Isobutane, Isoprene, Ligroin, Limonene, Mesitylene, Naphtha, Naphthalene, Nonane, Octane, Olefine, Paraffin, Pentane, Pentene, Pentylene, Phenanthrene, Phene, Pinene, Polyene, Propane, Pyrene, Retene, Squalene, Stilbene, Styrene, Terpene, Toluene, Triptane, Wax, Xylene, Xylol

Hydrogen Deut(er)on, Diplon, Ethene, H, Protium, Tritium

Hydrometer Salinometer

Hyena Aard-wolf, Earthwolf, Strand-wolf, Tiger-wolf

Hymn(s) Anthem, Benedictine, Bhajan, Canticle, Carol, Cathisma, Choral(e), Coronach, Dies Irae, Dithyramb, Doxology, Gloria, Hallel, Introit(us), Ithyphallic, Lay, Magnificat, Mantra, Marseillaise, Nunc dimittis, Ode, P(a)ean, Psalm, Recessional, Rigveda, Sanctus, Sequence, Stabat mater, Sticheron, Tantum ergo, Te deum, Trisagion, Troparion, Veda

Hymnographer, **Hymnologist** David, Faber, Heber, Moody, Neale, Parry, Sankey, Watts

Hype(d) Aflutter

Hypnosis, **Hypnotise**, **Hypnotic**, **Hypnotism**, **Hypnotist** Braidism, Chloral, Codeine, Entrance, Magnetic, Mesmerism, Svengali

Hypocrisy, **Hypocrite**, **Hypocritical** Archimago, Bigot, Byends, Cant, Carper, Chadband, Deceit, Dissembler, Heep, Holy Willie, Humbug, Mucker, Nitouche, Pecksniff, Pharisaic, Pharisee, Prig, Sepulchre, Tartuf(f)e, Two-faced, Whited sepulchre

Hypothesis, **Hypothetical** Biophor, Gluon, Graviton, Suppositious, Virtual

Hysteria, **Hysteric(al)** Conniption, Delirium, Frenzy, Meemie, Mother

Ii

I A, Ch, Cham, Che, Dotted, Ego, Ich, Indeed, India, Iodine, Italy, J, Je, Me, Self

Iberian Celtiberean

Ice(d), Ice-cream, Icing, Icy Alcorza, Anchor, Arctic, Ballicatter, Banana split, Berg, Black, Brash, Camphor, Cassata, Coconut, Cone, Cool, Cornet, Coupe, Cream, Crystal, Diamonds, Drift, Dry, Floe, Frappé, Frazil, Freeze, Frigid, Frore, Frosting, Frosty, Gelato, Gelid, Gems, Glacé, Glacial, Glacier, Glare, Glib, Granita, Graupel, Ground, Hailstone, Hok(e)y-pok(e)y, Knickerbocker glory, Kulfi, Lolly, Marzipan, Neapolitan, Pack, Pancake, Pingo, Polar, Popsicle®, Rime, Rink, Royal, Sconce, Serac, Shelf, Sherbet, Slay, Slider, Slob, Sludge, Sorbet, Spumone, Spumoni, Stream, Sugar, Tickly-benders, Topping, Tortoni, Tutti-frutti, Verglas, Wafer, Water, Wintry

Iceberg Calf, Floe, Growler

▶ **Ice-cream** *see* **ICE**

ID PIN

Idea(s) Archetype, Brainwave, Clou, Clue, Conceit, Concept, Fancy, Germ, Hunch, Idée fixe, Idolum, Image, Inkling, Inspiration, Interpretation, Light, > **NOTION**, Obsession, Plan, Plank, Rationale, Recept, Theory, Thought, Zeitgeist

Ideal(ise) A1, Abstract, Dream, Eden, Goal, Halo, Hero, Model, Monist, Nirvana, Notional, Paragon, Pattern, > **PERFECT**, Siddhi, Sidha, Sublimate, Utopian, Vision

Identical Alike, Clone, Congruent, Same, Selfsame, Verbatim

Identification, Identify Codeword, Credentials, Designate, Diagnosis, Differentiate, Discern, Document, Dog-tag, Earmark, Empathy, Espy, Finger(print), ID, Label, Mark, Name-tape, Password, Pin, Pinpoint, Place, Recognise, Reg(g)o, Spot, Swan-upping, Verify

Identity Alias, Appearance, Corporate, Credentials, Equalness, Likeness, Numerical, Oneness, Qualitative, Seity, Self, Selfhood

Idiom Argot, Cant, Expression, Jargon, Language, Pahlavi, Parlance, Pehlevi, Syri(a)cism, Syrism

Idiot(ic), Idiocy Congenital, Dingbat, Dolt, Eejit, Fool, Goose, Half-wit, Imbecile, Inane, Maniac, Moron, Natural, Nerk, Nidget, Noncom, Oaf, Ouph(e), > **STUPID (PERSON)**, Tony, Twit, Zany

Idle(ness), Idler Bum, Deadbeat, Dilly-dally, Drone, Farnarkel, Fester, Flaneur, Frivolous, Groundless, Indolent, Inert, Lackadaisical, Layabout, Laze, Lazy, Lead-swinger, Lie, Loaf, Lollop, Lounge, Mooch, Ride, Scapegrace, Shiftless, Skive, Sloth, Sluggard, Spiv, Stock-still, Stooge, Tarry, Truant, Twiddle, Unoccupied, Vain, Vegetate, Waste

Idol(ise) Adore, Adulate, Baal(im), Baphomet, Bel, Crush, Fetich(e), Fetish, God, Hero, Icon, Image, Joss, Juggernaut, Lion, Mammet, Manito, Manitou, Matinee, Maumet, Mawmet, Molech, Moloch, Mommet, Mumbo-jumbo, Swami, Teraph(im), Termagant, Vision, Wood, Worship

Idyll(ic) Arcady, Eclogue, Pastoral, Peneian

Igneous Pyrogenic

Ignite, Ignition Coil, Flare, Kindle, Lightning, Spark, Starter

Ignominious, Ignominy Base, Dishonour, Fiasco, Infamous, Scandal, > **SHAME**

Ignorance, Ignorant Analphabet, Anan, Artless, Benighted, Blind, Clueless, Darkness, Green, Hick, Illiterate, Inerudite, Ingram, Ingrum, Inscient, Know-nothing, Lewd, Lumpen, Misken, Nescience, Night, Oblivious, Oik, Philistine, Purblind, Red-neck, Unaware, Uneducated, Unlettered, Unread, Unschooled, Untold, Unversed, Unwist

Ignore Ba(u)lk, Blink, Bypass, Connive, Cut, Discount, Disregard, Forget, Neglect, Omit, Overlook, Overslaugh, Pass, Pass-up, Slight, Snub

Iguana Chuckwalla

Iliad Homeric

Ill Adverse, All-overish, Bad, Bilious, Cronk, Evil, Income, Off-colour, Poorly, Queer, Sea-sick, > **SICK**, Unweal, Unwell, Valetudinarian, Wog, Wrong

▷ **Ill** *may indicate* an anagram

Ill-adjusted Sad sack

Ill-bred Churlish, Plebeian, Uncouth, Unmannerly

▷ **Ill-composed** *may indicate* an anagram

Illegal, Illicit Adulterine, Black, Bootleg, Breach, Furtive, Ill-gotten, Malfeasance, Misbegotten, Pirated, Shonky, Unlawful

Illegitimate Bastard, By-blow, Come-o'-will, Fitz, Irregular, Natural, Scarp, Spurious

Ill-feeling, Ill-humour Bad blood, Bile, Curt, Dudgeon, Glum, Hate, Miff, Peevish, Pique, Rheumatic

▶ **Illicit** *see* ILLEGAL

Ill-mannered, Ill-natured Attercop, Crabby, Ethercap, Ettercap, Guttersnipe, Huffy, Stingy, Sullen, Ugly, Unkind

Illness Aids, Ailment, Attack, Autism, Brucellosis, Complaint, Croup, Diabetes, Disease, DS, Dwalm, Dwaum, Dyscrasia, Eclampsia, Grippe, Hangover, Hypochondria, Malady, ME, Scarlatina, Sickness, Toxaemia, Urosis, Weed, Weid, Wog

Ill-sighted Owl, Purblind

▶ **Ill-tempered** *see* ILL-MANNERED

Illuminate(d), Illumination Brighten, Clarify, Cul-de-lampe, Decorate, Enlighten, Floodlit, Lamplight, Langley, Light, Limn, Miniate, Nernst, Pixel, Radiate, Rushlight

Illusion, Illusory Air, Apparition, Barmecide, Deception, Fallacy, Fancy, Fantasy, Hallucination, Ignis-fatuus, Mare's-nest, Maya, Mirage, Optical, Phantom, Specious, Will o'the wisp

Illustrate(d), Illustration, Illustrator Case, Centrefold, Collotype, Demonstrate, Drawing, Eg, Elucidate, Epitomise, Exemplify, Explain, Figure, Frontispiece, Grangerize, Graphic, Half-tone, Illume, Illumin(at)e, Instance, Instantiate, Limner, Plate, Show, Sidelight, Spotlight, Tenniel, Vignette

Ill-will Animosity, Enmity, Grudge, Hostility, Malice, Spite

Image(s) Atman, Blip, Brand, Corporate, Discus, Effigy, Eidetic, Eidolon, Eikon, Emotion, Graphic, Graven, Hologram, Icon, Iconograph, Ident, Idol, Invultuation, Joss, Latent, Likeness, Matte, Mirror, Murti, Photogram, Photograph, Pic(ture), Pixel(l)ated, Pixil(l)ated, Poetic, Profile, Public, Recept, Representation, Scintigram, Search, Simulacrum, Spectrum, Spitting, Split, Stereotype, Symbol, Teraph(im), Tiki, Totem, Video, Virtual

Imaginary (land), Imagination, Imaginative, Imagine(d) Assume, Believe, Cloud-cuckoo-land, Conceive, Conjure, Cyborg, Dystopia, Envisage, Faery, Faine, Fancy, Feign, Fictional, Fictitious, Fictor, Figment, Figure, Hallucinate, Hobbit, Ideate, Invent, Oz, Picture, Poetical, Prefigure, Recapture, Replicant, Scotch mist,

> SUPPOSE, Surmise, Think, Visualise, Whangam

▷ **Imbecile** *may indicate* an anagram

Imbibe Absorb, Drink, Lap, Quaff, Suck, Swallow

Imitate, Imitation, Imitator Act, Ape, Copy(cat), Counterfeit, Dud, Echo, Echopraxia, Emulate, Epigon(e), Ersatz, Fake, False, Faux, Marinist, Me-too, Mime, Mimetic, Mimic(ry), Mockery, Monkey, Parody, Parrot, Paste, Pastiche, Pinchbeck, Potichomania, Rip-off, Sham, Simulate, Stumer, Take-off, Travesty

Immaculate Conception, Flawless, Lily-white, Perfect, Pristine, Spotless, Virgin

Immature(ly), Immaturity Callow, Crude, Embryo, Ergate(s), Green, Inchoate, Larval, Neotenic, Puberal, Pupa, Raw, Sophomoric, Tender, Unbaked, Unripe, Young

▷ **Immature** *may indicate* a word incompleted

Immediate(ly) At once, Direct, First-time, Forthwith, Imminent, Incontinent, Instantaneous, Near, > NOW, Outright, Present, Pronto, Right-off, Short-term, Slapbang, Spontaneous, Stat, Straight, Straight off, Sudden, Then

Immense Brobdingnag, Cosmic, Enormous, > GIGANTIC, Huge, Vast

Immerse Baptise, Demerge, Demerse, Drench, Emplonge, Enew, Engage, Plunge, Soak, Steep

Immobility, Immobilize Cataplexy, Catatonia, Hog-tie, Inertia, Pinion, Rigidity, Tether

Immodest Brash, Brazen, Forward, Indelicate, Unchaste

Immoral(ity) Corrupt, Dissolute, Evil, Lax, Libertine, Licentious, Nefarious, Peccable, Reprobate, Turpitude, Unsavoury, Wanton

Immortal(ity) Agelong, Amarant(h), Amritattva, Athanasy, > DIVINE, Enoch, Eternal, Famous, Godlike, Memory, Sin, Struldbrug, Timeless, Undying

Immune, Immunisation, Immunise(r), Immunity Acquired, Anamnestic, Anergy, Bar, Cree, Diplomatic, Free, Inoculate, Klendusic, Natural, Non-specific, Pasteurism, Pax, Premunition, Properdin, Serum, Vaccine

Imp(ish) Devilet, Elf, Flibbertigibbet, Gamin(e), Hobgoblin, Limb, Lincoln, Litherly, Nickum, Nis(se), Puck, Rascal, Sprite

Impact Bearing, Bump, Clash, Collision, Feeze, Impinge, Jar, Jolt, Pack, Percuss, Pow, Slam, Souse, Wham

Impartial Candid, Detached, Equitable, Even-handed, Fair, Just, Neutral, Unbiased

Impassable, Impasse Deadlock, Dilemma, Invious, Jam, Snooker, Stalemate, Zugzwang

Impatience, Impatient Chafing, Chut, Dysphoria, Fiddle-de-dee, Fiddlesticks, Fidgety, Fretful, Hasty, Irritable, Och, Peevish, Peremptory, Petulant, Pish, Till(e)y-vall(e)y, Tilly-fally, Tut

Impedance, Impede, Impediment Burr, Clog, Darn, Encumber, Halt, Hamstring, Handicap, > HINDER, Hog-tie, Let, Log, Obstacle, Obstruct, Reactance, Rub, Shackle, Snag, Stammer, Tongue-tie, Trammel, Veto, Z

Imperative Dire, Jussive, Mood, Need-be, Pressing, Vital

Imperfect(ion) Aplasia, Aplastic, Blotch, Defect, Deficient, Faculty, Flawed, Half-pie, Kink, Lame, Poor, Rough, Second

Imperial(ist), Imperious Beard, Commanding, Haughty, Majestic, Masterful, Mint, Peremptory, Regal, Rhodes, Royal

Imperishable Eternal, Immortal, Indestructible

Impersonal Abstract, Cold, Detached, Inhuman

Impersonate, Impersonation, Impersonator Amphitryon, Ape, As, Imitate, Impression, Mimic, Pose

Impertinence, Impertinent Crust, Flip(pant), Fresh, Impudent, Irrelevant, Rude, Sass, Sauce

Impetuous, Impetuosity Birr, Brash, Bullheaded, Elan, > HASTY, Headstrong, Heady, Hothead, Impulsive, Rash, Tearaway, Vehement, Violent

Impetus Birr, Drift, Incentive, Momentum, Propulsion, Slancio

Implant(ation) AID, Embed, Engraft, Enroot, Graft, Inset, Instil, Sow

Implement Agent, Flail, Fork, Hacksaw, Harrow, Hayfork, Muller, Pin, Pitchfork, Plectrum, Plough, Rest, Ripple, Seed drill, Spatula, Squeegee, Tongs, > TOOL, Toothpick, Utensil

Implicate, Implication Accuse, Concern, Connotation, Embroil, Incriminate, Innuendo, > INVOLVE, Overtone

Imply, Implied Hint, Insinuate, Involve, Predicate, Signify, > SUGGEST, Tacit

Importance, Important (person) Big, Big cheese, Big wheel, Calibre, Cardinal, Central, Cheese, Cob, Coming, Considerable, Core, Cornerstone, Count, Critical, Crucial, Crux, Earth-shaking, Earth-shattering, Eminent, Epochal, Grave, Gravitas, Greatness, Heavy, High, Honcho, Hotshot, Huzoor, Key, Keystone, Macher, Magnitude, Main, Major, Material, Matters, Megastar, Mighty, Milestone, Moment(ous), Nabob, Nib, Note, Numero uno, Obbligato, Personage, Pivotal, Pot, Preponderate, Prime, Principal, Salient, Seminal, Serious, Significant, Something, Special, Stature, Status, Stress, Substantive, Tuft, Urgent, VIP, Weight, Weighty, Worth

Importune, Importunate Beg, Coax, Flagitate, Press(ing), Prig, Solicit, Urgent

Impose, Imposing, Imposition Allocate, Assess, August, Burden, Charge, Diktat, Dread, Enforce, Enjoin, Epic, Fine, Flam, Foist, Fraud, Grand(iose), Hidage, Homeric, Hum, Impot, Inflict, Kid, Levy, Lumber, Majestic, Obtrude, Pensum, Pole, Scot, Sponge, Statuesque, Sublime, Whillywhaw

Impossible Hopeless, Incorrigible, Insoluble, Insurmountable, No-no, Unacceptable

Imposter, Impostor Bunyip, Charlatan, Disaster, > FAKE, Fraud, Idol, Pretender, Sham, Triumph, Warbeck

Impotent Barren, Helpless, Spado, Sterile, Weak

Impoverish(ed) Bankrupt, Bare, Beggar, Exhaust, Straiten

Impractical Absurd, Academic, Chim(a)era, Idealist, Laputan, Not on, Other-worldly, Quixotic, Useless

Imprecise Approximate, Inaccurate, Indeterminate, Loose, Nebulous, Rough, Sloppy, Vague

Impregnate Conceive, Imbue, Inseminate, Milt, Permeate

Impress(ive), Impression(able) Astonish, Awe, Effect, Feel(ing), Imprint, Pliable, Powerful, Press(gang), Print, Proof, Stamp, Strike, Watermark

Imprison(ment) Cape, Confine, Constrain, Custody, Durance, Immure, Incarcerate, Intern, Jail, Quad, Quod, Time

Impromptu Ad lib, Extempore, Improvised, Offhand, Spontaneous, Sudden, Unrehearsed

Improper, Impropriety Abnormal, Blue, Demirep, False, Indecent, Indecorum, Outré, Prurient, Solecism, Undue, Unmeet, Unseemly, Untoward

▷ **Improperly** *may indicate* an anagram

Improve(ment), Improver, Improving Advance, Ameliorate, Beet, Benefit, Bete, Break, Buck, Cap, Chasten, Conditioner, Détente, Didactic, Ease, Edify, Embellish, Emend, Enhance, Enrich, Eugenic, Euthenics, File, Gentrify, Kaizen, Meliorate, Mend, Potentiate, Promote, Rally, Refine, Reform, Resipiscence, Retouch, Slim, Surpass, Tart, Tatt, Titivate, Top, Touch-up, Turn round, Uptrend, Upturn

Improvise(d), **Improvisation** Adlib, Break, Devise, Extemporise, Invent, Knock-up, Lash-up, Noodle, Ride, Scratch, Sudden, Vamp, Wing

Impudence, **Impudent** Audacious, Backchat, Bardy, Bold, Brash, Brassy, Brazen, Cheeky, Cool, Crust, Effrontery, Forward, Gall, Gallus, Impertinent, Insolent, Jackanapes, Lip, Malapert, Neck, > **NERVE**, Pert, Sass(y), Sauce, Saucebox, Saucy, Temerity, Whippersnapper, Yankie

Impulse, **Impulsive** Compelling, Conatus, Dictate, Drive, Efferent, Headlong, Horme, Ideopraxist, Impetus, Instigation, > **INSTINCT**, Madcap, Nisus, Premature, Premotion, Send, Signal, Snap, Spontaneous, Tendency, Thrust, Tic, Urge, Whim

Impure, **Impurity** Adulterated, Donor, Faints, Feints, Indecent, Lees, Lewd, Regulus, Scum, Unclean

In A, Amid, Chic, Home, Hostel, I', Inn, Intil, Occupying, Pop(ular), Pub, Trendy, Within

Inaccurate Distorted, Erroneous, Faulty, Imprecise, Inexact, Out, Rough, Slipshod

Inactive, **Inaction**, **Inactivity** Acedia, Cabbage, Comatose, Dead, Dormant, Extinct, Fallow, Hibernate, Idle, Inert, Moratorium, Passive, Quiescent, Rusty, Sluggish, Torpid, Veg(etate)

Inadequate Derisory, Feeble, Inapt, Inferior, Pathetic, Poor, Ropy, Thin

▷ **In a flap** *may indicate* an anagram

Inane Empty, Fatuous, Foolish, Imbecile, Silly, Vacant

Inappropriate Amiss, Infelicitous, Malapropos, Off-key, Unapt, Unbecoming, Undue, Unsuitable, Untoward

Inattentive, **Inattention** Asleep, Deaf, Distrait, Dwaal, Dwa(l)m, Dwaum, Heedless, Loose, Slack, Unheeding, Unobservant

Inaugurate Han(d)sel, Initiate, Install, Introduce

Inauspicious Adverse, Ominous, Sinister

▷ **In a whirl** *may indicate* an anagram

▷ **In a word** *may indicate* two clue words linked to form one

Inborn, **Inbred** Inherent, Innate, Native, Selfed, Sib

Inca Quechua, Quichua

Incandescent Alight, Bright, Brilliant, Excited

Incantation Charm, Magic, Mantra, Spell

Incendiary Arsonist, Firebug, Fire-lighter, Napalm

Incense(d), **Incenser** Anger, Aroma, Elemi, Enfelon, Enrage, Homage, Hot, > **INFLAME**, Joss-stick, Navicula, Onycha, Outrage, Pastil(le), Provoke, Thurible, Thus, Vex, Wrathful

Incentive Carrot, Fillip, Impetus, Motive, Spur, Stimulus

Inch(es) Ait, Edge, Isle, Sidle, Uncial

Incident(al) Affair, Baur, Bawr, Carry-on, Chance, Circumstance, Episode, Event, Facultative, Negligible, Occasion, Occurrent, Page, Scene

Incinerate, **Incinerator** Burn, Combust, Cremate

Incise, **Incision**, **Incisive(ness)** Bite, Cut, Engrave, Mordant, Phlebotomy, Slit, Surgical, Tracheotomy, Trenchant

Incite(ment) Abet, Drive, Egg, Fillip, Hortative, Hoy, Impassion, Inflame, Instigate, Kindle, Motivate, Prod, Prompt, Provoke, Put, Rouse, Sa sa, Sedition, Set, Sic(k), Sool, > **SPUR**, Sting, Suborn, Suggest, Tar, Urge

Incline(d), **Inclination** Acclivity, Angle, Aslope, Atilt, Bank, Batter, Bent, Bias, Bow, Camber, Clinamen, Declivity, Dip, Disposed, Drift, Enclitic, Glacis, > **GRADIENT**, Grain, Hade, Heel, Hill, Kant, Kip, Lean, Liking, List, Maw, Minded, Nod, On, Partial, Peck, Penchant, Proclivity, Prone, Propensity, Rake, Ramp,

Ready, Rollway, Set, Shelve, Slant, > **SLOPE**, Steep, Steeve, Stomach, Supine, Tend, Tilt, Tip, Trend, Upgrade, Velleity, Verge, Weathering, Will

Include(d) Add, Bracket, Compass, Comprise, Connotate, Contain, Cover, Embody, Embrace, Enclose, Involve, Therein

Incognito Anonymous, Disguised, Faceless, Secret, Unnamed

Income Annuity, Disposable, Dividend, Earned, Entry, Living, Meal-ticket, Milch cow, Penny-rent, Prebend, Primitiae, Proceeds, Rent, Rent-roll, Returns, Revenue, Salary, Stipend, Unearned, Wages

Incomparable Supreme, Unequalled, Unmatched

Incompatible, Incompatibility Contradictory, Dyspathy, Inconsistent, Mismatched, Unsuited

Incompetent Bungler, Deadhead, Helpless, Ill, Inefficient, Inept, Palooka, Unable, Unfit

Incomplete Cagmag, Catalectic, Deficient, Inchoate, Lacking, Partial, Pendent, Rough, Unfinished

▷ **In confusion** *may indicate* an anagram

Incongruous, Incongruity Absurd, Discordant, Irish, Ironic, Sharawadgi, Sharawaggi

Inconsiderate High-handed, Petty, Presumptuous, Roughshod, Thoughtless, Unkind

Inconsistency, Inconsistent Alien, Anacoluthon, Anomaly, Contradictory, Discrepant, Oxymoronic, Paradoxical, Variance

Inconvenience, Inconvenient Awkward, Bother, Discommode, Fleabite, Incommodious, > **TROUBLE**

Incorporate(d), Incorporation Absorb, Embody, Inc, Integrate, Introgression, Join, Merge, Subsume

Incorrect Catachresis, False, Improper, Naughty

Incorruptible Honest, Immortal, Pure, Sea-green

Increase, Increasing Accelerando, Accelerate, Accession, Accrue, Add, Additur, Aggrandise, Amplify, Amp up, Appreciate, Approve, Augment, Auxetic, Bolster, Bulge, Crank up, Crescendo, Crescent, Crescive, Deepen, Dilate, Double, Ech(e), Eech, Eik, Eke, Enhance, Enlarge, Escalate, > **EXPAND**, Explosion, Greaten, > **GROW**, Heighten, Ich, Increment, Interbreed, Jack, Jack up, Lift, Magnify, Mark up, Mount, Multiply, Plus, Proliferate, Propagate, Ramp up, Redshift, Reflation, Regrate, Rise, Snowball, Swell, Thrive, Up, Upswing, Wax

Incredible Amazing, Cockamamie, Extraordinary, Fantastic, Steep, Stey, Tall

Incredulity, Incredulous Distrust, Suspicion, Thunderstruck

Incriminate Accuse, Implicate, Inculpate

Incumbent Lying, Obligatory, Occupier, Official

Incursion Foray, Inroad, Invasion, Raid, Razzia

Indecent Bare, Blue, Free, Immodest, Immoral, Improper, Lewd, Obscene, Racy, Scurril(e), Unproper, Unseem(ly)

Indecision, Indecisive Demur, Dithery, Doubt, Hamlet, Hung jury, Suspense, Swither, Weakkneed

Indecorous Graceless, Immodest, Outré, Unbecoming

Indefinite(ly) A, An, Any, Evermore, Hazy, Nth, Some, Undecided, Vague

Indelicate Broad, Coarse, Improper, Vulgar, Warm

Indent(ed), Indentation Apprentice, Contract, Crenellate, Dancetty, Dimple, Impress, Niche, Notch, Order, Subentire

Independence, Independent Autocephalous, Autogenous, Autonomy, Crossbencher, Detached, Extraneous, Free(dom), Free-lance, I, Liberty, Maverick,

Mugwump, Perseity, Self-sufficient, Separate, Separatist, Swaraj, Udal, UDI, Uhuru

Indestructible Enduring, Impenetrable, Inextirpable

Index Alidad(e), Catalogue, Cephalic, Colour, Cranial, Dial, Dow Jones, Exponent, Facial, Finger, Fist, Fog, Footsie, Forefinger, Gazetteer, Glycaemic, Hang Seng, Kwic, Margin, Nasal, Nikkei, Power, Price, Refractive, > **REGISTER**, Rotary, Share, Table, Thumb, TPI, UV, Verborum

India(n) Adivisi, Ayah, Baboo, Babu, Bharat(i), Canarese, Chin, Dard, Dravidian, File, Gond(wanaland), Gujarati, Harijan, Harsha, Hindu, Ink, Jain, Jat, Jemadar, Kanarese, Kannada, Khalsa, Kisan, Kolarian, Kshatriyas, Lepcha, Ma(h)ratta, Maratha, Mazhbi, Mofussil, Mogul, Munda, Munshi, Nagari, Nair, Nasik, Nation, Nayar, Ocean, Oriya, Pali, Parsee, Parsi, Peshwa, Prakrit, Punjabi, Sanskrit, Sepoy, Shri, Sikh, Sind(h), Sowar, Summer, Swadeshi, Tamil, Telegu, Vakeel, Vakil

Indiana, Indianian Hoosier

Indicate, Indication, Indicative, Indicator Adumbrate, Allude, Argue, Cite, Clue, Cursor, > **DENOTE**, Design, Desine, Dial, Endeixis, Evidence, Evince, Gesture, Gnomon, Litmus, Manifest, Mean, Mood, Nod, Notation, Pinpoint, Point, Portend, Proof, Ray, Register, Remarque, Representative, Reveal, > **SIGN**, Signify, Specify, Symptom, Tip, Token, Trace, Trait, Winker

Indifference, Indifferent Adiaphoron, Aloof, Apathetic, Apathy, Blasé, Blithe, Callous, Cavalier, Cold, Cool(th), Dead, Detached, Disdain, Easy-osy, Empty, Incurious, Insouciant, Jack easy, Mediocre, Neutral, Nonchalant, Perfunctory, Phlegm, Pococurante, Sangfroid, So-so, Stoical, Supercilious, Supine, Tepid, Unconcerned

Indignant, Indignation Anger, Annoyed, Incensed, Irate, Resentful, Wrathful

Indigo Anil, Blue, Bunting, Carmine, Indole, Isatin(e)

Indirect Back-handed, By(e), Devious, Implicit, Mediate, Oblique, Remote, Roundabout, Sidelong, Zig-zag

Indiscreet, Indiscretion Folly, Gaffe, Imprudence, Indelicate, Injudicious, Loose cannon, Rash, Unguarded

Indiscriminate Haphazard, Random, Scattershot, Sweeping

Indispensable Basic, Essential, King-pin, Necessary, Vital

Indispose(d), Indisposition Adverse, Disincline, Ill, Incapacitate, Sick, Unwell

Indistinct Ambiguous, Bleary, Blur, Bumble, Bummle, Faint, Fuzzy, Hazy, Pale, Sfumato, > **VAGUE**

▷ **In distress** *may indicate* an anagram

Indite Compose, Pen, Write

Individual(ist), Individuality Being, Discrete, Exclusive, Free spirit, Gemma, Haecceity, Identity, Ka, Libertarian, Loner, Man, Man-jack, One-to-one, Own, Particular, Person, Poll, Respective, Separate, Single, Singular, Solo, Soul, Special, Unit, Zoon

Indolence, Indolent Bone idle, Fainéance, Inactive, Languid, Lazy, Otiose, Sloth, Sluggish, Supine

Indomitable Brave, Dauntless, Invincible

Indubitably Certainly, Certes, Manifestly, Surely

Induce(ment) Bribe, Carrot, Cause, Coax, Draw, Encourage, Get, Inveigle, Lead, Motivate, > **PERSUADE**, Prevail, Suasion, Suborn, Tempt

Induct(ion), Inductance Epagoge, Henry, Inaugurate, Initiate, Install, L, Logic, Prelude, Remanence

Indulge(nce), Indulgent Absolution, Binge, Coddle, Drink, Favour, Gratify, Humour, Luxuriate, Oblige, Pamper, Pander, Pardon, Pet, Pettle, Please, > **SATISFY**, Splurge, Spoil, Spoonfeed, Surfeit, Tolerant, Venery, Voluptuous, Wallow

Industrial, Industrious, Industry Appliance, Application, Business, Busy, Cottage, Deedy, Diligence, Eident, Energetic, Labour, Ocnus, Ruhr, Service, Technical, Tourism, Zaibatsu

▶ **Inebriate** *see* INTOXICATE

Ineffective, Ineffectual Clumsy, Deadhead, Drippy, Droob, Dud, Empty, Fainéant, Fruitless, Futile, Idle, Ill, Impotent, Mickey Mouse, Neutralised, Powerless, Resty, Sterile, Toothless, > USELESS, Void, Weak, Wet

Inefficient Clumsy, Incompetent, Lame, Shiftless, Slack

Inept Absurd, Anorak, Farouche, Nerd, Otaku, Sad sack, Schlimazel, Unskilled, Wet

Inert(ia) Catatonia, Comatose, Dead, Dull, Excipient, Inactive, Leaden, Mollusc, Neon, Oblomovism, Potato, Sluggish, Stagnant, Stagnation, Thowless, Torpid

Inevitable, Inevitably Automatic, Certain, Fateful, Inexorable, Needs, Perforce, TINA, Unavoidable

Inexact(itude) Cretism, Incorrect, Terminological, Wrong

Inexpedient Impolitic, Imprudent, Unwise

Inexpensive Bargain, Cheap, Dirt-cheap, Economic

Inexperience(d), Inexpert Amateur, Callow, Colt, Crude, Fresh, > GREEN, Ham, Ingénue, Jejune, Raw, Rookie, Rude, Tender, Unseasoned, Unversed, Youthful

Inexplicable Magical, Mysterious, Paranormal, Unaccountable

Infamous, Infamy Base, Ignominious, Notorious, Opprobrium, Shameful, Villainy

Infant Babe, Baby, Innocent, Lamb, Minor, Oral, Rug rat

Infantry(man) Buff, Foot, Grunt, Jaeger, Phalanx, Pultan, Pulto(o)n, Pultun, > SOLDIER, Tercio, Turco

▷ **Infantry** *may refer to babies*

Infatuate(d), Infatuating, Infatuation Assot, Besot, Crush, Enamoured, Engou(e)ment, Entêté, Fanatic, Foolish, Lovesick, > OBSESSION, Rave, Turn

Infect(ed), Infecting, Infection, Infectious Angina, Anthrax, Catching, Catchy, Cholera, Communicable, Contagious, Contaminate, Corrupt, Cowpox, Diseased, Fester, Gonorrhoea, Herpes, Listeria, Lockjaw, Overrun, Poison, Polio(myelitis), > POLLUTE, Ringworm, Roup, Salmonella, Septic, Shingles, Taint, Tetanus, Thrush, Tinea, Typhoid, Typhus, Virulent, Whitlow

Infer(ence), Inferred Conclude, Deduce, Divine, Educe, Extrapolate, Generalise, Guess, Illation, Imply, Judge, Surmise

▷ **Infer** *may indicate* 'fer' *around another word*

Inferior Base, Bodgier, Cheap-jack, Cheesy, Coarse, Crummy, Degenerate, Dog, Ersatz, Gimcrack, Grody, Grub-street, Indifferent, Infra, Jerkwater, Less, Lo-fi, Lower, Low-grade, Minor, Naff, Nether, One-horse, Ornery, Paravail, Petty, Poor, Rop(e)y, Schlock, Second, Second-best, Shlock, Shoddy, Sprew, Sprue, Subjacent, Subordinate, Substandard, Surat, Tatty, Tinpot, Trashy, Underneath, Untermensch, Waste, Worse

Infest(ed), Infestation Beset, Blight, Dog, Hoatching, Overrun, > PLAGUE, Swarm, Torment

Infidel Atheist, Caffre, Heathen, Heretic, Kafir, Pagan, Saracen

Infiltrate Encroach, Enter, Instil, Intrude, Pervade

Infirm Decrepit, Doddery, Feeble, Lame, Shaky

▷ **Infirm** *may indicate* 'co' *around another word*

Inflame(d), Inflammable, Inflammation Acne, Adenitis, Afire, Ancome, Anger, Angina, Aortisis, Appendicitis, > AROUSE, Arteritis, Arthritis, Asbestosis, Balanitis, Blepharitis, Bloodshot, Bronchitis, Bronchopneumonia, Bubonic, Bunion, Bursitis, Carditis, Catarrh, Cellulitis, Cervicitis, Cheilitis, Colitis,

Conjunctivitis, Coryza, Croup, Cystisis, Dermatitis, Diverticulitis, Ecthyma, Eczema, Enamoured, Encephalitis, Encephalomyelitis, Enchafe, Endocarditis, Enfire, Enkindle, Enteritis, Enterocolitis, Erysipelas, Farmer's lung, Felon, Fever, Fibrosis, Fibrositis, Fire, Folliculitis, Founder, Garget, Gastritis, Gastroenteritis, Gingivitis, Gleet, Glossitis, Hepatitis A, Hepatitis B, Hyalitis, Ignatis, Ignite, Incense, Infection, Intertrigo, Ire, Iritis, Keratitis, Labyrinthitis, Laminitis, Laryngitis, Mastitis, Mastoiditis, Meningitis, Meningocephalitis, Metritis, Misenteritis, Mycetoma, Myelitis, Myocarditis, Myositis, Napalm, Naphtha, Nephritis, Neuritis, Noma, Onychia, Oophoritis, Ophthalmia, Orchitis, Osteitis, Osteoarthritis, Osteomyelitis, Osteoporosis, Otitis, Ovaritis, Pancreatitis, Paronychia, Parotitis, Pericarditis, Perihepatitis, Perinephritis, Periodontisis, Peritonitis, Perityphlitis, Pharyngitis, Phlebitis, Phlegmasia, Phlegmon, Phlogistic, Phrenitis, Pinkeye, Pleurisy, Pneumonia, Polyneuritis, Proctitis, Prostatitis, Prurigo, Pyelitis, Pyorrhoea, Quinsy, Rachitis, > **RED**, Retinitis, Rhinitis, Salpingitis, Scleritis, Shin splints, Sinusitis, Splenitis, Spondylitis, Stimulate, Stomatitis, Strumitis, Sty(e), Sunburn, Swelling, Swimmer's itch, Sycosis, Synovitis, Tendinitis, Tenosynovitis, Thoroughpin, Thrombosis, Thrush, Thyroiditis, Tonsillitis, Touchwood, Tracheitis, Tylosis, Typhlitis, Ulitis, Urethritis, Uvulitis, Vaginitis, Valvulitis, Vasculitis, Vincent's angina, Whitlow, Windburn

Inflate(d), **Inflation** Aerate, Aggrandise, Bloat, Bombastic, Dilate, Distend, Distent, Increase, Pneumatic, Pump, Remonetise, RPI, Spiral, Stagnation, Swell

Inflexible, **Inflexibility** Adamant(ine), Byzantine, Doctrinaire, Hard-ass, Hard-liner, Iron, Obstinate, Ossified, Relentless, Resolute, Rigid, Rigour, Set, Stubborn

Inflict(ion) Force, Give, Impose, Subject, Trouble, Visit, Wreak

Inflorescence Bostryx, Catkin, Ci(n)cinnus, Drepanium, Glomerule, Panicle, Pleiochasium, Raceme, Umbel

Influence(d), **Influential** Act, Affect, After, Backstairs, Charm, Clout, Credit, Determine, Drag, Earwig, Embracery, Eminence grise, Factor, Force, Govern, Hold, Impact, Impress, Incubus, Inspire, Interfere, Lead, Leverage, Lobby, Mastery, Militate, Mogul, Octopus, Operation, Power, Pressure, Prestige, > **PULL**, Push, Reach, Rust, Say, Seminal, Significant, Star, Star-blasting, Stimulus, Suggest, Svengali, Sway, Swing, Telegony, Undue, Will, Work, Wull

Influx Inbreak

Inform(ation), **Informed**, **Informer** Acquaint, Advise, Agitprop, Apprise, Au fait, Aware, Beagle, Bit, Burst, Canary, Ceefax®, Clype, Contact, Datum, Delate, Dob(ber), Dope, Education, Facts, Feedback, Fink, Fisgig, Fiz(z)gig, Gen, Genome, Grapevine, Grass, Griff, Gunsel, Hep, Input, Inside, Instruct, Izvesti(y)a, Light, Lowdown, Media, Moiser, Nark, Nepit, Nit, Nose, Occasion, Peach, Pem(m)ican, Poop, Prestel®, Prime, Propaganda, Prospectus, Rat, Read-out, Revelation, Rheme, Rumble, Shelf, Shop, Sidelight, Sing, Sneak, Snitch, Squeak, Squeal, Stag, Stoolie, Stool-pigeon, Supergrass, Sycophant, Tell, Tidings, Tip-off, Up, Whistle(-blower), Wire

Informal Casual, Intimate, Irregular, Outgoing, Unofficial

Infuriate Anger, Bemad, Bepester, Enrage, Exasperate, Incense, Madden, Pester, Provoke

Ingenious, **Ingenuity** Adept, Adroit, Art, Artificial, Clever, Cunning, Cute, Inventive, Natty, Neat, Resourceful, Smart, Subtle, Wit

Ingenuous Artless, Candid, Green, Innocent, Naive, Open

Ingot Bar, Billet, Bullion, Lingot, Sycee

Ingratiate, **Ingratiating** Butter, Court, Flatter, Greasy, Smarm(y)

Ingredient(s) Additive, Admixture, Basis, Content, Element, Factor, Formula, Makings, Staple

Inhabit(ants) Affect, Children, Denizen, Dweller, Inholder, Inmate, Live, Native, Occupant, People, Resident

Inhale, Inhalation Aspirate, Breath(e), Draw, Gas, Inspire, Sniff, Snort, Snuff, Take

Inherit(ance), Inherited, Inheritor Accede, Birthright, Congenital, Gene, Genom, Heirloom, Inborn, Legacy, Legitim, Meek, Patrimony, Portion, Succeed

Inhibit(ing), Inhibition, Inhibitor Captopril, Chalone, Chalonic, Deter, Enalapril, Forbid, Hang-up, Protease, Restrain, Retard, Retroactive, Stunt, Suppress

Initial Acronym, First, Letter, Monogram, Paraph, Prelim(inary), Primary, Rubric

▷ **Initially** *may indicate* first letters

Initiate(d), Initiation, Initiative Begin, Bejesuit, Blood, Bora, Bring, Ceremony, Debut, Enter, Enterprise, Epopt, Esoteric, Gumption, Induct, Instigate, Instruct, > LAUNCH, Nous, Spark, > START

Inject(or), Injection Bang, Booster, Collagen, Enema, Epidural, Fuel, Hypo, Implant, Innerve, Inoculation, Instil, Introduce, Jab, Mainline, Pop, Reheat, Serum, Shoot, Skin-pop, Solid, Syringe, Transfuse, Venipuncture

Injunction Command, Embargo, Mandate, Mareva, Writ

Injure(d), Injury, Injurious, Injustice ABH, Abuse, Aggrieve, Bale, Bled, Bruise, Contrecoup, Damage, De(a)re, Frostbite, Gash, GBH, Harm, > HURT, Ill-turn, Impair, Iniquity, Lesion, Malign, Mar, Mayhem, Mistreat, Mutilate, Nobble, Nocuous, Noxal, Nuisance, Oppression, Outrage, Packet, Paire, Prejudice, Rifle, RSI, Scaith, Scath(e), Scotch, Sore, Sprain, Tene, Tort, Trauma, Umbrage, Whiplash, Wound, Wrong

▶ **Injury** *see* AFTER INJURY

Ink(y) Black, Cyan, Indian, Invisible, Marking, Sepia, Stained

Inlaid, Inlay(er) Boulle, Buhl, Damascene, Emblemata, Empaestic, Enamel, Enchase, Incrust, Intarsia, Intarsio, Marquetrie, Marquetry, Piqué, Set, Tarsia, Veneer

Inlet Arm, Bay, Cove, Creek, Entry, Fiord, Firth, Fjord, Fleet, Geo, Gio, Gusset, Infall, Sullom Voe, Table Bay, Wash

▷ **Inlet** *may indicate* 'let' around another word

Inn(s), Innkeeper Albergo, Alehouse, Auberge, Barnard's, Boniface, Caravanserai, Coaching, Gray's, Halfway-house, Host, Hostelry, Hotel, House, Imaret, In, Inner Temple, Khan, Ladin(ity), Law, Licensee, Lincoln's, Lodging, Luckie, Lucky, Middle Temple, Padrone, Parador, Patron, Porterhouse, Posada, Posthouse, Pothouse, Publican, Roadhouse, Ryokan, Serai, Tabard, Tavern(er), Victualler

▷ **Inn** *may refer to* the law

Innards Entrails, Giblets, Gizzard, Guts, Harigals, Harslet, Haslet, Rein, Viscera

▶ **Innkeeper** *see* INN

Innocent Absolved, Angelic, Arcadian, Babe, Blameless, Canny, Chaste, Cherub, Childlike, Clean, Doddypoll, Dodipoll, Dove, Encyclical, Green, Idyllic, Ingenue, Lamb, Lily-white, Maiden, Naive, Opsimath, Pope, > PURE, Sackless, Seely, Simple, St, White

Innu Naskapi

Inoperative Futile, Nugatory, Silent, Void

Inordinate Excessive, Irregular, Undue

▷ **Inordinately** *may indicate* an anagram

In place of For, Qua, Vice, With

Inquest Debriefing, Hearing, Inquiry, Investigation

Inquire, Inquiring, Inquiry Ask, Demand, Investigation, Nose, Organon, Probe, Query, Question, See, Speer, Speir

Inquisition, Inquisitive, Iniquisitor Curious, Interrogation, Meddlesome, Nosy, Prying, Rubberneck, Snooper, Stickybeak, Torquemada

▷ **In revolt, In revolution** *may indicate* an anagram

Insane, Insanity Absurd, Batty, Crazy, Deranged, Loco, Mad, Manic, Paranoia, Pellagra, Psycho, Schizo

Inscribe(d), Inscription Chisel, Colophon, Dedicate, Emblazon, Engrave, Enter, Epigraph, Epitaph, Graffiti, Hic jacet, Hierograph, Lapidary, Legend, Lettering, Writ

Insect(s) Entomic, Nonentity, Non-person

Insectivore Agoura, Desman, Donaea, Drosera, Hedgehog, Jacamar, Nepenthaceae, Tanrec, Tenrec(idae), Venus flytrap, Zalambdodont

Insecure Infirm, > **LOOSE**, Precarious, Shaky, Unsafe, Unstable, Unsteady, Vulnerable

Insert(ed), Insertion, Inset Cue, Empiecement, Enchase, Enter, Entry, Foist, Fudge, Godet, Gore, Graft, Gusset, Immit, Imp, Implant, Inject, Inlay, Input, Interject, Interpolate, Interpose, Intersperse, Introduce, Intromit, Mitre, Pin, Sandwich

Inside(r) Content, Core, Entrails, Gaol, Heart, Indoors, Interior, Internal, Interne, Inward, Inwith, Mole, Tum, > **WITHIN**

Insignia Armour, Arms, Badger, Charge, Chevron, Mark, Regalia, Ribbon, Roundel, Tab

Insignificant (person) Dandiprat, Fico, Fiddling, Flea-bite, Fractional, Gnat, Inconsiderable, Insect, Mickey Mouse, Minimus, Miniscule, Minnow, Nebbich, Nobody, Nominal, Nonentity, One-eyed, Petit, Petty, Pipsqueak, Quat, Scoot, Scout, Scrub, Shrimp, Slight, Small potatoes, Small-time, Squirt, Squit, Tenuous, Trifling, Trivial, Two-bit, Unimportant, Venial, Warb, Whippersnapper

Insincere Affected, Artificial, Barmecide, Cant, Double, Double-faced, Empty, Factitious, Faithless, False, Glib, Greenwash, Hollow, Janus-faced, Lip service, Mealy-mouthed, Meretricious, Mouth-made, Pseudo, Shallow, Synthetic, Two-faced

Insipid Banal, Blab, Bland, Fade, Flat, Insulse, Jejune, Lash, Mawkish, Shilpit, Tame, Tasteless, Vapid, Weak, Wearish

Insist(ent) Assert, Demand, Dogmatic, Exact, > **STIPULATE**, Stress, Swear, Threap, Threep, Urge

Insolence, Insolent Audacity, Bardy, Brassy, Cheek, Contumely, Effrontery, Gum, Hubris, Hybris, Impudence, Lip, Rude, Snash, Stroppy, Wanton

Insolvent Bankrupt, Broke, Destitute, Penniless

Inspect(ion), Inspector Alnage(r), Auditor, Comb, Conner, Examine, Government, Investigator, Jerque, Keeker, Muster, Once-over, Peep, Perlustrate, Proveditor, Rag-fair, Recce, Review, Scrutinise, Survey, Test, Vet, Vidimus, Visitation

Inspiration, Inspire(d), Inspiring Actuate, Aerate, Afflatus, Aganippe, Animate, Brainstorm, Brainwave, Breath(e), Castalian, Draw, Elate, Exalt, Fire, Flash, Hearten, Hunch, Idea, Illuminate, Impulse, Induce, Inflatus, Infuse, Move, Muse, Pegasus, Prompt, Prophetic, Satori, Sniff(le), Stimulus, Taghairm, Theopneust(y), Uplift, Vatic

Install(ation) Enchase, Enthrone, Inaugurate, Induction, Infrastructure, Insert, Invest, Put (in)

Instalment Episode, Fascicle, Heft, Livraison, Never-never, Part, Serial, Tranche

Instance, Instant As, Case, Example, Flash, Jiffy, Moment, Present, Say, Shake, Spur, Tick, Trice, Twinkling, Urgent

Instead (of) Deputy, For, Lieu, Locum, Vice

Instigate Arouse, Foment, Impel, Incite, Prompt, Spur

Instinct(ive) Automatic, Flair, Herd, Id, Impulse, Inbred, Innate, Intuition, Nature, Nose, Talent, Tendency, Visceral

Institute, Institution Academy, Activate, Asylum, Bank, Begin, Bring, Charity, College, Erect, Found(ation), I, Inaugurate, MORI, Orphanage, Poorhouse, Raise, Redbrick, Retraict, Retrait(e), Retreat, Smithsonian, Start, University, Women's, Workhouse

Instruct(ed), Instruction, Instructor Advice, Apprenticeship, Brief, Catechism, Clinic, Coach, Course, Didactic, Direct(ive), Document, Edify, Educate, Ground(ing), Inform, Lesson, Manual, Notify, Order, Percept, Recipe, Rubric, Swami, > TEACH, Train, Tutelage, Tutorial, Up

Instrument(al) Ablative, Act, Agent, Helpful, Mean(s), > MUSICAL INSTRUMENT, Negotiable, > RESPONSIBLE, > TOOL, > UTENSIL

Insubordinate Contumacious, Faction, Mutinous, Rebel, Refractory

Insubstantial Airy, Brief, Flimsy, Frothy, Illusory, Jackstraw, Slight, Thin, Wispy, Ye(a)sty

Insult(ing) Abuse, Affront, Aspersion, Barb, Contumely, Cut, Dyslogistic, Embarrass, Facer, Fig, Lese-majesty, Mud, Mud-pie, Offend, Opprobrious, Skit, Slagging, Slight, Slur, Snub, Trauma, Uncomplimentary, Verbal, Yenta, Yente

Insurance, Insure(r) Abandonee, Cover, Fire, Guarantee, Hedge, Indemnity, Knock-for-knock, Life, Lloyds, Medicare, Mutual, National, Policy, Reversion, Security, Underwrite

Insurgent, Insurrection Cade, Mutiny, Outbreak, Rebel, Revolt, Sedition

▷ **Insurgent** *may indicate* 'reversed'

Intact Complete, Entire, Inviolate, Unused, Whole

Integrate(d), Integration Amalgamate, Assimilate, Combine, Fuse, Harmonious, Mainstream, Merge

Integrity Honesty, Principle, Rectitude, Strength, Uprightness, Whole

Intellect, Intellectual(s) Academic, Aptitude, Brain, Cerebral, Dianoetic, Egghead, Eggmass, Far-out, Genius, Highbrow, Intelligent, Intelligentsia, -ist, Learned, Literati, Luminary, Mastermind, Mental(ity), Mind, Noesis, Noetic, Noology, Nous, Profound, Reason, Titan

Intelligence, Intelligent Advice, Artificial, Boss, Brains, Bright, CIA, Discerning, Dope, Eggmass, Emotional, Esprit, G, Grey matter, GRU, Info, Ingenious, IQ, Knowledgeable, Machiavellian, Machine, MI, Mossad, Mother wit, News, Pate, Pointy-headed, Rational, Sconce, Sense, Sharp, Shrewd, Spetsnaz, Spetznaz, Tidings, Wit

Intend(ed), Intending Allot, Contemplate, Design, Destine, Ettle, Fiancé(e), Going, > MEAN, Meditate, Propose, Purpose

Intense, Intensify, Intensity Acute, Aggravate, Ardent, Earnest, Earthquake, Emotional, Enhance, Escalate, Excess, Extreme, Fervent, Keen, Luminous, Might, Profound, Radiant, Redouble, Sharpen, Vehement, Vivid

Intent, Intention(al) A dessein, Animus, Deliberate, Dole, Earnest, Hellbent, Manifesto, Mens rea, Mind, Purpose, Rapt, Resolute, Set, Studious, Systematic, Thought, Witting, Yrapt

Interaction Enantiodromia, Solvation

Intercede, Intercession Mediate, Negotiate, Plead, Prayer

Intercom Entryphone®

Interdict Ban, Forbid, Prohibit, Taboo

Interest(ed), Interesting Amusive, APR, Attention, Behalf, Benefit, Clou,

Compound, Concern, Contango, Coupon, Dividend, Ear-grabbing, Engage, Engross, Enthusiasm, Fad, Fee-simple, Fee-tail, Grab, Hot, Human, Import, Income, Insurable, Int(o), Intrigue, Landed, Life, Line, Negative, Part, Partisan, Percentage, Readable, Rente, Respect, Revenue, Scene, Share, Side, Sideline, Simple, Spice, Stake, Topical, Usage, Usance, Usure, Usury, Vested, Vig(orish), Warm

Interfere(r), **Interference** Busybody, Clutter, Disrupt, Hamper, Hinder, Intrude, Mar, Molest, Officious, Pry, Shash, Static, Tamper, Teratogen

Interim Break, Meanwhile, Temporary

Interior Backblocks, Cyclorama, Domestic, Innards, Innate, Inner, Inside, Outback, Plain, Up-country, Vitals

Interject(ion) Ahem, Begorra(h), Haith, Hoo-oo, Interpolate, Lumme, Nation, Sese(y), Sessa, 'Sheart, 'Slid, Tarnation, Tush

Interlace Mingle, Weave, Wreathe

Interloper Gate-crasher, Intruder, Trespasser

Interlude Antimask, Antimasque, Divertimento, Entr'acte, Interruption, Kyogen, Lunch-hour, Meantime, Pause, Verset

Intermediary, **Intermediate** Agent, Bardo, Comprador(e), Go-between, Instar, Mean, Medial, Mesne, Mezzanine, Middleman, Middle-of-the-road

Intermission Apyrexia, Break, Interval, Pause, Recess

Intermittent Broken, Fitful, Periodic, Random, Spasmic, Spasmodic, Sporadic

Intern(e) Confine, Doctor, Impound, Restrict, Trainee

Internal Domestic, Inner, Internecine, Inward, Within

International Cap, Cosmopolitan, Lion, UN, Universal

Interpret(er) Conster, Construe, Decipher, Decode, Dragoman, Exegete, Explain, Exponent, Expositor, Expound, Glossator, Hermeneutist, Jehovist, Linguistic, Linkster, Medium, Prophet, Read, Rede, Render, Represent, Spokesman, Textualist, > TRANSLATE, Ulema

Interpretation Anagoge, Anagogy, Construction, Copenhagen, Eisegesis, Exegesis, Exegete, Gematria, Gloss(ary), Gospel, Halacha(h), Halakah, Hermeneutics, Midrash, Portray, Reading, Rede, Rendition, Targum, Translation

Interrogate, **Interrogation** Catechism, Debrief(ing), Enquire, Examine, Grill, Pump, > QUESTION, Quiz

Interrupt(ion), **Interrupter** Ahem, Blip, Break, Butt, Chequer, Chip in, Disturb, Entr'acte, Heckle, Hiatus, Intercept, Interfere, Interpellate, Interpolate, Interpose, Interregnum, Intrusion, Pause, Portage, Rheotome, Stop, Suspend

Intersect(ion) Carfax, Carfox, Chiasm(a), Cross, Crunode, Cut, Decussate, Divide, Groin, Metacentre, Orthocentre, Trace

Intersperse Dot, Interpose, Scatter, Sprinkle

Intertwine Braid, Knit, Lace, Plait, Splice, Twist, Writhe

Interval Between, Break, Breather, Class, Closed, Comma, Diesis, Distance, Duodecimo, Entr'acte, Fifth, Gap, Half-time, Hiatus, Hourly, Interim, Interlude, Interregnum, Interspace, Interstice, Meantime, Meanwhile, Ninth, Octave, Ottava, Pycnon, Respite, Rest, Schisma, Semitone, Sixth, Space, Span, Spell, Wait

Intervene, **Intervention** Agency, Arbitrate, Interfere, Interjacent, Interrupt, Mediate, Mesne, Theurgy, Up

Interview Audience, Audition, Conference, Examine, Hearing, Oral, Press conference, See, Vox pop

Interweave, **Interwoven**, **Interwove** Entwine, Interlace, Monogram, Plait, Plash, Pleach, Raddle, Wreathed

Intestinal, **Intestine(s)** Bowel, Chit(ter)lings, Derma, Duodenum, Enteric,

Entrails, Guts, Harigals, Innards, Jejunum, Kishke, Large, Mesenteron, Omenta, Rectum, Small, Splanchnic, Thairm, Viscera

Intimacy, Intimate(ly) Achates, Boon, Bosom, Communion, Connote, Familiar, Friend, Inmost, Innuendo, Intrigue, Nearness, Opine, Pack, Private, Signal, Special, Thick, Throng, Warm, Well

Intimidate, Intimidating Browbeat, Bulldoze, Bully, Cow, Daunt, Dragon, Hector, Psych, Threaten, Unnerve

Intolerable, Intolerant Allergic, Bigotry, Excessive, Illiberal, Impossible, Ombrophobe, Self-righteous

Intone, Intonation Cadence

Intoxicant, Intoxicate(d), Intoxicating, Intoxication Bhang, Swacked, Zonked

Intractable Disobedient, Kittle, Mulish, Obdurate, Perverse, Surly, Unruly, Wilful

Intransigent Adamant, Inflexible, Rigid, Uncompromising

Intrepid Aweless, Bold, Brave, Dauntless, Doughty, Firm, > **RESOLUTE**, Valiant

Intricate Complex, Daedal(ian), Daedale, Dedal, Gordian, Intrince, Involute, Knotty, Pernickety, Tricky, Vitruvian

Intrigue(r), Intriguing Affaire, Artifice, Brigue, Cabal, Camarilla, Cloak and dagger, Collogue, Conspiracy, Fascinate, Hotbed, Ignatian, Jesuit, Jobbery, Liaison, Machinate, Plot, Politic, Rat, > **SCHEME**, Strategy, Traffic, Trinketer

▷ **Intrinsically** *may indicate* something within a word

Introduce(r), Introduction, Introductory Acquaint, Anacrusis, Curtain-raiser, Emcee, Enseam, Exordial, Foreword, Immit, Import, Induct, Initiate, Inject, Insert, Instil(l), Intercalate, Interpolate, Introit, Isagogic, Lead-in, Opening, Plant, Preamble, Preface, Preliminary, Prelude, Prelusory, Preparatory, Present, Proem, Prolegomena, Prolegomenon, Prologue, Proponent, Referral, Start, Usher

▷ **Introduction** *may indicate* a first letter

▷ **In trouble** *may indicate* an anagram

Intrude(r), Intrusion, Intrusive Abate, Aggress, Annoy, Bother, Burglar, > **ENCROACH**, Gatecrash, Interloper, Invade, Meddle, Nosey, Porlocking, Presume, Raid, Sorn, Trespass

Intuition, Intuitive Belief, ESP, Hunch, Insight, Instinct, Noumenon, Premonition, Seat-of-the-pants, Telepathy

▷ **In two words** *may indicate* a word to be split

Inundate, Inundation Flood, Overflow, Overwhelm, Submerge, Swamp

Inure Acclimatise, Accustom, Harden, Season, Steel

Invade(r), Invasion Angle, Attack, Attila, Dane, Descent, Encroach, Hacker, Hengist, Horsa, Hun, Infest, Inroad, Intruder, Jute, Lombard, Martian, Norman, Norsemen, Ostrogoth, Overrun, Permeate, Raid, Trespass, Vandal

Invalid(ate), Invalidation Bad, Bogus, Bunbury, Cancel, Chronic, Clinic, Defunct, Diriment, Erroneous, Expired, False, Inauthentic, Inform, Inoperative, Irritate, Lapsed, Nugatory, Null, Nullify, Refute, Shut-in, Terminate, Vitiate, Void

Invaluable Essential, Excellent, Precious, Useful

Invariable, Invariably Always, Constant, Eternal, Habitual, Perpetual, Steady, Uniform

Invective Abuse, Billingsgate, Diatribe, Philippic, Reproach, Ribaldry, Tirade

Invent(ion), Inventive Adroit, Babe, Baby, Brainchild, Chimera, Coin, Contrive, Cook up, > **CREATE**, Daedal, Design, Device, Excogitate, Fabricate, Fain, Fantasia, Feign, Figment, Imaginary, Improvise, Ingenuity, Mint, Originate, Patent,

Pretence, Resourceful, Synectics, Whittle, Wit

Inventor Archimedes, Arkwright, Artificer, Author, Babbage, Baird, Bell, Biro, Boys, Bramah, Cartwright, Celsius, Coiner, Creator, Crompton, Daedalus, Edison, Engineer, Galileo, Geiger, Hansom, Jubal, Marconi, Maxim, Minié, Mint-master, Morse, Nernst, Newcomen, Nobel, Patentee, Savery, Siemens, Tesla, Torricelli, Tull, Watt, Wheatstone, Whitney

Inventory Account, Index, Itemise, List, Register, Stock

Inversion, Invert(ed) Capsize, Chiasmus, Entropion, Entropium, Opposite, Overset, Reverse, Turn, Upset

Invertebrate Annelida, Anthozoan, Arthropod, Brachiopod, Crinoid, Ctenophore, Decapod, Echinoderm, Echinoid, Euripterid, Feather star, Gast(e)ropod, Globigerina, Hydrozoan, Mollusc, Onychophoran, Parazoan, Pauropod, Peritrich, Polyp, Poriferan, Protostome, Rotifer, Roundworm, Scyphozoan, Sea-cucumber, Sea-lily, Spineless, Starfish, Tardigrade, Trepang, Trochelminth, Water bear, Worm, Zoophyte

Invest(or), Investment Ambient, Angel, Beleaguer, Besiege, Bet, Blockade, Blue-chip, Capitalist, Contrarian, Dignify, Dub, Embark, Enclothe, Endow, Enrobe, Ethical, Financier, Flutter, Gilt, Girt, Holding, Infeft, Install, On, Pannicle, Parlay, Place, Portfolio, Put, Ring, Robe, Saver, Share, Siege, Sink, Spec, Speculation, Stag, Stake, Stock, Tessa, Trust, Trustee, Venture

▷ **Invest** *may indicate* one word surrounding another

Investigate, Investigator, Investigation Canvass, Case, CID, Delve, Examine, Explore, Fed, Fieldwork, Hunt, Inquest, Inquirendo, Inquiry, Inquisition, McCarthyism, Nose, Organon, Organum, Probe, Pry, Quester, Rapporteur, Research, Scan, Scrutinise, Search, Sleuth, Snoop, Study, Suss, Tec, Test, T-man, Track, Try, Zetetic

Inveterate Chronic, Dyed-in-the-wool, Habitual, Hardened

Invidious Harmful, Hostile, Malign

Invigorate, Invigorating, Invigoration Analeptic, Brace, Brisk, Cheer, Elixir, Energise, Enliven, Fortify, Insinew, Pep, Refresh, Renew, Stimulate, Tonic, Vital

Invincible Almighty, Brave, Stalwart, Valiant

Invisible Hidden, Imageless, Infra-red, Secret, Tusche, Unseen

Invite, Invitation, Inviting Ask, Attract, Bid, Call, Card, Overture, > REQUEST, Solicit, Stiffie, Summons, Tempt, Woo

Invocation, Invoke Appeal, Call, Conjure, Curse, Entreat, Epiclesis, Solicit

Invoice Account, Bill, Itemise, Manifest, Pro forma

Involve(d), Involvement Commitment, Complicate, Complicit, Concern, Embroil, Engage, Entail, Envelop, Imbroglio, Immerse, > IMPLICATE, Include, Intricate, Meet, Necessitate, Tangle

▷ **Involved** *may indicate* an anagram

Inward(s) Afferent, Homefelt, Introrse, Mental, Private, Varus, Within

Iolanthe Peri

Iota Atom, Jot, Subscript, Whit

IOU Cedula, Market, PN, Vowels

Iran(ian) Babist, Kurd, Mede, Parsee

Irascible Choleric, Crusty, Fiery, Peevish, Snappy, Tetchy

Irate Angry, Cross, Infuriated, Wrathful

Ire Anger, Cholera, Fury, Rage, Wrath

Irenic Peaceful

Iridescence, Iridescent Chatoyant, Opaline, Reflet, Shimmering, Shot, Water-gall

Iris Areola, Eye, Flag, Fleur-de-lis, Gladdon, Ixia, Lily, Lis, Orris, Rainbow, Sedge, Seg, Sunbow

Irish(man) Bark, Bog-trotter, Boy, Celt(ic), Clan-na-gael, Defender, Dermot, Dubliner, Eamon(n), Eirann, Erse, Fenian, Gaeltacht, Goidel, Greek, Keltic, Kern(e), Mick(e)(y), Milesian, Mulligan, Ogamic, Orange(man), Ostmen, Paddy(-whack), Partholon, Pat(rick), Rapparee, Redshank, Reilly, Riley, Rory, Sean, Shoneen, Teague, Ultonian

Iron(s), Ironwork(s) Airn, Alpha, Angle, Beta, Carron, Cautery, Chains, Chalybeate, Chancellor, Channel, Climbing, Coquimbite, Corrugated, Cramp(on), Crampon, Crimp, Cross, Curling, Curtain, Delta, Derringer, Dogs, Eagle-stone, Fayalite, Fe, Ferredoxin, Ferrite, Fetter, Fiddley, Flip-dog, Galvanised, Gamma, Gem, Golfclub, Goose, Grappling, Grim, Grozing, > **GUN**, Gyve, Horse, Ingot, Italian, Kamacite, Laterite, Lily, Maiden, Malleable, Marcasite, Mars, Martensite, Mashie, Mashy, Meteoric, Pea, Pig, > **PRESS**, Pro-metal, Rabble, Rations, Rod, Sad, Shooting, Smoother, Soft, Soldering, Spiegeleisen, Steam, Stirrup, Stretching, Strong, Taconite, Taggers, Terne, Tin terne, Toggle, Tow, Wafer, Waffle, Wear, Wedge, White, Wrought

Ironic, Irony Antiphrasis, Asteism, Dramatic, Meiosis, Metal, Ridicule, Sarcasm, Satire, Socratic, Tongue-in-cheek, Tragic, Trope, Wry

▶ **Ironwork(s)** *see* **IRON**

Irrational Absurd, Brute, Delirious, Foolish, Illogical, Superstitious, Surd, Wild

Irregular(ity) Abnormal, Anomaly, A salti, Asymmetric, Bashi-bazouk, Blotchy, Crazy, Erratic, Evection, Fitful, Flawed, Formless, Guerilla, Heteroclitic, Incondite, Inordinate, Kink, Occasional, Orthotone, Para-military, Partisan, Patchy, Random, Scalene, Sebundy, Solecism, Sporadic, TA, Uneven, Unsteady, Variable, Wayward, Zigzag

▷ **Irregular** *may indicate* an anagram

Irrelevant Digression, Gratuitous, Immaterial, Inept

Irreproachable Blameless, Spotless, Stainless

Irresistible Almighty, Endearing, Inevitable, Mesmeric, Overwhelming

Irresolute, Irresolution Doubtful, Hesitant, Timid, Unsure

Irresponsible Capricious, Feckless, Flighty, Slap-happy, Strawen, Trigger-happy, Wanton, Wildcat

Irreverent Disrespectful, Impious, Profane

Irrigate, Irrigation Colonic, Enema, Flood, Water

Irritable, Irritability, Irritant, Irritate(d), Irritation Acerbate, Anger, Annoy, Bête noire, Blister, Bug, Chafe, Chauff, Chippy, Chocker, Crabby, Cross-grained, Crosspatch, Crotchety, Crusty, Dod, Dyspeptic, Eat, Edgy, Enchafe, Erethism, Ewk, Exasperate, Fantod, Feverish, Fiery, Fleabite, Frabbit, Fractious, Fraught, Fretful, Gall, Get, Goad, Grate, Gravel, Hasty, Heck, Intertrigo, Irk, Itch, Jangle, Livery, Mardy, Narky, Needle, Nettle, Niggly, Ornery, Peckish, Peevish, Peppery, Pesky, Pestilent(ial), Pet, Petulance, Pinprick, Pique, Prickly, Provoke, Rag'd, Ragde, Rankle, Rasp, Rattle, Ratty, Rile, Roil, Rub, Ruffle, Savin(e), Scratchy, Shirty, Snappy, Snit, Snitchy, Splenetic, Sting, Tease, Techy, Testy, Tetchy, Thorn, Tickle, Toey, Touchy, Uptight, > **VEX**, Waxy

▷ **Irritated** *may indicate* an anagram

Islam(ic) Crescent, Druse, Druz(e), Kurd(ish), Senus(si), Sheriat, Shia(h), Shiite, Wah(h)abi

Island, Isle(t) Ait, Archipelago, Atoll, Cay, Char, Desert, Eyot, Floating, Holm, I, Inch, Is, Key, Lagoon, Mainland, Motu, Refuge, Traffic

Isn't Aint, Nis, Nys

Isolate(d) Ancress, Backwater, Cut off, Enclave, Enisle, Incommunicado, Inisle,

In vacuo, Island, Lone, Maroon, Pocket, Quarantine, Sea-girt, Seclude, Secret, Segregate, Separate, Sequester, Solitary, Sporadic, Stray

Isopod Gribble

Isotope Actinon, Deuterium, Muonium, Protium, Strontium-90, Thoron, Tritium

Issue(s) Children, Come, Crux, Debouch, Denouement, Derive, Disclose, Dispense, Edition, Effluence, Egress, Emerge, Emit, Escape, Exit, Exodus, Family, Feigned, Fiduciary, Flotation, Fungible, General, Government, Gush, Ish, Litter, Material, Number, Offspring, Outflow, Part, Proof, Publish, Result, Rights, Sally, Seed, Side, Son, Spawn, Special, Spring, Stream, Subject, Topic, Turn, Utter

Isthmus Darien, Karelian, Kra, Neck, Panama

It A, Chic, Hep, Id, Italian, Oomph, SA, 't, Vermouth

Italian, Italy Alpini, Ausonia, Bolognese, Calabrian, Chian, Dago, Ding, Este, Etnean, Etrurian, Etruscan, Eyeti(e), Eytie, Faliscan, Florentine, Genoese, Ghibelline, Guelf, Guelph, Hesperia, Irredentist, It, Latian, Latin, Lombard, Medici, Moro, Oscan, Paduan, Patarin(e), Roman, Sabine, Samnite, Sicel, Sienese, Signor(i), Sikel, Spag, Tuscan, Umbrian, Venetian, Vermouth, Volscian, Wop

Itch(ing), Itchiness Annoy, Cacoethes, Dhobi, Prickle, Prurience, Prurigo, Pruritis, Psora, Scabies, Scrapie, Seven-year, Tickle, > URGE

Item(ise) Also, Article, Bulletin, Detail, Entry, Flash, List, Number, Piece, Point, Spot, Too, Topic

Itinerant, Itinerary Ambulant, Didakai, Didakei, Did(d)icoy, Gipsy, Gypsy, Journey, Log, Pedlar, Peripatetic, Pie-powder, Roadman, Roamer, Romany, Rootless, Route, Stroller, Traveller

Ivory (tower) Bone, Dentine, Distant, Eburnean, Impractical, Incisor, Key, Solitude, Teeth, Tusk, Vegetable

Ivy Ale-hoof, Aralia, Boston, Bush, Climber, Creeper, Grape, Hedera, Helix, Japanese, Poison, Shield, Weeping

Izzard Z

Jj

Jab(ber) Chatter, Foin, Gabble, Immunologist, Inject, Jaw, Jook, Nudge, Poke, Prattle, Prod, Proke, Punch, Puncture, Sook, Sputter, Stab, Venepuncture, Yak

Jack(s) AB, Apple, Ass, Ball, Boot, Bowl(s), Boy, Card, Cheap, Coatcard, Crevalle, Deckhand, Dibs(tones), Five stones, Flag, Frost, Hoist, Honour, Horner, Hydraulic, Idle, J, Jock, Ketch, Kitty, Knave, London, Lumber, Mark, Matlow, Mistress, Nob, Noddy, Pilot, Point, Pot, Pur, Rabbit, Raise, Rating, Ripper, Robinson, Russell, Sailor, Salt, Screw, Sprat, Spring-heeled, Springtail, Steeple, Sticker, Straw, Tar, Tee, Tradesman, Turnspit, Union, Uplift, Wood, Yellow

Jacket Acton, Afghanistan, Amauti(k), Anorak, Baju, Bania(n), Banyan, Barbour®, Basque, Battle, Bed, Blazer, Blouson, Body-warmer, Bolero, Bomber, Brigandine, Bumfreezer, Bush, Cagoul(e), Camisole, Cardigan, Carmagnole, Casing, > **COAT**, Dinner, Dolman, Donkey, Drape, Dressing, Duffel coat, Duffle coat, Dust-cover, Dustwrapper, Fearnought, Flak, Fleece, Gambeson, Gendarme, Grego, Habergeon, Hacking, Ha(c)queton, Half-kirtle, Hug-me-tight, Jerkin, Jupon, Kagool, Life, Life preserver, Lumber, Mackinaw, Mae West, Mandarin, Mao, Matinée, Mess, Monkey, Nehru, Newmarket, Norfolk, Parka, Pea, Pilot, Polka, Potato, Reefer, Safari, Shell, Shortgown, Simar(re), Slip-cover, Smoking, Spencer, Sports, Steam, Strait, Tabard, Tailcoat, Toreador, Tunic, Tux(edo), Tweed, Vareuse, Waistcoat, Wam(m)us, Wampus, Water, Windbreaker®, Windcheater, Windjammer, Wrapper, Zouave

Jackknife Dive, Fold, Jockteleg, Pike

Jade(d) Axe-stone, Cloy, Crock, Exhaust, Fatigue, Greenstone, Hack, Hag, Horse, Hussy, Limmer, Minx, Nag, Nephrite, Sate, Screw, Slut, Stale, Tired, Trite, Weary, Yu(-stone)

Jaeger Skua

Jag(ged) Barbed, Cart, Drinking, Erose, Gimp, Injection, Laciniate, Ragde, Ragged, Serrate, Snag, Spree, Spur, Tooth

Jaguar Car, Caracal, Cat, E-type, Ounce, Tiger

Jail(er) Adam, Alcatraz, Bedford, Bin, Can, Clink, Cooler, Gaol, Hoosegow, Imprison, Incarcerate, Jug, Keeper, Lockup, Marshalsea, Newgate, Nick, Pen, Pokey, > **PRISON**, Screw, Shop, Strangeways, Turnkey, Warder

Jailbird Con, Lag, Lifer, Trusty

Jalopy Banger, Boneshaker, Buggy, Car, Crate, Heap, Stock-car

Jam(my) Block, Choke, Clog, Confiture, Crush, Cushy, Dilemma, Gridlock, Hold-up, Jeelie, Jeely, Lock, Log, Plight, > **PREDICAMENT**, Preserve, Press, Quince, Seize, Snarl-up, Spot, Squeeze, Stick, Tailback, Traffic, Vice, Vise, Wedge

Jamb Doorpost, Durn, Sconcheon, Scontion, Scuncheon, Upright

Jane Austen, Calamity, Eyre, Seymour, Shore, Sian

Jangle Clank, Clapperclaw, Clash, Rattle, Wrangle

Japan(ese), Japanese drama Ainu, Burakumin, Daimio, Eta, Geisha, Genro, Gloss, Haiku, Heian, Hondo, Honshu, Issei, Kabuki, Kami, Kana, Kirimon, Lacquer, Mandarin, Mikado, Mousmé, Mousmee, Nippon, Nisei, No(h), Resin, Sansei, Satsuma, Shinto, Shogun, Togo, Tycoon, Yamato

Jar(ring) Albarello, Amphora, Bell, Canopus, Churr, Clash, Crock, Cruet, Din, Dolium, Enrough, Gallipot, Grate, Greybeard, Gride, Grind, Gryde, Humidor, Hydria, > JOLT, Kalpis, Kang, Kilner®, Leyden, Mason, Off-key, Olla, Pint, Pithos, Pot(iche), Rasp, Shelta, Shock, Stamnos, Start, Stean, Steen, Stein, Tankard, Tinaja, Turn, Vessel, Water-monkey

Jargon Argot, Baragouin, Beach-la-mar, Buzzword, Cant, Chinook, Eurobabble, Eurospeak, Gobbledegook, Gobbledygook, Jive, Kennick, Legalese, Lingo, Lingoa geral, Lingua franca, Mumbo-jumbo, Newspeak, Parlance, Patois, Patter, Shelta, Shoptalk, > SLANG, Technospeak, Vernacular

Jaundice(d) Cynical, Icterus, Prejudiced, Sallow, Yellow

Jaunt Journey, Outing, Sally, Stroll, Swan, Trip

Jaunty Airy, Akimbo, Chipper, Debonair, Perky, Rakish

▷ **Jaunty** *may indicate* an anagram

Javelin Dart, Gavelock, Harpoon, Jereed, Jerid, Pile, Pilum, Spear

Jaw(s), Jawbone Blab, Chaft, Chap, Chat, Chaw, Cheek, Chide, Chin, Entry, Glass, Gnathite, Gonion, Jobe, Lantern, Mandible, Maxilla, Mesial, Muzzle, Mylohyoid, Natter, Opisthognathous, Overshot, Phossy, Pi, Premaxillary, Prognathous, Ramus, Shark, Stylet, Underhung, Undershot, Wapper-jaw, Ya(c)kety-Ya(c)k

Jazz(er), Jazzman Acid, Barber, Barrelhouse, Bebop, Blues, Boogie, Boogie-woogie, Bop, Cat, Cool, Dixieland, Enliven, Gig, Gutbucket, Hipster, Jive, Latin, Lick, Mainstream, Modern, Progressive, Ragtime, Riff, Scat, Skiffle, Stomp, Swinger, Trad, Traditional

Jealous(y) Envious, Green(-eyed), Grudging, Zelotypia

Jeer(ing) Barrack, Belittle, Birl, Boo, Burl, Digs, Fleer, Flout, Gird, Hoot, Jape, Jibe, > MOCK, Rail, Razz, Ridicule, Scoff, Sneer, Taunt

Jehovah God, Lord, Yahve(h), Yahwe(h)

Jelly Agar(-agar), Aspic, Brawn, Calf's foot, Chaudfroid, Comb, > EXPLOSIVE, Flummery, Gel, Isinglass, Jam, Medusa, Mineral, Mould, Napalm, Petroleum, Royal, Vaseline®

▷ **Jelly** *may indicate* an anagram

Jellyfish Aurelia, Box, Cnidaria, Medusa, Portuguese man-of-war, Sea-blubber, Sea-nettle, Sea-wasp

Jenny Ass, Lind, Mule, Spinner, Spinster, Wren

Jeopardise, Jeopardy Danger, Expose, Hazard, Peril, Risk

Jerk(y), Jerkily, Jerking, Jerks Aerobics, A salti, Bob, Braid, Cant, Diddle, Ebrillade, Flirt, Flounce, Gym(nastics), Hike, Hitch, Hoi(c)k, Jut, Kant, PE, Peck, Physical, Saccade, Shove, Spasm, Start, Surge, Sydenham's chorea, Tic, Toss(en), Tweak, > TWITCH, Wrench, Yank

Jerry, Jerry-built Boche, Flimsy, Fritz, Hun, Kraut, Mouse, Po(t)

Jersey(s) Cow, Frock, Gansey, Guernsey, Kine, Lily, Maillot, Polo, Roll-neck, Singlet, > SWEATER, Sweatshirt, Yellow, Zephyr

Jest(er), Jesting Badinage, Barm, Buffoon, Clown, Cod, Comic, Droll, Jape, Joker, Josh, Miller, Motley, Patch, Quip, Raillery, Ribaldry, Rigoletto, Sport, Toy, Wag, Wit, Yorick

Jesus > CHRIST, Emmanuel, IHS, INRI, Jabers, Lord

Jet Airbus®, Aircraft, Beadblast, Black, Burner, Chirt, Douche, Fountain, Geat, Harrier, Jumbo, Plane, Pump, Soffione, Spirt, Spout, Spray, Spurt, Squirt, Stream, Turbine, Turbo, Vapour

Jettison Discard, Dump, Flotsam, Jetsam, Lagan, Ligan

Jew(ish), Jews Ashkenazi, Chas(s)id, Diaspora, Essene, Falasha, Has(s)id, Hebrew, Kahal, Karaite, Levite, Lubavitch, Maccabee, Mitnag(g)ed, Pharisee,

Sadducee, Semite, Sephardim, Shemite, Shtetl, Tobit, Wandering, Yid(dish)

Jewel(s), Jeweller(y) Agate, Almandine, Artwear, Beryl, Bijouterie, Brilliant, Chrysoprase, Cloisonné, Cornelian, Costume, Crown, Diamond, Earbob, Ear-drop, Emerald, Ewe-lamb, Fabergé, Fashion, Ferron(n)ière, Finery, Garnet, > **GEM**, Girandole, Gracchi, Jade, Junk, Lherzolite, Marcasite, Navette, Olivine, Opal, Parure, Paste, Pavé, Pearl, Pendant, Peridot, Rivière, Rubin(e), Ruby, Sapphire, Sard, Scarab, Smaragd, Solitaire, Stone, Sunburst, Tom, Tomfoolery, Topaz, Torc, Treasure, Trinket

Jib Ba(u)lk, Boggle, Face, Foresail, Genoa, Milk, Reest, Reist, Stay-sail

Jibe Bob, Correspond, Fling, > **JEER**, Mock, Sarcasm, Slant, Taunt

Jig(gle) Bob, Bounce, Dance, Fling, Frisk, Hornpipe, Jog, Juggle

Jilt Discard, Reject, Shed, Throw-over

Jingle(r) Clerihew, Clink, Ditty, Doggerel, Rhyme, Tambourine, Tinkle

Jinx Curse, Hex, Jonah, Kibosh, Spoil, Voodoo, Whammy

Jitter(s), Jittery Coggly, DT, Fidgets, Funk, Jumpy, Nervous, Willies

▷ **Jitter(s)** *may indicate* an anagram

Job(bing) Appointment, Berth, Career, Chore, Comforter, Crib, Darg, Errand, Gig, Homer, Inside, Metier, Oratorio, Patient, Pensum, Plum, Position, Post, Problem, Put-up, Sinecure, Spot, Steady, > **TASK**, Ticket, Trotter, Undertaking, Work

▷ **Job** *may indicate* the biblical character

Jockey Carr, Cheat, Diddle, Jostle, Jump, Lester, Manoeuvre, Rider, Steve, Swindle, Trick, Video, Winter

▷ **Jockey** *may indicate* an anagram

Jocose, Jocular, Jocund Cheerful, Debonair, Facete, Facetious, Jesting, Lepid, Scurril(e), Waggish

Joe(y), Joseph Addison, Dogsbody, GI, Kangaroo, Pal, Roo, Sloppy, Stalin, Surface, Trey

Jog(ger), Joggle, Jog-trot Arouse, Canter, Dunch, Dunsh, Heich-how, Heigh-ho, Hod, Jiggle, Jolt, Jostle, Mosey, Nudge, Prompt, Ranke, Remind, Run, Shake, Shog, Tickle, Trot, Whig

Johannesburg Jozi

Johnny-come-lately Upstart

Join(er), Joined, Joining Accompany, Add, Annex, Associate, Attach, Combine, Conglutinate, Connect, Cope, > **COUPLE**, Dovetail, Engraft, Enlist, Enrol, Enter, Fuse, Glue, Graft, Include, Inosculate, Link, Marry, Meet, Member, Merge, Mix, Regelation, Rivet, Seam, Sew, Solder, Splice, Staple, Tenon, Unite, Wed, Weld, Yoke

Joint(ed) Ankle, Bar, Butt, Carpus, Chine, Clip, Co, Cogging, Colonial goose, Conjunction, Cuit, Cup and ball, Cut, Dive, Dovetail, Drumstick, Elbow, Entrecôte, Fish, Haunch, Heel, Hinge, Hip, Hough, Huck, J, Joggle, Jolly, Junction, Knee, Knuckle, Loin, Marijuana, Meat, Mitre, Mortise, Mutton, Phalange, Phalanx, Pin, Rabbet, Rack, Reefer, Ribroast, Roast, Saddle, Scarf, Seam, Shoulder, Silverside, Sirloin, Splice, Stifle, Straight, Strip, Syndesmosis, T, Tarsus, T-bone, Tenon, Together, Toggle, Tongue and groove, Topside, Undercut, Universal, Water, Weld, Wrist

Joist Bar, Beam, Dormant, Groundsill, I-beam, Rib, Sleeper, Solive, String

Joke(r), Joke-book Banter, Bar, Booby-trap, Card, Chaff, Chestnut, > **CLOWN**, Cod, Comedian, Comic, Crack, Cut-up, Farceur, Farceuse, Fool, Fun, Funster, Gab, Gag, Glike, Guy, Have-on, Hazer, Hoax, Hum, Humorist, Jape, Jest, Jig, Lark, Legpull, Merry-andrew, Merryman, One-liner, Practical, Prank(ster), Pun, Punchline, Quip, Sally, Scherzo, Sick, Skylark, Squib, Standing, Wag, Wheeze, Wild, Wisecrack, Wit

Jollity, Jolly 'Arryish, Bally, Convivial, Cordial, Do, Festive, Galoot, Gaucie, Gaucy,

Gawcy, Gawsy, Gay, Hilarious, Jocose, Jovial, Marine, Mirth, Rag, RM, Roger, Sandboy, Tar, Very

Jolt Bump, Jar, Jig-a jig, Jostle, Jounce, Shake, Shog, Start

▶ **Joseph** see JOE

Josh Chaff, Kid, Rib, Tease

Jostle Barge, Bump, Compete, Elbow, Hustle, Push, Shoulder

Journal Daily, Daybook, Diary, Gazette, Hansard, Lancet, Log, Organ, Paper, Periodical, Pictorial, Punch, Rag, Record, Trade

Journalism, Journalist Cheque-book, Columnist, Commentariat, Contributor, Diarist, Ed, Fleet St, Freelance, (GA) Sala, Gonzo, Hack, Hackery, Hackette, Investigative, Keyhole, Lobby, Muckraker, Newshound, Northcliffe, NUJ, Pepys, Press(man), Reporter, Reviewer, Scribe, Sob sister, Stead, Stringer, Wireman, > WRITER, Yellow

Journey Circuit, Cruise, Errand, Expedition, Eyre, Foray, Hadj, Jaunce, Jaunse, Jaunt, Mush, Odyssey, Passage, Periegesis, Ply, Raik, Rake, Red-eye, Ride, Run, Sentimental, Tour, Travel, Trek, Walkabout

Journeyman Artisan, Commuter, Craftsman, Sterne, Yeoman

Joust Tilt, Tournament, Tourney

Jovial Bacchic, Festive, Genial, Jolly

Joy(ful), Joyous Blithe, > DELIGHT, Dream, Ecstasy, Elation, Exulting, Fain, Felicity, Festal, Frabjous, Glad, Glee, Gloat, Hah, Hey, Jubilant, Nirvana, Rapture, Schadenfreude, Sele, Tra-la, Transport, Treat, Yippee

Jubilant, Jubilation, Jubilee Celebration, Cock-a-hoop, Diamond, Ecstatic, Elated, Holiday, Joy, Triumphant

Judas Double-crosser, Traitor, Tree

Judder Put-put, Shake, Vibrate

Judge(ment), Judges Adjudicator, Arbiter, Assess, Assize, Calculate, Connoisseur, Consider, Coroner, Court, Critic(ise), Decide, Dempster, Estimate, Evaluate, Gauge, Guess, Hearing, Honour, Interlocutor, J, Justice, Opinion, Puisne, Reckon(ing), Recorder, Ref(eree), Regard, Sentence, Sheriff, Sober, Solomon, Suppose, Think, Touch, Try, Umpire, Verdict, Wig, Wisdom, Worship

Judicious Critical, Discreet, Politic, Rational, Sage, Sensible, Shrewd, Sound

Jug(s) Amphora, Bird, Blackjack, Can, Cooler, Cream(er), Crock, Ewer, Gaol, Gotch, Pitcher, Pound, Pourer, Pourie, > PRISON, Quad, Quod, Shop, Stir, Toby

Juice, Juicy Bacca, Cassareep, Cassaripe, Cremor, Current, Fluid, Fruity, Gastric, Hypocist, Ichor, La(b)danum, Laser, Latex, Lush, Must, Oil, Pancreatic, Perry, Rare, Sap, Soma, Spanish, Succ(o)us, Succulent, Thridace, Vril, Zest

Jumble Chaos, Conglomeration, Farrago, Garble, Huddle, Jabble, Lumber, Mass, Medley, Mingle-mangle, Mish-mash, Mixter-maxter, Mixture, Pastiche, Raffle, Ragbag, Scramble, Shuffle, Wuzzle

▷ **Jumbled** may indicate an anagram

Jumbo Aircraft, Elephant, Jet, Large-scale, Mammoth, OS

Jump(er), Jumping, Jumpy Aran, Assemble, Axel, Bate, Batterie, Boomer, Bound, Bungee, Bungy, Caper, Capriole, Cicada, Cicata, Crew-neck, Cricket, Croupade, Daffy, Desultory, Entrechat, Euro, Eventer, Flea, Fosbury flop, Gansey, Gazump, Gelande (sprung), Guernsey, Halma, Helicopter, Hurdle, Impala, Itchy, Jersey, Joey, Kangaroo, Katydid, Knight, Lammie, Lammy, Leap(frog), Lep, Lope, Lutz, Nervous, Nervy, Ollie, Parachute, Pig, Pogo, Polo-neck, Pounce, Prance, Prank, Pronking, Puissance, Quantum, Quersprung, Rap, Salchow, Saltatory, Saltigrade, Saltus, Scissors, Scoup, Scowp, Skip, Skipjack, Skydiver, > SPRING, Start, Sweater, Toe (-loop), Trampoline, Triple, Turtle-neck, Vau(l)t, Water, Western roll

Junction Abutment, Alloyed, Box, Bregma, Carfax, Clover-leaf, Connection, Crewe, Crossroads, Intersection, Joint, Josephson, Knitting, Meeting, Point, Raphe, Spaghetti, Suture, T, Union

Jungle Asphalt, Blackboard, Boondocks, Bush, Concrete, Forest

Junior Cadet, Dogsbody, Fils, Petty, Scion, Sub(ordinate), Underling, Younger

Junk(shop) Bric-a-brac, Jettison, Litter, Lorcha, Lumber, Refuse, Ship, Tatt, Trash

▷ **Junk** *may indicate* an anagram

Junket(ing) Beano, Creel, Custard, Feast, Picnic, Rennet, Spree

Juno Lucina

Jurisdiction Authority, Bailiwick, Domain, Province, Soke(n)

Juror(s), Jury Assize, Dicast, Grand, Hung, Inquest, Judges, Mickleton, Old Fury, Pais, Panel, Party, Petit, Petty, Sail, Special, Tales, Tribunal, Venire, Venireman, Venue

Just(ice) Alcalde, All, Aristides, Astraea, Balanced, Condign, Cupar, Deserved, Equal, Equity, E(v)en, Fair, Fair-minded, Forensic, Honest, Impartial, J, Jasper, Jeddart, Jethart, Jurat, Mere, Natural, Nemesis, Newly, Nice, Only, Palm-tree, Piso, Poetic, Provost, Puisne, Pure and simple, Recent, Restorative, Right(ful), Righteous, Rightness, Rough, Shallow, Silence, Simply, Sommer, Street, Themis, Tilt, Upright

Justifiable, Justification, Justify Apology, Autotelic, Avenge, Aver, Avowry, Clear, Darraign(e), Darrain(e), Darrayn, Defend, Deraign, Excusable, Explain, Grounds, Rationale, Vindicate, Warrant

Jut Beetle, Bulge, Overhang, Project, Protrude, Sail

Juvenile Childish, Teenage(r), Yonkers, Young, Younkers

Kk

K Kelvin, Kilo, King, Kirkpatrick

Kangaroo Bettong, Boomer, Boongary, Bounder, Cus-cus, Diprotodont, Euro, Forester, Joey, Macropodidae, Nototherium, Old man, Potoroo, Rat, Steamer, Tree, Troop, Wallaby, Wallaroo

Karate Kung Fu, Wushu

Karma Destiny, Fate, Predestination

Kebab Cevapcici, Gyro, Satay, Sate, Shashli(c)k, Souvlakia

Keel Bilge, Bottom, Carina, Centreboard, Faint, False, Fin, List, Overturn, Skeg(g), Sliding

Keen(ness), Keener Acid, Acute, Agog, Argute, Aspiring, Astute, Athirst, Avid, Aygre, Bemoan, Bewail, Breem, Breme, Cheap, Coronach, Dash, Devotee, Dirge, Eager, Elegy, Enthusiastic, Fanatical, Fell, Greet, Grieve, Hone, Hot, Howl, Into, Lament, Mourn, Mustard, Mute, Narrow, Ochone, Ohone, Partial, Peachy, Perceant, Persant, Raring, Razor, Ready, Red-hot, Rhapsodic, Sharp, Shrewd, Shrill, Snell, Thirsting, Threnodic, Thrillant, Trenchant, Ululate, Wail, Whet, Zeal(ous)

Keep(er), Keeping Ames, Armature, Austringer, Castellan, Castle, Celebrate, Chatelain(e), Citadel, Conceal, Conserve, Curator, Custodian, Custody, Depositary, Depository, Detain, Donjon, Escot, Finder, Fort, Gaoler, Goalie, Guardian, Have, Hoard, > **HOLD**, Maintain, Nab, Net, Observe, Ostreger, Park, Pickle, Preserve, Retain, Safeguard, Stay, Stet, Stock, Store, Stow, Stumper, Support, Sustain, Tower, Warden, Withhold

Keepsake Memento, Souvenir, Token

Keg Barrel, Cask, Tub, Tun, Vat

Kennel(s) Guard, Home, House, Shelter

Kerb Edge, Gutter, Roadside

Kernel Copra, Core, Grain, Nucleus, Praline, Prawlin

Kestrel Bird, Hawk, Keelie, Stallion, Staniel, Stannel

Kettle Boiler, Cauldron, Dixie, Dixy, Drum, Fanny, Pot, Turpin

Key(s), Keyhole A, Ait, Ash, B, C, Cay, Clue, D, E, Essential, F, Flat, Function, G, Ignition, Important, Inch, Index, Islet, Ivory, Linchpin, Major, Minor, Note, Opener, Shift, Signature, Skeleton, Yale®

Keyboard, Keypad Azerty, Console, Digitorium, DVORAK, Manual, Martenot, Piano, Pianola®, Qwerty, Spinet

Kick(ing) Back-heel, Bicycle, Boot, Buzz, Corner, Dribble, Drop, Fling, Flutter, Fly, Free, Frog, Garryowen, Goal, Grub, Hack, Hitch, Hoof, Lash, Nutmeg, Pause, Penalty, Pile, Punce, Punt, Recalcitrate, Recoil, Recoyle, Savate, Scissors, Sixpence, Speculator, Spot, Spur, Spurn, Squib, Stab, Tanner, Tap, Thrill, Toe, Up and under, Vigour, Volley, Wince, Yerk, Zip

Kid(s) Arab, Befool, Billy, Brood, Cheverel, Chevrette, Child, Chit, Con, Delude, Goat, Hoax, Hocus, Hoodwink, Hum, Joke, Leather, Misguide, Nipper, Offspring, Pretend, Rag, Rib, Spoof, Suede, Sundance, > **TEASE**, Tot, Trick, Whiz(z), Wiz

Kidnap Abduct, Hijack, Plagium, Snatch, Spirit, Steal

Kildare Dr

Kill(ed), **Killer**, **Killing** Assassin, Behead, Butcher, Carnage, Category, Choke, Croak, Crucify, Cull, Despatch, Destroy, Electrocute, Euthanasia, Execute, Exterminate, Garotte, Gun, Handsel, Hatchet man, Hilarious, Homicide, Ice, Knacker, Knock off, Liquidate, Lynch, Mactation, Mercy, Mortify, Murder, Necklace, Penalty, Pesticide, Pick off, Predator, Quell, Sacrifice, Serial, Slaughter, Slay(er), Slew, Smite, Spike, Strangle, Thagi, Thug(gee), Top, Toreador, Total, Veto, Waste, Zap

Kilt Drape, Filabeg, Fustanella, Plaid, Tartan

Kin(sman) Ally, Family, Kith, Like, Nearest, Relation

Kind(ly) Akin, Amiable, Avuncular, Benefic, Benevolent, Benign, Boon, Breed, Brood, Brotherly, Category, Class, Clement, Considerate, Favourable, Gender, Generic, Generous, Genre, Gentle, Genus, Good, Humane, Ilk, Kidney, Kin, Lenient, Manner, Modal, Nature, Sisterly, Species, Strain, Strene, Trine, Type, Understanding, Variety, Well-disposed, Ylke

Kindle, **Kindling** Accend, Fire, Ignite, Incense, Incite, Inflame, > LIGHT, Litter, Lunt, Stimulate, Teend, Tind, Tine

King(s), **Kingly** Cobra, English, ER, Evil, Highness, Kong, Majesty, Monarch, Pearly, Penguin, Potentate, R, Ransom, Reigner, Rex, Rial, Roi, Royalet, Ruler, Ryal, Seven, Shilling, Sovereign, Stork

Kingdom, **Kingship** Animal, Aragon, Barataria, Bhutan, Bohemia, Brunel, Dominion, Edom, Elam, Fife, Heptarchy, Jordan, Lydia, Mercia, Meroe, Mineral, Moab, Navarre, Nepal, Noricum, Parthia, Pontic, Realm, Reign, Royalty, Sphere, Throne, Tonga, Vegetable, Wessex, World

Kink(y) Bent, Buckle, Crapy, Enmeshed, Flaw, Gasp, Knurl, Null, Nurl, Odd, Perm, Perverted, Quirk, Twist, Wavy

▷ **Kink(y)** *may indicate* an anagram

Kip(per) Cure, Dosser, Doze, Limey, Nap, > SLEEPER, Smoke

Kiss(er), **Kissing** Buss, Butterfly, Caress, Contrecoup, Cross, French, Lip, Neck, Osculate, Pax(-board), Pax-brede, Peck, Pet, Plonker, Pree, Salue, Salute, Smack(er), Smooch, Smouch, Snog, Spoon, Thimble, X, Yap

Kitchen Caboose, Cookhouse, Cuisine, Galley, Scullery, Soup

Kitty Ante, Cat, Fisher, Float, Fund, Jackpot, Pool, Pot, Tronc

Knack Art, Flair, Forte, Gift, Hang, Instinct, > TALENT, Trick

Knead Massage, Mould, Pug, Pummel, Work

Kneel(er) Defer, Genuflect, Hassock, Kowtow, Truckle

Knicker(bocker), **Knickers** Bloomers, Culottes, Directoire, Irving, Panties, Plus-fours, Shorts, Trousers

Knick-knack Bagatelle, Bibelot, Bric-a-brac, Gewgaw, Pretty(-pretty), Quip, Smytrie, Toy, Trangam, Trifle, Victoriana

Knife Anelace, Barlow, Barong, Bistoury, Blade, Boline, Bolo, Bolster, Bowie, Carver, Carving, Case, Catling, Chakra, Clasp, Cleaver, Couteau, Cradle, Cuttle, Cutto(e), Da(h), Dagger, Fleam, Flick, Fruit, Gull(e)y, Hay, Hunting, Jockteleg, Kard, Keratome, Kukri, Lance(t), Machete, Matchet, Moon, Oyster, Palette, Pallet, Panga, Paper, Parang, Pen, Pigsticker, Pocket, Putty, Scalpel, Scalping, Sgian-dubh, Sheath, Shiv, Simi, Skean-dhu, Slash, Snee, Snickersnee, Spade, Stab, Stanley, Steak, Sticker, Switchblade, Table, Tranchet, Trench

Knight Accolon, Aguecheek, Alphagus, Artegal, Banneret, Bayard, Bedivere, Black, Bliant, Bors, Britomart, Caballero, Calidore, Cambel, Caradoc, Carpet, Cavalier, Chevalier, Companion, Crusader, Douceper, Douzeper, Dub, Equites, Errant, Galahad, Gallant, Gareth, Garter, Gawain, Guyon, Hospitaller, Kay, KB, KBE, KG, La(u)ncelot, Launfal, Lionel, Lochinvar, Lohengrin, Maecenas,

Malta, Medjidie, Melius, Modred, N, Noble, Orlando, Paladin, Palmerin, Parsifal, Perceforest, Perceval, Percival, Pharamond, Pinel, Ritter, Samurai, Sir, Tannhauser, Templar, Teutonic, Trencher, Tristan, Tristram, Valvassor, Vavasour, White

Knit(ting), **Knitwear** Contract, Crochet, Entwine, Hosiery, Mesh, Porosis, Purl, Seam, Set, Stockinet, Weave, Wrinkle

Knob(by) Berry, Boll, Boss, Botoné, Bottony, Bouton, Bur(r), Cam, Caput, Cascabel, Croche, Handle, Hill, Inion, Knur(r), Node, Noop, Pellet, Pommel, Protuberance, Pulvinar, Snib, Snub, Snuff, Stud, Torose, Tuber, Tuner

Knock(er), **Knock down, off, out** Bang, Beaut, Biff, Blow, Bonk, Bump, Ca(a), Chap, Clash, Clour, Collide, Con, Criticise, Daud, Dawd, Degrade, Denigrate, Deride, Dev(v)el, Ding, Dinnyhauser, Etherise, Eyeful, Floor, Grace-stroke, > HIT, Innings, KO, Lowse, Lowsit, Mickey Finn, Pan, Pink, Quietus, Rap, Rat-tat, Skittle, Spat, Steal, Stop, Strike, Stun(ner), Tap, Technical, Thump, Tonk, Wow

Knot(ted), **Knotty** Apollo, Baff, Bend, Blackwall hitch, Bow, Bowline, Bur(r), Burl, Carrick-bend, Cat's paw, Clinch, Clove hitch, Cluster, Crochet, Diamond hitch, Englishman's, Entangle, Figure of eight, Fisherman's (bend), Flat, French, Gnar, Gordian, Granny, Half-hitch, Harness hitch, Hawser-bend, Herculean, Hitch, Interlace, Knag, Knap, Knar, Knur(r), Loop, Love(r's), Macramé, Macrami, Magnus hitch, Marriage-favour, Matthew Walker, Mouse, Nirl, Node, Nowed, Nub, Nur(r), Overhand, Picot, Porter's, Problem, Prusik, Quipu, Reef, Rolling hitch, Rosette, Running, Seizing, Sheepshank, Sheetbend, Shoulder, Shroud, Sleave, Slip, Slub, Spurr(e)y, Square, Stevedore's, Surgeon's, Sword, Tangle, Tat, Thumb, Tie, Timberhitch, Torose, Truelove, Tubercle, Turk's head, Virgin, Wale, Wall, Weaver's (hitch), Windsor, Witch

Know(how), **Knowing(ly)**, **Knowledge(able)**, **Known** Acquaintance, Autodidactic, Aware, Cognition, Compleat, Comprehend, Cred, Epistemics, Erudite, Expertise, Famous, Fly, Gnosis, Gnostic, Have, Hep, Hip, Info, Information, Insight, Intentional, Intuition, Jnana, Ken, Kith, Kydst, Lare, Light, Lore, Mindful, Omniscience, On, Pansophy, Party, Polymath, Positivism, Privity, Recherché, > RECOGNISE, Sapient, Savvy, Science, Scilicet, Sciolism, Shrewd, Smattering, Understand(ing), Up, Versed, Wat(e), Weet(e), Well-informed, Well-read, Wise, Wist, Wit, Wot

Ll

L Latitude, League, Learner, Left, Length, Liberal, Lima, Litre, Long, Luxembourg, Pound

Label Band, Book-plate, Brand, Designer, Docket, File, Mark, Own, Seal, Sticker, Style, Tab, Tag, Tally, Ticket, Trace

Laboratory Lab, Language, Skylab, Space-lab, Studio, Workshop

Labour(er), Laboured, Laborious Arduous, Begar, Birth, Carl, Casual, Chirl, Chore, Coolie, Corvée, Cottager, Cottar, Culchie, Dataller, Dwell, Gandy-dancer, Ganger, Gibeonite, Grecian, Grind, Hard, Hercules, Hodge, Ida, Job, Journeyman, Kanaka, Katorga, Leaden, Manpower, Moil, Navvy, Okie, Operose, Pain, Peon, Pioneer, Prole, Redneck, Roll, Roustabout, Rouster, Sisyphean, Slave, Stint, Strive, Sudra, Sweated, Task, > TOIL(S), Toss, Travail, Uphill, Vineyard, > WORK(ER), Workmen

Labyrinth Daedalus, Maze, Mizmaze, Warren, Web

▷ **Labyrinthine** *may indicate* an anagram

Lace, Lacy Alençon, Babiche, Beat, Blonde, Bobbin, Bone, Bourdon, Brussels, Chantilly, Cluny, Colbertine, Dash, Dentelle, Duchesse, Filet, Galloon, Guipure, Honiton, Inweave, Irish, Jabot, Lash, Macramé, Malines, Mechlin, Mignonette, Mode, Net, Orris, Pearlin, Picot, Pillow, Point, Reseau, Reticella, Ricrac, Rosaline, Seaming, Shoestring, Shoe-tie, Spike, Stay, Tat(ting), Tawdry, Thrash, Thread, Torchon, Trim, Trol(le)y, Valenciennes, Venise, Weave, Welt, Window-bar

Lack(ing), Lacks Absence, Aplasia, Bereft, Dearth, Famine, Ha'n't, Manqué, Minus, > NEED, Poverty, Privation, Remiss, Sans, Shortfall, Shy, Void, Want

Lackey Boots, Flunkey, Moth, Page, Poodle

Lacquer Coromandel, Enamel, Japan, Shellac, > VARNISH

Lad Boy(o), Bucko, Callan(t), Chiel(d), Child, Geit, Gyte, Knight, Loonie, Master, Nipper, Shaver, Stableman, Stripling, Tad, Whipper-snapper

Ladder(y) Accommodation, Bucket, Companion, Companionway, Etrier, Jack, Jacob's, Pompier, Potence, Rope, Run, Salmon, Scalado, Scalar, Scaling, Stie, Sty, Trap, Turntable

▶ **Lade** *see* LOAD

Ladle Bail, Dipper, Scoop

Lady Baroness, Bevy, Bountiful, Burd, Dame, Dark, Don(n)a, Duenna, Female, Frau, Frow, Gemma, Godiva, Hen, Khanum, Luck, Maam, Madam(e), Memsahib, Nicotine, Peeress, Senora, Signora, Tea, Windermere

▷ **Lady** *may indicate* an '-ess' ending

▷ **Ladybird** *may indicate* a female of a bird family

Lair Couch, Den, Earth, Haunt, Hideaway, Kennel, Lodge, Warren

Lake(s) Alkali, Basin, Bayou, Carmine, Crater, Crimson, Finger, L, Lacustrine, Lagoon, Lagune, > LOCH, Lochan, Lough, Madder, Mead, Mere, Nyanza, Ox-bow, Poets, Pool, Red, Reservoir, Salt, Shott, Tarn, Vlei

Lamb(skin) Baa, Barometz, Budge, Bummer, Cade, Canterbury, Caracul, Cosset, Ean(ling), Elia, Innocent, Keb, Larry, Noisette, Paschal, Persian, Rack, Shearling, Target, Yean(ling)

Lame(ness) Accloy, Claude, Cripple, Crock, Game, Gammy, Gimp(y), Halt, Hamstring, Hirple, Hors de combat, Maim, Main, Spavined, Springhalt, Stringhalt, Weak

Lament(able), **Lamentation**, **Lamenter** Bemoan, Bewail, Beweep, Complain, Croon, Cry, Dirge, Dumka, Elegy, Funest, Jeremiad, Jeremiah, Keen, Meane, Mein, Mene, Moon, Mourn, Ochone, Paltry, Piteous, Plain, Repine, Sorry, Threne, Threnody, Ululate, > WAIL, Welladay, Wel(l)away, Yammer

Lamina(te) Film, Flake, Folium, Formica®, Lamella, Layer, Plate, Scale, Table

Lamp(s) Aldis, Anglepoise, Arc, Argand, Bowat, Bowet, Buat, Cru(i)sie, Crusy, Davy, Eye, Eyne, Flame, Fluorescent, Fog, Geordie, Glow, Head, Hurricane, Incandescent, Induction, Kudlik, Lampion, Lantern, Lava, Lucigen, Mercury vapour, Miner's, Moderator, Neon, Nernst, Nightlight, Padella, Photoflood, Pilot, Platinum, Quartz, Reading, Riding, Safety, Sanctuary, Scamper, Searchlight, Signal, Sodium, Sodium-vapour, Spirit, Standard, Street, Stride, Stroboscope, Sun, Tail, Tantalum, Tiffany, Tilley, Torchier(e), Tungsten, Uplight(er), Veilleuse, Xenon

Lampoon Caricature, Parody, Pasquil, Pasquin(ade), Satire, Skit, Squib

Lance Dart, Harpoon, Morne, Pesade, Pike, Prisade, Prisado, Rejôn, Spear, Speisade, Thermic

Land(s), **Landed** Acreage, Alight, Alluvion, Bag, Beach, Byrd, Corridor, Country, Croft, Crown, Demain, Demesne, Disbark, Disembark, Ditch, Dock, Earth, Enderby, Estate, Fallow, Farren, Farthingland, Fee, Feod, Feoff, Feud, Fief, Freeboard, Gair, Glebe, Gore, Graham, Ground, Hide, Holding, Holm, Holy, Horst, Ind, Innings, Isthmus, Kingdom, La-la, Lea, Leal, Ley, Light, Link, Maidan, Manor, Marginal, Marie Byrd, Mesnalty, Moose pasture, Mortmain, Nation, Never-never, Nod, No man's, Odal, Onshore, Oxgang, Oxgate, Pakahi, Palmer, Panhandle, Parcel, Pasture, Peneplain, Peneplane, Peninsula, Piste, Plot, Point, Polder, Promised, Property, Purlieu, Queen Maud, Real estate, Realm, Realty, Reservation, Rupert's, Set-aside, Settle, Spit, Tack, Terra(e), Terra-firma, Terrain, Territory, Tie, Touchdown, Udal, Unship, Ure, Van Diemen's, Veld(t), Victoria, Waste, Wilkes

Landing (craft, stair, system) Autoflare, Forced, Gha(u)t, Halfpace, LEM, Module, Pancake, Pier, Quay, Soft, Solar, Splashdown, Three-point, Touchdown, Undercarriage

Landlord, **Land owner** Absentee, Balt, Boniface, Copyholder, Fiar, Franklin, Herself, Host, Innkeeper, Junker, Laird, Lessor, Letter, Patron, Proprietor, Publican, Rachman, Rentier, Squattocracy, Squire

Landscape Karst, Paysage, Picture, Saikei, Scene

Landslide, **Landfall** Avalanche, Earthfall, Eboulement, Lahar, Scree

Lane Boreen, Bus, Corridor, Crawler, Drury, Express, Fast, Fetter, Gut, Loan, Lois, Loke, Memory, Mincing, Passage, Petticoat, Pudding, Ruelle, Sea-road, Twitten, Twitting, Vennel, Wynd

Language(s) Argot, Artificial, Assembly, Auxiliary, Basic, Body, Cant, Dialect, Georgian, Humanities, Idioglossia, Idiom, Inclusive, Jargon, Lingo, Lingua franca, Macaroni, Neo, Newspeak, Object, Parlance, Pidgin, Pragmatics, Procedural, Programming, Prose, Rhetoric, Sign, > SPEECH, Style, Symbolic, Target, Technobabble, Telegraphese, Tone, > TONGUE, Verbiage, Vernacular, Vocabulary, Words, World

Languid, **Languish** Die, Divine, Droop, Feeble, Flagging, Listless, Lukewarm, Lydia, Melancholy, Quail, Torpid, Wilt

Lanky Beanpole, Gangly, Gawky, Spindleshanks, Windlestraw

Lantern Aristotle's, Bowat, Bowet, Buat, Bull's eye, Chinese, Dark(e)y, Epidiascope, Episcope, Glim, Jaw, Lanthorn, Magic, Sconce, Stereopticon, Storm

Lap Gremial, Leg, Lick, Lip, Luxury, Override, Pace, Sypher

▷ **Lapdog** *may indicate* 'greyhound'

Lapse Drop, Error, Expire, Fa', Fall, Nod, Sliding, Trip

Large(ness), Largest Ample, Astronomical, Big, Boomer, Bulky, Buster, Colossus, Commodious, Decuman, Enormous, Epical, Extensive, Gargantuan, > GIGANTIC, Ginormous, Great, Grit, Gross, Hefty, Helluva, Huge, Hulking, Humdinger, Humongous, Humungous, Kingsize, L, Lunker, Macrocephaly, Massive, Maximin, Maximum, Outsize, Plethora, Prodigious, Rounceval, Rouncival, Skookum, Slew, Slue, Sollicker, Spacious, Spanking, Stonker, Stout, Swingeing, Tidy, Titanic, Vast, Voluminous, Whopping

Largess Alms, Charity, Frumentation

Lark Adventure, Aunter, Caper, Dido, Dunstable, Exaltation, Fool, Giggle, Guy, Laverock, Mud, Pipit, Prank

Larva Army-worm, Axolotl, Bagworm, Bloodworm, Bot(t), Budworm, Caddice, Caddis, Cankerworm, Caterpillar, Chigger, Chigoe, Doodlebug, Grub, Jigger, Jointworm, Leather-jacket, Maggot, Mealworm, Measle, Muckworm, Naiad, Nauplius, Ox-bot, Planula, Pluteus, Shade, Silkworm, Tadpole, Wireworm, Witchetty, Woodworm, Zoea

Lascivious(ness) Crude, Goaty, Horny, Lewd, Lubric, Paphian, Satyric, Sotadic, Tentigo

Lash(ed), Lashings Cat, Cilium, Firk, Flagellum, Frap, Gammon, Knout, Mastigophora, Oodles, Oup, Quirt, Riem, Rope's end, Scourge, Secure, Sjambok, Stripe, Swinge, Tether, Thong, Trice, Whang, > WHIP

Lass(ie) Damsel, Maid, Quean, Queyn, Quin(i)e

Lasso Lariat, Reata, Rope

Last(ing) Abide, Abye, Aftermost, > AT LAST, Boot-tree, Bottom, Chronic, Dernier, Dure, Endurance, Endure, Extend, Extreme, > FINAL, Hinder, Latest, Linger, Live, Long-life, Model, Nightcap, Outstay, Perdure, Permanent, Perpetuate, Persist, Spin, Stable, Stay, Supper, Survive, Swan-song, Thiller, Thule, Tree, Trump, Ult(imate), Ultimo, Utmost, Wear, Weight, Whipper-in, Z

Last word(s) Amen, Envoi, Farewell, Ultimatum, Zythum

Latch Bar, Clicket, Clink, Espagnolette, Lock, Sneck

Late(r), Latest After(wards), Afterthought, Behindhand, Chit-chat, Dead, Ex, Former, Gen, Infra, Lag, Lamented, New(s), Overdue, Past, Recent, Sine, Slow, Stop-press, Syne, Tardive, Tardy, Trendy, Umquhile

Latent Concealed, Delitescent, Dormant, Maieutic, Potential

Lateral Askant, Edgeways, Sideways

Lathe Capstan, Mandrel, Mandril, Turret

Lather Flap, Foam, Froth, Sapples, Suds, Tan

Latin(ist) Biblical, Criollo, Dago, Dog, Erasmus, Eyeti, Greaseball, High, Humanity, Italiot, L, Late, Law, Low, Medieval, Neapolitan, New, Pig, Romanic, Romish, Scattermouch, Silver, Spic, Vulgar, Wop

Latitude Breadth, Celestial, Free hand, Horse, L, Leeway, Liberty, Licence, Meridian, Parallel, Play, Roaring forties, Scope, Tropic, Width

Latrine Ablutions, Bog, Cloaca, Furphy, Garderobe, Loo, Privy, Rear

Lattice Bravais, Clathrate, Espalier, Grille, Treillage, Trellis

Laugh(ing), Laughable, Laughter Belly, Cachinnate, Cackle, Chortle, Chuckle, Cod, Corpse, Democritus, Deride, Derision, Fit, Fou rire, Gelastic, Giggle, Goster, Guffaw, Ha, He-he, Ho-ho, Homeric, Hoot, Horse, Hout, Howl, Irrision, Lauch, Leuch, Levity, Mock, Nicker, Peal, Present, Riancy, Riant, Rich, Rident, Ridicule, Risus, Scream, Snigger, Snirt(le), Snort, Tehee, Titter, Yo(c)k

Launch(ing), **Launch pad** Begin, Blast-off, Catapult, Chuck, Fire, Float, Hurl, Initiate, Lift-off, Pioneer, Presentation, Release, Shipway, Slipway, Unstock, Upsend, VTO

Launder, **Laundry** Bagwash, Clean, Lav, Steamie, Tramp, Transfer, Wash, Washhouse, Whites

Laurel(s) Aucuba, Bay, Camphor, Daphne, Kalmia, Kudos, Pichurim, Sassafras, Spicebush, Spurge, Stan, Sweet-bay

Lava Aa, Bomb, Coulee, Cysticercus, Dacite, Lahar, Lapllll, Magma, Nuée ardente, Pahoehoe, Palagonite, Pitchstone, Pumice, Pyroclast, Scoria, Tephra, Toadstone

Lavatory Ajax, Bogger, Brasco, Can, Carsey, Carzey, Cludgie, Comfort station, Convenience, Cottage, Dike, Dunnakin, Dunny, Dyke, Earth closet, Elsan®, Facilities, Forica, Furphey, Gents, Heads, Jakes, Jane, John, Kars(e)y, Karzy, K(h)azi, Kleinhuisie, Kybo, Ladies, Lat(rine), Loo, Necessary, Netty, Office, Outhouse, Privy, Rear(s), Reredorter, Shithouse, Shouse, Siege, Smallest room, Throne, Thunderbox, Toot, Tout, Urinal, Washroom, WC

Lavish Barmecidal, Copious, Excessive, Exuberant, Flush, Free, Fulsome, Generous, Lucullan, Lush, Prodigal, Shower, Sumptuous, Wanton, Waste

Law(s) Act, Agrarian, Anti-trust, Ass, Association, Avogadro's, Bar, Barratry, > BILL, Biogenetic, Bonar, Boyle's, Bragg's, Brewster's, Brocard, Byelaw, Cain, Canon, Capitulary, Case, Chancery, Charles's, Civil, Code, Common, Constitution, Corn, Coulomb's, Criminal, Cupar, Curie's, Cy pres, Dalton's, Dead-letter, Decree, De Morgan's, Dharma, Dictate, Digest, Din, Distributive, Dry, Edict, Einstein's, Enact, Excise, Forest, Fundamental, Game, Gas, Gresham's, Grimm's, Grotian, Halifax, Henry's, Homestead, Hooke's, Hubble's, Hume's, International, Irade, Iure, Joule's, Jura, Jure, Jus, Kain, Kepler's, Kirchhoff's, Labour, Lay, Leibniz's, Lemon, Lenx's, Lien, Lor(d), Losh, Lydford, Lynch, Magdeburg, Mariotte's, Martial, May, Mendel's, Mercantile, Military, Moral, Mosaic, Murphy's, Natural, Newton's, Nomistic, Ohm's, Oral, Ordinance, Parity, Parkinson's, Pass, Penal, Periodic, Planck's, Plebiscite, Poor, Principle, Private, Public, Roman, Rubric, Rule, Salic, Salique, Scout, Sharia(h), Sheria(t), Shield, Shulchan Aruch, Snell's, Sod's, Stefan's, Stokes, Sumptuary, Sunna, Sus(s), Sword, Table, Talmud, Tenet, Thorah, Thorndike's, Torah, Tort, Tradition, Ulema, Unwritten, Use, Verner's, Vigilante, Written

Lawmaker, **Lawman**, **Lawyer** Alfaqui, Attorney, AV, Barrack room, Barrister, Bencher, BL, Bluebottle, Bramble, Bush, Coke, Counsel, DA, Defence, Doge, Draco, Enactor, Fiscal, Greenbag, Grotius, Hammurabi, Jurisconsult, Jurist, Legist, Mooktar, Moses, MP, Mufti, Mukhtar, Nomothete, Notary, Penang, Pettifoggers, Rabbi, Shirra, Shyster, Silk, Solicitor, Spenlow, Stratopause, Talmudist, Templar

Lawn Cloth, Grass, Green, Linen, Sward, Turf

Lawsuit Case, Cause, Plea, Trover

▸ **Lawyer(s)**, **Lawman** *see* **LAWMAKER**

▹ **Lax** *may indicate* an anagram

Lax(ity) Freedom, Inexact, Laissez-aller, Latitude, Loose, Remiss, > SLACK, Wide

Lay(ing), **Layman**, **Laic**, **Laid** Air, Aria, Ballad, Bed, Bet, Blow, Chant, Ditty, Drop, Earthly, Egg, Embed, Fit, Impose, Lied, Lodge, Man, Minstrel, Oat, Oblate, Ode, Outsider, Oviparous, Oviposit, Parabolanus, Secular, Set, Sirvente, > SONG, Sypher, Tertiary, Tribal, Wager, Warp

Layer(s) Abscission, Ancona, Appleton, Battery, Boundary, Cake, Caliche, Cladding, Coating, Crust, D, Depletion, E, Ectoplasm, Ectosarc, Ekman, Epiblast, Epilimnion, Epitaxial, Epithelium, Erathem, Exine, Exocarp, Film, Flake, Friction, Ganoin, Germ, Gossan, Gozzan, Granum, Ground, Heaviside, > HEN, Herb, Kennelly(-Heaviside), Kerf, Lamella, Lamina, Lap, Leghorn, Lie, Malpighian, Media, Miocene, Ozone, Pan, Patina, Paviour, Photosphere, Ply, Retina, Scale,

Sclerite, Screed, Skin, Sliver, Spathic, Stratify, Stratum, Substratum, Tabular, Tapetum, Tier, Tremie, Trophoblast, Trophoderm, Varve, Vein, Velamen, Veneer

Lay-off Dismiss, Hedge, Redundance

Lay-out Ante, Design, Fell, Format, Map, Mise, Pattern, Spend, Straucht, Straught, Streak, Streek, Stretch

Laze, Laziness, Lazy (person) Bed-presser, Bummer, Cabbage, Faineant, Hallian, Hallion, Hallyon, Indolent, Inert, Lackadaisical, Languid, Layabout, Lie-abed, Lig(ger), Lime, Lither, Loaf, Lotus-eater, Lusk, Sloth, Slouch, Slug(-a-bed), Sluggard, Susan, Sweer, Sweir, Workshy

▷ **Lazily** *may indicate* an anagram

Lead(er), Leading, Leadership Ag(h)a, Ahead, Akela, Article, Atabeg, Atabek, Ayatollah, Bab, Bellwether, Black, Bluey, Brand, Cable, Cade, Calif, Caliph, Came, Capitano, Capo, Captain, Castro, Caudillo, Centre, Cheer, Chieftain, Chin, China white, CO, Codder, Condottiere, Conducive, Conduct, Coryphaeus, Coryphee, Demagogue, Dictator, Duce, Dux, Editorial, Escort, Ethnarch, Extension, Figurehead, Floor, Foreman, Foremost, Frontrunner, Fu(e)hrer, Gaffer, Garibaldi, Gerent, Go, Graphite, Guide(r), Halter, Hand, Headman, Headmost, Headnote, Hegemony, Hero, Hetman, Honcho, Idi, Imam, Imaum, Jason, Jump, Juve(nile), King, Ksar, Leam, Livid, Loss, Lost, Lyam, Mahatma, Mahdi, Main, Market, Marshal, Massicot, Mayor, Meer, Mehdi, Minium, Mir, No1, Nomarch, Nose, Numero uno, Open, Pacemaker, Pacesetter, Padishah, Pb, Pilot, Pioneer, Pit, Plummet, PM, Precentor, Premier(e), President, Price, Ratoo, Rebbe, Rebecca, Red, Role, Ruler, Sachem, Sagamore, Saturn, Saturn's tree, Scotlandite, Scout, Scudler, Sharif, Sheik(h), Sixer, Skipper, Skudler, Soaker, Soul, Sounding, Spearhead, Staple, Star, Sultan, Supremo, Taoiseach, Tetraethyl, Top banana, Trail(blazer), Tribune, Up, Usher, Vaivode, Van(guard), Va(u)nt, Vaunt-courier, Voivode, Waivode, Warlord, White, Whitechapel, Wulfenite, Youth

▷ **Lead(s), Leaders** *may indicate* first letters of words

Leaf(y), Leaves Acanthus, Acrospire, Amphigastrium, Amplexicaul, Betel, Blade, Bract, Carpel, Cataphyll, Cladode, Consent, Corolla, Costate, Cotyledon, Drop, Duff, Fig, Finial, Foil, Foliage, Foliar, Folio(se), Folium, Frond, Glume, Gold, Holiday, Induviae, Jugum, K(h)at, Megaphyll, Needle, Nervate, Out, P, Pad, Page, Phyllid, Phyllome, Qat, Repair, Riffle, Rosula, Scale, Sclerophyll, Secede, Sepal, Siri(h), Skip, Spathe, Stipule, Tea, TTL, Valve, Vert, Withdraw

Leaflet At(t)ap, Bill, Bracteole, Circular, Dodger, Fly-sheet, Foliolose, Handbill, Pinna, Pinnula, Prophyll, Stipel, > **TRACT**

League Alliance, Band, Bund, Compact, Delian, Entente, Federation, Gueux, Guild, Hanse(atic), Holy, Ivy, Land, Major, Parasang, Primrose, Redheaded, Rugby, Super, Union, Zollverein, Zupa

Leak(y) Bilge, Drip, Escape, Extravasate, Gizzen, Holed, Holey, Ooze, Pee, Porous, Seepage, Sype, Trickle, Wee, Weep

Lean(ing) Abut, Barren, Batter, Bend, Careen, Carneous, Carnose, Griskin, Heel, > **INCLINE**, Lie, Lig(ge), Minceur, Propend, Rake, Rely, Rest, Scraggy, Scrawny, Skinny, Spare, Stoop, Taste, Tend, Tilt, Tip, Walty

Leap(ing), Leapt Assemblé, Bound, Brise, Cabriole, Caper, Capriole, Cavort, Clear, Croupade, Curvet, Echappé, Entrechat, Falcade, Fishdive, Frisk, Gambado, Gambol, Jeté, Jump, Loup, Luppen, Over, Pronk, Quantum, Sally, Salto, Somersa(u)lt, Somerset, > **SPRING**, Transilient, Vault, Volte

Learn(ed), Learner Beginner, Blue, Bluestocking, Chela, Con, Discover, Distance, Doctor, Don, Erudite, Gather, Get, Glean, Hear, Instrumental, Kond, L, Lear(e), Leir, Lere, Literate, Literati, Literato, Lucubrate, Master, Memorise, Mirza, Mug up, > **NOVICE**, Pandit, Programmed, Pundit, Pupil, Rookie, Savant, Scan, Scholar, See, Starter, Student, > **STUDY**, Tiro, Trainee, Tutee, Tyro, Wise

Learning Culture, Discipline, Erudition, Insight, Lore, Opsimathy, Rep, Wit

Lease(-holder) Charter, Farm, Feu, Gavel, Hire, Let, > **RENT**, Set(t), Tack, Tacksman

Leash Lead, Lyam, Lym(e), Slip, Three, Trash, Triplet

Leather(y) Artificial, Bouilli, Bouilly, Box-calf, Buckskin, Buff, Cabretta, Calf, Capeskin, Chammy, Chamois, Checklaton, Cheverel, Chevrette, Cordovan, Cordwain, Corium, Cowhide, Crispin, Cuir(-bouilli), Deacon, Deerskin, Diphthera, Doeskin, Dogskin, Durant, Fair, Goatskin, Hide, Hog-skin, Horsehide, Japanned, Kid, Kip(-skin), Lamp, Levant, Marocain, Maroquin, Mocha, Morocco, Mountain, Nap(p)a, Neat, Nubuck®, Ooze, Oxhide, Paste-grain, Patent, Pigskin, Plate, Rand, Rawhide, Rexine®, Riem(pie), Roan, Rock, Rough-out, Russia, Saffian, Shagreen, Shammy, Sharkskin, Shecklaton, Sheepskin, Shoe, Skiver, Slinskin, Spetch, Split, Spur, Stirrup, Strand, Strap, Suede, Tan, Taw, Thong, Upper, Wallop, Wash, Waxed, White, Whitleather, Yuft

Leave(r), **Leavings**, **Leave off** Abandon, Abiturient, Abscond, Absit, Absquatulate, Acquittal, Adieu, Bequeath, Blessing, Bug, Compassionate, Congé, Congee, Decamp, Depart, Desert, Devisal, Devise, Ditch, Exeat, Exit, Exodus, Forego, Forgo, Forsake, French, Furlough, Garlandage, > **GO**, Inspan, Ish, Legate, Licence, Maroon, Mizzle, Omit, Orts, Pace, Park, Part, > **PERMISSION**, Permit, > **QUIT**, Residue, Resign, Sabbatical, Scapa, Scat, Scram, Shore, Sick, Skedaddle, Skidoo®, Strand, Vacate, Vade, Vamo(o)se

Leaven Barm, Ferment, Yeast

Lecher(ous), **Lechery** Gate, Goaty, Lascivious, Libertine, Lickerish, Lustful, Profligate, Rake, Roué, Salaciousness, Satirisk, Satyr, Silen, Wolf

Lecture(r), **Lectures**, **Lecturing** Address, Aristotelian, Creed, Curtain, Dissert(ator), Don, Earful, Erasmus, Expound, Homily, Hulsean, Jaw, Jawbation, Jobe, L, Lector, Prelect, Prone, Rate, Read(er), Rede, Reith, Sententious, > **SERMON**, Spout, Talk, Teacher, Teach-in, Wigging, Yaff

Ledge Altar, Berm, Channel, Fillet, Linch, Misericord(e), Scarcement, Settle

Ledger Book, Purchase, Register

Left(-handed), **Left-hander**, **Left-winger** Balance, Bolshy, Corrie-fisted, Hie, High, L, Laeotropic, Laevorotation, Larboard, Links, Lorn, Near, Other, Over, Pink, Port, Quit, Rad, Red, Relic, Residuum, Resigned, Sinister, Soc(ialist), Southpaw, Thin, Titoism, Trot, Verso, Vo, Went, West, Wind, Yet

Leg(s), **Leggings**, **Leggy**, **Leg-wear** Antigropelo(e)s, Bandy, Breeches, Cabriole, Cannon, Chaparajos, Chaparejos, Chaps, Crural, Crus, Dib, Drumstick, Fine, Gaiter, Galligaskins, Gam(b), Gamash, Gambado, Garter, Gaskin, Gigot, Gramash, Gramosh, Haunch, Jamb, Limb, Long, Member, Myriapod, Oleo, On(side), Peg, Peraeopod, Periopod, Pestle, Pin, Podite, Proleg, Puttees, Pylon, Relay, Section, Shanks, Shanks's pony, Shaps, Shin, Short, Spats, Spatterdash, Spindleshanks, Square, Stage, Stump, Thigh, Tights

Legacy Bequest, Dowry, Entail, Heirloom

Legal(ism), **Legally**, **Legitimate** Bencher, Forensic, Halacha, Halaka(h), Halakha, Lawful, Licit, Nomism, Scienter

Legend Arthurian, Caption, Edda, Fable, Folklore, Motto, Myth, Saga, Story

▷ **Legend** *may indicate* leg-end, (e.g. foot, talus)

Legible Clear, Lucid, Plain

Legion(ary), **Legionnaire** Alauda, Army, British, Cohort, Countless, Deserter, Foreign, Geste, Honour, > **HOST**, Maniple, Many, Throng, Zillions

Legislate, **Legislator**, **Legislature** Assemblyman, Congress, Decemvir, Decree, MP, Nomothete, Oireachtas, > **PARLIAMENT**, Persian

Legume, **Leguminous** Bean, Guar, Lentil, Pea, Pod, Pulse

Leisure(ly) Adagio, Ease, Liberty, Moderato, Otium, Respite, Rest, Vacation

Lemming Morkin

Lemon Answer, Cedrate, Citron, Citrus, Yellow

Lemur Angwantibo, Aye-aye, Babacoote, Bush-baby, Colugo, Galago, Half-ape, Indri(s), Loris, Macaco, Malmag, Mongoose, > MONKEY, Potto, Ringtail, Sifaka, Tana, Tarsier

Lend Advance, Loan, Prest, Vaunce

Length(y), Lengthen(ing), Lengthwise Archine, Arsheen, Arshin(e), Aune, Cable, Chain, Cubit, Distance, Eke, Ell, > ELONGATE, Endways, Epenthetic, Expand, Extensive, Foot, Furlong, Inch, Ley, Mile, Nail, Passus, Perch, Piece, Plethron, Pole, Prolix, Prolong, Protract, Reach, Remen, Rod, Rope, Slow, Span, Stadium, Toise, Vara, Verbose, Yard

Lenient Clement, Exurable, Lax, Mild, Permissive, Tolerant

Lens Achromatic, Anamorphic, Anastigmat, Bifocal, Contact, Corneal, Crookes, Crown, Crystalline, Dielectric, Diopter, Dioptre, Diverging, Electron, Eye, Eyeglass, Eye-piece, Fish-eye, Gravitational, Hard, Lentil, Macro, Magnetic, Metallic, Mirror, Optic, Pantoscope, Soft, Stanhope, Sunglass, Telephoto, Toric, Trifocal, Wide-angle, Zoom

Leopard Clouded, Leap, Libbard, Ounce, Panther, Pard, Snow, Spots

Lesbian Bull dyke, Crunchie, Diesel, Dike, Dyke, Homophile, Lipstick, Sapphist, Tribade

Lese-majesty Treason

Lesion Cut, Gash, Scar, Serpiginous, Sore

Less(en), Lesser, Lessening Abate, Alaiment, Bate, Contract, Deaden, Decline, Deplete, Derogate, Dilute, > DWINDLE, Extenuate, Fewer, Junior, Littler, Minus, Reduce, Relax, Remission, Subordinate, Subsidiary, Under

Lesson Example, Lear(e), Lection, Leir, Lere, Moral, Object, Period, Sermon, Tutorial

Let (go, off, out), Letting Allow, Cap, Charter, Conacre, Displode, Divulge, Enable, Entitle, Explode, Hire, Impediment, Indulge, Lease, Litten, Loot(en), Luit(en), Lutten, Obstacle, Obstruct, > PERMIT, Rent, Reprieve, Sett, Unhand, Warrant

Lethal Deadly, Fatal, Fell, Mortal

Lethargic, Lethargy Accidie, Apathy, Coma, Drowsy, Ennui, Hebetude, Inertia, Lassitude, Listless, Passive, Sleepy, Sluggish, Stupor, Supine, Torpid

Letter(s) Ache, Aerogam, Aesc, Airgraph, Aleph, Alif, Alpha, Bayer, Begging, Beta, Beth, Block, Breve, Capital, Capon, Chain, Cheth, Chi, Circular, Col, Collins, Consonant, Covering, Cue, Cuneiform, Dead, Dear John, Delta, Digamma, Digraph, Dominical, Edh, Ef(f), Emma, Encyclical, Ep(isemon), Epistle, Epsilon, Eta, Eth, Fan, Favour, French, Gamma, Gimel, He, Heth, Initial, Iota, Izzard, Jerusalem, Kaph, Kappa, Koppa, Labda, Lambda, Lamed(h), Landlady, Landlord, Lessee, Lessor, Literal, Love, Mail, Mail-shot, Majuscule, Mem, Memo, Missive, Monogram, Mu, Night, Note, Notelet, Nu, Nun, Og(h)am, Omega, Omicron, Open, Pastoral, Patent, Pe, Phi, Pi, Plosive, Poison-pen, Polyphone, Postbag, Psi, Pythagorean, Rho, Rom, Runestave, Sad(h)e, Samian, Sampi, San, Scarlet, Screed, Screwtape, Script, See, Shin, Sigma, Sign, Signal, Sin, Sort, Swash, Tau, Tav, Taw, Teth, Theta, Thorn, Toc, Typo, Uncial, Upsilon, Vau, Vav, Versal, Vowel, Waw, Wen, Xi, Yod(h), Yogh, Ypsilon, Zed, Zeta

Lettuce Chicon, Corn-salad, Cos, Iceberg, Lactuca, Lamb's, Lollo rosso, Romaine, Salad, Thridace

Level(ler) A, Abney, Abreast, Aclinic, Aim, Base, Break even, Champaign, Countersink, Degree, Dumpy, Echelon, Equal, > EVEN, Extent, Flat, Flush, Grade,

O, Par, Plane, Plat(eau), Point, Race, Rank, Rase, Raze, Savanna, Spirit, Split, > SQUARE, Stratum, Strew, Strickle, Tier, Trophic, Water

Lever(age) Backfall, Bell-crank, Cock, Crampon, Crowbar, Dues, Gear, Handspike, Jemmy, Joystick, Key, Knee-stop, Landsturm, Pawl, Peav(e)y, Pedal, Prise, Prize, Pry, Purchase, Stick, Sweep, Swipe, Tappet, Tiller, Treadle, Tremolo arm, Trigger, Tumbler, Typebar

Levy Impose, Imposition, Leave, Militia, Octroi, Raise, Scutage, Talliate, Tax, Tithe

Lewd(ness) Bawdy, Blue, Impure, Libidinous, Lubricity, Obscene, Priapism, Prurient, Silen(us), Unclean

Lexicographer, Lexicon Compiler, Craigie, Drudge, Etymologist, Florio, Fowler, Grove, Johnson(ian), Larousse, Liddell, Murray, OED, Thesaurus, Vocabulist, Webster, Words-man

Liability, Liable Anme, Apt, Debt, Incur, Limited, Open, Prone, Subject, Susceptible

Liaison Affair, Contact, Link

Libel(lous) Defamatory, Malign, Slander, Smear, Sully, Vilify

Liberal(ity) Abundant, Adullamites, Ample, Besant, Bounteous, Bountiful, Breadth, Bright, Broad, Free(hander), Free-hearted, > GENEROUS, Giver, Grey, Grimond, Handsome, Indulgent, L, Largesse, Lavish, Octobrist, Open, > PROFUSE, Rad(ical), Samuelite, Simonite, Steel, Tolerant, Trivium, Unstinted, Verlig, Verligte, Whlg

Liberate(d), Liberation, Liberator Bolivar, Deliver, Emancipate, Fatah, > FREE, Inkatha, Intolerant, Messiah, PLO, Release, Save, Sucre, Unfetter, UNITA, Women's

Liberty Bail, Discretion, Franchise, Freedom, Hall, Mill, Sauce

Library Bibliothecary, BL, Bodleian, Bookmobile, Cottonian, Harleian, Laurentian, Lending, Mazarin, Public, Radcliffe, Reference, Tauchnitz

Licence, License Abandon, Allow, Authorisation, Carnet, Charter, Dispensation, Driving, Enable, Exequatur, Fling, Franchise, Free(dom), Gale, Imprimatur, Indult, > LATITUDE, Let, Marriage, Occasional, Passport, > PERMIT, Poetic, Pratique, Provisional, Road-fund, Rope, Slang, Special, Table

Lichen Apothecia, Archil, Corkir, Crotal, Crottle, Epiphyte, Epiphytic, Graphis, Korkir, Lecanora, Litmus, Orchel, Orchil(la), Orcine, Orseille, Parella, Parelle, Roccella, Rock tripe, Stone-rag, Stone-raw, Tree-moss, Usnea, Wartwort

Lick(ing) Bat, Beat, Deer, Lambent, Lap, Leather, Salt, Slake, Speed, Whip

Lid Cover, Hat, Kid, Maximum, Opercula, Screwtop, Twist-off

Lie(s), Liar, Lying Abed, Accubation, Accumbent, Ananias, Bam, Bare-faced, Bask, Billy, Bounce(r), Braide, Cau(l)ker, Cellier, Clipe, Clype, Concoction, Contour, Couchant, Cracker, Cram(mer), Cretism, Cumbent, Deception, Decubitous, Decumbent, Direct, Doggo, Fable, False(r), Falsehood, Falsify, Falsity, Fib, Fiction, Figment, Flam, Gag, Gonk, Incumbent, Invention, Inveracity, Kip, Lair, Leasing, Lee(ar), Lig(ge), Lurk, Mythomania, Obreption, Oner, Perjury, Plumper, Porky, Porky (pie), Procumbent, Prone, Prostrate, Pseudologia, Recline, Recumbent, Repent, Repose, Reptant, Ride, Romance(r), Sham, Sleep, Strapper, Stretcher, Supine, Swinger, Tale, Tappice, Tar(r)adiddle, Thumper, Tissue, Try, Untruth, Whacker, Whid, White, Whopper, Yanker

Lieutenant Flag, Loot, Lt, No 1, Sub(altern)

Life Age, Animation, Being, Bio, Biog(raphy), Brio, Clerihew, Esse, Existence, Good, Heart, Plasma, Span, Spirit, Still, Subsistence, Time, Vita, Zoe

Lifeless(ness) Abiosis, Algidity, Amort, Arid, Azoic, Barren, Cauldrife, > DEAD, Dull, Flat, Inanimate, Inert, Log, Mineral, Possum, Sterile, Stonen, Wooden

Lift(ed), Lifter, Lifting Arayse, Arsis, Attollent, Bone, Cable-car, Camel, Chair,

Cly, Copy, Crane, Davit, Dead, Dumb waiter, Elate, Elevator, Enhance, Extol, Filch, Fillip, Heave, Heeze, Heezie, Heft, Heist, Hitch, Hoise, Hoist, Hove, Jack, Jigger, Kleptomania, Leaven, Lefte, Lever, Lewis, Nab, Nap, Paternoster, Pilfer, Pulley, > **RAISE**, Ride, Scoop, Ski, Sky, Snatch, Steal, T-bar, Thumb, Up, Winch, Windlass

Light(en), **Lighting**, **Lighter**, **Lights** Aerate, Airy, Albedo, Ale, Alow, Apenglow, Amber, Ancient, Ans(wer), Arc, Aurora, Beacon, Beam, Bengal, Bezel, Bleach, Brake, Bulb, Candle, Casement, Chiaroscuro, Cierge, Clue, Courtesy, Day, Dewali, Diffused, Direct, Diwali, Drop, Eddystone, Electrolier, Ethereal, Fairy, Fall, Fan, Fantastic, Fastnet, Fetch-candle, Fill, Fire, First, Fixed, Flambeau, Flame, Flare, Flicker, Flippant, Flit(t), Floating, Flood, Fluorescent, Fog (lamp), Frothy, Fuffy, Gleam, Glim(mer), Glow, Gossamer, Green, Guiding, Hazard, Head, House, Ignite, Illum(in)e, Incandescence, Indirect, Induction, Inner, Irradiate, Junior, Key, Kindle, Klieg, Lamp, Land, Lantern, Lanthorn, Laser, Leading, Leerie, Levigate, Lime, Link, Loadstar, Lodestar, Lucarne, Lucigen, Luminaire, Lumine, Luminescence, Luminous, Lustre, Lux, Mandorla, Match, Mercurial, Mithra(s), Moon, Naphtha, Navigate, Neon, Nit, Northern, Obstruction, Od(yl), Optics, Pale, Pane, Parhelion, Pavement, Phosphorescence, Phot, Photon, Pilot, Pipe, Polar, Portable, Range, Rear, Red, Reflex, Rembrandt, Reversing, Riding, Rocket, Running, Rush, Scoop, Sea-dog, Search, Shy, Southern-vigil, Spill, Spot, Spry, Steaming, Strip, Strobe, Stroboscope, Subtle, Sun, Sunshine, Svelte, Tail, Tally, Taper, Taps, Threshold, Tind, Tine, Torch, Torchère, Touchpaper, Traffic, Trivial, Ultraviolet, Unchaste, Unoppressive, UV, Ver(e)y, Vesica, Vesta, Vigil, Watch, Wax, White, Window, Zodiacal

▷ **Light** *may indicate* an anagram

Lighter Barge, Birlinn, Casco, Gas-poker, Keel, Linstock, Lunt, Match, Pontoon, Pra(a)m, Spill, Taper

Lighthouse Beacon, Caisson, Eddystone, Fanal, Fastnet, Phare, Pharos, Signal

Lightning Ball, Catequil, Eclair, Enfouldered, Forked, Fulmination, Levin, Sheet, Thunderbolt, Wildfire, Zigzag

Like(ness), **Liking** As, Broo, Care, Corpse, Dig, Duplicate, Effigy, Eg, Egal, Enjoy, Equal, Fancy, Fellow, Lich, Palate, Parallel, Peas, Penchant, Please, Predilection, Semblant, Shine, Similar, Simile, Sort, Speaking, Taste, Tiki

Likely, **Likelihood** Apt, Fair, Odds-on, On, Plausible, Possible, Probable, Probit, Prone

Lily African, Agapanthus, Aloe, Amaryllis, Annunciation, Arum, Asphodel, Aspidistra, Belladonna, Calla, Camas(h), Camass, Canada, Candock, Chincherinchee, Colchicum, Colocasia, Convallaria, Corn, Crinum, Dale, Day, Easter, Elaine, Fawn, Fleur de lys, Fritillary, Galtonia, Haemanthus, Hemerocallis, Herb-paris, Jacob's, Kniphofia, Laguna, Lent, Leopard, Lote, Lotus, Madonna, Martagon, Nelumbo, Nenuphar, Nerine, Nuphar, Padma, Phormium, Plantain, Quamash, Regal, Sarsa, Scilla, Sego, Skunk cabbage, Smilax, Solomon's seal, Spider, Star of Bethlehem, Stone, Sword, Tiger, Trillium, Tritoma, Turk's cap, Victoria, Water, Yucca, Zephyr

Limb Arm, Bough, Branch, Crural, Exapod, Flipper, Hindleg, Imp, Leg, Leg-end, Member, Proleg, Ramus, Scion, Shin, Spald, Spall, Spaul(d), Wing

Lime Bass(wood), Beton, Calc, Lind(en), Malm, Mortar, Slaked, Soda, Teil, Tilia, Trap, Viscum, Whitewash

Limit(ation), **Limited**, **Limiting** Ambit, Bind, Border, Bound, Bourn(e), Brink, Cap, Cash, Ceiling, Circumscribe, Climax, Compass, Confine, Deadline, Define, Demark, Determine, Earshot, Eddington, Edge, End, Entail, Esoteric, > **EXTENT**, Extreme, Finite, Frontier, Gate, Goal, Impound, Insular, Limes, Lynchet, March, Maximum, Mete, Minimum, Nth, Outedge, Pale, Parameter, Perimeter, Periphery, Predetermine, Qualify, Range, Rate-cap, Ration, Reservation, Restrict, Rim, Roof, Scant, Shoestring, Sky, Speed, Stint, String, Tail(lie), Tailye, Term(inus),

Tether, Three-mile, Threshold, Thule, Tie, Time, Tropic, Twelve-mile, Utmost, Utter, Verge

▷ **Limit** *may indicate* 'surrounding'

Limp Claudication, Dot, Droopy, Flabby, Flaccid, Flimsy, Floppy, Hobble, Hop, Lifeless, Spancel, Tangle

Line(d), Lines, Lining Abreast, Agate, Agonic, Allan, > **ANCESTRY**, Anent, Angle, Apothem, Arew, Assembly, Axis, Bakerloo, Bar, Barcode, Battle, Baulk, Becket, Bikini, Bluebell, Bob, Bombast, Bottom, Boundary, BR, Brail, Branch, Bread, Bush, Canal, Carriage, Casing, Cell, Ceriph, Chord, Ciel, Club, Coach, Colour, Column, Contour, Cord(on), Course, Crease, Credit, Crocodile, Crowsfoot, Curve, Cushion, Dancette, Date, Datum, Deadball, Delay, Descent, DEW, Diagonal, Diameter, Diffusion, Distaff, Dotted, Downhaul, Dress, Dynasty, Earing, E-la-mi, Encase, Equator, Equinoctial, Equinox, Faint, Fall(s), Fault, Feint, Fess(e), Fettle, File, Finishing, Firing, Firn, Flex, Flight, Frame, Front, Frontier, Frost, Furr(ow), Germ, Gimp, Giron, Goal, graph, Grass, Green, Gridiron, Gymp, Gyron, Hachure, Halyard, Hard, Hatching, Hawser, Hemistich, Heptameter, Hexameter, High-watermark, Hockey, Hot, House, Impot, Inbounds, Inbred, Incase, Intima, Isallobar, Isobar, Isobath, Isochron(e), Isoclude, Isogloss, Isogonal, Isogram, Isohel, Isohyet, Isomagnetic, Isonome, Isophote, Isopiestic, Isopyenal, Isotherm, Knittle, L, Land, Lane, Lansker, Lap, Lariat, Latitude, Lead, Leash, Le(d)ger, Ley, Lie, Linq, LMS, Load, Log, Longitude, Loxodrome, Lubber, Lye, Macron, Maginot, Main, Mainsheet, Mark, Marriage, Mason-Dixon, Median, Meridian, Mesal, Monorail, Naman, Noose, Norsel, Northern, Number, Oche, Octastichon, Ode, Oder-Meisse, Og(h)am, Omentum, Onedin, Ordinate, Orphan, Painter, Parallel, Parameter, Parastichy, Party, Paternoster, Path, Penalty, Pencil, Phalanx, Picket, Pinstripe, Plimsoll, Plumb, Poetastery, Police, Policy, Popping-crease, Poverty, Power, Product(ion), Profession, Punch, Pure, Queue, Race, Radial, Radius, Rail, Rank, Raster, Ratlin(e), Ratling, Rattlin, Ray, Red, Retinue, Rew, Rhumb, Ripcord, Rope, Route, Row, Rule, Ry, Scazon, Score, Script, Secant, Seperatrix, Serif, Seriph, Service, Set, Siding, Siegfried, Sight, Silver, Slur, Snow, Soft, Solidus, Sounding, Spectral, Spring, Spunyarn, Squall, SR, Staff, Stance, Stanza, Starting, Static, Stave, Stean, Steen, Stein, Stem, Stich(os), Stock, Story, Strap, Streak, Striate, String, Stripe, Stuff, Symphysis, Tag, Tailback, Talweg, Tangent, Teagle, Tea lead, Terminator, Tetrameter, Thalweg, Thin blue, Thin red, Thread, Throwaway, Tidemark, Tie, Timber, Touch, Trade, Transmission, Transoceanic, Transversal, Tree, Trimeter, Trot, Trunk, Tudor, Variety, Verse, Virgule, Wad, Wallace's, Washing, Water(shed), White, Widow, Wire, Wrinkle, Zag, Zip

Linen Amice, Amis, Barb, Bed, Byssus, Cambric, Crash, Damask, Dornick, Dowlas, Ecru, Harn, Lawn, Lint, Napery, Percale, Seersucker, Sendal, Silesia, Toile

Liner Artist, Bin-bag, RMS, Ship, Sleeve, Steamer, Steen, Titanic

Linger(ing) Dawdle, Dwell, Hang, Hove(r), Lag, > **LOITER**, Straggle, Tarry, Tie

Linguist(ic), Linguistics Glottic, Philological, Phonemics, Polyglot, Semantics, Stylistics, Taxeme

Link(ing), Links Associate, Between, Bond, Bridge, Chain, Cleek, Colligate, Concatenation, Copula, Couple, Desmid, Drag, Ess, Flambeau, Hookup, Hotline, Incatenation, Interface, Internet, Intertwine, Karabiner, Krab, Liaise, Machair, Missing, Nexus, Pons, Preposition, Relate, Tead(e), > **TIE**, Tie-in, Tie-line, Torch, Unite, Yoke

Lion(ess) Androcles, Aphid, Chindit, Elsa, Glitterati, Hero, Leo, Maned, Nemean, Opinicus, Personage, Pride, Simba

Lip(py), Lips Cheek, Fat, Fipple, Flews, Helmet, Jib, Labellum, Labiate, Labret, Labrum, Ligula, Muffle, > **RIM**, Rubies, Sass, Sauce, Slack-jaw, Submentum

Lipase Steapsin

Liqueur, **Liquor** Abisante, Absinthe, Advokaat, Ale, Almondrado, Amaretto, Anise, Anisette, Apry, Benedictine, Bree, Brew, Broo, Broth, Calvados, Cassis, Cerise, Chartreuse, Chasse, Cherry marnier, Cher-suisse, Chicha, Choclair, Chococo, Cocoribe, Cointreau®, Creature, Crème, Crème de menthe, Curaçao, Drambuie®, Eau des creoles, Elixir, Enzian, Feni, Fenny, Fraises, Framboise, Fumet, Fustian, Galliano, Geropiga, Grand Marnier, Hogan, Hogan-mogen, Hooch, John Barleycorn, Jungle juice, Kahlua, Kaoliang, Kir, Kirschwasser, Kirsh(wasser), Kummel, Lager, Lap, Malt, Maraschino, Mastic, Metheglin, Mickey Finn, Midori, Mirabelle, Mobbie, Mobby, Noyau, Oedema, Ooze, Ouzo, Parfait d'amour, Pasha, Pastis, Pernod, Persico, Pot, Potation, Pousse-café, Prunelle, Rakee, Raki, Ratafia, Roiano, Roncoco, Rose, Rotgut, Rum, Sabra, Sambuca, Samshoo, Schnapps, Sciarada, Shypoo, Skink, Stingo, Stock, Stout, Strega®, Strunt, Stuff, Supernaculum, Tape, Taplash, Tequila, Tia Maria, Tickle-brain, Tiff, Van der Hum, White lightning, Wine

Liquid(ate), **Liquidity**, **Liquids**, **Liquefaction** Acetal, Amortise, Annihilate, Apprize, Bittern, Bouillon, Bromine, Cash, Court-bouillon, Creosol, Decoction, Dope, Eluate, Erase, Ethanol, Ether, Eucalyptol, Fluid, Fural, Furfural, Jaw, Lye, Mess, Minim, Pipe, Potion, Protoplasm, Ptisan, Serum, Solution, Solvent, Syrup, Titre, Tuberculin, Ullage, Whey

▷ **List** *may indicate* 'listen'

List(s), **Listing** Active, Agenda, Antibarbarus, Appendix, Army, Atilt, Barocco, Barrace, Bead-roll, Bibliography, Canon, Cant, Catalog(ue), Categorise, Catelog, Cause, Check, Civil, Class, Compile, Credits, Danger, Debrett, Docket, Entry, Enumerate, Front, Glossary, Hark, Hearken, Heel, Hit, Hit-parade, Honours, Index, Indian, Interdiction, Inventory, Itemise, Lean, Leet, Line-up, Linked, Lloyds, Mailing, Manifest, Navy, Notitia, Official, Panel, Paradigm, Party, Prize, Register, Repertoire, Reserved, Roin, Roll, Roon, Roster, Rota, Rund, Schedule, Short, Sick, Slate, Slope, Strip, Syllabus (of Errors), Table, Tariff, Tick, Ticket, Tilt, Timetable, Tip, Transfer, Union, Waiting, Waybill, White, Wine, Wish

Listen(er) Attend, Auditor, Auscultate, Ear, Eavesdropper, Gobemouche, Hark, > HEED, Lithe, Lug, Monitor, Oyez, Wire-tap

▷ **Listen to** *may indicate* a word sounding like another

Listless(ness) Abulia, Accidie, Acedia, Apathetic, Atony, Dawney, Indolent, Lackadaisical, Languor, Mooning, Mope, Mopus, Sloth, Thowless, Torpor, Waff

▷ **Lit** *may indicate* an anagram

Literary Academic, Bas bleu, Booksie, Erudite, Lettered

Literature Belles lettres, Corpus, Fiction, Gongorism, Midrash, Page, Picaresque, Prose, Responsa, Wisdom

Litter Bed, Brancard, Brood, Cacolet, Cubs, Debris, Doolie, Emu-bob, Farrow, Jampan, Kago, Kajawah, Kindle, Mahmal, Nest, Norimon, Palankeen, Palanquin, Palkee, Palki, Pup, > REFUSE, Scrap, Sedan, Stretcher, Team

Little Brief, Chota, Curn, Dorrit, Drib, Drop, Fewtrils, Insect, Iota, John, Jot, Leet, Lilliputian, Limited, Lite, Lyte, Mini, Miniscule, Minnow, Minuscule, > MINUTE, Modicum, Morceau, Nell, Paltry, Paucity, Petite, Pink, Scant, Scut, Shade, Shoestring, Shred, Shrimp, Slight, Sma', > SMALL, Smattering, Smidge(o)n, Smidgin, Some, Soupçon, Spot, Tad, Tich, Tine, Titch, Touch, Tyne, Vestige, Wee, Weedy, Whit, Women

Littoral Coast(al)

Live(d), **Livelihood**, **Living**, **Liveliness**, **Lively**, **Lives** Active, Alert, Allegro, Animated, Animation, Animato, AV, Awake, Be, Bouncy, Breezy, Brio, Brisk, Cant(y), Cheery, Chipper, Chirpy, Cohabit, Con moto, Crouse, Durante vita, Ebullient, Entrain, Exist, Feisty, Frisky, Gamy, Gay, Giocoso, Hang-out, Hard, High jinks, Hijinks, Is, Jazz, Kedge, Lad, Lead, Mercurial, Merry, Outgo, Pacey,

Peart, Pep, Piert, Quicksilver, Rackety, Racy, Reside, Rousing, Salt, Saut, Scherzo, Skittish, Spiritoso, Spirituel(le), Sprack, Spry, Spunky, Swinging, Vibrant, Vital, Vitality, Vive, > VOLATILE, Zappy, Zingy, Zippy, Zoe

▶ **Livelihood** *see* LIVE(D)

Living Advowson, Benefice, Biont, Bread, Canonry, Crust, Glebe, Inquiline, Lodging, Quick, Resident, Simony, Subsistence, Symbiotic, Vicarage, Vital

Lizard Abas, Agama, Amphisboena, Anguis, Anole, Basilisk, Bearded, Blindworm, Blue-tongued, Brontosurus, Chameleon, Chuckwalla, Dinosaur, Draco, Eft, Evet, Frilled, Galliwasp, Gecko(ne), Gila, Gila monster, Glass snake, Goanna, Guana, Hatteria, Hellbender, Horned, Iguana, Jew, Kabaragoya, Komodo (dragon), Lacerta, Legua(a)n, Lounge, Mastigure, Menopome, Moloch, Monitor, Mosasaur(us), Newt, Perentie, Perenty, Reptile, Sand, Sauria, Scincoid, Seps, Skink, Slow-worm, Snake, Stellio(n), Sungazer, Tegu(exin), Tokay, Tuatara, Tuatera, Varan, Wall, Whiptail, Worm, Worral, Worrel, Zandoli

Load(ed), **Loader**, **Loading**, **Loads** Accommodation, Affluent, Ballast, Base, Boot-strap, Burden, Cargo, Charge, Cobblers, Dead weight, Disc, Dope, Drunk, Dummy, Fardel, Fother, Freight, Front-end, Fulham, Full, Gestant, Heap, Input, Jag, Lade, Lard, Last, Live, Onus, Pack, Packet, Pay, Peak, Power, Prime, Rich, Seam, Shipment, Some, Span, Super, Surcharge, > TIGHT, Tod, Traction, Ultimate, Useful, Wealthy, Weight, Wharfinger, Wing

Loaf(er), **Loaves** Baguette, Baton, Bloomer, Bludge, Brick, Bum, Bu(r)ster, Cad, Cob, Coburg, Cottage, Farmhouse, Hawm, Hoe-cake, Idle, > LAZE, Long tin, Lusk, Manchet, Miche, Mouch, Pan(h)agia, Roll, Roti, Shewbread, Showbread, Slosh, Split tin, Sugar, Tin, Vantage, Yob

Loan(s) Advance, Balloon, Benevolence, Bottomry, Bridging, Debenture, Imprest, Lane, Mutuum, Omnium, Out, Prest, Respondentia, Roll-over, Start-up, Sub

Loathe, **Loathing**, **Loathsome** Abhor(rent), Abominate, Carrion, Detest, Hate, Nauseate, Scunner, Ug(h)

Lobby Demo, Entry, Foyer, Gun, Hall, Press, Urge

Lobster Cock, Crawfish, Crayfish, Crustacean, Decapoda, Langouste, Norway, Pot, Scampo, Spiny, Thermidor, Tomalley

Local(ity) Area, Endemic, Home, Inn, Landlord, Native, Near, Nearby, Neighbourhood, Number, Parochial, Pub, Regional, Resident, Tavern, Topical, Vicinal

▷ **Local** *may indicate* a dialect word

Locate Connect, Find, Fix, Lay, Pinpoint, Plant, Site, Spot

Location Address, Milieu, Place, Recess, Site, Situation, Sofar, Ubiety, Website, Zone

Loch, **Lough** Ashie, Awe, Derg, Earn, Eil, Erne, Etive, Fine, Gare, Garten, Holy, Hourn, Katrine, > LAKE, Larne, Leven, Linnhe, Lomond, Long, Moidart, Morar, More, Nakeel, Neagh, Ness, Rannoch, Ryan, Shiel, Strangford, Tay, Torridon

Lock(ing), **Locker**, **Locks**, **Lock up** Bar, Bolt, Canal, Central, Chubb®, Clinch, Combination, Cowlick, Curlicue, Davy Jones, Deadbolt, Detent, Drop, Fastener, Fermentation, Foretop, Gate, Haffet, Haffit, Handcuff, Hasp, Hold, Intern, Key, Latch, Lazaretto, Man, Mortise, Percussion, Prison, Quiff, Ragbolt, Ringlet, Sasse, Scalp, Scissors, > SECURE, Sluice, Snap, Spring, Stock, Strand, Tag, Talon, Time, Trap, Tress, Tuft, Vapour, Villus, Ward, Wheel, Wrestle, Yale®

Locomotive Banker, Bogie, Bul(l)gine, Engine, Iron horse, Mobile, Rocket, Steamer, Train

Locust, **Locust tree** Anime, Carob, Cicada, Hopper, Nymph, Robinia, Seventeen-year, Voetganger

Lodge(r) Billet, Board(er), Box, Cosher, Deposit, Dig, Doss, Entertain, Freemason, Grange, Guest, Harbour, Host, Inmate, Layer, Lie, Masonic, Nest, Orange,

Parasite, PG, Quarter, Rancho, Room(er), Stay, Storehouse, Stow, Tenant, Tepee, Wigwam

Lodging(s) Abode, B and B, Chummage, Dharms(h)ala, Digs, Dosshouse, Ferm, Grange, Grove, Hostel, Inquiline, Kip, Minshuku, Pad, Pension, Pied-à-terre, Quarters, Resiant, Rooms, Singleen, YHA

Loft(iness), Lofty Aerial, Airy, Arrogant, Attic, Celsitude, Chip, Garret, Grand, Haymow, High, Jube, Lordly, Magniloquent, Noble, Rarefied, Rigging, Rood, Roost, Tallat, Tallet, Tallot

Log Billet, Black box, Cabin, Chock, Diarise, Diary, Hack, Mantissa, Nap(i)erian, Neper, Patent, > **RECORD**, Stock, Yule

Logic(al) Alethic, Aristotelian, Chop, Dialectic(s), Doxastic, Epistemics, Modal, Organon, Ramism, Rational(e), Reason, Sequacious, Sorites, Symbolic, Trivium

Loiter(ing) Dally, Dare, Dawdle, Dilatory, Dilly-dally, Idle, Lag, Lallygag, Leng, Lime, > **LINGER**, Mooch, Mouch, Potter, Saunter, Scamp, Suss, Tarry

London(er) 'Arry, Big Smoke, Cockaigne, Co(c)kayne, Cockney, East-ender, Flat-cap, Jack, Roseland, Smoke, Town, Troynovant, Wen

Lone(r), Lonely Remote, Rogue, Secluded, Sole, Solitary, Unked, Unket, Unkid

Long(er), Longing, Longs Ache, Aitch, Ake, Appetent, Aspire, Brame, Covet, Desire, Die, Earn, Erne, Far, Greed, Green, Grein, > **HANKER**, Huey, Hunger, Island, Itch, L, Lanky, Large, Lengthy, Longa, Lust, Macron, Miss, More, Nostalgia, Option, Pant, Parsec, > **PINE**, Prolix, Side, Sigh, Tall, Thirst, Trews, Weary, Wish, Wist, Yearn, Yen

Longitude Celestial, Meridian

Longshoreman Hobbler, Hoveller, Wharfinger

Loo Ajax, Bog, Can, Chapel, Dike, Game, Gents, Jakes, John, Privy, Toilet

Loofah Towel gourd

Look(s), Look at Air, Aspect, Behold, Belgard, Bonne-mine, Busk, Butcher's, Butcher's hook, Clock, Close-up, Crane, Daggers, Decko, Deek, Dekko, Ecce, Ecco, Expression, Eye, Face, Facies, Gander, Gawp, Gaze, Geek, Glance, Glare, Gledge, Glimpse, Glom, Goggle, Good, Grin, Hallo, Hangdog, Hey, Iliad, Inspect, Keek, La, Leer, Lo, Mien, New, Ogle, Peek, Peep, Prospect, Ray, Recce, Refer, > **REGARD**, Scan, Scrutinise, Search, See, Seek, Shade, Sheep's eyes, Shufti, Shufty, Spy, Squint, Squiz, Survey, Toot, V, Vista, Wet

Look-out (man) Cockatoo, Crow's nest, Huer, Mirador, Sangar, Sentry, Sungar, Toot(er), Watch, Watchtower

▷ **Look silly** *may indicate* an anagram

Loom Beamer, Dobby, Emerge, Impend, Jacquard, Lathe, Menace, Picker, Temple, Threaten, Tower

Loop(ed), Loophole, Loopy Becket, Bight, Billabong, Bouclé, Carriage, Chink, Closed, Coil, Eyelet, Eyesplice, Fake, Frog, Frontlet, Grom(m)et, Grummet, Hank, Henle's, Hysteresis, Infinite, Kink, Knop, Lasket, Lug, Noose, Oillet, Parral, Parrel, Pearl(-edge), Picot, Purl, Staple, Stirrup, Terry, Toe, Twist

Loose(n), Loose woman Absolve, Abstrict, Afloat, Anonyma, Baggage, Bail, Besom, Bike, Chippie, Chippy, Cocotte, Demi-mondaine, Demirep, Desultory, Dissolute, Dissolve, Doxy, Draggletail, Dratchell, Drazel, Emit, Flirt-gill, Floosie, Floozie, Floozy, Floppy, Franion, Free, Gangling, Gay, Hussy, Insecure, Jade, Jezebel, Lax, Loast, Mob, Mort, Pinnace, Profligate, Quail, Ramp, > **RELAX**, Sandy, Scrubber, Slag, Slapper, Streel, Tart, Tramp, Trull, Unhasp, Unhitch, Unlace, Unpin, Unreined, Unscrew, Untie, Vague, Wappend, Whore

Loot Boodle, Booty, Cragh, Creach, Foray, Haul, Mainour, Peel, Pluck, > **PLUNDER**, Ransack, Rape, Reave, Rieve, Rob, Sack, Smug, Spoils, Spoliate, Swag, Treasure, Waif

Lop Behead, Clop, Curtail, Detruncate, Droop, Shroud, Sned, Trash

Lord(s), **Lordship**, **Lordly** Adonai, Arrogant, Boss, Byron, Dieu, Domineer, Dominical, Duc, Earl, Elgin, Gad, God, Haw-haw, Herr, Imperious, Jim, Justice, Kami, Kitchener, Landgrave, Law, Ld, Liege, Lonsdale, Losh, Lud, Misrule, Mynheer, Naik, Oda Nobunaga, Omrah, Ordinary, Ormazd, Ormuzd, Peer, Seigneur, Seignior, Shaftesbury, Sire, Spiritual, Taverner, Temporal, Tuan, Ullin

Lore Cab(b)ala, Edda, Lair, Lare, Riem, Upanis(h)ad

Lorry Artic(ulated), Camion, Crummy, Drag, Flatbed, Juggernaut, Low-loader, Rig, Tipper, Tonner, > **TRUCK**, Wagon

Lose(r) Also-ran, Decrease, Drop, Elude, Forfeit, Leese, Misère, Mislay, Misplace, Nowhere, Tank, Throw, Tine(r), Tyne, Underdog, Unsuccessful, Waste, Weeper

Loss, **Lost** Anosmia, Aphesis, Aphonia, Apocope, Apraxia, Astray, Attainder, Boohai, Chord, Cost, Dead, Decrease, Depreciation, Detriment, Disadvantage, Elision, Extinction, Foredamned, Forfeited, Forgotten, Forlorn, Gone, Lore, Lorn, Lurch, Missing, Omission, Outage, Pentimento, Perdition, Perdu, Perished, Preoccupied, Privation, Psilosis, Tine, Tinsel, Tint, Toll, Traik, Tribes, Tyne(d), Ullage, Unredeemed, Wastage, Wasted, Will, Wull

▷ **Lost** *may indicate* an anagram or an obsolete word

Lot(s) Abundant, Amount, Aret(t), Badly, Batch, Boatload, Caboodle, Cavel, Chance, Deal, Dole, Doom, Due, > **FATE**, Fortune, Hantle, Hap, Heaps, Horde, Host, Item, Job, Kevel, Kismet, Lashings, Legion, Luck, Manifold, Many, Mass, Moh, Moira, Mony, Mort, Myriad, Oceans, Omnibus, Oodles, Pack, Parcel, Plenitude, Plenty, Portion, Power, Purim, Raft, Scads, Set, Sight, Slather, Slew, Slue, Sortilege, Stack, Sum, Tall order, Tons, Vole, Wagonload, Weird

Lothario Lady-killer, Libertine, Rake, Womaniser

Lotion After-shave, Blackwash, Calamine, Collyrium, Cream, Humectant, Suntan, Unguent, Wash

Lottery, **Lotto** Bingo, Cavel, Draw, Gamble, Pakapoo, Pools, Punchboard, Raffle, Rollover, Scratchcard, Sweepstake, Tombola

Loud(ness), **Loudly** Bel, Big, Blaring, Booming, Brassy, Decibel, F, FF, Flashy, Forte, Fracas, Full-mouthed, Garish, Gaudy, Glaring, Hammerklavier, High, Lumpkin, Noisy, Orotund, Plangent, Raucous, Roarie, Siren, Sone, Stentor(ian), Strident, Tarty, Vocal, Vociferous, Vulgar

Loudspeaker Action, Boanerges, Bullhorn, Hailer, Megaphone, Stentor, Subwoofer, Tannoy®, Tweeter, Woofer

Lounge(r) Da(c)ker, Daiker, Departure, Hawm, Idle, Laze, Lizard, Loll, Lollop, Parlour, Slouch, Sun, Transit

Louse (up), **Lousy**, **Lice** Acrawl, Argulus, Bolix, Bollocks, Chat, Cootie, Crab, Crummy, Head, Isopod(a), Kutu, Nit, Oniscus, Pedicular, Phthiriasis, Psocoptera, Psylla, Slater, Snot, Sowbug, Sucking, Vermin

Lout Clod(hopper), Coof, Cuif, Hallian, Hallion, Hallyon, Hick, Hob, Hobbledehoy, Hooligan, Hoon, Jack, Jake, Keelie, Lager, Larrikin, Lob(lolly), Loord, Lubber, Lumpkin, Oaf, Oik, Rube, Swad, Tout, Yahoo, Yob(bo)

Louvre Shutter

Love(r) Abelard, Adore, Adulator, Affection, Agape, Amant, Amateur, Ami(e), Amoret, Amoroso, Amour, Antony, Ardour, Ariadne, Aroha, Aucassin, Beau, Bidie-in, Blob, Calf, Care, Casanova, Chamberer, Cicisbeo, Concubine, Coquet, Court, Courtly, Cupboard, Cupid, Dotard, Dote, Doxy, Duck(s), Ducky, Dulcinea, Eloise, Eloper, Emotion, Enamorado, Eros, Fan, Flame, Frauendienst, Free, Goose-egg, Idolise, Inamorata, Inamorato, Isolde, Jo, Lad, Leman, Like, Lochinvar, Loe, Loo, Lurve, Nihility, Nil, Nothing, Nought, O, Pairs, Paramour, Pash, Passion, Philander, Platonic, Protestant, Psychodelic, Puppy, Revere, Romance, Romeo, Spooner, Stale, Storge, Suitor, Swain, Thisbe, Toyboy, Troilus, True, Turtle(-dove), Valentine, Venus, Virtu, Zeal, Zero

Lovely Adorable, Belle, Dishy, Dreamy, Nasty

Love-making Kama Sutra, Sex, Snog

Low(est), Low-cut, Lower(ing) Abase, Abate, Abysmal, Amort, Area, Avail(e), Avale, B, Basal, Base(-born), Bass(o), Beneath, Cartoonist, Cheap, Church, Condescend, Contralto, Cow, Croon, Crude, Darken, Debase, Décolleté, Degrade, Demean, Demit, Demote, Depress, Devalue, Dim, Dip, Dispirited, Doldrums, Drawdown, Drop, Early, Embase, Flat, Foot, Frown, Gazunder, Glare, Guernsey, Gurly, Hedge, Humble, Ignoble, Imbase, Inferior, Jersey, Laigh, Lallan, Law, Mass, Mean, Menial, Moo, Mopus, Morose, Nadir, Net, Nether, Nett, Ostinato, Paravail, Plebeianise, Profound, Prole, Relegate, Ribald, Rock-bottom, Sad, Scoundrel, Scowl, Shabby, Short, Soft, Stoop, Subordinate, Sudra, Undermost, Vail, Vulgar, Weak, Wretched

▷ **Lower** *may refer to* cattle

Loyal(ty) Adherence, Allegiant, Brick, Dependable, Faithful, Fast, Fidelity, Gungho, Leal, Patriotic, Stalwart, Staunch, > TRUE, Trusty

Lozenge Cachou, Catechu, Fusil, Jujube, Mascle, Pastille, Pill, Rhomb, Rustre, Tablet, Troche

Lubricant, Lubricate, Lubrication Carap-oil, Coolant, Derv, Fluid, Force-feed, Grease, Oil, Petrolatum, Sebum, Unguent, Vaseline®, Wool-oil

Lucid Bright, Clear, Perspicuous, Sane

Lucifer Devil, Match, Proud

Luck(y) Amulet, Auspicious, Beginner's, Bonanza, Break, Caduac, Cess, Chance, Charmed, Chaunce, Daikoku, Dip, Fate, Fluke, > FORTUNE, Godsend, Hap, Heather, Hit, Jam(my), Joss, Lady, Lot, Mascot, Mozzle, Prosit, Providential, Pudding-bag, Purple patch, Seal, Seel, Serendipity, Sess, Sonsie, Sonsy, Star(s), Streak, Success, Talisman, Tinny, Tough, Turn-up, Windfall

Ludicrous Absurd, Bathetic, Bathos, Farcical, Inane, Irish, Jest, Laughable, Risible

Luggage Bags, Carryon, Cases, Dunnage, Excess, Grip, Hand, Kit, Petara, Suiter, Traps, Trunk

Lull, Lullaby Berceuse, Calm, Cradlesong, Hushaby, Respite, Rock, Sitzkreig, Soothe, Sopite

Lumber(ing) Clump, Galumph, Jumble, Pawn, Ponderous, Raffle, Saddle, Scamble, Timber

Luminance, Luminous, Luminosity, Luminescence Aglow, Arc, Glow, Ignis-fatuus, L, Light, Nit, Phosphorescent, Sea-dog, Wildfire, Will o' the wisp

Lump(y) Aggregate, Bubo, Bud, Bulge, Bur(r), Caruncle, Chuck, Chunk, Clat, Claut, Clod, Clot, Cob, Combine, Dallop, Da(u)d, Dollop, Enhydros, Epulis, Flocculate, Ganglion, Geode, Gnarl, Gob(bet), Goiter, Goitre, Grape, Hunch, Hunk, Inium, Knarl, Knob, Knub, Knur(r), Knurl, Lob, Lunch, Malleolus, Mass, Mote, Mott, Myxoma, Neuroma, Nibble, Nirl, Node, Nodule, Nodulus, Nub, Nubble, Nugget, Nur(r), Nurl, Osteophyte, Plook, Plouk, Quinsy, Raguly, Sarcoma, Scybalum, Sitfast, Slub, Strophiole, Tragus, Tuber(cle), Wart, Wodge

Lunacy, Lunatic Bedlam, Dementia, Demonomania, Folly, Insanity, Mad(ness), Psychosis

▷ **Lunatic** *may indicate* an anagram

Lunch(time) Dejeune, Déjeuner, L, Nacket, Nuncheon, Packed, Piece, Ploughman, Pm, Tiff(in), Working

Lung(s) Bellows, Coalminer's, Farmer's, Iron, Lights, Pulmo, Pulmonary, Soul

Lunge Breenge, Breinge, Dive, Stab, Thrust, Venue

Lurch Reel, Stoit, Stumble, Swee

Lure Bait, Bribe, Carrot, Decoy, Entice, Horn, Inveigle, Jig, Judas, Roper, Spinner, Stale, Temptation, Tice, Tole, Toll, Train, Trepan

Lurgi Illness

Lurk(ing) Dare, Latitant, Skulk, Slink, Snoke, Snook, Snowk

Lush Drunk, Fertile, Green, Juicy, Lydian, Sot, Tosspot, Verdant

Lust(ful), Lusty Cama, Concupiscence, Corflambo, Desire, Eros, Frack, Greed, Kama, Lech(ery), Lewd, Megalomania, Obidicut, Randy, Rank, Raunchy, Salacious, Venereous

Lustre, Lustrous Brilliance, Census, Galena, Gaum, Gilt, Gloss, Gorm, Inaurate, Lead-glance, Pentad, Reflet, Satiny, Schiller, Water

Lute, Lutist Amphion, Chitarrone, Cither, Dichord, Orpharion, Pandora, Theorbo, Vielle

Luxuriant, Luxuriate, Luxurious, Luxury (lover) Bask, Clover, Cockaigne, Cockayne, Copious, Deluxe, Dolce vita, Extravagant, Fleshpots, Lavish, Lucullan, Lush, Mollitious, Ornate, Pie, Plush, Posh, Rank, > RICH, Ritzy, Sumptuous, Sybarite, Wallow

▶ **Lying** *see* LIE

Lyre Cithern, Harp, Psaltery, Testudo

Lyric(al), Lyricist, Lyrist Cavalier, Dit(t), Epode, Gilbert, Melic, Ode, Orphean, Paean, Pean, Poem, Rhapsodic, Song

Mm

M Married, Member, Metre, Mike, Mile, Thousand

Macabre Gothic, Grotesque, Sick

Machine(ry) Apparat(us), Appliance, Automaton, Bathing, Bulldozer, Calender, Centrifuge, Cycle, > DEVICE, Dialyser, Dredge(r), Drum, Engine, Enginery, Facsimile, Fax, Fruit, Gin, Hawk-eye®, Heck, Hopper, Hot-press, Instrument, Jawbreaker, Lathe, Life-support, Loom, Milling, Moulinet, Mule, Nintendo®, Party, Planer, Plant, Press, Processor, Propaganda, Pulsator, Robot, Rowing, Sewing, Slicer, Slot, Spinning jenny, Tape, Tedder, Throstle, Time, Transfer, Turbine, Turing, Twin tub, Typewriter, Vending, Virtual, War, Washing, Weighing, Wimshurst, Wind(mill), Wringer

Mackintosh Burberry®, Mac, Mino, Oilskin, Slicker, Waterproof

Mad(den), Madman, Madness Angry, Balmy, Bananas, Barking, Barmy, Bedlam, Besotted, Bonkers, Crackbrained, Crackpot, Crazy, Cuckoo, Cupcake, Delirious, Dement, Distract, Dotty, Enrage, Fay, Fey, Folie, Folly, Frantic, Frenetic(al), Fruitcake, Furioso, Fury, Gelt, Gyte, Harpic, Hatter, Idiotic, Insane, Insanie, Insanity, Into, Irritate, Kook, Loco, Lunatic, Lycanthropy, Madbrained, Maenad, Mania, Mental, Meshug(g)a, Midsummer, Mullah, Psycho, Rabid, Raving, Redwood, Redwud, Scatty, Screwy, Short-witted, Starkers, Tonto, Touched, Troppo, Unhinged, Wood, Wowf, Wrath, Wud, Xenomania, Yond, Zany

▷ **Mad(den)** *may indicate* an anagram

▷ **Madly** *may indicate* an anagram

Madonna Lady, Lily, Mary, Pietà, Virgin

Madras Chennai

Mafia Camorra, Capo, Cosa nostra, Godfather, Mob, Ndrangheta, Omerta

Magazine Arsenal, Clip, Colliers, Cornhill, Cosmopolitan, Digizine, Economist, Field, Girlie, Glossy, Granta, Lady, Lancet, Listener, Magnet, Organ, Periodical, Pictorial, Playboy, Pulp, Punch, She, Slick, Spectator, Store, Strand, Tatler, Time, Vogue, Warehouse, Weekly, Yoof

Magic(al), Magician, Magic square Art, Black, Charm, Conjury, Diablerie, Diablery, Enchanting, Faust, Genie, Goetic, Goety, Gramary(e), Houdini, Illusionist, Incantation, Math, Medea, Merlin, Mojo, Moly, Morgan le Fay, Necromancer, Powwow, Prospero, Rhombus, Sorcery, Spell, Speller, Supernatural, Talisman, Voodoo, White, Wizard

Magistracy, Magistrate Aedile, Amman, Amtman, Archon, Avoyer, Bailie, Bailiff, Bailli(e), Burgess, Burgomaster, Cadi, Censor, Consul, Corregidor, Demiurge, Doge(ate), Edile, Effendi, Ephor, Field cornet, Finer, Foud, Gonfalonier, JP, Judiciary, Jurat, Kotwal, Landamman(n), Landdrost, Maire, Mayor, Mittimus, Novus homo, Podesta, Portreeve, Pr(a)efect, Pr(a)etor, Prior, Proconsul, Propraetor, Provost, Qadi, Quaestor, Recorder, Reeve, Shereef, Sherif, Stad(t)holder, Stipendiary, Syndic, Tribune, Worship

Magnate Baron, Bigwig, Industrialist, Mogul, Tycoon, VIP

Magnet(ic), Magnetism Animal, Artificial, Attraction, Bar, Charisma, Field, Gauss, Horseshoe, It, Loadstone, Lodestone, Maxwell, Od, Oersted, Permanent, Personal, Polar, Pole, Pole piece, Poloidal, Pull, Remanence, Retentivity, Solenoid,

Terrella, Terrestrial, Tesla, Tole

Magnificence, Magnificent Gorgeous, Grandeur, Imperial, Laurentian, Lordly, Noble, Pride, Regal, Royal, Splendid, State, Superb

Magnifier, Magnify(ing) Aggrandise, Augment, Binocle, > **ENLARGE**, Exaggerate, Increase, Loupe, Microscope, Teinoscope, Telescope

Magnolia An(n)ona, Beaver-tree, Champac, Champak, Mississippi, Sweet bay, Umbrella-tree, Yulan

Magpie Bell, Bird, Chatterer, Madge, Mag, Margaret, Outer, Pica, Piet, Pyat, Pyet, Pyot

Maid(en) Abigail, Aia, Amah, Biddy, Bonibell, Bonne, Bonnibell, Chamber, Chloe, Clothes-horse, Damosel, Dell, Dey, First, Girl, Guillotine, Ignis-fatuus, Imago, Inaugural, Io, Iras, Iron, Lorelei, M, Marian, May, Miss, Nymph, Opening, Over, Pucelle, Rhine, Skivvy, Soubrette, Suivante, Thestylis, Tirewoman, Tweeny, Valkyrie, Virgin, Wench

Mail Air, > **ARMOUR**, Byrnie, Cataphract, Chain, Da(w)k, E(lectronic), Express, Fan, Habergeon, Hate, Hauberk, Helm, Junk, Letter, Panoply, Pony express, Post, Ring, Send, Snail, Spam, Surface, Tuille(tte), Voice

Mailbag Pouch

Main(s) Brine, Briny, > **CENTRAL**, Chief, Cockfight, Conduit, Essential, Foremost, Generally, Grid, Gross, Head, > **KEY**, Lead(ing), Palmary, Predominant, Prime, Principal, Ring, > **SEA**, Sheer, Spanish, Staple, Water

Maintain, Maintenance Alimony, Allege, Ap(p)anage, Argue, Assert, Aver, Avouch, Avow, Claim, Contend, Continue, Defend, Escot, Insist, Preserve, Run, Sustain, Upbear, Uphold, Upkeep

Maize Corn, Hominy, Indian, Mealie, Popcorn, Samp

Majestic, Majesty August, Britannic, Dignity, Eagle, Grandeur, Imperial, Maestoso, Olympian, Regal, SM, Sovereign, Stately, Sublime, Tuanku

Major (domo) Drum, > **IMPORTANT**, PM, Seneschal, Senior, Sergeant, Star, Trumpet, Wig

Majority Absolute, Age, Body, Eighteen, Landslide, Latchkey, Maturity, Moral, Most, Preponderance, Relative, Silent, Working

Make(r), Make do, Making Amass, Brand, Build, Clear, Coerce, Coin, Compel, Compulse, Concoct, Creant, Create, Devise, Earn, Execute, Fabricate, Factive, Fashion, Faute de mieux, Fet(t), Forge, Form, Gar(re), God, Halfpenny, Mail(e), Manage, Marque, Prepare, Production, Reach, Render, Shape, Sort

▷ **Make** *may indicate* an anagram

Make believe Fantasy, Fictitious, Pretend, Pseudo

Make up Ad lib, Compose, Concealer, Constitution, Cosmetics, Gaud, Gawd, Gene, Identikit®, Kohl, Liner, Lipstick, Maquillage, Mascara, Metabolism, Paint, Pancake, Powder, Reconcile, Rouge, Slap, Tidivate, Titivate, Toiletry, White-face

Male Arrhenotoky, Buck, Bull, Dog, Ephebe, Ephebus, Gent, Hob, John Doe, Macho, Mansize, Masculine, Ram, Rogue, Spear(side), Stag, Stamened, Telamon, Tom

Malfunction Glitch, Hiccup

Malice, Malicious Bitchy, Catty, Cruel, Despiteous, Envy, Malevolent, Malign, Narquois, Schadenfreude, Serpent, Snide, Spite, Spleen, Venom, Virulent

Malign(ant), Malignity Asperse, Backbite, Baleful, Defame, Denigrate, Gall, Harm, Hate-rent, Hatred, Libel, Sinister, Slander, Spiteful, Swart(h)y, Toxin, Vicious, Vilify, Vilipend, Viperous, Virulent

Malleable Clay, Ductile, Fictile, Pliable

▷ **Malleable** *may indicate* an anagram

Mallet Beetle, Club, Hammer, Mace, Maul, Stick

Mammal Animal, Armadillo, Artiodactyl, Binturong, Bobcat, Cacomistle, Cacomixle, Caracal, Cervid, Cetacean, Charronia, Chevrotain, Chiropteran, Ciscus, Colugo, Creodont, Dhole, Dinothere, Dolphin, Dugong, Eutheria, Fisher, Glires, Glutton, Grison, Guanaco, Hydrax, Hyrax, Indri, Jaguarondi, Jaguarundi, Kinkajou, Lagomorph, Leporid, Linsang, Loris, Lynx, Manatee, Margay, Marten, Meerkat, Mongoose, Monotreme, Musteline, Numbat, Olungo, Otter, Pachyderm, Pangolin, Peccary, Pekan, Perissodactyl, Pika, Pine marten, Pinniped, Platypus, Polecat, Porpoise, Primate, Pronghorn, Pudu, Raccoon, Rasse, Rhytina, Sable, Shrew, Sirenian, Skunk, Sloth, Solenodon, Springhaas, Taguan, Tahr, Takin, Tamandu(a), Tanrec, Tapir, Tayra, Teledu, Tenrec, Theria(n), Titanothere, Tylopod, Uintathere, Vicuna, Viverrid, Weasel, Whale, Wolverine, Zorilla

Mammoth Epic, Gigantic, Huge, Jumbo, Mastodon, Whopping, Woolly

Man(kind) Ask(r), Best, Betty, Bimana(l), Biped, Bloke, Bo, Boxgrove, Boy, Cad, Cairn, Calf, Castle, Cat, Chal, Chap, Checker, Chequer, Chiel, Cockey, Cod, Contact, Continuity, Crew, Cro-Magnon, Cuffin, Cully, Dog, Don, Draught, Dude, Emmanuel, Essex, Everyman, Family, Fancy, Fella, Feller, Fellow, Folsom, Friday, Front, G, Gayomart, Geezer, Gent, Grimaldi, Guy, He, Heidelberg, Himbo, Hombre, Hominid, Homme, Homo, Homo sapiens, Inner, IOM, Iron, Isle, Jack, Java, Joe (Bloggs), Joe Blow, Joe Sixpack, John(nie), John Doe, Josser, Limit, Lollipop, M, Male, Medicine, Microcosm, Mister, Mon, Mondeo, Mr, Muffin, Mun, Neanderthal, Nutcracker, Oreopithecus, Organisation, Ou, Paleolithic, Party, Pawn, Peking, Person, Piece, Piltdown, Pin, Pithecanthropus, Property, Raff, Remittance, Renaissance, Resurrection, Rhodesian, Right-hand, Rook, Sandwich, Servant, Servitor, Ship, Sinanthropus, Sodor, Soldier, Solo, Spear, Staff, Stag, Straw, Third, Thursday, Trinil, Twelfth, Tyke, Type, Utility, Valet, Vir, White van, Wight

Manage(r), Manageable, Management, Managing Administer, Amildar, Attain, Aumil, Behave, Boss, Chief, Conduct, Contrive, Control, Cope, Darogha, Direct, Docile, Exec(utive), Fare, Find, Govern, Grieve, Handle, Honcho, IC, Impresario, Intendant, Logistical, MacReady, Maitre d('hotel), Manipulate, Manoeuvre, Proctor, Procurator, Regisseur, Rig, Roadie, > RUN, Scrape, Shift, Steward, Succeed, Suit, Superintend, Tawie, Tractable, Treatment, Trustee, Wangle, Wield(y), Yare

Mandate Authority, Decree, Fiat, Order

Mandela Madiba, Nelson

Mangle Agrise, Butcher, Distort, Garble, Hack, Hackle, Haggle, Wring(er)

▷ **Mangle** *may indicate* an anagram

Mania Cacoethes, Craze, Frenzy, Passion, Rage

Manifesto Plank, Platform, Policy, Pronunciamento

Manipulate, Manipulative, Manipulator, Manipulation Chiropractor, Control, Cook, Demagogic, Diddle, Fashion, Gerrymander, Handle, Jerrymander, Juggle, Logodaedalus, Osteopath, Ply, Rig, Tweeze, Use, Wangle

▷ **Manipulate** *may indicate* an anagram

Manner(ism), Mannerly, Manners Accent, A la, Appearance, Attitude, Bedside, Behaved, Behaviour, Bon ton, Breeding, Carriage, Conduct, Couth, Crew, Custom, Deportment, Ethos, Etiquette, Farand, Farrand, Farrant, Habit, How, Mien, Mode, Morality, Mores, Of, Ostent, Panache, Politesse, Presentation, P's & Q's, Quirk, Rate, Sort, Style, Thew(s), Thewe(s), Trick, Urbanity, Way, Wise

Manoeuvre(s) Campaign, Castle, Engineer, Exercise, Faena, Fianchetto, Fork, Gambit, Heimlich, Hot-dog, Jink(s), Jockey, Manipulate, Op(eration), Pesade, Ploy, Ruse, Skewer, Use, U-turn, Valsalva, Wheelie, Whipstall, Wile, Zigzag

▷ **Manoeuvre** *may indicate* an anagram

Manor (house) Area, Demain, Demesne, Estate, Hall, Vill(a)

Mansion Casa, Knole, Luton Hoo, Mentmore, Penshurst Place, Queen's House, Seat, Stourhead, Stowe

Mantle Asthenosphere, Authority, Burnous(e), Capote, Caracalla, Dolman, Elijah, Gas, Pall, Pallium, Paludament, Pelisse, Rochet, Sima, Toga, Tunic, Veil

Manual Blue collar, Bradshaw, Cambist, Console, Enchiridion, Guide, Hand, Handbook, How-to, Portolan(o), Positif

Manure Compost, Dressing, Dung, > FERTILISER, Guano, Hen-pen, Lime, Muck, Sha(i)rn, Tath

Manuscript(s) Codex, Codicology, Folio, Hand, Holograph, Longhand, MS, Opisthograph, Palimpsest, Papyrus, Parchment, Script, Scroll, Scrowl(e), Vellum

▷ **Manx** *may indicate* a last letter missing

Many C, CD, Countless, D, Hantle, Herd, Horde, Host, L, Lot, M, Manifold, Mony, Multi(tude), Myriad, Scad, Sight, Stacks, Tons, Umpteen

▷ **Many** *may indicate* the use of a Roman numeral letter

Map(ping) Atlas, Card, Cartogram, Chart, Chorography, Cognitive, Contour, Face, Genetic, Inset, Key, Loxodromic, Mappemond, OS, Plan, Plot, Relief, Sea-card, Sea-chart, Topography, Weather

Maple Acer, Mazer, Norway, Plane, Sugar, Sycamore, Syrup

Map-maker Cartographer, OS, Speed

Marble(s), Marbling Agate, All(e)y, Arch, Bonce, Bonduc, Bool, Boondoggle, Bowl, Chequer, Devil's, Dump, Elgin, Humite, Knicker, Languedoc, Marl, Marmoreal, Mottle, Nero-antico, Nicker, Onychite, Paragon, Parian, Petworth, Plonker, Plunker, Purbeck, Rance, Ringer, Ring-taw, Sanity, Scagliola, Taw, Variegate

March(ing) Abut, Adjoin, Advance, Anabasis, Border(er), Borderland, Dead, Defile, Demo, Etape, File, Footslog, Forced, Freedom, Fringe, Galumph, Go, Goosestep, Hunger, Ides, Jarrow, Lide, Limes, Lockstep, Meare, Music, > PARADE, Progress, Protest, Quick, Route, Slow time, Step, Strunt, Strut, Trio, Tromp, Wedding, Yomp

▷ **March** *may indicate* 'Little Women' character, Amy, Beth, Jo, Meg

Marge, Margin(al) Annotate, Border, Brim, Brink, Curb, Edge, Hair's breadth, Lean, Limit, Littoral, Neck, Nose, Profit, Rand, Repand, > RIM, Selvedge, Sideline, Tail, Term

Marijuana Alfalfa, Camberwell carrot, Dagga, Gage, Ganja, Grass, Greens, Hay, Herb, Jive, Kaif, Kef, Kif, Leaf, Locoweed, Mary-Jane, Pot, Roach, Rope, Shit, Sinsemilla, Splay, Spliff, Tea, Toke, Weed

Marinade Chermoula, Escabeche

Mariner AB, Ancient, MN, RM, Sailor, Salt, Seafarer, Tar

Mark(ing), Marked, Marks Accent, Antony, Apostrophe, Asterisk, Astrobleme, Badge, Banker, Bethumb, Birth, Blaze, Blot, Blotch, Brand, Bruise, Bull, Butt, Cachet, Caract, Caret, Caste, CE, Cedilla, Charter, Chequer, Cicatrix, Class, Clout, Colon, Comma, Coronis, Crease, Criss-cross-row, Dash, Denote, Dent, Diacritic, Diaeresis, Dieresis, Distinction, DM, Duckfoot quote, Ensign, Enstamp, Exclamation, Expression, Feer, Fleck, Glyph, Gospel, Grade, Guillemet, Hacek, Hair-line, Hash, Hatch, Heed, High water, Hyphen, Impress(ion), Indicium, Ink, Inscribe, Insignia, Interrogation, Keel, Kite, Kumkum, Lentigo, Line, Ling, Livedo, Logo, Lovebite, Low water, M, Macron, MB, Merk, Mottle, NB, Notal, Note, Notice, Obelisk, Observe, Oche, Paginate, Paraph, Period, Pilcrow, Pit, Plage, Pling, Point, Popinjay, Port wine, Post, Presa, Printer's, Proof, Punctuation, Question, Quotation, Record, Reference, Register, Regulo, Ripple, Roundel, Sanction, Scar, Score, Scratch, Section, See, Service, Shadow, Shilling, Sigil, Sign, Smit, Smut, Smutch, Speck, Splodge, Splotch, Stain, Stencil, Stigma(ta),

Strawberry, Stress, Stretch, Sucker, Swan-upping, Symbol, Tag, Target, Tatow, Tattoo, Tee, Theta, Thread, Tick, Tika, Tikka, Tilak, Tilde, Tittle, Token, Touchmark, Trace, Track, Trout, Tug(h)ra, Twain, Umlaut, Ure, Victim, Wand, Warchalking, Watch, Weal, Welt

Market(ing), Market day, Market place, Market garden Agora, Alcaiceria, Baltic, Bazaar, Bear, Billingsgate, Black, Borgo, Bull, Buyer's, Capital, Captive, Cattle, Change, Chowk, Common, Denet, Direct, Discount, Dragon, EC, Emerging, Emporium, Errand, Exchange, Fair, Feeing, Flea, Forum, Forward, Free, Grey, Growth, Internal, Kerb, Lloyds, Main, Mandi, Mart, Mercat, Money, Niche, Nundine, Open, Outlet, Piazza, Relationship, Sale, Sellers', Share, Shop, Single, Social, Sook, Souk, Spot, Stance, Staple, Stock, Stock Exchange, Tattersall's, Terminal, Test, Third, Tiger, Trade, Tron, Truck-farm , Tryst, Vent, Viral, Wall Street

Maroon Brown, Castaway, Enisle, Firework, Inisle, Isolate, Strand

Marriage > ALLIANCE, Bed, Beenah, Bigamy, Bridal, Coemption, Confarreation, Conjugal, Connubial, Digamy, Endogamy, Espousal, Exogamy, Gandharva, Genial, Hetaerism, Hetairism, Hymen(eal), Jugal, Ketubah, Knot, Levirate, Match, Mating, Matrilocal, Matrimony, Mésalliance, Monandry, Monogamy, Morganatic, Noose, Nuptial, Pantagamy, Punalua, Sacrament, Shidduch, Tie, > UNION, Wedding, Wedlock

Marrow Courgette, Friend, Gist, Medulla, Myeloid, Pith, Pumpkin, Squash, Vegetable

Marry, Married Ally, Amate, Buckle, Cleek(it), Confarreate, Couple, Coverture, Espouse, Feme covert, Forsooth, Hitch, Join, Knit, M, Mate, Matron, Memsahib, Pair, Pardie, Quotha, Splice, Tie, Troggs, Troth, Unite, W, Wed, Wive

Marsh(y) Bayou, Bog, Chott, Corcass, Emys, Everglades, Fen, Hackney, Maremma, Merse, Mire, Morass, Ngaio, Paludal, Plashy, Pontine, Pripet, Quagmire, Romney, Salina, Salt, Shott, Slade, Slough, Sog, Spew, Spue, Swale, Swamp, Taiga, Terai, Vlei, Wetlands

Marshal Arrange, Array, Commander, Earp, Foch, French, Hickok, MacMahon, Muster, Neil, Ney, Order, Pétain, Provost, Shepherd, Tedder, Usher

Marsupial Bandicoot, Bilby, Cuscus, Dasyure, Dibbler, Didelphia, Diprotodont, Dunnart, Honey mouse, Honey possum, Kangaroo, Koala, Macropod, Metatheria, Notoryctes, Notothenium, Numbat, Opossum, Pad(d)ymelon, Pademelon, Petaurist, Phalanger, Polyprodont, Possum, Potoroo, Pouched mouse, Pygmy glider, Quokka, Quoll, Roo, Tammar, Tasmanian devil, Theria, Thylacine, Tuan, Wallaby, Wambenger, Wombat, Yapo(c)k

Martial (arts) Bellicose, Budo, Capoeira, Capuera, Chopsocky, Dojo, Iai-do, Judo, Ju-jitsu, Karate, Kung Fu, Militant, Ninjutsu, Shintaido, Tae kwon do, T'ai chi (chuan), Warlike, Wushu

Martyr(dom), Martyrs Alban, Alphege, Colosseum, Donatist, Justin, Latimer, MM, Passional, Persecute, Sebastian, Stephen, Suffer, Tolpuddle, Wishart

Marvel(lous) Epatant, Fab, Marl, Miracle, Mirific, Phenomenon, Prodigious, Superb, Super-duper, Terrific, Wonder

Marx(ism), Marxist Aspheterism, Chico, Comintern, Commie, Groucho, Gummo, Harpo, Karl, Menshevik

Mary Bloody, Celeste, Madonna, Moll, Morison, Tum(my), Typhoid, Virgin

Mascot Charm, Talisman, Telesm, Token

Masculine, Masculinity He, He-man, Linga(m), M, Machismo, Macho, Male, Manly, Virile

Mash(er) Beau, Beetle, Brew, Lady-killer, Pap, Pestle, Pound, Sour, Squash

Mask(ed) Bird cage, Camouflage, Cloak, Cokuloris, Death, Disguise, Dissemble, Domino, False face, Gas, Hide, Larvated, Life, Loo, Loup, Mascaron, Matte, Oxygen, Persona, Respirator, Screen, Semblance, Shadow, Stalking-horse,

Stocking, Stop out, Template, Visor, Vizard

Mass(es) Aggregate, Agnus dei, Anniversary, Banket, Bezoar, Bike, Body, Bulk, Cake, Chaos, Clot, Congeries, Conglomeration, Consecration, Core, Crith, Critical, Crowd, Demos, Density, Flake, Flysch, Folk, Geepound, Gravitational, Great, Herd, High, Horde, Hulk, Inertial, Jud, Kermesse, Kermis, Kilo(gram), Kirmess, Low, Lump, M, Majority, Missa, Month's mind, Mop, Nest, Phalanx, Pile, Plumb, Pontifical, Populace, Proper, Raft, Requiem, Rest, Ruck, Salamon, Salmon, Scrum, Sea, Serac, Service, Shock, Sicilian, Size, Slub, Slug, Solar, Solemn, Solid, Stack, Stroma, Sursum corda, Te Igitur, Tektite, Trental, Vesper, Vigil, Volume, Wad, Weight, Welter

Massacre Amritsar, Blood-bath, Butcher, Carnage, Glencoe, Havock, Manchester, Peterloo, Pogrom, Purge, Scullabogue, Scupper, September, Sicilian vespers, Slaughter, Slay

Massage, Masseur An mo, Chafer, Do-in, Effleurage, > **KNEAD**, Malax, Palp, Petrissage, Physio, Rolf(ing), Rubber, Shampoo, Shiatsu, Swedish, Tapotement, Thai, Tripsis, Tui na

Massif Makalu

Massive Big, Bull, Colossal, Heavy, Herculean, Huge, Monumental, Strong, Titan

Mast(ed), Masthead Acorn, Crosstree, Hounds, Jigger, Jury, Mizzen, Pannage, Pole, Racahout, Royal, Ship-rigged, Spar, Top-gallant

Master(ly) Artful, Baalebos, Baas, Beak, Beat, Boss, Buddha, Bwana, Careers, Checkmate, Conquer, Control, Dan, Dominate, Dominie, Employer, Enslave, Exarch, Expert, Gov, Grand, Harbour, Herr, Himself, International, Learn, Lord, MA, Maestro, Mas(s), Mes(s), Nkosi, Old, Ollamh, Ollav, Oner, Oppress, Original, Overcome, Overlord, Overpower, Overseer, Passed, Past, Pedant, Rabboni, Seigneur, Seignior, Signorino, Sir(e), Skipper, > **SUBDUE**, Subjugate, Superate, Surmount, Swami, Tame, Task, Thakin, Towkay, Tuan, Usher, Vanquish, Virtuoso

Mastersinger Sachs

Mat(ted), Matting Bast, Coaster, Doily, Dojo, Doyley, Felt, Inlace, Pad, Paunch, Plat, Rug, > **TANGLE**, Tat(ami), Tatty, Taut, Tawt, Tomentose, Welcome, Zarf

Match(ed) Agree, Alliance, Amate, Balance, Besort, Bonspiel, Bout, Carousel, Compare, Congreve, Contest, Cope, Correlate, Correspond, Counterpane, Doubles, Emulate, Engagement, Equal(ise), Equate, Even, Exhibition, Fellow, Fit, Fixture, Four-ball, Friction, Friendly, Fusee, Fuzee, Game, Go, Greensome, International, Joust, Light, Locofoco, Love, Lucifer, Main, Marrow, Marry, Meet, Mouse, Needle, Pair(s), Paragon, Parti, Pit, Prizefight, Promethean, Reproduce, Return, Rival, Roland, Rubber, Safety, Shield, Singles, Slanging, Slow, Spunk, Striker, Suit, Sync, > **TALLY**, Team, Test, Tie, Twin, Union, Venue, Vesta, Vesuvian, Wedding

Mate, Mating Achates, Adam, Amigo, Amplexus, Bedfellow, Bo, Breed, Buddy, Buffer, Butty, Chess, China, Chum, Cobber, Comrade, Consort, Crony, Cully, Digger, Eve, Feare, Feer, Fellow, Fere, Fiere, Fool's, Husband, Maik, Make, Marrow, Marry, Match, Mister, Oldster, Oppo, > **PAIR**, Pal, Paragon, Partner, Pheer(e), Pirrauru, Scholar's, Serve, Sex, Skaines, Smothered, Soul, > **SPOUSE**, Tea, Wack, Wife, Wus(s)

Material Agalmatolite, Aggregate, Agitprop, Apt, Armure, Ballast, Blastema, Bole, Borsic, Byssus, Celluloid, Cellulose, Ceramic, Cermet, > **CLOTH**, Cob, Compo, Copy, Corfam®, Corporeal, Data, Documentation, Earthy, > **FABRIC**, Factual, Fallout, Fettling, Fibrefill, Fibreglass, Fines, Flong, Frit(t), Fuel, Gang(ue), Germane, Hylic, Illusion, Illuvium, Interfacing, Lambskin, Macintosh, Matter, Metal, Oilskin, Papier-maché, Pertinent, Physical, Pina-cloth, Plasterboard, Positive, Pug(ging), Raw, Relevant, Sackcloth, Sagathy, Skirting, Stuff, Substance,

Swish, Tangible, Tape, Textile, Thingy, Towelling, Tusser, Wattle and daub

Mathematician Apollonius, Archimedes, Archytas, Bernoulli, Bessel, Boole, Briggs, Cantor, Cocker, Descartes, Diophantus, Dunstable, Eratosthenes, Euclid, Euler, Fermat, Fibonacci, Fourier, Gauss, Godel, Goldbach, Gunter, Hawking, Laplace, Leibniz, Lie, Mercator, Napier, Newton, Optime, Pascal, Penrose, Playfair, Poisson, Ptolemy, Pythagoras, Pytheas, Riemann, Torricelli, Turing, Wrangler, Zeno

Mathematics, **Mathematical**, **Maths** Algebra, Arithmetic, Arsmetrick, Calculus, Geometry, Logarithms, Mechanics, Numbers, Trig

Matter Alluvium, Bioblast, Biogen, Body, Concern, Consequence, Dark, Degenerate, Empyema, Epithelium, Gear, Gluon, Go, Grey, Hyle, Impost(h)ume, Issue, Mass, Material, Molecule, Phlegm, Pith, Point, Positron, Protoplasm, Pulp, Pus, Quark, Reck, Reke, Scum, Shebang, Signify, Solid, Subject, > **SUBSTANCE**, Thing, Topic, Tousle, Touzle, White, Ylem

Mattress Bed(ding), Biscuit, Foam, Futon, Lilo®, Pallet, Palliasse, Tick

Mature, **Maturity** Adult, Age, Blossom, Bold, Concoct, Develop, Mellow, Metaplasis, Puberty, Ripe(n), Rounded, Seasoned, Upgrow(n)

Maul Hammer, Manhandle, Paw, Rough

Maximum All-out, Full, Highest, Most, Peak, Utmost

May Blossom, Can, Hawthorn, Merry, Might, Month, Mote, Quickthorn, Shall, Whitethorn

Maybe Happen, Mebbe, Perchance, Perhaps, Possibly

▷ **May become** *may indicate* an anagram

Mayor Alcaide, Burgomaster, Casterbridge, Councilman, Porteeve, Provost, Whittington

Maze Labyrinth, Meander, Warren, Wilderness

MC Compere, Host, Ringmaster

Mead(ow) Flood, Grass, Haugh, Inch, Lea(se), Ley, Meath(e), > **PASTURE**, Runnymede, Saeter, Salting, Water

Meagre Bare, Exiguous, Measly, Paltry, Pittance, Scant, Scrannel, Scranny, Skimpy, Skinny, Spare, Stingy, Thin

Meal(s) Banquet, Barbecue, Barium, Beanfeast, Blow-out, Board, Breakfast, Brunch, Buffet, Cassava, Cereal, Cholent, Chota-hazri, Collation, Corn, Cornflour, Cottoncake, Cottonseed, Cou-cou, Cribble, Dejeune(r), Deskfast, Dinner, Drammock, Ervalenta, Fare, Farina, Feast, Flour, Food, Grits, Grout, Hangi, High tea, Iftar, Indian, Lock, Lunch, Mandioc, Mandioc(a)a, Mani(h)oc, Matzo, Melder, Meltith, Mensal, Mess, Mush, No-cake, Nosh, Nuncheon, Obento, Ordinary, Picnic, Piece, Plate, Poi, Polenta, Porridge, Prandial, Prix fixe, Rac(c)ahout, Refection, Repast, Revalenta, Rijst(t)afel, Salep, Scambling, Scoff, Seder, Smorgasborg, Snack, Spread, Square, Supper, Table d'hote, Takeaway, Tea, Thali, Tiffin, Tightener, Twalhours, Undern

Mean(ing), **Meant** Aim, Arithmetic(al), Average, Base, Betoken, Bowsie, Caitiff, Connotation, Curmudgeon, Definition, Denotate, Denote, Design, Dirty, Drift, Essence, Ettle, Feck, Footy, Foul, Geometric(al), Gist, Golden, Hang, Harmonic, Humble, Hunks, Ignoble, Illiberal, Imply, Import, Inferior, Insect, Intend, Intermediate, Lexical, Low, Mang(e)y, Marrow, Medium, Mesquin, Method, Mid, Miserly, Narrow, Near, Norm, Nothing, One-horse, Ornery, Paltry, Par, Penny-pinching, Petty, Piker, Pinch-penny, Pith, Point, Purport, > **PURPOSE**, Quadratic, Ratfink, Revenue, Roinish, Roynish, Scall, Scrub, Scurvy, Semanteme, Semantic(s), Sememe, Sense, Shabby, Signify, Slight, Small, Sneaky, Snoep, Snot, Sordid, Sparing, Spell, Stingy, Stink(ard), Stinty, Substance, Symbol, Thin, Threepenny, Tightwad, Two-bit, Value, Whoreson

Means Agency, Dint, Income, Media, Method, Mode, Opulence, Organ, Private,

Resources, Staple, Substance, Tactics, Visible, Ways

Measure(d), **Measuring**, **Measurement** By(e)law, Calibre, Circular,
Crackdown, > DANCE, > DIMENSION, Distance, Dose, Dry, Gavotte, Gross, Imperial,
Limit, Linear, Moratorium, Of, Offset, Precaution, Prophylactic, Quickstep,
Ration, Share, > SIZE, Standard, Statute, Step, Strike, Struck, Survey, Token, Wine

Meat(s) Bacon, Bard, Beef, Biltong, Brawn, Brisket, Brown, Burger, Cabob,
Carbonado, Carrion, Charcuterie, Chop, Collop, Confit, Croquette, Cut, Devon,
Easy, Edgebone, Entrecote, Escalope, Essence, Fanny Adams, Fleishig, Fleishik,
Flesh, Flitch, Force, Galantine, Gigot, Gobbet, Gosht, Griskin, Ham, Haslet,
Jerky, Joint, Junk, Kabab, Kabob, Kebab, Kebob, Lamb, Loin, Luncheon, Mart,
Mince, Mutton, Noisette, Offal, Olive, Pastrami, Pem(m)ican, Piccata, Pith,
Pork, Processed, Rack, Red, Rillettes, Roast, Saddle, Sasatie, Satay, Scaloppino,
Schnitzel, Scran, Scrapple, Sey, Shashlik, Shishkebab, Side, Sirloin, Sosatie,
Spam®, Spare rib, Spatchcock, Spaul(d), Steak, Tenderloin, Tongue, Variety, Veal,
Venison, Vifda, Virgate, Vivda, Weiner schnitzel, White, Wurst

Mechanic(s) Apron-man, Artificer, Artisan, Banausic, Engineer, Fitter, Fundi,
Hand, Journeyman, Kinematics, Kinetics, Operative, Statics, Technician

▷ **Mechanic(al)** *may indicate* characters from 'A Midsummer Night's Dream'

Mechanical, **Mechanism** Action, Apparatus, Auto, Banausic, Derailleur,
Escapement, Gimmal, Instrument, Machinery, Movement, Organical, Pulley,
Pushback, Servo, Trippet, Works

Medal(lion)(s) Award, Bar, Bronze, Decoration, Dickin, DSM, GC, George, Gold,
Gong, Gorget, MM, Numismatic, Pan(h)agia, Purple Heart, Putty, Roundel, Silver,
Touchpiece, VC, Vernicle

Mediate, **Mediator** ACAS, Arbitrate, Intercede, Interpose, Intervene, Liaison,
Muti, Referee, Thirdsman, Trouble-shooter

Medical, **Medicament**, **Medication**, **Medicine (chest)** Alternative, Anodyne,
Antacid, Antibiotic, Antidote, Antisepsis, Antiseptic, Arnica, Bi, Bismuth, Charm,
Chiropody, Chlorodyne, Clinician, Complementary, Cordial, Corpsman, Cubeb,
Curative, Defensive, Diapente, Dose, Draught, Drops, > DRUG, Dutch drops,
Electuary, Elixir, Empirics, Enema, Excipient, Expectorant, Fall-trank, Febrifuge,
Folk, Forensic, Fringe, Galen, Galenism, Genitourinary, Gutta, Herb, Herbal,
Holistic, Hom(o)eopathy, Iatric(al), Industrial, Inhalant, Inro, Internal, Iodine,
Iron, Ko cycle, Lariam®, Laxative, Leechcraft, Legal, Loblolly, Lotion, Magnesia,
Menthol, Mishmi, Mixture, Moxar, Muti, Nephritic, Nervine, Nostrum, Nuclear,
Nux vomica, Officinal, Oporice, Orthopoedics, Osteopath, Palliative, Panacea,
Paregoric, Patent, Pathology, Pharmacy, Physic, Physical, Pill, Placebo, Potion,
Poultice, Preparation, Preventive, Psionic, Psychiatry, Quinine, Quin(quin)a,
Radiology, Relaxative, > REMEDY, Salve, Sanative, Senna, Serology, Simple, Space,
Specific, Sports, Steel, Stomachic, Stupe, Suppository, Synergast, Syrup, Tablet,
Tar-water, Therapeutics, TIM, Tisane, Tonic, Totaquine, Trade, Traditional Chinese,
Treatment, Troche, Valerian, Veronal, Veterinary, Virology

Medieval Archaic, Feudal, Gothic, Med, Old, Trecento

Meditate, **Meditation**, **Meditator**, **Meditative** Brood, Chew, Cogitate,
Muse, Mystic, Ponder, Reflect, Reverie, Revery, Ruminate, Transcendental,
Vipassana, Weigh, Zazen

Medium Agency, Average, Channel, Clairvoyant, Contrast, Culture, Dispersive,
Element, Ether, Even, Happy, Home, Intermediary, Interstellar, M, Magilp, Mean,
Megilp, Midsize, Midway, Milieu, Oils, Organ, Ouija, Planchette, Press, Radio,
Regular, Shaman, Spiritist, Spiritualist, Television, Telly, TV, Vehicle

Medley Charivari, Collection, Gallimaufry, Jumble, Macedoine, Melange, Mix,
Pastiche, Patchwork, Pi(e), Pot-pourri, Quodlibet, Ragbag, Salad, Salmagundi,
Series

▷ **Medley** *may indicate* an anagram

Meek Docile, Griselda, Humble, Milquetoast, Patient, Tame

Meerkat Suricate

Meet(ing), Meeting place Abide, Abutment, AGM, Appointment, Apropos, Assemble, Assembly, Assignation, Audience, Baraza, Bosberaad, Camporee, Caucus, Chapterhouse, Chautauqua, Clash, Conclave, Concourse, Concur, Confluence, Confrontation, Congress, Connivance, Consistory, Consulta, Contact, Conterminous, Convene, Convent(icle), Convention, Converge, Conversazione, Convocation, Correspond, Cybercafé, Defray, Demo, EGM, Encounter, Ends, Experience, Face, Find, Fit, For(e)gather, Forum, Fulfil, Gemot, Giron, Gorsedd, Guild, Gyeld, Gymkhana, Gyron, Howf(f), Hunt, Hustings, Imbizo, Indaba, Infall, Interface, Interview, Join, Junction, Kgotla, Korero, Lekgotla, Liaise, Marae, Moot, Obviate, Occlusion, Occur, Oppose, Overflow, Pay, Plenary, Plenum, Pnyx, Pow-wow, Prayer, Prosper, Quadrivial, Quaker, Quorate, Quorum, Race, Races, Rally, Rencontre, Rencounter, Rendezvous, Reunion, Sabbat(h), Satisfy, Seance, See, Seminar, Session, Sit, Social, Sports, Suitable, Summit, Symposium, Synastry, Synaxis, Synod, Tackle, Talkfest, Town, Track, Tryst, Venue, Vestry, Wapinshaw, Wardmote, Wharepuni, Workshop

Mellow Genial, Mature, Ripe, Smooth

Melody, Melodious Air, Arioso, Cabaletta, Cantabile, Cantilena, Cantus, Conductus, Counterpoint, Descant, Dulcet, Euphonic, Fading, Musical, Orphean, Plainsong, Ranz-des-vaches, Strain, Theme, Tunable, > **TUNE(S)**

Melon(like) Cantaloup(e), Cas(s)aba, Gourd, Honeydew, Mango, Musk, Nar(r)as, Ogen, Pepo, Persian, Rock

Melt(ed), Melting Ablate, Colliquate, > **DISSOLVE**, Eutectic, Eutexia, Flux, Found, Fuse, Fusil(e), Liquescent, Liquid, Run, Smectic, Syntexis, Thaw, Touch

Member Adherent, Arm, Branch, Bro(ther), Chin, Confrère, Cornice, Crossbeam, Crypto, Direction, Felibre, Fellow, Forearm, Forelimb, Gremial, Insider, Leg, Limb, Longeron, M, MBE, Montant, MP, Organ, Part, Partisan, Private

Membrane, Membranous Amnion, Arachnoid, Axilemma, Caul, Chorioallantois, Chorion, Choroid (plexus), Chromoplast, Conjunctiva, Cornea, Decidua, Dissepiment, Dura (mater), Endocardium, Endometrium, Endosteum, Ependyma, Exine, Extine, Film, Frenulum, Haw, Hyaloid, Hymen, Indusium, Intima, Intine, Involucre, Mater, Mediastinum, Meninx, Mesentery, Mucosa, Mucous, Nictitating, Patagium, Pellicle, Pericardium, Pericarp, Perichondrium, Pericranium, Periost(eum), Periton(a)eum, Pia mater, Pleura, Putamen, Rim, Sarcolemma, Scarious, Schneiderian, Sclera, Serosa, Serous, Synovial, Tela, Third eyelid, Tissue, Tonoplast, Trophoblast, Tympan(ic), Vacuolar, Velum, Vitelline, Web

Memento, Memoir Keepsake, Locket, Relic, Remembrancer, Souvenir, Token, Trophy

Memo(randum) Bordereau, Cahier, Chit, IOU, Jot, Jurat, Minute, Note, Notepad, > **REMINDER**

Memorable, Memorise, Memory Bubble, Cache, Catchy, Collective, Con, Core, Echoic, Engram(ma), Extended, Flash (bulb), Folk, Get, Historic, Iconic, Immortal, Immunological, Learn, Living, Long-term, Main, Memoriter, Mind, Mneme, Mnemonic, Mnemosyne, Non-volatile, Notable, Pelmanism, Photographic, RAM, Recall, Recovered, > **REMEMBER**, Retention, Retrospection, Ro(a)te, ROM, Samskara, Screen, Semantic, Short-term, Souvenir, Sovenance, Static, Virtual, Volatile, Word, Working

Memorial Cenotaph, Cromlech, Ebenezer, Gravestone, Hatchment, Marker, Monument, Mount Rushmore, Obelisk, Plaque, Relic, Statue, Tomb, Trophy

Menace, Menacing Danger, Endanger, Foreboding, Minatory, Peril, Pest, Threat(en)

Mend Beet, Bete, Bushel, Cobble, Correct, Darn, Fix, Heal, Improved, Patch, Piece, Recover, Remedy, > REPAIR, Set, Sew, Solder, Trouble-shoot

Menial Drudge, Drug, Eta, Fag, Flunkey, Lowly, Scullion, Servile, Toady, Underling

▷ **Mental** *may indicate* the chin

Mention(ed) Allusion, Bename, Benempt, Broach, Bynempt, Citation, Hint, Name, Notice, Quote, Refer, Speech, State, Suggest, Touch

Menu Card, Carte, Carte du jour, Cascading, Fare, List, Table d'hôte, Tariff

Mercenary Arnaout, Condottiere, Freelance, Greedy, Hack, Hessian, Hireling, Landsknecht, Legionnaire, Pindaree, Pindari, Rutter, Sordid, Spoilsman, Venal, Wildgeese

Merchandise Cargo, Goods, Line, Produce, Ware(s)

Merchant(man) Abudah, Antonio, Broker, Bun(n)ia, Burgher, Chandler, Chap, Crare, Crayer, Dealer, Factor, Flota, Hoastman, Importer, Jobber, Magnate, Marcantant, Mercer, Monger, Négociant, Pedlar, Polo, Retailer, Shipper, Speed, Stapler, Trader, Vintner, Wholesaler

Merciful, Mercy Amnesty, Charity, Clement, Compassionate, Corporal, Grace, Humane, Kind, Kyrie, Lenient, Lenity, Miserere, Misericord(e), Pacable, Pity, Quarter, Ruth, Sparing, Spiritual

Merciless Cruel, Hard, Hard-hearted, Inclement, Pitiless

Mere(ly) Allenarly, Bare, Common, Lake, Pond, Pool, Pure, Sheer, Tarn, Very

Merge(r), Merging Amalgamate, Blend, Coalesce, Conflate, Consolidate, Die, Elide, Fusion, Incorporate, Interflow, Liquesce, Meld, Melt, Mingle, Syncretism, Synergy, Unify, Unite

Merit(ed) CL, Condign, Deserve, Due, Earn, Found, Rate, Virtue, Worth(iness)

Mess(y) Balls-up, Bedraggled, Boss, Botch, Canteen, Caudle, Chaos, Clamper, Clutter, Cock-up, Failure, Farrago, Fiasco, Flub, Garboil, G(l)oop, Glop, Gory, Guddle, Gunge, Gunk, Gun-room, Hash, Horlicks, Hotch-potch, Hugger-mugger, Imbroglio, Lash-up, Louse, Mash, Meal, Mismanage, Mix, Mixter-maxter, Modge, Muck, Muff, Muss, Mux, Pi(e), Piss-up, Plight, Pollute, Pottage, Screw-up, Scungy, Shambles, Shambolic, Shemozzle, Sight, Slaister, Smudge, Snafu, Soss, Sty, Sully, Untidy, Wardroom, Whoopsie, Yuck(y)

Message(s) Aerogram, Bull, Bulletin, Cable, Contraplex, Dépêche, Despatch, Dispatch, Errand, Flame, Missive, News, Note, Pager, Posting, Postscript, Radiogram, Rumour, Signal, Slogan, SOS, Subtext, Telegram, Telephone, Telex, Tidings, Wire, > WORD

Messenger Angel, Apostle, Azrael, Caddie, Caddy, Chaprassi, Chuprassy, Courier, Culver, Despatch-rider, Emissary, Envoy, Gaga, Gillie Whitefoot, Hatta, Herald, Hermes, Internuncio, Iris, Ladas, Mercury, Nuncio, Peon, Post, Pursuivant, Runner, Send

Messiah Christ, Emmanuel, Immanuel, Mahdi, Mashiach, Saviour, Son of man

Metal(s), Metallic, Metalware Ag, Aglet, Aiglet, Aiguillette, Al, Aluminium, Antimony, Babbitt, Base, Bell, Billon, Brassy, Britannia, Cadmium, Chrome, Chromium, Cobalt, Copper, Death, Dutch, Dysprosium, Er(bium), Europium, Expanded, Filler, Foil, Fusible, Gallium, Germanium, Gib, Heavy, Hot, Ingot, Invar®, Iridium, Iron, Jangling, Leaf, Magnolia, Manganese, Mineral, Misch, Mitis, Monel(l), Muntz, Natrium, Nickel, Noble, Nonferrous, Ore, Osmium, Parent, Perfect, Planchet, Platinum, Precious, Prince's, Protore, Regulus, Rhenium, Road, Ruthenium, Samarium, Scrap, Sheet(-iron), Slug, Sm, Sn, Sodium, Speculum, Speiss, Sprue, Steel, Strontium, Taggers, Tantalum, Terbic, Terbium, Terne, Thallium, Thorium, Thrash, Tin, Tole, Tramp, Transition, Tutania, Tutenag, Type, White, Wolfram, Yellow, Zinc

▷ **Metamorphosing** *may indicate* an anagram

Metaphor Conceit, Figure, Image, Kenning, Mixed, Symbol, Trope, Tropical

Meteor(ic), Meteorite Achondrite, Aerolite, Aerosiderite, Bolide, Chondrite, Comet, Drake, Fireball, Germinid, Leonid, Perseid, Siderite, Siderolite, Star(dust), Stony

Method(ology), Methodical Art, Billings, Formula, Gram's, Line, Manner, Mode, Modus, Modus operandi, Monte Carlo, Montessori, Neat, Orderly, Painstaking, Ploy, Procedure, Process, Stanislavski, > **SYSTEM**, Tactics, Technique, Way

Metre Alexandrine, Amphibrach, Amphimacer, Anapaest, Antispast, Arsis, Ballad, Cadence, Choliamb, Choree, Choriamb, Common, Dipody, Galliambic, Iambic, Long, M, Prosody, Rhythm, Sapphic, Scansion, Scazon, Service, Short, Spondee, Strophe, Tripody, Trochee

Microphone Bug, Crystal, Mike, Radio, Throat

Microwave Nuke

Mid(st) Amongst

Midday Meridian, N, Noon

Middle, Middling Active, Basion, Centre, Core, Crown, Enteron, Eye, Girth, Heart, Loins, Median, Mediocre, Meridian, Meseraic, Mesial, Mesne, Meso, Midriff, Moderate, Noon, Passive, Turn, Twixt, Wa(i)st

Middleman Broker, Comprador(e), Diaphragm, Interlocutor, Intermediary, Jobber, Median, Navel, Regrater, Regrator

Midget Dwarf, Homunculus, Lilliputian, Pygmy, Shrimp

Midlander Brummie

▶ **Midnight** *see* PAST MIDNIGHT

▶ **Midst** *see* MID

Might(iness), Mighty Force, Main, Mote, Nibs, Potence, > **POWER**, Prowess, Puissant, Should, Strength

Migrate, Migration, Migratory Colonise, Diapedesis, Diaspora, Drift, Eelfare, Exodus, Fleet, Run, Tre(c)k

Mild(ly) Balmy, Benign, Bland, Clement, Euphemism, Genial, Gentle, Lenient, Litotes, Mansuete, Meek, > **MODERATE**, Pacific, Patient, Sarcenet, Sars(e)net, Temperate

Mile(s) Admiralty, Coss, Coverdale, Food, Geographical, Knot, Kos, Li, Milliary, Nautical, Passenger, Roman, Royal, Sea, Soldier, Square, Standish, Statute, Swedish, Train

Militant, Military Activist, Aggressive, Battailous, Commando, Hawkish, Hezbollah, Hizbollah, Hizbullah, Hostile, Ireton, Landwehr, Mameluke, Martial, Presidio, Soldatesque, West Point

Militia Guard, Minuteman, Reserve, Trainband, Yeomanry

Milk(er), Milky Acidophilus, Beestings, Bland, Bleed, Bonny-clabber, Bristol, Casein, Colostrum, Condensed, Creamer, Crud, Curd, Emulge, Evaporated, Exploit, Galactic, Glacier, Goat's, Jib, Kefir, Kephir, K(o)umiss, Lactation, Lacteal, Latex, Madzoon, Magnesia, Matzoon, Mess, Opaline, Pinta, Posset, Sap, Shedder, Skim(med), Soya, Squeeze, Strippings, Stroke, Suckle, UHT, Whig, Yaourt, Yogh(o)urt

Mill(ing), Mills Aswarm, Barker's, Boxing, Coffee, Economist, Gang, Gastric, Grind(er), Hayley, Kibble, Knurl, Mano, Melder, Molar, Nurl, Paper, Pepper, Post, Powder, Press, Pug, Quern, Reave, Rob, Rolling, Satanic, Scutcher, Smock, Stamp, Stamping, Strip, Sugar, Surge, Thou, Tide, Tower, Tuck, Water, Wool(len), Works

Mime, Mimic(ry) Ape, Batesian, Copycat, Farce, Imitate, Impersonate, Mina, Mullerian, Mummer, Sturnine

Mind(er) Aide, Beware, Brain, Genius, Handler, > HEED, Herd, Id, Intellect, Psyche, Psychogenic, Resent, Sensorium, Tabula rasa, Tend, Thinker, Wit, Woundwort

Mine, Mining Acoustic, Antenna, Bomb, Bonanza, Bottom, Bouquet, Burrow, Camouflet, Chemical, Claymore, Colliery, Contact, Creeping, Dane-hole, Data, Dig(gings), Drifting, Egg, Eldorado, Excavate, Explosive, Floating, Flooder, Fougade, Fougasse, Gallery, Gob, Golconda, Gold, Gopher, Grass, Homing, Land, Limpet, Magnetic, Naked-light, Nostromo, Open-cast, Open-cut, Ophir, Pit, Placer, Pressure, Prospect, Rising, Sap, Set(t), Show, Sonic, Stannary, Stope, Strike, Strip, Undercut, Wheal, Win, Workings

Miner, Mine-worker, Mine-working Butty-gang, Collier, Cutter, Digger, Forty-niner, Geordie, Leaf, Molly Maguire, NUM, Oncost(man), Pitman, Shot-firer, Stall, Tributer, UDM

Mineral Accessory, Index

Mingle Blend, Consort, Interfuse, Mell, > MIX, Participate, Socialise, Unite

Minimise, Minimum (range) Bare, Downplay, Fewest, Least, Neap, Shoestring, Stime, Styme, Threshold, Undervalue

▷ **Minimum of** may indicate the first letter

Minister Ambassador, Attend, Buckle-beggar, Chancellor, Chaplain, Cleric, Coarb, Commissar, Deacon, Dewan, Diplomat, Divine, D(i)wan, Dominee, Dominie, Envoy, Mas(s)john, Mes(s)john, Moderator, Nurse, Officiant, Padre, Parson, Peshwa, Preacher, Predikant, Presbyter, Rector, Secretary, Seraskier, > SERVE, Stickit, Tend, Visier, Vizier

Ministry Defence, Department, Dept, DoE, MOD, MOT, Orders, Service

▷ **Ministry** may indicate some government department

Minor(ity) Child, Comprimario, Ethnic, Faction, Few, Infant, Junior, Less, Minutia, Nonage, One-horse, Petty, Pupillage, Slight, Trivial, Ward

Mint Aim, Bugle-weed, Catnip, Coin, Ettle, Fortune, Herb, Horse, Humbug, Labiate, Monarda, Monetise, Nep, New, Penny-royal, Polo®, Poly, Selfheal, Stamp, Strike, Unused, Utter

Minute(s), Minutiae Acta, Alto, Degree, Detailed, Diatom, Entry, Infinitesimal, Little, Micron, Mo, Mu, Nano-, Resume, Small, Teen(t)sy, Teeny, Tine, Tiny, Trivia, Tyne, Wee

Miracle, Miraculous Cana, Marvel, Merel(l), Meril, Morris, Mystery, Phenomenon, Thaumaturgic, Theurgy, Wonder

Mirror(ed) Alasnam, Busybody, Cambuscan, Catoptric, Cheval, Claude Lorraine glass, Coelostat, Conde, Dare, Enantiomorph, Glass, Image, Imitate, Lao, Magnetic, Merlin, One-way, Pierglass, Primary, Psyche, Rearview, > REFLECT, Reynard, Sign, Specular, Speculum, Stone, Two-way, Vulcan, Wing

▷ **Misalliance** may indicate an anagram

Miscellaneous, Miscellany Assortment, Chow, Collectanea, Diverse, Etceteras, Misc, Odds and ends, Odds and sods, Olio, Omnium-gatherum, Potpourri, Raft, Ragbag, Sundry, Varia, Variety, Various

Mischance Misfare

Mischief(-maker), Mischievous Ate, Bale, Bane, Cantrip, Cloots, Devilment, Diablerie, Dido, Disservice, Gremlin, Harm, Hellery, Hellion, Hob, Imp, Injury, Jinks, Larrikin, Malicho, Mallecho, Nickum, Owl-spiegle, Pestilent, Pickle, Prank, Puckish, Rascal, Scally(wag), Scamp, Scapegrace, Shenanigans, Spriteful, Tricksy, Wag, Wicked

Misconception Delusion, Idol(on), Idolum, Misunderstanding

▷ **Misdelivered** may indicate an anagram

Miser(ly) Carl, Cheapskate, Cheese-parer, Close, Curmudgeon, Gare, Grasping, Harpagon, Hunks, Marner, Meanie, Mingy, Niggard, Nipcheese, Nipfarthing,

Pennyfather, Pinch-commons, Puckfist, Runt, Scrape-good, Scrape-penny, Screw, Scrimping, Scrooge, Skinflint, Snudge, Storer, Tightwad, Timon

Miserable, **Misery**, **Miserably** Abject, Bale, Distress, Dole, Forlorn, Gloom, Grief, Hell, Joyless, Lousy, Perdition, Sorry, Sourpuss, Tragic, Triste, > **UNHAPPY**, Woe(begone), Wretched

Misfortune Accident, Affliction, Bale, Calamity, Curse, Disaster, Distress, Dole, Hex, Ill, Reverse, Rewth, Ruth, Wroath

▷ **Misguided** *may indicate* an anagram

Misheard Mondegreen

Mislead(ing) Blind, Cover-up, Deceive, Delude, Dupe, Equivocate, Fallacious, False, Gag, Red herring, Runaround

▷ **Misled** *may indicate* an anagram

Mismanage Blunder, Bungle, Muddle

Misprint Error, Literal, Slip, Typo

Misrepresent(ation) Abuse, Belie, Calumny, Caricature, Colour, Distort, Falsify, Garble, Lie, Slander, Traduce

Miss(ing) Abord, Avoid, Colleen, Desiderate, Dodge, Drib, Err(or), Fail, Forego, Gal, > **GIRL**, Kumari, Lack, Lass, Link, Lose, Mademoiselle, Maid, Maiden, Mile, Muff(et), Neglect, Negligence, Omit, Otis, Overlook, Senorita, Skip, Spinster, Unmeet, Wanting

▷ **Miss** *may refer to* Missouri

Missile Air-to-air, Ammo, Anti-ballistic, Arrow, Artillery, Atlas, Ball, Ballistic, Beam Rider, Blue streak, Bolas, Bolt, Bomb, Boomerang, Brickbat, Bullet, Condor, Cruise, Dart, Dingbat, Doodlebug, Dum-dum, Exocet®, Falcon, Fléchette, Genie, Grenade, Guided, HARM, Harpoon, Hawk, Hellfire, Hound Dog, ICBM, Interceptor, Jired, Kiley, Kyley, Kylie, Lance, Mace, MARV, Maverick, Minuteman, MIRV, Missive, Mx, Onion, Patriot, Pellet, Pershing, Phoenix, Polaris, Poseidon, Qual, Quarrel, Rocket, SAM, Scud, Sea Skimmer, Sergeant, Shell, Shillelagh, Shot, Shrike, Side-winder, Smart bomb, Snowball, Sparrow, Spartan, Spear, Sprint, SSM, Standard Arm, Standoff, Styx, Subroc, Surface to air, Surface to surface, Talos, Tartar, Terrier, Thor, Titan, Tomahawk, Torpedo, Tracer, Trident, UAM, Warhead

Mission(ary) Aidan, Alamo, Antioch, Apostle, Assignment, Bethel, Caravan, Charge, Delegation, Embassage, Embassy, Errand, Evangelist, Iona, Legation, Livingstone, LMS, Message, NASA, Op, Paul, Quest, Reclaimer, Task, Vocation

Mist(y) Blur, Brume, Cloud, Dew, Drow, Fog, Haar, Haze, Hoar, Miasma, Moch, Nebular, Niflheim, Rack, Roke, Scotch, Sfumato, Smir(r), Smog, Smur, Vapour

Mistake(n) Barry (Crocker), Bish, Bloomer, Blooper, Blunder, Boner, Boob, Booboo, Boss, Botch, Clanger, Clinker, Confound, Deluded, Domino, Erratum, Error, Fault, Floater, Flub, Fluff, Gaffe, Goof, Howler, Identity, Incorrect, Lapse, Malapropism, Miss, Muff, Mutual, Nod, Off-beam, Oversight, Plonker, Pratfall, Screw-up, > **SLIP**, Slip-up, Solecism, Stumer, Trip, Typo

▷ **Mistake(n)** *may indicate* an anagram

Mistress Amie, Aspasia, Canary-bird, Chatelaine, Concubine, Courtesan, Goodwife, Herself, Hussif, Inamorata, Instructress, Lady, Leman, Maintenon, Montespan, Mrs, Natural, Paramour, Stepney, Teacher, Wardrobe, Wife

Mistrust(ful) Doubt, Gaingiving, Suspect, Suspicion

Misunderstand(ing) Disagreement, Discord, Mistake

Misuse Abuse, Defalcate, Malappropriate, Malapropism, Maltreat, Perversion, Torment

Mix(ed), **Mixer**, **Mixture**, **Mix-up** Alloy, Amalgam, Associate, Assortment, Attemper, Balderdash, Bigener, Bland, Blend, Blunge, Bordeaux, Brew, Carburet,

Card, Caudle, Chow, Cocktail, Co-meddle, Compo, Compound, Conglomerate, Consort, Cross, Cut, Disperse, Dolly, Drammock, Embroil, Emulsion, Entectic, Farrago, Fold-in, Freezing, Garble, Grill, Griqua, Heather, Hobnob, Hotchpotch, Hybrid, Imbroglio, Interlace, Intermingle, Isomorphous, Jumble, Lace, Lard, Lignin, Linctus, Load, Macedoine, Matissé, Meddle, Medley, Melange, Mell, Meng(e), Ment, Mess, Mestizo, Metis, Ming(le), Miscellaneous, Miscellany, Mishmash, Mong, Motley, Muddle, Muss(e), Neapolitan, Octaroon, Octoroon, Olio, Olla, Pi(e), Potin, Pousowdie, Powsowdy, Praiseach, Promiscuous, Raggle-taggle, Ragtag, Salad, Scramble, Spatula, Stew, Stir, Temper, Through-other, Trail, Vision, Yblent

▷ **Mixed** *may indicate* an anagram

Moan(ing) Beef, Bleat, Groan, Hone, Keen, > **LAMENT**, Meane, Plangent, Sough, Wail, W(h)inge

Mob(ster) Army, Assail, Canaille, Crew, Crowd, Gang, Herd, Hoi-polloi, Hoodlum, Lynch, Ochlocrat, Press, Rabble, Raft, Ragtag, Riff-raff, Rout, Scar-face

Mobile, Mobilise, Mobility Donna, Fluid, Movable, Plastic, Rally, Thin, Upward(ly), Vagile, Vertical

Mock(ery), Mocking Ape, Banter, Chaff, Chyack, Cod, Cynical, Deride, Derisory, Dor, Ersatz, False, Farce, Fleer, Flout, Gab, Geck, Gibe, Guy, Imitation, Irony, Irrisory, > **JEER**, Jibe, Lampoon, Mimic, Narquois, Paste, Pillorise, Rail(lery), Ridicule, Sacrilege, Sardonic, Satirise, Scout, Sham, Simulate, Slag, Travesty, Wry

Mode Convention, Fashion, Form, Manner, Rate, Step, Style, Ton

Model(ler), Modelling Archetype, Bozzeto, Cast, Copy, Demonstration, Diorama, Doll, Dummy, Ecorché, Effigy, Epitome, Example, Exemplar, Fictor, Figure, Figurine, Icon, Ideal, Image, Instar, Jig, Last, Lay-figure, Layman, Madame Tussaud, Manakin, Manikin, Mannequin, Maquette, Mark, Mock-up, > **MOULD**, Norm, Original, Orrery, Papier-mache, Parade, Paragon, Pattern, Phelloplastic, Pilot, Plasticine, Pose(r), Posture-maker, Prototype, Replica, Role, Scale, Sedulous, Sitter, Specimen, Standard, Superwaif, T, Template, Templet, Terrella, Toy, Type, Typify, Waif, Waxwork

▷ **Model(s)** *may indicate* an anagram

Moderate(ly), Moderation Abate, Allay, Alleviate, Average, Centre, Chasten, Continent, Diminish, Discretion, Ease, Gentle, Girondist, Ho, Lessen, Lukewarm, Measure, Medium, Menshevik, Mezzo, Middling, Mild, Mitigate, OK, Politique, Reason(able), Slake, So-so, Temper(ate), Tolerant, Tone, Via media, Wet

Modern(ise) AD, Aggiornamento, Contemporary, Fresh, Latter(-day), Neonomian, Neoterical, > **NEW**, Present-day, Progressive, Recent, Swinger, Update

Modest(y) Aidos, Blaise, Chaste, Decent, Demure, Humble, Ladylike, Maidenly, Mim, Mussorgsky, Propriety, Prudish, Pudency, Pure, Reserved, Shame, Shy, Unpretending, Unpretentious, Verecund

Modifiable, Modification, Modifier, Modify Adapt, Alter, Backpedal, Change, Enhance, Extenuate, H, Leaven, Plastic, Qualify, Retrofit, Soup, Streamline, Temper, Vary

Moist(en), Moisture Baste, Bedew, Damp, Dank, De(a)w, Humect, Latch, Love-in-a-mist, Madefy, Mesarch, Nigella, Sponge, Wet

▷ **Moither** *may indicate* an anagram

Molecular, Molecule Acceptor, Atom, Buckyball, Carbene, Cavitand, Chiral, Chromophore, Closed chain, Cobalamin, Codon, Coenzyme, Cofactor, Dimer, DNA, Enantiomorph, Footballene, Fullerene, Gram, Hapten, Iota, Isomer, Kinin, Ligand, Long-chain, Metabolite, Metameric, Monomer, Peptide, Polymer, Polysaccharide, Quark, Replicon, Semantide, Stereoisomer, Trimer, Uridine

Mollusc(s) Ammonite, Amphineura, Arca, Argonaut, Ark-shell, Belemnite, Bivalve, Bulla, Capiz, Cephalopod, Chiton, Clam, Cockle, Conch, Cone-shell,

Cowrie, Cowry, Cuttle(fish), Dentalium, Doris, Gaper, Gast(e)ropod, Goniatite, Heart-cockler, Heart-shell, Helix, Horse mussel, Lamellibranch, Limpet, Malacology, Marine boxer, Money cowry, Murex, Mussel, Mya, Nautilus, Neopilina, Octopod, Octopus, Olive, Opisthobranch, Oyster, Pandora, Paper nautilus, Paper-sailor, Pearly nautilus, Pecten, Pelican's-foot, Pholas, Piddock, Pinna, Polyp, Poulpe, Pteropod, Quahaug, Quahog, Razor-clam, Razor-fish, Razorshell, Saxicava, Scallop, Scaphopoda, Sea-hare, Sea-lemon, Sea-slug, Sepia, > **SHELLFISH**, Shipworm, Slug, Snail, Solen, Spat, Spirula, Spoot, Squid, Strombus, Tectibranch, Tellen, Tellin, Teredo, Toheroa, Top-shell, Triton, Trochophore, Trochus, Trough-shell, Turbo, Tusk-shell, Unio, Univalve, Veliger, Venus, Venus shell, Vitrina, Wentletrap, Whelk, Wing-shell, Winkle

Moment(s), Momentous Bit, Flash, Import, Instant, Jiffy, > **MINUTE**, Mo, Nonce, Pun(c)to, Sands, Sec, Shake, Stound, Stownd, Tick, Time, Trice, Twinkling, Weighty, Wink

Momentum Impetus, L, Speed, Thrust

Monarch(y) Autocrat, Butterfly, Crown, Emperor, HM, Karling, King, Potentate, Queen, Raine, Reign, Ruler, Tsar

Monastery Abbey, Abthane, Charterhouse, Chartreuse, Cloister, Community, Gompa, Hospice, Lamaserai, Lamasery, Laura, Priory, Vihara, Wat

Monastic Abthane, Celibate, Holy, Monkish, Oblate, Secluded

Monetary, Money Ackers, Akkas, Allowance, Annat, Ante, Appearance, Assignat, Banco, Batta, Blood, Blunt, Boodle, Bottle, Brass, Bread, Bread and honey, Broad, Cabbage, Capital, Cash, Caution, Change, Chink, Cob, > **COIN**, Collateral, Conscience, Crackle, Cranborne, Crinkly, Currency, Danger, Dib(s), Dingbat, Dosh, Dust, Earnest, Easy, Even, Fat, Fee, Fiat, Float, Folding, Fonds, Fund, Funny, Gate, Gelt, Gilt, Gold, Grant, Gravy, Greens, Hard, Head, Hello, Hoot, Hot, Housekeeping, Hush, Idle, Ingots, Investment, Kale, Key, L, Lolly, Loot, Lucre, M, Mammon, Maundy, Mazuma, Means, Mint, Monopoly, Moola(h), Narrow, Necessary, Needful, Nest-egg, Note, Numismatic, Nummary, Oaker, Ochre, Offertory, Oof, Option, Outlay, P, Packet, Paper, Passage, Payroll, Peanuts, Pecuniary, Pelf, Pin, Pine-tree, Pittance, Plastic, Plum, Pocket, Posh, Press, Prize, Proceeds, Profit, Protection, Purse, Push, Ready, Rebate, Resources, Revenue, Rhino, Rogue, Rowdy, Salt(s), Scratch, Scrip, Seed, Shin-plaster, Ship, Short, Siller, Silly, Silver, Slush, Smart, Soap, Soft, Spondulicks, Stake, Sterling, Stipend, Stuff, Subsistence, Sugar, Sum, Table, Takings, Tender, Tin, Toea, Token, Tranche, Treaty, Tribute, Turnover, Viaticum, Wad, Wealth, Wonga

Monitor Detect, Goanna, Iguana, Lizard, Observe, Prefect, Record, Track, Warship, Watchdog, Worral, Worrel

Monk(s) Abbey-lubber, Abbot, Acoemeti, Archimandrite, Arhat, Augustinian, Austin, Basilian, Bede, Beghard, Benedictine, Bernardine, Bethlehemite, Bhikhu, Black, Bonaventura, Bonze, Brother, Bruno, Caedmon, Caloyer, Carthusian, Celestine, Cellarist, Cenobite, Cistercian, Cluniac, Coenobite, Cowl, Culdee, Dan, Dervish, Dom, Dominican, Félibre, Friar, General, Gyrovague, Hegumen, Hermit, Hesychast, Hildebrand, Ignorantine, Jacobin, Jacobite, Jerome, Lama, Maurist, Mechitharist, Mekhitarist, Mendel, Norbertine, Oblate, Olivetan, Order, Pelagian, Prior, Rakehell, Rasputin, Recluse, Recollect, Roshi, Salesian, Sangha, Savonarola, Sub-prior, Talapoin, Theatine, Thelemite, Thelonius, Thomas à Kempis, Tironensian, Trappist, Votary

Monkey Anger, Ape, Aye-aye, Baboon, Bandar, Bobbejaan, Bonnet, Bushbaby, Capuchin, Catar(r)hine, Cebidae, Cebus, Chacma, Coaita, Colobus, Cynomolgus, Diana, Douc, Douroucouli, Drill, Durukuli, Entellus, Galago, Gelada, Gibbon, Gorilla, Grease, Green, Grison, Grivet, Guenon, Guereza, Hanuman, Hoolock, Howler, Hylobates, Indri, Jacchus, Jackey, Jocko, Kippage, Langur, Leaf, Lemur, Loris, Macaco, Macaque, Magot, Malmag, Mandrill, Mangabey, Marmoset,

Meddle, Meerkat, Mico, Midas, Mona, Mycetes, Nala, Nasalis, NewWorld, Old World, Orang-utang, Ouakari, Ouistiti, Phalanger, Platyrrhine, Powder, Primate, Proboscis, Pug, Puzzle, Rage, Ram, Rhesus, Sago(u)in, Saguin, Sai(miri), Sajou, Saki, Sapajou, Satan, Semnopithecus, Siamang, Sifaka, Silen(us), Silverback, Simian, Simpai, Slender loris, Spider, Squirrel, Talapoin, Tamarin, Tamper, Tana, Tarsier, Tee-tee, Titi, Toque, Trip-hammer, Troop, Tup, Uakari, Vervet, Wanderoo, White-eyelid, Wistiti, Wou-wou, Wow-wow, Wrath, Zati

Monologue Patter, Rap, Recitation, Soliloquy, Speech

Monopolise, Monopoly Appalto, Bloc, Cartel, Corner, Engross, Octroi, Régie, Trust

Monorail Aerobus

Monosyllable Proclitic

▷ **Monsoon** *may indicate* weekend (Mon soon)

Monster, Monstrous Alecto, Asmodeus, Bandersnatch, Behemoth, Bunyip, Caliban, Cerberus, Cete, Chichevache, Chim(a)era, Cockatrice, Colossal, Cyclops, Deform, Dinoceras, Div, Dragon, Echidna, Enormous, Erebus, Erl-king, Eten, Ettin, Fiend, Fire-drake, Frankenstein, Freak, Geryon, Ghost, Giant, Gila, Golem, Gorgon, Green-eyed, Grendel, Harpy, Hippocampus, Hippogriff, Huge, Hydra, Jabberwock, Kraken, Lamia, Leviathan, Mastodon, Medusa, Minotaur, Moloch, Nessie, Nicker, Nightmare, Ogre, Ogr(e)ish, Opinicus, Orc, Outrageous, Pongo, Sarsquatch, Satyral, Scylla, Shadow, Simorg, Simurq(h), Siren, Skull, Snark, Spectre, Sphinx, Spook, Stegodon, Stegosaur, Succubus, Taniwha, Teras, Teratoid, Triceratops, Troll, Typhoeus, Typhon, Unnatural, Vampire, Vast, Wasserman, Wendego, Wendigo, Wer(e)wolf, Wyvern, Yowie, Ziffius

Monstrance Ostensory

Month(ly) Ab, Abib, Adar, April, Asadha, Asvina, August, Bhadrapada, Brumaire, Bul, Cheshvan, Chislev, December, Dhu-al-Hijjah, Dhu-al-Qadah, Elul, February, Floreal, Frimaire, Fructidor, Germinal, Hes(h)van, Iy(y)ar, January, July, Jumada, June, Jysaitha, Kartuka, Kisleu, Kislev, Lide, Lunar, Magha, March, Margasirsa, May, Messidor, Mo, Moharram, Moon, Muharram, Muharrem, Nisan, Nivose, November, October, Periodical, Phalguna, Pluviose, Prairial, Rabia, Rajab, Ramadan, Safar, Saphar, September, Sha(a)ban, Shawwal, S(h)ebat, Sivan, Solar, Tammuz, Tebeth, Thermidor, Tisri, Vaisakha, Veadar, Vendemiaire, Ventose

Monument Ancient, Arch, Archive, Cenotaph, Column, Cromlech, Dolmen, Henge, Megalith, Memorial, Menhir, National, Pantheon, Pyramid, Stele(ne), Stone, Stonehenge, Stupa, Talayot, Tombstone, Trilith, Trilithon, Urn

Mood(y) Active, Anger, Atmosphere, Attitude, Capricious, Dudgeon, Enallage, Fit, Glum, Grammar, Humour, Hump, Imperative, Morale, Optative, Passive, Peat, Pet, Revivalist, Sankey, Spleen, Subjunctive, Temper, Tid, Tone, Tune, Vein, Vinegar, Whim

Moon(light), Moony Aah, Alignak, Aningan, Apogee, Artemis, Astarte, Blue, Callisto, Calypso, Cheese, Cynthia, Diana, Epact, Eye, Flit, Full, Gander, Ganymede, Gibbous, Glimmer, Grimaldi, Harvest, Hecate, Hunter's, Hyperion, Inconstant, Juliet, Leda, Lucina, Luna(r), Mani, Mascon, McFarlane's Buat, Midsummer, Mock, Month, Mope, New, Nimbus, Nocturne, Octant, Oliver, Paddy's lantern, Paraselene, Paschal, Pasiphaë, Phoebe, Plenilune, Proteus, Raker, Satellite, Selene, Set, Shepherd, Shot, Sickle, Sideline, Silvery, Sonata, Stargaze, Stone, Syzygy, Thebe, Thoth, Titan, Triton, Umbriel, Wander

Mop(ping) Dwile, Flibbertigibbet, Girn, Glib, Shag, Squeegee, Squilgee, Swab, Swob, Thatch, > WIPE

Moral(ity), Morals Apologue, Deontic, Ethic(al), Ethos, Everyman, Fable, High-minded, Integrity, Precept, Principled, Puritanic, Righteous, Tag, Upright, Virtuous

Morale Ego, Mood, Spirit, Zeal

Morbid(ity) Anasarca, Ascites, Cachaemia, Dropsy, Ectopia, Ghoul(ish), Gruesome, Pathological, Plethora, Prurient, Religiose, Sick, Sombre

More Additional, Else, Extra, Increase, Less, Mae, Merrier, Mo(e), Over, Piu, Plus, Stump, Utopia

Morning Ack-emma, Am, Antemeridian, Dawn, Daybreak, Early, Matin(al), Morrow

Morose Acid, Boody, Churlish, Cynical, Gloomy, Glum, Grum, Moody, Sour-eyed, Sullen, Surly

Morsel Bit, Bite, Bouche, Canape, Crumb, Dainty, Morceau, Ort, Scrap, Sippet, Sop, Tidbit, Titbit

Mortal(ity) Averr(h)oism, Being, Deathly, > FATAL, Grave, Human, Lethal, Yama

Mortgage(e) Balloon, Bond, Cedula, Debt, Dip, Encumbrance, Endowment, Hypothecator, Loan, Pledge, Wadset(t)

Mosaic Buhl, Cosmati, Inlay, Intarsia, Musive, Pietra dura, Screen, Terrazzo, Tessella(te), Tessera

▶ **Moslem** *see* MUSLIM

Mosque Dome of the Rock, El Aqsa, Jami, Masjid, Medina

Moss(y) Acrogen, Agate, Bryology, Carrag(h)een, Ceylon, Club, Fog, Fontinalis, Hag(g), Hypnum, Iceland, Irish, Lecanoram, Lichen, Litmus, Long, Lycopod, Marsh, Musci, Muscoid, Parella, Peat, Polytrichum, Reindeer, Rose, Scale, Selaginella, Spanish, Sphagnum, Staghorn, Usnea, Wolf's claw

Most Largest, Major, Maxi(mum), Optimum

Moth(s) Abraxas, Antler, Arch, Arctiidae, Atlas, Bag, Bee, Bell, Bobowler, Bogong, Bombycid, Brown-tail, Buff-tip, Bugong, Burnet, Cabbage, Cactoblastus, Carpenter, Carpet, Cecropia, Cinnabar, Clearwing, Clifden nonpareil, Clothes, Codlin(g), Corn (-borer), Dagger, Dart-moth, Death's head, Diamondback, Drepanid, Drinker, Eggar, Egger, Emerald, Emperor, Ermine, Flour, Fox, Geometer, Geometrid, Ghost, Giant peacock, Gipsy, Goat, Goldtail, Gooseberry, Grass, Gypsy, Hawk, Herald, Honeycomb, Hook-tip, House, Hummingbird, Imago, Io, Kentish glory, Kitten, Lackey, Lappet, Large Emerald, Lasiocampidae, Leafroller, Leopard, Lepidoptera, Lichen, Lobster, Luna, Lymantriidae, Magpie, Meal, Mother of pearl, Mother Shipton, Muslin, Noctua, Noctuid, Notodonta, Nun, Oak-egger, Owl, Owlet, Peppered, Pine-beauty, Pine-carpet, Plane, Plume, Polyphemus, Privet hawk, Processionary, Prominent, Psyche, Pug-moth, Purple Emperor, Puss, Pyralidae, Red underwing, Sallow-kitten, Saturnia, Saturniid, Scavenger, Silkworm, Silver-Y, Sphingid, Sphinx, Swift, Tapestry, Thorn, Tiger, Tinea, Tineidae, Tortrix, Turnip, Tussock, Umber, Underwing, Unicorn, Vapourer, Veneer, Wainscot, Wave, Wax, Wheat, Winter, Woodborer, Yellow underwing, Y-moth, Zygaena

Mother Bearer, Church, Cognate, Cosset, Courage, Dam(e), Dregs, Ean, Earth, Eve, Generatrix, Genetrix, Goose, Hubbard, Lees, Ma, Machree, Mam(a), Mamma, Mater, Maya, Minnie, Mom, Multipara, Mum, Native, Nature, Nourish, Parity, Pourer, Reverend, Shipton, Superior, Surrogate, Wit

▷ **Mother** *may indicate* a lepidopterist (moth-er)

Motion Contrary, Diurnal, Early day, Fast, Gesture, Harmonic, Impulse, Kepler, Kinematics, Kinetic, Link, Move, Oblique, Offer, Parallactic, Peculiar, Perpetual, PL, Proper, Proposal, Rack and pinion, Rider, Similar, Slow, Spasm, Wave

Motionless Doggo, Frozen, Immobile, Quiescent, Stagnant, Stasis, Still, Stock-still

Motive, Motivate, Motivation Actuate, Cause, Ideal, Impel, Incentive, Intention, Mainspring, Mobile, Object, > PURPOSE, Spur, Ulterior

Motor(boat) Auto, Car, Dynamo, Engine, Hot rod, Inboard, Induction, Jato, Linear, Outboard, Scooter, Thruster, Turbine

Motorway Autobahn, Autopista, Autoput, Autoroute, Autostrada, Expressway, M(1)

Motto Device, Epigraph, Gnome, Impresa, Imprese, Impress(e), Legend, Maxim, Mot, Poesy, Posy, Saw

Mould(ed), Mouldable, Moulding, Mouldy Accolade, Architrave, Archivolt, Astragal, Baguette, Beading, Bend, Black, Bread, Briquet(te), Cabling, Casement, Cast(ing), Chessel, Chill, Cornice, Coving, Cyma, Dariole, Die, Dripstone, Echinus, Egg and dart, Flong, > FORM, Foughty, Fungus, Fust, Gadroon, Godroon, Hood-mould, Hore, Humus, Injection, Matrix, Mildew, Model, Mool, Mucid, Must, Noble rot, Ogee, Ovolo, Palmette, Papier-mâché, Phycomycete, Pig, Plasm(a), Plastic, Plat, Prototype, Prunt, Reglet, Rot, Rust, Sandbox, Scotia, Shape, Smut, Soil, Stringcourse, Tailor, Talon, Template, Templet, Timbale, Tondino, Torus, Water table

Mound Agger, Bank, Barp, Barrow, Berm, Cone, Dike, Dun, Embankment, Heap, Hog, Kurgan, Mogul, Monticule, Mote, Motte, Orb, Pile, Pingo, Pome, Rampart, Rampire, Tuffet

Mount(ed), Mounting, Mountain (peak), Mountains > ALPINE, Aspiring, Back, Barp, Ben, Berg, Board, Breast, Butter, Chain, Charger, > CLIMB, Colt, Cordillera, Cradle, Dew, Display, Djebel, Dolly, Escalade, Frame, Hinge, Horse, Inselberg, Jebel, Massif, Monture, Mt, Nunatak, Orography, Orology, Passe-partout, Pike, Pile, Pin, Pownie, Quad, Ride, Saddlehorse, Scalado, Scale, Set, Soar, Stage, Stie, Strideways, Tel, Tier, Tor, Turret, Upgo, Volcano

Mountaineer(ing) Abseil, Alpinist, Arnaut, Climber, Hunt, Sherpa, Smythe, Upleader

Mourn(er), Mournful, Mourning Adonia, Black, Dirge, Dole, Elegiac, Grieve, Grone, Hatchment, Keen, Lament, Niobe, Omer, Ovel, Plangent, Saulie, Shivah, Shloshim, Sorrow, Tangi, Threnetic, Threnodial, Weeds, Weep, Willow

Mouse(like), Mousy Black eye, Deer, Dun(nart), Flitter, Harvest, Honey, Icon, Jumping, Meadow, Muridae, Murine, Pocket, Rodent, Shiner, > SHREW, Vermin, Waltzer

Mousetrap Samson's post

Mouth(piece) Aboral, Bazoo, Brag, Buccal, Cakehole, Chapper, Check, Crater, Debouchure, Delta, Embouchure, Estuary, Fipple, Gab, Gam, Gills, Gob, Gum, Hard, Kisser, Labret, Lawyer, Lip, Manubrium, Maw, Neb, Orifex, Orifice, Os, Oscule, Ostium, Outfall, Port, Potato trap, Speaker, Spokesman, Spout, Stoma, Swazzle, Swozzle, Teat, Trap, Uvula

Move(d), Mover, Movable, Moving Act, Actuate, Affect, Andante, Astir, Budge, Carry, Catapult, Chattel, Coast, Counter-measure, Coup, Decant, Démarche, Displace, Disturb, Ease, Eddy, Edge, Evoke, False, Flit, Flounce, Fluctuate, Forge, Frogmarch, Gambit, Gee, Go, Gravitate, Haulier, Hustle, Inch, Instigate, Jee, Jink, Kedge, Kinetic, Knight's progress, Link, Mill, Mobile, Mosey, Motivate, Nip, Opening, Overcome, Pan, People, Poignant, Prime, Proceed, Progress, Prompt, Propel, Quicken, Qui(t)ch, Rearrange, Redeploy, Relocate, Remuage, Retrocede, Roll, Rouse, Roust, Sashay, Scoot, Scramble, Scroll, Scuttle, Sealed, Sell, Shift, Shog, Shoo, Shunt, Sidle, Skelp, Slide, Soulful, Spank, Steal, Steer, Step, Stir, Styre, Sway, Swish, Tack, Tactic, Taxi, Transfer, Translate, Translocate, Transplant, Transport, Travel, Troll, Trundle, Turn, Unstep, Up, Upsticks, Vacillate, Vagile, Veronica, Vire, Volt(e), Waft, Wag, Wapper, Whirry, Whish, Whisk, Whiz, Wuther, Yank, Zoom, Zwischenzug

Movement(s) Action, Allegro, Allemande, Almain, Andantino, Antic, Bandwagon, Cadence, Capoeira, Cell, Charismatic, Chartism, Course, Crusade,

Dadaism, Diaspora, Diastole, Ecumenical, Enlightenment, Eoka, Eurhythmics, Expressionism, Faction, Feint, Fianchetto, Fris(ka), Gait, Geneva, Gesture, Groundswell, Hip-hop, Honde, Imagism, Indraught, Intermezzo, Jor, Kata, Kin(a)esthetic, Kinesis, Kinetic, Larghetto, Largo, Lassu, Ligne, Logistics, Manoeuvre, Mudra, Nastic, Naturalism, Naziism, New Wave, Nihilism, Official, Operation, Orchesis, Oxford, Pantalon, Parallax, Pase, Passade, Photokinesis, Photonasty, Piaffer, Pincer, Play, Populist, Poule, Poulette, Procession, Progress, Provisional, Punk, Puseyism, Reformation, REM, Renaissance, Resistance, Ribbonism, Risorgimento, Romantic, Rondo, Scherzo, Sinn Fein, Spuddle, Stir(e), Swadeshi, Swing, Symbolist, Tamil Tigers, Tantrism, Taxis, Tectonic, Telekinesis, Tide, Trend, Ultramontanism, UNITA, Verismo, Veronica, Wheel, Women's, Zionism

Mow(er), Mowing Aftermath, Cut, Grimace, Lattermath, Math, Rawing, Rawn, Rowan, Rowen, Rowing, Scytheman, Shear, Sickle, Tass, Trim

MP Backbencher, Commoner, Gendarme, Member, Provost, Redcap, Retread, Snowdrop, Stannator, Statist, TD

Much Abundant, Far, Glut, Great, Lots, Mickle, Scad, Sore, Viel

Muck (up), Mucky Bungle, Dirt, Dung, Island, Leep, Manure, Midden, Mire, Rot, Soil, Sordid, Spoil, Stercoral

Mud(dy) Adobe, Clabber, Clart, Clay, Cutcha, Dirt, Drilling, Dubs, Fango, Glaur, Glob, Gutter, Kacha, Lahar, Lairy, Limous, Moya, Ooze, Peloid, Pise, Riley, Roily, Salse, Slab, Slake, Sleech, Slime, Slob, Slough, Sludge, Slur(ry), Slush, Stulch, Tocky, Trouble, Turbid, Volcanic

Muddle Befog, Bemuse, Botch, Cock up, Confuse, Disorder, Embrangle, Fluster, Gump, Mash, Mêlée, Mess, Mix, Mull, Pickle, Puddle, Shemozzle, Stupefy, Tangle

▷ **Muddled** *may indicate* an anagram

Muffle(d), Muffler Damp, Envelop, Hollow, Mob(b)le, Mute, Scarf, Silencer, Sourdine, Stifle

Mug(ger), Muggy Assault, Attack, Bash, Beaker, Bock, Can, Club, Con, Croc(odile), Cup, Dial, Dupe, Enghalskrug, Face, Fool, Footpad, Gob, Humid, Idiot, Latron, Learn, Mou, Noggin, Pan, Pot, Puss, Rob, Roll, Sandbag, Sap, Sconce, Simpleton, Steamer, Stein, Sucker, Swot, Tankard, Tax, Thief, Thug(gee), Tinnie, Tinny, Toby, Trap, Ugly, Visage, Yap

Mule Ass, Bab(o)uche, Barren, Donkey, Funnel, Hybrid, Mocassin, Moccasin, Moyl(e), Muffin, Muil, Rake, Shoe, Slipper, Sumpter

Multiple, Multiplication, Multiplied, Multiplier, Multiply Augment, Breed, Double, > **INCREASE**, Modulus, Populate, Product, Proliferate, Propagate, Severalfold

Multitude Army, Crowd, Hirsel, Horde, Host, Legion, Populace, Shoal, Sight, Throng, Zillion

Mumble Grumble, Moop, Moup, Mouth, Mump, Mushmouth, Mutter, Royne, Slur

Munch Champ, Chew, Chomp, Scranch

Mundane Banal, Common, Earthly, Nondescript, Ordinary, Prosaic, Quotidian, Secular, Trite, Workaday, Worldly

Munition(s) Arms, Artillery, Matériel, Ordnance

Murder(er), Murderess, Murderous Aram, Assassin, Blue, Bluebeard, Bravo, Burke, Butcher, Butler, Cain, Cathedral, Crackhalter, Crippen, Cutthroat, Do in, Eliminate, Filicide, First degree, Fratricide, Genocide, Hare, Hitman, Homicide, Internecine, > **KILL**, Liquidate, Locusta, Made man, Massacre, Matricide, Modo, Parricide, Patricide, Poison, Red, Regicide, Ripper, Ritual, Ritz, Second degree, Sikes, Slaughter, Slay, Strangle(r), Take out, Thagi, Throttle, Thug(gee), Whodun(n)it

Murk(y) Black, Dirk(e), Gloom, Obscure, Rookish, Stygian

Muscle, Muscular Abductor, Abs, Accelerator, Accessorius, Adductor, Anconeus, Aryepiglottic, Arytaenoid, Athletic, Attollens, Beef(y), Beefcake, Biceps, Bowr, Brachialus, Brawn, Buccinator, Ciliary, Clout, Complexus, Corrugator, Creature, Cremaster, Deltoid, Depressor, Diaphragm, Digastric, Dilat(at)or, Duvaricator, Effector, Elevator, Erecter, Erector, Evertor, Extensor, Eye-string, Flexor, Force, Gastrocnemius, Gemellus, Glut(a)eus, Gluteus maximus, Gracilis, Hamstring, Hiacus, Iliacus, Intrinsic, Involuntary, Kreatine, Lat, Latissimus dorsi, Laxator, Levator, Lumbricalis, Masseter, Mesomorph, Might, Motor, Mouse, Myalgia, Mylohyoid, Nasalis, Oblique, Occlusor, Omohyoid, Orbicularis, Pathos, Pec(s), Pectoral, Perforans, Perforatus, Peroneus, Plantaris, Platysma, Popliteus, > **POWER**, Pronator, Protractor, Psoas, Pylorus, Quad(riceps), Quadratus, Rambo, Rectus, Retractor, Rhomboid, Risorius, Rotator, Sarcolemma, Sarcous, Sartorius, Scalene, Scalenus, Serratus, Sinew, Smooth, Soleus, Sphincter, Spinalis, Splenial, Sthenic, Striated, Striped, Supinator, Temporal, Tenaculum, Tendon, Tensor, Teres, Thenar, Thew, Tibialis, Tonus, Trapezius, Triceps, Vastus, Voluntary, Zygomatic

Muse(s), Muse's home, Musing Aglaia, Aonia(n), Attic, Calliope, Clio, Cogitate, Consider, Erato, Euphrosyne, Euterpe, Helicon, Inspiration, IX, Melpomene, Nine, Nonet, Pensée, Pierides, Poly(hy)mnia, Ponder, > **REFLECT**, Ruminate, Study, Teian, Terpsichore, Thalia, Tragic, Urania, Wonder

Museum Ashmolean, BM, British, Fitzwilliam, Gallery, Guggenheim, Hermitage, Louvre, Metropolitan, Parnassus, Prado, Repository, Smithsonian, Tate, Uffizi, VA, V and A

Mushroom Agaric, Blewits, Burgeon, Button, Cep, Champignon, Darning, Enoki, Expand, Fly agaric, > **FUNGUS**, Gyromitra, Horse, Hypha(l), Ink-cap, Liberty cap, Magic, Matsutake, Meadow, Morel, Oyster, Parasol, Penny-bun, Porcino, Russula, Sacred, Scotch bonnet, Shaggymane, Shiitake, Sickener, Spread, Start-up, Straw, Truffle, Upstart, Velvet shank, Waxcap

Music Absolute, Light, Medieval, Minstrelsy, > **MUSICAL INSTRUMENTS**, Phase, Piece, Pop(ular), Post-rock, Score

Musical Arcadian, Azione, Brigadoon, Cats, Chess, Euphonic, Evergreen, Evita, Gigi, Grease, Hair, Harmonious, Kabuki, Kismet, Lyric, Mame, Melodic, Oliver, Opera, Operetta, Orphean, Revue, Showboat

Musical instrument(s) Tabla

Musician(s), Musicologist Accompanist, Arion, Arist, Brain, Chanter, Combo, > **COMPOSER**, Conductor, Crowder, Ensemble, Executant, Flautist, Gate, Grove, Guslar, Handel, Jazzer, Jazzman, Joplin, Mahler, Mariachi, Menuhin, Minstrel, Muso, Orphean, Pianist, Rapper, Reed(s)man, Répétiteur, Rubinstein, Sideman, Spohr, String, Tortelier, Trouvère, Violinist, Waits

Musket Brown Bess, Caliver, Carabine, Eyas, Flintlock, Fusil, Hawk, Nyas, Queen's-arm, Weapon

Muslim (ritual), Moslem Alaoulte, Ali, Almohad(e), Balochi, Baluchi, Berber, Caliph, Dato, Dervish, Fatimid, Ghazi, Hadji, Hafiz, Hajji, Iranian, Islamic, Ismaili, Karmathian, Khotbah, Khotbeh, Khutbah, Mahometan, Mogul, Moor, Morisco, Moro, Mufti, Mus(s)ulman, Mutazilite, Nawab, Paynim, Pomak, Said, Saracen, Say(y)id, Senus(s)i, Shafiite, Shia(h), Shiite, Sofi, Sonnite, Sufi, Sulu, Sunna, Sunni(te), Turk, Wahabee, Wahabi(te)

Must(y) Amok, Essential, Foughty, Froughy, Frowsty, Frowy, Funky, Fust, Man, Maun(na), Mote, Mould, Mucid, Mun, Need(s)-be, Shall, Should, Stum, Wine

▷ **Must** *may indicate* an anagram

Mustard Black, Charlock, Cress, English, Erysimum, French, Garlic, Nitrogen, Praiseach, Quinacrine, Runch, Sauce-alone, Senvy, Treacle, Wall, White, Wild

Musteline Skunk

▷ **Mutation** *may indicate* an anagram

Mute(d) Deaden, Dumb, Noiseless, Silent, Sordino, Sordo, Sourdine, Stifle

Mutilate(d), Mutilation Castrate, Concise, Deface, Dismember, Distort, Garble, Hamble, Injure, Maim, Mangle, Mayhem, Obtruncate, Riglin, Tear

▷ **Mutilate(d)** *may indicate* an anagram

Mutineer, Mutiny Bounty, Caine, Curragh, Indian, Insurrection, Nore, Pandy, > REVOLT, Rising, Sepoy

Mutter(ing) Chunter, Fremescent, Mumble, Mump, Murmur, Mussitate, Rhubarb, Roin, Royne, Rumble, Witter

Muzzle Decorticate, Gag, Jaw, Mouth, Restrain, Snout

Mysterious, Mystery Abdabs, Abdals, Acroamatic, Arcane, Arcanum, Cabbala, Closed book, Craft, Creepy, Cryptic, Dark, Deep, Delphic, Eleusinian, Enigma, Esoteric, Grocer, G(u)ild, Incarnation, Inscrutable, Miracle, Mystagogue, Numinous, Occult, Original sin, Orphic, Penetralia, Riddle, > SECRET, Telestic, Trinity, UFO, Uncanny, Whodunit

▷ **Mysterious(ly)** *may indicate* an anagram

Mystic (word), Mystical Abraxas, Agnostic, Cab(e)iri, Epopt, Fakir, Familist, Hesychast, Mahatma, Occultist, Rasputin, Secret, Seer, Sofi, Sufi, Swami, Theosophy, Transcendental

Mystify Baffle, Bamboozle, Bewilder, Metagrabolise, Metagrobolise, Puzzle

Myth(ology), Mythical (beast) Allegory, Behemoth, Bunyip, Centaur, Cockatrice, Dragon, Euhemerism, Fable, Fantasy, Fictitious, Folklore, Garuda, Geryon, Griffin, Hippocampus, Impundulu, Kelpie, Kylin, Legend, Leviathin, Lore, Otnit, Pantheon, Pegasus, Phoenix, Sea horse, Selkie, Solar, Speewah, Sphinx, Sun, Thunderbird, Tokoloshe, Unicorn, Urban, Wivern, Wyvern, Yale, Yeti

Nn

N Name, Nitrogen, Noon, North, November

Nadir Bottom, Depths, Dregs, Minimum

Nag(ging) Badger, Bidet, Brimstone, Callet, Cap, Captious, Complain, Fret, Fuss, Harangue, Harp, Henpeck, Horse, Jade, Jaw, Keffel, Peck, Pester, Plague, Rosinante, Rouncy, > **SCOLD**, Tit, Yaff

Nail(ed) Brad, Brod, Catch, Clinker, Clout, Fasten, Hob, Keratin, Onyx, Pin, Rivet, Sisera, Sparable, Sparrow-bill, Spick, Spike, Sprig, Staple, Stub, Stud, Tack(et), Talon, Tenterhook, Thumb, Tingle, Toe, Unguis

Naive(té) Artless, Green, Guileless, Ingenuous, Innocence, Open, Simplistic, Unsophisticated, Wide-eyed

Naked Adamical, Artless, Bare, Blunt, Buff, Clear, Cuerpo, Defenceless, Encuerpo, Exposed, Gymno-, Nuddy, Nude, Querpo, Raw, Scud, Simple, Stark(ers), Uncovered

Name(d), Names Agnomen, Alias, Anonym, Appellation, Appoint, Baptise, Byline, Call, Celeb(rity), Christen, Cite, Cleep, Clepe, Cognomen, Day, Designate, Dinges, Dingus, Dit, Domain, Dub, Epithet, Eponym, Exonym, Family, First, Generic, Given, Handle, Hete, Hight, Identify, Identity, Label, Maiden, Marque, Masthead, Mention, Metronymic, Middle, Moni(c)ker, Mud, N, Nap, Nemn, Nom, Nomen(clature), Noun, Patronymic, Pennant, Personage, Pet, Place, Proper, Proprietary, Pseudonym, Quote, Red(d), Repute, Sign, Signature, Sir, Specify, Stage, Street, Substantive, Tag, Term, > **TITLE**, Titular, Titule, Trade, Trivial

Nap(py) Bonaparte, Diaper, Doze, Drowse, Fluff, Frieze(d), Fuzz, Kip, Moze, Oose, Ooze, Oozy, Put(t), Shag, Siesta, > **SLEEP**, Slumber, Snooze, Tease, Teasel, Teaze, Tipsy, Tuft

Napkin Cloth, Diaper, Doily, Sanitary, Serviette

▷ **Napoleon** *may indicate* a pig

Narcotic Ava, Benj, B(h)ang, Charas, Churrus, Coca, Codeine, Datura, Dope, > **DRUG**, Heroin, Hop, Kava, Laudanum, Mandrake, Marijuana, Meconium, Methadone, Morphia, Opiate, Pituri, Sedative

Narrate, Narration, Narrative, Narrator Allegory, Anecdote, Cantata, Describe, Diegesis, Fable, History, Periplus, Plot, Raconteur, Récit, Recite, Recount, Saga, Scheherazade, Splatterpunk, Story, Tell

Narrow(ing), Narrow-minded Alf, Bigoted, Borné, Constringe, Cramp, Ensiform, Grundy(ism), Hidebound, Illiberal, Insular, Kyle, Limited, Meagre, Nary, One-idead, Parochial, Phimosis, Pinch, Prudish, Puritan, Scant, Shrink, Slender, Slit, Specialise, Squeak, Stenosed, Strait, Suburban, Verkramp, Waist

Nastiness, Nasty Disagreeable, Drevill, Filth, Fink, Ghastly, Lemon, Lo(a)th, Malign(ant), Noxious, Obscene, Odious, Offensive, Ribby, Sordid, Vile

Nation(s), National(ist) Anthem, Baathist, Casement, Chetnik, Country, Cuban, Debt, Eta, Federal, Folk, Grand, Indian, IRA, Jingoist, Land, Mexican, Pamyat, Patriot, > **PEOPLE**, Polonia, Race, Risorgimento, Scottish, Subject, Swadeshi, United, Wafd, Yemini, Young Ireland, Zionist

Native(s) Abo(rigin), Aborigine, African, Amerind, Annamese, Arab, Ascian, Australian, Autochthon, Aztec, Basuto, Belonging, Bengali, Boy, Cairene, Carib, Carioca, Chaldean, Citizen, Colchester, Conch, Creole, Criollo, Domestic,

Dyak, Edo, Enchorial, Eskimo, Fleming, Genuine, Habitual, Inborn, Indigene, Indigenous, Inhabitant, Intuitive, Kaffir, Libyan, Local, Malay, Maori, Micronesian, Moroccan, Norwegian, Oyster, Polack, Portuguese, Son, Spaniard, Te(i)an, Thai, Tibetan, Uzbeg, Uzbek, Whitstable, Yugoslav

Natural(ly), Naturalised, Naturalism Artless, Ass, Easy, Genuine, Homely, Idiot, Illegitimate, Inborn, Inbred, Indigenous, Ingenerate, Inherent, Innate, Moron, Native, Nidget, Nitwit, Nude, Ordinary, Organic, Prat, Real, Sincere, True, Untaught

Nature Adam, Character, Disposition, Esse(nce), Ethos, Inscape, Mould, Quintessence, Second, SN, Temperament

Naught Cypher, Failure, Nil, Nothing, Zero

Naughty Bad, Girly, Improper, Light, Marietta, Rascal, Remiss, Spright, Sprite, Wayward

Nausea, Nauseous Disgust, Fulsome, Malaise, Queasy, Sickness, Squeamish, Wamble, Wambly

Nave Aisle, Apse, Centre, Hub, Nef

Navigate, Navigator Albuquerque, Bougainville, Cabot, Cartier, Columbus, Control, Da Gama, Dias, Direct, Franklin, Frobisher, Gilbert, Hartog, Haul, Henry, Hudson, Keel, Magellan, Navvy, Orienteer, Pilot, Sail, Star-read, > STEER

Navy, Naval AB, Armada, Blue, Fleet, French, Maritime, Merchant, N, Red, RN, Wren

Near(er), Nearest, Nearby, Nearly, Nearness About, Adjacent, All-but-, Almost, Anigh, Approach, Approximate, Beside, By, Close, Cy pres, Degree, Even, Ewest, Feckly, Forby, Gain, Handy, Hither, Imminent, Inby(e), Mean, Miserly, Narre, Neist, Next, Nie, Niggardly, Nigh, Outby, Propinquity, Proximity, Short-range, Stingy, Thereabout(s), To, Upon, Warm, Well-nigh

Neat(ly) Bandbox, Cattle, Clean-cut, Clever, Dainty, Dapper, Deft, Dink(y), Doddy, Donsie, Elegant, Feat(e)ous, Featuous, Gayal, Genty, Gyal, Intact, Jemmy, Jimpy, Nett, Ninepence, Orderly, Ox(en), Preppy, Pretty, Rother, Shipshape, Short, Smug, Snod, Spruce, Straight, > TIDY, Trig, Trim, Unwatered

Necessary, Necessarily Bog, Cash, De rigueur, > ESSENTIAL, Estovers, Important, Indispensable, Intrinsic, Money, Needful, Ought, Perforce, Requisite, Vital, Wherewithal

Necessitate, Necessity Ananke, Compel, Constrain, Cost, Emergency, Entail, Exigent, Fate, Indigence, Logical, Mathematical, Must, Natural, Need, Need-be, Oblige, Perforce, Require, Requisite

Neck(ed) Bottle, Brass, Canoodle, Cervical, Cervix, Channel, Col, Crag, Craig, Crop, Embrace, Gall, Gorgerin, Halse, Hawse, Inarm, Inclip, Isthmus, Kiss, Mash, Nape, Pet, Polo, Rubber, Scrag, Scruff, Smooch, Snog, Strait, Swan, Swire, Theorbo, Torticollis, Trachelate, Vee

▷ **Necking** *may indicate* one word around another

Necklace Anodyne, Chain, Choker, Collar, Corals, Pearls, Rope, Sautoir, String, Torc, Torque

Neckline Boat, Collar, Cowl, Crew, Décolletage, Plunging, Sweetheart, Turtle, Vee

Neckwear Ascot, Barcelona, Boa, Bow, Collar, Cravat, Fur, Steenkirk, Stock, Tie

Nectar Ambrosia, Amrita, Honey, Mead

Need(ed), Needy Call, Demand, Desiderata, Egence, Egency, Exigency, Gap, Gerundive, Impecunious, Indigent, > LACK, Mister, Pressing, PRN, Require, Strait, Strapped, Want

Needle(s) Acerose, Acicular, Aciform, Between, Bodkin, Cleopatra's, Darning, Dip, Dry-point, Electric, Goad, Gramophone, Hagedorn, Hype, Hypodermic, Ice, Icicle, Inoculate, Leucotome, Magnetic, Miff, Monolith, Neeld, Neele, Netting, Obelisk, Pine, Pinnacle, Pique, Pointer, Prick, R(h)aphis, Sew, Sharp, Spanish, Spicule, Spike, Spine, Stylus, Tattoo, Tease, Thorn, Wire

Needlework Baste, Crewel, Embroidery, Mola, Patchwork, Rivière, Sampler, Tapestry, Tattoo

Negation, Negative Anion, Apophatic, Cathode, Denial, Enantiosis, Ne, No, Non, Nope, Nullify, Photograph, Refusal, Resinous, Unresponsive, Veto, Yin

Neglect(ed), Neglectful, Negligence, Negligent Careless, Casual, Cinderella, Cuff, Default, Dereliction, Disregard, Disuse, Failure, Forget, Forlorn, Heedless, Inattention, Incivism, Laches, Malpractice, Misprision, Omission, Oversight, Pass, Pass-up, Shirk, Slight, Slipshod, Undone

▷ **Neglected** *may indicate* an anagram

Negligee Déshabillé, Manteau, Nightgown, Robe

Negotiate, Negotiator Arbitrate, Arrange, Bargain, Clear, Confer, Deal, Diplomat, Intermediary, Liaise, Manoeuvre, Mediator, Parley, Trade, Transact, Treat(y), Weather

Neigh Bray, Hinny, Nicker, Whicker, Whinny

Neighbour(ly), Neighbouring, Neighbours, Neighbours Abut(ter), Alongside, Amicable, Bor, Border, But, Friendly, Joneses, Nearby, Next-door

Neighbourhood Area, Community, District, Environs, Locality, Precinct, Vicinage, Vicinity

Nerve(s), Nervous(ness), Nervure, Nerve centre, Nervy Abdabs, Accessory, Acoustic, Afferent, Aflutter, Afraid, Alveolar, Auditory, Axon, Baroreceptor, Bottle, Bouton, Buccal, Chord, Chutzpah, Collywobbles, Column, Commissure, Cones, Courage, Cranial, Cyton, Depressor, Edgy, Effector, Efferent, Electrotonus, Epicritic, Excitor, Facial, Gall, Ganglion, Glossopharyngeal, Grit, Guts, Habdabs, Heart-string, High, Highly-strung, Hyp, Impudence, Jitters, Jittery, Median, Mid-rib, Motor, Myelon, Nappy, Neck, Nidus, Octulomotor, Olfactory, Optic, Pavid, Perikaryon, Proprioceptor, Rad, Radial, Receptor, Restiform, Restless, Sacral, Sangfroid, Sauce, Sciatic, Screaming abdabs, Sensory, Shaky, Solar plexus, Splanchnic, Spunk, Steel, Strung-up, Synapse, Tense, Tizzy, Toey, Tongue-tied, Trembler, Tremulous, Trigeminal, Trochlear, Twitchy, Ulnar, Uptight, Vagus, Vapours, Vestibulocochlear, Wandering, Willies, Windy, Yips

▷ **Nervously** *may indicate* an anagram

Nest Aerie, Aery, Airey, Ayrie, Bike, Bink, Brood, Byke, Cabinet, Cage, Caliology, Clutch, Dray, Drey, Eyrie, Eyry, Lodge, Nid, Nide, Nidify, Nidus, Sett, Termitarium, Wurley

Nestle Burrow, Cose, Cuddle, Nuzzle, Snug(gle)

Net(ting), Nets, Network Bamboo, BR, Bunt, Butterfly, Cast, Casting, Catch, Caul, Clap, Clear, Cobweb, Crinoline, Crossover, Drift, Earn, Eel-set, Enmesh, Equaliser, Ethernet, Fetch, Filet, Final, Fish, Flew, Flue, Fyke, Gill, > GRID, Hammock, Internet, Intranet, JANET, Kiddle, Lace, LAN, Land, Landing, Lattice, Leap, Line, Linin, Mains, Maze, Mosquito, Neural, Neuropic, Old boys', PCN, Plexus, Portal system, Pound, Pout, Purse-seine, Quadripole, Reseau, Rete, Retiary, Reticle, Reticulate, Reticulum, Ring, Safety, Sagene, Screen, Sean, Seine, Set(t), Shark, Snood, System, Tangle, Tela, Telex, Toil, Torpedo, Trammel, Trap, Trawl, Tulle, Tunnel, Usenet, WAN, Web, Wide-area, Wire

Nettle(rash) Anger, Annoy, Day, Dead, Hemp, Hives, Horse, Irritate, Labiate, Nark, Pellitory, Pique, Ramee, Rami, Ramie, Rile, Ruffle, Sting, Urtica(ceae), Urticaria

Neuter Castrate, Gib, Impartial, Neutral, Sexless, Spay

Neutral(ise) Alkalify, Buffer zone, Counteract, Grey, Impartial, Inactive, Schwa, Sheva, Shiva, Unbiased

Never(more) Nary, Nathemo(re), No more

Nevertheless Algate, Anyhow, But, However, Still, Yet

▷ **New** *may indicate* an anagram

New(s), News agency Bulletin, Copy, Coranto, Dope, Euphobia, Evangel,

Flash, Forest, Fresh, Fudge, Gen, Green, Griff, Info, Innovation, Intelligence, Item, Kerygma, Latest, Mint, Modern, N, Novel, Oil(s), Original, PA, Paragraph, Pastures, Pristine, Propaganda, Recent, Report, Reuter, Scoop, Span, Tass, Teletext®, Tidings, Ultramodern, Unco, Word

Newcomer Dog, Freshman, Griffin, Immigrant, Jackaroo, Jackeroo, Jillaroo, Johnny-come-lately, Novice, Parvenu, Pilgrim, Settler, Tenderfoot, Upstart

Newsman, **News-reader** Announcer, Editor, Journalist, Press, Reporter, Sub, Sysop

Newspaper Blat(t), Broadsheet, Courier, Daily, Express, Fanzine, Feuilleton, Freesheet, Gazette, Guardian, Herald, Journal, Jupiter, Le Monde, Mercury, National, Organ, Patent inside, Patent outside, Post, Pravda, Press, Print, Rag, Red-top, Sheet, Spoiler, Squeak, Sun, Tabloid, Today

Newt(s) Ask(er), Eft, Evet, Swift, Triton, Urodela

New Zealand(er) Aotearoa, Enzed, Kiwi, Maori, Moriori, Pakeha, Pig Island, Shagroon

Next Adjacent, Adjoining, After, Alongside, Beside, Following, Immediate, Later, Nearest, Neist, Proximate, Proximo, Sine, Subsequent, Syne

Nib J, Pen, Point, Tip

Nibble Bite, Brouse, Browse, Byte, Crop, Eat, Gnaw, Knap(ple), Moop, Moup, Munch, Nag, Nepit, Nosh, Peck, Pick, Snack

Nice(ty) Accurate, Amene, Appealing, Dainty, Fastidious, Fine, Finical, Genteel, Lepid, Ninepence, Pat, Pleasant, Precise, Quaint, Rare, Refined, Subtil(e), Subtle, Sweet, T

Niche Alcove, Almehrahb, Almery, Ambry, Apse, Aumbry, Awmrie, Awmry, Columbarium, Cranny, Exedra, Fenestella, Mihrab, Recess, Slot

Nick(ed) Appropriate, Arrest, Bin, Blag, Can, Chip, Cly, Colin, Copshop, Cut, Denay, Dent, Deny, > DEVIL, Erose, Groove, Hoosegow, Kitty, Knock, Nab, Nap, Nim, Nock, Notch, Pinch, Pook, Pouk, Prison, Scratch, > STEAL, Steek, Swan-upping, Swipe, Thieve, Wirricow, Worricow, Worrycow

Nickname Alias, Byname, Byword, Cognomen, So(u)briquet

Night(s), **Nightfall** Acronychal, Arabian, Darkmans, First, Gaudy, Guest, Guy Fawkes, Hen, Leila, Nacht, Nicka-nan, Nutcrack, Nyx, School, Stag, Twelfth, Twilight, Walpurgis, Watch, White

Night-cap Biggin, Cocoa, Nip, Pirnie, Sundowner

Nightingale Bulbul, Florence, Jugger, Lind, Philomel, Scutari, Swedish, Watch

Nightmare, **Nightmarish** Cacod(a)emon, Ephialtes, Incubus, Kafkaesque, Oneirodynia, Phantasmagoria

Nightshade Belladonna, Bittersweet, Circaea, Dwale, Henbane, Morel, Solanum

Nil Nothing, Nought, Zero

Nimble, **Nimbly** Active, > AGILE, Alert, Deft, Deliver, Fleet, Light, Light-footed, Lissom(e), Lithe, Quiver, Sciolto, Springe, Spry, Supple, Swack, Wan(d)le, Wannel, Wight, Ya(u)ld

Nip(per) Bite, Check, Chela, Chill, Claw, Dram, Gook, Jap, Lad, Lop, Nep, Nirl, Peck, Pincers, Pinch, Pook, Scotch, Sneap, Susan, Taste, Tot, Tweak, Urchin, Vice, Vise

Nipple Dug, Mastoid, Pap, Teat

No Aikona, Denial, Na(e), Nah, Negative, Nix, Nope, Nyet, O, Refusal

Nob(by) Grandee, Parage, Prince, Swell, Toff

▷ **Nobbled** *may indicate* an anagram

Noble(man), **Noblewoman**, **Nobility** Adeline, Aristocrat, Atheling, Baron(et), Bart, Boyar, Brave, Bt, Burgrave, Childe, Count, County, Daimio, Dom, Don, Doucepere, Douzeper(s), Duc, Duke, Duniwassal, Earl, Empress, Eorl, Ethel, Eupatrid, Fine, Gent, Glorious, Graf, Grandee, Grandeur, Great, Heroic, Hidalgo, Highborn, Infant, Jarl, Junker, King, Landgrave, Lord, Magnate, Magnifico,

Manly, Margrave, Marquis, Nair, Nayar, Palatine, Patrician, Peer, Rank, Seigneur, Seignior, Sheik(h), Stately, Sublime, Thane, Thegn, Titled, Toiseach, Toisech, Vavasour, Vicomte, Vidame, Viscount

Noble gas(es) Argon, Helium, Krypton, Neon, Radon, Xenon

Nobody Gnatling, Jack-straw, Nebbish, Nemo, None, Nonentity, Nyaff, Pooter, Quat, Schlepp, Scoot, Shlep

Nod(ding) Agree, Assent, Beck(on), Bob, Browse, Catnap, Cernuous, Doze, Mandarin, Nutant, Somnolent

Node, Nodular, Nodule Boss, Enhydros, Geode, Knot, Lump, Lymph, Milium, Pea-iron, Ranvier, Swelling, Thorn

Noise, Noisy Ambient, Babel, Bedlam, Big, Blare, Bleep, Blip, Bobbery, Boing, Boink, Bruit, Cangle, Charm, Chellup, Clamant, Clamour, Clangour, Clash, Clatter, Clitter, Clutter, Coil, Crackle, Creak, Deen, Din, Dirdum, Euphonia, Euphony, F, Flicker, Fuss, Hewgh, Hubbub, Hue, Hullabaloo, Hum, Hurly-burly, Knocking, Loud, Mush, Obstreperous, Ping, Pink, Plangent, Quonk, Racket, Report, Roar, Robustious, Rorie, Rort, Rory, Row(dow-dow), Rowdedow, Rowdy(dow)(dy), Rucous, Schottky, Scream, Screech, Shindig, Shindy, Shot, Shreek, Shreik, Shriech, Shriek, Solar, Sone, Sonorous, Sound, Stridor, Surface, Thermal, Thunder, Tinnitus, Top, Tumult, > UPROAR, VIP, Vociferous, White, Zoom

Nomad(ic) Bedawin, Bed(o)uin, Bedu, Berber, Chal, Edom(ite), Fula(h), Gypsy, Hottentot, Kurd, Kyrgyz, Rom, Rootless, Rover, Saracen, Sarmatian, Strayer, Tsigane, Tsigany, Tuareg, Vagabond, Vagrant, Zigan

No man's land Tom Tiddler's ground

Nomenclature Term

Nominate, Nomination Appoint, Baptism, Designate, Elect, Present, > PROPOSE, Slate, Specify, Term

Non-Aboriginal Wudjula

Nonchalance, Nonchalant Blasé, Casual, Cool, Debonair, Insouciant, Jaunty, Poco

Non-Christian Saracen

Non-conformist, Non-conformity Beatnik, Bohemian, Chapel, Deviant, Dissent(er), Dissident, Ebenezer, Heresiarch, Heretic, Maverick, Odd-ball, Outlaw, Pantile, Patarine, Rebel, Recusant, Renegade, Renegate, Sectarian, Wesleyan

Non-drip Thixotropic

None Nada, Nary, Nil, Nought, Zero

Nonentity Cipher, Nebbich, Nebbish(er), Nebish, Nobody, Pipsqueak, Quat

▷ **Nonetheless** *may indicate* an 'o' to be omitted

Non-existent Unbeing, Virtual

Nonsense Absurdity, Amphigory, Balderdash, Baloney, Bilge, Bizzo, Blague, Blah, Blarney, Blat(her), Blether, Bollocks, Boloney, Borax, Bosh, Bull, Bulldust, Bullshit, Bull's wool, Buncombe, Bunkum, Clamjamfr(a)y, Clamjamphrie, Claptrap, Cobblers, Cock, Cockamamie, Cod, Codswallop, Crap, Crapola, Drivel, Dust, Eyewash, Faddle, Fandangle, Fiddlededee, Fiddle-faddle, Fiddlesticks, Flannel, Flim-flam, Footling, Fudge, Gaff, Gammon, Get away, Gibberish, Guff, Gum, Hanky-panky, Haver, Hogwash, Hokum, Hooey, Horsefeathers, Humbug, Jabberwocky, Kibosh, Kidstakes, Malark(e)y, Moonshine, Mouthwash, My eye, Phooey, Piffle, Pshaw, Pulp, Ratbaggery, Rats, Rhubarb, Rigmarole, Rot, Rubbish, Scat, Shenanigans, Shit(e), Squit, Stuff, Tom(foolery), Tommy-rot, Tosh, Trash, Tripe, Tush, Twaddle, Unreason, Waffle

Noodle(s) Capellini, Crispy, Daw, Fool, Head, Laksa, Lokshen, Manicotti, Mee, Moony, Pasta, Sammy, Simpleton

Nook Alcove, Angle, Corner, Cranny, Niche, Recess, Rookery

Noose Fank, Halter, Lanyard, Loop, Necktie, Rope, Rope's end, Snare, Twitch

▶ **Nor** see NOT

▶ **Nordic** see NORWAY, NORWEGIAN

Norm Canon, Criterion, Rule, Standard

Normal Average, Everyday, Natural, Norm, Ordinary, Par, Perpendicular, Regular, Standard, Usu(al)

▶ **Norse** see NORWAY, NORWEGIAN

North(ern), Northerner Arctic, Boreal, Cispontine, Copperhead, Doughface, Eskimo, Hyperborean, Magnetic, N, Norland, Runic, Septentrion, True, Up

North American (Indian) Ab(e)naki, Algonki(a)n, Algonqui(a)n, Apache, Arapaho, Assiniboine, Basket Maker, Blackfoot, Brave, Caddoan, Cajun, Cayuga, Cherokee, Cheyenne, Chibcha, Chickasaw, Chinook, Chipewyan, Choctaw, Comanche, Copperskin, Creek, Crow, Delaware, Dene, Erie, Fox, Galibi, Geronimo, Haida, Hiawatha, Hopi, Huron, Injun, Iroquois, Kiowa Apache, Kootenai, Kootenay, Kutenai, Kwakiuti, Lakota, Mahican, Malecite, Mandan, Manhattan, Massachuset(ts), Melungeon, Menominee, Mescalero, Micmac, Mikasuki, Miniconjou, Minneconjou, Mission, Mogollon, Mohave, Mohawk, Mohegan, Mohican, Montagnais, Montagnard, Mound Builder, Mugwump, Muskogee, Narraganset, Natchez, Navaho, Nez Percé, Nootka, Northern P(a)iute, Oglala, Ojibwa(y), Okanagon, Okinagan, Omaha, Oneida, Onondaga, Osage, P(a)iute, Palouse, Papago, Papoose, Pawnee, Pequot, Pima, Plains, Pocahontas, Pomo, Ponca, Pontiac, Potawatom, Pueblo, Quapaw, Red(skin), Sachem, Sagamore, Sahaptan, Sahapti(a)n, Salish, Sannup, Sauk, Scalper, Seminole, Senecan, Serrano, Shawnee, Shoshone, Sioux, Sitting Bull, Siwash, Southern P(a)iute, Status, Suquamash, Susquehannock, Tahitan, Taino, Tarahumara, Teton, Tewa, Tiwa, Tlingit, Tribe, Tsimshian, Tuscarora, Ute, Wampanoag, Wichita, Winnebago, Wyandot(te), Yalkama, Yanqui, Yuman, Zuni

Northern Ireland NI, Six Counties

Nose, Nosy A(d)jutage, Aquiline, Beak, Bergerac, Boko, Bouquet, Conk, Cromwell, Curious, Desman, Droop, Fink, Gnomon, Grass, Grecian, Honker, Hooter, Index, Informer, Meddle, Muffle, Muzzle, Nark, Neb, Nozzle, Nuzzle, Proboscis, Prying, Pug, Rhinal, Roman, Schnozzle, Shove, Smelly, Sneb, Sniff, Snoot, Snout, Snub, Squeal, Stag, Stickybeak, Toffee

Nostalgia Longing, Retrophilia, Yearning

Not, Nor Dis-, Na(e), Ne, Neither, Never, No, Pas, Polled, Taint

Notable, Notability Conspicuous, Distinguished, Eminent, Especial, Landmark, Large, Lion, Memorable, Signal, Striking, Unco, VIP, Worthy

▷ **Not allowed** *may indicate* a word to be omitted

Notation(al) Benesh, Entry, Memo, Polish, Positional

Notch(ed) Crena(l), Crenel, Cut, Dent, Erode, Erose, Gain, Gap, Gimp, Indent, Jag, Kerf, Nick, Nock, Raffle, Sinus, Snick, Tally, Vandyke

Note(s), Notebook A, Accidental, Advice, Apostil(le), Apparatus, Arpeggio, Auxiliary, B, Bill(et), Bradbury, Breve, C, Cedula, Chit(ty), Chord, Cob, Comment, Conceit, Continental, Cover, Credit, Crotchet, Currency, D, Debit, Delivery, Demand, Dig, Dominant, E, E-la, F, Fa(h), Fame, Fiver, Flat, Flim, G, Gamut, Gloss(ary), Gold, Grace, Greenback, Heed, Identic, Index rerum, IOU, Item(ise), Jot(tings), Jug(-jug), Key, Kudos, La, Large, Leading, Line, Log, Long, Longa, Marginalia, Masora(h), Me, Melisma, Melody, Memo(randum), Mese, Mi, Minim, Minute, > MONEY, Mordent, Natural, NB, Nete, Neum(e), Oblong, Observe, Octave, Oncer, Ostmark, Outline, Passing, Post-it®, Pound, Promissory, Prompt, Protocol, PS, Quarter, Quaver, Rag-money, Re, Record, Remark, Renown, Request, Root, Scholion, Semibreve, Semiquaver, Semitone, Sextolet, Sharp, Shoulder, Si, Sick, Smacker, Sol, Stem, Strike, Subdominant, Submediant, Subtonic, Supertonic, Te, Ten(ner), Third, Tierce, Tonic, Treasury, Treble, Ut, Verbal, Wad, Whole

▷ **Notes** *may indicate* the use of letters A-G

Noteworthy Eminent, Extraordinary, Memorable, Particular, Signal, Special

Nothing, Nought Cipher, Devoid, Diddlysquat, Emptiness, FA, Gratis, Nada, Naught, Nihil, Niks-nie, Nil, Nix(-nie), Noumenon, Nowt, Nuffin, O, Rap, Rien, Sweet FA, Void, Zero, Zilch, Zip(po)

Notice(able) Ad(vertisement), Advice, Affiche, Apprise, Attention, Avis(o), Banns, Bill, Blurb, Caveat, Circular, Cognisance, Crit, D, Descry, Discern, Dismissal, Enforcement, Gaum, Get, Gorm, Handbill, > **HEED**, Intimation, Marked, Mensh, Mention, NB, No(t)chel, Obit, Observe, Oyez, Placard, Plaque, Playbill, Poster, Press, Proclamation, Prominent, > **REMARK**, Review, See, Short, Si quis, Spot, Spy, Sticker, Tent, Whip

Notify Acquaint, Advise, Apprise, Awarn, Inform, > **TELL**

Notion(al) Conceit, Crotchet, Fancy, Hunch, Idea, Idolum, Inkling, Opinion, Reverie, Vapour, Whim

Notoriety, Notorious Arrant, Byword, Crying, Egregious, Esclandre, Fame, Flagrant, Infamous, Infamy, Proverbial, Reclame, Repute

▶ **Nought** *see* **NOTHING**

Noumenon Thing-in-itself

Noun Agent, Aptote, Collective, Common, Count, Gerund, Mass, N, Proper, Substantive, Tetraptote, Verbal

Nourish(ing), Nourishment Aliment, Cherish, Cultivate, Feed, Ingesta, Meat, Nurse, Nurture, Nutrient, Promote, Replenish, Sustenance, Trophic

Novel(ty) Aga-saga, Bonkbuster, Book, Campus, Change, Different, Dime, Dissimilar, Epistolary, Fad, Fiction, Fresh, Gimmick, Gothic, Graphic, Historical, Horror, Idiot, Innovation, > **NEW**, Newfangled, Original, Outside, Page-turner, Paperback, Penny dreadful, Picaresque, Pot-boiler, Primeur, Pulp, Roman-à-clef, Romance, Roman fleuve, Sex and shopping, Shilling-dreadful, Shilling-shocker, Ulysses, Unusual, Whodun(n)it, Yellowback

▷ **Novel** *may indicate* an anagram

▶ **Novelist** *see* **WRITER**

Novice Acolyte, Apprentice, Beginner, Chela, Colt, Cub, Greenhorn, Griffin, Jackaroo, Jillaroo, Kyu, L, Learner, Neophyte, Patzer, Postulant, Prentice, Rookie, Tenderfoot

Now(adays) AD, Alate, Anymore, Current, Here, Immediate, Instanter, Interim, Nonce, Nunc, Present, Pro tem, This

Nozzle A(d)jutage, Fishtail, Nose, Nose-piece, Rose, Spout, Stroup, Syringe, Tewel, Tuyere, Tweer, Twier, Twire, Twyer(e)

Nuance Gradation, Nicety, Overtone, Shade

Nub Crux, Gist, Knob, Lump, Point

Nuclear, Nucl(e)ide, Nucleus Cadre, Calandria, Centre, Core, Crux, Daughter, Deuteron, Eukaryon, Euratom, Heartlet, Hub, Isomer, Isotone, Karyon, Kernel, Linin, Mushroom, Nuke, Pith, Prokaryon, Triton

▷ **Nucleus** *may indicate* the heart of a word

Nude, Nudism, Nudist, Nudity Adamite, Altogether, Aphylly, Bare, Buff, Eve, Exposed, Gymnosophy, > **NAKED**, Nuddy, Scud, Stark, Stripped, Undress

Nudge Dunch, Dunsh, Elbow, Jostle, Poke, Prod

Nuisance Bore, Bot, Bugbear, Chiz(z), Drag, Impediment, Inconvenience, Mischief, Pest, Plague, Public, Terror, Trial

Null(ification), Nullify Abate, Cancel, Counteract, Defeasance, Destroy, Diriment, Disarm, Invalid(ate), Negate, Neutralise, Recant, Terminate, Undo, Veto, Void

Numb(ness) Asleep, Blunt, Dead(en), Stun, Stupor, Torpefy, Torpescent, Torpid

Number(s) Abundant, Accession, Air, Algebraic, Algorithm, Aliquant, Aliquot,

Amicable, Anaesthetic, Antilog, Army, Atomic, Babylonian, Binary, Box, Calculate, Cardinal, Cetane, Chromosome, Class, Cocaine, Coefficient, Cofactor, Complex, Composite, Concrete, Constant, Coordination, Count, Cyclic, Decillion, Deficient, Deficit, Diapason, Digit, Drove, E, Edition, Epidural, Ether, Eucaine, Ex-directory, F, Feck, Frost(bite), Gas, Gobar, Golden, Googol, Handful, Hash(mark), Hemlock, Host, Imaginary, Include, Index, Integer, Irrational, Item, Lac, Lakh, Legion(s), Lepton, Livraison, Local, Mach, Magazine, Magic, Mass, Melodic, Milliard, Minyan, Mixed, Mort, Muckle, Multiple, Multiplex, Multiplicity, Multitude, Myriadth, Natural, Neutron, No(s), Nonillion, Nth, Num, Numerator, Numerical, Octane, Octillion, Opiate, Opium, Opposite, Opus, Ordinal, OT, Paginate, Par, Paucal, Peck, Perfect, Pile, PIN, Plural, Prime, Proton, Quantum, Quorum, Quotient, Random, Rational, Real, Reckon, Registration, Regulo®, Scads, Serial, Sight, Slew, Slue, Some, Square, Strangeness, Strength, Summand, Surd, T, Tale, Telephone, Tell, Thr(e)ave, Totient, Totitive, Transcendental, Troop, Turn-out, Umpteen, Umpty, Urethane, Verse, Wave, Whole, Wrong

▷ **Number** *may indicate* a drug

Numeral(s) Arabic, Chapter, Figure, Ghubar, Gobar, Integer, Number, Roman

Nun Beguine, Bhikkhuni, Clare, Cluniac, Conceptionist, Dame, Minim, Minoress, Mother Superior, Pigeon, Poor Clare, Religeuse, Sister, Top, Vestal, Vowess, Zelator, Zelatrice, Zelatrix

▷ **Nun** *may indicate* a biblical character, father of Joshua

Nurse(ry) Aia, Alice, Amah, Ayah, Bonne, Caledonia, Care(r), Cavell, Charge, Cherish, Crèche, Day, Deborah, District, Dry, EN, Flo(rence), Foster, Gamp, Glumdalclitch, Harbour, Karitane, Mammy, Midwife, Minister, Mother, Mrs Gamp, Nan(n)a, Nanny, Night, Nightingale, Nourice, Nourish, Parabolanus, Phytotron, Playroom, Playschool, Plunket, Probationer, RN, Seminary, SEN, Sister, Staff, Suckle, Tend, VAD, Visiting, Wet

Nursery(man) Conservatory, Crèche, Garden, Hothouse, Rhyme, Seedsman, Slope

▷ **Nursing** *may indicate* one word within another

Nut(s), Nutcase, Nutshell, Nut tree, Nutty Acajou, Acorn, Almond, Amygdalus, Aphorism, Arachis, Areca, Arnut, Babassu, Barcelona, Barking, Barmy, Bats, Beech-mast, Bertholletia, Betel, Brazil, Briefly, Buffalo, Butterfly, Butternut, Cashew, Cob, Coffee, Cola, Coquilla, Coquina, Core, Cranium, Cuckoo, Dukka(h), En, Filberd, Filbert, Gelt, Gilbert, Gland, Glans, Goober, Gum, Hazel, Head, Hickory, Illipe, Ivory, Kernel, Kola, Lichee, Li(t)chi, Litchi, Loaf, Lug, Lunatic, Lychee, Macadamia, Macahuba, Macaw-palm, Macoya, Manic, Marking, Mast, Mockernut, Monkey, Noisette, Noodle, Palmyra, Para, Pate, Pecan, Philippina, Philippine, Philopoena, Physic, Pili, Pine, Pistachio, Praline, Prawlin, Quandang, Quantong, Queensland, Rhus, Sapucaia, Sassafras, Shell, Skull, Slack, Sleeve, Stuffing, Supari, Thumb, Tiger, Walnut, Weirdo, Wing, Zany, Zealot

▷ **Nut** *may indicate* Egyptian god, father of Osiris

Nutcracker Cosh

Nutrient, Nutriment, Nutrition Eutrophy, Food, Ingesta, Protein, Sustenance, Trace element, Trophic

▷ **Nuts** *may indicate* an anagram

Nymph(et) Aegina, Aegle, Amalthea, Arethusa, Callisto, Calypso, Camenae, Carme, Clytie, Constant, Cymodoce, Daphne, Doris, Dryad, Echo, Egeria, Eurydice, Galatea, Hamadryad, Hesperides, Houri, Hyades, Ida, Insect, Larva, Liberty, Lolita, Maelid, Maia, Maiden, Mermaid, Naiad, Nereid, Oceanid, Oenone, Oread, Pupa, Rusalka, Sabrina, Scylla, Siren, Sylph, Syrinx, Tessa, Tethys, Thetis, Water, Wood

Oo

O Blob, Duck, Nought, Omega, Omicron, Oscar, Oxygen, Spangle, Tan, Zero

Oar(s), Oarsmen Blade, Ctene, Eight, Leander, Organ, Paddle, Propel, Rower, Scull, Spoon, Sweep

Oat(meal), Oats Ait, Athole brose, Avena, Brome-grass, Fodder, Grain, Grits, Groats, Gruel, Haver, Loblolly, Parritch, Pilcorn, Pipe, Porridge, Quaker®, Rolled, Wild

Oath Affidavit, Begorrah, Curse, Dang, Demme, Doggone, Drat, Ecod, Egad, Expletive, God-so, Halidom, Hippocratic, Igad, Imprecation, Jabers, Lumme, Lummy, Nouns, Oons, Promise, Sacrament, Sal(a)mon, Sheart, Strewth, Stygian, Swear, Tarnation, Tennis-court, Voir dire, Vow, Zbud

Obedient, Obedience, Obey Bridlewise, Comply, Dutiful, Follow, Hear, Mindful, Obsequious, Observe, Obtemper, Perform, Pliant, Servant, Yielding

Obese, Obesity Bariatrics, Corpulent, Fat, Stout

Object(s), Objection(able), Objective(ness), Objector Ah, Aim, Ambition, Argue, Article, Bar, Beef, Case, Cavil, Challenge, Clinical, Complain(t), Conchy, Conscientious, Cow, Demur, Direct, End, Exception, Fuss, > **GOAL**, Her, Him, Impersonal, Improper, Indifferent, Indirect, Intensional, Intention, It, Item, Jib, Loathe, Mind, Moral, Niggle, Non-ego, Noumenon, Obnoxious, Offensive, Oppose, Outness, Plan, Plot, Point, Protest, Question, Quibble, Quiddity, Rebarbative, Recuse, Refuse, Resist, Retained, Sake, Scruple, Sex, Subject, Sublime, Target, Thing, Transitive, Tut, Ultimate, Unbiased, Virtu, Wart

▷ **Object** *may indicate* a grammatical variant

Oblige, Obliging, Obligation, Obligatory Accommodate, Affable, Behold, Binding, Burden, Charge, Compel, Complaisant, Compliant, Contract, Corvée, Debt, De rigueur, Duty, Easy, Encumbent, Force, Giri, Gratify, Impel, Incumbent, IOU, Mandatory, Must, Necessitate, Obruk, Promise, Sonties, Synallagmatic, Tie, Wattle

Oblique(ly) Askance, Askew, Awry, Cross, Diagonal, Perverse, Separatrix, Skew, Slanting, Solidus, Squint, Virgule

▷ **Oblique** *may indicate* an anagram

Oblivion, Oblivious Forgetful, Lethe, Limbo, Nirvana, Obscurity

Obloquy Opprobrium

Obnoxious Foul, Horrid, Offensive, Pestilent, Repugnant

Obscene(ly), Obscenity Bawdy, Blue, Fescennine, Gross, Hard-core, Indecent, Lewd, Lubricious, Paw(paw), Porn(o), Salacious, Smut, Vulgar

Obscure, Obscurity Abstruse, Anheires, Becloud, Befog, Blend, Blot out, Cloud, Cobweb, Conceal, Cover, Cryptic, Darken, Deep, Dim, Disguise, Eclipse, Encrypt, Envelop, Esoteric, Filmy, Fog, Hermetic, Hide, Indistinct, Mantle, Mist, Murk, Nebular, Night, Nubecula, Obfuscate, Obnubilate, Opaque, Oracular, Overcloud, Overshade, Overshadow, Recherché, Recondite, Shadowy, Tenebrific, Twilit, Unclear, > **VAGUE**, Veil, Vele, Wrap

▷ **Obscure(d)** *may indicate* an anagram

Observance, Observant, Observation Adherence, Alert, Attention,

Observe(d) | 262

Comment, Custom, Empirical, Espial, Eyeful, Holy, Honour, Lectisternium,
> NOTICE, Obiter dicta, Percipient, Recce, Remark, Right, Rite, Ritual, Vising

Observe(d), Observer Behold, Bystander, Celebrate, Commentator, Detect,
Espy, Eye, Heed, Keep, Mark, NB, Note, Notice, Obey, Onlooker, Optic, Regard(er),
Remark, Rite, Scry, See, Sight, Spectator, Spial, Spot, Spy, Study, Take, Twig, View,
Voyeur, Witness

Obsess(ed), Obsession, Obsessive Besot, Bug, Craze, Dominate, Fetish,
Fixation, Hang-up, Haunt, Hobbyhorse, Hooked, Idée fixe, Infatuation, Mania,
Monomania, Necrophilia, Neurotic, One-track, Preoccupy, Thing

Obsidian Pe(a)rlite

Obsolete, Obsolescence, Obsolescent Abandoned, Antique, Archaic,
Dated, Dead, Defunct, Disused, Extinct, Latescent, Obs, Outdated, Outworn,
Passé

Obstacle Barrage, Barrier, Boyg, Cheval de frise, Chicane, Dam, Drag, Dragon's
teeth, Drawback, Gate, Handicap, Hindrance, Hitch, Hurdle, Node, Oxer, Remora,
Rock, Sandbank, Snag, Stimie, Stumbling-block, Stymie

Obstinacy, Obstinate Asinine, Buckie, Bullish, Contumacious, Cussed, Dour,
Froward, Headstrong, Inflexible, Intractable, Intransigent, Mule, Persistent,
Perverse, Pervicacious, Pig-headed, Recalcitrant, Refractory, Restive, Rusty,
Self-will, Stiff(-necked), Stubborn, Wilful

Obstruct(ion) Bar, Block, Bottleneck, Chicane, Clog, Crab, Cross, Cumber, Dam,
Embolus, Fil(l)ibuster, Gridlock, Hamper, Hedge, Hinder, Hurdle, Ileus, Impede,
Let, Obstacle, Occlude, Sab(otage), Snooker, Stall, Stap, Stonewall, Stop, Stymie,
Sudd, Thwart, Trammel, Trump

Obtain Achieve, Acquire, Cop, Exist, Gain, Get, Land, Pan, Prevail, Procure,
Realise, Secure, Succeed, Wangle, Win

Obvious Apparent, Axiom, Blatant, Brobdingnag, Clear, Distinct, Evident,
Flagrant, Frank, Inescapable, Kenspeck(le), Manifest, Marked, Open(ness),
Open and shut, Overt, Palpable, Patent, Pikestaff, Plain, Pronounced, Salient,
Self-evident, Stark, Transparent, Truism, Visible

Occasion Call, Cause, Ceremony, Encheason, Event, Fete, Field day, Nonce,
> OPPORTUNITY, Reason, Ride, Tide, Time

Occasional(ly) Casual, Chance, Daimen, Intermittent, Irregular, Motive, Orra,
Periodic, Sometimes, Sporadic, While

Occupant, Occupation, Occupy(ing) Absorb, Activity, Avocation, Beset,
Business, Busy, Denizen, Embusy, Employ, Engage, Engross, Hold, In, Incumbent,
Indwell, Inhabitant, Inmate, Involve, Line, Metier, People, Profession, Pursuit,
Resident, Runrig, Sideline, Squat, Stay, Tenancy, Tenant, Tenure, Thrift, Trade,
Upon, Use, Vocation, Walk of life

Occur(rence) Arise, Be, Betide, Betime, Case, Event, Fall, Happen, Incident,
Instance, Outbreak, Outcrop, Pass, Phenomenon

Ocean(ic), Oceania Abundance, Abyssal, Antarctic, Arctic, Atlantic, Blue,
Deep, German, Hadal, Herring-pond, Indian, Melanesia, Micronesia, Pacific,
Panthalassa, Pelagic, Polynesia, Sea(way), Southern, Thalassic, Waves, Western

Octopus Cephalopod, Devilfish, Scuttle, Squid

Odd (person), Oddity Abnormal, Anomaly, Bizarre, Card, Cure, Curio, Droll,
Eccentric, Eery, Erratic, Gink, Impair, Imparity, Jimjam, Offbeat, Original, Orra,
Outré, Paradox, Parity, Peculiar, Queer, Quiz, Random, Rare, Remote, Rum,
Screwball, Singular, > STRANGE, Unequal, Uneven, Unmatched, Unusual, Weird,
Whims(e)y

▷ **Odd(s)** *may indicate* an anagram or the odd letters in words

Oddfellow OF

Odds, **Oddments** Bits, Carpet, Chance, Gubbins, Handicap, Line, Price, SP, Tails, Variance

Ode Awdl, Dit, Epicede, Epicedium, Epinicion, Epinikion, Genethliacon, Horatian, Hymn, Lay, Lyric, Monody, Paeon, Pindaric, Poem, Sapphic, Song, Stasimon, Threnody, Verse

Odium, **Odious** Comparison, Disestimation, Disgrace, Foul, Hatred, Heinous, Invidious, Repugnant, Stigma

Odorous, **Odour** Air, BO, Flavour, Funk, Hum, Opopanax, Perfume, Quality, Redolence, Sanctity, Scent, Smell

▷ **Of** *may indicate* an anagram

Of course Certainly, Natch, Yes

Off Absent, Agee, Ajee, Away, Discount, Distance, Far, From, High, Inexact, Licence, Odd, Reasty, Reesty, Relache, Start

▷ **Off** *may indicate* an anagram

▷ **Off-colour** *may indicate* an anagram

Offence Attack, Crime, Delict, Delinquency, Distaste, Fault, Huff, Hurt, Lapse, Miff, Misdemeanour, Misprision, Outrage, Peccadillo, Pip, Pique, Piracy, Regrate, Sedition, > **SIN**, Summary, Trespass, Umbrage, Violation

Offend(ed), **Offender** Affront, Anger, Annoy, Bridles, Culprit, Default, Disoblige, Displease, Distaste, Hip, Huff, Hurt, Hyp, Infringe, Inveigh, Miffy, Miscreant, Nettle, Nonce, Nuisance, Peeve, Provoke, Sin(ner), Stray, Twoccer, Violate, Wrongdoer

Offensive Affront, Aggressive, Alien, Attack, Bombardment, Campaign, Cruel, Embracery, Execrable, Eyesore, Foul, Indelicate, Nasty, Noisome, Obnoxious, Obscene, Peccant, Personal, Push, Putrid, Rank, Repugnant, > **RUDE**, Scandalous, Scurrilous, Sortie, Storm, Ugly, Unbecoming

Offer(ing) Alms, Altarage, Anaphora, Bargain, Bid, Bode, Bouchée, Cadeau, Corban, Deodate, Dolly, Epanophora, Extend, Ex voto, Gift, Godfather, Hold, Inferiae, Invitation, Oblation, Overture, Peddle, Plead, Potla(t)ch, Present, Propine, > **PROPOSAL**, Propose, Propound, Sacrifice, Shewbread, Shore, S(h)raddha, Special, Stamp, Stand, Submit, Tender, Utter, Volunteer, Votive, Wave, Xenium

Offhand Airy, Banana, Brusque, Casual, Cavalier, Curt, Extempore, Impromptu, Indifferent, Snappy

Office(s) Agency, Box, Branch, Broo, Bucket shop, Bureau, Buroo, Chair, Colonial, Complin(e), Consulate, Crown, Dead-letter, Deanery, Den, Divine, Employment, Evensong, Foreign, Function, Holy, Home, Job, Land, Last, Left luggage, Lieutenancy, Little, Mayoralty, Met(eorological), Ministry, Mistery, Nocturn, Nones, Obit, Oval, Palatinate, Papacy, Patent, Personnel, Pipe, Place, Plum, Portfolio, Position, Post, Prelacy, Press, Prime, Printing, Record, Regency, Register, Registry, Rite, See, Sinecure, Situation, Stationery, Tariff, Terce, Ticket, Tierce, Tol(l)booth, Vespers, War

Officer(s) Acater, Adjutant, Admiral, Ag(h)a, Agistor, Aide, Bailiff, Beatty, Black Rod, Blimp, Bombardier, Bos(u)n, Brass-hat, Brigadier, Bumbailiff, Capt(ain), Catchpole, Catchpoll, Cater, Centurion, Chamberlain, Chancellor, CIGS, Colonel, Commander, Commissioner, Commodore, Compliance, Constable, Cop(per), Co-pilot, Cornet, Coroner, Counter-round, Cursitor, Datary, Deacon, Decurion, Duty, Earl Marshal, Ensign, Equerry, Exciseman, Executive, Exon, Field Marshal, Filacer, First, Flag, Flying, Gallant, Gazetted, Gen(eral), GOC, Group, Gunner, Havildar, Incumbent, Intendant, Janty, Jaunty, Jonty, Jurat, Justiciar, Lance-sergeant, Liaison, Lictor, Lord High Steward, Lt, Marshal, Mate, Moderator, NCO, Number one, Nursing, Official Solicitor, Orderly, Oxon, Petty, Pilot, Pipe major, PO, Posse, Prefect, Prison, Probation, Proctor, Provost, Provost-marshal, Purser, Pursuivant, Quartermaster, Relieving, Returning, Rodent, Rupert, Sbirro,

Sea Lord, Second mate, Select-man, Serang, Sergeant-major, Sewer, Sexton, Sheriff, Skipper, SL, SM, Speaker, Staff, Striper, Sub(altern), Sublieutenant, Superintendent, Tindal, Tipstaff, Treasurer, Tribune, Usher, Varlet, Waldgrave, Warden, Wardroom, Warrant, Watch, Yeoman

Official(s), Officiate, Officious Aga, Agent, Amban, Amtman, Atabeg, Atabek, Attaché, Authorised, Beadle, Bossy, Bureaucrat, Catchpole, Censor, Chamberlain, Chancellor, Commissar, Commissioner, Consul, Count, Dean, Diplomat, Dogberry, Ephor, Equerry, Escheater, Eurocrat, Executive, > **FORMAL**, Functionary, Gauleiter, Gymnasiarch, Hayward, Incumbent, Inspector, Intendant, Jack-in-office, Jobsworth, Keeper, Landdrost, Lictor, Linesman, Mandarin, Marplot, Marshal, Mayor, MC, Meddlesome, Mirza, Mueddin, Notary, Ombudsman, Palatine, Paymaster, Plenipotentiary, Polemarch, Pontificate, Poohbah, Postmaster, Pragmatic, Prefect, Proctor, Procurator, Prog, Proveditor, Reeve, Regisseur, Registrar, Remembrancer, Shammash, Shammes, Sherpa, Souldan, Staff, Steward, Suit, Timekeeper, Tipstaff, Tribune, Trier, Trior, Turncock, Valid, Valuer General, Verderer, Verger, Vizier, Walla(h), Whip, Yamen, Yeoman

Offset Balance, Cancel, Compensate, Counter(act), Counterbalance

Offspring Boy, Burd, Chick, Children, Daughter, Descendant, Family, Fry, Get, Girl, Heir, Procreation, Product, Progeny, Seed, Sient, Son, Spawn

Often Frequent, Habitual, Repeated

▷ **Often** *may indicate* 'of ten'

Oil(y), Oil producer Aj(o)wan, Anele, Anoint, Argan, Attar, Balm, Balsam, Banana, Bath, Beech-mast, Ben, Benne, Benni, Bergamot, Bittern, Bone, BP, Bribe, Brilliantine, Butter, Cajeput, Cajuput, Camphire, Camphor, Camphorated, Canola, Carapa, Carron, Castor, Chaulmoogra, Chinese wood, Clove, Coal, Coconut, Cod-liver, Colza, Copra, Corn, Cotton-seed, Creosote, Croton, Crude, Derv, Diesel, Dittany, Drying, Elaeis, El(a)eoptene, Essence, Essential, Ethereal, Eucalyptus, Evening primrose, Extra virgin, Fatty, Fish, Fixed, Fuel, Fusel, Gas, Gingelli, Gingelly, Gingili, Good, Grapeseed, Grass, Groundnut, Hazelnut, Heavy, Jojoba, Kerosene, Kerosine, Lamp, Lavender, Linalo(o)l, Linseed, Lipid, Long, Lubricant, Lumbang, Macassar, Magilp, Megilp, Menthol, Midnight, Mineral, Mirbane, Multigrade, Musk, Mustard, Myrbane, Myrrhol, Naphtha, Neat's-foot, Neem, Neroli, Niger, Nim, Nimb, Nut, Oint, Oiticica, Oleo, Olive, Ottar, Otto, Palm, Paraffin, Parathion, Patchouli, Peanut, Petroleum, Picamar, Pomade, Poon, Poppy, Pristane, Pulza, Ramtil, Rape, Rapeseed, Retinol, Ricinus, Rock, Rose, Rosin, Rusa, Safrole, Sandalwood, Sassafras, Savin(e), Seed, Semsem, Sesame, Shale, Short, Sleek, Slick, Slum, Smalmy, Smarmy, Smeary, Snake, Spearmint, Sperm, Spike(nard), Spindle, Stand, Star-anise, Sunflower, Sweet, Tall(ow), Tolu, Train, Tung, Turpentine, Unction, Vegetable, Verbena, Virgin, Vitriol, Volatile, Wallaba, Walnut, Whale, Wintergreen, Wood, Wool, Ylang-ylang, Yolk

Ointment Balm, Basilicon, Boracic, Boric, Cerate, Cream, Nard, Pomade, Pomatum, Salve, Spikenard, Unguent, Vaseline®, Zinc

OK Agree(d), Approve, Authorise, Clearance, Copacetic, Copesettic, Go-head, Green light, Hunky-dory, Initial, Kosher, Right(o), Sanction, Sound, U, Vet

Old(er), Oldie Ae(t), Aged, Aine(e), Ancient, Antique, Auld, Bean, Decrepit, Dutch, Fogram, Former, Gaffer, Geriatric, Glory, Golden, Gray, Grey, Hills, Hoary, Immemorial, Major, Methuselah, Moore, Nestor, Nick, O, OAP, Obsolete, Off, Ogygian, One-time, Outworn, Palae-, Passé, Primeval, Ripe, Rugose, Sen(escent), Senile, Senior, Shot, Signeur, Stale, Trite, Venerable, Veteran, Victorian(a), Worn

Old-fashioned Aging, Ancient, Antediluvian, Arch(aic), Arriere, Bygone, Corn(y), Dated, Dowdy, Fuddy-duddy, Medieval, No tech, Obsolete, Ogygian, Outmoded, Passé, Primeval, Quaint, Relic, Retro, Rinky-dink, Schmaltzy, Shot, Square, Steam, Stick-in-the-mud, Traditional, Uncool

Old man, **Old woman** Anile, Aunty, Bodach, Burd, Cailleach, Crow, Faggot, Fantad, Fantod, Fogey, Fogramite, Fogy, Fussy, Gammer, Geezer, Grannam, Greybeard, Greyhen, Husband, Kangaroo, Luckie, Lucky, Methuselah, Mort, Mzee, OAP, Oom, Presbyte, Trout, Wife, Wight, Woopie, Wrinkly

Oleander Nerium

Omelette Crepe, Foo yong, Foo yung, Frittata, Fu yung, Pancake, Spanish, Tortilla

Omen Abodement, Absit, Augury, Auspice, Foreboding, Forewarning, Freet, Freit, Portent, Presage, Prodrome, Sign, Token, Warning

Ominous Alarming, Baleful, Bodeful, Dire, Dour, Forbidding, Grim, Inauspicious, Oracular, Sinister, Threatening

Omission, **Omit** Aph(a)eresis, Apocope, Apospory, Apostrophe, Caret, Disregard, Drop, Elide, Elision, Ellipse, Ellipsis, Failure, Haplography, Haplology, Lipography, Loophole, Miss, Neglect, Nonfeasance, Oversight, Paral(e)ipomenon, Senza, Skip

On (it) Aboard, About, Agreed, An, An't, At, Atop, By, Game, In, Leg, O', Of, Oiled, Over, Pon, Re, Tipsy, Up(on)

▷ **On** *may indicate* an anagram

▷ **On board** *may indicate* chess, draughts, or 'SS' around another word

Once(r) Ance, Bradbury, Earst, Erst(while), Ever, Ex, Fore, Former, Jadis, Oner, Onst, Secular, Sole, Sometime, Whilom

One(self) A, Ace, Ae, Alike, An(e), Any, Body, Chosen, Eeny, Ego, Ein, Individual, Integer, Me, Monad, Per se, Single(ton), Singular, Solo, Tone, Un, Unit(y), Unitary, United, Yin, You

One o'clock 1 am, NNE

Onion(s) Bengi, Bonce, Bulb, Chibol, Chive, Cibol, Cive, Eschalot, Head, Ingan, Jibbons, Leek, Lyonnaise, Moly, Pearl, Ramp, Ramson, Rocambole, Ropes, Scallion, Scilla, Shal(l)ot, Spanish, Spring, Squill, Sybo(e), Sybow

Onlooker Bystander, Kibitzer, Rubberneck, Spectator, Witness

Only Allenarly, Anerly, But, Except, Just, Meer, Merely, Nobbut, Seul, Singly, Sole

Onward Advance, Ahead, Away, Forth, Forward, Progress

Ooze Drip, Exhale, Exude, Gleet, Mud, Percolate, Pteropod(a), Seep, Sew, Sipe, Slime, Slob, Spew, Spue, Sweat

Opaque, **Opacity** Dense, Dull, Leucoma, Obscure, Obtuse, Onycha, Roil, Thick

Open(er), **Opening**, **Openness** Adit, Ajar, Antithesis, Anus, Apert(ure), Apparent, Apse, Autopsy, Bald, Bare, Bat, Bay, Bole, Breach, Break, Broach, Buttonhole, Candid, Cardia, Cavity, Chance, Chasm, Chink, Clear, Crevasse, Dehisce, Deploy, Door, Dup, Embrasure, Exordium, Expansive, Eyelet, Fair, Fenestra, Fissure, Fistula, Flue, Fontanel(le), Foramen, Frank, Free, Gambit, Gap, Gaping, Gat, Gate, Give, Glasnost, Glottis, Hagioscope, Hatch, Hatchback, Hiatus, Hilus, > HOLE, Inaugural, Intake, Interstice, Intro, Key, Lacy, Lance, Lead, Loid, Loophole, Loose, Manhole, Meatus, Mofette, Mouth, Oillet, Orifice, Oscule, Osculum, Ostiole, Ostium, Overture, Patent, Peephole, Pert, Pervious, Pick(lock), Placket, Plughole, Pore, Port(age), Porta, Porthole, Preliminary, Premiere, Prise, Pro-am, Public, Pylorus, Rent, Room, Scuttle, Sesame, Sicilian, Sincere, Slit, Spare, Spirant, Squint, Start, Stoma, Syrinx, Thereout, Touchhole, Trapdoor, Trema, Trou, Truthful, Unbar, Unbolt, Unbutton, Uncork, Undo, Unfurl, Unhasp, Unlatch, Unscrew, Unsubtle, Untie, Unzip, Vent, Vulnerable, Window

Opera Aida, Ariadne, Ballad, Bouffe, Burletta, Comic, ENO, Ernani, Falstaff, Faust, Fedora, Fidelio, Glyndebourne, Grand, Hansel and Gretel, Horse, Idomineo, Iolanthe, Light, Lohengrin, Lulu, Met, Musical, Nabucco, Norma, Oater, Oberon, Onegin, Orfeo, Otello, Parsifal, Pastorale, Patience, Pinafore, Rigoletto, Ruddigore, Savoy, Scala, Seria, Singspiel, Soap, Space, Tell, The Met, Threepenny,

Tosca, Turandot, Verismo, Work, Zarzuela

Operate, Operation(s), Operative Act(ion), Activate, Actuate, Agent, Artisan, Attuition, Barbarossa, Caesarean, Campaign, Conduct, Couching, Current, Desert Storm, Detective, Exercise, Function, Game, Hobday, Holding, Keystroke, Liposuction, Logical, Manipulate, Mechanic, Mules, Overlord, Practice, Run, Sealion, Shirodkar's, Sortie, Strabotomy, Ure, Valid, Wertheim, Work

Operator Agent, Conductor, Dealer, Manipulator, Nabla, Sparks, Surgeon

Opiate, Opium Dope, Drug, Hop, Laudanum, Meconin, Narcotic, Religion, Soporific, Thebaine

Opinion, Opinionative Attitude, Belief, Bet, Consensus, Cri, Dictum, Dogma, Doxy, Entêté, Esteem, Feeling, Guess, Judgement, Mind, Private, Public, Pulse, Say, Second, Sense, Sentence, Sentiment, Tenet, Utterance, View, Viewpoint, Voice

Opponent(s) Adversary, Antagonist, Anti, E-N, Enemy, E-S, Foe, Gainsayer, N-E, N-W, S-E, S-W, W-N, W-S

Opportune, Opportunist, Opportunity Appropriate, Apropos, Break, Carpetbagger, > **CHANCE**, Day, Equal, Facility, Favourable, Ganef, Ganev, Ganof, Godsend, Go-go, Golden, Gonif, Gonof, Heaven-sent, Occasion, Opening, Pat, Photo, Room, Seal, Seel, Sele, Snatcher, Tide, Timely, Timous, Well-timed, Window

Oppose(d), Opposer, Opposing, Opposite, Opposition Against, Agin, Anti, Antipathy, Antipodes, Antiscian, Antithesis, Antithetic, Antonym, Argue, At, Au contraire, Averse, Battle, Black, Breast, Colluctation, Combat, Confront, Contradict, Contrary, Converse, Counter, Diametric, Dissent, Distance, E contrario, Face, Foreanent, Fornen(s)t, Hinder, Hostile, Impugn, Inimical, Inverse, Militate, Noes, Object, Overthwart, Polar, Reaction, Reluct, Repugn, Resist, Retroact, Reverse, Rival, Shadow, Subtend, Syzygy, Teeth, Terr, Thereagainst, Thwart, Toto caelo, Traverse, V, Versus, Vis-a-vis, Withstand

Oppress(ion), Oppressive Airless, Bind, Burden, Close, Crush, Despotic, Incubus, Jackboot, Onerous, Overpower, Persecute, Ride, Stifling, Sultry, Tyrannise

Opt, Option(al) Alternative, > **CHOICE**, Choose, Default, Elect, Facultative, Fine, Menu, Pick, Plump, Select, Soft, Voluntary, Votive, Wale, Zero(-zero)

Optimism, Optimist(ic) Chiliast, Expectant, Hopeful, Morale, Pangloss, Pollyanna, Rosy, Sanguine, Upbeat

Or Au, Either, Ere, Gold, Ossia, Otherwise, Sol

Orange An(n)atta, Annatto, Arnotto, Aurora, Bergamot, Bigarade, Blood, Blossom, Chica, Clockwork, Croceate, Flame, Flamingo, Fulvous, Jaffa, Kamala, Kamela, Kamila, Karaka, Mandarin, Mock, Naartje, Nacarat, Nartjie, Navel, Osage, Pig, Roucou, Ruta, Satsuma, Seville, Shaddock, Tangerine, Tenné, Ugli, Ulsterman

Orate, Oration Address, Eloge, Elogium, Elogy, Eulogy, Harangue, Panegyric, Speech

Oratorio, Orator(y) Boanerges, Brompton, Brougham, Cantata, Cicero, Creation, Demosthenes, Diction, Elijah, Hwyl, Isocrates, Morin, Nestor, Prevaricator, Proseucha, Proseuche, Rhetor, Samson, Spellbinder, Stump, Tub-thumper, Windbag

Orbit Apse, Apsis, Circuit, Dump, Eccentric, Ellipse, Eye, Path, Revolution, Stationary

Orchestra(te), Orchestration Ensemble, Gamelan, Hallé, LPO, LSO, Ripieno, Score, Symphony

Orchid Adam and Eve, Adder's mouth, Arethusa, Bee, Bird's nest, Bog, Burnt-tip, Calanthe, Calypso, Cattleya, Coralroot, Cymbidium, Disa, Epidendrum, Fly,

Fragrant, Frog, Helleborine, Lady, Lady's slipper, Lady's tresses, Lizard, Man, Marsh, Military, Monkey, Musk, Naked lady, Odontoglossum, Oncidium, Puttyroot, Salep, Slipper, Snakemouth, Swamp pink, Twayblade, Vanda, Vanilla

Ordain Arrange, Command, Decree, Destine, Enact, Induct, Japan, Priest

Ordeal Corsned, Disaster, Preeve, Test, > TRIAL

Order(ed), Orderly, Orders Adjust, Affiliation, Alphabetical, Anton Piller, Apollonian, Apple-pie, Arrange, Array, Attendant, Attention, Attic, Avast, Bade, Banker's, Bankruptcy, Bath, Batman, Battalia, Bed, Behest, Benedictine, Bespoke, Bid, Book, Call, Camaldolite, Canon, Category, Caveat, CB, Charter, Cheque, Chit, Class, Coherent, Command(ment), Committal, Compensation, Composite, Court, Decorum, Decree, Demand, Dictate, Diktat, Direct(ion), Directive, Dispone, Dominican, Doric, DSO, Edict, Embargo, Enclosed, Enjoin, En règle, Establishment, Eviction, Exclusion, Fiat, Firing, Firman, Form(ation), Franciscan, Fraternity, Freemason, Garnishee, Garter, Gilbertine, Ginkgo, Grade, Habeas corpus, Hest, Holy, Indent, Injunction, Interdict, Ionic, Irade, Khalsa, Kilter, Kosmos, Language, Lexical, Loose, Mail, Mandamus, Mandate, Marching, Market, Marshal, Masonic, Merit, Methodical, Minor, Monastic, Monitor, Natural, Neatness, Nunnery, OBE, Oddfellows, Official, OM, Open, Orange, Ord, Ordain, Organic, Pecking, Possession, Postal, Precedence, Precept, Premonstrant, Prescribe, Preservation, Provisional, Rank, Receiving, Reception, Règle, Regular, Religious, Restraining, Return, Right, Rule, Ruly, Sailing, Sealed, Search, Series, Settle, Shipshape, Short, Side, Standing, State, Statutory, Stop(-loss), Straight, Subpoena, Summons, Supervision, System, Tabulate, Tall, Taxis, Tell, Templar, Third, Thistle, Tidy, Trim, Ukase, Uniformity, Warison, Warrant, Word, Writ

▷ **Ordering** *may indicate* an anagram

Ordinary Average, Banal, Bog standard, Canton, Chevron, Comely, Common (or garden), Commonplace, Cot(t)ise, Everyday, Fess(e), Flanch, Flange, Folksy, Grassroots, Hackneyed, Mediocre, Middling, Mundane, > NORMAL, O, OR, Plain, Prosy, Pub, Rank and file, Run-of-the-mill, Saltier, Saltire, Simple, Tressure, Trivial, Unexceptional, Uninspired, Usual, Workaday, Your

Ore Alga, Babingtonite, Bauxite, Bornite, Calamine, Calaverite, Cerusite, Chalcocite, Chalcopyrite, Coffinite, Coin, Copper, Crocoite, Element, Galenite, Glance, Haematite, Hedyphane, Horseflesh, Ilmenite, Iridosmine, Ironstone, Limonite, Mat, Melaconite, Middlings, Mineral, Minestone, Niobite, Oligist, Peacock, Phacolite, Pitchblende, Proustite, Psilomelane, Pyrargyrite, Pyromorphite, Realgar, Schlich, Seaweed, Slug, Smaltite, Sphalerite, Stephanite, Stilpnosiderite, Stream-tin, Tenorite, Tetrahedrite, Tin, Wad(d)

Organ(s), Organic Adnexa, Appendix, Archegonium, Barrel, Biogenic, Calliope, Carpel, Chair, Chamber, Chemoreceptor, Chord, Claspers, Clave, Conch(a), Console, Corti's, Cribellum, Ctene, Ear, Echo, Electric, Electronic, Electroreceptor, End, Essential, Exteroceptor, Feeler, Fin, Flabellum, Fundus, Gametangium, Gill, Glairin, Gonad, Hammond®, Hand, Hapteron, Harmonica, Harmonium, House, Hydraulos, Imine, Isomere, Kerogen, Kidney, Lien, Light, Liver, Lung-book, Means, Mechanoreceptor, Media, Medulla, Melodion, Ministry, Nasal, Natural, Nectary, Nephridium, Newspaper, Oogonia, Ovipositor, Palp, Pancreas, Parapodium, Part, Pedal, Photophore, Photoreceptor, Physharmonics, Pipe, Pipeless, Placenta, Plastid, Portative, Positive, Prothallus, Pulmones, Purtenance, Radula, Receptor, Recit, Reed, Regal, Relict, Sang, Saprobe, Scent, Sense, Sensillum, Serra, Siphon, Spinneret, Spleen, Sporangium, Sporophore, Stamen, Steam, Swell, Syrinx, Tentacle, Theatre, Theca, Thymus, Tongue, Tonsil, Tool, Tympanum, Uterus, Vegetative, Velum, Viscera, Viscus, Vitals, Voice, Voluntary, Womb, Wurlitzer®

Organelle Peroxisome

Organise(d), Organisation, Organiser Activate, Anatomy, > ARRANGE, Association, Brigade, Caucus, Collect, Comecon, Company, Constitution,

Coordinate, Design, Embody, Entrepreneur, Fascio, Firm, Impresario, Infrastructure, Jaycee, Ku Klux Klan, Logistics, Machine, Mafia, Marshal, Mobilise, Octopus, Orchestrate, Outfit, Personal, Quango, Rally, Regiment, Resistance, Rosicrucian, Run, Setup, Social, Soroptimist, Sort, Stage, Steward, System, Tidy, Together, UN

▷ **Organise(d)** *may indicate* an anagram

Organism Aerobe, Agamic, Being, Biont, Biotic, Cell, Chimeric, Ciliate, Clade, Coral, Diplont, Ecad, Entity, Epizoon, Germ, Incross, Infauna, Infusoria(n), Lichen, Medusa, Microbe, Moneron, Nekton, Neuston, Pathogen, Phenetics, Plankton, Protist, Protozoan, Saprobe, Streptococcus, Symbion(t), Volvox

Orgy Bacchanalia(n), Binge, Bust, Carousal, Dionysian, Feast, Revel, Saturnalia, Spree, Wassail

Orient(al) Adjust, Annamite, Chinoiserie, Dawn, Dayak, E, East(ern), Fu Manchu, Hindu, Levant, Leyton, Malay, Mongolian, Shan, Sunrise, Tatar, Thai, Tibetan, Turk(o)man

Origin(al), **Originate**, **Originating** Abo, Adam, Arise, Beginning, Birth, Come, Cradle, Creation, Derive, Editio princeps, Elemental, Emanate, Epicentre, Etymon, Extraction, First, Firsthand, Focus, Found, Generic, Genesis, Genetical, Germ, Grow, Hatch, Incunabula, Innovate, Invent, Master, Mother, Nascence, Natality, New, Novel, Ord, Primal, Primary, Primigenial, Primordial, Pristine, Prototype, Provenance, Rise, Root, Seminal, Source, Spring, Start, Ur, Ylem, Zoism

Ornament(al), **Ornamentation** Adorn, Anaglyph, Anthemion, Arabesque, Barbola, Baroque, Barrette, Bead, Bedeck, Billet, Blister, Boss, Bracelet, Broider, Bugle, Bulla, Cartouche, Chase, Clock, Cockade, Corbeil(le), Cornice, Crocket, Cross-quarters, Curlicue, Decorate, Decoration, Diamanté, Die-work, Diglyph, Dog's-tooth, Doodad, Embellish, Emblem(a), Enrich, Epaulet(te), Epergne, Fallal, Fandangle, Fiddlehead, Figuration, Figurine, Filagree, Filigrain, Filigree, Fleuret, Fleurette, Fleuron, Florid, Fret, Fretwork, Frill, Frounce, Furbelow, Furnish, Gadroon, Gaud, Headwork, Helix, Illustrate, Inlay, Knotwork, Labret, Leglet, Macrome, Mantling, Millefleurs, Mordent, Moresque, Motif, Nail-head, Netsuke, Nicknackery, Niello, O, Ovolo, Palmette, Parure, Paternoster, Pectoral, Pendant, Picot, Pipe, Pompom, Pounce, Prettify, Prunt, Quatrefoil, Rel(l)ish, Rococo, Spangle, Tassel, Tool, Torque, Torsade, Tracery, Trappings, Trill, Trimming, Trinket, Turn

▷ **Ornate** *may indicate* an anagram

Orthodox Cocker, Conventional, Hardshell, Proper, Sound, Standard

Oscillate, **Oscillation**, **Oscillator** Fluctuate, Librate, Rock, Seiche, Squeg, Swing, Vibrate, Waver

Osseous Bony, Hard, Skeletal, Spiny

Ostensibly Apparent, External, Seeming

Ostentation, **Ostentatious** Camp, Display, Dog, Eclat, Epideictical, Extravagant, Fantoosh, Flamboyant, Flash(y), Flaunt, Florid, Flourish, Garish, Gaudy, Highfalutin(g), Parade, Pomp, Pretence, Puff, > SHOW(ING), Side, Splash, Swank, Tacky, Tulip

Ostler Stabler

Ostracise, **Ostracism** Banish, Blackball, Boycott, Cut, Exclude, Exile, Potsherd, Snub, Taboo

Other(wise), **Others** Additional, Aka, Alia, Alias, Allo-, Alternative, Besides, Different, Distinct, Else, Et al, Etc, Excluding, Former, Further, Rest, Significant

▷ **Otherwise** *may indicate* an anagram

Ought All, Should

Our(selves) Us, We

▶ **Ousel** *see* OUZEL

Oust Depose, Dislodge, Eject, Evict, Expel, Fire, Supplant

Out Absent, Aglee, Agley, Asleep, Aus, Begone, Bowl, Dated, En ville, Exposed, External, Forth, Haro, Harrow, Hors, Oust, Skittle, Striking, Stump, Taboo, Uit, Unfashionable, Up, York

▷ **Out** *may indicate* an anagram

Out and out Absolute, Arrant, Sheer, Stark, Teetotal, Thorough, Totally, Utter

Outbreak Epidemic, Eruption, Explosion, Plague, Putsch, Rash, Recrudescence

Outburst Access, Blurt, Bluster, Boutade, Evoe, Explosion, Fit, Flaw, Furore, Fusillade, Gush, Gust, Paroxysm, Passion, Salvo, Storm, Tantrum, Tumult, Volley

Outcast Cagot, Discard, Exile, Exul, Ishmael, Leper, Mesel, Pariah, Rogue

Outcome Aftermath, Consequence, Dénouement, Effect, Emergence, End, Event, > RESULT, Sequel, Upshot

Outcry Bray, Howl, Hue, Protest, Racket, Steven, Uproar, Utas

Outdated Archaic, Dinosaur, Effete, Feudal, Fossil, Obsolete, Outmoded, Passé, Square

Outdoor(s) Alfresco, External, Garden, Open air, Plein-air

Outer External, Extrogenous, Magpie, Top

Outfit(ter) Catsuit, Ensemble, Equipage, Fitout, Furnish, Get-up, Haberdasher, Habit, Kit, Rig, Samfoo, Samfu, Strip, Suit, Team, Trousseau, Weed(s)

Outflank Overlap

Outgoing Egression, Exiting, Extrovert, Open, Retiring

Outgrowth Ala(te), Aril, Bud, Enation, Epiphenomenon, Exostosis, Offshoot, Root-hair, Sequel, Trichome

Outhouse Lean to, Privy, Shed, Skilling, Skipper, Stable

Outing Excursion, Jaunt, Junket, Picnic, Sortie, Spin, Spree, Treat, Trip, Wayzgoose

Outlandish Barbarous, Bizarre, Exotic, Foreign, Peregrine, Rum

Outlaw Allan-a-Dale, Attaint, Badman, Ban, Bandit(ti), Banish, Exile, Fugitive, Hereward, Horn, Proscribe, Robin Hood, Rob Roy, Ronin, Tory, Waive

Outlet Débouché, Egress, Estuary, Exit, Femerall, Market, Opening, Outfall, Sluice, Socket, Tuyere, Tweer, Twier, Twyer(e), Vent

Outline Adumbration, Aperçu, Circumscribe, Configuration, Contorno, Contour, Delineate, Digest, > DRAFT, Footprint, Layout, Note, Perimeter, Plan, Profile, Relief, Scenario, Schematic, Shape, Silhouette, Skeletal, Skeleton, Sketch, Summary, Syllabus, Synopsis, T(h)alweg, Trace

Outlook Casement, Perspective, Prospect, View, Vista

▷ **Out of** *may indicate* an anagram

▷ **Out of sorts** *may indicate* an anagram

Output Data, Get, Produce, Production, Turnout, Yield

▷ **Output** *may indicate* an anagram

Outrage(ous) Affront, Atrocity, Desecrate, Disgust, Egregious, Enorm(ity), Flagrant, Insult, OTT, Rich, Sacrilege, Scandal, Shocking, Ungodly, Violate

▷ **Outrageously** *may indicate* an anagram

Outright Clean, Complete, Entire, Point-blank, Utter

Outside Ab extra, Crust, Exterior, External, Front, Furth, Hors, Periphery, Rim, Rind, Rine, Surface

Outsider Alien, Bolter, Bounder, Cad, Extern, Extremist, Foreigner, Incomer, Oustiti, Pariah, Ring-in, Stranger, Stumer, Unseeded, Upstart

Outskirts Edge, Fringe, Periphery, Purlieu

Outspoken Bluff, Blunt, Broad, Candid, Explicit, Forthright, Frank, Plain, Rabelaisian, Round, Vocal

Outstanding Ace, Beaut(y), Belter, Billowing, Bulge, Chief, Eminent, Especial, Exceptional, Extant, First, Fugleman, Highlight, Humdinger, Impasto, Jut, Lulu, Marked, Matchless, Oner, Owing, Paragon, Phenomenal, Prince, Prize, Prominent, Promontory, Prosilient, Proud, Relief, Relievo, Salient, Signal, Special, Squarrose, Star, Stellar, Strout, Superb, Tour de force, Unpaid, Unsettled

Outward Efferent, Extern(e), External, Extrinsic, Extrorse, Extrovert, Posticous, Postliminary, Superficial

Outwit Baffle, Best, Circumvent, Dish, Euchre, Fox, Over-reach, > THWART, Trick

Ouzel Ring, Water

Oval(s) Cartouche, Ellipse, Henge, Navette, Ooidal

Oven(-like) Aga®, Calcar, Convection, Cul-de-four, Dutch, Furnace, Haybox, Horn(it)o, Kiln, Lear, Leer, Lehr, Lime kiln, Microwave, Muffle, Oast, Oon, Stove

Over Above, Across, Again, Atop, C, Clear, Done, Finished, Hexad, Left, Maiden, Of, On, Ore, Ort, Owre, Sopra, Spare, Superior, Surplus, Uber, Yon

Overcast Cloudy, Lowering, Sew, Sombre

Overcharge Clip, Extort, Fleece, Gyp, OC, Rack-rent, Rook, Rush, Soak, Sting

Overcome Beat, Bested, Conquer, Convince, Defeat, Kill, Master, Mither, Prevail, Quell, Speechless, Subjugate, Surmount, Vanquish, Win

▷ **Overdrawn** *may indicate* 'red' outside another word

Overdue Behindhand, Belated, Excessive, Late

Overflow Lip, Nappe, Ooze, Redound, Spillage, Surfeit, Teem

Overhang(ing) Beetle, Bulge, > JUT, Project, Shelvy

Overhaul Bump, Catch, Overtake, Recondition, Revision, Service, Strip

Overhead(s) Above, Aloft, Ceiling, Cost, Exes, Hair(s), Headgear, Oncost, Rafter, Upkeep, Zenith

Overhear Catch, Eavesdrop, Tap

Overheat Enrage

Overlap(ping) Correspond, Equitant, Imbricate, Incubous, Kern(e), Limbous, Obvolute, Tace, Tasse

Overlay Ceil, Smother, Stucco, Superimpose, Veneer

Overload Burden, Plaster, Strain, Surcharge, Tax

Overlook Condone, Disregard, Excuse, Forget, Miss, Pretermit, Superintend, Waive

Overpower(ing) Crush, Evince, Mighty, Onerous, Oppress, Overwhelm, Subdue, Surmount, Swelter, Whelm

Overrule Abrogate, Disallow, Veto

Overrun Exceed, Extra, Infest, Inundate, Invade, Swarm, Teem

Overseas Abroad, Colonial, Outremer

Oversee(r) Baas, Boss, Captain, Care, Deputy, Direct, Eyebrow, Foreman, Grieve, Handle, Induna, Periscope, Steward, Supercargo, Survey(or)

Overshadow Cloud, Dominate, Eclipse, Obscure, Outclass

Oversight Blunder, Care, Error, Gaffe, Lapse, Neglect

Overstate(ment) Embroider, Exaggerate, Hyperbole

Overt Manifest, Patent, Plain, Public

Overtake Catch, For(e)hent, Lap, Leapfrog, Overget, Overhaul, > PASS, Supersede

Overthrow Dash, Defeat, Demolish, Depose, Down, Labefact(at)ion, Ruin, Smite, Stonker, Subvert, Supplant, Unhorse, Vanquish, Whemmle, Whommle, Whummle, Worst

Overture Advance, Carnival, Egmont, Hebrides, Intro, Leonora, Offer, > OPENING, Prelude, Propose, Sinfonia, Toccata, Toccatella, Toccatina

Overturn(ing) Catastrophe, Quash, Reverse, Tip, Topple, Up(set), Upend, Whemmle

Overwhelm(ed), Overwhelming Accablé, Assail, > CRUSH, Inundate, KO, Mind-boggling, Overcome, Scupper, Smother, Submerge, Swamp

Overwork(ed) Fag, Hackneyed, Ornament, Sloq, Stale, Supererogation, Tax, Tire, Toil

Owe(d), Owing Attribute, Due, OD

Owl(s) Barn, Barred, Blinker, Boobook, Brown, Bubo, Bunter, Eagle, Elegant, Fish, Glimmergowk, Hawk, Hoo(ter), Horned, Jenny, Little, Long-eared, Longhorn, Madge, Moper, Mopoke, Mopus, Night, Ogle, Parliament, Ruru, Saw-whet, Scops, Screech, Snowy, Strich, Striges, Strigiformes, Tawny, Wood

Own(er), Owning, Ownership Admit, Agnise, Confess, Domain, Dominium, Fess, Have, Hold, Mortmain, Nain, Of, Possess, Proper, Proprietor, Recognise, Reputed, Title, Use

Ox(en) Anoa, Aquinas, Aurochs, Banteng, Banting, Bison, Bonas(s)us, Buffalo, Bugle, Bullock, Cat(t)alo, Fee, Gaur, Gayal, Gyal, Kouprey, Mart, Musk, Neat, Ovibos, Rother, Sapi-utan, S(e)ladang, Steare, Steer, Taurus, Ure, Urus, Yak, Yoke, Zebu

▷ **Oxtail** *may indicate* 'x'

Oxygen (and lack of) Anoxia, Epoxy, Liquid, Lox, Loxygen, O

Oyster (bed), Oyster disease, Oyster-eater Avicula, Bivalve, Bush, Cul(t)ch, Kentish, Lay, Mollusc, Native, Ostrea, Ostreophage, Pandore, Pearl, Plant, Prairie, Scalp, Scaup, Seed(ling), Spat, Spondyl, Vegetable

Oz Amos, Australia

Ozone Air, Atmosphere, Oxygen

Pp

Pace, **Pacemaker** Canter, Clip, Cracking, Dog-trot, Easter, Gait, Jog-trot, Lope, Measure, Pari passu, Pioneer, > **RATE**, Snail's, Spank, Speed, Stroll, Tempo, Tramp, Tread, Trot

Pacific, **Pacify** Appease, Bromide, Conciliate, Dove, Ease, Irenic, Lull, Mild, Moderate, Ocean, Placid, Quiet, Serene, Soothe, Subdue, Sweeten, Tranquil

Pack(age), **Packed**, **Packing** Bale, Blister, Bobbery, Box, Bubble, Bundle, Cards, Cold, Compress, Congest, Cram, Crate, Crowd, Cry, Deck, Dense, Dunnage, Embox, Entity, Everest, Excelsior, Face, Fardel, Floe, Gasket, Gaskin, Glut, Hamper, Hunt, Ice, Jam, Kennel, Knapsack, Load, Matilda, Pair, > **PARCEL**, Pikau, Power, Pun, Rout, Rucksack, Set, Shiralee, Steeve, Stow, Suits, Tamp, Tread, Troop, Truss, Wad, Wet, Wolf, Wrap

Packet Boat, Bundle, Liner, Mailboat, Mint, Parcel, Roll, Sachet, Steamboat, Wage

Pact Agreement, Alliance, Bargain, Bilateral, Cartel, Contract, Covenant, Locarno, > **TREATY**, Warsaw

Pad(ding) Batting, Bombast, Brake, Bustle, Compress, Crash, Cushion, Dabber, Damper, Dossil, Enswathe, Expand, Falsies, Filler, Flat, Frog, Gumshield, Hard, Hassock, Horse, Ink, Launch, Leg-guard, Lily, Nag, Note, Numnah, Patch, Paw, Ped, Pillow, Pincushion, Plastron, Pledget, Plumper, Pouf(fe), Protract, Pudding, Pulvillus, Scratch, Shoulder, Stamp, Stuff, Sunk, Tablet, Thief, Touch, Tournure, Tylopod, Tympan, Velour(s), Velure, Wad, Wase, Writing

Paddle, **Paddle boat**, **Paddle-foot** Canoe, Dabble, Doggy, Oar, Pinniped, Seal, Side-wheel, Spank, Splash, Wade

Pagan Animist, Atheist, Gentile, Gentoo, Godless, Heathen, Idolater, Infidel, Odinist, Paynim, Saracen

Page(s), **Pageboy** Back, Bellboy, Bellhop, Bleep, Boy, Buttons, Callboy, Centrefold, Flyleaf, Folio, Foolscap, Front, Gate-fold, Groom, Haircut, Home, Hornbook, Leaf, Messenger, Moth, Octavo, Op-ed, P, Pane, PP, Problem, Quarto, Ream, Recto, Ro, Servant, Sheet, Side, Squire, Tear sheet, Tiger, Title, Varlet, Verso, Web, Yellow

Pageant Cavalcade, Pomp, Spectacle, Tattoo, Triumph

▶ **Paid** *see* PAY

Pain(ful), **Pains** Ache, Aggrieve, Agony, Ake, Angina, Anguish, Bad, Bale, Bitter, Bore, Bot(t), Bother, Colic, Cramp, Crick, Distress, Dole, Doleur, Dolour, Dool(e), Dysury, Excruciating, Gip, Grief, Gripe, Gyp, Harrow, Heartburn, > **HURT**, Ill, Kink, Laborious, Mal, Migraine, Misery, Myalgia, Neuralgia, Pang, Persuant, Pest, Prick, Pungent, Rack, Raw, Referred, Sair, Sciatica, Smart, Sore, Sorrow, Sten(d), Sting, Stitch, Teen(e), Tene, Throe, Torment, Torture, Twinge, Wrench, Wring

▷ **Pain** *may indicate* bread (French)

Painkiller Aminobutene, Analgesic, Bute, Cocaine, Distalgesic, Enkephalin, Meperidine, Metopon, Morphine, Number, Pethidine

Paint(ed), **Painting** Abstract, Acrylic, Action, Airbrush, Aquarelle, Art autre, Art deco, Artificial, Art nouveau, Ash Can School, Bice, Canvas, Cellulose, Chiaroscuro, Clair-obscure, Clobber, Coat, Colour, Cubism, Dadaism, Daub, Dayglo, Decorate,

Depict, Diptych, Distemper, Eggshell, Emulsion, Enamel, Fard, Finery, Finger, Flemish, Fore-edge, Fresco, Genre, Gild, Gloss, Gouache, Grease, Hard-edge, Historical, Impasto, Impressionism, Intumescent, Lead, Limn, Luminous, Matt, Mehndi, Miniate, Miniature, Modello, Mona Lisa, Monotint, Mural, Naive, Neo-Impressionism, Nightpiece, Nocturne, Non-drip, Oaker, Ochre, Oil, Old Master, Oleo(graph), Op art, Orphism, Paysage, Pentimento, Pict, Picture, Pigment, Pinxit, Plein air, Pointillism(e), Portray, Poster, Post-Impressionism, Primitive, Raddle, Rosemaling, Roughstuff, Sand, Scenography, Scumble, Secco, Sfumato, Sien(n)ese, Skyscape, Spray, Stencil, Stereochrome, Still life, Stipple, Tablature, Tempera, Tondo, Umber, Umbrian, War, Wax

Painter > ARTIST, Colourist, Cubist, Decorator, Gilder, Illusionist, Impressionist, Limner, Miniaturist, Paysagist, Plein-airist, Pre-Raphaelite, Primitive, Sien(n)ese

Pair(ing) Brace, Couple(t), Duad, Duo, Dyad(ic), Fellows, Geminate, Jugate, Link, Match, Mate, Ocrea, Pigeon, Pr, Span, Synapsis, Syndyasmian, Syzygy, Tandem, Thummim, Twa(e), Tway, Two, Urim, Yoke

Pal Ally, Amigo, Bud(dy), China, Chum, Comrade, Crony, Cully, Mate

Palace Alhambra, Basilica, Blenheim, Buckingham, Court, Crystal, Edo, Elysee, Escorial, Escurial, Fontainebleau, Gin, Holyrood, Hotel, Istana, Lambeth, Lateran, Louvre, Mansion, Nonsuch, Palatine, Pitti, Quirinal, Sans Souci, Schloss, Seraglio, Serail, Shushan, Topkapi, Trianon, Tuileries, Valhalla, Vatican, Versailles

Palatable, Palatalized, Palate Dainty, Relish, Roof, Sapid, Savoury, Soft, Taste, Toothsome, Uranic, Uraniscus, Uvula, Velum

Pale, Paling Ashen, Blanch, Bleach, Cere, Dim, Etiolate(d), Fade, > FAINT, Fence, Ghostly, Haggard, Insipid, Lily (white), Livid, Mealy, Ox-fence, Pastel, Peelie-wally, Picket, Sallow, Shilpit, Stang, Verge, Wan, Whey-faced, White, Wishy-washy

Palestine, Palestinian Amorite, Gadarene, Intifada, Israel, Pal, PLO, Samaria

Pall Bore, Cloy, Damper, Glut, Mantle, Satiate, Shroud

Pallet Bed, Cot, Couch, Mattress, Tick

Palm Accolade, Areca, Assai, Atap, Babassu, Betel, Buriti, Burrawang, Bussu, Cabbage, Calamus, Carna(h)uba, Carnauba, Chamaerops, Chiqui-chiqui, Coco, Conceal, Coquito, Corozo, Corypha, Date (tree), Doom, Doum, Elaeis, Euterpe, Fan, Feather, Fob, Foist, Gomuti, Gomuto, Groo-groo, Gru-gru, Hand, Ita, Itching, Ivory, Jip(p)i-Jap(p)a, Jipyapa, Jupati, Kentia, Laurels, Loof, Macahuba, Macaw, Macoya, Moriche, Nikau, Nipa, Oil, Palmyra, Paxiuba, Peach, Pupunha, Raffia, Raphia, Rat(t)an, Royal, Sabal, Sago, Sugar, Talipat, Talipot, Thenar, Toddy, Triumph, Troelie, Troolie, Trooly, Trophy, Vola, Washingtonia, Wax, Wine

Paltry Bald, Cheap, Exiguous, Mean, Measly, Peanuts, Pelting, Petty, Poor, Puny, Scalled, Sorry, Tin(-pot), Tinny, Trashy, Trifling, Two-bit, Vile, Waff, Whiffet

Pamper(ed) Cocker, Coddle, Cosher, Cosset, Cuiter, Feather-bed, Gratify, High-fed, > INDULGE, Mollycoddle, Pet, Spoon-fed

Pamphlet Brochure, Catalogue, Leaflet, Notice, Sheet, Tract

Pan Agree, Auld Hornie, Bainmarie, Balit, Basin, Betel(-pepper), Braincase, Chafer, Dent, Dial, Drip, Dripping, Goat-god, Goblet, God, Hard, Ice-floe, Iron, Karahi, Ladle, Lavatory, Muffin, Nature-god, Pancheon, Panchion, Patella, Patina, Peter, Poacher, Preserving, Prospect, Roast, Salt, Search, Skid, Skillet, Slag, Slate, Spider, Vessel, Warming, Wo(c)k, Work

Pancake Blin(i), Blintz(e), Burrito, Crêpe (suzette), Drop(ped)-scone, Flam(m), Flapjack, Flaune, Flawn, Fraise, Fritter, Froise, Pikelet, Poppadum, Quesadilla, Slapjack, Suzette, Taco, Tortilla, Tostada, Waffle

Pane Glass, Light, Panel, Quarrel, Quarry, Sheet

Panel(ling) Board, Cartouche, Dashboard, Fa(s)cia, Gore, Hatchment, Inset, Instrument, Jury, Mandorla, Mimic, Orb, Patch(board), Rocker, Screen, Skreen, Solar, Stile, Stomacher, Tablet, Valance, Volet, Wainscot

Pang Achage, Ache, Qualm, Spasm, Stab, Twinge, Wrench

Panic Alar(u)m, Amaze, Consternation, Fear, Flap, Flat-spin, Fright, Funk, Guinea-grass, Millet, Raggee, Raggy, Ragi, Scarre, Stampede, Stampedo, Stew, Tailspin

Pannier Basket, Cacolet, Corbeil, Dosser, Skip, Whisket

Panorama, **Panoramic** Range, Scenery, Veduta, View, Vista

Pant(s) Bags, Breeches, Capri, Cargo, Chaps, Chinos, Culottes, Deck, Dhoti, Drawers, Fatigues, Flaff, Gasp, Gaucho, Harem, Longjohns, Longs, Parachute, Pech, Pedal-pushers, Pegh, Puff, Slacks, Smalls, Stovepipe, Sweat, Throb, Toreador, Trews, Trousers, Wheeze, Yearn

Panther Bagheera, Black, Cat, Cougar, Jaguar, Leopard, Pink

Pantomime, **Pantomime character** Charade, Cheironomy, Dumb-show, Farce, Galanty, Harlequinade, Play

Pantry Buttery, Closet, Larder, Spence, Stillroom

Papal, **Papist** Catholic, Clementine, Concordat, Guelf, Guelph, Pontifical, RC, Roman, Vatican

Paper(s), **Paperwork**, **Papery** Art, Atlas, Ballot, Baryta, Bible, Blotting, Bond, Broadsheet, Broadside, Bromide, Brown, Building, Bumf, Bumph, Carbon, Cartridge, Cellophane®, Chad, Chinese, Chiyogami, Cigarette, Command, Commercial, Confetti, Corrugated, Cream-laid, Cream-wove, Credentials, Crepe, Crown, Daily, Decorate, Demy, Document, Dossier, Elephant, Emery, Emperor, Essay, Exam, File, Filter, Final, Flock, Folio, Foolscap, FT, Galley, Garnet, Gem, Glass(ine), Grand Jesus, Graph, Greaseproof, Green, Guardian, Hieratica, India, Jesus, Journal, Kraft, Lace, Laid, Lavatory, Legal cap, Linen, Litmus, Manifold, Manil(l)a, Marble, Mercantile, Mirror, MS, Music(-demy), News(print), Note, Oil, Onion-skin, Order, Packing, Pad, Page, Papillote, Papyrus, Parchment, Pickwick, Plotting, Position, Post, Pot(t), Pravda, Press, Print, Quair, Quarto, Quire, Rag, Ramee, Rami(e), Ream, Retree, Rhea, Rice, Rolled, Rolling, Royal, Satin, Saxe, Scent, Scotsman, Scrip, Scroll, Scrowl, Sheaf, Sheet, Silver, Slipsheet, Spoilt, Stamp, State, Sugar, Sun, Tabloid, Taffeta, Tar, TES, Test, Thesis, Thread, Tiger, Tissue, Today, Toilet, Torchon, Touch, Tracing, Trade, Transfer, Treatise, Treeware, Turmeric, Vellum, Velvet, Voucher, Walking, Waste, Watch, Wax(ed), Web, Whatman®, White, Willesden, Wood(chip), Worksheet, Wove, Wrapping, Writing

Paper-cutting, **Paper-folding** Decoupage, Kirigami, Origami, Psaligraphy

Paprika Spanish

Par Average, Equate, Equivalent, > **NORMAL**, Scratch

Parable Allegory, Fable, Proverb

Parachute, **Parachutist** Aigrette, Drogue, Float, Jump, Para, Parabrake, Red Devil, Silk, Skyman, Thistledown, Umbrella

Parade (ground) Air, Arcade, Cavalcade, Church, Display, Dress, Drill, Easter, Emu, Flaunt, Gala, Hit, Identification. Procession, Identity, Maidan, March-past, Pageantry, Pomp, Prom(enade), Show, Sick, Ticker tape

Paradise Arcadia, Avalon, Bliss, Eden, Elysium, Garden, Heaven, Lost, Malaguetta, Nirvana, Park, Regained, Shangri-la, Svarga, Swarga, Swerga, > **UTOPIA**

Paradox(ical) Absurdity, Cantor's, Contradiction, Dilemma, Electra, Gilbertian, Koan, Olber's, Puzzle, Russell's, Zeno's

Paraffin Earthwax, Kerosene, Kerosine, Liquid, Ozocerite, Ozokerite, Photogen(e), Propane

Parallel Analog, Collimate, Corresponding, Equal, Even, Forty-ninth, Like

Paralysis, **Paralyse** Apoplexy, Cataplexy, Cramp, Curarise, Cycloplegia, Diplegia, Halt, Hemiplegia, Infantile, Monoplegia, Numbness, Palsy, Paraplegia, Paresis,

Polio, Quadriplegia, Scram, Shock, Shut, Spastic, Spina bifida, Stun

Parapet (space) Bartisan, Bartizan, Battlement, Brisure, Bulwark, Crenel, Flèche, Machicolation, Merlon, Rampart, Redan, Surtout, Terreplein, Top, Wall

Parasite, Parasitic Ascarid, Autoecious, Babesiasis, Bilharzia, Biogenous, Biotroph, Bladder-worm, Bloodsucker, Bonamia, Bot, Candida, Coccus, Conk, Copepod, Cryptosporidium, Cryptozoite, Dodder, Ectophyte, Endamoeba, Endophyte, Entophyte, Entozoon, Epiphyte, Epizoon, Filarium, Flea, Giardia, Gregarinida, Haematozoon, Hair-eel, Heartworm, Heteroecious, Hook-worm, Ichneumon, Inquiline, Isopod, Kade, Ked, Lackey, Lamprey, Leech, Licktrencher, Liverfluke, Louse, Lungworm, Macdonald, Mallophagous, Mistletoe, Monogenean, Nematode, Nit, Orobanche, Pinworm, Plasmodium, Puccinia, Rafflesia, Rhipidoptera, Rickettsia, Roundworm, Schistosoma, Scrounger, Shark, Smut-fungus, Sponge(r), Sporozoa(n), Strepsiptera, Strongyle, Strongyloid, Stylops, Sucker, Symphile, Tapeworm, Tick, Toady, Toxoplasma, Trematode, Trencher-friend, Trencher-knight, Trichina, Tryp(anosoma), Vampire, Viscum, Worms

Parcel Allocate, Allot, Aret, Bale, Bundle, Holding, Lot, Package, Packet, Sort, Wrap

Parch(ed) Arid, Bake, Dry, Graddan, Roast, Scorched, Sere, Thirsty, Torrid

Parchment Diploma, Forel, Mezuzah, Papyrus, Pell, Pergameneous, Roll, Roule, Scroll, Sheepskin, Vellum

Pardon(able), Pardoner Absolve, Amnesty, Anan, Assoil, Clear, Condone, Eh, Excuse, > **FORGIVE**, Grace, Mercy, Qu(a)estor, Release, Remission, Remit, Reprieve, Venial, What

Parent(al) Ancestral, Father, Forebear, Genitor, Maternal, Mother, Paternal, Storge

Parish District, Flock, Kirkto(w)n, Parischan(e), Parishen, Parochin(e), Peculiar, Province, Title

Park(ing) Amusement, Battery, Brecon Beacons, Business, Common, Country, Dales, Dartmoor, Enclosure, Everglades, Exmoor, Forest, Fun, Game, Garage, Gardens, Grand Canyon, Green, Green lung, Grounds, Hyde, Jasper, Jasper National, Jurassic, Kruger, Lake District, Lung, Mansfield, Motor, Mungo, Nairobi, National, Northumberland, Osterley, P, Paradise, Peak District, Pitch, Pittie-ward, Preserve, Rec, Regent's, Safari, Sanctuary, Sandown, Science, Sequoia, Sequoia National, Serengeti, Shenandoah National, Siding, Snowdonia, Stand, Stop, Theme, Trailer, Valet, Wildlife, Wind, Yard, Yellowstone, Yosemite

Parka Atigi

Parliament Addled, Althing, Barebones, Black, Bundestag, Commons, Congress, Cortes, Council, Cross-bench, Dail, Diet, Drunken, Eduskunta, Folketing, House, Imperial, Knesset, Lack-learning, Lagt(h)ing, Landst(h)ing, Lawless, Legislature, Lok Sabha, Long, Lords, Majlis, Merciless, Mongrel, Odelst(h)ing, Rajya Sabha, Reichstag, Riksdag, Rump, St Stephens, Sanhedrin, Seanad, Seanad Eireann, Sejm, Short, Stannary, Stirthing, Stormont, Stort(h)ing, Thing, Tynwald, Unicameral, Volkskammer, Westminster

Parliamentarian Cabinet, Fairfax, Ireton, Leveller, Member, MP, Roundhead, Whip

Parlour Beauty, Funeral, Lounge, Massage, Salon, Snug

Parochial Insular

Parody Burlesque, Lampoon, Mock, Piss-take, Satire, Sendup, Skit, Spoof, Travesty

Parrot Amazon, Cockatoo, Conure, Copy, Flint, Green leek, Imitate, Kaka(po), Kea, Lorikeet, Lory, Lovebird, Macaw, Mimic, Nestor, Owl, Parakeet, Paroquet, Poll(y), Popinjay, Psittacine, Quarrion, Repeat, Rosella, Rote, Stri(n)gops, T(o)uraco

Parson(age) Clergyman, Cleric, Glebe, Manse, Minister, Non juror, Pastor, Priest, Rector, Rectory, Rev, Sky-pilot, Soul-curer, Vicarage , Yorick

Part(s), Parting Accession, Aliquot, Antimere, Area, Aught, Bulk, Bye, Cameo, Character, Chunk, Cog, Component, Constituent, Crack, Cue, Dislink, Diverge, Dole, Element, Episode, Escapement, Farewell, Fascicle, Fork, Fraction, Goodbye, Half, Instalment, Into, Lathe, Lead, Leave, Leg, Lill, Lilt, Lines, List, Livraison, Member, Meronym, Parcel, Passus, > **PIECE**, Portion, Primo, Principal, Private, Proportion, Pt, Quota, Rape, Ratio, Region, Rive, Role, Scena, Scene, Secondo, Section, Sector, Segment, Separate, Serial, Sever, Shade, Share, Shed, Sleave, Sle(i)ded, > **SOME**, Spare, Split, Stator, Sunder, Synthon, Tithe, Unit, Vaunt, Voice, Walk on, Wrench

Partial(ity), Partially Biased, Ex-parte, Fan, Favour, Halflins, Imbalance, Incomplete, One-sided, Predilection, Slightly, Unequal, Weakness

Particle(s) Alpha, Antineutron, Atom, Baryon, Beta, Bit, Boson, Corpuscle, Dander, Delta, Deuteron, Elementary, Fleck, Fragment, Fundamental, Gauge boson, Gemmule, Globule, Gluon, Grain, Granule, Heavy, Ion, J, Jot, J/psi, Lambda, Lepton, Meson, Mite, Molecule, Mote, Muon, Neutrino, Neutron, Nibs, Omega-minus, Parton, Photon, Pion, Platelet, Positron, Preon, Proton, Psi(on), Quark, Radioactivity, Shower, Sigma, Sinter, Smithereen, Spark, Speck, Strange, W, Whit, WIMP, Z

Particular Choosy, Dainty, > **DETAIL**, Endemic, Especial, Essential, Express, Fiky, Fog, Fussy, Item, Itself, London fog, Nice, Niffy-naffy, Own, Pea-souper, Peculiar, Pernickety, Pet, Point, Prim, Proper, > **RESPECT**, Special, Specific, Stickler, Strict, Stripe

Partisan Adherent, Axe, Biased, Carlist, Champion, Devotee, Factional, Fan, Irregular, Partial, Provo, Sider, Spear, Supporter, Yorkist

Partition(ed) Abjoint, Bail, Barrier, Bretasche, Bulkhead, Cloison, Cubicle, Diaphragm, Dissepiment, Division, Hallan, Mediastinum, Parpane, Parpen(d), Parpent, Parpoint, Perpend, Perpent, Replum, > **SCREEN**, Scriene, Septum, Tabula, Wall, With

Partner(ship) Accomplice, Ally, Associate, Butty, Cahoot(s), Coachfellow, Colleague, Comrade, Confederate, Consort, Couple, Dutch, Escort, E-W, Firm, Gigolo, Mate, N-S, Pal, Pard, Sidekick, Silent, Sleeping, Sparring, Spouse, Stablemate, Stand, Symbiosis

▷ **Part of** *may indicate* a hidden word

Party Acid house, Alliance, Assembly, At-home, Ball, Band, Barbecue, Bash, Beano, Bee, Bloc, Blowout, Body, Bottle, Bunfight, Bust, Caboodle, Camp, Carousal, Carouse, Caucus, Celebration, Clambake, Cocktail, Commando, Communist, Concert, Congress, Conservative, Contingent, Cooperative, Coterie, Cult, Democratic, Detail, Ding, Discotheque, Do, Drum, Faction, Fest, Fianna Fáil, Fine Gael, Firing, Funfest, Gala, Gang, Garden, Green, Greenback, Grumbletonian, Guilty, Hen, Hoedown, Hooley, Hootenanny, House, Housewarming, Hurricane, Jol(lities), Junket, Junto, Knees-up, L, Labour, Launch, Lib, Liberal, Love-in, Low heels, Mallemaroking, Musicale, National, Neck-tie, Octobrist, Opposition, Orgy, People's, Person, Petting, Plaid, Progressive, Prohibition, Pyjama, Rage, Rave, Rave-up, Razzle(-dazzle), Reception, Republican, Revel, Ridotto, Rocking, Rort, Rout, SDP, Search, Sect, Set, Shindig, Shine, Shower, Side, Slumber, Smoker, SNP, Soc(ialist), Social, Social credit, Social Democratic, Soiree, Spree, Squad(rone), Squadrone volante, Stag, Symposium, Tea, Teafight, Third, Thrash, Tory, Treat, Unionist, United, Whig, Wine, Wingding, Working

Pass(ed), Passing, Pass on, Past Ago, Agon, Annie Oakley, Aorist, Approve, Arise, Arlberg, Before, Behind, Beyond, Botte, Brenner, Brief, By, Bygone, Caudine Forks, Cerro Vordo, Chine, Chit(ty), Clear, Col, Cote, Cross, Cursory, Death, Defile, Delate, Demise, Die, Disappear, Double, Elapse, Emit, Enact, End, Ensue,

Ephemeral, Exceed, Exeat, Foist, Forby, Forgone, Former, Forward, Gap, Gate, Gha(u)t, Glencoe, Glide, Go, Great St Bernard, Gulch, Halse, Hand, Happen, Hause, Hospital, Impart, Impermanent, In transit, Khyber, Killiecrankie, La Cumbre, Lap, Late, Lead, Migrate, Nek, Notch, Nutmeg, Occur, Oer, OK, Okay, Oke, Omit, One-time, Overhaul, Overshoot, Overtake, Pa, Palm, Participle, Perish, Permeate, Permit, Perpetuate, Poll, Poort, Predicament, Pretty, Proceed, Propagate, Pun(c)to, Qualify, Railcard, Reach, Reeve, Refer, Relay, Retroactive, Retrospect, Reverse, Safe conduct, St Gotthard, San Bernardino, Senile, Serve, Simplon, Since, Skim, Skip, Skirt, Slap, Sling, Snap, Spend, Stab, State, Thermopylae, Thread, Through, Ticket, Tip, Transient, Transilient, Transitory, Transmit, Transude, Travel, Troop, Uspallata, Veronica, Vet, Visa, Visé, Wall, Wayleave, Weather, While, Yesterday, Yesteryear

Passage Adit, Airway, Aisle, Alley(way), Alure, Apostrophe, Arcade, Archway, Areaway, Arterial, Breezeway, Bylane, Cadenza, Career, Channel, Chute, Citation, Clause, Close, Coda, Conduit, Corridor, Creep, Crossing, Crush, Dead-end, Defile, Drake, Drift, Duct, Eel-fare, Episode, Excerpt, Extract, Fare, Fat, Flat, Flight, Flue, Gallery, Gangway, Gap, Gat, Gate, Gut, Hall, Head, Inlet, Journey, Lane, Lapse, Loan, Lobby, Locus, Meatus, Middle, Mona, Movement, Northeast, Northwest, Para(graph), Path, Pend, Phrase, Pore, Portion, Prelude, Prose, Purple, Ride, Ripieno, Rite, Rough, Route, Sailing, Screed, Shaft, Shunt, Slap, Snicket, Strait, Street, Stretta, Stretto, Subway, Sump, Text, Thorough(fare), Throat, Tour, Trachea, Trance, Transe, Transit(ion), Travel, Tunnel, Tutti, Undercast, Unseen, Ureter, Voyage, Way, Windpipe

▷ **Passage of arms** *may indicate* 'sleeve'

Passenger(s) Cad, Commuter, Fare, Pillion, Rider, Slacker, Steerage, Straphanger, Traveller, Voyager, Wayfarer

Passion(ate), Passionately Anger, Appetite, Ardour, Con fuoco, Fervour, Fire, Flame, Frampold, Fury, Gust, Heat, Hot, Hunger, Hwyl, Ileac, Iliac, Intense, Ire, Irish, Kama, Love, Lust, Mania, Obsession, Oestrus, Rage, Stormy, Sultry, Torrid, Violent, Warm, Wax, Wrath, Yen, Zeal

Passive (stage) Apathetic, Dormant, Inert, Pathic, Patient, Pupa, Supine, Yielding

Passport Access, Clearance, Congé(e), Key, Laissez-passer, Nansen, Navicert, Sea-letter, Visa

Password Code, Countersign, Logon, Nayword, Parole, Sesame, Shibboleth, Tessera, Watchword

▶ **Past** *see* PASS

Pasta Agnolotti, Cannelloni, Capelletti, Conchiglie, Durum, Farfal, Farfel, Fedelini, Fettuc(c)ine, Fusilli, Lasagna, Lasagne, Linguini, Macaroni, Manicotti, Noodles, Orzo, Penne, Perciatelli, Ravioli, Rigatoni, Spaghetti, Spaghettina, Tagliarini, Tagliatelle, Tortelli(ni), Vermicelli, Ziti

Paste, Pasty Ashen, Batter, Beat, Botargo, Boule, Bridie, Cerate, Clobber, Cornish, Dentifrice, Dough, Electuary, Fake, Filler, Fondant, Frangipane, Glue, Guarana, Harissa, Knish, Lute, Magma, Marzipan, Masala, Mastic, Miso, Mountant, Pale, Pallid, Pâté, Patty, Pearl-essence, Pie, Piroshki, Pirozhki, Poonac, Punch, Putty, Rhinestone, Slip, Slurry, Spread, Strass, Tahina, Tahini, Tapenade, Taramasalata, Wan

Pastor(al) Arcadia, Bucolic, Curé, Eclogue, Endymion, Idyl(l), Minister, Priest, Rector, Rural, Shepherd, Simple

Pastry Baclava, Bakemeat, Baklava, Beignet, Brik, Chausson, Choux, Coquile, Creamhorn, Cream puff, Croustade, Cruller, Crust, Danish, Dariole, Dough, Eclair, Filo, Flaky, Flan, French, Millefeuille, Phyllo, Pie, Pie-crust, Profiterole, Puff, Quiche, Rough-puff, Samosa, Shortcrust, Strudel, Tart, Turnover, Vol-au-vent

Pasture Alp, Eadish, Eddish, Feed, Fell, Fodder, Grassland, Graze, Herbage, Kar(r)oo, Lair, Lare, Lea, Lease, Leasow(e), Leaze, Ley, Machair, Mead(ow), Pannage, Potrero, Raik, Rake, Soum, Sowm, Tie, Transhume, Tye

▶ **Pasty** *see* PASTE

Patch(y) Bed, Bit, Cabbage, Clout, Coalsack, Cobble, Cooper, Court plaster, Cover, Friar, Fudge, > MEND, Mosaic, Nicotine, Pasty, Piebald, Piece, Plage, Plaque, Plaster, Pot, Purple, Shinplaster, Shoulder, Solder, Tingle, Tinker, Vamp, Variegated

Path(way) Aisle, Allée, Alley, Arc, Berm, Berme, Boreen, Borstal(l), Bridle, Causeway, Causey, Clickstream, Course, Eclipse, Flight, Gate, Ginnel, Glide, Lane, Ley, Locus, Orbit, Pad, Parabola, Primrose, Ride, Ridgeway, Route, Runway, Sidewalk, Spurway, Stie, Sty(e), Swath(e), Track, Trail, Trajectory, Trod, Walkway, > WAY, Xystus

Pathetic(ally) Doloroso, Drip, Forlorn, Piteous, Poignant, Sad, Touching

Patience Calm, Endurance, Forbearance, Fortitude, Indulgence, Monument, Solitaire, Stoicism, Virtue

Patient(s) Calm, Case, Clinic, Forbearing, Grisel(da), Grisilda, Invalid, Job, Long-suffering, Passive, Resigned, Stoic, Subject, Ward

Patriot(ic), **Patriotism** Cavour, Chauvinist, DAR, Emmet, Flag-waving, Flamingant, Garibaldi, Hereward, Irredentist, Jingoism, Loyalist, Maquis, Nationalist, Tell

Patrol Armilla, Guard, Outguard, Picket, Piquet, Prowl-car, Reconnaissance, Scout, Sentinel, Sentry-go, Shark, Shore, Turm

Patron(age), **Patronise(d)**, **Patronising** Advowson, Aegis, Auspices, Benefactor, Business, Champion, Client, Customer, Donator, Egis, Fautor, Maecenas, Nepotic, Protector, Protégé, Provider, Shopper, > SPONSOR, Stoop, Stoup

Pattern(ed) Argyle, Bird's eye, Blueprint, Branchwork, Check, Chequer, Clock, Design, Diaper, Diffraction, Dog's tooth, Draft, Epitome, Example, Exemplar, Fiddle, Figuration, Format, Fret, Grain, Greek key, Herringbone, Holding, Hound's tooth, Intonation, Koru, Matrix, Meander, > MODEL, Moire, Mosaic, Norm, Paisley, Paradigm, Paragon, Pinstripe, Plan, Polka-dot, Pompadour, Precedent, Prototype, Queenstitch, Radiation, Raster, Shawl, Stencil, Symmetry, Syndrome, Tangram, Template, Tessera, Tracery, Traffic, Tread, Type, Willow

Pause Break, Breakpoint, Breather, Caesura, Cessation, Cesura, Comma, Desist, Er, Fermata, Hesitate, Interkinesis, Interval, Limma, Lull, Pitstop, Rest, Selah, Stop

Pave(ment), **Paving** Causeway, Clint, Diaper, Granolith, Path, Roadside, Set(t), Sidewalk, Travolator, Trottoir

Pawn(shop) Agent, Betel, Chessman, Counter, Derby, Dip, Gage, Gallery, Hanging, Hock, Hostage, Leaving-shop, Lumber, Monte-de-piété, Monti di pieta, Pan, Passed, Peacock, Piece, Pignerate, Pignorate, Pledge, Pop, Security, Siri, Spout, Tiddleywink, Tool, Wadset, Weed

Pawnbroker, **Pawnee** Hockshop, Lumberer, Moneylender, Nunky, Sheeny, Uncle, Usurer

Pay(master), **Payment**, **Paid**, **Pay off**, **Pay out** Advertise, Amortise, Annat, Annuity, Ante, Arles, Atone, Basic, Batta, Blench, Bonus, Bukshee, Cain, Cashier, Cheque, COD, Commute, Compensate, Consideration, Damage, Defray, Disburse, Discharge, Dividend, Down, Dub, Emolument, Endow, Equalisation, Eric, Escot, Farm, Fee, Feu-duty, Finance, Foot, Fork out, Fund, Gale, Gate, Give, Grave, Greenmail, Han(d)sel, Hazard, Hire, HP, Imburse, Kain, Kickback, Mail, Meet, Modus, Overtime, Payola, Pension, Pittance, Pony, Posho, Premium, Primage, Pro, Pro forma, Progress, Purser, Quit(-rent), Ransom, Redundancy,

Refund, Remittance, Remuneration, Rent, Requite, Residual, Respects, Royalty, Salary, Satisfaction, Scot, Screw, Scutage, Settle, Severance, Shell, Shell out, Sick, Sink, Sold(e), > SPEND, Square, Stipend, Strike, Stump, Sub, Subscribe, Sweetener, Table, Take-home, Tar, Tender, Token, Tommy, Transfer, Treasure, Treat, Tribute, Truck, Veer, Wage

PE Aerobics, Gym

Pea(s) Carling, Chaparral, Chickling, Desert, D(h)al, Dholl, Garbanzo, Goober, Hastings, Legume, Mangetout, Marrowfat, Passiform, Pigeon, Pulse, Rounceval, Split, Sugar

Peace(ful), **Peace-keeper**, **Peace organisation**, **Peace symbol** Ahimsa, Ataraxy, Calm, Ease, Frith, Halcyon, Interceder, Irenic(on), King's, Lee, Lull, Nirvana, Olive, Pacific, Pax, Queen's, Quiet, Repose, Rest, Salem, Serene, Sh, Shalom, Siesta, Still, Tranquil, Truce, UN

Peach Blab, Cling, Clingstone, Dish, Dob, Freestone, Inform, Laetrile, Malakatoone, Melocoto(o)n, Nectarine, Oner, Quandang, Shop, Sneak, Split, Squeak, Stunner, Tattle, Tell, Victorine

Peacock Coxcomb, Dandy, Fop, Junonian, Muster, Paiock(e), Pajock(e), Pavo(ne), Pawn, Payock(e), Pown, Sashay

Peak(y) Acme, Aiguille, Alp, Apex, Ben, Comble, Communism, Crag, Crest, Darien, Drawn, Eiger, Gable, Gannett, Horn, Matterhorn, Mons, > MOUNTAIN, Nib, Nunatak, Optimum, Pale, Pin, Pinnacle, Rainier, Sallow, Snowdon, Spire, Top, Tor, Visor, Widow's, Zenith

Pear Aguacate, Alligator, Anchovy, Anjou, Asian, Avocado, Bartlett, Bergamot, Beurré, Blanquet, Carmelite, Catherine, Colmar, Conference, Cuisse-madame, Jargonelle, Muscadel, Muscatel, Musk, Nelis, Perry, Poperin, Poppering, Poprin, Prickly, Pyrus, Queez-maddam, Seckel, Seckle, Warden, William

Pearl(s), **Pearly** Barocco, Barock, Baroque, Cultured, False, Gem, Imitated, Jewel, Mabe, Margaret, Margaric, Nacrous, Olivet, Orient, Prize, Rope, Seed, Simulated, String, Sulphur, Unio(n)

Peasant Bonhomme, Boor, Bumpkin, Chouan, Churl, Clodhopper, Contadino, Cossack, Cottar, Cott(i)er, Fellah(s), Fellahin, Hick, Jungli, Kern(e), Kisan, Kulak, M(o)ujik, Muzhik, Raiyat, Roturier, Rustic, Ryot, Swain, Tyrolean, Whiteboy, Yokel

Pebble(s), **Pebbly** Banket, Calculus, Cobblestone, Dreikanter, Gallet, Gooley, Gravel, Psephism, Pumie, Pumy, Scree, Shingle

Peck Bill, Bushel, Dab, Forpet, Forpit, Gregory, Kiss, Lip, Lippie, Nibble, Tap

Peculiar(ity) Appropriate, Characteristic, Distinct, Eccentric, Especial, Exclusive, Ferly, Funny, Idiosyncratic, Kink, Kooky, Odd, Own, Proper, Queer, Quirk, Singular, > SPECIAL, Specific, Strange, Unusual

▷ **Peculiar** *may indicate* an anagram

Pedal Bike, Chorus, Cycle, Damper, Lever, P, Rat-trap, Soft, Sostenuto, Sustaining, Treadle, Treddle

Peddle, **Pedlar** Bodger, Boxwallah, Camelot, Chapman, Cheapjack, Colporteur, Drummer, Duffer, Hawk, Huckster, Jagger, Packman, Pedder, Pether, Sell, Smouch, Smouse(r), Sutler, Tallyman, Tink(er), Yagger

▷ **Peddling** *may indicate* an anagram

Pedestrian Banal, Commonplace, Dull, Ganger, Hack, Hike, Itinerant, Jaywalker, Laborious, Mundane, Trite, Walker

Pedigree(s) Ancestry, Blood, Breeding, Descent, House, Lineage, Phylogeny, Stemma(ta), Stirps, Thoroughbred

Peel(er) Bark, Bobby, Candied, Decorticate, Exfoliate, Flype, Pare, PC, Rind, Rine, Scale, Shell, Skin, > STRIP, Tirr, Zest

▷ **Peeled** *may indicate* outside letter(s) to be removed from a word

Peep(er), Peephole Cheep, Cook, Glance, Gledge, Keek, Kook, Lamp, Nose, Peek, Pink, Pry, Spy, Squeak, Squint, Stime, Styme, Voyeur

Peer(age), Peers Life, Representative, Spiritual, Temporal

Peevish(ness) Capernoited, Captious, Crabby, Cross, Doddy, Frabbit, Frampal, Frampold, Franzy, Fretful, Lienal, Moody, Nattered, Petulant, Pindling, Protervity, Shirty, Sour, Teachie, Testy, Te(t)chy

Peg Cheville, Cleat, Cotter-pin, Die, Fix, Freeze, Knag, Leg, Margaret, Nail, Nog, Pin, Piton, Snort, Spigot, Spile, Square, Stengah, Stinger, Support, Tap, Tee, Thole, Tholepin, Thowel, Toggle, Tot, Woffington

Pelican Alcatras, Bird, Crossing, Golden Hind, LA, Louisiana

Pellet Bolus, Buckshot, Bullet, Pill, Prill, Slug

Pelmet Valance

Pelt Assail, Clod, Fleece, Fur, Hail, Hide, Hie, Lam, Pepper, Random, Shower, Skin, Squail, Stone

Pen Ballpoint, Bamboo, Bic®, Biro®, Cage, Calamus, Cartridge, Catching, Confine, Coop, Corral, Crawl, Crow-quill, Cru(i)ve, Cub, Cyclostyle, Dabber, Data, Enclosure, Fank, Farm, Felt(-tipped), Fold, Fountain, Gaol, Gladius, Hen, Highlighter, Hoosegow, J, > **JAIL**, Keddah, Kraal, Lair, Light, Marker, Mew, Mure, Music, Piggery, Poison, Pound, Quill, Ree, Reed, Ring, Rollerball, Scribe, Stell, Stie, Stir, Sty(e), Stylet, Stylo, Stylograph, Stylus, Submarine, Swan, Tank, Write

▷ **Pen** *may indicate* a writer

Penal(ize) Cost, Fine, Gate, Handicap, Huff, Mulct, Punitive, Servitude

Penalty Abye, Amende, Cost, Eric, Fine, Forfeit, Han(d)sel, Huff, Pain, Price, Punishment, Sanction, Wide

Pencil Beam, Ca(l)m, Caum, Charcoal, Chinagraph®, Crayon, Draft, Draw, Eyebrow, Fusain, Grease, Harmonic, Ink, Keelivine, Keelyvine, Lead, Outline, Propelling, Slate, Stump, Styptic

Pendant Albert, Chandelier, Drop, Girandole, Laval(l)ière, Necklace, Poffle

Pending Imminent, In fieri, Unresolved, Until

Penetrate, Penetrating, Penetration Acumen, Acuminate, Bite, Bore, Cut, Enpierce, Enter, Imbue, Impale, Incisive, Indent, Indepth, Infiltrate, Insight, Into, Intrant, Lance, Permeate, Pierce, Probe, Sagacious, Shear, Thrust, Touch, X-ray

Penguin Aeroplane, Anana, Auk, Emperor, Fairy, Gentoo, King, Korora, Macaroni, Rock-hopper

Peninsula Alaska, Antarctic, Arabian, Ards, Arm, Avalon, Baja California, Balkan, Bataan, Boothia, Cape, Cape Cod, Cape Verde, Chalcidice, Chersonese, Chukchi, Crimea, Deccan, Delmarva, East Cape, Eyre, Florida, Gallipoli, Gaspé, Gower, Iberia(n), Indo-China, Istria, Jutland, Kamchatka, Kathiawar, Kintyre, Kola, Kowloon, Labrador, Leizhou, Lleyn, Malay, Melville, Neck, Nova Scotia, Otago, Palmer, Peloponnese, Promontory, Scandinavian, Sinai, Spit, Spur, Tasman, The Lizard, Wilson's Promontory, Wirral, Yorke

Penny Bean, Cartwheel, Cent, Copper, D, Dreadful, P, Sen, Sou, Sterling, Stiver, Win(n), Wing

Pension(er) Allowance, Ann(at), Annuitant, Board, Chelsea, Cod, Cor(r)ody, Gratuity, Guest-house, Half-board, Occupational, Payment, Personal, Retire, Serps, Stakeholder, Stipend, Superannuation

People Bods, Body, Chosen, Commonalty, Commons, Demos, Ecology, Enchorial, Flower, Folk, Fraim, Gens, Guild, Human, Inca, Inhabit, Janata, Kin, Land, Lapith, Lay, Man(kind), Men, Mob, Nair, Nation(s), Nayar, One, Peculiar, Personalities, Phalange, Populace, Proletariat(e), Public, Punters, Quorum, Race, Settle, Society, Souls, They, Tribe, Volk

Pepper Alligator, All-spice, Ava, Bird, Black, Capsicum, Cayenne, Chilli, Condiment, Cubeb, Devil, Dittander, Dittany, Ethiopian, Green, Guinea, Jalapeno, Jamaica, Kava, Malaguetta, Matico, Negro, Paprika, Pelt, Pim(i)ento, Piper, Red, Riddle, Sambal, Spice, Sprinkle, Szechwan, Tabasco®, Yaqona, Yellow

Peptide Substance P

Perceive, Perception, Perceptive Acumen, Alert, Anschauung, Apprehend, Astute, Clairvoyance, Clear-eyed, Cryptaesthetic, Descry, Dianoia, Discern, Divine, ESP, Extrasensory, Feel, Insight, Intelligence, Intuit(ion), Kinaesthesia, Notice, Observe, Pan(a)esthesia, Remark, > SEE, Sense, Sensitive, Sentience, Shrewd, Subliminal, Tact, Taste, Understanding

Percentage Agio, Commission, Contango, Cut, Proportion, Royalty, Share, Vigorish

Perch(ing) Aerie, Alight, Anabis, Bass, Comber, Eyrie, Fish, Fogash, Gaper, Insessorial, Lug, Perca, Pole, Roost, Ruff(e), Seat, Serranid, > SIT, Zingel

Percussion (cap) Amorce, Idiophone, Impact, Knee, Knock, Thump, Timbrel

Perennial Continual, Enduring, Flower, Livelong, Perpetual, Recurrent

Perfect(ly), Perfection(ist) Absolute, Accomplish, Accurate, Acme, Apple-pie, Bloom, Complete, Consummation, Cross-question, Dead, Develop, Fare-thee-well, Finish, Flawless, Fulfil, Full, Holy, Ideal(ist), Impeccable, Intact, It, Mint, Par, Paragon, Past, Pat, Peace, Pedant, Point-device, Practice, Present, Pure, Quintessential, Refine, Siddha, Soma, Sound, Spot-on, Stainless, Sublime, The nines, Thorough, Three-pricker, Unblemished, Unqualified, Utopian, Utter, Whole, Witeless

Perform(ed), Performer, Performing Achieve, Act(or), Appear, Artist(e), Basoche, Busk, Chansonnier, Discharge, Do, Enact, Entertainer, Execute, Exert, Exhibit, Fancy Dan, Fulfil, Function, Geek, Hand, Headliner, Hersall, Implement, Interlocutor, Majorette, Make, Moke, On, Player, Praxis, Recite, Render, Ripieno, Sword-swallower, Throw, Vaudevillian, Virtuoso

Performance Accomplishment, Achievement, Act, Auto, Bravura, Broadcast, Command, Concert, Dare, Deed, Demonstration, Discharge, Entracte, Execution, Gas, Gig, Hierurgy, Holdover, Hootenanny, Masterstroke, Matinee, One-night stand, Operation, Perpetration, Practice, Première, Production, Recital, Rehearsal, Rendering, Rendition, Repeat, Repertoire, Rigmarole, Scene, Show, Sneak preview, Solo, Specific, Spectacle, Stunt, Turn

Perfume (box) Aroma, Attar, Bergamot, Cassolette, Chypre, Civet, Cologne, Enfleurage, Fragrance, Frangipani, Incense, Ionone, Lavender (water), Linalool, Myrrh, Opopanax, Orris, Orrisroot, Patchouli, Patchouly, Pomander, Potpourri, Redolence, > SCENT, Terpineol

Perhaps A(i)blins, Belike, Haply, Happen, May(be), Peradventure, Percase, Perchance, Possibly, Relative, Say

▷ **Perhaps** *may indicate* an anagram

Perimeter Boundary, Circuit, Circumference, Limits

Period(ic) Abbevillian, AD, Age, Alcher(ing)a, Annual, Cambrian, Carboniferous, Chukka, Chukker, Climacteric, Cooling off, Cretaceous, Critical, Curse, Cycle, Day, Devonian, Diapause, Dot, Dreamtime, > DURATION, Eocene, Epoch, Excerpt, Full-stop, Glacial, Grace, Incubation, Innings, Interregnum, Jurassic, Kalpa, Latency, Latent, Lesson, Liassic, Limit, Meantime, Meanwhile, Mesolithic, Mesozoic, Miocene, Monthly, Neocomian, Neolithic, Octave, Olde-worlde, Oligocene, Ordovician, Paleolithic, Phase, Phoenix, Pre-Cambrian, Quarter, Quarternary, Reformation, Refractory, Regency, Rent, Riss, Romantic, Safe, Season, Session, Sidereal, Span, Spell, Stage, Stop, Stretch, Synodic, Term, Tertiary, Trecento, Triassic, Trimester, Usance, Window

Periodic(al) Comic, Digest, Economist, Etesian, Journal, Liassic, Listener, Mag,

New Yorker, Organ, Paper, Phase, Publication, Punch, Rambler, Regency, Review, Spectator, Strand, Stretch, Tatter, Tract

Perish(able), Perished, Perishing Brittle, > DIE, End, Ephemeral, Expire, Fade, Forfair, Fungibles, Icy, Tine, Tint, Transitory, Tyne, Vanish

Perm(anent) Abiding, Durable, Eternal, Everlasting, Fixed, Full-time, Indelible, > LASTING, Marcel, Stable, Standing, Stative, Wave

Permeability, Permeate Infiltrate, Leaven, Osmosis, Penetrate, Pervade, Seep

Permission, Permit(ted) Allow, Authorise, Carnet, Chop, Clearance, Congé(e), Consent, Copyright, Enable, Grant, Lacet, Laisser-passer, Latitude, Leave, Legal, Let, Liberty, Licence, License, Lief, Luit, Nihil obstat, Ok(e), Pace, Pass, Placet, Planning, Power, Pratique, Privilege, Sanction, Stamp-note, Suffer, Ticket, Triptyque, Visa, Vouchsafe, Way-leave, Wear

Perpendicular Aplomb, Apothem, Atrip, Cathetus, Erect, Normal, Orthogonal, Plumb, Sheer, Sine, > UPRIGHT, Vertical

Perplex(ed), Perplexity Anan, Baffle, Bamboozle, Beset, Bewilder, Bother, Buffalo, Bumbaze, Cap, Confound, Confuse, Embarrass, Feague, Floor, Flummox, Knotty, Meander, Mystify, Nonplus, Out, Puzzle, Quizzical, Stump, Tangle, Tickle, Tostication

Persecute, Persecution Afflict, Annoy, Badger, Crucify, Dragon(n)ades, Harass, Haze, Intolerant, Oppress, Pogrom, Ride, Torture

Persevere, Perseverance Assiduity, Continue, Fortitude, Insist, Patience, Persist, Plug, Stamina, Steadfastness, Stick, Stickability, Tenacity

Persia(n) Babee, Babi, Bahai, Cyrus, Farsi, Iran(ian), Mazdean, Mede, Pahlavi, Parasang, Parsee, Pehlevi, Pushtu, Samanid, Sassanid, Sohrab, Xerxes, Zoroaster

Persist(ence), Persistent Adhere, Assiduity, Chronic, Continual, Diligent, Doggedness, Endure, Importunate, Labour, Longeval, Lusting, Persevere, Press, Sedulous, Sneaking, Stick, Tenacity, Urgent

Person(s), Personal(ly) Alter, Being, Bird, Bod(y), Chai, Chal, Chi, Cookie, Entity, Everymen, Figure, Fish, Flesh, Head, Human, Individual, One, Own, Party, Passer-by, Private, Quidam, Selfhood, Sod, Soul, Specimen, Tales

Personage, Personality Anima, Celeb(rity), Character, Charisma, Dignitary, Ego, Grandee, Identity, Noble, Notability, Panjandrum, Presence, Sama, Seity, Sel, Self, Sell, Star, Tycoon

Personified, Personification, Personify Embody, Incarnate, Prosopop(o)eia, Represent

Perspective Attitude, Distance, Point of view, Proportion, View, Vista

Persuade(d), Persuasion, Persuasive Cajole, Coax, Cogent, Conviction, Convince, Disarm, Eloquent, Faith, Feel, Forcible, Geed, Get, Induce, Inveigle, Move, Plausible, > PREVAIL, Religion, Soft sell, Suborn, Truckled, Wheedle, Winning

Pert(ness) Bold, Cocky, Dicacity, Flippant, Forward, Fresh, Impertinent, Insolent, Jackanapes, Minx, Saucy, Tossy

Pertinent Apropos, Apt, Fit, Germane, Relevant, Timely

Perturb(ation) Aerate, Confuse, Dismay, Disturb, Dither, State, Trouble, Upset, Worry

Pervade, Pervasion, Pervasive(ness) Diffuse, Drench, Immanence, Permeate, Saturate

Perverse, Perversion, Pervert(ed) Aberrant, Abnormal, Algolagnia, Awry, Cam(stairy), Camsteary, Camsteerie, Cantankerous, > CONTRARY, Corrupt, Cussed, Deviate, Distort, Donsie, False, Gee, Kam(me), Kinky, Licentious, Misuse, Nonce, Paraphilia, Refractory, Sadist, Sicko, Stubborn, Thrawn, Traduce, Unnatural, Untoward, Uranism, Warp(ed), Wayward, Wilful, Wrest, Wry

▷ **Perverted** *may indicate* an anagram

Pessimism, Pessimist(ic) Alarmist, Bear, Crapehanger, Crepehanger, Cynic, Defeatist, Doomwatch, Doomy, Doubter, Downbeat, Fatalist, Glumbum, Jeremiah, Killjoy, Negative

Pest(er) Badger, Bedbug, Blight, Bot, > **BOTHER**, Brat, Breese, Bug, Dim, Disagreeable, Earbash, Fly, Fowl, Harass, Irritate, Mither, Mouse, Nag, Nudnik, Nuisance, Nun, Pize, Plague, Rotter, Scourge, Tease, Terror, Thysanoptera, Vermin, Weevil

Pesticide DDT, Derris, Heplachlor, Mouser, Permethrin, Synergist, Warfarin

Pestilence, Pestilent Curse, Epidemic, Evil, Lues, Murrain, Noxious, Pernicious, Plague

Pet Aversion, Cade, Canoodle, Caress, Chou, Coax, Cosset, Dandle, Daut(ie), Dawt(ie), Dod, Dort, Ducky, Favourite, Fondle, Glumps, Hamster, Huff, Hump, Ire, Jarta, Jo, Lallygag, Lapdog, Miff, Mouse, Neck, Pique, Rabbit, Smooch, Snog, Spat, Strum, Sulk(s), Tantrum, Teacher's, Tiff, Tout, Towt, Umbrage, Virtual, Yarta

Petition(er) Appeal, Beg, Boon, Crave, Entreaty, Millenary, Orison, Plaintiff, Postulant, Prayer, Representation, Request, Round robin, Solicit, Sue, Suit(or), Suppli(c)ant, Vesper

Petrify(ing) Fossilise, Frighten, Lapidescent, Niobe, Numb, Ossify, Scare, Terrify

Petrol(eum) Cetane, Diesel, Esso®, Ethyl, Fuel, Gas, High-octane, Ligroin, Maz(o)ut, Octane, Olein, Rock-tar, Unleaded

Petticoat Balmoral, Basquine, Crinoline, Female, Filabeg, Fil(l)ibeg, Jupon, Kilt, Kirtle, Phil(l)abeg, Phil(l)ibeg, Placket, Sarong, Shift, Underskirt, Wylie-coat

Petty, Pettiness Baubling, Bumbledom, Childish, Little, Mean, Minor, Narrow, Niggling, Nyaff, One-horse, Parvanimity, Picayunish, Pimping, Puisne, Shoestring, Small, Stingy, Tin, Trivial, Two-bit

Petulance, Petulant Fretful, Huff, Moody, Peevish, Perverse, Procacity, Sullen, Toutie, Waspish

Phaeton Spider

Phantom Apparition, Bogey, Bugbear, Eidolon, Idol, Incubus, Maya, Shade, Spectre, Tut, Wraith

Pharmacist > **CHEMIST**, Dispenser, MPS, Preparator

Phase Cycle, Form, Period, Post-boost, REM, Stage, State, Synchronise

Phenomenon Blip, Effect, Event, Flying saucer, Marvel, Miracle, Mirage, Paranormal, Psi, Synergy

Philanthropist, Philanthropy Altruist, Benefactor, Carnegie, Charity, Coram, Donor, Nobel, Rockefeller, Samaritan, Shaftesbury, Tate, Wilberforce

Philistine, Philistinism Artless, Ashdod, Barbarian, Foe, Gath, Gaza, Gigman, Goliath, Goth, Lowbrow, Vandal

Philosopher, Philosophy Activism, Ahimsa, Analytical, Animism, Anthrosophy, Antinomianism, Attitude, Averr(h)oism, Comtism, Conceptualism, Cracker-barrel, Deontology, Empiricism, Enlightenment, Epistemology, Ethics, Existentialism, Fatalism, Hedonism, Hobbism, Humanism, Idealism, Ideology, -ism, Linguistic, Logical atomism, Logos, Marxism, Materialism, Metempiricism, Monism, Moral(ist), Natural, Neoplatonism, Nihilism, Nominalism, Opinion, Peripatetic, Phenomenology, Populism, Positivism, Rationalism, Realism, Scientology, Shankara(-charya), Stoic, Synthetic, Taoism, Theism, Theosophy, Transcendentalism, Ultraism, Utilitarianism, Utopianism, Voluntarism, Yoga

Phone Bell, Blower, Call, Cellular, Dial, Intercom, Mobile, Ring

Phonetic(s) Oral, Palaeotype, Spoken, Symbol

▷ **Phonetically** *may indicate* a word sounding like another

Phon(e)y Bogus, Charlatan, Counterfeit, Fake, Impostor, Poseur, > **SHAM**, Specious, Spurious

▷ **Phony** *may indicate* an anagram

Photo(copy), **Photograph(y)**, **Photographic**, **Photo finish** Close-up, Composite, Duplicate, Exposure, Film, Flash, Headshot, Hologram, Microdot, Mugshot, Negative, Panel, Picture, Positive, Print, Rotogravure, Sepia, Shoot, Shot, Snap, Still, Take, Topo, Vignette, X-ray

Phrase Buzzword, Catch(word), Cliché, Comma, Expression, Heroic, Laconism, Leitmotiv, Locution, Mantra, Phr, Refrain, Riff, Slogan, Tag, Term

Physic(s) Cryogenics, Culver's, Cure, Dose, Kinematics, Medicine, Nuclear, Nucleonics, Particle, Purge, Remedy, Rheology, Science, Thermodynamics

Physician Allopath, Doctor, Galen, Hakim, Harvey, Hippocrates, Internist, Leech, Linacre, Lister, Medic(o), Mesmer, Mindererus, Paean, Paracelsus, Practitioner, Quack, Roget, Therapist, Time

Physicist Alfren, Ampere, Angstrom, Appleton, Archimedes, Avogadro, Becquerel, Bohr, Born, Bose, Bragg, Brewster, Carnot, Cockcroft, Coulomb, Crookes, Curie, Dalton, Davisson, Debye, Einstein, Faraday, Fermi, Galileo, Gauss, Geiger, Giorgi, Hahn, Hawking, Heaviside, Heisenberg, Henry, Hertz, Huygens, Joliot-Curie, Josephson, Joule, Kirchhoff, Landau, Lawe, Lodge, Lorentz, Mach, Marconi, Newton, Oersted, Ohm, Oppenheimer, Pauli, Pic(c)ard, Planck, Popov, Reaumur, Ro(e)ntgen, Scientist, Stark, Torricelli, Van Allen, Volta, Young

Pi, **Pious** Devotional, Devout, Fraud, Gallio, God-fearing, Godly, Holy, Mid-Victorian, Sanctimonious, Savoury, Smug

Piano Bechstein, Celesta, Celeste, Concert grand, Cottage, Flugel, Forte, Grand, Honkytonk, Keyboard, Overstrung, P, Player, Softly, Steinway, Stride, Upright

Picaresque Roman à tiroirs

Pick(er), **Pickaxe**, **Picking**, **Pick up** Break, Choice, Cream, Cull, Elite, Flower, Gather, Glean, Hack, Hopper, Mattock, Nap, Nibble, Oakum, Plectrum, Pluck, Plum, Select, Single, Sort, Steal, Strum, Tong, Wale

▷ **Picked** *may indicate* an anagram

Pickle(r) Achar, Brine, Cabbage, Caper, Chow-chow, Chutney, Corn, Cure, Dilemma, Dill, Eisel, Esile, Gherkin, Girkin, Jam, Kimchi, Marinade, Marinate, Mess, Mull, Olive, Onion, Peculate, Peregrine, Piccalilli, Samp(h)ire, Scrape, Souse, Vinegar, Wolly

Pickpocket(s) Adept, Bung, Cly-faker, Cutpurse, Dip, Diver, Fagin, File, Nipper, Wire

Picnic Alfresco, Braaivleis, Clambake, Fun, Outing, Push-over, Spread, Wase-goose, Wayzgoose

Picture(s) Anaglyph, Art, Canvas, Collage, Decoupage, Depict, Describe, Diptych, Drawing, Drypoint, Emblem, Epitome, Etching, Film, Flick, Fresco, Gouache, Graphic, Histogram, Icon, Identikit®, Imagery, Inset, Landscape, Likeness, Lithograph, Montage, Motion, Movie, Moving, Movy, Mugshot, Oil, Photo, Photofit, Photogram, Pin-up, Pix, Plate, Portrait, Prent, Presentment, Print, Retrate, Scene, Shadowgraph, Shot, Slide, Snapshot, Stereochrome, Stereogram, Stereograph, Stevengraph, Still-life, Table(au), Talkie, Thermogram, Tone, Topo, Transfer, Transparency, Vectograph, Vision, Votive, Word, Zincograph

Pie(s) Anna, Banoffee, Battalia, Bridie, Camp, Chewet, Cobbler, Cottage, Curry puff, Custard, Deep-dish, Easy, Flan, Hash, Humble, Madge, Mess, Mince, Mud, Mystery bag, Pandowdy, Pastry, Pasty, Patty, Périgord, Pica, Piet, Pirog, Pizza, Pyat, Pyet, Pyot, Quiche, Rappe, Resurrection, Shepherd's, Shoofly, Spoil, Squab, Stargaz(e)y, Star(ry)-gazy, Sugar, Tart, Tarte tatin, Torte, Tourtiere, Turnover, Tyropitta, Umble, Vol-au-vent, Warden

▷ **Pie** *may indicate* an anagram

Piece(s) Add, Bishop, Bit, Blot, Cameo, Cannon, Cent, Charm, > **CHESSMAN**, Chip,

Chunk, Coin, Companion, Component, Concerto, Conversation, Crumb, Domino, End, Extract, Flitters, Fragment, Gat, Goring, > **GUN**, Haet, Hait, Hunk, Item, Join, Mammock, Medaillons, Mite, Money, Morsel, Museum, Nip, Novelette, Oddment, Off-cut, Ort, Part, Party, Patch, Pawn, Period, Peso, Pistareen, Pole, > **PORTION**, Recital, Scrap, Section, Set, Shard, Sherd, Slice, Sliver, Sou, Speck, String, Stub, Swatch, Tait, Tate, Tile, Toccata, Wedge

Pier(s) Anta, Groyne, Jetty, Jutty, Landing, Mole, Plowman, Quay, Slipway, Swiss roll, Wharf

Pierce(d), **Piercer**, **Piercing** Accloy, Awl, Broach, Cleave, Dart, Drill, Endart, Fenestrate(d), Gimlet, Gore, Gride, Gryde, Hull, Impale, Jag, Keen, Lance, Lancinate, Lobe, Move, Needle, Penetrate, Perforate, Pike, Poignant, Punch, Puncture, Riddle, Rive, Shrill, Skewer, Slap, Sleeper, Spear, Spike, Spit, Stab, Steek, Stiletto, Sting, Thirl, Thrill(ant)

Pig(s), **Piggy**, **Pigskin** Anthony, Babe, Barrow, Bartholomew, Bland, Boar, Bush, Doll, Elt, Farrow, Fastback, Football, Gadarene, Gilt, Glutton, Gride, Guinea, Gus, Ham, Hog, Ingot, Iron, Kentledge, Kintledge, Landrace, Large black, Large white, Long, Napoleon, Peccary, Policeman, Pork(er), Razorback, Rosser, Runt, Saddleback, Shoat, Shot(e), Shott, Slip, Snowball, Sounder, Sow, Squealer, Suid(ae), Tamworth, Tithe, Toe, Warthog, Yelt

Pigeon Archangel, Barb, Bird, Cape, Carrier, Clay, Cropper, Culver, Dove, Fantail, Goura, Gull, Homer, Homing, Horseman, Jacobin, Kuku, Manumea, Nun, Owl, Passenger, Peristeronic, Pouter, Ringdove, Rock(er), Roller, Ront(e), Ruff, Runt, Scandaroon, Solitaire, Spot, Squab, Squealer, Stock-dove, Stool, Talkie-talkee, Tippler, Tumbler, Turbit, Wonga-wonga, Zoozoo

Pig-headed Self-willed

Pigment(ation) Anthoclore, Anthocyan(in), Argyria, Betacyanin, Bilirubin, Biliverdin, Bister, Bistre, Cappagh-brown, Carmine, Carotene, Carotenoid, Carotin, Carotinoid, Chlorophyll, Chrome, Chromogen, Cobalt, Colcothar, Colour, Dye, Etiolin, Flavin(e), Fucoxanthin, Gamboge, Gossypol, Haem, H(a)emocyanin, H(a)emoglobin, Hem(e), Iodopsin, Lamp-black, Lithopone, Liverspot, Lutein, Luteolin, Madder, Melanin, Naevus, Nigrosine, Ochre, Opsin, Orpiment, Paris-green, Phthalocyanine, Phycoerythrin, Phycoxanthin, Phytochrome, Porphyrin, Pterin, Quercetin, Realgar, Retinene, Rhiboflavin, Rhodopsin, Sepia, Sienna, Sinopia, Smalt, Tapetum, Tempera, Terre-verte, Tincture, Umber, Urochrome, Verditer, Viridian, Xanthophyll, Xanthopterin(e)

Pike Assegai, Crag, Dory, Fogash, Gar(fish), Ged, Gisarme, Glaive, Hie, Holostei, Javelin, Lance, Luce, Partisan, Pickerel, Ravensbill, Scafell, Snoek, Spear, Speed, Spontoon, Vouge, Walleyed

Pile(d), **Piles**, **Piling** Agger, Amass, Atomic, Bing, Bomb, Camp-sheathing, Camp-shedding, Camp-sheeting, Camp-shot, Clamp, Cock, Column, Crowd, Deal, Down, Emerods, Farmers, Fender, Fig, Floccus, Fortune, Galvanic, Hair, Haycock, Heap, Hept, Historic, Hoard, Load, Lot, Marleys, Mass, Nap, Post, Pyre, Raft, Reactor, Ream(s), Rouleau, Screw, Shag, Sheet, > **STACK**, Starling, Stilt, Trichome, Upheap, Voltaic, Wealth, Windrow, Wodge

Pilgrim(age) Aske, Childe Harold, Expedition, Fatima, Hadj(i), Hajj(i), Loreto, Lourdes, Mecca, Palmer, Pardoner, Reeve, Scallop-shell, Shrine, Voyage, Yatra

Pill(s) Abortion, Ball, Beverley, Bitter, Bolus, Caplet, Capsule, Dex, Doll, Dose, Globule, Lob, Medication, Medicine, Number nine, Peel, Pellet, Pep, Pilula, Pilule, Placebo, Poison, Protoplasmal, Radio, Sleeping, Spansule, Tablet, Troche, Trochisk, Upper

Pillar(ed), **Pillars** Anta, Apostle, Atlantes, Baluster, Balustrade, Boaz, Canton, Caryatides, Cippus, Columel, Column, Eustyle, Gendarme, Hercules, Herm, Impost, Islam, Jachin, Lat, Man, Modiolus, Monolith, Newel, Obelisk, Pedestal, Peristyle, Pier, Post, Respond, Stalactite, Stalagmite, Stoop, Telamon, Trumeau

Pillow(case) Bear, Beer, Bere, Bolster, Cod, Cow, Cushion, Headrest, Hop, Lace, Pad, Pulvinar

Pilot Ace, Airman, Auto(matic), Aviator, Captain, > CONDUCT, Experimental, George, Govern, Guide, Hobbler, Lead, Lodesman, Palinure, Palinurus, Pitt, Prune, Shipman, Steer, Test, Tiphys, Trial, Usher, Wingman

Pimpernel Bastard, Bog, Scarlet, Water, Wincopipe, Wink-a-peep, Yellow

Pimple, Pimply Blackhead, Botch, Gooseflesh, Grog-blossom, Hickey, Horripilation, Papula, Plook, Plouk, Pock, Pustule, Quat, Rumblossom, Rum-bud, Spot, Uredinial, Wen, Whelk, Whitehead, Zit

Pin Bayonet, Belaying, Bolt, Brooch, Cotter, Curling, Dowel, Drawing, Drift, End, Fasten, Fid, Firing, Fix, Gam, Gudgeon, Hair, Hairgrip, Hob, Joggle, Kevel, King, Nail, Needle, Nog, Panel, Peg, Pintle, Pivot, Preen, Rivet, Rolling, Safety, Scarf, SCART, Scatter, Shear, Skewer, Skittle, Skiver, Spike, Spindle, Split, Staple, Stick, Stump, Swivel, Taper, Thole, Thumbtack, Tre(e)nail, U-bolt, Woolder, Wrest, Wrist

Pinball Pachinko

Pinch(ed) Arrest, Bit, Bone, Chack, Constrict, Cramp, Crisis, Emergency, Gaunt, Misappropriate, Nab, Nick, Nim, Nip, Peculate, Peel, Pilfer, Pocket, Pook(it), Prig, Pugil, Raft, Rob, Scrimp, Scrounge, Skimp, Smatch, Snabble, Snaffle, Sneak, Sneap, Sneeshing, Snuff, Squeeze, > STEAL, Swipe, Tate, Tweak, Twinge

Pine(s), Pining Arolla, Bristlecone, Celery, Cembra, Chile, Cluster, Cone, Conifer, Cypress, Droop, Dwine, Earn, Erne, Fret, Ground, Hone, Hoop, Huon, Jack, Japanese umbrella, Jeffrey, Kauri, Languish, Languor, Loblolly, Lodgepole, Long, Longleaf, Monkey-puzzle, Moon, Norfolk Island, Norway, Nut, Oregon, Parana, Picea, Pitch, Radiata, Red, Scotch, Scots, Screw, Softwood, Spruce, Starve, Stone, Sugar, Tree, Umbrella, Urman, Waste, White, Yearn

Pink Blush, Carolina, Castory, Clove, Colour, Coral, Dianthus, Dutch, Emperce, FT, Fuchsia, Gillyflower, Knock, Lake, Lychnis, Moss, Mushroom, Oyster, Peach-blow, Peak, Perce, Pierce, Pompadour, Pounce, Rose(ate), Ruddy, Salmon, Scallop, Shell, Shocking, Shrimp, Spigelia, Spit, Stab, Tiny

Pin-point Focus, Identify, Isolate, Localise

Pioneer Baird, Bandeirante, Blaze, Boone, Colonist, Emigrant, Explore, Fargo, Fleming, Frontiersman, Harbinger, Innovator, Lead, Marconi, Oecist, Pathfinder, Rochdale, Sandgroper, Settler, Spearhead, Trail-blazer, Trekker, Voortrekker, Wells

▶ **Pious** *see* PI

Pipe(s), Piper, Pipeline, Piping Aorta, Aulos, Balance, Barrel, Blub, Boatswain's, Bong, Briar, Bubble, Calabash, Call, Calumet, Chanter, Cheep, Cherrywood, Chillum, Churchwarden, Clay, Cob, Conduit, Corncob, Crane, Cutty, Down, Drain, Drill, Dry riser, Duct, Escape, Exhaust, Faucet, Feed, Fistula, Flue, Flute, Gage, Hawse, Hod, Hogger, Hooka(h), Hose, Hubble-bubble, Hydrant, Indian, Irish, Jet, Mains, Manifold, Meerschaum, Montre, Narghile, Narg(h)il(l)y, Nargile(h), Oat(en), Oboe, Organ, Ottavino, Pan, Peace, Pepper, Pibroch, Piccolo, Pied, Pitch, Pule, Quill, Rainwater, Recorder, Ree(d), Rise, Riser, Serpent, Service, Sewer, Siphon, Skirl, Sluice, Soil, Stack, Standpipe, Stopcock, Tail, Throttle, Tibia, Tootle, Trachea, Tremie, Tube, Tweet, U-bend, Union, Uptake, Vent, Volcanic, Waste, Water(-spout), Weasand, Whistle, Woodnote

Piracy, Pirate, Piratical Algerine, Barbarossa, Blackbeard, Boarder, Bootleg, Brigand, Buccaneer, Buccanier, Cateran, Condottier, Conrad, Corsair, Crib, Dampier, Fil(l)ibuster, Flint, Hijack, Hook, Kidd, Lift, Loot, Morgan, Picaro(on), Pickaroon, Plagiarise, Plunder, Rakish, Rover, Sallee-man, Sallee-rover, Sea-king, Sea-rat, Sea-robber, Silver, Smee, Steal, Teach, Viking, Water-rat, Water-thief

Pistol Air, Ancient, Automatic, Barker, Colt®, Dag, Derringer, Gat, > GUN, Hackbut, Horse, Luger®, Pepperbox, Petronel, Revolver, Rod, Shooter, Starter, Starting, Very, Water, Weapon

Pit(ted) Abyss, Alveolus, Antrum, Bottomless, Catch, Cave, Cesspool, Chasm, Cloaca, Colliery, Crater, Den, Depression, Depth, Dungmere, Ensile, Fossa, Fovea, Foxhole, Hangi, Heapstead, Hell, Hole, Hollow, Inferno, Inspection, Khud, Lacunose, Lime, Mark, Match, Measure, > **MINE**, Mosh, Orchestra, Parterre, Pip, Play, Pock-mark, Potato, Punctate, Putamen, Pyrene, Ravine, Scrobicule, Silo, Soakaway, Solar plexus, Stone, Sump, Tar, Tear, Trap, Trou-de-loup

Pitch(ed) Absolute, Asphalt, Atilt, Attune, Bitumen, Burgundy, Coal-tar, Concert, Crease, Diamond, Dive, Ela, Elect, Encamp, Erect, Establish, Fever, Fling, Fork, Ground, International, Intonation, Key, Labour, Length, Level, Lurch, Maltha, Mineral, Nets, Neume, Patter, Peck, Perfect, Philosophical, Piceous, Pight, Pin, Plong(e), Plunge, Pop, Resin, Rock, Ruff(e), Sales, Scend, Seel, Send, Shape, Sling, Slope, Soprarino, Spiel, Stoit, Tar, Tessitura, Tilt, Tone, Tonemic, Tonus, Tremolo, Tune, Vibrato, Wicket, Wood

Pith(y) Ambatch, Aphorism, Apo(ph)thegm, Core, Down, Essence, Gnomic, Hat-plant, Heart, Marrow, Medulla, Moxa, Nucleus, Rag, Succinct, Terse

Pitiless Flint-hearted, Hard, Ruthless

Pity, **Piteous**, **Pitiful** Ah, Alack, Alas, Commiseration, > **COMPASSION**, Mercy, Pathos, Rue, Ruth(ful), Seely, Shame, Sin, Sympathy

Pivot(al) Ax(i)le, Central, Focal, Fulcrum, Gooseneck, Gudgeon, Kingbolt, Revolve, Rotate, Slue, > **SWIVEL**, Trunnion, Turn, Wheel

Place Aim, Allocate, Berth, Bro, Decimal, Deploy, Deposit, Fix, Habitat, Hither, Howf, Identify, Impose, > **IN PLACE OF**, Install, Job, Joint, Juxtapose, Lay, Lieu, Locality, Locate, Locus, Pitch, Plat, Plaza, Point, Posit, > **POSITION**, Put, Realm, Region, Scene, Second, Set, Site, Situate, Situation, Spot, Stead, Sted(e), Stedd(e), Stratify, Town, Vendome

Plagiarise, **Plagiarist** Copy, Crib, Lift, Pirate, Steal

Plague (spot) Annoy, Bane, Bedevil, Black death, Boil, Bubonic, Burden, Curse, Dog, Dun, Goodyear, Goujeers, Harry, Infestation, Locusts, Lues, Murrain, Murran, Murrin, Murrion, Pest, Pester, Pox, Press, Scourge, Tease, Token, Torture, Try, Vex

Plain(s) Abraham, Artless, Ascetic, Au naturel, Bald, Bare, Blatant, Broad, Campagna, Candid, Ceará, Clear, Dowdy, Downright, Dry, Esdraelon, Evident, Explicit, Flat, Flood, Girondist, Gran Chaco, Great, Homely, Homespun, Inornate, Llano, Lombardy, Lowland, Manifest, Mare, Marathon, Mare, Obvious, Ocean of storms, Olympia, > **ORDINARY**, Outspoken, Overt, Packstaff, Pampa(s), Patent, Pikestaff, Prairie, Prose, Sailing, Salisbury, Savanna(h), Secco, Serengeti, Sharon, Simple, Sodom, Spoken, Staked, Steppe, Tableland, Thessaly, Tundra, Vega, Veldt, Visible, Walled

Plainchant Canto fermo

Plaint(ive) Complaint, Dirge, Lagrimoso, Lament, Melancholy, Sad, Whiny

Plan(ned), **Planner**, **Planning** Aim, American, Angle, Architect, Arrange, Blueprint, Brew, Budget, Care, Chart, Commission, Contingency, Contrive, Dalton, Dart, Deliberate, Delors, Design, Device, Devise, Diagram, Draft, Drawing, Elevation, Engineer, European, Family, Five-Year, Floor, Format, Galveston, Game, Ground, Hang, Idea, Idée, Instal(l)ment, Intent, Lay(out), Leicester, Map, Marshall, Master, Mastermind, Mean, Outline, Pattern, Pipe-dream, Plot, Ploy, Policy, Premeditate, Procedure, Programme, Project, Projet, Proposal, Rapacki, Scenario, Schedule, Scheme, Schlieffen, Spec(ification), Stratagem, Strategy, Subterfuge, System, Tactician, Wheeze

Plane Aero(dyne), Air, > **AIRCRAFT**, Airliner, Airship, Bandit, Boeing, Bomber, Bus, Camel, Canard, Cartesian, Chenar, Chinar, Comet, Concorde, Crate, Dakota, Datum, Delta-wing, Even, Facet, Fault, Fillester, Fillister, Flat, Glider, Gotha, Hurricane, Icosahedron, Icosohedra, Jack, Jet, Jointer, Jumbo, Level, MIG, Mirage,

Mosquito, Moth, Octagon, Platanus, Polygon, Rocket, Router, Shackleton, Shave, Smooth, Sole, Spitfire, Spokeshave, STOL, Surface, Sycamore, Taube, Thrust, Trainer, Tree, Trident, Viscount

Planet(s), Planetary Alphonsine, Ariel, Asteroid, Body, Cabiri, Ceres, Chiron, Constellation, Earth, Eros, Extrasolar, Georgian, Giant, Hyleg, Inferior, Inner, Jovian, Jupiter, Major, Mars, Mercury, Minor, Moon, Neptune, Pluto, Primary, Psyche, Quartile, Red, Satellitium, Saturn, Sphere, Starry, Sun, Superior, Terrestrial, Uranus, Venus, Vista, Vulcan, World

Plank Board, Chess, Duckboard, Garboard, Plonk, Sarking, Slab, Spirketting, Straik, Strake, Stringer, Wood

Plant(s), Plant part Annual, Anther, Bed, Biennial, Biota, Cultigen, Cultivar, Dibble, Ecad, Embed, Endogen, Enrace, Epiphyte, Establish, Factory, Fix, Growth, Herbarium, Insert, Instil, Inter, Labiate, Land, Lathe, Machinery, Ornamental, Phloem, Sere, Shrub, Sow, Succulent, Tree, Works

Plantation Arboretum, Bosket, Bosquet, Estate, Grove, Hacienda, Pen, Pinetum, Ranch, Tara, Vineyard

Plaster(ed) Bandage, Blister, Blotto, Butterfly clip, Cake, Cataplasm, Clam, Clatch, Compo, Court, Daub, Diachylon, Diachylum, Drunk, Emplastrum, Fresco, Gesso, Grout, Gypsum, Intonaco, Leep, Lit, Mud, Mustard, Oiled, Parge(t), Porous, Poultice, Render, Roughcast, Scratch-coat, Screed, Secco, Shellac, Sinapism, Smalm, Smarm, Smear, Sowsed, Staff, Sticking, Stookie, Stucco, Teer

Plastic Ductile, Fictile, Laminate, Loid, Pliant, Polythene, PVC, Vinyl, Wet-look, Yielding

▷ **Plastic** *may indicate* an anagram

Plate(s), Plated, Platelet, Plating Acierage, Ailette, Angle, Anode, Armadillo, Armour, Ashet, Baffle, Baleen, Batten, Brass, Butt, Chape, Charger, Chrome, Coat, Communion, Copper, Ctene, Deadman, Denture, Diaphragm, Disc, Dish, Echo, Electro, Electrotype, Elytron, Elytrum, Enamel, Escutcheon, Face, Fashion, Fine, Fish, Flatware, Foil, Frog, Gold, Graal, Ground, Half, Horseshoe, Hot, Illustration, L, Lame, Lamina, Lanx, Latten, Licence, Mascle, Mazarine, Nail, Nef, Neural, Nickel, Number, Paten, Patina, Petri, Phototype, Planometer, Plaque, Plastron, Platter, Poitrel, Print, Quarter, Race, Registration, Rove, Salamander, Scale, Screw, Scrim, Scutcheon, Scute, Scutum, Selling, Sheffield, Shield, Sieve, Silver, Slab, Soup, Spacer, Spoiler, Steel, Stencil, Stereo(type), Sternite, Surface, Swash, T, Tablet, Tace, Tasse(l), Tectonic, Tergite, Terne, Theoretical, Tin(ware), Torsel, Touch, Trade, Trencher, Trophy, Tsuba, Vane, Vanity, Vassail, Vessel, Wall, Water, Web, Wet, Whirtle, Whole, Wrap(a)round, Zincograph

Plateau Altiplano, Deccan, Fjeld, Highland, Highveld, Horst, Kar(r)oo, La Mancha, Langres, Mat(t)o Grosso, Mesa Verde, Meseta, Nilgiris, Ozark, Paramo, Piedmont, Puna, Tableland

Platform Accommodation, Bandstand, Base, Bema, Catwalk, Crane, Crow's nest, Dais, Deck, Dolly, Drilling, Estrade, Exedra, Exhedra, Flake, Footpace, Footplate, Foretop, Gangplank, Gantry, Gravity, Hustings, Landing stage, Machan, Oil, Pad, Paint-bridge, Pallet, Perron, Plank, Podium, Predella, Production, Programme, Pulpit, Raft, Rig, Rostrum, Round-top, Scaffold, Shoe, Skidway, Soapbox, Space, Sponson, > STAGE, Stand, Stoep, Tee, Terminal, Ticket, Top, Tribunal, Tribune, Turntable, Wharf

Play(ing) Accompany, Active, Amusement, Antic, Caper, Charm, Clearance, Curtain-raiser, Dandle, Drama, Echo, Endgame, Escapade, Everyman, Extended, Fair, Finesse, Frisk, Frolic, Fun, Gamble, Gambol, Game, Holiday, Inside, Interlude, Jam, Jape, Jest, Jeu, Lake, Latitude, Lear, Leeway, Licence, Long, Mask, Masque, Medal, Melodrama, Miracle, Morality, Mummers, Mysteries, Nativity, Nurse, Oberammergau, Parallel, Passion, Perform, Personate, Portray, Prank, Pretend, Recreation, Represent, Riff, Rollick, Romp, Room, Rope, RUR, Saw, Sketch,

Sport, Stage, Strain, Stroke, Strum, Tolerance, Tonguing, Toy, Tragedy, Trifle, Twiddle, Vamp, Word

▷ **Play** *may indicate* an anagram

Player(s) Actor, Athlete, Back, Black, Brass, Bugler, Busker, Cast, CD, Centre, Colt, Contestant, DVD, E, East, ENSA, Equity, Fiddle, Flanker, Fullback, Ghetto-blaster, Goalie, Half, Half-back, Half-forward, Hooker, Infielder, It, Juke-box, Kest, Linebacker, Lineman, Lion, Lock, Longstop, Lutanist, Lutenist, Man, Midfield, Mid-on, Mime, Musician, Musician(er), N, North, Ombre, Onside, Participant, Pianola®, Pitcher, Pocket, Pone, Pro, Prop, Quarterback, Record, Rover, S, Scrape, Scratch, Scrum half, Seed, Shamateur, Shortstop, Side, South, Stand-off, Stand-off half, Stereo, Striker, Strings, Strolling, Super, Sweeper, Team, Thespian, Tight end, Troubador, Troupe, Upright, Utility, Virtuosi, W, Walkman®, West, White, Wing, Winger, Wingman

Playful Arch, Coy, Frisky, Humorous, Kittenish, Ludic, Merry, Piacevole, Scherzo, Skittish, Sportive

Playwright Aeschylus, Albee, Arden, Ayckbourn, Barrie, Barry, Beaumarchais, Beaumont, Beckett, Behan, Bellow, Bennett, Besier, Bolt, Brecht, Chekhov, Congreve, Corneille, Coward, Dekker, Delaney, Dramaturge, Dramaturgist, Drinkwater, Euripides, Fletcher, Fry, Gems, Genet, Goldoni, Gorky, Harwood, Hay, Ibsen, Jonson, Marlowe, Massinger, Menander, Miller, Molière, Mortimer, O'Casey, Odets, O'Neill, Orton, Osborne, Pinero, Pinter, Pirandello, Priestley, Racine, Rattigan, Scriptwriter, Shaw, Sheridan, Sherry, Simpson, Sophocles, Stoppard, Storey, Strindberg, Synge, Tate, Terence, Thespis, Travers, Vanbrugh, Webster, Wesker, Wilde

Plea Appeal, Claim, Defence, Entreaty, Excuse, Exoration, Orison, Placitum, Prayer, Rebuttal, Rebutter, Rogation, Suit

Plead(er) Answer, Argue, Beg, Entreat, Intercede, Litigate, Moot, Vakeel, Vakil

Please(d), Pleasant, Pleasing, Pleasure(-seeker) Aggrate, Agreeable, Alcina, Algolagnia, Amene, Amuse, Arride, Benign, Bitte, Braw, Cheerful, Chuffed, Comely, Comfort, Content, Cute, Delectation, Delice, Delight, Do, Euphonic, Fair, Felicitous, Fit, Flatter, Fun, Genial, Glad, Gladness, Gratify, Hedonism, Jammy, Joy, Kama, Kindly, Lepid, List, Oblige, Piacevole, Primrose path, Prithee, Prythee, Queme, Satisfy, Suit, Tasty, Tickle, Tickle pink, Treat, Vanity, Voluptuary, Wally, Will, Winsome, Wrapped, Xanadu List

Pleat Accordion, Box, Crimp, Fold, French, Frill, Goffer, Gusset, Kick, Knife, Plait, Pranck(e), Prank, Sunburst, Sunray

Pledge Affidavit, Arles, Band, Betroth, Bond, Borrow, Bottomry, Dedicate, Deposit, Earnest(-penny), Engage, Fine, Gage, Guarantee, Hock, Hypothecate, Impignorate, Mortgage, Oath, Pass, Pawn, Pignerate, Pignorate, Plight, Propine, Sacrament, Security, Stake, Surety, Teetotal, Toast, Troth, Undertake, Vow, Wad, Wed

Plentiful, Plenty Abounding, Abundance, Abundant, Ample, Bags, Copious, Copy, Easy, Excess, Foison, Fouth, Ful(l)ness, Fushion, Galore, Goshen, Lashings, Lots, Oodles, Pleroma, Profusion, Quantity, Riches, Rife, Routh, Rowth, Scouth, Scowth, Slue, Sonce, Sonse, Umpteen

▶ **Pliers** *see* PLY

Plimsoll(s) Dap, Gutty, Gym-shoe, Line, Mutton-dummies, Sandshoe, Tacky

Plot(s) Allotment, Babington, Bed, Brew, Carpet, Chart, Cliché, Connive, Conspiracy, Conspire, Covin, Covyne, Engineer, Erf, Erven, Frame-up, Graph, Gunpowder, Imbroglio, Intrigue, Locus, Lot, Machination, Map, Meal-tub, Odograph, Pack, Patch, Plan, Plat, Rye-house, Scenario, > SCHEME, Sect(ion), Shot, Site, Story, Taluk, Terf, Turf, Web

Plough(man), Ploughed, Ploughing Arable, Ard, Arval, Big Dipper, Breaker,

Bull tongue, Chamfer, Charles's wain, Contour, Dipper, Disc, Drall, Drill, Ear, Earth-board, Ere, Fail, Fallow, Farmer, Feer, Flunk, Gadsman, Gang, Great bear, Harrow, Lister, Middlebreaker, Middlebuster, Mouldboard, Piers, Pip, Push, Rafter, Rib, Ridger, Rive, Rotary, Rove, Sand, Scooter, Septentrion(e)s, Sill, Sow, Stump-jump, Swing, Till(er), Trench, Triones, Wheel

Ploy Brinkmanship, Dodge, Manoeuvre, Stratagem, Strike, Tactic, Wile

Pluck(ing), Plucky Avulse, Bare, Carphology, Cock, Courage, Deplume, Epilate, Evulse, Floccillation, Gallus, Game, > **GRIT**, Guts, Loot, Mettle, Pick, Pinch, Pip, Pizzicato, Plectron, Plectrum, Ploat, Plot, Plunk, Pook(it), Pouk(it), Pull, Race, Scrappy, Snatch, Spin, Spirit, Spunk, Summon, Tug, Twang, Tweak, Tweeze, Yank

Plug Ad, Banana, Block, Bung, Caulk, Chew, Commercial, Dam, DIN, Dook, Dossil, Dottle, Douk, Fipple, Fother, Gang, Glow, Go-devil, Hype, Jack, Lam, Operculum, Pessary, Phono, Prod, Promote, Publicity, Ram, Rawlplug®, Recommendation, Safety, Spark(ing), Spile, Spiling, Stop(per), Stopple, Strobili, Suppository, Tampion, Tap, Tent, Tompion, Vent, Wage, Wander, Wedge

Plum Bullace, Cherry, Choice, Damson, Gage, Greengage, Ground, Japanese, Kaki, Mammee-sapota, Marmalade, Maroon, Mirabelle, Mussel, Myrobalan, Naseberry, Persimmon, Proin(e), Pruin(e), Prune, Quetsch, Raisin, Sapodilla, Sebesten, Victoria

Plumage, Plume Aigrette, Crest, Egret, Feather, Hackle, Panache, Preen, Ptilosis, Quill

Plumb(er) Bullet, Dredge, Fathom, Lead(sman), Perpendicular, Plummet, Sheer, Sound, Test, True, Vertical

Plump(er) Bold, Bonnie, Bonny, Buxom, Choose, Chubbed, Chubby, Cubby, Dumpy, Embonpoint, Endomorph, Fat, Fleshy, Flop, Fubsy, Full, Lie, Matronly, Opt, Plank, Plonk, Plop, Podgy, Portly, Roll-about, Rolypoly, Rotund, Round, Rubenesque, Sonsie, Sonsy, Soss, Souse, Squab, Squat, Stout, Swap, Swop, Tidy, Well-fed

Plunder(er) Berob, Booty, Depredate, Despoil, Devastate, Escheat, Fleece, Forage, Freebooter, Gut, Harry, Haul, Herriment, Herryment, Hership, Loot, Maraud, Peel, Pill(age), Privateer, > **RANSACK**, Rape, Rapparee, Ravine, Reave, Reif, Reive, Rieve, Rifle, Rob, Sack, Scoff, Shave, Skoff, Spoil(s), Spoliate, Sprechery, Spuilzie, Spuly(i)e, Spulzie, Swag

Plunge(r) Demerge, Dive, Douse, Dowse, Duck, Enew, Immerge, Immerse, La(u)nch, Nose-dive, Plummet, Raker, Send, Sink, Souse, Swoop, Thrust

Ply, Plier(s) Bend, Birl, Cab, Exercise, Exert, Gondoliers, Importune, Layer, Practise, Run, Trade, Wield

▷ **Plying** *may indicate* an anagram

Plymouth Brethren Darbyite

PM Addington, Afternoon, Attlee, Autopsy, Bute, Cabinet-maker, Disraeli, Gladstone, Major, Melbourne, Peel, Pitt, Portland, Premier, > **PRIME MINISTER**, Salisbury, Taoiseach

Pocket Air, Appropriate, Bag, Bin, Cavity, Cly, Cup, Enclave, Fob, Glom, Hideaway, Hip, Jenny, Misappropriate, Patch, Placket, Plaid-neuk, Pot, Pouch, Purloin, Purse, Sac, Sky, Slash, Sling, Slit, Steal, Take, Watch

Pod(s) Babul, Bean, Belly, Carob, Chilli, Dividivi, Gumbo, Lomentum, Neb-neb, Okra, Pipi, Pregnant, Siliqua, Tamarind, Vanilla

Poem(s), Poetry Acmeism, Acrostic, Anthology, Ballad(e), Dit(t), Dithyramb, Doggerel, Elegy, Epic(ede), Haiku, Heroic, Hokku, Lay, Limerick, Mahabharata(m), Mahabharatum, Metre, Mock-heroic, Ode, Pastoral, Poesy, Prelude, Prose, Punk, Quatorzain, Quatrain, Ramayama, Rhapsody, Rig-Veda, Rime, Rondeau, Song, Sonnet, Stanza, Tetrastich, Title, Verse

Poet(s) Bard(ling), Cumberland, Cyclic, Elegist, Georgian, Iambist, Imagist,

Laureate, Layman, Lyrist, Maker, Meistersinger, Metaphysical, Metrist, Minnesinger, Minstrel, Mistral, Monodist, Odist, Parnassian, PL, Pleiade, Poetaster, Rhymer, Rhymester, Rhymist, Rymer, Scald, Scop, Skald, Smart, Sonneteer, Spasmodic, Thespis, Tragic, Trench, Troubadour, Trouvère, Trouveur

▶ **Poetry** *see* POEM

Po-faced Stolid

Point(ed), Pointer, Points Ace, Aim, Antler, Apex, Apogee, Appui, Bar, Barb, Boiling, Break(ing), Brownie, Cape, Cardinal, Cash, Centre, Choke, Clou, Clue, Colon, Comma, Cone, Conic, Corner, Cover, Crisis, Crux, Curie, Cursor, Cusp, Cuss, Decimal, Degree, Detail, Direct, Dot, E, Epee, Fang, Feature, Fitch(e), Focal, Focus, Foreland, Freezing, Fulcrum, Germane, Gist, Gnomon, Hastate, Head, Hinge, Index, Indicate, Indicator, Ippon, Jester, Knub, Lance, Lead, Limit, Lizard, Locate, Locus, Mark, Melting, Metacentre, Moot, N, Nail, Neb, Needle, Ness, Nib, Node, Now, Nub, Obelisk, Opinion, Ord, Particle, Peak, Perigee, Pin, Pinnacle, Place, Power, Pressure, Prong, Prow, Punctilio, Punctual, Ras, S, Saturation, Scribe, Seg(h)ol, Set, Shaft, Show, Shy, Silly, Socket, Sore, Spearhead, Spicate, Spick, Spike, Stage, Sticking, Stiletto, Sting, Strong, Sum, Talking, Taper, Technicality, Tine, > TIP, Tongue, Trig, Triple, Turning, Use, Vane, Vantage, Verge, Verse, Vertex, Vowel, W

Pointless Blunt, Curtana, Flat, Futile, Inane, Inutile, Muticous, Otiose, Stupid, Vain

Poison(er), Poisoning, Poisonous Abron, Aconite, Acrolein, Adamsite, Aflatoxin, Aldrin, Amanita, Antiar, Apocynum, Aqua-tofana, Arsenic, Aspic, Atropia, Atropin(e), Bane, Barbasco, Belladonna, Boletus, Borgia, Botulism, Brom(in)ism, Brucine, Bufotalin, Cacodyl, Cadaverine, Calabar-bean, Cannabin, Cicuta, Colchicine, Coniine, Contact, Cowbane, Coyotillo, Curare, Curari, Cyanide, Cyanuret, Datura, Daturine, Deadly nightshade, Digitalin, Dioxin, Dumbcane, Durban, Echidnine, Embolism, Emetin(e), Envenom, Ergotise, Fluorosis, Flybane, Flypaper, Food, Formaldehyde, Gelsemin(in)e, Gila, Gossypol, Hebenon, Hebona, Hemlock, Henbane, Hydragyrism, Hydrastine, Hyoscyamine, Iodism, Lead, Lewisite, Limberneck, Lindane, Lobeline, Locoweed, Malevolent, Manchineel, Mandragora, Mephitic, Mezereon, Miasma, Mineral, Monkshood, Muscarine, Mycotoxin, Nerve gas, Neurine, Neurotoxin, Neutron, Nicotine, Noogoora burr, Noxious, Obeism, Ouabain, Ourali, Ourari, Paraquat®, Paris green, Phallin, Phalloidin, Phosphorism, Picrotoxin, Pilocarpine, Plumbism, Ptomaine, Py(a)emia, Raphania, Ratsbane, Rot, Safrole, Salicylism, Samnitis, Santonin, Sapraemia, Sarin, Sassy wood, Saturnism, Saxitoxin, Septic(aemia), Solanine, Solpuga, Soman, Stibine, Stibium, Stonefish, Strophanthus, Strychnine, Sugar of lead, Surinam, Systemic, Tanghin, Tanghinin, Tetro(do)toxin, Thebaine, Thorn-apple, Timbo, Toxaphene, Toxic, Toxicology, Toxicosis, Toxin, Toxoid, Trembles, Tropine, Tutu, Upas, Urali, Uroshiol, Venefic, Venin, Venom(ous), Veratridine, Veratrin(e), Viperous, Virose, Virous, Virulent, Wabain, Warfarin, Wolfsbane, Woorali, Woorara, Wourali, Yohimbine

Poke, Poky Bonnet, Broddle, Garget, Itchweed, Jab, Meddle, Mock, Nousle, Nudge, Nuzzle, Ombu, Peg, Pick, Pote, Pouch, Powter, > PRISON, Prog, Proke, Punch, Root(le), Rout, Rowt, Stab, Thrust

Polar, Pole(s), Poler Anode, Antarctic, Arctic, Boom, Bowsprit, Caber, Celestial, Crossbar, Extremity, Fizgy, Flagstaff, Galactic, Geomagnetic, Lug, Magnetic, Mast, May, N, Nadir, Negative, Nib, North, Po, Polack, Positive, Punt, Quant, Quarterstaff, Range, Rood, S, Shaft, Slav, South, Spar, Sprit, Staff, Starosta, Stilt, Sting, Telegraph, Terrestrial, Topmast, Totem, Zenith

▷ **Polar** *may indicate* with a pole

Police(man), Policewoman Bluebottle, Bobby, Busy, Catchpole, CID, Constable, Cop(per), Detective, Dibble, Europol, Flatfoot, Flying Squad, Force,

Fuzz, Garda, Gendarme, Gestapo, G-man, Guard, Inspector, Interpol, Keystone, Kitchen, Mata-mata, Met(ropolitan), Military, Morse, Mountie, MP, Officer, Patrolman, PC, Peeler, Porn squad, Provincial, Redcap, Riot, Robert, Rozzer, RUC, Secret, Special, State trooper, Super, Sweeney, Texas Rangers, The Bill, The Law, Vice squad, Vigilante, Zabtieh

Police station Copshop, Lock-up, Watchhouse

Policy Assurance, Ballon d'essai, CAP, Comprehensive, Course, Demesne, Endowment, Expedience, Insurance, Knock for knock, Laisser-faire, Lend-lease, Line, Method, Open(-sky), Plank, Platform, Pork-barrel, Practice, Programme, Revanchism, Scorched earth, Stop-go, Tack, Tactics, Ticket

Polish(ed), Polisher Beeswax, Black, Blacklead, Bob, Buff, Bull, Burnish, Chamois, Complaisant, Edit, Elaborate, Elegant, Emery, Enamel, Finish, French, Furbish, Gentlemanly, Glass, Gloss, Heelball, Hone, Inland, Lap, Lustre, Nail, Perfect, Planish, Polite, Refinement, Refurbish, Rottenstone, Rub, Sand, Sandblast, Sandpaper, Sejm, Sheen, Shellac, Shine, Slick, Supercalender, Urbane, Veneer, Wax

Polite Civil, Courteous, Genteel, Grandisonian, Mannered, Suave, Urbane, Well-bred

Politic(al), Politics Apparat, Body, Chartism, Civic, Diplomacy, Discreet, Expedient, Falange, Fascism, Gesture, Leftism, Party, Poujadism, Power, Practical, Public, Radicalism, Rightism, State, Statecraft, Tactful, Wise

Politician(s) Bright, Carpet-bagger, Catiline, Chesterfield, Congressman, Demagogue, Demo(crat), Diehard, Disraeli, Eden, Evita, Green, Incumbent, Independent, Ins, Isolationist, Laski, Left, Legislator, Liberal, Log-roller, MEP, Minister, Moderate, MP, Parliamentarian, Parnell, Politico, Polly, Puppet, Rad, Rep, Senator, Socialist, Statesman, Statist, Tadpole, Taper, TD, Tory, Trotsky, Unionist, Veep, Warhorse, Whig, Wilberforce

Poll(ing) Ballot, Bean, Canvass, Count, Cut, Deed, Dod, Election, Exit, Gallup, Head, Humlie, Hummel, MORI, Nestor, Not(t), Opinion, Parrot, Pineapple, Pow, Scrutiny, Straw, Votes

▷ **Poll** *may indicate* a first letter

Pollen, Pollinate(d), Pollination Anemophilous, Beebread, Dust, Errhine, Farina, Fertilised, Witch-meal, Xenia

Pollute(d), Pollutant, Pollution Adulterate, Contaminate, Defile, Dirty, File, Foul, Impure, Infect, Miasma, Nox, Rainout, Soil, Soilure, Stain, Sully, Taint, Violate

Pomp(ous) Big, Bombastic, Budge, Ceremonial, Display, Dogberry, Euphuistic, Fustian, Grandiloquent, Grandiose, Heavy, Highfalutin(g), High-flown, High-muck-a-muck, High-sounding, Hogen-mogen, Inflated, Orotund, Ostentatious, Pageantry, Parade, Pretentious, Solemn, Splendour, Starchy, State, Stilted, Stuffy, Turgid

Pond(s) Dew, Dub, Hampstead, Lakelet, Pool, Pound, Puddle, Slough, Stank, Stew, Tank, Turlough, Vivarium, Viver

Ponder(ous) Brood, Cogitate, Contemplate, Deliberate, Heavy, Laboured, Mull, Muse, Perpend, Poise, Pore, Reflect, Ruminate, > **THINK**, Vise, Volve, Weight(y), Wonder

Pontiff, Pontifical, Pontificate Aaron, Aaronic, Antipope, Dogmatise, Papal

Pontoon Blackjack, Bridge, Caisson, Chess, Game, Vingt-et-un

Pony Canuck, Cayuse, Cow, Dales, Dartmoor, Eriskay, Exmoor, Fell, Garran, Garron, Gen(n)et, GG, Griffin, Griffon, Gryfon, Gryphon, Jennet, Jerusalem, Mustang, New Forest, One-trick, Pit, Polo, Pownie, Sable Island, Shanks', Sheltie, Shetland, Show, Tangun, Tat(too), Timor, Welsh, Welsh mountain, Western Isles

Pool Backwater, Bank, Bethesda, Billabong, Bogey hole, Cenote, Cess, Collect,

Combine, Dub, Dump, Flash, Flow, Jackpot, Kitty, Lido, Lin(n), Meer, Mere, Mickery, Mikvah, Mikveh, Moon, Natatorium, Piscina, Piscine, Plash, Plesh, Plunge, > **POND**, Reserve, Snooker, Spa, Stank, Sump, Tank, Tarn, Wave

Poor(ly) Bad, Bare, Base, Bijwoner, Breadline, Buckeen, Bywoner, Catchpenny, Conch, Cronk, Destitute, Gritty, Hard-up, Have-nots, Hopeless, Humble, Hungry, Ill(-off), Impecunious, Indigent, Lazarus, Lean, Low, Low-downer, Meagre, Mean, Needy, Obolary, Pauper, Peaky, Poxy, Roinish, Rop(e)y, Roynish, Sad, Scrub, Shabby, Shitty, Sober, Sorry, Sub, Thin, Third-rate, Trashy, Undeserving, Unwell

▷ **Poor** *may indicate* an anagram

Pop (off), Popper, Popping Bang, Brit, Burst, Cloop, Crease, Die, Father, Fr, Gingerbeer, Hip-hop, Hock, Insert, Lumber, Mineral, Nip, Pater, Pawn, Pledge, Population, Press-stud, Punk, Sherbet, Soda, Splutter, Weasel

▷ **Pop** *may indicate* an anagram

Pope(s) Adrian, Alexander, Atticus, Boniface, Clement, Dunciad, Eminence, Fish, Great Schism, Gregory, Hildebrand, Holiness, Innocent, Joan, Leo, Papa, Pius, Pontiff, Ruff(e), Schism, Theocrat, Tiara, Urban, Vatican, Vicar of Christ

Poppy Argemone, Bloodroot, California, Chicalote, Coquelicot, Corn, Diacodin, Eschscholtzia, Flanders, Horned, Iceland, Matilija, Mawseed, Opium, Papaver, Ponceau, Prickly, Puccoon, Rhoeadales, Shirley, Tall, Welsh

Popular(ity) Common, Demotic, General, Heyday, Hit, In, Laic, Lay, Mass, Plebeian, Prevalent, Public, Successful, Tipped, Trendy, Vogue

Population, Populace Catchment, Census, Demography, Inhabitants, Malthusian, Mass, Mob, > **PEOPLE**, Public, Universe

Porcelain Arita, Artificial, Bamboo, Celadon, Chelsea, China, Coalport, Crackle(ware), Crown Derby, Dresden, Eggshell, Famille, Famille jaune, Famille noir, Famille rose, Famille verte, Goss, Hard-paste, Hizen, Imari, Jasper, Jasper(ware), Limoges, Lithophane, Meissen, Minton, Parian, Sèvres, Softpaste, Spode, Sung

Pore Browse, Hole, Hydrathode, Lenticel, Muse, Ostium, Outlet, Ponder, Stoma, Study

Pork Bacon, Boar, Brawn, Chap, Crackling, Flitch, Griskin, Ham, Pancetta, Scrapple, Spare-rib

Porridge Berry, Bird, Brochan, Brose, Busera, Crowdie, Drammach, Drammock, Gaol, Grits, Grouts, Gruel, Hominy, Kasha, Mahewu, Mealie pap, Oaten, Oatmeal, Parritch, Pease-brose, Polenta, Pottage, Praiseach, Sadza, Samp, Sentence, Skilly, Stirabout, Stretch, Sup(p)awn, Time, Ugali

Port(s) Beeswing, Carry, Cinque, Entrepot, Free, Gate, Geropiga, > **HARBOUR**, Haven, Hithe, Hythe, Larboard, Left, Manner, Mien, Parallel, Tawny, Treaty, Wine

Porter Ale, Bearer, Bellboy, Bummaree, Caddie, Caddy, Cole, Concierge, Coolie, Door-keeper, Doorman, Dvornik, Entire, Hamaul, Ham(m)al, Humper, Janitor, October, Ostiary, Red-cap, Stout

Portion Ann(at), Bit, Deal, Distribute, Dole, Dose, Dotation, Fragment, Helping, Heritage, Hunk, Jointure, Lot, Modicum, Nutlet, Ounce, > **PART**, Piece, Ratio, Scantle, Scantling, Section, Segment, Serving, Share, Size, Slice, Something, Tait, Taste, Tate, Tittle, Tranche, Wodge

Portrait(ist) Depiction, Drawing, Eikon, Icon, Ikon, Image, Kit-cat, Lely, Likeness, Painting, Retraitt, Retrate, Sketch, Vignette

Portray(al) Caricature, Depict, Describe, Feature, Image, Limn, Paint, Render, Represent, > **SHOW**

Pose(r), Poseur Aesthete, Affect(ation), Arabesque, Asana, Ask, Contrapposto, Drape, Lotus, Masquerade, Model, Place, Plastique, Posture, Pretend, Problem, Propound, Pseud, Sit, Stance, Sticker, Tickler

Position Asana, Attitude, Bearing(s), Close, Codille, Delta, Emplacement, Enfilade, False, Fixure, F(o)etal, Foothold, Fowler's, Grade, Instal, Lay, Lie, Location, Locus, Lodg(e)ment, Lotus, Missionary, Mudra, Office, Open, Pass, Peak, Place, Plant, Point, Pole, Post, Put, Recumbent, Root, Seat, Set(ting), Sextile, Sims, Site, Situ, Situs, Stance, Standing, Standpoint, Station, Status, Strategic, Syzygy, Tagmeme, Thesis, Tierce, Trendelenburg's, Viewpoint

Positive, Positivist Absolute, Anode, Assertive, Categorical, > CERTAIN, Comte, Definite, Emphatic, Plus, Print, Sure, Thetic, Upbeat, Yang, Yes

Possess(ed), Possession(s), Possessive Adverse, Apostrophe, Asset, Aver, Bedevil, Belonging(s), Demonic, Driven, Energumen, Estate, Have, Haveour, Haviour, Heirloom, His, Hogging, Know, Lares (et) penates, Mad, Obsessed, Occupation, > OWN, Sasine, Seisin, Sprechery, Substance, Tenancy, Usucap(t)ion, Vacant, Worth

Possible, Possibility, Possibly Able, Contingency, Feasible, Likely, Maybe, Mayhap, Peradventure, Perchance, Perhaps, Posse, Potential, Prospect, Resort, Viable, Will

▷ **Possibly** *may indicate* an anagram

Post(s), Postage Affix, After, Assign, Bitt, Bollard, Command, Correspondence, Delivery, Excess, Finger, First, Flagpole, Graded, Gradient, Guardhose, Hitching, Jamb, Joggle, King, Last, Listening, Log, Mail, Mast, Newel, Observation, Outstation, Pale, Paling, Parcel, Pendant, Penny, Picket, Pile, Piling, Piquet, Placard, Place, Plant, Plum, Pole, Position, Puncheon, Pylon, Quoin, Registered, Remit, RM, Seat, Send, Snubbing, Staff, Staging, Stake, Starting, Station, Term(inal), Tool, Trading, Upright, Vacancy, Waymark, Winning

Postman, Postmaster, Postwoman Carrier, Courier, Emily, Hill, Messenger, Nasby, Pat, Portionist, Sorter

Post-modern Po-mo

Postpone(ment) Adjourn, Contango, Defer, Delay, Frist, Hold over, Long-finger, Moratorium, Mothball, Pigeon-hole, Postdate, Prorogue, Reprieve, Respite, Shelve, Stay, Suspend, Withhold

Posture(r), Posturing Affectation, Asana, Attitude, Decubitus, Deportment, Mudra, Pose, Pretence, Site, Stance, Vorlage

Pot(s), Potting, Potty Bankroll, Basil, Belly, Cafetière, Cannabis, Casserole, Ca(u)ldron, Ceramic, Chamber, Chanty, Chimney, Cocotte, Crewe, Crock(ery), Crucible, Cruse(t), Delf(t), Dixie, Ewer, Flesh, Gage, Grass, Hash(ish), Helmet, Hemp, In off, Kettle, Kitty, Lobster, Lota(h), Maiolica, Majolica, Marijuana, Marmite, Melting, Ming, Olla, Olpe, Pan, Pat, Pipkin, Planter, Pocket, Poot, > POTTERY, Pout, Prize, Samovar, Shoot, Skeet, Skillet, Steamer, Stomach, Tea, Test, Throw, Trivet, Tureen, Urn

Potato(es) Batata, Chat, Couch, Datura, Duchesse, Early, Fluke, Hashbrowns, Hog, Hole, Hot, Irish, Jersey, Kidney, Kumara, Lyonnaise, Mash, Murphy, Parmentier, Peel-and-eat, Pratie, Praty, Roesti, Rumbledethump(s), Seed, Solanum, Stovies, Sweet, Tatie, Tattie, Teddy, Tuber, Ware, White, Yam

Potential(ly) Action, Capacity, Making(s), Manqué, Possible, Promise, Resting, Scope, Viable

▷ **Potentially** *may indicate* an anagram

Potter Cue, Dabbity, Dacker, Daidle, Daiker, Dibble, Dilly-dally, Dodder, Etruscan, Fettle, Fiddle, Footer, Footle, Fouter, Gamesmanship, Idle, Mess, Minton, Muck, Niggle, One-upmanship, Plouter, Plowter, Spode, Thrower, Tiddle, Tink(er), Troke, Truck, Wedgwood

▷ **Potter** *may indicate* a snooker-player

Pottery Agatewear, Bank, Basalt, Bisque, Celadon, Ceramet, Ceramic, China, Creamware, Crock, Crouch-ware, Dabbity, Delf(t), Earthenware, Encaustic,

Etruria, Faience, Flatback, Gombroon, Granitewear, Hollowware, Jomon, Lustreware, Maiolica, Majolica, Ming, Pebbleware, Raku, Red-figured, Satsuma, Scroddled, Sgraffito, Slab, Slipware, Smalto, Spode, Spongeware, Stoneware, Studio, Sung, Terra sigillata, Ware, Wedgwood®, Wemyss, Whieldon

Pouch(ed) Bag, Brood, Bum-bag, Bursa, Caecum, Cheek, Cisterna, Codpiece, Diverticulum, Fanny pack, Gill, Jockstrap, Marsupial, Poke, Purse, Sac, Scrip, Scrotum, Spleuchan, Sporran

Pound(er) Ache, As, Bar, Bash, Batter, Beat, Bombard, Bradbury, Bray, Broadpiece, Bruise, Contund, Coop, Drub, Embale, Enclosure, Ezra, Fold, Green, Hammer, Hatter, Imagist, Intern, Iron man, Jail, Kiddle, Kidel, Kin, Knevell, L, Lam, Lb, Lock, Mash, Nevel, Nicker, Oncer, One-er, Oner, Pale, Pen, Penfold, Pestle, Pin, Pindar, Pinfold, Powder, Pulverise, Pun, Quop, Rint, Smacker, Sov(ereign), Stamp, Strum, Thump, Tower, Weight

Pour Birl(e), Bucket, Cascade, Circumfuse, Decant, Diffuse, Flood, Flow, Jaw, Jirble, Libate, Rain, Seil, Shed, Sile, Skink, Spew, Stream, Teem, Turn, Vent, Weep, Well

Poverty Beggary, Dearth, Deprivation, Illth, Indigence, > **LACK**, Need, Penury, Poortith, Squalor, Want

Powder(ed), Powdery Alumina, Baking, Boracic, Calamine, Chalk, Cosmetic, Culm, Curry, Custard, Cuttlefish, Dentifrice, Dust, Dusting, Explosive, Face, Floury, Fulminating, Giant, Gregory, Grind, Gun, Hair, Kohl, Litmus, Meal, Mould-facing, Percussion, Persian, Plate, Pollen, Pounce, Priming, Prismatic, Projecting, Pulver, Putty, Rachel, Rochelle, Rouge, Seidlitz, Sherbet, Sitosterol, Smokeless, Snuff, Talc(um), Toner, Tooth, Tutty, Washing

Power(ful), Powers Ability, Able, Almighty, Arm, Attorney, Authority, Axis, Big, Cham, Charisma, Clairvoyance, Clout, Cogency, Command, Corridor, Cube, Danger, Despotic, Diadem, Dominion, Effective, Eminence, Eminence grise, Empathy, Energy, Eon, Exponent, Facility, Faculty, Fire, Flower, Force, Geothermal, Grey, Hefty, High, Horse, Hot, Hp, Hydroelectric, Influence, Kilowatt, Log, Logarithm, Mastery, Might, Mogul, Motive, Motor, Muscle, Nature, Nth, Nuclear, Od-force, Omnificent, Omnipotent, Option, P, Panjandrum, People, Pester, Posse, Potency, Puissant, Punch, Regime, Resolving, Sinew, Solar, Soup, Stamina, Staying, Steam, Stiff, Stopping, Strength, > **STRONG**, Supercharge, Supreme, Teeth, Telling, Throne, Tidal, Tycoon, Vertu(e), Vigour, Vis, Volt, Vroom, Water, Watt, Wattage, Wave, Weight, Wind, World

Practical, Practicable Active, Brass tacks, Doable, Easy-care, Hard-boiled, Joker, No-nonsense, Nuts and bolts, On, Pragmatic, Realist(ic), Realpolitik, Rule of thumb, Sensible, Shrewd, Useful, Utilitarian, Viable, Virtual

Practice, Practise, Practitioner, Practised Abuse, Adept, Custom, Distributed, Do, Drill, Enure, Exercise, General, Group, Habit, Inure, Ism, Keep, Knock-up, Massed, Meme, Nets, Operate, Order, Ply, Policy, Praxis, Private, Prosecution, Pursuit, Rehearsal, Rehearse, Restrictive, Rite, Rut, Sadhana, Sharp, Target, Teaching, Test-run, Trade, Tradition, Train, Trial, Ure, Usage, Use

Prairie IL, Illinois, Llano, Plain, Savanna, Steppe, Tundra, Veldt

Praise(worthy) Acclaim, Adulation, Alleluia, Allow, Anthem, Applause, Belaud, Bless, Blurb, Bouquet, Butter, Carol, Citation, CL, Commend(ation), Compliment, Dulia, Encomium, Envy, Eulogise, Eulogium, Eulogy, Exalt, Extol, Gloria, Glory, Herry, Hery(e), Hosanna, Hype, Incense, Laud, Lip service, Lo(o)s, Meritorious, Panegyric, Rap, Roose, Tribute

Prance Brank, Canary, Caper, Cavort, Galumph, Gambol, Jaunce, Jaunse, Prank(le), Swagger, Tittup, Trounce

Prank(s) Attrap, Bedeck, Bedizen, Caper, Dido, Escapade, Fredaine, Frolic, Gaud, Jape, Lark, Mischief, Rag, Reak, Reik, Rex, Rig, Spoof, Trick, Vagary

Prattle Babble, Blat(her), Chatter, Gab(nash), Gas, Gibber, Gossip, Gup, Lalage, Patter, Yap

Pray(ing) Appeal, Beg, Beseech, Daven, > ENTREAT, Impetrate, Intone, Invoke, Kneel, Mantis, Solicit, Wrestle

Prayer (book), Prayers Acoemeti, Act, Angelus, Ave (Maria), Bead, Beadswoman, Bede, Bene, Bidding, Breviary, Collect, Common, Cry, Devotion, Eleison, Entreaty, Evensong, Grace, Hail Mary, Intercession, Invocation, Kaddish, Khotbah, Kol Nidre, Kyrie, Kyrie eleison, Lauds, Litany, Lord's, Mantis, Mat(t)ins, Missal, Novena, Orant, Orarium, Orison, Our Father, Paternoster, Patter, Petition, Phylactery, Placebo, Plea, Requiem, Requiescat, Rogation, Rosary, Salat, Secret, Shema, State, Suffrage, Venite, Yajur-Veda

▷ **Prayer** *may indicate* one who begs

Preach(er) Ainger, Boanerges, Devil-dodger, Donne, Ecclesiastes, Evangelist, Exhort, Gospeller, Graham, Holy Roller, Itinerant, Knox, Lecture, Mar-text, Minister, Patercove, Postillate, Predicant, Predicate, Predikant, Priest, Prophet, Pulpiteer, Rant, Spintext, Spurgeon, Teach

Prearrange(d) Stitch up

Pre-Cambrian Torridonian

Precaution Care, Fail-safe, Guard, In case, Prophylaxis, Safeguard

Precede(nce), Precedent Antedate, Example, Forego, Forerun, Herald, Pas, Predate, Preface, Priority, Protocol

Precinct(s) Ambit, Area, Banlieue, Close, Courtyard, District, Environs, Pedestrian, Peribolos, Region, Shopping, Temenos, Verge, Vihara

Precious Adored, Chary, Chichi, Costly, Dear, Dearbought, Ewe-lamb, La-di-da, Murr(h)a, Owre, Precise, Rare, Valuable

Precipitate, Precipitation, Precipitous Abrupt, Accelerate, Cause, Deposit, Hailstone, Headlong, Impetuous, Launch, Lees, Pellmell, Pitchfork, Rash, Sca(u)r, Sheer, Shoot, Sleet, Snowflake, Start, > STEEP

Precise(ly), Precisian, Precision Absolute, Accurate, Dry, Exact, Explicit, Fine-drawn, Literal, Minute, Nice(ty), Particular, Perfect, Plumb, Point-device, Prig, Prim, Punctilious, Spang, Specific, Starchy, Stringent, Succinct, Surgical, Tight, Very

Predator(y) Carnivore, Eagle, Fox, Glede, Harpy-eagle, Jackal, Kestrel, Kite, Lycosa, Marauder, Predacious, Puma, Tanrec, Tarantula, Tenrec

Predecessor Ancestor, Forebear, Foregoer

Predicament Box, Dilemma, Embroglio, Hobble, Hole, Jam, Pass, Peril, Pickle, Plight, Quandary, Scrape, Spot

Predict(ion), Predictable, Predictor Augur, Belomancy, Bet, Damn, Divination, Forecast, Foreordain, Foresay, Foreshadow, Foreshow, Forespeak, Foretell, Forsay, Horoscope, Nap, Necromancy, Portend, Presage, Previse, Prognosis, Prophecy, Prophesy, Regular, Second-guess, Soothsayer

Pre-eminence, Pre-eminent Arch, Foremost, Palm, Paramount, Primacy, Supreme, Topnotch, Unique

Preface Foreword, Herald, Intro, Preamble, Precede, Proem, Prolegomenon, Usher

Prefer(ence), Preferred Advance, Choose, Discriminate, Elect, Faard, Faurd, Favour, Imperial, Incline, Lean, Liquidity, Predilect(ion), Prefard, Priority, Proclivity, Promote, Sooner, Stocks, Taste, Will

Pregnancy, Pregnant Big, Clucky, Cyesis, Ectopic, Enceinte, Fertile, Gestation, Gravid(a), Great, Heavy, Knocked-up, Pseudocyesis

Prehistoric Ancient, Azilian, Beakerfolk, Brontosaurus, Cambrian, Clovis, Cro-magnon, Eocene, Folsom, Primeval, Primitive, Pteranodon, Pterodactyl(e),

Pterosaur, Saurian, Sinanthropus, Titanosaurus, Trilith(on)

Prejudice(d) Bias, Derry, Discrimination, Down, Illiberal, Impede, Injure, Insular, Intolerance, Partiality, Parti pris, Preoccupy, Prepossession, Racism

Preliminary Draft, Exploration, Heat, Initial, Introductory, Precursory, Previous, Prodrome, Prolusion, Rough, Title-sheet

Prelude Entree, Forerunner, Intrada, Overture, Proem(ial), Ritornell(e), Ritornello

Premature Early, Precocious, Pre(e)mie, Premy, Previous, Slink, Untimely, Untimeous

Premier Chief, Leader, Main, PM, > **PRIME MINISTER**, Tojo

Premise(s) Assumption, Datum, Epicheirema, Ground, Hypothesis, Inference, Lemma, Postulate, Property, Proposition, Reason

Premium Ap, Bond, Bonus, Discount, Grassum, Pm, Reward, Scarce, Share

Preoccupation, Preoccupied, Preoccupy Absorb, Abstracted, Distrait, Engross, Hang-up, Intent, Obsess, Thing

Prepare(d), Preparation Address, A la, Arrange, Attire, Boun, Bowne, Busk, Calver, Cock, Concoct, Cooper, Countdown, Decoct, Did, Do, Dress, Edit, Forearm, Game, Groom, Ground, Inspan, Key, Lay, Legwork, Lotion, Measure, Mobilise, Parasceve, Prime, Procinct, Prothesis, Provide, Psych, > **READY**, Rehearsal, Ripe, Set, Spadework, Stand-to, Suborn, Train, Truss, Warm-up, Yare

▷ **Prepare(d)** *may indicate* an anagram

Preposterous Absurd, Chimeric, Foolish, Grotesque, Unreasonable

▷ **Preposterous** *may indicate* a word reversed

Prerequisite Condition, Essential, Necessity, Sine qua non

Presbyter(ian) Berean, Blue, Cameronian, Covenanter, Elder, Knox, Macmillanite, Moderator, Sacrarium, Whig(gamore)

Prescribe Appoint, Assign, Dictate, Enjoin, Impose, Ordain, Rule, Set

Prescription Cipher, Decree, Direction, Formula, Medicine, R, Rec, Receipt, Ritual, Specific

Presence Aspect, Bearing, Closeness, Company, Debut, Hereness, Shechinah, Shekinah, Spirit

Present(ation), Presented, Presenter, Presently Anchorman, Anon, Assists, Award, Bestow, Bonsela, Boon, Bounty, Box, Cadeau, Congiary, Coram, Current, Debut, Dee-jay, Deodate, DJ, Donate, Dotal, Douceur, Dower, Endew, Endow, Endue, Enow, Etrenne, Existent, Fairing, Feature, Front-man, Gie, > **GIFT**, Give, Going, Grant, Gratuity, Hand, Here, Hodiernal, Inst, Introduce, Largess(e), Linkman, MC, Mod, Nonce, Now, Nuzzer, Porrect, Potlach, Pr, Produce, Proffer, Pro-tem, Put, Render, Show, Slice, Tip, Today, Vee-jay, Xenium, Yeven

Preserve(d), Preservative, Preserver Bottle, Burnettize, Can, Chill, Confect, Corn, Creosote, Cure, Dehydrate, Dry, Eisel, Embalm, Fixative, Formaldehyde, Formalin, Freeze, Guard, Hain, Hesperides, Jam, Jerk, Keep, Kinin, Kipper, Konfyt, Kyanise, > **MAINTAIN**, Marmalade, Mummify, Pectin, Peculiar, Piccalilli, Pickle, Pot, Powellise, Salt, Salve, Saut, Souse, Store, Stuff, Tanalized, Tar, Tin, Vinegar, Waterglass

Preshrunk Sanforized®

Preside(nt) Abe, Adams, Banda, Carter, Chair, Childers, Cleveland, Coolidge, Coty, Dean, Director, Eisenhower, Ford, Garfield, Grant, Harding, Harrison, Hoover, Ike, Kennedy, Kruger, Lead, Lincoln, Madison, Moderator, Nixon, P, Peron, Polk, Pr(a)eses, Prexy, Roosevelt, Sa(a)dat, Speaker, Superintendent, Supervisor, Taft, Tito, Truman, Tyler, Veep, Washington

Press(ed), Pressing, Pressure Acute, Atmospheric, Bar, Bench, Blackmail, Blood, Cabinet, Chivvy, Closet, Clothes, Coerce, Cram, Crease, Crimp, Critical, Crowd, Crush, Cupboard, Cylinder, Dragoon, Drill, Dun, Durable, Duresse,

Enforcement, Enslave, Exigent, Filter, Fluid, Fly, Force, Fourth estate, Goad, Gutter, Hasten, Head, Heat, Herd, Hie, Hug, Hustle, Hydraulic, Impact, Important, Importune, Inarm, Iron, Jam, Jostle, Knead, Leverage, Lie, Lobby, Mangle, Mill, Minerva, Newspapers, Obligate, Onus, PA, Partial, Pascal, Peer, Permanent, Persist, Ply, Printing, Private, Pump, > **PUSH**, Racket, Ram, Ratpack, Record, Recruit, Reporter, Roll, Rotary, Rush, Screw, Scrum, Serr(e), Sit, Speed, Spur, Squash, Squeeze, Stop, Strain(t), Straint, Stress, Tension, Throng, Throttle, Thrutch, Tourniquet, Turgor, > **URGE**, Urgence, Urgency, Vanity, Vapour, Vice, Wardrobe, Weight, Wine, Wring, Yellow

Prestige, **Prestigious** Cachet, Credit, Distinguished, Fame, Influence, Kudos, Notable, Status

Presume, **Presumably**, **Presumption**, **Presumptuous** Allege, Arrogant, Audacity, Believe, Bold, Brass, Cocksure, Cocky, Doubtless, > **EXPECT**, Familiar, Forward, Gall, Impertinent, Insolent, Liberty, Outrecuidance, Pert, Probably, Suppose, Uppish, Whipper-snapper

Pretence, **Pretend(er)**, **Pretext** Act, Affect(ation), Afflict, Assume, Blind, Bluff, Charade, Charlatan, Claim, Cover, Cram, Dissemble, Dissimulate, Excuse, Feign, Feint, Gondolier, Hokum, Humbug, Hypocrisy, Impostor, Jactitation, Lambert Simnel, Let-on, Make-believe, Malinger, Masquerade, Obreption, Old, Parolles, Perkin Warbeck, Pose, Profess, Pseud(o), Quack, Sham, Simulate, Stale, Stalking-horse, Subterfuge, Suppose, Warbeck, Young

Pretension, **Pretentious(ness)** Arty, Bombast, Fantoosh, Fustian, Gaudy, Grandiose, High-falutin(g), Kitsch, La-di-da, Orotund, Ostentatious, Overblown, Paraf(f)le, Pompous, Pseud(o), Sciolism, Showy, Snobbish, Squirt, Tat, Tinhorn, Uppity

Pretty Attractive, Becoming, Chocolate-box, Comely, Cute, Dear, Decorate, Dish, Elegant, Fair(ish), Fairway, Inconie, Incony, Keepsaky, Looker, Moderately, Pass, Peach, Picturesque, Primp, Quite, Sweet, Twee, Winsome

Prevail(ing) Dominate, Endure, Go, Induce, Persist, Persuade, Predominant, Preponderate, Reign, Ring, Triumph, Victor, Win

Prevalent Catholic, Common, Dominant, Endemic, Epidemic, Obtaining, Rife, Widespread

Prevent(ive) Avert, Bar, Debar, Deter, Embar, Estop, Foreclose, Forfend, Help, Impound, Inhibit, Keep, Let, Obstruct, Obviate, Preclude, Prophylactic, Stop, Theriac, Trammel

Previous(ly) Afore, Already, Before, Earlier, Ere(-now), Fore, Former, Hitherto, Once, Prior

Prey Booty, Feed, Kill, Pelt, Plunder, Predate, Proul, Prowl, Quarry, Raven, Ravin(e), Soyle, Spreagh, Victim

Price(d), **Pricing**, **Price-raising** Appraise, Assess, Charge, Consequence, Contango, > **COST**, Dearth, Due, Evens, Exercise, Expense, Fee, Fiars, Hammer, Hire, Intervention, Issue, Limit, List, Loco, Market, Offer, Packet, Perverse, Predatory, Prestige, Quotation, Quote, Rate, Regrate, Reserve, Shadow, Song, Spot, Starting, Street value, Striking, Trade, Unit, Upset, Value, Vincent, Weregild, Wergeld, Wergild, Worth, Yardage

Prick(ed), **Prickle**, **Prickly** Acanaceous, Accloy, Argemone, Arrect, Bearded, Brakier, Bramble, Brog, Bunya, Cactus, Cloy, Cnicus, Echinate, Goad, Gore, Hedgehog, Hedgepig, Impel, Inject, Jab, Jook, Juk, Kali, Penis, Pierce, Prod, Puncture, Rubus, Ruellia, Seta, Setose, Smart, Spinate, Stab, Star-thistle, Stimulus, Sting, Tattoo, Tatu, Teasel, Thistle, Thorn, Tingle, Urge

Pride Bombast, Brag, Conceit, Elation, Esprit de corps, Glory, Hauteur, Hubris, Inordinate, Lions, London, Machismo, Plume, Preen, Purge, Triumphalism, Vainglory, Vanity

Priest(ess), Priests Abbot, Becket, Brahmin, Cardinal, Clergyman, Cleric, Curé, Dalai Lama, Druid, Father, Flamen, High, H(o)ungan, Lama, Mage, Mallet, Metropolitan, Minister, Missionary, Monsignor, Padre, Parson, Pastor, Père, Pontiff, Pope, Pope's knight, Preacher, Prelate, Presbyter, Prior(ess), Rabbi, Rector, Rev, Salian, Seminarian, Sky pilot, Spoiled, Vicar

Primacy, Primate Ape, Aye-aye, Bandar, Bigfoot, Biped, Bishop, Bush baby, Cardinal, Ebor, Gibbon, Hanuman, Hominid, Jackanapes, King-kong, Loris, Macaque, Magot, Mammal, Marmoset, > **MONKEY**, Orang, Pongid, Potto, Prosimian, Quadruman, Ramapithecus, Rhesus, Sifaka

Prime(r), Primary, Priming Arm, Basic, Bloom, Cardinal, Charging, Chief, Choice, Claircolle, Clearcole, Clerecole, Closed, Detonator, Direct, Donat, Donet, Election, Enarm, First, Flower, Heyday, Mature, Open, Original, Paramount, Peak, Radical, Remex, Sell-by-date, Supreme, Thirteen, Tip-top, Totient, Totitive, Valuable, Windac, Windas, Ylem

Prime Minister Asquith, Attlee, Baldwin, Balfour, Begin, Bute, Canning, Chamberlain, Chatham, Dewan, Disraeli, Diwan, Eden, Grand Vizier, Grey, Home, Leaderene, North, Number Ten, Peel, Pitt, PM, Premier, Shastri, Tanaiste, Taoiseach, Thatcher, Walpole

Primitive Aborigine, Amoeba, Antediluvian, Arabic, Archaic, Atavistic, Barbaric, Caveman, Crude, Early, Evolué, Fundamental, Naive, Neanderthal, Neolithic, Old, Persian, Primordial, Pro, Prothyl(e), Protomorphic, Protyl(e), Radical, Rudimentary, Savage, Subman, Turkish, Uncivilised, Ur

Prince(ly) Albert, Amir, Arjuna, Black, Caliph, Charming, Crown, Elector, Florizel, Fortinbras, Gospodar, Highness, Igor, Ksar, Maharaja, Merchant, Noble, Pantagruel, Pirithous, Potentate, Rajah, Regal, Rudolph, Serene, Sherif, Student, Tereus

Princess Begum, Di(ana), Infanta, Rani

Principal Arch, Capital, Central, > **CHIEF**, Decuman, Especial, First, Foremost, Head, Leading, Main(stay), Major, Mass, Protagonist, Ringleader, Staple, Star

Principle(s), Principled Animistic, Anthropic, Archimedes, Axiom, Basis, Bernouilli, Brocard, Canon, Carnot, Code, Cosmological, Criterion, Cui bono, Cy pres, Doctrine, Dogma, Element, Essential, Exclusion, First, Fourier, Generale, Germ, Ground rule, Guideline, Heisenberg, Honourable, Key, Law, Least time, Logos, Methodology, Organon, Peter, Plank, Platform, Pleasure, Precept, Prescript, Rationale, Reality, Reason, Reciprocity, Relativity, Remonstrance, Rudiment, Rule, Spirit, Tenet, Theorem, Ticket, Uncertainty, Verification, Vital, Yang, Yin

Print(er), Printing Baskerville, Batik, Calotype, Caxton, Chapel, Chromo, Cicero, Collotype, Contact, Copperplate, Dab, Dot matrix, Electrothermal, Elzevir, Engrave, Etching, Ferrotype, Fine, Font, Gravure, Half-tone, Hectograph, Heliotype, Image, Impact, Impress, India, Ink-jet, Intaglio, Italic, Jobbing, Laser, Letterpress, Letterset, Line, Line-engraving, Lino-cut, Lithograph, Logotype, Lower-case, Matrix, Mimeograph®, Monotype®, Moon, Non-impact, Off-line, Offset, Old-face, Oleo, Oleograph, Opaline, Phototype, Plate, Platinotype, Positive, Press, Publish, Remarque, Report, Reproduction, Retroussage, Rotogravure, Screen, Ship, Silk-screen, Small, Splash, Spore, Stamp, Stonehand, Strike, Thermal, Three-colour, Trichromatic, Typesetter, Typothetae, Whorl, Woodburytype, Woodcut, Xylograph

Prior(ity) Abbot, Afore, Antecedent, Earlier, Former, Hitherto, Monk, Overslaugh, Pre-, Precedence, Prefard, Preference, Previous, Privilege, Triage

Prison Alcatraz, Bastille, Bin, Bird, Boob, Bridewell, Brig, Brixton, Bullpen, Cage, Can, Cell, Chok(e)y, Clink, Club, College, Confine, Cooler, Coop, Counter, Dartmoor, Dispersal, Dungeon, Durance, Fleet, Fotheringhay, Gaol, Glass-house, Gulag, Hokey, Holloway, Hulk(s), Internment, > **JAIL**, Jug, Kitty, Limbo,

Lock-up, Marshalsea, Mattamore, Maze, Newgate, Nick, Oflag, Open, Pen, Penitentiary, Pentonville, Pit, Poke(y), Porridge, Pound, Princetown, Quad, Quod, Reformatory, Roundhouse, Scrubs, Shop, Sing-sing, Slammer, Spandau, Stalag, State, Stir, Strangeways, Tol(l)booth, Tower, Wandsworth, Wormwood Scrubs

Prisoner Canary-bird, Captive, Collegian, Collegiate, Con(vict), Detainee, Detenu, Inmate, Internee, Lag, Lifer, Political, POW, Trustee, Trusty, Yardbird, Zek

Private(ly) Ain, Aside, Atkins, Auricular, Buccaneer, Byroom, Clandestine, Close, Closet, Confidential, Enisle(d), Esoteric, Homefelt, Hush-hush, In camera, Individual, Inner, Intimate, Non-com, Own, Personal, Piou-piou, Poilu, Proprietary, Pte, Rank(er), Retired, Sanction, Sapper, Secret, Several, > **SOLDIER**, Sub rosa, Tommy

Privileg(ed) Birthright, Blest, Charter, Curule, Enviable, Exempt, Favour, Franchise, Freedom, Indulgence, Liberty, Mozarab, Nomenklatura, Octroi, Patent, Prerogative, Pryse, Regale, Regalia, Right, Sac

Privy Apprised, Can, Closet, Intimate, Jakes, John, Loo, Necessary, Reredorter, Secret, Sedge, Siege

Prize(s), Prizewinner, Prized Acquest, Apple, Archibald, Assess, Award, Best, Booby, Booker, Bravie, Capture, Champion, Consolation, Creach, Cup, Dux, Efforce, > **ESTEEM**, Force, Garland, Goncourt, Grice, Honour, Jackpot, Jemmy, Lever, Lot, Money, Nobel, Palm, Pearl, Pewter, Pie, Plum, Plunder, Pot, Pulitzer, Purse, Ram, Reprisal, > **REWARD**, Scalp, Ship, Spreaghery, Sprechery, Stakes, Tern, Treasure, Trophy, Turner, Value

Pro Aye, Coach, For, Harlot, Moll, Paid, Tramp, Yea, Yes

▶ **Pro** *see* **PROSTITUTE**

Probable, Probability Apparent, Belike, Ergodic, Feasible, Likely, Possible

Probe Antenna, Bore, Cassini, Delve, Dredge, Explore, Fathom, Feeler, Fossick, Inquire, Investigate, Pelican, Poke, Pump, > **SEARCH**, Seeker, Sound, Space, Stylet, Tent, Thrust, Tracer

Problem(s) Acrostic, Boyg, Brainteaser, Crux, Dilemma, Egma, Enigma, Facer, Glitch, Handful, Hang-up, Headache, Hitch, Hurdle, Indaba, Knot(ty), Koan, Miniature, Musive, Net, Nuisance, Obstacle, Pons asinorum, Poser, Quandary, Question, Re, Rebus, Riddle, Rider, Snag, Sorites, Sum, Teaser, Thing, Tickler, Toughie, Tsuris, Yips

Proceed(s), Proceeding, Procedure Acta, Afoot, Algorithm, Continue, Course, Drill, Emanate, Fand, Flow, Fond, Goes, Haul, Issue, Machinery, March, Mechanics, Mine, MO, Modal, Move, On, Pass, Practice, Praxis, Process, Profit, Punctilio, Pursue, Put, Rake, Return, Rite, Routine, Sap, Steps, System, Take, Use, Yead(s), Yede, Yeed

Process(ing), Procession, Processor Acromion, Action, Ala, Ambarvalia, Axon, Ben Day, Bessemer, Catalysis, Cortège, Demo, Haber, Handle, Markov, Method, Moharram, Mond, Motorcade, Muharram, Open hearth, Pageant, Parade, Paseo, Photosynthesis, Pipeline, Pomp, Recycle, Series, Skimmington, Solvay, Speciation, String, Train, Treat, Trial

Proclaim, Proclamation Announce, Annunciate, Ban, Blaze, Blazon, Boast, Broadsheet, Cry, Edict, Enounce, Enunciate, Herald, Indiction, Kerygma, Oyez, Preconise, Profess, Publish, Ring, Shout, Trumpet, Ukase

Prodigious, Prodigy Abnormal, Amazing, Huge, Immense, Monster, Monument, Mozart, Phenomenal, Portentous, Tremendous, Wonder, Wonderwork, Wunderkind

Produce(r), Producing Afford, Breed, Cause, Create, Crop, Ean, Edit, Effect, Engender, Evoke, Exhibit, Extend, Fruit, Generate, Get, Grow, Impresario, Issue, Kind, Make, Offspring, Onstream, Originate, Output, Propage, Propound, Raise, Son, Stage, Supply, Teem, Throw, Wares, Whelp, Yield

▷ **Produces** *may indicate* an anagram

Product(ion), **Productive(ness)**, **Productivity** Actualities, Apport, Artefact, Ashtareth, Ashtaroth, Astarte, Bore, Coefficient, Commodity, Drama, End, Factorial, Fecund, Fertile, Fruit, Genesis, Global, Handiwork, Harvest, Net domestic, Net national, Output, Outturn, Pair, Partial, Profilic, Result, Rich, Scalar, Show, Speiss, Uberous, Uberty, Vector, Waste, Work, Yield

▷ **Production** *may indicate* an anagram

Profane, **Profanation**, **Profanity** Coarse, Coprolalia, Desecrate, Impious, Irreverent, Sacrilege, Unholy, Violate

Profess(ed), **Professor** Absent-minded, Academic, Adjoint, Admit, Asset, Challenger, Claim, Declare, Disney, Emeritus, Higgins, Hodja, Kho(d)ja, Know-all, Ostensible, Own, Practise, Pundit, Regent, Regius, RP, STP

Profession(al) Admission, Assurance, Buppy, Business, Career, Creed, Expert, Métier, Practitioner, Pretence, Pursuit, Regular, Salaried, Skilled, Trade, Vocation, Yuppie

Proficiency, **Proficient** Adept, Alert, Dan, Expert, Forte, Past master, Practised, Skill, Technique

Profile Analysis, Contour, Half-face, Loral, Outline, Silhouette, Sketch, Statant, T(h)alweg, Vignette

Profit(able), **Profiteer**, **Profits** Advantage, Arbitrage, Asset, Avail, Benefit, Boot, Bunce, Cere, Divi(dend), Economic, Edge, Emblements, Emoluments, Exploit, Fat, Gain, Graft, Gravy, Grist, Gross, Income, Increment, Issue, Jobbery, Juicy, Leech, Lucrative, Makings, Margin, Melon, Milch cow, Mileage, Moneymaker, Net, Pay(ing), Perk, Pickings, Preacquisition, Rake-off, Return, Reward, Royalty, Spoils, Use, Usufruct, Utile, Utility, Vail

Profuse, **Profusion** Abundant, Copious, Excess, Free, Galore, Lavish, Liberal, Lush, Quantity, Rank, Rich, Two-a-penny

Program(ming), **Programming language**, **Programmer** Ada, Algol, Applet, Basic, BIOS, Bloatware, Boot, Bot, Cancelbot, Chatbot, Cobol, Coder, Columbus, CU See Me, Debugger, Dictionary, Est, Executive, Firmware, Fortran, Freeware, Inputter, Java®, Linear, Linker, LISP, Loader, Logic, LOGO, Object, Package, Parser, Pascal, PROLOG, PROM, Router, Screensaver, Search engine, Shell, Small-talk, SNOBOL, Software, Source, Spellchecker, Spreadsheet, SQL, Sustaining, Systems, Telnet, Translator, Utility, Web browser, Web crawler, Worm

Programme Agenda, Broadcast, Card, Chat show, Code, Documentary, Docusoap, Dramedy, Est, Event, Faction, Fly-on-the-wall, Infotainment, Linear, Mockumentary, PDL, Phone-in, Plan, Playbill, Prank, Regimen, Report, Schedule, Scheme, Sepmag, Show, Sitcom, Sked, Soap, Software, Syllabus, System, Telecast, Telethon, Timetable

Progress(ive), **Progression** > ADVANCE, Afoot, Arithmetic, Avant garde, Course, Fabian, Flow, Forge, Forward, Gain, Geometric, Go, Growth, Headway, Incede, Liberal, Move, Onwards, Paraphonia, Pilgrim's, Prosper, Rack, Rake's, Reformer, Roll, Run, Sequence, Series, Step, Vaunce, Way, Yead, Yede, Yeed

Prohibit(ed), **Prohibition(ist)** Ban, Block, Debar, Dry, Embargo, Estop, Forbid, Hinder, Index, Injunct, Interdict, Noli-me-tangere, Off-limits, Prevent, Pussyfoot, Rahui, Suppress, Taboo, Tabu, Verboten, Veto

Project(ile), **Projecting**, **Projection**, **Projector** Aim, Ammo, Assignment, Astral, Astrut, Ball, Ballistic, Beetle, Bullet, Butt, Buttress, Cam, Cast, Catapult, Channel, Cinerama®, Cog, Conceive, Console, Discus, Eaves, Enterprise, Episcope, Excrescence, Exsert, Extrapolate, Fet(ter)lock, Flange, Gore, Guess, Hangover, Helicity, Hoe, Homolosine, Hurtle, Inion, Jut, Kern, Knob, Ledge, Lobe, Lug, Magic lantern, Mucro, Nab, Nose, Opaque, Orthogonal, Orthographic, Outcrop, Outjet, Outjut, Outshot, Overhang, Overhead, Oversail, Peter's, Pitch,

Planetarium, Planisphere, Prickle, Promontory, Proud(er), Quillon, Roach, Rocket, Sail, Salient, Sally, Sanson-Flamsteed, Scheme, Screen, Shelf, Shrapnel, Sinusoidal, Snag, Snout, Spur, Stand out, Stick out, Tang, Tappet, Tenon, Throw, Toe, Tracer, Trimetric, Trippet, Turnkey, Turtleback, Tusk, Umbo, Undertaking, Zenithal

Prolong(ed) Extend, Lengthen, Protract, Sostenuto, Spin, Sustain

Prom(enade) Alameda, Boulevard, Cakewalk, Catwalk, Crush-room, Esplanade, Front, Mall, Parade, Paseo, Pier, Sea-front, Stroll, > **WALK**

Prominence, Prominent Antitragus, Blatant, Bold, Colliculus, Condyle, Conspicuous, Egregious, Emphasis, Featured, Gonion, High profile, Important, Insistent, Luminary, Manifest, Marked, Obtrusive, Outstanding, Salient, Signal, Teat, Toot, Tragus

Promise, Promising Accept, Assure, Augur, Auspicious, Avoure, Behest, Behight, Behote, Bode, Coming, Compact, Covenant, Engagement, Foretaste, Guarantee, Hecht, Hest, Hete, Hight, IOU, Likely, Manifest, Parole, Pledge, Plight, Pollicitation, Potential, Recognisance, Recognizance, Rosy, Sign, Sponsor, Swear, Tile, Undertake, Vow, Warranty, Word

Promote(r), Promotion Adman, Advance, > **ADVERTISE**, Advocate, Aggrandise, Aid, Assist, Blurb, Boost, Campaign, Dog and pony show, Elevate, Encourage, Exponent, Foment, Foster, Further, Help, Hype, Increase, Make, Pracharak, Prefer, Prelation, Promulgate, Provoke, Queen, Rear, Remove, Run, Salutary, Sell, Sponsor, Spruik, Stage, Step, Subserve, Tendencious, Tendentious, Upgrade, Upload, Uprate

Prompt(er), Promptly, Promptness Actuate, Alacrity, Autocue®, Believe, Celerity, Chop-chop, Cue, Egg, Expeditious, Frack, Idiot-board, Immediate, Incite, Inspire, Instigate, Move, Pernicious, Premove, Punctual, Quick, Ready, Speed(y), Spur, Stimulate, Sudden, Tight, Tit(e), Titely, Tyte, Urgent

Prone Apt, Groof, Grouf, Grovel, Liable, Lying, Prostrate, Recumbent, Subject, Susceptible

Pronounce(d), Pronouncement Adjudicate, Affirm, Articulate, Assert, Asseveration, Clear, Conspicuous, Declare, Definite, Dictum, Emphatic, Enunciate, Fiat, Indefinite, Marked, Opinion, Palatalise, Pontificate, Recite, Utter, Velarise, Vocal, Voice, Vote

Proof Apagoge, Argument, Bona fides, Confirmation, Direct, Evidence, Firm, Foundry, Galley, Godel's, Indirect, Positive, Preif(e), Probate, Pull, Quality, Refutation, Remarque, Reproduction, Resistant, Revision, Secure, Slip, Strength, Test, Tight, Token, Trial, Upmake, Validity

Prop Airscrew, Bolster, Buttress, Crutch, Dog-shore, Fulcrum, Leg, Loosehead, Misericord(e), Punch(eon), Rance, Rest, Shore, Sprag, Spur, Staff, Stay, Stempel, Stemple, Stilt, Stoop, Stoup, Stull, > **SUPPORT**, Tighthead, Underpin

Propaganda, Propagandist Agitprop, Ballyhoo, Brainwashing, Chevalier, Doctrine, Promotion, Psyop, Psywar, Publicity, Slogan

Propel(ler) Airscrew, Ca', Drive, Fin, Launch, Leg, Lox, > **MOVE**, Oar, Paddle, Pedal, Project, Push, Rotor, Row, Screw, Throw

Proper(ly) Ain, Convenance, Correct, Decent, Decorous, Due, Eigen, En règle, Ethical, > **FIT**, Genteel, Governessy, Kosher, Noun, Ought, Own, Pakka, Pathan, Prim, Pucka, Pukka, Puritanic, Real, Seemly, Suitable, Tao, Trew, True, Veritable, Well

Property Assets, Attribute, Aver, Belongings, Chattel, Chose, Contenement, Dead-hand, Demesne, Des res, Dowry, Effects, Enclave, Escheat, Escrow, Estate, Fee, Feu, Flavour, Fonds, Freehold, Goods, Hereditament, Hot, Hotchpot, Immoveable, Inertia, Intellectual, Jointure, Leasehold, Living, Means, Mortmann, Paraphernalia, Peculium, Personal, Personalty, Premises, Private, Public, Quale,

Quality, Real, Stock, Stolen, Theft, Time-share, Timocracy, Trait, Usucapion, Usucaption

Prophesy, **Prophet(ess)**, **Prophetic** Amos, Augur, Bab, Balaam, Cassandra, Daniel, Deborah, Divine, Elias, Elijah, Elisha, Ezekiel, Ezra, Fatal, Forecast, Foretell, Hosea, Is, Isa, Is(a)iah, Jeremiah, Joel, Jonah, Mahdi, Major, Malachi, Mani, Mantic, Micah, Minor, Mohammed, Mormon, Moses, Nahum, Nathan, Nostradamus, Obadiah, Ominous, Oracle, Portend, Predictor, Prognosticate, Pythoness, Seer, Sibyl, Zephaniah, Zoroaster

Proportion(ate) Commensurable, Dimension, Portion, Pro rata, Quantity, Quota, Ratio, Reason, Regulate, Relation, Sine, Size, Soum, Sowm

Proposal, **Propose** Advance, Bid, Bill, Eirenicon, Feeler, Irenicon, Mean, Motion, Move, Nominate, Offer, Overture, Plan, Pop, Proffer, Propound, Recommend, Resolution, Scheme, Slate, Submission, > **SUGGEST**, Table, Tender, Volunteer, Woot, Would

Proposition Axiom, Corollary, Deal, Disjunction, Ergo, Hypothesis, Lemma, Overture, Pons asinorum, Porism, Premise, Premiss, Rider, Sorites, Spec, Superaltern, Theorem, Thesis

Proprietor, **Propriety** Correctitude, Decorum, Etiquette, Grundy, Keeper, Lord, Master, Owner, Patron, Rectitude

Prose, **Prosy** Haikai, Polyphonic, Saga, Stich, Verbose, Version, Writing

Prosecute, **Prosecutor**, **Prosecution** Allege, Avvogadore, Charge, Crown, Fiscal, Furtherance, Impeach, Indict, Practise, Public, Sue, Wage

Prospect(or) Explore, Forty-niner, Fossick, Look-out, Mine, > **OUTLOOK**, Panorama, Perspective, Pleases, Reefer, Scenery, Search, Sourdough, View, Vista, Visto, Wildcatter

Prosper(ity), **Prosperous** Blessed, Blossom, Boom, Fair, Fat cat, Flourish, Get ahead, Heyday, Mérimée, Palmy, > **SUCCEED**, Thee, Thrift, Thrive, Up, Warison, Wealth, Welfare, Well-heeled, Well-to-do

Prostitute, **Prostitution** Brass, Catamite, Chippie, Cocotte, Debase, Dell, Dolly-mop, Doxy, Harlot, Hetaera, Hetaira, Jailbait, Loose woman, Madam, Magdalen(e), Moll, Mutton, Pro, Rent-boy, Rough trade, Scrubber, Slap, Stew, Streetwalker, Strumpet, Tart, Trull, Whore

Protect(ed), **Protection**, **Protector** Adonise, Aegis, Arm, Armour, Asylum, Auspice, Bastion, Buckler, Chaffron, Chain mail, Chamfrain, Chamfron, Charm, Cherish, Cloche, Coat, Cocoon, Conserve, Cover, Covert, Cromwell, Cushion, Danegeld, Data, Defend, Defilade, Egis, Enamel, Entrenchment, Escort, Flank, Groundsheet, Guard(ian), Gumshield, Hedge, House, Hurter, Immune, Indemnify, Insure, Keep, Kickback, Lee, Mac(k)intosh, Mail, Male, Mollycoddle, Mother, Mouthpiece, Mudguard, Noll, Nosey, Oliver, Overall, Parados, Patent, Patron, Police, Pomander, Preserve, Revetment, Ride shotgun, Safeguard, Sandbag, Save, Screen, Scug, Shadow, Sheathing, Sheeting, Shelter, > **SHIELD**, Skug, Splashback, Splashboard, Splasher, Starling, Sunscreen, Talisman, Tribute, Tutelar, Umbrella, Underseal, Vaccine, Ward(ship), Weatherboard, Weatherstrip, Windbreaker, Windshield, Write

Protein Abrin, Actin, Actomyosin, Adipsin, Alanine, Albumen, Albumin, Aleuron(e), Allergen, Amandine, Analogon, Angiotensin, Antibody, Avidin, Bradykinin, Calmodulin, Capsid, Capsomere, Caseinogen, Ceruloplasmin, Collagen, Complement, Conchiolin, Conjugated, Cytokine, Dystrophin, Elastin, Enzyme, Factor VIII, Ferritin, Fibrin, Fibrinogen, Fibroin, Flagellin, Gelatin, Gliadin(e), Glob(ul)in, Gluten, Haemoglobin, Haptoglobin, Histone, Hordein, Immunoglobulin, Incaparina, Interferon, Interleukin, Lactalbumin, Lectin, Legumin, Leptin, Leucin(e), Luciferin, Lysin, Meat, Mucin, Myogen, Myoglobin, Myosin, Opsin, Opsonin, Ovalbumin, Pepsin(e), Phaseolin, Prion, Prolamin(e),

Protamine, Proteose, Prothrombin, Quorn®, Renin, Repressor, Ribosome, Sclerotin, Sericin, Serum albumin, Serum globulin, Single-cell, Soya, Spectrin, Spongin, Tempeh, Toxalbumin, Transferrin, Tropomyosin, Troponin, Tubulin, Vitellin, Zein

Protest(er) Aver, Avouch, Clamour, Come, Démarche, Demo, Demonstrate, Demur, Deprecate, Dissent, Expostulate, Hartal, Inveigh, Lock-out, Luddite, March, Object, Outcry, Picket, Plea, Refus(e)nik, Remonstrate, Sit-in, Squawk, Squeak, Squeal, Work-to-rule

Protestant Amish, Anabaptist, Anglo, Calvin, Congregationalism, Covenanter, Cranmer, Dissenter, Evangelic, Gospeller, Huguenot, Independent, Lady, Lutheran, Mennonite, Methodist, Moravian, Nonconformist, Oak-boy, Orangeman, Pentecostal, Pietism, Prod, Puritan, Stundist, Swaddler, Wesleyan

Protract(ed) Delay, > EXTEND, Lengthen, Livelong, Prolong

Proud Arrogant, Boaster, Cocky, Conceited, Dic(k)ty, Elated, Flush, Haughty, Haut, Level, Lordly, Orgulous, Superb, Vain

Prove(d), Proving Apod(e)ictic, Argue, Ascertain, Assay, Attest, Authenticate, Aver, Confirm, Convince, Evince, Justify, > PROOF, > SHOW, Substantiate, Test

Proverb Adage, Axiom, Byword, Gnome, Maxim, Paroemia, Saw

▷ **Proverbial** *may refer to* the biblical Proverbs

Provide(d), Provident(ial) Afford, Allow, Arrange, Besee, Bring, Cater, Compare, Conditional, Endow, Equip, Far-seeing, Fend, Find, Furnish, Generate, Give, Grubstake, If, Lay on, Maintain, Proviso, Purvey, Serve, So, Sobeit, > SUPPLY, Suttle

Province, Provincial(ism) Area, District, Exclave, Land, Regional, Suburban, Territory, Ulster

Provision(s), Provisional Acates, A(p)panage, Board, Fodder, Insolvency, Jointure, Larder, Makeshift, Proggins, Scran, Skran, Stock, Supply, Suttle, Viands, Viaticum, Victuals

Proviso, Provisional Caution, Caveat, Clause, Condition, Interim, IRA, On trial, Reservation, Salvo, Stipulation, Temporary, Tentative

Provocation, Provocative, Provoke Agacant, Alluring, Egg, Elicit, Erotic, Exacerbate, Excite, Flirty, Harass, Incense, Induce, Inflame, Instigate, Irk, Irritate, Needle, Nettle, Occasion, Pique, Prompt, Raise, Red rag, Sedition, Spark, Stimulate, Tar, Tease, Urge, Vex, Wind up

Prowl(er) Hunt, Lurch, Lurk, Mooch, Prole, Ramble, Roam, Rove, Snoke, Snook, Snowk, Tenebrio, Tom

Proxy Agent, Attorn, Deputy, PP, Regent, Sub, Surrogate, Vicar, Vice

Prude(nce), Prudent, Prudery Bluenose, Canny, Caution, Circumspect, Comstocker, Conservative, Discreet, Discretion, Foresight, Frugal, Grundyism, Metis, Mrs Grundy, Politic, Prig, Prissy, Provident, Sage, Sensible, Sparing, Strait-laced, Strait-lacer, Thrifty, Vice-nelly, Victorian, Ware, Wary, Well-advised, Wise

Prune(r) Bill-hook, Dehorn, Lop, Plum, Proign, Proin(e), Reduce, Reform, Secateur, Sned, Thin, Trim

Pry Ferret, Force, Lever, Meddle, Nose, Paul, Peep, Question, Search, Snoop, Toot

Psalm Anthem, Cantate, Chant, Chorale, Hallel, Hymn, Introit, Jubilate, Metrical, Miserere, Neck-verse, Paean, Proper, Ps, Song, Tone, Tract, Venite

Pseudonym Aka, Alias, Allonym, Anonym, Pen-name, Stage-name

Psychiatrist, Psychologist Adler, Alienist, Clare, Coué, Ellis, Freud, Headshrinker, Jung, Laing, Reich, Shrink, Trick-cyclist

Psychic, Psychosis ESP, Lodge, Medium, Seer, Telekinesis

Psychological, Psychology, Psychologist Analytical, Behaviourism, Clinical,

Depth, Dynamic, Educational, Experimental, Eysenck, Gestalt, Hedonics, Humanistic, Industrial, Latah, Occupational, Organisational, Piaget, Social, Structural

Psychotherapy Rebirthing

Pub Bar, Boozer, Free-house, Gin-palace, Houf(f), House, Howf(f), Inn, Joint, Local, Pothouse, Potshop, Shanty, Tavern, Tiddlywink

Public Apert, Bar, Civil, Common, Demos, General, Inn, Lay, Limelight, National, Open, Out, Overt, Populace, State, Vulgar, World

Publican Ale-keeper, Bung, Host, Landlord, Licensee, Tapster, Taverner

Publication Announcement, Broadsheet, Edition, Exposé, Issue, > JOURNAL, Lady, Mag, Organ, Pictorial, Samizdat, Tabloid, Tatler, Tract, Tribune, Yearbook

Publicist, Publicity Ad(vert), Airing, Ballyhoo, Coverage, Exposure, Flack, Glare, Headline, Hype, Leakage, Limelight, Notoriety, Plug, PRO, Promotion, Propaganda, Réclame, Spin-doctor, Splash

Publish(er), Published, Publishing, Publicise Air, Blaze, Cape, Delator, Desktop, Disclose, Edit, Evulgate, Issue, Noise, OUP, Out, Pirate, Plug, Post, Print(er), Proclaim, Propagate, Release, Run, Vanity, Vent, Ventilate

Pudding Afters, Black, Blancmange, Brown Betty, Cabinet, Charlotte, Christmas, Clootie dumpling, College, Custard, > DESSERT, Duff, Dumpling, Eve's, Flummery, Fritter, Fromenty, Frumenty, Furme(n)ty, Furmity, Haggis, Hasty, Milk, Nesselrode, Panada, Pandowdy, Parfait, Pease, Plum, Popover, Rice, Roly-poly, Sowens, Sponge, Spotted dick, Stickjaw, Stodge, Suet, Summer, Sundae, Sweet, Tansy, Tapioca, Umbles, White hass, White hause, White hawse, Yorkshire, Zabaglione

Puff(ed), Puffer, Puffy Advertise, Blouse, Blow, Blowfish, Blurb, Bouffant, Breath, Chuff, Chug, Drag, Encomist, Eulogy, Exsufflicate, Fag, Flaff, Flatus, Fluffy, Fuff, Globe-fish, Grampus, Gust, Hype, Lunt, Pech, Pegh, Pluffy, Plug, Powder, Recommend, Skiff, Slogan, Steam, Swell, Toke, Waff, Waft, Waif, Whiff, Whiffle

Pull (up) Adduce, Attraction, Crane, Drag, Draw, Force, Haul, Heave, Heeze, Hook, > INFLUENCE, Lug, Mousle, Pluck, Rein, Ring, Rove, Rug, Saccade, Sally, Sole, Sool(e), Sowl(e), Stop, Tit, Tow, Trice, Tug, Undertow, Wrest, Yank

Pulp Cellulose, Chyme, Chymify, Crush, Flong, Kenaf, Marrow, Mash, Mush, Pap, Paste, Pomace, Pound, Puree, Rot, Rubbish, Squeeze, Squidge

Pulpit(e) Ambo(nes), Lectern, Mimbar, Minbar, Pew, Rostrum, Tent, Tub, Wood

Pulsar Geminga

Pulse Alfalfa, Beat, Calavance, Caravance, Chickpea, D(h)al, Dholl, Dicrotic, Garbanzo, Gram, Groundnut, Ictus, Lentil, Lucerne, Pea, Rhythm, Sain(t)foin, Soy beans, Sphygmus, Sync, Systaltic, Systole, Throb

▷ **Pummelled** *may indicate* an anagram

Pump Bellows, Bowser, Centrifugal, Chain, Compressor, Cross-question, Donkey, Drive, Electromagnetic, Elicit, Feed, Filter, Force, Grease-gun, Grill, Heart, Heat, Hydropult, Inflate, Knee-swell, Lift, Mud, Nodding-donkey, Parish, Petrol, Piston, Pulsometer, Question, Rotary, Scavenge, Shoe, Stirrup, Stomach, Suction, Turbine, Vacuum, Water, Wind

Pumpernickel Rye (bread)

Pun Calembour, Clinch, Equivoque, Paragram, Paronomasia, Quibble, Ram

Punch(ed) Biff, Blow, Box, Bradawl, Card, Centre, Chad, Check, Chop, Clip, Cobbler's, Fist(ic), Gang, Haymaker, Hit, Hook, Horse, Jab, Key, Kidney, Knobble, Knubble, KO, Lander, Milk, One-er, Overhand, Perforate, Planter's, Plug, Poke, Polt, Pommel, Pounce, Prod, Pummel, Rabbit, Roundhouse, Rum, Slosh, Sock, Sting(o), Stoush, Suffolk, Upper-cut, Wap, Wind, Zest

Punctuate, Punctuation (mark) Bracket, Colon, Comma, Emphasize,

Interabang, Interrobang, Interrupt, Mark, Semicolon

Puncture(d) Bore, Centesis, Criblé, Cribrate, Deflate, Drill, Flat, Hole, Lumbar, Perforate, Pierce, Prick

Pungency, Pungent Acid, Acrid, Acrolein, Alum, Ammonia, Bite, Bitter, Caustic, Hot, Mordant, Nidorous, Piquant, Poignant, Point, Racy, Salt, Spice, Sting, Tangy, Witty

Punish(ed), Punishing, Punishment Amerce, Baffle, Bastinado, Beat, Birch, Cane, Capital, Cart, Castigate, Chasten, Chastise, Come-uppance, Corporal, Correct, Dam(nation), Defrock, Desert(s), Detention, > DISCIPLINE, Fatigue, Fine, Flog, Gate, Gauntlet, Gruel, Hellfire, Hiding, Hot seat, Imposition, Impot, Interdict, Jankers, Keelhaul, Knout, Lambast(e), Lines, Necklace, Nemesis, Pack-drill, Penalise, Penance, Perdition, Picket, Pillory, Pine, Rap, Reprisal, Retribution, Scaffold, Scourge, Sentence, Six of the best, Smack, Smite, Spank, Stocks, Strafe, Strap, Strappado, Tar and feather, Toco, Toko, Treadmill, Trim, Trounce, What for, Whip

▷ **Punish** may indicate an anagram

Punt(er), Punting Antepost, Back, Bet, Gamble, Kent, Kick, Pound, Quant, Turfite

Pupil Abiturient, Apple, Apprentice, Boarder, Cadet, Catechumen, Disciple, Etonian, Eyeball, Follower, Gyte, Junior, L, Monitor, Prefect, Protégé(e), Scholar, Senior, Student, Tutee, Ward

▷ **Pupil** may refer to an eye

Puppet(eer) Creature, Doll, Dummy, Fantoccini, Glove, Guignol, Judy, Marionette, Mawmet, Mommet, Pawn, Pinocchio, Punch(inello), Rod, Tool

Purchase(r), Purchasing Acquisition, Bargain, Buy, Coff, Compulsory, Earn, Emption, Gadsden, Get, Grip, Halliard, Halyard, Hold, Layaway, > LEVERAGE, Louisiana, Parbuckle, Perquisitor, Secure, Shop, Toehold

Pure, Purity Absolute, Cando(u)r, Cathy, Chaste, Chiarezza, Clean(ly), Cosher, Fine, Good, Holy, Immaculate, Incorrupt, Innocent, Intemerate, Inviolate, Kathy, Kosher, Lily, Lilywhite, Maidenhood, Me(a)re, Net(t), Pristine, Quintessence, Sanctity, Sheer, Simon, Simple, Sincere, Snow-white, Stainless, True, Unalloyed, Vertue, Virgin, Virtue, White

Purgative, Purge Aloes, Cascara, Castor-oil, Catharsis, Delete, Drastic, Elaterium, Eliminate, Emetic, Erase, Evacuant, Expiate, Flux, Hydragogue, Ipecacuanha, Jalop, Laxative, Physic, Pride's, Relaxant, Scur, Senna

Purification, Purifier, Purify(ing) Absolve, Bowdlerise, Catharsis, Clay, Clean(se), Depurate, Dialysis, Distil, Edulcorate, Elution, Exalt, Expurgate, Filter, Fine, Gas-lime, Lustre, Lustrum, Refine, Retort, Samskara, Sanctify, Scorify, Scrub, Try

Puritan(ical) Bible belt, Bluenose, Digger(s), Ireton, Ironsides, Pi, Pilgrim, Precisian, Prude, Prynne, Roundhead, Seeker, Traskite, Waldenses, Wowser, Zealot

Purloin Abstract, Annex, Appropriate, Lift, Nab, Pilfer, Snaffle, Sneak, Steal

Purple Amarantin(e), Amethyst, Aubergine, Burgundy, Cassius, Claret, Eminence, Heather, Heliotrope, Hyacinthine, Indigo, Lavender, Lilac, Magenta, Mulberry, Pansy, Plum, Puce, Purpurin, Royal, Violet

Purpose Advertent, Aim, Avail, Cautel, Design, Ettle, Goal, Here-to, > INTENT, Mean(ing), Meant, Mint, Motive, Object, Plan, Point, Raison d'être, > REASON, Resolution, Resolve, Sake, Telic, Telos, Tenor, Use

Purse Ad crumenam, Bag, Bung, Caba, Clutch, Crease, Crumenal, Fisc, Fisk, Long Melford, Pocket, Prim, Privy, Prize, Pucker, Spleuchan, Sporran, Wallet, Whistle

▷ **Pursed** may indicate one word within another

Purslane Sea, Water

Pursue(r), Pursuit Alecto, Business, Chase, Chivvy, Course, Dog, Follow, Follow up, Hobby, Hot-trod, Hound, Hunt, Line, Practice, Practise, Proceed, Prosecute, Quest, Scouring, Stalk, Trivial

Pursuivant Blue Mantle

Push(er), Push in Barge, Birr, Boost, Bunt, Detrude, Drive, Edge, Effort, Elbow, Fire, Horn, Hustle, Impulse, Invaginate, Jostle, Nose, Nudge, Nurdle, Obtrude, Pitchfork, Plod, Ply, Press, Promote, Propel, Railroad, Ram, Sell, Snoozle, Subtrude, Thrust, Urge

Put (off; on; out; up) Accommodate, Add, Bet, Cup, Daff, Defer, Dish, Do, Don, Douse, Implant, Impose, Incommode, Inn, Lade, Lodge, Lump, Oust, Pit, Place, Plonk, Set, Smore, Station, Stow

Put down Abase, Degrade, Demean, Disparage, Floor, Humiliate, Land, Snuff, Write

▷ **Put off** *may indicate* an anagram

Putty Glaziers', Jewellers', Painters', Plasterers', Polishers'

Puzzle(r) Acrostic, Baffle, Bemuse, Bewilder, Brainteaser, Chinese, Confuse, Conundrum, Crossword, Crux, Egma, Elude, Enigma, Fox, Glaik, Gravel, Intrigue, Jigsaw, Kittle, Logogriph, Magic pyramid, Mind-bender, Monkey, Mystify, Nonplus, Perplex, Ponder, Pose(r), Rebus, Riddle, Rubik's cube®, Sorites, Sphinx, Stick(l)er, Stump, Tangram, Tickler, Wordsearch, Wordsquare

Pyramid Cheops, Chephren, Frustum, Stack, Teocalli

Quack Charlatan, Crocus, Dulcamara, Empiric, Fake, > IMPOSTOR, Katerfelto, Mountebank, Pretender, Saltimbanco

Quadrilateral Lambeth, Tetragon, Trapezium, Trapezoid

Quagmire Bog, Fen, Imbroglio, Marsh, Morass, Swamp, Wagmoire

Quahog Clam

Quail Asteria, Bevy, Bird, Blench, Bob-white, Button, Caille, Colin, Flinch, Harlot, Hen, Quake, Shrink, Tremble

Quaint Cute, Naive, Odd, Old-world, Picturesque, Strange, Twee, Wham, Whim(sy)

Quake(r), Quaking Aminadab, Broad-brim, Dither, Dodder, Fox, Friend, Fry, Hicksite, Obadiah, Penn, Quail, Seism, Shake(r), Shiver, > TREMBLE, Tremor, Trepid

Qualification, Qualified, Qualify Able, Adapt, Adverb, Capacitate, Caveat, Competent, Condition, Degree, Diplomatic, Entitle, Fit, Graduate, Habilitate, Meet, Pass, Proviso, Restrict, Temper, Versed

Quality Aroma, Attribute, Body, Calibre, Cast, Charisma, Essence, Fabric, Fame, First water, Five-star, Flavour, Grade, Inscape, It, Kite-mark, Long suit, Mystique, Pitch, Premium, Primary, Property, Q, Quale, Reception, Sort, Standard, Stature, Style, Substance, Suchness, Thew, Thisness, Timbre, Tone, Up-market, Vinosity, Virgin, Virtu(e), Water, Worth

Quantity > AMOUNT, Analog(ue), Batch, Bundle, Capacity, Deal, Dose, Feck, Fother, Hundredweight, Idempotent, Intake, Jag, Lock, Lot, Mass, Measure, Melder, Myriad, Nonillion, Number, Ocean(s), Operand, Parameter, Parcel, Peck, Plenty, Posology, Pottle, Qs, Qt, Quire, Quota, Quotient, Ream, Scalar, Slather, Slew, Slue, Sum, Surd, Tret, Unknown, Vector, Warp, Whips

Quarrel(some) Altercate, Barney, Bate, Bicker, Brawl, Bust-up, Cantankerous, Cat and dog, Clash, Contretemps, Difference, Disagree, Dispute, Dust-up, Fall out, Feisty, Fracas, Fray, Hassle, Loggerheads, Pugnacious, Squabble, Tiff, Tink, Vendetta, Wrangle

Quarry, Quarry face Chalkpit, Game, Mine, Pit, Prey, Scabble, Scent, Stone pit, Victim

Quarter(ing), Quarters Airt, Barrio, Billet, Canton(ment), Casern(e), Chinatown, Clemency, Close, Coshery, District, Dorm, E, Empty, Enclave, Fardel, Farl, First, Focsle, Forecastle, Forpet, Forpit, Fourth, Ghetto, Ham(s), Harbour, Haunch, Last, Latin, Medina, > MERCY, N, Note, Oda, Pity, Point, Principium, Quadrant, Region, S, Season, Sector, Tail, Trimester, W, Wardroom, Warp, Winter

▷ **Quarterdeck** *may indicate* a suit of cards

Quarto Crown, Demy, Foolscap, Imperial, Medium, Royal, Small

Quartz Agate, Amethyst, Bristol diamond, Buhrstone, Cacholong, Cairngorm, Chalcedony, Chert, Citrine, Flint, Granophyre, Jasp(er), Morion, Onyx, Plasma, Prase, Rainbow, Rose, Rubasse, Sapphire, Silex, Silica, Smoky, Stishovite, Tiger-eye, Tonalite, Whin Sill

Quash Abrogate, Annul, Quell, Recant, Scotch, Subdue, Suppress, Terminate, Void

Quaver(ing) Shake, Trill, Vibrate, Warble

Quay Bund, Levee, Wharf

Queasy Delicate, Nauseous, Squeamish

Queen(ly) Adelaide, Alcestis, Alexandra, Anna, Anne, Artemesia, Atossa, Balkis, Beauty, Bee, Begum, Bess, Boadicea, Boudicca, Brunhild(e), Camilla, Candace, Card, Caroline, Cleopatra, Dido, Drag, Eleanor(a), Ellery, Esther, Gertrude, Guinevere, Hatshepset, Hatshepsut, Hecuba, Helen, Hermione, Hippolyta, Isabel, Ishtar, Isolde, Jocasta, Juno, Leda, Maam, Mab, Maeve, Marie Antoinette, Mary, Matilda, May, Monarch, Nefertiti, Omphale, Pansy, Pearly, Penelope, Persephone, Phaedram, Proserpina, Qu, R, Ranee, Regal, Regina(l), Semiramis, Sheba, Titania, Victoria, Virgin

Queer(ness) Abnormal, Berdash, Bizarre, Crazy, Cure, Curious, Fey, Fie, Fifish, Gay, Nance, Nancy, > ODD, Outlandish, Peculiar, Pervert, Poorly, Quaint, Rum, Spoil, Uranism, Vert

Quench Assuage, Cool, Extinguish, Satisfy, Slake, Slo(c)ken, Sta(u)nch, Yslake

▶ **Query** *see* QUESTION

Quest Goal, Graal, Grail, Hunt, Pursuit, Venture

Question(ing), Questionnaire Appose, Ask, Bi-lateral, Burning, Catechise, Chin, Contest, Conundrum, Cross-examine, Debrief, Dichotomous, Direct, Dispute, Dorothy Dixer, Doubt, Erotema, Eroteme, Erotesis, Examine, Fiscal, Good, Grill, Heckle, Impeach, Impugn, Indirect, Information, Innit, Interpellation, Interrogate, Interview, Koan, Leading, Loaded, Maieutic, Matter, Open, Oppugn, Pop, Pose, Previous, Probe, Problem, Pump, Q, Qu, Quaere, Quiz, Rapid-fire, Refute, Rhetorical, Riddle, Speer, Speir, Survey, Suspect, Tag, Teaser, Tickler, Vexed, West Lothian, WH, What, Worksheet

Queue Braid, Breadline, Cercus, Crocodile, Cue, Dog, File, > LINE, Pigtail, Plait, Plat, Tail(back), Track

Quibble(r), Quibbling Balk, Carp, Carriwitchet, Casuist, Cavil, Chicaner, Dodge, Elenchus, Equivocate, Hairsplitting, Nitpick, Pedantry, Pettifoggery, Prevaricate, Pun, Quiddity, Quillet, Quirk, Sophist

Quick(en), Quickening, Quicker, Quickly, Quickness Accelerate, Acumen, Adroit, Agile, Alive, Animate, Breakneck, Brisk, Celerity, Chop-chop, Cito, Deft, Enliven, Existent, Expeditious, Express, Fastness, Hasten, Hie, Hotfoot, Impulsive, Jiffy, Keen, Living, Mercurial, Mistress, Mosso, Nailbed, Nimble, Nippy, Pdq, Piercing, Post-haste, Prestissimo, Presto, Prompt, Pronto, Rapid, Ready, Sharp, Slippy, Smart, Snappy, Soon, Spry, Streamline, Sudden, Swift, Tout de suite, Trice, Up tempo, Veloce, Vital, Vite

Quid Chaw, Chew, L, Nicker, Plug, Pound, Quo, Sov, Tertium, Tobacco

Quiet(en), Quietly Accoy, Allay, Appease, Barnacle, Calm, Compose, Doggo, Ease, Easeful, Easy, Encalm, Entame, Gag, Grave, Kail, Laconic, Loun(d), Low, Lown(d), Low-profile, Lull, Meek, Muffle, Mute, P, Pacify, Pause, Peace, Piano, Pipe down, QT, Reserved, Reticent, Sedate, Settle, Sh, Shtoom, Silence, Sober, Soothe, Sotto voce, Still, Subact, Subdued, Tace, Taciturn, Tranquil, Whisht, Whist

Quilt(ed), Quilting Comfort(er), Counterpane, Cover, Doona®, Duvet, Echo, Eiderdown, Futon, Kantha, Matel(l)asse, Patchwork, Trapunto

Quip Carriwitchet, Crack, Epigram, Gibe, Jest, Jibe, Joke, Taunt, Zinger

Quirk Concert, Foible, Idiosyncrasy, Irony, Kink, Twist

Quit(s) Abandon, Absolve, Ap(p)ay, Cease, Desert, Even(s), Go, Leave, Meet, Resign, > STOP

Quite Actually, All, Ap(p)ay, Clean, Dead, Enough, Enow, Fairly, Fully, Precisely, Real, Right, Sheer, Very

Quiver(ing) Aspen, Quake, Shake, Sheath, The yips, Tremble, Tremolo, Tremor, Tremulate, Trepid, Vibrant, Vibrate

Quiz Bandalore, Catechism, Examine, Interrogate, I-spy, Mastermind, Oddity, Probe, Question, Smoke, Trail, Yo-yo

Quota Proportion, Ration, Share

Quotation, **Quote(d)**, **Quote** Adduce, Citation, Cite, Co(a)te, Duckfoot, Epigraph, Evens, Extract, Forward, Instance, Name, Price, Recite, Reference, Say, Scare, Soundbite, Tag, Verbatim, Wordbite

Quotient Intelligence, Kerma, Quaternion, Ratio, Respiratory

Rr

Rabbit Angora, Astrex, Brer, Buck, Bun(ny), Chat, Con(e)y, Cottontail, Daman, Dassie, Doe, Harp, Hyrax, Jack, Klipdas, Marmot, Muff, Nest, Novice, Oarlap, Patzer, Prate, Rattle, Rex, Snowshoe, Tapeti, Terricole, Waffle, Yak, Yap, Yatter

Rabble Canaille, Clamjamphrie, Clanjamfray, Colluvies, Crowd, Doggery, Herd, Hoi-polloi, Horde, Legge, Mob, Raffle, Rag-tag, Rascaille, Rascal, Riff-raff, Rout, Scaff-raff, Shower, Tag, Tagrag

Race(course), **Racing**, **Race meeting** Aintree, Ancestry, Arms, Ascot, Autocross, Belt, Boat, Breed, Bumping, Career, Caucus, Cesarewitch, Chantilly, Chase, Claiming, Classic, Contest, Country, Course, Current, Cursus, Cyclo-cross, Dash, Derby, Doggett's Coat and Badge, Dogs, Doncaster, Drag, Egg and spoon, Epsom, Event, Fastnet, Flat, Flow, Fun-run, Generation, Ginger, Goodwood, Grand National, Grand Prix, Handicap, Harness, Hialeah, Human(kind), Hurry, Inca, Indy, Kind, Leat, Leet, Leger, Le Mans, Lick, Lignage, Line(age), Longchamps, Madison, Man, Marathon, Master, Meets, Mile, Motocross, > **NATIONAL**, Newmarket, Nursery, Nursery stakes, Oaks, Obstacle, One-horse, Picnic, Plate, Point-to-point, Potato, Pursuit, Rallycross, Rallying, Rapids, Redcar, Regatta, Relay, Rill, Rod, Sack, St Leger, Scramble, Scratch, Scud, Scurry, Seed, Selling, Slalom, Slipstream, Slot-car, Speedway, Sprint, Stakes, Steeplechase, Stem, Stock, Strain, Streak, Sweepstake, Tail, Tear, Thousand Guineas, Three-legged, Tide, Torch, Torpids, Towcester, Tribe, Trotting, TT, Turf, Two-horse, Two Thousand Guineas, Walking, Walk-over, Waterway, Wetherby, Welter, White, Wincanton

Racehorse, **Racer** Eclipse, Filly, Hare, Maiden, Plater, Red Rum, Steeplechaser, Trotter

Rack Bin, Cloud, Cratch, Drier, Flake, Frame, Hack, Hake, Pulley, Roof, Stretcher, Toast, Torment, Torture

Racket(eer) Bassoon, > **BAT**, Battledore, Bloop, Brattle, Caterwaul, Chirm, Clamour, Crime, Deen, Din, Discord, Earner, > **FIDDLE**, Gyp, Hubbub, Hustle, > **NOISE**, Noisiness, Protection, Ramp, Rort, Sokaiya, Stridor, Swindle, Tumult, Uproar, Utis

Radar Angel, AWACS, Beacon, DEW line, Doppler, Gadget, Gee, Gull, Lidar, Loran, Monopulse, Navar, Rebecca-eureka, Shoran, Surveillance, Teleran®, Tracking

Radiance, **Radiant** Actinic, Aglow, Aureola, Beamish, Brilliant, Glory, Glow, Happy, Lustre, Refulgent, Sheen

Radiate, **Radiating**, **Radiation**, **Radiator** Actinal, Air-colour, Beam, Bremsstrahlung, C(h)erenkov, Effuse, Emanate, Fluorescence, Glow, Heater, Infrared, Isohel, Laser, Millirem, Pentact, Photon, Pulsar, Quasar, Rem(s), Rep, Roentgen, > **SHINE**, Sievert, Spherics, Spoke, Stellate, SU, Sun, Ultra violet, Van Allen

Radical Amyl, Aryl, Bolshevist, Bolshie, Butyl, Ester, Extreme, Fundamental, Innate, Leftist, Methyl, Phenyl, Pink, Propyl, Red, Revolutionary, Root, Rudiment, Trot(sky), Vinyl, Whig

Radio Boom-box, Cat's whisker, CB, Cellular, Citizen's band, Crystal set, Digital, Ether, Gee, Ghetto-blaster, Local, Loudspeaker, Marconigraph, Receiver, Reflex, Set, Simplex, Sound, Steam, Talkback, Tranny, Transceiver, Transistor, Transmitter,

Transponder, Walkie-talkie, Walkman®, Walky-talky, Wireless

Radioactive, Radioactivity Actinide, Americium, Astatine, Bohrium, Cobalt 60, Emanation, Hot, Nucleonics, Steam, Thorium, Uranite

Radiology Interventional

Raft(ing) Balsa, Catamaran, Float, Kontiki, Life, Pontoon

Rafter Barge-couple, Beam, Chevron, Jack, Joist, Ridge, Spar, Timber

Rag(ged), Rags Bait, Bate, Clout, Coral, Deckle, Dud(s), Duddery, Duddie, Duster, Fent, Figleaf, Glad, Guyed, Haze, Kid, Lap(pie), Lapje, Mop, Paper, Red, Remnant, Revel, Rivlins, Roast, Rot, S(c)hmatte, Scold, Scrap, > **SHRED**, Slate, Slut, Splore, Tat(t), Tatter(demalion), Tatty, Taunt, > **TEASE**, Tiger, Tongue, Uneven

▷ **Rag(ged)** *may indicate* an anagram

Rage, Raging > **ANGER**, Ardour, Bait, Bate, Bayt, Chafe, Conniption, Explode, Fashion, Fierce, Fit, Fiz(z), Fume, Furibund, Furore, Fury, Gibber, Go, Ire, Mode, Paddy(-whack), Passion, Pelt, Pet, Rabid, Ramp, Rant, Road, Snit, Storm, Tear, Temper, Ton, Utis, Wax, Wrath

Raid(er) Assault, Attack, Bodrag, Bust, Camisado, Chappow, Commando, Do, For(r)ay, Imburst, Incursion, Inroad, Inrush, Invade, Jameson, Maraud, March-treason, Mosstrooper, Pict, Pillage, Plunder, Ransel, Razzia, Reive, Sack, Scrump, Skrimp, Skrump, Smash-and-grab, Sortie, Spreagh, Storm, Viking

Rail(er), Railing Abuse, Arm, Arris, Balustrade, Ban, Banister, > **BAR**, Barre, Barrier, Bird, Conductor, Coot, Corncrake, Crake, Criticise, Dado, Fender, Fiddle, Flanged, Flat-bottomed, Flow, Gush, Insult, Inveigh, Light, Live, Metal, Picture, Pin, Plate, Post, Pulpit, Rag, Rate, Rave, Rung, Scold, Slate, Slip, Sora, Soree, Spar, T, Taffrail, Takahe, Taunt, Third, Towel, Train

Railroad, Railway Amtrak, BR, Bulldoze, Cable, Cash, Coerce, Cog, Cremaillère, Dragoon, El, Elevated, Funicular, GWR, Inclined, L, Light, Lines, LMS, LNER, Loop-line, Maglev, Marine, Metro, Monorail, Mountain, Narrow-gauge, Rack, Rack and pinion, Rly, Road, Rollercoaster, Ropeway, ROSCO, Ry, Scenic, SR, Stockton-Darlington, Switchback, Telpher-line, Track, Train, Tramline, Tramway, Trans-Siberian, Tube, Underground

Rain(y) Acid, Brash, Deluge, Drizzle, Hyad(e)s, Hyetal, Mistle, Mizzle, Oncome, Onding, Onfall, Pelt, Pluviose, Pluvious, Pour, Precipitation, Right, Roke, Scat, Seil, Serein, Serene, Shell, Shower, Sile, Skiffle, Skit, Smir(r), Smur, Soft, Spat, Spet, Spit, Storm, Thunder-plump, Virga, Weep, Wet

Raise(d), Raising Advance, Aggrade, Attollent, Boost, Build, Cat, Coaming, Cock, Collect, Elate, > **ELEVATE**, Emboss, Enhance, Ennoble, Erect, Escalate, Exalt, Fledge, Grow, Heave, Heezie, Heft, High, Hike, Hoist, Increase, Jack, Key, Leaven, Lift, Mention, Overcall, Perk, Rear, Regrate, Repoussé, Revie, Rouse, Saleratus, Siege, Sky, Snarl, Sublimate, Upgrade, Weigh

Rake, Raker, Rakish Casanova, Comb, Corinthian, Dapper, Dissolute, Enfilade, Jaunty, Lecher, Libertine, Lothario, Raff, Reprobate, Rip, Roué, Scan, Scour, Scowerer, Scratch, Strafe, Swash-buckler, Swinge-buckler, Wagons

Rally, Rallying-point Autocross, Autopoint, Badinage, Banter, Demo, Gather, Jamboree, Meeting, Mobilise, Monte Carlo, Muster, Oriflamme, Persiflage, Recover, Rely, Rest, Risorgimento, Roast, Rouse, Scramble

Ram Aries, Battering, Buck, Bunt, Butter, Corvus, Crash, Drive, Hidder, Hydraulic, Mendes, Pun, Sheep, Stem, Tamp, Tup, Wether

Ramble(r), Rambling Aberrant, Aimless, Digress, Incoherent, Liana, Liane, Rigmarole, Roam, Rose, Rove, Skimble-skamble, Sprawl, Stray, Vagabond, Wander

Ramp Bank, Gradient, Helicline, Incline, Slipway, Slope

▷ **Rampant** *may indicate* an anagram or a reversed word

Rampart Abat(t)is, Brisure, Butt, Defence, Fortification, Parapet, Terreplein, Vallum, Wall

Ranch Bowery, Corral, Farm, Hacienda, Spread

Rancid Frowy, Reast(y), Reest(y), Sour, Turned

Rancour Gall, Hate, Malice, Resentment, Spite

Random Accidental, Aleatoric, Arbitrary, > **AT RANDOM**, Blind, Casual, Desultory, Fitful, > **HAPHAZARD**, Harvest, Hit-or-miss, Indiscriminate, Scattershot, Sporadic, Stochastic

▷ **Random(ly)** *may indicate* an anagram

Range(r), Rangy Align, Ambit, Andes, Atlas, AZ, Band, Bushwhack, Capsule, Carry, Cheviot, Compass, Cotswolds, Course, Darling, Diapason, Dolomites, Dynamic, Err, > **EXTENT**, Eye-shot, Forest, Gamut, Gunshot, Harmonic, Himalayas, Interquartile, Ken(ning), Kolyma, Limit, Line, Long, Massif, > **MOUNT**, Orbit, Oven, Owen Stanley, Palette, Point-blank, Prairie, Purview, Rake, Reach, Register, Repertoire, Roam, Rocket, Scale, Scope, Sc(o)ur, Selection, Short, Sierra, Sloane, Spectrum, Sphere, Urals, Wasatch, Waveband, Woomera

Rank(s) Arrant, Begum, Brevet, Caste, Category, Cense, Classify, Cornet, Degree, Dignity, Downright, Earldom, Estate, Etat(s), Grade, Gross, High, Olid, Place, Range, Rate, Rooty, Row, Sergeant, Serried, Sort, > **STATION**, Status, Taxi, Tier, > **TITLE**, Utter, Viscount

Ransack Fish, Loot, Pillage, Plunder, Rifle, Ripe, Rob, Rummage

Rant(er), Ranting Bombast, Declaim, Fustian, Ham, Harangue, Rail, Rodomontade, Scold, Spout, Spruik, Stump, Thunder, Tub-thump

Rap(ped) Blame, Censure, Clour, Gangsta, Halfpenny, Knock, Ratatat, Shand, Strike, Swapt, Tack, Tap

Rape Abuse, Assault, Belinda, Cole-seed, Colza, Creach, Creagh, Date, Deflower, Despoil, Gangbang, Hundred, Lock, Lucretia, Navew, Oilseed, Plunder, Stuprate, Thack, Violate

Rapid(ity), Rapidly Chute, Dalle, Express, Fast, Meteoric, Mosso, Presto, Pronto, Quick-fire, Riffle, Sault, Shoot, Speedy, Stickle, Swift, Veloce, Wildfire

Rapport Accord, Affinity, Agreement, Harmony

Rapture, Rapturous Bliss, > **DELIGHT**, Ecstasy, Elation, Joy, Trance

Rare, Rarity Blue moon, Curio, Earth, Geason, Infrequent, Intemerate, One-off, Rear, Recherché, Scarce, Seeld, Seld(om), Singular, > **UNCOMMON**, Uncooked, Underdone, Unusual

Rascal(ly) Arrant, Bad hat, Cad, Cullion, Cur, Devil, Gamin, Hallian, Hallion, Hallyon, Limner, Loon, Low, Rip, Rogue, Scallywag, Scamp, Scapegrace, Schelm, Skeesicks, Skellum, Skelm, Smaik, Spalpeen, Tinker, Toe-rag, Varlet, Varmint, Villain

Rash(er) Acne, Bacon, Brash, Collop, Daredevil, Eruption, Erysipelas, Fast, Foolhardy, Harum-scarum, > **HASTY**, Headlong, Hives, Hotspur, Impetigo, Impetuous, Imprudent, Impulsive, Lichen, Madbrain, Madcap, Nettle, Outbreak, Overhasty, Precipitate, Reckless, Roseola, Rubella, Sapego, Serpigo, Spots, Thoughtless, Unheeding, Unthinking, Urticaria

Rat(s), Ratty Agouta, Bandicoot, Blackleg, Blackneb, Boodie, Brown, Bug-out, Camass, Cane, Cur, Defect, Desert, Fink, Footra, Foutra, Geomyoid, Gym, Heck, Hydromys, Informer, Kangaroo, Mall, Maori, Mole, Moon, Norway, Pack, Poppycock, Potoroo, Pshaw, Pup(py), Renegade, Renegate, Rice, Rink, Rodent, Roland, Rot(ten), Scab, Sewer, Shirty, Squeal, Stinker, Turncoat, Vole, Water, Wharf, Whiskers, White, Wood

Rate(s), Rating A, Able, Apgar, Appreciate, Assess, Base, Basic, Bit, Carpet, Castigate, Cess, Classify, Cost, Count, Credit, Deserve, Erk, Estimate, Evaluate,

Exchange, Grade, Headline, Hearty, Hurdle, Incidence, ISO, Lapse, Leading, Mate's, Mortality, Mortgage, MPH, Octane, Ordinary, OS, Pace, Penalty, Percentage, PG, Piece, Poor, Prime (lending), Rag, Rebuke, Red, Refresh, Reproof, Rocket, Row, Sailor, Scold, Slew, > **SPEED**, Standing, Starting, Surtax, TAM, Tax, Tempo, Tog, U, Upbraid, Value, Water, Wig, World-scale, X

Rather Degree, Gey, Instead, Lief, Liever, Loor, More, Prefer, Pretty, Some(what), Sooner

Ratio Advance, Albedo, Aspect, Bypass, Cash, Compression, Cosine, Distinctiveness, Duplicate, Focal, Fraction, Golden, Gyromagnetic, Inverse, Liquidity, Loss, Mass, Neper, PE, Pi, Pogson, Poisson's, Position, Proportion, Protection, Quotient, Reserve, Savings, Signal-to-noise, Sin(e), Slip, Tensor, Trigonometric

Ration(s) Allocate, Apportion, Compo, Dole, Etape, Iron, K, Quota, Restrict, Scran, Share, Size

Rational(isation) Dianoetic, Level-headed, Logical, Lucid, Matter-of-fact, Sane, Sensible, Sine, Sober, Tenable

Rattle (box), Rattling Chatter, Clack, Clank, Clap, Clatter, Conductor, Death, Demoralise, Disconcert, Gas-bag, Hurtle, Jabber, Jangle, Jar, Natter, Nonplus, Rale, Rap, Reel, Rhonchus, Ruckle, Shake, Sistrum, Tirl, Upset

Ravage Depredation, Desecrate, Despoil, Havoc, Pillage, Prey, Ruin, Sack, Waste

Raven(ous) Black, Corbel, Corbie, Corvine, Croaker, Daw, Grip, Hugin, Munin, Unkindness

Ravine Arroyo, Barranca, Barranco, Canada, Chasm, Chine, Clough, Coulee, Couloir, Dip, Flume, Ghyll, Gorge, Grike, Gulch, Gully, Kedron, Khor, Khud, Kidron, Kloof, Lin(n), Nal(l)a, Nallah, Nulla(h), Pit

Ravish Constuprate, Debauch, Defile, Devour, Rape, Stuprate, Transport, Violate

Raw Brut, Chill, Coarse, Crude, Crudy, Damp, Fresh, Greenhorn, Natural, Recruit, Rude, Uncooked, Wersh

Ray(s), Rayed Actinic, Alpha, Beam, Beta, Canal, Cathode, Cosmic, Delta, Diactine, Dun-cow, Eagle, Electric, Fish, Gamma, Grenz, Guitarfish, Homelyn, Manta, Medullary, Monactine, Polyact, R, Radius, Re, Roentgen, Roker, Röntgen, Sawfish, Sea-devil, Sephen, Shaft, Skate, Stick, Sting, Stingaree, Tetract, Thornback, Torpedo

Reach(ed) Ar(rive), Attain, Boak, Boke, Carry, Come, Get out, Hent, Hit, Key-bugle, Lode, Octave, Peak, Raught, Rax, Retch, Ryke, Seize, Stretch, Touch, Win

React(or), Reaction(ary) Allergy, Answer, Backlash, Backwash, Behave, Blimp, Blowback, Breeder, Bristle, Catalysis, Chain, Convertor, Core, Counterblast, Dibasic, Falange, Fast(-breeder), Feedback, Furnace, Gut, Interplay, Kickback, Knee-jerk, Nuclear, Outcry, Pile, Reciprocate, Recoil, Repercussion, Respond, Reversible, Rigid, Sensitive, Sprocket, Thermal

▷ **Reactionary** *may indicate* reversed or an anagram

Read(ing) Bearing, Browse, Decipher, Decode, Exegesis, First, Grind, Grounden, Haftarah, Haphtarah, Interpret, Learn, Lection, Lesson, Lu, Maftir, Maw, Pericope, Peruse, Pore, Rad, Rennet-bag, Scan, Second, See, Solve, Speed, Stomach, > **STUDY**, Third, Vell, Ycond

Reader(s) ABC, Alidad(e), Bookworm, Editor, Epistoler, Lay, Lector, Primer, Silas Wegg, Taster

Readiest, Readily, Readiness, Ready Alacrity, Alamain, Alert, Amber, Apt, Atrip, Available, Boun, Bound, Brass, Cash, Conditional, Dough, Eager, Early, Eftest, Fettle, Fit, Forward, Game, Geared-up, Gelt, Go, Keyed, Latent, Lolly, Masterman, Money, On, Predy, Prepared, Present, Prest, Primed, Prompt, Reckoner, Ripe, Set, Soon, Spot, Turnkey, Usable, Wherewithal, Willing, Yare, Yark

Readymade Bought, Precast, Prepared, Prêt-à-porter, Slops, Stock, Store

Real, Reality, Realities, Really Actual, Bona-fide, Coin, Deed, De facto, Dinkum, Dinky-di(e), Earnest, Echt, Ens, Entia, Entity, Essence, > **GENUINE**, Honest, Indeed, Mackay, McCoy, McKoy, Naive, Ontic, Quite, Royal, Simon Pure, Sooth, Sterling, Substantial, Tangible, Tennis, Thingliness, True, Verismo, Verity, Very, Virtual

Realise, Realisation, Realism, Realistic Achieve, Attain, Attuite, Cash, Dirty, Down-to-earth, Embody, Encash, Fetch, Fruition, Fulfil, Learn, Magic, Naive, Practical, Sell, Sense, Suss, Understand

▶ **Realities, Reality** *see* **REAL**

Realm Dominion, Field, Kingdom, Land, Region, Special(i)ty, UK

Ream Bore, Foam, Froth, Paper, Rime, Screed

Reap(er) Binder, Crop, Death, Earn, Gather, Glean, Harvest, Scythe, Shear, Sickleman, Solitary, Stibbler

Rear(ing) Aft, Back(side), Baft, Behind, Bring-up, Bunt, Cabré, Derrière, Foster, Haunch, Hind, Loo, Nousell, Nurture, Prat, > **RAISE**, Serafile, Serrefile, Tonneau

Reason(able), Reasoning A fortiori, Analytical, Apagoge, A priori, Argue, Argument, Basis, Call, Cause, Colour, Consideration, Deduce, Expostulate, Fair, Ground(s), Ijtihad, Inductive, Intelligent, Logic, Logical, Logistics, Mind, Moderate, Motive, Noesis, Petitio principii, Plausible, Point, Pretext, Pro, Proof, Purpose, Rational(e), Sanity, Sense, Sensible, Settler, Syllogism, Synthesis, Think, Why, Wit

Rebate Diminish, Lessen, Refund, Repayment

Rebel(lion), Rebellious Apostate, Beatnik, Bolshy, Boxer, Cade, Contra, Danton, Diehard, Fifteen, Forty-five, Iconoclast, Insurgent, Insurrection, IRA, Jacobite, Kick, Luddite, Mutine(er), Mutiny, Oates, Putsch, Recalcitrant, Recusant, Resist, Revolt, Rise, Sedition, Straw, Tyler, Warbeck, Zealot

▷ **Rebellious** *may indicate* a word reversed

Rebuff Check, Cold-shoulder, Noser, Quelch, Repulse, Retort, Rubber, Sneb, Snib, Snub

Rebuke Admonish, Berate, Check, Chide, Earful, Lecture, Neb, Objurgate, Rap, Rate, Razz, Reprimand, Reproof, Reprove, Rollick, Scold, Slap, Slate, Snub, Strop, Threap, Threep, Tick off, Trim, Tut, Upbraid, Wig

Recall(ing) Annul, Eidetic, Encore, Evocative, Reclaim, Recollect, Redolent, Remember, Remind, Reminisce, Repeal, Retrace, Revoke, Total, Withdraw

▷ **Recast** *may indicate* an anagram

Recede Decline, Ebb, Lessen, Regress, Shrink, Withdraw

Receipt(s) Acknowledge, Chit, Docket, Recipe, Revenue, Take, Voucher

Receive(d), Receiver Accept, Accoil, Admit, Antenna, Assignee, Bailee, Dipole, Dish, Donee, Ear, Fence, Get, Grantee, Greet, Hydrophone, Inherit, Pernancy, Phone, Pocket, Radio, Reset, Roger, Set, Take, Tap, Transistor

Recent(ly) Alate, Current, Fresh, Hot, Just, Late, Modern, New, Yesterday, Yestereve, Yesterweek

Receptacle Ash-tray, Basket, Bin, Bowl, Box, Ciborium, Container, Cyst, Hell-box, Monstrance, Reliquary, Relique, Sacculus, Spermatheca, Tank, Thalamus, Tidy, Tore, Torus

Reception, Receptive Accoil, At home, Bel-accoyle, Couchée, Court, Durbar, Greeting, Infare, Kursaal, Levée, Open, Ovation, Ruelle, Saloon, Sensory, Soirée, Teleasthetic, Welcome

Receptor(s) Metabotropic, Steroid

Recess(ion) Alcove, Apse, Bay, Break, Cove, Dinette, Ebb, Embrasure, Fireplace, Grotto, Inglenook, Interval, > **NICHE**, Nook, Respite, Rest, Withdrawal

▷ **Recess** *may indicate* 'reversed'

▷ **Recidivist** *may indicate* 'reversed'

Recipient Assignee, Beneficiary, Disponee, Grantee, Heir, Legatee, Receiver

Reciprocal, Reciprocate Corresponding, Elastance, Exchange, Inter(act), Mutual, Repay, Return

Recital, Recitation(ist), Recite(r) Ave, Declaim, Diseuse, Enumerate, Litany, Monologue, Parlando, Quote, Reading, Reel, Relate, Rhapsode, Say, Sing, Tell

Reckless(ness) Blindfold, Careless, Catiline, Desperado, Desperate, Devil-may-care, Gadarene, Harum-scarum, Hasty, Headfirst, Headlong, Hell-bent, Irresponsible, Madcap, Perdu(e), Ramstam, Rantipole, > RASH, Slapdash, Temerity, Ton-up, Wanton, Wildcat

▷ **Reckless** *may indicate* an anagram

Reckon(ing) Assess, Bet, Calculate, Cast, Census, Computer, Consider, Count, Date, Doomsday, Estimate, Fancy, Figure, Guess, Number, Rate, Settlement, Shot, Tab

Reclaim(ed), Reclamation Assart, Empolder, Impolder, Innings, Novalia, Polder, Recover, Redeem, Restore, Swidden, Tame, Thwaite

Recognise(d), Recognition Accept, Acknow(ledge), Admit, Anagnorisis, Appreciate, Ascetic, Cit(ation), Exequatur, Identify, Isolated, Ken, > KNOW, Nod, Oust, Own, Reward, Salute, Scent, Standard, Voice, Wat, Weet

Recoil Backlash, Bounce, Kick(back), Quail, Rebound, Redound, Repercussion, Resile, Reverberate, Shrink, Shy, Spring, Start

Recollect(ion) Anamnesis, Memory, Pelmanism, Recall, > REMEMBER, Reminisce

▷ **Recollection** *may indicate* an anagram

Recommend(ation) Advise, Advocate, Counsel, Direct, Endorse, Nap, Promote, Rider, Suggest, Testimonial, Tip, Tout

Recompense Cognisance, Deodand, Deserts, Expiate, Guerdon, Pay, Remunerate, Repayment, Requite, Restitution, Reward

Reconcile(d) Adapt, Adjust, Affrended, Atone, Harmonise, Henotic, Make up, Mend

Record(er), Record company, Recording Album, Ampex, Annal(ist), Archive, Audit trail, Bench-mark, Black box, Blue Riband, Book, Can, Casebook, CD, Chart, Chronicle, Clickstream, Coat(e), Daybook, Diary, Dictaphone®, Dictograph®, Digital, Disc, Document, Dossier, Elpee, EMI, Endorsement, English flute, Enter, Entry, EP, Ephemeris, Estreat, Ever, File, Film, Flight, Flute, Form, Forty-five, Gram, Hansard, Incremental, Indie, Journal, Ledger, List, Log, Logbook, LP, Mark, Maxi-single, Memento, Memo(randum), Memorial, Memorise, Meter, Minute, Mono, Notate, Notch, Note, Pass book, Platter, Playback, Pressing, Previous, Protocol, Public, Quote, Rapsheet, Rec, Register, Release, Roll, Score(board), Seven-inch, Seventy-eight, Single, Stenotype®, Tachograph, Tally, Tallyman, Tape, Thirty-three, Toast, Trace, Track, Transcript, Travelog, Trip, Twelve-inch, VERA, Vid(eo), Videotape, Vote, Wax, Wire, Worksheet, Write

Recover(y) Amend, Clawback, Comeback, Convalescence, Cure, Dead cat bounce, Lysis, Over, Perk, Rally, Reclaim, Recoup, Redeem, Regain, Repaint, Replevin, Replevy, Repo(ssess), Rescript, Rescue, Resile, > RETRIEVE, Revanche, Salvage, Salve, Upswing

Recruit(s) Attestor, Bezonian, Choco, Conscript, Crimp, Draft, Employ, Engage, Enlist, Enrol, Headhunt, Intake, Muster, Nignog, Nozzer, Rookie, Sprog, Volunteer, Wart, Yobbo

Rectifier, Rectify Adjust, Amend, Dephlegmate, Redress, Regulate, > REMEDY, Right

Recur(rent), Recurring Chronic, Quartan, Quintan, Recrudesce, Repeated, Repetend, Return

▷ **Recurrent** *may indicate* 'reversed'

Recycler, Recycling Freegan

Red(den), Redness Admiral, Angry, Ashamed, Auburn, Beet, Blush, Bolshevik, Brick, Burgundy, C, Carmine, Carroty, Cent, Cerise, Cherry, Chinese, Claret, Commo, Communist, Copper, Coral, Corallin(e), Crimson, Crocoite, Debit, Duster, Embarrassed, Eosin, Eric, Erik, Erythema, Flame, Flaming, Florid, Flush, Foxy, Garnet, Geranium, Ginger, Gory, Gu(les), Guly, Hat, Henna, Herring, Indian, Inflamed, Infra, Inner, Lake, Left(y), Lenin, Letter, Magenta, Maoist, Maroon, Marxist, Murrey, Neaten, Oxblood, Pillar-box, Plum, Pompeian, Poppy, Raddle, Radical, Raspberry, Raw, Realgar, Rhodamine, Rhodopsin, Ridinghood, Roan, Rosaker, Rose, Rot, Rouge, Rubefy, Rubella, Ruby, Ruddy, Russ(e), Russet, Russian, Rust(y), Sanguine, Santalin, Sard, Scarlet, Setter, Tape, Tidy, Tile, Titian, Trot, Trotsky, Turkey, Venetian, Vermilion, Vinaceous, Wine

▷ **Red** *may indicate* an anagram

Redeem(er), Redemption Cross, Liberate, Mathurin, Ransom, Retrieve, Salvation, Save

▶ **Red Indian** *see* NORTH AMERICAN INDIAN

▷ **Rediscovered** *may indicate* an anagram

Reduce(r), Reduced, Reduction Abatement, Allay, Alleviate, Attenuate, Beggar, Clip, Commute, Condense, Contract, Cut, Cutback, Damping, Debase, Decimate, Decrease, Decrement, Demote, Deplete, Detract, Devalue, Diminish, Diminuendo, Discount, Downsize, Draw-down, Epitomise, Grind, > LESSEN, Lite, Markdown, Mitigate, Moderate, Palliate, Pot, Pulp, Put, Remission, Retrench, Rundown, Scant, Shade, Shorten, Shrinkage, Slash, Strain, Taper, Telescope, Thin, Weaken, Write-off

Redundancy, Redundant Frill, Futile, Needless, Otiose, Pleonasm, Superfluous, Surplus

Reef Atoll, Barrier, Bombora, Cay, Coral, Fringing, Great Barrier, Key, Knot, Lido, Motu, Sca(u)r, Skerry, Witwatersrand

Reel Bobbin, Dance, Eightsome, Hoolachan, Hoolican, Pirn, Spin, Spool, Stagger, Strathspey, Sway, Swift, Swim, Totter, Wheel, Whirl, Wintle

Refer Advert, Allude, Assign, Cite, Direct, Mention, Pertain, Relate, Remit, Renvoi, Renvoy, See, Submit, Touch, Trade

Referee Arbiter, Commissaire, Mediate, Oddsman, Ref, Umpire, Voucher, Whistler, Zebra

Reference Allusion, Apropos, Character, Coat, Grid, Index, Innuendo, Mention, Passion, Quote, Regard, Renvoi, Respect, Retrospect, Testimonial, Vide

Refine(d), Refinement, Refiner(y) Alembicate, Attic, Catcracker, Couth, Cultivate, Culture, Distinction, Elaborate, Elegance, Exility, Exquisite, Genteel, Grace, Nice, Nicety, Polish(ed), Polite, Précieuse, Pure, Rare(fy), Recherché, Saltern, Sift, Smelt, Spirituel, Subtilise, Try, U, Urbane, Veneer

Reflect(ing), Reflection, Reflective, Reflector Albedo, Blame, Cat's eye®, Cats-eye, Chew, Cogitate, > CONSIDER, Echo, Glass, Glint, Image, Meditate, Mirror, Muse, Ponder, Ruminate, Thought

Reform(er) Amend, Apostle, Bloomer, Calvin, Chastise, Correct, Enrage, Fry, Ghandi, Howard, Improve, Knox, Lollard, Luther, Mend, PR, Progressionist, Protestant, Puritan, Rad(ical), Recast, Reclaim, Reconstruction, Rectify, Regenerate, Ruskin, Transmute

▷ **Reform(ed)** *may indicate* an anagram

Refrain Abstain, Alay, Avoid, Bob, Burden, Chorus, Desist, Epistrophe, Fa-la,

Forbear, Hemistich, Repetend, Ritornello, Rumbelow, Rum(p)ti-iddity, Rum-ti-tum, Spare, Tag, Tirra-lirra, Tirra-lyra, Undersong, Wheel

Refresh(ment), Refresher Air, Bait, Be(a)vers, Buffet, Cheer, Elevenses, Enliven, Food, Four-hours, Nap, New, Nourishment, Purvey, Refection, Reflect, Refocillate, Reinvigorate, Renew, Repast, Restore, Revive, Seltzer, Shire, Slake, Water

Refrigerator Chill, Chiller, Cooler, Deep freeze, Esky®, Freezer, Freon, Fridge, Ice-box, Minibar, Reefer

Refuge Abri, Asylum, Bolthole, Dive, Fastness, Funkhole, Girth, Grith, Harbour, Haven, Hideaway, Hole, Holt, Home, Hospice, Oasis, Port, Reefer, Resort, Retreat, Sheet-anchor, > **SHELTER**, Soil, Stronghold

▷ **Refurbished** *may indicate* an anagram

Refusal, Refuse Bagasse, Ba(u)lk, Bilge, Bin, Black, Blackball, Boycott, Bran, Brash, Breeze, Brock, Bull, Bunkum, Cane-trash, Chaff, Clap-trap, Crane, Crap, Debris, Decline, Deny, Disown, Draff, Drivel, Dross, Dunder, Dung, Fag-end, Fenks, Finks, First, Frass, Garbage, Guff, Hogwash, Hold-out, Husk, Interdict, Jib, Junk, Knub, Lay-stall, Leavings, Litter, Lumber, Mahmal, Marc, Megass(e), Midden, Mush, Nay(-say), Nill, No, Noser, Nould, Nub, Offal, Off-scum, Orts, Pigwash, Pot all, Punk, Raffle, Rape(cake), Rat(s), Rebuff, Red(d), Reest, Regret, Reneg(u)e, Renig, Rot, > **RUBBISH**, Ruderal, Scaff, Scrap, Scree, Scum, Sewage, Shant, Shell heap, Slag, Spurn, Sullage, Sweepings, Swill, Tinpot, Tip, Tosh, Trade, Trash, Tripe, Trumpery, Turndown, Twaddle, Unsay, Utter, Wash, Waste

▷ **Re-fused** *may indicate* an anagram

▶ **Regal** *see* **ROYAL**

Regard(ing) As to, Attention, Care, Consider, > **ESTEEM**, Eye, Gaum, Look, Observe, Odour, Pace, Rate, Re, Respect, Revere, Sake, Steem, Value, Vis-à-vis

Regardless Despite, Heedless, Irrespective, Notwithstanding, Rash, Uncaring, Willy-nilly

Regiment Black Watch, Buffs, Colour(s), Discipline, Greys, Ironsides, Lifeguard, Monstrous, Nutcrackers, Organise, RA, RE, REME, Rifle, Royals, Tercio, Tertia

▷ **Regiment** *may indicate* an anagram

Region Arctogaea, > **AREA**, Belt, Brittany, Bundu, Camargue, Chiasma, Climate, Clime, District, E, End, Hinterland, Hundred, Midi, Offing, Pargana, Part, Pergunnah, Piedmont, Province, Quart(er), Realm, Refugium, Ruthenia, Sector, Stannery, Subtopia, Tagma, Territory, Tetrarchate, Tract, Tundra, Umbria, Vaud, Weald, Zone

Register(ing), Registration, Registry Actuarial, Almanac, Annal, Cadastral, Cadastre, Calendar, Cartulary, Cash, Census, Check-in, Diptych, Enlist, Enrol, Enter, Gross, Handicap, Index, Indicate, Inscribe, Inventory, Land, Ledger, List, Lloyd's, Log, Matricula, Menology, NAI, Net, Note, Notitia, Parish, Park, Patent, Read, Record, Reg(g)o, Rent-roll, Roll, Roule, Score, Ship's, Soprano, Terrier, Voice

Regret(ful), Regrettable Alack, Alas, Apologise, Deplore, Deprecate, Ewhow, Forthwink, Ichabod, Lackaday, Lament, Mourn, Otis, Pity, Remorse, Repentance, Repine, Ruth, Sorrow, Tragic

Regular(ity), Regularly Clockwork, Constant, Custom, Episodic, Even, Giusto, Goer, Habitual, Habitué, Hourly, Insider, Methodic, Nine-to-five, Normal, Often, Orderly, Orthodox, Patron, Peloria, Periodic, Rhythmic, Routine, Set, Smooth, > **STANDARD**, Stated, Statutory, Steady, Strict, Symmetric, Uniform, Usual, Yearly

Regulate, Regulation, Regulator Adjust, Appestat, Bye-law, Code, Control, Correction, Curfew, Customary, Direct, Gibberellin, Governor, Guide, Logistics, Metrostyle, Order, Ordinance, Police, Rule, Snail, Square, Standard, Statute, Stickle, Sumptuary, Thermostat, Valve

Rehearsal, Rehearse Band-call, Dress, Drill, Dry-block, Dry-run, Dummy-run,

Practice, Practise, Preview, Recite, Repeat, Trial

Reign Era, Govern, Meiji, Prevail, Raine, Realm, Restoration, > RULE

Rein(s) Bearing, Check, Control, Curb, Free, Lumbar, Restrain

Reinforce(ment) Aid, Augment, Bolster, Boost, Brace, Buttress, Cleat, Line, Plash, Pleach, Recruit, Reserve, > STRENGTHEN, Support, Tetrapod, Underline

Reject(ion) Abhor, Abjure, Athetise, Bin, Blackball, Cast, Deny, Dice, Discard, Disclaim, Disdain, Diss, Flout, Frass, Jilt, Kest, Kill, Knock-back, Ostracise, Oust, Outcast, Outtake, Pip, Plough, Rebuff, Recuse, Refuse, Reny, Reprobate, Repudiate, Repulse, Scout, Scrub, Spet, Spin, Spit, Sputum, Thumbs-down, Turndown, Veto

Rejoice, **Rejoicing** Celebrate, Exult, Festivity, Gaude, Glory, Joy, Maffick, Sing

Rejoin(der), **Rejoined** Answer, Counter, Relide, Reply, Response, Retort, Reunite

Relate(d), **Relation(ship)**, **Relative** Account, Affair, Agnate, Akin, Allied, Appertain, Associate, Blood, Cognate, Concern, Connection, Connexion, Consanguinity, Cousin, Coz, Dispersion, Eme, Enate, False, Formula, German(e), Granny, Impart, Item, Kin, Kinsman, Labour, Liaison, Link, Love-hate, Mater, Material, Matrix, Narrative, One-to-one, Pertain, Phratry, Pi, Plutonic, Poor, > PROPORTION, Proxemics, Public, Race, Rapport, Ratio, Recite, Recount, Refer(ence), Relevant, Respect(s), Sib(b), Sibling, Sine, Symbiosis, Syntax, Tale, Tell, Who

Relax(ation), **Relaxant**, **Relaxed** Abate, Atony, Calm, Com(m)odo, Degage, Detente, Diversion, Downbeat, Ease, Easy-going, Flaccid, Laid-back, Leisured, > LOOSEN, Mitigate, Peace, Relent, Relief, Remit, Rest, Slacken, Sleep, Toneless, Unbend, Unknit, Untie, Unwind

▷ **Relaxed** *may indicate* an anagram

▷ **Relay(ing)** *may indicate* an anagram

Release Abreact, Announcement, Bail, Catharsis, Clear, Day, Death, Deliver(y), Desorb, Disburden, Discharge, Disclose, Disengage, Disimprison, Dismiss, Disorb, Emancipate, Enfree, Excuse, Exeem, Exeme, Extricate, Exude, Free, Handout, Happy, > LIBERATE, Manumit, Merciful, Moksa, Parole, Press, Quietus, Quittance, Relinquish, Ripcord, Soft, Spring, Tre corde, Unconfine, Uncouple, Undo, Unhand, Unleash, Unloose, Unpen, Unshackle, Unteam, Untie

Relevance, **Relevant** Ad rem, Applicable, Apposite, Apropos, Apt, Germane, Material, Pertinent, Point, Valid

▶ **Reliable**, **Reliance** *see* RELY

Relic Antique, Ark, Artefact, Fossil, Leftover, Memento, Neolith, Remains, Sangraal, Sangrail, Sangreal, Souvenir, Survival

Relief, **Relieve(d)** Aid, Air-lift, Allay, Alleviate, Alms, Anodyne, Assistance, Assuage, Bas, Cameo, Cavo-relievo, Comfort, Cure, Détente, Ease(ment), Emboss, Emollient, Free, High, Indoor, Let-up, Lighten, Low, Mafeking, On the parish, Outdoor, Palliate, Phew, Photo, Pog(e)y, Reassure, Redress, Remedy, Replacement, Repoussé, Reprieve, > RESCUE, Respite, Retirement, Rid, Spare, Spell, Stand-in, Succour, Taper, Tax, Whew, Woodcut

Religion, **Religious (sect)** Baha'i, Biblist, Bogomil, Camaldolite, Carthusian, Celestine, Christadelphian, Cistercian, Coenobite, Congregant, Creed, Culdee, Denomination, Devout, Doctrine, Druse, Druz(e), Faith, Gilbertine, God-squad, Gueber, Guebre, Hadith, Hare Krishna, Has(s)id, Hieratic, Hospital(l)er, Ignorantine, Islam, Ismaili, Jain(a), Jansenism, Jehovah's Witness, Jesuit, Jewry, Judaism, Lamaism, Loyola, Lutheran, Mahatma, Manichee, Mazdaism, Mazdeism, Missionary, Missioner, Mithraism, Mormonism, Nun, Opium, Pantheist, Parsism, Pi, Piarist, Pietà, Postulant, Progressive, Reformation, Sabbatarian, Sabian, Sacramentarian, Santeria, Scientology®, Serious,

Shaker, Shamanism, Shango, Shinto(ism), Sikhism, Sodality, Sons of Freedom, Spike, Sunna, Taoism, Theatine, Theology, Tractarianism, Tsabian, Utraquist, Voodooism, Whore, Zabian, Zarathustric, Zealous, Zend-avesta, Zoroaster

Relish(ing) Botargo, Catsup, Chow-chow, Condiment, Enjoy, Flavour, Gentleman's, Gout, Gust(o), Ketchup, Lap(-up), Lust, Opsonium, Palate, Sapid, Sar, Sauce, Savour, Seasoning, Tang, Tooth, Worcester sauce, Zest

Reluctant Averse, Backward, Chary, Circumspect, Grudging, Laith, Loth, Nolition, Renitent, Shy, Unwilling

Rely, **Reliance**, **Reliant**, **Reliable** Addiction, Authentic, Bank, Confidence, Constant, > COUNT, Dependent, Found, Hope, Jeeves, Lean, Loyal, Mensch, Presume, Pukka, Rest, Safe, Secure, Solid, Sound, Sponge, Stand-by, Staunch, Trustworthy, Trusty, Unfailing

Remain(der), **Remaining**, **Remains** Abide, Ash(es), Balance, Bide, Continue, Corse, Dreg(s), Dwell, Embers, Estate, Exuviae, Fag-end, Kreng, Last, Late, Lave, Left, Lie, Locorestive, Manet, Nose, Oddment, Orts, Other, Outstand, Persist, Relic(ts), Reliquae, Residue, Rest, Ruins, Scourings, Scraps, Stay, Stick, Stub, Surplus, Survive, Tag-end, Talon, Tarry, Wait

Remark Aside, Barb, Bromide, Comment(ary), Descry, Dig, Generalise, Mention, Noise, > NOTE, Notice, Obiter dictum, Observe, Platitude, Reason, Sally, Shot, State

Remarkable, **Remarkably** Amazing, Arresting, Beauty, Bodacious, Conspicuous, Dilly, Egregious, Extraordinary, Heliozoan, Legendary, Lulu, Mirable, Notendum, Noteworthy, Phenomenal, Rattling, > SIGNAL, Singular, Some, Striking, Tall, Unco, Uncommon, Visible

Remedial, **Remedy** Aid, Antacid, Antibiotic, Antidote, Arnica, Calomel, Corrective, Cortisone, > CURE, Drug, Elixir, Feverfew, Fumitory, Ginseng, Heal, Ipecac, Medicate, Medicine, Nostrum, Palliative, Panacea, Paregoric, Poultice, Rectify, Redress, Repair, Salve, Simple, Specific, Therapeutic, Treatment

Remember(ing), **Remembrance** Bethink, Commemorate, Con, Mem, Memorial, Memorise, Mention, Mneme, Recall, Recollect, Remind, Reminisce, Retain, Rosemary, Souvenir

▷ **Remember** *may indicate* RE-memberviz. Sapper

Remind(er) Aftertaste, Aide-memoire, Bookmark, Evocatory, Evoke, Jog, Keepsake, Mark, Memento, Memo, Mnemonic, Mnemotechnic, Monition, Nudge, Phylactery, Prod, Prompt, Souvenir, Token

Remission Abatement, Absolution, Acceptilation, Indulgence, Pardon, Pause

Remnant Butt, End, Fent, Heeltap, Left-over, Odd-come-short, Offcut, Relic, > REMAINDER, Rump, Trace, Vestige

Remorse Angst, Ayenbite, Breast-beating, Compunction, Contrition, Had-i-wist, Pity, > REGRET, Rue, Ruing, Ruth, Sorrow

Remote Aloof, Aphelion, Backveld, Backwater, Backwood, Bullamakanka, Bundu, > DISTANT, Forane, Inapproachable, Insular, Irrelevant, Jericho, Long(inquity), Out(part), Outback, Scrub, Secluded, Shut-out, Slightest, Surrealistic, Unlikely, Withdrawn

Removal, **Remove(d)** Abduct, Abstract, Banish, Blot, Circumcision, Clear, Couch, Declassify, Dele(te), Depilate, Depose, Detach, Detract, Dislodge, Dispel, Doff, Efface, Eject, Eloi(g)n, Emend, Eradicate, Erase, Estrange, Evacuate, Evict, Exalt, Excise, Extirpate, Far, Flit, Huff, Nick, Rid, Scratch, Shift, Spirit, Subtract, Supplant, Transfer, Transport, Unseat, Uproot

Render(ing) Construe, Deliver, Do, Gie, Give, Interpretation, Make, Melt, Pebble-dash, Plaster, Provide, Recite, Represent, Restore, Setting, Tallow, Try, Yeve

Rendezvous Date, Meeting, Philippi, Tryst, Venue

Rendition Account, Delivery, Interpretation, Translation

Renegade, **Renege** Apostate, Default, Defector, Deserter, Rat(ton), Traitor, Turncoat

▷ **Renegade** *may indicate* a word reversal

Renew(al) Instauration, Neogenesis, Palingenesis, Refresh, Replace, Resumption, Retrace, Revival, Urban

Renounce, **Renunciation** Abandon, Abdicate, Abjure, Abnegate, Disclaim, Disown, For(e)go, For(e)say, Forfeit, Forisfamiliate, Forsake, Forswear, Kenosis, Recede, Relinquish, Renay, Retract, Sacrifice

Renovate(d), **Renovation** Duff, Face-lift, Instauration, Makeover, Refurbish, Renew, Repair, Restore, Revamp

Rent(er), **Renting** Broken, Charge, Cornage, Cost, Crack, Cranny, Cuddeehih, Cuddy, Division, Economic, Fair, Farm, Fee, Fissure, Gale, Gavel, Ground, > HIRE, Lease, Let, List, Mail, Market, Occupy, Peppercorn, Quit-rent, Rack, Rip, Rived, Riven, Screed, Seat, Slit, Split, Stallage, Subtenant, Tare, Tenant, Tithe, Tore, Torn, Tythe, White

▷ **Reorganised** *may indicate* an anagram

Repair(s), **Repairer**, **Reparation** Amend(s), Anaplasty, Botch, Cobble, Damages, Darn, Doctor, Fettle, Fitter, Go, Haro, Harrow, > MEND, Overhaul, Patch, Recompense, Redress, Refit, Reheel, Remedy, Renew, Repoint, Resort, Restore, Retouch, Satisfaction, Stitch, Ulling, Vamp, Volery

Repartee Backchat, Badinage, Banter, Persiflage, Rejoinder, Retort, Riposte, Wit

Repast Bever, Collection, Food, Meal, Tea, Treat

Repay(ment) Avenge, Compensate, Quit, Refund, Requite, Retaliate, Reward, Satisfaction

Repeat(edly), **Repetition**, **Repetitive** Again, Alliteration, Belch, Bis, Burden, Burp, Copy, Ditto(graphy), Duplicate, > ECHO, Echolalia, Encore, Eruct, Facsimile, Habitual, Harp, Image, Imitate, Iterate, Leit-motiv, Parrot, Passion, Perpetuate, Playback, Recite(r), Redo, Refrain, Regurgitate, Reiterate, Renew, Rep, Repetend, Rerun, Retail, Rote, Same(y), Screed, Tautology, Thrum

Repel(lent) Estrange, Harsh, Offensive, Rebarbative, Reject, Repulse, Revolt, Squalid, Turn-off, Ug(h), Ward

▶ **Repetition** *see* REPEAT

Replace(ment), **Replaceable**, **Replacing** Change, Deputise, Diadochy, For, Pre-empt, Raincheck, Refill, Replenish, Restore, Stand-in, Substitute, Supersede, Supplant, Surrogate, Taxis, Transform, Transliterate, Understudy

Replete, **Repletion** Awash, Full, Gorged, Plenitude, Plethora, Sated, Satiation

Replica Clone, Copy, Duplicate, Facsimile, Image, Repetition, Spit

Reply Accept, Answer, Churlish, Duply, Rejoinder, Rescript, Response, Retort, Surrebut, Surrejoin

Report(er) Account, Announce, Auricular, Bang, Blacksmith, Bruit, Bulletin, Cahier, Clap, Columnist, Comment, Commentator, Correspondent, Court, Cover, Crack, Crump, Cub, Debrief, Disclose, Dispatch, Explosion, Fame, Fireman, Grapevine, Hansard, Hearsay, Jenkins, Journalist, Legman, Libel, News, Newshawk, Newshound, Newsman, Noise, Pop, Pressman, Protocol, Relate, Relay, Representation, Repute, Return, Roorback, Rumour, Sitrep, Sound(bite), Staffer, State(ment), Stringer, Tale, > TELL, Thesis, Transcribe, Tripehound, Troop, Update, Weather, Whang, Wolfenden, Write up

▷ **Reported** *may indicate* the sound of a letter or word

Represent(ation), **Representative**, **Represented** Agent, Ambassador, Caricature, Client, Commercial, Cross-section, Delegate, Depict, Deputation, Describe, Display, Drawing, Drummer, Effigy, Elchee, Eltchi, Emblem, Embody,

Emissary, Example, Image, John Bull, Legate, Lobby, Map, Mouthpiece, MP, Personate, Personify, Portray, Proportional, Quintessence, Rep, Resemble, Salesman, Senator, Shop steward, Simulacrum, Spokesman, Stand-in, Steward, Symbolic, Tableau, Transcription, Typical

▷ **Represented** *may indicate* an anagram

Reprimand Bounce, Carpet, > CENSURE, Chide, Dressing-down, Earful, Jobe, Lace, Lecture, Rating, Rebuke, Reproof, Rocket, Rollicking, Slate, Strafe, Targe, Tick off, Tongue-lashing, Wig

Reproach Blame, Braid, Byword, Chide, Discredit, Dispraise, Exprobate, Gib, Mispraise, Odium, Opprobrium, Rebuke, Ronyon, Runnion, Scold, Shend, Sloan, Stigma, Taunt, Truant, Upbraid, Upcast, Yshend

Reproduce(r), Reproduction, Reproductive (organ) Clone, Copy, Counterfeit, Depict, Edition, Etch, Eugenics, Megaspore, Mono, Multiply, Oogamy, Parthenogenesis, Phon(e)y, Propagate, Refer, Replica, Roneo®, Seminal, Simulate, Stereo

▷ **Reproduce** *may indicate* an anagram

Reproof, Reprove Admonish, Berate, Chide, Correction, Corruption, Lecture, Rate, Rebuff, Rebuke, Scold, Sloan, Tut, Upbraid

Reptile, Reptilian Agamid, Alligarta, Alligator, Base, Basilisk, Caiman, Cayman, Chameleon, Chelonian, Creeper, Crocodile, Diapsid, Dicynodont, Dinosaur, Goanna, Herpetology, Lacertine, Lizard, Mamba, Pteranodon, Pterodactyl, Rhynchocephalian, Sauroid, > SNAKE, Squamata, Synapsid, Tegu(exin), Thecodont, Therapsid, Tortoise, Tuatara, Tuatera, Turtle, Worm

Republic Banana, State

Republican Antimonarchist, Democrat, Fenian, Fianna Fail, Girondist, IRA, Iraqi, Leveller, Montagnard, Mugwump, Plato, Red, Sansculotte, Sansculottic, Sinn Fein, Whig

Repudiate Abjure, Deny, Discard, Disclaim, Disown, Ignore, Recant, Reject, Renounce, Repel

Repugnance, Repugnant Abhorrent, Alien, Disgust, Distaste, Fulsome, Horror, Loathing, Revulsion

Reputable, Reputation, Repute(d) Bubble, Dit, Estimate, Fame, Good, Izzat, Loos, Los, Name, Note, Notoriety, Odour, Opinion, Prestige, Putative, Regard, Renown, Said, Sar, > STANDING, Stink, Trustworthy

Request Adjure, Appeal, Apply, Ask, Beg, Desire, Entreaty, Invite, Petition, Plea, Prayer, Solicit, Supplication

Require(d), Requirement Charge, Crave, De rigueur, Desire, Enjoin, Exact, Expect, Incumbent, Lack, Necessity, Need, Prerequisite

Requisite, Requisition Commandeer, Due, Embargo, Essential, Indent, Necessary, Needful, Order, Press

Rescue Aid, Air-sea, Deliver, Free, Liberate, Ransom, Recover, Recower, Redeem, Regain, Relieve, Reprieve, Retrieve, Salvage, Salvation, > SAVE

Research(er) Boffin, Delve, Dig, Enquiry, Explore, Fieldwork, Investigate, Legwork, Market, Operational, Pioneer, Sus(s)

Resemblance, Resemble, Resembling Affinity, Apatetic, Approach, Assonant, Likeness, -oid, -opsis, Replica, Similitude, Simulate

Resent(ful), Resentment Anger, Bridle, Choler, Cross, Dudgeon, Grudge, Indignation, Ire, Malign, Miff, Pique, Rankle, Smart, Spite, Umbrage

Reservation, Reserve(d), Reservist(s) Aloof, Arrière-pensée, Backlog, Bashful, Book, By, Caveat, Central, Cold, Demiss, Detachment, Distant, Earmark, Engage, Ersatz, Except, Fall-back, Fort Knox, Gold, Hold, Husband, Ice, Indian, Introvert, Landwehr, Layby, Locum, Mental, Militiaman, Nature, Nest-egg,

Nineteenth man, Proviso, Qualification, Reddendum, Res, Rest, Restraint, Retain, Reticence, Retiring, Rez, Salvo, Sanctuary, Save, Scenic, Scruple, Set aside, Special, Stand-by, Stand-offishness, Starch, Stash, Stock(pile), TA(men), Uncommunicate, Understudy, Warren, Waves, Withhold

Reservoir Basin, Cistern, G(h)ilgai, Gilgie, Repository, Stock, Sump, Tank

Reside(nce), Resident(s) Abode, Address, Amban, Chequers, Commorant, Consulate, Denizen, Dwell, Embassy, Establishment, Expatriate, Exurbanite, Gremial, Guest, Home, Indweller, Inholder, Inmate, Intern, Ledger, Lei(d)ger, Lieger, Lodger, Metic, Pad, Parietal, Resiant, Settle, Sojourn, Stay, Tenant, Villager, Yamen

Residual, Residue Ash, Astatki, Calx, Caput, Chaff, Cinders, Crud, Draff, Dregs, Expellers, Greaves, Leavings, Mazout, Mortuum, Remainder, Remanent, Remnant, Slag, Slurry, Snuff, Vinasse

Resign(ed), Resignation Abandon, Abdicate, Demit, Fatalism, Heigh-ho, Leave, Meek, > QUIT, Reconcile, Stoic, Submit

Resin Acaroid, Amber, Amine, Amino, Arar, Asaf(o)etida, Bakelite®, Balsam, Benjamin, Benzoin, Cannabin, Caranna, Carauna, Charas, Churrus, Colophony, Conima, Copai(ba), Copaiva, Copal(m), Courbaril, Dam(m)ar, Dammer, Dragon's blood, Elemi, Epoxy, Frankincense, Galbanum, Galipot, Gambi(e)r, Gamboge, Glyptal, Guaiacum, Gum, Hasheesh, Hashish, Hing, Jalapin, Kino, Lac, Ladanum, Mastic, Melamine, Myrrh, Olibanum, Opopanax, Phenolic, Podophyllin, Polyester, Polymer, Propolis, Retinite, Roset, Rosin, Rosit, Rozet, Rozit, Sagapenum, Sandarac(h), Saran®, Scammony, Shellac, Storax, Styrax, Synthetic, Takamaka, Urea, Xylenol

Resist Bristle, Buck, Contest, Defy, Face, Fend, Gainstrive, Impede, Oppose, Redound, Reluct, Stand (pat)

Resistance, Resistant, Resistor Barretter, Bleeder, Ceramal, Cermet, Chetnik, Coccidiostat, Combat, Drag, Element, Friction, Hostile, Immunity, Impediment, Internal, Invar, Klendusic, Klepht, Maquis, Maraging, Megohm, Microhm, Negative, Obstacle, Ohm, Passive, Pull, R, Radiation, Reluctance, Renitent, Resilient, Rheostat, Sales, Satyagraha, Soul-force, Specific, Stability, Stand, Stonde, Stubborn, Tough

Resolute, Resolution Analysis, Bold, Cast-iron, Courage, Decided, Decision, Denouement, Determined, > FIRM, Fortitude, Granite, Grim, Grit, Hardiness, Insist, Pertinacity, Promotion, Rede, Resolve, Stable, Stalwart, Staunch, Stout, Strength, Sturdy, Tenacity, Unbending, Valiant, Willpower

Resolve(d), Resolver Analyse, Calculate, Decide, Declare, > DETERMINE, Deux et machina, Factorise, Fix, Hellbent, Intent, Nerve, > PURPOSE, Settle, Steadfast, Tenacity, Vow

▷ **Resolved** *may indicate* an anagram

Resort Centre, Dive, Etaples, Expedient, Frame, Frequent, Haunt, Hove, Hydro, Invoke, Lair, Last, Las Vegas, Morecambe, Nassau, Pau, Pis aller, Rapallo, Recourse, Repair, Riviera, Southend, Spa(w), Use

▷ **Resort(ing)** *may indicate* an anagram

Resource(s), Resourceful Assets, Beans, Bottom, Chevisance, Clever, Faculty, Funds, Gumption, Ingenious, Input, Inventive, Means, Sharp, Stock-in-trade, > VERSATILE, Wealth

Respect(ed), Respectable, Respectful Admire, Ahimsa, Aspect, Behalf, Consider, Decent, Deference, Devoir, Duty, Esteem, Gigman, Homage, > HONOUR, Kempt, Latria, Obeisant, Officious, Pace, Particular, Preppy, Prestige, Proper, Reference, Regard, Relation, Reputable, Revere, Sir, S(t)irrah, U, Venerate, Wellborn, Well-thought-of, Wise, Worthy

Respirator, Respire, Respiration Artificial, Blow, Breathe, Exhale, Gasmask,

Inhale, Iron lung, Pant, Snorkel

Respond, Response, Responsive Amenable, Answer, Antiphon, Comeback, Conditioned, Echo, Feedback, Flechman, Grunt, Immune, Kneejerk, Kyrie, Litany, Nastic, Pavlovian, Photonasty, React(ion), Reflex, Reply, Repost, Retort, Rheotaxis, Rheotropism, Rise, Synapte, Syntonic, Tender, Thigmotropic, Tic, Tropism, Unconditioned, Voice, Warm

Responsibility, Responsible Anchor, Answerable, Baby, Blame, Buck, Charge, Culpable, Dependable, Diminished, Duty, Frankpledge, Hot seat, Incumbent, Instrumental, Liable, Mea culpa, Onus, Pigeon, Sane, Solid, Stayman, Trust

Rest (day) Anchor, Balance, Bed, Break, Breather, Calm, Catnap, Depend, Dwell, Ease, Easel, Etc, Feutre, Gite, Halt, Inaction, Jigger, Lave, Lean, Lie, Lie-in, Light, Lodge, Loll, Lound, Nap, Others, Pause, Quiescence, Quiet, Relache, Relax, Rely, Remainder, Repose, Requiem, Respite, Sabbath, Siesta, > SLEEP, Slumber, Spell, Spider, Stopover, Support, Surplus

Restaurant, Restaurateur Automat, Beanery, Bistro, Brasserie, British, Cabaret, Cafe, Canteen, Chew'n'spew, Chip-shop, Chophouse, Commissary, Cook shop, Creperie, Diner, Eatery, Eating-house, Estaminet, Greasy spoon, Grill, Grillroom, Grub shop, Luncheonette, Maxim's, Noshery, Padrone, Rathskeller, Ratskeller, Roadhouse, Rotisserie, Slap-bang, Steakhouse, Takeaway, Taqueria, Taverna, Teahouse, Tearoom, Teashop, Trattoria

Restive, Restless(ness) Chafing, Chorea, Fikish, Free-arm, Itchy, Jactitation, Toey, Unsettled

▷ **Restless** *may indicate an anagram*

Restoration, Restorative, Restore(d) Cure, Descramble, Heal, Mend, Pentimento, Pick-me-up, Postliminy, Rally, Recondition, Redeem, Redintegrate, Redux, Refurbish, Regenerate, Rehabilitate, Rejuvenate, Remedial, Renew, Renovate, Repone, Restitute, Resuscitate, Retouch, Revamp, Revive, Stet, Tonic

Restrain(ed), Restraint Abstinence, Ban, Bate, Bit, Bottle, Branks, Bridle, Cage, Chain, Chasten, > CHECK, Cohibit, Compesce, Confinement, Contain, Control, Cramp, Curb, Dam, Decorum, Detent, Dry, Duress, Embargo, Enfetter, Freeze, Halt, Hamshackle, Handcuffs, Harness, Heft, Hinder, Hopple, Impound, Inhibit, Jess, Lid, Low-key, Manacle, Measure, Mince, Moderation, Muzzle, Quiet, Rein, Repress, Restrict, Ritenuto, Shackle, Sober, Sobriety, Squeeze, Stay, Stent, Stint, Straitjacket, Temper, Tether, Tie, Trash

Restrict(ed), Restriction Band, Bar, Bind, Bit, Burden, Cage, Catch, Censorship, Chain, Circumscribe, Closet, Condition, Cord, Corset, Cramp, Curb, DORA, Fence, Fold, Gate, Ground, Guard, Hamper, Hidebound, Hobble, Inhibit, Intern, Kennel, Let, > LIMIT, Lock, Mere, Narrow, Net, Nick, Pale, Parochial, Pen, Pent, Pier, Pin, Pot-bound, Private, Proscribed, Qualify, Regulate, Rein, Rope, Safety belt, Scant, Seal, Section, Selected, Shackle, Snare, Squeeze, Stenopaic, Stent, Stint, Stop, Straiten, Stunt, Tether, Tie

Result(s) Aftermath, Ans(wer), Bring, Causal, Consequence, Effect, Emanate, End, Ensue, Entail, Event, Eventuate, Finding, Fruict, Fruits, Issue, Karmic, Lattermath, > OUTCOME, Outturn, Pan, Proceeds, Quotient, Sequel, Side-effect, Sum, Upshot, Wale

Retain(er), Retains Brief, Contain, Deposit, Fee, Hold, Keep, Panter, Pantler, Reserve, Retinue, Servant

Retaliate, Retaliation Avenge, Counter, Lex talionis, Quit(e), Redress, Repay, Reprisal, Requite, Retort, Talion

Reticence, Reticent Clam, Coy, Dark, Reserve, Restraint, Secretive, Shy, Taciturn

Retinue Company, Cortège, Equipage, Following, Meiney, Meinie, Meiny, Sowarry, Suite

Retire(d), **Retiree**, **Retirement**, **Retiring** Abed, Aloof, Baccare, Backare, Backpedal, Blate, Bowler-hat, Cede, Coy, Depart, Ebb, Emeritus, Essene, Former, Leave, Lonely, Modest, Mothball, Nun, Outgoing, Pension, Private, Quit, Recede, Recluse, Reserved, Resign, Retract, Retreat, Retrocedent, Roost, Rusticate, Scratch, Shy, Superannuate, Unassertive, Withdraw

▷ **Retirement** *may indicate* 'bed' around another word, or word reversed

Retort Alembic, Comeback, Courteous, Quip, Repartee, > **REPLY**, Retaliate, Riposte, Still

Retract(ion) Disavow, Epanorthosis, Palinode, Recall, Recant, Renounce, Revoke

Retreat Abbey, Arbour, Ashram(a), Asylum, Backwater, Bower, Bug, Cell, Cloister, Convent, Dacha, Departure, Donjon, Girth, Grith, Hermitage, Hideaway, Hide-out, Hole, Ivory-tower, Lair, Lama(sery), Mew, Monastery, Nest, Nook, Recede, Recoil, Redoubt, Reduit, Refuge, Retire, Retraite, Right-about, Rout, Shelter, Skedaddle, Stronghold, Withdraw

Retribution Come-uppance, Deserts, Nemesis, Revenge, Reward, Utu, Vengeance

Retrieve(r), **Retrieval** Access, Bird-dog, Field, Gundog, Labrador, Read-out, Recall, Recoup, Recover, Redeem, Rescue, Salvage

Return(s) Agen, Bricole, Census, Comeback, Day, Diminishing, Dividend, Elect, Er, Extradite, Gain, Pay, Proceeds, Profit, Rebate, Rebound, Recur, Redound, Regress, Reject, Render, Rent, Repay, Replace, Reply, Requital, Respond, Restitution, Restore, Retour, Revenue, Reverse, Revert, Riposte, Takings, Tax, Traffic, > **YIELD**

Reveal(ing), **Revelation** Advertise, Air, Apocalyptic, Bare, Betray, Bewray, Confess, Descry, Disclose, Discover, Discure, > **DIVULGE**, Epiphany, Exhibit, Explain, Expose, Giveaway, Hierophantic, Impart, Indicate, Ingo, Kythe, Leak, Manifest, Open, Satori, > **SHOW**, Spill, Tell-tale, Unclose, Uncover, Unfold, Unheal, Unmask, Unveil

Revel(ling), **Revelry** Ariot, Bacchanalia, Bend, Carnival, Carouse, Comus, Dionysian, Feast, Gloat, Glory, Joy, Merriment, Orgy, Rant, Rejoice, Riot, Roister, Rollicks, Rout, Saturnalia, Splore, Swig, Upsee, Ups(e)y, Wallow, Wassail, Whoopee

Revenge(ful) Aftergame, Avenge, Commination, Goel, Grenville, Montezuma's, Reprise, Requite, Retaliation, Revanche, Ultion, Utu, Vindictive

Revere(nce) Admire, Awe, Bostonian, Dread, Dulia, Esteem, Hallow, Hery, Homage, > **HONOUR**, Hyperdulia, Latria, Obeisance, Paul, Respect, Venerate

Reversal, **Reverse**, **Reversing**, **Reversion** Antithesis, Antonym, Arsy-versy, Atavism, Back(slide), Change-over, Chiasmus, Counter(mand), Escheat, Evaginate, Exergue, Flip, Inversion, Misfortune, > **OPPOSITE**, Overturn, Palindrome, Pile, Regress, Revoke, Rheotropic, Switchback, Tails, Throwback, Transit, Turn, Un-, Undo, U-turn, Verso, Vice versa, Volte-face

Review(er) Appeal, Censor, Critic, Critique, Editor, Feuilleton, Footlights, Inspect, Judicial, Magazine, March-past, Notice, Pan, Recapitulate, Repeat, Revise, Rundown, Spithead, Summary, Survey, Write-up

▷ **Review** *may indicate* an anagram or a reversed word

Revise(r), **Revision** Alter, Amend, Correct, Diaskeuast, Edit, Peruse, Reappraise, Reassess, Recense, Reform, Rev, Update

▷ **Revise(d)** *may indicate* an anagram

Revival, **Revive**, **Revivify**, **Reviving** Araise, Enliven, Gothic, Rally, Reanimate, Reawake(n), Rebirth, Redintegrate, Refresh, Rekindle, Renaissance, Renascent, Renew, Renovate, Restore, Resurrect, Resuscitate, Risorgimento, Romantic, Rouse, Wake

Revolt(ing), Revolution(ary) Agitator, American, Anarchist, Apostasy, Bloodless, Bolshevik, Boxer, Cade, Castro, Chartist, Che, Chinese, Circle, Coup d'etat, Cultural, Cycle, Dervish, Disgust, Enrage, February, French, Girondin, Glorious, Green, Grody, Gyration, Industrial, > **IN REVOLT**, Insurgent, Insurrection, IRA, Lenin, Marat, Marx, Maximalist, Montagnard, Mutiny, Nauseating, Orbit, Palace, Paris commune, Peasants, Putsch, > **REBEL(LION)**, Red Shirt, Reformation, Riot, Robespierre, Roll, Rotation, Russian, Sedition, Sicilian vespers, Syndicalism, Trot(sky), > **UPRISING**, Velvet, Weatherman, Whirl

▷ **Revolutionary** *may indicate* 'reversed'

Revolve(r), Revolving Carrier, Catherine wheel, Centrifuge, Colt®, Gat, Girandole, Grindstone, > **GUN**, Gyrate, Iron, Klinostat, Lathe, Maelstrom, Peristrephic, Pistol, Pivot, Roller, Rotate, Rotifer, Rotor, Roundabout, Run, Tone, Turn(stile), Turntable, Turret, Wheel, Whirl(igig), Whirlpool

Reward Albricias, Bonus, Bounty, Compensate, Consideration, Desert, Emolument, Fee, Guerdon, Head money, Meed, Payment, Premium, Price, Prize, Profit, Purse, Recompense, Reguerdon, Remuneration, Requital, Requite, S, Shilling, Wage, War(r)ison

Rhetoric(al) Anaphora, Apophasis, Aureate, Bombast, Chiasmus, Eloquence, Enantiosis, Epistrophe, Erotema, Eroteme, Erotesis, Euphemism, Hendiadys, Oratory, Paral(e)ipsis, Peroration, Pleonasm, Syllepsis, Trivium

Rhyme(s), Rhymer, Rhyming Assonance, Clerihew, Closed couplet, Couplet, Crambo, Cynghanedd, Doggerel, Eye, Feminine, Head, Internal, Masculine, Measure, Nursery, Perfect, Poetry, Rondel, Runic, Sight, Slang, Slant, Tercet, Terza-rima, Thomas, Triple, > **VERSE**, Virelay

Rhythm(ic) Agoge, Alpha, Asynartete, Backbeat, Beat, Beta, Bo Diddley beat, Breakbeat, Cadence, Circadian, Duple, In-step, Meter, Movement, Oompah, Pyrrhic, Rubato, Sdrucciola, Singsong, Sprung, Swing, Syncopation, Tala, Talea, Time, Voltinism

Rib(bed), Ribbing, Rib-joint Bar, Chaff, Cod, Costa, Cross-springer, Dutch, Eve, False, Floating, Futtock, Groin, Intercostal, Lierne, Nervate, Nervular, Nervure, Ogive, Persiflage, Rally, Spare, Springer, Subcosta, Tease, Tierceron, Tracery, True, Wife

Ribbon Band, Bandeau, Blue, Bow, Braid, Caddis, Caddyss, Cordon, Fattrels, Ferret, Fillet, Grosgrain, Hatband, Infula, Pad, Petersham, Radina, Rein, Soutache, Taenia, Tape, Teniate, Tie, Torsade

Rice Arborio, Basmati, Brown, Elmer, Entertainer, Indian, Kedgeree, Patna, Pilaf, Pilau, Pilaw, Reis, Risotto, Sushi, Twigs, Wild

Rich(es) Abounding, Abundant, Affluent, Amusing, Bonanza, Comic, Copious, Croesus, Dives, Edmund, Edwin, Fat, Feast, Fertile, Flush, Fruity, Full, Golconda, Haves, Heeled, High, Loaded, Lush, Luxurious, Mammon, Moneybags, Moneyed, Nabob, Oberous, Plenteous, Plush, Plutocrat, Rolling, Sumptuous, Toff, Vulgarian, > **WEALTHY**, Well-heeled, Well-to-do

▷ **Rickety** *may indicate* an anagram

Riddle Boulter, Charade, Colander, Dilemma, Enigma, Koan, Logogriph, Pepper, Perforate, Permeate, Puzzle, Screen, Searce, Search, Sieve, Sift, Siler, Sorites, Strain, Tems(e), Trommel

Ride, Riding Annoy, Bareback, Bestride, Bruise, Canter, Coast, Cycle, District, Division, Drive, Equitation, Field, Hack, Harass, Haute école, Hitchhike, Merry-go-round, Mount, Pick(-a-)back, Piggyback, Postil(l)ion, Rape, Revere's, Roadstead, Rollercoaster, Sit, Spin, Stang, Switchback, Third, Trot, Weather, Welter, Wheelie, White-knuckle

Rider(s) Addendum, Adjunct, Appendage, Attachment, Boundary, Cavalier, Charioteer, Circuit, Codicil, Condition, Corollary, Dispatch, Equestrian, Eventer,

Freedom, Gaucho, Godiva, Guidon, Haggard, Horseman, Jockey, Lochinvar, Messenger, Peloton, Postil(l)ion, Proviso, PS, Revere, Spurrer, Walkyrie

Ridge Arete, As(ar), Bank, Baulk, Chine, Crease, Crest, Dune, Esker, Hoe, Ledge, Promontory, Wale, Weal, Whorl

Ridicule, Ridiculous Absurd, Badinage, Bathos, Chaff, Cockamamie, Deride, Derisory, Egregous, Foolish, Gibe, Gird, Guy, Haze, Jibe, Josh, Laughable, Ludicrous, Mimic, Mock, Paradox, Pasquin, Pillory, Pish, Pooh-pooh, Raillery, Rich, Roast, Satire, Scoff, Scout, Screwy, Sight, Silly, Skimmington, Taunt, Travesty

Rifle Air, Armalite®, Bone, Browning, Bundook, Burgle, Carbine, Chassepot, Enfield, Enfield musket, Express, Garand, > **GUN**, Kalashnikov, Loot, Martini®, Mauser®, Minié, Pilfer, Ransack, Repeater, Rob, Springfield, Winchester®

Rig(ging) Accoutre, Attire, Bermuda, Drilling, Equip, Feer, Gaff, Get-up, Gunter, Hoax, Jack-up, Manipulate, Marconi, Martingale, Outfit, Panoply, Ratline, Ropes, Schooner, Sport, Stack, Swindle, Tackle, Trull

▷ **Rigged** *may indicate* an anagram

Right(en), Rightness, Rights Ancient lights, Appropriate, Befit, Blue-pencil, Cabotage, Civil, Claim, Competence, Conjugal, Conservative, > **CORRECT**, Cure, Direct, Divine, Droit, Due, Equity, Ethical, Exactly, Fascist, Fitting, Forestage, Franchise, Freedom, Gay, Germane, Hedge-bote, Human, Interest, Liberty, Lien, Meet, Miner's, Moral, New, Offside, OK, Okay, Option, Patent, Performing, Prerogative, Priority, Privilege, Proper, Property, Pukka, R, Rain, Reason, Rectify, Redress, Remedy, Repair, Rt, So, Stage, Tenants', True, Women's

Rigid(ity) Acierated, Catalepsy, Craton, Extreme, Fixed, Formal, Hidebound, Inflexible, Renitent, Set, Slavish, Starch(y), Stern, Stiff, Stretchless, Strict, Stringent, Tense, Turgor

Rigorous, Rigour Accurate, Austere, Cruel, Exact, Firm, Hard, Inclement, Iron-bound, Stern, Strait, Strict, Stringent

▷ **Rile(y)** *may indicate* an anagram

Rim Atlantic, Border, Chimb, Chime, Edge, Felloe, Felly, Flange, > **LIP**, Margin, Strake, Verge

Ring(ed), Ringer, Ringing, Rings Anchor, Angelus, Annual, Annulus, Arena, Band, Bangle, Bell, Call, Cambridge, Carabiner, Cartel, Change, Chime, Circle, Circlet, Circlip, Circus, Clang, Clink, Coil, Cordon, Corona, Corral, Cycle, Dead, Death's head, Dial, Ding, Disc, Dong, D(o)uar, Echo, Encircle, Encompass, Engagement, Enhalo, Enlace, Environ, Enzone, Eternity, Extension, Eyelet, Fairy, Ferrule, Gas, Gird(le), Girr, Gloriole, Grom(m)et, Growth, Halo, Hob, > **HOOP**, Hoop-la, Hula-hoop, Ideal, Inner, Inorb, Keeper, Key, Knell, Knock-out, Kraal, Lifebelt, Link, Loop, Lute, Magpie, Manacle, Mourning, Napkin, Nose, O, Orb, Outer, Peal, Pen, Phone, Ping, Piston, Potato, Price, Prize, Quoit, Resonant, Resound, Retaining, Round, Rove, Runner, Scarf, Seal, Signet, Slinger, Slip, Snap-link, Solomon, Sound, Spell, Split, Stonehenge, Surround, Swivel, Syndicate, Tang, Tattersall, Teething, Thimble, Timbre, Ting, Tingle, Tink, Tintinnabulate, Toe, Token, Toll, Tore, Torquate, Torques, Torret, Torus, Trochus, Vice, Vortex, Wagnerian, Washer, Wedding, Woggle, Zero

Riot(er), Riotous(ly), Riots Anarchy, Brawl, Clamour, Demo, Deray, Gordon, Hilarious, Hubbub, Luddite, Medley, Melee, Orgy, Pandemonium, Peterloo, Porteous, Profusion, Quorum, Rag, Rebecca, Rebel, Roister, Rout, Rowdy, Ruffianly, Swing, Tumult

▷ **Rioters, Riotous** *may indicate* an anagram

Rip(ping) Basket, Buller, Cur, Grand, Handful, Horse, Lacerate, Rent, Rep, Splendid, Tear, Tide, Topnotch, To-rend, Unseam

Ripe, Ripen(ing) Auspicious, Full, Mature, Mellow, Rathe, Ready

▷ **Rippling** *may indicate* an anagram

Rise(r), Rising Advance, Appreciate, Ascend, Assurgent, Bull, Butte, Cause, Easter, Eger, Elevation, Emerge, Emeute, Eminence, Erect, Escalate, Hance, Hauriant, Haurient, Heave, Hike, Hill, Hummock, Hunt's up, Improve, Increase, Insurgent, Intumesce, Jibe, Knap, Knoll, Lark, Levee, Levitate, Lift, Mount, Mutiny, Orient, Peripety, Putsch, Rear, Resurgent, Resurrection, > **REVOLT**, Saleratus, Scarp, Soar, Stand, Stie, Sty, Surface, Surge, Tor, Tower, Transcend, Up, Upbrast, Upburst, Upgo, Uprest, Upsurge, Upswarm, Upturn, Well

Risk(y) Actuarial, Adventure, Back, Calculated, Chance, Compromise, > **DANGER**, Daring, Dice, Dicy, Emprise, Endanger, Fear, Gamble, Game, Hairy, Hazard, Imperil, Jeopardy, Liability, Peril, Precarious, Security, Spec, Unsafe, Venture

Rite(s) Asperges, Bora, Ceremony, Exequies, Initiation, Liturgy, Nagmaal, Obsequies, Powwow, Ritual, Sacrament, Sarum use, Superstition, York

Ritual Agadah, Arti, Ceremony, Chanoyu, Customary, Formality, Haggada, Lavabo, Liturgy, Rite, Sacring, Seder, Social, Use

Rival(ry), Rivals Absolute, Acres, Aemule, Compete, Emulate, Emule, Envy, Fo(n)e, > **MATCH**, Needle, Opponent, Touch, Vie

River Ea, Estuary, Flood, Flower, Fluvial, Potamic, R, Riverain, Runner, Stream, Tributary, Waterway

Road(s), Roadside, Road surface A, A1, Access, Anchorage, Arterial, Asphalt, Autobahn, Autopista, Autostrada, Ave(nue), B, Beltway, Boulevard, Burma, Carriageway, Causeway, Cloverleaf, Coach, Concession, Corduroy, Corniche, Course, Cul-de-sac, Dirt, Driveway, Escape, Exit, Expressway, Fairway, Feeder, Fly-over, Fly-under, Foss(e) Way, Freeway, Grid, Hampton, Highway, Horseway, Kerb, Lane, Loan, Loke, Mall, Metal, M1, Motorway, Orbital, Overpass, Parkway, Path, Pike, Post, Private, Rd, Relief, Ride, Ridgeway, Ring, Royal, Service, Shoulder, Shunpike, Skid, Slip, Speedway, Spur(way), St(reet), Switchback, Tarmac, Tar-seal, Thoroughfare, Tobacco, Toby, Track(way), Trunk, Turning, Turnpike, Underpass, Unmade, Verge, Via, Way

Roadstead La Hogue

Roam Extravagate, Peregrinate, Rake, Ramble, Rove, Stray, Wander, Wheel

Roar(ing) Bawl, Bell(ow), Bluster, Boom, Boys, Cry, Forties, Guffaw, Laugh, Roin, Rote, Rout, Royne, Thunder, Tumult, Vroom, Wuther, Zoom

Roast Bake, Barbecue, Baste, Birsle, Brent, Cabob, Cook, Crab, Crown, Decrepitate, Grill, Kabob, Pan, Ridicule, Scald, Scathe, Sear, Slate, Tan, Torrefy

Rob(bed), Robber(y) Abduct, Bandit, Bereave, Brigand, Burgle, Bust, Cateran, Clyde, Dacoit, Daylight, Depredation, Do, Fake, Filch, Fleece, Footpad, Heist, Highjack, High toby, Highwayman, Hijack, Hold-up, Hustle, Job, Ladrone, Land-pirate, Larceny, Latron, Loot, Pad, Pillage, Pinch, Piracy, Pluck, Plunder, Rapine, Reave, Reft, Reive, Rieve, Rifle, Robertsman, Roll, Roy, Rustler, Sack, Screw, Short change, Skinner, Smash and grab, > **STEAL**, Steaming, Stick-up, Sting, Swindle, Thief, Toby, Turn-over, Turpin

Robe(s) Alb, Amice, Amis, Attrap, Camis, Camus, Cassock, Chimer, Chrisom(-cloth), Christom, Dalmatic, Dolman, > **DRESS**, Gown, Ihram, Kanzu, Khalat, Khilat, Kill(a)ut, Kimono, Mantle, Parament, Parliament, Pedro, Peplos, Pontificals, Regalia, Rochet, Saccos, Sanbenito, Soutane, Sticharion, Stola, Stole, Talar, Tire, Vestment, Yukata

Robot Android, Automaton, Cyborg, Dalek, Golem, Nanobot, Puppet, RUR, Telechir

Rock(s), Rocker, Rocking, Rocky Acid, Ages, Agitate, Astound, Cap, Cock, Country, Cradle, Dogger, Edinburgh, Erathem, Erratic, Garage, Gib(raltar), Heavy metal, Mantle, Marciano, Matrix, Native, Nunatak(kr), Permafrost, Petrology, Platform, Plymouth, Punk, Quake, Reggae, Reservoir, Rip-rap, Sally, Sedimentary, > **SHAKE**, Shoogle, Showd, Soft, Stonehenge, Stun, Sway, Swee, Swing, Ted, Teeter,

Totter, Unstable, Unsteady, Wall, Weeping, Wind, Windsor

Rocket Arugula, Booster, Capsule, Carpet, Congreve, Delta, Drake, Dressing down, Engine, Flare, Jato, Onion, Posigrade, Reprimand, Reproof, Retro, SAM, Skylark, Soar, Sounding, Stephenson, Thruster, Tourbillion, Upshoot, V1, Vernier, Warhead, Weld

▷ **Rocky** *may indicate* an anagram

Rod(-shaped), **Rodlike**, **Rods** Aaron's, Bar, Barbel(l), Barre, Birch, Caduceus, Caim, Can, Cane, Cue, Cuisenaire, Dipstick, Divining, Dowser, Drain, Firearm, Fisher, Fly, Fuel, Gun, Handspike, Laver, Linchpin, Lug, Moses, Newel, Perch, Pin, Pistol, Piston, Pitman, Pointer, Pole, Pontie, Pontil, Ponty, Puntee, Punty, Raddle, Rood, Shaft, Spindle, Spit, Stair, Staple, Stave, Stay-bolt, Stick, Switch, Tie, Twig, Verge, Virgate, Virgulate, Wand, Withe

Rodent Acouchi, Acouchy, Ag(o)uti, Bandicoot, Bangsring, Banxring, Beaver, Biscacha, Bizcacha, Bobac, Bobak, Boomer, Capybara, Cavy, Chickaree, Chincha, Chinchilla, Chipmunk, Civet, Coypu, Cricetus, Dassie, Deer-mouse, Delundung, Dormouse, Fieldmouse, Gerbil(le), Glires, Glutton, Gnawer, Gopher, Groundhog, Guinea pig, Ham(p)ster, Hedgehog, Hog-rat, Hutia, Hyrax, Jerboa, Jird, Lemming, Marmot, Mole rat, Mouse, Murid, Mus, Musk-rat, Musquash, Ochotona, Ondatra, Paca, Porcupine, Potoroo, Rat, Ratel, Ratton, Renegade, Runagate, Sciurine, Sewellel, Shrew, S(o)uslik, Spermophile, Springhaas, Springhase, Squirrel, Taguan, Taira, Tuco-tuco, Tucu-tuco, Vermin, Viscacha, Vole, Woodchuck, Woodmouse

Rogue, **Roguish(ness)** Arch, Bounder, Charlatan, Chiseller, Drole, Dummerer, Elephant, Espiegle(rie), Ganef, Ganev, Ganof, Gonif, Gonof, Greek, Gypsy, Hedge-creeper, Hempy, Herries, Imp, Knave, Latin, Limmer, Monkey, Panurge, Picaresque, Picaroon, Pollard, Poniard, Rapparee, Ra(p)scal(l)ion, Riderhood, Savage, Scamp, Schellum, Schelm, Skellum, Sleeveen, Slip-string, Sly, Swindler, Varlet, Villain, Wrong'un

Roll(ed), **Roller**, **Roll-call**, **Rolling**, **Rolls** Absence, Bagel, Bap, Bolt, Bridge, Brioche, Calender, Cambridge, Comber, Cop, Couch, Court, Croissant, Cylinder, Dandy, Drum, Dutch, Electoral, Eskimo, Even, Forward, Furl, Go, Hotdog, Labour, List, Loaded, Mangle, Moving, Music, Muster, Opulent, Patent, Pay, Petit-pain, Piano, Pigeon, Pipe, Platen, Ragman, Record, Reef, Reel, Register, Ren, Rent, Revolute, Revolve, Ring, Road, Rob, Rolag, Roster, Rota, Rotate, Roulade, RR, Rumble, Run, Sausage, Skin up, Snap, Somersault, Spool, Spring, Sway, Swell, Swiss, Table, Tandem, Taxi, Temple, Tent, Terrier, Toilet, Tommy, Trill, Trindle, Trundle, Victory, Volume, Wad, Wallow, Wave, Western

▷ **Rollicking** *may indicate* an anagram

Roman Agricola, Agrippa, Calpurnia, Candle, Catholic, Cato, Consul, CR, Crassus, Decemviri, Decurion, Empire, Flavian, Galba, Holiday, Italian, Jebusite, Latin, Maecenas, Papist, Patrician, PR, Quirites, Raetic, RC, Retarius, Rhaetia, Road, Scipio, Seneca, Sulla, Tarquin, Tiberius, Type, Uriconian

Romance, **Romantic (talk)** Affair, Amorous, Byronic, Casanova, Catalan, Dreamy, Fancy, Fantasise, Fib, Fiction, Gest(e), Gothic, Invention, Ladin(o), Ladinity, Langue d'or(ian), Langue d'oil, Langue d'oui, Lie, Neo-Latin, Novelette, Poetic, Quixotic, R(o)uman, Stardust, Tale

▶ **Romany** *see* GYPSY

Rome Holy See, Imperial City

Ronnie Biggs

Roof (edge), **Roofing** Belfast, Bell, Ceil, Cl(e)ithral, Cover, Curb, Divot, Dome, Drip, Eaves, French, Gable, Gambrel, Hardtop, Hip(ped), Home, Imperial, Jerkin-head, Leads, Mansard, Monopitch, Palate, Pavilion, Pop-top, Porte-cochère, Rigging, Saddle, Shingle, Skirt, Tectiform, Tectum, Tegula, Thatch,

Thetch, Tiling, Top, Uraniscus

Room(s), **Roomy** Anteroom, Apartment, Assembly, Attic, Ben, Berth, Boardroom, Boiler, Boudoir, Bower, But, Cabin(et), Camera, Capacity, Casemate, CC, Ceiling, Cell, Cellar, Chamber, Changing, Chat, Closet, Commodious, Compartment, Consulting, Control, Cubicle, Cutting, Dark, Day, Delivery, Digs, Dissecting, Divan, Drawing, Dressing, Elbow, End, Engine, Extension, Foyer, Gap, Garret, Green, Grill, Gun, Herbarium, Incident, Lab, Latitude, Laura, Lavra, Leeway, Library, Living, Locker, Lodge, Loft, Loo, Lounge, Margin, Mould-loft, Music, Oda, Operations, Orderly, Oriel, Pad, Panic, Parlour, Powder, Priesthole, Private, Projection, Property, Public, Pump, Reception, Recitation, Recovery, Recreation, Rest, Rm, Robing, Rumpus, Salle, Salon, Scope, Scullery, Serdab, Servery, Shebang, Single, Single-end, Smoking, Snug, Solar, > **SPACE**, Spacious, Spare, Spence, Spheristerion, Staff, Standing, Steam, Still, Stock, Stowage, Street, Strong, Studio, Study, Suite, Sun, Tap, Tea, Tiring, Tool, Twin, Utility, Vestiary, Vestry, Waiting, Ward, Wash, Wiggle, Work

Root(ing), **Roots** Cassava, Cheer, Cube, Delve, Dig, Eddo, Eradicate, Foundation, Ginseng, Grass, Grub, Heritage, Horseradish, Hurrah, Mandrake, Nuzzle, Poke, Pry, Radish, Rhizome, Snuzzle, Source, Square, Tap, Taro, Tuber, Tulip, Turnip, Turpeth, Zedoary

Rope(s) Backstay, Ba(u)lk, Bind, Bobstay, Boltrope, Brail, Breeching, Bunt-line, Cable, Cablet, Cord, Cordage, Cordon, Cringle, Downhaul, Drag, Earing, Fall, Flemish coil, Fore-brace, Foresheet, Forestay, Futtock-shroud, Gantline, Guest, Guide, Guy, Halliard, Halser, Halter, Halyard, Hawser, Hawser-laid, Headfast, Inhaul, Jack-stay, Jeff, Jump, Kernmantel, Ladder, Lanyard, Lasher, Lasso, Line, Longe, Lunge, Mainbrace, Mainsheet, Manil(l)a, Marlin(e), Monkey, Mooring, Nip, Noose, Outhaul, Painter, Pastern, Prolonge, Prusik, Rawhide, Reef point, Riata, Roband, Robbin, Rode, Runner, Sally, Seal, Selvagee, Sennit, Sheet, Shroud, Sinnet, Span, Spun-yarn, Stay, Sternfast, Stirrup, String, Sugan, Swifter, Tackle, Tail, Tether, Tie, Timenoguy, Tow(line), Trace, Trail, Triatic, Triatic stay, Vang, Wanty, Widdy, Wire

Rose(-red), **Rosie**, **Rosy** Albertine, Avens, Blooming, Bourbon, Briar, Brier, Cabbage, Canker, China, Christmas, Compass, Damask, Dog, Eglantine, England, Floribunda, Geum, G(u)elder, Hybrid, Lancaster, Lee, Moss, Multiflora, Musk, Noisette, Peace, Pink, Promising, Rambler, Red(dish), Rugosa, Snowball, Sprinkler, Standard, Tea, Tokyo, Tudor, York

Rosemary Rosmarine

Rot(ten), **Rotting** Addle, Baloney, Boo, Bosh, Botrytis, Bull, Caries, Carious, Corrode, Corrupt, Daddock, Decadent, > **DECAY**, Decompose, Degradable, Dotage, Dry, Eat, Erode, Fester, Foul, Kibosh, Manky, Mildew, Noble, Nonsense, Poppycock, Poxy, Punk, Putid, Putrefy, Putrid, Rail, Rancid, Rank, Rat, Ret, Rust, Sapropel, Septic, Sour, Squish, Twaddle, Wet

Rotate, **Rotating**, **Rotation**, **Rotator** Gyrate, Pivot, Pronate, Rabat(te), Reamer, Revolve, Roll, Selsyn, Trundle, Turn, Wheel, Windmill

▶ **Rotten** *see* ROT

▷ **Rotten** *may indicate* an anagram

Rough(en), **Roughly**, **Roughness** About, Approximate, Asper(ate), Burr, C, Ca, Choppy, Circa, Coarse, Craggy, Crude, Frampler, Grained, Gross, Gruff, Gurly, Gusty, Hard, Harsh, Hispid, Hoodlum, Hooligan, Impolite, Imprecise, Incondite, Inexact, Irregular, Jagged, Karst, Keelie, Kokobeh, Muricate, Push, Ragged, Ramgunshoch, Raspy, Raucle, Rip, Risp, Robust, Row, Rude, Rugged, Rusticate, Rusty, Scabrid, Sea, Shaggy, Sketchy, Some, Spray, Spreathe, Squarrose, Stab, Strong-arm, Swab, Tartar, Tearaway, Ted, Textured, Uncut, Violent, Yahoo

▷ **Roughly** *may indicate* an anagram

Round(ness) About, Ammo, Ball, Beat, Bout, Cartridge, Catch, Circle, Complete, Cycle, Dome, Doorstep, Figure, Full, Global, Hand, Jump-off, Lap, Leg, Milk, O, Oblate, Orb, Orbit, Patrol, Peri-, Pirouette, Plump, Qualifying, Quarter, Rev, Ring, Robin, Roly-poly, Rota, Rotund, Route, Routine, Rung, Salvo, Sandwich, Sarnie, Semi-final, Shot, Skirt, Slice, Sphere, Step, Table, Tour, Tubby, U-turn

▷ **Round** *may indicate* a word reversed

Roundabout Ambages, Approximately, Bypass, Carousel, Circuit, Circumambient, Circumbendibus, Circus, Devious, Eddy, > INDIRECT, Peripheral, Rotary, Tortuous, Turntable, Waltzer, Whirligig

Routine Automatic, Day-to-day, Drill, Everyday, Grind, Groove, Habitual, Ho-hum, Jogtrot, Pattern, Perfunctory, Pipe-clay, Red tape, Rota, Rote, Round, Rut, S(c)htick, Schtik, Treadmill, Workaday

Rove(r), Roving Car, Errant

Row(er) Align, Altercation, Arew, Argue, Argument, Bank, Barney, Bedlam, Bow, Cannery, Colonnade, Death, Debate, Din, Dispute, Dust-up, Feud, File, Fireworks, Food, Hullabaloo, Line(-up), Noise, Oar, Paddle, Parade, Pull, Quarrel, Range, Rank, Rew, Rotten, Ruction, Rumpus, Scene, Scull, Series, Set, Shindig, Shindy, Shine, Skid, Spat, Stern, Street, Stroke, Sweep, Terrace, Tier, Tiff, Torpid, Wetbob, Wherryman

Rowdy, Rowdiness Hooligan, Loud, Noisy, Rorty, Rough, Roughhouse, Ruffian, Scourer, Skinhead, Stroppy, Unruly, Uproarious

Royal(ty), Royalist Academy, Angevin, Basilical, Battle, Bourbon, Emigré, Exchange, Fee, Hanoverian, Imperial, Imposing, Inca, Kingly, Majestic, Malignant, Palatine, Payment, Pharaoh, Plantagenet, Prince, Purple, Queenly, Regal, Regis, Regius, Regnal, Sail, Sceptred, Society

Rub(bing), Rubber(y), Rub out Abrade, Buff, Bungie, Bungy, Calk, Caoutchouc, Chafe, Cold, Condom, Corrode, Cow gum®, Crepe, Destroy, Ebonite, Efface, Elastic, Embrocate, Emery, Erase, Fawn, Foam, Fray, Fret, Friction, Frottage, Grate, Graze, Grind, Gum elastic, Gutta-percha, Hard, India, Irritate, Jelutong, Latex, Masseur, Obstacle, Polish, Root, Safe, Sandpaper, Scour, Scrub, Scuff, Seringa, Smoked, Sorbo®, Sponge, Synthetic, Towel, Trace, Ule, Wipe

▷ **Rubbed** *may indicate* an anagram

Rubbish Balls, Brack, Bull, Bunkum, Clap-trap, Cobblers, Debris, Dre(c)k, Drivel, Fiddlesticks, Garbage, Grot, Grunge, Hogwash, Kak, Landfill, Leavings, Litter, Mullock, Nonsense, Phooey, Raff, Raffle, > REFUSE, Stuff, Tinpot, Tip, Tom(fool), Tosh, Trade, Tripe, Trouch, Twaddle

Rude Abusive, Barbaric, Bestial, Bumpkin, Callow, Churlish, Coarse, Discourteous, Elemental, Goustrous, Green, Ill-bred, Impolite, Indecorous, Inficete, Ingram, Ingrum, Insolent, Ocker, Offensive, Peasant, Raw, Risque, Rough, Simple, Surly, Unbred, Uncomplimentary, Uncourtly, Unlettered, Unmannered, Vulgar

▷ **Ruffle** *may indicate* an anagram

Rug Afghan, Bearskin, Carpet, Drugget, Ensi, Flokati, Gabbeh, Hearth, Herez, Heriz, Kelim, K(h)ilim, Kirman, Lap robe, Mat, Maud, Numdah, Oriental, Prayer, Runner, Rya, Scatter, Travelling

Ruin(ed), Ruins Annihilate, Blast, Blight, Blue, Carcase, Collapse, Corrupt, Crash, Crock, Damn, Decay, Defeat, Demolish, Despoil, Destroy, Devastate, Disfigure, Dish, Disrepair, Dogs, Doom, Downcome, Downfall, End, Fordo, Hamstring, Heap, Hell, Insolvent, Inure, Kaput(t), Kibosh, Loss, Mar, Mocers, Mother's, Overthrow, Petra, Pot, Puckerood, Ravage, Reck, Relic, Scotch, Scupper, Scuttle, Shatter, Sink, Smash, Spill, > SPOIL, Stramash, Subvert, Undo, Unmade, Ur, Violate, Whelm, Woe, Wrack

▷ **Ruined** *may indicate* an anagram

Rule(r), **Rules**, **Ruling** Abbasid, Alexander, Align, Ameer, Amir, Archduke, Ardri(gh), Aristocrat, Atabeg, Atabek, Autocrat, Bajayet, Bajazet, Ban, Bey, Bismarck, Bodicea, Boudicca, Bretwalda, Britannia, Burgrave, Bylaw, Caesar, Caligula, Caliph, Calliper, Canon, Castro, Catapan, Caudillo, Chagan, Chain, Cham, Charlemagne, Chogyal, Cleopatra, Club-law, Code, Condominium, Constitution, Control, Cosmocrat, Criterion, Cromwell, Czar, Decree, Dergue, Despot, Dewan, Dey, Dictator, Diwan, Doge, Domineer, Dominion, Duce, Dynast, Elector, Emir, Emperor, Empire, Establishment, Ethnarch, Etiquette, Exarch, Fatwa, Feint, Fetwa, Formation, Formula, Franco, Fuhrer, Gaekwar, Gag, Gaikwar, Genghis Khan, Gerent, Global, Golden, Govern, Ground, Haile Selassie, Heptarch, Herod, Hespodar, Hierarch, Hitler, Home, Hoyle, Imam, Inca, Jackboot, Jamshid, Jamshyd, Judges, K, Kabaka, Kaiser, Khan, Khedive, King, Law, Leibniz's, Lesbian, Lex, Lindley, Liner, Maharaja, Majority, Mameluke, Manchu, Maxim, Mede, Method, Mikado, Mir, Miranda, Mistress, Mogul, Monarch, Montezuma, Motto, Mpret, Mudir, Napoleon, Nawab, Negus, Nero, Nizam, Norm(a), Ochlocrat, Oligarch, Ordinal, Overlord, Padishah, Parallel, Parallelogram, Pasha, Pendragon, Pericles, Peshwa, Pharaoh, Phase, Phrase-structure, Plantocrat, Plumb, Plutocrat, Podesta, Pope, Potentate, Precedent, Precept, President, Prevail, Prince, Principle, Protocol, Queen, Queensberry, R, Rafferty's, Raj(ah), Rajpramukh, Rana, Realm, Rector, Regal, Regent, Reign, Rewrite, Rex, Ring, Rubric, Sachem, Sagamore, Saladin, Sassanid, Satrap, Serkali, Setting, Shah, Shaka, Sheik, Sherif, Shogun, Sirdar, Slide, Sophi, Sophy, Souldan, Sovereign, Squier, Squire, Stadtholder, Stalin, Standard, Statute, Stratocrat, Suleiman, Sultan, Suzerain, Swaraj, Sway, Ten-minute, Tenno, Ten-yard, Tetrarch, Three, Thumb, Toparch, Transformation(al), Trapezoid, Tsar, T-square, Tutankhamun, Tycoon, Tyrant, Vali, Viceroy, Wali, Wield

Rumble, **Rumbling** Borborygmus, Brool, Curmurring, Drum-roll, Groan, Growl, Guess, Lumber, Mutter, Rumour, Thunder, Tonneau, Twig

Rumour Breeze, Bruit, Buzz, Canard, Cry, Fame, Furphy, > GOSSIP, Grapevine, Hearsay, Kite, Noise, On-dit, Pig's-whisper, Report, Repute, Say-so, Smear, Talk, Underbreath, Unfounded, Vine, Voice, Whisper, Word

Run(ning), **Run away**, **Run into**, **Run off**, **Runny**, **Runs** Admin(ister), Arpeggio, Bleed, Bolt, Break, Bunk, Bye, Career, Chase, Coop, Corso, Course, Cresta, Cross-country, Current, Cursive, Cut, Dash, Decamp, Direct, Double, Drive, Dry, Dummy, Escape, Extra, Fartlek, Flee, Flit, Flow, Fly, Follow, Fun, Fuse, Gad, Gallop, Gauntlet, Go, Green, Ground, Hare, Haste(n), Hennery, Hie, Home, Idle, Jog, Jump bail, Ladder, Lauf, Leg, Leg bye, Lienteric, Lope, Manage, Marathon, Melt, Milk, Mizzle, Mole, Molt, Neume, Now, On, On-line, Operate, Pace, Paper chase, Pelt, Ply, Pour, Print, Purulent, R, Race, Range, Red, Renne, Rin, Romp, Roulade, Rounder, Ruck, Scamper, Scapa, Scarper, Schuss, Scud, Scutter, Scuttle, See, Sequence, Shoot, Single, Skate, Skedaddle, Ski, Skid, Skirr, Skitter, Slalom, Slide, Smuggle, Spew, Split, Spread, Sprint, Sprue, Squitters, Stampede, Straight, Streak, Stream, Taxi, Tear, Tenor, Tie-breaker, Trial, Trickle, Trill, Trot

Runner(s) Atalanta, Bean, Blade, Bow Street, Carpet, Coe, Courser, Deserter, Emu, Field, Geat, Gentleman, Harrier, Internuncio, Leg bye, Legman, Messenger, Miler, Milk, Owler, > RUN(NING), Scarlet, Series, Slipe, Smuggler, Stolon, Stream, Trial

▷ **Running**, **Runny** *may indicate* an anagram

Rural Agrarian, Agrestic, Boo(h)ai, Boondocks, Bucolic, Country, Forane, Georgic, Mofussil, Platteland, Praedial, Predial, Redneck, Rustic, Sticks, The Shires, Wops-wops

Rush(ed) Accelerate, Barge, Bolt, Bustle, Career, Charge, Dart, Dash, Expedite, Feese, Fly, Gold, Hare, Hasten, High-tail, > HURRY, Hurtle, Jet, Lance, Leap, Onset, Pellmell, Phase, Plunge, Precipitate, Railroad, Rampa(u)ge, Rash, Reed, Rip,

Scamp(er), Scour, Scud, Scurry, Sedge, Spate, Speed, Stampede, Star(r), Streak, Streek, Surge, Swoop, Swoosh, Tear, Thrash, Thresh, Tilt, Torrent, Tule, Zap, Zoom

Russia(n), Russian headman, Russian villagers Apparatchik, Ataman, Belorussian, Beria, Bolshevik, Boris, Boyar, Byelorussian, Circassian, Cossack, D(o)ukhobor, Dressing, Esth, Igor, Ivan, Kabardian, Kalmuk, Kalmyck, Leather, Lett, Mari, Menshevik, Minimalist, Mir, Muscovy, Octobrist, Osset(e), Red, Romanov, Rus, Russ(niak), Russki, Ruthene, Salad, Serge, Slav, Stakhanovite, SU, Thistle, Udmurt, Uzbeg, Uzbek, Vladimir, Vogul, Yuri, Zyrian

Rust(y) Aeci(di)um, Brown, Corrode, Cor(ro)sive, Erode, Etch, Ferrugo, Iron-stick, Maderise, Oxidise, Rubiginous, Soare, Stem, Teleutospore, Telium, Uredine, Uredo, Verdigris

Rustic Arcady, Bacon, Bor(r)el(l), Bucolic, Bumpkin, Chawbacon, Churl, Clodhopper, Clown, Corydon, Damon, Doric, Forest, Georgic, Hayseed, Hick, Hillbilly, Hind, Hob, Hobbinoll, Hodge, Homespun, Idyl(l), Pastorale, Peasant, Pr(a)edial, Put(t), Rube, Rural, Strephon, Swain, Villager, Villatic, Yokel

▷ **Rustic** *may indicate* an anagram

Rustle(r), Rustling Abactor, Crinkle, Duff, Fissle, Frou-frou, Gully-raker, Poach, Speagh(ery), Sprechery, Steal, Stir, Susurration, Swish, Thief, Whig

Rut Channel, Furrow, Groove, Heat, Routine, Track

Ruthless Brutal, Cruel, Dog eat dog, Fell, Hard, Hardball, Hard-bitten

Ss

S Ogee, Saint, Second, Sierra, Society, South, Square

SA It, Lure

Sabotage, Saboteur Destroy, Frame-breaker, Ratten, Spoil, Wrecker

Sack(cloth), Sacking Bag, Bed, Boot, Bounce, Budget, Burlap, Can, Cashier, Chasse, Congé, Congee, Dash, Depredate, Despoil, Discharge, Doss, Fire, Gunny, Havoc, Jute, Knap, Loot, Mailbag, Maraud, Mitten, Pillage, Plunder, Poke, Push, Rapine, Reave, Road, Rob, Sanbenito, Sherris, Sherry, Spoliate, Vandalise

▷ **Sacks** *may indicate* an anagram

Sacrifice Forego, Gambit, Immolate, Lay down, Oblation, > **OFFERING**, Relinquish, Suttee

Sad(den), Sadly, Sadness Alas, Attrist, Blue, Con dolore, Dejected, Desolate, Disconsolate, Dismal, Doleful, Dolour, Downcast, Drear, Dull, Dumpy, Heartache, Lovelorn, Low, Lugubrious, Mesto, Oh, Plangent, Sorrowful, Sorry, Tabanca, Tearful, Tear-jerker, Threnody, Tragic, Triste, Tristesse, Unhappy, Wan, Wo(e)begone

Saddle (bag, cloth, girth, pad) Alforja, Aparejo, Arson, Burden, Cantle, Cinch, Col, Crupper, Demipique, Lumber, Numnah, Oppress, Pack, Panel, Pigskin, Pilch, Pillion, Seat, Sell(e), Shabrack, Side, Stock, Tree, Western

▷ **Sadly** *may indicate* an anagram

Safe(ty) Active, Copper-bottomed, Deposit, Harmless, Immunity, Impunity, Inviolate, Night, Passive, Peter, Reliable, Roadworthy, Sanctuary, Secure, Sound, Strong-box, Strongroom, Sure, Whole-skinned, Worthy

Safeguard Bulwark, Caution, Ensure, Fail-safe, Frithborh, Fuse, Hedge, Palladium, Protection, Register, Ward

Saga Aga, Chronicle, Edda, Epic, Icelandic, Legend

Sago Portland

▷ **Said** *may indicate* 'sounding like'

Sail(s), Sailing Bunt, Canvas, Cloth, Coast, Course, Cruise, Fan, Gaff(-topsail), Genoa, Head, Jib, Jut, Lateen, Leech, Luff, Lug, Moonraker, Muslin, Navigate, Peak, Ply, Rag, Reef, Rig, Ring-tail, Royal, Sheet, Spanker, Spencer, Spinnaker, Spritsail, Square, Staysail, Steer, Studding, Top(-gallant), Yard

Sailor(s) AB, Admiral, Argonaut, Blue-jacket, Boatman, Boatswain, Bosun, Budd, Commodore, Crew, Deckhand, Drake, Evans, Freshwater, Gob, Greenhand, Hat, Hearties, Helmsman, Hornblower, Hydronaut, Jack, Jaunty, Lascar, Leadsman, Limey, Lt, Lubber, Mariner, Matelot, Matlo(w), Middy, MN, Nelson, Noah, NUS, Oceaner, OS, Polliwog, Pollywog, Popeye, Privateer, Rating, RN, Salt, Seabee, Seacunny, Sea-dog, Sea-lord, > **SEAMAN**, Serang, Sin(d)bad, Submariner, Tar, Wandering, Yachtsman

Saint(ly), Saints Agatha, Agnes, Aidan, Alban, Alexis, Alvis, Ambrose, Andrew, Anselm, Anthony, Asaph, Audrey, Augustine, Barbara, Barnabas, Bartholomew, Basil, Bees, Benedict, Bernard, Boniface, Brandan, Brendan, Bridget, Canonise, Canonize, Catharine, Cecilia, Chad, Christopher, Clement, Columba(n), Crispian, Crispin(ian), Cuthbert, Cyr, David, Denis, Denys, Diego, Dominic, Dorothea, Dunstan, Dymphna, Elmo, Eloi, Elvis, Eulalie, Francis, Genevieve, George,

Gertrude, Giles, Hagiology, Hallowed, Helena, Hilary, Hilda, Hugh, Ignatius, James, Jerome, John, Joseph, Jude, Kentigern, Kevin, Kilda, Latterday, Lawrence, Leger, Leonard, Linus, Loyola, Lucy, Luke, Malo, Margaret, Mark, Martha, Martin, Matthew, Michael, Monica, Mungo, Nicholas, Ninian, Odyl, Olaf, Oswald, Pancras, Patrick, Patron, Paul(inus), Peter, Pillar, Plaster, Polycarp, Quentin, Regulus, Ride, Rishi, Roch, Ronan, Roque, Rosalie, Rule, S, Sebastian, Severus, Simeon, Simon, SS, St, Stanislaus, Stephen, Swithin, Templar, Teresa, Thecia, Theresa, Thomas, Tobias, Ursula, Valentine, Veronica, Vincent, Vitus, Walstan, Wilfred, William, Winifred

Sake Account, Behalf, Cause, Drink

Salad Caesar, Chef's, Cos, Cress, Cucumber, Days, Endive, Fennel, Finoc(c)hio, Frisée, Fruit, Greek, Guacamole, Lettuce, Lovage, Mixture, Niçoise, Purslane, Radicchio, Radish, Rampion, Rocket, Russian, Slaw, Tabbouli, Tomato, Waldorf

▷ **Salad** *may indicate* an anagram

Salary Emolument, Fee, Hire, Pay, Prebend, Screw, Stipend, > WAGE

Sale(s) Auction, Cant, Car-boot, Clearance, Farm-gate, Fire, Garage, Jumble, Market, Outroop, Outrope, Raffle, Retail, Roup, Rummage, Subhastation, Trade, Turnover, Venal, Vend, Vendue, Vent, Voetstoets, Voetstoots, Warrant, Wash, White, Wholesale

Salisbury Cecil, Sarum

Salmon Atlantic, Chinook, Chum, Cock, Coho(e), Grav(ad)lax, Grilse, Kelt, Keta, Par(r), Pink, Redfish, Rock, Smelt, Smolt, Smowt, Sockeye

Salt(s), Salty AB, Acid, Alginate, Aluminate, Andalusite, Aspartite, Attic, Aurate, Azide, Base, Bath, Bicarbonate, Bichromate, Borate, Borax, Brackish, Brine, Bromate, Bromide, Capr(o)ate, Caprylate, Carbamate, Carbonate, Carboxylate, Cerusite, Chlorate, Chlorite, Chromate, Citrate, Complex, Corn, Cure(d), Cyanate, Cyclamate, Datolite, Deer lick, Diazonium, Dichromate, Dioptase, Dithionate, Double, Enos, Epsom, Ferricyanide, Formate, Glauber, Glutamate, Halite, Halo-, Health, Hydrochloride, Hygroscopic, Iodide, Ioduret, Isocyanide, Lactate, Lake-basin, Lithate, Liver, Magnesium, Malate, Malonate, Manganate, Matelot, Microcosmic, Monohydrate, Mucate, Muriate, NaCl, Nitrate, Nitrite, Oleate, Osm(i)ate, Oxalate, Palmitate, Pandermite, Perchlorate, Periodate, Phosphate, Phosphite, Phthalate, Picrate, Piquancy, Plumbate, Plumbite, Potassium, Powder, Propionate, Pyruvate, Rating, Resinate, Rochelle, Rock, Rosinate, Sailor, Sal ammoniac, Salify, Sal volatile, Saut, Sea-dog, Seafarer, Seasoned, Sebate, Selenate, Smelling, Soap, Sodium, Solar, Stannate, Stearate, Suberate, Succinate, Sulfite, Sulphate, Sulphite, Sulphonate, Table, Tannate, Tantalate, Tartrate, Tellurate, Thiocyanate, Thiosulphate, Titanate, Tungstate, Uranin, Urao, Urate, Vanadate, Volatile, Water-dog, White, Wit(ty), Xanthate

Salutation, Salute Address, Ave, Banzai, Barcoo, Bid, Cap, Cheer, Command, Coupé(e), Curtsey, Embrace, Feu de joie, Fly-past, Genuflect, Greet, Hail, Hallo, Halse, Homage, Honour, Jambo, Kiss, Present, Salaam, Salvo, Sieg Heil, Toast, Tribute, Wassail

Salvage Dredge, Lagan, Ligan, Reclaim, Recover, Recycle, Rescue, Retrieve, Tot

Salve Anele, Anoint, Assuage, Ave, Lanolin(e), Lotion, Ointment, Remedy, Saw, Tolu, Unguent

Same(ness) Ae, Agnatic, Contemporaneous, Do, Egal, Equal, Ib(id), Ibidem, Id, Idem, Identical, Identity, Ilk, Iq, Like, One, Thick(y), Thilk, Uniform, Ylke

Sample, Sampling Biopsy, Blad, Browse, Example, Foretaste, Handout, Muster, Pattern, Pree, Prospect, Quadrat, Scantling, Specimen, Swatch, Switch, > TASTE, Transect, Try

▷ **Sam Weller** *may indicate* the use of 'v' for 'w' or vice versa

Sanction Allow, Appro, Approbate, Approof, Approve, Authorise, Bar, Countenance, Endorse, Imprimatur, Mandate, OK, Pass, Pragmatic, Ratify, Sustain

Sanctuary, Sanctum Adytum, Asylum, By-room, Cella, Ch, Church, Frithsoken, Frithstool, Girth, Grith, Holy, Lair, Naos, Oracle, Penetralia, Preserve, Refuge, Sacellum, Sacrarium, > SHELTER, Shrine, Temple

Sandhopper Amphipod

Sandwich Bruschetta, Butty, Club, Croque-monsieur, Cuban, Doorstep, Earl, Hamburger, Island, Open, Roti, Round, Sarney, Sarnie, Smorbrod, Smorgasbord, Smorrebrod, Sub, Submarine, Thumber, Toastie, Triple-decker, Twitcher, Victoria

▷ **Sandwich(es)** *may indicate* a hidden word

Sane, Sanity Compos mentis, Formal, Healthy, Judgement, Rational, Reason, Sensible, Wice

Sanguine Confident, Hopeful, Optimistic, Roseate, Ruddy

Sap Benzoin, Bleed, Cremor, Drain, Enervate, Entrench, Ichor, Juice, Laser, Latex, Lymph, Mine, Mug, Pulque, Ratten, Resin, Roset, Rosin, Rozet, Rozit, Secretion, Soma, Sura, Swot, Undermine, Weaken

Sarcasm, Sarcastic Biting, Cutting, Cynical, Derision, Irony, Mordacious, Mordant, Pungent, Quip, Sarky, Satire, Sharp, Snide, Sting, Wisecrack

Sardonic Cutting, Cynical, Ironical, Scornful

Sash Baldric(k), Band, Belt, Burdash, Cummerbund, Obi, Scarf, Window

Satan Adversary, Apollyon, Arch-enemy, Cram, > DEVIL, Eblis, Lucifer, Shaitan

Satellite Adrastea, Ananke, Ariel, Artificial, Astra, Atlas, Attendant, Aussat, Belinda, Bianca, Bird, Callisto, Calypso, Camenae, Carme, Charon, Communications, Comsat®, Cordelia, Cosmic, Cressida, Deimos, Desdemona, Despina, Dione, Disciple, Early bird, Earth, Echo, Elara, Enceladus, Europa, Explorer, Fixed, Follower, Galatea, Galilean, Ganymede, Geostationary, Helene, Henchman, Himalia, Hipparchus, Hyperion, Iapetus, Intelsat, Io, Janus, Lackey, Larissa, Leda, Lysithea, Meteorological, Metis, Mimas, Miranda, Moon, Mouse, Nereid, Oberon, Ophelia, Orbiter, Pan, Pandora, Pasiphae, Phobos, Phoebe, Portia, Prometheus, Puck, Rhea, Rosalind, Sinope, Sputnik, Syncom, Telesto, Telstar, Tethys, Thalassa, Thebe, Tiros, Titan, Titania, Triton, Umbriel, Weather

▶ **Satin** *see* SILK

Satisfaction, Satisfactory, Satisfy(ing), Satisfactorily Agree, Ah, Ap(p)ay, Appease, Assuage, Atone, Change, Compensation, Complacent, > CONTENT, Defrayment, Enough, Feed, Fill, Fulfil, Glut, Gratify, Indulge, Jake, Job, Liking, Meet, OK, Pacation, Palatable, Pay, Please, Propitiate, Qualify, Redress, Repay, Replete, Sate, Satiate, Serve, Settlement, Slake, Square, Suffice, Tickety-boo, Well

Saturate(d) Drench, Glut, Imbue, Impregnate, Infuse, Permeate, > SOAK, Sodden, Steep, Waterlog

Sauce, Saucy Alfredo, Allemanse, Apple, Arch, Baggage, Barbecue, Béarnaise, Béchamel, Bigarade, Bold(-faced), Bolognese, Bordelaise, Bourguignonne, Bread, Brown, Caper, Carbonara, Catchup, Catsup, Chasseur, Chaudfroid, Cheek, Chilli, Condiment, Coulis, Cranberry, Cream, Cumberland, Custard, Dapper, Dip, Dressing, Enchilada, Espagnole, Fenberry, Fondue, Fu yong, Fu yung, Gall, Garum, Gravy, Hard, Hoisin, Hollandaise, Horseradish, HP®, Impudence, Jus, Ketchup, Lip, Malapert, Marinade, Marinara, Matelote, Mayonnaise, Melba, Meunière, Mint, Mirepoix, Mole, Mornay, Mousseline, Nam pia, Nerve, Newburg, Nuoc mam, Oxymal, Oyster, Panada, Parsley, Passata, Peart, Pert, Pesto, Piri-piri, Pistou, Ravigote, Relish, Remoulade, Rouille, Roux, Sabayon, Sal, Salpicon, Salsa, Salsa verde, Sambal, Sass, Satay, Shoyu, Soja, Soubise, Soy, Soya, Stroganoff, Sue, Supreme, Sweet and sour, Tabasco®, Tamari, Tartar(e), Tomato, Topping, Tossy, Velouté, Vinaigrette, White, Wine, Worcester, Worcestershire

Sausage(s) Andouillette, Banger, Black pudding, Boerewors, Bologna, Bratwurst, Cervelat, Cheerio, Chipolata, Chorizo, Cumberland, Devon, Drisheen, Frankfurter, Knackwurst, Knockwurst, Liver(wurst), Mortadella, Pep(p)eroni,

Polony, Salami, Sav(eloy), Snag(s), String, White pudding, Wiener(wurst), Wienie, Wurst, Zampone

Savage Barbarian, Boor, Brute, Cruel, Fierce, Grim, Immane, Inhuman, Maul, Sadistic, Truculent, Vitriolic, Wild

Save, **Saving(s)** Bank, Bar, Besides, But, Capital, Conserve, Deposit, Economy, Except, Hain, Hoard, Husband, ISA, Keep, Layby, Nest egg, Nirlie, Nirly, PEPS, Preserve, Put by, Reclaim, Redeem, Relieve, Reprieve, > **RESCUE**, Reskew, Sa', Salt, Salvage, Scrape, Scrimp, Shortcut, Slate club, Spare, Stokvel, Succour, TESSA, Unless

Saw Adage, Aphorism, Apothegm, Azebiki, Back, Band, Beheld, Bucksaw, Buzz, Chain, Circular, Cliché, Compass, Coping, Cross-cut, Crown, Cut, Dictum, Dovetail, Dozuki, Flooring, Frame, Fret, Gang, Glimpsed, Gnome, Grooving, Hack, Hand, Jig, Keyhole, Legend, Log, Maxim, Met, Motto, Pad, Panel, Paroemia, Pitsaw, Proverb, Pruning, Quarter, Rabbeting, Rack, Ribbon, Rip, Ryoba, Sash, Saying, Scroll, Serra, Skil®, Skip-tooth, Slogan, Span, Spied, Stadda, Stone, Sweep, Tenon, Trepan, Trephine, Whip, Witnessed

Say, **Saying(s)** Adage, Agrapha, Allege, Aphorism, Apophthegm, Apostrophise, Articulate, Axiom, Beatitude, Bon mot, Bromide, Byword, Cant, Catchphrase, Cliché, Declare, Dict(um), Eg, Enunciate, Epigram, Express, Fadaise, Gnome, Impute, Logia, Logion, Mean, Mot, Mouth, Observe, Predicate, Pronounce, Proverb, Put, Quip, Recite, Rede, Relate, Remark, Report, Saine, Saw, Sc, Sententia, > **SPEAK**, Suppose, Sutra, Utter, Voice, Word

▷ **Say**, **Saying(s)** *may indicate* a word sounding like another

Scale, **Scaly** API gravity, Ascend, Balance, Beaufort, Brix, Bud, Burnham, Celsius, Centigrade, Chromatic, > **CLIMB**, Diagonal, Diatonic, Escalade, Fahrenheit, Flake, Full, Gamme, Gamut, Gapped, Gauge, Gravity, Hexachord, Humidex, Indusium, Interval, Kelvin, Ladder, Lamina, Layer, Leaf, Lepid, Libra, Ligule, Magnitude, Major, Mercalli, Mesel, Minor, Mohs, Natural, Nominal, Ordinal, Palet, Peel, Pentatonic, Plate, Platform, > **RANGE**, Rankine, Ratio, Réaumur, Regulo, Richter, Scan, Scent, Scurf, Shin, Sliding, Submediant, Tegula, Tonal, Tron(e), Vernier, Wage, Wentworth, Wind

Scan(ning), **Scanner** CAT, CT, Examine, Helical, OCR, Peruse, PET, Rake, Raster, Scrutinise, SEM, SPET, Survey, Tomography, Ultrasound, Vet

Scandal(ous), **Scandalise** Belie, Canard, Commesse, Disgrace, Gamy, Hearsay, Muck-raking, Opprobrium, Outrage, Shame, Slander, Stigma, Watergate

Scant(y) Bare, Brief, Exiguous, Ihram, Jejune, Jimp, Poor, Scrimpy, Short, Shy, Slender, Spare, Sparse, Stingy

Scapegoat Butt, Fall-guy, Hazazel, Joe Soap, Patsy, Stooge, Target, Victim, Whipping-boy

Scarce(ly), **Scarcity** Barely, Dear, Dearth, Famine, Few, Hardly, Ill, Lack, Rare, Scanty, Seldom, Short, Strap, Uncommon, Want

Scarecrow Bogle, Bugaboo, Dudder, Dudsman, Gallibagger, Gallibeggar, Gallicrow, Gallybagger, Gallybeggar, Gallycrow, Malkin, Mawkin, Potato-bogle, Ragman, S(h)ewel, Tattie-bogle

Scarf Babushka, Belcher, Cataract, Comforter, Cravat, Curch, Doek, Dupatta, Fichu, Hai(c)k, Haique, Hyke, Lambrequin, Madras, Mantilla, Muffettee, Muffler, Neckatee, Nightingale, Orarium, Pagri, Palatine, Rail, Rebozo, Sash, Screen, Stole, Tallith, Tippet, Trot-cosy, Trot-cozy, Vexillum

Scatter(ed), **Scattering** Bestrew, Broadcast, Diaspora, Disject, Dispel, Dissipate, Flurr, Litter, Rout, Scail, Skail, Sow, Sparge, Splutter, Sporadic, Spread, Sprinkle, Squander, Straw, Strew

Scavenge(r) Dieb, Forage, Hunt, Hy(a)ena, Jackal, Rake, Ratton, Rotten, Scaffie, Sweeper, Totter

Scene(ry) Arena, Boscage, Coulisse, Decor, Flat(s), Landscape, Locale, Prop, Prospect, Set, Sight, Site, Sketch, Stage, Tableau, Tormenter, Tormentor, Venue, View

Scent Aroma, Attar, Chypre, Cologne, Essence, Fragrance, Frangipani, Fumet(te), Gale, Moschatel, Nose, Odour, Orris, Ottar, Otto, Perfume, Sachet, Smell, Spoor, Vent, Waft, Wind

Sceptic(al), Scepticism Cynic, Doubter, Incredulous, Infidel, Jaundiced, Nihilistic, Pyrrho(nic), Sadducee

Schedule Agenda, Calendar, Itinerary, Prioritise, Programme, Register, Slot, Table, Timetable

Scheme(r), Scheming Colour, Concoct, Conspire, Crafty, Cunning, Dare, Darien, Dart, Decoct, Devisal, Diagram, Dodge, Draft, Gin, Honeytrap, Intrigue, Jezebel, Machiavellian, Machinate, Manoeuvre, Nostrum, Pilot, > **PLAN**, Plat, Plot, Project, Proposition, Purpose, Put-up job, Racket, Ruse, Stratagem, System, Table, Wangle, Wheeze

Scholar, Scholiast Abelard, Academic, Alumni, BA, Bookman, Clergy, Clerk, Commoner, Demy, Disciple, Erasmus, Erudite, Etonian, Exhibitioner, Extern(e), Graduate, Literate, MA, Pauline, Plutarch, Polymath, Pupil, Rhodes, Sap, Savant, Schoolboy, Soph, > **STUDENT**, Tom Brown

School Academy, Ampleforth, Approved, Barbizon, Bauhaus, Beacon, Benenden, Board, Boarding, Charm, Charterhouse, Chartreux, Cheder, Choir, Church, Classical, Coed, Community, Composite, Comprehensive, Conservative, Conservatoire, Conservatory, Cool, Correspondence, Council, Crammer, Cult, Dada, Day, Direct grant, Downside, Drama, Drill, Driving, Dual, Educate, Elementary, Eton, Exercise, External, Faith, Fettes, Finishing, First, Flemish, Frankfurt, Free, Gam, Giggleswick, Gordonstoun, Grade, Grammar, Grant-aided, Grant-maintained, Group, Gymnasium, Harrow, Heder, Hedge, High, Historical, Honour, Hospital, Hostel, Hypermodern, Independent, Industrial, Infant, Institute, Integrated, Intermediate, Ionic, Jim Crow, Junior, Kindergarten, Lake, Lancing, Language, Life, List D, Loretto, Lower, Mahayana, Maintained, Maintaining, Manchester, Mannheim, Marlborough, Middle, National, Night, Normal, Nursery, Oundle, Parochial, Pensionnat, Perse, Piano, Play, Pod, Poly, Prep, Preparatory, Primary, Private, Provided, Public, RADA, Ragged, RAM, Real, Reformatory, Repton, Residential, Rhodian, Roedean, Rossall, Rydal, Satanic, Secondary(-modern), Sect, Seminary, Separate, Single-sex, Ski, Slade, Song, Spasmodic, Special, State, Stonyhurst, Stowe, Style, Summer, Sunday, Teach, Tonbridge, Trade, > **TRAIN**, Tutor, Upper, Voluntary(-aided), Voluntary-controlled, Wellington, Whales, Winchester

Science Anatomy, Anthropology, Art, Astrodynamics, Astrophysics, Atmology, Axiology, Biology, Botany, Chemistry, Cognitive, Computer, Dismal, Domestic, Earth, Electrodynamics, Eth(n)ology, Euphenics, Exact, Geology, Information, Life, Mechanics, Natural, Noble, Nomology, Ology, Ontology, Optics, Pedagogy, Physical, Physics, Policy, Political, Rocket, Rural, Skill, Social, Soft, Soil, Sonics, Stinks, Stylistics, Tactics, Technics, Technology

Scoff Belittle, Boo, Chaff, Deride, Dor, Eat, Feast, Flout, Food, Gall, Gibe, Gird, Gobble, > **JEER**, Mock, Rail, Rib, Ridicule, Roast, Scaff, Scorn, Sneer, Taunt

Scold(ing) Admonish, Berate, Callet, Catamaran, Chastise, Chide, Clapperclaw, Do, Earful, Flite, Flyte, Fuss, Jaw(bation), Jobation, Lecture, Nag, Objurgate, Philippic, Rant, Rate, > **REBUKE**, Reprimand, Reprove, Revile, Rouse on, Row, Sas(s)arara, Sis(s)erary, Slang, Slate, Termagant, Tick-off, Tongue-lash, Trimmer, Upbraid, Virago, Wig, Xant(h)ippe, Yaff, Yankie, Yap

Scooter Vespa®

Scope Ambit, Diapason, Domain, Elbow-room, Extent, Freedom, Gamut, Ken, Latitude, Leeway, Purview, Range, Remit, Room, Rope, Scouth, Scowth, Size, Sphere

Scorch(er) Adust, Blister, Brasero, > BURN, Char, Destroy, Frizzle, Fry, Parch, Scouther, Scowder, Scowther, Sear, Singe, Soar, Speed, Swale, Swayl, Sweal, Sweel, Torrefy, Torrid, Wither

Score Apgar, Behind, Bill, Birdie, Bradford, Bye, Capot, Chase, Conversion, Count, Crena, Debt, Eagle, Etch, Full, Groove, Hail, Honours, Ingroove, Ippon, Law, Magpie, Make, Music, Net, Nick, Notation, Notch, Partitur(a), Peg, Pique, Point, Record, Repique, Rit(t), Rouge, Run, Rut, Scotch, Scratch, Scribe, Scrive, Set, Single, Spare, Stria, String, Sum, Tablature, > TALLY, Twenty, Vocal, Waza-ari, Win

▷ **Scorer** *may indicate* a composer

▷ **Scoring** *may indicate* an anagram

Scorn(ful) Arrogant, Bah, Contempt, Contumely, Deride, Despise, Dis(s), Disdain, Dislike, Flout, Geck, Haughty, Insult, Meprise, Mock, Opprobrium, Putdown, Rebuff, Ridicule, Sarcastic, Sardonic, Sarky, Scoff, Scout, Sdaine, Sdeigne, Sneer, Spurn, Wither

Scot(sman), Scots(woman), Scottish Blue-bonnet, Fingal, Shetlander, Tartan, Tax

Scotland Alban(y), Albion, Caledonia, Lallans, Lothian, NB, Norland, Scotia

Scoundrel Cur, Knave, Reprobate, Scab, Smaik, Varlet, > VILLAIN

▷ **Scour** *may indicate* an anagram

Scout Akela, Beaver, Bedmaker, Colony, Disdain, Explorer, Flout, Guide, Outrider, Pathfinder, Pickeer, Pioneer, Reconnoitre, Rover, Runner, Scoff, Scorn, Scourer, Scurrier, Sixer, Talent, Tenderfoot, Tonto, Venture

Scrap(s), Scrappy Abandon, Abrogate, > BIT, Cancel, Conflict, Discard, Dump, > FIGHT, Fisticuffs, Fragment, Fray, Iota, Jot, Mêlée, Mellay, Morceau, Morsel, Odd, Off-cut, Ort, Ounce, Patch, Piece, Pig's-wash, Rag, Rase, Raze, Remnant, Scarmoge, Scissel, Scissil, Scrub, Set-to, Shard, Sherd, Shred, Skerrick, Skirmish, Snap, Snippet, Spall, Tait, Tate, Tatter, Titbit, Trash, Truculent, Whit

Scrape(r) Abrade, Agar, Bark, Clat, Claw, Comb, Curette, D and C, Escapade, Grate, Graze, Harl, Hoe, Hole, Jar, Kowtow, Lesion, Lute, Predicament, Racloir, Rake, Rasorial, Rasp, Rasure, Raze, Razure, Saw, Scalp, Scart, Scrat(ch), Scroop, Scuff, Shave, Skimp, Skive, Squeegee, Strake, Strigil, Xyster

Scratch(es), Scratched Cracked heels, Grabble, Score, Scrawp, Scrooch, Scrorp, Streak, Striation

▷ **Scratch(ed)** *may indicate* an anagram

Scream(er) Bellow, Cariama, Caterwaul, Comedian, Comic, Cry, Eek, Headline, Hern, Kamichi, Laugh, Priceless, Primal, Riot, Scare-line, Screech, Seriema, Shriek, Skirl, Squall, Sutch, Yell

Screen(s) Arras, Backstop, Blind(age), Block, Blue, Boss, Camouflage, Chancel, Check, Chick, Cinerama®, Cloak, Cornea, Cover, Curtain, Divider, Dodger, Eyelid, Fire, Fluorescent, Glib, Grille, Hallan, Help, Hide, Hoard, Hoarding, Intensifying, Lattice, Mantelet, Mask, Nintendo, Nonny, Obscure, Organ, Parclose, Partition, Pella, Purdah, Radar, Retable, Riddle, Rood, Scog, Sconce, Scope, > SHADE, Shelter, Shield, Show, Sift, Sight, Silver, Skug, Small, Smoke, Split, Sunblock, Televise, Tems, Touch, Traverse, Umbrella, VDU, Vet, Wide, Windbreak, Window, Windshield

Screw Adam, Allen, Archimedes, Butterfly, Cap, Coach, Countersunk, Double-threaded, Dungeoner, Extort, Female, Grub, Ice, Interrupted, Jailer, Jailor, Lag, Lead, Levelling, Lug, Machine, Male, Micrometer, Miser, Monkey-wrench, Niggard, Perpetual, Phillips®, Prop(ellor), Robertson, Salary, Skinflint, Spiral, Thumb(i)kins, Twin, Twist, Vice, Worm

Script Book, Gurmukhi, Hand, Hiragana, Italic, Jawi, Kana, Libretto, Linear A, Linear B, Lines, Lombardic, Miniscule, Nagari, Nastalik, Nastaliq, Ogam, Ronde, Scenario, Screenplay, Writing

Scripture(s), **Scriptural version** Adi Granth, Agadah, Antilegomena, Avesta, Bible, Gemara, Gematria, Gospel, Granth (Sahib), Guru Granth, Haggada(h), Hermeneutics, Hexapla, Holy book, Holy writ, Koran, K'thibh, Lesson, Lotus Sutra, Mishna(h), OT, Rig-veda, Smriti, Tantra, Targum, Testament, Upanishad, Veda, Vedic, Verse, Vulgate

Scrotum Oscheal

Scrounge(r) Blag, Bludge(r), Borrow, Bot, Cadge, Forage, Freeload, Layabout, Ligger, Scunge, Sponge

Scrub(ber) Cancel, Chaparral, Cleanse, Dele(te), Gar(r)igue, Loofa(h), Luffa, Masseur, Negate, Pro, Rub, Scour, Tart

▷ **Scrub** *may indicate* 'delete'

Scrutinise, **Scrutiny** Check, Docimasy, Examine, Inspect, Observe, Peruse, Pore, Pry, > **SCAN**, Study

▷ **Scuffle** *may indicate* an anagram

Sculpt(ure) Bas-relief, Bronze, Carve, Della-robbia, Figure, Kouros, Mobile, Nude, Pieta, Relievo, Shape, > **STATUARY**, Topiary

Scum Dregs, Dross, Epistasis, Scorious, Slag, Slime, Spume, Sullage

Scurf, **Scurvy** Dander, Dandriff, Dandruff, Furfur, Horson, Lepidote, Leprose, Scabrous, Scall, Scorbutic, Whoreson, Yaw(e)y, Yaws

Sea(s) Adriatic, Aegean, Amundsen, Andaman, Arabian, Arafura, Aral, Azov, Baltic, Banda, Barents, Beaufort, Bellingshausen, Benthos, Bering, Billow, Biscay, Black, Blue, Bosp(h)orus, Brine, Briny, Caribbean, Caspian, Celebes, Celtic, Ceram, Channel, China, Chukchi, Coral, Dead, Ditch, Drink, Euripus, Euxine, Flores, Galilee, Greenland, Head, Herring-pond, High, Hudson Bay, Icarian, Inland, Ionian, Irish, Japan, Kara, Labrador, Laptev, Ler, Ligurian, Main, Mare, Marmara, Med, Mediterranean, Nordenskjold, North, Norwegian, > **OCEAN**, Offing, Offshore, Oggin, Okhotsk, Pelagic, Philippine, Polynya, Quantity, Red, Ross, Sargasso, Seven, Skagerrak, South, South China, Spanish main, Strand, Sulu, Tasman, Tethys, Thalassic, Tiberias, Tide, Timor, Tyrrhenian, Water, Weddell, White, Yellow, Zee

Seaman, **Seamen** AB, Crew, Jack, Lascar, Lubber, Mariner, OD, Ordinary, PO, RN, > **SAILOR**, Salt, Swabby, Tar

Sear Brand, Burn, Catch, Cauterise, Frizzle, Parch, Scath(e), Scorch, Singe, Wither

Search(ing) Beat, Comb, Dragnet, Examine, Ferret, > **FORAGE**, Fossick, Frisk, Grope, Home, Hunt, Indagate, Inquire, Jerk, Jerque, Kemb, Manhunt, Perscrutation, Probe, Proll, Prospect, Proul, Prowl, Quest, Rake, Rancel, Ransack, Ransel, Ranzel, Ravel, Ripe, Root, Rootle, Rummage, Scan, Scour, Scur, Sker, Skirr, Snoop, Strip, Thumb, Trace, Zotetic

Season(able), **Seasonal**, **Seasoned**, **Seasoning** Accustom, Age, Aggrace, Autumn, Betimes, Christmas, Close, Condiment, Devil, Dress, Duxelles, Easter, Enure, Etesian, Fall, Fennel, Festive, Flavour, Garlic, G(h)omasco, Growing, Hiems, High, In, Inure, Lent, Marjoram, Master, Mature, Nutmeg, Open, Paprika, Pepper, Powellise, Practised, Ripen, Salt, Sar, Seal, Seel, Sele, Silly, Solstice, Spice, Spring, Summer(y), Tahini, Ticket, Tide, Time, Whit, Winter

Seat Bosun's chair, Bunker, Sagbag, Sedile, Siege Perilous, Window

Sea-weed Agar, Alga(e), Arame, Badderlock, Bladderwort, Bladderwrack, Carrag(h)een, Ceylon moss, Chondrus, Conferva, Coralline, Cystocarp, Desmid, Diatom, Dulse, Enteromorpha, Fucus, Gulfweed, Heterocontae, Kelp, Kilp, Kombu, Laminaria, Laver, Nori, Nullipore, Oarweed, Ore, Peacock's tail, Porphyra, Redware, Rockweed, Sargasso, Seabottle, Sea-furbelow, Sea-lace, Sea-lettuce, Sea-mat, Sea-moss, Sea-tangle, Seaware, Sea-whistle, Sea-wrack, Tang, Ulva, Varec(h), Vraic, Wakame, Wakane, Ware, Wrack

Seclude, **Seclusion** Cloister, Incommunicado, Isolate, Maroon, Nook, Privacy, Purdah, Quarantine, Retiracy, Retreat, Secret, Sequester, Shyness, Solitude

Second(s), **Secondary** Abet, Alternative, Another (guess), Appurtenance, Assist, Back(er), Beta, Coming, Comprimario, Deuteragonist, Flash, Friend, Imperfect, Indirect, Inferior, Instant, Jiffy, Latter, Lesser, Minor, Mo(ment), Nature, Other, Pig's-whisper, Runner-up, Sec, Shake, Share, Side(r), Sight, Silver, Split, Subsidiary, Support, Tick, Trice, Twinkling, Wind

Second-hand Hearsay, Reach-me-down, Used

Secrecy, **Secret(s)**, **Secretive** Apocrypha, Arcana, Arcane, Backstairs, Cabbalistic, Cagey, Clam, Clandestine, Closet, Code, Covert, Cryptic, Dark, Deep, Deep-laid, Devious, Esoteric, Hidden, Hole and corner, Hush-hush, Inly, Inmost, Latent, Mysterious, Mystical, Mystique, Open, Oyster, Password, Penetralia, > PRIVATE, Privy, QT, Rune, Shelta, Silent, Sly, State, Stealth, Sub rosa, Tight-lipped, Top, Trade, Unbeknown, Undercover, Underhand, Unknown, Unre(a)d, Unrevealed, Untold

Secretary Aide, Amanuensis, Chancellor, Chronicler, CIS, Desk, Desse, Famulus, Minuteman, Moonshee, Munshi, Notary, Permanent, Scrive, Social, Stenotyper, Temp

Sect(arian), **Secret society** Ahmadiy(y)ah, Albigenses, Covenantes, Cynic, Encratite, Familist, Hassid, Hemerobaptist, Hesychast, Ismaili, Ophites, Patripassian, Paulician, Pietist, Plymouth Brethren, Pure Land, Sandeman, Schwenkfelder, Seventh Day Adventist, Shembe, Soka Gakkai, Sons of Freedom, Utraquist, Zealot

Section, **Sector** Caesarian, Chapter, Classify, Conic, Cross, Cut, Division, Ellipse, Eyalet, Gan, Golden, Gore, Hyperbola, Lith, Lune, Meridian, Metamere, Mortice, Movement, Octant, Outlier, Panel, Passus, > PIECE, Platoon, Private, Public, Quarter, Rhythm, Rib, Segment, Severy, Slice, Stage, Ungula, Unit, Zone

Secure, **Security** Anchor, Assurance, Bag, Bail, Band, Bar, Batten, Belay, Bellwether, Bolt, Bond, Buck Rogers, Calm, Catch, Cement, Chain, Cinch, Clamp, Clasp, Clench, Clinch, Close, Cocoon, Collateral, Collective, Consols, Cushy, Debenture, Engage, Ensure, Equity, Establishment, Fasten, Fastness, Fortify, Fungibles, Gilt, Guarantee, Guy, Immune, Indemnity, Invest(ment), Knot, Lace, Land, Lash, Latch, Lien, Listed, Lock, Lockaway, Longs, Mortgage, Nail, National, Obtain, Patte, Pin, Pledge, Pot, Pre-empt, Preference, Protect, Quad, Rope, Rug, > SAFE, Safety, Settle, Snell, Snug, Social, Sound, Stable, Staple, Stock, Strap, Sure(ty), Tack, Take, Tie, Tight, Trap, Warrant, Watertight, Wedge, Win

Sedative Amytal®, Anodyne, Aspirin, Barbitone, Bromide, Chloral, Depressant, Hypnic, Lenitive, Lupulin, Meprobamate, Metopryl, Miltown, Narcotic, Nembutal®, Opiate, Paraldehyde, Pethidine, Phenobarbitone, Premed(ication), Scopolamine, Seconal®, Soothing, Thridace, Veronal

Sediment Alluvium, Chalk, Deposit, Dregs, F(a)eces, Fecula, Foots, Grounds, Lees, Molasse, Placer, Residue, Salt, Sapropel, Silt, Sludge, Terrigenous, Till, Varve, Warp

Seduce(r), **Seductive** Bewitch, Debauch, Dishonour, Honeyed, Honied, Jape, Lothario, Luring, Mislead, Siren, Tempt

▷ **Seduce** *may indicate* one word inside another

See(ing) Behold, Bishopric, Consider, Descry, Diocesan, Discern, Episcopal, Eye, Glimpse, Holy, Lo, Notice, Observe, Papal, Perceive, Realise, Spot, Spy, Twig, Understand, Vatican, Vid(e), View, Vision, Voila, Witness

Seed(s), **Seedy** Achene, Argan, Arilli, Arillode, Ash-key, Bean, Ben, Best, Bonduc, Cacoon, Caraway, Carvy, Cebadilla, Cevadilla, Chickpea, Coriander, Corn, Cum(m)in, Dragon's teeth, Embryo, Endosperm, Ergot, Favourite, Germ, Grain, Gritty, Issue, Ivory-nut, Kernel, Lomentum, Mangy, Miliary, Nucellous, Nut, Offspring, Ovule, Pea, Piñon, Pip, Poorly, Poppy, Sabadilla, Scuzz, Semen, Seminal,

Sesame, Shabby, Silique, Sorus, Sow, Sperm, Spore, Zoosperm

Seek(er) Ask, Beg, Busk, Chase, Court, Endeavour, Pursue, Quest, Scur, Search, Skirr, Solicit, Suitor

Seem(ingly) Appear, Look, Ostensible, Purport, Quasi, Think

Seemly Comely, Decent, Decorous, Fit, Suitable

Seer Eye, Nahum, Observer, Onlooker, Prescience, Prophet, Sage, Sibyl, Soothsayer, Witness, Zoroaster

Segment Antimere, Arthromere, Cut, Division, Gironny, Gyronny, Intron, Lacinate, Lobe, Merome, Merosome, Metamere, Pig, Prothorax, Scliff, Share, Shie, Skliff, Somite, Split, Sternite, Syllable, Tagma, Telson, Urite, Uromere

Segregate, **Segregation** Apartheid, Exile, Insulate, Intern, > **ISOLATE**, Jim Crow, Seclude, Separate

Seize, **Seizure** Angary, Apprehend, Areach, Arrest, Attach(ment), Bag, Bone, Capture, Claw, Cleek, Cly, Collar, Commandeer, Confiscate, Distrain, Distress, For(e)hent, > **GRAB**, Grip, Hend, Impound, Impress, Maverick, Na(a)m, Nab, Nap, Nim, Poind, Possess, Pot, Raid, Replevy, Rifle, Sequestrate, Smug, Tackle, Wingding

Select(ion), **Selecting**, **Selector** Assortment, Bla(u)d, Cap, Casting, Choice, Choose, Classy, Cull, Darwinism, Discriminate, Draft, Draw, Eclectic, Edit, Elite, Excerpt, Exclusive, Extract, Favour, Garble, Inside, K, Nap, Natural, Pericope, > **PICK**, Pot-pourri, Prefer, Recherché, Sample, Seed, Single, Sort, Stream, Tipster, Triage, UCCA

Self Atman, Auto, Character, Ego, Person, Psyche, Seity, Sel, Soul

Self-conscious Guilty

▶ **Self-defence** see **MARTIAL (ARTS)**

Self-esteem Amour-propre, Conceit, Confidence, Egoism, Pride

Self-important, **Self-indulgent**, **Self-interested** Aristippus, Arrogant, Conceited, Immoderate, Jack-in-office, Licentious, Narcissistic, Pompous, Pragmatic, Profligate, Solipsist, Sybarite

Selfish(ness) Avaricious, Egoist, Greedy, Hedonist, Mean, Solipsism

Self-possession Aplomb, Composure, Cool, Nonchalant

Self-satisfied, **Self-satisfaction** Complacent, Narcissism, Smug, Tranquil

Sell(er), **Selling** Apprize, Auction, Barter, Bear, Betray, Catch, Chant, Chaunt, Cope, Costermonger, Direct, Dispose, Do, Fancier, Flog, Go, Hard, Have, Hawk, Hustle, Inertia, Knock down, Market, Marketeer, Menage, Merchant, Missionary, Oligopoly, Pardoner, Peddle, Peddler, Pick-your-own, Purvey, Push, Pyramid, Rabbito(h), Realise, Rep, Retail, Ruse, Simony, Soft, Stall-man, Sugging, Switch, > **TRADE**, Vend

Semblance Aspect, Likeness, Sign, Verisimilitude

Semi-circular D, Hemicycle

Senator Antiani, Cicero, Elder, Legislator, Solon

Send, **Sent** Consign, > **DESPATCH**, Disperse, Emit, Entrance, Issue, Launch, Order, Post, Rapt, Ship, Transmit, Transport

Send up Chal(l)an, Lampoon, Promote

Senile, **Senility** Caducity, Dementia, Disoriented, Doddery, Doitit, Dotage, Eild, Eld, Gaga, Nostology, Twichild

Senior Aîné, Doyen, Elder, Father, Grecian, Mayor, Père, Primus, Superior, Upper

Sensation(al) Acolouthite, Anoesis, Aura, Blood, Commotion, Emotion, Empfindung, Feeling, Gas, Lurid, Melodrama, Pyrotechnic, Shocker, Shock-horror, Splash, Stir, Styre, Synaesthesia, Thrill, Tingle, Vibes, Wow, Yellow

Sense, **Sensual**, **Sensing** Acumen, Aura, Carnal, Coherence, Common, Dress, ESP, Faculty, Feel, Gross, Gumption, Gustation, Hearing, Horse, Idea, Import,

Instinct, Intelligence, Intuition, Lewd, Meaning, Nous, Olfactory, Palate,
Perceptual, Rational, Receptor, Remote, Rumble-gumption, Rumgumption,
Rum(m)el-gumption, Rum(m)le-gumption, Sight, Sixth, Slinky, Smell, Sybarite,
Synesis, Taste, Touch, Voluptuary, Voluptuous, Wisdom, Wit

Senseless Absurd, Anosmia, Illogical, Mad, Numb, Stupid, Stupor, Unconscious,
Unwise

Sensible Aware, Dianoetic, Prudent, Raisonné, Rational, Sane, Solid,
Well-balanced

Sensitive, **Sensitivity** Alive, Allergic, Dainty, Delicate, Keen, Passible,
Sympathetic, Tactful, Tender, Thin-skinned, Ticklish, Touchy(-feely), Vulnerable

Sentence(s) Assize, Bird, Carpet, Clause, Commit, Condemn, Custodial,
Death, Decree(t), Deferred, Doom, Fatwah, Indeterminate, Judgement, Life,
Matrix, Paragraph, Period(ic), Porridge, Predicate, Rap, Rheme, Rune, Stretch,
Suspended, Swy, Tagmene, Verdict, Versicle

Sentiment(al), **Sentimentality** Byronism, Corn, Cornball, Drip, Feeling,
Goo, Govey, Gucky, Gush, Maudlin, Mawkish, Mind, Mush, Opinion, Romantic,
Rose-pink, Rosewater, Saccharin, Schmaltzy, Sloppy, Smoochy, Soppy, Spoony,
Tear-jerker, Traveller, Treacly, Twee, View, Weepy, Yucky

Sentry Picket, Sentinel, Vedette, Watch

Separate(d), **Separation**, **Separately** Abstract, Asunder, Comma,
Compartmentalise, Cull, Cut, Decollate, Decompose, Decouple, Deduct,
Demarcate, Demerge, Detach, Dialyse, Disally, Disconnect, Disjunction,
Dissociate, Distance, Distinct, Disunite, Divide, Division, Divorce, Eloi(g)n, Elute,
Elutriate, Esloin, Estrange, Filter, Grade, Heckle, Hive, Hyphenate, Insulate,
Intervene, Isolate, Judicial, Laminate, Lease, Legal, Part, Particle, Peel off, Piece,
Prescind, Red(d), Rift, Scatter, Screen, Segregate, Sequester, Sever, Several, Shed,
Shore, Shorn, Sift, Sleave, Sle(i)ded, Solitary, Sort, > **SPLIT**, Stream, Sunder, Sundry,
Tems(e), Tmesis, Try, Twin(e), Unclasp, Unravel, Winnow, Wrench

Sepulchral, **Sepulchre** Bier, Cenotaph, Charnel, Crypt, Funeral, Monument,
Pyramid, Tomb, Vault, Whited

Sequence Agoge, Algorithm, Byte, Chronological, Continuity, Continuum,
Fibonacci, Intron, Line, Order, Program(me), Run, Seriatim, Series, Succession,
Suit, Suite, Train, Vector

Serene, **Serenity** Calm, Composed, Placid, Repose, Sangfroid, Sedate, Smooth,
> **TRANQUIL**

Serf(dom) Adscript, Bondman, Ceorl, Churl, Helot, Manred, > **SLAVE**, Thete,
Thrall, Vassal, Velle(i)nage

Sergeant Buzfuz, Cuff, Drill, Havildar, Kite, Platoon, RSM, Sarge, SL, SM, Staff,
Technical, Troy

Series Actinide, Actinium, Chain, Concatenation, Continuum, Course, Cycle,
Cyclus, Electromotive, Enfilade, En suite, Episode, Ethylene, Geometric,
Gradation, Harmonic, Homologous, Lanthanide, Line, Loop, Methane,
Neptunium, Partwork, Power, > **PROGRESSION**, Radioactive, Rest, Routine,
Rubber, Run, Sequence, Ser, Sitcom, String, Succession, Suit, Thorium, Time,
Tone, Train, Uranium, World

Serious(ly) Critical, Earnest, Grave, Gravitas, Important, Major, Momentous,
Pensive, Sad, Serpentine, Sober, Solemn, Sombre, Staid, Straight(-faced), Very

Sermon Address, Discourse, Gatha, Homily, Lecture, Preachment, Spital

Serpent(ine) Adder, Anguine, Asp, Aspic(k), Basilisk, Boa, Cockatrice, Dipsas,
Firedrake, Nagas, Sea-snake, > **SNAKE**, Traitor, Viper

Serum Antilymphocyte, Antitoxin, ATS, Fluid, Humoral, Opsonin, Senega

Servant, **Serve(r)** Attendant, Ayah, Batman, Bearer, Bedder, Bedmaker,
Between-maid, Boot-catcher, Boots, Boy, Butler, Caddie, Civil, Columbine, Cook,

Daily, Domestic, Dromio, Drudge, Employee, Factotum, File, Flunkey, Footboy, Footman, Friday, G(h)illie, Gip, Gully, Gyp, Handmaid, Helot, Henchman, Hireling, Jack, Jack-slave, Kitchen-knave, Lackey, Lady's maid, Maid, Major-domo, Man, Man Friday, Menial, Minion, Myrmidon, Obedient, Page, Pantler, Public, Retainer, Retinue, Scout, Scullion, Servitor, Slavey, Soubrette, Steward, Tiger, Tweeny, Underling, Valet, Valkyrie, Varlet, Vassal, Waiter

Serve, Service(s) Ace, Act, Active, Amenity, Answer, Assist, Attendance, Avail, Benediction, Breakfast, Candlemas, Cannonball, China, Civil, Communion, Community, Complin(e), Credo, Devotional, Dinnerset, Diplomatic, Divine, Drumhead, Duty, Ecosystem, Employ, Evensong, Facility, Fault, Fee, Feudal, Fish, Foreign, Forensic, Forward, > **FUNCTION**, Help, Helpline, Kol Nidre, Lip, Litany, Liturgy, Mass, Mat(t)ins, Memorial, Mincha, Minister, Ministry, Missa, National, Nocturn, Nones, Oblige, Office, Oracle, Overarm, Overhaul, Pass, Pay, Personal, Pit stop, Possum, Pottery, Prime, Proper, Public, RAF, Requiem, Rite, Sacrament, Secret, Selective, Senior, Sext, Shacharis, Shaharith, Shuttle, Silver, Social, Sue, Tableware, Tea, Vespers, Wait, Watch-night, Worship, Yeoman('s)

▷ **Serviceman** *may indicate* a churchman

Servile, Servility Abasement, Base, Crawling, Knee, Lickspittle, Menial, Obsequious, Slavish, Slimy, Suck-hole, Sycophantic, Truckle

Session(s) Bout, Executive, Galah, Jam, Kirk, Meeting, Nightshift, Petty, Poster, Quarter, Rap, Round, Séance, Sederunt, Settle, Sitting, Term

Set(ting) (down; in; off; out; up) Activate, Brooch, Cabal, Coagulate, Cyclorama, Data, Dead, Detonate, Explode, Film, Flash, Infinite, Jet, Open, Ordered, Ouch, Permanent, Power, Saw, Smart, Subscriber, Televisor, Tiffany, Toilet, Truth

Setback Checkmate, Hiccup, Jolt, Relapse, Retard, Retreat, Reversal, Scarcement, Sickener, Tes, Vicissitude

Settle(d), Settler, Settlement Adjust, Agree, Alight, Appoint, Arrange, Ascertain, Avenge, Balance, Bed, Bench, Boer, Borghetto, Camp, Clear, Clench, Clinch, Colonial, Colonise, Colony, Compose, Compound, Compromise, Decide, Defray, Determine, Discharge, Dispose, Dowry, Encamp, Endow, Ensconce, Entail, Establish, Expat, Faze, Fix, Foot, Foreclose, Gravitate, Guilder, Habitant, Illegitimate, Informal, Jointure, Kibbutz, Land, Ledge, Light, Manyat(t)a, Merino, Mission, Nest, Nestle, Opt, Outpost, Over, Pa(h), Pale, Patroon, Pay, Penal, Perch, Pilgrim, Pioneer, Placate, Planter, Populate, Port Arthur, Port Nicholson, Pueblo, Readjust, Reduction, Reimburse, Remit, Reside, Resolve, Rest, Sate, Satisfaction, Secure, Sedimentary, Set fair, Silt, Sofa, Soldier, Solve, Soweto, Square, State, Still, Straits, Subside, Township, Vest(ed), Viatical, Voortrekker

▷ **Settlement** *may indicate* an anagram

▷ **Settler** *may indicate* a coin

Seven(th) Ages, Days, Dials, Great Bear, Hebdomad, Hepta-, Hills, Nones, Pleiad(es), S, Sages, Seas, Septenary, Septimal, Sins, Sisters, Sleepers, Stars, Wonders, Zeta

Seven-week Omer

Several Divers, Many, Multiple, Some, Sundry

Severe(ly), Severity Acute, Bad, Chronic, Cruel, Dour, Draconian, Drastic, Eager, Extreme, Grave, Grievous, Gruel(ling), Hard, > **HARSH**, Ill, Inclement, Morose, Penal, Rhadamanthine, Rigo(u)r, Roundly, Serious, Sharp, Snell(y), Sore, Spartan, Stern, Strict

Sew(ing), Sew up Baste, Cope, Embroider, Fell, Machine, Mitre, Overlock, Run, Seam, Seel, Stitch, Tack, Whip

Sewage, Sewer Cesspool, Cloaca, Culvert, Dorcas, > **DRAIN**, Effluence, Jaw-box, Jaw-hole, Mimi, Needle, Privy, Shore, Soil, Sough, Soughing-tile, Waste

Sex(y) Bed-hopping, Coupling, Erotic, Favours, Female, Gam(ic), Gender, Hump, Incest, Intercourse, Kind, Libidinous, Libido, Lingam, Lumber, Male, Mate, Nookie, Oomph, Oral, Paedophilia, Pederasty, Phat, Priapean, Race, Randy, Raunchy, Rut(ish), Salacious, Screw, Sect, Steamy, Sultry, Teledildonics, Venereal, Venery, VI, Voluptuous

Shabby Base, Buckeen, Dog-eared, Down-at-heel, Fusc(ous), Grotty, Mean, Moth-eaten, Oobit, Oorie, Oubit, Ourie, Outworn, Owrie, Raunch, Scaly, Scruffy, Seedy, Shoddy, Squalid, Tatty, Worn, Woubit

Shackle(s) Bind, Bracelet, Chain, Entrammel, Fetter(lock), Hamper, Irons, Manacle, Restrict, Tie, Trammel, Yoke

Shade(d), **Shades**, **Shading**, **Shadow**, **Shady** Adumbrate, Arbour, Awning, Blend, Blind, Bongrace, Bowery, Brocken spectre, Buff, Cast, Chiaroscuro, Chroma, Cloche, Cloud, Cross-hatch, Degree, Dis, Dog, Dubious, Eclipse, Eye, Five o'clock, Galanty, Gamp, Ghost, Gradate, Gray, Hachure, Hell, Herbar, Hint, Hue, Inumbrate, Larva, Lee, Mezzotint, Nuance, Opaque, Overtone, Parasol, Phantom, Presence, Ray-Bans®, Satellite, Screen, Shroud, Sienna, Silhouette, Silvan, Skia-, Soften, Spectre, Spirit, Stag, Sunglasses, Swale, Swaly, Tail, Tinge, Tint, Tone, Ugly, Umbra(tile), Umbrage(ous), Underhand, Velamen, Velar(ium), Velum, Visor

Shaft(ed), **Shafting** Arbor, Arrow, Barb, Barrow-train, Beam, Capstan, Cardan, Chimney, Column, Crank, Cue, Disselboom, Dolly, Drive, Fil(l), Fust, Incline, Journal, Limber, Loom, Mandrel, Mandril, Moulin, Parthian, Passage, Pile, Pit, Pitch, Pole, Propeller, Ray, Scape, Scapus, Shank, Snead, Spindle, Staff, Stale, Steal(e), Steel, Stele, Stulm, Sunbeam, Thill, Tige, Trave, Upcast, Winning, Winze

Shaggy Ainu, Comate, Hairy, Hearie, Hirsute, Horrid, Horror, Rough, Rugged, Shock, Shough, Tatty, Untidy

Shake(n), **Shakes**, **Shaky** Ague(-fit), Astonish, Brandish, Coggle, Concuss, Dabble, Dick(e)y, Didder, Dither, Dodder, Feeble, Groggy, Hod, Hotch, Jar, Jiggle, Joggle, Jolt, Jounce, Judder, Jumble, Milk, Mo, Nid-nod, Press flesh, Quake, Quiver, Quooke, Rattle, Rickety, Rickle, > ROCK, Rouse, Shimmer, Shiver, Shock, Shog, Shoogle, Shudder, Succuss(ation), Sweat, Tremble, Tremolo, Tremor, Tremulous, Trill(o), Tumbledown, Undulate, Vibrate, Vibrato, Wag, Waggle, Wind, Wobble, Wonky

▷ **Shake** *may indicate* an anagram

Shallow(s) Ebb, Flat, Fleet, Flew, Flue, Justice, Neritic, Shoal, Slight, Superficial

Sham Apocryphal, Bluff, Bogus, Braide, Charade, Counterfeit, Deceit, Fake, > FALSE, Hoax, Idol, Impostor, Mimic, Mock, Phony, Pinchbeck, Pretence, Pseudo, Repro, Snide, Spurious

Shame(ful), **Shame-faced** Abash, Aidos, Contempt, Crying, Degrade, Discredit, Disgrace, Dishonour, Embarrass, Fie, Gross, Hangdog, Honi, Humiliate, Ignominy, Infamy, Inglorious, Modesty, Mortify, Pity, Pudor, Pugh, Shend, Sin, Slander, Stain, Stigma, Yshend

Shape(d), **Shapely**, **Shaping** Blancmange, Boast, Cast, Contour, Face, Fashion, Figure, Form, Format, Geoid, Gnomon, Headquarters, Hew, Jello, Model, > MOULD, Ream, Rhomb(us), Scabble, Sculpt, Wrought

Share(d), **Shares**, **Sharing** Allocation, Allotment, Apportion, Blue-chip, Chop, Co, Cohabit, Coho(e), Common, Communal, Contango, Culter, Cut, Deferred, Divi(dend), Divide, Divvy, Dole, Dutch, Equity, Finger, Golden, Impart, Interest, Job, Kaffer, Kaf(f)ir, Kangaroo, Lion's, Market, Moiety, Odd lot, Ordinary, > PART, Partake, Participate, Penny, PIBS, Plough, Plough-iron, Portion, Prebend, Pref(erred), Preference, Pro rata, Prorate, Quarter, Quota, Rake off, Ration, Rug, Scrip, Security, Shr, Slice, Snack, Snap, Sock, Split, Stock, Taurus, Time, Tranche, Two-way, Whack

Shark Angel, Basking, Beagle, Blue, Bonnethead, Carpet, Cestracion, Cow,

Demoiselle, Dog(fish), Hammerhead, Houndfish, Huss, Lemonfish, Loan, Mackerel, Mako, Noah, Nurse, Penny-dog, Plagiostomi, Porbeagle, Requiem, Rhin(e)odon, Rigg, Sail-fish, Sea-ape, Sharp, Shovelhead, Smoothhound, Squaloid, Swindler, Thrasher, Thresher, Tiger, Tope, Usurer, Whale, Wobbegong, Zygaena

Sharp(er), Sharpen(er), Sharpness Abrupt, Accidental, Acerose, Acidulous, Acrid, Aculeus, Acumen, Acuminate, Acute, Alert, Angular, Arris, Bateless, Becky, Bitter, Brisk, Cacuminous, Cheat, Clear, Coticular, Cutting, Dital, Edge(r), Fine, Gleg, Grind, Hone, Hot, Keen, Kurtosis, Massé, Oilstone, Peracute, Piquant, Poignant, Pronto, Pungent, Razor, Rogue, Rook, Set, Shrewd, Snap, Snell, Sour, Spicate, Strop, Swindler, Tart, Tomium, Vivid, Volable, Whet

Shawl Afghan, Buibui, Cashmere, Chuddah, Chuddar, Dopatta, Dupatta, Fichu, India, Kaffiyeh, Kashmir, Mantilla, Maud, Paisley, Partlet, Prayer, Serape, Stole, Tallis, Tallit(ot), Tallith, Tonnag, Tozie, Tribon, Whittle, Wrap(per), Zephyr

Shed(ding), Shedder Autotomy, Barn, Cast, Cho(u)ltry, Coducity, Depot, Discard, Doff, Drop, Effuse, Exuviate, Hangar, Hovel, Hut, Infuse, Lair, Lean-to, Linhay, Linny, Mew, Moult, Pent, Potting, Salmon, Shippen, Shuck, Skeo, Skillion, Skio, Slough, Sow, Spend, Spent, Spill, Tilt, Tool

Sheep(ish) Ammon, Ancon(es), Aoudad, Argali, Barbary, Bell(wether), Bharal, Bident, Bighorn, Black, Blackface, Blate, Border Leicester, Broadtail, Burhel, Burrel(l), Caracul, Cheviots, Coopworth, Corriedale, Cotswold, Coy, Crone, Dinmont, Dorset Down, Dorset Horn, Down, Drysdale, Embarrassed, Ewe, Exmoor, Fank, Fat-tailed, Flock, Fold, Hair, Hampshire, Hampshire Down, Hangdog, Herdwick, Hidder, Hirsel, Hog(g), Hogget, Jacob, Jemmy, Jumbuck, Karakul, Kent, Kerry Hill, Lamb, Lanigerous, Leicester, Lincoln, Lo(a)ghtan, Loghtyn, Lonk, Marco Polo, Masham, Merino, Mor(t)ling, Mouf(f)lon, Mountain, Muflon, Mug, Mus(i)mon, Mutton, Oorial, Ovine, Oxford Down, Perendale, Portland, Ram, Rambouillet, Romeldale, Romney Marsh, Rosella, Ryeland, Scottish Blackface, Shearling, Shorthorn, > SHY, Soay, Southdown, Spanish, Stone('s), Suffolk, Sumph, Swaledale, Teeswater, Teg(g), Texel, Theave, Trip, Tup, Two-tooth, Udad, Urial, Vegetable, Welsh Mountain, Wensleydale, Wether, Wiltshire Horn, Woollyback, Yow(e), Yowie

Sheet(s), Sheeting Balance, Cere-cloth, Cerement, Charge, Chart, Crime, Cutch, Dope, Expanse, Film, Folio, Foolscap, Heft, Leaf, Membrane, Nappe, Out-hauler, Page, Pot(t), Pour, Proof, Prospectus, Ream, Rope, Sail, Scandal, Shroud, Stern, Stratus, Taggers, Tarpaulin(g), Tear, Tentorium, Terne, Thunder, Time, Web, Winding

Shell(ed), Shellfish Abalone, Acorn-shell, Admiral, Ambulacrum, Ammo, Argonaut, Balamnite, Balanus, Balmain bug, Bivalve, Blitz, Boat, Bombard, Buckie, Camera, Capiz, Capsid, Carapace, Cartridge, Casing, Chank, Chelonia, Chitin, Clam, Clio, Coat-of-mail, Cochlea, Cockle, Cohog, Conch, Cone, Copepoda, Cover, Cowrie, Cowry, Crab, Crustacea, Cuttlefish, Dariole, Deerhorn, Dentalium, Dop, Drill, Electron, Escallop, Eugarie, Foraminifer, Framework, Frustule, Globigerina, Haliotis, Hull, Husk, Hyoplastron, Isopoda, Lamp, Langouste, Limacel, Limpet, Lobster, Lorica, Lyre, Malacostraca, Midas's ear, Mollusc, Monocoque, Moreton Bay bug, Mother-of-pearl, Murex, Music, Mussel, Nacre, Nautilus, Ormer, Ostracod, Ostrea, Otter, Oyster, Paua, Pawa, Peag, Peak, Pea(s)cod, Pecten, Pereia, Periostracum, Periwinkle, Pipi, Pipsqueak, Plastron, Pod, Prawn, Projectile, Purple, Putamen, Quahog, Razor, Sal, Scalarium, Scallop, Scollop, Sea-ear, Sea-pen, Shale, Shard, Sheal, Sheel, Shiel, Shill, Shock, Shot, Shrapnel, Shrimp, Shuck, Sial, Smoke-ball, Spend, Spindle, Star, Stomatopod, Stonk, Straddle, Strafe, Stromb(us), Swan-mussel, Tear, Test(a), Thermidor, Toheroa, Tooth, Top, Torpedo, Trivalve, Turbo, Turritella, Tusk, Univalve, Valency, Venus, Wakiki, Wampum, Whelk, Whiz(z)bang, Winkle, Xenophya, Yabbie, Yabby, Zimbi

▷ **Shelled** *may indicate* an anagram

Shelter Abri, Anderson, Asylum, Awn, Awning, Belee, Bender, Bield, Billet, Blind, Blockhouse, Booth, Bunker, Burladero, Butt, Cab, Carport, Casemate, Cot(e), Cove, Covert, Coverture, Defence, Dodger, Donga, Dripstone, Dug-out, Fall-out, Garage, Gunyah, Harbour, Haven, Hithe, Hospice, Hostel, House, Hovel, Humpy, Hut, Hutchie, Kipsie, Lee, Lee-gage, Loun, Lound, Lown, Lownd, Mai mai, Mission, Morrison, Nodehouse, > **REFUGE**, Retreat, Roof, Sanctuary, Scog, Sconce, Scoog, Scoug, Screen, Scug, Shed, Shiel(ing), Shroud, Skug, Snowshed, Stell, Storm-cellar, Succah, Sukkah, Summerhouse, Tax, Tent, Testudo, Tortoise, Tupik, Twigloo, Umbrage, Weather, Wheelhouse, Wi(c)kiup, Wickyup, Wil(t)ja, Windbreak

Shepherd(ess) Abel, Acis, Amaryllis, Amos, Bergère, Bo-peep, Chloe, Clorin, Conduct, Corin, Corydon, Cuddy, Daphnis, Dorcas, Drover, Endymion, Escort, Ettrick, German, Grubbinol, Gyges, Herdsman, Hobbinol, Lindor, Marshal, Menalcas, Padre, Pastor(al), Pastorella, Phebe, Sheepo, Strephon, Tar-box, Thenot, Thyrsis, Tityrus

Sherry Amoroso, Cobbler, Cyprus, Doctor, Fino, Gladstone, Jerez, Manzanilla, Oloroso, Sack, Solera, Whitewash, Xeres

Shiah Ismaili

Shield(s), **Shield-shaped** Ablator, Achievement, Aegis, Ancile, Armour, Arms, Baltic, Biological, Bodyguard, Box, Buckler, Canadian, Cartouche, Clypeus, Defend, Dress, Escutcheon, Fence, Gobo, Guard, Gyron, Hatchment, Heat, Hielaman, Insulate, Laurentian, Lozenge, Mant(e)let, Mask, Pavis(e), Pelta, Protect, Ranfurly, Riot, Rondache, Scandinavian, Screen, Scute, Scutum, Sheffield, Sternite, Targe(t), Thyroid, Vair, Visor

Shift(er), **Shifty** Amove, Astatic, Blue, Budge, Change, Chemise, Core, Cymar, Devious, Displace, Doppler, Evasive, Expedient, Fend, Graveyard, Hedging, Landslide, Linen, Move, Night, Nighty, Red, Relay, Remove, Ruse, Scorch, Shirt, Shovel, Shunt, Simar(re), Slicker, Slip(pery), Spell, Stagehand, Stint, Tour, Transfer, Tunic, Turn, Vary, Veer, Warp

▷ **Shift(ing)** *may indicate* an anagram

▷ **Shimmering** *may indicate* an anagram

Shin Clamber, Climb, Cnemial, Leg, Shank, Skink, Swarm

Shine(r), **Shining**, **Shiny** Aglow, Beam, Buff, Burnish, Deneb, Effulge, Excel, Flash, Gleam, Glisten, Gloss, > **GLOW**, Irradiant, Japan, > **LAMP**, Leam, Leme, Lucent, Luminous, Lustre, Mouse, Nitid, Phosphoresce, Polish, Radiator, Relucent, Resplend, Rutilant, Skyre, Sleek, Twinkle, Varnish

▷ **Shiny** *may indicate* a star

Ship(ping) Boat, Container, Convoy, > **DISPATCH**, Embark, Export, Her, Hulk, Jolly, Keel, Man, MV, Post, Privateer, Prize, Prow, Raft, Ram, Sail, Saique, She, SS, Tall, Tub, Vessel, Weather

Shipshape Apple-pie, Neat, Orderly, Tidy, Trim

Shirt Boiled, Brown, Calypso, Camese, Camise, Chemise, Choli, Cilice, Dasheki, Dashiki, Dick(e)y, Dress, Fiesta, Garibaldi, Grandad, Hair, Hawaiian, Jacky Howe, Kaftan, Kaross, K(h)urta, Nessus, Non-iron, Parka, Partlet, Polo, Red, Safari, Sark, Serk, Shift, Smock, Stuffed, Subucula, T

Shiver(ing), **Shivers**, **Shivery** Aguish, Break, Chitter, Crumble, Dash, Dither, Fragile, Frisson, Grew, Grue, Malaria, Oorie, Ourie, Owrie, Quake, Quiver, > **SHAKE**, Shatter, Shrug, Shudder, Smash, Smither, Smithereens, Splinter, Timbers, Tremble

▷ **Shiver(ed)** *may indicate* an anagram

Shock(ed), **Shocker**, **Shocking** Acoustic, Aghast, Agitate, Anaphylactic, Appal, Astound, Bombshell, Bunch, Culture, Defibrillate, Disgust, Dreadful,

Drop, Earthquake, ECT, Egregious, Electric, Epatant, Fleg, Floccus, Galvanism, Gobsmack, Hair, Horrify, Impact, Infamous, Insulin, Jar, Jolt, Live, Mane, Mop, Outrage, Poleaxe, Putrid, Recoil, Return, Revolt, Rick(er), Scandal(ise), Seismic, Shake, Sheaf, Shell, Stagger, Start(le), Stun, Thermal, Trauma, Turn

▷ **Shocked** *may indicate* an anagram

Shoe(s) Accessory, Arctic, Athletic, Ballet, Balmoral, Bauchle, Blocked, Boat, Boot, Brake, Brogan, Brogue, Brothel creepers, Buskin, Calceate, Calk(er), Calkin, Casuals, Caulker, Cawker, Charlier, Chaussures, Chopin(e), Clodhopper, Clog, Co-respondent, Court, Creeper, Dap, Deck, Espadrille, Flattie, Galoche, Galosh, Gatty, Geta, Ghillie, Golosh, Gumshoe, Gym, High-low, High tops, Hot, Hush-puppies®, Jandal®, Jellies, Kletterschue, Kurdaitcha, Launch(ing), Loafer, Mary-Janes®, Mocassin, Moccasin, Muil, Mule, Open-toe, Oxford, Oxonian, Panton, Patten, Peeptoe, Pennyloafer, Pile, Plate, Plimsole, Plimsoll, Poulaine, Pump, Rivlin, Rope-soled, Rubbers, Rullion, Sabaton, Sabot, Saddle, Safety, Sandal, Sandshoe, Sannie, Scarpetto, Shauchle, Skid, Skimmer, Slingback, Slip-on, Slipper, Slip-slop, Sneaker, Snow, Sock, Soft, Solleret, Spike, Stoga, Stogy, Suede, Tackies, Takkies, Tennis, Tie, Topboot, Track, Trainer, Upper, Vamp(er), Veld-schoen, Veldskoen, Velskoen, Vibram®, Vibs, Wagon lock, Wedgie, Welt, Winkle-picker, Zori

Shoemaker Blacksmith, Clogger, Cobbler, Cordiner, Cordwainer, Cosier, Cozier, Crispi(a)n, Farrier, Leprechaun, Sachs, Smith, Snob, Soutar, Souter, Sowter, Sutor

Shoot(er), Shooting Ack-ack, Airgun, Arrow, Bine, Bostryx, Braird, Breer, Bud, Bulbil, Catapult, Chit, Cyme, Dart(le), Delope, Discharge, Drib, Elance, Enate, Eradiate, Film, Fire, Germ, Germain(e), Germen, Germin(ate), Glorious twelfth, > **GUN**, Gunsel, Head-reach, Hurl, Imp, Layer, Limb, Loose, Offset, Photograph, Pluff, Plug, Poot, Pop, Pot, Pout, Ramulus, Rapids, Ratoon, Riddle, Rod, Rove, Runner, Septembriser, Skeet, Snipe, Spire, Spirt, Spout, Spray, Sprout, Spurt, Spyre, Start, Stole, Stolon, Strafe, Sucker, Tellar, Teller, Tendril, Tiller, Turion, Twelfth, Twig, Udo, Vimen, Wand, Weapon, Wildfowler

Shop(s), Shopper Agency, Arcade, Atelier, Betray, Boutique, Bucket, Buy, Chain, Charity, Chippy, Closed, Coffee, Commissary, Co-op, Cop, Corner, Cut-price, Dairy, Delicatessen, Denounce, Dolly, Duddery, Duka, Duty-free, Emporium, Factory, Galleria, Gift, Grass, In bond, Inform, Luckenbooth, Machine, Mall, Mall-rat, Market, Megastore, Muffler, Off-licence, Open, Opportunity, Outlet, Parlour, Patisserie, Personal, Precinct, Print, PX, Retail, RMA, Salon, Sex, Shambles, Share, Shebang, Spaza, Squat, > **STORE**, Studio, Sundry, Superette, Supermarket, Superstore, Swap, Tally, Tea, Thrift, Tommy, Tuck, Union, Vintry, Warehouse, Works

Shopkeeper British, Butcher, Chemist, Gombeen-man, Greengrocer, Grocer, Haberdasher, Hosier, Ironmonger, Merchant, Newsagent, Provisioner, Retailer, Stationer

Shore Bank, Beach, Buttress, Coast, Coste, Landfall, Littoral, Offing, Prop, Rivage, Seaboard, Strand, Strandline

Short(en), Shortly Abbreviate, Abridge, Abrupt, Anon, Brief, Brusque, Commons, Concise, Contract, Crisp, Cross, Curt, Curtail, Curtal, Diminish, Drink, Epitomise, Ere-long, Inadequate, Lacking, Laconical, Light, Limited, Low, Mini, Near, Nip, Nutshell, Punch, Reduce, Reef, Scanty, Scarce, Shrift, Shy, Soon, Sparse, Spirit, Squab, Squat, Staccato, Stint, Stocky, Strapped, Stubby, Succinct, Taciturn, Teen(s)y, Terse, Tight, Tot, Wee

Shortage Dearth, Deficit, Drought, Famine, Lack, Need, Paucity, Scarcity, Sparsity, Wantage

Shorts Bermuda, Board, Boxer, Briefs, Culottes, Hot pants, Kaccha, Lederhosen, Plus-fours, Stubbies®, Trunks

Shot(s) Ammo, Approach, Attempt, Backhand, Ball, Barrage, Blank, Blast,

Bull, Bullet, Burl, Canna, Cannonball, Cartridge, Case, Chain, Chip, Cover, Crab, Crack, Daisy cutter, Dink, Dolly, Dram, Draw, Drop, Dunk, Exhausted, Forehand, Gesse, Glance, Go, Grape, Guess, Hook, Jump, Marksman, Massé, Matte, Money, Mulligan, Noddy, Parthian, Parting, Passing, Pellet, Penalty, Photo, Plant, Pop, Pot, Puff, Rid, Round, Safety, Salvo, Scratch, Shy, Silk, Six, Slam-dunk, Slap, Slice, Slug, Slung, Sped, Spell, Spent, Square cut, Stab, Still, Throw, Tonic, Tracking, Trial, Try, Turn, Volley, Warning, Wrist

Shout(er), Shouting Barrack, Bawl, Bellow, Boanerges, Call, Claim, Clamour, Cry, Din, Exclaim, Heckle, Hey, Hoi(cks), Holla, Holla-ho(a), Holler, Hollo, Holloa, Hooch, Hosanna, Howzat, Hue, Rah, Rant, Root, Round, Sa sa, Treat, Trumpet, Vociferate, Whoop, Yell(och), Yippee, Yoohoo

Shovel Backhoe, Dustpan, Hat, Main, Peel, Power, Scoop, Shool, Spade, Steam, Trowel, Van

Show(ing), Shown, Showy Appearance, Aquacade, Bench, Betray, Branky, Broadcast, Burlesque, Cabaret, Chat, Circus, Come, Con, Cruft's, Demo(nstrate), Depict, Diorama, Display, Do, Dressy, Dumb, Effere, Entertainment, Establish, Evince, > **EXHIBIT**, Expo, Extravaganza, Exude, Facade, Fair, Fangled, Farce, Flamboyant, Flash, Flaunt, Floor, Game, Garish, Gaudy, Gay, Give, Glitz(y), Gloss, Horse, Indicate, Jazzy, Light, Loud, Manifest, Matinée, Minstrel, Musical, Ostentatious, Pageant, Panel game, Pantomime, Parade, Patience, Performance, Phen(o), Point, Pomp, Portray, Pretence, Pride, Procession, Prog(ramme), Project, Prominence, Prove, Pseudery, Puff, Puppet, Quiz, Raree, Razzmatazz, Reality, Represent, Reveal, Revue, Road, Rushes, Screen, Shaw, Sight, Sitcom, Slang, Soap, Son et lumière, Specious, Spectacle, Splash, Splay, Stage, Stunt, Talk, Tattoo, Tawdry, Telethon, Theatrical, Three-man, Tinhorn, Unbare, Uncover, Usher, Vain, Variety, Vaudeville, Veneer, Wear, Wild west

Shower Douche, Exhibitor, Flurry, Hail, Indicant, Indicator, Meteor, Party, Pelt, Pepper, Precipitation, Rain, Scat, Scouther, Scowther, Skit, Snow, Spat, Spet, Spit, Splatter, Spray, Sprinkle, Ticker tape

▷ **Showing, Shown in** *may indicate* a hidden word

Shred Clout, Filament, Grate, Mammock, Mince, Rag, Screed, Swarf, Tag, Tatter, Thread, Wisp

Shrewd Acute, Arch, Argute, Artful, Astucious, Astute, Callid, Canny, Clued-up, Cute, File, Gnostic, Gumptious, Judicious, Knowing, Pawky, Politic, Sagacious, Sapient(al), Wily, Wise

Shriek Cry, Scream, Shright, Shrike, Shrill, Shritch, Skirl, Yell

Shrine Adytum, Altar, Dagoba, Dargah, Delphi, Fatima, Feretory, Harem, Holy, Joss house, Kaaba, Marabout, Naos, Pagoda, Reliquary, Scrine, Scryne, Stupa, Tabernacle, Temple, Tope, Vimana, Walsingham

Shrink(age), Shrinking, Shrunk Alienist, Blanch, Blench, Cling, Compress, Contract, Cour, Cower, Creep, Crine, Cringe, Dare, Decrew, Depreciate, Dread, Dwindle, Flinch, Funk, Less, Nirl, > **PSYCHIATRIST**, Quail, Recoil, Reduce, Sanforised, Shrivel, Shy, Violet, Wince, Wizened

Shrub(bery) Aalii, Acacia, Alhagi, Andromeda, Arboret, Arbutus, Aucuba, Azalea, Barberry, Beautybrush, Bottlebrush, Brere, Brush, Buaze, Buazi, Buckthorn, Buddleia, Bullace, > **BUSH**, Camellia, Caper, Cascara, Clianthus, Cola, Coprosma, Coyotillo, Crossandra, Cytisus, Daphne, Epacris, Fatsia, Feijoa, Firethorn, Frutex, Fynbos, Gardenia, Garrya, Gorse, Hardhack, Hebe, Henna, Hibiscus, Hop-tree, Horizontal, Inkberry, Jaborandi, Jasmine, Jessamine, Jetbread, Jojoba, Joshua tree, Juniper, Kat, Lantana, Laurustine, Lavender, Lignum, Manoao, Maqui(s), Matico, Melaleuca, Mesquit, Mimosa, Mistletoe, Monte, Myrica, Myrtle, Nabk, Ninebark, Ocotillo, Olea(cea), Parkleaves, Patchouli, Pituri, Plant, Poinsettia, Privet, Protea, Pyracantha, Pyxie, Qat, Rhatany, Rhododendron, Rhus, Rock rose, Romneya, Rue, Ruta, Salal, Savanna(h), Savin(e), Senna, Shadbush, Shallon, Skimmia,

Southernwood, Spekboom, Spicebush, Steeplebush, Sumach, Supplejack, Sweetsop, Tamarisk, Tea-tree, Thyme, Titi, Toyon, Tutsan, Tutu, Undergrowth, Wahoo, Waratah, Ya(u)pon, Yupon, Zamia

▷ **Shuffle(d)** *may indicate* an anagram

Shuttle Alternate, Commute, Drawer, Flute, Go-between, Shoot, Shunt, Space, Tat(t), Weave

Shy Bashful, Blate, Blench, Cast, Catapult, Chary, Coy, Deficient, Demure, Farouche, Flinch, Funk, Heave, Jerk, Jib, Laithfu', Lob, Mim, Rear, Recoil, Reserved, Sheepish, Shrinking, Skeigh, Start, Throw, Timid, Tongue-tied, Toss, Try, Violet, Withdrawn

Shyster Ambulance chaser

Sick(en), **Sickening**, **Sickliness**, **Sickly**, **Sickness** Affection, Ague, Ail, Bad, Bends, Cat, Chunder, Colic, Crapulence, Crook, Decompression, Delicate, Disorder, Gag, Hangover, Icky, Ill, Infection, Leisure, Mal, Mawkish, Morbid, Morning, Motion, Mountain, Nauseous, Pale, Peaky, Pestilent, Pindling, Plague, Queasy, Radiation, Regorge, Repulsive, Retch, Serum, Sleeping, Space, Spue, Squeamish, Sweating, Travel, Twee, Valetudinarian, Virus, Vomit, Wan

Side Abeam, Airs, Beam, Border, Camp, Distaff, Edge, Effect, Eleven, English, Epistle, Facet, Flank, Flip, Gunnel, Hand, Hypotenuse, Iliac, Lateral, Lee(ward), Left, Off, On, OP, Pane, Part, Partisan, Party, Port, Pretension, Profile, Prompt, Rave, Reveal, Right, Rink, Silver, Slip, Spear, Starboard, Swank, > **TEAM**, Windward, Wing, XI

Sidekick Right-hand man, Satellite

Sienese Tuscan

Sienna Burnt, Raw

Sight(ed) Aim, Barleycorn, Bead, Conspectuity, Eye(ful), Eyesore, Glimpse, Ken, Long, Oculated, Prospect, Range, Riflescope, Scene, Scotopia, Second, See, Short, Spectacle, Taish, Vane, > **VIEW**, Visie, Vision, Vista

Sign(s), **Signing**, **Signpost** Accidental, Addition, Ampersand, Aquarius, Archer, Aries, Arrow, Auspice, Autograph, Badge, Balance, Beck, Beckon, Board, Brand, Bull, Bush, Call, Cancer, Capricorn, Caract, Caret, Chevron, Clue, Crab, Cross, Cue, Di(a)eresis, Division, DS, Earmark, Emblem, Endorse, Endoss, Enlist, Evidence, Exit, Fascia, Fish, Gemini, Gesture, Goat, Hallmark, Harbinger, Hex, Hieroglyphic, Hint, Ideogram, Indian, Indicate, Indication, Initial, Inscribe, Ivy-bush, Leo, Libra, Local, Logogram, Minus, Multiplication, Negative, Nod, Notice, Obelisk, Obelus, Omen, Peace, Pisces, Plus, Positive, Presage, Radical, Ram, Rest, Rune, Sacrament, Sagittarius, Sain, Scorpio, Segno, Semeion, Shingle, Show, Sigil, Sigla, Signal, Star, Subscribe, Subtraction, Superscribe, Symbol, Symptom, Syndrome, Tag, Taurus, Tic(k)tac(k), Tilde, Titulus, Token, Trace, Twins, Umlaut, V, Vestige, Virgo, Vital, Warning, Waymark, Word, Zodiac

Signal(ler) Alarm, Alert, Amber, Assemble, Beacon, Bell, Bleep, Bugle, Buzz, Code, Cone, Cue, Detonator, Distress, Earcon, Flag, Flagman, Flare, Flash, Fog, Gantry, Gesticulate, Gong, Griffin, Gun, Harmonic, Heliograph, Heliostat, Herald, Hooter, Icon, Important, Interrupt, Interval, Luminance, Mark, Message, Modem, Morse, NICAM, Notation, Noted, Output, Password, Peter, Pinger, Pip, Radio, Renowned, Reveille, Robot, Salient, Semaphore, Singular, Smoke, Sonogram, SOS, Spoiler, Squawk, Taps, Target, Telegraph, Thumb, Tic(k)-tac(k), Time, Traffic, Troop, Very, Video, V-sign, Waff, Waft, Wave

Signature Alla breve, Autograph, By-line, Digital, Hand, John Hancock, John Henry, Key, Mark, Onomastic, Specimen, Subscription, Time

Significance, **Significant** Cardinal, Consequence, Emblem, Impact, Important, Indicative, Key, Magnitude, Matter, Meaningful, Moment(ous), Noted, Noteworthy, Paramount, Pith, Pregnant, Salient, Special, Telling

Silence(r), **Silent** Choke-pear, Clam, Clamour, Creepmouse, Dumbstruck,

Earplug, Gag, Hist, Hush, Hushkit, Mim(budget), Muffler, Mum(p), Mute, Omertà, Quench, Quiesce, > QUIET, Reticence, Shtoom, Shush, Speechless, Still, Sulky, Tace(t), Tacit(urn), Throttle, Tight-lipped, Wheesh(t)

Silk(y), **Silk screen** Alamode, Atlas, Barathea, Brocade, Bur(r), Charmeuse®, Chenille, Chiffon, Cocoon, Corn, Crape, Crepe, Duchesse, Dupion, Faille, Filoselle, Florence, Florentine, Flosh, Floss, Flox, Foulard, Gazar, Georgette, Glossy, Kincob, Lustrine, Lustring, Lutestring, Makimono, Marabou(t), Matelasse, Ninon, Organza, Ottoman, Paduasoy, Parachute, Peau de soie, Pongee, Prunella, Prunelle, Prunello, Pulu, Raw, Samite, Sars(e)net, Satin, Schappe, Sendal, Seric, Sericeous, Serigraph, Shalli, Shantung, Sien-tsan, Sleave, Sleek, Smooth, Spun, Surah, Tabaret, Tabby, Taffeta, Tasar, Thistledown, Tiffany, Tram, Tulle, Tussah, Tusseh, Tusser, Tussore, Velvet

Silly, **Silliness** Absurd, Brainless, Crass, Cuckoo, Daft, Ditsy, Divvy, Dumb, Fatuous, Folly, Fool, Footling, Frivolous, Goopy, Goosey, Gormless, Idiotic, Imbecile, Inane, Inept, Infield(er), Mid-off, Mid-on, Mopoke, Puerile, Season, Simple, Soft(y), Spoony, > STUPID, Tripe, Wacky

▷ **Silver** *may indicate* a coin

Similar(ity) Analog(ue), Analogical, Corresponding, Equivalent, Etc, Homoeoneric, Homogeneous, Homologous, Homonym, Kindred, > LIKE, Parallel, Resemblance, Samey

Simile Epic

Simple(r), **Simplicity**, **Simplify**, **Simply** Arcadian, Artless, Austere, Bald, Bare, Basic, Crude, Doddle, Doric, > EASY, Eath(e), Elegant, ESN, Ethe, Fee, Folksy, Gotham, Green, Herb(alist), Homespun, Idyllic, Incomposite, Inornate, Mere, Naive(té), Naked, Niaiserie, One-fold, Open and shut, Ordinary, Paraphrase, Pastoral, Peter, Plain, Pleon, Provincial, Pure, Reduce, Rustic, Sapid, Semplice, Sheer, Silly, Simon, Spartan, Stupid, Woollen

Sin(ful) Aberrant, Anger, Avarice, Besetting, Bigamy, Covetousness, Crime, Deadly, Debt, Envy, Err, Evil, Folly, Gluttony, Hamartiology, Harm, Hate, Impious, Lapse, Lust, Misdeed, Misdoing, Mortal, > OFFENCE, Original, Peccadillo, Piacular, Pride, Scape, Scarlet, Sine, Sloth, Transgress, Trespass, Unrighteous, Venial, Vice, Wicked, Wrath, Wrong

Sincere(ly), **Sincerity** Bona-fide, Candour, Earnest, Entire, Frank, Genuine, Heartfelt, Honest, Open, Real(ly), True, Verity, Whole-hearted

▶ **Sinful** *see* SIN

Sing(ing) Barbershop, Bel canto, Carol, Chant, Cheep, Chorus, Coloratura, Community, Cough, Croon, Crow, Diaphony, Diddle, Glee club, Hum, Inform, Intone, Karaoke, La-la, Lilt, Melic, Parlando, Peach, Pen(n)illion, Pipe, Plainchant, Rand, Rant, Rap, Record, Render, Scat, Second(o), Squeal, Tell, Thrum, Trill, Troll, Vocalise, Warble, Yodel

Singer Alto, Bard, Baritone, Bass, Bing, Bird, Canary, Cantatrice, Cantor, Car, Castrato, Chanteuse, Chantor, Chazan, Cher, Chorister, Coloratura, Crooner, Diva, Falsetto, Gleeman, Kettle, Lark, Lauder, Lorelei, Melba, Minstrel, Siren, Songstress, Soprano, Soubrette, Succentor, Tenor, Torch, Treble, Troubador, Vocalist, Voice, Warbler

Single, **Singly** Ace, Aefa(u)ld, Aefawld, Alone, Azygous, Bachelor, Celibate, Discriminate, EP, Exclusive, Feme sole, Matchless, Monact, Mono, Odd, One-off, Only, Pick, Run, Sole, Solitary, Spinster, Unattached, Uncoupled, Unique, Unwed, Versal, Yin

Singular(ity) Curious, Especial, Exceptional, Extraordinary, Ferly, Odd, Once, One, Peculiar, Queer(er), Rare, > UNIQUE, Unusual

Sink(ing), **Sunken** Basin, Bog, Cadence, Carbon, Cower, Delapse, Depress, Descend, Devall, Dip, Down, Drain, Draught-house, Drink, Drop, Drown, Ebb, Flag, Founder, Gravitate, Heat, Hole, Immerse, Invest, Jawbox, Kitchen, Lagan,

Laigh, Lapse, Ligan, Merger, Pad, Pot, Prolapse, Put(t), Relapse, Sag, Scupper, Scuttle, Set, Settle, Shipwreck, Slump, Steep-to, Sty, Submerge, Subside, Swag, Swamp

Siren Alarm, Alert, Hooter, Houri, Ligea, Lorelei, Mermaid, Oceanides, Parthenope, Salamander, Teaser, Temptress, Vamp

Sister(s) Anne, Beguine, Minim, > NUN, Nurse, Religeuse, Sib, Sibling, Sis, Sob, Soul, Swallow, Titty, Ursuline, Verse, Weird

Sit(ter), Sitting Bestride, Clutch, Dharna, Duck, Gaper, Model, Perch, Pose, Reign, Roost, Séance, Session, Squat

Site, Siting Area, Camp, Feng shui, Greenfield, Home-page, Location, Lot, Pad, Place, Plot, Rogue, Silo, Spot, Stance

Situation Ballpark, Berth, Cart, Case, Catch, Catch-22, Cliff-hanger, Contretemps, Cow, Dilemma, Galère, Hole, Job, Lie, Location, Lurch, Matrix, Niche, No-win, Office, Plight, Position, Post, Scenario, Schmear, Schmeer, Set-up, Shebang, Showdown, Status quo, Sticky wicket, Strait, Where, Worst case

Size(able) Amplitude, Area, Bulk, Calibre, Countess, Demy, > EXTENT, Format, Girth, Glair, Glue, Gum, Imperial, Measure, Physique, Pot(t), Princess, Proportion, Tempera, Tidy

Skate(r), Skateboarder, Skating Blade, Figure, Fish, In-line, Maid, Mohawk, Rock(er), Roller, Rollerblade®, Runner

Skeleton, Skeletal Anatomy, Atomy, Axial, Bones, Cadaverous, Cadre, Cage, Coenosteum, Corallum, Framework, Key, Ossify, Outline, Scenario, Sclere

Sketch(y) Cameo, Character, Charade, Croquis, Delineate, Diagram, Draft, > DRAW, Ebauche, Esquisse, Illustration, Limn, Line, Maquette, Modello, Outline, Pencilling, Playlet, Pochade, Précis, Profile, Skit, Summary, Thumbnail, Trick, Vignette, Visual

Ski(ing) Aquaplane, Glide, Glissade, Hot-dog, Langlauf, Nordic, Schuss, Super G, Telemark, Vorlage, Wedeln

Skill(ed), Skilful Ability, Able, Ace, Address, Adept, Adroit, Art, Bravura, Canny, Chic, Competence, Craft, Deacon, Deft, Dextrous, Enoch, Expertise, Facility, Feat, Finesse, Flair, Gleg, Habile, Hand, Handicraft, Handy, Hend, Hot, Ingenious, Knack, Know-how, Knowing, Lear(e), Leir, Lere, Masterly, Masterpiece, Mean, Mistery, Mystery, Mystique, Practised, Proficient, Prowess, Quant, Resource, Savvy, Science, Skeely, Sleight, Soft, Speciality, Tactics, Talent, Technic, Technique, Touch, Trade, Trick, Versed, Virtuoso

Skin(s) Agnail, Armour, Bark, Basan, Basil, Box-calf, Calf, Callus, Case, Cere, Chevrette, Coat, Cortex, Crackling, Cutaneous, Cuticle, Cutis, Deacon, Deer, Derm(a), Dermis, Dewlap, Disbark, Ectoderm, Enderon, Epicarp, Eschar, Excoriate, Exterior, Fell, Film, Flaught, Flay, Flench, Flense, Flinch, Fourchette, Goldbeater's, Hangnail, Hide, Jacket, Kip, Leather, Membrane, Muktuk, Pachyderm, Peau, Peel, Pell, Pellicle, Pelt, Plew, Prepuce, Rack, Rape, Rind, Scalp, Scarskin, Serosa, Shell, Spetch, Strip, Tegument, Veneer, Wattle, Woolfell

Skin disease, Skin trouble Boba, Boil, Buba, Chloasma, Chloracne, Cowpox, Cyanosis, Dartre, Dermatitis, Dermatosis, Dyschroa, Ecthyma, Erysipelas, Exanthem(a), Favus, Framboesia, Herpes, Hives, Ichthyosis, Impetigo, Leishmaniasis, Livedo, Lupus vulgaris, Mal del pinto, Mange, Miliaria, Morula, Pemphigus, Pinta, Pityriasis, Prurigo, Psoriasis, Pyoderma, Rash, Ringworm, Rosacea, Rose-rash, Sapego, Scabies, Sclerodermia, Scurvy, Seborrhoea, Serpigo, Strophulus, Tetter, Tinea, Vaccinia, Verruca, Verruga, Vitiligo, Xanthoma, Yaws

Skinless Ecorché

Skip(ped), Skipper Boss, Caper, Captain, Cavort, Drakestone, Elater, Frisk, Hesperian, Jump, Jumping-mouse, Lamb, Luppen, Miss, Omit, Patroon, Ricochet, Saury, Scombresox, Spring, Tittup, Trounce(r)

Skirt(ing) Fil(l)ibeg, Grass, Petticoat, Philibeg, Pinafore, Stringboard, Wrapover

Skull Bregma(ta), Calvaria, Cranium, Head, Malar, Obelion, Occiput, Pannikell, Phrenology, Scalp, Sinciput

Sky(-high) Air, Azure, Blue, Canopy, Carry, E-layer, Element, Empyrean, Ether, Firmament, Heaven, Lift, Loft, Mackerel, Occident, Octa, Welkin

Slab Briquette, Bunk, Cake, Chunk, Dalle, Hawk, Ledger, Metope, Mihrab, Mud, Plank, Slice, Stela, Tab, Tile

Slack(en), Slackness Abate, Careless, Crank, Dilatory, Dross, Ease, Easy-going, Idle, Lax(ity), Loose, Malinger, Nerveless, Relax, Release, Remiss, Shirk, Skive, Slow, Surge, Unscrew, Veer

Slander(ous) Asperse, Backbite, Calumny, Defame, Derogatory, Disparage, Libel, Malediction, Malign, Missay, Mud, Obloquy, Sclaunder, Smear, Traduce, Vilify, Vilipend

Slang Abuse, Argot, Back, Berate, Cant, Colloquial, Ebonics, Flash, Jargon, Lingo, Nadsat, Rhyming, Slate, Zowie

Slant(ed), Slanting Angle, Asklent, Atilt, Bevel, Bias, Brae, Cant, Careen, Chamfer, Clinamen, Diagonal, Escarp, Oblique, Prejudice, Slew, > SLOPE, Splay, Talus, Tilt, Virgule

Slash(ed) Chive, Cut, Gash, Jag, Laciniate, Leak, Oblique, Rash, Rast, Reduce, Scorch, Scotch, Separatrix, Slit, Solidus, Wee

Slaughter(house), Slaughterer Abattoir, Bleed, Bloodshed, Butcher, Carnage, Decimate, Hal(l)al, Holocaust, Jhatka, Kill, Mactation, > MASSACRE, S(c)hechita(h), Scupper, Shambles, Shechita(h), Shochet, Smite

Slave(ry), Slaves Addict, Aesop, Aida, Androcles, Barracoon, Blackbird, Bond, Bond(s)man, Bondwoman, Boy, Caliban, Contraband, Dogsbody, Drudge, Drug, Dulosis, Esne, Galley, Helot, Mameluke, Mamluk, Marmaluke, Maroon, Minion, Odalisk, Odali(s)que, Peasant, Pr(a)edial, Rhodope, Serf, Servitude, Spartacus, Terence, Theow, Thersites, Thete, Thrall, Topsy, Vassal, Villein, Wage, White, Yoke

Slay(er), Slaying Destroy, Execute, Ghazi, > KILL, Mactation, Murder, Quell, Saul, Slaughter

Sled(ge), Sleigh(-ride) Bob, Dray, Hurdle, Hurly-hacket, Kibitka, Komatik, Lauf, Luge, Polack, Pulk(h)(a), Pung, Skidoo®, Slipe, Stoneboat, Tarboggin, Toboggan, Travois

Sleep, Sleeper(s), Sleepiness, Sleeping, Sleepy Beauty, Bed, Bivouac, Blet, Car, Catnap, Coma, Couchette, Crash, Cross-sill, Cross-tie, Dormant, Dormient, Doss, Doze, Drowse, Gum, Hibernate, Hypnology, Hypnos, Kip, Lethargic, Lie, Morpheus, Nap, Narcolepsy, Nod, Over, Paradoxical, Petal, REM, Repast, Repose, Rest, Rip Van Winkle, Sandman, Shuteye, Skipper, Sloom, Slumber, Snooz(l)e, Somnolent, Sopor(ose), Sownd, Tie, Torpid, Twilight, Wink, Zizz

Sleeping sickness Trypanosomiasis

Sleeve (opening) Arm(hole), Batwing, Bishop's, Bush, Collet, Cover, Dolman, Gatefold, Gigot, Gland, Leg-o'-mutton, Liner, Magyar, Manche, Pagoda, Pudding, Querpo, Raglan, Sabot, Scye, Slashed, Trunk, Turnbuckle, Wind

▶ **Sleigh** see SLED

Slender(ness) Asthenic, Ectomorph, Elongate, Exiguity, Exility, Fine, Flagelliform, Flimsy, Gracile, Jimp, Leptosome, Loris, Narrow, Skinny, Slight, Slim, Small, Spindly, Stalky, Styloid, Svelte, Sylph, Tenuous, Trim, Waif

Slice Cantle, Chip, Collop, Cut, Doorstep, Fade, Frustrum, Piece, Rasure, Round, Sector, Segment, Share, Sheave, Shive, Slab, Sliver, Tranche, Wafer, Whang

Slide Chute, Cursor, Diapositive, Drift, Glissando, Hirsle, Ice-run, Illapse, Lantern, Mount, Pulka, Schuss, Skid, Skite, Slip, Slither, Snowboard, Transparency

Slight(ly) Affront, Belittle, Cold shoulder, Cut, Detract, Disparage, Disregard, Facer, Flimsy, Halfway, Insult, Misprise, Neglect, Nominal, Pet, Petty, Rebuff,

Remote, > **SLENDER**, Slim, Slimsy, Slur, Small, Smattering, Sneaking, Snub, Subtle, Superficial, Sylphine, Tenuous, Thin, Tiny, Wee, Wispy

Slime, Slimy Glair, Glit, Guck, Gunk, Mother, Muc(o)us, Oily, Ooze, Sapropel, Slake, Sludge, Uliginous

Sling Balista, Catapult, Drink, Fling, Hang, Parbuckle, Prusik, Support, Toss, Trebuchet

Slip(ped), Slipping, Slips Boner, Cutting, Disc, Docket, Drift, EE, Elapse, Elt, Error, Faux pas, Fielder, Form, Freudian, Glide, Glissade, Infielder, Label, Landslide, Lapse, Lath, Mistake, Muff, Nod, Oversight, Petticoat, Prolapse, Quickset, Rejection, Relapse, Run, Scape, Sc(h)edule, Scoot, Set, Shim, Sin, Ski, Skid, Skin, Skite, Slade, Slidder, Slide, Slither, Slive, Spillican, Stumble, Surge, Ticket, Trip, Tunicle, Underskirt, Unleash

Slipper(s) Baboosh, Babouche, Babuche, Calceolate, Carpet, Eel, Mocassin, Moccasin, Moyl, Mule, Pabouche, Pampootie, Pantable, Pantof(f)le, Panton, Pantoufle, Pump, Rullion, Runner, Ski, Sledge, Sneaker, Sock

Slippery Foxy, Glid, Icy, Lubric, Shady, Shifty, Skidpan, Slick

▷ **Slipshod** *may indicate* an anagram

Slit Cranny, Cut, Fent, Fissure, Fitchet, Gash, Loop, Pertus(at)e, Placket, Race, Rit, Scissure, Spare, Speld(er), Vent

Slogan Amandla, Byword, Catchword, Jai Hind, Mot(to), Phrase, Rallying-cry, Slughorn(e), Warcry, Watchword

Slope(s), Sloping Acclivity, Angle, Anticline, Bahada, Bajada, Bank, Batter, Bevel, Borrow, Borstal(l), Brae, Breast, Chamfer, Cuesta, Declivity, Delve, Diagonal, Dry, Escarp, Fla(u)nch, Geanticline, Glacis, Grade, Gradient, Heel, Hill, Incline, Kant, Lean, Natural, Nursery, Oblique, Pent, Periclinal, Pitch, Rake, Ramp, Rollway, Scarp, Schuss, Scrae, Scree, Shelve, Sideling, Skewback, Slant, Slippery, Slipway, Splay, Steep, Stoss, Talus, Tilt, Verge, Versant, Weather

Sloppily, Sloppy Lagrimoso, Lowse, Madid, Mushy, Remiss, Schmaltzy, Slapdash, Slipshod, Sloven, Slushy, Untidy

▷ **Sloppy** *may indicate* an anagram

Sloth(ful) Accidie, Acedia, Ai, Bradypus, Edentate, Ground, Idle, Inaction, Indolent, Inertia, Lazy, Lie-abed, Megatherium, Sweer(t), Sweir(t), Three-toed

Slough(ing) Cast, Despond, Ecdysis, Eschar, Exuviae, Lerna, Marsh, Morass, Paludine, Shed, Shuck, Swamp

Sloven(ly) Careless, Dag(gy), D(r)aggle-tail, Frowsy, Grobian, Jack-hasty, Slattern, Sleazy, Slipshod, Slummock, Untidy

Slow(ing), Slower, Slowly Adagio, Allargando, Andante, Brady, Brake, Broad, Calando, Crawl, Dawdle, Deliberate, Dilatory, Dull, Dumka, ESN, Flag, Gradual, Inchmeal, Lag, Langram, Larghetto, Largo, Lash, Lassu, Late, Leisurely, Lentando, Lento, Lifeless, Loiter, Meno mosso, Obtuse, Pedetentous, Rall(entando), Rein, Reluctant, Retard, Ribattuta, Ritardando, Ritenuto, Slack, Slug, Sluggish, Snaily, Solid, Stem, Tardigrade, Tardive, Tardy

Slowcoach Slowpoke, Slug

Slug(s) Ammo, Bêche-de-mer, Blow, Bullet, Cosh, Drink, Limaces, Limax, Mollusc, Nerita, Pellet, Shot, Snail, Trepang

Sluggish Dilatory, Drumble, Idler, Inert, Jacent, Lacklustre, Laesie, Languid, Lazy, Lentor, Lethargic, Lug, Phlegmatic, Saturnine, Sleepy, > **SLOW**, Stagnant, Tardy, Torpid, Unalive

Slumber Doze, Drowse, Nap, Nod, Sleep, Sloom, Snooze

Slump Decrease, Depression, Deteriorate, Dip, Flop, Recession, Sink, Slouch

Slur(ring) Defame, Drawl, Innuendo, Opprobrium, Slight, Smear, Synaeresis, Tie

Sly Christopher, Clandestine, Coon, Covert, Cunning, Foxy, Leery, Peery, Reynard, Shifty, Sleeveen, Stealthy, Subtle, Tinker, Tod, Tricky, Weasel, Wily

▷ **Slyly** *may indicate* an anagram

Smack(er) Buss, Cuff, Flavour, Foretaste, Fragrance, Hooker, Kiss, Lander, Lips, Pra(h)u, Relish, Salt, Saut, Skelp, Slap, Slat, Smatch, Smouch, Soupçon, Spank, Spice, Splat, Tack, Taste, Thwack, Tincture, Trace, X, Yawl

Small (thing) Atom, Bantam, Beer, Bijou, Bittie, Bitty, Denier, Diminutive, Dinky, Drib, Elfin, Few, Fry, Grain, Haet, Ha'it, Half-pint, Handful, Holding, Insect, Ion, Leet, Lilliputian, Limited, Lite, > LITTLE, Lock, Low, Meagre, Measly, Midget, Mignon, Miniature, Minikin, Minute, Mite, Modest, Modicum, Peerie, Peewee, Petit(e), Petty, Pigmy, Pink(ie), Pinky, Pint-size, Pittance, Pocket, Poky, Rap, Reduction, Runt, S, Scattering, Scrump, Scrunt, Scut, Shrimp, Single, Slight, Slim, Smattering, Smidge(o)n, Smidgin, Smithereen, Smout, Soupçon, Sprinkling, Spud, Stim, Stunted, Tad, Thin, Tidd(l)y, Tiny, Titch(y), Tittle, Tot(tie), Totty, Trace, Trivial, Wee, Weedy, Whit

Smart(en), **Smartest** Ache, Acute, Alec, Astute, Best, Bite, Chic, Classy, Clever, Cute, Dandy, Dapper, Dressy, Elegant, Flash, Flip, Fly, Groom, Kookie, Kooky, Natty, Neat, Nifty, Nip, Nobby, Pac(e)y, Pacy, Posh, Preen, Primp, Prink, Pusser, Raffish, Rattling, Ritzy, Saucy, Slick, Sly, Smoke, Smug, Snappy, Soigné(e), Spiff, Sprauncy, Sprightly, Spruce, Sprush, Spry, Sting, Swagger, Sweat, Swish, Tiddley, Tippy, Titivate, Toff, U

Smash(ed), **Smasher**, **Smashing** Atom, Brain, Break, Crush, Demolish, Devastate, Dish, High, Kaput, Kill, Lulu, Shatter, Shiver, Slam, Stave, Super, Terrific, Tight, > WRECK

▷ **Smash(ed)** *may indicate* an anagram

Smear Assoil, Besmirch, Blur, Cervical, Clam, Daub, Defile, Denigrate, Discredit, Drabble, Enarm, Gaum, Gorm, Lick, Oil, Pay, Plaster, Slairg, Slaister, Slather, Slime, Slubber, Slur, Smalm, Smarm, Smudge, Sully, Teer, Traduce, Wax

Smell(ing), **Smelly** Aroma, BO, Effluvium, Fetor, F(o)etid, Fug, Gale, Gamy, Graveolent, Guff, Hing, Honk, Hum, Mephitis, Miasm(a), Musk, Niff, Nose, Odour, Olent, Olfact(ory), Osmatic, Perfume, Pong, Ponk, Pooh, Rank, Redolent, Reech, Reek, Sar, Savour, > SCENT, Sniff, Snifty, Snook, Snuff, Steam, Stench, Stifle, Stink, Tang, Whiff

Smile(s), **Smiling** Agrin, Beam, Cheese, Favour, Gioconda, Grin, Rictus, Self-help, Simper, Smirk

Smoke(r), **Smoking**, **Smoky** Blast, Bloat, Censer, Chain, Chillum, > CIGAR(ETTE), Cure, Fog, Fuliginous, Fume, Funk, Gasper, Hemp, Incense, Indian hemp, Inhale, Kipper, Latakia, Lum, Lunt, Manil(l)a, Nicotian, Pother, Pudder, Puff, Reech, Reek, Reest, Roke, Smeech, Smeek, Smoor, Smoulder, Smudge, Snout, Toke, Vapour, Viper, Whiff, Wreath

Smooth(e), **Smoother**, **Smoothly** Bland, Brent, Buff, Chamfer, Clean, Clockwork, Dress, Dub, Easy, Even, Fettle, File, Flat, Fluent, Glabrous, Glare, Glassy, Glib, Goose, Iron, Legato, Level, Levigate, Linish, Mellifluous, Oil, Plane, Plaster, Rake, Roll, Rub, Sand(er), Satiny, Scrape, Sleek, Slick, Slickenslide, Slur, Smug, Snod, Sostenuto, Streamlined, Suave, Swimmingly, Terete, Terse, Trim, Urbane

Smother Burke, Choke, Muffle, Oppress, Overlie, Smoor, Smore, Stifle, Suppress

Smug Complacent, Conceited, Goody-two-shoes, Neat, Oily, Pi, Self-satisfied, Trim

Smuggle(d), **Smuggler**, **Smuggling** Bootleg, Contraband, Donkey, Fair trade, Gunrunning, Moonshine, Mule, Owler, Rum-runner, Run, Secrete, Steal, Traffic

Smut(ty) Bawdy, Blight, Blue, Brand, Burnt-ear, Coom, Filth, Grime, Racy, Soot, Speck

Snack Bever, Bhelpuri, Bite, Blintz, Breadstick, Brunch, Butty, Canapé, Chack, Crudités, Elevenses, Entremets, Four-by-two, Gorp, Meze, Nacket, Nibble, Nocket,

Nooning, Nuncheon, Padkos, Pie, Popcorn, Rarebit, Refreshment, Samo(o)sa, Sandwich, Sarnie, Savoury, Tapa, Taste, Toast(y), Vada, Voidee, Wada, Zakuska

Snag Catch, Contretemps, Drawback, Hindrance, Hitch, Impediment, Knob, Nog, Obstacle, Remora, Rub, Tear

Snail Brian, Cowrie, Cowry, Dodman, Escargot, Gasteropod, Helix, Hodmandod, Limnaea, Lymnaea, Nautilus, Nerite, Roman, Slow, Slug, Strombus, Unicorn-shell, Univalve, Wallfish, Whelk

Snake Adder, Aesculapian, Amphisbaena, Anaconda, Anguine, Anguis, Apod(e), Asp, Bandy-bandy, Berg-adder, Blacksnake, Blind, Blue-racer, Boa, Boma, Boomslang, Brown, Bull, Bush-master, Camoodi, Carpet, Cerastes, Clotho, Coachwhip, Cobra, Coluber, Congo, Constrictor, Copperhead, Coral, Corn, Cottonmouth, Cribo, Crotalidae, Daboia, Death-adder, Dendrophis, Diamond(-back), Dipsas, Dugite, Elaps, Ellops, Fer-de-lance, Garter, Glass, Grass, Habu, Hamadryad, Hognose, Homorelaps, Hoop, Horned viper, Horsewhip, Hydra, Indigo, Jararaca, Jararaka, Joe Blake, Kaa, K(a)rait, King (cobra), Lachesis, Langaha, Mamba, Massasauga, Meander, Milk, Mocassin, Moccasin, Mulga, Naga, Naia, Naja, Ophidian, Pipe, Pit-viper, Plumber's, Puff-adder, Python, Racer, Rat, Rattler, Reptile, Ribbon, Ringhals, Ringneck, Rinkhals, Riverjack, Rock, Sand viper, Seps, > **SERPENT**, Sidewinder, Slowworm, Smooth, Spitting, Squamata, Sucuruju, Surucucu, Taipan, Takshaka, Thirst, Thread, Tiger, Timber rattlesnake, Tree, Uraeus, Vasuki, Viper, Water (moccasin), Whip, Wind, Worm

Snap(per), Snappy, Snap up Autolycus, Bite, Break, Brittle, Camera, Click, Cold, Crack, Cross, Curt, Edgy, Fillip, Girnie, Glom, Gnash, Hanch, Knacker, Knap, Livery, Mugshot, Photo, Photogene, Scotch, Snack, Snatch, Spell, Still, Tetchy, Vigour

Snare Bait, Benet, Engine, Entrap, Gin, Grin, Hook, Illaqueate, Inveigle, Net, Noose, Rat-trap, Springe, Toil, > **TRAP**, Trapen, Trepan, Web, Weel, Wire

Snarl(ing) Chide, Complicate, Cynic, Enmesh, Gnar(l), Gnarr, Growl, Grumble, Knar, Knot, Snap, Tangle, Yirr

Sneak(y) Area, Carry-tale, Clipe, Clype, Inform, Lurk, Mumblenews, Nim, Peak, Scunge, Skulk, Slip, Slyboots, Snitch, Snoop, Split, Steal, Stoolie, Tell(-tale)

Sneeze (at), Sneezing Atishoo, Sternutation

Sniff Inhale, Nose, Nursle, Nuzzle, Scent, Smell, Snivel, Snort, Snuffle, Vent, Whiff

Snob(bery), Snobbish Cobbler, Crispin, High-hat, Scab, Side, Snooty, Soutar, Souter, Sowter, Toffee-nose, Vain, Vamp

Snore, Snoring Rhonchus, Rout, Snort, Stertorous, Zz

Snort(er) Drink, Grunt, Nare, Nasal, Roncador, Snore, Toot

Snout Bill, Boko, Cigar, Informer, Muzzle, Nose, Nozzle, Proboscis, Schnozzle, Tinker, Tobacco, Wall

Snow(y), Snowstorm Marine, Powder, Red, Spotless, Virga, Yellow

Snub Cut, Diss, Go-by, Lop, Pug, Quelch, Rebuff, Reproof, Retroussé, Short, Slap, Slight, Sloan, Sneap, Snool, Wither

Snuff(le) Asarabacca, Dout, Errhine, Extinguish, Maccaboy, Ptarmic, Pulvil, Rappee, Smother, Snaste, Sneesh(an), Sniff, Snift, Snush, Tobacco, Vent

Snuffbox Mill, Mull

Snug(gle) Burrow, Cose, > **COSY**, Couthie, Couthy, Croodle, Cubby, Cuddle, Embrace, Lion, Neat, Nestle, Nuzzle, Rug, Snod, Tight, Trim

So Ergo, Hence, Sic(h), Sol, Therefore, Thus, True, Very, Yes

Soak Bate, Bath(e), Beath, Bewet, Bloat, Blot, Buck, Cree, Deluge, Drench, Drink, Drook, Drouk, Drown, Drunk, Duck, Dunk, Embay, Embrue, Fleece, Grog, Imbrue, Infuse, Lush, Macerate, Marinate, Mop, Oncome, Permeate, Rait, Rate, Ret(t), Saturate, Seep, Sipe, Sog, Sop, Souce, Souse, Sows(s)e, Steep, Sype, Thwaite, Toper, Wet

Soap(y), Soap opera Cake, Carbolic, Eluate, Flake, Flannel, Flattery, Green, Joe, Lather, Marine, Metallic, Moody, Mountain, Pinguid, Saddle, Saponaceous, Saponin, Sawder, Slime, Soft, Spanish, Suds, Sudser, Sugar, Tablet, Toilet, Washball, Yellow

Soar(ing) Ascend, Essorant, Fly, Glide, Rise, Tower, Zoom

Sociable, Sociability Affable, Cameraderie, Chummy, Cosy, Extravert, Folksy, Friendly, Genial, Gregarious

Socialism, Socialist Champagne, Chartist, Dergue, Fabian, Fourierism, ILP, International, Lansbury, Left(y), Marxism, Nihilism, Owen(ist), Owenite, Pinko, Red, Revisionist, Sandinista, Spartacist, Utopian, Webb

Society Affluent, Association, Benefit, Body, Building, Camorra, Class, Club, College, Company, Co-op, Cooperative, Culture, Dorcas, Elite, Elks, Fabian, Fashion, Foresters, Freemans, Freemasons, Friendly, Friends, Glee club, Group, Guilds, Haut monde, High, Humane, Institute, Invincibles, John Birch, Ku-klux-klan, Law, Linnean, Lodge, Mafia, Masonic, Mau-mau, Menage, Molly Maguire, National, Oddfellows, Oral, Orangemen, Oratory, Order, Permissive, Plural, Pop, Provident, Repertory, Rotary, Royal, S, School, Secret, Soc, Soroptomist, Sorority, Stakeholder, Tammany, Theosophical, Toc H, Ton, Tong, Triad, U, Whiteboy

Socket Acetabulum, Alveole, Budget, Gudgeon, Hollow, Hosel, Hot shoe, Jack, Nave, Ouch, Pod, Port, Power-point, Strike

Sod Clump, Delf, Delph, Divot, Gazo(o)n, Mool, Mould, Mouls, Scraw, Sward, Turf

Sofa Canapé, Chesterfield, Couch, Daybed, Divan, Dos-à-dos, Dosi-do, Ottoman, Settee, Squab, Tête-à-tête

Soft(en), Softener, Softening, Softly Amalgam, Anneal, B, BB, Blet, Boodle, Cedilla, Cree, Dim, Doughy, Emolliate, Emollient, Flabby, Gentle, Hooly, Humanise, Lash, Lax, Lenient, Limp, Low, Mease, Mellow, Melt, Mild, Milksop, Mitigate, Modulate, Mollify, Morendo, Mulch, Mush(y), Mute, Neale, Nesh, Option, P, Palliate, Pastel, Piano, Plushy, Porous, Propitiate, Rait, Rate, Relent, Sentimental, Silly, Slack, Squashy, Squidgy, Squishy, Temper, > TENDER, Tone, Velvet, Weak

Soil(ed), Soily Acid, Adscript, Agrology, Agronomy, Alkali(ne), Alluvium, Azonal, Bedraggle, Chemozem, Clay, Cohesive, Defile, Desecrate, Desert, Dinge, Dirt(y), Discolour, Earth, Edaphic, Frictional, Gault, Glebe, Grey, Grimy, Ground, Gumbo, Hotbed, Humus, Illuvium, Intrazonal, Lair, Land, Latosol, Lithosol, Loam, Loess, Lome, Loss, Mire, Mool, Mo(u)ld, Mud, Mulch, Mull, Night, Peat, Ped, Pedology, Phreatic, Planosol, Podsol, Podzol, Prairie, Pure, Regar, Regolith, Regosol, Regur, Rendzina, Rhizosphere, Root-ball, Sal, Sedentary, Smudge, Smut, Solonchak, Solonetz, Solum, Soot, Stain, Stonebrash, Sub, Sully, Tarnish, Tash, Terrain, Terricolous, Tilth, Top, Udal, Umber, Virgin, Zonal

Soldier(s) Alpini, Amazon, Ant, Anzac, Army, Arna(o)ut, Atkins, ATS, Battalion, Bombardier, Borderer, Brigade, Cadet, Campaigner, Centurion, Chindit, Chocolate, Cohort, Colonel, Colours, Commando, Confederate, Cornet, Corp(s), Cossack, Crusader, Ded, Desert rat, Doughboy, Draftee, Dragoon, Emmet, Fighter, Foot, Fusilier, General, GI, Grenadier, Grim dig, Guardsman, Guerilla, Gurkha, Hussar, Inf(antry), Ironside, Irregular, Joe, Lancer, Legionary, Legionnaire, Line, Militiaman, Minuteman, Musketeer, Non-com, Old moustache, OR, Orderly, Paratroop, Partisan, Phalanx, Platoon, Point man, POW, Private, Rank(er), Rank and file, Rapparree, Regiment, Regular, Rifleman, Sabre, Saddler, Samurai, SAS, Sepoy, Serviceman, Squaddy, Stormtrooper, Subaltern, Tarheel, Terrier, Territorial, Tommy, Toy, Trooper, Troops, Unknown, Vet(eran), Voltigeur, Volunteer, Wagon, Warrior, Whitecoat, Yeoman

▷ **Soldiers** *may indicate* bread for boiled eggs

Sole, Solitaire, Solitary Alone, Anchoret, Anchorite, Clump, Fish,

Incommunicado, Lemon, Lonesome, Megrim, Merl, Meunière, Monkish, Only, Pad, Palm, Patience, Pelma, Planta(r), Plantigrade, Platform, Recluse, Scaldfish, Single(ton), Skate, Slip, Smear-dab, Tap, Thenar, Unique, Vibram®, Vola

Solemn Austere, Devout, Earnest, Grave, Gravitas, Owlish, Po-faced, Sacred, Sedate, Serious, Sober, Sobersides

Solicit Accost, Approach, Ask, Attract, Bash, > BEG, Canvass, Cottage, Importun(at)e, Plead, Ply, Speer, Speir, Tout, Woo

Solid(arity), Solidify Cake, Chunky, Clot, Clunky, Compact, Comradeship, Concrete, Cone, Congeal, Consolidate, Cube, Cylinder, Dense, Enneahedron, Firm, Foursquare, Freeze, Frustrum, Fuchsin(e), Gel, Hard, Holosteric, Impervious, Merbromin, Octahedron, Pakka, Petrarchan, Platonic, Polyhedron, Prism, Pucka, Pukka, Robust, Set, Stilbene, Sublimate, Substantial, Tetrahedron, Thick, Unanimous

Solitary Antisocial, Friendless

Solo Aria, Cadenza, Cavatine, Concertante, Lone, Monodrama, Monody, Ombre, One-man, Scena, Variation

Solution Amrit, Colloidal, Electrolyte, Final, Reducer, Soup, Standard, Viscose

▷ **Solution** *may indicate* an anagram

Solve(d), Solver Assoil, Casuist, Clear, Crack, Decode, Loast, Loose, Read(er), Troubleshoot, Unclew, Unriddle

Solvent Acetaldehyde, Acetone, Alcahest, Aldol, Alkahest, Anisole, Aqua-regia, Banana oil, Cleanser, Decalin, Diluent, Dioxan(e), Eleunt, Eluant, Ether, Funded, Furan, Hexane, Ligroin, Megilp, Menstruum, Methanol, Methylal, Naphtha, Paraldehyde, Picoline, Protomic, Pyridine, Sound, Stripper, Terebene, Terpineol, Tetrachloromethane, Thiophen, Toluene, Toluol, Trike, Trilene, Turpentine

Sombre Dark, Drab, Drear, Dull, Gloomy, Grave, Morne, Subfusc, Subfusk, Sullen, Triste

Some Any, Arrow, Ary, Certain, Divers, Few, One, Part, Portion, Quota, These, They, Wheen

▷ **Some** *may indicate* a hidden word

▷ **Somehow** *may indicate* an anagram

Sometime(s) Erstwhile, Ex, Former, Occasional, Off and on, Quondam

Son Boy, Disciple, Epigon(e), Fils, Fitz, Lad, Lewis, M(a)c, Offspring, Prodigal, Progeny, Scion

Song Air, Amoret, Anthem, Aria, Art, Aubade, Ballad, Barcarol(l)e, Berceuse, Blues, Burden, Cabaletta, Calypso, Canticle, Carol, Catch, Chanson, Cha(u)nt, Conductus, Cycle, Descant, Dirge, Ditty, Flamenco, Folk, Glee, Hillbilly, Hymn, Internationale, Lament, Lay, Lied(er), Lilt, Lullaby, Lyric, Madrigal, Marseillaise, Melody, Negro spiritual, Number, Nunc dimittus, Paean, Part, Plain, Plantation, Psalm, Rap, Rhapsody, Roulade, Roundelay, Rune, Scat, Sea-shanty, Serenade, Shanty, Siren, Sososholoza, Spiritual, Stave, Strain, Strophe, Swan, Taps, Theme, Torch, Trill, Tune, Villanella, Warble, Yodel

Sonnet Amoret, Italian, Petrarch(i)an, Shakespearean, Shakespearian, Spenserian

Soon(er) Anon, Directly, Erelong, OK, Oklahoma, Presently, Shortly, Tight, Timely, Tit(ely), Tite, Tyte

Soothe, Soothing Accoy, Allay, Anetic, Appease, Assuage, Bucku, Calm, Compose, Demulcent, Emollient, Irenic, Lenitive, Lull, Mellifluous, Mollify, Pacific, Paregoric, Poultice, Quell, Rock

Sophisticate(d) Blasé, Boulevardier, City slicker, Civilised, Cosmopolitan, Couth, Doctor, High-end, Patrician, Polished, Sative, Slicker, Svelte, Urbane, Worldly

▷ **Sophoclean** *may indicate* Greek (alphabet, etc)

Sorbet Water ice

Sorcerer, **Sorceress**, **Sorcery** Angakok, Ashipu, Circe, Conjury, Diablerie, Hoodoo, Kadaitcha, Kurdaitcha, Lamia, Mage, Magic(ian), Magus, Medea, Merlin, Morgan le Fay, Mother Shipton, Necromancer, Obi, Pishogue, Shaman, Sortilege, Voodoo, Warlock, Witch, Wizard

Sore(ly), **Sores** Abrasion, Bitter, Blain, Boil, Canker, Chancre, Chap, Chilblain, Cold, Dearnly, Felon, Gall, Impost(h)ume, Ireful, Kibe, Quitter, Quittor, Raw, Rupia(s), Saddle, Sair, Shiver, Sitfast, Surbate, Ulcer(s), Whitlow, Wound

Sorrow(ful) Affliction, Distress, Dole, Dolour, > GRIEF, Lament, Misery, Nepenthe, Penance, Pietà, Remorse, Rue, Triste, Wae, Waugh, Wirra, Woe, Yoop

Sorry Ashamed, Contrite, Miserable, Oops, Penitent, Pitiful, Poor, Regretful, Relent, Wretched

▷ **Sorry** *may indicate* an anagram

▶ **Sorts** *see* OUT OF SORTS

▷ **So to speak** *may indicate* 'sound of'

Soul(ful) Alma, Ame, Anima, Animist, Atman, Ba, Brevity, Deep, Eschatology, Expressive, Heart, Inscape, Larvae, Manes, Person, Psyche, Saul, Shade, Spirit

Sound(ed), **Soundness**, **Sound system** Accurate, Ach-laut, Acoustic, Albemarle, Alveolar, Audio, Bleep, Blow, Bong, Cacophony, Chime, Chirr(e), Chord, Chug, Clam, Clang, Clink, Clop, Clunk, Dah, Dental, Dit, Dive, Echo, Fast, Fathom, Fettle, Fit, Good, Hale, Harmonics, Healthy, Hearty, Hi-fi, Inlet, Knell, Lo-fi, Long Island, Lucid, Mach, Madrilene, Mersey, Milford, Music, Narrow, > NOISE, Onomatopaeia, Oompah, Optical, Orthodox, Palatal, Paragog(u)e, Peal, Phone(me), Phonetic, Phonic, Phonology, Pitter(-patter), Plap, Plink, Plonk, Plop, Plosion, Plumb, Plummet, Plunk, Probe, Put-put, Quadraphonic(s), Rale, Rational, Real, Reliable, Ring, Robust, Rumble, Rustle, Safe, Sandhi, Sane, S(c)hwa, Sensurround®, Skirl, Solid, Sone, Souffle, Sough, Splat, Stereo, Stereophony, Strait, Surround, Swish, Tannoy®, Thorough, Timbre, Ting, Tone, Toneme, Trig, Triphthong, Trumpet, Twang, Ultrasonic(s), Unharmed, Uvular, Valid, Voice, Vowel, Watertight, Well, Whistle, Whole(some), Wolf

Sounding board Abat-voix

Soup Alphabet, Bird's nest, Bisque, Borsch, Bouillabaisse, Bouillon, Broth, Chowder, Cock-a-leekie, Consommé, Gazpacho, Gumbo, Minestrone, Mock turtle, Mulligatawny, Oxtail, Pot-au-feu, Pot(t)age, Primordial, Puree, Ramen, Rubaboo, Sancoche, Skink, Stock, Turtle, Vichyssoise

▷ **Soup** *may indicate* an anagram

Sour(puss) Acerb, Acescent, Acid, Acidulate, Alegar, Bitter, Citric, Crab, Esile, Ferment, Moody, Stingy, Turn, Verjuice, Vinegarish

Source Authority, Basis, Bottom, Centre, Database, Derivation, Egg, Fons, Font, Fount, Fountain-head, Germ, Head-stream, Literary, Mine, Mother, Origin, Parent, Pi, Pion, Point, Provenance, Quarry, Reference, Rise, Root, Seat, Seed, Spring, Springhead, Urn, Well, Wellhead, Wellspring, Ylem

South(ern), **Southerner** Austral, Dago, Decanal, Decani, Dixieland, Meridian, S

South Africa(n) Bantu, Caper, Grikwa, Griqua, Hottentot, Kaf(f)ir, SA, Springbok, Swahili, Xhosa, ZA, Zulu

Souvenir Keepsake, Memento, Relic, Remembrance, Scalp, Token, Trophy

Sovereign(ty), **Sovereign remedy** Anne, Autocrat, Bar, Condominium, Couter, Dominant, ER, Goblin, Haemony, Harlequin, Imperial, Imperium, James, King, L, Liege, Nizam, Pound, Quid, Royalty, Ruler, Shiner, Supreme, Swaraj, Synarchy

Sow(ing) Catchcrop, Elt, Foment, Gilt, Inseminate, Plant, Scatter, Seed, Sprue, Strew, Yelt

Spa Baden, Baden-Baden, Bath, Evian, Harrogate, Hydro, Kurhaus, Kursaal, Leamington, Vichy

Space(d), **Spacing**, **Spacious**, **Space man** Abyss, Acre, Area, Areola, Bay, Bracket, Breathing, Cellule, Cishinar, Clearing, Concourse, Cubbyhole, Deep, Distal, Distance, Elbow-room, Esplanade, Ether, Exergue, Expanse, Extent, Footprint, Freeband, Gap, Glade, Glenn, Goaf, Gob, Gutter, Hair, Hash(mark), Headroom, Indention, Inner, Intergalactic, Interplanetary, Interstellar, Interstice, Invader, Kneehole, Lacuna, Lair, Legroom, Life, Logie, Lumen, Lunar, Lung, Maidan, Metope, Muset, Musit, Orbit, Outer, Personal, Proportional, Quad, Retrochoir, > **ROOM**, Ruelle, Sample, Sheets, Shelf room, Slot, Spandrel, Spandril, Step, Storage, Third, Topological, Tympanum, Ullage, Uncluttered, Vacuole, Vacuum, Vast, Vector, Void

Spacecraft, **Space agency**, **Space object**, **Spaceship**, **Space station** Apollo, Capsule, Columbia, Deep Space, Explorer, Galileo, Genesis, Giotto, Lander, LEM, Luna, Lunik, Mariner, MIR, Module, NASA, Orbiter, Pioneer, Probe, Quasar, Ranger, Salyut, Shuttle, Skylab, Soyuz, Sputnik, Starship, Tardis, Viking, Vostok, Voyager, Zond

Spade Breastplough, Caschrom, Cas crom, Castrato, Detective, Graft, Loy, Negro, Paddle, Pattle, Pettle, Pick, S, Shovel, Slane, Spit, Suit, Tus(h)kar, Tus(h)ker, Twiscar

Span Age, Arch, Attention, Bestride, Bridge, Chip, Ctesiphon, Extent, Life, Range

Spaniard, **Spanish** Alguacil, Alguazil, Barrio, Basque, Cab, Caballero, Carlist, Castilian, Catalan, Chicano, Dago, Don, Fly, Grandee, Hidalgo, Hispanic, Jose, Main, Mestizo, Mozarab, Pablo, Señor, Spic(k), Spik

Spaniel Cavalier, Field, Irish water, King Charles, Toady, Toy, Water, Welsh springer

Spar Barytes, Blue John, Boom, Bowsprit, Box, Cauk, Cawk, Fight, Gaff, Iceland, Jib-boom, Mainyard, Martingale, Mast, Nail-head, Outrigger, Rafter, Rail, Ricker, Shearleg, Sheerleg, Snotter, Spathic, Sprit, Steeve, Stile, Triatic, Yard

Spare, **Sparing** Angular, Cast-off, Dup(licate), Economical, Free, Frugal, Gash, Gaunt, Hain, Lean, Lenten, Other, Pardon, Reserve, Rib, Save, Scant, Slender, Stint, Subsecive, Thin

Spark Animate, Arc, Beau, Blade, Bluette, Dandy, Flash, Funk, Ignescent, Kindle, Life, Scintilla, Smoulder, Spunk, Trigger, Zest

Sparkle(r), **Sparkling** Aerated, Coruscate, Diamanté, Effervesce, Elan, Emicate, Fire, Fizz, Flicker, Frizzante, Glint, Glisten, Glitter, Pétillant, Scintillate, Seltzer, Seltzogene, Spangle, Spritzig, Spumante, Twinkle, Verve, Witty, Zap

Spartan(s) Austere, Basic, Enomoty, Hardy, Helot, Laconian, Lysander, Menelaus, Severe, Valiant

Spasm(odic) Blepharism, Chorea, Clonus, Cramp, Crick, Fit(ful), Hiccup, Hippus, Intermittent, Irregular, > **JERK**, Kink, Laryngismus, Nystagmus, Paroxysm, Periodical, Start, Tetany, Throe, Tonic, Tonus, Trismus, Twinge, Twitch

▷ **Spasmodic** *may indicate* an anagram

Speak(er), **Speaking** Address, Articulate, Broach, Chat, Cicero, Collocuter, Communicate, Converse, Coo, Declaim, Dilate, Discourse, Diseur, Dwell, Effable, Elocution, Eloquent, Expatiate, Express, Extemporise, Filibuster, Intercom, Intone, Inveigh, Jabber, Jaw, Lip, Loq, Mang, Mention, Mike, Mina, Mouth, Mouthpiece, Nark, Open, Orate, Orator, Palaver, Parlance, Parley, Pontificate, Prate, Preach, Prelector, Rhetor, > **SAY**, Sayne, Spout, Spruik, Stump, Talk, Tannoy®, Tongue, Trap, Tweeter, Utter, Voice, Waffle, Witter, Word

Spear Ash, Asparagus, Assagai, Assegai, Dart, Gad, Gavelock, Gig, Gungnir, Hastate, Impale, Javelin, Lance(gay), Launcegaye, Leister, Morris-pike, Partisan, Pierce, Pike, Pilum, Skewer, Spike, Trident, Trisul(a), Waster

Special Ad hoc, Constable, Designer, Distinctive, Extra, Important, Notable, Notanda, Particular, Peculiar, Specific

Specialise, **Specialist(s)** Authority, Concentrate, Connoisseur, Consultant, ENT,

Expert, Illuminati, Maestro, Major, Quant, Recondite, Technician

Specific(ally), **Specified**, **Specify** As, Ascribe, Assign, Cure, Define, Detail, Explicit, Itemise, Medicine, Namely, Precise, Remedy, Sp, Special, Stipulate, The, Trivial

Speck(led) Atom, Bit, Dot, Fleck, Floater, Freckle, Muscae volitantes, Particle, Peep(e), Pip, Spreckle, Stud

Spectacle(d), **Spectacles**, **Spectacular** Bifocals, Blinks, Colourful, Epic, Escolar, > **GLASSES**, Goggles, Horn-rims, Optical, Pageant, Pince-nez, Pomp, Preserves, Scene, Show, Sight, Son et lumière, Sunglasses, Tattoo, Trifocal, Varifocals

Spectator(s) Bystander, Dedans, Etagère, Eyer, Gallery, Gate, Groundling, Kibitzer, Observer, Onlooker, Standerby, Witness

Spectral, **Spectre** Apparition, Boggle, Bogy, Eidolon, Empusa, Ghost, Idola, Iridal, Malmag, Phantasm, Phantom, Phasma, Spirit, Spook, Tarsier, Walking-straw, Wraith

Speculate, **Speculative**, **Speculator**, **Speculation** Arbitrage, Bear, Better, Bull, Conjecture, Flier, Flyer, Gamble, Guess, Ideology, If, Imagine, Meditate, Notional, Operate, Pinhooker, Shark, Stag, Theoretical, Theorise, Theory, Thought, Trade, Wonder

Speech, **Speech element** Accents, Address, Argot, Articulation, Bunkum, Burr, Curtain, Delivery, Dialect, Diatribe, Diction, Direct, Discourse, Dithyramb, Drawl, Floge, English, Eulogy, Filibuster, Free, Gab, Glossolalia, Harangue, Idiolect, Idiom, Inaugural, Indirect, Jargon, Keynote, King's, > **LANGUAGE**, Lallation, Lingua franca, Litany, Maiden, Monologue, Morph(eme), Musar, Oblique, Oral, Oration, Parabasis, Parle, Peroration, Phasis, Philippic, Phonetics, Prolog(ue), Queen's, Reported, Rhetoric, Sandhi, Scanning, Screed, Sermon, Side, Slang, Soliloquy, Stemwinder, Stump, Tagmeme, Talk, Taxeme, Tirade, Tongue, Vach, Visible, Voice, Wawa, Whistle-stop

Speed(ily), **Speedy** Accelerate, Alacrity, Amain, Amphetamine, Apace, Average, Bat, Belive, Belt, Breakneck, Burn, Celerity, Clip, Dart, Despatch, DIN, Dispatch, Expedite, Fangy, Fast, Film, Fleet, Further, Gait, Gallop, Goer, Group, Gun, Haste, Hie, Hotfoot, Hypersonic, Induce, Instantaneous, Knot, Landing, Lick, Mach, Merchant, MPH, > **PACE**, Phase, Pike, Post-haste, Pronto, Race, Rapidity, Rate, RPS, Rush, Scorch, Scud, Scurr, Skirr, Soon, Spank, Split, Stringendo, Supersonic, Swift, Tach, Tear, Tempo, Ton up, V, Velocity, Vroom, Wave, Whid, Wing

Spell(ing) Abracadabra, Bewitch, Bout, Cantrip, Charm, Conjuration, Do, Elf-shoot, Enchantment, Entrance, Fit, Go, Gri(s)-gri(s), Hex, Incantation, Innings, Jettatura, Juju, Knur, > **MAGIC**, Need-fire, Nomic, Orthography, Period, Philter, Philtre, Pinyin, Relieve, Ride, Romaji, Run, Rune, Scat, Shot, Signify, Snap, Snatch, Sorcery, Sp, Spasm, Splinter, Stint, Stretch, Tack, Tour, Trick, Turn, Weird, Whammy, Witchcraft

Spend(er), **Spending** Anticipate, Birl, Blue, Boondoggling, Consume, Deplete, Disburse, Exhaust, Fritter, Live, Outlay, Pass, Pay, Splash, Splurge, Ware

Spendthrift Prodigal, Profligate, Profuser, Wastrel

Sphere, **Spherical** Armillary, Celestial, Discipline, Element, Field, Firmament, Globe, Mound, Orb(it), Planet, Prolate, Province, Realm, Theatre, Wheel

Spice, **Spicy** Anise, Aniseed, Cardamom, Cinnamon, Clove, Clow, Coriander, Cum(m)in, Dash, Devil, Garam masala, Ginger, Mace, Marjoram, Masala, Myrrh, Nutmeg, Oregano, Paprika, Peppercorn, Pimento, Piquant, Season, Tansy, Tarragon, Taste, Turmeric, Vanilla, Variety

Spider(s) Arachnid, Aranea, Araneida, Attercop, Bird, Black widow, Bobbejaan, Cardinal, Cheesemite, Citigrade, Diadem, Epeira, Ethercap, Ettercap, Funnel-web, Harvester, Harvestman, House, Hunting, Huntsman, Jumping,

Katipo, Lycosa, Mite, Money, Mygale, Orb-weaver, Pan, Phalangid, Podogona, Pycnogonid, Red, Redback, Rest, Ricinulei, Saltigrade, Scorpion, Solpuga, Spinner, Strap, Tarantula, Telary, Trapdoor, Violin, Water, Wolf, Zebra

Spike(d) Barb, Brod, Calk, Calt(h)rop, Chape, Cloy, Crampon, Ear, Fid, Foil, Gad, Goad, Grama, Herissé, Impale, Lace, Locusta, Marlin(e), Nail, > **PIERCE**, Point, Pricket, Prong, Puseyite, Rod, Sharp, Shod, Skewer, Spadix, Spear, Spicate, Spicule, Strobiloid, Tang, Thorn, Tine

Spill(age) Divulge, Drop, Fidibus, Jackstraw, Lamplighter, Leakage, Let, Overflow, Overset, Scail, Scale, Shed, Skail, Slop, Stillicide, Taper, Tumble

Spin(ner), Spinning Aeroplane, Arabian, Arachne, Bielmann, Birl, Camel, Centrifuge, Cribellum, Cut, Day trip, Dextrorse, DJ, Flat, Flip, Gimp, Googly, Gymp, Gyrate, Gyre, Gyroscope, Hurl, Isobaric, Lachesis, Mole, Nun, Peg-top, Pirouette, Pivot, PR, Precess, Prolong, Purl, Rev(olve), Ride, Rotate, Royal, Screw, Side, Sinistrorse, Slide, Spider, Stator, Strobic, Swirl, Swivel, Throstle, Tirl, Toss, Trill, Twirl, Twist, Wheel, Whirl, Work

Spinal (chord), Spine, Spiny Acromion, Aculeus, Areole, Backbone, Barb, Chine, Coccyx, Column, Doorn, Epidural, Muricate, Myelon, Notochord, Ocotillo, Prickle, Quill, Rachial, Ray, R(h)achis, Thorn, Tragacanth

▸ **Spine** *see* **SPINAL**

Spirit(s), Spirited Akvavit, Alcohol, Ammonia, Angel, Animal, Animation, Applejack, Apsaral, Aquavit, Aqua vitae, Arak, Ardent, Ariel, Arrack, Astral, Bitters, Blithe, Boggart, Bogle, Brandy, Bravura, Brio, Brollachan, Cant, Cherub, Courage, Creature, Daemon, Dash, Distillation, Div, Djinn(i), > **DRINK**, Dryad, Eblis, Elan, Element(al), Emit, Empusa, Entrain, Erdgeist, Esprit, Essence, Ethos, Fachan, Faints, Familiar, Feints, Fetich(e), Fetish, Fettle, Fight, Firewater, Fuath, Gamy, Geist, Geneva, Genie, Genius, > **GHOST**, Ghoul, Ginger, Ginn, Gism, Glastig, Go, Grappa, Gremlin, Grit, Grog, Gumption, Hartshorn, Heart, Hollands, Holy, Imp, Incubus, Jinn(i), Ka, Kelpie, Kindred, Kobold, Larva, Lemur(e), > **LIQUOR**, Lively, Loki, Manes, Manito(u), Manitu, Mare, Metal, Meths, Methyl(ated), Mettle, Mobby, Morale, Neutral, Nix, Nobody, Numen, Ondine, Panache, Party, Pecker, Pep, Peri, Pernod®, Petrol, Phantom, Pluck(y), Pneuma, Poltergeist, Potato, Poteen, Presence, Proof, Psyche, Puck, Python, Racy, Rakee, Raki, Rectified, Ruin, Rye, Salt, Saul, Schnapps, Seraph, Shade, Shadow, Short, Soul, Spectre, Spright, Sprite, Spunk, Steam, Surgical, Sylph, Team, Tequila, Ton, Turpentine, Turps, Undine, Verve, Vigour, Vim, Vodka, Voodoo, Water horse, White, Wili, Wine, Wood, Wraith, Zing, Zombie

Spiritual(ism), Spiritualist Aerie, Aery, Coon-song, Ecclesiastic, Ethereous, Eyrie, Eyry, Incorporeal, Negro, Planchette

Spit(ting), Spittle Barbecue, Broach, Chersonese, Dead ringer, Dribble, Drool, Emptysis, Eructate, Expectorate, Fuff, Gob, Golly, Gooby, Grill, Hawk, Impale, Jack, Lookalike, Peninsula, Ras, Ringer, Rotisserie, Saliva, Skewer, Slag, Spade(ful), Spawl, Sputter, Sputum, Tombolo, Yesk, Yex

Spite(ful) Backbite, Bitchy, Catty, Grimalkin, Harridan, Irrespective, Malevolent, Malice, Mean, Petty, Pique, Rancour, Spleen, Venom, Waspish

Splash Blash, Blue, Dabble, Dash, Dog, Drip, Feature, Flouse, Fl(o)ush, Gardyloo, Jabble, Ja(u)p, Jirble, Paddle, Plap, Plop, Plowter, Sket, Slosh, Soda, Sozzle, Spairge, Spat(ter), Spectacle, Splat(ch), Splatter, Splodge, Splosh, Splotch, Spray, Spree, Squatter, Swash, Swatter, Water, Wet

Splendid, Splendour Braw, Brilliant, Bully, Capital, Champion, Clinker, Dandy, Eclat, Effulgent, Excellent, Fine, Finery, Fulgor, Gallant, Garish, Glittering, Glorious, Glory, Gorgeous, Grand(eur), Grandiose, Heroic, Lustrous, Majestic, Noble, Palatial, Panache, Pomp, Proud, Radiant, Rich, Ripping, Royal, Stunning, Super(b), Wally

▷ **Spliced** *may indicate* an anagram

Splinter(s) Flinder, Fragment, Matchwood, Shatter, Shiver, Skelf, Sliver, Spale, Spicula, Spill

Split Axe, Banana, Bifid, Bifurcate, Bisect, Break, Burst, Chasm, Chine, Chop, Clint, Clove(n), Crack, Crevasse, Cut, Disjoin, Distrix, > **DIVIDE**, Division, Divorce, End, Fissile, Fissure, Flake, Fork(ed), Fragment, Grass, Lacerate, Partition, Red(d), Rift(e), Rip, Rive, Russian, Ryve, Schism, Scissor, Segregate, Separate, Sever, Share, Skive, Slit, Sliver, Spall, Spalt, Speld, Tattle, Tmesis, Told, Wedge

▷ **Split** *may indicate* a word to become two; one word inside another; or a connection with Yugoslavia

Spoil(s), **Spoilt** Addle, Blight, Booty, Botch, Bribe, Coddle, Corrupt, > **DAMAGE**, Dampen, Deface, Defect, Deform, Dish, Foul, Hames, Harm, Impair(ed), Indulge, Loot, Maltreat, Mar, Muck, Mutilate, Mux, Pamper, Pet, Pickings, Pie, Plunder, Prize, Queer, Rait, Rate, Ravage, Ret, Rot, Ruin, Scupper, Swag, Taint, Tarnish, Vitiate, Winnings

▷ **Spoil(ed)**, **Spoilt** *may indicate* an anagram

▷ **Spoken** *may indicate* the sound of a word or letter

Sponge(r), **Spongy** Battenburg, Bum, Cadge, Cake, Diact, Free-loader, Lig, Loofa(h), Madeira, Madeleine, Mooch, Mop, Parasite, Scrounge, Sop, Sucker, Swab, Sycophant, Tetract, Tiramisu, Wangle, Wipe, Zoophyte

Sponsor(ship) Aegis, Angel, Backer, Egis, Finance, Godfather, Godparent, Gossip, Guarantor, Lyceum, Patron, Surety

Spontaneous Autonomic, Gratuitous, Immediate, Impromptu, Impulsive, Instant, Intuitive, Natural

Spoof Chouse, Cozenage, Deception, Delusion, Fallacy, > **HOAX**, Imposture, Ramp, Swindle, Trick

Spoon(ful), **Spoon-shaped** Apostle, Canoodle, Cochlear, Dollop, Dose, Gibby, Labis, Ladle, Mote, Neck, Rat-tail, Runcible, Scoop, Scud, Server, Spatula, Sucket, Woo, Wooden

Sport(s), **Sporting**, **Sportive** Aikido, Amusement, Angling, Aquatics, Autocross, Basho, Blood, Bonspiel, Breakaway, Brick, Bungee-jumping, By-form, Contact, Curling, Cyclo-cross, Daff, Dalliance, Dally, Deviant, Drag-racing, Extreme, Field, Freak, Frisky, Frolic, Fun, > **GAME**, Gent, Gig, Hang-gliding, In, Joke, Karate, Kickboxing, Korfball, Laik, Lake, Langlauf, Lark, Merimake, Merry, Morph, Mutagen, Octopush, Orienteering, Pal, Pancratium, Paragliding, Parakiting, Parapenting, Parasailing, Parascending, Paraskiing, Polo, Rallycross, Recreate, Rogue, RU, Rules, Shinny, Shinty, Skijoring, Snowboarding, Softball, Spectator, Speedball, Speed-skating, Speedway, Squash, Steeplechase, Sumo, Tailing, Tournament, Tourney, Toy, Trampolining, Trapshooting, Wakeboarding, Water polo, Wear, Weightlifting, Windsurfing, Winter, Wrestling

▷ **Sport(s)** *may indicate* an anagram

Spot(s), **Spotted**, **Spotting**, **Spotty** Ace, Acne, Area, Areola, Areole, Bead, Beauty, Befoul, Blackhead, Blain, Blemish, Blind, Blip, Blob, Blot, Blotch(ed), Blur, Brind(l)ed, Carbuncle, Caruncle, Cash, Check, Cloud, Colon, Comedo, Corner, Cyst, Dance, Dapple(-bay), Dick, Discern, Discover, Dot, Drop, Eruption, Eye, Flat, Fleck, Floater, Foxed, Freak, Freckle, Furuncle, G, Gay, High, Hot, Jam, Leaf, Lentago, Location, Loran, Mackle, Macle, Macul(at)e, Mail, Meal, Measly, Microdot, Moil, Mole, Mote, Motty, Naevoid, Note, Notice, Ocellar, Ocellus, Paca, Papule, Parhelion, Patch, Peep(e), Penalty, Pied, Pimple, Pin, Pip, Place, Plot, Pock, Punctuate, Pupil, Pustule, Quat, Radar, Rash, Recognise, Red, Situation, Skewbald, Smut, Soft, Speck(le), Speculum, Splodge, Spy, Stigma, Sully, Sun, Taint, Tar, Tight, Touch, Trouble, Weak, Whelk, Whitehead, X, Yellow, Zit

Spouse Companion, Consort, F(i)ere, Hubby, Husband, Mate, Oppo, Partner, Pheer, Pirrauru, Wife, Xant(h)ippe

Spout(er) Adjutage, Erupt, Gargoyle, Geyser, Grampus, Gush, Impawn, Jet, Mouth, Nozzle, Orate, Pawn, Pourer, Raile, Rote, Spurt, Stream, Stroup, Talk, Tap, Vent

Sprain(ed) Crick, Reckan, Rick, Stave, Strain, Wrench, Wrick

Spray Aerosol, Aigrette, Atomiser, Buttonhole, Corsage, Egret, Hair, Posy, Rose, Rosula, Shower, Sparge, Spindrift, Splash, Sprent, Sprig, Sprinkle, Spritz, Strinkle, Syringe, Twig

▷ **Spray** *may indicate* an anagram

Spread(ing), **Spreader** Air, Apply, Banquet, Bestrew, Beurre, Blow-out, Branch, Bush, Butter, Carpet, Centre, Contagious, Couch, Coverlet, Coverlid, Deploy, Diffract, Diffuse, Dilate, Disperse, Dissemination, Distribute, Divulge, Double, Drape, Dripping, Elongate, Emanate, Expand, Extend, Fan, Feast, Flare, Guac(h)amole, Honeycomb, Jam, Lay, Marge, Marmite®, Metastasis, Multiply, Nutter, Oleo, Open, Overgrow, Paste, Pâté, Patent, Patulous, Perfuse, Pervade, Picnic, Propagate, Radiate, Ran, Run, Scale, Set, Sheet, Slather, Smear, Smorgasbord, Sow, Span, Speld, Spelder, Spillover, Splay, Sprawl, Spray, Straddle, Straw, Stretch, Strew, Strow, Suffuse, Systemic, Tath, Teer, Unfold, Unguent, Vegemite®, Widen, Wildfire

▷ **Spread** *may indicate* an anagram

Spring(s), **Springtime**, **Springy** Arise, Bolt, Bounce, Bound, Box, Bunt, Cabriole, Caper, Capriole, Cavort, Cee, Coil, Dance, Elastic, Eye, Fount(ain), Gambado, Germinate, Geyser, Grass, Hair, Helix, Hop, Hot, Jump, Leaf, Leap, Lent, May, Mineral, Originate, Persephone, Pierian, Pounce, Prance, Primavera, Prime, Resilient, Ribbon, Rise, Saddle, Season, Skip, Snap, Spa, Spang, Spaw, Stem, Stot, Submarine, Sulphur, Thermae, Thermal, Valve, Vault, Vernal, Ware, Watch, Waterhole, Weeping, Well(-head), Whip

▷ **Spring(y)** *may indicate* an anagram

Sprinkle(r), **Sprinkling** Asperge, Aspergill(um), Bedash, Bedrop, Bescatter, Caster, Dredge, Dust, Hyssop, Lard, Pouncet, Rose, Scatter, Shower, Sow, Spa(i)rge, Spatter, Splash, Spray, Spritz, Strinkle

Sprout Braird, Breer, Bud, Burgeon, Chit, Crop, Eye, Germ(inate), Grow, Pullulate, Shoot, Spire, Tendron, Vegetate

Spruce Dapper, Engelmann, Natty, Neat, Norway, Picea, Pitch-tree, Prink, Shipshape, Sitka, Smart, Spiff, Tidy, Tree, Trim, Tsuga

Spur Accourage, Activate, Calcar(ate), Encourage, Fame, Fire, Goad, Heel, Incite, Limb, Lye, Needle, Prick, Rippon, Rowel, Shoot, Spica, Stimulus, Strut, Stud, Tar, Urge

▷ **Spurious** *may indicate* an anagram

Spy(ing), **Spies** Agent, Beagle, Caleb, CIA, Descry, Dicker, Emissary, Fink, Informer, Keeker, Mata Hari, MI, Mole, Mouchard, Nark, Nose, Operative, Pimp, Plant, Pry, Recce, Scout, See, Setter, Shadow, Sinon, Sleeper, Spetsnaz, Spook, Tout, Wait

Squalid, **Squalor** Abject, Colluvies, Dinge, Dingy, Filth, Frowsy, Grungy, Poverty, Scuzzy, Seedy, Sleazy, Slum(my), Slurb, Sordid

Squall Blast, Blow, Commotion, Cry, Drow, Flaw, Flurry, Gust, Sumatra, Wail, Yell, Yowl

Squander Blow, Blue, Fritter, Frivol, Mucker, Slather, Splash, Splurge, Ware, > **WASTE**

Square(d), **Squares** Agree, Anta, Ashlar, Ashler, Bang, Barrack, Belgrave, Berkeley, Block, Bribe, Chequer, Compone, Compony, Corny, Deal, Dinkum, Even(s), Fair, Fog(e)y, Forty-nine, Fossil, Four, Gobony, Grey, Grosvenor, Latin, Least, Leicester, Level, Magic, Market, Meal, Mitre, Nasik, Neandert(h)aler, Nine, Norma, Old-fashioned, Palm, Passé, Pay, Perfect, Piazza, Place, Platz, Plaza, Quad(rangle), Quadrate, Quarry, Quits, Red, Rood, S, Set(t), Sloane, Solid, Squier, Squire, Straight, T, Tee, Times, Traditionalist, Trafalgar, Try, Unhip

Squash(y) Adpress, Butternut, Conglomerate, Crush, Gourd, Kia-ora, Knead, Marrow, Mash, Obcompress, Oblate, Pattypan, Press, Pulp, Shoehorn, Silence, Slay, Slew, Slue, Soft, Squeeze, Squidge, Squidgy, Suppress, Torpedo

Squeeze Bleed, Chirt, Coll, Compress, Concertina, Constrict, Cram, Crowd, Crush, Dispunge, Exact, Express, Extort, Hug, Jam, Mangle, Milk, Preace, Press, Sandwich, Sap, Scrooge, Scrouge, Scrowdge, Scruze, Shoehorn, Squash, Squish, Sweat, Thrutch, Wring

Squid Calamari, Calamary, Cephalopod, Ink-fish, Loligo, Mortar, Nautilus, Octopus

▷ **Squiggle** *may indicate* an anagram

Squill Sea, Spring

Squint(ing) Boss-eyed, Cast, Cock-eye, Cross-eye, Glance, Gledge, Glee, Gley, Heterophoria, Louche, Proptosis, Skellie, Skelly, Sken, Squin(n)y, Strabism, Swivel-eye, Vergence, Wall-eye

Squire Armiger(o), Beau, Donzel, Escort, Hardcastle, Headlong, Land-owner, Scutiger, Swain, Western

Squirm(ing) Fidget, Reptation, Twist, Worm, Wriggle, Writhe

Squirt(er) Chirt, Cockalorum, Douche, Jet, Scoosh, Scoot, Skoosh, Spirt, Spout, Spritz, Urochorda, Wet, Whiffet, Whippersnapper

Stab Bayonet, Crease, Creese, Dag, Effort, Go, Gore, Guess, Jab, Knife, Kreese, Kris, Lancinate, Pang, Pierce, Pink, Poniard, Prick, Prong, Stick, Stiletto, Wound

Stabilise(r), **Stability** Aileron, Balance, Emulsifier, Even, Maintain, Peg, Permanence, Plateau, Poise, Steady

Stable(s) Augean, Balanced, Barn, Byre, Certain, Constant, Durable, Equerry, Equilibrium, Firm, Livery, Loose box, Manger, Mews, Poise, Secure, Solid, Sound, Stall, Static(al), Steadfast, Steady, Stud, Sure

Stack(s) Accumulate, Chimney, Clamp, Cock, End, Funnel, Heap, Lum, > **PILE**, Rick, Shock, Staddle

Stadium Arena, Ballpark, Bowl, Circus, Circus Maximus, Coliseum, Hippodrome, Velodrome

Staff Alpenstock, Ash-plant, Bato(o)n, Bourdon, Burden, Caduceus, Cane, Crook, Crosier, Cross(e), Crozier, Crutch, Cudgel, Entourage, Equerry, Etat-major, Faculty, Ferula, Ferule, Flagpole, General, Linstock, Lituus, Mace, Omlah, Pastoral, Personnel, Pike, Pole, Rod, Runic, Sceptre, Seniority, Skeleton, Stave, Stick, Taiaha, Tapsmen, Tau, Thyrsus, Truncheon, Verge, Wand, Workers, Workforce

Stage Act, Anaphase, Apron, Arena, Bema, Boards, Catasta, Chrysalis, Committee, Diligence, Dog-leg, Estrade, Fargo, Fit-up, Grade, Juncture, Key, Landing, Leg, Level, Metaphase, Milestone, Moment, Mount, Oidium, Phase, Phasis, Pier, Pin, Platform, Point, Prophase, PS, Puberty, Report, Rostrum, Scene, Sensorimeter, Sound, Stadium, Step, Stor(e)y, Subimago, Theatre, Thrust, Transition, Trek, Yuga

Stagger(ed) Alternate, Amaze, Astichous, Falter, Floor, Lurch, Recoil, Reel, Rock, Shock, Stoiter, Stot(ter), Stumble, Sway, Teeter, Thunderstruck, Titubate, Tolter, Totter

▷ **Staggered** *may indicate* an anagram

Stain(er) Aniline, Bedye, Besmirch, Blemish, Blob, Blot, Blotch, Discolour, Dishonour, Dye, Embrue, Ensanguine, Eosin, Fox, Gram's, Grime, Imbrue, Iodophile, Keel, Maculate, Mail, Meal, Mote, Portwine, Slur, Smirch, Smit, Soil, Splodge, Splotch, Stigma, Sully, Taint, Tarnish, Tinge, Tint, Vital, Woad

Stair(case), **Stairs** Apples, Apples and pears, Caracol(e), Cochlea, Companionway, Escalator, Flight, Perron, Rung, Spiral, Step, Tread, Turnpike, Vice, Wapping

Stake(s) Ante, Bet, Claim, Gage, Holding, Impale, Impone, Interest, Lay, Loggat,

Mark, Mise, Paal, Pale, Paling, Palisade, Peel, Peg, Pele, Picket, Pile, Play, Post, Pot, Punt, Rest, Revie, Risk, Spike, Spile, Stang, Stob, Sweep, Tether, Vie, Wager

Stale Aged, Banal, Flat, Fozy, Frowsty, Hackneyed, Handle, Hoary, Mouldy, Musty, Old, Pretext, Rancid, Urine, Worn

▷ **Stale** *may indicate* an obsolete word

Stalemate Deadlock, Dilemma, Hindrance, Impasse, Mexican standoff, Saw-off, Standoff, Tie, Zugswang

Stalk(s) Bun, Cane, Follow, Funicle, Ha(u)lm, Pedicel, Pedicle, Peduncle, Petiole, Petiolule, Phyllode, Pursue, Scape, Seta, Shaw, Spear, Spire, Stem, Stipe(s), Stride, Strig, Strut, Stubble, Stump, Trail, Yolk

Stall(s) Arrest, Bay, Booth, Box, Bulk, Crib, > DELAY, Floor, Flypitch, Hedge, Kiosk, Loose-box, Orchestra, Pen, Pew, Prebendal, Seat, Shamble, Sideshow, Stand, Stasidion, Temporise, Trap, Traverse, Travis, Trevis(s)

Stamina Endurance, Fibre, Fortitude, Guts, Last, Stay, Steel

Stammer(ing) Hesitate, Hum, Stumble, Waffle

Stamp(s), Stamped Appel, Cast, Character, Date(r), Die, Enface, Frank, Imperforate, Impress, Imprint, Incuse, Label, Matchmark, Mint, Pane, Penny black, Perfin, Philately, Pintadera, Postage, Press(ion), Rubber, Seal, Seebeck, Se-tenant, Signet, Spif, Strike, Swage, Tête-bêche, Touch, Touchmark, Trading, Trample, Tread, Tromp, Type

Stand(ing), Stand for, Stand up Apron, Arraign, Attitude, Base, Be, Bear, Bide, Binnacle, Bipod, Bristle, Brook, Caste, Cradle, Crease, Dais, Degree, Desk, Dock, Dree, Dumb-waiter, Easel, Etagère, Face, Foothold, Freeze, Gantry, Gueridon, Hard, Hob, Insulator, Last, Lazy Susan, Lectern, Leg, Music, Nef, Odour, One-night, Ovation, Pedestal, Place, Plant, Podium, Pose, Position, Prestige, Promenade, Protest, Qua, Rack, Rank, Regent, Remain, Represent, Repute, Rise, Stall, Statant, Station, Stay, Stillage, Stock, Stool, Straddle, Stroddle, Strut, Table, Tantalus, Taxi, Teapoy, Terrace, > TREAT, Tree, Tripod, Trivet, Umbrella, Upright, Whatnot

Standard(s) Banner, Base, Baseline, Basic, Benchmark, Bogey, British, Canon, CAT, Classic(al), Cocker, Colour(s), Criterion, Double, Eagle, English, Ethics, Examplar, Example, Exemplar, Flag, Ga(u)ge, Gold, Gonfalon, Guidon, Ideal, Labarum, Level, Living, Model, Norm(a), Normal, Numeraire, Old Glory, Oriflamme, Par, Parker Morris, Pennon, Principle, Rate, Regular, Rod, Rose, Routine, Royal, > RULE, Silver, Spec(ification), Staple, Sterling, Stock, Time, Touchstone, Tricolour, Troy, Two-power, Usual, Valuta, Vexillum, Yardstick

Stanza Ballad, Elegiac, Envoi, Envoy

Star(s) Aster(isk), Body, Celebrity, Constant, Constellation, Cynosure, Double, Exploding, Falling, Feather, Feature, Film, Fixed, Flare, Giant, Headline, Hero, Hexagram, Idol, Lead, Lion, Mogen David, Movie, Multiple, Pentacle, Personality, Pip, Pointer, Principal, Pulsating, Shell, Shine, Shooting, Sidereal, Solomon's seal, Spangle, Starn(ie), Stellar, Stern, Swart, (The) Pointers, Top-liner, Ultraviolet, Variable, Vedette

Stare Eyeball, Fisheye, Gape, Gapeseed, Gawp, Gaze, Goggle, Gorp, Look, Outface, Peer, Rubberneck

Stark Apparent, Austere, Bald, Bare, Gaunt, Harsh, Naked, Nude, Sheer, Stiff, Utterly

Start(ed), Starter Abrade, Abraid, Abray, Activate, Actuate, Begin, Boggle, Bot, Broach, Bug, Bump, Chance, Commence, Crank, Create, Crudites, Dart, Ean, Embryo, Face-off, False, Fire, Flinch, Float, Flush, Flying, Found, Gambit, Gan, Genesis, Getaway, Gun, Handicap, Head, Hot-wire, Impetus, Imprimis, Incept(ion), Initiate, Instigate, Institute, Intro, Jerk, Jump, Jump-off, Kick-off, L, Lag, Launch, Lead, Off, Offset, Onset, Ope(n), Ord, Origin, Outset, Preliminary, Prelude, Put-up, Reboot, Resume, Roll, Rouse, Scare, Set off, Shy, Slip, Snail,

Spring, Spud, String, Tee-off, Wince

▷ **Start** *may indicate* an anagram or first letter(s)

Starvation, **Starve(d)**, **Starving** Anorexia, Anoxic, Cold, Diet, Famish, Perish, Pine, Undernourished

▷ **Starving** *may indicate* an 'o' in the middle of a word

Stash Secrete

State(s) Affirm, Alabama, Alaska, Alle(d)ge, Andorra, Aread, Arizona, Ark(ansas), Arrede, Assert, Assever, Attest, Aver, Avow, Bahar, Balkan, Belize, Benin, Brunei, Buffer, California, Carolina, Case, Chad, Cite, Client, Colorado, Commonwealth, Condition, Confederate, Conn(ecticut), Country, Critical, Cutch, Dakota, Declare, Del(aware), Dependency, Dixie, Dubai, Durango, Emirate, Empire, Etat, Ethiopia, Federal, Fettle, Fla, Flap, Florida, Free, Ga, Gabon, Georgia, Ghana, Guatemala, Gulf, Habitus, Hawaii, Hesse, Honduras, Humour, Ia, Idaho, Illinois, Indiana, Iowa, Jalisco, Jamahiriya, Jharkand, Jigawa, Johore, Jumhouriya, Kalat, Kano, Kansas, Karnataka, Kashmir, Kedah, Kelantan, Kentucky, Kerala, Khelat, Kingdom, Kogi, Kutch, Kuwait, Kwara, Land, Lesh, Louisiana, Madras, Maine, Malawi, Malay, Manipur, Maranhao, Maryland, Mass(achusetts), Md, Me, Meghalaya, Mess, Mewar, Mi(chigan), Michoacán, Minas Gerais, Minnesota, Mississippi, Missouri, Mizovam, Montana, Morelos, Mysore, Nagaland, Name, Nanny, Nation, Native, Nayarit, NC, Nebraska, Negri Sembilan, Nevada, New Hampshire, New Jersey, New Mexico, New South Wales, New York, Nirvana, Nuevo Léon, NY, Oaxaca, Ogun, Ohio, Oklahoma, Oman, Ondo, Orange Free, Oregon, Orissa, Osun, Oyo, Pa, Pahang, Palatinate, Papal, Para, Paraiba, Parana, Penang, Pennsylvania, Perak, Perlis, Pernambucio, Piaui, Plateau, Plight, Police, Pradesh, Predicament, Predicate, Premise, Pronounce, Protectorate, Prussia, Puebla, Punjab, Puppet, Qatar, Quantum, Queensland, Queretaro, Quintana Roo, Rajasthan, Realm, Reich, Republic, RI, Rivers, Rogue, Rondonia, Roraima, Saarland, Sabah, St Kitts and Nevis, St Vincent, Samoa, San Luis Potosi, Santa Catarina, Sao Paulo, Sarawak, Satellite, Saxony(-Anholt), Say, Schleswig-Holstein, Selangor, Sergipe, Sikkim, Slave, Sokoto, Sonora, Sorry, South Australia, South Carolina, South Dakota, Sparta, Standing, Steady, Styria, Succession, Swat, Tabasco, Tamaulipas, Tamil Nadu, Tanganyika, Tasmania, Tennessee, T(e)rengganu, Texas, Threeness, Thuringia, Tiaxcala, Tocantina, Togo, Ton(g)kin(g), Travancore, Tripura, Trucial, Udaipur, UK, Uncle Sam, Union, United, US, Ut, Utah, Uttaranchai, Utter Pradesh, Va, Vatican City, Venezuela, Veracruz, Vermont, Victoria, Virginia, Washington, Welfare, West Virginia, Wis(consin), Wyoming, Yucatan, Zacatecas

▷ **Stated** *may indicate* a similar sounding word

Stately, **Stately home** August, Dome, Grand, Imposing, Majestic, Mansion, Noble, Regal

Statement Account, Affidavit, Aphorism, Assertion, Attestation, Avowal, Bill, Bulletin, Communiqué, Deposition, Dictum, Diktat, Encyclical, Evidence, Expose, Factoid, Grand remonstrance, Invoice, Jurat, Manifesto, Mission, Outline, Pleading, Press release, Profession, Pronouncement, Proposition, Quotation, Release, Report, Sentence, Soundbite, Sweeping, Testimony, Truism, Utterance, Verb

Station(s) Action, Base, Berth, Birth, Camp, Caste, CCS, Comfort, Crewe, Deploy, Depot, Dressing, Euston, Filling, Fire, Garrison, Gas, Halt, Head, Hill, Hilversum, Ice, Lay, Location, Marylebone, Outpost, Panic, Petrol, Pitch, Place, Plant, Point, Police, Polling, Post, Power, Quarter, Radio, Rank, Relay, Rowme, Seat, Service, Sheep, Sit, Space, Stance, Stand, Status, Stond, Subscriber, Tana, Tanna(h), Terminus, Testing, Thana(h), Thanna(h), Tracking, Triangulation, Victoria, Waterloo, Waverley, Way, Weather, Work

Statuary, **Statue(tte)** Acrolith, Bronze, Bust, Discobolus, Effigy, Figure, Figurine, Galatea, Idol, Image, Kore, Kouros, Liberty, Memnon, Monument, Oscar,

Palladium, Pietà, Sculpture, Sphinx, Stonework, Tanagra, Torso, Xoanon

Staunch Amadou, Leal, Resolute, Steady, Stem, Stout, Styptic, Watertight

Stay(s) Alt, Avast, Bide, Bolster, Cohab(it), Corselet, Corset, Embar, Endure, Fulcrum, Gest, Guy, Hawser, Indwell, Jump, Lie, Lig, Linger, Moratorium, Prop, > REMAIN, Reprieve, Restrain, Settle, Sist, Sleepover, Sojourn, Strut, Sustain, Tarry

Steadfast Constant, Firm, Implacable, Resolute, Sad, Stable

Steady Andantino, Ballast, Beau, Boyfriend, Composer, Constant, Even, Faithful, Firm, Girlfriend, Measured, Regular, Stabilise, Stable, Unswerving

Steak Chateaubriand, Chuck, Fillet, Flitch, Garni, Mignon, Minute, Pope's eye, Porterhouse, Rump, Slice, Tartare, T-bone, Tenderloin, Tournedos, Vienna

Steal(ing) Abstract, Bag, Bandicoot, Bone, Boost, Cabbage, Cly, Convey, Creep, Crib, Duff, Embezzle, Filch, Glom, Grab, Half-inch, Heist, Joyride, Kidnap, Knap, Lag, Liberate, Lift, Loot, Mag(g), Mahu, Mill, Naam, Nam, Nap, Nick, Nim, Nip, Nym, Peculate, Pilfer, Pillage, Pinch, Piracy, Plagiarise, Plunder, Poach, Prig, Proll, Purloin, Ram-raid, Remove, Rifle, Rob, Rustle, Scrump, Skrimp, Smug, Snaffle, Snatch, Sneak, Snitch, Souvenir, Swipe, Take, Theft, Thieve, Tiptoe, TWOC, Whip

Steam(ed), Steamy Boil, Condensation, Cushion, Dry, Fume, Gaseous, Het, Humid, Live, Mist, Porn, Radio, Roke, Sauna, Spout, Vapor, Vapour, Wet

Steel(y) Cast, Chrome, Chromium, Cold, Concrete, Damascus, Damask, High-carbon, High-speed, Magnet, Manganese, Mild, Spray

Steep Abrupt, Arduous, Brent, Embay, Expensive, Hilly, Krans, Krantz, Kranz, Macerate, Marinade, Marinate, Mask, Precipice, Precipitous, Rait, Rapid, Rate, Ret, Saturate, Scarp, Soak, Sog, Souse, Stey, Stickle

Steer(er), Steering Ackerman, Airt, Buffalo, Bullock, Cann, Castor, Con(n), Cox, Direct, > GUIDE, Helm, Navaid, Navigate, Ox, Pilot, Ply, Rudder, Stot, Whipstaff, Zebu

Stem Alexanders, Arrow, Axial, Bine, Bole, Caudex, Caulicle, Caulome, Check, Cladode, Cladophyll, Confront, Corm, Culm, Dam, Epicotyl, Floricane, Ha(u)lm, Kex, Pedicle, Peduncle, Pin, Rachis, Rhizome, Rise, Sarment, Scapus, Seta, Shaft, Shank, Spring, Stalk, Staunch, Stipe, Stolon, Sympodium, Tail

Step(s) Act, Balancé, Chassé, Choctaw, Corbie, Curtail, Dance, Démarche, Echelon, Escalate, False, Flight, Fouetté, Gain, Gait, Glissade, Goose, Grecian, Greece, Grees(e), Greesing, Grese, Gressing, Griece, Grise, Grize, Halfpace, Lavolt, Lock, Measure, Move, Notch, Pace, Pas, Pas de souris, Phase, Pigeon's wing, Quantal, Raiser, Ratlin(e), Rattlin(e), Rattling, Roundel, Roundle, Rung, Shuffle, Slip, Stage, Stair, Stalk, Stile, Stope, Stride, Toddle, Trap, Tread, Trip, Unison, Waddle, Walk, Whole, Winder

Stereotype(d) Hackney, Ritual

Sterile, Sterilise(r), Sterility Barren, Dead, Fruitless, Impotent, Infertile, Neuter, Pasteurise, Spay

Stern Aft, Austere, Counter, Dour, Flinty, Grim, Hard, Implacable, Iron, Isaac, Nates, Poop, Rear, Relentless, Rugged, Stark, Strict, Tailpiece

Stew(ed), Stews Bath, Blanquette, Boil, Bouillabaisse, Bouilli, Braise, Bredie, Brothel, Burgoo, Carbonade, Casserole, Cassoulet, Chowder, Coddle, Colcannon, Compot(e), Daube, Flap, Fuss, Goulash, Haricot, Hash, Hell, Hot(ch)pot(ch), Irish, Jug, Lobscouse, Matelote, Mulligan, Navarin, Olla podrida, Osso bucco, Paddy, Paella, Pepperpot, Pot-au-feu, Pot-pourri, Ragout, Ratatouille, Salmi, Sass, Scouse, Seethe, Simmer, Squiffy, Stie, Stove, Stovies, Sty, Succotash, Sweat, Swelter

Steward Chiltern Hundreds, Sewer, Smallboy

▷ **Stewed** *may indicate* an anagram

Stick(ing) (out), Sticks, Sticky, Stuck Adhere, Affix, Aground, Ash, Ashplant, Attach, Bamboo, Bastinado, Bat, Baton, Bauble, Bayonet, Bludgeon, Bond,

Boondocks, Cambrel, Cane, Celery, Cement, Chalk, Chapman, Clag, Clam(my), Clarty, Clave, Cleave, Cling, Clog, Club, Cocktail, Cohere, Coinhere, Composing, Control, Crab, Crosier, Cross(e), Crotch, Crozier, Cue, Distaff, Divining-rod, Dog, Dure, Endure, Fag(g)ot, Firewood, Flak, Founder, Fuse, Gad(e), Gambrel, Gelatine, Glair, Glit, Glue, Goad, Gold, Goo, Gore, Ground-ash, Gum, Gunge, Gunk, Harpoon, Hob, Hurley, Immobile, Impale, Inhere, Isinglass, Jab, Jam, Jut, Kebbie, Kid, Kindling, Kip, Kiri, Knitch, Knobkerrie, Lance, Lath(i), Lug, Message, Minder, Orange, Parasitic, Paste, Penang-lawyer, Persist, Pierce, Plaster, Pogo, Pole, Posser, Protrude, Protuberant, Quarterstaff, Rash, Ratten, Rhubarb, Rhythm, Rod, Ropy, Scouring, Seat, Shillela(g)h, Shooting, Size, Ski, Smudge, Spanish windlass, Spear, Spurtle, Staff, Stand, Stang, Stob, Stodgy, Swagger, Switch, Swizzle, Swordstick, Tack(y), Tally, Tar, Thick, Throwing, Toddy, Truncheon, Twig, Viscid, Viscous, Waddy, Wait, Walking, Wand, White, Woomera(ng)

Sticker Barnacle, Bur, Glue, Label, Limpet, Poster

Stiff, **Stiffen(er)**, **Stiffening**, **Stiffness** Anchylosis, Angular, Ankylosis, Baleen, Bandoline, Brace, Buckram, Budge, Corpse, Corpus, Dear, Defunct, Expensive, Formal, Frore(n), Goner, Gut, Hard, Mort, Petrify, Pokerish, Prim, Ramrod, Rigid, Rigor, Rigor mortis, Sad, Set, Size, Solid, Starch, Stark, Stay, Steeve, Stieve, Stilted, Stoor, Stour, Stowre, Sture, Unbending, Whalebone, Wigan, Wooden

Still Accoy, Airless, Alembic, Assuage, Becalm, Calm, Check, Current, Doggo, Ene, Even(ness), Howbe, However, Hush, Illicit, Inactive, Inert, Kill, Languid, Limbec(k), Lull, Motionless, Nevertheless, Patent, Peaceful, Photograph, Placate, Placid, Posé, Quiescent, Quiet, Resting, Silent, Snapshot, Soothe, Stagnant, Static, Stationary, Though, Yet

Stimulant, **Stimulate**, **Stimulus** Activate, Adrenaline, Antigen, Arak, Arouse, Benny, Caffeine, Cinder, Coca, Conditioned, Cue, Dart, Digitalin, Digoxin, Egg, Energise, Evoke, Excitant, Fillip, Fuel, Galvanize, Ginger, Goad, Hormone, Incite, Innerve, Inspire, Irritate, Jog, Key, K(h)at, Kick, Mneme, Motivate, Oestrus, Pep, Philtre, Pick-me-up, Piquant, Prod, Promote, Provoke, Psych, Qat, Rim, Roborant, Rowel, Rub, Sassafras, Sensuous, Spur, Sting, Stir, Tannin, Tar, Theine, Tickle, Titillate, Tone, Tonic, Unconditioned, Upper, Whet(stone), Winter's bark

Sting(ing) Aculeate, Barb, Bite, Cheat, Cnida, Goad, Nematocyst, Nettle(tree), Overcharge, Perceant, Piercer, Poignant, Prick, Pungent, Rile, Scorpion, Sephen, Smart, Spice, Stang, Stimulus, Surcharge, Tang, Trichocyst, Urent, Urtica

Stingy Cheeseparing, Chintzy, Close, Costive, Hard, Illiberal, Mean, Miserly, Narrow, Near, Nippy, Parsimonious, Snippy, Snudge, Tight(wad), Tight-arse

▷ **Stingy** *may indicate* something that stings

Stipulate, **Stipulation** Clause, Condition, Covenant, Insist, Provision, Proviso, Rider, Specify

Stir(red), **Stirring** Accite, Admix, Ado, Afoot, Agitate, Amo(o)ve, Animate, Annoy, Bother, Bustle, Buzz, Can, Churn, Cooler, Excite, Foment, Furore, Fuss, Gaol, Hectic, Impassion, Incense, Incite, Inflame, Insurrection, Intermix, Jee, Jog, Kitty, Limbo, Live, > MIX, Move, Noy, Poss, Pother, > PRISON, Prod, Provoke, Quad, Quatch, Quetch, Quinche, Qui(t)ch, Quod, Rabble, Rear, Roil, Rouse, Roust, Rummage, Rustle, Sod, Steer, Styre, Swizzle, To-do, Upstart, Wake

▷ **Stir(red)**, **Stirring** *may indicate* an anagram

Stitch (up) Bargello, Basket, Baste, Blanket, Blind, Box, Buttonhole, Cable, Chain, Couching, Crewel, Crochet, Cross, Daisy, Embroider, Feather, Fell, Flemish, Florentine, Garter, Gathering, Grospoint, Hem, Herringbone, Honeycomb, Insertion, Kettle, Knit, Lazy daisy, Lock, Monk's seam, Moss, Needle, Open, Overlock, Pearl, Petit point, Pinwork, Plain, Purl, Queen, Rag, Railway, Rib, Rope, Running, Saddle, Satin, Screw, Sew, Slip, Spider, Stab, Stay, Steek, Stem, Stockinette, Stocking, Straight, Sutile, Suture, Tack, Tailor's tack, Tent, Topstitch, Whip, Whole

Stock(ed), **Stocks**, **Stocky** Aerie, Aery, Ambulance, Barometer, Blue-chip, Bouillon, Bree, Breech, Buffer, But(t), Capital, Carry, Cattle, Choker, Cippus, Congee, Court-bouillon, Cravat, Dashi, Debenture, Delta, Die, Endomorph, Equip, Fumet, Fund, Gamma, Gear(e), Government, Graft, Gun, Handpiece, He(a)rd, Hilt, Hoosh, Industrial, Intervention, Inventory, Joint, Just-in-time, Kin, Larder, Laughing, Line, Little-ease, Omnium, Pigeonhole, Preferred, Pycnic, Race, Ranch, Recovery, Rep(ertory), Replenish, Reserve, Rolling, Root, Scrip, Seed, Shorts, Soup, Squat, Staple, Steale, Steelbow, Stirp(e)s, > **STORE**, Strain, Stubby, Supply, Surplus, Talon, Tap, Team, Tie, Utility, Virginia

Stocking(s) Fishnet, Hogger, Hose, Leather, Moggan, Netherlings, Nylons, Seamless, Sheer, Sock, Spattee, Tights

Stole(n) Bent, Epitrachelion, Hot, Maino(u)r, Manner, Manor, Nam, Orarion, Orarium, Reft, Scarf, Staw, Tippet

Stomach(ic) Abdomen, Abomasum, Accept, Appetite, Belly, Bible, Bingy, Bonnet, Bread-basket, Brook, C(o)eliac, Corporation, Epiploon, Gaster, Gizzard, Gut, Heart, Jejunum, King's-hood, Kite, Kyte, Little Mary, Manyplies, Mary, Maw, Mesaraic, Midriff, Omasum, Paunch, Potbelly, Psalterium, Pylorus, Rennet, Reticulum, Rumen, Stick, Swagbelly, > **SWALLOW**, Tripe, Tum, Tun-belly, Urite, Vell, Venter, Wame, Washboard, Wem

Stoneware Crouch-ware

Stool Buffet, Coppy, Cracket, Creepie, Cricket, Cucking, Curule, Cutty, Faeces, Hassock, Milking, Piano, Pouf(fe), Seat, Sir-reverence, Step, Stercoral, Sunkie, Taboret, Tripod, Turd

Stop(page), **Stopcock**, **Stopper**, **Stopping** Abort, Arrest, Avast, Bait, Ba(u)lk, Bide, Block, Brake, Buffer, Bung, > **CEASE**, Cessation, Chapter, Check, Checkpoint, Cheese, Clarabella, Clarino, Clarion, Clog, Close, Colon, Comfort, Comma, Conclude, Cork, Coupler, Cremo(r)na, Cut, Deactivate, Debar, Demurral, Desist, Deter, Devall, Diapason, Diaphone, Discontinue, Discourage, Dit, Dolce, Dot, Echo, Embargo, End, Field, Fifteenth, Flag, Flue, Flute, Foreclose, Foundation, Freeze, Full, Gag, Gamba, Gemshorn, Glottal, Gong, Halt, Hartal, Hinder, Hitch, Ho, Hold, Hoy, Intermit, Jam, Kibosh, Let-up, Lill, Lin, Lute, Media, Mutation, Nasard, Oboe, Obturate, Occlude, Oppilate, Organ, Outspan, Pause, Period, Piccolo, Pit, Plug, Point, Poop, Preclude, Prevent, Principal, Prorogue, Pull-in, Pull over, Pull-up, Punctuate, Quash, Quint, Quit, Racket, Red, Reed, Refrain, Register, Rein, Remain, Request, Rest, Scotch, Screw-top, Semi-colon, Sext, Sist, Snub, Solo, Spigot, Stall, Stanch, Standstill, Stash, Stasis, Station, Staunch, Stay, Stive, Strike, Subbase, Suction, Supersede, Suppress, Suspend, Tab, Tamp(ion), Tap, Tenuis, Terminate, Toby, Truck, Voix celeste, Waypoint, When, Whistle, Whoa

Storage, **Store(house)**, **Store** Accumulate, Arsenal, Backing, Barn, Bin, Bottle, Bottom drawer, Boxroom, Bunker, Buttery, Cache, Cell, Cellar, Chain, Clamp, Clipboard, Convenience, Co-op(erative), Co-operative, Core, Cupboard, Cutch, Database, Deli, Dene-hole, Dépanneur, Department(al), Depository, Depot, Dime, Discount, Dolly-shop, Elevator, Emporium, Ensile, Entrepot, Etape, Fund, Garner, Girnal, Glory hole, Go-down, Granary, > **HOARD**, Hold, Hope chest, House, Humidor, Husband, Hypermarket, Larder, Lastage, Liquor, Lumber room, Magazine, Main, Mart, Memory, Mine, Morgue, Mothball, Mow, Multiple, Nest-egg, Off-licence, Package, Pantechnicon, Pantry, Pithos, Provision, Pumped, Rack(ing), RAM, Repertory, Reposit, ROM, Sector, > **SHOP**, Silage, Silo, Spence, Springhouse, Squirrel, Stack, Stash, Stock, Stockroom, Stow, Superbaza(a)r, Superette, Supermarket, Supply, Tack-room, Tank, Thesaurus, Tithe-barn, Tommy-shop, Virtual, Warehouse, Woodshed, Woodyard, Wool (shed)

▶ **Storey** *see* **STORY**

Storm(y) Ablow, Adad, Assail, Attack, Baguio, Blizzard, Bluster, Brouhaha, Buran, Charge, Cyclone, Devil, Dirty, Dust, Electric, Enlil, Expugn, Furore, Gale,

Gusty, Haboob, Hurricane, Ice, Magnetic, Monsoon, Onset, Rage(ful), Raid, Rain, Rampage, Rant, Rave, Red spot, Rugged, Rush, Shaitan, Snorter, Squall, Tea-cup, Tempest, Tornade, Tornado, Tropical, Unruly, Violent, Weather, Willy-willy, Zu

▷ **Stormy** *may indicate* an anagram

Story, **Storyline**, **Storey**, **Stories** Account, Allegory, Anecdote, Apocrypha, Attic, Bar, Basement, Baur, Biog, Blood and thunder, Chestnut, Clearstory, Clerestory, Cock and bull, Conte, Cover, Decameron, Edda, Epic, Episode, Etage, Exclusive, Fable, Fabliau, Fib, Fiction, Flat, Floor, Folk-tale, Gag, Geste, Ghost, Hard-luck, Heptameron, Horror, Idyll, Iliad, Jataka, Lee, Legend, Lie, Marchen, Mezzanine, Myth(os), Mythus, Narrative, Nouvelle, Novel(la), Oratorio, Parable, Passus, Pentameron, Plot, Rede, Report, Romance, Rumour, Saga, Scoop, Script, Serial, SF, Shaggy dog, Shocker, Short, Smoke-room, Sob, Spiel, Spine-chiller, Splash, Stage, Success, Tale, Tall, Thread, Thriller, Tier, Upper, Version, Yarn

Story-teller Aesop, Fibber, Griot, Liar, Munchausen, Narrator, Raconteur, Shannachie, Tusitala

Stout(ness) Ale, Burly, Chopping, Chubby, Embonpoint, Endomorph, Entire, Fat, Fubsy, Hardy, Humpty-dumpty, Lusty, Manful, Milk, Obese, Overweight, Porter, Portly, Potbelly, Robust, Stalwart, Stalworth, Sta(u)nch, Strong, Stuggy, Sturdy, Substantial, Tall

Stove Baseburner, Break, Calefactor, Cockle, Cooker, Furnace, Gasfire, Oven, Potbelly, Primus®, Range, Salamander

Straggle(r), **Straggly** Estray, Gad, Meander, Ramble, Rat-tail, Spidery, Sprawl, Stray, Wander

Straight(en), **Straightness** Align, Bald, Beeline, Correct, Die, Direct, Downright, Dress, Frank, Gain, Het(ero), Honest, Lank, Legit, Level, Normal, Rectilineal, Rectitude, Righten, Sheer, Slap, Tidy, True, Unbowed, Unlay, Upright, Veracious, Virgate

Straightfaced Agelast

Straightforward Candid, Direct, Easy, Even, Forthright, Honest, Jannock, Level, Plain sailing, Pointblank, Simple

Strain(ed), **Strainer**, **Straining** Agonistic, Ancestry, Aria, Breed, Carol, Clarify, Colander, Distend, Drawn, Effort, Exert, Filter, Filtrate, Fit, Fitt(e), Force, Fray, Fytt(e), Intense, Kind, Melody, Milsey, Molimen, Music, Note, Overtask, Passus, Percolate, Pressure, Pull, Rack, Raring, Reck(an), Retch, Rick, Seep, Seil(e), Set, Shear, Sieve, Sift, Sile, Stape, Start, Stock, Streak, Stress, Stretch, Sye, Tamis, Tammy, Tax, Tenesmus, Tense, Tension, Threnody, Try, Vein, Vice, Work, Wrick

Strait(s) Bab el Mandeb, Basilan, Desperate, Drake Passage, Golden Gate, Kerch, Mackinac, Mona Passage, North Channel, Soenda, Sumba, Tatar, Tiran, Tsugaru, Windward Passage

Strange(ness), **Stranger** Alien, Aloof, Amphitryon, Curious, Eerie, Exotic, Foreign, Fraim, Frem(d), Fremit, Frenne, Funny, Guest, Malihini, New, Novel, Odd(ball), Outlandish, Outsider, Quare, Queer, Rum, S, Screwy, Selcouth, Singular, Tea-leaf, Uncanny, Unco, Uncommon, Unked, Unket, Unkid, Unused, Unusual, Wacky, Weird, Wondrous

▷ **Strange** *may indicate* an anagram

Strap(ping) Able-bodied, Band, Barber, Beat, Bowyangs, Brail, Braw, Breeching, Browband, Crupper, Cuir-bouilli, Curb, Deckle, Girth, Halter, Harness, Holdback, Jess, Jock(ey), Larrup, Lash, Ligule, Lorate, Lore, Manly, Martingale, Nicky-tam, Octopus, Pandy, Rand, Rein, Robust, Shoulder, Sling, Spider, Strop, Surcingle, Suspender, T, Tab, Taws(e), T-bar, Thong, Throatlash, Throatlatch, Trace, Tump-line, Wallop, Watch

Stratagem, **Strategist**, **Strategy** Artifice, Clausewitz, Coup, Deceit, Device, Dodge, Exit, Fetch, Finesse, Fraud, Heresthetic, Kaupapa, Masterstroke, Maximum, Minimax, Plan, Rope-a-dope, Scheme, Scorched earth, Sleight,

Subterfuge, Tactic(s), Tactician, Trick, Wile

Straw(s), **Strawy** Balibuntal, Boater, Buntal, Chaff, Cheese, Halm, Hat, Haulm, Hay, Insubstantial, Last, Leghorn, Nugae, Oaten, Panama, Parabuntal, Pedal, Stalk, Stramineous, Strammel, Strummel, Stubble, Trifles, Wisp, Ye(a)lm

Stray Abandoned, Chance, Depart, Deviate, Digress, Err, Forwander, Foundling, Maverick, Meander, Misgo, Pye-dog, Ramble, Roam, Sin, Straggle, Streel, Traik, Unowned, Waff, Waif, Wander

Streak(ed), **Streaker**, **Streaky** Bended, Blue, Brindle, Comet, Flaser, Flash, Fleck, Freak, Hawked, Highlights, Lace, Layer, Leonid, Lowlight, Mark, Merle, Mottle, Primitive, Race, Run, Schlieren, Seam, Shot, Striate, Striga, Strip(e), Vein, Venose, Vibex, Waif, Wake, Wale, Yellow

Stream Acheron, Beam, Beck, Bourne, Burn, Consequent, Course, Current, Driblet, Fast, Flow, Flower, Freshet, Gulf, Gush, Headwater, Influent, Jet, Kill, Lade, Lane, Leet, Logan, Meteor, Nala, Obsequent, Pokelogan, Pour, Pow, Riffle, Rill, River, Rivulet, Rubicon, Run, Runnel, Sike, Slough, Spruit, Star, Streel, Subsequent, Syke, The Fleet, Thrutch, Tide-race, Torrent, Tributary, Trickle, Trout, Watercourse, Water-splash, Winterbourne

Streamer Banner(all), Ribbon, Tape

Street Alley, Ave(nue), Bowery, Broad, Carey, Carnaby, Cato, Causey, Cheapside, Civvy, Close, Corso, Court, Crescent, Downing, Drive, Easy, Fleet, Gate, Grub, Harley, High(way), Lane, Meuse, Mews, One-way, Parade, Paseo, Queer, Road, Side, Sinister, St, Strand, Terrace, Thoroughfare, Threadneedle, Throgmorton, Wall, Wardour, Watling, Way, Whitehall

Strength(en), **Strengthening** Afforce, Bant, Beef, Brace, Brawn, Build, Confirm, Consolidate, Enable, Energy, Foison, Force, Forte, Fortify, Freshen, Grit, Herculean, Horn, Intensity, Iron, Line, Main, Man, Might, Munite, Muscle, Nerve, > POWER, Prepotence, Pre-stress, Proof, Reinforce, Roborant, Sinew, Spike, Stamina, Steel, Sthenia, Stoutness, > STRONG, Tensile, Thews, Titration, Unity, Vim

Stress(ed) Paroxytone, Post-traumatic, Primary, Rhythm, Sentence, Shear, Wind shear, Word, Yield (point)

Stretch(able), **Stretched**, **Stretcher**, **Stretching** Belt, Brick, Crane, Distend, Draw, Ectasis, Eke, Elastic, Elongate, Expanse, Extend, Extensile, Farthingale, Fib, Frame, Give, Gurney, Lengthen, Litter, Narrows, Outreach, Pallet, Porrect, Procrustes, Prolong, Protend, Pull, Rack, Rax, > REACH, Sentence, Shiner, Spell, Spread, Strain, Taut, Tend, Tense, Tensile, Tenter, Term, Time, Tract, Tractile, Tree, Trolley

Stretcher-bearer Fuzzy-wuzzy angel

Strict Dour, Harsh, Literal, Orthodox, Penal, Puritanical, Rigid, Rigorous, Severe, Spartan, Stern, Strait(-laced)

Stride Gal(l)umph, Leg, Lope, March, Pace, Piano, Stalk, Sten, Straddle, Stroam, Strut, Stump

Strident Brassy, Grinding, Harsh, Raucous, Screech

Strife Bargain, Barrat, Conflict, Contest, Discord, Disharmony, Dissension, Feud, Food, Friction, Ignoble, Scrap(ping)

Strike(r), **Striking**, **Strike out** Air, Alight, Annul, Arresting, Attitude, Backhander, Baff, Band, Bang, Bash, Bat, Baton, Batsman, Batter, Beat, Belabour, Better, Biff, Black, Bla(u)d, Bonanza, Bop, Buff, Buffet, Butt, Cane, Catch, Chime, Chip, Clap, Clash, Clatch, Clip, Clock, Clout, Club, Cob, Collide, Constitutional, Coup, Cue, Cuff, Dad, Dent, Dev(v)el, Ding, Dint, Dismantle, Douse, Dowse, Dramatic, Drive, Dush, Eclat, Fet(ch), Fillip, Firk, Fist, Flail, Flog, Frap, General, Get, Go-slow, Gowf, Hail, Hartal, Head-butt, > HIT, Horn, Hour, Hunger, Ictus, Illision, Impact, Impinge, Impress, Jarp, Jaup, Jole, Joll, Joule, Jowl, Knock, Lam, Lambast, Laser, Lay(-off), Lightning, Match, Middle, Notable, Noticeable, Official,

Out, Pash, Pat(ter), Pat, Peen, Percuss, Picket, Plectrum, Pronounced, Pummel, Punch, Ram, Rap, Remarkable, Rolling, Salient, Scrub, Scutch, Shank, Sideswipe, Sitdown, Sit-in, Slam, Slap, Slat, Slog, Slosh, Smack, Smash, Smite, Sock, Souse, Spank, Stayaway, Stop(page), Stub, Swap, Swat, Swinge, Swipe, Swop, Sympathy, Tan, Tat, Thump, Tip, Token, Tripper, Unconstitutional, Unofficial, Walk-out, Wallop, Wap, Whack, Whang, Whap, Wherrit, Who does what, Wildcat, Wipe, Wondrous, Zap

String(s), Stringy Band, Beads, Bootlace, Bow, Cello, Chalaza, Chanterelle, Cord, Cosmic, Drill, Enfilade, Fiddle, First, G, Glass, Gut, Henequin, Hypate, Idiot, Injection, Keyed, Lace, Lag, Lichanos, Macramé, Mese, Necklace, Nete, Nicky-tam, Production, Proviso, Purse, Quint, Ripcord, Rope, Second, Series, Shoe(-tie), Sinewy, Snare, Straggle, Strand, Sympathetic, Team, Tendon, Thairm, Tie, Tough, Train, Trite, Viola, Violin, Wreathed

Strip(ped), Stripper, Striptease Airfield, Armband, Band, Bare, Bark, Batten, Belt, Bereave, Blowtorch, Chippendale, Comic, Cote, Defoliate, Denude, Deprive, Derobe, Despoil, Devest, Disbark, Dismantle, Dismask, Disrobe, Divest, Drag, Ecorché, Fannel(l), Fiche, Film, Flashing, Flaught, Flay, Fleece, Flench, Flense, Flight, Flinch, Flounce, Flype, Furring, Gaza, Goujon, Hatband, Infula, Jib, Label, Landing, Lap-dancer, Lardon, Lath, Ledge, Linter, List, Littoral, Loading, Maniple, Median, Mobius, Panhandle, Parting, Peel, Pillage, Pluck, Pull, Puttee, Puttie, Rand, Raunch, Raw, Ribbon, Roon, Royne, Rumble, Rund, Runway, Screed, Scrow, Shear, Shed, Shim, Shuck, Skin, Slat, Slit, Sliver, Spellican, Spilikin, Spill(ikin), Splat, Splent, Spline, Splint, Splinter, Spoil, Straik, Strake, Strap, Streak, Strop, Sugar soap, Swath, Sweatband, Tack, Tee, Thong, Tirl, Tirr, Uncase, Undeck, Undress, Unfrock, Unrig, Unrip, Valance, Weather, Zone

Strive, Striving Aim, Aspire, > ATTEMPT, Contend, Endeavour, Enter, Kemp, Labour, Nisus, Pingle, Press, Strain, Struggle, Toil, Try, Vie

Stroke Apoplex(y), Backhander, Bat, Bisque, Blow, Boast, Breast, Butterfly, Caress, Carom, Chip, Chop, Counterbuff, Coup, Coy, Crawl, Dash, Dint, Dog(gy)-paddle, Down-bow, Drear(e), Dropshot, Effleurage, Exhaust, Feat, Flick, Fondle, Forehand, Glance, Ground, Hairline, Hand(er), Ictus, Jenny, Jole, Joll, Joule, Jowl, Knell, Knock, Lash, Lightning, Like, Line, Loft, Long jenny, Loser, Oarsman, Oblique, Odd, Off-drive, Outlash, Palp, Paw, Pot-hook, Pull, Punto reverso, Put(t), Reverso, Ridding straik, Roquet, Rub, Scart, Scavenge, Sclaff, Scoop, Seizure, Sheffer's, Short jenny, Sider, Sixte, Slash, Smooth, Solidus, Spot, Strike, Stripe, Sweep, Swipe, Tact, Tittle, Touch, Touk, Trait, Trudgen, Trudgeon, Tuck, Upbow, Virgule, Wale, Whang

Strong(est) Able, Brawny, Cast-iron, Doughty, Durable, F, Fit, Forceful, Forcible, Forte, Hale, Hercules, Humming, Husky, Intense, Mighty, Nappy, Pithy, Pollent, Potent, Powerful, Pungent, Racy, Rank, Robust, Samson, Solid, Stalwart, Stark, Steely, Sthenic, Stiff, Stout, Str, Strapping, > STRENGTH, Sturdy, Substantial, Suit, Tarzan, Thesis, Thickset, Trusty, Vegete, Vehement, Vigorous, Violent, Well-set, Ya(u)ld

Stronghold Acropolis, Aerie, Bastion, Castle, Citadel, Eyrie, Fastness, Fortress, Keep, Kremlin, Redoubt, Tower

Structural, Structure Analysis, Anatomy, Armature, Building, Edifice, Erection, Fabric, Fairing, Format(ion), Frame, Ice-apron, Lantern, Mole, Organic, Pediment, Pergola, Physique, Shape, Skeleton, Squinch, Starling, Syntax, System, Texas, Texture, Trochlea, Undercarriage

Struggle Agon(ise), Agonistes, Buckle, Camp, Chore, Class, Conflict, Contend, Contest, Cope, Debatement, Effort, Endeavour, Fight, Flounder, Grabble, Grapple, Kampf, Labour, Luctation, Mill, Pingle, Rat-race, Reluct, Scrape, Scrimmage, Scrum, Scrummage, Scuffle, Slugfest, Sprangle, > STRIVE, Toil, Tug, Tussle, Uphill, Vie, War(sle), **Wrestle**

▷ **Struggle** *may indicate* an anagram

Stubborn(ness) Adamant, Bigoted, Contumacious, Cussed, Diehard,
Entêté, Hard(-nosed), Hidebound, Intransigent, Inveterate, Moyl(e), Mulish,
Mumpsimus, Obdurate, Obstinate, Opinionated, Ornery, Ortus, Pertinacious,
Perverse, Recalcitrant, Reesty, Refractory, Rigwiddie, Rigwoodie, Self-willed,
Stiff, Tenacious, Thrawn, Wrong-headed

Stud(ded) Farm, Frost, Press, Shear, Stop

Student(s) Alumnus, Apprentice, Bajan, Bejant, Bursar, Cadet, Class, Coed,
Commoner, Dan, Dig, Disciple, Dresser, Dux, Exchange, Exhibitioner, External,
Form, Fresher, Freshman, Gownsman, Graduand, Greenwelly, Gyte, Ikey,
Internal, Junior, > **LEARNER**, Magistrand, Matie, Mature, Medical, NUS,
Opsimath, Ordinand, Oxonian, Plebe, Poll, Postgraduate, Preppy, Pupil, Reader,
Sap, > **SCHOLAR**, Self-taught, Semi, Seminar, Shark, Sizar, Sizer, Smug, Softa,
Soph(omore), Sophister, Subsizar, Swot, Templar, Tiro, Tosher, Trainee, Tuft,
Tukkie, Tutee, Wooden wedge, Wrangler, Year

Study, **Studied**, **Studies**, **Studious** Analyse, Bone, Brown, Carol, Case, Classics,
Con(ne), Conscious, Consider, Course, Cram, Den, Dig, Etude, Feasibility, Field,
Gen up, Learn, Liberal, Media, Motion, Mug, Mull, Muse, Nature, Perusal, Peruse,
Pilot, Pore, Post-doctoral, Probe, Read, Recce, Reconnoitre, Research, Revise,
Sanctum, Sap, Scan, Scrutinise, Swot, Take, Time and motion, Trade-off, Tutorial,
Typto, Voulu, Work

Stuff(iness), **Stuffing**, **Stuffy** Airless, Canvas, Close, Cloth, Codswallop,
Cram, Crap, Dimity, Farce, Feast, Fiddlesticks, Fill, Force, Forcemeat, Frows(t)y,
Frowzy, Fug, Gear, Gobble, Gorge, Guff, Havers, Hooey, Horsehair, Lard, Line,
Linen, > **MATERIAL**, Matter, No-meaning, Nonsense, Overeat, Pad, Pang, Panne,
Pompous, Ram, Replete, Rot, Sate, Scrap, Sob, Stap, Steeve, Stew, Taxidermy,
Trig, Upholster, Wad, Youth

Stumble Blunder, Err, Falter, Flounder, Founder, Lurch, Peck, Snapper, Stoit,
Titubate, Trip

Stun(ning), **Stunned** Astonish, Astound, Awhape, Bludgeon, Concuss, Cosh,
Daze, Dazzle, Deafen, Dove, Drop-dead, Glam, KO, Shell-shocked, Shock, Stoun,
Stupefy

Stunt(ed) Aerobatics, Confine, Droichy, Dwarf, Feat, Gimmick, Hot-dog, Hype,
Jehad, Jihad, Loop, Nirl, Puny, Ront(e), Runt, Ruse, Scroggy, Scrub(by), Scrunt(y),
Stub, Trick, Wanthriven

Stupid, **Stupid person** Dense, Dull(ard), Fatuous, Gormless, Gross, Inane,
Insensate, Mindless, Natural, Obtuse, Silly, Thick, Torpid

Sturdy Burly, Dunt, Gid, Hardy, Hefty, Lusty, Stalwart, Staunch, Steeve, Strapping,
Strong, Thickset, Turnsick, Vigorous

Style(s), **Stylish**, **Stylist** Adam, A la, A-line, Band, Barocco, Barock, Baroque,
Blow-dry, Burin, Call, Chic, Chippendale, Class, Cultism, Cut, Dapper, Dash, Decor,
Decorated, Demotic, Diction, Dub, Elan, Elegance, Empire, Entitle, Execution,
Face, Farand, > **FASHION**, Finesse, Flamboyant, Flossy, Form(at), Genre, Gnomon,
Gothic, Grace, Gr(a)ecism, Grand, Groovy, Hair-do, Hand, Hepplewhite, Hip,
Homeric, House, International (Gothic), Katharev(o)usa, Manner, Mod(e),
Modish, Natty, New, Nib, Nifty, Old, Panache, Pattern, Pen, Perm, Perpendicular,
Personal, Phrase, Pistil, Pointel, Port, Post-modernism, Preponderant, Probe,
Queen Anne, Rakish, Rank, Regency, Rococo, Romanesque, Sheraton, Silk,
Snazzy, Spiffy, Sporty, Street, Swish, Taste, Term, Title, Ton, Tone, Touch,
Traditional, Tuscan, Uncial, Vogue, Way

Subconscious Inner, Instinctive, Not-I, Subliminal, Suppressed

Subcontract Outsource

Subdue(d) Abate, Allay, Chasten, Conquer, Cow, Dominate, Lick, Low-key, Master,
Mate, Mute, Quieten, Reduce, Refrain, Slow, Sober, Suppress, Tame, Under

Subject(s), **Subjection**, **Subject to** Amenable, Art, Bethrall, Caitive, Case, Citizen, Core, Cow, Enthrall, Gist, Hobby, Hobby-horse, Inflict, Liable, Liege(man), Matter, National, On, Overpower, PE, People, Poser, RE, RI, Serf, Servient, Servitude, Sitter, Slavery, Snool, Submit, Suit, > THEME, Thirl, Thrall, Topic, Under, Vassal

Sublime August, Empyreal, Grand, Great, Lofty, Majestic, Outstanding, Perfect, Porte, Splendid

Submarine Diver, Nautilus, Polaris, Sub, U-boat, Undersea

▷ **Submarine** *may indicate* a fish

Submerge(d) Dip, Dive, Drown, Embathe, Engulf, Imbathe, Lemuria, Overwhelm, Ria, Sink, Take, Whelm

Submissive, **Submit** Acquiesce, Bow, Capitulate, Comply, Defer, Docile, Knuckle, Meek, Obedient, Passive, Pathetic, Refer, Render, Resign, Snool, Stoop, Succumb, Truckle, > YIELD

Subordinate Adjunct, Dependent, Flunky, Inferior, Junior, Minion, Myrmidon, Offsider, Postpone, Secondary, Servient, Stooge, Subject, Subservient, Surrender, Under(ling), Underman, Under-strapper, Vassal

Subscribe(r), **Subscription** Approve, Assent, Conform, Due, Pay, Sign(atory), Signature, Undersign, Underwrite

Subsequent(ly) Anon, Consequential, Future, Later, Next, Postliminary, Since, Then

Subside, **Subsidence**, **Subsidy** Abate, Adaw, Aid, Assuage, Bonus, Diminish, Ebb, Grant, Sink, Sit, Swag

Substance, **Substantial** Ambergris, Antitoxin, Body, Cermet, Chalone, Chitin, Colloid, Considerable, Content, Ectoplasm, Elemi, Essential, Exudate, Fabric, Fixative, Getter, Gist, Gluten, Gossypol, Gravamen, Hearty, Hefty, Indol, Inhibitor, Isatin(e), Isomer, Linin, Material, Matter, Meaning, Meat(y), Mineral, Mole, Orgone, Polymer, Protyl(e), Quid, Reality, Resin, Sense, Solid, Stuff, Sum, Tangible

▶ **Substantial** *see* SUBSTANCE

Substitute, **Substitution** Acting, Change, Changeling, Commute, Creamer, Deputy, Emergency, Ersatz, -ette, Euphemism, Exchange, Fill-in, Improvise, Instead, Lieu(tenant), Locum, Makeshift, Pinch-hit, Proxy, Regent, Relieve, Replace, Represent, Reserve, Resolution, Ringer, Stand-in, Stead, Stopgap, Surrogate, Switch, Swop, Understudy, Vicarious

Subterfuge Artifice, Chicane, Evasion, Hole, Manoeuvre, Off-come, Ruse, Strategy, Trick

Subtle(ty) Abstruse, Alchemist, Crafty, Fine(spun), Finesse, Ingenious, Nice, Nice(ty), Refinement, Sly, Thin, Wily

Subtract(ion) Deduct, Discount, Take, Tithe, Withdraw

Suburb Environs, Exurbia, Outskirts, Purlieu

Subversion, **Subvert** Fifth column, Overthrow, Reverse, Sabotage, Sedition, Treasonous, Undermine, Upset

Succeed, **Success(ful)**, **Success(ful)** Accomplish, Achieve, Arrive, Blockbuster, Boffo, Breakthrough, Chartbuster, Contrive, Coup, Eclat, Effective, Efficacious, Fadge, Felicity, Flourish, Follow, Fortune, Gangbuster, Get, Go, Hit, Hotshot, Inherit, Killing, Landslide, Luck, Made, Manage, Masterstroke, Mega, Midas touch, Offcome, Pass, Prevail, Procure, Prosper, Purple patch, Reach, Replace, Riot, Score, Seal, Seel, Sele, Sell out, Soaraway, Socko, Speed, Stardom, Superstar, Sure thing, Tanistry, Triumph, Up, Up and coming, Upstart, Vault, Weather, W(h)iz(z)kid, Win, Wow, Wunderkind

Successor Co(m)arb, Deluge, Descendant, Ensuite, Epigon(e), Heir, Incomer, Inheritor, Khalifa, Next, Syen

Succulent Cactus, Echeveria, Juicy, Lush, Rich, Saguaro, Sappy, Spekboom, Tender, Toothy

Suck(er), Sucking Absorb, Aspirator, Ass, Dracula, Drink, Dupe, Fawn, Gnat, Graff, Graft, Gull, Hoove, Lamia, Lamprey, Leech, Liquorice, Mammal, Mouth, Mug, Patsy, Plunger, Shoot, Siphon, Slurp, Smarm, Swig, Sycophant, Toad-eater, Vampire

Sudden(ly) Abrupt, Astart, Astert, Extempore, Ferly, Fleeting, Foudroyant, Hasty, Headlong, Impulsive, Overnight, Rapid, Slap, Sodain, Subitaneous, Swap, Swop, Unexpected

Sue Ask, Beseech, Dun, Entreat, Implead, Implore, Petition, Pray, Process, Prosecute, Woo

Suffer(er), Suffering Abide, Aby(e), Ache, Affliction, Agonise, Auto, > BEAR, Brook, Calvary, Cop, Die, Distress, Dree, Endurance, Endure, Feel, Gethsemane, Golgotha, Grief, Hardship, Have, Incur, Let, Luit, Martyr, Pain, Passible, Passion, Passive, Patible, Patience, Pellagrin, Permit, Pine, Plague, Purgatory, Stand, Stomach, Sustain, Thole, Tolerate, Toll, Torment, Trial, Tribulation, Undergo, Use, Victim

Suffice, Sufficient Adequate, Ample, Basta, Do, Due, Enough, Enow, Satisfy, Serve

Suffocate Asphyxiate, Choke, Smother, Stifle, Strangle, Throttle

Sugar(y), Sugar cane Aldohexose, Aldose, Amygdalin, Arabinose, Barley, Beet, Blood, Brown, Candy, Cane, Caramel, Cassonade, Caster, Cellobiose, Cellose, Confectioner's, Daddy, Demerara, Deoxyribose, Dextrose, Disaccharide, Flattery, Fructose, Fucose, Furanose, Galactose, Gallise, Glucose, Glucosoric, Goo(r), Granulated, Grape, Gur, Heroin, Hexose, Honeydew, Hundreds and thousands, Iced, Icing, Inulin, Invert, Jaggary, Jaggery, Jagghery, Lactose, Laevulose, Loaf, Lump, Maltose, Manna, Mannose, Maple, Money, Monosaccharide, Muscovado, Nectar, Palm, Panocha, Pentose, Penuche, Raffinose, Rhamnose, Ribose, Saccharine, Saccharoid, Simple, Sis, Sorbose, Sorg(h)o, Sorghum, Sparrow, Spun, Sweet, Trehalose, Triose, White, Wood, Xylose

Suggest(ion), Suggestive Advance, Advice, Advise, Connote, Cue, Hint, Idea, Imply, Innuendo, Insinuate, Intimate, Mention, Modicum, Moot, Posit, Prompt, Proposal, Propound, Provocative, Racy, Raise, Recommend, Redolent, Reminiscent, Risqué, Smacks, Soft core, Suspicion, Touch, Trace

Suicide Felo-de-se, Hara-kiri, Hari-kari, Kamikaze, Lemming, Lethal, Sati, Seppuku, Suttee

Suit Action, Adapt, Adjust, Agree, Answer, Apply, Appropriate, Become, Befit, Beho(o)ve, Bequest, Birthday, Cards, Case, Cat, Clubs, Conform, Courtship, Demob, Diamonds, Dittos, Diving, Do, Dress, Etons, Fashion, Fit, G, Garb, Gee, Gree, Hearts, Hit, Jump, Lis pendens, Long, Lounge, Major, Mao, Match, Minor, Monkey, NBC, Noddy, Orison, Outcome, Paternity, Petition, Plaint, Play, Plea, Please, Point, Prayer, Pressure, Process, Pyjama, Quarterdeck, Queme, Romper(s), Safari, Sailor, Salopettes, Satisfy, Serve, Shell, Siren, Skeleton, Slack, Space, Spades, Strong, Sun, Sunday, Supplicat, Sweat, Swim, Tailleur, Three-piece, Track, Trouser, Trumps, Tsotsi, Twin, Two-piece, Uniform, Union, Wet, Zoot

Suitable Apposite, Appropriate, Apt, Becoming, Capable, Congenial, Consonant, Convenance, Convenient, Due, Expedient, > FIT, Keeping, Meet, Opportune, Relevant, Seemly, Worthy

Suite Allemande, Apartment, Chambers, Ensemble, Entourage, Hospitality, Lounge, Nutcracker, Partita, Retinue, Rooms, Serenade, Set, Tail, Three-piece, Train, Two-piece

Suitor Beau, Gallant, Lover, Petitioner, Pretender, Swain

Sulk(y), Sulkiness B(r)oody, Dod, Dort, Gee, Glout(s), Glower, Glum, Grouchy, Grouty, Grumps, Huff, Hump, Jinker, Mope, Mump, Pet, Pique, Pout, Spider, Strunt, Sullen

Sullen Dorty, Dour, Farouche, Glum(pish), Grim, Moody, Peevish, Stunkard, Sulky, Surly

Sully Assoil, Bedye, Besmirch, Blot, Defile, Glaur(y), Smear, Smirch, Soil, Tarnish, Tar-wash

Sultry Humid, Sexy, Smouldering, Steamy, Tropical

Sum(s), **Sum up** Add(end), Aggregate, All, Amount, Bomb, Encapsulate, Foot, Logical, Lump, Number, Perorate, > QUANTITY, Re-cap, Refund, Remittance, Reversion, Solidum, Total, Vector

Summarize, **Summary** Abridge, Abstract, Aperçu, Bird's eye, Brief, Compendium, Condense, Conspectus, Digest, Docket, Epitome, Gist, Instant, Minute, Offhand, Outline, Overview, Precis, Recap, Resume, Résumé, Round-up, Syllabus, Synopsis, Tabloid, Tabulate, Tabulation, Wrap-up

Summer(time) Aestival, August, BST, Computer, Estival, Indian, Lintel, Luke, Prime, St Luke's, St Martin's, Season, Solstice, Totter

Summit Acme, Acri-, Apex, Brow, Climax, Conference, > CREST, Crown, Height, Hillcrest, Jole, Peak, Pike, Pinnacle, Spire, Vertex, Vertical, Yalta

Summon(s) Accite, Arrière-ban, Azan, Beck(on), Call, Cist, Cital, Citation, Command, Convene, Drum, Evoke, Garnishment, Gong, Hail, Invocation, Muster, Order, Page, Post, Preconise, Rechate, Recheat, Reveille, Signal, Sist, Ticket, Warn, Warrant, Whoop, Writ

Sun(-god), **Sunlight**, **Sunny**, **Sunshine** Amen-Ra, Amon-Ra, Apollo, Aten, Bright, Cheer, Day(star), Dry, Earthshine, Glory, Heater, Helio(s), Helius, Horus, Mean, Midnight, New Mexico, Parhelion, Phoebean, Photosphere, Ra, Radiant, Rays, Re, Rising, Shamash, Sol(ar), Soleil, Sonne, Surya, Svastika, Swastika, Tabloid, Tan, Titan, UV

Sunblock Parasol

Sunder Divide, Divorce, Part, Separate, Sever, Split

▶ **Sun-god** *see* SUN

▶ **Sunken** *see* SINK

Sunshade Awning, Canopy, Parasol, Umbrella

Sup Dine, Eat, Feast, Sample, Sip, Swallow

Super A1, Arch, Extra, Fab(ulous), Great, Grouse, Ideal, Lulu, Paramount, Superb, Terrific, Tip-top, Tops, Walker-on, Wizard

Superb A1, Fine, Grand, Majestic, Splendid, Top-notch

Supercilious Aloof, Arrogant, Bashaw, Cavalier, Haughty, Lordly, Snide, Sniffy, Snooty, Snotty, Snouty, Superior

Superficial Cosmetic, Cursenary, Cursory, Exterior, Facile, Glib, Outside, Outward, Overlying, Perfunctory, Shallow, Sketchy, Skindeep, Smattering, Veneer

▷ **Superficial(ly)** *may indicate* a word outside another

Superfluous, **Superfluity** De trop, Extra, Lake, Mountain, Needless, Otiose, Redundant, Spare, Unnecessary

Superhuman Bionic, Herculean, Heroic, Supernatural

Superintend(ent) Boss, Director, Foreman, Guide, Janitor, Oversee(r), Preside, Sewer, Surveillant, Warden, Zanjero

Superior(ity) Abbess, Abeigh, Above, Advantage, Aloof, Atop, Better, Brahmin, Choice, Condescending, Custos, De luxe, Dinger, Eminent, Excellent, Exceptional, Finer, Herrenvolk, High-grade, Lake, Liege, Mastery, Morgue, Mother, Nob, Outstanding, Over, Paramount, Predominance, Prestige, Pretentious, Prior, Superordinate, Supremacy, Swell, Top(-loftical), Transcendent(al), U, Udal, Upper(most), Uppish, Upstage

Superlative Best, Exaggerated, Peerless, Supreme, Utmost

Supernatural Divine, Eerie, Fey, Fie, Fly, Gothic, Mana, Paranormal, Sharp, Siddhi, Unearthly

Supernumerary Additional, Corollary, Extra, Mute, Orra

Supersede Replace, Stellenbosch, Supplant

Supervise(d), Supervision, Supervisor Administer, Chaperone, Check, Direct, Engineer, Foreman, Grieve, Handle, Honcho, Invigilate, Manager, Officiate, Overman, Oversee(r), Probation, Shopwalker, Targe, Under, Walla(h)

Supper Dinner, > DRINK(ER), Hawkey, Hockey, Horkey, Last, Meal, Nagmaal, Repast, Soirée

Supplant Displace, Exchange, Replace, Substitute, Supersede

Supple Compliant, Leish, Limber, Lissom(e), Loose, Loose-limbed, Pliable, Souple, Wan(d)le, Wannel, Whippy

Supplement(ary) Addend(um), Addition, And, Annex(e), Appendix, Auxiliary, Colour, Eche, Eke, Extra, Paralipomena, Postscript, Relay, Ripienist, Ripieno, Weighting

Supplier, Supplies, Supply Accommodate, Advance, Afford, Cache, Cater, Commissariat, Contribute, Crop, Endue, Equip, Excess, Exempt, Feed, Fill, Find, Fit, Foison, Fund, Furnish, Give, Grist, Grubstake, Heel, Holp(en), Indue, Issue, Lend, Lithely, Mains, Materiel, Pipeline, Plenish, Ply, > PROVIDE, Provision, Purvey, RASC, Retailer, Serve, Source, Stake, Stock, > STORE, Viands, Vintner, Water, Widow's cruse, Yield

Support(er), Supporting Abet, Adherent, Advocate, Affirm, Aficionado, Aid, Ally, Ancillary, Andiron, Anta, Arch, Arm, Assistant, Axle, Back(bone), Back-up, Baluster, Banister, Bankroll, Barrack, Barre, Base, Batten, Beam, Bear, Befriend, Belt, Bier, Bolster, Boom, Bra, Brace, Bracket, Brassiere, Breadwinner, Bridge, Buttress, C(ee)-spring, Chair, Champion, Clientele, Column, Confirm, Console, Cornerstone, Countenance, Cradle, Cross-beam, Crutch, Dado, Doula, Easel, Encourage, Endorse, Endow, Engager, Espouse, Family, Fan, Favour, Fid, Finance, Flying buttress, Fly-rail, Footrest, Footstool, For, Gamb, Gantry, Garter, Girder, Groundswell, Headrest, Help, Henchman, Impost, Income, Jack, Jockstrap, Joist, Keep, Kingpost, Knee, Lectern, Leg, Lifebelt, Lifebuoy, Lobby, Loyalist, Mainstay, Maintain, Makefast, Miserere, Misericord(e), Moral, -nik, Nourish, Partisan, Partners, Patronage, Pedestal, Pier, Pillar, Pin, Plinth, Poppet, Post, Potent, Price, Prop, Proponent, PTA, Pull-for, Pylon, Raft, Rally round, Reinforce, Relieve, Respond, Rest, Rind, Rod, Root, Royalist, Samaritan, Sanction, Sawhorse, Second, Shore, Skeg, Skeleton, Skid, Sleeper, Sling, Socle, Solidarity, Splat, Splint, Sponson, Sprag, Spud, Staddle, Staddlestone, Staff, Staging, Stake, Stalwart, Stanchion, Stand(-by), Stay, Steady, Step, Stick, Stirrup, Stool, Stringer, Strut, Subscribe, Subsidy, Succour, Summer, Suspender, Sustain, Tee, Tendril, Third, Tie, Tige, Torsel, Trestle, Tripod, Trivet, Truss, Underlay, Underpin, Understand, Uphold, Upkeep, Viva, Waterwings, Zealot

Suppose(d), Supposition An, Assume, Believe, Expect, Guess, Hypothetical, Idea, If, Imagine, Imply, Opine, Presume, Putative, Sepad, Theory

Suppository Pessary

Suppress(ion) Abolish, Adaw, Burke, Cancel, Censor, Clampdown, Crush, Ecthlipsis, Elide, Elision, Gleichschaltung, Mob(b)le, Quash, Quell, Quench, Restrain, Silence, Smother, Squash, Stifle, Submerge, Subreption

Supreme, Supremacy, Supremo Baaskap, Caudillo, Consummate, Kronos, Leader, Napoleon, Overlord, Paramount, Peerless, Regnant, Sovereign, Sublime, Sudder, Top, Utmost

Sure(ly) Assured, Ay, Bound, Cert(ain), Confident, Definite, Doubtless, Firm, Know, Pardi(e), Pardy, Perdie, Positive, Poz, Safe, Secure, Shoo-in, Sicker, Syker, Uh-huh, Yes

Surety Bail, Guarantee, Mainprise, Security, Sponsional

Surface Aerofoil, Appear, Area, Arise, Camber, Control, Day, Dermal, Dermis, Emerge, Epigene, Exterior, External, Face, Facet, Flock, Macadam, Meniscus, Outcrop, Outward, Paintwork, Patina, Pave, Plane, Reveal, Rise, Salband, Side, Skin, Soffit, Spandrel, Superficial, Superficies, Tarmac®, Tar-seal, Texture, Top, Toroid, Worktop

Surfeit(ed) Blasé, Cloy, Excess, Glut, Overcloy, Plethora, Satiate, Stall, Staw

Surge Billow, Boom, Drive, Gush, Onrush, Seethe, Sway, Swell

Surgeon Abernethy, BCh, BS, CHB, CM, Doctor, Lister, Medic, Operator, Orthopod, Plastic, Sawbones, Tang, Vet(erinary)

Surgery Anaplasty, Cosmetic, Facelift, Keyhole, Knife, Laparotomy, Laser, Medicine, Nip and tuck, Nose job, Op, Open-heart, Osteoplasty, Plastic, Prosthetics, Reconstructive, Repair, Spare-part, Zolatrics

Surly Bluff, Cantankerous, Chough, Chuffy, Churl(ish), Crusty, Cynic, Glum, Gruff, Grum, Grumpy, Rough, Sullen, Truculent

Surpass Bang, Beat, Best, Cap, Ding, Eclipse, Efface, Exceed, Excel, Outdo, Outgun, Out-Herod, Outshine, Outstrip, Overtop, Transcend

Surplus Excess, Extra, Glut, Lake, Mountain, Out-over, Over, Overcome, Remainder, Rest, Spare, Surfeit

Surprise(d), Surprising Alert, Amaze, Ambush, Astonish, Bewilder, Blimey, Bombshell, By Jove, Caramba, Catch, Confound, Coo, Cor, Crikey, Criminé, Cripes, Dear, Eye-opener, Gadso, Gee, Geewhiz, Gemini, Gobsmacked, Golly, Good-lack, Gorblimey, Gordon Bennett, Gosh, Ha, Hah, Hallo, Heavens, Heck, Heh, Hello, Hey, Ho, Jeepers, Jeez(e), Law, Lawks, Lor, Lordy, Lummy, Marry, Musha, My, Och, Odso, Omigod, Oops, Open-mouthed, Overtake, Phew, Pop-eyed, Really, Sheesh, Shock, Singular, Spot, Stagger, Startle, Strewth, Stun, Sudden, Treat, Turn-up, Uh, Whew, Whoops, Wonderment, Wow, Wrongfoot, Yikes, Yow, Zowie

Surrender Capitulate, Cave-in, Cession, Enfeoff, Extradite, Fall, Forego, Forfeit, Handover, Hulled, Recreant, Release, Relinquish, Submit, Succumb, Waive, > YIELD

Surround(ed), Surrounding(s) Ambient, Architrave, Background, Bathe, Bego, Beset, Bundwall, Circumvallate, Circumvent, Compass, Doughnutting, Ecology, Embail, Encase, > ENCIRCLE, Enclave, Enclose, Encompass, Enfold, Environ, Enwrap, Fence, Gherao, Gird, Hedge, Impale, Invest, Mid, Orb, Orle, Outflank, Outside, Perimeter, Setting, Wall

Surveillance, Survey(ing), Surveyor Behold, Cadastre, Case, Conspectus, Domesday, Doomwatch, Espial, Examination, Eye, Geodesy, Groma, Look-see, Once-over, Ordnance, Poll, Recce, Reconnaissance, Regard, Review, Scan, Scrutiny, Stakeout, Straw poll, Supervision, Terrier, Theodolite, Triangulate, Vigil, Watch

Survival, Survive, Surviving, Survivor Cope, Die hard, Endure, Extant, Finalist, Hibakusha, Last, Leftover, Outlast, Outlive, Overlive, Persist, Relic(t), Ride, Weather

Suspect, Suspicion, Suspicious Askance, Breath, Dodgy, Doubt, Dubious, Fishy, Grain, Guess, Hint, Hunch, Jalouse, Jealous, Leery, Misdeem, Misdoubt, Misgiving, Mistrust, Modicum, Notion, Paranoia, Queer, Scent, Smatch, Soupçon, Thought, Tinge, Whiff

▷ **Suspect, Suspicious** *may indicate* an anagram

Suspend(ed), Suspense, Suspension Abate, Abeyance, Adjourn, Anti-shock, Cliffhanger, Colloid, Dangle, Defer, Delay, Dormant, Freeze, Ground, > HANG, Hydraulic, Independent, Intermit, Mist, Moratorium, Nailbiter, Pensile, Poise, Prorogue, Put on ice, Reprieve, Respite, Rub out, Rusticate, Sideline, Sol, Stand off, Swing, Tenterhooks, Truce, Withhold

▷ **Suspended** *may indicate* 'ice' (on ice) at the end of a down light

Sustain(ed), **Sustaining**, **Sustenance** Abide, Aliment, Bear, Constant, Depend, Endure, Food, Keep, Last, Maintain, Nutriment, Pedal, Prolong, Sostenuto, Succour, Support

Suture Lambda, Pterion, Stitch

Swab Dossil, Dry, Mop, Pledget, Scour, Sponge, Squeegee, Stupe, Tampon, Tompon, Wipe

Swagger(er), **Swaggering** Birkie, Bluster, Boast, Brag, Bragadisme, Bravado, Bucko, Cock, Crow, Jaunty, Matamore, Nounce, Panache, Pra(u)nce, Roist, Roll, Rollick, Roul, Royster, Ruffle, Side, Strive, Swank, Swash(-buckler)

Swallow(able), **Swallowing** Barn, Bird, Bolt, Consume, Devour, Down, Drink, Eat, Endue, Engulf, Esculent, Glug, Gobble, Gulp, Incept, Ingest, Ingulf, Ingurgitate, Itys, Lap, Martin, Martlet, Progne, Quaff, Shift, Sister, Slug, Stomach, Swig, Take

Swamp(y) Bog, Bunyip, Cowal, Deluge, Dismal, Drown, Engulf, Everglade, Flood, Inundate, Lentic, Lerna, Lerne, Loblolly, Mar(i)sh, Morass, Muskeg, Overrun, Overwhelm, Paludal, Quagmire, Slash, Slough, Sudd, Vlei, Vly

▷ **Swap(ped)** *may indicate* an anagram

Swarm(ing) Abound, Alive, Bike, Bink, Byke, Cast, Cloud, Crowd, Flood, Geminid, Host, Hotter, Infest, Pullulate, Rife, Shin, Shoal, Throng

Sway(ing) Careen, Carry, Command, Diadrom, Domain, Dominion, Flap, Fluctuate, Govern, Hegemony, Influence, Lilt, Oscillate, Prevail, Reel, Reign, Rock, Roll, Rule, Shog, Shoogle, Swag, Swale, Swee, Swing(e), Teeter, Titter, Totter, Vacillate

Swear(ing), **Swear word** Attest, Avow, Coprolalia, Curse, Cuss, Depose, Execrate, Jurant, Juratory, Oath, Pledge, Plight, Rail, Sessa, Tarnal, Tarnation, Verify, Vow

Sweat(ing), **Sweaty** Apocrine, Clammy, Diaphoresis, Excrete, Exude, Forswatt, Glow, Hidrosis, Lather, Ooze, Osmidrosis, Secretion, Slave, Stew, Sudament, Sudamina, Sudate, Swelter

Sweater Aran, Argyle, Circassian, Circassienne, Cowichan, Fair Isle, Gansey, Guernsey, Indian, Jersey, Polo, Pullover, Roll-neck, Siwash, Skivvy, Slip-on, Slop-pouch, Sloppy Joe, Turtleneck, Woolly

Sweep(er), **Sweeping(s)** Besom, Broad, Broom, Brush, Chimney, Chummy, Clean, Curve, Debris, Detritus, Expanse, Extensive, Lash, Lottery, Net, Oars, Pan, Phasing, Range, Scavenger, Scud, Sling, Snowball, Soop, Street, Stroke, Surge, Swathe, Vacuum, Waft, Well, Wide

Sweet(s), **Sweetener**, **Sweetmeat**, **Sweetness** Adeline, Afters, Barley sugar, Bombe, Bonbon, Bonus, Brandyball, Bribe, Bull's eye, Burnt-almonds, Butterscotch, Candy, Candyfloss, Caramel, Charity, Charming, Cherubic, Choc(olate), Choccy, Cloying, Coconut ice, Comfit, Confect(ion), Confetti, Confit, Conserve, Crème, Cute, Dolce, Dolly, Dolly mixture, Douce(t), Dragée, Dulcet, Dulcitude, Flummery, Fondant, Fool, Fragrant, Fresh, Fudge, Glycerin, Gob-stopper, Goody, Gum(drop), Hal(a)vah, Halva, Honey(ed), Humbug, Hundreds and thousands, Ice, Jelly baby, Jelly bean, Jube, Jujube, Kiss, Lavender, Lemon drop, Licorice, Liquorice, Lollipop, Lolly, Lozenge, Luscious, Marshmallow, Marzipan, Melodious, Mint, Mousse, Muscavado, Nectared, Noisette, Nonpareil, Nougat, Pandrop, Pastille, Pea, Peardrop, Pet, Pick'n'mix, Pie, Praline, Pud(ding), Redolent, Rock, Seventeen, Sillabub, Sixteen, Soot(e), Sop, Sorbet, Spice, Split, Stickjaw, Sucker, Sucrose, Sugar, Sugarplum, Syllabub, Syrupy, Tablet, Taffy, Tart, Toffee, Torte, Trifle, Truffle, Turkish delight, Twee, Uses, William, Winsome, Zabaglione

Sweetheart Amoret, Amour, Beau, Dona(h), Dowsabel(l), Doxy, Dulcinea, Flame, Follower, Honey(bunch), Honeybun, Jarta, Jo(e), Lass, Leman, Lover, Masher, Neaera, Peat, Romeo, Steady, Toots(y), True-love, Valentine, Yarta, Yarto

Swell(ing) Adenomata, Ague-cake, Anasarca, Aneurysm, Apophysis, Bag, Bellying, Berry, Billow, Blab, Blister, Bloat, Blow, Boil, Boll, Bolster, Botch, Braw, Bubo, Bulb, Bulge, Bump, Bunion, Capellet, Cat, Chancre, Chilblain, Cratches, Cyst, Dandy, Diapason, Dilate, Dom, Don, Eger, Elephantiasis, Enhance, Entasis, Epulis, Excellent, Farcy-bud, Frog, Gall, Gathering, Gent, Goiter, Goitre, Gout, Grandee, Ground, H(a)ematoma, Heave, Heighten, Hove, Hydrocele, Increase, Inflate, Intumesce, Kibe, L, Lampas(se), Lampers, Lump, Macaroni, Mouse, Nodule, Odontoma, Oedema, OK, Onco-, Ox-warble, Parotitis, Plim, Plump, Protrude, Proud, Pulvinus, Rise, Roil, Scirrhus, Scleriasis, Sea, Strout, Struma, Stye, Surge, Teratoma, Toff, Tuber(cle), Tumour, Tympany, Upsurge, Venter, Warble, Wen, Whelk, Windgall, Xanthoma

▷ **Swelling** *may indicate* a word reversed

Swerve, Swerving Bias, Broach, Careen, Deflect, Deviate, Lean, Sheer, Shy, Stray, Swing, Warp, Wheel

Swift(ly) Apace, Bird, Dean, Dromond, Fleet, Flock, Hasty, Martlet, Newt, Nimble, Presto, Prompt, Quick, > RAPID, Slick, Spanking, Velocipede, Wight

▷ **Swilling** *may indicate* an anagram

Swim(ming) Bathe, Bogey, Bogie, Crawl, Dip, Float, Naiant, Natatorial, Paddle, Reel, Run, Skinny-dip, Soom, Synchro(nized), Trudgen, Whirl

▷ **Swim** *may indicate* an anagram

▷ **Swimmer** *may indicate* a fish

Swindle(r) Beat, Bunco, Cajole, Champerty, > CHEAT, Con, Defraud, Diddle, Do, Escroc, Fiddle, Finagle, Fleece, Fraud, Gazump, Gip, Graft, Grifter, Gyp, Hocus, Hustler, Leg, Leger, Mulct, Nobble, Peter Funk, Plant, Racket, Ramp, Rig, Rogue, Scam, Sell, Shark, Sharper, Shicer, Shyster, Skin, Sting, Stitch-up, Suck, Swiz(z), Trick, Twist, Two-time

Swing(er), Swinging Colt, Dangle, Flail, Hang, Hep, Kip(p), Lilt, Metronome, Mod, Music, Oscillate, Pendulate, Pendulum, Rock, Rope, Shoogie, Shuggy, Slew, Swale, Sway, Swee, Swerve, Swey, Swipe, Trapeze, Vibratile, Voop, Wave, Wheel, Whirl, Yaw

▷ **Swirling** *may indicate* an anagram

Switch(ed), Switches, Switching Birch, Change, Convert, Crossbar, Cryotron, Dimmer, Dip, Exchange, Gang, Hairpiece, Knife, Legerdemain, Mercury, Message, Pear, Replace, Retama, Rocker, Rod, Scutch, Thyristor, Time, Toggle, Trip, Tumbler, Twig, Wave, Zap

▷ **Switched** *may indicate* an anagram

Swivel Caster, Pivot, Root, Rotate, Spin, Terret, Territ, Torret, Turret, Wedein

Swollen Blown, Bollen, Bulbous, Full, Gourdy, Gouty, Incrassate, Nodose, Puffy, Tumid, Turgescent, Turgid, Varicose, Ventricose, Vesiculate

Swoon Blackout, Collapse, Dwa(l)m, Dwaum, Faint

▶ **Swop** *see* SWAP

Sword(-like), Swordplay Andrew Ferrara, Anelace, Angurvadel, Anlace, Arondight, Assegai, Balisarda, Balmung, Bilbo, Blade, Brand, Brandiron, Broad(sword), Brondyron, Cemitare, Claymore, Court, Curtal-ax, Curtana, Curtax, Cutlass, Damascene, Damocles, Dance, Dirk, Dance, Ensiform, Epée, Espada, Estoc, Excalibur, Falchion, Faulchi(o)n, Foil, Gladius, Glaive, Gleave, Glorious, Hanger, Iai-do, Jacob's staff, Joyeuse, Katana, Kendo, Khanda, Kirpan, Kreese, Kris, Kukri, Machete, Morglay, Parang, Rapier, Sabre, Samurai, Schiavone, Schlager, Scimitar, Semita(u)r, Shabble, Shamshir, Sharp, Sigh, Simi, Skene-dhu, Smallsword, Spadroon, Spirtle, Spit, Spurtle(blade), Steel, Toledo, Tulwar, Two-edged, Whinger, Whiniard, Whinyard, White-arm, Yatag(h)an

Sycophant(ic) Brown-nose, Claqueur, Crawler, Creeper, Fawner, Lickspittle, Parasite, Toad-eater, Toady, Yesman

Syllable(s) Acatalectic, Anacrusis, Aretinian, Om, Tonic

Syllabus Program(me), Prospectus, Résumé, Summary, Table

Symbol(ic), **Symbols**, **Symbolism**, **Symbolist** Agma, Algebra, Allegory, Ampersand, Ankh, Asterisk, Badge, Cachet, Caret, Cedilla, Character, Chord, Cipher, Clef, Colon, Decadent, Del, Diesis, Dingbat, Eagle, Emblem, Equal, Fertility, Grammalogue, Hash, Hieroglyph, Icon, Iconography, Ideogram, Index, Lexigram, Logo(gram), Mark, Metaphor, Minus, Moral, Motif, Mystical, Neum(e), Nominal, Notation, Obelus, Om, Pentacle, Phonetic, Phonogram, Pi, Plus, Rose, Rune, Segno, Semicolon, Shamrock, Sign, Slur, Status, Swastika, Syllabary, Synthetism, Tag, Talisman, Thistle, Tiki, Tilde, Token, Totem, Trademark, Triskele, Type, Wild card

Symmetric(al), **Symmetry** Balance, Digonal, Diphycercal, Even, Harmony, Isobilateral, Radial, Regular

Sympathetic, **Sympathise(r)**, **Sympathy** Approval, Commiserate, Compassion, Condole(nce), Condone, Congenial, Crypto, Empathy, Fellow-traveller, Humane, Par, Pity, Rapport, Ruth, Side, Vicarious

Symphony Concert, Eroica, Fifth, Jupiter, Manfred, Music, New World, Opus, Pastoral, Sinfonia, Unfinished

Symptom(s) Epiphenomenon, Feature, Indicia, Merycism, Mimesis, Prodrome, Semiotic, Sign, Syndrome, Token, Trait, Withdrawal

Syncopated, **Syncopation**, **Syncope** Abridged, Breakbeat, Revamp, Zoppa, Zoppo

Syndrome Adams-Stokes, Asperger's, Carpal tunnel, Cerebellar, Characteristic, China, Chronic fatigue, Compartment, Cri du chat, Crush, Cushing's, Down's, Empty nest, Fetal alcohol, Fragile X, Goldenhar's, Gorlin, Guillain-Barré, Gulf War, Hutchinson-Gilford, Jerusalem, Klinefelter's, Korsakoff's, Locked-in, Marfan, ME, Menières, Munch(h)ausen's, Nonne's, Overuse, Pattern, POS, Postviral, Prader-Willi, Premenstrual, Proteus, Reiter's, Reye's, SARS, Sezary, Sick building, Sjogren's, Stevens-Johnson, Stockholm, Stokes-Adams, Sturge-Weber, Tall-poppy, Temperomandibular, TMJ, Tourette's, Toxic shock, Turner's, Wag the Dog, Wernicke-Korsakoff, Wobbler, XYY

Synopsis Abstract, Blurb, Conspectus, Digest, Outline, Résumé, Schema, > SUMMARY

Synthetic Ersatz, Fake, False, Mock, Polyamide, Spencerian

Syringe(s) Douche, Flutes, Harpoon, Hypo, Needle, Reeds, Spray, Squirt, Wash

Syrup Cassis, Corn, Flattery, Grenadine, Linctus, Maple, Molasses, Orgeat, Rob, Sugar, Treacle

System(s), **Systematic** ABO, An mo, Binary, Braille, Code, Compander, Continental, Cosmos, Course, Crystal, Decimal, Dewey (Decimal), Distributed, Early warning, Economy, Eocene, Establishment, Expert, Feudal, Formal, Grading, Harvard, HLA, Immune, Imprest, Imputation, Inertial, Kalamazoo, Life-support, Limbic, Linear, Loop, Lymphatic, Madras, Merit, > METHOD, Metric, Midi, Nervous, Network, Nicam, Notation, Octal, Operating, Order, Organon, Panel, Periodic, Plenum, Points, Process, Purchase, Quota, Realtime, Regime, Regular, Respiratory, Root, Scheme, Scientific, Servo, SI, Sofar, Solar, Sonar, Sound, Spoils, Sprinkler, Squish lip, Stack(ing), Staff, Star, Structure, Studio, Tally, Ternary, Theory, Tommy, Touch, Truck, Turnkey, Tutorial, Two-party, Universe, Vestibular, Warehousing, Water, Weapon

Tt

Table(-like) Altar, Board, Bradshaw, Breakfast, Calendar, > **CHART**, Coffee, Console, Counter, Decision, Desk, Diagram, Dinner, Draw-leaf, Draw-top, Dressing, Drop-leaf, Drum, Experience, Food, Gateleg, Glacier, Graph, Green-cloth, High, Imposing, Index, Key, League, Life, Light, > **LIST**, Lord's, Mahogany, Matrix, Mensa(l), Mesa, Mortality, Multiplication, Occasional, Operating, Pembroke, Periodic, Piecrust, Pier, Plane, Platen, Pool, Pythagoras, Reckoner, Refectory, Roll, Round, Sand, Schedule, Scheme, Slab, Sofa, Spoon, Stall, Statistical, Stone, Tea, Te(a)poy, Tide, Times, Toilet, Trestle, Trolley, Truth, Twelve, Washstand, Water, Whirling, Wool, Workbench, Writing

Tablet Abacus, Album, Aspirin, Caplet, Eugebine, Medallion, Opisthograph, Osculatory, Ostracon, Ostrakon, > **PAD**, > **PILL**, Plaque, Slate, Stele, Stone, Tombstone, Torah, Triglyph, Triptych, Troche, Trochisk, Ugarit

Taboo, Tabu Ban(ned), Bar, Blackball, Forbidden, No-no

Tachograph Spy-in-the-cab

Tack(y) Baste, Beat, Brass, Cinch, Clubhaul, Cobble, Gybe, Leg, Martingale, Nail, Saddlery, Salt-horse, > **SEW**, Sprig, Stirrup, Veer, White-seam, Yaw, Zigzag

Tackle Accost, Approach, Attempt, Beard, Bobstay, Burton, Claucht, Claught, Clevis, Collar, Dead-eye, Garnet, Gear, Haliard, Halyard, Harness, Jury-rig, Rig, Rigging, Scrag

Tact, Tactful Delicacy, Diplomacy, Diplomatic, Discreet, Discretion, Politic, Savoir-faire

Tactic(s) Audible, Hardball, Manoeuvre, Masterstroke, Plan, Ploy, Salami, Shock, > **STRATEGY**, Strong-arm

Tactless(ness) Blundering, Brash, Crass, Gaffe, Gauche, Indelicate

Tail, Tailpiece > **APPENDAGE**, Bob, Brush, Caudal, Coda, Colophon, Cue, Dock, Fan, Fee, > **FOLLOW**, Fud, Liripoop, Parson's nose, Pole, Pope's nose, PS, Queue, Scut, Seat, Stag, Stern, Telson, > **TIP**, Train, Women

Tailor(ed) Bespoke, Bushel, Cabbager, Couturier, Cutter, Darzi, Durzi, Epicene, Feeble, Nine, Outfitter, Pick-the-louse, Pricklouse, Sartor, Seamster, Snip, Starveling, Style, Whipcat, Whipstitch

▷ **Tailor** *may indicate* an anagram

Taint(ed) Besmirch, Blemish, Fly-blown, High, Infect, Leper, Off, Poison, > **SPOIL**, Stain, Stigma, Trace, Unwholesome

Take(n), Take in, Taking(s), Take over Absorb, > **ACCEPT**, Adopt, Assume, Attract, Bag, Beg, Bite, Bone, Borrow, Bottle, > **CAPTURE**, Catch, Claim, Cop, Coup, Detract, Dishy, Entr(y)ism, Exact, Expropriate, Get, Grab, Handle, Haul, Hent, House, Howe, Huff, Incept, Ingest, Mess, Misappropriate, Nick, Occupy, Pocket, Quote, R, Rec, Receipt, Receive, Recipe, Reverse, Rob, Seise, Sequester, Ship, Smitten, Snatch, Sneak, > **STEAL**, Stomach, Subsume, Swallow, Sweet, Swipe, Toll, Trump, Turnover, Usher, Usurp, Wan, Winsome, Wrest

▷ **Taken up** *may indicate* reversed

Tale(s) Allegory, Blood, Conte, Decameron, Edda, Fable, Fabliau, Fairy, Fiction, Gag, Geste, Hadith, Iliad, Jataka, Jeremiad, Legend, Lie, Mabinogion, Maise,

Ma(i)ze, Marchen, Narrative, Odyssey, Rede, Saga, Score, Sinbad, Spiel, > **STORY**, Tradition, Traveller's, Weird

Talent(ed) Accomplishment, Aptitude, Bent, Dower, Faculty, Flair, Genius, Gift, Knack, Nous, Prodigy, Schtick, Strong point, Versatile, Virtuoso, W(h)iz(z), Whiz-kid

Talk(ing), **Talking point**, **Talker**, **Talks** Ana, Articulate, Babble, Blab, Blat, Blather, Blether-skate, Cant, Chalk, Chat, Chinwag, Chirp, Commune, Confer, Converse, Coo, Cross, Descant, Dialog(ue), Diatribe, Dilate, Discourse, Diseur, Dissert, Double, Earbash, Earful, Express, Fast, Froth, Gab, Gabble, Gabnash, Gas, Gibber, Gossip, Guff, Harp, Imparl, Jabber, Jargon, Jaw, Jazz, Lip, Mang, Maunder, Mince, Monologue, Nashgab, Natter, Noise, Palaver, Parlance, Parley, Patter, Pawaw, Pep, Pidgin, Pillow, Pitch, Potter, Powwow, Prate, Prattle, Presentation, Prose, Proximity, Ramble, Rap, Rigmarole, Rote, SALT, Shop, Slang(-whang), Small, Soliloquy, > **SPEAK**, Spiel, Spout, Straight, Sweet, Table, Tachylogia, Topic, Turkey, Twaddle, Twitter, Up(s), Utter, Vocal, Waffle, Witter, Wrangle, Yabber, Yack, Yak, Yalta, Yammer, Yap, Yatter

Talkative Chatty, Fluent, Gabby, Garrulous, Gash, Glib, Loquacious, Vocular, Voluble

Tall Etiolated, Exaggerated, Hie, High, Hye, Lanky, Lathy, Leggy, Lofty, Long, Procerity, Randle-tree, Tangle, Taunt, Tower, Towery

Tally > **AGREE**, Census, Correspond, Count, Match, Nickstick, Notch, Record, > **SCORE**, Stick, Stock, Tab, Tag

Tame Amenage, Break, Docile, Domesticate, Mansuete, Meek, Mild, Safe, Snool, Subdue

Tamper(ing) Bishop, Cook, Doctor, Fake, Fiddle, Meddle, Medicate, Monkey, Nobble, Phreaking

Tan(ned), **Tanned skin**, **Tanning** Adust, Bablah, Babul, Bark, Basil, Beige, Bisque, Bronze, > **BROWN**, Catechu, Insolate, Lambast, Leather, Neb-neb, Paste, Pipi, Puer, Pure, Spank, Sun, Tenné, Umber, Val(l)onia, Valonea, Ybet

Tangle Alga, Badderlock, Burble, Dulse, Embroil, Entwine, Fank, Fankle, Heap, Implication, Ket, > **KNOT**, Labyrinth, Laminaria, Lutin, Mat, Mix, Nest, Oarweed, Ore, Perplex, Pleach, Sea-girdle, Seaweed, Skean, Skein, Snarl, Taigle, Taut(it), Tawt, Thicket, Varec

▷ **Tangled** *may indicate* an anagram

Tank Abrams, Alligator, Amphibian, Aquarium, Belly, Casspir, Centurion, Cesspool, Challenger, Chieftain, Cistern, Drop, Feedhead, Float, Flotation, Gasholder, Header, Keir, Kier, Panzer, Pod, Quiescent, > **RESERVOIR**, Ripple, Sedimentation, Septic, Sherman, Shield pond, Sponson, Sump, Surge, Think, Tiger, Vat, Ventral, Vivarium

Tantalise Entice, Tease, Tempt, Torture

Tantrum Paddy, Pet, Rage, Scene, Tirrivee, Tirrivie

Tap(ping), **Taps** Accolade, Blip, Broach, Bug, Cock, Drum, Faucet, Flick, Hack, Mixer, Paracentesis, Pat, Patter, Percuss, Petcock, > **RAP**, Spigot, Stopcock, Tack, Tat, Tit

Tape Chrome, DAT, > **DRINK**, Duct, Ferret, Finish, Gaffer, Grip, Idiot, Incle, Inkle, Insulating, Magnetic, Masking, Measure, Metal, Narrowcast, Paper, Passe-partout, Perforated, Punched, Record, Red, Scotch, Sellotape®, Shape, Sticky, Ticker, Video, Welding

Taper(ed), **Tapering** Diminish, Fastigiate, Featheredge, Fusiform, Lanceolate, Narrow, Nose, Subulate, Tail

Tapestry Alentous, Arras(ene), Bayeux, Bergamot, Crewel-work, Dosser, Gobelin, Hanging, Oudenarde, Tapet

Target > **AIM**, Blank, Butt, Clout, Cockshy, Dart, Drogue, End, Hit, Home, Hub,

Inner, Magpie, Mark, Motty, > **OBJECT**, Outer, Pelta, Pin, Prey, Prick, Quintain, Sitter, Sitting, Tee, Victim, Wand

Tarry Bide, Dally, Leng, > **LINGER**, Stay, Sticky

Tartar Argal, Argol, Beeswing, Crust, Hell, Plaque, Rough, Scale, Tam(b)erlane, Zenocrate

Task Assignment, Aufgabe, Duty, Errand, Exercise, Fag, Imposition, Mission, Ordeal, Stint, Thankless, Vulgus

Taste(ful), Taster, Tasty Acquired, Aesthetic, Appetite, Degust, Delibate, Delicious, Discrimination, > **EAT**, Fashion, Flavour, Form, Gout, Gust, Gustatory, Hint, Lekker, Lick, Palate, Penchant, Pica, Pree, Refinement, Relish, > **SAMPLE**, Sapor, Sar, Savour, S(c)hme(c)k, Sip, Smack, Smatch, Snack, Soupçon, Stomach, Succulent, Tang, Titbit, Toothsome, > **TRY**, Vertu, Virtu, Wine

Tasteless Appal, Fade, Flat, Insipid, Stale, Vapid, Vulgar, Watery, Wearish, Wersh

Tattle(r) Blab, Chatter, > **GOSSIP**, Prate, Rumour, Sneak, Snitch, Totanus, Willet

Taunt Dig, Fling, Gibe, Gird, > **JEER**, Rag, Ridicule, Twight, Twit

Tavern Bar, Bodega, Bousing-ken, Bush, Fonda, > **INN**, Kiddleywink, Kneipe, Mermaid, Mitre, Mughouse, Pothouse, Shebeen, Taphouse

Tawdry Catchpenny, > **CHEAP**, Flashy, Gaudy, Sleazy, Tatty

Tax(ing), Taxation ACT, Agist, Aid, Alms-fee, Assess, Capitation, Carbon, Cense, Cess, > **CHARGE**, Corporation, Council, Custom, Danegeld, Direct, Duty, Energy, EPT, Escot, Escuage, Exact, Excise, EZT, Geld, Gift, Head, Impose, Imposition, Impost, Impute, Indirect, Inheritance, IR, Land, Levy, Lot, Negative, Octroi, Operose, Overwork, PAYE, Poll, Poundage, Primage, Property, Proportional, PT, Punish, Purchase, Rate, Regressive, Road, Sales, Scat(t), Scot (and lot), Scutage, Sess, SET, Sin, Single, Skat, Stealth, Stent, Stumpage, Super, Tariff, Task, Teind, Tithe, Tobin, Toilsome, Toll, Tonnage, Tribute, Try, Turnover, Unitary, Value-added, VAT, Wattle, Wealth, Weary, White rent, Windfall, Window, Withholding

Tax-collector, Taxman Amildar, Cheater, Exciseman, Farmer, Gabeller, Inspector, IR(S), Publican, Stento(u)r, Tithe-proctor, Tollman, Undertaker, Zemindar

Tea Afternoon, Assam, Beef, Black, Bohea, Brew, Brick, Bush, Cambric, Camomile, Caper, Ceylon, Cha, Chamomile, Chanoyu, China, Chirping-cup, Congo(u), Cream, Cuppa, Darjeeling, Earl Grey, Grass, Green, Gunfire, Gunpowder, Herb(al), High, Hyson, Indian, Jasmine, K(h)at, Kitchen, Labrador, Lapsang, Lapsang Souchong, Leaves, Ledum, Lemon, Malt, Manuka, Marijuana, Maté, Mexican, Mint, Morning, New Jersey, Oolong, Orange pekoe, Oulong, Paraguay, Pekoe, Post and rail, Pot, Qat, Red-root, Rooibos, Rosie Lee, Russian, Senna, Souchong, Stroupach, Stroupan, Switchel, Tay, Thea, Theophylline, Twankay, Yerba (de Maté)

Teach(er), Teaching (material), Teachings Adjoint, Agrege, Apostle, Beale, BEd, Buss, > **COACH**, Con(ne), Didactic, Doctrine, Dogma, Dominie, Dressage, Edify, > **EDUCATE**, Educationalist, Edutainment, Explain, Faculty, Froebel, Gospel, Governess, Guru, Head, Inculcate, Indoctrinate, Inform, Instil, Instruct, Ism, Kumon (Method), Lair, Lear(e), Lecturer, Leir, Lere, Maam, Magister, Marker, Marm, Master, Mentor, Miss, Mistress, Molla(h), Monitor, Mufti, Mullah, Munshi, Nuffield, Pedagogue, Pedant, Pr(a)efect, Preceptor, Proctor, Prof, Prog, PT, Pupil, Rabbi, Rebbe, Remedial, Rhetor, Scholastic, Schoolman, Scribe, Show, Sir, Socrates, Sophist, Staff, Sunna, Supply, Swami, Tantra, Team, Train(er), Tutelage, Tutor, Usher

Team Colts, Crew, Dream, Ecurie, Eleven, Equipe, Fifteen, Outfit, Oxen, Panel, Possibles, Relay, Scrub, > **SIDE**, Span, Squad, Squadron, Staff, Troupe, Turnout, Unicorn, United, XI

Tear(s), Tearable, Tearful, Tearing Beano, Claw, Crocodile, Drop, Eye-drop,

Eye-water, Greeting, Hurry, Lacerate, Laniary, Pelt, Ranch, Rash, Reave, Rheum, Rip, Rive, Rume, Screed, Shred, Snag, Split, Spree, Tire, Wet, Worry, Wrench, Wrest

Tease, Teasing Arch, Backcomb, Badinage, Bait, Banter, Chap, Chiack, Chip, Cod, Grig, Guy, Hank, Imp, Ironic, Itch, Josh, Kemb, Kid, Mag, Nark, Persiflage, > RAG, Raillery, Rally, Razz, Rib, Rot, Strip, > TANTALISE, Torment(or), Twit

Teat Dug, Dummy, Mamilla, Mastoid, Nipple, Pap, Soother, Tit

Technical, Technician, Technique Adept, Alexander, Artisan, Brushwork, College, Delphi, Execution, Foley artist, Footsteps editor, Kiwi, Know-how, Manner, > METHOD, Operative, Salami, Sandwich, Science, Toe and heel

Tedium, Tedious Boring, Chore, Deadly, Drag, Dreich, Dull, Ennui, Heaviness, Long, Longspun, Monotony, Operose, Prosy, Soul-destroying, > TIRING, Wearisome, Yawn

Teem(ing) Abound, Bustling, Empty, Great, Pullulate, Swarm

Teenager Adolescent, Bobbysoxer, Junior, Juvenile, Minor, Mod, Rocker, Sharpie

▶ **Teeth** *see* TOOTH

Teetotal(ler) Abdar, Blue Ribbon, Nephalist, Rechabite, Temperate, TT, Water-drinker, Wowser

Telegram, Telegraph Bush, Cable, Ems, Grapevine, Greetings, Message, Moccasin, Telex, Wire

Telephone Ameche, ATLAS, Bell, Blower, BT, Call, Cellphone, Centrex, Cordless, Dial, GRACE, Handset, Horn, Intercom, Line, Mercury, Pdq, Ring, STD, Touch-tone, Vodafone®, Wire

Telescope Altazimuth, Binocle, Cassegrain(ian), Collimator, Coudé, Electron, Finder, Galilean, Gemini, Glass, Gregorian, Heliometer, Hubble, Intussuscept, Meniscus, Newtonian, Night-glass, Optical, Palomar, Perspective, Radio, Reflector, Refractor, Schmidt, Shorten, Snooperscope, Spyglass, Stadia, Terrestrial, Tube, X-ray, Zenith

Television, Telly Box, Digital, Diorama, Goggle box, ITV, MAC, PAL, RTE, Set, Small screen, Tube, > TV, Video

Tell Acquaint, Announce, Apprise, Beads, Blab, Clipe, Clype, Direct, > DISCLOSE, Divulge, Grass, Impart, Inform, > NARRATE, Noise, Notify, Number, Recite, Recount, Relate, Report, Retail, Rumour, Sneak, Snitch, Spin, Teach, William

Temper, Temperate Abstinent, Allay, Anneal, Assuage, Attune, Balmy, Bile, Blood, Calm, Choler, Continent, Dander, Delay, Ease, Fireworks, Flaky, Irish, Leaven, > MILD, Mitigate, Moderate, Modify, > MOOD, Neal, Paddy, Pet, Rage, Season, Sober, Soften, Spitfire, Spleen, Strop, Tantrum, Techy, Teen, Teetotal, Tetchy, Tiff, Tone, Trim, Tune

Temperament(al) Bent, Blood, Choleric, Crasis, Disposition, Equal, Just, Kidney, Mean-tome, Melancholy, Mettle, Moody, > NATURE, Neel, Over-sensitive, Phlegmatic, Prima donna, Sanguine, Unstable, Viscerotonia

Temperature Absolute, Celsius, Centigrade, Chambré, Curie, Fahrenheit, Fever, Flashpoint, Heat, Heterothermal, Hyperthermia, Kelvin, Regulo, Room, T, Weed, Weid

Temple, Temple gate Capitol, Chapel, Church, Delphi, Delubrum, Ephesus, Fane, Gurdwara, Heroon, Inner, Masjid, Middle, Mosque, Museum, Naos, Pagod(a), Pantheon, Parthenon, > SHRINE, Shul(n), Teocalli, Teopan, Torii, Vihara, Wat

Temporal Petrosal, Petrous

Temporary Acting, Caretaker, Cutcha, Ephemeral, Hobjob, Interim, Kutcha, Locum, Makeshift, Pro tem, Provisional, Short-term, Stopgap, Temp, Transient, Transitional

Tempt(ation), Tempting, Tempter, Temptress Allure, Apple, Bait, Beguile,

Beset, Dalilah, Decoy, Delilah, > ENTICE, Eve, Groundbait, Impulse, Lure, Providence, Satan, Seduce, Siren, Snare, Tantalise, Test, Tice, Trial

Ten Commandments, Decad, Iota, Tera-, Tribes, X

Tenacious, Tenacity Clayey, Determined, Dogged, Fast, Guts, Hold, Intransigent, Persevering, Persistent, Resolute, Retentive, Sticky

Tenancy, Tenant(s) Censuarius, Cosherer, Cottar, Cotter, Cottier, Dreng, Feuar, Feudatory, Homage, Ingo, Inhabit, Leaseholder, Lessee, > LODGER, Metayer, Occupier, Rentaller, Renter, Shorthold, Sitting, Socager, Socman, Sokeman, Suckener, Tacksman, Valvassor, Vassal, Vavasour, Visit

Tend Care, Dress, Herd, Incline, Lean, Liable, Nurse, Prone, Run, Shepherd, Verge

Tendency Apt, Bent, Bias, Conatus, Drift, Import, Militant, Penchant, Proclivity, Propensity, Trend

Tender(iser), Tenderly, Tenderness Affettuoso, Amoroso, Bid, Bill, Coin, Con amore, Crank, Dingey, Ding(h)y, Fond, Frail, Gentle, Green, Humane, Jolly-boat, Legal, Nesh, Nurse, > OFFER, Papain, Pinnace, Prefer, Present, Proffer, Proposal, Quotation, Red Cross, Sair, Shepherd, > SOFT, Sore, SRN, Submit, Sympathy, Tendre

Tendon Achilles, Aponeurosis, Hamstring, Leader, Paxwax, Sinew, String, Vinculum, Whitleather

Tenor Course, > DRIFT, Effect, Gigli, Gist, Purport, Singer, T, Timbre, Trial, Vein

Tense Aor, Aorist, Case, Clench, Drawn, Edgy, Electric, Essive, Imperfect, Keyed up, Mood(y), Nervy, Overstrung, Past, Perfect, Pluperfect, Preterite, Rigid, Stiff, Stressed(-out), Strict, T, Uptight

Tension Creative, High, Isometrics, Isotonic, Meniscus, Nerviness, Premenstrual, > STRAIN, Stress, Stretch, Surface, Tone, Tonicity, Tonus, Yips

Tent Bell, Bivvy, Cabana, Douar, Duar, Kedar, Kibitka, Marquee, Oxygen, Pavilion, Probe, Ridge, Shamiana(h), Shamiyanah, Shelter, Tabernacle, Teepee, Tepee, Tipi, Top, Topek, Trailer, Tupek, Tupik, Wigwam, Y(o)urt

Term(s), Terminal, Termly Air, Anode, Buffer, Cathode, Coast, Coste, Designate, Desinant, Distal, Distributed, Euphemism, Expression, Final, Gnomon, Goal, Half, Hilary, Inkhorn, Intelligent, Law, Lent, Major, Michaelmas, Middle, Minor, > PERIOD, Rail(head), Real, Removal, Sabbatical, Semester, Session, Stint, Stretch, Trimester, Trimestrial, Trinity, Waterloo, > WORD, Workstation

Terminate, Termination, Terminus Abort, Axe, Conclude, Depot, Desinent, Earth, > END, Expiry, > FINISH, Goal, Liquidate, Naricorn, Railhead, Suffix

Terpene Squalene

Terrace Barbette, Beach, Bench, Linch, Lynchet, Perron, Shelf, Stoep, Tarras, Undercliff, Veranda(h)

Terrible, Terribly Awful, Deadly, Fell, Frightful, Ghastly, Horrible, Much, Odious, Very

Terrier Bedlington, Cesky, Dandie Dinmont, Fox, Irish, Jack Russell, Scotch, Scottish, Soft-coated wheaten, Staffordshire bull, Sydney silky, West Highland white, Westie, Wire-haired

Terrific, Terrified, Terrify(ing) Affright, Aghast, Agrise, Agrize, Agryze, Appal, Awe, Enorm, Fear, Fine, Fley, Gast, Helluva, Huge, Overawe, > PETRIFY, Scare, Superb, Unman, Yippee

Territory Abthane, Ap(p)anage, Colony, Domain, Dominion, Duchy, Emirate, Enclave, Exclave, Goa, Lebensraum, Manor, Margravate, No-man's-land, Northern, Nunavut, Panhandle, Principate, Protectorate, Province, Realm, > REGION, Sphere, Sultanate, Ter(r), Trust, Yukon

Test(er), Testing Achievement, Acid, Alpha, Ames, Appro, Aptitude, Assay, Audition, Barany, Bench, Bender, Benedict, Beta, Blood, Breath, Breathalyser®,

Candle, Canopy, Check, Chi-square, Cis-trans, Cloze, Conn(er), Coomb's, Crash, Criterion, Crucial, Crucible, Crunch, Dick, Driving, Dummy-run, Examine, Exercise, Experiment, Field, Flame, Frog, Ink-blot, Intelligence, International, Litmus, Mazzin, Means, Medical, MOT, Mug, Neckverse, Needs, Objective, Oral, > ORDEAL, Pale, Pap, Paraffin, Patch, Paternity, Performance, Personality, PH, Pilot, Pons asinorum, Pree, Preeve, Preve, Probe, Projective, Proof, Prove, Pyx, Q-sort, Qualification, Quiz, Rally, Reagent, Road, Rorschach, SAT, Schutz-Charlton, Scratch, Screen, Shadow, Shibboleth, Showdown, Shroff, Sign, Significance, Sixpence, Skin, Slump, Smear, Smoke, Snellen, Sound, Spinal, Stress, Tempt, Tensile, Touch, Touchstone, Trial, Trier, Trior, Try, Turing, Ultrasonic, Viva

Testament Bible, Heptateuch, Hexateuch, New, Old, Pentateuch, Scripture, Septuagint, Tanach, Targum, Will

Testicle(s) Ballocks, Balls, Bollix, Bollocks, Cojones, Gool(e)y, Goolie, Knackers, Monorchid, Nuts, Ridgel, Ridgil, Rig(gald), Rocks, Stone

Testify, **Testimonial**, **Testimony** Character, Chit, Declare, Depone, Deposition, > EVIDENCE, Rap, Scroll, Viva voce, Witness

Tether Cord, Endurance, Noose, Picket, Seal, Stringhalt, > TIE

Text(s), **Textbook** ABC, Body, Brahmana, Church, Codex, Donat, Ennage, Greeked, Harmony, Libretto, Mandaean, Mantra, Mezuzah, Octapla, Op-cit, Philology, Plain, Pyramid, Quran, Responsa, Rubric, Script, S(h)astra, Shema, > SUBJECT, Sura, Sutra, Tefillin, Tephillin, Tetrapla, Thesis, Topic, Tripitaka, Typography, Upanis(h)ad, Variorum, Vulgate, Zohar

Thank(s), **Thankful**, **Thanksgiving** Appreciate, Collins, Deo gratias, Gloria, Grace, Gramercy, Grateful, Gratitude, Kaddish, Mercy, Roofer

Thatch(er), **Thatching** At(t)ap, Hair, Heard, Hear(i)e, Hele, Hell, Mane, PM, Reed, Straw, Thack, Theek, Wig

▷ **Thaw** *may indicate* 'ice' *to be removed from a word*

Theatre(s), **Theatrical(ity)** Abbey, Adelphi, Balcony, Broadway, Camp, Cinema, Circle, Coliseum, Criterion, Crucible, Drama, Event, Everyman, Field, Fringe, Gaff, Gaiety, Globe, Grand Guignol, Great White Way, Hall, Haymarket, Hippodrome, Histrionic, House, Kabuki, La Scala, Legitimate, Little, Lyceum, Melodramatic, Mermaid, Music-hall, National, News, Nickelodeon, Noh, Odeon, Odeum, Operating, OUDS, Palladium, Panache, Pennygaff, Pit, Playhouse, Political, Rep(ertory), Sadler's Wells, Shaftesbury, Sheldonian, Shop, Stage, Stalls, Stoll, Straw-hat, Street, Summer stock, Total, Touring, Vic, Windmill, Zarzuela

Theft, **Thieving** Appropriation, Burglary, Heist, Identity, Kinchinlay, Larceny, Maino(u)r, Manner, Petty larceny, Pilfery, Plagiarism, Plunder, Pugging, Ram-raid, Robbery, Stealth, Stouth(rief), > THIEF, Touch, TWOC

Theme Crab canon, Donnée, Fugue, Idea, Leitmotiv, Lemma, Lemmata, > MELODY, Motif, Peg, Question, > SUBJECT, Text, Topic, Topos

Theologian, **Theologist**, **Theology** Abelard, Aquinas, Calvin, Christology, Colet, DD, Divine, Erastus, Eschatology, Eusebius, Exegetics, Hase, Irenics, Jansen, Kierkegaard, Knox, Mullah, Newman, Niebuhr, Origen, Paley, Pelagius, Pusey, Rabbi, Religious, Schoolman, Softa, STP, Tertullian, Ulema

Theorem, **Theoretical**, **Theorist**, **Theory** Academic, Atomic, Automata, Big bang, Binomial, Boo-hurrah, Catastrophe, Chaos, Conspiracy, Corpuscular, Decision, Deduction, Dependency, Dictum, Domino, Dow, Einstein, Empiricism, Exponential, Fermat's (last), Galois, Game, Gauge, Germ, Grotian, Guess, Holism, Hypothesis, Ideal, Identity, Ideology, Information, Ism(y), Kinetic, Lemma, MAD, Model, Mythical, Nernst heat, Notion, Number, Object relations, Perturbation, Probability, Proof, Pure, Pythagoras, Quantity, Quantum, Relativity, Satisfaction, Set, Steady state, String, System, Tychism, Wave

Therapeutic, **Therapy** Aversion, Behaviour, Cellular, Chavuttithirumal,

Chelation, Cognitive, Cognitive-behavioural, Colour, Combination, Craniosacral, Crystal (healing), Curative, Curietherapy, Deep, Electric shock, Family, Faradism, Fever, Flotation, Gemstone, Gene, Gestalt, Group, Hellerwork, HRT, Hypnosis, Implosive, Insight, Larval, Light, Live cell, Magnetic, Metamorphic technique, MLD, Movement, Music, Narco, Natal, Natural, Non directive, Occupational, ORT, Osteopathy, Past life, Pattern, Physical, Polarity, Pressure, Primal, Primal (scream), Psychodrama, Radiation, Radio, Radium, Rainbow, Reflexology, Regression, Reichian, Reiki, Relaxation, Retail, Rogerian, Rolfing, Root-canal, Sanatory, Scientology®, Scream, Sex, SHEN, Shiatsu, Shiatzu, Shock, Sound, Speech, Speleotherapy, Supportive, Thalassotherapy, Theriacal, Thermotherapy, Touch, > **TREATMENT**, Water cure, X-ray, Zone

Thermodynamic Enthalpy, Entropy

Thermometer Aethrioscope, Centesimal, Glass, Pyrometer, Wet and dry bulb

Thick(en), **Thickening**, **Thickener**, **Thickness**, **Thickset** Abundant, Algin, Burly, Bushy, Callosity, Callus, Clavate, Cloddy, Cruddle, Curdle, Dense, Dextrin(e), Dumose, Engross, Grist, Grume, Guar, Gum, Hyperostosis, Incrassate, Inspissate, Kuzu, Liaison, Panada, Roux, Sclerosis, > **SOLID**, Soupy, Squat, Stumpy, > **STUPID**, Thieves, This, Thixotropic, Waulk, Wooden, Xantham

Thicket Bosk, Brake, Brush, Cane-brake, Chamisal, Coppice, Copse, Dead-finish, Greve, Grove, Macchie, Maquis, Queach, Reedrand, Reedrond, Salicetum, Shola

Thief, **Thieves**, **Thievish** Autolycus, Blood, Chummy, Coon, Corsair, Cutpurse, Filcher, Flood, Footpad, Freebooter, Heist, Hotter, Ice-man, Jackdaw, Kiddy, Larcener, Light-fingered, Looter, Mag, Nip(per), Pad, Pilferer, Pirate, Plagiarist, Poacher, Prig, Raffles, > **ROBBER**, Rustler, Shark, Shop-lifter, Sneak, Taffy, Taker, Tea-leaf, Thick

Thin(ner) Acetone, Bald, Bony, Cull, Dilute, Emaciated, Enseam, Fine, Fine-drawn, Flimsy, Gaunt, Hair('s-)breadth, Inseem, Lanky, Lean, Puny, Rangy, Rare, Rarefied, Reedy, Scant, Scraggy, Scrawny, Sheer, Sieve, Skeletal, Skimpy, Skinking, Slender, Slim, Slimline, Slink, > **SPARE**, Sparse, Spindly, Stilty, Stringy, Subtle, Taper, Tenuous, Turps, Wafer, Washy, Waste, Watch, Water(y), > **WEAK**, Weedy, Wiry, Wispy, Wraith

Thing(s) Alia, Article, Chattel, Chose, Doodah, Doofer, Entia, Fetish, Fixation, It, Item, Jingbang, Job, Last, Material, Matter, Noumenon, > **OBJECT**, Obsession, Paraphernalia, Phobia, Res, Tool, Vision, Whatnot

Thingummy Dingbat, Dinges, Doodah, Doofer, Doohickey, Gubbins, Whatsit, Yoke

Think(er), **Thinking** Associate, Believe, Brain, Brood, Casuistry, Cogitate, Conjecture, Consider, Contemplant, Deem, Deliberate, Descartes, Dianoetic, Divergent, Esteem, Fancy, Fear, Feel, Fogramite, Ghesse, Gnostic, Guess, Hegel, Hold, > **IMAGINE**, Judge, Lateral, Meditate, Mentation, Mindset, Mull, Muse, Opine, Pensive, Philosopher, Phrontistery, Ponder, Pore, Presume, Ratiocinate, Rational, Reckon, Reflect, Reminisce, Ruminate, Synectics, Trow, Vertical, Ween, Wishful

Third, **Third rate** Bronze, C, Eroica, Gamma, Gooseberry, Interval, Mediant, Picardy, Quartan, Tertius, Tierce, Trisect

Thirst(y) > **CRAVE**, Dives, Drought, Drouth, Dry, Hydropic, Nadors, Pant, Polydipsia, Thrist

Thirteen Baker's dozen, Long dozen, Riddle, Unlucky

Thistle Canada, Carduus, Carline, Cnicus, Echinops, Musk, Safflower, Sow, Star, Thrissel, Thistle

Thomas Arnold, Christadelphian, De Quincey, Didymus, Doubting, Dylan, Erastus, Hardy, Loco, Parr, Rhymer, Tompion, True, Turbulent

Thomas Aquinas Angelic Doctor

Thorn(y) Acantha, Bael, Bel, Bhel, Bramble, Briar, Coyotillo, Doom, Edh, Eth, Irritation, Jerusalem, Mahonia, Mayflower, Nabk, Nebbuk, Nebe(c)k, > **NEEDLE**, Prickle, Slae, Spine, Spinescent, Spinulate, Trial, Wagn'bietjie, Ye, Zare(e)ba, Zariba, Zeriba

Thorough(ly) A fond, Complete, Even-down, Firm, Fully, Ingrained, Inly, Out, Out and out, Painstaking, Pakka, Pucka, Pukka, Ripe, Sound, Strict, Total, Tout à fait, Up

Thought(s), Thoughtful(ness) Avisandum, Broody, Censed, Cerebration, Cogitation, Concept, Considerate, Contemplation, Dianoetic, Felt, Idea, Innate, Kind, Maieutic, Mind, Musing, Notion, Opinion, Pensée, Pensive, Philosophy, Reflection, Rumination, Second

Thoughtless Blindfold, Careless, Heedless, Inconsiderate, Pillock, > **RASH**, Reckless, Remiss, Scatter-brained, Vacant

Thousand(s) Chiliad, Gorilla, K, Lac, Lakh, M, Millenary, Millennium, Plum, Toman

Thrash(ing) > **BEAT**, Belabour, Belt, Bepelt, Binge, Bless, Cane, Dress, Drub, Flail, Flog, Jole, Joll, Joule, Jowl, Lace, Laidie, Laidy, Lambast, Larrup, Lather, Leather, Lick, Marmelise, Paste, Ploat, Quilt, Slog, Smoke, Strap-oil, Swat, Targe, Towel, Trim, Trounce, Whale, Whap

Thread, Threadlike Acme screw, Ariadne, Bar, Bottom, Bride, Buttress, Chalaza, Chromosome, Clew, Clue, Cord, Coventry blue, Eel-worm, End, Fibre, Filament, File, Filiform, Filose, Float, Flourishing, Gold, Gossamer, Heddle, Ixtle, Lace, Lap, Lingel, Lingle, Link, Lisle, Lurex®, Meander, Organzine, Pack, Pearlin(g), Pick, Ravel, Reeve, Sacred, Screw, Sellers screw, Seton, Silver, Single, Stroma, Suture, Tassel, Tendril, Theme, Thrid, Thrum, Trace, Tram, Trundle, Tussore, Twine, Warp, Wax(ed), Weft, Wick, > **WIND**, Wisp, Worm

Threat(en), Threatened, Threatening Baleful, Blackmail, Bluster, Coerce, Comminate, Face, Fatwa, Fraught, Greenmail, Greymail, Hazard, Impend, Imperil, Loom, > **MENACE**, Minacious, Minatory, Mint, Omen, Overcast, Overhang, Parlous, Peril, Portent, Ramp, Shore, Strongarm, Ugly, Veiled, Warning

Three, Threefold, Three-wheeler, Thrice Graces, Har, Harpies, Jafenhar, Leash, Muses, Musketeers, Pairial, Pair-royal, Prial, Ter, Tern, Terzetta, Thrice, Thridi, Tid, T.i.d, Tierce, Tray, Trey, Triad, Tricar, Triennial, Trifid, Trigon, Trilogy, Trinal, Trine, Trinity, Trio, Triple, Triptote, Troika

Three-quarter Wing

Threshold Absolute, Brink, Cill, Difference, Doorstep, Limen, Liminal, Sill, Tax, Verge

▶ **Thrice** *see* **THREE**

Thrift(y) Economy, Frugal, Husbandry, Oeconomy, Sea-grass, Sea-pink, Virtue

Thrill(er), Thrilling Atingle, Buzz, Delight, Dindle, Dinnle, Dirl, Dread, Dynamite, Emotive, > **ENCHANT**, Excite, Film noir, Frisson, Gas, Jag, Kick, Page-turner, Perceant, Plangent, Pulsate, Pulse, Quiver, Sensation, Thirl, Tinglish, Tremor, Vibrant, Whodunit

Thrive Batten, Blossom, Boom, Do, Fl, > **FLOURISH**, Flower, Grow, Mushroom, > **PROSPER**, Succeed, Thee

Throat(y) Craw, Crop, Deep, Dewlap, Fauces, Gorge, Gular, Gullet, Guttural, Jugular, Maw, Pereion, Pharynx, Prunella, Quailpipe, Roopit, Roopy, Strep, Swallet, Thrapple, Thropple, Throttle, Weasand, Wesand, Whistle, Windpipe

Throb(bing) Beat, Palpitate, Pant, Pit-a-pat, Pulsate, Quop, Stang, Tingle, Vibrato

▷ **Throbbing** *may indicate* an anagram

Throne Bed-of-justice, Cathedra, Episcopal, Gadi, Rule, Seat, See, Siege, Tribune

Throttle > CHOKE, Gar(r)otte, Gun, Mug, Scrag, Silence, Stifle, Strangle, Strangulate, We(a)sand

Through, **Throughout** Along, Ana, By, Dia-, During, Everywhere, Over, Passim, Per, Pr, Sempre, Sic passim, To, Trans, Via, Yont

▶ **Throw(n)** *see* TOSS

Throw (up), **Thrower**, **Throw-out** Bin, Cast-off, Chunder, Egesta, Jettison, Puke, Spew, Squirt, Squit

Thrust, **Thruster** Aventre, Bear, Boost, Botte, Burn, Detrude, Dig, Drive, Elbow, Exert, Extrude, Foin, > FORCE, Gist, Hay, Impulse, Job, Lunge, Obtrude, Oust, Pass, Passado, Peg, Perk, Pitchfork, Poke, Potch(e), Pote, Probe, Propel, Pun, Punto, > PUSH, Put, Remise, Repost, Run, Shoulder, Shove, Sock, Sorn, Squat, Stap, Stick, Stoccado, Stoccata, Stock, Stuck, Thrutch, Tilt, Tuck

Thug(s) Goon(da), Gorilla, Gurrier, Hoodlum, Loord, Ninja, Ockers, Phansigar, Roughneck, SS, Strangler, Ted, Tityre-tu, Tsotsi

Thump(ing) Blow, Bonk, Cob, Crump, Drub, Dub, Hammer, Knevell, Knock, Nevel, Oner, Paik, > POUND, Pummel, Slam, Slosh, Swat, Swingeing, Thud, Tund

Thunder(ing), **Thunderstorm** Bolt, Boom, Clap, Donnerwetter, Foudroyant, Foulder, Fulminate, Intonate, Lei-king, Pil(l)an, Raiden, > ROAR, Rumble, Summanus, Tempest, Thor, Tonant

Thwart Baffle, Balk, > CROSS, Dish, Foil, Frustrate, Hamstring, Hogtie, Obstruct, Outwit, Pip, Prevent, Scotch, Snooker, Spike, Spite, Stonker, Stymie, Transverse

Tick, **Tick off** Acarida, Acarus, Beat, Click, Cr, > CREDIT, Deer, HP, Idle, Instant, Jar, Ked, Mattress, Mile, Mo, Moment, Ricinulei, Second, Strap, Worm

Ticket(s) Billet, Bone, Brief, Carnet, Commutation, Complimentary, Coupon, Day, Docket, Dream, Excursion, Kangaroo, Label, Meal, One-day, One-way, Parking, Pass, Pass-out, Pawn, Platform, Raffle, Raincheck, Return, Scratchcard, Season, Single, Soup, Split, Straight, Stub, Supersaver, Tempest, Tessera(l), Through, Tix, Transfer, Tyburn, Unity, Voucher, Walking, Zone

Tickle, **Ticklish** Amuse, Delicate, Divert, Excite, Gratify, Gump, > ITCH, Kittle, Queasy, Thrill, Titillate

Tide, **Tidal** Current, Drift, Eagre, Easter, Eger, Estuary, Flood, High, Low, Marigram, Neap, Roost, Sea, Seiche, Slack water, Spring, Trend, Wave

Tidy Comb, Considerable, Curry, Fair, Fettle, Kempt, Large, Neat, > ORDER, Pachyderm, Predy, Preen, Primp, Red(d), Slick, Snug, Sort, Spruce, Trim

Tie, **Tying** Ascot, Attach, Barcelona, Berth, Bind, Black, > BOND, Bootlace, Bow, Bowyang, Cable, Cope, Cravat, Cup, Dead-heat, Drag, Draw, Four-in-head, Frap, Halter, Handicap, Harness, Holdfast, Kipper, > KNOT, Lash, Level, Ligament, Ligate, Ligature, Link, Marry, Match, Moor, Neck and neck, Oblige, Obstriction, Old School, Oop, Oup, Overlay, Raffia, Restrain, Rod, Scarf, School, Score draw, Semifinal, Shackle, Shoelace, Shoestring, Sleeper, Slur, Solitaire, Soubise, Splice, Stake, Strap, String, Tawdry-lace, Tether, Trice, Truss, Unite, White, Windsor

Tiff Bicker, Contretemps, Difference, Dispute, Feed, Feud, Huff, Miff, Skirmish, Spat, Squabble

Tiger Bengal, > CAT, Clemenceau, Demoiselle, Lily, Machairodont, Machairodus, Margay, Paper, Sabre-tooth, Smilodon, Tasmanian, Woods

Tight(en), **Tightness**, **Tights** Boozy, Bosky, Brace, Cinch, Close(-hauled), Constriction, Cote-hardie, Fishnet, Fleshings, High, Hose, Jam, Leggings, Leotards, Lit, Loaded, Maillot, Mean, Merry, Niggardly, Oiled, Pang, Pantihose, Phimosis, Pickled, Pinch(penny), Plastered, Prompt, Proof, Rigour, Snug, Squiffy, Stenosis, > STINGY, Stinko, Strict, Stringent, Swift, Swig, Taut, Tense, Tipsy, Trig, Woozy

Tile(d), **Tiles** Antefix, Arris, Azulejo, Dalle, Derby, Encaustic, > HAT, Imbrex,

Imbricate, Lid, Ostracon, Ostrakon, Peever, Quarrel, Quarry, Rag(g), Rooftop, Sclate, Shingle, Slat, Tegula, Tessella, Tessera, Titfer, Topper, Wall, Wally

Till Cashbox, Checkout, Coffer, Ear, Eulenspiegel, Farm, Hasta, Hoe, Husband, Lob, Peter, > **PLOUGH**, Set, Unto

Tilt Awning, Bank, Camber, Cant, Cock, Dip, Heel, Hut, Joust, Just, > **LIST**, Quintain, Rock, Tip, Unbalance

Timber Apron, Balk, Batten, Beam, Bond, Bridging, Cant-rail, Chess, Clapboard, Compass, Cross-tree, Cruck, Elmwood, Flitch, Four-by-two, Greenheart, Hardwood, Harewood, Intertie, Iroko, Ironwood, Joist, Knee, Ligger, Lintel, Log, Lumber, Nogging, Purlin(e), Putlock, Putlog, Rib, Ridgepole, Roundwood, Rung, Sandalwood, Sapele, Sapodilla, Satinwood, Scantling, Shook, Shorts, Skeg, Sneezewood, Softwood, Souari, Stemson, Stere, Sternpost, Sternson, Straddle, Stull, Summer, Swing-stock, Towing-bitts, Transom, Two-by-four, Wale, Wallplate, Weatherboard, Whitewood, > **WOOD**, Yang

Time(s), Timer Access, Agoge, Apparent, Assymetric, Astronomical, Autumn, Awhile, Bird, BST, Central, Chronic, Chronometer, Chronon, Clock, Closing, Common, Compound, Connect, Core, Counter, Date, Day, Dead, Decade, Dimension, Double, Duple, Duration, Early, Eastern, Eastern Standard, Egg-glass, Enemy, Eon, Ephemeris, Epoch, Equinox, Era, European, Eve(ning), Extra, Father, Fleximte, Forelock, Free, Full, Gest, Glide, Half, Healer, High, Hour, Hourglass, Hr, Idle, Imprisonment, Injury, Innings, Instant, Interlude, Jiff, Juncture, Kalpa, Latent, Lead, Lean, Leisure, Life, Lighting-up, Lilac, Local, Mean, Menopause, Metronome, Multiple, Needle, Nonce, Nones, Occasion, Oft, Opening, Pacific, Paralysis, Part, Period, Phanerozoic, Pinger, Porridge, Post, Prime, Proper, Quadruple, Quality, Question, Quick, Reaction, Real, Reaper, Recovery, Response, Reverberation, Rhythm, Sandglass, Seal, > **SEASON**, Seel, Seil, Serial, Session, Shelf-life, Sidereal, Sight, Simple, Sith(e), Slow, Solar, Solstice, Space, Span, Spare, Spell, Spin, Split, Spring, Standard, Stoppage, Stopwatch, Stound, Stownd, Stretch, Summer, Sundial, Sundown, Sythe, T, Tem, Tempo, Tempore, Tense, Thief, Three-four, Thunderer, Tick, Tid, Tide, Trice, Triple, Two-four, Universal, Usance, While, Winter, X, Yonks, Zero

Time-keeper, Timepiece Ben, Clock, Hourglass, Ref, Sand-glass, Sundial, Ticker, Tompion, Watch

Timely Appropriate, Apropos, Happy, Opportune, Pat, Prompt

Timetable Bradshaw, > **CHART**, Schedule

Timid, Timorous Afraid, Aspen, Bashful, Blate, Chicken, Cowardly, Eerie, Eery, Faint-hearted, Fearful, Hare, Hen-hearted, Milquetoast, Mouse, Mous(e)y, Pavid, Pigeon-hearted, Pusillanimous, Quaking, Shrinking, > **SHY**, Skeary, Sook, Yellow

Tin(ned), Tinfoil, Tinny Argentine, Britannia metal, Can, Cash, Debe, Dixie, Maconochie, > **MONEY**; Moola(h), Ochre, Plate, Rhino, Sn, Stannary, Stannic, Tain, Tole

Tincture Arnica, Bufo, Chroma, Elixir, Fur, Infusion, Laudanum, Metal, Or, Sericon, Sol, Spice, Taint, Tenné, Vert

Tinder Amadou, Faggot, Fuel, Funk, Punk, Spark, Spunk, Touchwood

Tingle, Tingling Dinnle, Dirl, Paraesthesia, Prickle, Thrill, Throb, Tinkle

Tinker Bell, Caird, Coster, Didicoy, Didikoi, > **FIDDLE**, Gypsy, Mender, Pedlar, Potter, Prig, Putter, Repair, Sly, Snout, Tamper, Tramp, Traveller

Tiny Atto-, Baby, Diddy, Dwarf, Ha'it, Infinitesimal, Itsy-bitsy, Lilliputian, Minikin, Minim, Mite, Negligible, Petite, Small, Smidgeon, Teeny, Tim, Tine, Toy, Wee

Tip, Tipping Apex, Arrowhead, Asparagus, Backshish, Baksheesh, Batta, Beer-money, Cant, Cert, Chape, Counsel, Coup, Cowp, Crown, Cue, Cumshaw, Douceur, Dump, Extremity, Fee, Felt, Ferrule, Filter, Forecast, Glans, Gratuity,

Heel, > **HINT**, Hunch, Inkle, Iridise, Largess(e), List, Mess, Nap, Noop, Ord, Perk, Perquisite, Point, Pointer, Pour, Previse, Suggestion, Summit, Tag, Tail, Tilt, Toom, Touch, Tronc, Vail, Vales, Whisper, Wrinkle

Tipsy Bleary, Boozy, Bosky, Elevated, Moony, Nappy, Oiled, On, Rocky, Screwed, Slewed, Slued, Squiffy, Wet

▷ **Tipsy** *may indicate* an anagram

Tirade Diatribe, Invective, Jobation, Laisse, Philippic, Rand, Rant, Screed, Slang

Tire(d), **Tiredness**, **Tiring** All-in, Beat, Bore, Bushed, Caparison, Dress, Drowsy, > **EXHAUST**, Fag, Fatigue, Flag, Fordid, Fordod, Forjeskit, Frazzle, Gruel, Irk, Jade, Lassitude, Limp, ME, Poop, Puggled, > **ROBE**, Rubber, Sap, Shagged, Sicken, Sleepry, Sleepy, Swinkt, Tax, Tedious, Wabbit, Wappend, Weary, Wrecked

▶ **Tiro** *see* TYRO

Tissue Adenoid, Adhesion, Adipose, Aerenchyma, Aponeurosis, Archesporium, Callus, Carbon, Cartilage, Cementum, Chalaza, Cheloid, Chlorenchyma, Coenosarc, Collagen, Collenchyma, Commissure, Conducting, Connective, Cortex, Dentine, Diploe, Epimysium, Epineurium, Epithelium, Eschar, Evocator, Fabric, Fascia, Flesh, Gamgee, Gauze, Gleba, Glia, Granulation, Gum, Heteroplasia, Histogen, Histoid, Infarct, Keloid, Kleenex®, Lamina, Lies, Ligament, Luteal, Lymphoid, Macroglia, Marrow, Matrix, Mechanical, Medulla, > **MEMBRANE**, Meristem, Mesophyll, Mestom(e), Mole, Myelin(e), Myocardium, Neuroglia, Nucellus, Olivary, Pack, Palisade, Pannus, Paper, Papilla, Parenchyma, Periblem, Perichylous, Peridesmium, Perimysium, Perinephrium, Perineurium, Perisperm, Phellogen, Phloem, Pith, Placenta, Plerome, Polyarch, Pons, Primordium, Prosenchyma, Prothallis, Pterygium, Pulp, Radula, Sarcenet, Sars(e)net, Scar, Sclerenchyma, Sequestrum, Sinew, Soft, Somatopleure, Stereome, Stroma, Submucosa, Suet, Tarsus, Tela, Tendon, Tonsil, Tunica, Vascular, Velum, Web, Wound, Xylem, Zoograft

Tit, **Tit-bit(s)** Analecta, Currie, Curry, Delicacy, Dug, Nag, Nipple, Pap, Quarry, Sample, Scrap, Snack, Teat, Tug, Twitch, Zakuska

Titan(ic), **Titaness** Atlas, Colossus, Cronos, Enormous, Giant, Huge, Hyperion, Kronos, Leviathan, Liner, Oceanus, Phoebe, Prometheus, Rhea, Themis, Vast

Title Abbe, > **ADDRESS**, Ag(h)a, Appellative, Baroness, Baronet, Bart, Bhai, Calif, Caliph, Caption, Charta, Chogyal, Claim, Conveyance, Count(ess), Courtesy, Credit, Dan, Datin, Dauphin, Dayan, Deeds, Devi, Dom, Don, Don(n)a, Dowager, Dub, Duchess, Duke, Earl, Effendi, Eminence, Epithet, Esquire, Excellency, Fra, Frau(lein), Handle, Header, Heading, Headline, Hojatoleslam, Hon, Honour, Imperator, Interest, Kalif, Kaliph, King, Lady, Lala, Lemma, Lord, Mal(l)am, Marchesa, Marchese, Marquess, Marquis, Master, Masthead, Memsahib, Meneer, Miladi, Milady, Milord, Mr(s), Name, Nizam, Nomen, Padishah, Peerage, Pir, Polemarch, Prefix, Prince(ss), Queen, > **RANK**, Reb, Reverence, Reverend, > **RIGHT**, Rubric, Sahib, Sama, San, Sardar, Sayid, Senhor(a), Señor(a), Shri, Singh, Sir, Sirdar, Son, Sowbhaqyawati, Sri, Stratum, Tannie, Tenno, Torrens, Tycoon, U, Worship

To(wards) At, Beside, Inby, Onto, Shet, Shut, Till

Toad(y) Bootlicker, Bufo, Bumsucker, Cane, Clawback, Crawler, Fawn, Frog, Horned, Jackal, Jenkins, Knot, Lackey, Lickspittle, Midwife, Minion, Natterjack, Nototrema, Paddock, Parasite, Pipa, Placebo, Platanna, Puddock, Sook, Spade-foot, Surinam, Sycophant, Tuft-hunter, Xenopus, Yesman

Toadstool Amanita, Death-cap, Death-cup, > **FUNGUS**, Grisette, Paddock-stool, Parrot, Sulphur tuft

Toast(er) Bacchus, Bell, Birsle, Brindisi, > **BROWN**, Bruschetta, Bumper, Cheers, Chin-chin, Crostini, Crouton, French, Gesundheit, Grace-cup, Grill, Health, Iechyd da, Kiaora, L'chaim, Lechayim, Loyal, Melba, Pledge, Propose, Prosit,

Round, Scouther, Scowder, Scowther, Sentiment, Sippet, Skoal, Slainte, Soldier, Sunbathe, Zwieback

Tobacco, Tobacco-field Alfalfa, Bacchi, Baccy, Bird's eye, Broadleaf, Burley, Canaster, Capa, Caporal, Cavendish, Chew, Dottle, Honeydew, Killikinnick, Kinnikinick, Latakia, Mundungus, Nailrod, Navy-cut, Negro-head, Nicotine, Niggerhead, Perique, Pigtail, Plug, Quid, Régie, Returns, Shag, Sneesh, Snout, Snuff, Stripleaf, Turkish, Twist, Vega, Virginia, Weed

Today Hodiernal, Now, Present

Toddle(r) Baim, Gangrel, Mite, Tot, Totter, Trot, Waddle

Toe(s) Dactyl, Digit, Hallux, Hammer, Piggy, Pinky, Pointe, Poulaine, Prehallux, Tootsie

Toffee Butterscotch, Caramel, Cracknel, Gundy, Hard-bake, Hokey-pokey, Humbug, Tom-trot

Together Among, At-one, Atone, Attone, Gathered, Infere, > **JOINT**, Pari-passu, Sam, Unison, Wed, Y, Yfere, Ysame

Toil(s) Drudge, Fag, Industry, > **LABOUR**, Mesh, Net, Seine, Sisyphus, Sweat, Swink, Tela, Tew, Trap, Travail, Tug, Web, > **WORK**, Wrest, Yacker, Yakka, Yakker

Toilet Can, Chemical, Coiffure, John, Lat(rine), > **LAVATORY**, Loo, Necessary house, Necessary place, Pot, Powder room, WC

Token Buck, Counter, Coupon, Disc, Double-axe, Emblem, Gift, Indication, > **MEMENTO**, Nominal, Portend, Seal, Sign, Signal, Symbol, Symptom, Tessera, Valentine

Tolerable Acceptable, Bearable, Mediocre, Passable, So-so

Tolerance, Tolerant, Tolerate(d) Abear, Abide, > **ALLOW**, Bear, Broadminded, Brook, Endure, Enlightened, Hack, Had, Immunological, Latitude, > **LENIENT**, Lump, Mercy, Permit, Stand, Stick, Stomach, Studden, Suffer, Support, Thole, Wear, Zero

Toll Chime, Customs, Due, Duty, Excise, Joll, Joule, Jowl, Octroi, Pierage, Pike, Pontage, Rates, > **RING**, Scavage, Streetage, Tariff, Tax

Tom(my) Atkins, Bell, Bowling, Bread, Brown, > **CAT**, Collins, Edgar, Gib, Grub, Gun, He-cat, Jerry, Jones, Mog(gy), Nosh, Peeping, Private, Pte, Puss, Ram-cat, Sawyer, Snout, Soldier, Stout, Thos, Thumb, Tiddler, Tucker

Tomato Beef(steak), Cherry, Husk, Love-apple, Plum, Strawberry, Tamarillo, Wolf's peach

Tomb(stone) Burial, Catacomb, Catafalque, Cenotaph, Cist, Coffin, Dargah, Durgah, Grave, Hypogeum, Kistvaen, Marmoreal, Mastaba, Mausoleum, Megalithic, Monument, Pyramid, > **SEPULCHRE**, Sepulture, Serdab, Shrine, Speos, Tholos, Tholus, Through-stone, Treasury, Vault

Tomboy Gamine, Gilpey, Gilpy, Hoyden, Ladette, Ramp, Romp

Tomorrow Future, Manana, Morrow

Ton(nage) C, Chic, Displacement, Freight, Gross, Hundred, Long, Measurement, Metric, Register, Shipping, Short, T

Tone, Tonality Brace, Fifth, Harmonic, Inflection, Key, Klang, Ninth, Partial, Qualify, > **SOUND**, Strain, Temper, Tenor, Timbre, Trite, Whole

Tongue Brogue, Burr, Chape, Clack, Clapper, Doab, Final, Forked, Glossa, Glossolalia, Jinglet, > **LANGUAGE**, Languet(te), Lap, Ligula, Lill, Lingo, Lingulate, Mother, Organ, Radula, Ranine, Rasp, Red rag, Spit, Tab, Voice

Tonic Bracer, C(h)amomile, Doh, Key, Mease, Medicinal, Mishmee, Mishmi, Oporice, Pick-me-up, Quassia, Refresher, Roborant, Sarsaparilla, Solfa

▷ **Tonic** *may indicate* a musical note

Too Als(o), Besides, Eke, Excessive, Item, Likewise, Moreover, Oer, Over, Overly, Plus, Troppo

Tool Adze, Auger, Awl, Ax(e), Beetle, Bevel, Billhook, Bit, Broach, Brog, Bur(r), Burin, Calipers, Catspaw, Chaser, Chisel, Chopper, Clippers, Croze, Dibber, Dibble, Die, Dolly, Drawknife, Drift(pin), Edge, Elsin, Eolith, Facer, Fid, File, Firmer, Float, Former, Fraise, Froe, Frow, Fuller, Gad, Gimlet, Gouger, Grapnel, Graver, Hammer, Hardy, Hob, Hoe, Husker, > IMPLEMENT, > INSTRUMENT, Iron, Jemmy, Jim Crow, Jointer, Laster, Loom, Lute, Machine, Mallet, Marlin(e)spike, Mitre square, Muller, Nippers, Outsiders, Pattle, Pawn, Penis, Percussion, Pestle, Pick, Picklock, Pitchfork, Piton, Plane, Pliers, Plunger, Power, Pricker, Property, Punch, Puncheon, Rabble, Rasp, Reamer, Ripple, Roll(er), Rounder, Router, Sander, Saw, Scalpel, Scissors, Scraper, Screwdriver, Scythe, Secateurs, Sickle, Slater, Sleeker, Snake, Spanner, Spirit-level, Spokeshave, Strickle, Strike, Strimmer®, Swage, Swingle, Swipple, Tint, Triblet, Trowel, Tweezers, Twibill, Upright, Vibrator, Vice, Wrench

Tooth(ed), Toothy, Teeth Bicuspid, Bit, Buck, Bunodont, Canine, Carnassial, Chactodon, Cheek tooth, Cog, Cott's, Crena(te), Ctenoid, Cusp, Denticle, Dentin(e), Dentures, Egg, Eye, False, Fang, Gam, Gat, Gnashers, Grinder, Heterodont, Impacted, Incisor, Ivory, Joggle, Laniary, Milk, Mill, Molar, Nipper, Odontoid, Orthodontics, Overbite, Pawl, Pearly gates, Pectinate, Peristome, Permanent, Phang, Plate, Pre-molar, Prong, Ratch, Scissor, Secodont, Sectorial, Serration, Set, Snaggle, Sprocket, Store, Sweet, Trophi, Tush, Tusk, Uncinus, Upper, Wallies, Wang, Wiper, Wisdom, Wolf, Zalambdodont

Top (drawer; hole; line; notcher), Topmost, Topper Ace, Acme, A1, Altissimo, Apex, Apical, Behead, Best, Better, Big, Blouse, Blouson, Boob tube, Brow, Bustier, Cap, Capstone, Ceiling, Coma, Cop, Coping, Corking, Cream, > CREST, Crista, Crop, Crown, Culmen, De capo, Decollate, Diabolo, Dog, Dome, Double, Drawer, Elite, Execute, Fighting, Finial, Flip, Gentry, Gyroscope, Halterneck, Hard, Hat, > HEAD, Height, Hummer, Humming, Imperial, Jumper, Lid, Nun, One-er, Optimate, Orb, Parish, > PEAK, Peerie, Peery, Peg, Peplos, Peplus, Pinnacle, Pitch, Replenish, Ridge, Roof, Sawyer, Screw, Secret, Shaw, Shirt, Skim, Slay, Soft, Spinning, Star, Summit, Superb, Supreme, Supremo, Surface, Sweater, Tambour, Targa, Teetotum, Texas, Tile, Trash, T-shirt, Up(most), Uppermost, V, Vertex, Whipping, Whirligig

▷ **Top** *may indicate* first letter

Topic(al) Head, Item, Motion, Subject, Text, > THEME

Topping Grand, Icing, Meringue, Pepperoni, Piecrust, Streusel

Topple Oust, Overbalance, Overturn, Tip, Upend, > UPSET

Topsy-turvy Careen, Cockeyed, Inverted, Summerset, Tapsalteerie, Tapsleteerie

Torah Maftir

Torch Brand, Cresset, Flambeau, Lamp, Lampad, Link, Plasma, Tead(e), Wisp

Toreador Escamillo, Matador, Picador, Torero

Torment(ed), Tormentor Agony, Anguish, Bait, Ballyrag, Bedevil, Butt, Cruciate, Crucify, Curse, Distress, Excruciate, Frab, Grill, Harass, Hell, Martyrdom, Molest, Nag, Nettle, Pang, Pine, Plague, > RACK, Sadist, Tantalise

Torpedo Bangalore, Bomb, Ray, Weapon

Torpid, Torpor Comatose, Dormant, Languid, Lethargic, Sluggish, Slumbering

Torrid Amphiscian, Hot, Sultry, Tropical

Torso Body, Midriff, Trunk

Tortoise Chelonia, Emydes, Emys, Galapagos, Hic(c)atee, Kurma, Pancake, Snapping-turtle, Terrapin, Testudo, Timothy, Turtle

Tortoiseshell Epiplastra, Hawksbill, Testudo

▷ **Tortuous** *may indicate* an anagram

Torture, Torture chamber, Torture instrument Agonise, Auto-da-fé, Bastinade, Bastinado, Boot, Bootikin, Catasta, Chinese burn, Chinese water,

Crucify, Engine, Excruciate, Flageolet, Fry, Gadge, Gauntlet, Gyp, Iron maiden, Knee-cap, Naraka, Persecute, Pilliwinks, Pine, Pinniewinkle, Pinnywinkle, > **RACK**, Sadism, Scaphism, Scarpines, Scavenger, Scavenger's daughter, Scourge, Strappado, Tantalise, Third degree, Thumbscrew, Tumbrel, Tumbril, Water, Wheel, Wrack

▷ **Tortured** *may indicate* an anagram

Toss(ing), Throw(n) Abject, Bandy, Bounce, Buck, Bung, Buttock, Cant, Canvass, Cast, Catapult, Crabs, Cross-buttock, Dad, Daud, Deal, Disconcert, Elance, Estrapade, Falcade, > **FLING**, Flip, Flump, Flutter, Flying (head)-mare, Gollum, Haunch, Heave, Hipt, Hoy, > **HURL**, Jact(it)ation, Jaculation, Jeff, Jump, Lance, Lob, Loft, Pash, Pitch, Purl, Round-arm, Seamer, Shy, Slat, Sling, Unhorse, Unseat, Upcast

Tot Add, Babe, Bairn, > **CHILD**, Dop, Dram, Infant, Mite, Nightcap, Nip(per), Nipperkin, Slug, Snifter, Snort, Tad

Total, Toto Absolute, Aggregate, All(-out), Amount, Balance, Be-all, > **COMPLETE**, Entire, Gross, Lot, Sum, Tale, Tally, Unqualified, Utter, Whole

Totter Abacus, Daddle, Daidle, Didakai, Didakei, Did(d)icoy, Didicoi, Halt, Ragman, Rock, > **STAGGER**, Swag, Sway, Topple, Waver

Touch(ed), Touching, Touchy Accolade, Adjoin, Affect, Anent, Badass, Barmy, Cadge, Captious, Carambole, Caress, Carom, Common, Concern, Connivent, Contact, Contiguous, Emove, > **FEEL**, Finger, Finishing, Flick, Fondle, Haptic, Huffy, Iracund, Irascible, J'adoube, Liaison, Libant, Loan, Loco, Midas, Miffy, Near, Nie, Nigh, Nudge, Palp, Pathetic, Paw, Potty, Re, Sense, Shade, Skiff, Soft, Sore, Spice, > **SPOT**, Tactile, Tactual, Tag, Tangible, Tap, Taste, Tat, Tickle, Tig, Tinderbox, Tinge, Titivate, Trace, Trait, Tuck, Vestige

Touchstone Basanite, Criterion, Norm, Standard

Tough(en) Adamantine, Anneal, Apache, Arduous, Ballsy, Burly, > **HARD**, Hard-boiled, Hardy, Heavy duty, He-man, Hood, Husky, Indurate, Knotty, Leathern, Leathery, Nut, Pesky, Rambo, Rigwiddie, Rigwoodie, Roughneck, Sinewy, Spartan, Steely, Stiff, String, Sturdy, Teuch, Thewed, Tityre-tu, Virile

Tour(er), Tourist Barnstorm, Circuit, Cook's, Emmet, Excursion, Grand, Grockle, GT, Holiday-maker, Itinerate, > **JOURNEY**, Lionise, Mystery, Outing, Posting, Roadie, Rubberneck, Safari, > **TRAVEL**, Trip(per), Viator, Whistle-stop

Tournament Basho, Carousel, Drive, Event, Joust, Just, Plate, Pro-am, Round robin, Royal, Tilt, Tourney, Wimbledon

Tow(ing) Button, Fibre, > **HAUL**, Pull, > **ROPE**, Skijoring, Stupe, Track

▶ **Towards** *see* **TO**

Towel Dry, Jack, Nappy, Roller, Rub, Sanitary, Tea, Terry, Turkish

Tower Aspire, Atalaya, Babel, Barbican, Bastille, Bastion, Belfry, Bell, Bloody, Brattice, Brettice, Brogh, Campanile, Conning, Control, Cooling, Donjon, Dungeon, Edifice, Eiffel, Fly, Fortress, Gantry, Garret, Gate, Horologium, Ivory, Keep, Leaning, Loom, Maiden, Martello, Minar(et), Monument, Mooring, Mouse, Nurhag, Overtop, Peel, Pinnacle, Pound, Pylon, Rear, Rise, Rood, Round, Sail, Sears, Shot, Silo, Ski-lift, Spire, Stealth, Steeple, Tête-de-pont, Texas, Tractor, Tugboat, > **TURRET**, Victoria, Watch, Water, Ziggurat

Town, Township Boom, Borgo, Borough, Bourg, Burg(h), City, Conurbation, County, Deme, Dormitory, Dorp, Favella, Ghost, Ham(let), Market, Municipal, Nasik, One-horse, Podunk, Pueblo, Satellite, Shanty, Tp, Twin, Urban, Wick

Townee, Townsman Cad, Cit(izen), Dude, Freeman, Oppidan, Philister, Resident

Toxic(ity), Toxin Abrin, Antigen, Botulin, Coumarin, Curare, Deadly, Dioxan, Eclampsia, Lethal, Muscarine, Phenol, Phenothiazine, Psoralen, Sepsis, Serology, Venin, Venomous

Toy Bauble, Bull-roarer, Cockhorse, Cyberpet, Dally, Dandle, Doll, Executive, Faddle, Finger, Flirt, Frisbee®, Gewgaw, Golly, Gonk, Jack-in-the-box, Jumping-jack, Kaleidoscope, Kickshaw, Knack, Lego®, Noah's ark, Novelty, Paddle, Pantine, Peashooter, Plaything, Praxinoscope, Rattle, Scooter, Shoofly, Skipjack, Taste, Teddy, Thaumatrope, > **TRIFLE**, Trinket, Tu(r)ndun, Whirligig, Yoyo, Zoetrope

Trace Atom, Cast, Derive, Describe, Draft, Draw, Dreg, Echo, Footprint, Ghost, > **HINT**, Mark, Outline, Relic, Relict, Remnant, Scintilla, Semblance, Sign, Smack, Soupçon, Strap, > **TOUCH**, Track, Vestige, Whit

Track(s), Tracker, Tracking, Trackman Aintree, Band, B-road, Caterpillar®, Cinder, Circuit, Course, Dog, DOVAP, Drift, Ecliptic, El, Fast, Fettler, Footing, Gaudy dancer, Hunt, Ichnite, Ichnolite, Inside, Lane, Ley, Line, Loipe, Loopline, Mommy, Monitor, Monza, > **PATH**, Persue, Piste, Pug, Pursue, Race, Raceway, Rail, Railway, Rake, Ridgeway, Route, Run, Rut, Siding, Sign, Skidway, Sleuth, Slot, Sonar, Speedway, Spoor, Tan, Tan-ride, Taxi, Tenure, Tideway, > **TRAIL**, Trajectory, Tram, Tramline, Tramroad, Tramway, Tread, Trode, Tug(boat), Twin, Wake, Wallaby, Way, Y

Tract(able), Tracts Area, Belt, Bench, Clime, Common, Dene, Enclave, Flysheet, Lande, Leaflet, Monte, Moor, > **PAMPHLET**, Prairie, Province, Purlieu, Pusey, Region, Taluk, Tawie, Terrain, Wold

Trade(r), Tradesman, Trading Arb(itrageur), Banian, Banyan, Bargain, Barter, Bricks and clicks, Burgher, Business, Cabotage, Calling, Carriage, Chaffer, Chandler, Chapman, Cheapjack, Coaster, > **COMMERCE**, Coster, Costermonger, Crare, Crayer, Deal(er), Errand, Exchange, Factor, Fair, Floor, Free, Handle, Horse, Hosier, Hot, Importer, Indiaman, Industry, Insider, Ironmonger, Jobber, Line, Merchant, Métier, Middleman, Mister, Monger, Mystery, Outfitter, Paralleling, Pitchman, Ply, Rag, Retailer, Roundtripping, Scalp, Screen, Sell, Simony, Slave, Stationer, Sutler, Suttle, > **SWAP**, Traffic, Transit, Trant, Truck, Union, Vaisya, Vend, Wholesaler, Wind

Trademark Brand, Chop, Idiograph, Label, Logo

Tradition(s), Traditional(ist) Ancestral, Classical, Convention, Custom(ary), Eastern, Folkway, Hadith, Heritage, Legend, Lore, Mahayana, Misoneist, Old guard, Old-school, Orthodox, Pharisee, Pompier, Practice, Purist, Suburban, Time-honoured, Trad, Tralaticious, Tralatitious

Traffic, Traffic pattern Barter, Broke, Cabotage, Clover-leaf, Commerce, Contraflow, Deal, Negotiate, Passage, Run, Smuggle, Trade, Truck, Vehicular

Tragedian, Tragedy, Tragic Aeschylus, Buskin, Calamity, Cenci, Corneille, Dire, > **DRAMA**, Euripides, Macready, Melpomene, Oedipean, Oresteia, Otway, Pathetic, Seneca, Sophoclean, Thespian, Thespis

Trail(er), Trailing Abature, Bedraggle, Caravan, Creep, Drag, Draggle, Follow, Ipomaea, Lag, Liana, Liane, Nature, Oregon, Path, Persue, Preview, Promo(tion), Pursue, Repent, Runway, Scent, Shadow, Sign, Sleuth, Slot, Spoor, Stream, Streel, Trace, > **TRACK**, Trade, Traipse, Trape, Trauchle, Trayne, Troad, Vapour, Vlne, Virga, Wake

Train(er), Training Advanced, APT, BR, Breed, Caravan, Cat, Cavalcade, Circuit, Coach, Commuter, Condition, Cortège, Diesel, Direct, Discipline, Dog, Dressage, Drill, Drive, Educate, Entourage, Enure, Eurostar®, Exercise, Express, Fartlek, Field, Flier, Flight simulator, Freightliner®, Fuse, Gear, Ghan, Ghost, Gravy, Grounding, GWR, Handle(r), Instruct, Intercity®, Interval, Journey, Liner, Link, LMS, LNER, Loco, Lunge, Maglev, Mailcar, Manège, Manrider, Mentor, Milk, Nopo, Nurture, Nuzzle, Omnibus, Orient Express, Owl, Pack, Paddy, PE, Pendolino, Potty, Practise, > **PREPARE**, Procession, PT, Puffer, Puff-puff, Push-pull, Q, Queue, Rattler, Rehearse, Retinue, Road, Roadwork, Rocket, Ry, Sack, > **SCHOOL**, Series, Shoe, Shuttle service, Siege, Skill centre, Sloid, Sloyd, Sowarry, Special, SR, Steer,

String, Suite, Tail, Tame, > TEACH, Through, Tire, Track shoe, Trail, Tube, Wage, Wagon, Wave, Way

▷ **Train(ed)** *may indicate* an anagram

Traitor Betrayer, Casement, Dobber-in, Joyce, Judas, Nid(d)ering, Nid(d)erling, Nithing, Proditor, Quisling, Renegade, Reptile, Tarpeian, Traditor, Treachetour, Turncoat, Viper, Wallydraigle, Weasel

▷ **Trammel** *may indicate* an anagram

Tramp, Trample Bog-trotter, Bum, Caird, Clochard, Clump, Derelict, Dero, Dingbat, Dosser, Estragon, Footslog, Freighter, Gadling, Gook, Hike, Hobo, Knight of the road, Override, Overrun, Pad, Piker, Plod, Poach, Potch(e), Rover, Scorn, Ship, Splodge, Sundowner, Swagman, > TINKER, Toe-rag(ger), Track, Traipse, Tread, Trek, Trog, Tromp, Truant, Trudge, Tub, Vagabond, Vagrant, Weary Willie

Trance Catalepsy, Cataplexy, Goa, Narcolepsy

Tranquil(lity) Ataraxy, Calm, Composure, Halcyon, Lee, Quietude, Sedate, > SERENE

Tranquillise(r) Appease, Ataractic, Ataraxic, > CALM, Diazepam, Downer, Hypnone, Hypnotic, Librium®, Nervine, Nitrazepam, Oxazepam, Placate, Satisfy, Soothe, Still, Valium®

Transcend(ent), Transcendental(ist) Excel, Mystic, Overtop, Surpass, Thoreau

Transfer Alien, Alienate, > ASSIGN, Attorn, Calk, Cede, Communize, Consign, Convey(ance), Credit, Crosstalk, Decal, Demise, Devolve, Download, Exchange, Explant, Hive off, Make over, Mancipation, Metathesis, Mortmain, Nuclear, On-lend, Pass, Photomechanical, Provection, Reassign, Redeploy, Remit, Remove, Repot, Second, Settlement, Transduction, Transfection, Uproot, Virement

▷ **Transferred** *may indicate* an anagram

Transform(ation), Transformer Alter, Balun, Change, Lorentz, Metamorphism, Metamorphose, Metamorphosis, Metaplasia, Metastasis, Morphing, Permute, Rectifier, Sea change, Tinct, Toupee, Transmogrify, Wig

▷ **Transform(ed)** *may indicate* an anagram

Transgress(ion) Encroach, Err, Infringe, Offend, Overstep, Peccancy, > SIN, Violate

Transient, Transit(ion), Transitory Brief, Ephemeral, Fleeting, Fly-by-night, Fugacious, Hobo, Metabasis, Passage, Passing, Provisional, Seque, T, Temporary

Translate, Translation, Translator Calque, Construe, Convert, Coverdale, Crib, Explain, Free, Horse, Interpret, In vitro, Jerome, Key, Linguist, Loan, Machine, Metaphrase, Paraphrase, Pinyin, Polyglot, Pony, Reduce, Render, Rendition, Rhemist, Simultaneous, Targum, Tr, Transcribe, Transform, Trot, Unseen, Version(al), Vulgate, Wycliffe

▷ **Translate(d)** *may indicate* an anagram

Transmit(ter), Transmitted, Transmission Air, Band, Beacon, > BROADCAST, Carry, CB, Communicate, Consign, Contagion, Convection, Convey, Forward, Gearbox, Gene, Heredity, Impart, Intelsat, Manual, Microphone, Modem, Nicol, Permittivity, Propagate, Racon, Radiate, Radio, Receiver, Simulcast, Sonabuoy, Tappet, Telecast, Telegony, Telemetry, Teleprinter, Telex, Tiros, Traduce, Traject, Tralaticious, Tralatitious, UART, Uplink, Upload, Walkie-talkie

Transparent, Transparency Adularia, Clear, Crystal(line), Diaphanous, Dioptric, Glassy, Glazed, Hyaloid, Iolite, Leno, Limpid, Lucid, Luminous, Patent, Pellucid, Sheer, Slide, Tiffany

Transport(ed), Transporter, Transportation Argo, Bear, Bike, Broomstick, BRS, Bus, Cargo, Carract, > CARRY, Cart, Charm, Convey, Delight, Ecstasy, Eloin,

Enrapt, Enravish, Entrain, Esloin, Estro, Freight, Haul(age), Helicopter, Jerrican, Joy, Kurvey, Maglev, Monorail, Palanquin, Pantechnicon, Public, Put, Rape, Rapine, Rapture, Roadster, Ship, Shuttle, Sledge, Supersonic, Tote, Trap, Tuktuk, Waft, Wheels, Wireway

Transpose, Transposition Anagram, Commute, Convert, Invert, Metathesis, Shift, Spoonerism, Switch, Tr

▷ **Transposed** *may indicate* an anagram

Trap(s), Trapdoor, Trapped, Trappings Ambush, > BAGGAGE, Bags, Belongings, Booby, Buckboard, Bunker, Carriage, Catch, Catch-pit, Clapnet, Corner, Cru(i)ve, Deadfall, Death, Decoy, Dogcart, Downfall, Eelset, Emergent, Ensnare, Entrain, Fall, Fit-up, Fly, Flypaper, Frame-up, Fyke, Gig, Gin, Gob, Grin, Hatch, Ice-bound, Jinri(c)ksha(w), Keddah, Kettle, Kheda, Kiddle, Kidel, Kipe, Kisser, Knur(r), Light, Lime, > LUGGAGE, Lure, Mesh, Mouth, Net, Nur(r), Paraphernalia, Pitfall, Plant, Police, Pot, Poverty, Putcheon, Putcher, Quicksand, Radar, Regalia, Sand, Scruto, > SNARE, Speed, Spell, Spider, Springe, Stake-net, Star, Steam, Stench, Sting, Stink, Sun, Tangle, Tank, Teagle, Toil, Tonga, Trou-de-loup, Two-wheeler, U, U-bend, Vampire, Web, Weel, Weir, Wire

Trash(y) Bosh, Deface, Dre(c)k, Garbage, Junk, Kitsch, Pulp, > RUBBISH, Schlock, Scum, Tinpot, Vandalise, Worthless

Travel(ler), Travelling Backpack, Bagman, Commercial, Commute, Crustie, Crusty, Drive, Drummer, Fare, Fellow, Fly, Fogg, Gipsen, Gipsy, Gitano, Globe-trotter, Go, Gulliver, Gypsy, Hike, Interrail, Itinerant, Journey, Long-haul, Marco Polo, Meve, Migrant, Motor, Move, Mush, Nomad, Passepartout, Peregrination, Peripatetic, Pilgrim, Ply, Polo, Range, Rep, Ride, Rom(any), Rove, Safari, Sail, Salesman, Samaritan, > TOUR, Trek, Tripper, Tsigane, Viator, Voyage, Wayfarer, Wend, Wildfire, Zigan

Travesty Burlesque, Charade, Distortion, Parody, Show, Skit

Tray Antler, Carrier, Case, Charger, Coaster, Gallery, Joe, Lazy Susan, Plateau, Tea, Trencher, Voider

Treacherous, Treachery Deceit, Delilah, Fickle, Ganelon, Guile, Insidious, Knife, Medism, Perfidious, Punic, Quicksands, Serpentine, Sleeky, Snaky, Trahison, Traitor, > TREASON, Two-faced, Viper

Tread Clamp, Clump, Dance, Pad, Step, Stramp, Track, Trample

Treadle Footboard

Treason Betrayal, Insurrection, Lèse-majesté, Lese-majesty, Perduellion, Sedition, > TREACHERY

Treasure(r), Treasury Banker, Bursar, Cache, Camerlengo, Camerlingo, Cherish, Chest, Cimelia, Coffer, Ewe-lamb, Exchequer, Fisc(al), Fisk, Godolphin, Golden, Heritage, Hoard, Montana, Palgrave, > PRIZE, Procurator, Purser, Relic, Riches, Steward, Thesaurus, Trove

Treat, Treatment Action, Acupuncture, Allopathy, Antidote, Aromatherapy, Beano, Besee, Capitulate, Care, Chemotherapy, Condition, Course, Cupping, Cure, Deal, Detox(ification), Dialysis, Do, > DOCTOR, Dose, Dress, Dutch, Entertain, Est, Facial, Faith-healing, Fango, Figuration, Foment, Frawzery, Handle, Holistic, Homeopathy, HRT, Hydrotherapy, Hypnotherapy, Intermediate, Kenny, Laser, Manage, Medicate, Naturopathy, Negotiate, Osteopathy, > OUTING, Pasteur, Pedicure, Pelotherapy, Physic, Physiotherapy, Pie, Process, Psychoanalysis, Psychotherapy, Radiotherapy, Regale, Rehab(ilitation), Rest cure, Root, Secretase, Serotherapy, Shout, Shrift, Smile, > STAND, Tablet, Themotherapy, Therapy, Titbit, Traction, Twelve-step, Usance, Use, Vet

▷ **Treated** *may indicate* an anagram

Treatise Almagest, Commentary, Didache, Discourse, Monograph, Pandect, Summa, Tract(ate), Upanishad, Vedanta

Treaty Agreement, Alliance, Assiento, Concordat, Covenant, Entente, Lateran, Maastricht, > PACT, Protocol, Utrecht

Treble Castrato, Choirboy, Chorist(er), Pairial, Soprano, > TRIPLE, Triune

Tree(s) Actor, > ANCESTRY, Axle, Beam, Boom, Bosk, Bottle, Conifer, Corner, Deciduous, Decision, Dendrology, Descent, Family, Fault, Fringe, Gallows, Grove, Hang, Hardwood, Jesse, Nurse, Pedigree, Pole, Sawyer, Shoe, Softwood, Staddle, Stemma, Summer, Timber, Tyburn, > WOOD

Tremble, Trembling, Tremor Aftershock, Butterfly, Dither, Dodder, Hotter, Judder, Palpitate, Quail, Quake, Quaver, Quiver, Seismal, > SHAKE, Shiver, Shock, Shudder, Stound, Temblor, Trepid, Twitchy, Vibrate, Vibration, Vibratiuncle, Vibrato, Wobble, Wuther, Yips

Tremendous Big, Enormous, Howling, Immense, Marvellous

▶ **Tremor** *see* TREMBLE

Trench(er) Boyau, Cunette, Cuvette, Delf, Delph, Dike(r), > DITCH, Dyke(r), Encroach, Fleet, Foss(e), Foxhole, Fur(r), Furrow, Grip, Gullet, Gutter, Leat, Line, Mariana, Moat, Oceanic, Outwork, Rill, Rille, Ring-dyke, Salient, Sap, Shott, Slit, Sod, Sondage

Trend(y) Bent, Bias, Chic, Climate, Drift, Fashion, Hep, In, Mainstream, Newfangled, Pop, Posey, Rage, Style, Swim, Tendency, Tendenz, Tenor, Tide, Tonnish

Trespass(ing) Encroach, Errant, Hack, Impinge, Infringe, Offend, Peccancy, Sin, Trench, Wrong

Trial Adversity, Affliction, Appro, Approbation, Approval, Assize, Attempt, Bane, Bernoulli, Bout, Corsned, Court-martial, Cow, Cross, Dock, Essay, > EXPERIMENT, Field, Fitting, Hearing, Nuremberg, Ordeal, Pilot, Pree, Probation, Proof, Rehearsal, Scramble, Taste

Triangle(d), Triangular Acute, Bermuda, Cosec, Deltoid, Equilateral, Eternal, Gair, Golden, Gore, Gyronny, Isosceles, Obtuse, Pascal's, Pedimental, Pyramid, Rack, Right-angled, Scalene, Similar, Trigon, Tromino, Warning

Tribe(s), Tribal, Tribesmen Clan(nish), Dynasty, Ephraim, Family, Gond, Issachar, Judah, Lost, Manasseh, Nation, > RACE, Schedule, Standloper, Zebulun

Tribune, Tribunal Aeropagus, Bema, Bench, > COURT, Divan, Forum, Hague, Industrial, Leader, Platform, Rienzi, Rota, Star-chamber

Tributary Affluent, Bogan, Branch, Creek, Fork

Tribute Cain, Citation, Commemoration, Compliment, Deodate, > DUE, Epitaph, Festschrift, Gavel, Heriot, Homage, Kain, Memento, Ode, Panegyric, Peter's pence, > PRAISE, Rome-penny, Scat(t), Tax, Toast, Wreath, Wroth

Trick(ed), Trickery, Tricks(ter), Tricky Antic, Art, Artifice, Attrap, Awkward, Bamboozle, Begunk, Book, Bunco, Bunko, Cantrip, Capot, Catch, Cheat, Chicane(ry), Chouse, Claptrap, Cod(-act), Cog, Confidence, Coyote, Crook, Davenport, Deception, Deck, Delicate, Delude, Device, Dirty, > DO, > DODGE, Dupe, Elf, Elfin, Elvan, Fard, Feat, Fetch, Fiddle, Finesse, Flam, Flim-flam, Fob, Fox, Fraud, Fun, Game, Gaud, Gleek, Glike, Guile, Had, Hey presto, Hoax, Hocus(-pocus), Hoodwink, Hum, Illude, Illusion, Jockey, John, Kittle, Knack, Lark, Magsman, Mislead, Monkey, Monkey-shine, Nap, Palter, Parlour, Pass, Pawk, Pleasantry, Prank, Prestige, Put-on, Quick, Ramp, Raven, Reak, Reik, Rex, Rig, Ropery, Ruse, Scam, Sell, Set-up, Shanghai, Shenanigan, Shifty, Shill, Skite, Skul(l)duggery, Skylark, Slam, Sleight, Slight, Spoof, Stall, Stint, Subterfuge, Three-card, Ticklish, Trap, Trump, Turn, Underplot, Vole, Wangle, Wheeze, Wile, Wrinkle

▷ **Trick** *may indicate* an anagram

Trifle(s), Trifling Bagatelle, Banal, Bauble, Bibelot, Birdseed, Bit, Cent, Chickenfeed, Coquette, Dabble, Dalliance, Denier, Do, Doit, Faddle, Falderal,

Fallal, Feather, Fewtril, Fiddle, Fig, Flamfew, Fleabite, Flirt, Folderol, Fool, Footle, Fribble, Frippery, Fritter, Frivol, Gewgaw, Idle, Iota, Kickshaw, Knick-knack, Mite, Nothing, Palter, Paltry, Peanuts, Peddle, Peppercorn, Petty, Philander, Piddle, Piffle, Pin, Pingle, Pittance, Play, Potty, Quelquechose, Quiddity, Quiddle, Slight, Small beer, Smatter, Song, Sport, Stiver, Strae, Straw, Sundry, Tiddle, Toy, Trinket, Trivia, Whit

Trigger Detent, Hair, Instigate, Pawl, Precipitate, Start

Trill(ed), **Triller**, **Trilling** Burr, Churr, Hirrient, Quaver, Ribattuta, Roll, Staphyle, Trim, Twitter, Warble

Trim(med), **Trimmer**, **Trimming** Ballast, Bleed, Braid, Bray, Chipper, Clip, Dapper, Dinky, Dress, Ermine, Face, Fettle, File, Froufrou, Garnish, Garniture, Gimp, Guimpe, Macramé, Macrami, Marabou, Neat, Net(t), Ornament, Pare, Pipe, Plight, Posh, Preen, Pruin(e), Prune, Robin, Ruche, Sax, Sett, Shipshape, Smirk, Smug, Sned, Snod, > **SPRUCE**, Straddle, Stroddle, Stylist, Svelte, > **TIDY**, Time-server, Torsade, Trick, Wig

Trinket(s) Bauble, Bibelot, Bijou(terie), Charm, Fallal, Nicknack, Toy, Trankum

Trip(per) Awayday, Cruise, Dance, Day, Ego, Errand, > **FALL**, Field, Flight, Flip, Guilt, Head, High, Jolly, Journey, Junket, Kilt, Link, Outing, Pleasure, Power, Ride, Round, Run, Sail, Sashay, Spin, Spurn, > **STUMBLE**, Tour, Trek, Trial, Voyage

▷ **Trip** *may indicate* an anagram

Triple, **Triplet** Codon, Hemiol(i)a, Sdrucciola, Ternal, Tiercet, Treble, Trifecta, Trilling, Trin(e), Tripling

Trite Banal, Boilerplate, Corny, Hackneyed, Hoary, Novelettish, Rinky-dink, Stale, Stock, Time-worn

Triumph(ant) Cock-a-hoop, Codille, Cowabunga, Crow, Exult, Glory, Impostor, Killing, Oho, Olé, Ovation, Palm, Victorious, > **WIN**

Trivia(l), **Triviality** Adiaphoron, Bagatelle, Balaam, Bald, > **BANAL**, Footling, Frippery, Frothy, Futile, Idle, Inconsequential, Light, Minutiae, Nitpicking, Nothingism, Paltry, Pap, Peppercorn, Pettifoggery, Petty, Picayune, Piddling, Piffling, Shallow, Small, Small beer, Small fry, Snippety, Squirt, Squit, Toy(s), Vegie

Trolley Brute, Cart, Dolly, Gurney, Shopping, Tea, Truck, Trundler

▶ **Trollop** *see* LOOSE WOMAN

Trompe l'oeil Quadratura, Quadrature

Troop(s), **Trooper** Alpini, Band, BEF, Brigade, Company, Depot, Detachment, Guard, Horde, Household, Logistics, Midianite, Militia, Pultan, Pulton, Pultoon, Pultun, SAS, School, Shock, Sowar, State, Storm, Subsidiary, Tp, Turm(e)

Trophy Adward, Ashes, > **AWARD**, Belt, Cup, Emmy, Memento, Palm, > **PRIZE**, Scalp, Schneider, Spoils, Tourist, TT

Trot(ter), **Trot out** Air, Crib, Crubeen, Job, Jog, Passage, Pettitoes, Piaffe, Pony, Ranke, Red(-shirt), Rising, Tootsie

Trouble(s), **Troublemaker**, **Troublesome** Ache, Ado, Affliction, Aggro, Agitate, Ail, Alarm, Annoy, Bale, Barrat, Beset, > **BOTHER**, Bovver, Brickle, Burden, Care, Coil, Concern, Debate, Disaster, Disquiet, Distress, Disturb, Dog, Dolour, Eat, Exercise, Fash, Finger, Firebrand, Gram(e), Grief, Harass, Harry, Hassle, Hatter, Heat, Heist, Hellion, Hot water, Howdyedo, Inconvenience, Infest, > **IN TROUBLE**, Jam, Mess, Mixer, Moil, Molest, Noy, Perturb, Pester, Plague, Poke, Reck, Rub, Scrape, Shake, Soup, Spiny, Stir, Storm, Sturt, Tartar, Teen, Teething, Thorny, Tine, Toil, Trial, Turn-up, Tyne, Unsettle, Vex, > **WORRY**

▷ **Troublesome** *may indicate* an anagram

Trough Back, Bed, Bucket, Buddle, Channel, Chute, Culvert, Graben, Hod, Hutch, Manger, Stock, Straik, Strake, Syncline, Troffer, Tundish, Tye

Trouser(s) Bags, Bell-bottoms, Bloomers, Breeches, Capri pants, Churidars,

Clam-diggers, Continuations, Cords, Corduroys, Cossacks, Culottes, Daks, Denims, Drainpipe, Drawers, Ducks, Dungarees, Eel-skins, Flannels, Flares, Galligaskins, Gaskins, Gauchos, Hip-huggers, Hipsters, Inexpressibles, Innominables, Jeans, Jodhpurs, Kaccha, Ke(c)ks, Knee cords, Lederhosen, Longs, Loons, Moleskins, Overalls, Oxford bags, Palazzo (pants), Palazzos, Pantaloons, Pants, Pedal pushers, Pegtops, Plus-fours, Plus-twos, Reach-me-downs, Salopettes, Shalwar, Ski pants, Slacks, Stovepipes, Strides, Strossers, Sweatpants, Trews, Trouse, Unmentionables, Unutterables, Utterless

Trout Aurora, Brook, Brown, Bull, Coral, Finnac(k), Finnock, Fish, Gillaroo, Herling, Hirling, Peal, Peel, Phinnock, Pogies, Quintet, Rainbow, Sewen, Sewin, Speckled, Splake, Steelhead, Togue, Whitling

Truant Absentee, AWOL, Dodge, Hooky, Kip, Mich(e), Mitch, Mooch, Mouch, Wag

Truce Armistice, Barley, Ceasefire, Fainites, Fains, Interlude, Pax, Stillstand, Treague, Treaty

Truck Bakkie, Bogie, Breakdown, Business, Cattle, Cocopan, Dealings, Dolly, Dumper, Flatbed, Forklift, Haul, Hopper, Journey, > **LORRY**, Low-loader, Pallet, Panel, Pick-up, Semi, Sound, Stacking, Tipper, Tow(ie), Traffic, Trolley, Trundle, Ute, Utility, Van, Wrecker

Trudge Footslog, Jog, Lumber, Pad, Plod, Stodge, Stramp, Taigle, Traipse, Trash, Trog, Vamp

True Accurate, Actual, Apodictic, Constant, Correct, Exact, Factual, Faithful, Genuine, Honest, Indubitable, Leal, Literal, Loyal, Platitude, Plumb, Pure, Real, Realistic, Sooth, Very

Truly Certainly, Certes, Fegs, Forsooth, Honestly, Indeed, Surely, Verily, Yea

Trump(s), Trumpet(er) Agami, Alchemy, Alchymy, Bach, Blare, Blast, Bray, Buccina, Bugle(r), Call, Card, Clarion, Conch, Cornet, Corona, Crow, Daffodil, Elephant, Fanfare, Hallali, Honours, > **HORN**, Invent, Jew's, Last, Lituus, Lur(e), Lurist, Manille, Marine, Megaphone, Proclaim, Ram's-horn, Resurrect, Ruff, Salpingian, Salpinx, Satchmo, Sennet, Shofar, Shophar, Slug-horn, Surpass, Tantara, Tantarara, Tar(at)antara, Theodomas, Tiddy, Triton, Triumph

Trunk(s) Aorta(l), A-road, Body, Bole, Box, Bulk, But(t), Carcase, Chest, Coffer, Hose, Imperial, Log, Peduncle, Pollard, Portmanteau, Portmantle, Proboscis, Ricker, Road, Saratoga, Shorts, STD, Stock, Stud, Synangium, Torso, Valise, Wardrobe

Trust(y), Trusting, Trustworthy Affy, Authentic, Belief, Care, Cartel, Charge, Combine, Confide, Credit, Dependable, Discretionary, > **FAITH**, Fiduciary, Gullible, Honest, Hope, Investment, Leal, Lippen, Loyal, National, NT, Reliable, Reliance, Rely, Repose, Reputable, Staunch, Tick, Trojan, Trow, True, Trump, Unit

Truth(ful), Truism Accuracy, Alethic, Axiom, Bromide, Cliché, Cold turkey, Dharma, Dialectic, > **FACT**, Facticity, Forsooth, Gospel, Home, Honesty, Idea(l), Logical, Maxim, Naked, Pravda, Reality, Sooth, Soothfast, Troggs, Veraity, Veridical, Verisimilitude, Verity, Vraisemblance

Try(ing) Aim, Approof, Assay, Attempt, Audition, Bash, Bid, Birl, Burden, Burl, Conative, Contend, Crack, Effort, Empiric(utic), > **ENDEAVOUR**, Essay, Examine, Experiment, Fand, Fish, Fling, Foretaste, Go, Harass, Hard, Hear, Importunate, Irk, Offer, Ordalium, Practise, Pree, Prieve, > **SAMPLE**, Seek, Shot, Sip, Stab, Strain, Strive, Taste, Tax, Tempt, Test, Touchdown, Whirl

Tub(by), Tubbiness, Tub-thumper Ash-leach, Back, Bath, Boanerges, Bran, Corf, Cowl, Dan, Diogenes, Endomorph, Firkin, Keeve, Kid, Kieve, Kit, Pin, Podge, Pudge, Pulpit, Tun, Vat, Wash

Tube, Tubing, Tubular Acorn, Arteriole, Artery, Barrel, Blowpipe, Bronchus, Burette, Calamus, Camera, Cannula, Capillary, Casing, Catheter, Cathode-ray, Cave, Conduit, Crookes, Digitron, Diode, Discharge, Drain, Drift, Dropper, Duct,

Electron, Endiometer, Eustachian, Extension, Fallopian, Fistula, Germ, Grommet, Hose, Inner, Kinescope, Macaroni, Matrass, Metro, Neural, Nixie, Orthicon, Oval, Oviduct, Pentode, Picture, Pilot-static, > PIPE, Pipette, Pitot, Pneumatic, Pollen, Promethean, Salpinx, Saticon®, Saucisse, Saucisson, Schnorkel, Shock, Sieve, Siphon, Siphonet, Sleeve, Snorkel, Speaking, Spout, Staple, Static, Stent, Storage, Straw, Subway, Sucker, Swallet, Telescope, Teletron, Television, Terete, Test, Tetrode, Tile, Torpedo, Torricellian, Trachea, Trocar, Trochotron, Trunk, Tunnel, Tuppenny, U, Underground, Ureter, Urethra, Vacuum, Vas, VDU, Vein, Vena, Venturi, Video, Vidicon®, Worm, X-ray

Tuber(s) Arnut, Arracacha, Bulb, Chufa, Coc(c)o, Dasheen, Earth-nut, Eddoes, Mashua, Oca, Potato, Salep, Taproot, Taro, Yam

Tuberculosis Consumption, Crewels, Cruel(l)s, Decline, Lupus, Phthisis, Scrofula

Tuck Dart, Friar, Gather, Grub, Kilt, Pin, Pleat, Scran

Tudor Stockbrokers'

Tuff Schalstein

Tuft(ed) Amentum, Beard, C(a)espitose, Candlewick, Catkin, Cluster, Coma, Comb, Cowlick, Crest, Dollop, Flaught, Floccus, Goatee, Hassock, Pappus, Penicillate, Quiff, Scopate, Shola, Tait, Tassel, Toorie, Toupee, Tourie, Tussock, Tuzz, Whisk

Tug Drag, Haul, Jerk, Lug, Pug, > PULL, Rive, Ship, Sole, Soole, Sowl(e), Tit, Tow, Towboat, Yank

Tumble, Tumbler Acrobat, Cartwheel, Drier, Fall, > GLASS, Pitch, Popple, Purl, Realise, Spill, Stumble, Topple, Trip, Twig, Voltigeur, Welter

▷ **Tumble** *may indicate* an anagram

Tumour Adenoma, Anbury, Angioma, Angiosarcoma, Astrocytoma, Burkitt('s) lymphoma, Cancer, Carcinoid, Carcinoma, Carcinosarcoma, Chondroma, Condyloma, Crab(-yaws), Dermoid, Encanthis, Encephaloma, Enchondroma, Endothelioma, Epulis, Exostosis, Fibroid, Fibroma, Ganglion, Gioblastoma, Glioma, Granuloma, Grape, > GROWTH, Gumma, Haemangioma, Haematoma, Hepatoma, Lipoma, Lymphoma, Medullablastoma, Melanoma, Meningioma, Mesothelioma, Metastasis, Mole, Myeloma, Myoma, Myxoma, Neoplasm, Neuroblastoma, Neuroma, -oma, Oncology, Osteoclastoma, Osteoma, Osteosarcoma, Papilloma, Polypus, Retinoblastoma, Sarcoma, Scirrhous, Seminoma, Steatoma, Struma, Talpa, Teratoma, Thymoma, Wart, Wen, Wilm's, Windgall, Wolf, Xanthoma, Yaw

Tumult Brattle, Brawl, Coil, Deray, Ferment, Fracas, Hirdy-girdy, Hubbub, Reird, Riot, > ROAR, Romage, Rore, Stoor, Stour, Stowre, Stramash, Tew, > UPROAR

Tuna Pear, Yellowfin

Tune(s), Tuneful, Tuner, Tuning Adjust, Air, Aria, Canorous, Carillon, Catch, Choral, Dump, Etude, Fork, Harmony, Hornpipe, Jingle, Key, Maggot, Measure, Melisma, > MELODY, Old Hundred, Peg, Port, Potpourri, Raga, Rant, Ranz-des-vaches, Signature, Snatch, Song, Spring, Strain, Sweet, Syntonise, Temper, Theme, Tone, Tweak

Tungstate, Tungsten Scheelite, W, Wolfram

Tunic Ao dai, Caftan, Chiton, Choroid, Cote-hardie, Dalmatic, Dashiki, Gymslip, Hauberk, Kabaya, Kaftan, Kameez, K(h)urta, Tabard, Toga

Tunnel(ler) Bore, Channel, Condie, Countermine, Culvert, Cundy, Gallery, Head, Mine, Qanat, Simplon, Stope, Subway, Syrinx, Tube, Underpass, Wind, Wormhole

Turban Bandanna, Hat, Mitral, Pagri, Puggaree, Puggery, Puggree, Sash, Scarf

Turbulence, Turbulent Becket, Bellicose, Buller, Factious, Fierce, Rapids, Stormy

▷ **Turbulent** *may indicate* an anagram

Turf Caespitose, Clod, Divot, Earth, Fail, Feal, Flaught, > **GRASS**, Greensward, Peat, Screw, > **SOD**, Sward

Turk(ish) Anatolian, Bashaw, Bashkir, Bey, Bimbashi, Bostangi, Byzantine, Caimac(am), Crescent, Effendi, Gregory, Horse(tail), Irade, Kaimakam, Kazak(h), Kurd, Mameluke, Mutessarif(at), Omar, Osman(li), Ottamite, Ottoman, Ottomite, Rayah, Scanderbeg, Selim, Seljuk(ian), Seraskier, Spahi, Tatar, Timariot, Usak, Uzbeg, Uzbek, Yakut

Turkey, Turkey-like Anatolia, Brush, Bubbly(-jock), Curassow, Eyalet, Flop, Gobbler, Norfolk, Sultanate, Talegalla, TR, Trabzon, Vulturn

Turkish delight Rahat lacoum, Trehala

Turmoil Chaos, Din, Ferment, Stoor, Stour, Tornado, Tracasserie, Tumult, > **UPROAR**, Welter

▷ **Turn(ing)** *may indicate* an anagram

Turn(ing), Turned away, Turned up, Turns Act, Addle, Advert, Antrorse, Avert, Bad, Bank, Become, Bend, Bump, Career, Cartwheel, Cast, Change, Char(e), Chore, Christiana, Christie, Christy, Churn, Cock, Coil, Crank(le), Cuff, Curd(le), Curve, Defect, Deflect, Detour, Deviate, Dig, Digress, Divert, Ear, Earn, Elbow, Evert, Fadge, Flip, Forfend, Go, Good, Hairpin, Handbrake, Head-off, Hie, High, Hinge, Hup, Influence, Innings, Invert, Jar, Jink, Keel, Kick, Lodging, Lot, Luff, Mohawk, Number, Obvert, Parallel, Parry, Penchant, Pivot, Plough, Pronate, Prove, PTO, Quarter, Rebut, Refer, Refract, Retroflex, Retroussé, Retrovert, Rev, Revolt, Ride, Riffle, Rocker, Roll, Root, > **ROTATE**, Rote, Roulade, Rout, Routine, Screw, Sheer, > **SHOT**, Shout, Sicken, Skit, Slew, Slue, Solstice, Sour, > **SPELL**, Spin, Spot, Sprain, Star, Start, Stem, Step, Swash, Swing, Swivel, Telemark, Three-point, Throw, Tiptilt, Tirl, Transpose, Trend, Trick, Trie, Turtle, Twiddle, Twist, U, Uey, Up, Veer, Versed, Version, Vertigo, Volta, Volte-face, Volutation, Wap, Warp, Wend, Went, > **WHEEL**, Whelm, Whirl, Whorl, Wimple, Wind, Wrest, Wriggle, Zigzag

Turn-coat Apostate, Cato, Defector, Quisling, Rat, Renegade, Tergiversate, Traitor

Turner Axle, Lana, Lathe, Painter, Pivot, Rose-engine, Spanner, Worm, Wrench

Turning point Crisis, Crossroads, Landmark, Watershed

Turnip(-shaped) Baggy, Bagie, Hunter, Napiform, Navew, Neep, Rutabaga, > **STUPID PERSON**, Swede, Tumshie

Turn over Capsize, Careen, Flip, Inversion, Production, PTO, Somersault, TO, Up-end

Turret(ed) Barmkin, Bartisan, Garret, Louver, Louvre, Pepperbox, Sponson, > **TOWER**, Turriculate

Turtle, Turtle head Bale, Calipash, Calipee, Chelone, Diamondback, Emys, Floor, Green, Hawk(s)bill, Inverted, Leatherback, Loggerhead, Matamata, Mossback, Mud, Musk, Ridley, Screen, Snapper, Snapping, Soft-shelled, Stinkpot, Terrapin, Thalassian

Tuscany Chiantishire

Tusk Gam, Horn, Ivory, Tooth, Tush

Tussle Giust, Joust, Mêlée, Scrimmage, Scrum, Scuffle, Skirmish, Touse, Touze, Towse, Towze, Tuilyie, Wrestle

Tutor Abbé, Aristotle, Ascham, Bear, > **COACH**, Crammer, Don, Instruct, Leader, Preceptor, Répétiteur, Supervisor, Teacher

TV Baird, Box, Cable, Digital, Idiot-box, Lime Grove, Monitor, PAL, SECAM, Sky, Tele, Telly, Tube, Video

Twaddle Blether, Drivel, Rot, Slipslop, Tripe

Tweak Pluck, Twiddle, Twist, Twitch

Twelfth, Twelve Apostles, Dozen, Epiphany, Glorious, Grouse, Midday, Midnight,

N, Night, Noon, Ternion, Twal

▶ **Twice** *see* TWO

Twig(s) Besom, Birch, Cotton, Cow, Dig, Grasp, Kow, Osier, Realise, Reis, Rice, Rumble, Sarment, See, Sprig, Sticklac, Switch, Understand, Wand, Wattle, Wicker, Withe

Twilight Astronomical, Civil, Cockshut, Crepuscular, Demi-jour, Dusk, Gloam(ing), Gotterdämmerung, Nautical, Summerdim

Twin(s) Asvins, Castor, Coetaneous, Didymous, Dioscuri, Ditokous, Dizygotic, Double, Fraternal, Gemel, Identical, Isogeny, Kindred, Macle, Monozygotic, Pigeon-pair, Pollux, Siamese, Tweedledee, Tweedledum

Twine Braid, Coil, Cord, Inosculate, Packthread, Sisal, Snake, String, Twist, Wreathe

Twinkle, Twinkling Glimmer, Glint, Mo(ment), > SPARKLE, Starnie, Trice

▷ **Twirling** *may indicate* an anagram

Twist(ed), Twister, Twisting, Twisty Askant, Askew, Baccy, Becurl, Bought, Braid, Card-sharper, Chisel, Coil, Contort, Convolution, Crinkle, Crisp, Cue, Curl(icue), Cyclone, Deform, Detort, Distort, > DODGE, Entwine, Garrot, Helix, Kink, Mangulate, Mat, Oliver, Plait, Quirk, Raddle, Ravel, Rick, Rogue, Rotate, Rove, Serpent, Skew, Slew, Slub(b), Slue, Snake, Snarl, Spin, Spiral, Sprain, Squiggle, Squirm, Swivel, Tendril, Thrawn, Torc, Tornado, Torque, Torsade, Torsion, Tortile, Turn, Tweak, Twiddle, Twine, Twirl, Typhoon, Wamble, Warp, Wlnd, Wreathe, Wrench, Wrest, Wriggle, Wring, Writhe, Wry, Zigzag

▷ **Twisted, Twisting** *may indicate* an anagram

Twit, Twitter Chaff, Cherup, Chirrup, Dotterel, Gear(e), Giber, > JEER, Stupid, Taunt, Warble

Twitch(ing), Twitchy Athetosis, Clonic, Grass, Jerk, Life-blood, Start, Subsultive, Tic, Tig, Tit, Tweak, Twinge, Vellicate, Yips

Two(some), Twice Bice, Bis, Bisp, Both, Brace, Couple(t), Deuce, Double, Duad, Dual, Duet, Duo, Dyad, > PAIR, Swy, Tête-à-tête, Twain, Twins, Twister

Tycoon Baron, Magnate, Plutocrat, Shogun

Type(s), Typing A, Agate, Aldine, Antimony, Antique, B, Balaam, Baskerville, Bastard, Black-letter, Blood, Body, Bold face, Bourgeois, Braille, Brand, Brevier, Brilliant, Canon, Caslon, Category, Character, Chase, Cicero, Clarendon, Class, Columbian, Condensed, Cut, Egyptian, Elite, Elzevir, Em, Emblem, Emerald, English, Face, Font, Form(e), Founder's, Fount, Fraktur, Fudge, Garamond, Gem, Genre, Gent, Gothic, Great primer, Hair, Ilk, Image, Key, Kidney, Kind, Late-star, Ligature, Light-faced, Longprimer, Ludlow, Minion, Modern, Moon, Mould, Non-pareil, Norm, Old English, Old-face, Old Style, Paragon, Pattern, Pearl, Peculiar, Personality, Pi, Pica, Pie, Plantin, Point, Primer, Print, Quad(rat), Roman, Ronde, Ruby, Sanserif, Secretary, Semibold, Serif, Serological, Sp, Species, Spectral, Stanhope, Style, Times, Tissue, Touch, Version

▷ **Type of** *may indicate* an anagram

Typical Average, Characteristic, Classic, Normal, Representative, Standard, Symbolic, True-bred, Usual

Tyrant, Tyranny, Tyrannical Absolutism, Autocrat, Caligula, Despot, Dictator, Drawcansir, Gelon, Herod, Lordly, Nero, Oppressor, Pharaoh, Sardanapalus, Satrap, Stalin, Totalitarian, Tsar, Yoke

Tyre Balloon, Cross-ply, Cushion, Michelin, Pericles, Pneumatic, Radial, Radial(-ply), Recap, Remould, Retread, Shoe, Sidewall, Slick, Snow, Spare, Tread, Tubeless, Whitewall

Tyro Beginner, Ham, > NOVICE, Rabbit, Rookie, Rooky, Starter

Uu

Ugly Cow, Customer, Eyesore, Foul, Gorgon, Gruesome, Hideous, Homely, Huckery, Loth, Mean, Ominous, Plain

Ulcer(ous) Abscess, Aphtha, Canker, Chancroid, Decubitus, Duodenal, Gastric, Helcoid, Noma, Peptic, Phagedaena, Rodent, Rupia, Sore, Wolf

Ulster NI, Overcoat, Raincoat, Ulad

Ultimate Absolute, Basic, Deterrent, Eventual, Final, Furthest, Last, Maximum, So, Supreme, Thule

Ultrasound Lithotripsy

Umbrage Offence, Pique, Resentment, Shade

Umbrella(-shaped) Bumbershoot, Chatta, Gamp, Gingham, Gloria, Mush(room), Parasol, Sunshade, Tee

Umpire Arb(iter), Byrlawman, Daysman, Decider, Judge, Oddjobman, Odd(s)man, Overseer, Referee, Rule, Stickler, Thirdsman

Unable Can't, Incapable

Unacceptable Non-U, Not on, Out, Stigmatic

Unaccompanied A cappella, Alone, High-lone, Secco, Single, Solo, Solus

Unaffected Artless, Genuine, Homely, Natural, Plain, Sincere, Unattached

Unanswerable Erotema, Irrefragable, Irrefutable

Unappreciated Thankless

Unattached Freelance, Loose

Unattractive Drac(k), Lemon, Plain, Plug-ugly, Rebarbative, Seamy, Ugly

▷ **Unauthentic** *may indicate* an anagram

Unavail(able), Unavailing Bootless, Futile, Ineluctable, Lost, No use, Off, Vain

Unaware Heedless, Ignorant, Incognisant, Innocent, Oblivious

Unbalanced Asymmetric, Deranged, Doolalli, Doolally, Loco, Lopsided, Uneven

Unbecoming, Unbefitting Improper, Infra dig, Shabby, Unfitting, Unseemly, Unsuitable, Unworthy

Unbelievable, Unbeliever Agnostic, Atheist, Cassandra, Doubter, Giaour, Heathen, Incredible, Infidel, Pagan, Painim, Paynim, Sceptic, Tall, Zendik

Unbiased Fair, Impartial, Just, Neutral, Objective, Unattainted

Unbreakable Infrangible, Inviolate

Unbridled Fancy free, Footloose, Lawless, Uncurbed, Unrestricted, Unshackled, Untramelled

Uncanny Eerie, Eldritch, Extraordinary, Geason, Rum, Spooky, Weird

Unceasing Continuous

Uncertain(ty) Blate, Broken, Chancy, Chary, Contingent, Delicate, Dicey, Dither, Doubtful, Dubiety, Hesitant, Iffy, Indeterminate, Indistinct, Irresolute, Peradventure, Queasy, Risky, Slippery, Tentative, Vor

▷ **Uncertain** *may indicate* an anagram

Unchangeable, Unchanged, Unchanging As is, Enduring, Eternal, Idempotent, Immutable, Monotonous, Stable

Unchaste Corrupt, Immodest, Immoral, Impure, Lewd, Wanton

Uncivil(ised) Barbaric, Benighted, Boondocks, Discourteous, Disrespectful, Giant-rude, Heathen, Impolite, Military, Rude, Rudesby

Uncle Abbas, Afrikaner, Arly, Bob, Dutch, Eme, Nunky, Oom, Pawnbroker, Pop-shop, Remus, Sam, Tio, Tom, Usurer, Vanya

Unclean Defiled, Dirty, Impure, Obscene, Ordure, Squalid, Tabu, T(e)refa(h)

Unclear Ambitty, Hazy, Nebulous, Obscure

Uncommon Rare, Strange, Unusual

▷ **Uncommon(ly)** *may indicate* an anagram

Uncompromising Cutthroat, Hardline, Hardshell, Intransigent, Rigid, Strict, Ultra

Unconcerned Bland, Careless, Casual, Cold, Indifferent, Insouciant, Nonchalant, Strange

Unconditional Absolute, Free, Pure

Unconnected Asyndetic, Detached, Disjointed, Off-line

Unconscious(ness) Asleep, Catalepsy, Cold, Comatose, Instinctive, Non-ego, Subliminal, Trance, Under

Unconsummated Mariage blanc

Uncontrolled Atactic, Free, Incontinent, Loose, Wild

Unconventional Beatnik, Bohemian, Drop-out, Eccentric, Gonzo, Heretic, Heterodox, Informal, Irregular, Offbeat, Original, Outlandish, Outré, Raffish, Unorthodox

▷ **Unconventional** *may indicate* an anagram

Uncouth(ness) Backwoodsman, Bear, Crude, Gothic, Inelegant, Rube, Rude, Rugged, Uncivil

Uncover(ed) Bare, Disclose, Expose, Inoperculate, Open, Peel, Reveal, Shave, Shill, Shuck, Uncap

Unction, Unctuous(ness) Anele, Balm, Chrism, Extreme, Ointment, Oleaginous, Ooze, Smarm, Soapy

Uncultivated, Uncultured Artless, Bundu, Fallow, Ignorant, Philistine, Rude, Tramontane, Wild

Undecided Doubtful, Moot, Non-committal, Open-ended, Pending, Pendulous, Uncertain, Wavering

Under Aneath, Below, Beneath, Hypnotized, Sotto, Sub-, Unconscious

Undercoat Base, Primer

Undercover Espionage, Secret, Veiled

▶ **Undergarment** *see* **UNDERWEAR**

Undergo Bear, Dree, Endure, Sustain

Undergraduate Fresher, L, Pup, Sizar, Sophomore, Student, Subsizar

Underground (group) Basement, Catacomb, Cellar, Hell, Hypogaeous, Irgun, Kiva, Macchie, Maquis, Mattamore, Metro, Phreatic, Pict, Plutonia, Pothole, Secret, Souterrain, Subsoil, Subterranean, Subway, Tube

Undergrowth Brush, Chaparral, Firth, Frith, Scrub

Underhand Dirty, Haunch, Insidious, Lob, Oblique, Secret, Sinister, Sly, Sneaky, Surreptitious

Underline Emphasise, Insist

Underling Bottle-washer, Cog, Inferior, Jack, Menial, Munchkin, Subordinate

Undermine Erode, Fossick, Sap, Subvert, Tunnel, Weaken

Understand(able), Understanding Accept, Acumen, Agreement, Apprehend, Capeesh, Clear, Cognisable, Comprehend, Conceive, Concept, Cotton-on, Deal,

Dig, Enlighten, Entente, Exoteric, Fathom, Follow, Gather, Gauge, Gaum, Geddit, Gorm, Grasp, Have, Head, Heels, Insight, Ken, Kind, Knowhow, Learn, Light, Omniscient, Pact, Plumb, Rapport, Rapprochement, Realise, Savey, Savvy, See, Sense, Sole, Substance, Tolerance, Treaty, Tumble, Twig, Uptak(e), Wisdom, Wit

Understate(d), Understatement Litotes, M(e)iosis

Understood Implicit, OK, Perspicuous, Roger, Tacit, Unspoken

Understudy Deputy, Double, Stand-in, Sub

Undertake, Undertaking Attempt, Contract, Covenant, Enterprise, Guarantee, Pledge, Promise, Scheme, Shoulder, Warranty

Undertaker Entrepreneur, Mortician, Obligor, Sponsor, Upholder

Underwear Balbriggan, Bloomers, Bodice, Body, Body stocking, Body suit, Bra(ssiere), Briefs, Broekies, Camiknickers, Camisole, Chemise, Chemisette, Chuddies, Combinations, Combs, Corset, Dainties, Drawers, (French) knickers, Frillies, Girdle, Innerwear, Jump, Linen, Lingerie, Linings, Long Johns, Pantalets, Pantaloons, Panties, Pantihose, Panty girdle, Petticoat, Scanties, Semmit, Shift, Shorts, Singlet, Skivvy, Slip, Smalls, Stays, Step-ins, Subucula, Suspenders, Tanga, Teddy, Thermal, Underdaks, Undergarments, Underpants, Undershirt, Underthings, Undies, Unmentionables, Vest, Wyliecoat, Y-fronts®

Underworld Chthonic, Criminal, Hell, Lowlife, Mafia, Shades, Tartar(e), Tartarus, Tartary

Underwrite, Underwritten Assure, Endorse, Guarantee, Insure, Lloyds, PS

Undeveloped Backward, Depauperate, Green, Inchoate, Latent, Ridgel, Ridgil, Ridgling, Rig, Riggald, Riglin(g), Rudimentary, Seminal

Undiluted Neat, Pure, Sheer, Straight

Undivided Aseptate, Complete, Entire, Indiscrete, One

Undo(ing) Annul, Defeat, Destroy, Downfall, Dup, Poop, Poupe, Release, Ruin, Unravel

Undone Arrears, Left, Postponed, Ran, Ruined

Undoubtedly Certes, Positively, Sure

Undress(ed) Bare, Disarray, Disrobe, En cuerpo, Expose, Négligé, Nude, Nue, Peel, Querpo, Raw, Rough, Self-faced, Spar, Strip, Unapparelled

Undulate, Undulating Billow, Nebule, Ripple, Roll, Wave

▷ **Unduly** *may indicate* an anagram

Unearth(ly) Astral, Dig, Discover, Disentomb, Exhumate, Indagate

Unease, Uneasiness, Uneasy Angst, Anxious, Creeps, Inquietude, Itchy, Malaise, Restive, Shy, Tense, The willies, Uptight, Windy, Womble-cropped

Unemployed, Unemployment Drone, Idle, Latent, Lay-off, Redundant

Unending Chronic, Eternal, Lasting, Sempiternal

Unequal(led) Aniso-, Disparate, Non(e)such, Scalene, Unjust

Unerring Dead, Exact, Precise

Uneven(ness) Accident, Blotchy, Bumpy, Irregular, Jaggy, Patchy, Ragged, Scratchy

▷ **Unevenly** *may indicate* an anagram

Unexceptional Ordinary, Workaday

Unexpected(ly) Abrupt, Accidental, Adventitious, Fortuitous, Inopinate, Snap, Sodain(e), Sudden, Turn-up, Unawares, Unwary

Unexploded Live

Unfair Bias(s)ed, Crook, Dirty, Inclement, Invidious, Mean, Partial

Unfaithful Disloyal, Godless, Infidel, Traitor

Unfashionable Cube, Dowdy, Passe, Square

▷ **Unfashionable** *may indicate* 'in' to be removed

Unfasten Undo, Untie, Untruss

Unfathomable Bottomless

Unfavourable Adverse, Ill, Poor, Untoward

Unfeeling Adamant, Callous, Cold, Cruel, Dead, Hard, Inhuman(e), Insensate, Robotic

Unfinished Crude, Inchoate, Raw, Scabble, Scapple, Stickit

Unfit(ting) Disabled, Faulty, Ill, Impair, Inept, Outré, Unable

▷ **Unfit** *may indicate* an anagram

Unfold Deploy, Display, Divulge, Evolve, Interpret, Open, Relate, Spread

Unfortunate(ly) Accursed, Alack, Alas, Hapless, Ill-starred, Luckless, Shameless, Sorry, Unlucky

Unfriendly Aloof, Antagonistic, Asocial, Chill(y), Cold, Fraim, Fremd, Fremit, Hostile, Icy, Remote, Surly

Unfruitful Abortive, Barren, Sterile

Ungainly Awkward, Gawkish, Uncouth, Weedy

Ungracious Cold, Offhand, Rough, Rude

Unguent Nard, Pomade, Salve

Ungulate Antelope, Dinoceras, Eland, Equidae, Hoofed, Moose, Rhino, Ruminantia, Takin, Tapir, Tylopoda

Unhappily, Unhappy, Unhappiness Blue, Depressed, Disconsolate, Dismal, Doleful, Downcast, Down-hearted, Dysphoria, Glumpish, Love-lorn, Lovesick, Miserable, Sad, Sore, Tearful, Unlief, Upset

▷ **Unhappily** *may indicate* an anagram

Unhealthy Bad, Clinic, Diseased, Epinosic, Insalubrious, Morbid, Noxious, Peaky, Prurient, Sickly

Uniform Abolla, Battledress, Consistent, Dress, Equable, Equal, Even, Flat, Forage-cap, Homogeneous, Identical, Khaki, Kit, Livery, Regimentals, Regular, Rig, Robe, Same, Sole, Standard, Steady, Strip, Unvaried

Unimaginative Banausic, Literalistic, Pedestrian, Pooter

Unimportant Cog, Fiddling, Footling, Frivolous, Idle, Immaterial, Inconsequent, Inconsiderable, Insignificant, MacGuffin, Makeweight, Minnow, Minutiae, Negligible, Nugatory, Peripheral, Petty, Small-time, Trifling, Trivia(l)

Uninhabited Bundu, Deserted, Lonely

Uninspired Humdrum, Pedestrian, Pompier, Tame

Uninterested, Uninteresting Apathetic, Bland, Dreary, Dry, Dull, Grey, Incurious, Nondescript

Uninterrupted Constant, Continuous, Incessant, Running, Steady

Union(ist) Affiance, Allegiance, Alliance, Art, Association, Bed, Benelux, Bond, Close, Combination, Company, Concert, Confederacy, Craft, Credit, Customs, Diphthong, Economic, Enosis, Ensemble, Equity, EU, European, Federal, Federation, French, Frithgild, Fusion, Group, Guild, Heterogamy, Horizontal, Industrial, Liaison, Liberal, Link-up, Management, Marriage, Match, Merger, NUM, Nuptials, NUR, NUS, NUT, Pan-American, Pearl, RU, Rugby, Samiti, Sex, Sherman, Solidarity, Soviet, Splice, Sponsal, Student, Synthesis, Syssarcosis, Teamsters, TU, U, UNISON, USDAW, Uxorial, Vertical, Vienna, Wedding, Wedlock, Wield

Unique(ness) Alone, A-per-se, Hacceity, Inimitable, Lone, Matchless, Nonesuch, Nonpareil, Nonsuch, One-off, Only, Peerless, Rare, Singular, Sole, Sui generis

Unit Abampere, Absolute, Ace, Amp, Angstrom, Archine, Archiphoneme, Bar, Bargaining, Barn, Base, Baud, Becquerel, Bioblast, Biogen, Biophor(e),

Bit, Brigade, Byte, Cadre, Candela, Cell, Centimorgan, Centipoise, Chaldron, Congius, Corps, Coulomb, Crith, Cusec, Dalton, Daraf, Darcy, Debye, Degree, Denier, Derived, Dessiatine, Detachment, DIN, Dioptre, Division, Dobson, Dol, Dyne, Echelon, Electromagnetic, Electron, Electrostatic, Element, Em, EMU, En, Energid, Ensuite, Episome, Erg, Farad, Feedlot, Fermi, Field, Flight, Foot-candle, Foot-lambert, Foot-pound, Foot-ton, Fresnel, Fundamental, Gal, Gauss, Gestalt, GeV, Gigabit, Gigaflop, Gigahertz, Gigawatt, Gilbert, Glosseme, Gram, Grav, Gray, Henry, Hertz, Hide, Hogshead, Holon, Ion, Item, Jansky, Joule, K, Kelvin, Kilderkin, Kilerg, Kilowatt, Lambert, Last, League, Lexeme, Lumen, Lux, Magneton, Man-hour, Maxwell, Measure, Megabyte, Megahertz, Megaton, Megawatt, Megohm, Message, Metre, Mho, Micella, Micelle, Microcurie, Microinch, Micron, Mil, Module, Mole, Monad, Monetary, Mongo(e), Morgen, Morpheme, Neper, Nepit, Nest, Newton, Nit, Octa, Oersted, Ohm, Okta, Organ, Panzer, Parasang, Pascal, Ped, Pennyweight, Peripheral, Phoneme, Phot, Phyton, Pixel, Ploughgate, Point, Poise, Poundal, Power, Practical, Probit, Protoplast, RA, Radian, Rem, Remen, Rep, Ro(e)ntgen, Rutherford, Sabin, Sealed, Second, Secure, Semeion, Sememe, Shed, SI, Siemens, Sievert, Singleton, Sink, Slug, Sone, Steradian, Stere, Stilb, Stock, Stoke(s), Strontium, Syllable, Syntagm(a), TA, Tagmeme, Terabyte, Terminal, Tesla, Tetrapody, Tex, Therblig, Therm, Tog, Token, Torr, Vanitory, Vanity, Var, Vara, Volt, Wall, Watt, Weber, Wing, X, Yrneh

Unite(d) Accrete, Bind, Coalesce, Combine, Concordant, Connate, Connect, Consolidate, Consubstantiate, Covalent, Fay, Federal, Federate, Fuse, Gene, Injoint, Join, Kingdom, Knit, Lap, Link, Marry, Meint, Meng, Ment, Merge, Meynt, Ming, Nations, Oop, Oup, Siamese, Solid, States, Tie, > **WED**, Weld, Yoke

Unity Harmony, One, Solidarity, Sympathy, Togetherness

Universal, Universe All, Catholic, Cosmos, Creation, Ecumenic(al), Emma, General, Global, Infinite, Macrocosm, Mandala, Microcosm, Sphere, U, World(wide)

University Academe, Academy, Alma mater, Aston, Berkeley, Bonn, Brown, Campus, Civic, College, Columbia, Cornell, Exeter, Gown, Harvard, Ivy League, Open, OU, Oxbridge, Pennsylvania, Princeton, Reading, Redbrick, St Andrews, Sorbonne, Varsity, Yale

Unjust(ified) Groundless, Inequity, Iniquitous, Invalid, Tyrannical

Unknown Agnostic, Anon, A.N.Other, Hidden, Ign, Incog(nito), N, Nobody, Noumenon, Occult, Quantity, Secret, Soldier, Strange, Symbolic, Tertium quid, Warrior, X, Y

Unless Nisi, Save, Without

Unlike(ly) Difform, Disparate, Dubious, Far-fetched, Improbable, Inauspicious, Long shot, Outsider, Remote, Tall, Unlich

Unlimited Almighty, Boundless, Indefinite, Measureless, Nth, Universal, Vast

Unload Disburden, Discharge, Drop, Dump, Jettison, Land

Unlucky Donsie, Hapless, Ill(-starred), Inauspicious, Infaust, Jonah, Misfallen, S(c)hlimazel, Stiff, Thirteen, Untoward, Wanchancie, Wanchancy

Unmarried Bachelor, Common-law, Single, Spinster

Unmentionable(s) Bra, Foul, > **UNDERWEAR**, Undies

Unmindful Heedless, Oblivious

Unmistakable Clear, Manifest, Plain

Unnatural Abnormal, Affected, Cataphysical, Contrived, Eerie, Flat, Geep, Irregular, Strange

▷ **Unnaturally** *may indicate* an anagram

Unnecessary De trop, Extra, Gash, Gratuitous, Needless, Otiose, Redundant, Superfluous

Unobserved Backstage, Sly, Unseen
Unobtainable Nemesis
Unoccupied Empty, Idle, Vacant, Void
Unoriginal Banal, Copy, Derivative, Imitation, Plagiarised, Slavish
Unorthodox Heretic, Heterodox, Maverick, Off-the-wall, Unconventional
▷ **Unorthodox** *may indicate* an anagram
Unpaid Amateur, Brevet, Hon(orary), Voluntary
Unperturbed Bland, Calm, Serene
Unplanned Impromptu, Improvised, Spontaneous
Unpleasant, **Unpleasant person** Creep, God-awful, Grim, Grotty, Horrible,
Icky, Invidious, Nasty, Obnoxious, Odious, Offensive, Painful, Pejorative,
Rebarbative, Shady, Shitty, Shocker, Sticky, Toerag, Wart
Unpredictable Aleatory, Dicy, Erratic, Maverick, Wild card
Unprepared Ad lib, Extempore, Impromptu, Unready
Unprincipled Amoral, Dishonest, Irregular, Reprobate
Unproductive Arid, Atokal, Atokous, Barren, Dead-head, Eild, Fallow, Futile,
Lean, Poor, Shy, Sterile, Yeld, Yell
Unprofitable Bootless, Fruitless, Lean, Thankless
Unprotected Exposed, Nude, Vulnerable
Unqualified Absolute, Entire, Outright, Profound, Pure, Quack, Sheer, Straight,
Thorough, Total, Utter
Unquestionably, **Unquestioning** Absolute, Certain, Doubtless, Implicit
Unravel Construe, Disentangle, Feaze, Fray, Solve
Unreadable Poker-faced
Unreal(istic) Eidetic, En l'air, Escapist, Fake, Fancied, Illusory, Mirage, Oneiric,
Phantom, Phon(e)y, Pseudo, Romantic, Sham, Spurious
Unreasonable, **Unreasoning** Absurd, Bigot, Extreme, Illogical, Irrational,
Misguided, Perverse, Rabid
Unrecognised Incognito, Inconnu, Invalid, Thankless, Unsung
Unrefined Coarse, Common, Crude, Earthy, Gur, Rude, Vul(g), Vulgar
Unrelenting Implacable, Remorseless, Severe, Stern
Unreliable Dodgy, Erratic, Fickle, Flighty, Fly-by-night, Shonky, Unstable,
Wankle, Wonky
Unresponsive Cold, Frigid, Nastic, Rigor
Unrest Discontent, Ferment
Unrestrained Free, Hearty, Homeric, Immoderate, Incontinent, Lax, Lowsit,
Rampant, Wanton, Wild
Unruly Anarchic, Bodgie, Buckie, Camstairy, Camsteary, Camsteerie, Coltish,
Exception, Fractious, Lawless, Obstreperous, Ragd(e), Raged, Ragged,
Rambunctious, Rampageous, Rattlebag, Riotous, Tartar, Turbulent, Turk,
Wanton, Wayward, Zoo
▷ **Unruly** *may indicate* an anagram
Unsafe Deathtrap, Fishy, Insecure, Perilous, Precarious, Vulnerable
Unsatisfactory, **Unsatisfying** Bad, Lame, Lousy, Meagre, Rocky, Thin,
Wanting
Unseasonable, **Unseasoned** Green, Murken, Raw, Untimely
Unseemly Coarse, Improper, Indecent, Indign, Untoward
Unselfish Altruist, Generous
Unsettle(d) Homeless, Hunky, Indecisive, Nervous, Outstanding, Queasy,
Restive

▷ **Unsettled** *may indicate* an anagram

Unsight(ed), Unsightly Hideous, Repulsive, Ugly

Unskilled Awkward, Dilutee, Gauche, Green, Inexpert, Rude

Unsophisticated Alf, Boondocks, Boonies, Bushie, Cornball, Corny, Cracker-barrel, Direct, Down-home, Faux-naif, Hillbilly, Homebred, Homespun, Inurbane, Jaap, Jay, Naive, Provincial, Rube, Verdant

Unsound Barmy, Infirm, Invalid, Shaky, Wildcat, Wonky

▷ **Unsound** *may indicate* an anagram

Unspeakable Dreadful, Ineffable, Nefandous

Unspoiled, Unspoilt Innocent, Natural, Perfect, Pristine, Pure

Unstable, Unsteady Anomic, Astatic, Bockedy, Casual, Crank, Crank(y), Dicky, Erratic, Flexuose, Flexuous, Fluidal, Giddy, Groggy, Infirm, Insecure, Labile, Rickety, Shifty, Slippy, Tickle, Tottery, Totty, Variable, Walty, Wambling, Wankle, Warby, Wobbly

▶ **Unsteady** *see* UNSTABLE

▷ **Unstuck** *may indicate* an anagram

Unsubstantial Aeriform, Airy, Flimsy, Paltry, Shadowy, Slight, Thin, Yeasty

Unsuccessful Abortive, Futile, Manqué, Vain

Unsuitable Impair, Improper, Inapt, Incongruous, Inexpedient, Malapropos, Unfit

Untidy Daggy, Dowd(y), Frowzy, Litterbug, Ragged, Scruff(y), Slipshod, Slovenly, Tatty

▷ **Untidy** *may indicate* an anagram

Untie Free, Undo, Unlace

Untold Secret, Umpteen, Unread, Unred, Vast

Untouchable Burakumin, Dalit, Harijan, Immune, Sealed

▷ **Untrained** *may indicate* 'BR' to be removed

Untroubled Insouciant

Untrue, Untruth Apocryphal, Eccentric, Faithless, False(hood), Lie, Prefabrication, Unleal

Untrustworthy Dishonest, Fickle, Shifty, Sleeky, Tricky

Unused, Unusable Impracticable, New, Over, Wasted

Unusual(ly) Abnormal, Atypical, Exceptional, Extra(ordinary), Freak, New, Novel, Odd, Out-of-the-way, Outre, Particular, Rare, Remarkable, Singular, Special, > STRANGE, Unco, Unique, Untypical, Unwonted

▷ **Unusual** *may indicate* an anagram

Unvarying Constant, Eternal, Stable, Static, Uniform

Unwanted De trop, Exile, Gooseberry, Nimby, Outcast, Sorn

Unwashed Grubby

Unwelcome, Unwelcoming Frosty, Icy, Lulu, Obtrusive, (Persona) Non grata

Unwell Ailing, Crook, Dicky, Ill, Impure, Poorly, Seedy, Toxic

Unwholesome Miasmous, Morbid, Noxious

Unwilling(ness) Averse, Disinclined, Intestate, Loth, Nolition, Nolo, Perforce, Reluctant

Unwind Relax, Straighten, Unreave, Unreeve

▷ **Unwind** *may indicate* an anagram

Unwise Foolish, Ill-advised, Impolitic, Imprudent, Inexpedient, Injudicious, Rash

Unworthy Below, Beneath, Indign, Inferior

Unyielding Adamant, Eild, Firm, Inexorable, Intransigent, Obdurate, Rigid, Steely, Stubborn, Tough

Up(on), **Upturned**, **Upper**, **Uppish** A, Afoot, Antidepressant, Arrogant, Astir, Astray, Astride, Cloud-kissing, Euphoric, Heavenward, Hep, Horsed, Incitant, Off, On, Primo, Range, Ride, Riding, Skyward, Speed, > UPPER CLASS, Vamp, Ventral

Upbraid Abuse, Rebuke, Reproach, Reprove, Scold, Twit

Update Brief, Renew, Report

Upfront Open

Upheaval Cataclysm, Eruption, Seismic, Stir

▷ **Upheld** *may indicate* 'up' in another word

Uphill Arduous, Borstal, Sisyphean

Upholstery Lampas, Moquette, Trim

Uplift Boost, Edify, Elate, Elevation, Exalt, Hoist, Levitation, Sky

Upper class, **Upper crust** Aristocrat, County, Crachach, Nobility, Patrician, Posh, Sial, Top-hat, Tweedy, U

Upright(s), **Uprightness** Aclinic, Anend, Apeak, Apeek, Aplomb, Arrect, Erect, Goalpost, Honest, Jamb, Joanna, Merlon, Mullion, Orthograde, Perpendicular, Piano, Pilaster(s), Post, Rectitude, Roman, Splat, Stanchion, Stares, Stile, Stud, Vertical, Virtuous

Uprising Incline, Intifada, Rebellion, Revolt, Tumulus

Uproar(ious) Ballyhoo, Bedlam, Blatancy, Brouhaha, Charivari, Clamour, Collieshangie, Commotion, Cry, Din, Dirdam, Dirdum, Durdum, Emeute, Ferment, Flaw, Fracas, Furore, Garboil, Hell, Hoopla, Hubbub(oo), Hullabaloo, Hurly(-burly), Katzenjammer, Noise, Noyes, Outcry, Pandemonium, Racket, Raird, Reird, Riotous, Roister, Romage, Rowdedow, Rowdydow(dy), Ruckus, Ruction, Rumpus, Stramash, Turmoil, Whoobub

Uproot Eradicate, Evict, Outweed, Supplant, Weed

Upset(ting) Aggrieve, Alarm, Bother, Capsize, Catastrophe, Choked, Coup, Cowp, Crank, Derange, Dip, Discomboberate, Discombobulate, Discomfit, Discomfort, Discommode, Disconcert, Dismay, Disquiet, Distraught, Disturb, Dod, Eat, Fuss, Inversion, Keel, Miff, Nauseative, Offend, Overthrow, Overturn, Perturb, Pip, Pother, Purl, Rattle, Rile, Ruffle, Rumple, Sad, Seel, Shake, Sore, Spill, Tapsalteerie, Tip, Topple, Trauma, Undo

▷ **Upset** *may indicate* an anagram; a word upside down; or 'tes'

Upshot Outcome, Result, Sequel

Upside down Inverted, Resupinate, Tapsie-teerie, Topsy-turvy

▷ **Upstart** *may indicate* 'u'

Up to Till, Until

Up-to-date Abreast, Contemporary, Current, Mod, New-fashioned, Right-on, State-of-the-art, Swinging, Topical, Trendy

Upwards Acclivious, Aloft, Antrorse, Cabré

Urban Civic, Megalopolis, Municipal, Town

Urbane Civil, Debonair, Townly

Urchin Arab, Brat, Crinoid, Crossfish, Cystoid, Echinoidea, Echinus, Gamin, Gutty, Heart, Mudlark, Nipper, Ragamuffin, Sand-dollar, Sea-egg, Spatangoidea, Spatangus, Street-arab, Townskip

Urge, **Urgent** Admonish, Ca, Coax, Constrain, Crying, Dire, Drive, Egg, Enjoin, Exhort, Exigent, Goad, Hard, Hie, Hoick, Hunger, Hurry, Id, Immediate, Impel, Impulse, Incense, Incite, Insist(ent), Instance, Instigate, Itch, Kick, Libido, Nag, Peremptory, Persuade, Press(ing), Prod, Push, Set on, Spur, Strong, Wanderlust, Whig, Yen

▷ **Urgent** *may indicate* 'Ur-gent', viz. Iraqi

Urinal Bog, John, Jordan, > LAVATORY, Loo, Pissoir

Urinate, **Urine** Chamber-lye, Emiction, Enuresis, Lant, Leak, Micturition, Pee, Piddle, Piss, Slash, Stale, Strangury, Tiddle, Widdle

Urn(s), **Urn-shaped** Cinerarium, Ewer, Grecian, Olla, Ossuary, Samovar, Storied, Vase

Us 's, UK, Uns, We

Usage, **Use(r)**, **Used**, **Utilise** Application, Apply, Avail, Boot, Consume, Custom, Deploy, Dow, > EMPLOY, Ex, Exercise, Exert, Exploit, Flesh, Habit, Hand-me-down, Inured, Manner, Ply, Practice, Sarum, Spent, Sport, Tradition, Treat, Ure, Wield, With, Wont

Useful Asset, Availing, Commodity, Dow, Expedient, Invaluable

Useless Base, Bung, Cumber, Dead-wood, Dud, Empty, Futile, Gewgaw, Idle, Inane, Ineffective, Lame, Lemon, Otiose, Plug, Sculpin, Sterile, Swap, US, Vain, Void, Wet

Usher Black Rod, Chobdar, Commissionaire, Conduct(or), Doorman, Escort, Guide, Herald, Huissier, Macer, Rod, Show, Steward

Usual Common, Customary, Habit(ual), Natural, Normal, Ordinary, Routine, Rule, Solito, Stock, Typical, Wont

Usurer, **Usury** Gombeen, Loanshark, Moneylender, Note-shaver, Shark, Uncle

Utensil(s) Batterie, Battery, Chopsticks, Colander, Cookware, Corer, Fish-kettle, Fork, Funnel, Gadget, Grater, Gridiron, Implement, Instrument, Knife, Mandolin(e), Ricer, Scoop, Skillet, Spatula, Spoon, Things, Tool, Zester

▶ **Utilise** *see* USE

Utilitarian Benthamite, Mill, Practical, Useful

Utility Elec(tricity), Gas, Water

Utmost Best, Extreme, Farthest, Maximum

Utopia(n) Adland, Cloud-cuckoo-land, Ideal, Pantisocracy, Paradise, Perfect, Shangri-la

Utter(ance), **Uttered**, **Utterly** Absolute, Accent, Agrapha, Agraphon, Arrant, Cry, Dead, Deliver, Dictum, Dog, Downright, Ejaculate, Enunciate, Express, Extreme, Glossolalia, Issue, Judgement, Lenes, Lenis, Most, Oracle, Pass, Phonate, Pronounce, Pure, Quo(th), Rank, Rattle, Remark, Saw, > SAY, Sheer, Stark, State, Syllable, Tell, Vend, Vent, Very, Voice

Vv

V Anti, Bomb, Del, Five, Nabla, See, Sign, Verb, Verse, Versus, Victor(y), Volt, Volume

Vacancy, Vacant Blank, Empty, Glassy, Hole, Hollow, Inane, Place, Space, Vacuum

Vacation Holiday, Leave, Outing, Recess, Trip, Voidance

Vaccination, Vaccine Antigen, Cure, HIB, Jenner, Sabin, Salk, Serum, Subunit

Vacuum Blank, Cleaner, Dewar, Emptiness, Magnetron, Nothing, Plenum, Thermos®, Void

Vagabond Bergie, Gadling, > GYPSY, Hobo, Landlo(u)per, Rapparee, Romany, Rover, Runagate, Tramp

Vague(ness) Amorphous, Bleary, Blur, Confused, Dim, Equivocal, Hazy, Ill-defined, Ill-headed, Indeterminate, Indistinct, Loose, Mist, Nebulous, Shadowy, Woolly-minded

▷ **Vaguely** *may indicate* an anagram

Vain Bootless, Coxcomb, Coxcomical, Egoistic, Empty, Fruitless, > FUTILE, Hollow, Idle, Proud, Strutting, Useless, Vogie

Valet Aid, Andrew, Jeames, Jeeves, Man, Passepartout, Servant, Skip-kennel

Valiant Brave, Doughty, Heroic, Resolute, Stalwart, Stouthearted, Wight

Valid(ate) Confirm, Establish, Just, Legal, Sound

Valley Clough, Comb(e), Coomb, Cwm, Dale, Dean, Death, Defile, Dell, Den, Dene, Dingle, Dip, Drowned, Dry, Ghyll, Glen, Grindelwald, Hollow, Ravine, Ria, Rift, Silicon, Tempe, Vale

Valour Bravery, Courage, Heroism, Merit, Prowess

Valuable, Valuation, Value Absolute, Acid, Appraise, Appreciate, Apprize, Assess(ment), Asset, Bargain, Calibrate, Carbon, Checksum, Cherish, CIF, Cop, Cost, Crossover, Denomination, Equity, Esteem, Estimate, Expected, Face, Feck, Hagberg, Intrinsic, Limit, Market, Modulus, Net present, Net realizable, Nominal, Nuisance, Omnium, Par, pH, Place, Precious, Present, Price, Prize, Prys, Quartile, Rarity, Rate, Rateable, Rating, Regard, Residual, Respect, Rogue, Salt, Sentimental, Set, Steem, Stent, Store, Street, Surrender, Taonga, Time, Treasure, Valuta, > WORTH

Valve Air, Ball, Bicuspid, Bleed, Butterfly, Check, Clack, Cock, Dynatron, Flip-flop, Gate, Magnetron, Mitral, Non-return, Pentode, Petcock, Piston, Poppet, Puppet, Resnatron, Safety, Seacock, Semilunar, Shut-off, Sleeve, Sluice, Stopcock, Tap, Tetrode, Thermionic, Throttle, Thyratron, Triode, Ventil, Vibroton

Vampire Bat, Dracula, False, Ghoul, Lamia, Lilith, Pontianak

Van(guard) Advance, Box-car, Brake, Camper, Cart, Dormobile®, Forefront, Foremost, Front, Head, Kombi®, Lead, Leader(s), Lorry, Loudspeaker, Panel, Pantechnicon, Removal, Spearhead, Truck, Ute, Wagon

Vandal(ise), Vandalism Desecrate, Hooligan, Hun, Loot, Pillage, Ravage, Rough, Sab(oteur), Sack, Saracen, Skinhead, Slash, Trash

Vanish(ed) Cease, Disappear, Disperse, Dissolve, Evanesce(nt), Evaporate, Extinct, Faint(ed), Mizzle, Slope, Unbe

Vanity Amour-propre, Arrogance, Ego, Esteem, Futility, Pomp, Pretension, Pride, Self-esteem

Vaporise, Vapour Boil, Cloud, Fog, Fume, Halitus, Iodine, Miasma, Mist, Reek, Roke, > STEAM, Steme, Water

▶ **Variable, Variance, Variant, Variation** *see* VARY

▶ **Varied, Variety** *see* VARY

▷ **Varied** *may indicate* an anagram

Variegate(d) Dappled, Flecked, Fretted, Motley, Mottle, Pied, Rainbow, Skewbald, Tissue

▷ **Variety of** *may indicate* an anagram

Various Divers(e), Manifold, Multifarious, Several, Sundry

Varnish(ing) Arar, Bee-glue, Copal, Cowdie-gum, Dam(m)ar, Desert, Dope, Dragon's-blood, Glair, Japan, Lacquer, Lentisk, Nail, Nibs, Resin, Shellac, Spirit, Tung-oil, Tung-tree, Vernis martin, Vernissage

Vary(ing), Variable, Variance, Variant, Variation, Varied, Variety Ablaut, Alter, Amphoteric, Assortment, Breed, Brew, Cepheid, Change, Chequered, Colour, Contrapuntal, Counterpoint, Dependent, Differ, Discrepancy, Diverse, Diversity, Dummy, Eclectic, Enigma, Fickle, Fluctuating, Form, Grid, Iid, Inconsistent, Inconstant, Independent, Line, Medley, Mix, Morph, Multifarious, Multiplicity, Mutable, Nuance, Olio, Omniform, Parametric, Protean, Random, Remedy, Response, Smorgasbord, Sort, Species, Spice, Sport, Stirps, Stochastic, Strain, Timeserver, Tolerance, Twistor, Var, Versatile, Versiform, Version, Vicissitude, VI, Wane, Wax, X, Y, Z

Vase Bronteum, Canopus, Diota, Hydria, Jardiniere, Kalpis, Lecythus, Lekythos, Murr(h)a, Portland, Pot, Potiche, Stamnos, Urn, Vessel

Vasectomy Desexing

Vast(ness) Big, Cosmic, Enormous, Epic, Extensive, Huge(ous), Immense, Mighty, Ocean, Prodigious

Vat Back, Barrel, Blunger, Chessel, Copper, Cowl, Cuvee, Fat, Girnel, Keir, Kier, Tank, Tub, Tun

Vault(ed), Vaulting Arch, Barrel, Cavern, Cellar, Chamber, Clear, Cross, Crypt, Cul-de-four, Cupola, Dome, Dungeon, Fan, Firmament, Fornicate, Groin, Hypogeum, Jump, Kiva, Leap(frog), Lierne, Palm, Pend, Pendentive, Pole, Rib, Safe, Sepulchre, Severy, Shade, Souterrain, Tomb, Wagon, Weem

▷ **Vault** *may indicate* an anagram

Veda Yajurveda

Veer Bag, Boxhaul, Broach, Deviate, Gybe, Swerve, Tack, Turn, Wear, Yaw

Vegan Parev(e), Parve

Vegetable(s) Alexanders, Allium, Artichoke, Asparagus, Aubergine, Beans, Beet(root), Borecole, Brassica, Broccoli, Cabbage, Calabrese, Calaloo, Calalu, Cardoon, Carrot, Castock, Cauliflower, Celeriac, Celery, Chard, Chicory, Chiffonade, Chive, Choko, Chufa, Cocoyam, Colcannon, Cole, Collard, Corn-on-the-cob, Coulis, Courgette, Crout, Cucumber, Custock, Daikon, Endive, Escarole, Eschalot, Fennel, Finocchio, Flora, Gherkin, Greens, Guar, Hastings, Inert, Ingan, Jerusalem artichoke, Jicama, Kale, Kohlrabi, Kumara, Kumera, Lablab, Leek, Legume(n), Lettuce, Macedoine, Mangel(-wurzel), Mangetout, Mangold, Marrow(-squash), Mirepoix, Mooli, Navew, Neep, Oca, Okra, Okro, Olitory, Onion, Orach(e), Parsnip, Pea(se), Pepper, Pimento, Plant, Potato, Pottage, Pratie, Primavera, Pulse, Pumpkin, Quinoa, Radicchio, Radish, Rapini, Ratatouille, Rocambole, Root, Rutabaga, Sabji, Salad, Salsify, Samphire, Sauce, Sauerkraut, Savoy, Scorzonera, Shallot, Sibol, Sium, Skirret, Sorrel, Spinach(-beet), Spinage, Sprouts, Spud, Squash, Succotash, Swede, Sweet corn,

Sweet potato, Taro, Tomato, Tonka-bean, Triffid, Turnip, Udo, Wort, Yam, Zucchini

Vegetarian Herbivore, Meatless, Vegan, Veggie

Vegetate, Vegetator, Vegetation Alga, Flora, Greenery, Herb, Maquis, Quadrat, Scrub, Stagnate

Vehemence, Vehement(ly) Amain, Ardent, Fervid, Frenzy, Heat, Hot, Intense, Violent

Vehicle Ambulance, Amtrack, Artic, Articulated, ATV, Autocycle, Autorickshaw, Brake, Brancard, Buckboard, Buggy, Bus, Cab, Camper, Car, Caravan, Carry-all, Cart, Channel, Chariot, Commercial, Conveyance, Crate, Curricle, Cycle, Dennet, Dog-cart, Dormobile®, Dray, Duck, Dune buggy, Estate car, Fiacre, Float, Fly, Four-by-four, Four-seater, Gharri, Gharry, Gladstone, Go-cart, Go-kart, Go-Ped®, Gritter, Growler, Half-track, Hansom, Hatchback, Hearse, Hovercraft, Jeep®, Jeepney, Jet-Ski, Jingle, Jinker, Jitney, Juggernaut, Kago, Kart, Koneke, Landau, Land Rover, Launch, LEM, Limber, Litter, Lorry, Machine, Means, Medium, Micro-scooter, Minibus, Minicab, Minivan, Motor, Multipurpose, Norimon, Offroad, Paddock-basher, Pantechnicon, Pedicab, Penny-farthing, People carrier, People-mover, Perambulator, Personnel carrier, Phaeton, Pick-up, Quad, Recreational, Re-entry, Ricksha(w), Runabout, Samlor, Sand-yacht, Scow, Shay, Shuttle, Sidecar, Skibob, Skidoo®, Sled(ge), Sleigh, Sno-Cat®, Snowmobile, Snowplough, Soyuz, Spider, Stanhope, Station wagon, Steam-car, Sulky, Surrey, Tarantas(s), Taxi, Tempera, Three-wheeler, Tipcart, Tip-up, Tonga, Tracked, Tractor, Trailer, Tram, Transporter, Trap, Tricar, Tricycle, Trishaw, Troika, Trolley, Trolleybus, Truck, Tuk tuk, Tumble-car(t), Tumbril, Turbo, Two-seater, Two-wheeler, Unicycle, Ute, Utility, Vahana, Velocipede, Vespa, Volante, Wagon, Wheelbarrow, Wrecker

Veil Burk(h)a, Calyptra, Chad(d)ar, Chador, Chuddah, Chuddar, Cover, Curtain, Envelop, Hejab, Hijab, Humeral, Kalyptra, Kiss-me, Lambrequin, Mantilla, Mist, Obscure, Purdah, Scene, Veale, Volet, Weeper, Wimple, Yashmak

Vein Artery, Basilic, Coronary, Costa, Epithermal, Fahlband, Gate, Innominate, Jugular, Ledge, Lode, Mainline, Media, Midrib, Mood, Nervure, Percurrent, Portal, Postcava, Precava, Pulmonary, Rake, Rib, Saphena, Sectorial, Stockwork, Stringer, Style, Varicose, Varix, Vena, Venule

Velocity Muzzle, Radial, Rate, Speed, Terminal, V

Veneer Facade, Gloss, Varnish

Venerable Aged, August, Bede, Guru, Hoary, Sacred, Sage, Vintage

Venerate, Veneration Adore, Awe, Douleia, Dulia, Hallow, Homage, Idolise, Latria, Revere, Worship

Vengeance, Vengeful Erinyes, Reprisal, Ultion, Vindictive, Wannion, Wrack, Wreak

Venice La Serenissima

Venom(ous) Poison, Rancour, Spite, Toxic, Virus

Vent Aperture, Belch, Chimney, Emit, Express, Fumarole, Issue, Ostiole, Outlet, Solfatara, Spiracle, Undercast, Wreak

Ventilate, Ventilator Air, Air-brick, Air-hole, Discuss, Express, Louvre, Plenum, Shaft, Voice, Winze

Venture(d) Ante, Chance, Dare, Daur, Durst, Flutter, Foray, Handsel, Hazard, Opine, Presume, Promotion, Risk, Spec, Throw

Venue Bout, Locale, Place, Showground, Stadium, Tryst, Visne

Venus Cohog, Cytherean, Hesper(us), Love, Lucifer, Morning-star, Primavera, Quahog, Rokeby, Vesper

Veracity, Veracious Accurate, Factual, Sincere, Truth(ful)

Veranda(h) Balcony, Gallery, Lanai, Patio, Porch, Sleep-out, Stoep, Stoop, Terrace

Verb(al), **Verbs** Active, Auxiliary, Conative, Copula, Infinitive, Intransitive, Irregular, Passive, Phrasal, Preterite, Stative, Transitive, Vb, Word-of-mouth

Verbose, **Verbosity** Padding, Prolix, Talkative, Wordy

Verdict Decision, Judg(e)ment, Open, Opinion, Pronouncement, Resolution, Ruling

Verge Border, Brink, > EDGE, Hard shoulder, Incline, Rim

Verify Affirm, Ascertain, Check, Crosscheck, Prove, Validate

Vermin(ous) Lice, Mice, Ratty, > RODENT, Scum

Vernacular Common, Dialect, Idiom, Jargon, Lingo, Native, Patois

Versatile Adaptable, All-rounder, Flexible, Handy, Protean, Resourceful

Verse(s), **Versed** Dactyl, Free, Linked, Logaoedic, Passus, Poetry, Political, Reported, > RHYME

▷ **Versed** *may indicate* reversed

Version Account, Authorised, Cover, Edition, Form, Paraphrase, Rede, Rendering, Rendition, Revision, Translation

Vertical Apeak, Apeek, Atrip, Erect, Lapse, Ordinate, Perpendicular, Plumb, Sheer, Standing, Stemmed, Stile, Upright

Vertigo Dinic, Dizziness, Fainting, Giddiness, Megrim, Nausea, Staggers, Whirling

Very (good, well) A1, Ae, Assai, Awfully, Bonzer, Boshta, Boshter, Dashed, Def, Ever, Extreme(ly), Fell, Frightfully, Gey, Grouse, Heap, Hellova, Helluva, Highly, Jolly, Light, Mighty, Molto, Much, OK, Opt, Precious, Precise, Purler, Real, Self same, So, Sore, Stinking, Très, Utter, V, VG, Way

Vessel > BOAT, Capillary, Container, Craft, Dish, Motor, Pressure, Receptacle, Seed, > SHIP, Utensil, Vascular

Vest Beset, Confer, Gilet, Modesty, Semmit, Singlet, Skivvy, Spencer, Sticharion, String, Undercoat, Waistcoat

Vestibule Anteroom, Atrium, Entry, Exedra, Foyer, Hall, Lobby, Narthex, Porch, Portico, Pronaos, Tambour

Vestment Alb, Chasuble, Cotta, Dalmatic, Ephod, Fannel, Fanon, Garb, > GARMENT, Mantelletta, Omophorion, Pallium, Parament, Ph(a)elonian, Pontificals, Raiment, Rational, Rochet, Rocquet, Sakkos, Sticharion, Stole, Surplice, Tunic(le)

Vet(ting), **Veterinary**, **Vets** Check, Doc(tor), Examine, Inspect, OK, Screen, Veteran, Zoiatria, Zootherapy

Veteran BL, Expert, GAR, Master, Oldster, Old sweat, Old-timer, Old 'un, Retread, Seasoned, Soldier, Stager, Stalwart, Stalworth, Vet, War-horse

▷ **Veteran** *may indicate* 'obsolete'

Veto Ban, Bar, Debar, Item, Local, Negative, Pocket, Reject, Taboo, Tabu

Vex(ing), **Vexed** Anger, Annoy, Bother, Chagrin, Debate, Fret, Gall, Grieve, Harass, Irritate, Mortify, Pester, Rankle, Rile, Sore, Spite, Tease, Torment, Trouble

Via By, Per, Through

Viable Economic, Going, Healthy, Possible

Vibrate, **Vibration(s)** Atmosphere, Diadrom, Dinnle, Dirl, Flutter, Fremitus, Hotter, Jar, Judder, Oscillate, Pulse, Quake, Resonance, Seiche, Shimmy, Shudder, Thrill, Throb, Tingle, Tremble, Tremor, Trill, Twinkle, Wag, Whir(r)

Vicar Bray, Elton, Incumbent, Pastoral, Plenarty, Primrose, Rector, Rev(erend), Trimmer

Vice Clamp, Crime, Deputy, Eale, Evil, Greed, Iniquity, Instead, Jaws, Regent, Second (in command), > SIN

Viceroy Khedive, Nawab, Provost, Satrap, Willingdon

Vicinity Area, Environs, Locality, Neighbourhood, Region

Victim Abel, Butt, Casualty, Dupe, Frame, Host, Lay-down, Mark, Martyr, Nebbich, Neb(b)ish, Pathic, Patsy, Prey, Quarry, Sacrifice, Scapegoat

Victor(y) Banzai, Beater, Cadmean, Captor, Champ(ion), Conqueror, Conquest, Epinicion, Epinikion, Flagship, Fool's mate, Gree, Gris, Hugo, Jai, Kobe, Landslide, Lepanto, Ludorum, Mature, Nike, Palm, Philippi, Pyrrhic, Runaway, Scalp, Signal, Triumph, VE (day), Vee, Vic, Walkover, Win(ner)

Vie Compete, Contend, Emulate, Strive

Vietcong Charley, Charlie

View(er) Aim, Angle, Aspect, Belief, Bird's eye, Cineaste, Consensus, Consider, Cosmorama, Dekko, Dogma, Doxy, Endoscope, Eye, Facet, Gander, Glimpse, Grandstand, Idea, Introspect, Kaleidoscope, Landscape, Notion, Opinion, Optic®, Outlook, Pan, Panorama, Point, Private, Profile, > **PROSPECT**, Scan, Scape, Scene(ry), See, Sight, Slant, Specular, Standpoint, Stereoscope, Synop(sis), Tenet, Thanatopsis, Theory, Veduta, Vista, Visto, Watch, Witness, Worm's eye

Viewpoint Attitude, Belvedere, Grandstand, Perspective, Sight

Vigil, Vigilant(e) Awake, Aware, Deathwatch, Eve, Lyke-wake, Wake, Wake-rife, Wary, Watch

Vigorous(ly), Vigour Athletic, Bant, Billy-o, Billy-oh, Birr, Blooming, Brisk, Con brio, Drastic, Elan, Emphatic, Energetic, Flame, Forceful, Furioso, Go, Green, Heart(y), Heterosis, Hybrid, Lush, Lustihood, Lusty, P, Pep, Pith, Potency, Punchy, Pzazz, Racy, Rank, Robust, Round, Rude, Spirit, Sprack, Sprag, Steam, Sthenic, Stingo, Strength, Strong, Thews, Tireless, Tone, Tooth and nail, Trenchant, Vegete, Vim, Vitality, Vivid, Voema, Zip

▷ **Vigorously** *may indicate* an anagram

Vile Base, Corrupt, Depraved, Dregs, Durance, Earthly, Mean, Offensive, Scurvy, Vicious

Villa Bastide, Chalet, Dacha, House

Village Aldea, Auburn, Burg, Clachan, Dorp, Endship, Global, Gram, Greenwich, Hamlet, Kainga, Kampong, Kraal, Mir, Pueblo, Rancheria, Rancherie, Shtetl, Thorp(e), Vill, Wick

Villain(y) Baddy, Bluebeard, Bravo, Crim(inal), Crime, Dastard, Dog, Heavy, Iago, Knave, Macaire, Miscreant, Mohock, Nefarious, Ogre, Rogue, Scelerat, Scoundrel, Tearaway, Traitor

Vim Go, Vigour, Vitality, Zing

Vindicate, Vindication Absolve, Acquit, Apologia, Avenge, Clear, Compurgation, Darraign(e), Darrain(e), Darrayn, Defend, Deraign, Justify

Vindictive Hostile, Malevolent, Repay(ing), Spiteful

Vinegar Acetic, Alegar, Balsam, Eisel(l), Esile, Oxymel, Tarragon, Wine

Vintage Classic, Crack, Cru, Old, Quality

Viola, Violet African, Alto, Amethyst, Archil, Dame's, Dog, Dog's tooth, Gamba, Gentian, Gridelin, Ianthine, Indole, Ionone, Kiss-me, Mauve, Orchil, Pansy, Parma, Prater, Saintpaulia, Shrinking, Tenor

Violate, Violating, Violation Abuse, Breach, Contravene, Defile, Desecrate, Fract, Infraction, March-treason, Outrage, Peccant, Rape, Ravish, Stuprate, Transgress, Trespass

Violence, Violent(ly) Amain, Attentat, Berserk, Brutal, Drastic, Extreme, Fierce, Flagrant, Force, Frenzied, Furious, Heady, Het, High, Hot, Mighty, Onset, Rage, Rampage, Rampant, Rough, Rude, Severe, Slap, Stormy, Ta(r)tar, Tearaway, Thuggery, Tinderbox, Vehement, Vie

▶ **Violet** *see* VIOLA

Violin(ist), **Violin-maker**, **Violin-shaped** Alto, Amati, Cremona, Fiddle, Griddle, Guarneri(us), Guarnieri, Kit, Leader, Luthier, Nero, Paganini, Rebeck, Rote, Stradivarius

VIP Bashaw, Bigshot, Bigwig, Brass, Cheese, Cob, Effendi, Envoy, Imago, Magnate, Magnifico, Mugwump, Nabob, Nib, Nob, Pot, Snob, Someone, Swell, Tuft, Tycoon, Worthy

Virago Amazon, Battle-axe, Beldam(e), Harpy, Shrew

Virgin(al), **Virginity** Celibate, Chaste, Cherry, Intact, Maiden, Maidenhead, Maidenhood, May, New, Pietà, Pucel(l)age, Pucelle, Pure, Queen, Snood, Tarpeia, Vestal

Virile, **Virility** Energetic, Machismo, Macho, Manly, Red-blooded

Virtue(s), **Virtuous** Angelic, Assay-piece, Attribute, Cardinal, Caritas, Charity, Chastity, Continent, Dharma, Efficacy, Ethical, Excellent, Faith, Fortitude, Good, Grace, Hope, Justice, Moral(ity), Natural, Patience, Plaster-saint, Principal, Prudence, Qua, Say-piece, Temperance, Theological, Upright, Worth

Virulent Acrimonious, Deadly, Hostile, Malign, Noxious, Toxic, Vitriolic, Waspish

Viscera Bowels, Entrails, Giblets, Guts, Harigal(d)s, Haslet, Innards, Omentum, Umbles, Vitals

Viscous (liquid), **Viscosity** Glaireous, Gluey, Gummy, Slab, Sticky, Stoke, Tacky, Tar, Thick

Visible Clear, Conspicuous, Evident, Explicit, Obvious

Vision(ary) Aery, Aisling, Apparition, Bourignian, Double, Dream(er), Emmetropia, Fancy, Idealist, Image, Kef, Moonshine, Mouse-sight, Mystic, Ocular, Phantasm(a), Phantom, Pholism, Photopia, Romantic, Seeing, Seer, Sight, Stereo, Tunnel, Twenty-twenty

Visit(or) Affliction, Alien, Caller, ET, Event, First-foot, Guest, Habitue, Haunt, Kursaal, See, Sightseer, Stranger, Take

Visor, **Vizor** Eyeshade, Mesail, Mezail, Umbrel, Umbr(i)ere, Umbril, Vent(ayle)

Vital(ity) Alive, Central, Critical, Crucial, Energy, Esprit, Essential, Existent, Foison, Gusto, Indispensable, Key, Kick, Life-blood, Linchpin, Lung, Mites, Momentous, Necessary, Oomph, Organ, Pizzazz, Salvation, Sap, Viable, Vigour, Zing, Zoetic

Vitriol(ic) Acid, Acrimonious, Biting, Caustic, Mordant

Vituperate Abuse, Berate, Castigate, Censure, Defame, Inveigh, Lash, Rail, Scold

Vivid Bright, Brilliant, Dramatic, Eidectic, Fresh, Graphic, Keen, Live, Pictorial, Picturesque, Sharp, Violent

▸ **Vizor** *see* VISOR

Vocabulary Idiolect, Idioticon, Jargon, (Kata)kana, Lexicon, Lexis, Meta-language, Nomenclator, Wordbook

Vocation Call, Métier, Mission, Priesthood, Profession, Shop

Vogue Chic, Day, > FASHION, Mode, Rage, Style, Ton

Voice(d) Active, Air, Alto, Ancestral, Bass, Chest, Contralto, Countertenor, Edh, Emit, Eth, Express, Falsetto, Glottis, Harp, Head, Lyric, Mezzo-soprano, Mouth, Opinion, Passive, Phonic, Pipe, Presa, Quill, Say, Sonant, Soprano, Speak, Spinto, Sprechstimme, Steven, Syrinx, Tais(c)h, Tenor, Throat, Tone, > TONGUE, Treble, Utter, White

Voiceless Aphonia, Aphony, Dumb, Edh, Eth, Mute, Silent, Tacit

Void Abyss, Annul, Belch, Blank, Chasm, Defeasance, Defecate, Diriment, Empty, Evacuate, Gap, Hollow, Inane, Invalid, Irritate, Lapse, Nullify, Quash, Space, Vacuum

Volatile Excitable, Explosive, Latin, Live(ly), Mercurial, Temperamental, Terpene

Volcanic, **Volcano** Aa, Agglomerate, Amygdale, Andesite, Aniakchak, Antisana, Aragats, Ararat, Askja, Aso(san), Cameroon, Chimborazo, Citlaltépetl, Comoros, Cone, Conic, Corcovado, Cotopaxi, Demavend, Egmont, El Misti, Erclyas Dagi, Erebus, Etna, Fernando de Noronha, Fuji, Fumarole, Haleakala, Hekla, Hornito, Huasca(ra)n, Ice, Idocrase, Igneous, Ignimbrite, Iliamna, Ischia, Iwo Jima, Katmai, Kauai, Kazbek, Kilimanjaro, Krakatoa, Lassen Peak, Lipari, Maui, Mauna Kea, Mauna Loa, Mayon, Misti, Mofette, Montserrat, Mount Erebos, Mount Katmai, Mount St Helens, Mt Suribachi, Mud, National Park, Nevada de Colima, Nevada de Toluca, Nyamuragira, Nyiragongo, Obsidian, Okmok, Olympus Mons, Paricutin, Pele, Pelée, Pico de Teide, Pico de Teyde, Plinian, Popocatepetl, Pozz(u)olana, Pumice, Puy, Puzzolana, Ruapehu, St Helena, St Helens, St Kilda, Salse, Sandblow, Semeroe, Semeru, Shield, Soffioni, Solfatara, Soufrière Hills, Stromboli, Taal, Tambora, Tangariro, Taraniki, Thira, Tolima, Trass, Tuff, Vesuvius, Warrumbungle Range

Volley Barrage, Boom, Broadside, Platoon, Salvo, Tirade, Tire

Volume Band, Barrel, Book, Bushel, Capacity, CC, Code(x), Content, Cubage, Gallon, Hin, Loudness, Mass, Ml, Omnibus, Peck, Pint, Quart, Quart(o), Roll, Roul(e), Size, Space, Stere, Tome, Vol

Voluntary, **Volunteer** Enlist, Fencible, Free, Honorary, Offer, Postlude, Reformado, Spontaneous, Tender, Tennessee, Terrier, TN, Ultroneous, Yeoman

Voluptuary, **Voluptuous** Carnal, Hedonist, Luscious, Sensuist, Sensuous, Sybarite

Vomit(ing) Barf, Boak, Boke, Cascade, Cat, Chunder, Disgorge, Egist, Egurgitate, Emesis, Honk, Keck, Posset, Puke, Ralph, Retch, Rolf, Spew, Upchuck

Voracious, **Voracity** Bulimia, Edacity, Gluttony, Greed, Ravenous, Serrasalmo

Vote(r), **Votes**, **Voting** Alternative, Aye, Ballot, Block, Card, Casting, Choose, Colonist, Coopt, Cross, Cumulative, Division, Donkey, Fag(g)ot, Floating, Franchise, Free, Grey, Informal, Mandate, Nay, No, Opt, People, Placet, Plebiscite, Plump, Plural, Poll, Postal, PR, Preferential, Referendum, Return, Scrutiny, Side, Straw(-poll), Suffrage, Swinging, Tactical, Theta, Ticket, Token, Transferable, Voice, X, Yea, Yes

Vouch(er), **Vouchsafe** Accredit, Assure, Attest, Chit, Coupon, Endorse, Gift, Guarantee, Luncheon, Meal-ticket, Receipt, Ticket, Token, Warrant

Vow Baptismal, Behight, Behot(e), Earnest, Ex voto, Hecht, Hest, I do, Nuncupate, > OATH, Pledge, Plight, Promise, Simple, Solemn, Swear, Troth

Vowel(s) Ablaut, Anaptyxis, Aphesis, Breve, Cardinal, Diphthong, Indeterminate, Monophthong, S(c)hwa, Seg(h)ol, Svarabhakti, Triphthong

Voyage(r) Anson, Course, Cruise, Launch, Passage, Peregrinate, Sinbad, Travel

Vulgar(ian) Base, Gross, Plebby

Vulnerable Exposed, Open, Susceptible, Unguarded, Wide-open

Vulture Aasvogel, Bird, Buzzard, California (condor), Condor, Culture, Falcon, Gallinazo, Gier, Griffon, Gripe, Grype, Lammergeier, Lammergeyer, Ossifrage, Predator, Turkey, Urubu, Zopilote

Ww

Wad(ding) Batting, Lump, Pad, Pledget, Roll, Swab, Wodge

Wade(r), Wading Antigropelo(e)s, Curlew, Dikkop, Egret, Flamingo, Gallae, Grallatorial, Greenshank, Heron, Ibis, Jacksnipe, Limpkin, Paddle, Phalarope, Plodge, Sarus, Seriema, Shoebill, Splodge, Stilt(bird), Terek, Virginia

Wafer Biscuit, Cracker, Crisp, Gaufer, Gaufre, Gofer, Gopher, Host, Papad, Seal

Waffle Adlib, Blather, Equivocate, Gas, Gaufer, Gaufre, Gofer, Gopher, Hedge, Poppycock, Prate, Rabbit

Wag(gish), Waggle Arch, Card, Comedian, Joker, Lick, Nod, Rogue, Shake, Sway, Wit(snapper), Wobble

Wage(s) Ante, Fee, Hire, Living, Meed, Minimum, Pay, Portage, Practise, Prosecute, Rate, Salary, Screw, Subsistence

Wage-earner Breadwinner, Employee, Proletariat(e)

Wager Ante, Back, > BET, Gamble, Lay, Pascal's, Stake, Wed

Wagon(er) Ar(a)ba, Aroba, Bootes, Boxcar, Brake, Buck, Buckboard, Buggy, Caisson, Carriage, Cart, Cattle truck, Chuck, Cocopan, Conestoga, Corf, Covered, Democrat, Dray, Flatcar, Fourgon, Gambo, Go-cart, Hopper, Hutch, Low-loader, Mammy, Paddy, Palabra, Patrol, Plaustral, Police, Prairie schooner, Rave, Reefer, Rubberneck, Shandry, Station, Tank, Tartana, Telega, Tender, Trap, Trekker, Truck, Van, Victoria, Wain, Water

Wail(er) Banshee, Bawl, Blubber, Howl, Keen, Lament, Moan, Skirl, Threnody, Threnos, Ululate, Vagitus, Wah-wah, Yammer

Waist(band) Belt, Cummerbund, Girdlestead, Hour-glass, Middle, Midship, Obi, Sash, Shash, Wasp, Zoster

Waistcoat Gilet, Jerkin, Lorica, MB, Sayon, Vest, Weskit

Wait(er) Abid(e), Ambush, Barista, Bide, Busboy, Butler, Buttle, Carhop, Commis, Cupbearer, Dally, Delay, Estragon, Expect, Flunkey, Frist, Garçon, Hang on, Hesitate, Hover, Interval, Khidmutgar, Lime, Linger, Lurch, Maitre d', Maitre d'hôtel, Minority, Omnibus, Pannier, Pause, Remain, Serve(r), Sommelier, Stay, Steward, Suspense, Taihoa, Tarry, Tend(ance), Tray, Vladimir, Wine, Won

Waitress Hebe, Miss, Mousme(e), Nippy, Server

Waive Abandon, Defer, Overlook, Postpone, Relinquish, Renounce

Wake(n) Abrade, Abraid, Abray, Aftermath, Alert, Animate, Arouse, Astern, Deathwatch, Excite, Hereward, Keen, Prod, Rear, Train, Wash

Walk(er), Walking, Walkabout, Walkway Alameda, Alley, Alure, Amble, Ambulate, Arcade, Birdcage, Charity, Cloister, Clump, Constitutional, Dander, Emu, Esplanade, EVA, Flanerie, Gait, Gallery, Ghost, Go, Gradient, Hike, Hookey, Hump, Lambeth, Leg, Lumber, Mall, March, Mince, Mosey, Pace, Pad, Pasear, Paseo, Passage, Path, Ped, Perambulate, Pergola, Prance, Prom(enade), Rack, Ramble, Rampart, Random, Routemarch, Sashay, Shamble, Sidle, Slommock, Space, Spanish, Sponsored, Stalk, Step, Stroll, Strut, Stump, Terrace, Toddle, Tramp, Trash, Travolator, Tread, Trog, Truck, Trudge, Turn

Wall Bail, Bailey, Barrier, Berlin, Berm, Cavity, Cell, Chinese, Climbing, Curtain, Dado, Dam, Dike, Dry-stone, Fail-dike, Fourth, Frustule, Gable, Great, Hadrian's,

Hanging, Hangman, Head, Immure, Non-bearing, Parapet, Parpane, Parpen(d), Parpent, Partition, Party, Peribolos, Perpend, Perpent, Puteal, Retaining, Revet(ment), Ring, Roman, Roughcast, Sea, Septum, Side, Street, Tambour, Tariff, Vallation, Video, Wa', Wailing, Western

Wallaby Brusher, Dama, Kangaroo, Pad(d)ymelon, Pademelon, Quokka, Tammar

Wall-covering, **Wallpaper** Anaglypta®, Arras, Burlap, Lincrusta, Paper, Tapestry, Tapet

Wallet Billfold, Case, Notecase, Pochette, Purse, Scrip

Wallop Bash, Baste, Batter, Beat, Biff, Clout, Cob, > HIT, Lam, Lounder, Polt, Pound, Slog, Strap, Swinge, Tan, Tat, Trounce

Wallow(ing) Bask, Flounder, Luxuriate, Revel, Roll, Splash, Swelter, Tolter, Volutation, Welter

▶ **Wallpaper** *see* WALL-COVERING

Walrus Morse, Moustache, Pinniped, Rosmarine, Sea-horse, Tash

Wan Pale, Pallid, Pasty, Sanguine, Sorry

Wander(er), **Wandering** Bedouin, Berber, Bum, Caird, Delirious, Deviate, Digress, Drift, Errant, Estray, Excursive, Expatiate, Gad(about), Grope, Hobo, Jew, Landloper, Maunder, Meander, Mill, Moon, Nomad(e), Odysseus, Peregrine, Peripatetic, Ramble, Range, Romany, Room, Rove, Stooge, Straggle, Stray, Stroam, Stroll, Swan, Ta(i)ver, Tramp, Troll, Vagabond, Vagrant, Vague, Waif, Wend, Wheel, Wilder

▷ **Wandering** *may indicate* an anagram

Want(ing), **Wants** Absence, Conative, Covet, Crave, Dearth, Defect, Deficient, Derth, Desiderata, > DESIRE, Destitution, Envy, Hardship, Indigent, Itch, Lack, Long, Mental, Need, Penury, Require, Scarceness, Scarcity, Shortfall, Shy, Void, Wish, Yen

Wanton(ness) Bona-roba, Cadgy, Chamber, Cocotte, Deliberate, Demirep, Filly, Flirt-gill, Gammerstang, Giglet, Giglot, Gillflirt, Hussy, Jay, Jezebel, Jillflirt, Lewd, Licentious, Loose, Nice, Protervity, Roué, Slut, Smicker, Sportive, Sybarite, Toyish, Twigger, Unchaste, Wayward

War(fare), **Wars** American Civil, American Independence, Ares, Armageddon, Arms, Attrition, Bate, Battle, Biological, Chemical, Civil, Clash, Class, Cod, Cold, Combat, Conflict, Crimean, Crusade, Electronic, Emergency, Feud, > FIGHT, Flame, Food, Franco-Prussian, Fray, Germ, Great, Guer(r)illa, Gulf, Holy, Hostilities, Hot, Hundred Years', Information, Internecine, Jenkins' ear, Jihad, Korean, Mars, Mexican, Napoleonic, Nuclear, Opium, Peasants', Peloponnesian, Peninsular, Phony, Price, Private, Psychological, Punic, Push-button, Queen Anne's, Rebellion, Revolutionary, Roses, Russo-Japanese, Secession, Seven Years', Six Day, Social, Spanish-American, Spanish Civil, Star, Sword, Theomachy, Thirty Years', Total, Trench, Trojan, Turf, Vietnam, Winter, World, Yom Kippur

Warble(r) Carol, Chiff-chaff, Chirl, Fauvette, Peggy, Rel(l)ish, Trill, Vibrate, Yodel, Yodle

Ward (off) Artemus, Averruncate, Care, Casual, Charge, Defend, District, Fend, Guard, Maternity, Nightingale, Oppose, Parry, Protégé, Pupil, Soc, Soken, Vintry, Wear, Weir

Warden Caretaker, Concierge, Constable, Curator, Custodian, Game, Guardian, Keeper, Meter maid, Ranger, Septimus, Spooner, Steward, Traffic

Ware(s) Arretine, Beware, Biscuit, Cameo, Canton, Chelsea, China, Etruria, Faience, Goods, Lustre, Merchandise, Palissy, Samian, Sanitary, Satsuma, Shippo, Truck, Wemyss

Warehouse Bonded, Data, Depository, Entrepôt, Freight-shed, Go-down, Hong, Store

▶ **Warfare** *see* WAR

Wariness, Wary Ca'canny, Cagey, Careful, Cautel, Caution, Chary, Discreet, Distrust, Guarded, Leery, Mealy-mouthed, Prudent, Sceptical, Vigilant

Warlike Battailous, Bellicose, Gung-ho, Lachlan, Martial, Militant

Warm(er), Warming, Warmth Abask, Admonish, Air, Ardour, Balmy, British, Calefacient, Calid(ity), Chambré, Cordial, Empressement, Enchafe, Fervour, Foment, Genial, Global, Glow, > HEAT, Hot, Incalescent, Kang, Lew, Logic, Loving, Muff, Muggy, Mull, Tepid, Thermal, Toast, Toasty

Warn(ing) Admonish, Alarum, Alert, Amber, Apprise, Beacon, Bleep, Buoy, Caution, Caveat, Caveat emptor, Cone, Counsel, Document, Early, En garde, Example, Foghorn, Fore, Foretoken, Gardyloo, Garnishment, Harbinger, Hazchem, Heads up, Hoot, Horn, Klaxon, Larum, Lesson, Light, Maroon, Nix, Nota bene, Notice, Omen, Pi-jaw, Portent, Premonitory, Presage, Profit, Rumble strip, Scaldings, Signal, Storm, Tattler, Threat, Tip-off, Token, Yellow card

Warp(ed) Bias, Buckle, Cast, Contort, Distort, Kam, Kedge, Pandation, Time, Twist, Weft

▷ **Warped** *may indicate* an anagram

Warrant(y) Able, Authorise, Caption, Certificate, Detainer, Distress, Guarantee, Justify, Mittimus, Permit, Precept, Royal, Search, Sepad, Swear, Transire, Vouch, Warn

Warrior Achilles, Agamemnon, Ajax, Amazon, Anzac, Brave, Crusader, Eorl, Fighter, Geronimo, Impi, Myrmidon, Nestor, Samurai, Soldier, Tatar, Unknown, Warhorse, Zulu

Warship Battleship, Castle, Cog, Corvette, Cruiser, Destroyer, Drake, Dromon(d), Invincible, Man-o-war, Mine-layer, Monitor, Privateer, Ram

▶ **Wary** *see* WARINESS

Wash(ed), Washer, Washing (up), Wash out Ablution, Affusion, Alluvion, Bath, Bay(e), Bidet, Bur(r), Calcimine, Circlip, Clean(se), Cradle, D, Dashwheel, Dele(te), Dip, Edulcorate, Elute, Enema, Fen, Flush, Freshen, Gargle, Grommet, Grummet, Irrigate, Kalsomine, Lap, > LAUNDER, Lave, Leather, Lip, Lotion, Marsh, Maundy, Mop, Nipter, Pan, Pigswill, Poss, Purify, Rinse, Scrub, Shampoo, Shim, Sind, Sloosh, Sluice, Soogee, Soojee, Soojey, Squeegie, Sujee, Swab, Synd, Tie, Twin tub, Tye, Wake

Wasp(ish) Bembex, Bink, Bite, Chalcid, Cuckoo-fly, Cynipidae, Cynips, Digger, Fig, Fretful, Gall(-fly), Hornet, Horntail, Hoverfly, Irritable, Marabunta, Mason, Miffy, Muddauber, Paper, Peevish, Pompilid, Potter, Seed, Solitary, Spider, Vespa, Yellow jacket

▷ **Wasp** *may indicate* a rugby player

Wastage, Waste(d), Wasting, Wasteland Atrophy, Blue, Cesspit, Cirrhosis, Consume, Cotton, Crud, Culm, Decay, Desert, Detritus, Devastate, Dilapidate, Dissipate, Dross, Dung, Dwindle, Dwine, Dystrophy, Effluent, Egesta, Emaciate, Erode, Excrement, Exhaust, Expend, Faeces, Flue, Fribble, Fritter, Garbage, Gash, Gob, Gunge, Haggard, Havoc, Hazardous, Knub, Lavish, Loose, Lose, Loss, Low-level, Merino, Misspent, Moor, Muir, Mungo, Natural, Nub, Nuclear, Offal, Oller, Ordure, Pellagra, Pine, Prodigalise, Radioactive, Rammel, Ravage, Red mud, Red tape, > REFUSE, Rubble, Ruderal, Scissel, Scoria, Scrap, Sewage, Slag, Slurry, Spend, Spill, Spoil(age), Squander, Sullage, Tailing, Thin, Ureal, Urine, Vast, Wear, Wilderness

▷ **Wasted** *may indicate* an anagram

Watch(er) Accutron®, Analog(ue), Argus, Await, Bark, Behold, Bird-dog, Black, Clock, Coastguard, Digital, Dog, Espy, Fob, Gregory, Guard, Half-hunter, Huer, Hunter, Lever, Lo, Look, Look-out, Middle, Monitor, Morning, Nark, Neighbourhood, Night, Nit, Note, Observe, Overeye, Patrol, Posse, Quartz,

Regard, Repeater, Rolex®, Scout, Sentinel, Sentry, Shadow, Spectate, Spotter, Stemwinder, Surveillance, Tend, Ticker, Timekeeper, Timepiece, Timer, Tompion, Tout, Turnip, Vedette, > VIGIL, Voyeur, Wait, Wake, Wrist(let)

Watchman Bellman, Charley, Charlie, Chok(e)y, Cho(w)kidar, Guard, Sentinel, Sentry, Speculator, Tompion, Viewer

Watch-tower Atalaya, Barbican, Beacon, Mirador, Sentry-go

Water(ed), **Waters**, **Watery** Adam's ale, Adam's wine, Apollinaris, Aq(ua), Aquatic, Aqueous, Barley, Bayou, Bedabble, Bilge, Bound, Brine, Broads, Brook, Burn, Canal, Cancer, Chuck, Cold, Compensation, Conductivity, Dead, Deg, Dew, Dill, Dilute, Dribble, Drinking, Eau, Ebb, Element, Evian®, First, Flood, Ford, Fossil, Grey, Gripe, Ground, Hard, Heavy, Hellespont, High, Holy, Hot, Irrigate, Javel(le), Kyle, Lagoon, Lagune, Lake, Lavender, Leachate, Light, Lode, Lough, Low, Lubricated, Lymph, Meteoric, Mineral, Miner's inch, Moiré, Nappe, North, Oasis®, Oedema, Overfall, Pawnee, Pee, Perrier®, Pisces, Polly, Poppy, Potash, Potass, Pump, Purest, Quinine, Rain, Rapids, Rate, Reach, Rip, Riverine, Rose, Runny, Rydal, Saltchuck, Scorpio, Sea, Seltzer, Sera, Serous, Serum, Shower, Skinkling, Slack, Slick, Sluice, Soda, Sodden, Soft, Sound, Souse, Stream, Surface, Table, Tap, Tar, Territorial, Thin, Tide, Toilet, Tonic, Urine, Vichy, Viscous, Wash(y), Weak, Wee, Whey, White, White coal, Wild, Wishy-washy

Water-carrier Aqueduct, Bheestie, Bheesty, Bhistee, Bhisti, Bucket, Carafe, Chatty, Furphy, Hose, Hydra, Kirbeh, Pail, Pitcher

Water-course Arroyo, Billabong, Canal, Ditch, Dyke, Falaj, Furrow, Gutter, Khor, Lead, Nala, Nulla, Rean, Rhine, Shott, Spruit, Wadi

Watercress Nasturtium

Waterfall Angel (Falls), Cataract, Churchill, Chute, Cuquenan, Force, Foss, Kabiwa, Kile, Lasher, Lin(n), Mardel, Mtarazi, Niagara, Overfall, Rapid, Sault, Sutherland, Takakkaw, Tugela, Yosemite

Waterman Aquarius, Bargee, Ferryman, Oarsman

Water-plant Alisma, Aquatic, Cress, Crowfoot, Elodea, Gulfweed, Lace-leaf, Lattice-leaf, Nelumbo, Nenuphar, Nuphar, Ouvirandra, Pontederia, Quillwort, Reate, Sea-mat, Sedge, Seg, Stratiotes, Urtricularia, Vallisneria

Waterproof, **Water-tight** Caisson, Caulk, Cofferdam, Dampcourse, Dubbin(g), Groundsheet, Loden, Mac, Mino, Oilers, Oilskin, Pay, Seaworthy, Stank, Sta(u)nch, Waders

Water-sprite Kelpie, Kelpy, Nix(ie), Nixy, Tangie, Undine, Water-nymph

Waterway Aqueduct, Canal, Channel, Culvert, Ditch, Igarapé, Illinois, Intracoastal, Lode, River, Sound, Straight, Suez

Water-wheel Noria, Pelton, Sakia, Saki(y)eh

Wave(s), **Waved**, **Wavelength**, **Wavy** Alpha, Beachcomber, Beam, Beck, Beta, Billow, Bore, Bow, Brain, Brandish, Breaker, Carrier, Comber, Complex, Continuous, Crest, Crime, Crimp, Delta, Dominant, Dumper, Electromagnetic, Finger, Flap, Flaunt, Float, Flote, Flourish, Gesticulate, Gravitational, Gravity, Graybeard, Ground, Groundswell, Harmonic, Haystack, Heat, Internal, Ionospheric, Lee, Long, Longitudinal, Marcel, Matter, Medium, Mexican, New, Perm(anent), Plunger, Primary, Pulse, Radar, Radiation, Radio, Rip, Ripple, Roller, Rooster, Sea, Secondary, Seiche, Seismic, Shock, Short, Sine, Sky, Snaky, Sound, Spiller, Square, Squiggle, Standing, Stationary, Stream, Supplementary, Surf, Surge, Sway, Tabby, Theta, Third, Thought, Tidal, Tidal bore, Tide, Train, Transverse, Travelling, Tsunami, Ultrasonic, Undate, Unde, Undulate, Waffle, Waft, Wag, Waive, Wash, Waw, Whitecap, White-horse, Wigwag

▷ **Wave(s)** *may indicate* an anagram

Waver(ing), **Waverer** Dither, Falter, Flag, Gutter, Hesitate, Oscillate, Stagger, Sway, Swither, Teeter, Vacillate, Waffle, Wet, Wow

Wax(ed), **Waxing**, **Waxy** Ambergris, Appal, Bate, Bees, Bone, Brazilian, Cere, Ceresin, Cerumen, Chinese, Cobbler's, Cutin, Earth, Effuse, Enseam, Gr(e)aves, Grow, Heelball, Honeycomb, Increase, Increscent, Inseam, Ire, Japan, Kiss, Livid, Lost, Lyrical, Means, Mineral, Mummy, Paraffin, Pela, Petroleum, Rage, Seal, Sealing, Spermaceti, Tallow, Tantrum, Temper, Toxaphene, Vegetable, White, Yielding

Way(s), **Wayside** Access, Agate, Appian, Autobahn, Avenue, Borstal(l), Bypass, Companion, Course, Crescent, Direction, Door, Draw, E, Each, Entrance, Family, Fashion, Flaminian, Foss(e), Gate, Habit, Hatch, Hedge, High, Hither, How, Lane, Manner, Means, Method, Milky, Mo, Mode, N, Pass, Path, Permanent, Pilgrim's, Procedure, Railroad, Regimen, Ridge, > ROAD, Route, S, Sallypost, St(reet), Style, System, Thoroughfare, Thus, Trace, Trail, Troade, Turnpike, Underpass, Untrodden, Via, W, Wise

Way-out Advanced, Bizarre, Egress, Esoteric, Exit, Exotic, Extreme, Offbeat, Trendy

Wayward Capricious, Disobedient, Errant, Erratic, Loup-the-dyke, Obstreperous, Perverse, Stray, Unruly, Wilful

Weak(er), **Weaken(ing)**, **Weakest**, **Weakness** Achilles' heel, Appal, Arsis, Attenuate, Blot, Brittle, Chink, Cripple(d), Debile, Debilitate, Decrease, Delay, Delicate, Dilute, Disable, Effete, Emasculate, Enervate, Enfeeble, Entender, Fade, Faible, Failing, Faint, Fatigue, Feeble, Fissile, Flag, Flaw, Flimsy, Foible, Fragile, Frailty, Give, Gone, Ham, Helpless, Honeycomb, Impair, Impotence, Infirm, Knock-kneed, Lassitude, Low, Low ebb, Meagre, Mild, Milk and water, Namby-pamby, Pale, Pall, Paresis, Puny, Push-over, Pusillanimous, Reduce, Simp, Slack, Tenuous, Thesis, Thin, Thready, Tottery, Unable, Underdog, Undermine, Unnerve, Unstable, Vapid, Vessel, Vulnerability, W, Washy, Water(y), Wish(y)-wash(y)

Wealth(y) Abundance, Affluence, Bullion, Croesus, Fat-cat, Fortune, Golconda, Jet-set, Klondike, Klondyke, Loaded, Lolly, Mammon, Means, Mine, Mint, Moneyed, Nabob, Opulence, Ore, Pelf, Plutocrat, Reich, Rich, Ritzy, Solid, Substance, Treasure, Untold, Well-heeled, Well-off, Well-to-do

Weapon Airgun, Alderman, Arbalest, Arblast, Arm, Armalite®, Arquebus(e), Arrow, Arsenal, Assegai, Ataghan, Backsword, Ballista, Baton, Battleaxe, Bayonet, Bazooka, Bill, Binary, Blowgun, Blowpipe, Bludgeon, Bolo, Bomb, Bondook, Broadsword, Caliver, Calthrop, Caltrap, Caltrop, Carbine, Catapult, Catchpole, Cestus, Chainshot, Club, Co(e)horn, Cosh, Creese, Cudgel, Culverin, Cutlass, Dag(ger), Dart, Derringer, Deterrent, Doodlebug, Dragon, Dragoon, Duster, Elf-arrow, Enfield, Estoc, Excalibur, Flail, Flamethrower, Flintlock, Forty-five, Fougade, Fougasse, Gad(e), Gaid, Gingal(l), Gisarme, Glaive, Grenade, Halberd, Halbert, Harpoon, Harquebus, Hoplology, Howitzer, Javelin, Jingal, Katana, Knife, Knuckleduster, Kris, Lance, Life-preserver, Longbow, Long-range, Machete, Mangonel, Manrikigusari, Matchet, Mauser®, Maxim, Mere, Missile, Morgenstern, Mortar, Munition, Musket, Nuclear, Nuke, Nunchaku (sticks), Onager, Orgue, Partisan, Pea-shooter, Petrary, Petronel, Pike, Pilum, Pistol, Poleaxe, Quarterstaff, Revolver, Rifle, Sabre, Saker, Sandbag, Sarbacane, Shotgun, Sidearm, Skean-dhu, Skene-dhu, Slingshot, Smallsword, Snickersnee, Sparke, Sparth, Spat, Spontoon, Sten, Stiletto, Sting, Stinkpot, Sword, Taiaha, Taser®, Theatre, Throw-stick, Tomboc, Torpedo, Traditional, Trebuchet, Trident, Truncheon, V1, Vou(l)ge, Whirl-bat, Whorl-bat

Wear(ing), **Wear Out** Abate, Ablative, Abrade, Attrition, Chafe, Corrade, Corrode, Deteriorate, Detrition, Efface, Erode, Erosion, Fashion, For(e)spend, Fray, Frazzle, Fret, Garb, Impair, In, Pack, Scuff, Sport, Stand, Tedy

▷ **Wear** *may indicate* the NE (eg Sunderland)

Weariness, **Wearisome**, **Weary** Beat, Bejade, Bore, Cloy, Dog-tired, Ennui, Ennuyé, Exhaust, Fag, Fatigate, Fatigue, Harass, Hech, Irk, Jade, Lacklustre,

Lassitude, Pall, Puny, Ramfeezle, Sleepy, Spent, Tire, Trash, Try, Tucker, Wabbit, Worn

Weasel Beech-marten, Cane, Delundung, Ermine, Ferret, Glutton, Grison, Kolinsky, Marten, Mink, Mustela, Pekan, Polecat, Stoat, Taira, Tayra, Vermin, Whitterick, Whit(t)ret, Whittrick, Wolverine, Woodshock

Weather, **Weather forecast** Atmosphere, Cyclone, Discolour, Ecoclimate, Elements, Endure, Met, Sky, Stand, Survive, Tiros, Undergo, Withstand

Weatherboard Rusticating

Weave(r), **Weaves**, **Weaving** Arachne, Basket, Cane, Complect, Entwine, Finch, Heald, Heddle, Interlace, Lace, Lease, Leno, Lion, Loom, Marner, Plain, Raddle, Ripstop, Rya, Shuttle, Sparrow, Splice, Taha, Texture, Throstle, Tissue, Tweel, Twill, Twine, Wabster, Waggle, Webster, Zigzag

Web(bed), **Webbing**, **Web-footed**, **Web-site** Aranea, Food, Fourchette, Infomediary, Internet, Mat, Maze, Mesh(work), Offset, Palama, Palmate, Palmiped, Patagium, Pinnatiped, Skein, Snare, Tela, Tissue, Toil, Totipalmate, WorldWide

Wed(ding), **Wedlock** Alliance, Bet, Diamond, Espousal, Golden, Hymen, Join, Knobstick, Link, Marriage, Marry, Mate, Me(i)nt, Meng(e), Meynt, Ming, Nuptials, Pair, Penny, Ruby, Shotgun, Silver, Spousal, > **UNION**, Unite, White, Y

Wedge(d) Chock, Chunk, Cleat, Cotter, Cuneal, Doorstop, Feather, Forelock, Gagger, Gib, Jack, Jam, Key, Niblick, Prop, Quoin, Scotch, Shim, Sphenic, Stick, Trig, Vomerine, Whipstock

Weed(y) Adderwort, Agrestal, Alga, Allseed, Anacharis, Arenaria, Bedstraw, Bell-bind, Blinks, Burdock, Carpetweed, Catch, Charlock, Chickweed, Chlorella, Cigar(ette), Cissy, Clover, Cobbler's pegs, Cockle, Colonist, Coltsfoot, Corncockle, Couch, Daisy, Dallop, Darnel, Dock, Dollop, Dulse, Elodea, Ers, Fag, Fat hen, Femitar, Fenitar, Fucoid, Fumitory, Groundsel, Helodea, Hoe, Indian, Joe-pye, Knapweed, Knawel, Knot-grass, Lemna, Mare's-tail, Marijuana, Matfelon, Mayweed, Nard, Nettle, Nipplewort, Nostoc, Onion, Oxygen, Paterson's curse, Pearlwort, Pilewort, Piri-piri, Plantain, Potamogeton, Purslane, Ragi, Ragwort, Reate, Rest-harrow, Ribwort, Ruderal, Runch, Sagittaria, Sargasso, Scal(l)awag, Scallywag, Senecio, Softy, Sorrel, Spurge, Spurrey, Sudd, Sun-spurge, Swine's-cress, Tansy, Tare, Thistle, Tine, Tobacco, Tormentil, Twitch, Ulotrichale, Ulva, Vetch, Viper's bugloss, Wartcress, Widow's, Winnow, Yarr

▷ **Weed** *may indicate* 'urinated'

Weedkiller Arsenic, Atrazine, Dalapon, Diquat, Diuron, Herbicide, Paraquat®, Simazine

Week(ly) Ember, Expectation, Great, Hebdomadary, Holy, Orientation, Ouk, Oulk, Passion, Periodical, Rag, Rogation, Sennight, Working

Weep(er), **Weepy**, **Wept** Bawl, Blubber, Cry, Grat, Greet, Lachrymose, Lament, Loser, Maudlin, Niobe, Ooze, Pipe, Sob, Wail

Weigh(ing), **Weigh down**, **Weight(y)** All-up, Arroba, Artal, As, Atomic, Avoirdupois, Balance, Bantam, Bob, Bulk, Burden, Candy, Cantar, Carat, Catty, Cental, Clove, Consider, Count, Counterpoise, Cruiser, Ct, Dead, Decagram(me), Deliberate, Drail, Dumbbell, Emphasis, Equivalent, Feather, Fother, G, Gerah, Grain, Gram, Heft, Importance, Impost, Incumbent, Journey, Kandy, Kantar, Kerb, Khat, Kin, Kip, Last, Libra, Load, Mark, Massive, Maund, Metage, Mina, Mna, Molecular, Moment, Mouse, Nail, Obol, Oke, Onerous, Oppress, Ounce, Overpoise, Oz, Pease, Perpend, Plummet, Poise, Pood, Pound, Preponderance, Prey, Pud, Pudge, Quintal, Rod, Rotolo, Scruple, Seer, Sinker, Sit, Slang, Stone, Stress, Talent, Tare, Throw, Tical, Tod, Tola, Ton(nage), Tonne, Tophamper, Troy, Unce, Unmoor, Welter, Wey, Wt

Weir Cauld, Dam, Garth, Kiddle, Kidel, Lasher, Pen, Watergate

Weird Bizarre, Curious, Dree, Eerie, Eery, Eldritch, Kookie, Offbeat, Spectral, Strange, Supernatural, Taisch, Uncanny, Zany

Welch, Welsh Abscond, Cheat, Default, Embezzle, Levant, Rat, Reneg(u)e, Renig, Skedaddle, Weasel

Welcome, Welcoming Aloha, Ave, Bel-accoyle, Ciao, Embrace, Entertain, Glad-hand, Greet, Haeremai, Hallo, Halse, Hello, Hospitable, How, Hullo, Receive, Reception, Salute

Welfare Advantage, Alms, Benison, Ha(y)le, Heal, Health, Sarvodaya, Weal

Well (done) Artesian, Atweel, Aweel, Bien, Bore(hole), Bravo, Cenote, Development, Dry hole, Euge, Famously, Fine, Fit, Gasser, Good, Gosh, Gusher, Hale, > **HEALTHY**, Hot, Inkpot, Law, My, Namma hole, Odso, Oh, Oil, Phreatic, Potential, So, Source, Spa, Spring, Sump, Surge, Um, Upflow, Zemzem

Wellbeing Atweel, Bien-être, Comfort, Euphoria, Euphory, Good, Health, Welfare

Well-born Eugene

Well-known Famous, Illustrious, Notorious, Notour, Prominent

Well-off Affluent, Far, Rich, Wealthy

▶ **Welsh** *see* WELCH

Welsh(man) Briton, Brittonic, Brython, Cake, Cambrian, Celtic, Cog, Cym(ric), Cymry, Dai, Emlyn, Evan, Fluellen, Gareth, Harp, Idris, Ifor, Keltic, P-Celtic, P-Keltic, Rabbit, Rarebit, Rees, Rhys, Sion, Taffy, Tudor, W

West(ern), Westerly Ang mo, Favonian, Hesperian, Mae, Movie, Oater, Occidental, Ponent, Spaghetti, Sunset, W, Wild

▷ **West end** *may indicate* 't' or 'W'

Wet(ting) Bedabble, Bedraggled, Clammy, Daggle, Damp, Dank, Dew, Dip, Douse, Dowse, Drench, Drip(ping), Drook, Drouk, Embrue, Enuresis, Feeble, Humect, Humid, Hyetal, Imbue, Irrigate, Irriguous, Madefy, Madid, Marshy, Moil, Moist(en), Molly, Namby-pamby, Pee, Piddle, Pouring, Rainy, Ret(t), Roral, Roric, Runny, Saturate, Shower, Simp(leton), Sipe, Sluice, > **SOAK**, Sodden, Sopping, Sour, Steep, Tiddle, Tipsy, Urinate, Wat, Wee, Widdle, Wimpy, Wringing

Whale(meat), Whaling Baleen, Beaked, Beluga, Blower, Blubber, Blue, Bottlehead, Bottlenose, Bowhead, Cachalot, Calf, Cetacea(n), Cete, Dolphin, Fall, Fin(back), Finner, Gam, Glutton, Grampus, Greenland, Grey, Humpback, Killer, Kreng, Leviathan, Manatee, Minke, Monodon, Mysticeti, Paste, Pilot, Pod, Porpoise, Right, Rorqual, School, Scrag, Sei, Sperm, Thrasher, Toothed, Toothless, White

▷ **Whale** *may indicate* an anagram

What Anan, Eh, How, Pardon, Que, Siccan, That, Which

Whatnot, What's-its-name Dinges, Dingus, Doings, Etagère, Gismo, Jiggamaree, Jiggumbob, Thingamy, Thingumajig, Thingumbob, Thingummy, Timenoguy

Wheat Amelcorn, Blé, Bulg(h)ur, Cracked, Durum, Einkorn, Emmer, Federation, Fromenty, Frumenty, Furme(n)ty, Furmity, Grain, Hard, Mummy, Rivet, Sarrasin, Sarrazin, Seiten, Semolina, Sharps, Spelt, Triticum

Wheedle Banter, Barney, Blandish, Cajole, Coax, Cog, Cuiter, Cuittle, Flatter, Inveigle, Tweedle, Whilly(whaw)

Wheel(er) Balance, Bedel, Bevel, Bogy, Buff(ing), Caster, Castor, Catherine, Chain, Chark(h)a, Circle, Cistern, Crown, Cycle, Daisy, Disc, Driving, Emery, Epicycloidal, Escape, Fan, Felloe, Felly, Ferris, Fifth, Fortune, Gear, Grinding, Helm, Hurl, Idle(r), Jagger, Kick, Lantern, Magnate, Medicine, Nabob, Nose, Paddle, Pattern, Pedal, Pelton, Perambulator, Persian, Pin, Pinion, Pitch, Pivot, Planet, Potter's, Prayer, Pulley, Rag, Ratchet, Roll, Rotate, Roulette, Rowel, Sheave, Snail, Spider, Spinning, Sprocket, Spur, Star, Steering, Stitch, Tail, Throwing-table, Tread,

Trindle, Trolley, Truckle, Trundle, > TURN, Water, Web, Wire, Worm

Wheelwright Spokesman

Wheeze Asthma, Jape, Joke, Pant, Ploy, Rale, Reak, Reik, Rhonchus, Ruse, Stridor, Trick, Whaisle, Whaizle

Where(abouts) Location, Neighbourhood, Place, Site, Vicinity, Whaur, Whither

Wherewithal Finance, Means, Money, Needful, Resources

Whet(stone) Coticular, Excite, Hone, Sharpen, Stimulate

Whether Conditional, If

Which(ever), Which is Anyway, As, QE, Whatna, Whilk, Who

While Although, As, Interim, Since, Space, Span, Though, Throw, Time, When, Whenas, Yet

Whim(s), Whimsical, Whimsy Bizarre, Caprice, Conceit, Crotchet, Fad, Fancy, Fey, Flisk, Kicksy-wicksy, Kink, Notion, Quaint, Quirk, Tick, Toy, Vagary

Whine, Whinge Cant, Carp, Complain, Cry, Grumble, Kvetch, Mewl, Moan, Peenge, Pule, Snivel, Whimper, Yammer

Whip(ped), Whip out, Whipping Beat, Braid, Bullwhip, Cat, Cat o'nine tails, Chastise, Chief, Colt, Crop, Drive, Firk, Five-line, Flagellate, Flay, Gad, Hide, Jambok, Knout, Larrup, > LASH, Leather, Limber, Lunge, Quirt, Rawhide, Riem, Scourge, Sjambok, Slash, Steal, Stock, Swinge, Swish, Switch, Taw, Thong, Three-line, Trounce, Welt, West country, Whap

Whirl(er), Whirling Circumgyrate, Dervish, Eddy, Gyrate, > IN A WHIRL, Pivot, Reel, Spin, Swing, Swirl, Vortex, Vortical, Whirry

Whirlpool Eddy, Gulf, Gurge, Maelstrom, Moulin, Swelchie, Vorago, Vortex, Weel, Wiel

Whirlwind Cyclone, Dust devil, Eddy, Tornado, Tourbillion, Typho(o)n, Vortex, Willy-willy

Whirr Birr

Whisker(s) Beard, Beater, Burnsides, Cat's, Dundreary, Hackle, Hair, Moustache, Mutton-chop, Samuel, Side(-boards), Side-burns, Vibrissa

Whisk(e)y Alcohol, Bond, Bourbon, Canadian, Cape Smoke, Corn, Creature, Fife, Fire-water, Hoo(t)ch, Irish, Malt, Moonshine, Morning, Mountain dew, Nip, Peat-reek, Pot(h)een, Red eye, Rye, Scotch, Usquebaugh

▷ **Whisky** *may indicate an anagram*

Whisper Breath(e), Bur(r), Hark, Hint, Innuendo, Murmur, Round, Rumour, Rustle, Sigh, Stage, Susurrus, Tittle, Undertone

Whistle(r) Blow, Calliope, Feedback, Hiss, Marmot, Penny, Ping, Pipe, Ref, Siffle(ur), Sowf(f), Sowth, Steam, Stop, Stridor, Swab(ber), Tin, Toot, Tweedle, Tweet, Warbler, Wheeple, Wheugh, Whew, Wolf

White(n), Whitener, Whiteness Agene, Agenise, Alabaster, Albedo, Albescent, Albino, Albumen, Argent, Ashen, Au lit, Blameless, Blanch, Blanco, Bleach, Buckra, Cabbage, Calm, Cam, Camstone, Candid, Candour, Canescent, Canities, Caucasian, China, Chinese, Christmas, Cliffs, Collar, Company, Egg, Elephant, Ermine, European, Fang, Fard, Feather, Flag, Flake, French, Glair, Gwen(da), Gwendolen, Honorary, Hore, House, Innocent, Ivory, Large, Leucoma, Lie, Lily, Livid, Man, Marbled, Mealy, Opal, Oyster, Pale(face), Pallor, Paper, Paris, Pearl, Poor, Pure, Redleg, Russian, Sclerotic, Sheep, Silver, Small, Snow(y), Spanish, Taw, Wan, Wedding, Zinc

White man Ba(c)kra, Buckra, Caucasian, Gub(bah), Haole, Honkie, Honky, Larney, Mzungu, Occidental, Ofay, Pakeha, Paleface, Redleg, Redneck, WASP

Whole, Wholehearted, Wholeness, Wholly All, Eager, Entire(ty), Entity, Fully, Hale, Intact, Integer, Integrity, Largely, Lot, Sum, Systemic, Thoroughly, Total, Unbroken, Uncut

Wholesale(r) Cutprice, En bloc, Engrosser, Jobber, Sweeping

Whoop(er), Whooping cough Alew, Celebrate, Chincough, Crane, Cry, Excite, Kink(cough), Kink-hoast, Pertussis, Swan

Whopper, Whopping Barn, Crammer, Huge, Immense, Jumbo, Lie, Lig, Oner, Out and outer, Scrouger, Slapper, Slockdolager, Soc(k)dalager, Soc(k)dolager, Soc(k)doliger, Soc(k)dologer, Sogdolager, Sogdoliger, Sogdologer, Tale, Taradiddle

Whore Drab, Harlot, Loose woman, Pinnace, Pro, Quail, Road, Strumpet, Tart

Wicked(ness) Atrocity, > BAD, Candle, Criminal, Cru(i)sie, Crusy, Depravity, Devilish, Evil, Goaty, Godless, Heinous, Immoral, Impious, Improbity, Iniquity, Lantern, Nefarious, Night-light, Pravity, Rush, Satanic, Scelerate, Sin(ful), Taper, Turpitude, Unholy, Vile

▷ **Wicked** *may indicate* containing a wick

Wicket Gate, Hatch, Pitch, Square, Sticky, Stool, Stump, Yate

Wide, Widen(ing), Width Abroad, Ample, Bay, Broad, Dilate, Drib, Eclectic, Expand, Extend, Far, Flanch, Flange, Flare, Flaunch, Ga(u)ge, General, Miss, Prevalent, Roomy, Spacious, Spread, Sundry, Sweeping, Vast

Widespread Diffuse, Epidemic, Extensive, General, Pandemic, Panoramic, Prevalent, Prolate, Routh(ie), Sweeping

Widow(ed) Black, Dame, Dowager, Golf, Grass, Jointress, Relict, Sati, Sneerwell, Suttee, Vidual, Viduous, Whydah-bird, Widdy

Wife, Wives Bride, Concubine, Consort, Devi, Dutch, Enid, Evadne, Feme, Feme covert, Frau, Haram, Harem, Harim, Helpmate, Helpmeet, Hen, Her indoors, Kali, Little woman, Mate, Memsahib, Missis, Missus, Mrs, Partner, Penelope, Potiphar's, Rib, Seraglio, Spouse, Squaw, Trophy, Trouble and strife, Umfazi, Ux(or), W

Wig Bagwig, Bob(wig), Brutus, Buzz-wig, Campaign, Carpet, Cauliflower, Caxon, Chevelure, Chide, Cockernony, Dalmahoy, Full-bottomed, Gizz, Gregorian, Hair(piece), Heare, Jas(e)y, Jazey, Jiz, Major, Periwig, Peruke, Postiche, Ramil(l)ie(s), Rate, Reprimand, Rug, Scold, Scratch, Sheitel, Spencer, Targe, Tie, Toupee, Toupet, Tour

Wild Aberrant, Agrestal, Barbarous, Berserk, Bundu, Bush, Chimeric, Crazy, Earl, Errant, Erratic, Farouche, Feral, Frantic, Frenetic, Haggard, Hectic, Lawless, Mad(cap), Manic, Meshugge, Myall, Natural, Rampant, Raver, Riotous, > SAVAGE, Unmanageable, Unruly, Violent, Warrigal, West, Woolly

▷ **Wild(ly)** *may indicate* an anagram

Wile, Wily Art, Artful, Artifice, Astute, Braide, > CUNNING, Deceit, Foxy, Peery, Ruse, Shifty, Shrewd, Slee, > SLY, Spider, Stratagem, Streetwise, Subtle, Trick, Versute, Wide

Wilful Deliberate, Headstrong, Heady, Obstinate, Recalcitrant, Wayward

Will, Willing(ly) Alsoon, Amenable, Bard, Bequeath, Bewildered, Bill(y), Complaisant, Compliant, Conation, Content, Desire, Devise, Devote, Fain, Force, Free, Game, General, Hay, Holographic, Leave, Legator, Leve, Lief, Lieve, Living, Noncupative, Obedient, On, Please, Prone, Purpose, Raring, Rather, Ready, Receptive, Scarlet, Soon, Spirit, Swan, Testament, Testate, Volition, Voluntary, Volunteer, Way, Wimble, Woot

▷ **Will** *may indicate* an anagram

William(s) Bill(y), Conqueror, Occam, Orange, Pear, Rufus, Silent, Sweet, Tell, Tennessee

Willow(ing), Willowy Crack, Lissom(e), Lithe, Osier, Poplar, Pussy, Salix, Sallow, Sauch, Saugh, Supple, Twilly, Weeping, Withy

▶ **Wily** *see* WILE

Wimp(ish) Namby-pamby, Pantywaist, Weed

▷ **Wimple** *may indicate* an anagram

Win(ner), **Winning** Achieve, > BEAT, Capot, Champion, Conciliate, Conquer, Cup, Cute, Decider, Disarming, Dormie, Dormy, Earn, Endearing, First, Gain, Gammon, Hit, Jackpot, Land, Laureate, Lead, Medallist, Motser, Motza, Nice, Pile, Pot, Prevail, Profit, Purler, Repique, Result, Rubicon, Shoo-in, Slam, Snip, Success, Sweet, Take, > TRIUMPH, Up, Vellet, Velvet, Victor(y), Vole, Walk over, Wrest

Wind(er), **Winding(s)**, **Windy** Aeolian, Air, Airstream, Ambages, Anfractuous, Anti-trade, Aquilo(n), Argestes, Auster, Backing, Baguio, Bend, Berg, Bise, Blore, Blow, Bluster, Bora, Boreas, Bottom, Brass, Breeze, Brickfielder, Burp, Buster, Cape doctor, Capstan, Chili, Chill, Chinook, Coil, Colic, Cordonazo, Corus, Crank, Creeky, Curl, Cyclone, Downwash, Draught, Draw, Dust devil, Easterly, Etesian, Euraquilo, Euroclydon, Eurus, Evagation, Favonian, Favonius, Fearful, Firn, Flatulence, Flatus, Flaw, Fo(e)hn, Gale, Gas, G(h)ibli, Gregale, Gust, Haboob, Harmattan, Heaves, Hurricane, Hurricano, Jet stream, Kamseen, K(h)amsin, Knee-swell, Levant(er), Libecc(h)io, Libs, Link, Meander, Meltemi, Mistral, Monsoon, Muzzler, Nervous, Noreast, Norther, Nor(th)wester(ly), Noser, Notus, Pampero, Periodic, Ponent, Poop, Prevailing, Puna, Purl, Quill, Reeds, Reel, Rip-snorter, Roll, Samiel, Sciroc, Scirocco, Screw, Sea, Second, Series, Serpentine, Shamal, Shimaal, Simoom, Simoon, Sinuous, Sirocco, Slant, Snake, Snifter, Snorter, Solano, Solar, Sough, Souther, Southerly buster, Spiral, Spool, Squall, Stellar, Sumatra, Surface, Swirl, Tail, Tehuantepecer, Thread, Throw, Tornado, Tortuous, Tourbillon, Trade, Tramontana, Trend, Turn, Twaddle, Twine, Twister, Twisty, Typhon, Typhoon, Veer, Veering, Ventose, Volturnus, Waffle, Weave, Wester, Westerly, Whirlblast, White squall, Williwaw, Willy-willy, Winch, Wrap, Wreathe, Wrest, Zephyr(us), Zonda

Window(s) Atmosphere, Bay, Bow, Casement, Catherine-wheel, Companion, Compass, Day, Deadlight, Dormer, Dream-hole, Eye, Eyelids, Fanlight, Fenestella, Fenestra, French, Gable, Garret, Glaze, Guichet, Jalousie, Jesse, Judas, Lancet, Lattice, Launch, Loop-light, Louver, Louvre, Lozen, Lucarne, Lunette, Luthern, Lychnoscope, Marigold, Mezzanine, Mirador, Monial, Mullion, Oculus, Oeil-de-boeuf, Ogive, Orb, Oriel, Ox-eye, Pane, Pede, Picture, Porthole, Quarterlight, Radio, Re-entry, Rosace, Rose, Sash, Sexfoil, Spyhole, Storm, Transom, Trellis, Ventana, Weather, Wheel, Wicket, Windock, Winnock

Window-bar, **Window-fastening** Astragal, Espagnolette

Wine Bin, Cup, Essence, Fortified, Low, Must, Piece, Premier cru, Prisage, Rotgut, Rouge, The grape, Vat, Vintage

Wing(ed), **Winger**, **Wings**, **Wing-like** Aerofoil, Ala(r), Alula, Annexe, Appendage, Arm, Bastard, > BIRD, Branch, Canard, Cellar, Corium, Coulisse, Delta, Dipteral, El(l), Elevon, Elytral, Elytriform, Elytron, Elytrum, Fender, Flap, Flew, Flipper, Forward, Halteres, Hurt, Left, Limb, Parascenia, Parascenium, Patagium, Pennate, Pennon, Pinero, Pinion, Pip, Pterygoid, Putto, Right, Rogallo, Sail, Scent-scale, Segreant, Seraphim, Sweepback, Sweptback, Sweptwing, Swift, Swingwing, Tailplane, Tectrix, Tegmen, Transept, Van, Vol(et), Wound(ed)

▷ **Winger** *may indicate* a bird

Wink (at) Bat, Condone, Connive, Flicker, Ignore, Instant, Nap, Nictitate, Pink, Twinkle

Winnow Fan, Riddle, Separate, Sift, Van, Wecht

Winter, **Wintry** Bleak, Brumal, Cold, Dec, Fimbul, Frigid, Frore, Hibernate, Hiemal, Hiems, Hodiernal, Jasmine, Nuclear, Snowy

Wipe (out), **Wiping** Abolish, Abrogate, Absterge, Amortise, Cancel, Cleanse, Demolish, Destroy, Deterge, Dicht, Dight, Expunge, Hanky, Mop, Nose-rag, Null, Purge, Raze, Sponge, Tersion, Tissue

Wire(s), **Wiry** Aerial, Barb(ed), Cable, Cat's whiskers, Chicken, Coil, Earth,

Fencing, Filament, Filar, File, Heald, Heddle, High, Kirschner, Lean, Lecher, Live, Marconigram, Mil, Nichrome®, Nipper, Piano, Pickpocket, Razor, Sevice, Shroud, Sinewy, Snake, Solenoid, Spit, Staple, Stilet, Strand, String, Stylet, Telegram, Telegraph, Thoth, Thread, Trace

Wise(acre), Wisdom Advisedly, Athena, Athene, Canny, Depth, Ernie, Gothamite, Hep, Hindsight, Judgement, Learned, Long-headed, Lore, Manner, Mimir, Minerva, Norman, Oracle, Owl, Philosopher, Philosophy, Politic, Polymath, Prajna, Profound, Prudence, Sagacity, Sage, Salomonic, Sapience, Savvy, Shrewd, Smartie, Solon, Sophia, Wice

Wise man Balthazar, Caspar, Heptad, Melchior, Nestor, Sage, Sapient, Seer, Solomon, Swami, Thales, Worldly

Wish(es) Crave, Death, Desiderate, > **DESIRE**, Hope, List, Long, Pleasure, Precatory, Regards, Velleity, Want, Yearn

Wit(s), Witticism, Witty Acumen, Attic, Badinage, Banter, Brevity, Commonsense, Concetto, Cunning, Dry, Epigram, Esprit, Estimation, Eutrapelia, Eutrapely, Facetious, Fantasy, Hartford, Humour, Imagination, Intelligence, Irony, Jest, Jeu d'esprit, Joke, Marbles, Marinism, Memory, Mind, Mot, Mother, Native, Nous, Pawky, Pun, Repartee, Rogue, Sally, Salt, Saut, Sconce, > **SENSE**, Shaft, Smart, Videlicet, Viz, Wag, Weet, Wisecrack, Word-play

Witch(craft) Broomstick, Cantrip, Carline, Circe, Coven, Craigfluke, Crone, Cutty Sark, Ensorcell, Galdragon, Glamour, Goety, Gramary(e), Gyre-carlin, Hag, Hecat(e), Hex, Lamia, Magic, Medea, Myal(ism), Night-hag, Obeahism, Obiism, Pythoness, Salem, Selim, Sibyl, Sieve, Sorceress, Speller, Sycorax, Trout, Valkyrie, Vaudoo, Vilia, Voodoo, Weird, Wicca

With And, By, Con, Cum, Hereby, In, Mit, Of, W

Withdraw(al), Withdrawn Abdicate, Alienate, Aloof, Cold turkey, Cry off, Detach, Disengage, Distrait, Enshell, Evacuate, Hive off, Inshell, Introvert, Offish, Palinode, Preserve, Recant, Recoil, Repair, Resile, Reticent, Retire, Retract(ion), Retreat, Revoke, Revulsion, Scratch, Secede, Sequester, Shrink, Shy, Stand down, Subduct, Unreeve, Unsay

Wither(ed), Withering, Withers Arefy, Atrophy, Burn, Corky, Die, Droop, Dry, Evanish, Fade, Forpine, Googie, Languish, Marcescent, Miff, Nose, Scram, Sere, Shrink, Shrivel, Welk, Welt

▷ **With gaucherie** *may indicate* an anagram

Withhold(ing) Abstain, Conceal, Curt, Deny, Detain, Detinue, Hide, Keep, > **RESERVE**, Trover

Within Enclosed, Endo-, Immanent, Indoors, Inside, Interior, Intra

Without Bar, Beyond, Ex, Lack(ing), Less, Minus, Orb, Outdoors, Outside, Sans, Save, Sen, Senza, Sine, X

▷ **Without** *may indicate* one word surrounding another

▷ **Without restraint** *may indicate* an anagram

Witless Crass, > **STUPID PERSON**

Witness Attest, Bystander, Deponent, Depose, Evidence, Expert, Hostile, Jehovah's, Martyr, Material, Muggletonian, Observe, Obtest, Onlooker, Proof, > **SEE**, Testament, Teste, Testify, Testimony

▶ **Witticism** *see* **WIT**

Wizard (priest) Archimage, Carpathian, Conjuror, Expert, Gandalf, Hex, Magician, Merlin, Oz, Prospero, Shaman, Sorcerer, Super, Warlock

Wobble, Wobbling, Wobbly Chandler's, Coggle, Precess, Quaver, Rock, Shoggle, Shoogle, Totter, Tremble, Trillo, Wag, Waggle, Walty, Waver

Woe(ful) Alack, Alas, Bale, Bane, Distress, Doole, Dule, Ewhow, Gram, Grief, Jeremiad, Lack-a-day, Misery, Pain, Plague, > **SORROW**, Tribulation

Wolds Lincoln(shire), Yorkshire

Wolf(ish), **Wolf-like** Akela, Assyrian, Bolt, Cancer, Casanova, Coyote, Cram, Dangler, Earth, Engorge, Fenrir, Fenris, Gorge, Grey, Ise(n)grim, Lobo, Lone, Lothario, Lupine, Luster, Lycanthrope, MI, Michigan, Pack, Prairie, Rake, Ravenous, Red, Rip, Roué, Rout, Rye, Scoff, Sea, Strand, Tasmanian, Thylacine, Tiger, Timber, Wanderer, Were, Whistler

Woman(hood), **Women** Anile, Besom, Biddy, Bimbo, Bint, Boiler, Broad, Callet, Chai, Chook, Crone, Cummer, Dame, Daughter, Distaff, Doe, Dona(h), Dorcas, Doris, Drab, Eve, F, Fair, Fair sex, > **FEMALE**, Feme, Flapper, Floozy, Frail, Frow, Gammer, Gin, Girl, Gyno-, -gyny, Harpy, Harridan, Hen, Her, Inner, Jade, Jane, Lady, Liberated, Lilith, Lorette, Madam(e), Mademoiselle, Mary, Miladi, Milady, Mob, Mort, Ms, Pandora, Peat, Pict, Piece, Piece of goods, Placket, Popsy, Quean, Queen, Ramp, Rib, Ribibe, Rudas, Runnion, Sabine, Scarlet, She, Skirt, Sort, Squaw, Tail, Tib, Tiring, Tit, Tottie, Totty, Trot, Wahine, Weaker sex, Wifie

Wonder(s) Admire, Agape, Amazement, AR, Arkansas, Arrah, Awe, Colossus, Ferly, Grape-seed, Marle, > **MARVEL**, Meteor, Mirabilia, Miracle, Muse, Nine-day, Phenomenon, Prodigy, Speculate, Stupor, Suppose, Surprise, Wheugh, Whew, Wow

Wonderful(ly) Amazing, Bees' knees, Bitchin(g), Chinless, Épatant, Fantastic, Far-out, Ferly, Geason, Gee-whiz, Glorious, Gramercy, Great, Lal(l)apalooza, Magic, Mirable, Old, Purely, Ripping, Smashing, Sublime

Wood(en), **Woodland**, **Woody** Arboretum, Batten, Beam, Board, Boord(e), Brake, Cask, Channel, Chipboard, Clapboard, Conductor, Dead, Deadpan, Expressionless, Fathom, Fire, Fish, Funk, Furious, Gantry, Gauntree, Hanger, Hard, Hyle, Kindling, Knee, Lath, Lumber, Nemoral, Nemorous, Offcut, Pallet, Pulpwood, Punk, Silvan, Slat, Spinney, Splat, Spline, Splint, Stolid, Sylvan, Three-ply, Timber, Tinder, Touch, Treen, Trees, Twiggy, Vert, Xylem, Xyloid

▷ **Wood** *may indicate* an anagram (in sense of mad)

Woodpecker Bird, Flicker, Hickwall, Picarian, Rainbird, Sapsucker, Saurognathae, Witwall, Woodwale, Yaffle

Woodwind Bassoon, Clarinet, Cornet, Flute, Oboe, Piccolo, Pipe, Recorder, Reed

Wool(len), **Woolly** Alpaca, Angora, Aran, Beige, Berlin, Botany, Bouclé, Cardi(gan), Cashmere, Clip, Cotton, Dog, Doily, Down, Doyley, Drugget, Duffel, Fadge, Fingering, Fleece, Flock, Fuzz, Glass, Guernsey, Hank, Jaeger, Jersey, Kashmir, Ket, Lanate, Lock, Merino, Mineral, Noil(s), Offsorts, Oo, Pashm, Pelage, Persian, Rock, Say, Shetland, Shoddy, Skein, Slipe, Slip-on, Slub, Spencer, Staple, Steel, Swansdown, Tammy, Three-ply, Tod, Tricot, Tweed, Vicuna, Virgin, Wire, Yarn

Word(s), **Wording**, **Wordy** Buzz, Cheville, Claptrap, Clipped, Code, Comment, Content, Dick, Dit(t), Echoic, Embolalia, Epos, Etymon, Faith, Four-letter, Function, Ghost, Grace, Hard, Heteronym, Hint, Homograph, Homonym, Household, > **IN A WORD**, > **IN TWO WORDS**, Janus, Jonah, Key, Last, Lexeme, Lexicon, Lexis, Loan, Logia, Logos, Long-winded, Lyrics, Mantra, Message, Mot, Neologism, News, Nonce, Nonsense, Noun, Oracle, Order, Palabra, Paragram, Parole, Particle, Phrase, Piano, Pledge, Pleonasm, Polysemen, Portmanteau, Preposition, Prolix, Promise, Pronoun, Reserved, Rumour, Saying, Semantics, Signal, Subtitle, Surtitle, Term, Tetragram, Text, Trigger, Trope, Typewriter, Verb, Verbiage, Verbose, Vogue, Warcry, Weasel, Written

Workaholic, **Work(er)**, **Working(-class)**, **Workmen**, **Works**, **Workman(ship)** Act(ivate), Ant, Appliqué, Apronman, Artefact, Artel, Artifact, Artificer, Artisan, Beaver, Bee, Blue-collar, Bohunk, Bull, Business, Careerist, Casual, Char, Chargehand, Chore, Claim, Clock, Coolie, Corvée, Crew, Do, Dog, Dogsbody, Drudge, Drug, Earn, Effect, Effort, Em, Ergon, Ergonomics, Eta, Evince, Exercise, Exploit, Factotum, Facture, Fat, Fettler, Field, Fret, Fuller, > **FUNCTION**,

Gel, Go, Graft, Grass, Grind, Hand, Harness, Hat, Hobo, Horse, Hunky, Industry,
Innards, Job, Journeyman, Key, Knead, Labour, Laid, Luddite, Lump, Machinist,
Man, Manipulate, Manpower, Mechanic, Menial, Midinette, Mine, Ming,
MO, Moil, Moonlight, Movement, Navvy, Neuter, Number, Oeuvre, On, Op,
Opera(tion), Operative, Operator, Opus, Outside, Ouvrier, Ox, Part, Peasant, Peg,
Pensum, Peon, Ply, Portfolio, Potboiler, Practise, Production, Prole(tariat), Public,
Pursuit, Red-neck, Rep, Ride, Robot, Roughneck, Rouseabout, Roustabout,
Run, Satisfactory, Scabble, Serve, Service, Servile, Shift, Shop, Situation, Slogger,
Smithy, Social, Staff, Stevedore, Stint, Strap, Straw, Strive, Support, Surface,
Swaggie, Swagman, Sweat, Swink, Take, Tamper, Task, Temp, Tenail(le), Termite,
Tew, Tick, Till, Toccata, Toil, Travail, Treatise, Trojan, TU, Tut, Uphill, Walla(h),
White-collar

▷ **Working** *may indicate* an anagram

Works, **Workshop** Atelier, Engine, Factory, Forge, Foundry, Garage, Hacienda,
Hangar, Innards, Lab, Mill, Passage, Plant, Public, Shed, Shop, Skylab, Smithy,
Studio, Sweatshop, Telecottage, Time, Tin, Upper

World(ly), **Worldwide** Carnal, Chthonic, Cosmopolitan, Cosmos, Dream, Earth,
Fleshly, Fourth, Free, Ge, Globe, Kingdom, Lay, Lower, Mappemond, Microcosm,
Mondaine, Mondial, Mould, Mundane, Nether, New, Old, Orb, Other, Oyster,
Planet, Possible, Secular, Sensual, Society, Sphere, Spirit, Temporal, Terra, Terrene,
Terrestrial, Third, Universe, Vale, Web, Welt

Worm(-like), **Worms**, **Wormy** Acorn, Anguillula, Annelid, Annulata, Apod(e),
Apodous, Army, Arrow, Articulata, Ascarid, Bilharzia, Bladder, Blind, Blood,
Bob, Bootlace, Brandling, Bristle, Caddis, Capeworm, Caseworm, Catworm,
Cestode, Cestoid, Chaetopod, Clamworm, Copper, Dew, Diet, Diplozoon,
Edge, Enteropneust, Fan, Filander, Filaria, Flag, Flat, Fluke, Galley, Gape,
Gilt-tail, Gordius, Gourd, Guinea, Hair-eel, Hairworm, Heartworm, Helminth,
Hemichordata, Hookworm, Horsehair, Idle, Inchworm, Leech, Liver-fluke, Lob,
Lumbricus, Lytta, Maw, Measuring, Merosome, Miner's, Mopani, Nematoda,
Nematode, Nemertea, Nereid, Night-crawler, Oligochaete, Paddle, Palmer,
Palolo, Paste-eel, Peripatus, Piper, Planarian, Platyhelminth, Polychaete,
Ragworm, Ribbon, Roundworm, Sabella, Sand-mason, Schistosome,
Scoleciform, Scolex, Seamouse, Serpula, Servile, Ship, Sipunculacea,
Sipunculoidea, Stomach, Strawworm, Strongyl(e), Taenia, Tag-tail, Taint,
Tapeworm, Tenioid, Teredo, Termite, Threadworm, Tiger tail, Tongue, Toxocara,
Trematode, Trichina, Trichin(ell)a, Trichinosed, Triclad, Tube, Tubifex, Turbellaria,
Vermiform, Vinegar, Vinegar eel, Wheat-eel, Wheatworm, Whipworm

Worn (out) Attrite, Bare, Decrepit, Detrition, Effete, Epuisé, Exhausted, Forfairn,
Forfoughten, Forjaskit, Forjeskit, Frazzled, Old, On, Passé, Raddled, Rag, Seedy,
Shabby, Shot, Spent, Stale, Tired, Traikit, Trite, Used, Weathered, Whacked

Worried, **Worrier**, **Worry** Agonise, Annoy, Anxiety, Badger, Bait, Beset, Bother,
Care(worn), Cark, Chafe, Concern, Deave, Deeve, Distress, Disturb, Dog, Eat,
Exercise, Feeze, Frab, Fret, Fuss, Harass, Harry, Hyp, Inquietude, Knag, Nag,
Perturb, Pester, Pheese, Pheeze, Phese, Pingle, Pium, Rile, Sool, Stew, Tew, Touse,
Towse, Trouble, Vex, Wherrit, Worn

▷ **Worried** *may indicate* an anagram

Worse(n) Adversely, Degenerate, Deteriorate, Exacerbate, Impair, Inflame,
Pejorate, Regress, War(re), Waur

Worship(per) Adore, Adulation, Ancestor, Angelolatry, Autolatry, Bless,
Churchgoer, Cult, Deify, Devotion, Douleia, Dulia, Epeolatry, Exercise, Fetish,
Glorify, Gurdwara, Happy-clappy, Henotheism, Hero, Idolatry, Idolise, Latria,
Lauds, Lionise, Liturgics, Lordolatry, Mariolatry, Oncer, Orant, Praise, Puja,
Revere, Sabaism, Sakta, Service, Shacharis, Shakta, Sun, Synaxis, Thiasus,
Vaishnava, Venerate, Votary, Wodenism

Worst Beat, Best, Defeat, Get, Nadir, Outdo, Overpower, Pessimum, Rock-bottom, Scum, Severest, Throw, Trounce

Worsted Caddis, Caddyss, Challis, Coburg, Genappe, Lea, Ley, Serge, Shalli, Tamin(e), Whipcord

▷ **Worsted** *may indicate* an anagram

Worth(while), Worthy, Worthies Admirable, Asset, Be, Cop, Deserving, Eligible, Estimable, Feck, > MERIT, Notable, Substance, Tanti, Use, Value, Virtuous, Wealth

Worthless (person) Base, Beggarly, Bilge, Blown, Bodger, Bootless, Bum, Catchpenny, Cheapjack, Crumb, Cypher, Damn, Despicable, Doit, Dreck, Dross, Fallal, Frippery, Gimcrack, Gingerbread, Gubbins, Hilding, Jimcrack, Left, Light, Mud, Nugatory, Nyaff, Obol, Orra, Otiose, Paltry, Pin, Poxy, Punk, Raca, Rag, Rap, Riffraff, Rubbishy, Scabby, Scum, Shotten, Siwash, Sorry, Straw, Tinhorn, Tinpot, Tinsel, Tittle, Toerag, Trangam, Trashy, Trumpery, Tuppenny, Twat, Two-bit, Twopenny, Useless, Vain, Vile

Wound(ed) Battery, Bite, Bless, Blighty, Bruise, Chagrin, Coiled, Crepance, Cut, Dere, Engore, Ganch, Gash, Gaunch, Gore, Harm, Hurt, Injury, Lacerate, Lesion, Maim, Molest, Mortify, Offend, Pip, Sabre-cut, Scab, Scar, Scath, Scotch, Scratch, Shoot, Snaked, Snub, Sore, Stab, Sting, Trauma, Twined, Umbrage, Vuln, Vulnerary, Walking, Wing, Wint

Woundwort Clown's, Marsh

Wrangle(r), Wrangling Altercate, Argie-bargie, > ARGUE, Bandy, Bicker, Brangle, Broil, Dispute, Haggle, Mathematical, Rag, Vitilitigation

Wrap(per), Wrapping, Wrap up Amice, Amis, Bind, Bubble, Bundle, Cellophane®, Cere, Clingfilm, Cloak, Clothe, Cocoon, Conclude, Emboss, Enfold, Enrol(l), Ensheath(e), Envelop(e), Foil, Folio, Furl, Hap, Hem, Kimono, Kraft, Lag, Lap, Mail, Muffle, Negligee, Parcel, Roll, Rug, Shawl, Sheath(e), Stole, Swaddle, Swathe, Tinfoil, Tsutsumu, Velamen, Wap, Wimple

Wreath(e) Adorn, Anadem, Chaplet, Coronal, Crown, Entwine, Festoon, Garland, Laurel, Lei, Torse, Tortile, Twist

Wreck(age), Wrecked, Wrecker Crab, Debris, Demolish, Devastate, Flotsam, Founder, Goner, Hesperus, Hulk, Lagan, Ligan, Luddite, Mutilate, Ruin(ate), Sabotage, Shambles, Shatter, Sink, Smash, Subvert, Torpedo, Trash, Wrack

▷ **Wrecked** *may indicate* an anagram

Wrench Allen, Fit, Jerk, Lug, Mole, Monkey, Pin, Pull, Socket, Spanner, Sprain, Stillson®, Strain, Tear, Twist, Windlass, Wrest

Wrestle(r), Wrestling All-in, Arm, Basho, Catchweight, Clinch, Featherweight, Flying mare, Freestyle, Full-nelson, Grapple, Grovet, Half-nelson, Hammerlock, Haystacks, Headlock, Hip-lock, Indian, Judo, Knee-drop, Milo, Monkey climb, Mud, Nelson, Niramiai, Pinfall, Posting, Sambo, Stable, Struggle, Sumo, Tag, Tag (team), Tussle, Whip, Wristlock, Writhe

Wretch(ed) Blackguard, Blue, Caitiff, Chap-fallen, Cullion, Forlorn, Git, Hapless, Lorn, Measly, Miser, Miserable, Peelgarlic, Pilgarlick, Pipsqueak, Poltroon, Poor, Punk, Rat, Scoundrel, Scroyle, Seely, Snake, Unblest, Wo(e)

▷ **Wretched** *may indicate* an anagram

Wrinkle(d), Wrinkly Clue, Cockle, Corrugate, Crease, Crepy, Crimple, Crimpy, Crinkle, Crow's-foot, Crumple, Fold, Frounce, Frown, Frumple, Furrow, Gen, Groove, Headline, Hint, Idea, Line, Lirk, Plissé, Plough, Pucker, Purse, Ridge, Rimple, Rivel, Rop(e)y, Ruck(le), Rugose, Rumple, Runkle, Seamy, Shrivel, Sulcus, Time-worn, Tip, Whelk

Writ(s) Capias, Certiorari, Cursitor, Dedimus, Distringas, Elegit, Fieri facias, Filacer, Habeas corpus, Holy, Injunction, Latitat, Law-burrows, Mandamus, Mittimus, Noverint, Praemunire, Process, Replevin, Scirefacias, Significat,

Subpoena, Summons, Supersedeas, Tolt, Venire, Warrant

Write(r), Writing Amphigory, Apocrypha, > **AUTHOR**, Automatic, Ballpoint, Biographer, Biro®, Bloomsbury Group, Book-hand, Calligraphy, Causerie, Cento, Charactery, Clerk, Clinquant, Columnist, Copperplate, Creative, Cursive, Diarist, Dite, Draft, Endorse, Endoss, Engross, Epigrammatise, Epistle, > **ESSAYIST**, Expatiate, Fist, Form, Formulary, Freelance, Ghost, Graffiti, Graphite, Hack, Hairline, Hand, Haplography, Hieratic, Hieroglyphics, Hiragana, Indite, Ink, Inkhorn-mate, Ink-jerker, Inkslinger, Inscribe, Join-hand, Jot(tings), Journalese, Journalist, Journo, Kaleyard School, Kana, Leader, Lexigraphy, Lexis, Linear A, Lipogram, Litterateur, Longhand, Lucubrate, Mirror, Ms(s), Nib, Notary, Notate, Novelese, > **NOVELIST**, Pen, Pencil, Penmanship, Penny-a-liner, Pentel®, Picture, Planchette, > **POET**, Polemic, Pot-hook, Proser, Purana, Purple patch, Quill, Roundhand, Sanskrit, Sci-fi, Scratch, Screed, Screeve, Scribe, Scrip(t), Scripture, Scrivener, Secretary, Sign, Sling-ink, Space, Spirit, Stichometry, Style, Subscript, Superscribe, Sutra, Syllabary, Syllabic, Syllabism, Tantra, Transcribe, Treatise, Uncial, Wordsmith, Zend-Avesta

▷ **Writhing** *may indicate* an anagram

Wrong Aggrieve, Agley, Amiss, Astray, Awry, Bad, Chout, Delict, Disservice, Err, Fallacious, False, Harm, Ill, Immoral, Improper, Incorrect, Injury, Mischief, Misintelligence, Misled, Mistake(n), Misuse, Nocent, Offbase, Offend, Peccadillo, Perverse, Sin(ful), Tort, Transgress, Unethical, Unright, Unsuitable, Withershins, Wryly, X

▷ **Wrong** *may indicate* an anagram

Wry Askew, Contrary, Devious, Distort, Droll, Grimace, Ironic

X(-shaped) Buss, By, Chi, Christ, Cross, Decussate, Drawn, Kiss, Ten, Times, Unknown, X-ray

▶ **Xmas** *see* CHRISTMAS

X-ray Angiogram, Cholangiography, Emi-Scanner, Encephalogram, Encephalograph, Fermi, Grenz, Mammogram, Plate, Pyelogram, Radioscopy, Rem, Roentgen, Sciagram, Screening, Skiagram, Tomography, Venogram

Xylophone Marimba, Sticcado, Sticcato

Yy

Yacht Britannia, Dragon, Ice, Keelboat, Ketch, Knockabout, Land, Maxi, Sailboat, Sand

Yachtsman, Yachtsmen Chichester, RYS

Yank(ee) Bet, Carpetbagger, Hitch, Jerk, Jonathan, Lug, Northerner, Pluck, Pull, Rug, Schlep(p), So(o)le, Sowl(e), > **TUG**, Tweak, Twitch, Wrench, Wrest

▷ **Yank** *may indicate* an anagram

Yard Area, CID, Close, Court, Farm-toun, Garden, Haw, Hof, Kail, Knacker's, Main, Marshalling, Mast, Measure, Navy, Patio, Poultry, Prison, Ree(d), Scotland, Spar, Sprit, Steel, Stick, Stride, Switch, Tilt, Timber, Victualling, Y, Yd

Yarn(s) Abb, Berlin, Bouclé, Caddice, Caddis, Chenille, Clew, Clue, Cop, Cord, Crewel, Fib, Fibroline, Fingering, Genappe, Gimp, Gingham, Guimp(e), Gymp, Homespun, Jaw, Knittle, Knot, Lay, Lea, Ley, Line, Lisle, Lurex®, Marl, Merino, Nylon, Organzine, Orlon®, Ply, Rigmarole, Ripping, Saxony, Sennit, Sinnet, Skein, Story, Strand, Tale, Taradiddle, Thread, Thrid, Thrum(my), Tram, Warp, Weft, Woof, Wool, Worsted, Zephyr

Yawn(ing) Boredom, Chasmy, Fissure, Gant, Gape, Gaunt, Greys, Hiant, Oscitation, Pandiculation, Rictus

Year(ly), Years A, Age, Anno, Annual, Anomalistic, Astronomical, Calendar, Canicular, Civil, Common, Cosmic, Decennium, Donkey's, Dot, Ecclesiastical, Egyptian, Embolismic, Equinoctial, Financial, Fiscal, Gap, Great, Hebrew, Holy, Indiction, Julian, Leap, Legal, Light, Lunar, Lunisolar, Natural, PA, Perfect, Platonic, Riper, Sabbatical, School, Sidereal, Solar, Sothic, Summer, Sun, Tax, Theban, Time, Towmon(d), Towmont, Tropical, Twelvemonth, Vintage, Wander

Yearn(ing) Ache, Ake, Aspire, Brame, Burn, Covet, Crave, Curdle, Desire, Erne, Greed, Hanker, Hone, > **LONG**, Nostalgia, Pant, Pine, Sigh

▷ **Yearning** *may indicate* an anagram

Yeast Barm, Bees, Brewer's, Ferment, Flor, Leaven, Saccharomycete, Torula, Vegemite®

Yellow(ish) Amber, Auburn, Back, Beige, Bisque, Bistre, Buff, Butternut, Cadmium, Canary, Chicken, Chrome, Citrine, Cowardly, Craven, Daffodil, Etiolin, Fallow, Fever, Filemot, Flavin(e), Flaxen, Gamboge, Gold, Icteric, Isabel(le), Isabella, Jack, Jaundiced, Lemon(y), Mustard, Nankeen, Naples, Oaker, Ochre(y), Or(eide), Pages, Peril, Pink, Primrose, Queen's, River, Saffron, Sallow, Sand, Sear, Spineless, Straw, Sulphur, Tawny, Topaz, Tow, Weld, Xanthous, Yolk

Yes Ay(e), Da, Indeed, Ja, Jokol, Nod, OK, Oke, Quite, Sure, Truly, Uh-huh, Wilco, Yea, Yokul, Yup

Yesterday Démodé, Eve, Hesternal, Pridian

Yield(ing) Abandon, Afford, Bend, Bow, Breed, Capitulate, Catch, Cede, Come, Comply, Concede, Crack, Crop, Defer, Dividend, Docile, Ductile, Easy, Elastic, Facile, Flaccid, Flexible, Give, Harvest, Interest, Knuckle, Meek, Meltith, Mess, Output, Pan, Pay, Pliant, Produce, Relent, Render, Return, Sag, Soft, > **SUBMIT**, Succumb, Surrender, Susceptible, Truckle

Yoke Bow, Cang(ue), Collar, Couple, Harness, Inspan, Jugal, Pair, Span

Yokel Boor, Bumpkin, Chaw(-bacon), Clumperton, Hayseed, Hick, Jake, Jock, Peasant, Rustic

Yon(der) Distant, Further, O'erby, Thae, There, Thether, Thither

York(shire), **Yorkshireman** Batter, Bowl, Ebor, Pudding, Ridings, Tyke

You One, Sie, Thee, Thou, Usted, Ye

Young (person), **Youngster**, **Youth(ful)** Adolescent, Ageless, Bev(an), Boy, Boyhood, Bub, Calf-time, Ch, Charver, Chick, Chicken, Child, Chile, Cockerel, Cockle, Colt, Cub, DJ, Early, Ephebe, Ephebus, Esquire, Flapper, Fledgling, Foetus, Fry, Gigolo, Gilded, Gillet, Girl, Hebe, Hobbledehoy, Immature, Imp, Infant, Issue, Junior, Juvenal, Juvenesce, Juvenile, Kid, Kiddo, Kiddy, Kipper, Lad, Lamb, Latter-day, Leaping-time, Less, Litter, Little, Middle, Minor, Misspent, Mod, Mormon, Nance, Nestling, New, New Romantic, Nipper, Nymph, Plant, Progeny, Protégé(e), Punk, Pup, Sapling, Scent, Scion, Shaveling, Shaver, Skinhead, Slip, Son, Spawn, Sprig, Stripling, Swain, Ted, Teenager, Teens, Teenybopper, Toyboy, Well-preserved, Whelp, Whippersnapper, Wigga, Wigger

Younger, **Youngest** Baby, Benjamin, Cadet, Last born, Less, Minimus, Seneca, Wallydrag, Wallydraigle, Yr

▶ **Youth** *see* YOUNG PERSON

Zz

Z Izzard, Izzet, Zambia, Zebra
Zanzibar Swahili
Zeal(ous) Ardour, Bigotry, Devotion, Eager, Enthusiasm, Evangelic, Fervour, Fire, Perfervid, Study
Zealot Bigot, Devotee, Fan(atic), St Simon, Votary
Zenith Acme, Apogee, Height, Pole, Summit
Zephyr Breeze, Wind
Zeppelin Airship, Balloon, Dirigible
Zero Absolute, Blob, Cipher, Ground, Nil, Nothing, Nought, O, Z
Zest Condiment, Crave, Élan, Gusto, Pep, Piquancy, Relish, Spark, Spice, Tang, Zap, Zing
Zigzag Crémaillère, Crinkle-crankle, Dancette, Feather-stitch, Indent, Ric-rac, Slalom, Stagger, Tack, Traverse, Yaw
Zinc Blende, Gahnite, Mossy, Sherardise, Spelter, Sphalerite, Tutenag, Tutty, Willemite, Wurtzite, Zn
Zip(per) Dash, Energy, Fastener, Fly, Go, Oomph, Presto, Stingo, Vim, Vivacity, Whirry, Zero
Zodiac(al) Aquarius, Archer, Aries, Bull, Cancer, Capricorn, Counter-glow, Crab, Fish, Gegenschein, Gemini, Goat, Horoscope, Leo, Libra, Lion, Ophiuchus, Pisces, Ram, Sagittarius, Scales, Scorpio(n), Taurus, Twins, Virgin, Virgo, Watercarrier
Zone(s) Abyssal, Acid, Anacoustic, Area, Band, Bathyal, Belt, Benioff, Buffer, Canal, Climate, Collision, Comfort, Convergence, Crumple, Drop, Economic, Ecotone, End, Enterprise, Erogenous, Euro, Exclusion, F layer, Fracture, Free, Fresnel, Frigid, Hadal, Hot, Impact, Krumhole, Low velocity, Neutral, No-fly, Nuclear-free, Precinct, > REGION, Rift, Ring, Sahel, Sector, Shear, Skip, Smokeless, Stratopause, Strike, Subduction, Temperate, Time, Tolerance, Torrid, Tundra, Twilight